Human Behaviour

Human Behaviour

Compiled from:

Psychology
Fifth Edition
G. Neil Martin, Neil R. Carlson and William Buskist

Social Psychology
Seventh Edition
Michael A. Hogg and Graham M. Vaughan

Developmental Psychology
Second Edition
Rachel Gillibrand, Virginia Lam and Victoria L. O'Donnell

Cognitive Psychology
First Edition
Philip Quinlan and Ben Dyson

PEARSON

Harlow, England • London • New York • Boston • San Francisco • Toronto • Sydney • Auckland • Singapore • Hong Kong
Tokyo • Seoul • Taipei • New Delhi • Cape Town • Sao Paulo • Mexico City • Madrid • Amsterdam • Munich • Paris • Milan

Pearson Education Limited
KAO Two
KAO Park
Harlow
Essex CM17 9NA

And associated companies throughout the world

Visit us on the World Wide Web at:
www.pearson.com/uk

© Pearson Education Limited 2018

Compiled from:

Psychology
Fifth Edition
G. Neil Martin, Neil R. Carlson and William Buskist
ISBN 978-0-273-75552-4
© Pearson Education Limited 2013 (print and electronic)

Social Psychology
Seventh Edition
Michael A. Hogg and Graham M. Vaughan
ISBN 978-0-273-76459-5
© Pearson Education Limited 2014 (print and electronic)

Developmental Psychology
Second Edition
Rachel Gillibrand, Virginia Lam and Victoria L. O'Donnell
ISBN 978-1-292-00308-5
© Pearson Education Limited 2016 (print and electronic)

Cognitive Psychology
First Edition
Philip Quinlan and Ben Dyson
ISBN 978-0-13-129810-1
© Pearson Education Limited 2008

ISBN 978-1-787-26223-2

Printed and bound in Great Britain by CPI Group.

Contents

Preface

This text has been compiled to support students of Coventry University studying introductory modules on a psychology based course. These modules are key to building a strong knowledge base of Psychology as well as developing the skills needed to become successful students which can then be used in future careers in today's competitive job market.

The introductory modules are designed to provide a theme based approach to cognitive, social, developmental, biological and individual differences psychology. They are designed to give an overview of these key areas in psychology in a way which will provide the scaffolding required to understand how the different theoretical and methodological strands in psychology link together.

The modules aim to provide an opportunity to explore the application of psychological perspectives to solving real life problems. Topical themes will explore the context of core areas of study and students will be directed towards relevant theoretical frameworks and research areas but then will be expected to source their own academic resources in order to demonstrate an in depth understanding of key psychological principles and theories.

We wish you all the best in studies and hope that you enjoy your time with us at Coventry University.

Human Behaviour

CHAPTER 1

The science of psychology

It appears to be an almost universal belief that anyone is competent to discuss psychological problems, whether he or she has taken the trouble to study the subject or not, and that while everybody's opinion is of equal value, that of the professional psychologist must be excluded at all costs because he might spoil the fun by producing some facts which would completely upset the speculation and the wonderful dream castles so laboriously constructed by the layman.

Source: Eysenck, 1957, p. 13.

MyPsychLab

Explore the accompanying experiments, videos, simulations and animations on **MyPsychLab**.
This chapter includes activities on:

- Behaviourism
- Little Albert
- The Skinnerian learning process
- Fixed-interval and fixed ratio scheduling
- Check your understanding and prepare for your exams using the multiple choice, short answer and essay practice tests also available.

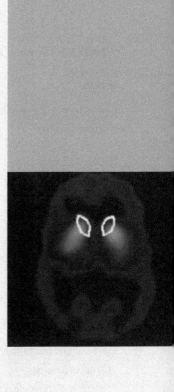

WHAT YOU SHOULD BE ABLE TO DO AFTER READING CHAPTER 1

- Define psychology and trace the history of the discipline.
- Be aware of the different methods psychologists use to study behaviour.
- Distinguish between the branches of psychology and describe them.
- Understand what is meant by the 'common-sense' approach to answering questions about psychology and outline its flaws.
- Describe and understand historical developments in psychology such as structuralism, behaviourism and the cognitive revolution.
- Be aware of how psychology developed in Europe and across the world.

QUESTIONS TO THINK ABOUT

- How would you define psychology and describe its subject matter? Once you have finished reading Chapter 1, see whether your view has changed.
- What types of behaviour do you think a psychologist studies?
- Are there any behaviours that a psychologist cannot or should not study?
- What do you think psychologists mean when they say they adopt the 'scientific approach'?
- Should psychological research always be carried out to help people?
- Are there different types of psychologist? If so, what are they and why?
- Do you think that much of what we know from psychology is 'common sense'? Why?
- Are some psychological phenomena universal, i.e. they appear across nations and cultures?
- How does psychology differ from other disciplines, such as biology, sociology and physics? Which discipline/subjects do you think it is closest to and why?

What is psychology?

If you asked this question of several people, you would probably receive several, very different answers. In fact, if you asked this question of several psychologists, you would still not receive complete agreement on the answer. Psychologists engage in research, teaching, counselling and psychotherapy; they advise industry and government about personnel matters, the design of products, advertising, marketing and legislation; they devise and administer tests of personality, achievement and ability. And yet psychology is a relatively new discipline; the first modern scientific psychology laboratory was established in 1878 and the first person ever to call himself a psychologist was still alive in 1920. In some European universities the discipline of psychology was known as 'mental philosophy' – not psychology – even as late as the beginning of the twentieth century.

Psychologists study a wide variety of phenomena, including physiological processes within the nervous system, genetics, environmental events, personality characteristics, human development, mental abilities, health and social interactions. Because of this diversity, it is rare for a person to be described simply as a psychologist; instead, a psychologist is defined by the sub-area in which they work. For example, an individual who measures and treats psychological disorders is called a clinical psychologist; one who studies child development is called a developmental psychologist; a person who explores the relationship between physiology and behaviour might call themselves a neuro psychologist (if they study the effect of brain damage on behaviour) or a biopsychologist/physiological psychologist/psychobiologist (if they study the brain and other bodily processes, such as heart rate). Modern psychology has so many branches that it is impossible to demonstrate expertise in all of these areas. Consequently, and by necessity, psychologists have a highly detailed knowledge of sub-areas of the discipline and the most common are listed in Table 1.1.

Table 1.1 The major branches of psychology

Branch	Subject of study
Psychobiology/Biological psychology	Biological basis of behaviour
Psychophysiology	Psychophysiological responses such as heart rate, galvanic skin response and brain electrical activity
Neuropsychology	Relationship between brain activity/structure and function
Comparative psychology	Behaviour of species in terms of evolution and adaptation
Ethology	Animal behaviour in natural environments
Sociobiology	Social behaviour in terms of biological inheritance and evolution
Behaviour genetics	Degree of influence of genetics and environment on psychological factors
Cognitive psychology	Mental processes and complex behaviour
Cognitive neuroscience	Brain's involvement in mental processes
Developmental psychology	Physical, cognitive, social and emotional development from birth to senescence
Social psychology	Individuals' and groups' behaviour
Individual differences	Temperament and characteristics of individuals and their effects on behaviour
Cross-cultural psychology	Impact of culture on behaviour
Cultural psychology	Variability of behaviour within cultures
Forensic and criminological psychology	Behaviour in the context of crime and the law
Clinical psychology	Causes and treatment of mental disorder and problems of adjustment
Health psychology	Impact of lifestyle and stress on health and illness
Educational psychology	Social, cognitive and emotional development of children in the context of schooling
Consumer psychology	Motivation, perception and cognition in consumers
Organisational or occupational psychology	Behaviour of groups and individuals in the workplace
Ergonomics	Ways in which humans and machines work together
Sport and exercise psychology	The effects of psychological variables on sport and exercise performance, and vice versa

Psychology defined

Psychology is the scientific study of behaviour. The word 'psychology' comes from two Greek words, *psukhe*, meaning 'breath' or 'soul', and *logos*, meaning 'word' or 'reason'. The modern meaning of psycho- is 'mind' and the modern meaning of -logy is 'science'; thus, the word 'psychology' literally means 'the science of the mind'. Early in the development of psychology, people conceived of the mind as an independent, free-floating spirit. Later, they described it as a characteristic of a functioning brain whose ultimate function was to control behaviour. Thus, the focus turned from the mind, which cannot be directly observed, to behaviour, which can. And because the brain is the organ that both contains the mind and controls behaviour, psychology very soon incorporated the study of the brain.

The study of physical events such as brain activity has made some psychologists question whether the word 'mind' has any meaning in the study of behaviour. One view holds that the 'mind' is a metaphor for what the brain does and because it is a metaphor it should not be treated as if it actually existed. In his famous book *The Concept of Mind*, the philosopher Gilbert Ryle describes this as the 'ghost in the machine' (Ryle, 1949). One might, for example, determine that the personality trait of extroversion exists and people will fall on different points along a dimension from not very extrovert to very extrovert. But does this mean that this trait really exists? Or is it a label used to make us understand a complex phenomenon in a simpler way? This is called the problem of **reification** in psychology: the assumption that an event or phenomenon is concrete and exists in reality because it is given a name.

The approach adopted by modern psychology is scientific, that is, it adopts the principles and procedures of science to help answer the questions it asks. Psychologists adopt this approach because it is the most effective way of determining 'truth' and 'falsity'; the scientific method, they argue, incorporates fewer biases and greater rigour than do other methods. Of course, not all approaches in psychology have this rigorous scientific leaning: early theories of personality, for example, did not rely on the scientific method (these are described in Chapter 14) and a minority of psychologists adopt methods that are not considered to be part of the scientific approach: qualitative approaches to human behaviour, for example (reviewed in Chapter 2).

How much of a science is psychology?

Psychology is a young science and the discipline has tried hard to earn and demonstrate its scientific spurs. Chemistry, physics or biology seem to have no such problems: their history is testament to their status as a science. Psychology, however, appears to be gaining ground.

Simonton (2004) compared the scientific status of psychology with that of physics, chemistry, sociology and biology, using a number of characteristics that typified a general science. These included the number of theories and laws mentioned in introductory textbooks (the higher the ratio of theory to law, the 'softer' – i.e. less scientific – the discipline); the discipline's publication rate (the more frequent the publications, the more scientific the discipline); appearance of graphs in journal papers (the 'harder' the discipline, the greater the number of graphs); the number of times publications were referred to by other academics; and how peers evaluated their colleagues. Simonton also looked at other measures of scientific standing such as 'lecture disfluency' (the number of pause words such as 'uh', 'er' and 'um': these are more common in less formal, structured and factual disciplines); and perceived difficulty of the discipline.

Not surprisingly, Simonton found that the natural sciences were judged to be more 'scientific' than were the social sciences. Psychology, however, fell right on the mean – at the junction between natural and social sciences, as you can see in Figure 1.1, and was much closer to biology than to sociology. The biggest gap in scores was found between psychology and sociology, suggesting that the discipline is closer to its natural science cousins than its social science acquaintances.

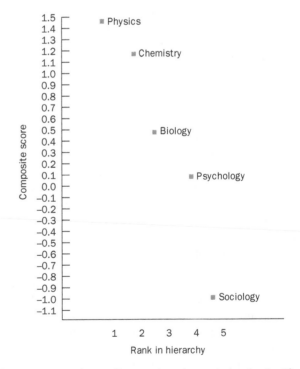

Figure 1.1 According to Simonton's study, psychology's scientific status was more similar to that of biology than other disciplines traditionally associated with it, such as sociology.

Source: D.K. Simonton, 'Psychology's status as a scientific discipline: its empirical placement within an implicit hierarchy of the sciences', *Review of General Psychology*, 2004, 8, 1, p. 65 (Fig. 2).

(a)   (b)

The stereotypical image of a psychologist **(a)** and a traditional scientist **(b)**.
Source: (a) Pelaez Inc./Corbis; (b) Tomas de Arno/Alamy Images.

A gap also separated chemistry and biology, suggesting that the sciences might be grouped according to three clusters: the physical sciences (chemistry and physics), life sciences (biology and psychology) and social science (sociology).

When does this understanding of a hierarchy of science develop? Researchers at Yale University sought to answer this question in a group of kindergarten children, school children and university students (Keil *et al.*, 2010). In one experiment, participants read a series of questions about a topic from each discipline and asked them to rate the difficulty of understanding these topics. For example, for physics one of the questions was 'How does a top stay spinning upright?', for chemistry, 'Why does paper burn but not aluminium foil?', for biology, 'Why are we allergic to some things but not others?', for psychology, 'Why is it hard to understand two people talking at once?' and for economics, 'Why do house prices go up and down over the years?' Children judged questions from the natural science to be more difficult to understand than those from psychology. The difficulty of economics subsided after late childhood.

In their second experiment, the researchers examined whether different branches of psychology were perceived as being more difficult than others (e.g., neuroscience, sensation and perception, cognitive psychology, social psychology, attention and memory, personality and emotions). Children regarded neuroscience as more difficult than cognitive psychology, and cognitive psychology as more difficult than social psychology. They were judged equally 'difficult' by adults.

Simonton concluded his study with an interesting observation. He argued that psychology's position in this hierarchy does not really reflect its scientific approach but its subject matter: because the subject matter of psychology can be viewed as not directly controllable or manipulable it may be perceived erroneously, despite its adoption of the scientific method, as neither scientific fish nor fowl.

For the moment, however, consider the value of the scientific approach in psychology. Imagine that you were allowed to answer any psychological question that you might want to ask: what is the effect of language deprivation on language development, say, or the effect of personality on the stability of romantic relationships, or the effect of noise on examination revision? How would you set about answering these questions? What approach do you think would be the best? And how would you ensure that the outcome of your experiment is determined only by those factors you studied and not by any others? These are the types of problem that psychologists face when they design and conduct studies.

Sometimes, the results of scientific studies are denounced as 'common sense': that they were so obvious as to be not worth the bother of setting up an experiment. The view, however, is generally ill-informed because, as you will discover throughout this book, psychological research frequently contradicts common-sense views. As the late, influential British psychologist Hans Eysenck noted in this chapter's opening quote, most people believe that they are experts in human behaviour. And to some extent we are all lay scientists, of a kind, although generally unreliable ones.

As Lilienfeld (2011) points out: people also overestimate their understanding of how toilets, zippers and sewing machines work. And humans are slightly more complicated than a lavatory. We are also likely to discount scientific explanations for phenomena, especially if they contradict our views of these phenomena. Munro (2010), for example, presented undergraduates with scientific research which either discounted their view of homosexuality or supported it. If the evidence was not to the participants'

liking, they were more dismissive of the scientific method. This attitude then carried over into another study in which the same participants were asked to make a judgement about whether science could assist making decisions about the retention of the death penalty. Those whose views had been challenged by science in the previous study were less likely to find science helpful in making decisions about other, unrelated topics. The Controversies section takes up this point.

Controversies in psychological science: Is psychology common sense?

The issue

Take a look at the following questions on some familiar psychological topics. How many you can answer correctly?

1 Patients with schizophrenia suffer from a split personality. Is this: (a) true most of the time; (b) true some of the time; (c) true none of the time; (d) true only when the individual is undergoing psychotherapy?

2 Under hypnosis, a person will, if asked by a hypnotist: (a) recall past life events with a high degree of accuracy; (b) perform physical feats of strength not possible out of hypnosis; (c) do (a) and (b); (d) do neither (a) nor (b)?

3 The learning principles applied to birds and fish also apply to: (a) humans; (b) cockroaches; (c) both (a) and (b); (d) neither (a) nor (b)?

4 Are physically attractive people: (a) more likely to be stable than physically unattractive people; (b) equal in psychological stability; (c) likely to be less psychologically stable; (d) likely to be much more unstable?

How well do you think you did? These four questions featured in the ten most difficult questions answered by first-year psychology undergraduates who completed a 38-item questionnaire about psychological knowledge (Martin *et al.*, 1997). In fact, when the responses from first- and final-year psychology, engineering, sociology, English and business studies students were analysed, no one group scored more than 50 per cent correct. Perhaps not surprisingly, psychologists answered more questions correctly than the other students, with sociologists following close behind. But why should psychology (and other) students perform so badly on a test of psychological knowledge?

The answer lies in the fact that the questionnaire was not really a test of psychological knowledge but of common-sense attitudes towards psychological research. Common-sense mistakes are those committed when a person chooses what they think is the obvious answer but this answer is incorrect. Some writers have suggested that 'a great many of psychology's basic

principles are self-evident' (Houston, 1983), and that 'much of what psychology textbooks purport to teach undergraduates about research findings in the area may already be known to them through common, informal experiences' (Barnett, 1986). Houston reported that although introductory psychology students answered 15 out of 21 questions about 'memory and learning' correctly, a collection of 50 individuals found in a city park on a Friday afternoon scored an average of 16. The 21 December 2008 edition of *The Sunday Times* featured a full-page article, boldly headed 'University of the bleedin' obvious', in which the journalist bemoaned what he perceived to be the triviality of (mostly) behavioural research. 'Why are we,' demanded the journalist or his angry sub-editor, 'deluged with academic research "proving" things that we know already?', citing a string of what was considered irritating, self-evident bons mots from various university departments.

Is the common-sense view of psychological research justified?

The evidence

Not quite. Since the late 1970s, a number of studies have examined individuals' false beliefs about psychology, and students' beliefs in particular. Over 76 per cent of first-year psychology students thought the following statements were true: 'Memory can be likened to a storage chest in the brain into which we deposit material and from which we can withdraw later', 'Personality tests reveal your basic motives, including those you may not be aware of', and 'Blind people have unusually sensitive organs of touch'. This, despite the fact that course materials directly contradicted some of these statements (Vaughan, 1977).

Furnham (1992, 1993) found that only half of such 'common-sense' questions were answered correctly by 250 prospective psychology students, and only 20 per cent of questions were answered correctly by half or more of a **sample** of 110 first-year psychology, fine arts, biochemistry and engineering students. In Martin *et al.*'s (1997) study, final-year students answered more questions correctly than did first-year students, but there was no

Controversies in psychological science: *Continued*

significant difference between first- and final-year psychology students. This suggests that misperceptions are slowly dispelled after students undergo the process of higher education and learning, but that studying specific disciplines does nothing to dispel these myths effectively. This is just one explanation.

What, then, is 'common' about 'common sense'? Some have likened common sense to fantastical thinking. This describes ways of reasoning about the world that violate known scientific principles (Woolley, 1997). For example, the beliefs that women can control breast cancer by positive thinking (Taylor, 1983), that walking under a ladder brings bad luck and that touching wood brings good luck (Blum and Blum, 1974) violate known physical laws, but people still believe in doing such things. People often draw erroneous conclusions about psychological knowledge because they rely on small sets of data, sometimes a very small set of data (such as a story in a newspaper or the behaviour of a friend).

Conclusion

As you work through your psychology course and through this book, discovering new and sometimes complicated ways of analysing and understanding human behaviour, you will realise that many of the beliefs and perceptions you held about certain aspects of psychology are false or only half right. Of course, no science is truly infallible and there are different ways of approaching psychological problems (and perhaps, sometimes, some problems are insoluble or we have no good method of studying them satisfactorily). Psychology, however, attempts to adopt the best of scientific approaches to understanding potentially the most unmanageable of subject matter: behaviour. And, for those of you who were wondering, the answers to the questions at the start of the box are c, d, c and a.

Explaining behaviour

The ultimate goals of research in psychology are to understand, predict and change human behaviour: to explain why people do what they do. Different kinds of psychologists are interested in different kinds of behaviour and different levels of explanation. How do psychologists 'explain' behaviour?

First, they must describe it accurately and comprehensively. We must become familiar with the things that people (or other animals) do. We must learn how to categorise and measure behaviour so that we can be sure that different psychologists in different places are observing the same phenomena. Next, we must discover the causes of the behaviour we observe – those events responsible for its occurrence. If we can discover the events that caused the behaviour to occur, we have 'explained' it. Events that cause other events (including behaviour) to occur are called **causal events** or **determinants.**

For example, one psychologist might be interested in visual perception and another might be interested in romantic attraction. Even when they are interested in the same behaviour, different psychologists might study different levels of analysis. Some look inside the organism in a literal sense, seeking physiological causes, such as the activity of nerve cells or the secretions of glands. Others look inside the organism in a metaphorical sense, explaining behaviour in terms of hypothetical mental states, such as anger, fear, curiosity or love. Still others look only for events in the environment (including things that other people do) that cause behaviours to occur.

Cutting edge: Are beautiful people good because they are desired?

Research has shown that beautiful people are rated more positively than their less attractively endowed counterparts. However, their beauty may also affect our perception of their interpersonal skills. Lemay *et al.* (2010) presented men and women with photographs of attractive or less attractive individuals and asked them to rate the person's interpersonal skills and how likely they (the participants) were to bond with that person. In two follow-on experiments, they asked the same of the participants in relation to attractive romantic partners and attractive friends.

They found that the owners of attractive faces were were regarded as interpersonally very receptive. More importantly, participants were more willing to bond with these individuals. This suggests one way in which beautiful people may get their own way: people want to desire them and get to know them.

Established and emerging fields of psychology

Throughout this book you will encounter many types of psychologist and many types of psychology. As you have already seen, very few individuals call themselves psychologists, rather they describe themselves by their specialism – cognitive psychologist, developmental psychologist, social psychologist, and so on. Before describing and defining each branch of psychology, however, it is important to distinguish between three general terms: psychology, **psychiatry** and **psychoanalysis**. A psychologist normally holds a university degree in a behaviour-related discipline (such as psychology, zoology, cognitive science) and usually possesses a higher research degree (a Ph.D. or doctorate) if they are teaching or a researcher.

Those not researching but working in applied settings such as hospitals or schools may have other, different qualifications that enable them to practise in those environments. Psychiatrists are physicians who have specialised in the causes and treatment of mental disorder. They are medically qualified (unlike psychologists, who nonetheless do study medical problems and undertake biological research) and have the ability to prescribe medication (which psychologists do not). Much of the work done by psychologists in psychiatric settings is similar to that of the psychiatrist, implementing psychological interventions for patients with mental illness. Psychoanalysts are specific types of counsellor who attempt to understand mental disorder by reference to the workings of the unconscious. There is no formal academic qualification necessary to become a psychoanalyst and, as the definition implies, they deal with a limited range of behaviour.

Most research psychologists are employed by colleges or universities, by private organisations or by government. Research psychologists differ from one another in two principal ways: in the types of behaviour they investigate and in the causal events they analyse. That is, they explain different types of behaviour, and they explain them in terms of different types of cause. For example,

two psychologists might both be interested in memory, but they might attempt to explain memory in terms of different causal events – one may focus on physiological events (such as the activation of the brain during memory retrieval) whereas the other may focus on environmental events (such as the effect of noise level on task performance). Professional societies such as the American Psychological Association and the British Psychological Society have numerous subdivisions representing members with an interest in a specific aspect of psychology. This section outlines some of the major branches or subdivisions of psychology. A summary of these can be found in Table 1.1.

Psychobiology/biological psychology is the study of the biological basis of behaviour (G.N. Martin, 2003). Other terms for the same branch include physiological psychology and biopsychology. It investigates the causal events in an organism's physiology, especially in the nervous system and its interaction with glands that secrete hormones. Psychobiologists study almost all behavioural phenomena that can be observed in non-human animals, including learning, memory, sensory processes, emotional behaviour, motivation, sexual behaviour and sleep, using a variety of techniques (see Chapter 4).

Psychophysiology is the measurement of people's physiological reactions, such as heart rate, blood pressure, electrical resistance of the skin, muscle tension and electrical activity of the brain (Andreassi, 2007). These measurements provide an indication of a person's degree of arousal or relaxation. Most psychophysiologists investigate phenomena such as sensory and perceptual responses, sleep, stress, thinking, reasoning and emotion.

Neuropsychology and **neuroscience** examine the relationship between the brain and **spinal cord**, and behaviour (Martin, 2006). Neuropsychology helps to shed light on the role of these structures in movement, vision, hearing, tasting, sleeping, smelling and touching as well as emotion, thinking, language and object recognition and perception, and others. Neuropsychologists normally (but not always) study patients who have suffered injury to the brain – through accident or disease – which disrupts functions such as speech

Cutting edge: Darkness and dishonesty

A group of Canadian and US researchers has suggested that darkness can not only produce anonymity for ne'er-do-wells but also provide the illusion of anonymity (Zhong *et al.*, 2010). In a series of experiments, people were more likely to cheat and accrue more unearned money when they were

in a slightly dimmed room than in a well-lit room. They also found that people who wore sunglasses behaved more selfishly than did those who wore clear glasses. Anonymity was a key mediator: those who thought that they were more anonymous behaved more dishonestly and selfishly.

Cutting edge: *Continued*

Utterly untrustworthy (see Zhong *et al.*, 2010).
Source: Rex Features: Miramax/Everett.

production or comprehension, object recognition, visual or auditory perception, and so on. **Clinical neuropsychology** involves the study of the effect of brain injury on behaviour and function.

Modern neuropsychology also relies on sophisticated brain imaging techniques such as positron emission tomography (PET) and functional magnetic resonance imaging (fMRI) which allow researchers to monitor the activity of processes in the brain as some psychological task is performed. This approach combines two approaches in psychology: neuroscience and cognitive psychology (see below). Because of this, the area of study is sometimes described as **cognitive neuroscience** (Gazzaniga, 1995) or behavioural neuroscience. A new development in this area has been the study of the psychobiological processes involved in social behaviour, a sub-branch called social neuroscience. Social neuroscientists examine the role of the brain in behaviours such as empathy, turn-taking, seeing things from another person's point of view, social interaction, political outlook, and so on. We look at the work of cognitive/behavioural/social

neuroscientists in more detail throughout this text (see in particular Chapter 4).

Comparative psychology is the study of the behaviour of members of a variety of species in an attempt to explain behaviour in terms of evolutionary adaptation to the environment. Comparative psychologists study behavioural phenomena similar to those studied by physiological psychologists. They are more likely than most other psychologists to study inherited behavioural patterns, such as courting and mating, predation and aggression, defensive behaviours and parental behaviours.

Closely tied to comparative psychology is **ethology**, the study of the biological basis of behaviour in the context of the evolution of development and function. Ethologists usually make their observations based on studies of animal behaviour in natural conditions and investigate topics such as instinct, social and sexual behaviour and cooperation. A sub-discipline of ethology is **sociobiology** which attempts to explain social behaviour in terms of biological inheritance and evolution. Ethology and sociobiology are described in more detail in Chapter 3. Evolutionary psychology studies 'human behaviour as a the product of evolved psychological mechanisms that depend on internal and environmental input for their development, activation, and expression in manifest behaviour' (Confer *et al.*, 2010, p. 110) (see Chapter 3). Although the basis of evolutionary psychology is found in the work of Charles Darwin (described in Chapter 3 and briefly below), as a sub-discipline it is relatively young having developed in the past 15 years.

Behaviour genetics is the branch of psychology that studies the role of genetics in behaviour (Plomin, 2008). The genes we inherit from our parents include a blueprint for the construction of a human brain. Each blueprint is a little different, which means that no two brains are exactly alike. Therefore, no two people will act exactly alike, even in an identical situation. Behaviour geneticists study the role of genetics in behaviour by examining similarities in physical and behavioural characteristics of blood relatives, whose genes are more similar than those of unrelated individuals. They also perform breeding experiments with laboratory animals to see what aspects of behaviour can be transmitted to an animal's offspring. Behavioural geneticists study the degree to which genetics are responsible for specific behaviours such as cognitive

ability. The work of behavioural geneticists is described in Chapter 3 and discussed in the context of intelligence research and personality in Chapters 11 and 14.

Cognitive psychology is the study of mental processes and complex behaviours such as perception, attention, learning, memory, concept formation and problem-solving. Explanations in cognitive psychology involve characteristics of inferred mental processes, such as imagery, attention, and mechanisms of language. Most cognitive psychologists do not study physiological mechanisms, but recently some have begun applying neuroimaging methods to studying cognitive function. A branch of cognitive psychology called **cognitive science** involves the modelling of human function using computer simulation or 'neural networks'. We briefly examine the contribution of such computer simulations to our understanding of behaviour in Chapters 7 and 10.

Developmental psychology is the study of physical, cognitive, emotional and social development, especially of children (Berk, 2009) but, more broadly, of humans from foetus to old age (these psychologists are sometimes called lifespan developmental psychologists). Some developmental psychologists study the effects of old age on behaviour and the body (a field called gerontology). Most developmental psychologists restrict their study to a

---

Cutting edge: See no evil? Not quite…

Turning a blind eye to something that is wrong, you would probably universally conclude, is morally indefensible. The fabled trio of monkeys (see no evil, hear no evil, . . . etc.) illustrates the dumb ignorance of a position where evil is allowed to prosper because it is ignored. But what if you could literally see no evil? How would your judgements of morality be made if, for example, you judged moral dilemmas with your eyes closed?

It sounds an odd question, but cast your mind back to the film *A Time to Kill*. Defence lawyer, Jake Brigance, asks the jury to close their eyes while he is summing up. The technique is adopted because lawyers think this helps people visualise events better. A study from a group of researchers from Harvard and Chicago Universities has now found that closing your eyes also influences your moral decision-making (Caruso and Gino, 2011).

In a series of four experiments, students were asked to make decisions when presented with a series of moral dilemmas. In one study, for example, people listened to a scenario where the participant was to hire a person in his company. A good friend rings up and suggests a potential candidate who is less qualified than the one the participant

has already considered. The friend offers the participant more business if the less-qualified candidate is employed. Should the participant accept the less-qualified person? Participants made the decision with eyes closed and open.

The researchers found that when eyes were closed, moral decisions were more black and white than when open: it discouraged dishonest behaviour strongly. Unethical behaviour was considered more unethical and ethical behaviour was considered more ethical when eyes were closed.

The effect was unrelated to attention (one argument suggested that people could visualise better with eyes closed and, therefore, pay more attention to detail). However, when attention was controlled for in another experiment, the same effect was found, suggesting that this factor does not influence the results. The authors suggest that there is something unique about having the eyes closed – they cite research showing how brain activation changes depending on whether a person listens to music with eyes open or the same music with eyes closed.

The message seems to be: don't turn a blind eye, close your eyes; then, think.

particular period of development, such as infancy, adolescence or old age. This field is described and illustrated in more detail in Chapter 12. The development of children's language is described in Chapter 10, and the effects of old age on cognition in Chapter 11.

Social psychology is the study of the effects of people on people. Social psychologists explore phenomena such as self-perception and the perception of others, cause-and-effect relations in human interactions, attitudes and opinions, interpersonal relationships, group dynamics and emotional behaviours, including aggression and sexual attraction (Hogg and Vaughan, 2007). Chapters 15 and 16 explore these issues and themes in social psychology. An example of how we interpret the social behaviour of others is considered in the Psychology in action section below.

Psychology in action: How to detect a liar

Take a look at this list of behaviours. Which do you think are characteristic of a person who is lying and why?

- Averting gaze
- Unnatural posture
- Posture change
- Scratching/touching parts of the body
- Playing with hair or objects
- Placing the hand over the mouth
- Placing the hand over the eyes

According to a standard manual of police interviewing, all of these features are characteristic of a liar (Inbau *et al.*, 1986). A study of participants in 75 countries found that 'averting gaze' was described as the best tell-tale sign of lying (Global Deception Research Team, 2006).

Unfortunately, despite the manual's exhortations and the international guesswork, none of these behaviours is actually reliably associated with deception and several studies have shown that general law enforcement officers are usually as poor as the average undergraduate at detecting truth and falsity. We can tell the difference between truth and falsity with 50% accuracy (Bond & DePaulo, 2006). Research by psychologists such as Aldert Vrij, for example, has highlighted how bad people are at detecting whether someone is telling the truth or is lying (Vrij, 2000, 2004b). They usually construct a false stereotype of a lying person which has little association with actual liars.

Studies of police officers and students report detection rates of between 40 and 60 per cent – a result no better than expected by chance (Vrij and Mann, 2001; Vrij, 2000). Police

Former American President Bill Clinton, British novelist Jeffrey Archer and former American President Richard Nixon. What features might have revealed that they were lying? Clinton claimed not to have had sexual relations with his intern, Monica Lewinsky, Jeffrey Archer was convicted of perjury and Richard Nixon authorised but denied the tapping of 17 government officials' and reporters' telephones and those of opponents at the Democratic National Committee headquarters at the Watergate apartments.

Source: Getty Images: Diana Walker/Time & Life Images (l); Matt Turner (c); Archive Photos (r).

officers and people who use the polygraph technique – the so-called lie detector – generally do no better than students (Ekman and O'Sullivan, 1991). The exception to this generally ignominious performance seems to be Secret Service agents (Ekman *et al.*, 1999). These groups tend to perform better than students and general law enforcement officers.

Perhaps the best detectors of dissembling would be those who routinely lie in order to get out of trouble. Researchers from the University of Gothenburg, Sweden (Hartwig *et al.*, 2004) found that criminals were significantly better than students at detecting liars. However, this finding was coloured by another – the criminals also detected fewer truth-tellers. The lie bias – that criminals are more likely to judge that someone is lying than telling the truth – might stem from the fact that criminals are naturally suspicious (because they are used to being lied to, whether in prison or in the context of their relationships with others) and because they themselves are practised liars (and, therefore, expect the worst of others).

In another study, adult male offenders from a medium security Canadian prison and a group of undergraduates were asked to recall four emotional events from their lives (Porter *et al.*, 2008) but lie about two of them. The researchers measured the number of illustrators (the use of hands to signify something), self-manipulations (touching/scratching the hand, head or body), frequency of head movement and number of smiles and laughs. Verbal indicators included the number of words spoken per minute, filled pauses ('umms' and 'ahs'), self-references and pauses that were longer than two seconds. Illustrators were higher when lying than when telling the truth in both groups. Offenders, however, used more self-manipulations when lying compared with non-offenders, a finding that seems to contradict previous studies. The authors suggest that this may be due to the specific context in which experiments take place, the type of lie, motivation, the consequences of the lie, and so on.

The offenders also smiled less than the students when lying about emotional events.

Of course, these deception studies are fairly artificial. Interviewing suspects, the police would argue, gives you much more information on which to base a judgement. So, does it? Studies have shown that people who observe such interviews are better at discriminating between truth-tellers and liars than are the interviewers themselves (Buller *et al.*, 1991; Granhag and Stromwall, 2001). Interviewers also showed evidence of truth bias – the tendency to declare that someone was saying the truth when they were not.

People tend to focus on different behavioural cues when deciding on whether a person is telling the truth or lying, with people relying on verbal cues when judging the truthfulness of a story and on non-verbal cues when the story is deceptive (Anderson *et al.*, 1999). A recent review suggests that the behaviours people claim to use when they detect lying are inaccurate, but the behaviours they actually use as cues show some overlap with objective clues (Hartwig and Bond, 2011).

So, what are the most reliable indices of lying? Is there a 'Pinocchio's nose'? Two of the most fairly reliable indicators appear to be a high-pitched voice and a decrease in hand movements. But the way in which people are asked to identify lying is also important. For example, people are less accurate detectors when asked, 'Is this person lying?' than when asked 'Does the person x sincerely like the person y?' (Vrij, 2001). When people are questioned indirectly they tend to focus on those behavioural cues that have been found to predict deception, such as decreased hand movement, rather than those that do not (Vrij, 2001).

New research on lying is presenting us with some counter intuitive and challenging findings about psychology and human behaviour. Often, as you saw in the Controversies in Psychological Science section earlier, these studies contradict 'received wisdom' and 'common sense'.

Individual differences is an area of psychology which examines individual differences in temperament and patterns of behaviour. Some examples of these include personality, intelligence, hand preference, sex and age. Chapters 11 and 14 describe some of these in detail.

Cross-cultural psychology is the study of the impact of culture on behaviour. The ancestors of people of different racial and ethnic groups lived in different environments which presented them with different problems and opportunities for solving those problems. Different cultures have, therefore, developed different strategies for adapting to their environments. These strategies show themselves in laws, customs, myths, religious beliefs and ethical principles as well as

in thinking, health beliefs and approaches to problem-solving. A slightly different name – **cultural psychology** – is given to the study of variations within cultures (not necessarily across cultures). Throughout the book, you will find a section entitled, '... An international perspective', which takes a topic in psychology and examines how it has been studied cross-culturally, e.g. Are personality traits, recognition of emotion, memory, mental illness, and so on culture-specific?

Forensic and **criminological psychology** applies psychological knowledge to the understanding, prediction and nature of crime and behaviour related to crime. There is a distinction between criminological and forensic psychology. Forensic psychologists can be commissioned by courts to prepare reports on the fitness of a defendant to stand trial, on the general psychological state of the defendant, on aspects of psychological research (such as post-traumatic stress disorders), on the behaviour of children involved in custody disputes, and so on. Criminological psychology refers to the application of psychological principles to the criminal justice system. The terms, however, are often used interchangeably.

Clinical psychology is probably the field most closely identified with applied psychology and psychology in general and aims 'to reduce psychological distress and to enhance and promote psychological well-being' (BPS Division of Clinical Psychology, 2012). It is an applied branch of psychology because clinical psychologists do not work in the laboratory under well-controlled experimental conditions but out in the field (usually clinic or hospital), applying the knowledge gained from practice and research. Clinical psychologists address problems caused by mental illnesses (see Chapter 18), and mental illness is one of the most widely misunderstood illnesses and the most peculiarly reported. It is also one of the most stigmatised – people feel embarrassed about mental illness and others may respond to sufferers unsympathetically because they do not understand the disorder. Hence, public figures such as the former UK government Director of Communications, Alastair Campbell, the comedian, Ruby Wax, and the actor and writer, Stephen Fry, have made their illnesses known and have promoted their public understanding.

Whether such promotion and the emphasis on illness succeeds in making the stigma less strident, however, is unclear. When Read and Harre (2001) asked psychology students questions such as would you be happy being romantically involved with someone who has spent time in a psychiatric hospital, those who were more likely to believe in biological/genetic causes of mental disorder were more likely to avoid mentally ill people and regard the mentally ill as unpredictable and dangerous. This finding was replicated in a study in which people saw a man hallucinating and expressing delusions – when his behaviour was given a biological or genetic explanation, people were more likely to regard him as dangerous and unpredictable (Walker and Read, 2002).

An analysis of the portrayal of mental illness in a week's worth of children's programmes on two television stations in New Zealand found that over 45 per cent contained reference to mental illness and most of these were: 'crazy', 'mad' and 'losing your mind', although 'mad' and 'crazy' were interchangeably used to mean 'angry' (Wilson *et al.*, 2000). Other terms included 'driven bananas', 'wacko', 'nuts', 'loony', 'cuckoo' and 'freak'. Mental illness was frequently portrayed as reflecting a loss of control. Characters at the receiving end of these epithets were routinely and invariably seen as negative, as objects of amusement or derision or as objects of fear. The characters were either comical or villainous. Psychologists have identified views such as these and proposed ways of changing them (see Chapter 18).

Alastair Campbell and Ruby Wax, two tireless campaigners for the public undertstanding of mental illness.
Source: Corbis: Robbie Jack (l); Reuters (r)

Health psychology is the study of the ways in which behaviour and lifestyle can affect health and illness (Sarafino, 2011). For example, smoking is associated with a number of illnesses and is a risk factor for serious illness and death. Health psychologists study what makes people initiate and maintain such unhealthy behaviour and can help devise strategies to reduce it. Health psychologists are employed in a variety of settings including hospitals, government, universities and private practice (see Chapter 17).

Educational psychology is another branch of applied psychology. Educational psychologists assess the behavioural problems of children at school and suggest ways in which these problems may be remedied. For example, the educational psychologist might identify a child's early inability to read (dyslexia) and suggest a means by which this may be overcome through special training. The educational psychologist might also deal with all aspects relevant to a child's schooling such as learning, social relations, assessment, disruptive behaviour, substance abuse, bullying and parental neglect.

Consumer psychology is the study of the motivation, perception, learning, cognition and purchasing behaviour of individuals in the marketplace and their use of products once they reach the home. Some consumer psychologists take a marketer's perspective, some take a consumer's perspective, and some adopt a neutral perspective, especially if they work at a university.

Organisational or occupational psychology is one of the largest and oldest fields of applied psychology and involves the study of the ways in which individuals and groups perform and behave in the workplace (Huczynski and Buchanan, 2010). Early organisational psychologists concentrated on industrial work processes (such as the most efficient way to shovel coal), but organisational psychologists now spend more effort analysing modern plants and offices. Most are employed by large companies and organisations.

A related branch, ergonomics or human factors psychology, focuses mainly on the ways in which people and machines work together. They study machines ranging from cockpits to computers, from robots to MP3/4 players, from transportation vehicles for the disabled to telephones. If the machine is well designed, the task can be much easier, more enjoyable and safer. Ergonomists help designers and engineers to design better machines; because of this, the terms ergonomics and engineering psychology are sometimes used interchangeably.

Sport and exercise psychology applies psychological principles to the area of sport. It also involves the study of the effects of sport and exercise on mood, cognition, well-being and physiology. This area is examined in more detail in Chapter 17.

Psychology: a European perspective

Psychology is one of the most popular degree courses in Europe. In 2009–10, psychology was the sixth most popular UK university degree in terms of applications (see Table 1.3). It is estimated that one in 850 people in the Netherlands has a degree in psychology (Van Drunen, 1995), and no course is more popular in Sweden (Persson, 1995).

Modern psychology has its origins in Europe: the first psychological laboratory was established in Europe and some of the first designated university degrees in psychology were established there. Research in North America

Psychology – An international perspective

Behind almost all research endeavours in psychology is a common aim: to discover a psychological universal. According to Norenzayan and Heine (2005), **psychological universals** are 'core mental attributes shared by humans everywhere'. That is, they are conclusions from psychological research that can be generalised across groups – ways of reasoning, thinking, making decisions, interpreting why people behave in the way that they do, recognising emotions and so on, are all examples of core mental attributes. A sound case for a psychological universal can be made if a phenomenon exists in a large variety of different cultures.

However, some differences may be more obvious in some groups than others – men and women, for example, the young and the old, the mentally ill and the mentally healthy, and so on. At this level of analysis, we cannot say that people in general behave in a particular way, but that a specific group of people behave in a particular way. Nowhere is this more relevant than when considering the role of culture in psychological studies. A variety of behaviours are absent or are limited in a variety of cultures and nations. Some recent research, for example, has highlighted significant differences between Western and Asian cultures in the types of autobiographical memory they recall, the parts of a landscape and photograph they focus on, and the way in which they draw and take a photograph (Varnum *et al.*, 2010). Table 1.2 summarises some of these differences.

Varnum *et al.* have noted that cultures can differ according to their social orientation so that some are independent and analytical and others are interdependent and holistic. Independent cultures emphasise the importance of self-direction, autonomy, the enhancement of self at the expense of others and they are self-expressive; interdependent cultures believe in being connected with others, working and living harmoniously and enhancement of the self at the expense of others is absent. The most common examples of such cultures are Western and East Asian, respectively, although these are very large categories and there will be considerable variation within them, let alone between them.

Northern Italians, for example, appear to be more independent than Southern Italians (Martella and Maass, 2000), are more analytic and categorise objects more taxonomically (Knight and Nisbett, 2007). Villages in the Black Sea region of Turkey also differ according to the type of economic activity they engage in. So, fishermen and farmers categorised objects more thematically and perceived scenes more contextually than did herders (Uskul *et al.*, 2008). People who move and move often are more likely to show a personal than a collective sense of identity (Oishi, 2010).

Some countries appear to bridge the two types of approach. Russians, for example, appear to be more interdependent than are Germans (Naumov, 1996) and they reason and visually perceive stimuli more holistically (looking at the whole and the context, rather than a part of a scene, say). Croats show a similar pattern of behaviour to Russians (Varnum *et al.*, 2008).

A way of demonstrating a psychological universal is to examine a behaviour in three or more cultures, two of which are very different, with a third falling between them, and see how each differs from, or is similar to, the other. The best way, however, is to examine a variety of cultures, as Daly and Wilson (1988) did. Their research examined sex differences in the international rates of homicide and found that men were more likely to kill men than women were to kill women across all cultures. Debate then ensues as to why this universal should be (and that debate is often heated, as most in psychology are).

In the book, examples of universals (and exceptions) are described in the sections: '. . . An international perspective'. These will help you put the findings you read about into some form of cultural or international context. They should also help demonstrate that although studies sometimes report findings as being absolute and generalisable to populations in general, sometimes these findings are not.

Table 1.2 Behaviours/concepts reported to vary across cultures, or which may be less evident in certain cultures. Unfamiliar terms are defined in the chapters referred to in brackets

- Memory for and categorisation of colours (see Chapter 6)
- Spatial reasoning (see Chapter 8)
- Autobiographical memory (see Chapter 8)
- Perception of the environment
- Appreciation of art
- Some types of category-based inductive reasoning (see Chapter 11)
- Some perceptual illusions
- Some ways of approaching reasoning
- Aspects of numerical reasoning
- Risk preferences in decision-making (see Chapter 11)
- Self-concept (see Chapters 15 and 16)
- Similarity-attraction effect (see Chapters 15 and 16)
- Approach-avoidance motivation (see Chapter 13)
- The fundamental attribution error (see Chapters 15 and 16)
- Predilection for aggression
- Feelings of control, dominance or subordination
- High subjective well-being and positive affect
- Communication style
- Prevalence of major depression
- Prevalence of eating disorders (see Chapter 13)
- Mental illness (see Chapter 18)
- Noun bias in language learning (see Chapter 10)
- Moral reasoning
- Prevalence of different attachment style (see Chapter 12)
- Disruptive behaviour in adolescence
- Personality types (see Chapter 14)
- Response bias (see Chapter 2)
- Recognition of emotion
- Perception of happiness
- Body shape preference

Source: Adapted from Norenzayan and Heine, 2005.

Table 1.3 The top degree subjects in the UK, as indexed by number of applications to study 2009/10

Business studies	43,785
Nursing	34,370
Design studies	24,805
Management studies	24,790
Computing science	24,485
Psychology	23,130
Law	17,480

and Europe accounts for the majority of psychological studies published in the world (Eysenck, 2001) and there continues to be debate over whether these two fairly large 'geographical' areas adopt genuinely different approaches to the study of psychological processes (G. N. Martin, 2001).

Psychology as a discipline occupies a different status in different European countries and each country has established its own degrees and societies at different times, for historical or political reasons. Almost all countries have a professional organisation which regulates the activity of psychologists or provides psychological training or licensing of psychologists. The first such association in Denmark was founded in 1929 (the Psychotechnical Institute in Copenhagen) and what we would now call educational psychology formed the basis of the professional training it provided: the job of the institute was to select apprentices for the printing trade (Foltveld, 1995). The Netherlands' first psychological laboratory was founded in 1892 at Gröningen, Denmark's in 1944 at the University of Copenhagen and Finland's in 1921 by Eino Kaila at the University of Turku (Saari, 1995). Coincidentally, 1921 was also the year in which the Netherlands passed a Higher Education Act allowing philosophy students to specialise in psychology.

The British Psychological Society (BPS) was formed in 1901, with laboratories established at the University of Cambridge and University College London in 1897, closely followed by the establishment of laboratories in Aberdeen, Edinburgh and Glasgow (Lunt, 1995). Sweden's professional association was founded in 1955 (Sveriges Psykologforbund), with the Netherlands' pre-dating that in 1938 (Nederlandsch Instituut van Practizeerende Psychologen, or NIPP). Portugal is one of the younger psychology nations – the first students of psychology graduated in 1982 (Pereira, 1995). Because of the history of the country, psychology was not acknowledged as a university subject in Portugal until after the democratic revolution of 1974.

Psychological training and status of psychology in Europe

The types of career that psychology graduates pursue are similar across most European countries. Most psychologists are employed in the public sector, with the majority of those working in the clinical, educational or organisational fields. Training for psychologists varies between countries and controversy surrounds the licensing or the legalisation of the profession. For example, psychologists in almost all countries wish for formal statutory regulation of the profession (the medical and legal professions are regulated). In Denmark, the title of psychologist was legally protected in 1993 so that no one could call themselves a psychologist unless they had received specified training. In Greece, a law was passed in 1979 licensing psychologists to practise (Georgas, 1995). These enlightened views have not extended to some other countries, however, despite the attempts of professional organisations in lobbying their legislators. Finland and the UK have faced obstacles in legalising the profession.

The BPS has its own regulatory system so that applied psychologists need to undergo an approved route of training (to go on to practise as forensic, clinical, educational, health psychologists, for example) before they are recognised as qualified professional psychologists by the Society. Most of these individuals choose to register themselves as Chartered Psychologists – a person using the services of a psychologist designated chartered can, therefore, be assured that the person is a recognised professional psychologist.

European views of psychology and psychologists

Non-psychologists' views of what psychology is and what psychologists do are encouragingly positive and generally accurate although their knowledge of psychological research (as you saw earlier) is flawed. Table 1.4 shows you the responses of an Austrian sample to the question, 'What do you expect a psychologist to do?', and to the sentence, 'Psychologists can . . .' (Friedlmayer and Rossler, 1995).

A Finnish study which asked adults to rate which of a number of professions was more knowledgeable about human nature found that 53 per cent believed doctors were more knowledgeable, with psychologists following behind in second place (29 per cent) (Montin, 1995). A Norwegian study, however, found the opposite: 49 per cent chose psychologists and 23 per cent chose doctors (Christiansen, 1986). Figures 1.2 (a)–(d) give some of the other illuminating responses to the other questions asked in the Finnish survey. These not only reveal how

Table 1.4 Austrian views of psychologists (based on a sample of 300 respondents)

Statement/question	%
'Psychologists can . . .'	
See through other people	68
Help other people to change	72
Help others to help themselves	90
Exert influence through reports	57
Release people from mental suffering	62
Listen patiently	88
Direct the attention of social policy-makers	53
Handle children well	55
Cause harm by making mistaken diagnoses	68
Make people happier	54
Statement/question	**%**
'What do you expect a psychologist to do?'	
Talk	97
Test	90
File a report	85
Treatment/therapy	91
Train children	46
Proposing interventions	86
Negotiate conflicts	65
Give guidance and advice	94
Solve problems	44

Source: Based on Friedlmayer, S. and Rossler, E., Professional identity and public image of Austrian psychologists. Reproduced with permission from *Psychology in Europe* by A. Schorr and S. Saari (eds), ISBN 0-88937-155-5, © Hogrefe & Huber Publishers, Seattle, Toronto, Göttingen, Bern.

people receive or obtain their information about psychology but also show that the discipline is still shrouded in some mystery – 49 per cent declare knowing only 'a little' about psychology. Mercifully, 75 per cent of respondents disagreed that psychologists could read minds.

Psychology: the development of a science

Although philosophers and other thinkers have been concerned with psychological issues for centuries, the science of psychology is comparatively young. To understand how this science came into being, it is useful to trace its roots back through philosophy and the natural sciences. These disciplines originally provided the methods we use to study human behaviour and took many centuries to develop.

Philosophical roots of psychology

Animism

Each of us is conscious of our own existence. Furthermore, we are aware of this consciousness. Although we often find ourselves doing things that we had not planned to do (or had planned not to do), by and large we feel that we are in control of our behaviour. That is, we have the impression that our conscious mind controls our behaviour. We consider alternatives, make plans, and then act. We get our bodies moving; we engage in behaviour.

Earlier in human history, philosophers attributed a life-giving animus, or spirit, to anything that seemed to move or grow independently. Because they believed that the movements of their own bodies were controlled by their minds or spirits, they inferred that the sun, moon, wind, tides and other moving entities were similarly animated. This primitive philosophy is called **animism** (from the Latin *animare*, 'to quicken, enliven, endow with breath or soul'). Even gravity was explained in animistic terms: rocks fell to the ground because the spirits within them wanted to be reunited with Mother Earth.

Obviously, animism is now of historical interest only. But note that different interpretations can be placed on the same events. Surely, we are just as prone to subjective interpretations of natural phenomena, albeit more sophisticated ones, as our ancestors were. In fact, when we try to explain why people do what they do, we tend to attribute at least some of their behaviour to the action of a motivating spirit – namely, a will. In our daily lives, this explanation of behaviour may often suit our needs. However, on a scientific level, we need to base our explanations on phenomena that can be observed and measured objectively. We cannot objectively and directly observe 'will'.

Dualism: René Descartes

Although the history of Western philosophy properly begins with the Ancient Greeks, a French philosopher and mathematician, René Descartes (1596–1650), is regarded as the father of modern philosophy. He advocated a sober, impersonal investigation of natural phenomena using sensory experience and human reasoning. He assumed that the world was a purely mechanical entity that, having once been set in motion by God, ran its course without divine interference. Thus, to understand the world, one had only to understand how it was constructed. This stance challenged the established authority of the Church, which believed that the purpose of philosophy was to reconcile human experiences with the truth of God's revelations.

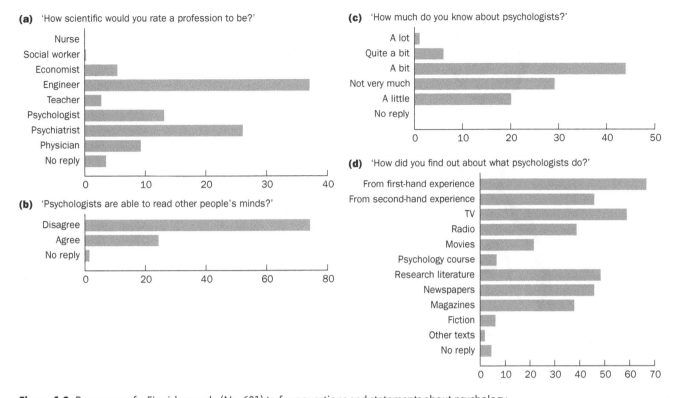

Figure 1.2 Responses of a Finnish sample (*N* = 601) to four questions and statements about psychology.

Source: Montin, S. The public image of psychologists in Finland. Reproduced with permission from *Psychology in Europe* by A. Schorr and S. Saari (eds), ISBN 0-88937-155-5, © 1995, Hogrefe & Huber Publishers, Seattle, Toronto, Göttingen, Bern.

RENÉ DESCARTES
Né à La Haye en 1596.

René Descartes (1596–1650).
Source: Corbis: Chris Hellier.

To Descartes, animals were mechanical devices; their behaviour was controlled by environmental stimuli. His view of the human body was much the same: it was a machine. Thus, Descartes was able to describe some movements as automatic and involuntary. For example, the application of a hot object to a finger would cause an almost immediate withdrawal of the arm away from the source of stimulation. Reactions like this did not require participation of the mind; they occurred automatically. Descartes called these actions **reflexes** (from the Latin *reflectere*, 'to bend back upon itself'). A stimulus registered by the senses produces a reaction that would be entirely physical and beyond voluntary control. There would be no intention or will to produce this physical reaction. Consider the well-known reflex of sensing the heat of a flame, as seen in Figure 1.3. The body recoils from flame in an involuntary way: we do not intentionally move away from the flame but our body reflexively puts in place a chain of muscle contractions which make us withdraw. The term 'reflex' is still in use today, but, of course, we explain the operation of a reflex differently (see Chapter 4).

What set humans apart from the rest of the world, according to Descartes, was their possession of a mind. This was a uniquely human attribute and was not

Figure 1.3 Descartes's diagram of a withdrawal reflex.
Source: Stock Montage, Inc.

subject to the laws of the universe. Thus, Descartes was a proponent of **dualism**, the belief that all reality can be divided into two distinct entities: mind and matter (this is often referred to as **Cartesian dualism**). He distinguished between 'extended things', or physical bodies, and 'thinking things', or minds. Physical bodies, he believed, do not think, and minds are not made of ordinary matter.

Although Descartes was not the first to propose dualism, his thinking differed from that of his predecessors in one important way: he was the first to suggest that a link exists between the human mind and its purely physical housing. Although later philosophers pointed out that this theoretical link actually contradicted his belief in dualism - the proposal of an interaction between mind and matter - **interactionism**, was absolutely vital to the development of the science of psychology.

From the time of Plato onwards, philosophers had argued that the mind and the body were different entities. They also suggested that the mind could influence the body but the body could not influence the mind, a little like a puppet and puppeteer with the mind pulling the strings of the body. Not all philosophers adopted this view, however. To some, such as Spinoza (1632–1677), both mental events (thinking) and physical events (such as occupying space) were characteristic of one and the

same thing, in the same way that an undulating line can be described as convex or concave – it cannot be described as exclusively one thing or another (this is called **double-aspect theory**).

Descartes hypothesised that this interaction between mind and body took place in the pineal body, a small organ situated at the top of the **brain stem**, buried beneath the large cerebral hemispheres of the brain. When the mind decided to perform an action, it tilted the pineal body in a particular direction, causing fluid to flow from the brain into the proper set of **nerves**. This flow of fluid caused the appropriate muscles to inflate and move.

How did Descartes come up with this mechanical concept of the body's movements? Western Europe in the seventeenth century was the scene of great advances in the sciences. This was the century, for example, in which William Harvey discovered that blood circulated around the body. It was not just the practical application of science that impressed Europeans, however, it was the beauty, imagination and fun of it as well. Craftsmen constructed many elaborate mechanical toys and devices during this period. The young Descartes was greatly impressed by the moving statues in the Royal Gardens (Jaynes, 1970) and these devices served as models for Descartes as he theorised about how the body worked. He conceived of the muscles as balloons. They became inflated when a fluid passed through the nerves that connected them to the brain and spinal cord, just as water flowed through pipes to activate the statues. This inflation was the basis of the muscular contraction that causes us to move.

Descartes's influence on the development of psychology was considerable. He proposed the revolutionary idea that the mind and the body were mutually interacting and suggested a method of studying 'the mind' which was based on reasoning and not metaphysical analysis. Descartes's notion of interactionism gave rise to two very influential but very different schools of thought in psychology at the end of the nineteenth and the beginning of the twentieth centuries: introspectionism and behaviourism. We consider these later in the chapter.

Empiricism: John Locke and David Hume

A prevalent belief in the seventeenth century was that ideas were innately present in our minds from birth. The English philosopher John Locke (1632–1704) rejected this belief. Instead, he proposed that all knowledge must come through experience: it is empirically derived. Descartes's rationalism – pursuit of truth through reason – was replaced by **empiricism** – pursuit of truth through observation and experience (in Greek, *empeiria* means experience). His model of the mind was a tablet of soft clay, a tabula rasa, smooth at birth and ready to accept the writings of experience imprinted upon it. Locke believed that our knowledge of complex experiences was nothing more than links between simple, primary sensations: simple ideas combined to form complex ones.

This idea was developed further by the Scottish philosopher David Hume (1711–76). In his book *A Treatise of Human Nature* (1739), Hume argued that the study of human nature could best be undertaken through experience and observation. Whereas Locke wrote of ideas, Hume wrote of perceptions which were composed of impressions and ideas. Impressions were what we would consider sensations – seeing print on a paper or hearing a loud bang; ideas were the less vivid recollection of such sense experiences. Impressions, according to Hume, were the most important perceptions because these were derived directly from observation. Any ideas based on content which was not derived empirically were not valuable and not trustworthy. Hume, therefore, espoused what is known as **positivism** – the school of thought which argues that all meaningful ideas can be reduced to observable material.

Perhaps Hume's greatest contribution to psychology was the **doctrine of the association of ideas**. In *An Inquiry Concerning Human Understanding* (1748), Hume argued that there were various types of connection or association between ideas. This was not itself a new idea. Aristotle had proposed the notion that two stimuli if paired frequently enough would result in the presentation of one event stimulating thoughts of the other. Hume suggested three specific types of association: resemblance (when we look at someone's photograph, for example, this triggers off thoughts about that person), contiguity (thoughts of an object or event will trigger thoughts related to those objects and events), and cause and effect (the idea that actions have identifiable causes). These associations were the 'cement' that helped bind the universe, and all complex human experiences were based on simple ideas derived from impressions. The most important of these associations was cause and effect, and Hume developed this theme by describing behaviour in terms of custom and habit. An act which produces an effect and which makes a repetition of that act likely is a habit or custom. Think of a simple behaviour such as switching on a light. Your knowledge that switching a light on will illuminate a room leads to the habitual pressing the switch if you need light. These notions of habit and causality became very important in the twentieth century with the development of behaviourism and the work of the Swiss developmental psychologist Jean Piaget (1896–1980) (see Chapter 12).

Idealism: Bishop Berkeley

In contrast to the empiricists, the Irish bishop, philosopher and mathematician George Berkeley (1685–1753) believed that our knowledge of events in the world did not come simply from direct experience. Instead, Berkeley (who gave his name to the famous university in California) argued that this knowledge is the result of inferences based on the accumulation of past experiences derived through the senses. In other words, we must learn how to perceive. For example, our visual perception of depth involves several elementary sensations, such as observing the relative movements of objects as we move our head and the convergence of our eyes (turning inward towards each other or away) as we focus on near or distant objects. Although our knowledge of visual depth seems to be immediate and direct, it is actually a secondary, complex response constructed from a number of simple elements. The aspect of Berkeley's philosophy which argues that all ideas come from the senses (*esse est percipi*) is called **idealism**.

Materialism: James Mill

With the work of the Scottish philosopher James Mill (1773–1836), the pendulum took its full swing from animism (physical matter animated by spirits) to materialism (mind composed entirely of matter). **Materialism** is the belief that reality can be known only through an understanding of the physical world, of which the mind is a part. Mill worked on the assumption that humans and animals were fundamentally the same. Both humans and animals were thoroughly physical in their make-up and were completely subject to the physical laws of the universe. He agreed in essence with Descartes's approach to understanding the human body but rejected the concept of an immaterial mind. Mind, to Mill, was as passive as the body. It responded to the environment in precisely the same way. The mind, like the body, was a machine.

In the nineteenth century, the philosophy of the past began to make way for the experimentation. In the latter part of the century, a part of Germany gave birth to modern psychology as we know it. Its midwife was Wilhelm Wundt.

Modern psychology: from the Leipzig laboratory to the cognitive revolution

Wilhelm Wundt (1832–1920) was the first person to call himself a psychologist and he shared the conviction of other German scientists that all aspects of nature, including the human mind, could be studied scientifically, an approach summarised in his book *Principles of Physiological Psychology*, the first textbook in psychology.

Wundt's approach was experimental in nature and his and his colleagues' work was conducted at the Leipzig laboratory, 200 km south of Berlin. Over 100 studies were conducted in the first 20 years of the laboratory's life. Initially, these were studies of the psychological and psychophysiological aspects of vision (seeing), audition (hearing) and somatosensation (feeling and touching). Later work focused on reaction time and the process involved in perceiving and then responding to a stimulus. Wundt also explored the nature of attention and emotional feeling as well as word association.

The fact that Germany was the birthplace of psychology had as much to do with social, political and economic influences as with the abilities of its scientists and scholars. The academic tradition in Germany emphasised a scientific approach to a large number of subject areas, such as history, phonetics, archaeology, aesthetics and literature. Thus, in contrast to French and British scholars, who adopted the more traditional, philosophical approach to the study of the human mind, German scholars were open to the possibility that the human mind could be studied scientifically. Experimental physiology, one of the most important roots of **experimental psychology**, was well established there. Eventually, Wundt's influence began to extend to other parts of Europe (especially the UK) and to the US.

Structuralism: Wilhelm Wundt

Wundt defined psychology as the 'science of immediate experience', and his approach was called **structuralism**,

Wilhelm Wundt (1832–1920).
Source: Corbis: Bettmann.

the first proper school of thought to emerge in the history of psychology. Its subject matter was the structure of the mind, built from the elements of consciousness, such as ideas and sensations. These elements could be constructed into a table of elements similar to the periodic table of elements. Structuralism's raw material was supplied by trained observers who described their own experiences under well-controlled conditions. The observers were taught to engage in **introspection** (literally, 'looking within'), the use of which was governed by strict rules. Introspectionists observed stimuli and described their experiences. It was intensive training: they had to produce approximately 10,000 introspective observations before their data were considered valid (Boring,1953).

Wundt's aims were threefold: to analyse the contents of conscious experience, to determine how the elements of consciousness are connected, and to devise a law which would explain such connections. Wundt and his associates, Edward Tichener (1867–1927) and Gustav Fechner (1801–87), made inferences about the nature of mental processes by seeing how changes in the stimuli caused changes in the verbal reports of their trained observers.

Wundt was particularly interested in the problem that had intrigued Berkeley: how did basic sensory information give rise to complex perceptions? His **doctrine of apperception** attempted to account for the fact that when we perceive, this perception is of a whole object and not separate elements of it. We see wholes, according to Wundt, because of the process of creative synthesis (or law of psychic resultants): a process which combines or synthesises elements to form a whole. Again, this process is very similar to a process in chemistry in which individual chemical elements when combined will form a new, wholly different entity. The whole would not be equivalent to the sum of its parts. Much of Wundt's work, however, aimed to break down and analyse the contents of the mind rather than determine how they are combined.

Wundt's method did not survive the test of time; structuralism died out in the early twentieth century. The major problem with his approach was the difficulty encountered by observers in reporting the raw data of sensation, data unmodified by experience. Although introspectionism aimed to establish well-controlled experimental conditions which would lead to reliable introspective observations, there was often little agreement between observers about their introspections. The method was also criticised for its reliance on retrospection; the recollection of an experience was frequently elicited some time after the experience itself had occurred and was, therefore, subject to error. In addition, attention began to shift from study of the human mind to the study of observable human behaviour. Behaviourism provided a devastating and critical alternative to introspectionism (see below).

Although structuralism has been supplanted, Wundt's contribution must be acknowledged. He was responsible for establishing psychology as a recognised, experimental science that was separate from philosophy. He used methods which involved observation and experimentation and trained a great number of psychologists, many of whom established their own schools and continued the evolution of the new discipline.

Memory: Hermann Ebbinghaus

Most of the pioneers of psychology founded schools, groups of people having a common belief in a particular theory and methodology. The exception to this trend was Hermann Ebbinghaus (1850–1909). In 1876, after receiving his Ph.D. in philosophy but still unattached to an academic institution, Ebbinghaus came across a second-hand copy of a book by Gustav Fechner describing a mathematical approach to the measurement of human sensation. Intrigued by Fechner's research, Ebbinghaus decided to attempt to measure human memory: the processes of learning and forgetting.

Working alone, Ebbinghaus devised methods to measure memory and the speed with which forgetting occurred. He realised that he could not compare the learning and forgetting of two prose passages or two poems because some passages would undoubtedly be easier to learn than others. Therefore, he devised a relatively uniform set of materials – nonsense syllables, such as 'juz', 'bul' and 'gof'. He printed the syllables on cards and read through a set of them, with the rate of presentation controlled by the ticking of a watch. After reading the set, he paused a fixed amount of time, then read the cards again. He recorded the number of times he had to read the cards to be able to recite them without error. He measured forgetting by trying to recite the nonsense syllables on a later occasion – minutes, hours or days later. The number of syllables he remembered was an index of the percentage of memory that had been retained.

Ebbinghaus's approach to memory was entirely empirical; he devised no theory of why learning occurs and was interested only in gathering facts through careful, systematic observation. However, despite the lack of theory, his work made important contributions to the development of the science of psychology. He introduced the principle of eliminating **variable errors** by making observations repeatedly on different occasions (using different lists each time) and calculating the average of these observations. Variable errors include errors caused by random differences in the subject's mood or alertness or by uncontrollable changes in the environment. He constructed graphs of the rate at which the memorised lists of nonsense syllables were forgotten, which provided a way to measure mental contents across time. Ebbinghaus's research provided a model of systematic, rigorous experimental procedures that modern psychologists still emulate (see Chapter 8).

Functionalism: William James and James Angell

After structuralism, the next major trend in psychology was **functionalism** which began in the US and was, in large part, a protest against the structuralism of Wundt. Structuralists were interested in what they called the *components* of consciousness (ideas and sensations); functionalists were more interested in the *process* of conscious activity (perceiving and learning). Functionalism grew from the new perspective on nature provided by Charles Darwin and his followers. Proponents of functionalism stressed the biological significance (the purpose, or function) of natural processes, including behaviours. The emphasis was on overt, observable behaviours, not on private mental events.

The most important psychologist to embrace functionalism was William James (1842–1910), brother of novelist Henry. As James said, 'My thinking is first, last, and always for the sake of my doing.' That is, thinking was not an end in itself; its function was to produce useful behaviours. Although James was a champion of experimental psychology, he did not appear to enjoy doing research, instead spending most of his time reading, thinking, teaching and writing during his tenure as professor of philosophy (later, professor of psychology) at Harvard University.

William James (1842–1910).
Source: Corbis: Bettmann.

Unlike structuralism, functionalism was not supplanted; instead, its major tenets were absorbed by its successor, behaviourism. One of the last of the functionalists, James Angell (1869–1949), described its basic principles:

- Functional psychology is the study of mental operations and not mental structures. It is not enough to compile a catalogue of what the mind does; one must try to understand what the mind accomplishes by doing this.
- Mental processes are not studied as isolated and independent events but as part of the biological activity of the organism. These processes are aspects of the organism's adaptation to the environment and are a product of its evolutionary history. For example, the fact that we are conscious implies that consciousness has adaptive value for our species.
- Functional psychology studies the relation between the environment and the response of the organism to the environment. There is no meaningful distinction between mind and body, they are part of the same entity.

Evolution and heritability: Charles Darwin and Francis Galton

While Wundt was developing the experimental basis of psychology in Leipzig, another thinker – not a psychologist – was on the verge of making one of the most important contributions to the understanding of behaviour. Charles Darwin (1809–82) proposed the theory of evolution in his book *On the Origin of Species by Means of Natural Selection,* published in 1859. His work, more than that of any other person, revolutionised biology. The concept of natural selection showed how the consequences of an animal's characteristics affect its ability to survive. Instead of simply identifying, describing and naming species, biologists began now to look at the adaptive significance of the ways in which species differed.

Darwin's theory suggested that behaviours, like other biological characteristics, could best be explained by understanding their role in the adaptation of an organism (a human or other animal) to its environment. Thus, behaviour has a biological context. Darwin assembled evidence that behaviours, like body parts, could be inherited. In *The Expression of the Emotions in Man and Animals*, published in 1873, he proposed that the facial gestures that animals make in expressing emotions were descended from movements that previously had other functions. New areas of exploration were opened for psychologists by the ideas that an evolutionary continuity existed among the various species of animals and that

behaviours, like parts of the body, had evolutionary histories. Darwin's notion of natural selection has had great impact on the way in which we view the genetic determinants of behaviour (see Chapter 3).

One of the first psychologists to study the influence of genetics on human behaviour was Sir Francis Galton (1822–1911), Darwin's first cousin. Galton was a polymath who made many other contributions to the field of science: he constructed the first weather maps of the British Isles, discovered and named the weather phenomenon known as anticyclone, invented the term 'correlation' (which describes the statistical relationships between two variables or factors), developed the technique of fingerprinting, founded the discipline of psychometrics, which applies statistical principles to the measurement of individual differences and the construction of psychological tests, and established the Anthropometric Laboratory in London in 1884, the birthplace of intelligence testing.

Galton was interested in discovering whether people's physical features correlated with each other and whether such correlations occurred for psychological features such as sensory capacity, reaction time, intellect and eminence. In fact, Galton did find that features such as height, arm length and weight were highly and positively correlated and argued from this that if one part of the body's dimensions were known then one could construct the rest of the body to scale.

Importantly, Galton was the first to provide statistical evidence for the heritability of psychological variables. In his study of eminent men, published in his book *Hereditary Genius* (Galton, 1869), Galton found that 31 per cent of illustrious men had eminent fathers and 48 per cent of these men had eminent sons. Of course, by today's standards, this study has several methodological shortcomings, not least of which is the collection of data from eminent men only (to make a valid comparison, you would also need to look at non-eminent men and their offspring). There is also the argument that eminence may not have been inherited but had been determined by the environment in which these men were raised (issues discussed in detail in Chapters 3 and 11). However, Galton remains an important figure in the history of psychology. His greatest contribution is the establishment of the study of individual differences as a scientific enterprise.

Psychodynamic theory: Sigmund Freud

While psychology was developing as a fledgling science, Sigmund Freud (1856–1939) was formulating a theory of human behaviour that would greatly affect psychology and psychiatry (not necessarily for the good) and radically influence intellectual thinking of all kinds.

Freud began his career as a neurologist, so his work was originally firmly rooted in biology. He soon became interested in behavioural and emotional problems and began formulating his psychodynamic theory of personality, which would evolve over his long career. Although his approach was based on observation of patients and not on scientific experiments, he remained convinced that the biological basis of his theory would eventually be established.

Freud and his theory are discussed in detail in Chapter 14 (Personality), but he is mentioned here to mark his place in the history of psychology. Freud's theory of the mind included structures, but his structuralism was quite different from Wundt's. He devised his concepts of ego, superego, id and other mental structures through talking with his patients, not through laboratory experiments. His hypothetical mental operations included many that were unconscious and hence not available to introspection. And unlike Wundt, Freud emphasised function; his mental structures served biological drives and instincts and reflected our animal nature.

For better or worse Freud's name is the one most closely allied to psychology in the mind of the public. In one study of eminent psychologists, as measured by citations in journals, introductory textbooks and nominations from self-selecting members of the American Psychological Society via an email survey, Freud was the most widely cited author in the discipline, as you can see in Tables 1.5 a–c (Hagbloom *et al.*, 2002). Second and third place were taken by Jean Piaget and Hans J. Eysenck.

Behaviourism: Edward Thorndike and Ivan Pavlov

The next major trend in psychology, behaviourism, followed directly from functionalism. It went further in its rejection of the special nature of mental events, denying that unobservable and unverifiable mental events were properly the subject matter of psychology. Behaviourists believed that because psychology is the study of observable behaviours, mental events – which cannot be observed – are outside the realm of psychology. **Behaviourism** is thus the study of the relation between people's environments and their behaviour; what occurs within their heads is irrelevant.

One of the first behaviourists was Edward Thorndike (1874–1949), an American psychologist who studied the behaviour of animals. He noticed that some events, usually those that one would expect to be pleasant, seemed to 'stamp in' a response that had just occurred. Noxious events seemed to 'stamp out' the response, or make it less likely to recur. We now call these processes reinforcement and punishment (see Chapter 7). Thorndike defined the law of effect as follows:

(a)   **(b)**

(c)

The three most widely cited psychologists of the 20th century: **(a)** Sigmund Freud; **(b)** Jean Piaget; **(c)** Hans J. Eysenck.
Source: (a) Illustrated London News Picture Library (b) AFP/Getty Images; (c) Popperfoto/Alamy Images.

> Any act which in a given situation produces satisfaction becomes associated with that situation, so that when the situation recurs the act is more likely than before to recur also. Conversely, any act which in a given situation produces discomfort becomes disassociated from that situation, so that when the situation recurs the act is less likely than before to recur. (*Source*: Thorndike, 1905, p. 203.)

The **law of effect** is in the functionalist tradition. It observes that the consequences of a behaviour act back upon the organism, affecting the likelihood that the behaviour that just occurred will occur again. An organism does something, and the consequences of this action make that action more likely. This process is very similar

Table 1.5 The top 10 psychologists (a) cited in the professional literature, (b) named as eminent by the American Psychological Society, and (c) most frequently cited in introductory textbooks.

(a)

Rank	Name	Citation frequency
1	Sigmund Freud	13 890
2	Jean Piaget	8 821
3	Hans J. Eysenck	6 821
4	B.J. Winer	6 206
5	Albert Bandura	5 831
6	S. Siegel	4 861
7	Raymond B. Cattell	4 828
8	B.F. Skinner	4 339
9	Charles E. Osgood	4 061
10	J.P. Guilford	4 006

(b)

Rank	Name	Citation frequency
1	B.F. Skinner	58
2	Jean Piaget	33
3	Sigmund Freud	28
4	John B. Watson	24
5	Albert Bandura	23
6.5	William James	21
6.5	Ivan P. Pavlov	21
8	Kurt Lewin/Roger Brown	17
9.5	Carl Rogers	14
9.5	Edward Thorndike	14

(c)

Rank	Name	Citation frequency
1	Sigmund Freud	560
2	B.F. Skinner	310
3	Albert Bandura	303
4	Jean Piaget	240
5	Carl Rogers	202
6	Stanley Schachter	200
7	Harry F. Harlow	175
8	Roger Brown	162
9	Neal E. Miller	154
10	D.C. McClelland	153

Source: Hagbloom, S.J., Warnick, R., Warnick, J.E., Jones, V.K., Yarbrough, G.L., Russell, T.M., Borecky, C.M., McGahhey, R., Powell, J.L., Beavers, J. and Monte, E., The 100 most eminent psychologists of the 20th century. *Review of General Psychology*, 2002, 6, 139–52, copyright © 2002 by the Educational Publishing Foundation, reprinted with permission.

to the principle of natural selection. Just as organisms that successfully adapt to their environments are more likely to survive and breed, behaviours that cause useful outcomes are more likely to recur.

Although Thorndike insisted that the subject matter of psychology was behaviour, his explanations contained mentalistic terms. For example, in his law of effect he spoke of 'satisfaction', which is certainly not a phenomenon that can be directly observed. Later behaviourists threw out terms like 'satisfaction' and 'discomfort' and replaced them with more objective terms that reflected the behaviour of the organism rather than any feelings it might have.

Another major figure in the development of behaviourism was not a psychologist but a physiologist: Ivan Pavlov (1849–1936), a Russian who studied the physiology of digestion (for which he later received a Nobel Prize). In the course of studying the stimuli that produce salivation, he discovered that hungry dogs would salivate at the sight of the attendant who brought in their dishes of food. Pavlov found that a dog could be trained to salivate at completely arbitrary stimuli, such as the sound of a bell, if the stimulus was quickly followed by the delivery of a bit of food into the animal's mouth.

Pavlov's discovery had profound significance for psychology. He showed that through experience an animal could learn to make a response to a stimulus that had never caused this response before. This ability, in turn, might explain how organisms learn cause-and-effect relations in the environment. In contrast, Thorndike's law of effect suggested an explanation for the adaptability of an individual's behaviour to its particular environment. So, from Thorndike's and Pavlov's studies two important behavioural principles had been discovered.

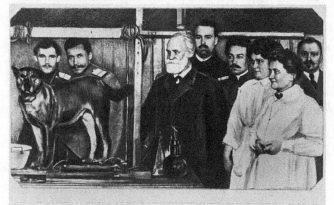

И. П. Павлов наблюдает за подопытной собакой
(1911 год)

Ivan Pavlov (1849–1936) in his laboratory with some of his collaborators. His research revealed valuable, though unsought, information about the principles of learning.

Source: Bettman/CORBIS, reprinted by permission.

Behaviourism: John B. Watson

Behaviourism as a formal school of psychology began with the publication of a book by John B. Watson (1878–1958), *Psychology from the Standpoint of a Behaviorist* (Watson, 1919). Watson was a charismatic professor of psychology at the Johns Hopkins University in the USA, a popular teacher and writer, the founding editor of the *Journal of Experimental Psychology*, and was a very convincing advocate of behaviourism. Even after leaving Johns Hopkins under mysterious circumstances and embarking on a highly successful career in advertising, he continued to lecture and write magazine articles about psychology.

According to Watson, psychology was a natural science whose domain was restricted to observable events: the behaviour of organisms. Watson's behaviourism can be best summed up by his definition published in an article entitled, 'Psychology as the behaviorist views it' (Watson, 1913):

> Psychology as the behaviorist views it is a purely objective experimental branch of natural science. Its theoretical goal is the prediction and control of behavior. Introspectionism forms no essential part of its methods, nor is the scientific value of its data dependent upon the readiness with which they lend themselves to interpretation in terms of consciousness. The behaviorist, in his efforts to get a unitary scheme of animal response, recognises no dividing line between man and brute.

Watson believed that the elements of consciousness studied by structuralists were too subjective to lend themselves to scientific investigation. He defined psychology as the objective study of behaviour and the stimuli which produce such behaviour. The important feature of behaviourism was its reliance only on observable behaviour. Even thinking was reduced to a form of behaviour – talking to oneself. Watson described visually observable behaviour as 'explicit behaviour' and those behaviours which could not be directly observed but potentially observed as 'implicit behaviour'. For example, we cannot see the body's cells transmitting electrical signals but we can observe such behaviour by using the correct electrical recording equipment.

Another important feature, tied to observation, was that the brain had very little to do with what was directly observed. What was important to Watson was the concept of stimulus and response, an idea suggested by Descartes and explicitly described by Pavlov. Watson argued that, given the correct stimuli, the organism could learn to behave (give responses) in a specific way (in the same way that Pavlov's dogs had 'learned' to associate the bell with the appearance of food). Watson, however, famously went further. In his book *Behaviorism* (1930), he argued:

> Give me a dozen healthy infants, well-formed, and my own specified world to bring them up in and I'll guarantee to take any one at random and train him to become any type of specialist I might select – doctor, lawyer, artist, merchant-chief and, yes, even beggar-man and thief, regardless of his talents, penchants, tendencies, abilities, vocations and race of his ancestors.

Evidence for this ambition came from his study of the 11-month-old Albert B – the first human being to be conditioned to fear an object in a laboratory (see Chapter 7). Many of Watson's ideas, such as the notion that reflexes can be conditioned, have been incorporated into the mainstream of psychology, although the central tenet that all behaviour that is studied must be observable has not. After Watson, a new form of behaviourism emerged which took Watson's ideas and developed them further. This new form became known as **neobehaviourism** or **radical behaviourism**.

Radical behaviourism: Edward Tolman and Clark Leonard Hull

The period 1930–1960 saw a tremendous surge not only in the description of the ways in which organisms behaved but also in the explanations for why they behaved in the way they did. This surge was generated largely by the work of a group of American psychologists, Edward Tolman (1886–1959), Clark Leonard Hull (1884–1952) and B.F. Skinner (1904–90). Each had a different view on how behaviour occurred but all

John B. Watson (1878–1958).
Source: Archives of the History of American Psychology.

used animal experiments and the procedures of learning experiments to support their theories. Hull, for example, proposed a highly detailed mathematical model of behaviour, based on his conditioning work with rats in his book *Principles of Behavior* (Hull, 1943). The basic feature of Hull's model was that all human (and any organism's) behaviour evolves through interaction with the environment. However, this interaction occurs within a wider frame of reference – the biological adaptation of the organism to the environment. The variable intervening between environment and organism was **drive** – a bodily need arising from deprivation or desire or another motivational spur. Although one of the more widely cited psychologists of his day, Hull has not made a lasting impact on psychology largely because his extremely detailed mathematical analyses were based on few experiments, the results of which were generalised well beyond the scope of the experimental context.

Tolman suggested that it was important not only to observe the stimulus and response but to take into account intervening variables. To Tolman, these intervening variables were cognitions and demands, and Tolman's theory became known as **purposive behaviourism**, so-called because all behaviour was goal-directed and had a purpose. Tolman's work did not bequeath any major principles or laws, however, although interest in his work continues (Reid and Staddon, 1998). You will find out more about Hull's and Tolman's approaches in Chapter 7.

Radical behaviourism: Burrhus Frederic Skinner

The bequest of a major framework of thinking in psychology was left to B.F. Skinner (1904–90), one of the most influential psychologists of the twentieth century whose entry into psychology's history was serendipitous. He originally wanted to be a writer, and later published novels in which he applied his research ideas. Skinner's work gave birth to the technology of teaching machines (which have since been replaced by computers), the use of behaviour modification in instruction of the mentally retarded, and the use of behaviour therapy to treat mental disorders.

Skinner's work focused on the idea of reinforcement and was based largely on observation of behaviour in pigeons. He found that a certain set of stimulus conditions (such as a box, hunger, food in sight) would elicit certain behaviours (strutting, random pecking). If the animal behaved in a certain way to obtain food then the food became the reinforcing stimulus or the reinforcer – a stimulus which increases the probability that behaviour will occur again. Using his observations of pigeons' behaviour, Skinner found that the pigeons could be trained to behave in a specific way when responding to specific signals from

B.F. Skinner (1904–90).
Source: Corbis: Bettmann.

their environment. For example, the pigeon would learn that it would receive food only if it pecked a food-dispensing lever a certain number of times; instead of randomly pecking at this lever it would then peck only the number of times necessary.

This form of learning, instrumental or operant learning, was of three types: positive reinforcement (e.g., the attention or approval given to a child from a teacher); punishment – a negative stimulus which is presented when a behaviour occurs (e.g., a rat receiving an electric shock whenever it presses a lever); and negative reinforcement – which reduces the likelihood of negative stimulation (e.g., a rat pressing a lever to avoid electric shock).

Reinforcement could also occur according to scheduling. For example, fixed-interval reinforcement involved a reinforcer that was given only after a set time; fixed-ratio reinforcement involved a reinforcer that was given only after a predetermined number of responses. Examples of fixed-interval reinforcement include receiving a wage at the end of the week or a salary at the end of the month; an example of fixed-ratio reinforcement would be the delivery of payment after, say, a certain number of items had been produced in a factory or after a specific number of products had been sold. Chapter 7 takes up these ideas.

Unlike Tolman and Hull, however, Skinner did not propose any intervening variables. To him, the behaving person or pigeon or rat was an 'empty organism'. He argued that humans were machines which behaved in lawful and predictable ways and his system was almost entirely descriptive with little in the way of theory emerging from it. In addition to his scientific work, Skinner published a novel, *Walden Two*, in which he described the way in which radical behaviourism could operate (Skinner, 1948).

Psychologists, including modern behaviourists, have moved away from the strict behaviourism of Watson and Skinner; mental processes such as imagery and attention are again considered to be proper subject matter for scientific investigation. But Watson's emphasis on objectivity in psychological research remains. Even those modern psychologists who most vehemently protest against what they see as the narrowness of behaviourism use the same principles of objectivity to guide their research.

Genetic epistemology: Jean Piaget

While American approaches to psychology were dominated by the new behaviourism, a different approach to the study of cognitive function was being pursued in Europe. The Swiss psychologist Jean Piaget (1896–1980) became interested in the question of human knowledge and how we begin to acquire knowledge. He believed that answers to such questions could be obtained by empirical, scientific research and he would measure the development of the acquisition of knowledge in children by presenting them with intellectual tasks at various stages of their lives (in fact, Piaget had worked with Theophile Simon, the collaborator of the man who designed the first IQ test, Alfred Binet). Piaget termed his approach to psychology as **genetic epistemology**: the study of the origin of knowledge in child development.

Apart from Piaget's focus on the acquisition of knowledge in groups of individuals, another difference between his European approach and that of his American counterparts was the lack of interest in the applied nature of research. Questions regarding the possibility of improving or accelerating children's learning did not interest Piaget, nor did it interest other European researchers (Leahey, 2003). Although his work made little impact on psychology at the time, the subsequent circulation of his work – with translations of his books – led to a considerable interest in his research (Smith, 1996), so much so, that few psychologists have dominated the study of child development in the way that Piaget has. Piaget's contribution to our understanding of child cognition is assessed in Chapter 12.

Gestalt psychology: Max Wertheimer

The structuralism of Wilhelm Wundt was not the only German influence on the development of psychology. In 1911, a German psychologist, Max Wertheimer (1880–1943), bought a toy that presented a series of pictures in rapid succession. Each picture was slightly different from the one that preceded it, and the resulting impression was that of continuous motion, like a film. Wundt and his followers insisted that if we want to understand the nature of human consciousness we must analyse it – divide it into its individual elements. But Wertheimer and his colleagues realised that the perception of a motion picture was not that of a series of individual still pictures. Instead, viewers saw continuity in time and space. They saw objects that retained their identity as they moved from place to place. Asking people to study these pictures one at a time and to describe what they saw (the structuralist approach) would never explain the phenomenon of the motion picture.

Wertheimer and his colleagues attempted to discover the organisation of cognitive processes, not their elements. They called their approach **Gestalt psychology**. Gestalt is a German word that roughly translates into 'unified form' or 'overall shape'. Gestalt psychologists insisted that perceptions resulted from patterns of interactions among many elements – patterns that could exist across both space and time. For example, a simple melody consists of a pattern of different notes, played one at a time. If the melody is played in different keys, so that the individual notes are different, people can still recognise it. Clearly, they recognise the relations the notes have to each other, not just the notes themselves.

Although the Gestalt school of psychology no longer exists, its insistence that elements of an experience interact – that the whole is not simply the sum of its parts – has had a profound influence on the development of modern psychology. Gestalt psychology did not disappear because of some inherent fatal flaw in its philosophy or methodology. Instead, many of its approaches and ideas were incorporated into other areas of psychology. Gestalt psychology is discussed in more detail in Chapter 6.

Humanistic psychology

Humanistic psychology developed during the 1950s and 1960s as a reaction against both behaviourism and psychoanalysis. Although psychoanalysis certainly dealt with mental phenomena that could not be measured objectively, it saw people as products of their environment and of innate, unconscious forces. Humanistic psychologists insist that human nature goes beyond environmental influences, and that conscious processes, not unconscious ones, are what psychologists should study. In addition, they note that psychoanalysis seems preoccupied with mental disturbance, ignoring positive phenomena such as happiness, satisfaction, love and kindness. **Humanistic psychology** is an approach to the study of human behaviour that emphasises human experience, choice and creativity, self-realisation and positive growth.

It emphasises the positive sides of human nature and the potential we all share for personal growth. In general, humanistic psychologists do not believe that we will understand human consciousness and behaviour through scientific research. Thus, the humanistic approach has not had a significant influence on psychology as a science. Its greatest impact has been on the development of methods of psychotherapy based on a positive and optimistic view of human potential.

The personality psychologists: Gordon Allport, Raymond Cattell, Hans Eysenck, Walter Mischel, Paul Costa and Robert McCrae

As the humanist movement was in full swing – or as swinging as it could manage – experimental psychologists had turned their attention to the scientific measurement of another important facet of behaviour: personality. This attention took the form of a search for universal **personality traits** – enduring personal characteristics which form a continuum along which we all fall. The earliest of these theorists was Gordon Allport (1897–1967) who, using dictionary terms as his starting point, suggested that personality comprised between three and 16 personality traits. Allport's scheme formed the basis for the model devised by Raymond Cattell (1905–98). He collected data from interviews and various questionnaires, and concluded that personality comprised 16 traits.

A more parsimonious account, based on a statistical technique called factor analysis, was proposed by Hans J. Eysenck (1916–97). Eysenck's model was, until recently, one of the most widely accepted views of personality traits. He proposed that personality comprised three dimensions – neuroticism–stability, extraversion–intraversion and psychoticism–normality – all of which had a biological basis, and that each of us scores somewhere along all three dimensions. Meanwhile, influential American psychologists such as Walter Mischel (b. 1930) argued that traits did not exist and that, when we behave, we are reacting to changes in our environment or situation (this approach is called situationism): that we may respond in a consistent way lulls us into thinking that we possess something called 'personality', characterised by a number of traits. The debate continues, but the situationists seem to be fighting a lost battle.

Considerable research supported Eysenck's model, but this was usurped in the 1980s by the Five Factor Model of personality, now most closely identified with the personality questionnaire developed by Paul T. Costa and

Paul T. Costa.
Source: Bo Mathisen.

Robert R. McCrae. The Big Five model is now the most widely accepted view of personality and argues that our personality comprises five traits which we possess to varying degrees: agreeableness, conscientiousness, extraversion, neuroticism and openness to experience. You'll find more information on all of these approaches in Chapter 14.

Robert R. McCrae.
Source: Robert McCrae.

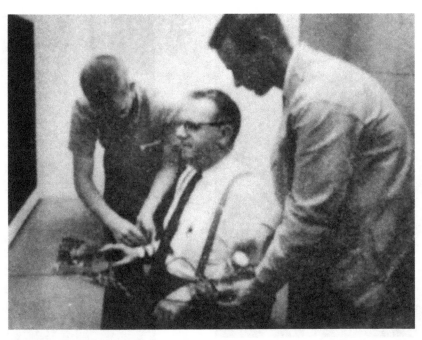

A photograph of Milgram's famous experiment, described in more detail in Chapter 16.
Source: Getty Images/Hulton Archive.

The social psychologists

In the middle of the twentieth century there also appeared a phenomenal body of research explaining how we view and influence other individuals. Here, there are too many significant figures to mention, but some of the most prominent that contributed significant new data and models which helped us understand social behaviour include Leon Festinger, Albert Bandura, Stanley Milgram, Philip Zimbardo, Elliot Aronson, Robert Zajonc, Richard Nisbett and Edward Jones. All Americans or working in the USA, these psychologists demonstrated how we could hold two seemingly contradictory views (Festinger), how **deindividuation** could strip us of our humanity (Zimbardo), how observation of others makes us imitate them (Bandura), how we become obedient to authority (Milgram), how we interpret the causes of our own behaviour differently from how we interpret that of others (Nisbett, Jones), amongst other things. You'll find descriptions of their research and the impact this has had on our understanding of social behaviour in Chapters 15 and 16.

Philip Zimbardo.
Source: Corbis: Lynn Goldsmith.

Elizabeth Loftus.
Source: Jodi Hilton/Pool/Reuters.

Alan Baddeley.
Source: Copyright UK Medical Research Council (2009) used by kind permission.

The cognitive revolution: beyond behaviourism

The emphasis on behaviourism in the first half of the twentieth century restricted the subject matter of psychology to observable behaviours. For many years, concepts such as consciousness were considered to be outside the domain of psychology. As one psychologist put it, 'psychology, having first bargained away its soul and then gone out of its mind, seems now . . . to have lost all consciousness' (Burt, 1962, p. 229).

In the decades that followed, many psychologists protested against the restrictions of behaviourism and turned to the study of consciousness, feelings, memory, imagery

Daniel Kahneman.
Source: Corbis: Reuters.

Amos Tversky.
Source: Barbara Tversky.

and other private events (although behaviourism was still a potent force and continues to run through much of today's experimental psychology like marble). Much of cognitive psychology uses an approach called **information processing** – information received through the senses is 'processed' by various systems in the brain. Some systems store the information in the form of memory, and other systems control behaviour. Some systems operate automatically and unconsciously, while others are conscious and require effort on the part of the individual. Because the information-processing approach was first devised to describe the operations of complex physical systems such as computers, the modern model of the human brain is, for most cognitive psychologists, the computer. Another model (neural networks) is now being used as an alternative to the computer (see Chapter 7).

Although cognitive psychologists study mental structures and operations, they have not gone back to the introspective methods that structuralists such as Wundt employed. Instead, they use experimental methods, under controlled conditions, to test hypotheses and discover facts about how we think and remember. Cognitive psychologists such as Donald Broadbent, Stanley Schachter, Neal Miller, Don McClelland, Alan Baddeley, Ulric Neisser, Allan Paivio, Stephen Kosslyn, Endel Tulving, Elizabeth Loftus, Daniel Kahneman and Amos Tversky (the last two won the Nobel Prize for economics in 2002) discovered new and important data about how we learn to learn, remember and reason. You'll find their research in Chapters 8 and 11 but also throughout the text.

The biological revolution

Biology has always been closely tied to psychology and as psychology began to flourish, it was against a backdrop of some quite staggering discoveries in the physical sciences. For example, Descartes's hydraulic model of muscular movement was shown to be incorrect by Luigi Galvani (1737–98), an Italian physiologist who discovered that muscles could be made to contract by applying an electrical current directly to them or to the nerves that were attached to them. The muscles themselves contained the energy needed for them to contract. They did not have to be inflated by pressurised fluid. This discovery is the source of a modern-day technique for helping people recover from serious, paralysing illnesses and injury: the use of brain electrical activity to control objects such as a computer cursor or a prosthetic limb.

Brain damage and behaviour: Paul Broca and Carl Wernicke

As discoveries in physiology and anatomy flourished, another medical endeavour was making itself felt slowly

throughout the later end of the 19th century: the study of the effect of brain injury on behaviour. In 1861, Paul Broca (1824–80), a French surgeon, reported the results of an autopsy on the brain of a man who had suffered a **stroke** several years previously. The stroke (damage to the brain caused, in this case, by a blood clot) had caused the man to lose the ability to speak. The patient, whose real name was Leborgne, was called Tan because this was the only word he uttered. He did not survive long at the hospital and Broca discovered that the stroke had damaged part of the brain on the left side near the front, as Figure 1.4 shows (although Marc Dax and others had reported similar findings earlier that century). Broca suggested that this region of the brain was a centre for speech – this part is now called Broca's area.

Broca's work was followed, independently, by that of Carl Wernicke (1848–1905), who noted that damage to an adjacent part of the brain impaired his patient's ability to comprehend speech but left speech production relatively intact. The language disorders produced by damage to the brain are described in Chapter 10.

Studying the effects of accidental brain damage on function has allowed neuroscientists to predict which regions of the brain may be involved in specific functions. A famous example of brain damage leading to speculation about the function of a brain region is that of Phineas Gage. Gage was an American railroad construction supervisor who, in the mid-nineteenth century, had an accident at work in which an iron rod shot through his face, through the front part of his brain and straight out of the top of his head. A reconstructed image of the trajectory of the rod through his skull can be seen in Figure 1.5a. Figure 1.5b is the

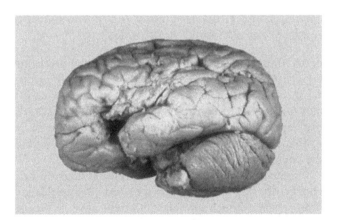

Figure 1.4 A photograph of Tan's brain. Note the egg-shaped cavity – this was thought to be responsible for his inability to speak fluently.

Source: T.E. Feinberg and M.J. Farah (1997) *Behavioral Neurology and Neuropsychology*. © The McGraw-Hill Companies.

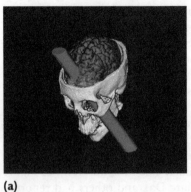

(a)

(b)

Figure 1.5 On a September afternoon in 1848, an unusual accident befell a young American railroad worker called Phineas Gage. An iron rod shot through his head as a result of an uncontrolled explosion at work. Almost 150 years later, Hannah Damasio and her colleagues at the University of Iowa took the medical reports of Gage's injury and plotted the course of the rod, using modern computer technology. **(a)** Shows one of the images of the rod's trajectory. **(b)** Shows a depiction of Gage himself.

Source: (a) From H. Damasio, T. Grabowski, R. Frank, A.M. Galaburda and A.R. Damasio, The return of Phineas Gage: Clues about the brain from a famous patient. *Science*, 1994, 264: 1102–05. Department of Neurology and Image Analysis Facility, University of Iowa. (b) From Macmillan, *An odd kind of fame* MIT: Bradford.

only existing image of Gage (with the rod tastefully superimposed).

Whereas before the injury, Gage had been a hard-working and conscientious individual, after the injury he became boorish, unpleasant and unreliable. The part of the brain damaged seemed to be that responsible for inhibiting inappropriate behaviour. We now know that patients with damage to this part of the brain have difficulty in inhibiting such behaviour (there is more on this phenomenon in Chapter 13).

Localisation of function: Gustav Fritsch and Eduard Hitzig, Franz Gall and Johann Spurzheim

In 1870, the German physiologists Gustav Fritsch and Eduard Hitzig discovered that applying a small electrical shock to different parts of the cerebral cortex caused movements of different parts of the body. In fact, the body appeared to be 'mapped' on the surface of the brain, so that the feet, hands, fingers and so on, had a part of the brain dedicated to them.

Originally, this work was conducted on dogs on Frau Hitzig's dressing table (because they had no available laboratory space). Such humble conditions gave rise to the first experiment in **localisation of function** in the brain – the ability to ascribe a particular function to a part of the brain, the goal of neuropsychology. No less elaborate, but ultimately doomed, was the attempt at localising function by Franz Gall (1758–1828) and Johann Spurzheim

(1776–1832). Their anatomical personology – or as it is commonly known, phrenology – suggested that if we were very adept at a function, the part of the brain responsible would be overactive. This overactivity caused an indentation in the skull and so a person's ability could be determined by palpating the head (there were thought to be 37 such functions in the brain, according to Gall and Spurzheim). If a person was mathematically gifted, therefore, the part responsible for this would be active and cause a bump in the skull, which the experimenter could palpate. This hypothesis was beautifully testable and it was not long before the edifice came crashing down when a person identified as a mathematically gifted genius transpired to be a mentally retarded criminal. It was, however, an attempt at localising function in the brain. Although Gall is best known for this, he also made more worthwhile contributions to neuroscience, such as identifying the importance of the left front part of the brain to speech.

Speed and magnitude of nerve impulses: Hermann von Helmholtz and Ernst Weber

A different and yet essentially physical approach to studying behaviour was also seen in the work of the German physicist and physiologist Hermann von Helmholtz (1821–94), who did much to demonstrate that mental phenomena could be explained by physiological means. This extremely productive scientist made contributions to both physics and physiology. He actively disassociated himself from natural philosophy, from which many assumptions about the nature of the mind had been derived. Helmholtz advocated a purely scientific approach, with conclusions based on objective investigation and precise measurement.

Until his time, scientists believed that the transmission of impulses through nerves was as fast as the speed of electricity in wires; under this assumption, transmission would be virtually instantaneous, considering the small distances that impulses have to travel within the human body. Helmholtz successfully measured the speed of the nerve impulse and found that it was only about 90 feet per second, which is considerably slower than the speed of electricity in wires. This finding suggested to later researchers that the nerve impulse is more complex than a simple electrical current passing through a wire, which is indeed true.

Helmholtz also attempted to measure the speed of a person's reaction to a physical stimulus, but he abandoned this attempt because there was too much variability from person to person. However, this variability interested scientists who followed him; they tried to explain the reason for individual differences in behaviour. Because both the velocity of nerve impulses and a person's reactions to stimuli could be measured, researchers theorised that mental events themselves could be the subject of scientific investigation. Possibly, if the proper techniques could be developed, one could investigate what went on within the human brain. Thus, Helmholtz's research was important in setting the stage for the science of psychology.

A contemporary of von Helmholtz's, Ernst Weber (1795–1878), began work that led to the development of a method for measuring the magnitude of human sensations. Weber, an anatomist and physiologist, found that people's ability to tell the difference between two similar stimuli – such as the brightness of two lights, the heaviness of two objects, or the loudness of two tones – followed orderly laws. This regularity suggested to Weber and his followers that the study of perceptual phenomena could be as scientific as that of physics or biology. The study of the relation between the physical characteristics of a stimulus and the perceptions they produce is a field called psychophysics or the physics of the mind (see Chapter 6).

Cognitive neuroscience: the future of the biology of the 'mind'?

The cognitive revolution did not lead to a renewed interest in biology. But the extraordinary advances in neurobiology in the late twentieth century have revolutionised psychology. Neurobiologists (biologists who study the nervous system) and scientists and engineers in allied fields have developed ways to study the brain that were unthinkable just a few decades ago. We can study fine details of nerve cells, discover their interconnections, analyse the chemicals they use to communicate with each other, produce drugs that block the action of these chemicals or mimic their effects.

More importantly, using neuroimaging techniques such as fMRI, MRI, PET, NIRS, MEG and various other technological abbreviations, we can see the internal structure of a living human brain, and measure the activity of different processes of the brain – in regions as small as a few cubic millimetres – while people are thinking, feeling, perceiving, comprehending and moving (Martin, 2006;

a Left parahippocampal gyrus

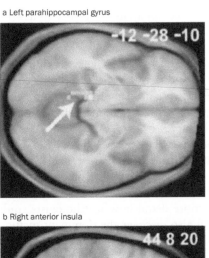

b Right anterior insula

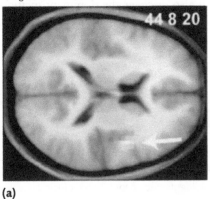

(a)

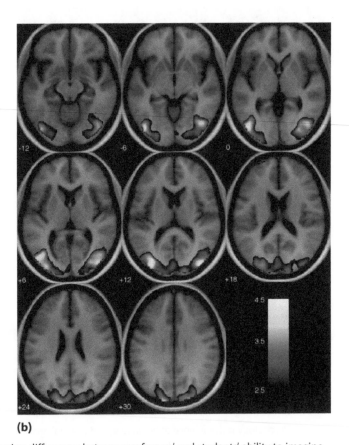

(b)

Figure 1.6 (a) These are two scans from two areas of the brain showing differences between perfumers' and students' ability to imagine an odour; **(b)** Scans showing areas of the brain activated in congenitally blind, but not sighted, individuals as they detected the scent of rose oil.

Source: (a) From Plailly, J., Delon-Martin, C. and Royet, J-P. (2012) Experience induces functional reorganization in brain regions involved in odor imagery in perfumers. *Human Brain Mapping*, 33, 224–34; (b) From Kupers, R., Bealieu-Lefebvre, M., Schneider, F.C., Kassuba, T., Paulson, O.B., Siebner, H.R., and Ptito, M. (2011) Neural correlates of olfactory processing in congenital blindness. *Neuropsychologia*, 49, 2037–44.

Raichle, 2008). An example of some of the research possible using neuroimaging can be seen in Figure 1.6. The first neuroimaging study of language was published in 1988 and involved listening to or reading aloud nouns. The studies illustrated in Figures 1.6a and 1.6b show how far research has developed

This combination of cognitive psychology and neuro science – cognitive neuroscience – provides a different way of studying behaviour and describing its causes. Currently, the endeavours in cognitive neuroscience are, because of the nature of the techniques used, directed towards studying basic, yet essential, behaviour such as rudimentary reading, recognising emotion, remembering and speaking. But this is changing and studies are now using neuroimaging to study how people converse, make moral decisions, appreciate television programmes, react to a lover's face and voice and even understand magic tricks. You'll find a review of many of these studies in Chapter 4.

Conceptual and historical issues in psychology

As this chapter has shown you, understanding a discipline's past can help you better understand its present and its future. Understanding a discipline's past shows you the stages – usually chaotic, not linear or orderly – that psychology has gone through to reach the status it has attained today and the body of knowledge it has accrued. The shifts in approach and subject matter across its history will be reflected in its future shifts. But these shifts will be gradual. The danger in highlighting stages in history, as is done here, is that that they are seen as discrete and self-contained. They are only discrete and self-contained because the prism of

historical retrospection makes them so and we can reflect back, soberly, on some of the momentous conceptual and experimental changes that psychology underwent. We are currently amidst an extraordinary boom in neuroimaging work. In 50 years' time, all of this work may seem quaintly obsolete. We don't know.

Historical milestones are one thing. Conceptual issues are another. The trends and schools described here arose when researchers operated in a different world and context to that in which we operate today. Much – if not most – research conducted in universities is funded by government, and government has priorities. Will these priorities see a shift in the types of topics psychologists study in the future?

On a grander scale, conceptual issues can be virtually synonymous with philosophical issues. For example, the question 'Is the scientific method the best method for establishing truth?' is a philosophical, rather than a psychological question, because it doesn't have an absolute answer. When we have answers to questions, philosophy is dead. In the chapters that follow you should be able to see how research arose and in what context – how some of the work in social psychology emerged from real-life events, such as the apparent reluctance to assist a person crying for help, or a soldier saying he was only obeying orders, for example. Or how cross-cultural research on facial expression led to a theory of emotion. Or how research on race differences in IQ became controversial. Or how we classify and diagnose mental illness. Or how sociobiology, according to some views, reduces human beings to self-interested savages.

So far, you have seen how psychology is a discipline that comprises a number of different branches. This survey of the history of psychology reveals a number of methodological approaches to the study of behaviour. The next chapter describes in more detail how psychologists study behaviour. You will also discover the dominant methodological approach to answering questions about psychology.

Chapter review

What is psychology?

- Psychology is the science of behaviour, and psychologists study a large variety of behaviours in humans and other animals.
- Psychology has many major branches:

- Psychobiologists study the biological basis of behaviour.
- Psychophysiologists study people's physiological reactions, such as changes in heart rate and muscle tension.
- Neuropsychologists study the relationship between central nervous system activity and structure and function.

- Comparative psychologists study the evolution of behaviour by comparing the behavioural capacities of various species of animals.
- Ethologists study the biological bases of behaviour through observation of animals in natural environments.
- Sociobiologists attempt to interpret human and animal behaviour in terms of evolution and biological inheritance.
- Behaviour geneticists study the degree of influence exerted by heredity and environment on behaviour.
- Cognitive psychologists study complex human behaviours such as cognition, memory and attention.
- Cognitive neuroscientists study the role of the human and animal brain in behaviour.
- Developmental psychologists study the development of behaviour throughout the lifespan.
- Social psychologists study the effects of people on the behaviour of other people.
- Individual differences involves the study of the effects of specific characteristics or traits on behaviour.
- Cross-cultural psychologists study the impact of culture on behaviour.
- Forensic and criminological psychologists study the ways in which psychological knowledge can be applied in criminal and legal settings.
- Clinical psychologists study the causes and treatment of mental disorders and problems of adjustment.
- Health psychologists study the ways in which lifestyle and behaviour affect illness and health.
- Educational psychologists assess the cognitive, social and emotional development of children in the school environment.
- Consumer psychologists study what motivates people to consume and how consumers' perceptions are formed.
- Organisational or occupational psychologists study the behaviour of individuals and groups in the workplace.
- Ergonomists help to design machines and workplace environments that enhance work performance.

The development of psychology as a science

- Psychology has its modern roots in the thinking of the French philosopher and mathematician René Descartes who argued that the mind and the body were two separate entities which interacted (dualism).
- The mid-nineteenth century gave rise to materialism and empiricism. Materialism maintained that the mind was made of matter; thus all natural phenomena, including human behaviour, could be explained in terms of physical entities: the interaction of matter and energy. Empiricism emphasised that all knowledge was acquired by means of sensory experience; no knowledge was innate. The concept of empiricism was developed by the philosophers John Locke and David Hume.

Modern psychology

- The first laboratory of experimental psychology was established in Leipzig in 1879 by Wilhelm Wundt.
- Wundt and his colleagues' work gave rise to structuralism: the idea that the mind was made up of components which could be broken apart and studied. The method of studying these components was introspection – the observation and recall of experience.
- At about the same time, Ebbinghaus contributed important methods for objectively measuring learning and forgetting.
- Darwin's ground-breaking theory of evolution, or theory of natural selection, argued that traits necessary for survival would be inherited and that only those adaptively useful traits would survive.
- Francis Galton founded the scientific study of individual differences in human behaviour and suggested that certain psychological characteristics could be inherited.
- Functionalism, which grew out of Darwin's theory of evolution, was concerned with the processes of consciousness such as perceiving and learning. Its major advocates were William James and James Angell.
- Functionalism gave rise to behaviourism, founded by John Watson, which still dominates the way we do research. The subject matter of behaviourism is observable behaviour; according to the behaviourists, mental events – because they were unobservable – should play no part in scientific psychology. Behaviourism developed a radical strain in the 1950s which viewed the organism's behaviour strictly in terms of stimulus and response.
- Humanistic psychology is concerned with the special nature of humanity and emphasises human experience, choice and creativity, and the potential for personal growth.
- The cognitive revolution arose from the belief that behaviourism's emphasis on observable behaviour missed some of the complexity of human cognition and behaviour. The cognitive revolution saw a rekindling of interest in phenomena such as memory, thinking, creativity, imagination and so on, and human behaviour was interpreted in terms of information processing.
- The biological revolution in psychology manifested itself in the increased interest of psychologists in all fields – not just physiological psychology – in the role of biological factors in behaviour. This has given rise to cognitive neuroscience in which the disciplines of neuropsychology and cognitive psychology have combined and used neuroimaging methods to create a greater understanding of the role of the brain in thinking, feeling and perceiving, specifically to localise function in the brain.

Suggestions for further reading

The history of psychology

Crivellato, E. and Ribatti, D. (2007) Soul, mind, brain: Greek philosophy and the birth of neuroscience. *Brain Research Bulletin*, 71, 327-36.

Hock, R. (2009) *Forty studies that changed psychology* (6th edn). Harlow: Pearson Education.

Leahey, T.H. (2003) *A History of Psychology* (6th edn). Englewood Cliffs, NJ: Prentice Hall International.

Mandler, G. (2011). *A history of modern experimental psychology.* Cambridge, MA: MIT Press.

Shepard, R.N. (2004) How a cognitive psychologist came to seek universal laws. *Psychonomic Bulletin and Review*, 11, 1, 1-23.

British Journal of Psychology, special issue, Supplement 1, April 2009.

Several sources describe the history of psychology, including its philosophical and biological roots, and these are some very good introductions. The special issue of the *British Journal of Psychology* reprints some of the most influential research papers of the past 100 years, with commentaries.

Concepts and controversies in psychology

Furnham, A. (1996) *All in the Mind*. London: Whurr Publishers.

Kassin, S., Briggs, K.H. and Tavris, C. (2008) *Current Directions in Introductory Psychology*. Boston, MA: Allyn & Bacon.

Lilienfeld, S.O. (2011). Public skepticism of psychology. *American Psychologist*, 67, 111-29.

Varnum, M.E.W., Grossmann, I., Kitayama, S., and Nisbett, R.E. (2010) The origin of cultural differences in cognition: The social orientation hypothesis. *Current Directions in Psychological Science*, 19, 9-13.

Excellent introductions to some controversial issues and major concepts in psychology.

Influential psychologists

Brockman, J. (2011) *The Mind: Leading Scientists Explore the Brain, Memory, Consciousness, and Personality*. London: Harper Perennial.

Cohen, D. (2004) *Psychologists on Psychology*. London: Hodder & Stoughton.

Fancher, R.E. (1996) *Pioneers of Psychology* (3rd edn). New York: W.W. Norton.

Kimble, G.A., Wertheimer, M. and White, C.L. (1991) *Portraits of Pioneers in Psychology*. Hillsdale, NJ: Lawrence Erlbaum Associates/American Psychological Association.

Cohen's book contains an excellent set of interviews with some of the leading psychologists of the time. The books by Brockman, Kimble *et al.* and Fancher contain biographical sketches of the major scientists who have contributed to psychology and so provide a good potted introduction to the personalities (and themes, ideas and developments) in psychology.

CHAPTER 3

Evolution, genetics and behaviour

Explore the accompanying experiments, videos, simulations and animations on **MyPsychLab**.
This chapter includes activities on:

- Chromosones
- Dominant and recessive traits
- Twin studies and adoption studies of heritability
- The inheritance of Huntington's disease and Phenylketonuria
- Check your understanding and prepare for your exams using the multiple choice, short answer and essay practice tests also available.

FOUND: GENES THAT MAKE BRITS FREE-THINKERS

They may seem like cultural stereotypes, but the traits of rugged British individualism compared with Chinese conformity may be rooted in genetic differences between races, say scientists.

Their study suggests that the individualism seen in Western nations, and the higher levels of collectivism and family loyalty found in Asian cultures, are caused by differences in the prevalence of particular genes.

The scientists looked at a gene that controls levels of serotonin, the brain chemical which regulates mood and emotions. They found one version of the gene was far more common in Western populations where, they said, it was associated with individualistic and free-thinking behaviour.

Such findings will need further confirmation but could provide tentative explanation of why the Japanese economy, for example, tends to be based around large companies showing high levels of loyalty between managers and employees.

Source: *The Sunday Times*, 11 March 2012.

WHAT YOU SHOULD BE ABLE TO DO AFTER READING CHAPTER 3

- Describe Darwin's theory of evolution.
- Outline the principles of genetic inheritance.
- Evaluate the contribution of genetics to psychology.
- Describe and evaluate sociobiology and evolutionary psychology's contribution to our understanding of behaviour.
- Discuss some of the reasons why we are sexually attracted to certain body types.
- Describe the psychological and evolutionary significance of altruism.

QUESTIONS TO THINK ABOUT

- What do you think is meant by the term 'evolution of behaviour'?
- When did the modern human being evolve?
- What are the implications of the theory of evolution for psychology?
- How do you think the process of evolution could explain modern behaviour such as romantic attraction, jealousy, language and marriage?
- Are we attracted to certain body types? If so, why? And is this preference universal?
- What do we mean when we say that a characteristic is heritable?
- Which has the more important effect on behaviour – genes or the environment? Or is the question not worth asking?
- Can any behaviour be studied at the genetic level?
- Why are we more altruistic to some people than others?

The development of evolutionary theory

From my early youth I have had the strongest desire to understand and explain whatever I observed, that is, to group all facts under some general laws . . . Therefore, my success as a man of science, whatever this may have amounted to, has been determined, as far as I can judge, by complex and diversified mental qualities and conditions. Of these, the most important have been – the love of science – unbounded patience in long reflecting over any subject – industry in observing and collecting facts – and a fair share of invention and common sense. With such moderate abilities as I possess, it is truly surprising that I should have influenced to a considerable extent the belief of scientific men on some important points.

(*Source*: Darwin, 1887, pp. 67–71).

These fairly humble words were written by a man who has influenced the course of scientific thought more than any other individual since Copernicus (who, in 1543, proposed that the sun, not the earth, was at the centre of the universe). Charles Darwin argued that, over time, organisms originate and become adapted to their environments by biological means. This concept is referred to as **biological evolution** – changes that take place in the genetic and physical characteristics of a population or group of organisms over time – and it stands as the primary explanation of the origin of life. The bicentenary of Darwin's birth was marked in 2009, together with the 150th anniversary of the publication of one of the most important books published in the past 300 years – *On the Origin of Species by Means of Natural Selection*. In this book, Darwin distilled his theory of evolution.

There is evidence of life on earth a billion years after the formation of the earth 4.5 billion years ago (Eiler, 2007) and the human race has existed, in various forms, for over 10 million years. This time-span has seen a tremendous change in our physical appearance, our biology and our behaviour. Our brains have developed, our societies have become more sophisticated, our intelligence has increased, our ability to communicate has improved, we have developed language systems. These processes illustrate the ways in which we have evolved and evolutionary theory seeks to explain why we have evolved in the way that we have. Why do birds have wings, giraffes have long necks, humans have bigger brains than other higher primates? How do changes in organic structure occur and how does this happen? The answers to questions such as these have important implications for the topics discussed in other

chapters in this book: intelligence, personality, social interaction, the use of language, the perception and expression of emotion, sex, hunger, mental disorder and so on.

Although it has its roots in biology, Darwin's work transcends biology and has influenced all the natural sciences, especially psychology (Dewsbury, 2009). In fact, Darwin himself had some aspirations for the young science. He wrote in 1859:

In the distant future, I see open fields for more important researches. Psychology will be based on a new foundation, that of the necessary acquirement of each mental power and capacity by gradation. Much light will be thrown on the origin of man and his history.

Since the 1970s, some psychologists have become increasingly aware of the various ways in which biology can influence behaviour. As you will see later in the chapter, many behavioural differences among organisms, both within and across species, correspond to genetic and other biological differences. Understanding these differences and their evolution allows psychologists to understand behaviour in terms of its possible origins and **adaptive significance** – its effectiveness in aiding the organism to adapt to changing environmental conditions.

Psychologists might research how past environmental conditions favoured gregariousness over a more solitary existence as a means of organising human culture and how the immediate environment influenced day-to-day sociability. They are interested in understanding both **ultimate causes** (from the Latin *ultimatus*, 'to come to an end') of behaviour – events and conditions that, over successive generations, have slowly shaped the behaviour of our species – and **proximate causes** (from the Latin *proximus*, 'near'), namely immediate environmental variables that affect behaviour.

By understanding how adaptive behaviour developed through the long-term process of evolution, psychologists are able to gain a more thorough understanding of our ability to adjust to changes in our immediate environment. To understand the present, we must understand the past – the history of the individual and the history of our species. We behave as we do because we are members of the human species – an ultimate cause – and because we have learned to act in special ways – a proximate cause. Both biology and environment contribute to our personal development.

Relatively recently, a field of psychology has emerged, **evolutionary psychology** (Tooby and Cosmides, 1989; Buss, 1995), which attempts to describe and explain how an organism's evolutionary history contributes to the behaviour patterns and cognitive strategies it uses for reproduction and survival during its lifetime. Evolutionary psychology's contribution to our understanding of human behaviour is assessed later in the chapter. First, however, we describe Darwin's theory of evolution. An understanding of this complex theory will help shed light on how behaviour has been interpreted, by some psychologists, in terms of evolution.

In the beginning: the voyage of the *Beagle*

The story of how Charles Darwin developed his theory illustrates the mix of hard work, intellect and good fortune that often makes scientific discovery possible. In fact, Darwin's work is an excellent example of how observation and experimentation can lead to scientific breakthroughs.

After receiving a degree in theology from the University of Cambridge, England, in 1831, Darwin met a Captain Robert FitzRoy who was looking for someone to serve as an unpaid naturalist and travelling companion during a five-year voyage on board HMS *Beagle*. The *Beagle*'s mission was to explore and survey the coast of South America and to make longitudinal measurements worldwide.

During the voyage, Darwin observed the flora and fauna of South America, Australia, South Africa and the islands of the Pacific, South Atlantic and Indian Oceans. He collected creatures and objects of every sort: marine animals, reptiles, amphibians, land mammals, birds, insects, plants, rocks, minerals, fossils and seashells. These specimens, which were sent back to England at various stages of the trip, were later examined by naturalists from all over Europe.

Charles Darwin (1809–82).
Source: Northwind Photo Library.

Darwin did not form his theory of evolution while at sea. Although he was impressed by the tremendous amount of diversity among seemingly related animals, he believed in creationism, the view that all living things were designed by God and are non-evolving (Gould, 1985).

The Origin of Species

On his return home to England in 1836, Darwin continued to marvel at the many ways animals and plants adapt to their environments. He sifted through his collections, often discussing his findings and ideas with other scientists. He carefully reviewed the work of earlier naturalists who had developed their own theories on evolution. Darwin was not the first person to propose a theory of evolution, but he was the first to amass considerable evidence in its favour. He became interested in artificial selection, a procedure in which particular animals are mated to produce offspring that possess desirable characteristics. For example, if a farmer wished to develop cattle that yielded the largest steaks, then they would examine the available breeding stock and permit only the 'beefiest' ones to reproduce. If this process is repeated over many generations of animals, the cattle should become beefier. In other words, in artificial selection, people select which animals will breed and which will not based on specific, desirable characteristics of the animals.

As he pondered on whether there might be a natural process corresponding to the role that humans play in artificial selection, Darwin's views on evolution began slowly to change. He believed that 'selection was the keystone of man's success in making useful races of animals and plants. But how selection could be applied to organisms living in a state of nature remained for some time a mystery to me' (Darwin, 1887, p. 53).

A year-and-a-half later, on reading Malthus's *Population*, Darwin proposed that because the 'struggle for existence' continued in plants and animals, then favourable variations would be preserved and unfavourable ones would die out. The result of such 'selection' would be the development of new species (Darwin, 1887).

This proposal contains the idea of natural selection: within any given population, some members of a species will produce more offspring than will others. Any animal that possesses a characteristic that helps it to survive or adapt to changes in its environment is likely to live longer and to produce more offspring than are animals that do not have this characteristic.

Darwin was well aware of the significance of his discovery but did not publish his theory until 20 years later, taking great pains to develop a clear, coherent and accurate case for his theory.

Darwin might have been even slower in publishing his theory had it not been for an intriguing coincidence. In 1858, he received a manuscript from the Welshman, Alfred Russell Wallace, another naturalist, outlining a theory of natural selection identical to his own. Darwin's colleagues suggested that he and Wallace make a joint presentation of their separate works before a learned society – the Linnean Society – so that each might lay equal claim to the theory of natural selection. This was done, and a year later Darwin published his 'abstract', which we know today as *The Origin of Species*. The book sold out on its first day of publication and has been selling steadily ever since. And although theories of evolution had existed before Darwin, he was the first to offer a systematic explanation for how evolution worked.

Darwin's theory of evolution

Two concepts are central to Darwin's theory of evolution: **adaptation** and **natural selection**. Adaptation refers to the ability of generations of species to adapt effectively to changes in the environment. Natural selection refers to the process whereby some variations in species will be transferred from one generation to the next but others will not. The zoologist, Richard Dawkins, has likened the process of natural selection to a sieve because it leaves out what is unimportant (Dawkins, 1996).

Darwin's theory has four basic premises:

1 The world's animal and plant communities are dynamic, not static: they change over time with new forms originating and others becoming extinct.

2 The evolutionary process is gradual and continuous. New species arise through slow and steady environmental changes that gradually 'perfect' each species to its surroundings. When sudden and dramatic changes occur in the environment, a species' ability to adapt is usually challenged. Some species adapt and live; others become extinct.

3 All organisms are descended from an original and common ancestor. Over time, the process of natural selection has created different species, each specifically adapted to its ecological niche.

4 Natural selection not only causes changes within populations during changing environmental conditions but also acts to maintain the status quo under relatively constant environmental conditions.

Natural selection

The essence of Malthus's essay, which Darwin was reading when the idea of natural selection first occurred to him, was that the earth's food supply grows more slowly than populations of living things. The resulting scarcity of food produces competition among animals, with the less fit individuals losing the struggle for life. For example, wolves who are agile are better able to capture prey than are slower packmates. Fast wolves will therefore tend to outlive and out-reproduce slower wolves. If a wolf's tendency to run fast is a genetically controlled trait, it will be passed on to its offspring. These offspring will be more likely to catch prey and will therefore live longer and have more opportunities to reproduce.

The ability of an individual to produce offspring defines that individual's **reproductive success** – the number of viable offspring it produces relative to the number of viable offspring produced by other members of the same species. Contrary to popular interpretation, 'survival of the fittest' does not always mean survival of the most physically fit or of the strongest. The evolutionary 'bottom line' is not physical strength but reproductive success. Physical strength is only one factor that might contribute to such success. In humans, for example, good looks, charm and intelligence play an important role in an individual's ability to attract a mate and reproduce. What is more, natural selection is not 'intentional'. Giraffes did not grow long necks in order to eat leaves from trees, but those with longer necks who were able to reach the leaves successfully reproduced while the others died out.

Two aspects of natural selection – variation and competition – are the critical factors that determine whether any particular animal and its offspring will enjoy reproductive success.

Variation

Variation includes differences among members of a species, such as physical characteristics (size, strength or physiology) and behavioural characteristics (intelligence or sociability). What factors are responsible for these sorts of variation?

First, an individual organism's genetic make-up – or its **genotype** – differs from that of all other individuals (except in the case of identical twins). As a result of these genetic differences, an individual organism's physical characteristics and behaviour, or its **phenotype**, also differs from that of every other individual.

Every individual's phenotype is produced by the interaction of its genotype with the environment. In essence, the genotype determines how much the environment can influence an organism's development and behaviour. For instance, identical twins have exactly the same genotype. If they are separated at birth and one twin has a better diet than the other, their phenotypes will be different: the better-fed twin is likely to be taller and stronger. However, regardless of diet, neither twin will ever become extremely tall or very muscular if they do not possess the genes for tallness and muscularity. Likewise, neither twin will realise their full potential for tallness and muscularity if they do not eat a nourishing diet. In this example, both the genotype (the genes related to tallness and muscularity) and a favourable environment (a well-balanced, nourishing diet) must be present for either twin to reach their full growth potential.

Phenotypes and the genotypes responsible for them may or may not be selected, depending on the particular advantage they confer. In a study that investigated the relationship between rainfall, food supply and finch population on one island, Grant (1986) discovered that the amount of rainfall and the size of the food supply directly affected the mortality of finches having certain kinds of beak. During droughts, small seeds became scarce. As a result, the finches having small, thin beaks died at a higher rate than finches having bigger, thicker beaks. During the next few years, the number of finches having bigger, thicker beaks increased – just as the principle of natural selection would predict. During times of plentiful rain, small seeds became abundant, and the number of finches having small, thin beaks became more plentiful in subsequent years.

Grant's study makes two important points. First, although evolution occurs over the long run, natural selection can produce important changes in the short run – in the space of only a few years. Secondly, phenotypic variation, in this case differences in beak size, can produce important selective advantages that affect survival. Imagine if all the finches had small, thin beaks: during the drought, most, if not all, of these finches might have died. None would be left to reproduce and these finches would have become extinct on this island. Fortunately, there was phenotypic variation in beak size among the finches, and because phenotypic variation is caused by genetic variation (different genotypes give rise to different phenotypes), some finches – those having large, thick beaks – had an advantage. Their food supply (the larger seeds) was relatively unaffected by the drought, enabling them to out-survive and out-reproduce the finches with small, thin beaks.

On the basis of this evidence, one might reasonably assume that all finches should have developed large, thick beaks. However, when rain is plentiful and small seeds are abundant, birds with small, thin beaks find it easier to feed. Under these environmental conditions, these birds have a phenotypic (and genotypic) advantage.

Competition

The second aspect of natural selection is **competition**. Individuals of a given species share a similar environment. Because of this, competition within a species for food, mates and territory is inevitable. Every fish captured and eaten by one bald eagle is a fish that cannot be captured and eaten by another bald eagle. If one bald eagle finds a suitable mate, then there is one fewer potential mates for other bald eagles and so on.

Competition also occurs between species when members of different species vie for similar ecological resources, such as food and territory. Competition for other resources indirectly influences reproductive success because the ability to find and court a suitable mate depends on the ability to stake out and defend a territory having an adequate food supply. The probability of a yellow-headed blackbird finding a mate and successfully rearing a family depends not only on its success in competing against other yellow-headed blackbirds, but also on its success in competing against red-winged blackbirds.

Natural selection works because the members of any species have different phenotypes. Because these phenotypes are caused by different genotypes, successful individuals will pass on their genes to the next generation. Over time, competition for food and other resources will allow only the best-adapted phenotypes (and their corresponding genotypes) to survive, thereby producing evolutionary change. This is what the theory would predict.

Knowledge and acceptance of evolution

How widespread do you think the acceptance of the theory of evolution is? In the US, it is law that science and religion are taught separately and that banning the teaching of evolution is unconstitutional (Scott and Matzke, 2007). In 2007, the Council of Europe's Parliamentary Assembly passed a resolution recommending that member states do not teach creationism as if it were the equivalent of science. One survey of over 1,000 students at a large American university, however, found that 25 per cent reported that their biology teacher had taught them creationism and 20 per cent were taught neither biology nor creationism (Moore, 2007). Creationism – the rejection of the theory of evolution in favour of the belief that the world was originated by a Creator – has gained some momentum in the USA, although recent legal rulings suggest that evolution is fighting back. Creationism's new incarnation is Intelligent Design but, to all intents and purposes, the terms are synonymous. The fierce and often acrimonious debate that exists between scientists and intelligent design advocates – see Dawkins's excoriating *The God Delusion* (2007) – could probably make a Controversies in Psychological Science section in itself.

Since 1985, American adults at various time intervals have been asked if the following statement is true or false: 'Human beings, as we know them, developed from earlier species of animals'. In 2002, US data were compared with those from nine European countries, with 32 countries in 2005 and with a survey of Japanese respondents in 2001 (Miller *et al.*, 2006). Figure 3.1 illustrates agreement/disagreement with the statement by nation.

Miller *et al.* found that over 20 years the percentage of Americans agreeing with the statement fell from 45 per cent to 40 per cent. Those who completely rejected the statement also fell from 48 per cent to 39 per cent. Those who were unsure jumped from 7 per cent in 1985 to 21 per cent in 2005. In later surveys, respondents were given the option of responding in a different way. They were asked whether the statement was definitely true, probably true, probably false, definitely false or don't know. A third of Americans considered the statement to be false and only 14 per cent regarded it as definitely true. European and Japanese respondents were more likely to accept the statement as true. In fact, the only country which was more sceptical than the US was Turkey. Eighty per cent of Iceland, Denmark, Sweden and France agreed; 78 per cent of the Japanese did. In European countries, the percentage absolutely disagreeing ranged from 7 per cent (Denmark, France, UK) to 15 per cent (the Netherlands).

Those who strongly believed in God, who prayed often and held pro-life beliefs were the most rejecting of the statement. All of these were more common in the US. Miller *et al.* explains the geographic disparity by suggesting that biblical fundamentalism – Genesis is to be read literally – is greater in the US, whereas in Europe Genesis is regarded as being more of a metaphor. A third of US respondents also agreed that half of the genes of mice and humans are identical and 38 per cent believed that we have half in common with chimps (as you'll see later, the percentage we share is a lot higher). Even if respondents disagreed with evolution, you might expect them to have a reasonable knowledge of the building blocks of life. Fewer than half of Americans surveyed were able to provide a passable definition of DNA.

Human evolution

Reconstruction of human evolution is a difficult job, something akin to assembling a giant jigsaw puzzle whose pieces have been scattered throughout the world. Some of the pieces may have been lost for ever; others have become damaged beyond recognition; and those few that are found force continual reinterpretation of how the other pieces might fit the puzzle. Another way in which we can date our remains is via carbon dating. Animals breathe a form of (naturally occurring) radioactive carbon called C14. When an animal dies, this carbon decays but at a constant rate. By examining the content of the carbon in the fossil or surrounding material, therefore, we can estimate the date of its existence. One problem here is that the amount of carbon found can be influenced by the amount in the air at the time.

We can also analyse the changes in DNA between similar fossils – the less the change in DNA, the closer the two fossils are in time. But the best we can do is make an educated guess about the evolution and lifestyles of our ancestors.

Many biologists and natural historians of Darwin's time believed that natural selection applied to all animals, including humans. Others insisted that although natural

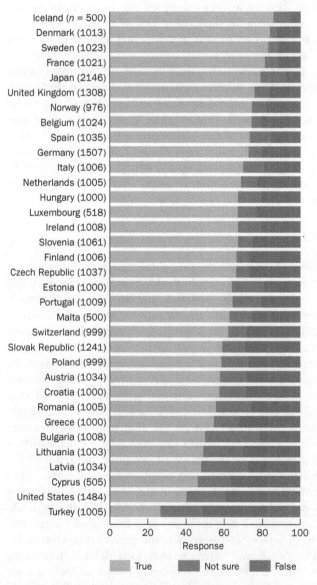

Figure 3.1 This graph shows 34 nations' degree of agreement with the statement 'Human beings, as we know them, developed from earlier species of animals'. The survey was undertaken in 2005.

Source: Miller, J.D., Scott, E. and Okamoto, S. (2006) Public acceptance of evolution. *Science*, 313, 765–6. Reprinted with permission from AAAS.

selection applied to other animals, it did not apply to humans. However, through study of the fossil record and recent developments in genetic research, we now know that our species is related genetically to other mammals. The gorilla and the chimpanzee are our closest living relatives, and together we appear to have descended from a common ancestor. You may have heard it said that we share 99 per cent of our genes with chimps. In fact, what we share is DNA involved in the production of proteins. Ninety-nine per cent of our DNA in this regard is identical (King and Wilson, 1975). Why, then, are we not exactly hirsute, whooping, tyre-swinging, banana-eaters? The reason is that 98 per cent of the human genome is not involved in the production of proteins. The remainder is involved in the timing of production and how much is produced (these are called regulatory genes – there is a more detailed description of genetics later in the chapter). It is this percentage which causes the great difference between the species (Demuth *et al.*, 2006). Humans also have multiple copies of genes that chimps do not (Pennisi, 2006). Therefore, while we have proteins in common, it is the way in which these proteins are organised which determines the differences between us.

Our dependence on information from fossil remains and other archaeological artefacts is problematic. As Byrne (1995) has colourfully pointed out, much of what we conclude about our ancestors' behaviour from archaeological findings is speculative; some is sensible speculation but it is speculation nonetheless. There is no way of empirically or conclusively demonstrating that artefacts were used in the way in which we suggest or that they indicate a specific way of living or behaving. In this sense, **paleoanthropology** – the study of human behaviour using information from fossil remains – is more like detective work than scientific work. 'The reality,' Byrne argues, 'is that we will never know with confidence the answers to many of the most important questions we would like to ask about what happened in the past five million years' (1995, p. 6).

With this caveat in mind, the general pattern of evolution is thought to occur something like this. Our evolution from a common ancestor appears to have begun in Africa about two to four million years ago (Clark, 1993).

The earliest humans have been labelled *Homo habilis* (literally 'handy man'). *Homo habilis* was small (only about 1.3 m tall and about 40 kg in weight), but was bipedal (able to walk upright on two feet). Compared with its predecessor – a species called *Australopithecus* ('apes from the South') – *Homo habilis* had a larger brain and more powerful hands. The strong hands were well suited to making simple stone tools; hence the name 'handy man'. A natural selection interpretation of such adaptively significant traits would argue that these early humans adapted to the environment in terms of creating shelter against the elements, catching and preparing food, and making weapons for self-defence.

Homo habilis was succeeded, about 400,000 years later, by *Homo erectus* ('upright man'). *Homo erectus* had a much larger brain and stood more erect than *Homo habilis* and had a more complex lifestyle. *Homo erectus* was the first of our ancestors to establish regular base camps, which probably served as centres for social activities, including the preparation and eating of food. We cannot be absolutely sure that these interpretations are the correct ones, however. *Homo erectus* created more efficient and stronger tools than did *Homo habilis*, successfully hunted big game, and discovered and used fire. Fire enabled these early humans to cook food, remain warm in cold weather and protect themselves from predators. *Homo erectus*'s use of fire, coupled with its apparent social nature and its ability to hunt and/or scavenge big game, permitted it to explore and settle new environments, including Europe, Asia, America and other parts of Africa (Spoor *et al.*, 2007).

The earliest known *Homo sapiens* ('intelligent man') appears to have arisen about 500,000 years ago. The best known of the early *Homo sapiens*, *Homo sapiens neanderthalensis* (so-called Neanderthals, named after the German valley in which the fossils were discovered), lived throughout Europe and Central Asia between approximately 300,000 and 35,000 years ago. Neanderthals constructed small huts from bones and animal skins and sometimes burned bones as fuel. They were skilled big game hunters, tool makers and clothiers, and they had cultural rituals for burying their dead. In one Neanderthal burial site unearthed in France, a small boy was found positioned on his left side with a small pillow of flints under his head and an axe positioned by his right hand. Similar Neanderthal burial sites have been discovered, suggesting that these humans possessed cultural traditions not previously found in the prehistoric record.

Informed speculation suggests that Neanderthals and modern humans (*Homo sapiens sapiens*) overlapped each other, although the origin of *Homo sapiens sapiens* is unclear. It seems to have arisen between 200,000 and 100,000 years ago. The Neanderthals became extinct around 25,000 years ago, with last evidence of their existence found in Gibraltar (Finlayson *et al.*, 2006). What is clear, though, is that the *Homo sapiens sapiens* line has survived to flourish in all parts of the world, despite the presence of hostile climate, terrain and predators. Figure 3.2 charts the suspected development of *Homo sapiens sapiens*. Some theorists have suggested that the variety of species is greater nearer the equator (Hillebrand, 2004) and that tropical environments create a museum and a cradle for species to flourish (McKenna and Farrell, 2006).

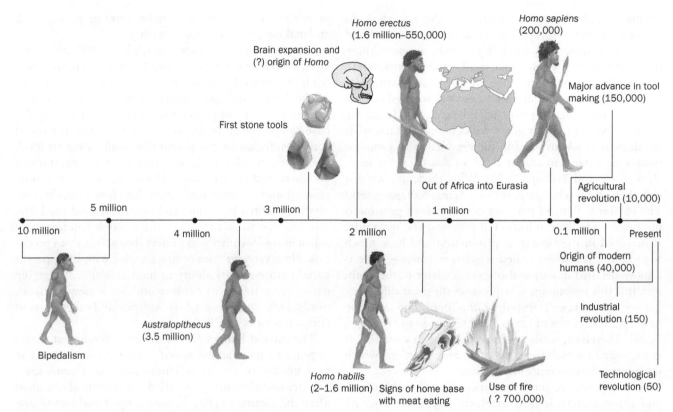

Figure 3.2 Major milestones in human evolution. The ability to walk upright freed the hands for tool use and other manipulative skills. Increased brain size accompanied increased intelligence. These two adaptations combined probably contributed significantly to all other major adaptations in human evolution.

Source: Adapted from Lewin, R., *Human Evolution: An illustrated introduction*. Cambridge, MA: Blackwell Scientific Publications, Inc., 1984.

Natural selection and human evolution

The apparent success of the human species in adapting to a variety of ecological niches stems from the fact that natural selection has favoured two important human characteristics: **bipedalism,** the ability to move about the environment on two feet, and **encephalisation,** increased brain size. The ability to walk upright, which appears to have evolved in our early hominid ancestors over 4 million years ago (Boaz, 1993; Ruff *et al.,* 1997), may have arisen from the need to stand on branches to reach food on other branches above (Thorpe *et al.,* 2007). Bipedalism allowed not only greater mobility, but also freed the hands for grabbing, holding and throwing objects. The ability to grasp objects, in combination with an expanding capacity for learning and remembering new skills provided by a larger brain, led to advances in tool making, food gathering, hunting and escaping predators (Eccles, 1989).

Early hominids had a brain volume of 650cm³ (and they were about 155cm tall). Current humans have a brain size of 1,500cm³ and are, on average, 175cm tall. It used to be thought that there was a relationship between body size and brain volume. However, the relationship is between relative size and brain volume and

Figures 3.3 (a)–(c) show the differences in brain and body size between various species. The increase in our brain relative to our size is called **positive brain allometry.** This began around 2 million years ago and has increased, more or less, since – from 450 cm³ (*Homo habilis*) to 1,000 cm³ (*Homo erectus*) to 1,350 cm³ 100,000 years ago (*Homo sapiens*). The increase may be attributable to better diet, better defence and, therefore, better survival. Children began to live longer, thus enabling the brain to be more fully developed when they conceived.

As the brain became larger, more of its volume – especially the front part which is the most recently evolved – appeared to become devoted to thinking, reasoning, decision-making and other complex cognitive, 'higher' functions. We will return to the role of this part of the brain in thinking in Chapter 11.

Another important ability that emerged from encephalisation was planning: the ability to anticipate future events and to consider the effects of these events on an individual or group of individuals. Such planning might have involved the organisation of hunts, the institution of social customs and events (such as weddings and funerals), and the planting and harvesting of crops. Over time, the interaction between bipedalism and

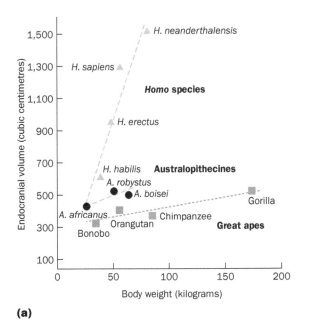

(a)

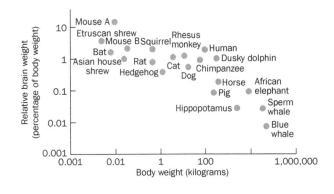

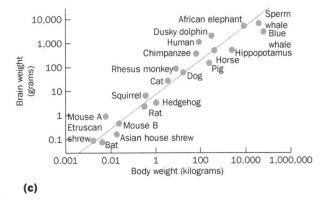

(c)

Brain weight (grams)

Sperm whale	9,000
African elephant	4,200
Bottlenose dolphin	1,350
Human	1,350
Horse	510
Gorilla	500
Ox	490
Chimpanzee	380
Lion	260
Rhesus monkey	64
Cat	25
Rat	2
Mouse	0.3

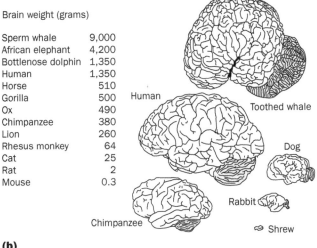

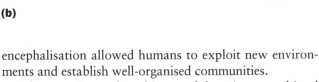

(b)

Figure 3.3 These three figures show the relationship between brain size and body weight in our human ancestors and non-human primates **(a)**; the weight of various species brains **(b)**; and the relationship between body weight and brain size in a variety of different species **(c)**.

Source: Dicke, U. and Roth, G. (2008). Intelligence evolved. *Scientific American Mind*.

encephalisation allowed humans to exploit new environments and establish well-organised communities.

Advances in tool making and hunting, combined with the use of fire for cooking, protection and warmth, were adaptive: they helped humans to live longer. The increased lifespan of humans may have aided the gradual accumulation of wisdom as the older members of early human communities began to share their knowledge with younger members through language. Although the fossil record cannot tell us when language first developed, we assume that those who were able to communicate with others through language had a distinct advantage over those who could not.

Language originated and subsequently evolved because of its immensely adaptive significance (Pinker, 1994). As Skinner (1986) noted, language not only provided a simple means of warning others of danger, but also provided a means of communicating important information to others, such as the location of a good hunting spot or instructions on how to craft a tool. Perhaps the most important advantage conferred by language was its ability to reinforce the already strong social tendencies of early humans. Language is the foundation upon which all human cultures are built (see Chapter 10).

Heredity and genetics

Darwin's work unveiled the process of natural selection and created new frontiers for exploration and experimentation. One of the most important of these frontiers is genetics, the study of 'the structure and function of genes and the way in which genes are passed from one generation to the next' (Russell, 1992, p. 2). Genetics, then, also involves the study of how the genetic make-up of an organism influences its physical and behavioural characteristics. Related to genetics are the principles of heredity, the sum of the traits and tendencies inherited from a person's parents and other biological ancestors. Although Darwin had built a strong case for natural selection, he could not explain a key tenet of his theory – inheritance. He knew that individual differences occurred within a given species and that those differences were subject to natural selection. But he did not know how adaptations were passed from parent to offspring.

Six years after *The Origin of Species* was published, Gregor Mendel, an Austrian monk who conducted experimental cross-breeding studies with pea plants, uncovered the basic principles of heredity. Mendel demonstrated conclusively how height, flower colour, seed shape and other traits of pea plants could be transmitted from one generation to the next. His work has since been applied to studying heredity in thousands of plants and animals.

The basic principles of genetics

Genes are segments of genetic material called **DNA** (deoxyribonucleic acid) – strands of sugar and phosphate that are connected by nucleotide molecules of

The Brit, Francis Crick, and the American, John Watson, who cracked the DNA code and were rewarded with a Nobel Prize in 1962, jointly with Marcus Williams.

Source: A. Barrington Brown/Science Photo Library Ltd.

adenine, thymine, guanine and cytosine. Each pairs up with another, but guanine always pairs with cytosine and adenine with thymine. These pairs form steps in a spiral staircase called a double helix. That is, the DNA is configured like a twisted ladder: the sugar and phosphate form the sides and the four nucleotides form the rungs. You can see this in Figure 3.4.

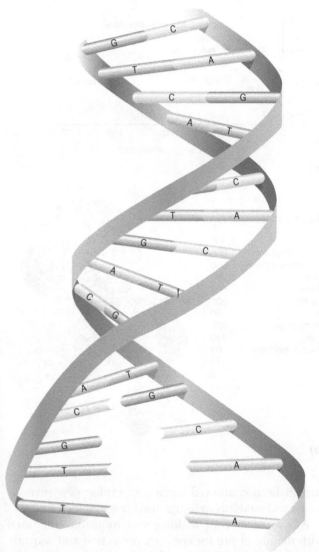

Figure 3.4 The structure and composition of DNA. DNA resembles a twisted ladder whose sides are composed of molecules of sugar and phosphate and whose rungs are made of combinations of four nucleotide bases: adenine (A), thymine (T), guanine (G) and cytosine (C). Genes are segments of DNA that direct the synthesis of proteins and enzymes according to the particular sequences of nucleotide bases that they contain. In essence, genes serve as 'recipes' for the synthesis of these proteins and enzymes, which regulate the cellular and other physiological processes of the body, including those responsible for behaviour.

Source: Based on Watson, J.D., *Molecular Biology of the Gene*. Menlo Park, CA: Benjamin, 1976.

The particular sequence of these nucleotide molecules directs the synthesis of protein molecules that regulate the biological and physical development of the body and its organs. Some protein molecules regulate cell development and others regulate the chemical interactions that occur within cells. Three billion pairs of these proteins form our genetic code (Plomin, 2008).

Protein synthesis

Genes can only influence our development and behaviour through protein synthesis. Proteins are strings of amino acids arranged in a chain. Each sequence of nucleotides (adenine, thymine, guanine and cytosine) specifies a particular amino acid. In a sense, genes are 'recipes' consisting of different nucleotide sequences. In this case, the recipe is for combining the proteins necessary to create and develop physiological structures and for behaviour – how those structures might function in response to environmental stimulation.

Strictly speaking, however, there are no genes for behaviour, only for the physical structures and physiological processes that are related to behaviour. For example, when we refer to a gene for schizophrenia (a mental disorder characterised by irrational thinking, delusions, hallucinations and perceptual distortions), we are really referring to a gene that contains instructions for synthesising particular proteins, which, in turn, are responsible for the development of specific physiological processes that are sensitive to certain stressful environmental conditions (we may even be wrong in specifying just one gene – there may be more than one).

Genes also direct the synthesis of **enzymes**, proteins which govern the processes that occur within every cell in the body, and thus control each cell's structure and function. In 2003, the Human Genome Project was completed and this mapped the sequence of approximately 3 billion pairs of molecules that make up the rungs of DNA. It found 25,000 genes in each human cell and it is these genes which make us what we are. It was an outstanding achievement, but what is left to do is probably very much harder: trying to associate genes with behaviour and expression in a consistent and reliable way. In the past 25 years there has been an enormous surge in the number of human genetic studies, as Figure 3.5 shows. How does the genotype manifest itself into the phenotype? How do these genes enable organs to be developed and to function (and specific organs at that)?

Chromosomes and meiosis

Genes are located on **chromosomes**, the rod-like structures made of DNA found in the nucleus of every cell. In essence, genes are particular regions of chromosomes that contain the recipes for particular proteins. Each set of chromosomes contains a different sequence of genes. We inherit 23 individual chromosomes from each of our parents, giving us 23 pairs – 46 individual chromosomes – in most cells of the body. One pair of chromosomes, the **sex chromosomes**, contains the instructions for the development of male or female sex characteristics – those characteristics that distinguish males from females.

Sexual reproduction involves the union of a sperm, which carries genetic instructions from the male, with an ovum (egg), which carries genetic instructions from the female. Sperms and ova differ from the other bodily cells in at least two important ways. First, new bodily cells are created by simple division of existing cells. Secondly, all 23 pairs of chromosomes divide in two, making copies of themselves.

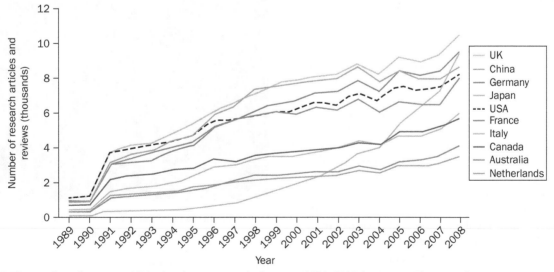

Figure 3.5 The number of papers published on human genetics between 1989–2008, by country. These are the top ten producers of genetics research.

Source: The Wellcome Trust.

The copies pull apart, and the cell splits into two cells, each having a complete set of 23 pairs of chromosomes. Sperms and ova are formed by a special form of cell division called **meiosis**. The 23 pairs of chromosomes break apart into two groups, with one member of each pair joining one of the groups. The cell splits into two cells, each of which contains 23 individual chromosomes. The assignment of the members of each pair of chromosomes to a particular group is a random process; thus, a single individual can produce 223 (8,388,608) different ova or sperms.

Although brothers and sisters may resemble each other, they are not exact copies. Because the union of a particular sperm with an ovum is apparently random, a couple can produce 8,388,608 × 8,388,608, or 70,368,774,177,664 different children. Only identical twins are genetically identical. Identical twins occur when a fertilised ovum divides, giving rise to two identical individuals. Fraternal twins are no more similar than any two siblings. They occur when a woman produces two ova, both of which are fertilised (by different sperms).

Sex is determined by the twenty-third pair of chromosomes: the sex chromosomes. There are two different kinds of sex chromosomes, X chromosomes and Y chromosomes. Females have a pair of X chromosomes (XX); males have one of each type (XY). Because women's cells contain only X chromosomes, each of their ova contains a single X chromosome (along with 22 other single chromosomes). Because men's cells contain both an X chromosome and a Y chromosome, half of the sperm they produce contain an X chromosome and half contain a Y chromosome. Thus, the sex of a couple's offspring depends on which type of sperm fertilises the ovum. A Y-bearing sperm produces a boy, and an X-bearing sperm produces a girl. Figure 3.6(a) illustrates this process; Figure 3.6(b) shows the human chromosomes.

Dominant and recessive alleles

Each pair of chromosomes contains pairs of genes: one gene in each pair is contributed by each parent. Individual genes in each pair can be identical or different. Alternative forms of genes are called **alleles** (from the Greek *allos*, 'other'). Consider eye colour, for example. The pigment found in the iris of the eye is produced by a particular gene. If parents each contribute the same allele for eye colour to their child, the gene combination is called homozygous (from the Greek *homo*, 'same', and *zygon*, 'yolk'). However, if the parents contribute different alleles, the gene combination is said to be heterozygous (from the Greek *hetero*, 'different'). Heterozygous gene combinations produce phenotypes controlled by the **dominant allele** – the allele that has a more powerful influence on the expression of the trait. The allele for brown eyes is dominant. When a child inherits the allele for brown eye

colour from one parent and the allele for blue eye colour from the other parent, the child will have brown eyes. Brown eye colour is said to be a dominant trait. The blue eye colour controlled by the **recessive allele** – the allele that

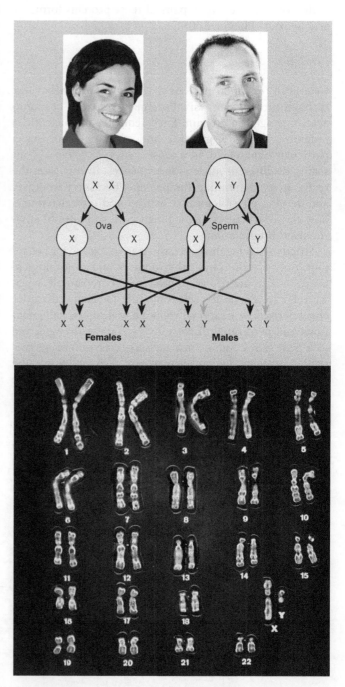

Figure 3.6 (a) Determination of sex: the sex of human offspring depends on whether the sperm that fertilises the ovum carries an X or a Y chromosome.
(b) Human chromosomes: the presence of a Y chromosome indicates that this sample came from a male. A sample from a female would include two X chromosomes.
Source: CNRI/Science Photo Library Ltd.

has a weaker effect on the expression of a trait – is not expressed. Only if both of a child's alleles for eye colour are of the blue type will the child have blue eyes. Thus, having blue eyes is said to be a recessive trait. Inheritance of two alleles for brown eyes will, of course, result in brown eyes. You can see this in Figure 3.7.

Other eye colours, such as hazel or black, are produced by the effects of other genes, which influence the dominant brown allele to code for more (black) or less (hazel) pigment in the iris.

It is important to remember that the genetic contributions to our personal development and behaviour are extremely complex. One reason for this complexity is that protein synthesis is often under polygenic control, that is, it is influenced by many pairs of genes, not just a single pair. The inheritance of behaviour is even more complicated, because different environments influence the expression of polygenic traits. Consider, for example, the ability to run. Running speed for any individual is the joint product of genetic factors that produce proteins for muscle, bone, blood, oxygen metabolism and motor coordination (to name but a few) and environmental factors such as exercise patterns, age, nutrition, accidents and so on.

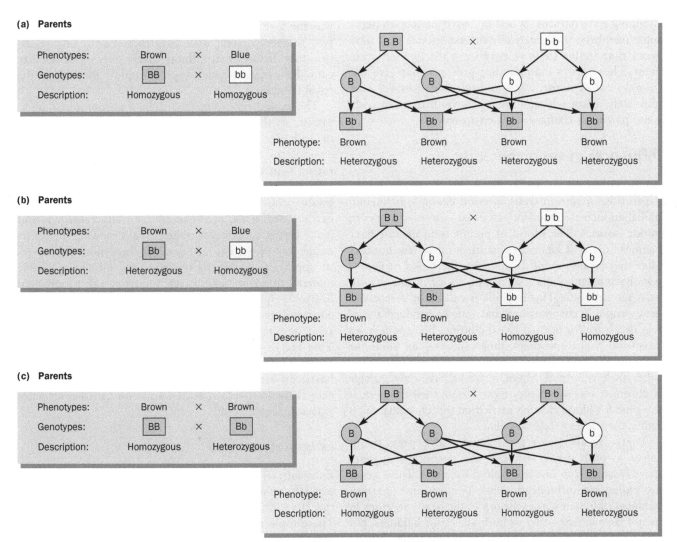

Figure 3.7 Patterns of inheritance for eye colour. **(a)** If one parent is homozygous for the dominant eye colour (BB), and the other parent is homozygous for the recessive eye colour (bb), then all their children will be heterozygous for eye colour (Bb) and will have brown eyes. **(b)** If one parent is heterozygous (Bb), and the other parent is homozygous recessive (bb), then their children will have a 50 per cent chance of being heterozygous (brown eyes) and a 50 per cent chance of being homozygous recessive (blue eyes). **(c)** If one parent is homozygous dominant (BB), and the other parent is heterozygous (Bb), then their children will have a 50 per cent chance of being homozygous for the dominant eye colour (BB) and will have brown eyes, and a 50 per cent chance of being heterozygous (Bb) for the trait and will have brown eyes.

Source: Based on Klug, W.S. and Cummings, M.R., *Concepts of Genetics* (2nd edn). Glenview, IL: Scott, Foresman, 1986. © 1986 Scott, Foresman & Co. Reprinted by permission of Addison Wesley Educational Publishers, Inc.

Genetic diversity

No two individuals, except identical twins, are genetically identical. Such genetic diversity is a characteristic of all species that reproduce sexually. Some organisms, however, reproduce asexually, such as yeast and fungi. Nurseries often reproduce plants and trees through grafting, which is an asexual process. But when we examine the world around us, we find that the overwhelming majority of species reproduce sexually. Why?

One answer is that sexual reproduction increases a species' ability to adapt to environmental changes. Sexual reproduction leads to genetic diversity, and genetically diverse species have a better chance of adapting to a changing environment. When the environment changes, some members of a genetically diverse species may have genes that enable them to survive in the new environment. These genes manufacture proteins that give rise to physical structures, physiological processes, and, ultimately, adaptively significant behaviour that can withstand particular changes in the environment.

Influences of sex on heredity

An individual's sex plays a crucial role in influencing the expression of certain traits. A good example is haemophilia, an increased tendency to bleed seriously from even minor injuries. The blood of people who do not have haemophilia will begin to clot in the first few minutes after they sustain a cut. In contrast, the blood of people who have haemophilia may not do so for 30 minutes or even several hours. Haemophilia is caused by a recessive gene on the X chromosome that fails to produce a protein necessary for normal blood clotting. Because females have two X chromosomes, they can carry an allele for haemophilia but still have normal blood clotting if the other allele is normal. Males, however, have only a single X chromosome, which they receive from their mothers. If the gene for blood clotting carried on this chromosome is faulty, they develop haemophilia.

There are also sex-related genes that express themselves in both sexes, although the phenotype appears more frequently in one sex than in the other. These genes are called **sex-influenced genes**. For example, pattern baldness (thin hair across the top of the head) develops in men if they inherit either or both alleles for baldness, but this trait is not seen in women, even when they inherit both alleles.

Mutations and chromosomal aberrations

Changes in genetic material are caused by **mutations** or **chromosomal aberrations**. Mutations are accidental alterations in the DNA code within a single gene. Mutations are the original source of genetic diversity. Although most mutations have harmful effects, some may produce characteristics that are beneficial in certain environments. Mutations can be either spontaneous, occurring naturally, or the result of human-made factors such as high-energy radiation.

Haemophilia provides one of the most famous examples of mutation. Although haemophilia has appeared many times in human history, no other case of haemophilia has had as far-reaching effects as the spontaneous mutation that was passed among the royal families of nineteenth-century Europe. Through genealogical analysis, researchers have discovered that this particular mutant gene arose with Queen Victoria (1819–1901). She was the first in her family line to bear affected children – two female carriers and an afflicted son. The tradition that dictates that nobility marry only other nobility caused the mutant gene to spread rapidly throughout the royal families.

The second type of genetic change, chromosomal aberration, involves either changes in parts of chromosomes or a change in the total number of chromosomes. An example of a disorder caused by a chromosomal aberration – in this case, a partial deletion of the genetic material in chromosome 5 – is the **cri-du-chat syndrome**. Infants who have this syndrome have gastrointestinal and cardiac problems, are severely mentally retarded, and make crying sounds resembling a cat's mewing (hence its name, 'cry of the cat'). In general, the syndrome's severity appears to be directly related to the amount of genetic material that is missing. Psychologists and developmental disability specialists have discovered that early special education training permits many individuals having this syndrome to learn self-care and communication skills. This fact highlights an important point about genetics and behaviour: even behaviour that has a genetic basis can often be modified through training or experience (Day and Sweatt, 2011), a notion called **epigenetics** (Masterpasqua, 2009).

Epigenetics

External events like trauma, drug abuse, lack of affection can affect the functioning of DNA. When these happen, the DNA does not alter, but is coated with molecules. These molecules alter the expression of the gene in two ways – either by preventing protein being constructed or by accelerating it. As you saw earlier, protein is essential to maintain the body and the brain. In the body, there is selective gene expression – each cell in the body may have the same gene but different cells use different types of gene. It does this via a molecule called ribonucleic acid (RNA), an intermediate molecule which is used by proteins attached to DNA to convert into other proteins.

This is why a cell from the lung, for example, is different from one from the brain or the heart.

A gene can be silenced; molecules can be prevented from accessing it and this is what epigenetic mechanisms do. They either facilitate or block access to the genes in cells. This, consequently, affects gene expression. In one experiment, the stress response of rats whose mothers had licked or groomed them consistently for up to 10 days after birth was compared with those who had not. The first group showed less anxiety and stress. The gene that allows the release of a hormone called corticosterone was examined in these pups and those who had not been licked had fewer corticosterone receptors in their brain (Weaver *et al.*, 2004). One proposed mechanism for this is that the hormone interacts with a structure in the brain called the hypothalamus to prevent it from overreacting to stressful events.

Another protein, brain-derived neurotrophic factor (BDNF), which is important for the growth, integrity and functioning of cells, is lower in women with depression and it has been suggested that distressing events or experiences can alter the DNA that encodes this protein. In one experiment, 'bully' mice and smaller, normal mice were placed in a cage together for five minutes and then separated by a mesh for 10 days (Berton *et al.*, 2006). As you might predict, the smaller mice showed the typical stress reaction – they would become submissive and anxious. However, when their brains were examined for levels of BDNF, these were lower in the bullied mice. More importantly, the molecule known to affect the expression of this protein was found in one region of the mice's brains. This molecule had shut off the BDNF protein. A course of antidepressants raised the levels of BDNF.

Similar to these genes are 'knockout genes', which work in a similar way. The animal is exposed to radiation which damages a gene. This inserts nucleotides in the gene which prevent it from expressing itself, hence, the gene has been 'knocked out'. When the gene which encodes for spatial learning had been knocked out in rats, their ability to learn to swim to a platform that was not visible underneath a pool of water was impaired (Nakazawa *et al.*, 2003).

Heredity and behaviour genetics

Each of us is born into a different environment and each of us possesses a unique combination of genetic instructions. As a result, we differ from one another. Consider your fellow undergraduates, for example. They come in different sizes and shapes, they vary in personality and intelligence, and they possess unequal artistic and athletic abilities. To what extent are these sorts of differences attributable to heredity or to the environment? If all your classmates had been reared in identical environments, any differences between them would necessarily be due to genetics. Conversely, if all your classmates had come from the same fertilised egg but were subsequently raised in different environments, any differences in their personal characteristics would necessarily be due only to the environment.

Heritability is a statistical term that refers to the amount of variability in a trait in a given population that is due to genetic differences among the individuals in that population. Heritability is sometimes confused with inheritance, the tendency of a given trait to be passed from parent to individual offspring. But heritability does not apply to individuals, it pertains only to the variation of a trait in a specific population. The more that a trait in a given population is influenced by genetic factors, the greater its heritability. The scientific study of heritability – of the effects of genetic influences on behaviour – is called behaviour genetics. As noted by one of this field's most prolific researchers, Robert Plomin, behaviour genetics is intimately involved with providing an explanation of why people differ (Plomin, 2008). As we will see below, behaviour geneticists attempt to account for the roles that both heredity and the environment play in individual differences in a wide variety of physical and mental abilities.

Behavioural genetics has begun to contribute to our biological understanding of a variety of psychological variables, including types of memory, the developmental disorders autism and developmental dyslexia, personality, ageing and emotional recognition and expression, although there is currently no agreement on the precise genes necessary for the phenotypes to be expressed (Bevilacqua and Goldman, 2011; Geschwind, 2011; Harris and Deary, 2011; Munafo and Flint, 2011; Papassotiropoulos and de Quervain, 2011). For example, twin studies (see below) suggest that the heritability for the ability to recall past experiences and their spatial and temporal context – a form of memory called episodic memory (described in Chapter 8) – is between 30 and 60 per cent. Variants of genes though to be implicated in memory include *HTR2A* and *BDNF* (de Quervain *et al.*, 2003), but others include *COMT, GRM3, PRNP, CHREAMTA, APOE, PDYN* and *CPEB3* (Papassotiropoulos and de Quervain, 2011) and *KIBRA* and *CLSTN2* (Papassotiropoulos *et al.*, 2006). *KIBRA* may be associated with the conscious recall of material and *BDNF*, which has received considerable attention, with learning that is dependent on the hippocampus, a structure which you will read about in the next chapter and in Chapter 8, and which is essential for the formation of new memories.

One particular gene, the *APOE E4* allele, appears to be important to cognitive decline and the possible development of dementia associated with Alzheimer's disease (see Chapter 11) although, again, the picture is mixed and is discussed in that chapter (Harris and Deary, 2011).

Studying genetic influences

Although farmers and animal breeders had experimented with artificial selection for thousands of years, only within the past 150 years has the relation between heredity and behaviour been formally studied in the laboratory. Mendel's careful analysis of genetic influences on specific characteristics gave us the first good clue that traits were actually heritable. Galton (1869) stimulated further interest in this field with his studies showing that intelligence tends to run in families (see Chapter 1): if parents are intelligent then, in general, so are their children. The search for genetic bases of behaviour has been active ever since. In fact, the search to understand the relative contributions of heredity and environment to human behaviour is among the most heavily researched areas in psychology.

Artificial selection in animals

Any heritable trait can be selected in a breeding programme. The heritability of many traits in animals, such as aggression, docility, preference for alcohol, running speed and mating behaviours, can be studied by means of artificial selection.

Consider, for example, Tryon's (1940) study of maze learning in rats. Tryon wished to determine whether genetic variables influenced learning. He began his study with a large sample of genetically diverse rats. He trained them to learn a maze and recorded the number of errors each rat made in the process. He then selected two groups of rats – those that learned the fastest (bright) and those that learned the slowest (dull). He mated 'bright' rats with other 'bright' rats and 'dull' rats with other 'dull' rats. To ensure that the rats were not somehow learning the maze from their mothers, he 'adopted out' some of the pups: some of the bright pups were reared by dull mothers and some of the dull pups were reared by bright mothers. He found that parenting made little difference in his results, so this factor can be discounted.

Tryon continued this sequence of having rats learn the maze and selectively breeding the best with the best (bright) and the worst with the worst (dull) over many generations. Soon, the maze performance of each group was completely different. He concluded that maze learning in rats could be manipulated through artificial selection.

Later studies showed that Tryon's results were limited by the standard laboratory cage environment in which rats lived when they were not running the maze. For example, Cooper and Zubek (1958) demonstrated that differences in maze ability were virtually eliminated when bright and dull strains of rats were reared in either enriched environments designed to stimulate learning (cages containing geometric objects, such as tunnels, ramps and blocks) or impoverished environments designed to inhibit learning (cages containing only food and water dishes).

However, Cooper and Zubek's rats that were reared in the standard laboratory cage performed similarly to Tryon's rats: the bright rats outperformed the dull rats. Thus, changing the environmental conditions in which the rats lived had an important result – reducing the effects of genetic differences between the bright and dull rats. This finding makes good sense when you consider the fact that genes are not expressed in the absence of an environment.

Tryon's research demonstrated that over successive generations a trait can be made to become more or less likely in a given population, but we do not know precisely why. We do not know whether genes related to learning or genes related to other traits were selected. Tryon's rats may have been neither especially bright nor especially dull. Perhaps each of these strains differed in its capacity to be motivated by the food reward that awaited it at the end of the maze.

Can gene manipulation ever occur in humans? Experiments involving the cloning of sheep illustrate the power of molecular genetics in radically altering nature's forms. Gene mapping may help us to understand how specific DNA sequences can influence physiological processes that affect behaviour, emotion, remembering and thinking and play a crucial role in identifying specific genes involved in psychological disorders (Plomin and DeFries, 1998). Some of these issues are discussed in the chapters on memory, intelligence and mental disorders (Chapters 8, 11 and 18).

Twin studies

There are two barriers to studying the effects of heredity on behavioural traits in humans. First, ethical considerations prevent psychologists and geneticists from manipulating people's genetic history or restricting the type of environment in which they are reared. For example, we cannot artificially breed people to learn the extent to which shyness, extraversion or any other personality characteristics are inherited or deprive the offspring of intelligent people of a good education to see if their intelligence will be affected. Secondly, in most cases, the enormous variability in human environments effectively masks any correlation that might exist between genetics and trait expression.

Psychologists have been able to circumvent these barriers by taking advantage of an important quirk of nature – multiple births. Recall that identical twins, also called **monozygotic (MZ) twins**, arise from a single fertilised ovum, called a zygote, that splits into two genetically identical cells. **Fraternal** or **dizygotic (DZ) twins** develop from the separate fertilisation of two ova. DZ twins are no more alike genetically than any two siblings. Because

MZ twins are genetically identical, they should be more similar to one another in terms of their psychological characteristics (such as personality or intelligence) than either DZ twins or non-twin siblings (see Figure 3.8).

Concordance research examines the degree of similarity in traits expressed between twins. Twins are concordant for a trait if both of them express it or if neither does, and they are discordant if only one expresses it. If concordance rates (which can range from 0 to 100 per cent) of any given trait are substantially higher for MZ twins than for DZ twins, heredity is likely involved in the expression of that trait. Tables 3.1(a) and (b) compare concordance values and correlations between MZ and DZ twins for several traits.

When we observe a trait exhibiting a high concordance for MZ twins but a low one for DZ twins, we can conclude that the trait may be strongly affected by genetics. This is especially true for a trait such as blood type, which has a heritability of 100 per cent. If the concordance rates are similar, the effect of heredity is low. Some research has extended this difference to psychological variables such as intelligence, attitudes and personality.

For example, pairs of identical twins have been found to hold more similar views on subjects such as religion, crime, punishment and so on than do pairs of DZ twins (Eaves et al., 1989), have fibres connecting parts of the brain that are more similar in volume (Jahanshad et al., 2010) and show greater asymmetry in the fibres connecting the front and the back of the brain. In a study of 195 pairs of MZ twins and 141 pairs of DZ twins, Olson et al. (2001) found that identical twins were more likely to share similar attitudes on 26 of 30 attitude items than were DZ twins (see Table 3.1b). Does this suggest that there are genes for such attitudes?

Figure 3.8 Monozygotic twins.
Source: Corbis: Outline.

Table 3.1 (a) Comparison of concordance rates and (b) correlations between monozygotic (MZ) and dizygotic (DZ) twins for various traits

(a)

| | Concordance % | |
Trait	MZ	DZ
Bood types	100	66
Eye colour	99	28
Mental retardation	97	37
Measles	95	87
Idiopathic epilepsy	72	15
Schizophrenia	69	10
Diabetes	65	18
Identical allergy	59	5
Tuberculosis	57	23

(b)

| | Correlations | |
Attitude	MZ	DZ
Doing crossword puzzles	0.46	0.11
Death penalty for murder	0.45	0.33
Sweets	0.36	0.23
Open-door immigration	0.47	0.20
Doing athletic activities	0.41	0.26
Voluntary euthanasia	0.45	0.21
Smoking	0.49	0.38
Being the centre of attention	0.31	0.14
Separate roles for men and women	0.27	0.26
Education	0.30	0.14
Making racial discrimination illegal	0.37	−0.01
Loud music	0.53	0.49
Getting along well with other people	0.20	0.19
Capitalism	0.41	0.19
Playing organised sports	0.52	0.10
Big parties	0.44	0.30
Playing chess	0.38	0.22
Looking my best all the time	0.42	0.14
Abortion on demand	0.53	0.28
Public speaking	0.34	0.26
Playing bingo	0.37	0.33
Wearing clothes that draw attention	0.38	0.28
Easy access to birth control	0.24	0.27
Exercising	0.35	0.17
Organised religion	0.43	0.21
Being the leader of groups	0.40	0.08
Reading books	0.55	0.24
Castration as punishment for sex crimes	0.39	0.29
Being assertive	0.28	0.27
Roller coaster rides	0.50	0.31

Source: **(a)** Table 7.4, p. 161 from *Concepts of Genetics*, 2nd edn, by William S. Klug and Michael R. Cummings. Copyright © 1986 by Scott, Foresman and Company. Reprinted by permission of Pearson Education, Inc. **(b)** Adapted from Olson, J.M., Vernon, P.A., Harris, J.A. and Jang, K.L. The heritability of attitudes: A study of twins. *Journal of Personality and Social Psychology*, 2001, 80(6) 845–60, copyright 2001 by the American Psychological Association, reprinted with permission.

This is highly unlikely. Instead, the authors suggest that there may be more general traits of factors which reflect specific attitudes. For example, when they took personality into account, they found that the trait of sociability was highly associated with five of the six attitude factors, perhaps suggesting that sociability may be the underlying 'cause' of such attitudes and which may be the heritable factor. Participants' attitudes towards leadership correlated with self-reported physical attractiveness, sociability and aggressiveness, but interpreting this relationship is difficult. Perhaps very attractive, sociable or aggressive people achieve leadership more easily and readily than do their less attractive, less sociable and less aggressive counterparts and that attitudes to leadership became more positive as a consequence. Conversely, participants may have been favourable towards leadership and made themselves more attractive, sociable or aggressive in order to achieve the status of leader.

Sociobiology and evolutionary psychology

Sociobiology has been defined as 'the systematic study of the biological basis of all social behaviour' (Wilson, 1975). It represents the synthesis of research findings regarding social behaviour from many other fields of science, including those from evolutionary psychology, anthropology and behaviour genetics. Evolutionary psychology and behaviour genetics are more specific fields than sociobiology in the sense that both are concerned with phenomena such as intelligence and cognition, in addition to social behaviour.

Sociobiologists are especially interested in understanding the evolutionary roots of our modern-day social actions. More often than not, sociobiologists study the evolutionary bases of social behaviour in non-human animals and then extrapolate from those species to humans (Barash, 1982). Sociobiology represents an interface between the biological sciences and psychology. However, not all psychologists are convinced of the sociobiologists' claims, arguing that sociobiology is too simplistic and that its emphasis on genetics inadequately explains the complexities of human behaviour.

Reproductive strategies and the biological basis of parenting

Perhaps the most important social behaviours related to the survival of a species are those related to reproduction and parenting. According to Puts (2010), around 75 per cent of the papers published in the journals *Evolution*,

Hormones and Behaviour and *Human Nature* between 1997 and 2007 were on mate choice. A focal point of sociobiological research and theory has been understanding more about the different kinds of social organisation that result from particular **reproductive strategies** – systems of mating and rearing offspring.

We assume that most Western sexual relationships are monogamous: the mating of one female and one male. If mating is successful, the individuals share in the raising of the child or children. But **monogamy** is just one of several reproductive strategies sexual creatures employ in mating and rearing of offspring (Barash, 1982). Three other major classes of reproductive strategy are also possible:

- **Polygyny:** one male mates with more than one female.
- **Polyandry:** one female mates with more than one male.
- **Polygynandry:** several females mate with several males.

According to Trivers (1972), these four reproductive strategies evolved because of important sex differences in the resources that parents invest in conceiving and rearing their offspring. Parental investment is the time, physical effort and risks to life involved in procreation and in the feeding, nurturing and protecting of offspring. According to sociobiologists, parental investment is a critical factor in mate selection. An individual who is willing and able to make a greater investment is generally more sought after as a mate and is often more selective or discriminating when selecting a mate (Trivers, 1972). Given that a human female will gestate for nine months, she should be highly selective about choosing a mate. On the basis of Trivers's theory, it is possible to predict that women will express an (evolved) preference for men who have high status and will divorce those who do not contribute the expected resources or who divert them to other women and children (Buss, 1995).

In some species, competition for mates leads to **sexual selection** – selection for traits specific to sex, such as body size or particular patterns of behaviour. For example, in some animals, such as buffalo, females select mates based on the male's ability to survive the skirmishes of the rutting (mating) season. In general, the larger and more aggressive males win these battles and gain access to more females and enjoy greater reproductive success.

This competition is assisted by the physical differences between men and women. For example, if fat is factored out, men are 40 per cent heavier and have 60 per cent more muscle than women, have 80 per cent greater arm muscle, 50 per cent lower body mass muscle (Lassek and Gaulin, 2008, 2009), and 90 per cent upper body strength. Their sprint times are 22 per cent faster, and they can leap 45 per cent higher; the average man is stronger than 99 per cent of women (Lassek and Gaulin, 2009). Men are also more likely to be aggressive, as are boys – they attack more, hit more and restrain more.

These factors, together with masculine features such as beards and deep voices, are important factors in mate choice and contribute to contest competition – a way in which men can eliminate (metaphorically) other men who compete for female attention. It is women who normally express choice for mates and so men vie for female attention using whatever means they believe will be successful and this means removing opposition. Therefore, men compete for sexual attention and women select based on so-called gene quality (which is what fitness, strength, masculinity are thought to convey).

Men prefer women with faces that are gracile – not lined, hirsute or masculine, and who have minimal body hair and high voices (Rilling *et al.*, 2009). These features all signify youthfulness and, therefore, reproductivity. They also prefer a particular waist to hip ratio, you will see later. It is interesting to note that no other primate has the fat distribution of women – on the breasts and hips (Pond and Mattacks, 1987).

Evolution, however, has led to the development of a male brain that can go beyond mere punch-ups and Tom Jones impersonations: men also use humour, music, poetry and other creative vehicles to attract a mate and these factors are considered important to women in a long-term relationship (Gangestad *et al.*, 2007; Prokosch *et al.*, 2009).

Polygyny is by far the most common reproductive strategy among humans. Eighty-four per cent of human societies practise polygyny or allow men who are either wealthy or powerful to practise it (Badcock, 1991). Monogamy is the next most popular reproductive strategy, with about 15 per cent of all human cultures practising it. Polyandry and polygynandry are both rare: combined, these two reproductive strategies dominate in fewer than 1 per cent of all human cultures.

Polygyny: high female and low male parental investment

In many species, the female makes the greater parental investment. According to sociobiological theory, whether one is an ova producer or a sperm producer defines the nature of one's parental investment.

Among most mammals (including humans), the costs associated with reproduction are higher for females than for males. First, females have fewer opportunities than males to reproduce. Generally, females produce only one ovum or a few ova periodically, whereas males produce vast quantities of sperm over substantially shorter time intervals. Secondly, females carry the fertilised ovum in their bodies during a long gestation period, continuously diverting a major portion of their own metabolic resources to nourish the rapidly growing foetus. Females also assume all the risks that accompany pregnancy and

childbirth, including physical discomfort and possible death. The male's contributions to reproduction are, at a minimum, the sperm and the time needed for intercourse. Thirdly, after the offspring is born, females may continue to devote some of their metabolic resources to the infant by nursing it. Just as important, they usually devote more time and physical energy than males to caring for the newborn.

In addition, a female can only bear a certain number of offspring in a lifetime, regardless of the number of males with whom she mates. In contrast, a male is limited in his reproductive success only by the number of females he can impregnate. For example, consider the differences between females and males in our species. If a woman became pregnant once a year for ten years, she would have ten children – only a fraction of the number of children that a man is capable of fathering over the same interval. If a man impregnated a different woman every month for ten years, he would have fathered 120 children. This example is hardly an exaggeration. According to the *Guinness Book of World Records*, the largest number of live births to one woman is 69 (she had several multiple births). In contrast, King Ismail of Morocco is reported to have fathered 1,056 children.

In many polygynous species, intense competition for the opportunity to mate occurs among males. The competition almost always involves some sort of physical confrontation: that is, males fight among themselves for the opportunity to mate. Usually, the larger, stronger and more aggressive male wins, which means that only he will mate with the available females in the vicinity. If one of the smaller, weaker males attempts to mate with a female, he is generally chased away by the victorious male.

Because females in polygynous species invest so heavily in their offspring, they are – according to sociobiologists – usually highly selective of their mates, choosing to mate only with those males who possess specific attributes, such as physical size, strength and aggressiveness. Such selectivity makes adaptive sense for both the female and her progeny.

Physical attractiveness

As the International Perspective and Controversies in Psychological Science sections below show, there is evidence that some aspects of our physical appearance are preferred more than others. Some studies find that body mass index (BMI) is important, especially when full-frontal images are judged; others suggest that shape is more important if a figure is seen in profile.

To test this hypothesis, Tovee and Cornelissen (2001) asked 40 male and 40 female undergraduates in the UK to rate a set of photographs of real women with obscured faces. There were 50 front-view figures and 50 in profile.

BMI, not **waist-to-hip ratio** (WHR), was the best predictor of attractiveness for figures seen from the front or in profile. Both men and women gave similar ratings, thus supporting the second hypothesis, and both sexes preferred the figures with the lowest WHR (a curvaceous figure). This suggests that BMI and WHR may reflect different aspects of female health and fitness. BMI may reflect general fitness and fertility whereas WHR is a 'more specific cue to fertility and pubertal status' although the authors acknowledge that this cue has its limitations. The WHR of anorexic and healthy women is similar, for example, although the anorexic group (which is amenorrheic, i.e. not menstruating) is not fertile whereas the healthy group is.

There is an analogous preference for low waist-to-chest ratio (WCR) in men (Maisey *et al.*, 1999). Unlike men, who prefer a certain body size, women prefer a certain shape. This is the 'inverted triangle' (narrow waist, broad shoulders). The researchers suggest that if the desirable WHR in women signifies health and reproductive potential, then a desirable WCR in men signifies physical strength.

Men's weight, however, can influence people's judgement of their personality. Wade *et al.* (2007) found that thinner men were rated as more socially desirable than overweight men. Thin men and men of normal weight also received higher ratings for friendliness, trustworthiness, intelligence and mate potential.

Bodies are often covered and we may not be able to perceive their exact shape. Faces, however, are almost always exposed and offer an immediate source of information about physical attractiveness. People with attractive faces are rated as healthier, sexier, more attractive and more fertile regardless of WHR (Furnham *et al.*, 2001). The evidence is contrary to what we would expect from the 'first pass filter' theory of mate selection. This refers to the notion that WHR is the first feature we focus on to determine our attraction to a partner; if it is acceptable, we then focus on other features and behaviours to further refine our choice.

People also find facial symmetry (where the left and right sides are almost totally symmetrical) attractive and healthy. Men with more symmetrical bodies have been reported to display more direct, sexual, competitive tactics when trying to win their date (Simpson *et al.*, 1999) and symmetrical movers are judged to be significantly better dancers than are asymmetrical ones (Brown *et al.*, 2005).

Of course, physical beauty is stereotypically (and self-evidently) skin-deep. A study by Swami *et al.* (2007) asked participants to rate line drawings of women which varied in body weight, WHR and personality (extravert, introvert). Extraverted 'women' were judged to be more attractive and sociable than introverted ones, indicating that non-physical features are also an important determinant of attractiveness. Women rate several characteristics as being more important in a partner than did men (Furnham, 2009). These included intelligence, stability, conscientiousness, height, education, social skills and compatibility in terms of politics and religion. For men, physical appearance was more important than it was for women. Men and women were more likely to like a mate who shared similar personality characteristics such as extraversion and conscientiousness.

The perils of being beautiful

Is there a disadvantage to being very attractive? Research suggests that there is. When female students were asked to judge the suitability of an attractive, average and unattractive man as a long-term partner in tandem with a lonely heart advertisement implying high, medium or low socio-economic status, who do you think the women chose? If you said high-status, attractive men, you'd be wrong. If you'd said attractive men of medium status, you'd be right. Why? According to the authors (Chu *et al.*, 2007) the women regarded attractive, high-status men as pursuing a mating strategy (simply put, they were after sex), rather than a parenting strategy (wanting to settle down). High-status, attractive men would, therefore, be far more likely to be the recipient of other women's attention (and, therefore, be at greatest risk of yielding to this attention). Women – well, UK undergraduates – it seems, don't want Mr Perfect, just Mr Almost Perfect.

They might also settle for Mr Average. In one study women engaged in speed-dating were asked how important they thought a man's physical attractiveness and earning prospects were (Eastwick and Finkel, 2008). In an ideal partner, these were considered to be important. However, this preference did not predict their mate choice at the dating evening, neither did it predict their choice of real-life partners when the researchers contacted them after the study.

One theory of attractiveness (the topic of romantic attraction is considered further in Chapter 16) suggests that we choose a mate who is similar in attractiveness to ourselves (even if we prefer busty blondes or six-packed hunks). This is called the matching phenomenon (Walster *et al.*, 1966), but no model can explain this satisfactorily – is it because we are more anxious or insecure, or fear rejection or have low self-esteem? Some social psychologists argue that we view others through our own egotistical lens. 'The self provides the frame of reference from which all else is observed,' state Combs and Snygg (1959). 'People are not really fat unless they are fatter than we.' This would suggest that our ratings of others' physical attractiveness is affected by our assessment of our own physical attractiveness (whether this view is shared by others or not). Montoya (2008) found that participants' ratings of another person's attractiveness

Controversies in psychological science: Are some body types universally attractive?

The issue

In the developed world, physically attractive women are considered to be those with a low WHR. This ratio is achieved because more fat is deposited on the buttocks and hips than the waist; this, in turn, is the result of women having higher levels of oestrogen than testosterone (Singh, 1995). This apparent universal preference for women with low WHR would seem to bolster the sociobiologist's argument that mates are selected for their health and fitness. But is such a preference genuinely universal?

The evidence

Yu and Shepard (1998) compared the body shape preferences of American men and men from the Matsigenka people in south-east Peru. The Matsigenka's culture is basically agrarian: they engage in slash and burn agriculture and supplement this food production with game and fruit gathered using traditional tools. None had been exposed

Source: Alamy Images.

Source: Getty Images.

to Western civilisation (no television, film, newspapers and so on). Whereas the Western sample predictably preferred those females with low WHR, the Matsigenka men preferred overweight females and those with high WHR, rating these as the more attractive, healthy and more desirable as a spouse. In a similar study, Frank Marlowe and Adam Wetsman, two American anthropologists, found that whereas American men in their study preferred a low WHR and especially liked the intermediate image showing a WHR of 0.7, Hazda men, a group of hunter-gatherers who inhabit mixed savannah woodland in Tanzania, preferred a higher WHR (Marlowe and Wetsman, 2001).

British and Malaysian participants, however, are less enamoured of WHR (Swami and Tovee, 2005a). The researchers asked 682 participants to rate the photographs of real women. The study found that those who lived in urban areas preferred lower BMIs than did those living in the country, perhaps reflecting the greater exposure of urbanites to slimmer women. People who lived in urban areas also

Controversies in psychological science: *Continued*

preferred men with low WCR (BMI or WHR were not good predictors) (Swami and Tovee, 2005b). In rural areas, however, BMI was the primary predictor of attractiveness. Urban raters preferred a men with an 'inverted triangle' shaped torso, whereas rural raters preferred heavier men with a less triangular shape. Swami and colleagues have also reported an interaction between WHR and breast size. South African men preferred high-WHR black figures with large breasts and high-WHR white figures with small breasts, whereas white British men and British Africans preferred high-WHR black figures with small breasts and high-WHR white figures with large breasts (Swami *et al.*, 2009).

A cross-cultural study of WHR preference in participants from Africa, Indonesia, Samoa and New Zealand has confirmed the universal trend: participants rated women low in WHR as being more attractive (even when BMI was controlled for) (Singh *et al.*, 2010). A new study has even extended this preference to the blind. Researchers from the USA and the Netherlands asked 19 men who had been blind since birth to rate their preference for the body shape of mannequins whose WHR ratio could be manipulated (Karremans *et al.*, 2010). The men did this by touch. They preferred figures with a low WHR. When sighted men performed the same task, the same effect was found but the preference was stronger.

Finally, one of the largest studies of its kind examined female body preferences of 7,434 respondents from 26 countries, grouped into 10 regions drawn from North America, South America, Western Europe, Eastern Europe, Scandinavia, Oceania (Australia, New Zealand), Southeast Asia, East Asia, South and West Asia and Africa (Swami *et al.*, 2010). Respondents from Eastern Europe, Scandinavia and Western Europe preferred heavier figures. There were significant differences between rural and urban sites in Malaysia and South Africa. The ideal body weight was heavier in societies that were less socially and economically developed.

Apart from East Asian men, other men chose a heavier figure as their preferred shape than did women, thereby highlighting a disparity about what women perceive as the ideal body shape preferred by men and men's own actual preference. 'Such misinterpretation of men's standards of bodily attractiveness on the part of women', Swami *et al.* conclude, 'may be near universal in contexts of high SES' (p. 320). One reason for the disparity may be that the media to which men are exposed feature curvier women whereas women's media idealise the thin.

American women expressed greater body dissatisfaction than women from any other region. At another level, individuals of low socio-economic status in Malaysia and South Africa also expressed low levels of body satisfaction. A correlation was found between exposure to Western media and preference for a thinner body type.

Conclusion

While a low waist-hip-ratio is considered the more appealing body shape in a large part of the world, even when controlling for weight, there are specific cultures and nations – although not many – which express a different preference.

---

decreased with the increasing, objective, physical attractiveness of the rater. People rating themselves moderate in attractiveness paired themselves with people they thought were attractive. There is support for his finding. One study found that people rated their partners as being significantly more attractive than themselves – there was no difference between men or women (Swami *et al.*, 2009).

Monogamy: shared, but not always equal, parental investment

Around 3 per cent of the relationships in mammals are monogamous. Monogamy has evolved in those species whose environments have favoured the contributions of both parents to the survival and reproductive success of their offspring. In other words, under some conditions, two individuals sharing parental duties enjoy more reproductive success than does one individual who must do it all alone.

Although both parents in monogamous species share offspring-rearing duties, each parent may not make an equal contribution towards that end. Like females in polygynous species, females in monogamous species generally have greater parental investment in the offspring, for many of the same reasons: the limited opportunity for mating relative to that for males, pregnancy and its accompanying risks, providing milk to the newborns, and the time and energy spent in caring for them. As a result, very few monogamous species, including our own, are exclusively monogamous. In fact, there is a strong tendency in most monogamous species towards patterns of reproductive behaviour and parental investment that resemble those of polygynous species.

For example, in monogamous species, females tend to be more careful than males in selecting a mate, and males tend to be more sexually promiscuous than females (Badcock, 1991). In our own species, men tend to engage in premarital sexual intercourse more often than do

Psychology in action: Menstrual cycle and attraction

Chemicals called hormones (discussed in the next chapter and Chapter 13), as well as a woman's point in her menstrual cycle, affect behaviour related to physical attraction and the perception of this behaviour. Women are judged to be more attractive when they are in the follicular stage of their menstrual cycle and men find their body odour more attractive at that point. Women's appetite decreases during ovulation and they also make themselves look more attractive during this period.

Haselton *et al.* (2007) asked men and women to judge the attractiveness of 30 women (who had partners) who were in the luteal or follicular stage of their cycle. More women in the follicular stage were judged as 'trying to look more attractive'. The closer the women were to ovulation (when the photograph was taken), the more likely the photograph was chosen as signifying someone attractive. These women were judged to wear more fashionable clothes, nicer clothes and show more upper body skin.

When women were asked to report to a laboratory on high- or low-fertility days (confirmed by a hormone test) and to pose for photographs and draw an outfit that they would prefer to wear that evening (Durante *et al.*, 2008), they were more likely to sketch sexier outfits during the high-fertility period – they drew more revealing outfits, as the example in Figure 3.9 shows. The more sexually experienced the woman, the skimpier the outfit. Single women drew more revealing outfits than those who had partners but the more satisfied the women were with their partners, the more revealing the outfit they drew (suggesting that they were confident to express their sexuality in the context of a secure relationship).

A separate study of 10 heterosexual women in their twenties and not on contraception asked them to rate their sexual interest in men's faces as brain activation was measured using fMRI (Rupp *et al.*, 2009). Activation was measured during the follicular and luteal stage of their cycle. Compared with the luteal phase, the follicular phase was associated with greater activation in the right front–middle part of the brain, a region which is involved in reward and reinforcement. Curiously, the effect was also found for photographs of houses (although the effect for faces was stronger). This suggests that either this region of the brain responds more strongly to visual images during the follicular stage or, given the stronger responses to faces, social stimuli are responded to more positively during the follicular stage.

The most fertile part of a woman's cycle occurs in the middle and lasts a few days near ovulation. In evolutionary terms, therefore, it may be important to maximise sexual behaviour (and attract a mate) during this period. Does this period influence men's behaviour towards women? And, if so, why might this be?

Miller and Maner (2011a) set up three experiments in which men's responses to women appeared to be influenced by the woman's point in her cycle. In one experiment,

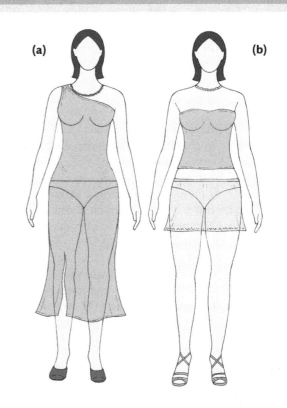

Figure 3.9 Example of an outfit illustration drawn by the same participant at low fertility **(a)** and high fertility **(b)**.

Source: Durante. K.M., Li, N.P. and Haselton, M.G. (2008) Changes in women's choice of dress across the ovulatory cycle: Naturalistic and laboratory task-based evidence. *Personality and Social Psychology Bulletin* 34 (11), 1451–60.

they found that men who smelled a T-shirt of an ovulating woman were more likely to think about sex-related words than when smelling a T-shirt from another part of the cycle. In the experiment, men completed a stem-completion task in which the missing letters from half of the words could form an obvious sex-related word. In a second experiment, the researchers found that men who were highly sensitive to odour and were asked to indicate how emotional a woman whose T-shirt they smelled was were more likely to show enhanced judgements of the women's degree of arousal. In a final study, they put men with a confederate who was highly fertile (or not) and observed their social interaction and their risk-taking (performance on a game of blackjack). Men exposed to the fertile confederate were more likely to mimic the behaviour of the confederate and to engage in riskier behaviour, as measured by the gambling task.

The studies appear to show that the point in the woman's menstrual cycle can influence men's behaviour at the lowest (word-stem completion, cognition) to the highest (behviour-mimicking, risk-taking) level. The behaviour is thought to be a subtle illustration of the motivation to engage in sexual activity.

females (Kinsey *et al.*, 1948, 1953; Hunt, 1974), although this gap appears to be decreasing. Men also tend to have more premarital and extramarital sexual partners (Symons, 1979), although recent studies show that over 90 per cent of male and female undergraduate respondents want to settle down with one partner exclusively at some point (Pedersen *et al.*, 2002).

Monogamy and hormones

Some scientists have hypothesised that monogamy may be attributable to chemicals called hormones, described in detail in the next chapter (Young *et al.*, 1998). These are generated by a region in the brain which sends signals to organs of the body to react in a certain way. The proposed relationship between hormones and monogamy has been based on studies of a type of rodent, the vole. Researchers have found that two types of vole show very different patterns of mating: the prairie vole is largely monogamous, forming lasting partnerships; the montane vole, however, is promiscuous and not a particularly social species. The male montane vole is not parental and does not form a bond with its partner; the female montane vole abandons its offspring around two to three weeks after birth (Young *et al.*, 1998).

Two key hormones have been identified that could underpin these behaviours: oxytocin (OT) and vasopressin (AVP). In prairie voles, vaginal–cervical copulation leads to an increase in the release of OT. This release may promote intense mating in females but has little effect on males. AVP, however, does affect male prairie voles. Administering this hormone in these male voles leads to a preference for an exclusive partner, aggression towards strangers and an increase in paternal care (Young *et al.*, 1998). In the montane male vole, the effect of the hormones is not aggression but self-grooming. The receptor distribution for these hormones in the brain of the prairie vole is similar to that in other monogamous types of vole; conversely, the distribution of receptors in montane voles is similar to other promiscuous vole types.

There is increasing evidence of a relationship between this chemical and caring behaviour in humans. For example, a study of intranasal administration of the chemical found that those who received it maintained eye contact more during relationship conflict resolution (Ditzen *et al.*, 2009). It is also associated with reductions in activity of a structure called the amygdala when people view negative and positive stimuli (e.g., Domes *et al.*, 2007).

Researchers from the University of Bristol sought to investigate whether these effects could extend to another psychological variable – trustworthiness (Theodoridou *et al.*, 2009). They administered a single intranasal dose of OT to an equal number of men and women and asked them to judge the trustworthiness and friendliness of a range of faces presented on a computer monitor. Trustworthiness and friendliness were rated more highly after OT administration, an effect found in men and women, suggesting that the presence of this chemical can enhance positive behaviour towards others.

Infidelity

For various evolutionary reasons, evolutionary psychologists suggest that men and women respond differently to different types of infidelity. Heterosexual men, for example, are more likely to show jealousy in response to sexual infidelity (a partner having sex with another man), whereas heterosexual women are more likely to show jealousy in response to emotional infidelity (a partner having a very deep, loving, yet non-sexual, relationship with another woman). A study in which male and female undergraduates were asked whether they would forgive the two types of infidelity in their partner conformed to the expected pattern and found that men were less likely to forgive sexual than emotional infidelity whereas women showed the opposite pattern (Shackelford *et al.*, 2002). Men were also more likely to terminate a relationship if their partner committed sexual infidelity.

Cutting edge: Boom and bust?

During ovulation, or peak fertility, women are known to alter their dress style to attract men. You have seen in this chapter how their drawings of their preferred dress was more revealing during this stage. A study has now examined the effect of menstruation on spending behaviour to see whether the 'impulsiveness' during this stage also extends to financial matters (Pine and Fletcher, 2011).

The online study asked 443 women aged between 18 and 50 years old to report their spending habits over the past seven days and to note their point on the menstrual cycle. Spending was less controlled and more impulsive during the luteal phase or later in their cycle, the point of the cycle in which women report mood swings, increased irritability and impulsivity, and impaired concentration.

Harris (2002) asked participants whether they would be more upset if they found out that their partner was trying different sexual positions with another person or if their partner was falling in love with another. Some 196 participants, with a **mean** age of 37, were recruited via newspaper advertisements and flyers. Harris was also interested in whether responses would be similar in homosexual and heterosexual men and women and so recruited roughly equal numbers of each. Participants were asked if they had been 'cheated' on, whether they focused on the emotional or sexual consequences of the cheating and whether the relationship ended as a result.

As predicted by evolutionary psychology, heterosexual men were more likely to find sexual infidelity more upsetting than they would emotional infidelity when responding to the forced-choice question. The reverse pattern was found for women. When participants recalled actual examples of infidelity, however, no sex differences

were found. Regardless of sexual orientation, both men and women were more likely to focus on a partner's emotional than sexual infidelity as the source of distress. No relationship was found between participants' responses to hypothetical and actual infidelity.

People who are married to disagreeable, undependable and emotionally unstable partners are less satisfied with their marriage (Shackelford and Buss, 2000). Low agreeableness, low emotional stability and low conscientiousness in women is associated with low marital satisfaction in men. Disagreeable, emotionally unstable men are also more likely to abuse their wives than their agreeable, emotionally stable counterparts. Furthermore, mate-guarding tactics such as threatening infidelity, threatening to punish infidelity and emotional manipulation (i.e. the factors which inflict costs on a relationship) are associated with lower marital satisfaction in the people at the receiving end of these tactics.

Infidelity – An international perspective

Evolutionary psychologists argue that the nature and degree of mate poaching/poachers should be similar across cultures but with some provisos. Studies show that men are more likely than women to engage in short-term mate poaching and so we might expect this finding across cultures.

In a study of 16,954 individuals from 53 nations, divided into 10 world regions (North America, South America, Western Europe, Eastern Europe, Southern Europe, the Middle East, Africa, Oceania, South/Southeast Asia and East Asia) mate poaching overall was very common – 70 per cent reported that they had been the object of a poaching attempt (Schmitt *et al.*, 2004). Eighty per cent of poaching attempts were apparently successful with 10 per cent of such attempts leading to a long-term relationship. Mate poaching was most common in Southern Europe, South America and Western Europe and was least common in Africa, South/Southeast Asia and East Asia, a finding that is consistent with the prediction regarding demanding environments. The number of attempts at mate poaching by members of various cultures can be seen in Figure 3.10.

Men were more vigorous mate poachers than were women, with 60 per cent of men reporting that they had attempted to mate poach and 40 per cent of women reporting so. In cultures where men and women were regarded as equals, this sex difference was smaller.

In keeping with previous studies discussed in this chapter, the personality measures showed that poachers were extraverted, disagreeable, unconscientious, slightly narcissistic and (no surprise here) unfaithful. The poached were likely to be

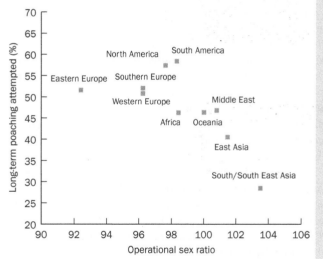

Figure 3.10 The degree of mate-poaching across nations and cultures. Europeans and Americans seem especially keen on it.

Source: D.P. Schmitt, Patterns and universals of mate poaching across 53 nations: The effects of sex, culture and personality on romantically attracting another person's partner, *Journal of Personality and Social Psychology*, 2004, 86 (4), 560–84, Figure 2.

extraverted, open, attractive and disagreeable. Both groups were likely to be highly sexual.

Of course, most of the study's participants were young undergraduates and the authors note that mate poaching may be more common in this younger group than it would be in an older sample.

What makes a person poach another's partner? One study found that 84 per cent of undergraduates reported that attempts had been made to poach them from their partners (Schmitt and Buss, 2001). Of those who were romantically linked (just over 55 per cent), 20 per cent of men and 28 per cent of women stated that their partners had been poached from someone else. In terms of personality, agreeable and conscientious people were least likely to be mate poachers, a finding that is found internationally (Schmitt, 2004). Those who did not regard relationships as exclusive and described themselves as having erotophilic tendencies – a constant desire to satisfy sexual needs – were more likely to poach. These individuals also scored high on sexual attractiveness: it appears that the poacher may have to be sexy, as well as adulterous. Extraverts were more likely than introverts to be recipients of poaching attempts. Those who rated themselves as sexually attractive, as not relationship exclusive and as emotionally investing (loving) were those who were most likely to be poached.

Physical attractiveness was more important for men than it was for women. Women, conversely, were more likely to view resource acquisition as a benefit of poaching, especially in short-term relationships. Because men value physical attractiveness in women, women pay greater attention to using physical characteristics as cues to attraction. Women, on the other hand, placed greater value on resources. Men, consequently, emphasised cues that indicate that they are resource-laden (such as expensive clothes, cars, jewellery and so on). For women, a strategy aimed at making themselves more attractive by disparaging the partner of the person they wanted to poach was not as effective as one based on enhancing their own physical attractiveness.

As predicted, men were found to be more successful than women at poaching when they displayed resources and were more effective at using humour as a poaching cue than were women in the short and long term. Women employed a tactic that was significantly more effective when used by them than by men: boosting the partner's ego.

Although based on a sample of undergraduates, and assessing perceived effectiveness rather than actual effectiveness of poaching, this series of studies shows that poaching is a common phenomenon and that men and women use different cues with varying degrees of success to poach a mate from their existing partner.

Jealousy

Jealousy has been defined as 'when individuals perceive a threat to their relationship because of an actual or imagined rival' (Massar and Buunk, 2010, p. 634). Although romantic jealousy seems more common in men than women, the sexes may also differ in what they become jealous about. Men are more likely to be jealous, angry and upset about sexual infidelity whereas women are more likely to be upset by emotional infidelity (their partner engaging in a warm and fulfilling friendship with another woman). These differences might have a neural basis (Takahashi et al., 2006).

Takahashi asked men and women to think about jealousy-arousing sentences such as 'My girlfriend stayed in a double-bed room in a hotel with her ex-boyfriend' and 'My girlfriend had her underwear taken off by another man' (sexual jealousy items) or 'My girlfriend wrote a love letter to another man' and 'My girlfriend gave gorgeous birthday presents to her ex-boyfriend' (emotional jealousy items) as well as neutral statements about their partner. The groups did not differ significantly in terms of the types of infidelity they felt jealous about – both sexes became equally jealous under both conditions (emotional or sexual infidelity). However, brain activation did differ by sex.

Men showed greater activation in the amygdala during sexual jealousy and in the hypothalamus during emotional infidelity. These are structures involved in sexuality and reproduction, amongst other functions. Women showed greater activation in the posterior superior temporal sulcus (STS), an area the authors suggest is implicated in 'the detection of others' intention or violation of social norms'.

Cutting edge: Facing jealousy

How easy can it be to induce jealousy and how subtle can the process be? Massar and Buunk (2010) exposed 40 young women to photographs of attractive or unattractive women for 60 ms. They then asked them to rate how jealous they felt when told to imagine placing themselves in a scenario designed to elicit jealousy (a rival being introduced). The researchers found that women who were exposed to their attractive counterparts reported significantly more jealousy than did those exposed to the unattractive ones. The study suggests that jealousy may be elicited without women being consciously aware of being primed.

Promiscuity

Promiscuity – the tendency to engage in sexual activity with multiple partners (not necessarily at the same time) – has been associated with specific personality types. Sensation-seekers, for example, have more partners than low sensation-seekers; and the unconscientious, extravert, the less agreeable and more antagonistic similarly report having more sexual partners than the conscientious, the less extravert and the more agreeable/less antagonistic. In a study of 105 young men and 105 young women, people who were dominant had significantly more sexual partners than did those who were less so (Markey and Markey, 2007). Curiously, people who were personally warm were also more likely to have had more sexual partners than the less warm.

A related study examined whether men who engaged in unrestricted sexual activity – engaging in transient sexual relations – perceived women's attractiveness differently from men who were more restricted (Swami *et al.*, 2008). Men self-described as restricted or unrestricted rated the attractiveness of drawings of women who differed according to BMI and WHR. The men, regardless of type, used BMI rather than WHR as the basis of their judgement but unrestricted men found women with lower BMI to be more attractive and healthy than did restricted men. The unrestricted men also preferred women with a low WHR.

Polyandry: high male and low female parental investment

Polyandry is a rare reproductive strategy among humans and non-existent in other mammals. It is more prevalent among species that lay eggs. Once the eggs are laid, then either the male or the female may take care of them, although in many instances the male makes the greater investment of time and effort.

An example of polyandry in humans is found among some of the people who live in remote Himalayan villages. These people are extremely poor and live in a harsh environment, which makes their primary livelihood, farming, difficult. In order to prevent the dissolution of family farms through marriage, families that have more than one son limit the number of marriages to only one per generation – several brothers may share the same wife. A female tends to marry more than one man (most often brothers) to guarantee that she will be adequately supported. In other words, the male's primary investment – the farm, which is the source of food and some income for the family – is guarded jealously through polyandry.

Polygynandry: group parental investment

Many primates, such as chimpanzees, live in colonies in which few or no barriers are placed on which female mates with which male. In other words, the colonies are promiscuous – during periods of mating, intercourse is frequent and indiscriminate. What is the advantage of such a reproductive strategy?

The primary advantage seems to be the cooperation of males and females in the colony with respect to rearing offspring. Because the males in the colony are not sure which offspring belong to them, it is in their best interest to help rear and protect all the offspring and defend their mothers. The unity in the colony and the lack of aggression among the males contributes directly to the general welfare of all colony members. Females and males have access to many mates, and the offspring are well cared for.

However, a form of monogamy called a consortship is sometimes observed in polygynandrous species. For instance, a particular male chimpanzee may ward off other male suitors from a particular female, resulting in an exclusive sexual union. If successful, he is guaranteed the certainty of which offspring are his, albeit at some cost. There is a chance that he could be seriously injured in protecting his mate from other males, and therefore he becomes less useful as a parental investor in his offspring or those of the colony.

Altruism and kin selection

A particularly interesting and important social behaviour in terms of evolution is **altruism,** the unselfish concern of one individual for the welfare of another. Examples of altruistic behaviour abound and its most extreme form is when one person risks their life to save the life of another. Examples of altruism are also common throughout the animal kingdom. The honey bee, for example, sacrifices its life on behalf of its hivemates by stinging an intruder. Here, the altruist's chances of survival and reproductive success are lowered while those of the other individuals are raised.

Sociobiologists seek out ultimate causes, especially the consequences of natural selection, to explain altruism. They assert that natural selection has favoured the evolution of organisms that show altruistic tendencies. However, there is an important problem here. On the surface, altruism poses an enigma to evolutionary theory. Recall that according to natural selection only phenotypes that enhance one's reproductive success are favoured. How could altruistic behaviour have evolved given that, by definition, it is less adaptive than selfish or competitive behaviour?

The geneticist William D. Hamilton (1964, 1970) suggested an answer to this question in a series of mathematical papers. Hamilton's ideas stemmed from examining natural selection from the perspective of the gene instead of from the perspective of the whole, living organism. He argued that natural selection does not favour mere reproductive success but rather **inclusive fitness,** or the reproductive success of those individuals who share many of the same genes. Altruistic acts are generally aimed at close relatives such as parents, siblings, grandparents and grandchildren. The closer the family relation is, the more likely the genetic similarity among the individuals involved. Such biological favouritism towards relatives is called **kin selection** (Maynard Smith, 1964).

The message here is clear: under the proper circumstances, individuals behave altruistically towards others with whom they share a genetic history, with the willingness to do so decreasing as the relative becomes more distant. In this view, altruism is not necessarily a conscious act but rather an act driven by a biological prompt that has been favoured by natural selection. Natural selection would favour this kind of altruism simply because organisms who share genes also help each other to survive.

Parenting is a special case of kin selection and an important contributor to one's survival and reproductive success. In the short run, parents' altruistic actions promote the continued survival of their offspring. In the long run, these actions increase the likelihood that the offspring, too, will become parents and that their genes will survive in successive generations. Such cycles continue according to biological schedule, generation after generation. In the words of sociobiologist, David Barash:

> It is obvious why genes for parenting have been selected: all living things are the offspring of parents who themselves were [the offspring of] parents! It is a guaranteed, unbroken line stretching back into time. [Genes] that inclined their bearers to be less successful parents left fewer copies of themselves than did those [genes] that were more successful. (*Source*: Barash, 1982, pp. 69–70.)

What is at stake is not the survival of individual organisms but the survival of the genes carried by those organisms. Genes allow organisms to maximise their inclusive fitness through altruistic behaviour directed at other organisms sharing the same genes (Dawkins, 1986). Inclusive fitness refers to the idea that reproduction and natural selection occurs because a species' success is measured through the production of offspring. You carry copies of genes that have been in your family line for thousands of years. When the opportunity presents itself, you will most likely carry on the tradition – reproducing and thus projecting your biological endowment into yet another generation. But you did not reach sexual

maturity on your own; the concern for your welfare by your parents, brothers, sisters, grandparents and perhaps an aunt or uncle has contributed to your chances of being reproductively successful. Genes not projected into the next generation simply disappear.

Another variable may mediate altruism, however: emotional closeness. Emotional closeness is defined as having a sense of concern and caring for another and enjoying a comforting, emotional relationship with them. One study asked participants to rate how willing they would be to behave altruistically towards members of their family when the family member could live or die, and when helping would be at a cost to the participant (Korchmaros and Kenny, 2001). Participants also indicated how emotionally close they were to these family members.

People were more likely to help family members with whom they shared a close relationship, regardless of the genetic closeness of the relationship, than with those with whom they shared a less close relationship. The findings suggest that emotional closeness may be a mediating cause of altruistic behaviour.

Evidence from step-relations' behaviour supports the idea of inclusive fitness. It has been reported, for example, that a disproportionate number of children in stepfamilies suffer physical harm, especially assault (Daly and Wilson, 1988). Child battering is more common in stepfamilies, as is the incidence of child abuse (Daly and Wilson, 1996). This evidence, the sociobiologists argue, supports the notion than non-genetic relatives are not disposed to invest resources in offspring that are genetically unrelated.

There is also evidence to suggest that cohabitation is a greater risk factor for spousal murder than is marriage. Canadian research published at the beginning of the 1990s suggested that women in cohabiting relationships were more likely than married women to be murdered by their partner (Wilson *et al.*, 1993, 1995). Data from specific US cities show the same pattern (e.g. Wilbanks, 1984). According to the Wilson *et al.* studies, women in their early twenties were at greater risk of homicide if they were married; for cohabiting women, women in their mid-thirties to forties were at greatest risk. A national study of over 400,000 US homicides committed between 1976 and 1994 found that women in cohabiting relationships were nine times more likely than married women to be murdered by their partner (Shackelford, 2001). The risk for married women decreased as they became older. Middle-aged women, however, were at greatest risk if they were in a cohabiting relationship. Young men were more likely to murder their wives whereas middle-aged men were more likely to murder their cohabiting partners.

One explanation for these findings is that men may tend to feel significantly and abnormally proprietorial about their partners, especially about their partner's sexuality. A man in a cohabiting relationship is more insecure than is a married man because the possibility of either partner leaving the relationship is more likely and is easier to do. The cohabiting man may, therefore, go to more extreme lengths to prevent his partner from leaving him than would a married man because cohabiting relationships are more likely to break down than are marriages. There is some evidence in support of this interpretation. Daly and Wilson (1988), for example, cite their partner data showing that men who kill their partners are more likely to do so because they suspect that their partner has been unfaithful or may be about to terminate their relationship.

Reciprocal altruism

Kin selection explains altruism towards relatives, but what about altruism directed towards non-relatives? According to Trivers (1971), this kind of altruism, called **reciprocal altruism**, exists because humans (and other organisms) can function more effectively if they work together. Human groups are hierarchical and cooperative (Buss, 1995), whether at the level of the family, canoe club or workplace. There is also evidence that kindness, dependability, emotional stability and intelligence (all traits one would associate with altruism) are the most valued personality characteristics in potential mates (Buss, 1995). Cooperation between groups is a fundamental survival strategy (Brewer and Caporael, 1990), and is seen in many higher primates (Byrne, 1995). For example, in order to win a mate from a dominant male savannah baboon, a male will engage the help of another baboon who will distract the dominant male and enter into a fight with him. This leaves the other, non-dominant male free to mate with the female. The altruism is reciprocal because the favour will be reciprocated by the successfully paired male in the future (Haufstater, cited in Byrne, 1995).

Sociobiology and evolutionary psychology as an explanation for human behaviour

So far in this chapter you have seen that sociobiologists attempt to explain social behaviour by reference to natural selection and genetic inheritance but it has been at the centre of a fierce scientific controversy ever since E.O. Wilson published *Sociobiology: The new synthesis* in 1975, the official birth date of the discipline. Wilson's *On Human Nature* (1978), which extended sociobiological theory to human affairs, ignited even more criticism. Most of the criticism focuses on the extension of the theory to human behaviour. Two issues which have caused greatest controversy are inclusive fitness and the mechanisms of adaptation.

Recall that inclusive fitness theory argues that reproduction and natural selection occur because species' survival success is measured through the production of offspring. Those characteristics which help promote the transmission of genes (either directly or indirectly) will be naturally selected, akin to Dawkins's sieve mentioned at the beginning of the chapter. Sociobiologists see humans as 'fitness maximisers', or 'fitness strivers' (Alexander, 1979), constantly applying the mechanisms for maximising inclusive fitness. The evolutionary psychologists, however, call this the 'sociobiological fallacy' (Buss, 1991, 1995) because it confuses the theory of origins of mechanisms with the theory of the nature of mechanisms. As Buss argues, if humans were 'fitness maximising blobs', why are men not queuing up at sperm banks to donate their sperm? Why do some couples forgo reproduction? We have developed a preference for fatty foods but this is known to be detrimental to us. If we know this food is unhealthy, why do we eat it? More to the point, we can look at individuals or their behaviour and easily find maximising fitness reasons for this behaviour. The inclusive fitness theory, therefore, cannot account for natural selection and, because of its breadth (one can interpret almost any behaviour in terms of maximising fitness), is virtually limitless in its application.

Instead of seeing humans as fitness maximisers, evolutionary psychologists see humans as 'adaptation executors' or 'mechanism activators' (Tooby and Cosmides, 1990). That is, humans apply evolved solutions to adaptive problems (Buss, 1995). These solutions are domain-specific. That is, the types of solution one would need to reach to select a mate are different from those one needs to obtain food or to parent children. Adaptive problems are large, complex and varied; the success of individuals in solving these problems depends on sex, species, age, context and individual circumstances (Buss *et al.*, 1998). Sociobiology, however, seems to ignore this psychological level of interpretation and goes from evolution straight to patterns of social organisation.

The most intense criticism of sociobiology is political, not scientific. Opponents argue that sociobiology sanctions the superiority of one group over another, be it a race, a gender or a political organisation. After all, they argue, if one group of individuals is genetically superior to another, then there are 'natural' grounds for justifying the 'survival of the fittest' and one group's unethical and immoral domination of another. An example is Hitler's quest for world domination in the name of Aryan superiority. Sociobiologists flatly deny such allegations and argue that it is the critics and not they who have confused the term 'natural' with the terms 'good' and 'superior'. Are political objections to sociobiology scientifically acceptable ones? Do you think that psychologists should be concerned with political objections to their findings or theories?

Given the broad-sweep nature of sociobiological theory, it is not surprising that the theory fails to account adequately for natural selection. Although kin selection and familial altruism could be interpreted as supporting the inclusive fitness theory, it is true that one could explain away a lot of behaviour by describing it as maximising fitness.

Evolutionary psychology is also aware of its limitations. Confer *et al.* (2010), for example, demonstrate how they believe evolutionary psychology can help us explain behaviour but also list a number of ways in which the discipline draws up short. For example, certain behaviours, such as those which limit reproductive success, are difficult to explain within the context of evolutionary psychology. Homosexuality – which does not increase an individual's reproductive success – and suicide are 'inexplicable on the basis of current evolutionary accounts' (p. 122). Another, more obvious limitation, is that we do not have the evidence required which would allow us to provide a full account of human nature – in short, we are hopelessly ill-informed about our evolution and our past and the specific pressures we encountered during evolution. The best we can do is make an educated guess, based on the techniques described in the earlier section. Confer *et al.* also note that explaining cultural and individual differences is problematic for the discipline and that is has been more effective at explaining species-typical and sex-differentiated behaviour. For example, although women are better than men at spatial location memory, the discipline cannot account for why there is so much variability in this ability in women.

Chapter review

Natural selection and evolution

- Understanding behaviour requires that psychologists learn more about both proximate causes of behaviour – how animals adapt to environmental changes through learning – and ultimate causes of behaviour – historical events and conditions in the evolution of a species that have shaped its behaviour.
- Darwin's voyage on the *Beagle* and his subsequent thinking and research in artificial selection led him to develop the idea of biological evolution, which explains how genetic and physical changes occur in groups of animals over time.
- The primary element of biological evolution is natural selection: the tendency of some members of a species to produce more offspring than other members do. Members of a species vary genetically; some possess specific traits to a greater or lesser extent than other individuals do. If any of these traits gives an animal a competitive advantage over other members of the species then that animal is also more likely to have greater reproductive success. Its offspring will then carry its genes into future generations.
- Two important adaptations during the course of human evolution are bipedalism – the ability to walk upright – and encephalisation – an increase in brain size. The combination of these two factors allowed early humans to explore and settle new environments and led to advances in tool making, hunting, food gathering and self-defence.

- Encephalisation appears to have been associated with language development. The study of the evolution of our species suggests the nature of the circumstances under which adaptive behaviour first emerged and those circumstances that have been important for its continued expression to the present time.

Heredity and genetics

- The instructions for the synthesis of protein molecules, which oversee the development of the body and all of its processes, are contained in genes. Genes are found on chromosomes, which consist of DNA and are found in every cell.
- Humans inherit 23 individual chromosomes, each of which contains thousands of genes, from each parent. This means that our genetic blueprint represents a recombination of the genetic instructions that our parents inherited from their parents.
- Such recombination makes for tremendous genetic diversity. Genetically diverse species have a better chance of adapting to a changing environment than do genetically non-diverse species because some members of the species may have genes that enable them to survive in a new environment.
- The expression of a gene depends on several factors, including its interaction with other genes (polygenic traits), the sex of the individual carrying the particular gene and the environmental conditions under which

that individual lives. Changes in genetic material caused by mutations or chromosomal aberrations lead to changes in the expression of a particular gene. For example, haemophilia, an increased tendency to bleed from even minor injuries, is the result of a mutation.
- Behaviour genetics is the study of how genes influence behaviour. Psychologists and other scientists use artificial selection studies of animals, twin studies, and adoption studies to investigate the possible relationship between genes and behaviour in humans.

Sociobiology and evolutionary psychology

- The discovery of the biological basis for social behaviour is the primary goal of sociobiology. Sociobiologists have been especially interested in studying social behaviour related to reproduction and the rearing of offspring.
- Evolutionary psychology is a relatively new sub-field of psychology (and sociobiology) that is devoted to the study of how evolution and genetic variables influence adaptive behaviour.
- Different reproductive strategies are believed to have evolved because of sex differences in the resources that parents invest in procreative and child-rearing activities. These resources include the time, physical efforts and risks to life involved in procreation and in the feeding, nurturing and protection of offspring.
- A low waist-to-hip ratio appears to be preferred by Western heterosexual men; a waist-to-chest ratio that emphasises narrow hips and broad shoulders is preferred by Western heterosexual women. In some cultures, however, there is a preference for heavier, larger women. One reason for this is that these cultures may not have been exposed to the Western ideals of physical beauty, those which emphasise the curvaceousness of women.
- Recent research suggests that facial attractiveness may be a more important determinant of mate selection than is waist-to-hip ratio.

- Men and women experience different types of jealousy and these feelings appear to be mirrored in different degrees of brain activation: men are more threatened by sexual infidelity whereas women are more threatened by emotional infidelity (a male partner having a very close, non-sexual relationship with a woman).
- Polygynous and monogamous strategies tend to require greater female investment, polyandrous strategies tend to require greater male investment, and polygynandrous strategies tend to require investment on the part of members of a large group, such as a colony of chimpanzees.
- Altruism is difficult to explain by appealing to natural selection. Altruistic behaviour generally involves one organism risking its life for others with whom it shares some genes (kin selection) or who are likely subsequently to be in a position to return the favour (reciprocal altruism).
- Inclusive fitness theory argues that reproduction and natural selection occur because species' survival success is measured through the production of offspring. Those characteristics which help promote the transmission of genes (either directly or indirectly) will be naturally selected.
- Sociobiology has been criticised on the grounds that natural selection is no longer a factor in human evolution, that research on animal social behaviour is not relevant to understanding human social behaviour, that environmental factors play a greater role in shaping human behaviour than genetic factors, and that sociobiology is simply a way to justify the superiority of one group over another. Sociobiologists reply that natural selection has shaped and continues to shape the evolution of culture, that findings from animal research can be generalised to humans, that genes and environment interact to determine behaviour, and, finally, that sociobiology is an attempt to understand human behaviour, not to justify it.

Suggestions for further reading

Evolution: Popular accounts

Brown, A. (2000) *The Darwin Wars*. London: Simon & Schuster.
Darwin, C. (1859) *The Origin of Species by Means of Natural Selection*. London: Murray.

Dawkins, R. (2009) *The Greatest Show on Earth: The Evidence for Evolution*. London: Bantam Press.
Scientific American Mind, special edition on 'Becoming Human: evolution and the rise of intelligence', 2006, 16, 2.
Some good introductions to evolutionary theory.

Behavioural genetics

Plomin, R. (2005) Finding genes in child psychology and psychiatry: When are we going to be there? *Journal of Child Psychology and Psychiatry*, 46, 10, 1030–38.

Plomin, R. (2008) *Behavioural Genetics*. London: Palgrave.

Scerif, G. and Karmiloff-Smith, A. (2005) The dawn of cognitive genetics? Critical developmental caveats. *Trends in Cognitive Sciences*, 9, 3, 126–36.

Special issue of *Trends in Cognitive Sciences*, 2011, vol. 15, on the genetics of cognition.

These items give a useful introduction to behavioural genetics (and objections to behavioural genetics).

Evolutionary psychology and sociobiology

Buss, D.M. (2008) *Evolutionary psychology: The new science of mind* (3rd edn). Boston, MA: Allyn & Bacon.

Buss, D.M. (2009) How can evolutionary psychology successfully explain personality and individual differences? *Perspectives in Psychological Science*, 4, 359–66.

Confer, J.C., Easton, J.A., Fleischman, D.S., Goetz, C.D., Lewis, D.M.G., Perilloux, C. and Buss, D.M. (2010) Evolutionary psychology. *American Psychologist*, 65, 2, 110–26.

Matsuzawa, T. (2008) *Primate origins of human cognition and behaviour*. New York: Springer.

Premack, D. (2010) Why humans are unique: Three theories. *Perspectives in Psychological Science*, 5, 22–32.

Vonk, J. and Shackelford, T.K. (2012) *The Oxford Handbook of Comparative Evolutionary Psychology*.Oxford: Oxford University Press.

Workman, L. and Reader, W. (2004) *Evolutionary psychology*. Cambridge: Cambridge University Press.

Some good introductions to sociobiology and evolutionary psychology.

CHAPTER 11

Intelligence and thinking

LESSONS FROM A TRAGEDY

St Anne's College, Oxford, 1962. I am on the sofa reading an essay to my English literature tutor. The door opens slowly and a woman with large blue-grey eyes and a helmet of rope-thick, not-so-clean hair appears with an old army blanket around her shoulders. She has a reputation for brilliance, eccentricity and lots of affairs of the heart. She is Iris Murdoch, distinguished philosopher, bestselling author, a noted teacher and student of human nature. As I expand on the character of Milton's Satan, I begin to quake under her gaze.

Cambridge University Department of Neurology, 2005. I am peering at a set of MRI scans of the grey matter belonging to the woman who once owned those fantastic blue-grey eyes . . . To a professional brain scientist's eye, the scans show that her neocortex is remarkably shrunken compared with a normal brain's. Slices of Iris Murdoch's brain, stored in a tissue bank in the same department, show protein deposits known as 'plaques' and 'tangles'.

It is probable that Iris Murdoch had Alzheimer's at 42 when, craving a cigarette, she walked into my tutor's room.

Source: John Cornwell, *The Sunday Times Magazine*, 15 May 2005.

WHAT YOU SHOULD BE ABLE TO DO AFTER READING CHAPTER 11

- Describe the ways in which intelligence has been defined.
- Understand the principles of intelligence testing.
- Describe the various models of reasoning.
- Evaluate the contribution of heredity and environment to intelligence.
- Be aware of and describe individual differences in intelligence.
- Describe and understand the effects of ageing on cognitive ability.
- Define and give examples of inductive and deductive reasoning.
- Appreciate the biases in human reasoning and why they occur.

QUESTIONS TO THINK ABOUT

- What is intelligence?
- How can intelligence be measured?
- Is it useful to invoke the concept of intelligence?
- Is there more than one 'intelligence'?
- Is there a difference between 'clever' and 'intelligent'?
- What factors contribute to the development of intelligent thought?
- Is intelligence heritable?
- What are the effects of ageing on functions such as language and remembering?
- What is dementia and are there different types of dementia with different symptoms?
- What causes dementia?
- How do we reason and are there effective and ineffective ways of reasoning?
- In which ways can our reasoning be irrational?
- Why do we sometimes violate various logical rules?
- What is creativity? Can we measure and facilitate creativity experimentally?

What is intelligence?

In general, if people do well academically or succeed at tasks that involve their heads rather than their hands, we consider them to be intelligent. If a politician makes a useful policy decision, we call it an intelligent decision. If an author writes an erudite book on an arcane subject, we might describe him as having written an intelligent appraisal. But if asked to give a precise definition of intelligence, psychologists – in common with non-scientists – come slightly unstuck. Sternberg and Detterman (1986) asked a dozen theorists to provide definitions of intelligence and received a dozen different descriptions. According to one of psychology's historians, writing in the 1920s, intelligence has come to represent whatever intelligence tests measure (Boring, 1923).

In general, however, psychologists agree that the term **intelligence** describes a person's ability to learn and remember information, to recognise concepts and their relations, and to apply the information to their own behaviour in an adaptive way (Neisser *et al.*, 1996a). Where they diverge is in describing the nature of intelligence and how it works. For example, some psychologists argue that there is a general factor called intelligence but no different subtypes of intelligence; others argue intelligence is a series of abilities; yet others adopt a combinative approach arguing that there is general intelligence but there are also specific abilities. The number of these abilities depends on the theory one examines.

Theories of intelligence

Most theories of intelligence are based on the analysis of performance on tests which seek to measure specific abilities such as non-verbal and verbal intellectual competence. Much of the debate in the psychology of intelligence has focused on whether there is a single intelligence or there are multiple intelligences. Is our intellectual ability a unitary factor or is it made up of a number of different abilities? Are these abilities, if they do exist, completely separate from each other or are they related?

Intelligence tests yield a single number, usually called an IQ score, although this does not itself mean that intelligence is a single, general characteristic. Some investigators have suggested that certain intellectual abilities are completely independent of one another. For example, a person can be excellent at spatial reasoning but poor at solving verbal analogies. But psychologists disagree over whether specific abilities are totally independent or whether one

general factor influences all abilities. The next sections consider some influential theories of intelligence.

Spearman's two-factor theory

Charles Spearman (1927) proposed that an individual's performance on a test of intellectual ability is determined by two factors: the **g factor**, which is a general factor, and the **s factor**, which is a factor specific to a particular test. Spearman did not call his g factor 'intelligence'; he considered the term too vague. He defined the g factor as comprising three 'qualitative principles of cognition': apprehension of experience, eduction of relations and eduction of correlates. A common task on tests of intellectual abilities – solving analogies – requires all three principles (Sternberg, 1985). For example, consider the following analogy:

LAWYER:CLIENT:DOCTOR:_____

This problem should be read as 'LAWYER is to CLIENT as DOCTOR is to _____'.

Apprehension of experience refers to people's ability to perceive and understand what they experience; thus, reading and understanding each of the words in the analogy requires apprehension of experience. Eduction (not 'education') is the process of drawing or bringing out, that is, making sense of, given facts. In this case, eduction of relations refers to the ability to perceive the relation between lawyer and client; namely, that the lawyer works for and is paid by the client. Eduction of correlates refers to the ability to apply a rule inferred from one case to a similar case. Thus, the person whom a doctor works for and is ultimately paid by is obviously a patient. Because analogy problems require all three of Spearman's principles of cognition, he advocated their use in intelligence testing.

Empirical evidence for Spearman's two-factor theory comes from correlations among various tests of particular intellectual abilities. The governing logic is as follows. If we administer ten different tests of intellectual abilities to a group of people and each test measures a separate, independent ability, the scores these people make on any one test will be unrelated to their scores on any other; the correlations among the tests will be approximately zero. However, if the tests measure abilities that are simply different manifestations of a single trait, the scores will be related; the intercorrelations will be close to 1.

In fact, the intercorrelations among a group of tests of intellectual abilities are neither zero nor 1. Instead, most of these tests are at least moderately correlated, so that a person who scores well on a vocabulary test also tends to score better than average on other tests, such as arithmetic or spatial reasoning. The correlations among various tests of intellectual ability usually range from 0.3 to 0.7, which means that they have between 9 per cent and 49 per cent of their variability in common (Ozer, 1985).

Spearman concluded that a general factor (*g*) accounted for the moderate correlations among different tests of ability. Thus, a person's score on a particular test depends on two things: the person's specific ability (*s*) on the particular test (such as spatial reasoning) and their level of the *g* factor, or general reasoning ability.

Evidence from factor analysis

Factor analysis is a statistical procedure developed by Spearman and Pearson that permits investigators to identify common factors among groups of tests. It is a form of data reduction in the sense that a large number of data can be reduced and explained by reference to two or three factors (Kline, 1993). In the case of intelligence tests, these common factors would be particular abilities that affect people's performance on more than one test. If a group of people take several different tests of intellectual ability and each person's scores on several of these tests correlate well with one another, the tests may (at least partly) be measuring the same factor. A factor analysis determines which sets of tests form groups. For example, Birren and Morrison (1961) administered the Wechsler Adult Intelligence Scale (WAIS, an intelligence test described in the next section) to 933 people. This test consists of 11 different subtests. Birren and Morrison calculated the correlations between subtests and then subjected these correlations to a factor analysis. Table 11.1 shows the results of the analysis.

Table 11.1 Three factors derived by factor analysis of scores on WAIS subtests

Subtest	Factors		
	A	**B**	**C**
Information	0.70	0.18	0.25
Comprehension	0.63	0.12	0.24
Arithmetic	0.38	0.35	0.28
Similarities	0.57	0.12	0.27
Digit span	0.16	0.84	0.13
Vocabulary	0.84	0.16	0.18
Digit symbol	0.24	0.22	0.29
Picture completion	0.41	0.15	0.53
Block design	0.20	0.14	0.73
Picture arrangement	0.35	0.18	0.41
Object assembly	0.16	0.06	0.59

Source: Adapted from Morrison, D.F. (1967) *Multivariate Statistical Methods*, New York: McGraw-Hill.

The factor analysis revealed three factors, labelled A, B and C. The numbers in the three columns in the table are called factor loadings; they are somewhat like **correlation coefficients** in that they express the degree to which a particular test is related to a particular factor. For the various subtests on factor A, the largest factor loading is for vocabulary, followed by information, comprehension and similarities. In the middle range are picture completion, arithmetic, picture arrangement and digit symbol. Digit span, object assembly and block design are the smallest. Verbal subtests make the most important contribution to factor A, so we might be tempted to call this factor verbal ability. But almost all tests make at least a moderate contribution, so perhaps this factor may reflect general intelligence. Digit span has a heavy loading on factor B (0.84), and arithmetic and digit symbol have moderate loadings. Factor B, therefore, is related to maintaining information in short-term memory and manipulating numbers. Factor C appears to be determined mainly by block design, object assembly, picture completion and picture arrangement, and might, therefore, represent the factor, spatial ability.

Although factor analysis can give hints about the nature of intelligence, it cannot provide definitive answers. The names given to factors are determined by the investigator and, although the names may appear to be quite appropriate, the process inevitably has a subjective element to it. There is also the danger of reification when conducting factor analysis. That is, the factors may wrongly be seen as concrete entities and not simply as labels used to describe a set of data as concisely and accurately as possible. Furthermore, factor analysis can never be more meaningful than the individual tests on which it is performed. To identify the relevant factors in human intelligence, one must include an extensive variety of tests in the factor analysis. The WAIS, for example, does not contain a test of musical ability. If it did, a factor analysis would undoubtedly yield an additional factor. Whether musical ability is a component of intelligence depends on how we decide to define intelligence; this question cannot be answered by a factor analysis.

Other psychologists employed factor analysis to determine the nature of intelligence. Louis Thurstone's study (1938) of students' performance on a battery of 56 tests extracted seven factors, which he labelled verbal comprehension, verbal fluency, number, spatial visualisation, memory, reasoning and perceptual speed. At first, Thurstone thought that his results contradicted Spearman's hypothesised *g* factor. However, Eysenck suggested a few years later that a second factor analysis could be performed on Thurstone's factors. If the analysis found one common factor, then Spearman's *g* factor would receive support. In other words, if Thurstone's seven factors themselves had a second-order factor in common, this factor might be conceived of as general intelligence.

Cattell performed a second-order factor analysis and found not one but two major factors. Horn and Cattell (1966) called these factors fluid intelligence (g_f) and crystallised intelligence (g_c). Fluid intelligence is reflected by performance on relatively culture-free tasks, such as those that measure the ability to see relations among objects or the ability to see patterns in a repeating series of items. Crystallised intelligence is defined by tasks that require people to have already acquired information, such as vocabulary and semantic information, and is therefore more culture-bound. Cattell regards fluid intelligence as closely related to a person's native capacity for intellectual performance; in other words, it represents a potential ability to learn and solve problems. In contrast, he regards crystallised intelligence as what a person has accomplished through the use of their fluid intelligence – what they have learned. Horn (1978) disagrees with Cattell by citing evidence suggesting that both factors are learned but are also based on heredity. He says that g_f is based on casual learning and g_c is based on cultural, school-type learning.

Figure 11.1 shows examples from four of the subtests that load heavily on fluid intelligence.

Tests that load heavily on the crystallised intelligence factor include word analogies and tests of vocabulary, general information and use of language. According to Cattell, g_c depends on g_f. Fluid intelligence supplies the native ability, whereas experience with language and exposure to books, school and other learning opportunities develop crystallised intelligence. If two people have the same experiences, the one with the greater fluid intelligence will develop the greater crystallised intelligence. However, a person with a high fluid intelligence exposed to an intellectually impoverished environment will develop a poor or mediocre crystallised intelligence. Table 11.2 presents a summary of tests that load on g_f and g_c.

No two investigators agree about the nature of intelligence. However, most believe that a small number of common factors account for at least part of a person's performance on intellectual tasks. The current view of g

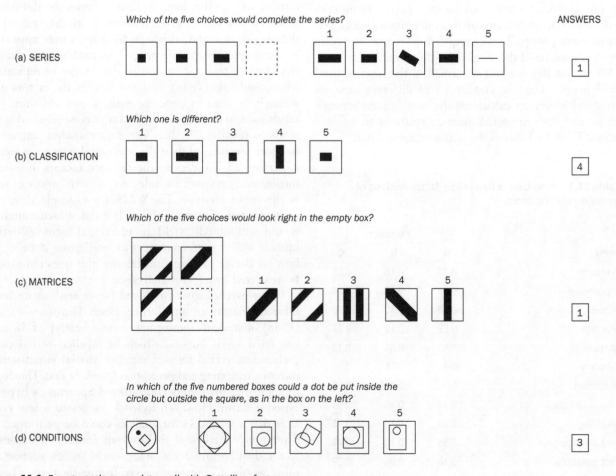

Figure 11.1 Four tests that correlate well with Cattell's g_f factor.

Source: from *Technical Supplement for the Culture Fair Intelligence Tests, Scales 2 and 3*, Institute for Personality and Ability Testing (Cattell, R.B., Krug, S.E., Barton, K. 1973), by permission of Hogrefe Ltd. © 2008 Hogrefe Ltd., Oxford, www.hogrefe.co.uk. All rights reserved.

Table 11.2 Summary of tests with large factor loadings on g_f or g_c

Test	Approximate factor loadings	
	g_f	g_c
Figural relations: Deduction of a relation when this is shown among common figures	0.57	0.01
Memory span: Reproduction of several numbers or letters presented briefly	0.50	0.00
Induction: Deduction of a correlate from relations shown in a series of letters, numbers, or figures, as in a letter series test	0.41	0.06
General reasoning: Solving problems of area, rate, finance, and the like, as in an arithmetic reasoning test	0.31	0.34
Semantic relations: Deduction of a relation when this is shown among words, as in an analogies test	0.37	0.43
Formal reasoning: Arriving at a conclusion in accordance with a formal reasoning process, as in a syllogistic reasoning test	0.31	0.41
Number facility: Quick and accurate use of arithmetical operations such as addition, subtraction and multiplication	0.21	0.29
Experimental evaluation: Solving problems involving protocol and requiring diplomacy, as in a social relations test	0.08	0.43
Verbal comprehension: Advanced understanding of language, as measured in a vocabulary reading test	0.08	0.68

Source: Adapted from Horn, J.L., Organization of abilities and the development of intelligence. *Psychological Review*, 1968, 75, 249. © 1968 by the American Psychological Association. Adapted by permission.

and its contribution to sub-factors of intelligence can be seen in Figure 11.2.

Sternberg's triarchic theory of intelligence

Sternberg (1985) has devised a theory of intelligence that derives from the information-processing approach used by many cognitive psychologists. Sternberg's theory has three parts; he calls it a triarchic theory (meaning 'ruled by three'). The three parts of the theory deal with three aspects of intelligence: componential intelligence, experiential intelligence and contextual intelligence. Taken together, these three components go beyond the abilities measured by most common tests of intelligence. They include practical aspects of behaviour that enable a person to adapt successfully to their environment. Table 11.3 provides a summary of the key concepts of Sternberg's triarchic theory.

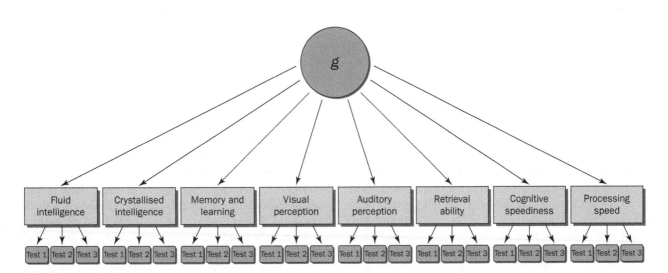

Figure 11.2 Intelligence researchers generally agree that all intellectual ability is underpinned by a general (g) intelligence. This contributes to other, specific abilities (which may be developed to a lesser or a greater extent depending on various factors such as education, interest, genes and environment).

Table 11.3 An outline of Sternberg's triarchic theory of intelligence

Componential intelligence

Meta components (e.g. planning)

Performance components (e.g. lexical access)

Knowledge acquisition components (e.g. ability to acquire vocabulary words)

Experimental intelligence

Novel tasks

Automated tasks

Contextual intelligence

Adaptation (adapting to the environment)

Selection (finding a suitable environment)

Shaping (changing the environment)

Componential intelligence consists of the mental mechanisms people use to plan and execute tasks. The components revealed by the factor analyses of verbal ability and deductive reasoning are facets of componential intelligence. Sternberg suggests that the components of intelligence serve three functions. Meta-components (transcending components) are the processes by which people decide the nature of an intellectual problem, select a strategy for solving it and allocate their resources. For example, good readers vary the amount of time they spend on a passage according to how much information they need to extract from it (Wagner and Sternberg, 1985; cited in Sternberg, 1985). This decision is controlled by a meta-component of intelligence. Performance components are the processes actually used to perform the task, for example word recognition and working memory. Knowledge acquisition components are those the person uses to gain new knowledge by sifting out relevant information and integrating it with what they already know.

The second part of Sternberg's theory deals with experiential intelligence. **Experiential intelligence** is the ability to deal effectively with novel situations and to solve automatically problems that have been previously encountered. According to Sternberg's theory, a person with good experiential intelligence is able to deal more effectively with novel situations than is a person with poor experiential intelligence. The person is better able to analyse the situation and to bring mental resources to bear on the problem, even if they have never encountered one like it before. After encountering a particular type of problem several times, the person with good experiential intelligence is also able to 'automate' the procedure so that similar problems can be solved without much

thought, freeing mental resources for other work. A person who has to reason out the solution to a problem every time it occurs will be left behind by people who can give the answer quickly and automatically. Sternberg suggests that this distinction is closely related to the distinction between fluid and crystallised intelligence (Horn and Cattell, 1966). According to Sternberg, tasks that use fluid intelligence are those that demand novel approaches, whereas tasks that use crystallised intelligence are those that demand mental processes that have become automatic.

The third part of Sternberg's theory deals with **contextual intelligence** – intelligence reflecting the behaviours that were subject to natural selection in our evolutionary history. Contextual intelligence takes three forms: adaptation, selection and shaping. The first form, adaptation, consists of fitting oneself into one's environment by developing useful skills and behaviours. In different cultures, adaptation will take different forms. For example, knowing how to distinguish between poisonous and edible plants is an important skill for a member of a hunter–gatherer tribe. Knowing how to present oneself in a job interview is an important skill for a member of an industrialised society. The second form of contextual intelligence, selection, refers to the ability to find one's own niche in the environment. That is, individuals will decide on careers or activities which they both enjoy doing and do well.

The third form of contextual intelligence is shaping. Adapting to the environment or selecting a new one may not always be possible or profitable. In such cases, intelligent behaviour consists of shaping the environment itself. For example, a person whose talents are not appreciated by their employer may decide to start their own business.

Gardner's multiple intelligences theory

Gardner's theory of intelligence is based on a neuropsychological analysis of human abilities (Gardner, 1983). It argues that intelligence falls into seven categories: linguistic intelligence, musical intelligence, logical/mathematical intelligence, spatial intelligence, bodily/kinesthetic intelligence and two types of personal intelligence. Bodily/kinesthetic intelligence includes the types of skill that athletes, typists, dancers or mime artists exhibit. Personal intelligence includes awareness of one's own feelings (intrapersonal intelligence) and the ability to notice individual differences in other people and to respond appropriately to them – in other words, to be socially aware (interpersonal intelligence).

Three of Gardner's types of intelligence – verbal intelligence, logical/mathematical intelligence and spatial intelligence – are not unusual, having been identified previously by many other researchers. The other four are

Linguistic

James Joyce

Other well-known exemplars:
Marcel Proust
Martin Amis
Virginia Woolf
Dorothy Parker
Henrik Ibsen
P.G. Wodehouse
Jane Austen

Logical/mathematical

Isaac Newton

Other well-known exemplars:
Stephen Hawking
Richard Feynman
Albert Einstein
Jules-Henri Poincaré
Marie Curie
Trevor Bayliss
Tim Berners-Lee

Musical

Paul McCartney

Other well-known exemplars:
Wolfgang Amadeus Mozart
Vivaldi
Ivor Novello
Vince Clarke
Shania Twain
Madonna
Cole Porter

Spatial

Salvador Dali

Other well-known exemplars:
Leonardo Da Vinci
Henry Moore
Norman Foster
Christopher Wren
Marcel Duchamp
Stephen Spielberg
Paul Smith

Body/kinetic/kinaesthetic

Chris Hoy

Other well-known exemplars:
Margot Fonteyn
Rudolph Nureyev
Michael Jordan
David Beckham

Interpersonal

Oprah Winfrey

Other well-known exemplars:
Anthony Clare
Bill Clinton
Jerry Springer
Ricki Lake

Intrapersonal

Nelson Mandela

Other well-known exemplars:
Dalai Lama
Mahatma Gandhi
Mother Teresa

Well-known exemplars of the type of individuals who would show high levels of each of Gardner's multiple intelligences.
Source: Press Association Images, Magnum Photos, Bettman/CORBIS.

rather unusual. According to Gardner, all seven abilities are well represented in the brain, in that specific brain damage can impair some of them but leave others relatively intact. For example, people with damage to the left parietal lobe can show apraxia, an inability to perform sequences of voluntary skilled movements. In contrast, people with damage to the right parietal lobe develop spatial neglect (see Chapter 6). Individuals with frontal lobe damage, as you will see later in this chapter, have difficulty evaluating the significance of social situations and making decisions about social matters (the frontal lobes used to be regarded as the region of the brain responsible for intelligence) (see also Chapters 4 and 13). These examples illustrate bodily/kinesthetic intelligence and both intrapersonal and interpersonal intelligence.

Emotional intelligence

A different type of intelligence, one not based on any particular cognitive ability, was proposed by Goleman (1995, 1998). This type of intelligence refers to the social and emotional components of interactions with others: the more socially sensitive and emotionally sensitive you were to the needs and behaviours of others, the more successful your interaction would be. Goleman referred to this as emotional intelligence but there is some controversy over whether this is a separate, valid and reliable type of intelligence (Sjoberg, 2001).

There is certainly evidence that social skill is a key factor in understanding others' thoughts and feelings and this is one of the factors that Goleman cites as being important to success in business. A recent study suggests that an interaction between intelligence and social skill may underlie some differences in job performance (Ferris *et al.*, 2001). Having low ability and social skill will do nothing for your career, but what if you had low ability and great social skill or great ability and low social skill?

The study asked 106 software engineers and programmers to complete a general ability scale which measured vocabulary, arithmetic, reasoning and spatial ability and also to rate their social skills, job performance and job dedication. These employees, their supervisors and their personnel managers were interviewed. A measure of personality was taken and salary level and sex were noted.

Neither high general mental ability nor high social skill was individually associated with high levels of performance or high salaries. Each factor seemed to influence the other. Social skill was highly correlated with performance and salary when workers were very mentally able; mental ability was highly correlated with job success when social skill was high. Having good social skill but low mental ability, however, resulted in lower salary levels. 'Perhaps individuals low in GMA [General Mental Ability]', the authors suggest, 'may attempt to overcompensate for their lack of intelligence by focusing a disproportionate amount of time and effort on social aspects of the job.'

It has been pointed out that Goleman's concept of emotional intelligence involves both social and emotional intelligence and that these may be separable. Measures of emotional intelligence seem to predict job success better than does interview performance (itself not a difficult achievement given the low correlation between interview performance and job performance), but empirical support for the concept is mixed (Mayer and Cobb, 2000).

Because the two factors involved in emotional intelligence may predict different behaviours, some researchers have developed specific scales to measure the emotional component only. Mayer *et al.* (1999), for example, have constructed such a scale and have defined emotional intelligence as 'the ability to perceive and express emotion, assimilate emotion in thought, understand and reason with emotion and regulate emotion in the self and others'. This scale seems to correlate well with questionnaires measuring empathy – a key feature of emotional intelligence – but its reliability and validity await more extensive testing. Some studies show that brief emotional intelligence measures predict commitment to a career but other authors have argued that the concept may not be as separate as some psychologists state. Sjoberg (2001), for example, argues that emotional intelligence may not be a measure of anything separate but is a factor that is 'secondary' to other concepts (which may be personality or cognitive ability).

Estimating intelligence – An international perspective

Although the proposition that men and women differ in intelligence is controversial, there is a great deal of evidence to suggest that males overestimate their own IQ more than do females (Beloff, 1992; Byrd and Stacey, 1993). These beliefs seem to be unrelated to actual cognitive performance. The actual IQ of males is significantly lower than their IQ estimate whereas that of females is also lower but not significantly so (Reilly and Mulhern, 1995).

A consistent finding is that participants of both sexes rate their fathers' IQ as being higher than their mothers' (Beloff, 1992; Furnham and Rawles, 1995). Not only are fathers rated as more intelligent than mothers, but sons are judged by their parents to have a higher IQ than daughters (Furnham and Gasson, 1998). These findings appear to generalise across cultures. Furnham *et al.* (1999a), for example, asked 400 participants from the UK, Hawaii and Singapore to estimate their own parents' and siblings' IQ score for each of Gardner's multiple intelligences, using the test described in Figure 11.3. There were no sex differences in the estimated intelligence of siblings and parents but men estimated their own mathematical, spatial and bodily/kinetic intelligence as well as their overall intelligence to be higher than did women.

A similar study asked 140 Belgian, 227 British and 177 Slovakian students to estimate their multiple intelligence

Estimating intelligence – *Continued*

How intelligent are you?

Intelligence tests attempt to measure intelligence. The average or mean score on these tests is 100. Most of the population (about $^2/_3$ people) score between 85 and 115. Very bright people score around 130 and scores have been known to go over 145.

The following graph shows the typical distribution of scores.

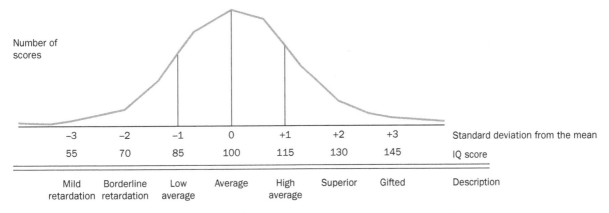

Figure 11.3 Example of a test used to examine individuals' perception of their own and their relatives' intelligence.

as well as that of their parents and siblings (Furnham *et al.*, 1999b). Men rated their own general intelligence, but not those of their parents or siblings, more highly than did women. When the researchers looked at specific types of intelligence, men rated their numerical (but not verbal or cultural) IQ higher than did women.

Few national differences were reported but those that were appeared to be attributable to the Slovakian women. They rated their own and their fathers' IQ more highly than did Slovakian men. They also rated their verbal intelligence more highly than numerical and cultural IQ (Slovakian men rated their cultural and numerical IQ to be similar but higher

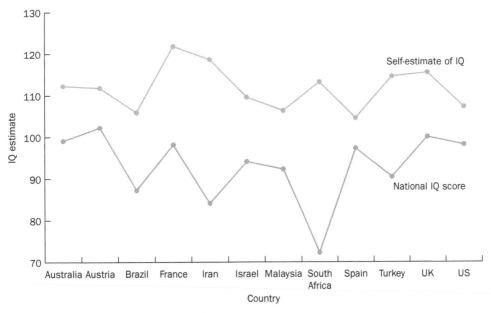

Figure 11.4 Self-estimates of intelligence and national IQ scores across nations.

Source: von Stumm, S., Chamorro-Premuzic, T. and Furnham, A. (2009). Decomposing self-estimates of intelligence: Structure and sex differences across 12 nations. *British Journal of Psychology*, 100, 429–42.

Estimating intelligence – *Continued*

than their cultural IQ). This is the first study of its kind to find that women rate their own intelligence more highly.

A study comparing British and Turkish respondents found that men rated their father's intelligence as being higher than their mother's (based on Gardner and Sternberg's models) and men rated their overall, verbal, logical, spatial, creative and practical intelligence higher than did women (Furnham *et al.*, 2009). Cultural differences were more pronounced than sex differences, however, with Turks rating their musical, body-kinesthetic, interpersonal, intrapersonal, naturalistic, creative, emotional and practical intelligence higher than did the Brits. Using the same intelligence measures, von Stumm *et al.* (2009) compared estimates of men and women from 12 nations – Australia, Austria, Brazil, France, Iran, Israel, Malaysia, South Africa, Spain, Turkey, UK and US. All nations overestimated their intelligence compared with actual scores and men overestimated their own intelligence pretty universally (see Figure 11.4).

In an intriguing study, Furnham *et al.* (2002a) asked British and American students to estimate their own overall intelligence and different types of intelligence, but also that of well-known figures such as Tony Blair, Bill Gates, Prince Charles and Bill Clinton. Men, as expected, estimated their verbal, logical and spatial IQ more highly than did women and women rated their male partners as having lower verbal IQ but higher spatial IQ than themselves. Of the famous figures, participants rated Bill Clinton and Prince Charles as less intelligent than themselves but Tony Blair and Bill Gates to be more intelligent.

A series of meta-analyses has confirmed the general pattern of findings reported in studies where men and women estimate their own, and male and female relatives' intelligence: males give higher estimates for all types of intelligence, apart from verbal ability (Symanowicz and Furnham, 2011). This asymmetry is not actually reflected in intelligence scores: they are comparable. But men believe they are more intelligent, indicating an over-inflation bias. The effect is seen cross-culturally, apart from in Uganda, Zimbabwe and Zambia where women give higher self-estimates.

'It is unclear,' the authors conclude, 'whether it is men who are arrogantly and conceitedly overestimating their intelligence, or that women are humbly and unconfidently under-estimating their intelligence, or that both are occurring to the same degree' (p. 502).

Are there consistent sex differences in cognitive ability?

Take a look at Figure 11.5. At the moment, the glass is empty but imagine that it is half full. Using a pencil, draw

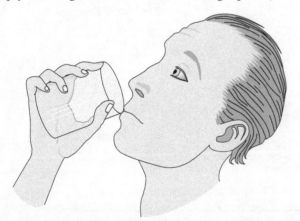

Figure 11.5 The Water Level Test. The glass is meant to be half full of water. The participant's task is to indicate where the top of the water should be.

Source: Kalichman, S.C., The effects of sex and context on paper and pencil spatial task performance, *Journal of General Psychology*, 1989, 116, 133–9. Reprinted with permission of the Helen Dwight Reid Educational Foundation. Published by Heldref Publications, 1319 Eighteenth St., NW, Washington, DC, 20036–1802, www.heldref .org, copyright © 1989.

a line across the glass where you think the top of the water should be. Do that now before you read on.

If you were a man, you probably drew the line horizontally across the glass; if you were a woman, you probably drew the line parallel to the direction in which the water glass is tipped. The correct line would be the horizontal one.

This phenomenon illustrates one of the most consistent sex differences in cognitive ability. The task is Piaget's Water Level Test, and men tend to be better at it than women (Halpern, 1992; Rilea, 2008). Other tests showing sex differences are summarised in Table 11.4.

Why should males tend to be better at this task? One explanation for the Water Level Test result is that men and boys are intrinsically superior at tests of spatial ability than are women and girls (we will come on to reasons why this should be a little later). Spatial ability refers to 'skills in representing, transforming, generating and recalling symbolic, nonlinguistic information' (Linn and Petersen, 1985). The test of spatial ability which shows the most consistent and reliable sex difference is mental rotation (Masters and Sanders, 1993). In this task, individuals are presented with three sets of cubes and have to match the target set with one of the other two. The task is not straightforward because the cubes

Table 11.4 Cognitive tests and tasks that usually show sex differences

Type of test/task	Example
Tasks and tests on which women obtain higher average scores	
Tasks that require rapid access to and use of phonological, semantic and other information in long-term memory	Verbal fluency – phonological retrieval
	Synonym generation – meaning retrieval
	Associative memory
	Spellings and anagrams
	Mathematical calculations
	Memory for spatial locations
Knowledge areas	Foreign languages
Production and comprehension of complex prose	Reading comprehension
	Writing
	Mirror tracing – novel, complex figures
Fine motor skills	Pegboard tasks
	Matching and coding tasks
Perceptual speed	Multiple speeded tasks
Speech articulation	Tongue-twisters
Tasks and tests on which men obtain higher average scores	
Tasks that require transformations in visual working memory	Mental rotation
	Piaget Water Level Test
Tasks that involve moving objects	Dynamic spatiotemporal tasks
Motor tasks that involve aiming	Accuracy in throwing balls or darts
Knowledge areas	General knowledge
	Maths and science knowledge
Test of fluid reasoning (especially in maths and science domain)	Promotional reasoning tasks
	Mechanical reasoning
	Verbal analogies
	Scientific reasoning

Source: Adapted with permission from Halpern, D.F., Sex difference in intelligence. *American Psychologist*, 1997, 52(10), 1091–102. © 1997 The American Psychological Association, reprinted with permission.

have to be mentally rotated before a match can be made (see Chapter 8).

The three-dimensional nature of the stimuli appears to be important. In one experiment the performance of 3- and 6-year-old boys and girls were compared on a two-dimensional task (a jigsaw puzzle) or a three-dimensional task (constructing Lego). It was found that although there was no difference between boys and girls on the two-dimensional task, boys performed better than girls at the three-dimensional task (McGuiness and Morley, 1991).

A different version of the standard mental rotation task was used in a study by Hirnstein *et al.* (2009). The researchers presented the well-known Vandeberg and Kuse mental rotation test in its original and in modified form. In the original, as you've seen, the participant is presented with one target and four sample sets of cubes and is asked to identify two samples that are identical, when rotated, to the target set. In the modified version, the participant has to compare each sample against the target, a modification that prohibits a leaping strategy – moving onto the next trial as soon as they think they've identified two matching samples (thereby ignoring the remaining, uncompared samples). Hirnstein *et al.* (2009) found that the performance of both men and women was poorer in the modified condition, but men's performance was more adversely affected than that of women. However, the better performance in men still remained.

Although superior mental rotation performance is a male preserve, object location memory is thought to be better in women, a finding that has been replicated internationally in 35 out of 40 countries (Silverman *et al.*, 2007). Honda and Nihei (2009) asked men and women to study a variety of objects and to recall the location

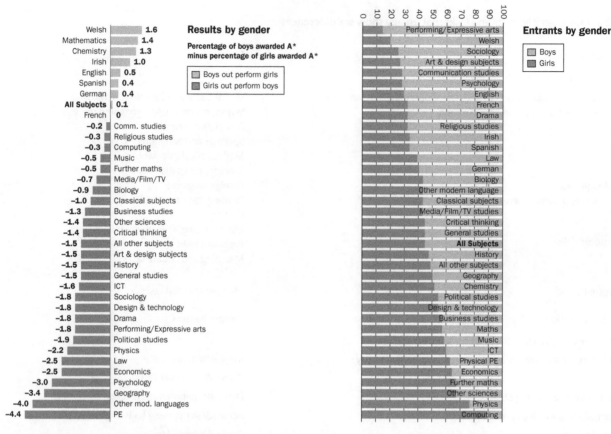

Figure 11.6 The percentage of boys and girls taking school subjects in England and Wales (right) and relative performance in each subject (left).

Source: from 'A-level results 2012: A and A* grades fall', *The Guardian*, 17/08/2012 (Vasagar, J), Copyright Guardian News & Media Ltd 2012.

of the objects either three minutes after presentation or one week later. Women were better than men after three minutes but not after a week. They were also better at locating objects whose locations had been swapped but, again, only in the three minute condition.

In other types of visuospatial test, women tend to outperform men. For example, women have been found to be consistently superior to men at tests involving visual recognition. It has been suggested that this may be so because of women's superior linguistic ability. Women, for example, are better than men at tests involving verbal fluency, such as naming as many objects as possible beginning with a specific letter (Halpern, 1997), and boys tend to be diagnosed with reading and speech disorders more commonly than are girls (Flynn and Rahbar, 1994).

The stimuli used can also be important. Rilea (2008) found that men were better at the Water Level Task but showed no advantage on mental rotation or paper folding. However, men were better at rotating polygons than stick figures (and they showed a right hemisphere advantage for the task; there was no right hemisphere advantage shown by women for either stimulus type). Contreras

et al. (2007) suggest a stimulus-specific complicating factor: the tests of spatial ability used are static, not dynamic. Therefore, they set up a study in which men and women performed a dynamic test of spatial ability – guiding two dots towards a destination in the shortest time. They found that even when performance factors were taken into account, men outperformed women (i.e. differences in performance style did not explain the sex difference). On average, men took longer to decide on the first move of the dots, then guided the dots more quickly.

These data suggest that 'spatial ability' is not an all-or-nothing concept but multidimensional. Different types of spatial ability test and different types of spatial stimuli produce sex differences; others do not.

Can sex differences be eliminated? There are some interesting answers. An experiment by McLoy and Koonce (1988, cited in Halpern, 1992) trained men and women on a standard simulated flight task and found that men were better at learning this task than were women. They also found that given sufficient training, women performed at about the same level as men; they simply needed more training to achieve this level of competence. Recently, a study manipulated participants' belief in performance and observed the consequences for behaviour. Men and women (in same sex groups) were asked to perform a mental rotation test but different groups were given different instructions (Moe, 2009). One group was told: 'men are better than women at this task'; another: 'women are better than men'; and a third were given instructions with no reference to sex. Each group was also told that the test was either quite easy or very difficult. Women performed better when given the sex-positive instruction but task difficulty priming had no discernible effect. Men performed better when given sex-positive instructions, when told the test was easy and, if given control instructions, when the task was described as difficult. The sex-negative instructions had no effect on performance of either sex.

Sex differences in visuospatial ability might also be due to different processing styles. Pena *et al.* (2008) asked men and women to complete a visuospatial exercise in which they had to guide two differently coloured dots on a monitor to a colour-appropriate target area. Participants did this by using a cursor to alter the direction of an arrow button which guided the dots. Two interesting findings emerged. Men, as expected, performed better than women but the type of strategy employed during the task affected success on the task. They also found that when one type of strategy was adopted, sex differences were reduced; when the other was employed, sex differences remained strong.

The two strategy styles were described as 'segmentary' or 'planned and feedback-dependent holistic'. Segmentary strategy involved focusing on a particular portion of the task, to the exclusion of other aspects of the task or the screen (hence, 'segment'). Followers of this strategy would change the course of the dot frequently. Holistic strategists did not make as many course changes. Some of these planned their actions before the task ('planned') and some acted on feedback from the screen ('feedback-dependent'). Men used the holistic strategy more often than did women; women were more likely to adopt the segmentary strategy. When men used planned holistic and segmentary strategies, they performed better than women using the same strategies. However, when both sexes employed the planned strategy, this sex difference narrowed.

Why should men outperform women on spatial tasks? Theories of sex differences in cognitive ability fall into four general categories: evolutionary, psychosocial, biological and cognitive.

Evolutionary theories

The evolutionary point of view suggests that spatial superiority in men is a throwback to the evolution of men and women as hunters and gatherers (Eals and Silverman, 1994). This theory suggests that because men originally roamed and hunted (activities which rely on the manipulation of visuospatial features in the environment), and because women stayed 'at home' and gathered, it is not surprising that men are spatially superior. The greater visual recognition performance seen in women is meant to reflect women's evolutionary role as foragers (Tooby and DeVore, 1987).

According to evolutionary psychologists, one reason why men are better at spatial cognition than women is that men were the hunters who ranged far and wide for their prey and would, therefore, need to develop a well-tuned set of navigational skills. Women, the child-bearers and rearers, stayed at home and foraged. Some argue that women's ranging was limited to picking plants; men would hunt for game.

According to Ecuyer-Dab and Robert (2004), however, this dichotomy suggests that rather than showing a superior spatial advantage by men over women it shows how context can affect the way in which each sex expresses its specific spatial skills: spatial cognition in men would be used to navigate the environment for a mate and food whereas women's spatial cognition developed to

Cutting edge: Boys, creatures of extremes?

Helen Cronin, the evolutionary psychologist, has pithily described the male species as having more Nobels but also more dumb-bells. That is, men are more likely to show extreme performances on measures of intelligence and cognitive ability whereas women may show a less extreme pattern. There is some evidence of this. An extensive study of 320,000 11–12-year-olds in the UK, found few strong differences between girls and boys on the Cognitive Abilities Test but boys were more strongly represented at the top and bottom of the distribution for the non-verbal measure scores and at the lower end of the verbal measure distribution (Strand *et al.*, 2006).

Lohman and Lakin (2009) administered the same test in three different versions to over 318,000 children from grades 3 to 11 in North America. They found almost identical results to those reported by the UK study, suggesting that the findings cannot be attributable to nation, age, education system or type of test. Instead, the results suggest a more universal finding.

deal with the immediate environment because they were more concerned with the survival of their offspring in the home. They, therefore, had no need to develop the navigational spatial skills that men did. In short, men developed and evolved large-scale navigation mechanisms and women evolved small-scale ones.

Ecuyer-Dab and Robert cite evidence from recent studies to support the hypothesis. Women, for example, were more likely than men to use landmarks when giving map directions. Men were more likely to provide more detail on direction and distance – although women are capable of doing this, they simply do not use these references as their primary source of information.

One objection to the theory that males are intrinsically superior to females on tests of mental rotation is that the results may be attributable to other causes. For example, because the task is timed, it has been argued that this is detrimental to women, who are more cautious when making decisions about rotation (Goldstein *et al.*, 1990). To test this hypothesis, Masters (1998) allowed male and female undergraduates either a short or unlimited time to perform a mental rotation task. She also used three different scoring procedures because previous studies had been criticised for basing their findings on using correct answers only (without looking at the number of incorrect responses too). Masters found that regardless of scoring procedure or time limit, men performed better than women. (Interestingly, however, some sex differences, such as female self-reported confusion over left and right, may be attributable to women rating themselves more critically than do men (Jordan *et al.*, 2006).)

However, evolutionary theories such as these are so broad as to be untestable (see Chapter 3). As Halpern (1997) also notes, you can explain almost any finding by indicating how it would be advantageous to hunters and gatherers.

Psychosocial theories

Psychosocial theories suggest that sex differences are learned through experience or imitation. Children, it is argued, fulfil sex-role stereotypes: boys are encouraged to play with toys which involve visuospatial manipulation; girls are not (we will come back to this in Chapter 12). It has also been suggested that boys and girls receive different models, rewards and punishment. One researcher has suggested that peer interaction is more likely to lead to stereotypical sex-role behaviour than is parent–child interaction, although this idea is controversial (Harris, 1995).

Another study, investigating the effect on spatial performance of the degree to which men and women internalise their sexual identity or behave in a stereotypically male or female way, on spatial test performance found a weak relationship between spatial ability and sex roles although the actual sex difference remained (Saucier *et al.*, 2002).

Halpern (1992) cites fairly strong evidence against a psychosocial explanation for sex differences in cognitive ability. She noted that among individuals with high reasoning ability, right-handed men outperformed left-handed men on tests of spatial ability but were poorer than left-handed men at verbal tasks. Conversely, left-handed females were better at spatial tasks than were right-handers but the opposite pattern applied to verbal tasks. Any theory of psychosocial influence would have difficulty in explaining these findings: why should right- and left-handed boys and girls be socialised differently? It would also have difficulty in explaining why boys are more likely than girls to suffer from stuttering and reading disorders.

Biological theories

Biological theories suggest that sex differences in cognitive ability may be due to biological factors such as hormonal regulation and brain organisation. There is evidence that anatomical differences exist between the brains of boys and girls and between those of men and women (Shaywitz *et al.*, 1995). Keller and Menon (2009) examined brain activation and structure in 25 men and women who performed various mathematical operations including subtraction and addition. While men and women were equally accurate and equally as fast at the tests, their brain activation during processing differed. There was greater activity in the right dorsal and ventral streams in men and in an area of the right parietal lobe known to be important for calculating arithmetical problems. In terms of structure, women had greater neuronal density in these areas compared with men. The authors suggest that the differences reflect women's more efficient use of neural resources.

Apart from neuroanatomical differences, there may also be differences in the amount of, or sensitivity to, hormones (Collaer and Hines, 1995). Cognitive ability, for example, appears to fluctuate across the menstrual cycle (Hampson, 1990), and the amount of testosterone appears to correlate with spatial skill (Moffat and Hampson, 1996). Brain activation during mental rotation varies depending on a woman's point in her menstrual cycle and with hormone secretion in both sexes (Schoning *et al.*, 2007). Twelve men and twelve women completed a three-dimensional mental rotation task and had their levels of testosterone and/or oestradiol measured. Women were tested during the early follicular and midluteal phase of their cycle. Men and women showed activation in frontal and parietal regions. In men, greater testosterone was associated with greater left parietal lobe activation. In women, there was also a correlation between testosterone levels and activation in the follicular phase. Women's estradiol levels in both phases were associated with increased activation in frontal and parietal areas.

In two interesting experiments, groups of individuals were given certain hormones for reasons other than enhancing cognitive ability. In one study, normal ageing men given testosterone to enhance their sex drive showed increased visuospatial performance (Janowsky *et al.*, 1994). In another, transsexuals given testosterone as part of their preoperative sex change programme were found to show increased visuospatial ability and decreased verbal ability over a period of three months (Van Goozen *et al.*, 1995).

Some studies have also found no relationship between hormone level and spatial ability (Liben *et al.*, 2002). This may not mean that steroids are not involved. 'It may be,' as the authors suggest, 'that such effects do occur but only under some as yet unidentified additional setting conditions (be they biological or experiential).'

Cognitive theories

Empathising and systemising are two ways of processing information, described by Simon Baron-Cohen (2003), in which people work at identifying someone's thoughts and feelings (perspective-taking, altruism, cooperativeness) or analysing relationships in non-social interactions (an interest in science, technology, the natural world, etc.). The approaches can be measured by two questionnaires, called the empathy quotient and the systemising quotient. Women are thought to be better at the former; men, the latter.

In a recent study, men were found to engage in higher levels of systemising than were women and non-heterosexual women higher than heterosexual women (Nettle, 2007). There were no differences between heterosexual and non-heterosexual men. Women did show a greater interest in the arts and culture, however, which may not be related to sociability/empathy.

Intelligence testing

Assessment of intellectual ability, or intelligence testing, is a controversial topic because of its importance in modern society. Unless people have special skills that suit them for a career in sports or entertainment, their economic success may depend heavily on formal education. Many employers use specialised aptitude tests to help them select among job candidates. Test scores correlate with school and university grades, the number of years in education and adult occupational status (Nisbett *et al.*, 2012). There are hundreds of tests of specific abilities, such as manual dexterity, spatial reasoning, vocabulary, mathematical aptitude, musical ability, creativity and memory. All these tests vary widely in reliability, validity and ease of administration.

Early intelligence tests

Intelligence testing has a long and chequered history. As early as 2200 BC, Chinese administrators tested civil servants (mandarins) periodically to be sure that their abilities qualified them for their job. In Western cultures, differences in social class were far more important than individual differences in ability until the Renaissance, when the modern concept of individualism came into being.

The term 'intelligence' is an old one, deriving from the Latin *intellectus* (meaning 'perception' or 'comprehension'). However, its use in the English language dates only from the late nineteenth century, when it was revived by the philosopher Herbert Spencer (1820–1903) and by the biologist/statistician Sir Francis Galton (1822–1911). Galton was the most important early investigator of individual differences in ability. He was strongly influenced by his cousin Charles Darwin, who stressed the importance of inherited differences in physical and behavioural traits related to a species' survival. Galton observed that there were family differences in ability and concluded that intellectual abilities were heritable. Having noted that people with low ability were poor at making sensory discriminations, he decided that tests involving such discriminations would provide valid measures of intelligence.

In 1884, Francis Galton established the Anthropometric Laboratory (meaning 'human-measuring') at the International Health Exhibition in London. His exhibit was so popular that afterwards his laboratory became part of the South Kensington Museum. He tested over 9,000 people on 17 variables, including height and weight, muscular strength and the ability to perform sensory discriminations. One task involved detecting small differences in the weights of objects of the same size and shape.

Galton made some important contributions to science and mathematics. His systematic evaluation of various large numbers of people and the methods of population statistics he developed served as models for the statistical tests now used in all branches of science. His observation that the distribution of most human traits closely resembles the normal curve (developed by the Belgian statistician Lambert Quételet, 1796–1874) is the foundation for many modern tests of statistical significance and can be seen in Figure 11.7.

Galton also outlined the logic of a measure he called correlation: the degree to which variability in one measure is related to variability in another. From this analysis, the British mathematician Karl Pearson (1857–1936) derived the correlation coefficient (r) used today to assess the degree of statistical relation between variables. In addition, Galton developed the logic of twin studies and adoptive parent studies to assess the heritability of a human trait.

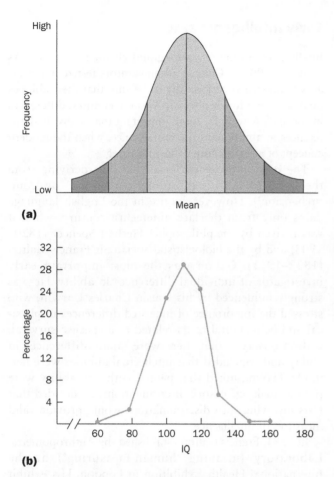

Figure 11.7 The normal curve and data from intelligence testing. **(a)** A mathematically derived normal curve. **(b)** A curve showing the distribution of IQ scores of 850 children of two-and-a-half years of age.
Source: Terman, L.M. and Merrill, M.A., *Stanford–Binet Intelligence Scale*. Boston MA: Houghton-Mifflin, 1960. Copyright © 1960 by Houghton Mifflin Company.

Modern intelligence tests

The Binet–Simon Scale

Alfred Binet (1857–1911), a French psychologist, and a colleague (Binet and Henri, 1896) suggested that a group of simple sensory tests could not adequately determine a person's intelligence. They recommended measuring a variety of psychological abilities (such as imagery, attention, comprehension, imagination, judgements of visual space, and memory for various stimuli) that appeared to be more representative of the traits that distinguished people of high and low intelligence.

To identify children who were unable to profit from normal classroom instruction and needed special attention, Binet and Theodore Simon assembled a collection of tests, many of which had been developed by other investigators, and published the **Binet–Simon Scale** in 1905. The tests

were arranged in order of difficulty, and the researchers obtained norms for each test. Norms are data concerning comparison groups that permit the score of an individual to be assessed relative to his or her peers. In this case, the norms consisted of distributions of scores obtained from children of various ages. Binet and Simon also provided a detailed description of the testing procedure, which was essential for obtaining reliable scores. Without a standardised procedure for administering a test, different testers can obtain different scores from the same child.

Binet revised the 1905 test in order to assess the intellectual abilities of both normal children and those with learning problems. The revised versions provided a procedure for estimating a child's **mental age** – the level of intellectual development that could be expected for an average child of a particular age. For example, if an 8-year-old child scores as well as average 10-year-old children, their mental age is 10 years. Binet did not develop the concept of IQ (intelligence quotient). Nor did he believe that the mental age derived from the test scores expressed a simple trait called 'intelligence'. Instead, he conceived of the overall score as the average of several different abilities.

The Stanford–Binet Scale

Lewis Terman of Stanford University translated and revised the Binet–Simon Scale in the USA. The revised group of tests, published in 1916, became known as the Stanford–Binet Scale. Revisions by Terman and Maud Merrill were published in 1937 and 1960. In 1985, an entirely new version was published. The **Stanford–Binet Scale** consists of various tasks grouped according to mental age. Simple tests include identifying parts of the body and remembering which of three small cardboard boxes contains a marble. Intermediate tests include tracing a simple maze with a pencil and repeating five digits orally. Advanced tests include explaining the difference between two abstract words that are close in meaning (such as fame and notoriety) and completing complex sentences.

The 1916 Stanford–Binet Scale contained a formula for computing the **intelligence quotient (IQ)**, a measure devised by Stern (1914). The (IQ) represents the idea that if test scores indicate that a child's mental age is equal to their chronological age (that is, calendar age), the child's intelligence is average; if the child's mental age is above or below their chronological age, the child is more or less intelligent than average. This relation is expressed as the quotient of mental age (MA) and chronological age (CA). The result is called the **ratio IQ**. The quotient is multiplied by 100 to eliminate fractions. For example, if a child's mental age is 10 and the child's chronological age is 8, then their IQ is (10 ÷ 8) × 100 = 125.

The 1960 version of the Stanford–Binet Scale replaced the ratio IQ with the deviation IQ. Instead of using the ratio of mental age to chronological age, the **deviation IQ** compares a child's score with those received by other children of the same chronological age (the deviation IQ was invented by David Wechsler, whose work is described in the next section). Suppose that a child's score is one **standard deviation** above the mean for their age. The standard deviation of the ratio IQ scores is 16 points, and the score assigned to the average IQ is 100 points. If a child's score is one standard deviation above the mean for their age, the child's deviation IQ score is 100 + 16 (the standard deviation) = 116. A child who scores one standard deviation below the mean receives a deviation IQ of 84 (100 – 16), as Figure 11.8 illustrates.

Wechsler Adult Intelligence Scale

When David Wechsler was chief psychologist at New York City's Bellevue Psychiatric Hospital he developed several popular tests of intelligence. The Wechsler–Bellevue Scale, published in 1939, was revised in 1942 for use in the armed forces and was superseded in 1955 by the **Wechsler Adult Intelligence Scale (WAIS)**. This test was revised again in 1981 (the WAIS-R), 1997 (the WAIS-III) and 2008 (WAIS-IV). The **Wechsler Intelligence Scale for Children** (WISC), first published in 1949 and revised in 1974 (the WISC-R), closely resembles the WAIS. Various versions of the WAIS-R have been devised for use with various populations (such as Irish, Scottish, Welsh and so on).

Previous versions of the scale provided a measure called 'full-scale IQ' which comprised scores from two separate subscales – performance IQ and verbal IQ. The current version, the WAIS-IV, however, has dispensed with the two subscales and now provides a total full-scale IQ score. It is a large collection of individual tests (the test is called a 'battery') currently validated on 2,200 individuals between 16 and 90 years of age. The tests

which form the WAIS-IV can be seen in Figure 11.9a. You can see that full-scale IQ is made up of scores from four separate subscales all of which have core components or subtests. It is these core components (10 tests) which contribute to full-scale IQ. Figures 11.9b and 11.9c show you examples of two of the new tests in the WAIS-IV that did not feature in WAIS-III.

The WAIS is the most widely administered adult intelligence test.

Reliability and validity of intelligence tests

The adequacy of a measure is represented by its reliability and validity (terms described in Chapter 2). In the case of intelligence testing, reliability is assessed by the correlation between the scores that people receive on the same measurement on two different occasions; perfect reliability is 1. High reliability is achieved by means of standardised test administration and objective scoring: all participants are exposed to the same situation during testing, and all score responses in the same way. The acceptable reliability of a modern test of intellectual ability should be at least 0.85. Validity is the correlation between test scores and the criterion – an independent measure of the variable that is being assessed.

However, most tests of intelligence correlate reasonably well with such measures as success in school (between 0.40 and 0.75). Thus, because intellectual ability plays at least some role in academic success, IQ appears to have some validity.

Are intelligence scores improving?

One of the most curious phenomena of intelligence measurement is that people appear to be getting significantly more intelligent or, more accurately, their IQ scores are increasing. This is called the Flynn effect after the psychologist James Flynn who noticed that the average level of intelligence has

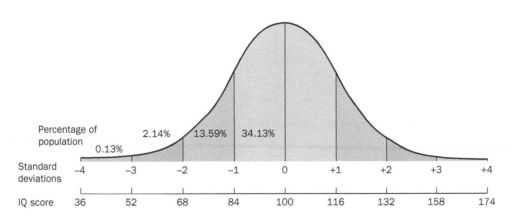

Figure 11.8 Calculating the deviation IQ score.

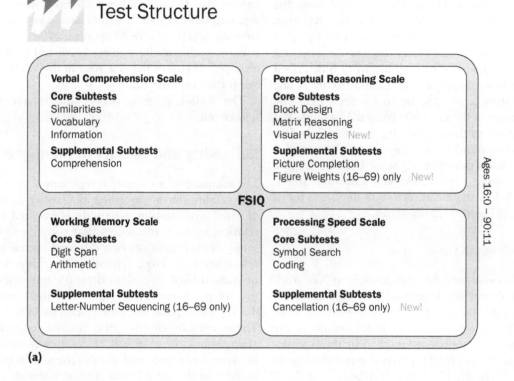

Test Structure

Verbal Comprehension Scale

Core Subtests
Similarities
Vocabulary
Information

Supplemental Subtests
Comprehension

Perceptual Reasoning Scale

Core Subtests
Block Design
Matrix Reasoning
Visual Puzzles New!

Supplemental Subtests
Picture Completion
Figure Weights (16–69) only New!

FSIQ

Working Memory Scale

Core Subtests
Digit Span
Arithmetic

Supplemental Subtests
Letter-Number Sequencing (16–69 only)

Processing Speed Scale

Core Subtests
Symbol Search
Coding

Supplemental Subtests
Cancellation (16–69 only) New!

Ages 16:0 – 90:11

(a)

New Subtests: Visual Puzzles

'Which 3 of these pieces go together to make this puzzle?'

(b)

New Subtests: Figure Weights

'Which one of these goes here to balance the scale?'

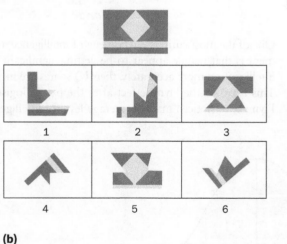

(c)

Figure 11.9 The new subtests which now form part of the latest revision of the WAIS(IV).

risen since the beginning of the twentieth century (Flynn, 1984, 1987). This is illustrated in Figure 11.10.

It has been estimated that people living in the 1930s would have IQ scores that were one to two standard deviations below those living in 2000. The US population appears to have made a 20-point acceleration in IQ in 60 years. Scores on tests of fluid intelligence have doubled compared with scores on crystallised intelligence. In one

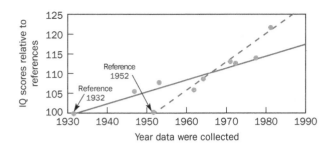

Figure 11.10 IQ increase over the twentieth century.

Source: Blair, C., Gamson, D., Thorne, S. and Baker, D., Rising mean IQ: Cognitive demand of mathematics education for young children, population exposure to formal schooling and the neurobiology of the PFC, *Intelligence*, 2005, 33, 93–106, p. 94, figure 1.

Dutch study, an 18–20 point increase in IQ was observed within a generation (Flynn, 1999). There has also been an increase in semantic and episodic memory performance (Rönlund and Nilsson, 2008). Why?

The most obvious explanation would be improved schooling and education, especially in primary or elementary school where the focus has shifted towards teaching cognitive skills that reflect fluid intelligence (Blair *et al.*, 2005a). Some suggest that this improvement may have halted in economically developed countries in the recent two decades. Lynn (2009) exploited the fact that measures of intelligent behaviour have been standardised in the past few years (standardisation is the process whereby a test's validity is tested to ensure that it is a measure of what it claims to measure for a given population). One, the well-known Raven's Coloured Progressive Matrices, was standardised in the UK in 2007 and 2008. In the task, participants have to select from several options the one which would complete a sequence with the final part missing.

Over the period 1982–2007, children between 4 and 11 years old improved by 8 IQ points. Children between 7 and 15 completing the Standard Progressive Matrices showed a 8.2 IQ point increase between 1979 and 2008.

Standardisations of two vocabulary tests – the Crichton Vocabulary Scale and the Mill Hill vocabulary scale in 2007 and 2008 in the UK – has shown that vocabulary knowledge declined in 4–11-year-olds on the Crichton scale and a small increase was recorded in 7–15 year-olds on the Mill Hill scale.

The improvement, Lynn suggests, is due to better nutrition, rather than education or greater cognitive stimulation because vocabulary showed negligible improvement across the decades.

There is a significant association between national IQ and educational achievement. Lynn and Mikk (2007) correlated published national IQs scores in 2002 and 2006 with the educational attainment scores of children in 25 (10-year-olds) and 46 (14-year-olds) countries. Maths and science achievement correlated significantly with national IQ. IQ was also associated with per capita income: the greater the IQ, the greater the income.

The roles of heredity and environment

Abilities – intellectual, athletic, musical and artistic – appear to run in families. Why? Are the similarities owing to heredity, or are they solely the result of a common environment, which includes similar educational opportunities and exposure to people having similar kinds of interests?

Cutting edge: Is there a relationship between cognitive ability test performance and career and academic success?

According to a review by Kuncel and Hezlett (2010), various persistent beliefs exist about cognitive test performance. These include: no relationship with leadership and creativity, independence from socioeconomic status and that personality may be a more important variable.

The review, however, appeared to debunk some of these beliefs. It found that standardised cognitive test scores predicted grade point average in American graduates but predicted less well the attainment of a degree (which involves a motivational component). As might be expected, scores on tests that are specific to the outcome measure are better predictors of performance than are general maths and verbal skill. Cognitive test performance predicted success in occupational training in civilian and military jobs as well as overall job performance, leadership effectiveness and creativity. The more complex the job and the training, the better the cognitive scores at predicting performance.

According to Sternberg and Grigorenko (1997), we know three facts about the roles of heredity and environment in intelligence: (1) both contribute to intelligence; (2) they interact in various ways; and (3) poor and enriched environments influence the development of intellectual ability regardless of heredity.

What these facts illustrate is that the typical nature–nurture debate in intelligence is no longer valid. The nature–nurture argument suggests that, in its most stark form, behaviour or function is determined solely by the environment or solely by genetics/heredity. Psychologists have discovered that this argument is too simplistic. In fact, it is inaccurate. Almost all psychologists agree that intelligence has a hereditary (as well as environmental) component. The debate now focuses on the degree to which each contributes to intelligence and the ways in which they interact to influence intellectual development.

The meaning of heritability

When we ask how much influence heredity has on a given trait, we are usually asking what the heritability of the trait is. Heritability is a statistical measure that expresses the proportion of the observed variability in a trait that is a direct result of genetic variability (GV). The value of this measure can vary from 0 to 1. The heritability of many physical traits in most cultures is very high; for example, eye colour is affected almost entirely by hereditary factors and little, if at all, by the environment. Thus, the heritability of eye colour is close to 1.

Heritability is a concept that many people misunderstand. It does not describe the extent to which the inherited genes are responsible for producing a particular trait; it measures the relative contributions of differences in genes and differences in environmental factors to the overall observed variability of the trait in a particular population. An example may make this distinction clear. Consider the heritability of hair colour in the Eskimo culture. Almost all young Eskimos have black hair, whereas older Eskimos have grey or white hair. Because all members of this population possess the same versions of the genes that determine hair colour, the GV with respect to those genes is in essence zero. All the observed variability in hair colour in this population is explained by an environmental factor – age. Therefore, the heritability of hair colour in the Eskimo culture is zero.

As with hair colour, we infer the heritability of a person's intelligence from their observed performance. Thus, looking at a person's IQ score is equivalent to looking at the colour of a person's hair. By measuring the correlation between IQ score and various genetic and environmental factors, we can arrive at an estimate of heritability. Clearly, even if hereditary factors do influence intelligence, the heritability of this trait must be considerably less than 1 because so many environmental factors also influence intelligence. The branch of psychology called behaviour genetics (see Chapters 1 and 3), predicts the degree of parental influence via genetic and environmental transmission on the development of the child's intellectual development. The proportion of the **variance** associated with genetic differences among individuals is called *h*; the remaining variation which is associated with environmental influences is referred to as 1–*h* (Neisser *et al.*, 1996a). The features which families share and have in common (such as choice of home) is sometimes referred to as *c*. Factor *h* can be subdivided into two types: additive *h*, which refers to the amount of hereditary variance that is passed from parent to child, and non-additive *h*, which refers to new, unique genetic expression in each generation. As children grow older, *h* increases and *c* decreases (McGue *et al.*, 1993). In childhood, the contribution of *h* and *c* to intelligence is similar; by adolescence, *h* predicts about three-quarters of intellectual ability.

The heritability of a trait depends on the amount of variability of genetic factors in a given population. If there is little GV, genetic factors will appear to be unimportant. Because the ancestors of people living in developed Western nations came from all over the world, GV is likely to be much higher there than in an isolated tribe of people in a remote part of the world. Therefore, if a person's IQ score is at all affected by genetic factors, the measured heritability of IQ will be higher in, say, Western European culture than in an isolated tribe.

The relative importance of environmental factors in intelligence depends on the amount of environmental variability (EV) that occurs in the population. If EV is low, then environmental factors will appear to be unimportant. In a society with a low variability in environmental factors relevant to intellectual development – one in which all children are raised in the same way by equally skilled and conscientious carers, all schools are equally good, all teachers have equally effective personalities and teaching skills, and no one is discriminated against – the effects of EV would be small and those of GV would be large. In contrast, in a society in which only a few privileged people receive a good education, environmental factors would be responsible for much of the variability in intelligence: the effects of EV would be large relative to those of GV.

Sources of environmental and genetic effects during development

Biological and environmental factors can affect intellectual abilities prenatally and post-natally. Newborn infants cannot be said to possess any substantial intellectual abilities; rather, they are more or less capable of developing these abilities during their lives. Therefore, prenatal influences can be said to affect a child's potential intelligence by affecting the development of the brain. Factors that impair brain development will necessarily also impair the child's potential intelligence.

As the axons of developing neurons grow, they thread their way through a tangle of other growing cells, responding to physical and chemical signals along the way. During this stage of prenatal development, differentiating cells can be misguided by false signals. For example, if a woman contracts German measles during early pregnancy, toxic chemicals produced by the virus may adversely affect the development of the foetus. Sometimes, these chemicals can misdirect the interconnections of brain cells and produce mental retardation. Thus, although development of a human organism is programmed genetically, environmental factors can affect development even before a person is born.

Educational influences in the environment, including (but not limited to) schooling, significantly affect the development of cognitive ability. Nisbett *et al.* (2012) note that children who miss a year of school demonstrate a drop in their IQ score, compared to attenders. A child who enters the 5th grade a year earlier than a child of the same age in the 4th grade has a verbal IQ that is five points higher at the end of the school year. In Norway, there are indications that adding two years beyond the 7th grade affects (improves) IQ at age 19 (Brinch and Galloway, 2011). According to Nisbett (2009), lengthening the school day, decreasing class sizes and using interactive computer games were all found to lead to an increase in academic skill.

Results of heritability studies

Estimates of the degree to which heredity influences a person's intellectual ability come from several sources. The two most powerful methods are comparisons between identical and fraternal twins and comparisons between adoptive and biological relatives (see Chapter 3).

Identical and fraternal twins

Current evidence indicates that the heritability of IQ is between 0.4 and 0.8. That is, highly heritable (Nisbett *et al.*, 2012). A comprehensive survey of the differences between identical (monozygotic, MZ) and fraternal (dizygotic, DZ) twins on tests of spatial and verbal ability is illustrated in Figure 11.11 (reported in Plomin and DeFries, 1998).

The figure illustrates the differences between the intelligence of groups across the lifespan from childhood to old age. What is remarkable about these data is that, across the lifespan, the similarity between identical twins is significantly greater than that between fraternal twins. Compare these results with those seen in Table 11.5. The table summarises data from a number of published studies of biological and adoptive families and adolescent and adult twins (Scarr, 1997). The table also shows that although identical twins reared in the same home show a

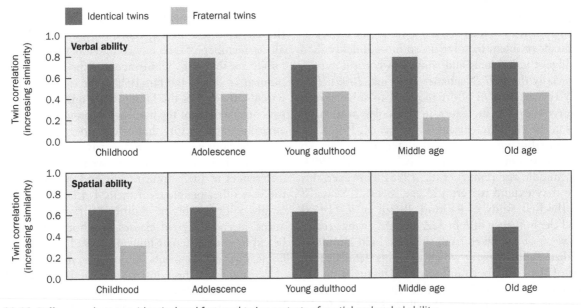

Figure 11.11 Differences between identical and fraternal twins on tests of spatial and verbal ability.

Source: Plomin, R. and DeFries, J.C., The genetics of cognitive abilities and disabilities. *Scientific American*, 1998, 287(5), pp. 40–47, reprinted by permission of Jennifer C. Christiansen.

Table 11.5 Intelligence test correlations of siblings from five behaviour-genetic studies of biological and adoptive families and twins (adolescents and adults).

Genetic r (correlation)	Relationship	Same home?	IQ correlation	Number of pairs
1.00	Same person tested twice	Yes	0.90	–
1.00	Identical twins	Yes	0.86	4672
1.00	Identical twins	No	0.76	158
0.50	Fraternal twins	Yes	0.55	8600
0.50	Fraternal twins	No	0.35	112
0.50	Biological siblings	Yes	0.47	26473
0.50	Biological siblings	No	0.24	203
0.00	Adoptive siblings	Yes	0.02	385

Source: Adapted with permission from Scarr, S. (1997). In *Intelligence, Heredity and Environments*, edited by R.J. Sternberg and E. Grigorenko. © 1997 Cambridge University Press, New York.

higher concordance rate than identical twins reared apart, these concordance rates are still higher (significantly so) than those of fraternal twins reared together.

MZ twins are also more comparable in terms of brain volume and activation. Grey matter in the frontal, parietal and occipital cortex is virtually identical in volume in MZ twins. There is also considerable similarity in volume between DZ twins but more variation in the posterio-occipital region and language-related frontal regions (Chiang *et al.*, 2009; van Leeuwen *et al.*, 2009). White matter volume is correlated in MZ twins but not in the frontal and parietal cortex in DZ twins. The structural pattern is mirrored in functional studies. For example, highly intelligent individuals given a simple or a moderately difficult problem to solve do so more quickly than less intelligent individuals and show less cortical activation, especially the PFC (Neubauer and Fink, 2009). This probably reflects lack of effort required to solve simple puzzles. As the task increases in difficulty activation increases in the highly intelligent (Larson *et al.*, 1995).

The contribution of *h* to intelligence appears to increase from 0.3 in early childhood (Cherny *et al.*, 1994) to 0.8 in middle age (Finkel *et al.*, 1995). However, this influence may extend to very old age (over 80 years of age). In the first study of its kind, Petrill *et al.* (1998) examined the influence of *h* in MZ and DZ twins greater than 80 years of age taken from the OctoTwin sample of the Swedish Twin Registry which contains details of 90 per cent of the twins born in Sweden. The mean age of the participants was 82.7 years and all were free from dementia and motor handicap. Petrill *et al.* (1998) found that there was a significant influence of *h* on ability, especially on memory performance.

At least half the total variance in IQ scores is accounted for by genetic variance (Chipuer *et al.*, 1990; Plomin *et al.*, 1997). The fact that, by most estimates, genetic factors account for approximately 50 per cent of the variability in IQ scores means that the other half of the variability is accounted for by environmental factors. However, when the data are taken from tables such as Table 11.5, contribution of the environment is less than 25 per cent. Some estimates, based on comparisons of parents and their offspring raised together or apart, suggest a value of only 4 per cent. Why are these figures so low?

Plomin (1988) suggests that estimates of the importance of environmental factors tend to be low because the environment in a given family is not identical for all its members. Some environmental variables within a family are shared by all members of the family, such as the number of books the family has, the examples set by the parents, the places the family visits on holiday, the noisiness or quietness of the home, and so on. But not all of the environmental factors that affect a person's development and behaviour are shared in this way. For example, no two children are treated identically, even by family members; differences in their appearances and personalities affect the way other people treat them. Different members of a family will probably have different friends and acquaintances, attend different classes in school and, in general, be exposed to different influences. And once people leave home, their environments become even more different.

Estimates of the contribution of EV to intelligence based on measurements made during childhood tend to be higher than similar estimates based on measurements made during adulthood. The reason for this difference may be that, during childhood, family members share a

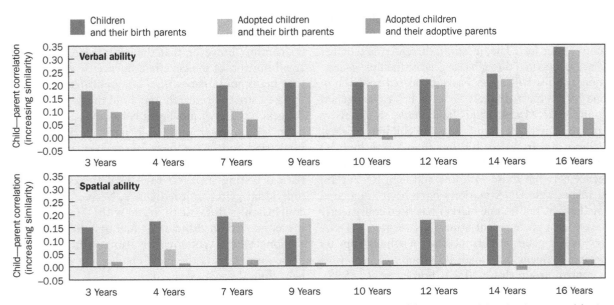

Figure 11.12 The Colorado Adoption Project monitored the spatial and verbal ability of (1) children and their birth parents; (2) adopted children and their birth parents; and (3) adopted children and their adoptive parents, from the child's third birthday to its sixteenth birthday. Notice how closely the adopted children's intelligence resembles that of their birth parents but that there is little resemblance between adopted children and their adopted parents.

Source: Plomin, R. and DeFries, J.C., The genetics of cognitive abilities and disabilities, *Scientific American*, 1998, 278, 5, 44, reprinted by permission of Jennifer C. Christiansen.

more similar environment, whereas during adulthood their environments become less similar. As Plomin (1997) notes, studies of genetically unrelated children (of a mean age of under 10 years) adopted and raised in the same families, suggest that up to 30 per cent of the variability in IQ scores is due to common environmental factors. However, when the comparison is made among young adults, the figure drops to less than 3 per cent. This can be seen in Figure 11.12, which summarises the correlations between children and their birth parents, adopted children and their birth parents, and adopted children and their adoptive parents for verbal and spatial ability from the time when the child was 3 years of age to adolescence (Plomin and DeFries, 1998). Adopted children appear to become more like their birth parents but do not become more like their adoptive parents, findings that were also reported in a study of the development of antisocial behaviour in twins (Pike *et al.*, 1996).

Thus, once children leave home and are exposed to different environmental variables, the effect of a common family environment almost disappears. What is left, in the case of related individuals, is their common genetic heritage.

Tucker-Drob *et al.* (2011) studied 750 twin pairs to examine the relationship between heritability and the socio-economic status (SES) of their parents. At 10 months, there was little effect of SES. At two years, there was much more variation especially in twins with parents of high SES. A re-analysis of data collected in the

1970s (and involving 839 twin pairs) found that 40 per cent of variance in IQ could be accounted for by genetics and shared environment in the families with lowest level of income and education (Harden *et al.*, 2007). This increased to 50 per cent accounted for by genetics and 30 per cent by shared environment in the richer and better educated families. Another study, of 548 adult twins and 207 older and younger siblings, found that older female siblings from educated families showed the largest effect of shared environment (Van der Sluis *et al.*, 2008). The amount of cortical white matter is also highly heritable. A study of 705 twins and siblings found that this increased with higher SES and higher IQ (Chliang *et al.*, 2011). Nisbett *et al.* conclude, however, that these effects of SES are much more common in North American than European populations.

If intelligence is inherited, how does inheritance occur?

Given that our DNA is what makes us what we are, the first and most obvious locus of any genetic cause would be our chromosomes (Plomin, 1997). The DNA contains sequences of information which are divided into sections by enzymes (called restriction enzymes). Sometimes these sequences are repeated. These enzymes act as markers which can be used to locate chromosomes and defects on chromosomes. Some **genetic disorders** of behaviour are single-gene disorders, that is, only one chromosome is affected. More complex behaviours, however, are likely to have multiple genetic loci called quantitative trait loci. The question, therefore, is whether intelligence is inherited through one gene or multiple genes.

Plomin and his colleagues have pioneered research in this, one of the most difficult areas in behaviour genetics. Plomin *et al.* (1994, 1995) have made an extensive study of DNA markers from Caucasian children of varying intelligence – from low IQ (less than 59) to high IQ (over 142) – and have found small genetic differences in intelligence between those with low and high IQ. Several of 100 identifiable DNA markers have been associated with intelligence, but no one marker has been consistently associated with it. A recent study has located a DNA marker for the gene on chromosome 6 which appears with greater frequency in a high IQ group (IQ over 136) than a control group (IQ = 103) (Chorney *et al.*, 1998).

This is an exciting finding because it was replicated in a group with even higher IQ (over 160). The researchers caution, however, that the gene accounted for only a small portion of the genetic influence on intelligence and that many more genes may be implicated. Nonetheless, this new area of research may hold the key to identifying the genetic basis of intelligent behaviour.

So far, however, only six genetic markers have been identified that have been associated with cognitive ability and only one of these withstood rigorous statistical testing. In their review of the contribution of individual genes in intelligence, Nisbett *et al.*'s (2012) conclusion is difficult to argue with: 'Figuring out why it has proved so difficult to identify the specific genes responsible for genetic variation in highly heritable behaviour traits is the most challenging problem facing behavioural genetics' (p. 6).

Psychology in action: Can low intelligence be improved?

Various projects, predominantly but not exclusively in the USA, have sought to discover whether early intervention in the schooling of poor children can lead to educational benefits beyond the period of intervention.

Some intervention programmes have shown that intervening early in a poor child's education can enhance their success at school (Johnson and Walker, 1991; Reynolds, 1994). Two such interventions include the Cognitive Acceleration Through Science Education programme (Adey and Shayer, 1994) and the Practical Intelligence for Schools Project (Sternberg and Wagner, 1986; Williams *et al.*, 1996). The former involves teaching children the pattern of thinking seen in science. In a two-year intervention study of 11–12-year-old children, there was a significant increase in science achievement test scores at the end of the intervention. The latter helps the child to build coping strategies based on knowing the strengths, weaknesses and demands of a task and applying the appropriate steps and strategies to complete these tasks. Again, intervention improved the intellectual skill of children when measured on practical and academic measures of writing, homework and test-taking. However, it is unclear whether these interventions make children think better or make them more intelligent.

In one study, children who received intervention were less likely to be placed in special needs classes while in school but (1) were not intellectually superior and (2) did not graduate any more quickly (Gray *et al.*, 1982). A second study, conversely, found that although intervention groups were less likely to be placed in special needs classes in school, they also performed better at school and, at 19 years old, performed better than the non-intervention group on tests of literacy (Weikart *et al.*, 1978).

The picture is clearly mixed, but if intervention programmes do show some evidence of success, why should this be? Campbell *et al.* (2001) suggest that intervention programmes directly affect a child's cognitive abilities by enabling it to 'meet the challenges of school'. The evidence, they argue, points towards a stronger role for these direct factors rather than indirect ones such as changes in motivation or the parents' perception of the child. The researchers explored some of these factors in a cohort of 104 largely African American children (98 per cent of total) from the Abecedarian project.

The Abecedarian project involved the study of the effects of educational intervention in children from low-income families. Fifty-seven of the infants were randomly assigned to the intervention group; the remainder to the control group. Intervention took the form of early education programmes in infancy for eight hours a day, five days a week, 50 weeks a year. A special curriculum was designed to promote cognitive, perceptual and social development. The control group did not receive such consistent education and attended various day-care centres for different periods, with no experimental intervention. The researchers (Campbell *et al.*, 2001) conducted follow-up assessments when the participants were 21 years old and these assessments included tests of intelligence and evaluations of achievement.

The researchers found that cognitive test performance increased more steeply in the treated group during early childhood when compared with controls. From 3 to 21 years, however, there was a generally better performance in the treated group than in the controls. Reading and mathematics performance was better in the treated group but both groups' performance remained fairly stable from

Psychology in action: *Continued*

middle childhood onwards: performance showed little change over time and both groups' achievement developed in parallel. It was evident, however, that both groups showed a gradual decline in scores between 12 and 21 years, when compared with standardised scores for the general population. While the treated group performed better than the untreated group, both groups' performance compared unfavourably with the population average.

There is also now considerable evidence that training in particular cognitive skills can lead to improved cognitive outcomes. For example, training on working memory tasks has been found to improve IQ significantly. Jaeggi *et al.* (2008, 2010) found that training on one working memory task for one month led to improved fluid intelligence scores

and reasoning after training. Mackey *et al.* (2011) gave children of low SES training on a working memory task and found a 10-point increase on a reasoning test after this. This effect has also been seen in elderly participants (Barella *et al.*, 2010; see later section).

The results suggest that early intervention in a child's education can be beneficial for children from low-income families with poor maternal education compared with no intervention at all. The period from birth to 3 years or 5 years may be the key to explaining why other intervention programmes do not show such success (Gray *et al.*, 1982). These intervention programmes began when the children were 3 or 4 years old; they were also less time-intensive than the Abecedarian project.

The effect of intelligence on health

In recent years, psychologists have turned to an unusual factor as a predictor of long-term good health: intelligence. Studies have shown that people with lower IQ are more likely to die earlier than those with higher IQ, whatever socio-economic class they belong to (Batty *et al.*, 2007). A new study of 1,181 Scottish people born in 1936 and followed by researchers from 1963 to 2003 has confirmed this finding (Deary *et al.*, 2008).

People with higher intelligence and who were most dependable had a significantly lower rate of mortality.

The 'hazard ratio' was 0.8 for intelligence and 0.77 for dependability (i.e. very low). Children who were in the lower half of the dependability/intelligence dimension were twice as likely to die as those in the upper half. The hazard ratio was 2.82. Smoking, high cholesterol and high blood pressure in middle age is associated with a hazard ratio of 2.34 in women and 3.2 in men (Lowe *et al.*, 1998).

The researchers suggest that a number of explanations could account for this association. There is a relationship between genetics and intelligence and longevity, for example. This relationship may be mediated by socio-economic status and engaging in healthy behaviour.

Controversies in psychological science: Is there a relationship between race and intelligence?

The issue

Of all the controversies in psychological science discussed in this book, perhaps the most controversial is that of the contribution of race to intelligence. *The Bell Curve*, a book written by a psychologist and a sociologist (Herrnstein and Murray, 1994), provoked a furore among psychologists and in the media across the world. The book asserted that psychologists agree that a general intelligence factor exists; that IQ tests measure what most people think of as intelligence; that IQ is almost impossible to modify through education and special training; that IQ is genetically determined; and that racial differences in IQ are the result of heredity. Whereas the chapter has so far discussed the first four assertions, this section addresses the last: whether race can influence IQ.

The evidence

Many studies have established the fact that there are racial differences in scores on various tests of intellectual abilities. For example, people who are identified as black generally score an average of 85 on IQ tests, whereas people who are identified as white score an average of 100 (Jensen, 1985; Lynn, 1991; Rushton, 1997). Although many blacks score better than many whites, on average whites do better on these tests. A statement endorsed by 52 professors indicated that, on average, whites' average IQ score is 100, African Americans' is 85, American-Hispanics' is somewhere between whites and African Americans', and Asians' is above 100 (Mainstream Science, 1994, cited in Suzuki and Valencia (1997)). Lynn's study (1996) of 2,260 children between 6 and

Controversies in psychological science: *Continued*

17 years of age found that Asian children scored an average of 107 IQ points, white children an average of 103 and black children an average of 89. Interestingly, black infants are more advanced than their white counterparts in the first 15 months of life (Lynn, 1998).

The controversy lies not in the facts themselves but in what these facts mean. Some authors have argued that the racial differences in scores on the tests are caused by heredity (Lynn, 1993; Rushton, 1995, 1997). *The Bell Curve* highlighted other racial aspects of intelligence such as the failure of intervention programmes to improve the IQs of black children.

The assertions made in *The Bell Curve* have not gone unchallenged. In response to the book and issues surrounding intelligence, the American Psychological Association set up a taskforce to report on the state of knowledge regarding the nature and determinants of intelligence (Neisser *et al.*, 1996a). In 2012, the APA published an update of Neisser *et al.'s* review (Nisbett *et al.*, 2012). Its conclusions were that (1) IQ heritability varied by social class, (2) no genetic polymorphisms were associated with variation in IQ, (3) crystallised and fluid intelligence are entirely separable abilities at the behavioural and biological level and that *g* is to all intents and purposes synonymous with IQ, (4) environment had an important effect in intelligence with 12–18 point improvement in IQ observed when (US) working class children were moved to (US) middle-class homes and (5) the gap between whites' and blacks' IQ had decreased by .33 standard deviations since Neisser *et al.'s* review. In 1996, they note, there was a 15 point difference between whites and blacks; between 1970 and 2002 there had been a 5.5 point gain (Dickens and Flynn, 2006)

Some investigators have attempted to use statistical methods to remove the effects of environmental variables, such as socio-economic status, that account for differences in performance between blacks and whites. However, these methods are controversial, and many statisticians question their validity. On the other hand, a study by Scarr and Weinberg (1976) provides unambiguous evidence that environmental factors can substantially increase the measured IQ of a black child. Scarr and Weinberg studied 99 black children who were adopted into white families of higher-than-average educational and socio-economic status. The expected average IQ of black children in the same area who were raised in black families was approximately 90. The average IQ of the adopted group was observed to be 105.

Other authors have flatly stated that there are no racial differences in biologically determined intellectual capacity. But this claim, like the one asserting that blacks are inherently less intelligent than whites, has not been determined scientifically. It is an example of what Jensen (1980) has called the egalitarian fallacy – the 'gratuitous assumption that all human populations are essentially identical in whatever trait or ability the test purports to measure' (p. 370). Although we know that blacks and whites have different environments and that a black child raised in an environment similar to that of a white child will receive a similar IQ score, the question of whether any racial hereditary differences exist has not been answered. When we point to group differences in races we are referring to general, average differences in intellectual performance; there are considerable within-group differences which may even be larger than between-group differences (Suzuki and Valencia, 1997).

There is also a problem with what we mean by race. We can define race biologically by gene frequencies (Loehlin *et al.*, 1975) or we can define it as a social construct. For many people, race is whatever they believe it to mean; they themselves ascribe meaning to it (Omi and Winant, 1994). In this sense, the concept of race makes very little scientific sense.

Conclusion

Although the issue of race and intelligence as currently conceived does not appear to be meaningful, it would be scientifically interesting to study the effects of different environments on inherited intellectual capacity. The interesting and more valid questions concerning race are those addressed by social psychologists and anthropologists – questions concerning issues such as the prevalence of prejudice, ethnic identification and cohesiveness, fear of strangers (xenophobia), and the tendency to judge something (or someone) that is different as inferior.

Intelligence, thinking and ageing

Ageing and cognitive ability

As the body and the brain grow older, certain changes occur. The acuity of the senses may begin to decline, the ability to move quickly is reduced. On the cognitive level, there is also a decline in various functions such as the manipulation of information in working memory, retrieval of names, reaction time, declarative memory, information processing. Functions such as vocabulary, however, see some improvement with age (Woodruff-Pak, 1997). General IQ scores will peak at around 25 years of age and decline up to 65 years. After 65, the score drops rapidly (Woods, 1994).

At the most severe end of cognitive decline, there is demen-tia – the gradual and relentless loss in intellectual function as the individual reaches the sixth decade of life and beyond.

Our categorisation of individuals into age groups is fairly arbitrary. In most developed countries, the age of retirement is set at 65 (an age originally set by Otto von Bismarck, the German chancellor from 1871 to 1890), although this does not mean that those people who are 65 or older are incapable of holding down a job or lack the cognitive and physical capacity to hold down such a job. The distribution of the elderly population in the Western world in 1950 was pyramid-shaped, that is, there were fewer people reaching old and very old (over 80 years) age. It has been estimated that by 2030, this distribution will be pillar-shaped, with roughly equal numbers in the old and very old categories.

Improvements in health care, sanitation, crime pre-vention and nutrition are thought to be responsible for this increase in the number of years we are living. Psychologically, therefore, the more we learn about the effects of ageing – and in reversing its negative effects – the more important this information will become in countries where we are living longer.

What is ageing?

From a strict point of view, we age as soon as we emerge from the womb. We are born with all the neurons we will have in life and they begin dying as soon as we grow. There is a massive shedding of neurons and synapses during childhood; this continues to old age. Of course, this shedding does not leave us intellectually helpless. Although neurons are lost, new connections are formed between existing neurons (this is why, although neurons are lost, the brain increases in weight during childhood) and the existing neurons work more efficiently. It has been suggested that psychological ageing begins after maturity and that this is measured by behaviour that includes the ability to acquire, remember and retrieve words, people and events and the ability to process and manipulate information. This scientific study of the ageing process is called **gerontology**.

One problem with studying the ageing process, how-ever, is the large variability between and within samples. For example, during a long period of study, older par-ticipants become susceptible to disease processes and illnesses which could directly affect the variables that ger-ontologists are interested in studying. This within-subject variation can also be seen in another capacity. If we take one age group, say the 50–60-year-old, and compare it with another on some cognitive measure, we are defining a group of individuals by an age category but all indi-viduals within this group may not show the same degree

of ageing. For example, although the ability to remem-ber strings of digits declines with age, some individuals perform badly, some stay the same and some actually get better (Holland and Rabbitt, 1991). Group variation becomes more of a problem when we look at data from cross-sectional studies.

Cross-sectional studies (see Chapter 2), compare inde-pendent groups on some measure. In ageing research, a cross-sectional design would involve assigning individu-als to age categories such as 18–25, 26–35, 36–45, 46–55 and so on. These groups would then complete a series of tests of cognitive ability, and differences between groups would be examined. If a difference in memory was found between the younger groups and the older groups, how-ever, we could not attribute this finding to ageing and cite ageing as a cause. Can you see why? (This question was posed in Chapter 2.) The reason is that we are not really looking at the effects of ageing but at the effect of age groups. We are not following one individual across all age ranges, but have sampled from several different age ranges. Because of this, our groups may differ on vari-ables that we had not anticipated, such as improvement in nutrition and healthcare. When one group influences the results in this way, the study is said to show a cohort effect. The conclusion we can draw is that age groups differ from each other.

A different type of design looks at age change and this is called a longitudinal design. Here, individuals are assessed across the lifespan and each individual acts as his/her own control (we could combine the two designs as well and compare individuals within one age group which vary on another characteristic, such as occupation or education level). A problem here is that with repeated testing, the individual will become increasingly famil-iar with the measures employed. When longitudinal and cross-sectional measures are compared, the longitudinal assessments show least decline in ability (Schaie, 1990).

However, recent studies suggest that cross-sectional designs such as these can be meaningful and provide simi-lar data to longitudinal studies. For example, Salthouse (2009) has summarised data showing the (fairly relentless decline) in cognitive ability as we get older, in a number of domains apart from vocabulary and general knowl-edge (which increase). You can see these data illustrated in Figure 11.13. The decline begins in adulthood and progresses thenceforth.

Memory decline

There is a gradual loss in performance for certain types of memory task with age. For example, older individu-als have difficulty in retrieving names (Rabbitt *et al.*, 1995) and putting names to famous faces (Burke *et al.*, 1991). In Burke *et al.*'s experiment, participants were

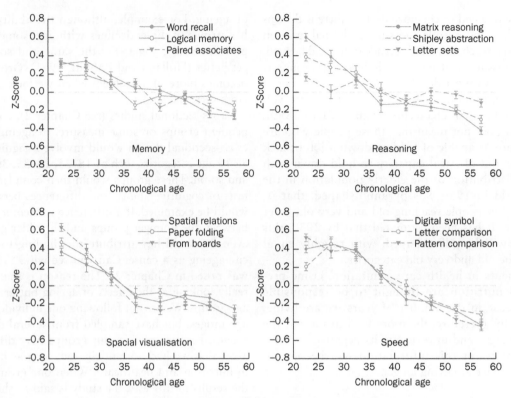

Figure 11.13 Mean scores and standard errors for 12 cognitive variables at 5-year age intervals.

Source: Salthouse, T.A. When does age-related cognitive decline begin? *Neurobiology of Aging*, 2009, 30, 507–14, figure 2.

allowed one minute in which to name famous faces. The number of tip-of-the-tongue responses as people tried to put names to faces increased with age. When participants were allowed to try to remember the names on the tips of their tongues, however, 95 per cent of their responses were correct, which suggests that the information had been stored but that the participants had difficulty in retrieving it.

Older people also have difficulty in recalling where, when or how an event occurred, despite knowing that an event has occurred. This type of memory is called **source memory** because the emphasis is on the recall of the context in which an event occurred, rather than of the content/knowledge of the event (Johnson *et al.*, 1993). This type of memory seems more affected in the elderly than is memory for facts or items (Trott *et al.*, 1997), possibly because it relies on the integrity of the frontal lobe and the integrity of this brain region is challenged in elderly individuals, as you will see later.

Age-related impairments have been reported for declarative memory, efficiency of processing information and metamemory (Woodruff-Pak, 1997). **Metamemory** refers to 'knowing about knowing'; this knowledge of skills necessary to complete a task may be absent in the elderly. For example, elderly individuals may not spend sufficient amounts of time on a task that requires time to be spent

on it (recall of digit names in serial order, for example). When they are instructed to spend a certain length of time on this task, however, they can recall accurately just as many series of digits as younger participants.

Prospective memory

Recent research on ageing and memory has focused on **prospective memory**, that is, remembering to perform an activity in the future (Maylor, 1996). This type of memory may be especially important to the elderly given that such monitoring is essential for taking medicine at particular times, for example (Park and Kidder, 1996; Einstein *et al.*, 1998). In experiments where a handkerchief or comb is borrowed by the experimenter at the beginning of a test session and/or hidden in a drawer and the individual has to remember to ask for the return of the item, there is an age-related decline in memory.

Studies of prospective memory can be either 'time based' or 'event based'. In time-based experiments, the participant engages in a task and has to inform the experimenter when a certain time has elapsed (Einstein *et al.*, 1995). This may be analogous to remembering to telephone someone in an hour's time (Maylor, 1996). In one study, Maylor (1990) asked 52–95-year-olds to telephone her once a day for a week. Three-quarters of those who adopted a memory strategy or used external cues for remembering were more reliable at telephoning than were those who did not use such mnemonics. In event-based experiments, participants must make a response when a particular event occurs in a sequence of events.

A study by Kliegel *et al.* (2000), however, suggests that the tests of prospective memory used in these experiments are not particularly realistic. These tests, they argue, usually require participants to make a single, isolated act within an experimental session. Everyday life, on the other hand, often involves more complicated planning than this. From cooking a three-course meal to air traffic control, the prospective memory required to perform these acts is complex.

The researchers asked 31 young (average age 26.5 years) and 31 older (average age 71.3 years) individuals to remind the experimenter to return to them a personal belonging (e.g. a wristwatch) at the end of the experiment. After having been given this instruction, participants were told that at some point they would complete a personal information questionnaire in the second part of the experiment after a short break and some tasks. This would be the cue for reminding the experimenter to return the belonging. Participants then completed various cognitive tasks that required them to follow a plan in order to perform these tasks successfully. They were then presented with the questionnaire.

While there was no difference between the two groups in their ability to remind the experimenter about the belonging, the older participants were significantly less likely to remember to initiate intended actions during the cognitive task phase of the experiment. The faithfulness with which participants executed their plans was no different between groups and both groups retained these plans equally well. The older participants, however, had difficulties in planning, initiating and executing the set of tasks.

A caveat

One note of caution, however, should be struck when interpreting these data. Some studies show that when memory instructions in some experiments are de-emphasised, age differences in performance disappear (Rahal *et al.*, 2001). Age is also affected by the content of the test. So, for example, if people have to recall a narrative that is character-based, older people perform more poorly at it than if they recalled a narrative that was based on perceptual features – referring to a man or a woman, rather than to a character (Fung and Carstencens, 2003). Older people also appear to perform better between 8 a.m. and 11 a.m. whereas younger participants give of their best between 1 p.m. and 5 p.m. (Hasher *et al.*, 1999).

Language

There are certain aspects of language processing that may not decline with age and may actually improve. One of the greatest gains is seen in vocabulary (Bayley and Oden, 1955; Jones, 1959). However, older individuals have difficulty in retrieving or accessing these words and exhibit a greater number of tip-of-the-tongue responses than do young individuals during retrieval (Bowles and Poon, 1985). According to LaRue (1992), the types of linguistic error made by elderly participants include: circumlocutions (giving inaccurate multi-word responses), nominalisations (describing functions not objects), perceptual errors (misidentifying stimuli) and semantic association errors (naming an object/feature associated with a target object). The elderly may also have difficulty in comprehending and initiating grammatically complex sentences (Kemper, 1992). Reasons for these, and other memory impairments, are discussed below.

Why does cognitive ability decline?

The evidence above indicates that cognitive ability, especially certain types of memory, declines with age. But is this the case? Ritchie (1997), for example, distinguishes between behaviour that is ageing-related and age-related. Ageing-related processes are the result of ageing; age-related processes occur only at a specific age. Is the decline seen in the elderly, therefore, not the result of ageing but of other age-related illnesses? Some European longitudinal data suggests that ageing may not be a factor (Leibovici *et al.*, 1996; Ritchie *et al.*, 1996). These researchers found that when controlling for physical illness, depression and signs of dementia, participants' cognitive performance improved over three years. They suggest that the decline that is commonly reported is due to pathology not ageing per se.

Processing speed and ageing

Several studies have shown a strong, positive association between our speed at processing information and intelligence. A new review of 172 studies, featuring over 53,000 participants, has now confirmed this association (Sheppard and Vernon, 2008). Intelligence measures were significantly associated with mental speed, an association which became stronger as the information processing task became more complex. Men and women also differed on some tests of information processing.

Over many years and several studies, Timothy Salthouse (1992, 1993; Craik and Salthouse, 2000) has argued that the elderly perform more poorly at cognitive tasks because they become slower at performing them. Older people have difficulty in activating, representing or maintaining information 'in mind', in attending to relevant stimuli in the environment and ignoring the irrelevant ones and in processing information speedily. If individual differences in speed are partialled out of these studies, then age-related differences disappear (Salthouse and Babcock, 1991). In fact, ageing could account for less than 1–2 per cent of the variance seen in such studies (Salthouse, 1993). This is a theory that has strong currency in gerontology. For example, several researchers have proposed that the cognitive decline seen in ageing may be attributable to reduced functioning of the frontal lobe (Parkin and Walter, 1992; West, 1996). The density of dopamine receptors declines in this area and dopamine is an important neurotransmitter in the performance of working memory tasks. The frontal cortex is also important for efficient information processing.

If there is significant frontal cortex decline with ageing, we might expect executive function, a key function of the frontal cortex, to be more significantly compromised in older participants. The support for this hypothesis, however, is mixed with some cross-sectional studies showing no differential decline and others showing decline on specific frontal lobe tests (one of these, a card sorting task, is described in the next major section on thinking) (Crawford et al., 2000).

The problem with suggesting that executive function may be specifically impaired, however, is that executive and non-executive task performance may be difficult to distinguish in elderly samples. The reason for this is the one cited by Salthouse (1996): all of these tasks may draw on a common resource such as speed of information processing.

But why does such slowing occur in the first place? Why is memory performance one of the most consistently affected cognitive abilities? One suggestion is that cognitive decline is the result of changes in the central nervous system (CNS) (Lowe and Rabbitt, 1997). In particular, researchers have focused on the hippocampus and the frontal cortex. There is a considerable loss in frontal lobe tissue over the course of the lifespan – around 17 per cent between the ages of 20 and 80 (Mittenberg et al., 1989; West, 1996). One PET study compared the encoding and retrieval of word pairs in young (mean age 26) and old (70 and over) adults (Cabeza et al., 1997). The young participants showed greater left prefrontal activation during encoding and right prefrontal activation during retrieval compared with the old sample. In fact, the old sample showed little frontal activation during encoding and more bilateral activation during retrieval. This pattern of activity suggested to the experimenters that the stimuli had been inefficiently processed or encoded. An fMRI study of recognition and encoding in young, middle-aged and older adults found that activation in brain areas involved in these memory processes declines across age groups but activation in areas that are irrelevant to the specific tasks increases (Grady et al., 2006).

An alternative (or complementary) view to the frontal lobe hypothesis suggests that ageing results in an impairment of cognitive differentiation – the degree to which behaviour is specialised for specific tasks. The decline, which is domain-independent, is reflected in neurons' inability to perform such differentiation. The cortical basis of visual differentiation may be the ventral visual cortex – this responds to faces, orthography and places – and shows less atrophy than other areas with age. In an fMRI study where 12-year-olds and 70-year-olds were asked to view faces, houses, pseudowords and chairs, less specialisation in activation in the ventral visual cortex was found in the elderly sample (Park et al., 2004). Given that perceptual processing speed declines with age, perhaps such a slowness might be the result of a ventral visual cortex that shows less differentiation. Because there is less differentiation, older participants who are asked to make the same/different decisions about geometric pairs or digits (a standard perceptual processing speed task) are slower at doing so.

Can the decline be halted?

We are living in a modern world, as all worlds are, and modern worlds present new technological challenges. Mobile phones, computers, broadband, the internet . . . to young people these are the meat and drink (or nut cutlet and alfalfa shake) of their lives. Older people have greater difficulty in adjusting to and using this technology (Charness and Boot, 2009). In one study, older people took twice as long to learn to use a new word processor at their own pace than did younger people, even if they had prior word processing experience (Charness et al., 2001).

However, all is not lost. Playing video games appears to result in a marked improvement in cognitive performance (Basak et al., 2008) and recent research involving cognitive training via computer has produced promising, positive results. For example, attention and memory have been found to improve through these interventions (Smith et al., 2009; Zehnder et al., 2009; Zeilinkski et al., 2011). Whether the effects extend beyond performance on the types of task trained in is still unclear. Short- and long-term memory do appear to improve, however (Gunther et al., 2003). In older people with mild cognitive impairment (MCI), training in memory exercises has improved episodic memory and led to improvements in prospective memory, quality of life and metamemory (Kinsella et al., 2009; Kurz et al., 2009). These cognitive changes are also correlated with changes (increases) in brain activation (Hampstead et al., 2011). Improvements in long-term episodic memory, for example, have been associated with increases in the frontal, temporal and parietal regions of the brain (Belleville et al., 2011). Using repetitive transcramial magnetic stimulation (rTMS), Turriziani et al. (2012) found that inhibition of the right dorsolateral prefrontal cortex (DLPFC) led to improvements in recognition memory in healthy participants and individuals with MCI.

Education may also be a protective factor. One Australian study of elderly blue-collar workers and academics found that the degree of education was associated with crystallised intelligence but not other types of cognitive ability (Christensen *et al.*, 1997) and a Dutch study has also shown that education was associated with a slower rate of memory decline (Schmand *et al.*, 1997). Andel *et al.* (2006) suggest that high levels of education and having a complex occupation may accelerate cognitive decline, arguably because the person's 'cognitive reserve' has been expended. However, a study of education in individuals with dementia (see below) found that the longer the individual was in education, the lower the risk of developing dementia (EClipsSE, 2010).

Dementia

Dementia refers to the gradual and relentless decline in cognitive ability and is characterised by impairment in short-term and long-term memory. There may also be confusion, change in personality and impaired abstract thinking and judgement. It has been estimated that 34.4 million people worldwide suffer from dementia, at a cost of \$422 billion (Wimo *et al.*, 2010). In the UK, 700,000 people suffer from dementia and the cost of caring for them is around £17 billion. Estimates of undiagnosed Alzheimer's disease suggest it may be as high as 80 per cent (Weimer and Sagar, 2009).

There are various types of dementia, such as **dementia of the Alzheimer type** (DAT, the commonest type), vascular dementia (the second commonest, caused by stroke), Pick's disease dementia and Lewy body dementia (both are characterised by neural abnormality). There are many causes of dementia: the most common is Alzheimer's disease. It is important to differentiate between Alzheimer's disease and DAT: the former is the disease, the latter is the psychological consequence of this illness.

Dementia of the Alzheimer type

According to **DSM-IV TR**, DAT is characterised by:

- Cognitive decline exemplified by memory impairment (learning new information and recalling previously learned information) and one or more of: aphasia, apraxia, agnosia and executive function problems.
- Symptoms which cause significant decline from previous level of functioning.
- Gradual onset and continuing cognitive decline.
- Symptoms that are not due to other progressive CNS diseases or conditions causing dementia.

(DSM-IV TR is the manual used by the majority of the world's clinicians to diagnose mental illness and mental disorder (you'll find this described in more detail in Chapter 18).)

The disease was named after Alois Alzheimer at the beginning of the last century who reported the case of a 56-year-old female patient who exhibited cognitive impairment as a result of abnormal brain formations. These formations (see Figure 11.14) are the characteristics of Alzheimer's disease and include neurofibrillary tangles – abnormal proteins which are found in various parts of the person's brain, especially the temporal, parietal and frontal cortices, neuritic senile plaques – abnormal nerve cell processes which surround the

(a)

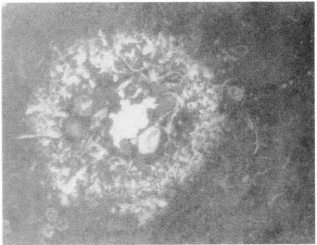

(b)

Figure 11.14 Images showing two of the characteristic neural features of Alzheimer's disease. **(a)** One of the neurofibrillary tangles that characterises brain cell abnormality in Alzheimer's disease. **(b)** The senile plaques seen in the nerve cell of a brain attacked by Alzheimer's disease.

Source: Beatty, J. (1995) *Principles of Behavioral Neuroscience*. New York: Brown and Benchmark/William C. Brown Communications Inc., 1995. Reprinted with permission.

protein and are found in the cortex – and granuovacuolar degeneration (Nelson *et al.*, 2010; Hyman *et al.*, 2012). The tangles are consistently associated with cognitive decline, with plaques having a greater effect on high-functioning individuals (Nelson *et al.*, 2010). Animal models suggest that the specific protein contributing to the cognitive decline in Alzheimer's disease may be an assembly called AB*56 which is found outside cells (Lesne *et al.*, 2006).

There is significant neuron loss in Alzheimer's disease. The frontal and temporal gyri are thought to shrink by approximately 20 per cent and atrophy is found in the hippocampus, amygdala and other subcortical areas such as the raphe nuclei and nucleus basalis of Meynert. Figures 11.15(a) and (b) and 11.16 and 11.17 show how extensive this atrophy can be.

The cortical regions affected in Alzheimer's disease invariably include the olfactory areas – the medial temporal lobe, the priform cortex, the prepiriform cortex, olfactory tubercle and entorhinal cortex, all of which have connections to (secondary) olfactory areas, the orbitofrontal cortex (OFC), insula and DlPFC. Some of the highest densities of plaques and tangles and the greatest pathology, for example, are found in the entorhinal cortex, subiculum, temporal pole, the piriform cortex, amygdala, OFC and prepiriform cortex. It is thought that it is for this reason that one of the earliest symptoms – if not the earliest – of Alzheimer's disease is impaired olfactory function (see Martin (2013) for a review of these studies). A study of Scandinavian participants found a significant relationship between the ability to identify odour and cognitive decline (Olofsson *et al.*, 2009).

The disease can occur sporadically or in a genetic form called familial Alzheimer's disease. The familial form is thought to be autosomal-dominant with the gene carried on chromosome 21 and, possibly, chromosome 19. The gene expresses itself by producing the amyloid precursor protein from which the protein associated with the senile plaques is formed. Early-onset Alzheimer's disease is associated with this marker and also with mutations on chromosomes 1 and 14 (Bird, 1999). The E4 allele of the apolipoprotein gene also appears to be a risk factor in Alzheimer's disease and for cognitive impairment (Deary *et al.*, 2002; Schieper's *et al.*, 2011) and the disease has been linked with genes including *CLU, CR1, TOMM40, BIN1* and *PICALM* (Weiner *et al.*, 2012). Another genetic risk factor, brain-derived neurotropic factor (BDNF), has been associated with hippocampal-dependent learning in normal ageing and the expression of this gene declines with age (Harris and Deary, 2011).

Clinical features of DAT

The major cognitive impairment in Alzheimer's disease is loss of memory. This impairment is gradual and occurs in the presence of a normal level of consciousness but in the absence of any other CNS disease that might account

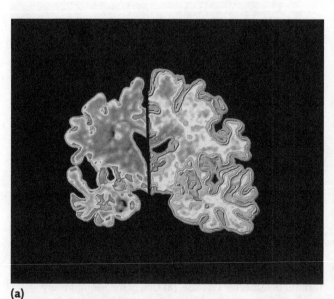

(a)

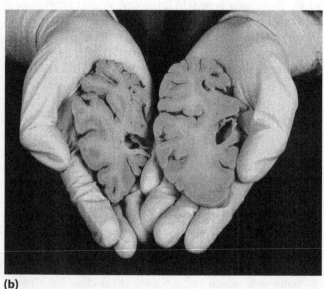

(b)

Figure 11.15 (a) Alzheimer's disease. A computer-enhanced photograph of a slice through the brain of a person who died of Alzheimer's disease (left) and a normal brain (right). Note that the grooves (sulci and fissures) are especially wide in the Alzheimer's brain, indicating degeneration of the brain. **(b)** Sections from a normal brain (right) and from a brain with Alzheimer's.

Source: (a) Alfred Pasieka/Science Photo Library (b) Plate 11.3 from *Human Neuropsychology*, 2nd edn, Pearson/Prentice Hall (Martin, G.N., 2006).

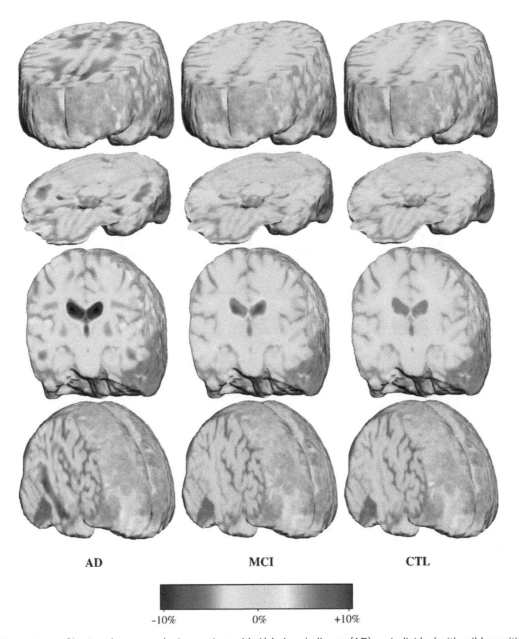

AD   **MCI**   **CTL**

-10%   0%   +10%

Figure 11.16 Comparison of brain volume atrophy in a patient with Alzheimer's disease (AD), an individual with mild cognitive impairment (MCI) and a healthy elderly control (CTL). The bluer the image, the greater the cell loss.

Source: Leow, A.D., Yanovsky, I., Parikshak, N. *et al*. Alzheimer's Disease Neuroimaging Initiative: A one-year follow-up study using tensor-based morphometry correlating degenerative rates, biomarkers and cognition. *NeuroImage*, 2009, 45, 645–55, figure 1.

for the symptoms. Some of the more marked deficits in memory include:

- An inability to recall autobiographical information from long-term memory (information about people, events and conversations, for example) is the major characteristic of the disease and appears early on in the disorder's development (Greene and Hodges, 1996a; Fleischman and Gabrieli, 1999).
- Impaired recall of previously learned information and, sometimes, memory for conceptual or factual information.

- Rapid forgetting.
- Explicit memory impairment (implicit memory is relatively preserved).
- Short- and long-term memory impairment (Fleischman and Gabrieli, 1998).
- Tendency to show a lack of a primacy effect but to show a recency effect – patients will more correctly recall items from the end of a list than the beginning (Bayley *et al*., 2000).
- Interference by previously learned information when new material is learned.

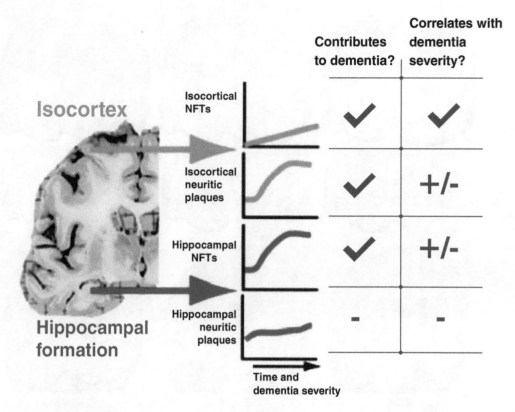

Figure 11.17 Areas of brain degeneration and its processes which contribute to dementia and its severity.

- Attention and working memory impairment.
- Semantic memory impairment – inability to recall over-learned information.
- Circumlocution and paraphrasic errors.
- Delayed-memory impairment – this appears to be best at discriminating DAT patients from controls (Zakzanis *et al.*, 1999).

One difficulty in diagnosing Alzheimer's disease is that senile plaques are seen with normal ageing (tangles tend not to be) whereas tangles are seen in other types of dementia (Ritchie, 1997). Although the effects of ageing and dementia may be distinguished by the fact that abnormalities in the elderly affect the superficial cortex, they go much deeper in Alzheimer's disease. There are also biochemical abnormalities seen in Alzheimer's disease.

In particular, there is significant loss of certain neurotransmitter pathways linking various brain structures, such as the cerebral cortex and the hippocampus, in Alzheimer's disease.

Memory decline in Alzheimer's disease

The major cognitive impairment in Alzheimer's disease is memory loss and episodic memory retrieval is thought to be one of the most seriously affected. A person's inability to recall autobiographical information from long-term memory (information about people and events, for example) is a major characteristic of the disease and appears early on in the disorder's development (Fleischman and Gabrieli, 1999). Figure 11.18 plots the decline in memory function in a patient with Alzheimer's disease and a matched control, across the lifespan. Figures 11.19(a) and (b) show brain scans of patients with Alzheimer's disease who tried to retrieve episodic memory.

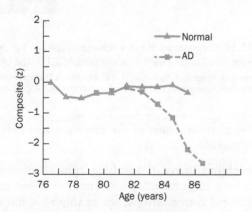

Figure 11.18 The decline in memory function in a patient with Alzheimer's disease and a matched control, across the lifespan.

Source: from Cognitive Deficits in the Early Stages of Alzheimer's Disease, *Current Directions in Psychological Science*, 17(3), Fig. 1, p.198 (Storandt, M. 2008), copyright © 2008 by Association for Psychological Science. Reprinted by Permission of SAGE Publication.

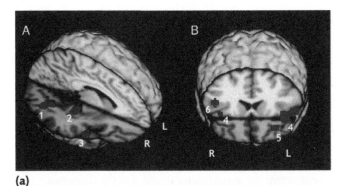

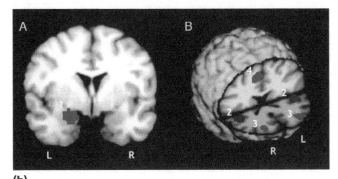

(b)

Figure 11.19 Comparison of brain activation between AD patients **(a)** across encoding studies, and **(b)** across retrieval studies.

Source: Schwindt, G.C. and Black, S.E. Functional imaging studies of episodic memory in Alzheimer's disease: a quantitative meta-analysis. *NeuroImage*, 2009, 45, 181–90, figures 2 and 3.

Explicit memory is more seriously affected than implicit memory and both short- and long-term memory are impaired (Fleischman and Gabrieli, 1998). Greene and Hodges (1996a, b), for example, found that patients with Alzheimer's disease performed poorly at naming, identifying and recognising famous faces from the present and past but also found that memory for personally meaningful events declined less rapidly than did public memory (memory for events in public life).

The cognitive decline seen in Alzheimer's patients is much more severe than that seen in disease-free individuals during the course of normal ageing, and various cognitive deficits correlate with a reduction in the volume of the hippocampus, the temporal cortex and thalamus. It can sometimes be difficult to distinguish between the effects of DAT and symptoms of MCI. MCI seems to occupy a half-way house between the cognitive decline seen with normal ageing and dementia. Sixty-one per cent of MCI patients begin with memory impairments (Storandt, 2008) and it, too, has some of the hallmarks of Alzheimer's disease, such as the amyloid-B deposits (Goedert and Spillantini, 2006). In a study of people who had not manifested the symptoms of dementia – the sample is the famous Framingham Study which follows a large cohort of people through life (Elias *et al.*, 2000) – two tests were associated with the

The author Terry Prachett, who has been diagnosed with dementia of the Alzheimer type.

Source: Getty Images/Peter Macdiarmid.

later development of dementia – verbal memory and the similarities test of the WAIS. Poor performance on these predicted later development of dementia. Other tests are thought to be good predictors, especially those which involve planning and sequencing (Storandt *et al.*, 2006).

Some psychologists have suggested that attention deficit may also be an early cognitive characteristic (Perry and Hodges, 1999) and may explain the deficit in episodic memory (Balota and Faust, 2001). What is unclear, however, is whether this deficit in attention is a global and unitary one – where all types of attention are impaired – or whether different types of attention are affected differently. Evidence suggests that divided attention is particularly affected (Baddeley *et al.*, 2001).

Memory impairments – such as disorientation over finding their homes, forgetting people's names and faces, and not being able to follow the flow of a conversation – are key features. In 2003, the journalist and critic Adrian Gill wrote an article about his father, who suffered from Alzheimer's disease. Gill wrote:

'Conversations with Daddy are like talking to someone who can travel through walls. In the middle of a sentence, he can be somewhere else. I have to open empirical, rational doors to follow him. He glides through time and subjects in a way that logic and language prevent me. It's a sort of itinerant freedom.'

Dementia and the novelist: the case of Iris Murdoch

Fellow novelist A.S. Byatt spared no sensitivity when she reviewed Iris Murdoch's last novel, *Jackson's Dilemma*. The book, Byatt averred, was 'an Indian rope trick . . . in which all the people have no selves and therefore there is no story and no novel'. Murdoch, however, was no novelistic novice. In 1978, she won the Booker Prize for *The Sea, The Sea* and was made Dame Commander of the British Empire in 1987 in recognition of her contribution to literature. Published criticism is an occupational hazard in the novelist's world but Byatt's criticism may have unwittingly reflected an organic, rather than creative, decline. Murdoch was diagnosed with Alzheimer's disease at the age of 76, just after she had finished writing *Jackson's Dilemma*; a post-mortem three years later confirmed the diagnosis.

Following the diagnosis of suspected Alzheimer's disease, Garrard *et al.* (2005) monitored structural changes in Murdoch's brain, as part of her neurological assessment. In 1997, there was evidence of global atrophy, especially in the hippocampus (bilaterally), as seen in Figure 11.20(a). You can see examples of her neuropsychological performance in Figure 11.20(b).

When *Jackson's Dilemma* was published in 1995, the author had suffered severe writer's block and had become unexpectedly inarticulate at a question and answer session with the public a year later. The following summer, she was only able to describe her surroundings by reference to a city name and was unable to subtract or spell backwards. Her picture naming became circumlocutory: a bus was described as 'something carried along'; and her spelling became regularised. She would spell cruise as 'crewse', for example. Her retrograde memory was profoundly impaired and her narrative speech was grammatical but lacked real content. For example: 'the girl is just holding a plate and various pieces of . . . well . . . something useful . . . standing at a window . . . whether the window is open is not quite clear to me. The thing where the water is running out. The girl doesn't bother. The window is open. Plate and two cups.'

Murdoch's disorder afforded Garrard *et al.* the opportunity to examine any relationship between the novelist's intellectual decline and the external manifestation of that decline – her final novel. The novelist regarded the work as being a true reflection of her output and requested no alterations be made to the text. Garrard *et al.* compared the vocabulary, syntax, grammatical class and lexical differences in this novel, in *Under the Net* (published in 1954) and in *The Sea, The Sea*.

The researchers found that her vocabulary was rich and innovative in the early work but was impoverished in the final novel. The number of words and class of words per sentence (ten sentences were taken from the first, middle and final chapters of each novel) was smallest in the last novel. There was no difference in word length between the novels but the final work contained more high frequency words, reflecting a decline in linguistic innovation. The use of high frequency words is, according to Garrard *et al.*, typical of temporal lobe pathology.

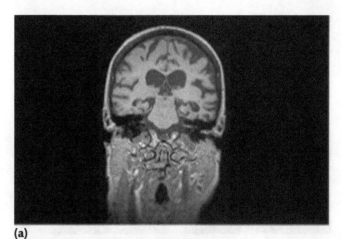

(a)

(b)

(c)

Figure 11.20 **(a)** A computer enhanced photograph of a slice through the brain of a patient with Alzheimer's disease; **(b)** Examples of Iris Murdoch's neuropsychological performance; **(c)** Iris Murdoch herself.

Sources: (a) PNAS: copyright 2008 National Academy of Sciences, USA. (b) From Garrard, P., Maloney, L.M., Hodges, J.R. and Patterson, K. The effects of very early Alzheimer's disease on the characteristics of writing by a renowned author, in *Brain*, 2005, 128, pp. 250–60, by permission of Oxford University Press and Peter Garrard. (c) Bassouls Sophie/CORBIS Sygma.

In a sense, of course, these data are correlational. The final novel exhibited the features described here and these features coincided with the development of the author's degenerative disease. Nonetheless, the data obtained from the analysis of the author's physical output reflects the behaviour observed by those closest to her.

Treatment for DAT

Is Alzheimer's disease reversible? Current treatments have focused on alleviating the memory impairments in DAT. The cholinergic hypothesis of Alzheimer's disease led to the development of drugs that specifically sought to redress the loss of cholinergic neurons and neurotransmitters (called cholinesterase inhibitors). There is currently no treatment that can reverse Alzheimer's disease or its effects.

Thinking

Human reasoning is not simple, neat and impeccable. It is not akin to a proof of logic . . . we build mental models which represent distinct probabilities or that unfold in time in a kinematic sequence, and we base our conclusions on them. (*Source*: Johnson-Laird, 2010.)

One of the most important components of cognition is thinking: categorising, reasoning and solving problems. When we think, we perceive, classify, manipulate, and combine information. When we are finished, we know something we did not know before (although our 'knowledge' may be incorrect).

The purpose of thinking is, in general, to solve problems. These problems may be simple classifications (What is that, a bird or a bat?); they may involve decisions about courses of actions (Should I buy a new car or pay to fix the old one?); or they may require the construction, testing and evaluation of complex plans of action (How am I going to manage to earn money to continue my education so that I can get out of this dead-end job, and still be able to enjoy life?). Much, but not all, of our thinking involves language. We certainly think to ourselves in words, but we also think in shapes and images. And some of the mental processes that affect our decisions and plans take place without our being conscious of them. Thus, we will have to consider non-verbal processes as well as verbal ones (Reber, 1992; Holyoak and Spellman, 1993).

Classifying

When we think, each object or event is not considered as a completely independent entity. Instead, we classify things – categorise them according to their characteristics. Then, when we have to solve a problem involving a particular object or situation, we can use information that we have already learned about similar objects or situations. To take a very simple example, when we enter someone's house for the first time, we recognise chairs, tables, sofas, lamps and other pieces of furniture even though we may never have seen these particular items before. Because we recognise these categories of objects, we know where to sit, how to increase the level of illumination, and so on.

Concepts are categories of objects, actions or states of being that share some attributes: cat, comet, team, destroying, playing, forgetting, happiness, truth, justice. Most thinking deals with the relations and interactions among concepts. For example, 'the hawk caught the sparrow' describes an interaction between two birds; 'studying for an examination is fun' describes an attribute of a particular action; and 'youth is a carefree time of life' describes an attribute of a state of being.

Concepts exist because the characteristics of objects have consequences for us. For example, angry dogs may hurt us, whereas friendly dogs may give us pleasure. Dangerous dogs tend to growl, bare their teeth and bite, whereas friendly dogs tend to prance around, wag their tails and solicit our attention. Thus, when we see a dog that growls and bares its teeth, we avoid it because it may bite us; but if we see one prancing around and wagging its tail, we may try to pat it. We have learned to avoid or approach dogs who display different sorts of behaviour through direct experience with dogs or through the vicarious experience of watching other people interact with them. The point is, we can learn the concepts of dangerous and friendly dogs from the behaviour of one set of dogs while we are young and respond appropriately to other dogs later in life. Our experiences with particular dogs generalise to others.

Formal and natural concepts

Formal concepts are defined by listing their essential characteristics, as a dictionary definition does. For example, dogs have four legs, a tail, fur and wet noses; are carnivores; can bark, growl, whine and howl; pant when they are hot; bear live young; and so on. Thus, a formal concept is a sort of category that has rules about membership and non-membership.

Psychologists have studied the nature of formally defined concepts, such as species of animals. Collins and

Quillian (1969) suggested that such concepts are organised hierarchically in semantic memory. Each concept has associated with it a set of characteristics. Consider the hierarchy of concepts relating to animals shown in Figure 11.21. At the top is the concept 'animal', with which are associated the characteristics common to all animals, such as 'has skin', 'can move around', 'eats', 'breathes' and so on. Linked to the concept 'animal' are groups of animals, such as birds, fish and mammals, along with their characteristics. These hierarchies are illustrated by Figure 11.21.

Collins and Quillian assumed that the characteristics common to all members of a group of related concepts (such as all birds) were attached to the general concept (in this case bird) rather than to all the members. Such an arrangement would produce an efficient and economical organisation of memory. For example, all birds have wings. Thus, we need not remember that a canary, a jay, a robin and an ostrich all have wings; we need only remember that each of these concepts belong to the category of bird and that birds have wings.

Collins and Quillian tested the validity of their model by asking people questions about the characteristics of various concepts. Consider the concept 'canary'. The investigators asked people to say true or false to statements such as, 'A canary eats'. When the question dealt with characteristics that were specific to the concept (such as 'can sing', or 'is yellow'), the subjects responded quickly. If the question dealt with a characteristic that was common to a more general concept (such as 'has skin' or 'breathes'), the subjects took a longer time in answering.

Presumably, when asked a question about a characteristic that applied to all birds or to all animals, the participants had to 'travel up the tree' from the entry for canary until they found the level that provided the answer. The further they had to go, the longer the process took.

The model above is attractive but it does not reflect realistically the way in which we classify concepts and their characteristics. For example, although people may conceive of objects in terms of a hierarchy, a particular person's hierarchy of animals need not resemble that compiled by a zoologist. For example, Rips *et al.* (1973) found that people said yes to 'A collie is an animal' faster than they did to 'A collie is a mammal'. According to Collins and Quillian's model, animal comes above mammal in the hierarchy, so the results should have been just the opposite.

Although some organisation undoubtedly exists between categories and subcategories, it appears not to be perfectly logical and systematic. For example, Roth and Mervis (1983) found that people judged Chablis to be a better example of wine than of drink, but they judged champagne to be a better example of drink than of wine. This inconsistency clearly reflects people's experience with the concepts. Chablis is obviously a wine: it is sold in bottles that resemble those used for other wines, it looks and tastes similar to other white wines, the word 'wine' is found on the label, and so on. By these standards, champagne appears to stand apart. A wine expert would categorise champagne as a particular type of wine. But the average person, not being particularly well acquainted with the fact that champagne is made of fermented grape juice, encounters champagne in the context

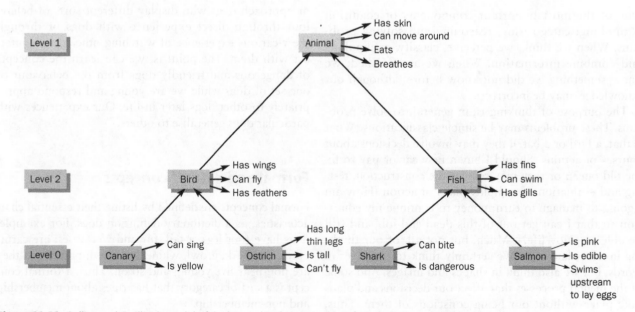

Figure 11.21 Collins and Quillian's model of the hierarchical organisation of concepts in semantic memory.

Source: From Robert L. Solso, *Cognitive Psychology*, 2nd edn. Published by Allyn & Bacon, Boston, MA. Copyright © 1988 by Pearson Education. By permission of the publisher.

of something to drink on a special occasion, something to launch ships with, and so on. Thus, its characteristics are perceived as being rather different from those of Chablis.

Rosch (1975; Mervis and Rosch, 1981) suggested that people do not look up the meanings of concepts in their heads in the way that they seek definitions in dictionaries. The concepts we use in everyday life are natural concepts, not formal ones discovered by experts who have examined characteristics we are not aware of. **Natural concepts** are based on our own perceptions and interactions with things in the world. For example, some things have wings, beaks and feathers, and they fly, build nests, lay eggs and make high-pitched noises. Other things are furry, have four legs and a tail, and run around on the ground. Formal concepts consist of carefully defined sets of rules governing membership in a particular category; natural concepts are collections of memories of particular examples that share some similarities. Formal concepts are used primarily by experts (and by people studying to become experts), whereas natural concepts are used by ordinary people in their daily lives.

Rosch suggests that people's natural concepts consist of collections of memories of particular examples, called **exemplars**, that share some similarities. The boundaries between formal concepts are precise, whereas those between natural concepts are fuzzy – the distinction between a member and a non-member is not always clear. Thus, to a non-expert, not all members of a concept are equally good examples of that concept. A robin is a good example of bird; a penguin or ostrich is a poor one. We may acknowledge that a penguin is a bird because we have been taught that it is, but we often qualify the category of membership by making statements such as 'strictly speaking, a penguin is a bird'. Exemplars represent the important characteristics of a category – characteristics that we can easily perceive or that we encounter when we interact with its members.

According to Rosch *et al.* (1976), natural concepts vary in their level of precision and detail. They are arranged in a hierarchy from very detailed to very general. When we think about concepts and talk about them, we usually deal with **basic-level concepts** – those that make important distinctions between different categories – but do not waste time and effort with those that do not matter. For example, chair and apple are basic-level concepts. Concepts that refer to collections of basic-level concepts, such as furniture and fruit, are called **superordinate concepts**. Concepts that refer to types of items within a basic-level category, such as deckchair and Granny Smith's, are called **subordinate concepts**. These can be seen in Figure 11.22.

The basic-level concept tends to be the one that people spontaneously name when they see a member of the category. That is, all types of chair tend to be called 'chair', unless there is a special reason to use a more precise label. People tend to use basic-level concepts for a very good

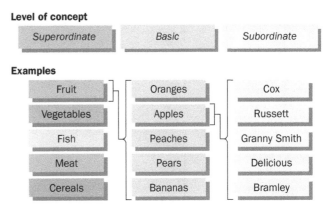

Figure 11.22 Examples of basic-level, subordinate and superordinate concepts.

reason: cognitive economy. The use of subordinate concepts wastes time and effort on meaningless distinctions, and the use of superordinate concepts loses important information. Rosch *et al.* (1976) presented people with various concepts and gave them 90 seconds to list as many attributes as they could for each of them. The subjects supplied few attributes for superordinate concepts but were able to think of many for basic-level concepts.

Subordinate concepts evoked no more responses than basic-level concepts did. Thus, because they deal with a large number of individual items and their characteristics, basic-level concepts represent the maximum information in the most efficient manner. When people think about basic-level concepts, they do not have to travel up or down a tree to find the attributes that belong to the concept. The attributes are directly attached to the exemplars that constitute each concept.

It is important to recognise that concepts can represent something more complex than simple exemplars or collections of attributes. Goldstone *et al.* (1991) showed participants groups of figures and asked them to indicate which were most similar to each other. When they showed the participants two triangles, two squares and two circles, the subjects said that the squares and triangles were most similar, presumably because both contained straight lines and angles. However, when they added a square to each of the pairs, the participants said that the two most similar groups were the triangles plus square and the circles plus square. The task is illustrated by Figure 11.23.

The concept this time was 'two things and a square'. If the participants were simply counting attributes, then the addition of a square to the pairs should not have changed their decision. As this study shows very clearly, concepts can include relations among elements that cannot be described by counting attributes.

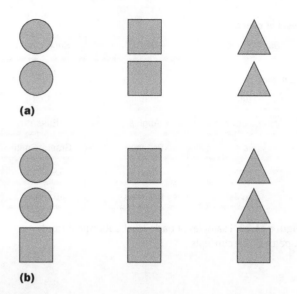

Figure 11.23 Concept formation. Participants were asked which of the groups of shapes were most similar. **(a)** Three pairs of geometrical shapes. **(b)** The same shapes with the addition of squares.

Concepts are the raw material of thinking; they are what we think about. But thinking itself involves the manipulation and combination of concepts. Such thinking can take several forms, but the most common forms are deductive reasoning and inductive reasoning.

Deductive reasoning

Deductive reasoning consists of inferring specific instances from general principles or rules. For example, the following two series of sentences express deductive reasoning:

> John is taller than Phil
>
> Sue is shorter than Phil
>
> Therefore, John is taller than Sue
>
> All mammals have fur
>
> A bat is a mammal
>
> Therefore, a bat has fur

Deductions consist of two or more statements from which a conclusion is drawn. The first group of sentences presented above involves the application of a simple mathematical principle. The second group presents a syllogism. The syllogism, a form of deductive logic invented by Aristotle, is often found in tests of intelligence. A syllogism is a logical construction that consists of a major premise (for example, 'all mammals have fur'), a minor premise ('a bat is a mammal'), and a conclusion ('a bat has fur'). The major and minor premises are assumed to be true. The problem is to decide whether the conclusion is true or false.

People differ widely in their ability to solve syllogisms. For example, many people would agree with the conclusion of the following syllogism:

> All mammals have fur
>
> A zilgid has fur
>
> Therefore, a zilgid is a mammal

These people would be wrong; the conclusion is not warranted. The major premise says only that all mammals have fur. It leaves open the possibility that some animals that have fur are not mammals.

Mental models

Why are some people better than others at solving syllogisms? Johnson-Laird (1985) notes that syllogistic reasoning is much more highly correlated with spatial ability than with verbal ability. Spatial ability includes the ability to visualise shapes and to manipulate them mentally. Why should skill at logical reasoning be related to this ability? Johnson-Laird and his colleagues (Johnson-Laird and Byrne, 1991; Johnson-Laird *et al.*, 1992) suggest that people solve problems involving logical deduction by constructing **mental models**, mental constructions based on physical reality. When faced with a reasoning problem, people will generate a mental model of the puzzle and see what conclusions they can draw from parts of the mental model. They search for alternative models that might contradict the conclusion reached from the initial model; but if this falsification is not forthcoming, the conclusion is accepted. If the alternative model does falsify the conclusion reached by previous reasoning, the search goes on for an alternative model which may help us to reach the correct conclusion. For example, if you consider the following problem:

> A is less than C
>
> B is greater than C
>
> Is B greater than A?

in order to compare A with B, you must remember the order of the three elements. One kind of mental model is an imaginary line going from small to large in which you mentally place each item on the line as you encounter it. Then, with all three elements in a row, you can answer the question. Figure 11.24 illustrates this.

In fact, when we solve problems concerning comparisons of a series of items, we tend to think about our own mental model that represents the information rather than about the particular facts given to us (Potts, 1972). For example, consider this passage:

> Although the four craftsmen were brothers, they varied enormously in height. The electrician was the very tallest, and the plumber was shorter than him. The plumber was taller than the carpenter, who, in turn, was taller than the painter. (*Source*: Just and Carpenter, 1987, p. 202.)

After reading this passage, people can more easily answer questions about pairs of brothers who largely differ in height. For example, they are faster to answer the question, 'Who is taller, the electrician or the painter?' than

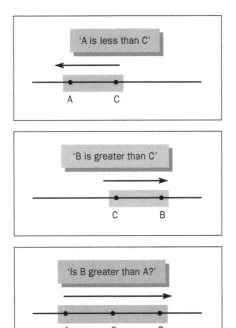

Figure 11.24 A mental model. Logical problems are often solved by imagining a physical representation of the facts.

Syllogistic reasoning – An international perspective

Several studies have suggested that illiterate, unschooled people in remote villages in various parts of the world are unable to solve syllogistic problems. Scribner (1977) visited two tribes of people in Liberia, West Africa – the Kpelle and the Vai – and found that tribespeople gave what Westerners would consider to be wrong answers. However, the people were not unable to reason logically but approached problems differently. For example, she presented the following problem to a Kpelle farmer. At first glance, the problem appears to be a reasonable one even for an illiterate, unschooled person because it refers to his own tribe and to an occupation he is familiar with.

> All Kpelle men are rice farmers
>
> Mr Smith is not a rice farmer
>
> Is he a Kpelle man?

The man replied:

Participant: I don't know the man in person. I have not laid eyes on the man himself.

Experimenter: Just think about the statement.

Participant: If I know him in person, I can answer that question, but since I do not know him in person, I cannot answer that question.

Experimenter: Try and answer from your Kpelle sense.

Participant: If you know a person, if a question comes up about him you are able to answer. But if you do not know the person, if a question comes up about him it's hard for you to answer.

Source: Scribner, 1977, p. 490.

The farmer's response did not show that he was unable to solve a problem in deductive logic. Instead, it indicated that as far as he was concerned, the question was unreasonable. In fact, his response contained an example of logical reasoning: 'If you know a person . . . you are able to answer.'

Scribner found that illiterate people would sometimes reject the premises of her syllogism, replace them with what they knew to be true, and then solve the new problem, as they had defined it. For example, she presented the following problem to a Vai tribesperson.

> All women who live in Monrovia are married
>
> Kemu is not married
>
> Does she live in Monrovia?

The answer was yes. The respondent said, 'Monrovia is not for any one kind of people, so Kemu came to live there.'

Syllogistic reasoning – *Continued*

The suggestion that only married women live in Monrovia was absurd, because the tribesperson knew otherwise. Thus, if Kemu wanted to live there, she could – and did.

Clearly, the intellectual ability of people in other cultures cannot be measured against Western standards.

In the world of traditional tribal people, problems are solved by application of logical reasoning to facts gained through direct experience. Their deductive-reasoning ability is not necessarily inferior, it is simply different, pragmatic.

the question, 'Who is taller, the plumber or the carpenter?' This finding is particularly important because the passage explicitly states that the plumber was taller than the carpenter, but one must infer that the electrician was taller than the painter. Just and Carpenter's study shows that the result of an inference can be more readily available than information explicitly given. How can this be? The most plausible explanation is that when people read the passage, they construct a mental model that represents the four brothers arranged in order of height. The painter is clearly the shortest and the electrician is clearly the tallest. Thus, a comparison between the extremes can be made very quickly.

The type of syllogistic reasoning described in the previous section does not always lead to an alternative model being sought. Many reasoners rarely go beyond the initial model they construct (Evans *et al.*, 1999). Participants in Evans *et al.*'s experiment, for example, were more likely to accept conclusions that were consistent with their original model and reject conclusions that were inconsistent rather than construct a more accurate, reasonable model. This lack of ability to search for alternative models and accept conclusions that are inconsistent with the original mental models can have serious consequences for us, especially if people are making judgements about our character, demeanour and conduct. Nowhere is this more important than when judgements are made against a person accused of a crime in a court trial. In a later section, you will see how juries appear to make their decisions (and the factors that can affect the nature of this decision-making) and how biases in jurors' reasoning can affect their verdict.

Many creative scientists and engineers report that they use mental models to reason logically and solve practical and theoretical problems (Krueger, 1976). For example, the American physicist and Nobel laureate Richard Feynman said that he used rather bizarre mental models to keep track of characteristics of complex mathematical theorems to see whether they were logical and consistent. Here is how Feynman described his thought processes:

When I'm trying to understand . . . I keep making up examples. For instance, the mathematicians would come in with a . . . theorem. As they're telling me the conditions of the theorem, I construct something that fits all the conditions. You know, you have a set [one ball] – disjoint [two balls]. Then the balls turn colours, grow hairs, or whatever, in my head as they [the mathematicians] put more conditions on. Finally, they state the theorem, which is some . . . thing about the ball which isn't true for my hairy green ball thing, so I say 'False!'
(*Source*: Feynman, 1985, p. 70.)

Inductive reasoning

Deductive reasoning involves applying the rules of logic to infer specific instances from general principles or rules. This type of reasoning works well when general principles or rules have already been worked out. **Inductive reasoning** is the opposite of deductive reasoning; it consists of inferring general principles or rules from specific facts. In one well-known laboratory example of inductive reasoning, participants are shown cards that contain figures differing in several dimensions, such as shape, number and colour (Milner, 1964). On each trial, they are given two cards and asked to choose the one that represents a particular concept. After they choose a card, the experimenter indicates whether the decision is correct or not. The task is illustrated in Figure 11.25.

One trial is not enough to recognise the concept. If the first trial reveals that a card is correct, then the concept could be red, or four or triangle, or some combination of these, such as red triangle, four red shapes, or even four red triangles. Information gained from the second trial allows the subject to rule out some of these hypotheses – for example, shape does not matter, but colour and number do. The participant uses steps to solve the problem in much the same way as a scientist does: they form a hypothesis on the basis of the available evidence and test that hypothesis

Figure 11.25 A card sorting task. Participants are asked to sort cards according to a given criterion, such as colour or shape, that is unknown to them. After they have successfully determined this criterion, it is unexpectedly and unknowingly changed and the participant has to determine the new sorting criterion.

Source: From Pinel, P.J., *Biopsychology*, 3rd edn © 1997. Published by Allyn and Bacon, Boston, MA. Copyright © by Pearson Education. By permission of the publisher.

on subsequent trials. If it is proved false, it is abandoned, a new hypothesis consistent with what went before is constructed and this new hypothesis is tested.

Logical errors in inductive reasoning

Psychologists have identified several tendencies that interfere with people's ability to reason inductively. These include the failure to select the information they need to test a hypothesis, the failure to seek information that would be provided by a comparison group, and the disinclination to seek evidence that would indicate whether a hypothesis is false.

Failure to select relevant information

When reasoning inductively, people often fail to select the information they need to test a hypothesis. For example, consider the following task, from an experiment by Wason and Johnson-Laird (1972):

Your job is to determine which of the hidden parts of these cards you need to see in order to answer the following question decisively:

For these cards is it true that if there is a vowel on one side there is an even number on the other side?

You have only one opportunity to make this decision; you must not assume that you can inspect the cards one at a time. Name those cards which it is absolutely essential to see.

The participants were shown four cards like those in Figure 11.26. Most people say that they would need to see card (a), and they are correct. If there was not an even number on the back of card (a), then the rule is not correct. However, many participants failed to realise that card (d) must also be inspected. True, there is no even number on this card, but what if there is a vowel on the other side? If there is, then the rule is (again) proved wrong. Many participants also wanted to see card (c), but there is no need to do so. The hypothesis says nothing about whether an even number can be on one side of the card without there being a vowel on the other side.

People have to be taught the rules of logic; they do not automatically apply them when trying to solve a problem. But under certain circumstances, most people do reason logically. For example, Griggs and Cox (1982) presented a slightly different version of this test. They asked people to decide which cards should be checked to see whether the following statement was true: 'If a person is drinking beer, she must be over age 19.' The cards represented people; their age was on one side and their drink (beer or Coke) was on the other. Which card(s) would you check? (See Figure 11.27.)

Most participants correctly chose cards (a) and (d). They knew that if someone were drinking beer, she must be old enough. Similarly, if someone were 16 years old, we must check to see what she was drinking. The subjects readily recognised the fact that we do not need to know the age of someone drinking Coke, and someone 22 years old can drink whatever beverage she prefers. This study

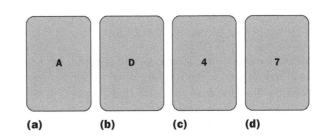

Figure 11.26 Cards used in a formal test of problem-solving.

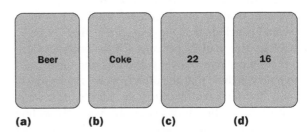

Figure 11.27 Cards used in a more realistic version of the problem-solving test.

shows that experiments using puzzles designed to test people's reasoning ability do not always assess their ability to apply a logical rule to a practical situation.

In everyday life, people may commit biases in reasoning despite evidence showing that their reasoning is incorrect. The controversy in the UK concerning the possible role of the triple MMR (measles, mumps and rubella) vaccine in autism is an example of this. Some parents regard the multiple vaccination as potentially dangerous to their child and request single vaccines (one each for each of the infections). The reasoning is based on evidence from a study in which 12 children who received the MMR vaccine developed gut problems and symptoms of a developmental disorder called autism in which the child becomes withdrawn and does not engage in social and emotional communication. Other, larger, more sophisticated studies reporting no negative effect of the vaccine on child development did little to dispel the belief that MMR might cause autism.

This real-life example mirrors findings from the laboratory. In fact, laboratory studies try to investigate why some people commit these biases in reasoning and decision-making. In one study, participants were presented with hypothetical social reforms that would benefit the majority of people but would leave a small minority less well off (Baron and Jurney, 1993). Although participants agreed that such social policy decisions would be beneficial to all people, they voted against the proposals because some people might be worse off. This type of reasoning may explain why politicians behave in the way that they do.

Failure to utilise a comparison group

Another tendency that interferes with people's ability to reason inductively is their failure to consider a comparison group. Imagine that you learn that 79 per cent of the people with a particular disease get well within a month after taking a new, experimental drug (Stich, 1990). Is the drug effective? The correct answer to this question is: we cannot conclude anything – we need more information. What we need to know is what happens to people with the disease if they do not take the drug. If we find that only 22 per cent of these people recover within a month, then we would conclude that the drug is effective; 79 per cent is much greater than 22 per cent. On the other hand, if we find that 98 per cent recover without taking the drug, then we would conclude that the drug is worse than useless – it actually interferes with recovery. In other words, we need a control group. But most people are perfectly willing to conclude that, because 79 per cent seems like a high figure, the drug must work. Seeing the necessity for a control group does not come naturally; unless people are deliberately taught about control groups, they will not realise the need for them.

Failure to seek or use information that would be provided by a control group has been called ignoring base rate information. As several researchers have suggested, the problem here may be that we engage in two types of reasoning (Reber, 1992; Evans and Over, 1996; Stanovich, 1999). One type of reasoning is deliberate and conscious and involves explicit memories of roles that we can describe verbally. The other type of reasoning is unconscious and uses information we have learned implicitly. Because the explicit and implicit memory systems involve at least some different brain mechanisms, information from one system cannot easily interact with information from the other system. One of the most serious consequences of this reasoning error can be seen in so-called pseudo-diagnosticity tasks (Doherty et al., 1979). This task involves making a medical diagnosis and is presented in the following way:

> A patient shows symptom A which is present in 95 per cent of patients suffering from disease B.
>
> Does this give grounds to suspect that the patient is suffering from disease B?

This decision can only be made by considering whether symptom A is also present in other illnesses; that is, the person must be aware of the base rate likelihood of disease B occurring relative to other diseases. If symptom A is present in other diseases, the data presented above do not give good grounds for an exclusive diagnosis of disease B. People who are untrained reasoners usually fail to consider this possibility: they are not sensitive to base rate information (Evans et al., 2002).

We are also more swayed by narrative, than numerical, evidence when making decisions and this leads to some erroneous decision-making. An online study examined the effects of narrative evidence and statistical evidence on men's perception of risk of contracting the hepatitis B virus and whether they would seek vaccination. All the participants were homosexual. Narrative evidence was more persuasive than statistical evidence in heightening awareness of the risk of contracting the illness and in predicting participants' intention to get vaccination.

If people are allowed to observe actual occurrences of certain events (that is, acquire the information about the base rate of occurrence automatically and implicitly), however, they can consider information about event frequency (Holyoak and Spellman, 1993). Furthermore, if people are given explicit instructions to consider alternative hypotheses, they will make decisions that take these alternative hypotheses into account (Klayman and Brown, 1993; Evans *et al.*, 2002).

Confirmation bias

Individuals may also show a disinclination to seek evidence that would indicate whether a hypothesis is false. Instead, people tend to seek evidence that might confirm their hypothesis; they exhibit the **confirmation bias**. For example, Wason (1968) presented people with the series of numbers '2, 4, 6' and asked them to try to figure out the rule to which they conformed. The participant was to test their hypothesis by making up series of numbers and saying them to the experimenter, who would reply yes or no. Then, whenever the participant decided that enough information had been gathered, they could say what the hypothesis was. If the answer was correct, the problem was solved. If it was not, the participant was to think of a new hypothesis and test that one.

Several rules could explain the series '2, 4, 6'. The rule could be 'even numbers', or 'each number is two more than the preceding one', or 'the middle number is the mean of the first and third number'. When people tested their hypotheses, they almost always did so by presenting several sets of numbers, all of which were consistent with their hypotheses. For example, if they thought that each number was two more than the preceding one, they might say '10, 12, 14' or '61, 63, 65'. Very few participants tried to test their hypotheses by choosing a set of numbers that did not conform to the rules, such as '12, 15, 22'. In fact, the series '12, 15, 22' does conform to the rule. The rule was so simple that few participants figured it out: each number must be larger than the preceding one.

The confirmation bias is very strong. Unless people are taught to do so, they tend not to think of possible non-examples of their hypotheses and to see whether they might be true – the way that scientists do. But, in fact, evidence that disconfirms a hypothesis is conclusive, whereas evidence that confirms it is not.

The confirmation bias in inductive reasoning has a counterpart in deductive reasoning. For example, consider the following sentences (Johnson-Laird, 1985):

> All the pilots are artists
>
> All the skiers are artists
>
> True or false: All the pilots are skiers

Many people say 'true'. They test the truth of the conclusion by imagining a person who is a pilot and an artist and a skier – and that person complies with the rules. Therefore, they decide that the conclusion is true. But if they would try to disconfirm the conclusion – to look for an example that would fit the first two sentences but not the conclusion – they would easily find one. Could a person be a pilot but not a skier? Of course; the first two sentences say nothing to rule out that possibility. There are artist–pilots and there are artist–skiers, but nothing says that there must be artist–pilot–skiers.

The tendency to seek (and to pay more attention to) events that might confirm our beliefs is demonstrated by the way we have distorted the original meaning of the saying, 'the exception proves the rule'. Most people take this to mean that we can still consider a rule to be valid even if we encounter some exceptions. But that conclusion is illogical: if there is an exception, the rule is wrong. In fact, the original meaning of the phrase was, 'the exception tests the rule', which it does. The word 'prove' comes from the Latin *probare*, 'to test'.

Sure-thing principle

The sure thing principle states that if you believe that you prefer A to B in all states of the world, then you should prefer A to B in any state of the world (Hardman and Harries, 2002). Usually, when people commit violations of the principle, it indicates an inability to think through a problem or situation. For example, Shafir *et al.* (1993) asked students to imagine they were waiting for exam results and to plan for two outcomes: making a deposit for a holiday and deferring a decision on whether to go on holiday until after the exam results are published, or booking a cheap holiday immediately. Students who were told their result booked a holiday, whether the result was a pass or a fail. Students who were not told, however, elected to pay a small deposit and decide whether to go when the results were published. The evidence showed that even if those who deferred their holiday knew they had failed or passed, they would have booked the holiday. If they booked the holiday whatever their results were, why did they defer the holiday when they did not know the results?

Who believes in spoon bending?

'Would any one in the audience who believes in telepathy, please put my hand up,' asked Emo Philips in one of his stand-up routines. This chapter (and Chapter 15 also) shows that people can make very poor reasoners and can make ineffective use of evidence to make judgements or inform decisions. Our decisions are affected by our own biases, personal beliefs and convictions. One review has highlighted some of these elementary reasoning errors in people who are convinced of their belief in something a little strange: psychic ability (Wiseman and Watt, 2006).

The two commonest types of psychic ability are extrasensory perception (ESP) and psychokinesis. ESP is the 'apparent ability to receive information via a channel of communication not presently recognised by mainstream science and includes alleged clairvoyance, telepathy and precognition (in which the information related to a future event)'. Psychokinesis is the 'apparent ability to influence physical objects and biological systems using unknown means, and encompasses a wide range of alleged phenomena, including causing objects to levitate, dice to roll at above chance levels and paranormal healing'. Is there something defective or unusual about the reasoning of the people who believe in such things?

Some psychologists have argued that believers in the paranormal have poor cognitive ability because they misattribute psychic causes to normal or natural phenomena – they cannot see a simple relationship between physical cause and effect (Alcock, 1981; Blackmore, 1992). There is some evidence of lower academic achievement in these individuals but the overall results are inconsistent.

People from the humanities are more likely to believe in psychic phenomena than are those with a science background but one study found that students of biology were greater believers than those from the humanities (Salter and Routledge, 1971). When asked to be critically evaluative of mock science papers, believers are less critical than non-believers (Gray and Mill, 1990). They are also poor at understanding probability. For example, if asked whether throwing 10 dice at the same time and getting 10 sixes is more or less likely than throwing one die 10 times and obtaining 10 sixes, believers underestimate the statistical likelihood (Musch and Ehrenberg, 2002). Believers are also more likely to see patterns in series of random dots (Blackmore and Moore, 1994) and to be prone to fantasy. 'The more the individual possesses the ability to find connections between their experiences and actual events,' writes Blackmore (1992), 'the more likely they are to view their experiences as psychic.'

Probability heuristic

The probability heuristic is similar to the confirmation bias in the sense that it shows how people can draw conclusions based on what they believe rather than on available evidence. The difference between them is that the probability heuristic shows how people can draw erroneous

Table 11.6 The Linda problem

Linda is 31 years old, single, outspoken and very bright. She majored in philosophy. As a student, she was deeply concerned with issues of discrimination and social justice, and also participated in anti-nuclear demonstrations.

Please rank the following by their probability, using 1 for the most probable and 8 for the least probable.

A   Linda is a teacher in primary school

B   Linda works in a bookstore and takes yoga classes

C   Linda is an attractive feminist

D   Linda is a psychiatric social worker

E   Linda is a member of Woman Against Rape

F   Linda is a bank teller

G   Linda is an insurance salesperson

H   Linda is a bank teller and is an active feminist

Source: Tversky, A. and Kahneman, D., Extensional versus intuitive reasoning: Conjunction fallacy in probability judgement. Psychological Review, 1983, 90, 293–315, © 1983 by the American Psychological Association, reprinted with permission.

conclusions by not taking into account the probability of an outcome (Kahneman et al., 1982; Tversky and Kahneman, 1983). The example in Table 11.6 illustrates the concept. Read through the example now and then come back to the text to see how you did.

In what position in life did you place Linda? If you responded like those participants in the original experiment, you would be significantly less likely to indicate that Linda was a bank teller than a bank teller and a feminist. For some reason, people were not likely to consider bank tellers to be active feminists (or vice versa), thereby ignoring the principles of probability. This type of error, called a conjunction error, is reduced when the initial description of the person is followed by text stating that 100 people fit the description they have read and the reader is asked how many of them are bank tellers and bank tellers and active feminists. When led in this way, people do not commit errors in reasoning that take little account of probability; without such guidance, these errors are committed.

An example of real-life decision-making is seen every time a juror reaches a verdict in a trial. Jurors' decisions carry great weight and in some cases can determine whether a person lives or dies. The Psychology in Action box describes some of the factors that can influence a juror's decision-making and tries to explain how jurors reach their decisions.

Psychology in action: Jury decision-making

> **Trial by jury itself, instead of being a security to persons who are accused, will be a delusion, a mockery and a snare.** Lord Denman, Lord Chief Justice.

The outcomes of many famous trials by jury in Europe and the USA in recent years may give some credence to Denman's thoughts. The verdict in the O.J. Simpson case in the USA and the acquittal of the Maxwell brothers of fraud in the UK have led to calls for a review of the jury system (Doran and Jackson, 1997). Jury systems exist in many countries. In England and Wales, for example, juries are considered part of the justice delivery system, but only 2 per cent of criminal cases go to trial by jury. In the UK, jurors are usually laypersons with no especial expertise in law or the subject of the trial; numbers vary between 12 (England and Wales) and 15 (Scotland). The lay nature of juries has made some question the verdicts of fraud trials, for example, where it is felt that the detailed evidence of fraud presented by the prosecution cannot be fully appreciated by a lay juror. In other countries, a jury may comprise a mixture of lay and expert jurors, called an 'escabinato jury'.

In Western societies, the jury symbolises all that is democratic, fair and just in a society. Jury decisions can call into question core values, and can have dramatic social consequences. For example, the 1992 Los Angeles riots, which left 50 dead and 2,300 injured, were sparked by the perception that an all-white jury had delivered an unjust verdict of 'not guilty' in the trial of white police officers accused of beating a black motorist. Several factors affect jury decision-making including the decision-making process itself, the number of people on a jury, jurors' prior beliefs, features specific to the case such as the sex, employment record and criminal history of the defendant, whether the crime involved the use of a weapon, and the availability of eyewitness testimony (Howitt, 2002).

Much of the research relies on experiments in which trials are simulated and mock juries hear (often genuine) court evidence, and draw their conclusions. The invented nature of much of these experiments obviously encourages us to be cautious when interpreting their results. However, many studies make their protocol as realistic as possible and encourage their participants to behave as if they were making real-life jury decisions.

Factors influencing juries' verdicts

The results make interesting reading. Allowing jurors to take notes or to ask questions leads to no significant change in the verdict reached or in the perception of the prosecution or defence (Penrod and Heuer, 1997), but makes the processing of complex evidence easier. The publicity given to a case (Otto et al., 1994), the attractiveness of the victim (Kerr, 1978) and the order of evidence (Kassin et al., 1990; Kerstholt and Jackson, 1998) have all been found to influence eventual verdicts. People who are anti-police are more likely to acquit than are those who do not hold anti-police views (Vidmar et al., 1997), and people are more persuaded by an expert witness when the evidence is complex (Cooper et al., 1996).

Jury size is important. In the case of Williams v. Florida, the US Supreme Court ruled that six jurors were as effective as twelve. Juries usually require unanimity: in the UK this may be required at first but if this is not forthcoming a 10/12 majority is required. In Spain, on the other hand, there is what is called qualified majority voting. To reach a verdict of not guilty, a majority of 5/9 must be reached; for a verdict of guilty, 7/9 is required.

Large juries tend to result in hung verdicts (Zeisel, 1971; Saks and Marti, 1997) and spend longer deliberating on the verdict, engage in more irrelevant deliberations, make more assertions, regard trial evidence less meaningfully and are more intransigent than their unanimous-verdict counterparts (Arce et al., 1998). Large juries are also likely to reach more guilty verdicts (Saks and Marti, 1997). Striking a note of caution, however, Saks and Marti found that although large mock juries reached more hung judgments, only 1 per cent of real juries were hung. When agreement between jurors is made compulsory, however, members do spend more time deliberating evidence in detail (Arce et al., 1998).

In a study of 1,000 defendants on felony charges, Myers (1979) found that there were some specific features of the case that influenced verdicts. These included whether: a weapon was recovered, a large number of witnesses gave testimony or were prepared to, the defendant had previous convictions and was employed, whether the defendant was young or old; and the seriousness of the crime was also a factor. Factors not associated with the final verdict were the eyewitness testimony of the defendant, the testimony of experts and the defendant's relation to the victim.

How do jurors reach a verdict?

Psychologists have suggested two models which might account for this type of decision-making (Honess and Charman, 2002). The story model argues that jurors evaluate evidence/information in a step-by-step manner and construct a meaningful narrative using the evidence they hear. During the course of the trial, the juror begins to form a story and evaluates subsequent evidence in light of this (Pennington and Hastie, 1986, 1992). The second model is the dual-process model. This model argues that the juror engages in two types of processing during decision-making. The first type, systematic processing, involves paying

Psychology in action: *Continued*

close attention to case detail and engaging in close scrutiny of information. The second type, heuristic processing, involves paying less attention to detail but paying more attention to the social, emotional, subjective aspects of the case such as the persuasiveness of expert evidence, and the belief that there is 'no smoke without fire' (Eagly and Chaiken, 1993).

Current evidence suggests that the story model best accounts for jury decision-making (Carlson and Russo, 2001). The model also suggests that because all jurors have access to evidence, their construction of stories will depend on the juror's own beliefs, predispositions and personal experiences.

Predecisional distortion'/bias

Failure to ignore a judge's instructions or to dismiss evidence deemed inadmissible is thought to contribute to bias in reasoning. Inadmissible evidence would still be evaluated, partially, according to the judgement the juror has already reached about the culpability of the defendant. Carlson and Russo call this 'predecisional distortion' because evidence is interpreted in a partial way before a verdict is reached. Carlson and Russo found that predecisional bias was greater in prospective mock jurors than it was in a group of students. These jurors distorted evidence twice as much, held stronger prior beliefs and were more confident in their judgements than were the student juror group, possibly because the prospective jurors were older than the students or because the students were more analytical and reflective. This is a reasonable hypothesis given

that the prospective group held strong prior beliefs that were not particularly susceptible to change.

If this bias is inherent in the system – because jurors are thinking individuals with differences in belief, thinking style and intellect – how can it be avoided? For a juror to reach a verdict before all the evidence is presented, and to interpret evidence in a way that is consistent with that verdict, is clearly problematic (Constantini and King, 1980). There is some evidence, however, that if people are given instructions not to develop biased thinking (either pro- or anti- an individual), then these biases can be removed. In mock jury settings, giving juries instructions before evidence is presented is more effective than instructing them after all the evidence has been heard (Bourgeois *et al.*, 1995).

There are some biases, however, that people would find very difficult to avoid. Pre-trial publicity is a good example of information presented prior to trial that could influence a juror's view of the evidence. Some judges in the UK consider such publicity could prejudice a defendant's case, as happened in 2001 when a judge ordered a retrial of two professional footballers accused of assaulting a man in Leeds city centre. A retrial was ordered after a national newspaper published an interview with the father of the assaulted man. The judge ruled that the defendants would not receive a fair trial. Although it seems intuitively reasonable, there is no systematic evidence to support the idea that pre-trial information could cause juror bias. More realistically, however, as Studebacker and Penrod (1997) note, there is no trial anywhere in the world where a juror would not be aware of some aspects of the crime.

One final note about factors associated with reasoning. Hodson and Busseri (2012) investigated the relationship between right-wing ideological thinking and reasoning in UK and US samples. The samples came from the 1958 National Child Development Study (8,000 participants) and the 1970 British Cohort Study (7,000). Cognitive ability was measured at 11 years of age and conservative ideology in their 30s. They found that lower *g* in childhood predicted racist thinking in adulthood and that this relationship was mediated by conservative ideology in the UK sample. Poor abstract reasoning skill predicted homophobia in adulthood.

Problem-solving

The ultimate function of thinking is to solve problems. We are faced with an enormous variety of them in our daily lives: fixing a television set, planning a picnic, choosing a

spouse, navigating across the ocean, solving a maths problem, tracking some game, designing a bridge, finding a job. The ability to solve problems is related to academic success, vocational success and overall success in life, so trying to understand how we do so is an important undertaking.

Algorithms and heuristics

Some kinds of problem can be solved by following a sequence of operators known as an algorithm. **Algorithms** are procedures that consist of a series of steps that, if followed in the correct sequence, will provide a solution. If you apply properly the steps of an algorithm (such as long division) to divide one number by another, you will obtain the correct answer. But many problems are not as straightforward as this. When there is no algorithm to follow, we must follow a heuristic to guide our search for a path to the solution. Heuristics (from the Greek *heuriskein*, 'to discover') are general rules that are useful in guiding our search for a path to the solution of a problem. Heuristics tell us what to pay attention to, what to ignore and what strategy to take.

Heuristic methods can be very specific, or they can be quite general, applying to large categories of problems. For example, management courses try to teach students problem-solving methods they can use in a wide variety of contexts. Newell and Simon (1972) suggest a general heuristic method that can be used to solve any problem: **means–ends analysis**. The principle behind means–ends analysis is that a person should look for differences between the current state and the goal state and seek ways to reduce these differences. The steps of this method are as follows (Holyoak, 1990, p. 121):

1 Compare the current state to the goal state and identify differences between the two. If there are none, the problem is solved; otherwise, proceed.

2 Select an operator that would reduce one of the differences.

3 If the operator can be applied, do so; if not, set a new subgoal of reaching a state at which the operator could be applied. Means–ends analysis is then applied to this new subgoal until the operator can be applied or the attempt to use it is abandoned.

4 Return to step 1.

At all times, the person's activity is oriented towards reducing the distance between the current state and the goal state. If problems are encountered along the way (that is, if operators cannot be applied), then subgoals are created and means–ends analysis is applied to solving that problem, and so on until the goal is reached.

Of course, there may be more than one solution to a particular problem, and some solutions may be better than others. A good solution is one that uses the smallest number of actions while minimising the associated costs. The relative importance of cost and speed determines which solution is best. Intelligent problem-solving involves more than trying out various actions (applying various operators) to see whether they bring you closer to the goal. It also involves planning. When we plan, we act vicariously, 'trying out' various actions in our heads. Obviously, planning requires that we know something about the consequences of the actions we are considering. Experts are better at planning than are novices. If we do not know the consequences of particular actions, we will be obliged to try each action (apply each operator) and see what happens. Planning is especially important when many possible operators are present, when they are costly or time-consuming, or when they are irreversible. If we take an irreversible action that brings us to a dead end, we have failed to solve the problem.

Reasoning, decision-making and the brain

For most of our complex, intelligent behaviour, a region in the front of the brain appears to be essential. Damage to the frontal lobes is associated with deficits in planning, putting stimuli in the correct order, behaving spontaneously and inhibiting incorrect responses (Adolphs *et al.*, 1996).

Damasio and colleagues' studies of patients with frontal lobe damage show that these individuals have great difficulty in making correct decisions (Damasio, 1995; Bechara *et al.*, 1996, 1997). Damasio suggests that the ability to make decisions leading to positive or potentially harmful consequences depends on the activation of somatic (that is, bodily) states. Damasio calls this the **somatic marker hypothesis** because such decisions involve automatic, endocrine and musculoskeletal routes. These routes mark events as important, but appear to be impaired in certain frontal lobe patients. When the decision can have a positive or negative outcome, the degree of physiological activity, such as heart rate and galvanic skin response (GSR) (see Chapter 4) that is normally seen in healthy individuals is absent in these patients (Bechara *et al.*, 1997).

In a typical experiment, patients were taught to play a card game (the Iowa Gambling Task) where they were told to make as much money as possible (Bechara *et al.*, 1997). There are four decks of cards and some have a high probability of delivering a large immediate monetary reward or a large delayed monetary loss or a low immediate monetary reward or a low delayed monetary loss. No participant was told which deck contained the greatest probability of obtaining these outcomes and, therefore, had to learn from experience, turning over cards and remembering the outcomes. They had hunches. When a decision involved a high degree of risk, for example, a healthy individual would show a characteristic increase in physiological arousal; the frontal lobe patient, however, would not. Neuroimaging studies of the same task are associated with increases in blood flow to the ventromedial region of the frontal cortex (Elliott *et al.*, 1997; Grant *et al.*, 2000).

Bechara *et al.* (1997) found that the ventromedial-damaged patients opted for the disadvantageous decks and failed to be sensitive to future consequences. Instead, they seemed to be guided by immediate reward. The researchers called this 'myopia for the future'. Even when the future consequences of behaving in a particular way were undesirable, these patients continued to behave in an inappropriate way. The group followed this up with a study showing that substance abusers performed within the same range as people with damage to the ventromedial cortex (Bechara *et al.*, 2001).

Manes *et al.* (2002) found that dorsolateral lesions were associated with working memory, set shifting and Iowa Gambling Task impairments; dorsomedial lesions were associated with planning and Iowa Gambling Task impairments, and orbitofrontal lesions were associated with performance at control level but showed prolonged deliberation on the Tower of London Task, a task that required forward planning (see Chapter 13 for an example of this task). However, the group with large frontal lesions showed great impairment and was the only group to show risky decision-making. According to Manes *et al.*'s criteria, patients in the Bechara studies would be classified as having large frontal lesions.

In healthy individuals, blood flow tends to increase in the frontal and parietal lobes during reasoning tasks (Goel *et al.*, 1997, 1998). According to theories of deduction, our ability to reason is either based on understanding the linguistic rules that underpin logic or based on whether visuospatial relations are involved in the reasoning (Goel, 2007). These two different interpretations probably explain why the results from neuroimaging have been inconsistent. Different types of reasoning tasks recruit different regions. For example, early studies, such as the PET studies of Goel – cited above – asked people to follow syllogisms such as:

> Some officers are generals
>
> No privates are generals
>
> Some officers are not privates

and found increased activation in the left frontal and temporal lobes.

Later studies, using fMRI, found increases in both sides of the PFC, the left temporal lobe and both sides of the parietal lobe (Goel *et al.*, 2000; Goel, 2003).

Differences in activation are seen depending on whether the reasoning task involves conditional reasoning (participants have to follow if–then relations), complex conditional reasoning (such as the card sorting task described earlier), and transitive inferences (e.g. understanding that the relationship between A and B or B and C can be transferred to A and C). Left prefrontal activation is seen during the first, bilateral occipital, parietal and frontal activation during the second and frontal and parietal activation in the last. Goel and Dolan (2001), for example, using the third type, asked people to reason problems such as:

> Graham is taller than Mike
>
> Mike is taller than Lynn
>
> Graham is taller than Lynn

Knauff *et al.* (2003) extended this to action sentences:

> A dog is cleaner than a cat
>
> An ape is dirtier than a cat
>
> A dog is cleaner than an ape

and found similar activation.

According to Goel (2007), these studies suggest that the frontal-temporal pathway provides us with a heuristic system for reasoning – it helps us process conceptually coherent material – whereas the parietal lobe underpins a more formal system based on universal reasoning rules – it is involved in processing non-conceptual, incoherent material.

There is an exception to this model, however. Take a look at the following statements:

1 Mary is cleverer than John; John is cleverer than George; Mary is cleverer than George

2 Mary is cleverer than John; John is cleverer than George; George is cleverer than Mary

3 Mary is cleverer than John; Mary is cleverer than George; John is cleverer than George

Patients with damage to the left PFC cannot process the first two types; patients with damage to the right are poor at processing the last, suggesting that there may be a degree of reasoning-related asymmetry in the brain.

In general, however, a small network of regions is involved in reasoning and, whatever the task, the PFC is involved.

Brain activation in the very intelligent

Would more or less activation in the frontal lobes be apparent in very bright individuals? An early PET study indicated that individuals with high IQ had lower metabolic rates than those with low IQ during problem-solving (Haier *et al.*, 1988). When high and low IQ individuals were trained on a computer game, both groups' brain activity declined but the decline in the high IQ group was more rapid, suggesting that the highly intellectually able may need to use less of their neural machinery to think (Haier *et al.*, 1992).

A study by Chinese researchers, however, has found that intelligence is not simply related to activity in the frontal lobe but to connections between this region and other brain areas (Song *et al.*, 2008). They used fMRI to study 59 healthy adults and correlated intelligence scores with the strength of connections between the orbitalateral prefrontal cortex (OLPFC) and other brain regions.

They found that the greater the intelligence score, the greater the strength between the prefrontal cortex and the OLPFC within it, and with the parietal, limbic and occipital cortices. The results suggest that intelligence can be correlated with increased brain activation, even when the brain is at rest.

Creative thinking

Creativity has almost as many definitions as intelligence. We recognise that the writing of a novel, the design of a sculpture and the construction of a painting are creative products but what does it mean to be creative? Feldhusen and Goh (1995) define creativity as a 'complex mix of motivational conditions, personality factors, environmental conditions, chance factors and end products'. Vernon (1989) suggests that creativity is a person's capacity to produce ideas, inventions, artistic objects, insight and products evaluated highly by experts. Torrance (1975) defines creativity as a set of abilities, skills, motivations and states linked to dealing with problems. Others define the components of creative thinking as involving a realisation that a problem exists, formulation of questions to clarify the problem, determining the causes of the problem, clarifying the desired goal or solution and selecting a way to achieve this goal (Feldhusen, 1993). Still others have suggested that creativity involves producing a recognised, important end-product, not rubbish.

All of these definitions seem to have a common feature – that creativity involves some form of end-product. However, this end-product need not be material. Albert (1990), for example, has suggested that creativity is expressed through decisions not products. There do, however, seem to be different degrees of creativity. The production of a novel, painting or sculpture is undoubtedly creative, but solving inductive and deductive problems also involves a degree of creative thinking. However, artistic production seems to require creativity plus talent. These are high-level creative behaviours as opposed to the basic creative behaviour involved in solving deductive reasoning puzzles.

Given that psychologists cannot measure high-level creativity directly in the laboratory – they cannot ask individuals to come into the laboratory and write full-length novels, for example – they have devised other tests which tap the capacity to engage in creative thinking. The Torrance Tests of Creativity, for example, measure performance on a series of verbal and figural tasks such as naming as many objects as possible beginning with a specific letter or creating as many designs as possible using the same basic design (for example a circle). Torrance (1975) reported that performance on these tests predicted creative achievement, occupation and creative writing. Other tests, such as those by Wallach and Kogan (1965), are verbal and measure verbal fluency – the ability to devise

In Greek mythology, Prometheus stole fire from the gods for mankind's use. Humans were thus able to use their own creativity and not rely on divine creation. The gods became displeased and released Pandora's Box on mankind – a casket of evil.

Source: Prometheus carrying fire (oil) Jan Crossiers (1600–71), Prado, Madrid, Spain. Index/Bridgeman Art Library Ltd.

many uses for objects and the ability to detect similarities between stimuli. There is little evidence that performance on tests such as the Wallach and Kogan and the Torrance Tests – called tests of divergent thinking – predicts creativity (Brown, 1989) and there is even doubt cast on whether they measure creative thinking at all (Kim, 2011).

Are there any features of the creative individual's personality that can predict creativity? Dacey (1989) has listed nine personality factors predictive of creativity and includes in this list flexibility, risk-taking and tolerance of ambiguity. Other factors suggested by other psychologists include: cognitive complexity, perceptual openness, field independence, autonomy and self-esteem (Woodman and Schoenfeldt, 1989), and fluency, flexibility, curiosity and humour (Treffinger *et al.*, 1990).

Creativity and romance

'In order to create,' said the great Russian violinist Igor Stravinsky, 'there must be a dynamic force – and what force is more potent than love?' Researchers at Arizona State University examined the relationship between romantic motives and creativity in a series of experiments (Griskevicius *et al.*, 2006).

Men and women looked at photographs of attractive people of the opposite sex, or imagined being in a romantic scenario, and then completed subjective (writing a short story) and objective (the Remote Associates Test) creativity tests. The Remote Associates Test asks people to come up with one word that links three others in 15 seconds. For example, 'sun' would correctly bring together 'dress', 'dial' and 'flower'.

For men, thinking about an attractive woman as a potential romantic partner increased creativity. Women's creativity only increased when the man was perceived as trustworthy and committed. Men's increased creativity was therefore associated with attraction to a short-term mate, whereas women's was associated with attraction to a long-term mate. Women did not show increased creativity when thinking about a short-term or long-term mate who could not demonstrate good long-term viability as a partner. Although both sexes reported increased positive mood and arousal after appraising a person who might become a short-term partner, mood was unrelated to creativity.

The next step would be to examine not only the relationship between creativity and actual courtship, but also the relationship between the quality of the relationship and creativity.

Creativity, cognition and mood

Does a person's emotional state affect his or her ability to perform cognitive operations or be creative? In a famous series of experiments, Isen and colleagues found that while positive mood led to undergraduates betting larger amounts in a gambling game than did controls, these bets were only large when the probability of winning was high (Isen and Patrick, 1983) and that those in a positive mood thought about loss more (Isen and Geva, 1987). Individuals in a positive mood are more likely to choose a risky treatment for back pain than are those in a control group (Deldin and Levin, 1986).

Positive mood appears to have a beneficial effect on creativity, however (Isen *et al.*, 1987). People who had watched some comedy which induced positive mood were better able to solve a creative problem which involved supporting a lighted candle on a door using tacks, some matches in a matchbox and the candle (the solution, just in case you are not in a positive mood, is to tack the box to the door and place the candle lit with the matches, on top of the box).

Oaksford *et al.* (1996) extended this study by having participants complete creative and reasoning tasks after watching either a comedy programme, a neutral, wildlife programme or a negative documentary about stress. Their aim was to test two hypotheses. The facilitation hypothesis suggests that positive mood benefits creative thinking by facilitating it; the suppression hypothesis suggests that positive and negative moods take up resources that would normally be available for performing the cognitive task. Although positive and negative mood impaired performance on a deductive reasoning task, the positive mood only was associated with poor performance on the Tower of London Task which involves forward planning and reasoning. Some examples from the task can be seen in Figure 11.28.

Australians in a negative mood appear to be more successful than those in a positive mood at convincing others to agree with statements such as 'Student fees should be increased/decreased' or 'Aboriginal land rights should be preserved/restricted in Australia' (Forgas, 2007). Those in a negative mood were more likely to persuade others to believe an unpopular view than were people in a positive mood. Why? When the content of the arguments were examined, people in a negative mood were more likely to use concrete messages in their persuasion. This, in turn, led to more effective persuasion. Mood had influenced participants' processing style.

A sad or negative mood is not necessarily a disadvantage – it tends to be associated with thinking that is systematic and careful and less reliant on heuristics (Blanchette and Richards, 2010). Another phrase for it is 'depressive realism' – people are less biased and more accurate in their judgements (Allan *et al.*, 2007).

Sometimes emotion can have unexpected consequences. A study of Londoners after the 7th July tube and bus bombings in the capital found that they were more emotional than Canadians (the comparison group) but were more accurate when reasoning about terrorism syllogisms (Blanchette *et al.*, 2007).

Anxiety, on the other hand, tends to be associated with risk aversion when making decisions (Maner and Gerend, 2007) especially when the risk is personally relevant. A review of anxiety and creativity suggests that some variables are uniformly associated with poor performance, especially when cognition involves creativity (Byron and Khazanchi, 2011). Anxiety impairs creativity, particularly if the person is characteristically anxious (the effects are less obvious if the person is temporarily anxious) presumably because this trait imposes cognitive demands that take thinking resources away from creativity and disrupt or interfere with creative production. The

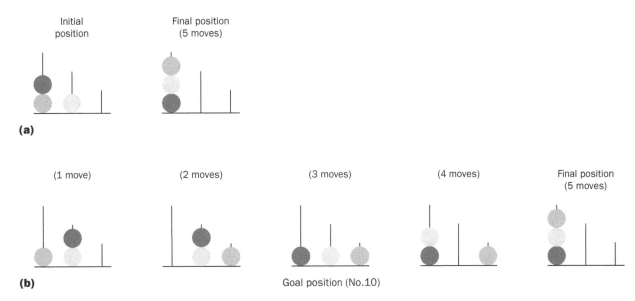

Figure 11.28 The Tower of London task. In **(a)** the participant is required to move the balls from the initial position to the target position in five moves; **(b)** shows how this is done.

more complex the creativity task, the greater the impairment, a finding that supports the demand/interference model. Anxiety also affected children more than it did adults.

Case studies in creativity

According to the theory of creativity proposed by Sternberg and Lubart (1991), there are three features of creativity that highly creative individuals possess. These features are: (1) domain-relevant skills – abilities the individual has in their domain and their knowledge of the domain; (2) creativity-relevant processes – the personality, cognitive style or other individual differences which promote creativity; and (3) intrinsic task motivation – the internal drive which motivates the individual and which can be influenced by the individual's environment. Domains for creative individuals such as John Irving, Charles Darwin and Claude Monet, for example, would be fiction, science and art, respectively.

Creative people are thought to produce products that are high in quality and novelty; intelligent, but not particularly creative, people can produce products of high quality but these may not be novel (Sternberg, 2001). The novel nature of creativity also suggests that its products 'defy the crowd' (Sternberg and Lubart, 1995): creative individuals produce unusual (sometimes) counter-intuitive products (ideas, as well as physical items), and some individuals, like Darwin, attempt to persuade the crowd with their ideas. Creatives also analyse the many ideas they have or may redefine problems or make unexpected connections between two things. As

the British artist Damien Hirst remarked, 'Put two things together that are meaningless; together, they create meaning.'

Sternberg and Lubart (1991) also suggest that the creative individual is a little like a successful market trader: they buy low and sell high. That is, they identify a problem needing a solution or find/pose an important question, and are then the first to provide the solution, leaving others to elaborate on these solutions and refine them. Some creatives may not be well known because they try to pose too many questions or attempt solutions to too many problems.

Curiosity is a trait which, according to some psychologists, marks out the creative from the non-creative (Kashdan and Fincham, 2002). But is there a more

'The physical impossibility of death in the mind of someone living' by Damien Hirst.
Source: Getty Images.

fundamental characteristic of creativity which psychology's current questionnaires and measures do not tap? According to Sternberg (2002), there is. It is

> the decision to be creative. People who create decide that they will forge their own path and follow it, for better or for worse. The path is a difficult one because people who defy convention often are not rewarded. Hence, at times, their self-esteem may be high, at other times, low. At times, they may work in groups, at other times individually. At times, they may feel curious, at other times, less so. But if psychologists are to understand and facilitate creativity, I suggest they must start, not with a kind of skill, not with a personality trait, not with a motivational set, and not with an emotional state, but rather, simply, with a decision . . . for creativity to occur, it must be preceded by a personal decision to think and act creatively, with all the risks attendant on doing so.'

Creativity and the brain

In an investigation of the role of the brain in creativity, Shamay-Tsoory (2011) examined the effect of brain injury on original creative thinking – defined as producing statistically infrequent ideas or connections between events and things – in patients with damage to the medial PFC, the inferior frontal gyrus, and the posterior and temporal cortex. They used the Torrance Test of creativity – where a person draws as many different, original, new objects from a circle as they can – and the Alternate uses test – where people devise as many alternate uses for six common objects – to measure originality.

Damage to the medial PFC was associated with greatest impairment in originality. However, there were some unusual asymmetries. Right-sided PFC lesions led to lower creativity scores but left-sided PFC damage was associated with slightly higher ones. The researchers found that the larger the lesion in the left inferior frontal and left parietal and temporal cortices, the greater the originality score (the opposite outcome was found for right-sided lesions).

These are areas involved in language production and the authors cite research showing that patients with injury to the left inferior frontal cortex show a previously undemonstrated artistic ability and motivation or

that increasing aphasia is accompanied by greater originality. Thus, creative thinking may rely on right frontal regions but linear, linguistic thinking – which impedes creative thinking – involves the left. 'It is possible,' the author suggests, 'that in order to produce an original response, as opposed to a more typical response, one would need to inhibit the typical, automatic responses most likely related to left hemisphere activation' (p. 184).

In terms of the regions of the brain that allow us to appreciate creativity – the neural substrates of aesthetic appreciation, if you will – a recent study compared people's brain activation while they observed sculptures or the bodies of athletes who struck the poses of the sculptures (Dio et al., 2011) (see Figure 11.29). The sculptures only activated the right antero-dorsal insula suggesting that perhaps this is the region that allows us to appreciate art, or at least art made of alabaster.

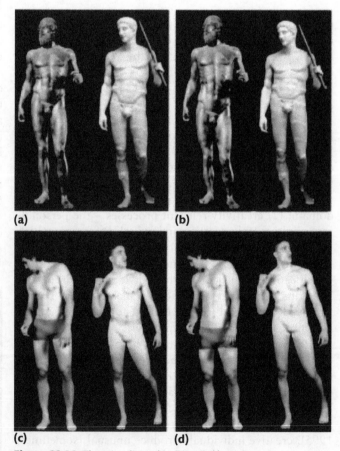

(a)   (b)

(c)   (d)

Figure 11.29 The stimuli used in Dio et al.'s study.

Controversies in psychological science: Are creativity and psychopathology related?

The issue

According to Dryden, 'Great wits are sure to madness near allied, and thin partitions do their bounds divide.' As if providing direct evidence for Dryden's poetic analysis, Lady Caroline Lamb once famously described Lord Byron as mad, bad and dangerous to know. But what empirical evidence is there to link psychopathology and creativity? If there is a relationship, does creativity cause psychopathology or does psychopathology cause creativity? Is it possible to determine this?

The evidence

Kraepelin (1921) had originally described a disorder called manic-depressive insanity in which the manic aspect of the disorder would produce changes in thought that would increase creativity and thinking. A number of authors report that increases in creativity are common during the manic episodes of bipolar disorder (Sutherland, 1987; Jamison, 1989; Goodwin and Jamison, 1990). Jamison (1989), for example, found that creative individuals, especially poets, reported states of mania during creation although she did not specify the direction of the change in behaviour (whether the poetry caused the mania or vice versa). There was also a high incidence of suicide in poets. Weisberg (1994), in studying the quantity and quality of the work of the composer Franz Schubert, who suffered what we would today call a bipolar disorder, found that although the quantity of the composer's work increased during manic episodes, the quality was not significantly improved.

In a famous study of the relationship between creativity and psychopathology, Ludwig (1994) compared 59 women writers from a Women Writers' Conference at the University of Kentucky and 59 women from a housewives' association, medical centre and university women's club. Ludwig found that the writers were more likely to suffer from mood disorders, drug abuse, panic attacks, general anxiety and eating disorders. The results of this study complement those of writers attending an Iowa writers' workshop, 90 per cent of whom were men (Andreasen, 1987). The study found a greater incidence of mood disorder in this group than in the general population (80 per cent v. 30 per cent) and a greater incidence of bipolar disorder. Shapiro and Weisberg (1999) sought to determine if the same relationship held for non-eminent samples. They gave a creativity and creativity personality questionnaire to 20 undergraduates (from a sample of 70) who met strict criteria for bipolar disorder. The presence of hypomanic or euphoric symptoms was found to be significantly associated with creativity, although depressive symptoms were not. The authors speculated that the depressed effect may be a part of the creative individual's behaviour because the inability to be creative (because of pressures in other areas of life) makes the individual depressed.

In two studies of creativity, Post (1994, 1996) analysed extensively the biographies of 291 world-famous creative men (visual artists, composers, creative writers, scientists, scholars and statesmen). He found that 90 per cent of the writers in his sample exhibited some traits which would be classified as a personality disorder according to mental disorder diagnostic manuals; only one scientist showed this profile (Henry Babbage, inventor of the first computer). In addition, 73.4 per cent of scientists exhibited unremarkable sexual behaviour whereas only 39 per cent of writers did. Depressive episodes occurred in 72 per cent of the writers. These data suggested to Post that, although the study was retrospective, a 'causal nexus' existed between creativity and psychopathology. In a subsequent study of 100 American and British writers (Post, 1996), there was a high prevalence of mood disorder, as seen in Table 11.7. Poets showed the greatest degree of bipolar disorder, although

Table 11.7 Mood disorders found in a sample of 100 writers

	N	Bipolar psychoses	Unipolar psychoses	Severely disabling depressions	Milder depressions	Brief reactions only	Cyclothymic traits only	Depressive traits only	Totals
Poets	35	2	1	4	11	4	5	1	28
Poets/ novelists	41	2	1	8	13	2	7	0	33
Playwrights	24	1	0	4	8	4	3	1	21
Totals	100	5	2	16	32	10	15	2	82

Source: Post, F., Verbal creativity, depression and alcoholism, *British Journal of Psychiatry*, 1996, 168, 545–55. Reproduced with permission of the Royal College of Psychiatrists.

Controversies in psychological science: *Continued*

Stephen Fry, Carrie Fisher, Richard Dreyfuss: creative individuals associated with manic-depression or clinical depression.
Source: Hugh Stewart/Corbis (t), Getty Images/WireImage (b).

the incidence of depression, marital/sexual problems and alcoholism in poets was low. Recently the degree of cognitive distortions found in the work of 36 eminent depressed and 36 non-depressed authors was analysed (Thomas and Duke, 2007).

There were more distortions in the depressed writers, and poets exhibited more than did novelists.

A study of 40 innovative American jazz musicians from the 1940s, 1950s and 1960s found that about 50 per cent were addicted to heroin, and 27 per cent became dependent on alcohol (Wills, 2003). Only one of the sample (Bud Powell) was schizophrenic but 28 per cent had 'probable' depression. This study, according to the author, 'adds weight to the finding that outstanding workers in the arts can suffer from above-average levels of mental health problems but manage to produce exceptional work despite this'.

If creativity and psychopathology are related, what creates this link? One personality trait which has been linked with creativity is **psychoticism** (Eysenck, 1995). Psychoticism refers to a cold, manipulative and indifferent personality style. A number of studies has shown that creative individuals score highly on tests of psychoticism (Fodor, 1994; Stavridou and Furnham, 1996). However, Aguilar-Alonso (1996) found no difference between high and low psychoticism on a measure of verbal and drawing creativity. Rawlings (1985) has suggested that individuals high in psychoticism show the same impulsive, non-conforming processes that underlie creative thinking ability. Perhaps what underlies creativity and psychoticism is disinhibition, the ability not to inhibit behaviour and thought.

Conclusion

Retrospective evidence suggests that there is a strong link between mental disorder and creativity. The problem with retrospective studies, however, is that we cannot empirically examine the personalities of creative individuals who are dead: we have to rely on books, anecdotes, personal reminiscences of creative individuals' relatives, friends or lovers. The findings of some recent empirical studies have been inconsistent. Modern studies employ creativity tests thought to tap specific forms of thinking but these may be far removed from the creativity seen in a visual artist, a poet or a novelist. While we may still be able to describe creative individuals as bad or dangerous, their madness is still open to question.

Chapter review

Theories of intelligence

- Although intelligence is often represented by a single score – the IQ – modern investigators do acknowledge the existence of specific abilities. What is controversial is whether a general factor also exists.
- Factor analysis is a data reduction technique that attempts to explain a large amount of data with reference to one or two factors.
- Spearman argued that a general intelligence factor existed (which he called g) and demonstrated that people's scores on a variety of specific tests of ability were correlated. He also believed that specific factors (s factors) also existed.
- Thurstone performed a factor analysis on 56 individual tests that revealed the existence of seven factors, not a single g factor.
- Cattell's factor analysis on such data obtained two factors. The nature of the tests that loaded heavily on these two factors suggested the names fluid intelligence (g_f) and crystallised intelligence (g_c), with the former representing a person's native ability and the latter representing what a person learns.
- Sternberg's triarchic theory of intelligence attempts to integrate laboratory research using the information processing approach and an analysis of intelligent behaviour in the natural environment.
- According to Sternberg, we use componential intelligence to plan and execute tasks. We use experiential intelligence to apply past strategies to new problems. Finally, we use contextual intelligence to adapt to, select or shape our environment.
- Gardner's multiple intelligences theory is based primarily on the types of skill that can be selectively lost through brain damage. His definition of intelligence includes many abilities that are commonly regarded as skills or talents.
- Like Sternberg's theory, Gardner's theory emphasises the significance of behaviours to the culture in which they occur.
- The most consistent sex difference in cognition is for mental rotation – men are better at it than are females.
- Men overestimate their own IQ but both sexes rate their fathers and male children as having higher IQs than their mothers or female children.

Intelligence testing

- Although the earliest known instance of ability testing was carried out by the ancient Chinese, modern intelligence testing dates from the efforts of Galton to measure individual differences.
- Galton made an important contribution to the field of measurement, but his tests of simple perceptual abilities were abandoned in favour of tests that attempt to assess more complex abilities, such as memory, logical reasoning and vocabulary.
- Binet developed a test that was designed to assess students' intellectual abilities in order to identify children with special educational needs.
- Although the test that superseded his, the Stanford–Binet Scale, provided for calculation of IQ, Binet believed that 'intelligence' was actually a composite of several specific abilities. For him, the concept of mental age was a convenience, not a biological reality.
- Wechsler's two intelligence tests, the WAIS-III for adults (and its variants) and the WISC-R for children, are the most widely used tests of intelligence.
- The reliability of modern intelligence tests is excellent, but assessing their validity is still difficult. Because no single criterion measure of intelligence exists, intelligence tests are validated by comparing the scores with measures of achievement, such as scholastic success.
- Tests also need to be intelligible and quick to complete.
- Intelligence tests can have both good and bad effects on the people who take them. The principal benefit is derived by identifying children with special needs (or special talents) who will profit from special programmes.

The roles of heredity and environment

- Variability in all physical traits is determined by a certain amount of genetic variability, environmental variability and an interaction between genetic and environmental factors.
- The degree to which genetic variability is responsible for the observed variability of a particular trait in a particular population is called heritability or h.
- Heritability is not an indication of the degree to which the trait is determined by biological factors; rather, it reflects the relative proportions of genetic and environmental variability found in a particular population.
- Intellectual development is affected by many factors, both prenatal and post-natal. Potential intelligence can be permanently reduced during prenatal or post-natal development by injury, toxic chemicals, poor nutrition or disease.
- Twin studies and studies comparing biological and adoptive relatives indicate that both genetic and

environmental factors affect intellectual ability, which is probably not surprising. These studies also point out that not all of a person's environment is shared by other members of the family; each person is an individual and is exposed to different environmental variables.

- The evidence suggests that biological children who are adopted are intellectually more like their biological parents; this finding applies across all age ranges.
- Although there are differences between races in terms of IQ score, it is unclear whether this is due to heredity.

Intelligence, thinking and ageing

- As we age, a decline is seen in working memory, retrieval of names, reaction time, declarative memory, information processing. Functions such as vocabulary, however, see some improvement with age.
- The cognitive decline is thought to be principally caused by poor processing speed, which means we perform tasks less quickly and efficiently than we did when younger.
- General IQ scores will peak at around 25 years of age and decline up to 65 years. After 65, the score drops rapidly.
- At the most severe end of cognitive decline, there is dementia – the gradual and relentless loss in intellectual function (especially memory) as the individual reaches the sixth decade of life and beyond.
- The major cause of dementia is Alzheimer's disease and the condition is called Dementia of the Alzheimer Type. The disease is characterised by abnormal protein deposits (plaques and tangles) in the brain. There is also a familial/genetic form and an early-onset form (which may have a genetic cause).

Thinking

- Formal concepts are defined as lists of essential characteristics of objects and events. In everyday life, we use natural concepts – collections of memories of particular examples, called exemplars.
- Concepts exist at the basic, subordinate and superordinate levels. We do most of our thinking about concepts at the basic level.

- Deductive reasoning consists of inferring specific instances from general principles.
- One of the most important skills in deductive reasoning is the ability to construct mental models that represent problems.
- Inductive reasoning involves inferring general principles from particular facts. This form of thinking involves generating and testing hypotheses.
- Without special training (such as learning the rules of the scientific method), people often ignore relevant information, ignore the necessity of control groups or show a confirmation bias – the tendency to look only for evidence that confirms one's hypothesis.
- Jury decision-making is one important real-life example of reasoning, and jurors can reach decisions that do not follow logic and that are influenced by factors other than trial evidence (such as jury size, pre-existing beliefs, aspects of the trial and so on).
- Current evidence suggests that jurors evaluate evidence in a step-by-step manner and construct a meaningful narrative using the evidence they hear.
- Problem-solving is best represented spatially: we follow a path in the problem space from the initial state to the goal state, using operators to get to each intermediate state. Sometimes a problem fits a particular mould and can be solved with an algorithm – a cut-and-dried set of operations.
- However, in most cases, a problem must be attacked by following a heuristic – a general rule that helps guide our search for a path to the solution of a problem. The most general heuristic is means–ends analysis, which involves taking steps that reduce the distance from the current state to the goal. If obstacles are encountered, subgoals are created and attempts are made to reach them.
- The regions of the brain recruited most consistently during reasoning and decision-making are the prefrontal cortex and parietal lobe.
- Creativity has been defined in many ways but most psychologists agree that it describes a person's capacity to produce novel ideas, inventions, objects or products and to engage in successful problem-solving.
- Studies suggest a link between psychopathology (such as manic depression and depression) and creativity, but whether the link is causal is open to question.

Suggestions for further reading

Intelligence

Carson, S. (2011) The unleashed mind. *Scientific American Mind*, 22, 22–9.

Cotelli, M., Manenti, R., Zanetti, O. and Miniussi, C. (2012) Non-pharmacological intervention for memory decline. *Frontiers in Human Neuroscience*, 6, 46.

Deary, I.J. *et al.* (2010) The neuroscience of human intelligence. *Nature Review Neuroscience*, 11, 201–11.

Ellis, L. (2011) Identifying and explaining apparent universal sex differences in cognition and behavior. *Personality and Individual Differences*, 51, 552–61.

Flynn, J.R. (2009) *What is Intelligence?* Cambridge: Cambridge University Press.

Halpern, D.F., Benbow, C.P., Geary, D.C., Gur, R.C., Hyde, J.S. and Gernsbacher, M.A. (2007) The science of sex differences in science and mathematics. *Psychological Science in the Public Interest*, 8, 1, 1–51.

Neurobiology of Aging (2009), 30. This special issue features a series of articles on age-related cognitive decline.

Nisbett, R.E., Aronson, J., Blair, C., Dickens, W., Flynn, J., Halpern, D.F. and Turkheimer, E. (2012) Intelligence: New findings and theoretical developments. *American Psychologist*, 67, 130–59.

Sternberg, R.J., Kaufman, J.C. and Grigorenko, E. (2008) *Applied Intelligence*. Cambridge: Cambridge University Press.

Some very good items on intelligence . . .

Thinking and reasoning

Andre, D. and Fernand, G. (2008) Sherlock Holmes – an expert's view of expertise. *British Journal of Psychology*, 99, 109–25.

Blanchette, I. and Richards, A. (2010) The influence of affect on higher level cognition: A review of research on interpretation, judgment, decision making and reasoning. *Cognition & Emotion*, 24, 561–95.

Gilhooly, K. (1996) *Thinking: Directed, undirected and creative*. Oxford: Academic Press.

Goel, V. (2007) Anatomy of deductive reasoning. *Trends in Cognitive Sciences*, 11, 10, 435–41.

Holyoak, K.J. and Morrison, R.G. (2012) *The Oxford Handbook of Thinking and Reasoning*. Oxford: Oxford University Press.

Johnson-Laird, P.N. (2010) Mental models and human reasoning. *PNAS*, 107, 18243–50.

Kahneman, D. (2012) *Thinking, fast and slow*. London: Penguin.

Sutherland, S. (1992) *Irrationality*. London: Penguin.

Tavris, C. and Aronson, E. (2008) *Mistakes Were Made (but not by me)*. London: Pinter & Martin.

. . . and thinking and reasoning.

CHAPTER 5
Attitudes

Chapter contents

Focus questions

1 What meanings do you give to *attitude*? An animal lover may say that an attitude is the body posture a hunting dog assumes when indicating the presence of prey. A sports coach may say that a certain team player has an 'attitude problem', which refers to the player's state of mind. Is the term worth keeping in our psychological dictionary if it has several quite different everyday meanings?

2 Citizens sometimes say that paying research companies to ask people about their political attitudes is a waste of money. One poll may contradict another carried out at the same time, and poll predictions of who will be voted into power have not always been very reliable. Is there any use, therefore, in trying to link people's attitudes to people's behaviour?

3 Rita polls people's attitudes and believes she knows what makes them tick. Her advice to psychologists is: if you want to find out what people's attitudes are, ask them! Is she right?

4 People can sometimes be unaware of or conceal their attitudes – how can we reveal these hidden attitudes? Mahzarin Banaji outlines the nature of implicit attitudes and introduces the Implicit Association Test (IAT), a technique that has been used to reveal them, in Chapter 5 of MyPsychLab at **www.mypsychlab.com** (watch *Attitudes and attitude change*).

will use which involves getting you to decide to buy a car by giving you a very low price

Go to **MyPsychLab** to explore video and test your understanding of key topics addressed in this chapter.

MyPsychLab

Structure and function of attitudes

A short history of attitudes

Attitude
(a) A relatively enduring organisation of beliefs, feelings and behavioural tendencies towards socially significant objects, groups, events or symbols.
(b) A general feeling or evaluation – positive or negative – about some person, object or issue.

Attitude is a word that is part of our commonsense language. Many years ago, the social psychologist Gordon Allport referred to attitude as social psychology's most indispensable concept. In the 1935 *Handbook of Social Psychology,* which was highly influential at the time, he wrote:

> The concept of attitudes is probably the most distinctive and indispensable concept in contemporary American social psychology. No other term appears more frequently in the experimental and theoretical literature.
>
> Allport (1935, p. 798)

In the historical context in which Allport was writing, his view is not remarkable. Others, such as Thomas and Znaniecki (1918) and Watson (1930), had previously equated social psychology and attitude research – actually defining social psychology as the scientific study of attitudes! The early 1930s also witnessed the first generation of questionnaire-based scales to measure attitudes. According to Allport, an attitude is:

> a mental and neural state of readiness, organised through experience, exerting a directive or dynamic influence upon the individual's response to all objects and situations with which it is related.
>
> Allport (1935, p. 810)

Allport was not to know that such a fashionable concept would become the centre of much controversy in the decades ahead. For example, a radical behavioural view would emerge to argue that an attitude is merely a figment of the imagination – people invent attitudes to explain behaviour that has already occurred.

In charting the history of attitude research in social psychology, McGuire (1986) identified three main phases separated by periods of waning interest:

1 A concentration on attitude measurement and how these measurements related to behaviour (1920s and 1930s).

2 A focus on the dynamics of change in an individual's attitudes (1950s and 1960s).

3 A focus on the cognitive and social structure and function of attitudes and attitude systems (1980s and 1990s).

The word 'attitude' is derived from the Latin *aptus,* which means 'fit and ready for action'. This ancient meaning refers to something that is directly observable, such as a boxer in a boxing ring. Today, however, attitude researchers view 'attitude' as a construct that, although not directly observable, precedes behaviour and guides our choices and decisions for action.

Attitude research in psychology and the social sciences has generated enormous interest and many hundreds, probably thousands, of studies covering almost every conceivable topic about which attitudes might be expressed. During the 1960s and 1970s attitude research entered a period of pessimism and decline. To some extent, this was a reaction to concern about the apparent lack of relationship between expressed attitudes and overt behaviour.

However, during the 1980s attitudes again became a centre of attention for social psychologists, stimulated by cognitive psychology's impact on social psychology (see reviews by Olson and Zanna, 1993; Tesser and Shaffer, 1990). This resurgence included a significant focus on how information processing and memory, and affect and feelings might affect attitude formation and change (Haddock and Zanna, 1999; Lieberman, 2000; Murphy, Monahan and Zajonc,

1995). There has also been extensive research on attitude strength and accessibility, on how attitudes relate to behaviour (Ajzen, 2001), and on implicit measures of attitude (Crano and Prislin, 2006; Fazio and Olson, 2003b). Most recently there has been a focus on biochemical dimensions of attitude phenomena (Blascovich and Mendes, 2010) and on neural activity associated with attitudes (Stanley, Phelps and Banaji, 2008).

Here, we take the view that attitudes are basic to and pervasive in human life. In doing this, we will not take McGuire's evolutionary sequence too literally, as the three foci he refers to have always been, and continue to be, of interest to social psychologists. Without having attitudes, people would have difficulty in construing and reacting to events, in trying to make decisions and in making sense of their relationships with other people in everyday life. Attitudes continue to fascinate researchers and remain a key, if sometimes controversial, part of social psychology. Let us now look at the anatomy of an attitude.

Attitude structure

One of the most fundamental psychological questions that can be asked about attitudes is whether they are a unitary construct or whether they have a number of different components.

One component

Thurstone preferred a one-component attitude model, defining an attitude as 'the affect for or against a psychological object' (1931, p. 261). A later text focusing on how one constructs scales to measure attitudes reiterated this view: an attitude is 'the degree of positive or negative affect associated with some psychological object' (Edwards, 1957, p. 2). How simple can you get – do you like the object or not? With hindsight, it can be argued that the dominant feature of affect became the basis of a more sophisticated sociocognitive model proposed by Pratkanis and Greenwald (1989) (see next section).

> **One-component attitude model**
> An attitude consists of affect towards or evaluation of the object.

Two components

Allport (1935) favoured a two-component attitude model. To Thurstone's 'affect' Allport added a second component – a state of mental readiness. Mental readiness is a predisposition which has a relatively consistent influence on how we decide what is good or bad, desirable or undesirable, and so on. An attitude is therefore a private event. Its existence is unobservable externally and can only be inferred, perhaps by examining our own mental processes introspectively. As we see later, we might also make inferences by examining what we say and what we do. You cannot see, touch or physically examine an attitude; it is a hypothetical construct.

> **Two-component attitude model**
> An attitude consists of a mental readiness to act. It also guides evaluative (judgemental) responses.

Three components

A third view is the three-component attitude model, which has its roots in ancient philosophy:

> The trichotomy of human experience into thought, feeling, and action, although not logically compelling, is so pervasive in Indo-European thought (being found in Hellenic, Zoroastrian and Hindu philosophy) as to suggest that it corresponds to something basic in our way of conceptualisation, perhaps . . . reflecting the three evolutionary layers of the brain, cerebral cortex, limbic system, and old brain.
>
> McGuire (1989, p. 40)

> **Three-component attitude model**
> An attitude consists of cognitive, affective and behavioural components. This threefold division has an ancient heritage, stressing thought, feeling and action as basic to human experience.

The three-component model of attitude was particularly popular in the 1960s (e.g. Krech, Crutchfield and Ballachey, 1962; Rosenberg and Hovland, 1960). It was also represented in the later work of Himmelfarb and Eagly (1974), who described an attitude as a relatively enduring organisation of beliefs about, and feelings and behavioural tendencies towards socially significant objects, groups, events or symbols. Note that this definition not only included the three components but also emphasised that attitudes are:

- relatively *permanent*: that is, they persist across time and situations. A momentary feeling is not an attitude;
- limited to *socially significant* events or objects;
- *generalisable* and at least some degree of abstraction. If you drop a book on your toe and find that it hurts, this is not enough to form an attitude, because it is a single event in one place and at one time. But if the experience makes you dislike books or libraries, or clumsiness in general, then that dislike is an attitude.

Each attitude, then, is made up of thoughts and ideas, a cluster of feelings, likes and dislikes, and behavioural intentions. Other theorists who have favoured the three-component model include Ostrom (1968) and Breckler (1984).

Despite the appeal of the 'trinity', this model presents a problem by prejudging a link between attitude and behaviour (Zanna and Rempel, 1988), itself a thorny and complex issue that is dealt with in detail later in this section. Suffice to say that most modern definitions of attitude involve both belief and feeling structures and are much concerned with how, if each can indeed be measured, the resulting data may help predict people's actions. (Based on what you have read so far, try to answer the first focus question.)

Attitude functions

Presumably attitudes exist because they are useful – they serve a purpose, they have a function. The approaches we have considered so far make at least an implicit assumption of purpose. Some writers have been more explicit. Katz (1960), for example, proposed that there are various kinds of attitude, each serving a different function, such as:

- knowledge;
- instrumentality (means to an end or goal);
- ego defence (protecting one's self-esteem);
- value expressiveness (allowing people to display those values that uniquely identify and define them).

An attitude saves cognitive energy, as we do not have to figure out 'from scratch' how we should relate to the object or situation in question (Smith, Bruner and White, 1956), a function that parallels the utility of a schema and fits the cognitive miser or motivated tactician models of contemporary social cognition, and of a stereotype (e.g. Fiske and Taylor, 2008; **see Chapter 2**).

Russell Fazio (1989) later argued that the main function of any kind of attitude is a utilitarian one: that of object appraisal. This should hold regardless of whether the attitude has a positive or negative valence (i.e. whether our feelings about the object are good or bad). Merely possessing an attitude is useful because of the orientation towards the object that it provides for the person. For example, having a negative attitude towards snakes (believing they are dangerous) is useful if we cannot differentiate between safe and deadly varieties. However, for an attitude truly to fulfil this function it must be accessible. We develop this aspect of Fazio's thinking about attitude function when we deal below with the link between attitude and behaviour.

Cognitive consistency

In the late 1950s and 1960s cognitive consistency theories came to dominate social psychology, and their emphasis on cognition dealt a fatal blow to simplistic reinforcement

---

Schema
Cognitive structure that represents knowledge about a concept or type of stimulus, including its attributes and the relations among those attributes.

Stereotype
Widely shared and simplified evaluative image of a social group and its members.

Cognitive consistency theories
A group of attitude theories stressing that people try to maintain internal consistency, order and agreement among their various cognitions.

Cognition
The knowledge, beliefs, thoughts and ideas that people have about themselves and their environment. May also refer to mental processes through which knowledge is acquired, including perception, memory and thinking.

explanations (e.g. by learning theorists such as Thorndike, Hull and Skinner) in social psychology (Greenwald, Banaji, Rudman, Farnham, Nosek and Mellott, 2002). The best known of these theories was cognitive dissonance theory (Cooper, 2007; Festinger, 1957), which, because of its importance in explaining attitude change we deal with later in the text (**see Chapter 6**). Another early example was balance theory.

As well as specifying that beliefs are the building blocks of attitude structure, this family of theories focused on inconsistencies among people's beliefs. Consistency theories differ in how they define consistency and inconsistency, but they all assume that people find inconsistent beliefs aversive. Two thoughts are inconsistent if one seems to contradict the other, and such a state of mind is bothersome. This disharmony is known as *dissonance*. Consistency theories argue that people are motivated to change one or more contradictory beliefs so that the belief system as a whole is in harmony. The outcome is restoration of consistency.

Balance theory

The consistency theory with the clearest implications for attitude structure is Fritz Heider's balance theory (Heider, 1946; also see Cartwright and Harary, 1956). Heider's ideas were grounded in *Gestalt* psychology, an approach to perception popular in Germany in the early twentieth century and applied by Heider to interpersonal relations. *Gestalt* psychologists believed that the human mind is a person's 'cognitive field', and it comprises interacting forces that are associated with people's perceptions of people, objects and events.

Balance theory focuses on the P–O–X unit of the individual's cognitive field. Imagine a triad consisting of three elements: a person (P), another person (O), and an attitude, object or topic (X). A triad is consistent if it is balanced, and balance is assessed by counting the number and types of relationships between the elements. For instance, P liking X is a positive (+) relationship, O disliking X is negative (−), and P disliking O is negative (−).

There are eight possible combinations of relationships between two people and an attitude object, four of which are balanced and four unbalanced (Figure 5.1). A triad is balanced if there are an odd number of positive relationships and can occur in a variety of ways. If P likes O, O likes X and P likes X, then the triad is balanced. From P's point of view, balance theory acts as a divining rod in predicting interpersonal relationships: if P likes the object X, then any compatible other, O, should feel the same way. Likewise, if P already likes O, then O will be expected to evaluate object X in a fashion similar to P. By contrast, if P likes O, O likes X and P dislikes X, then the relationship is unbalanced. The principle of consistency that underlies balance theory means that in unbalanced triads people may feel tense and be motivated to restore balance. Balance is generally restored in a manner requiring the least effort. So, in the last example, P could decide not to like O or to change his/her opinion about X, depending on which is the easier option.

Unbalanced structures are usually less stable and more unpleasant than balanced structures. However, in the absence of contradictory information, people assume that others will like what they themselves like. Further, we often prefer to agree with someone else – or in balance-theory language, P and O seek structures where they agree rather than disagree about how they evaluate X (Zajonc, 1968). Again, people do not always seek to resolve inconsistency. Sometimes they organise their beliefs so that elements are kept isolated and are resistant to change (Abelson, 1968). For example, if P likes opera and O does not, and if P and O like each other, P may decide to isolate the element of opera from the triad by listening to opera when O is not present.

Overall, research on balance theory has been extensive and mostly supportive. For a more recent example of a study in this tradition, see Gawronski, Walther and Blank (2005).

Cognition and evaluation

We noted above the existence of a one-component view of attitudes – initially one in which affect reigns supreme (Thurstone, 1931), but subsequently focusing on evaluation as the core

Balance theory
According to Heider, people prefer attitudes that are consistent with each other, over those that are inconsistent. A person (P) tries to maintain consistency in attitudes to, and relationships with, other people (O) and elements of the environment (X).

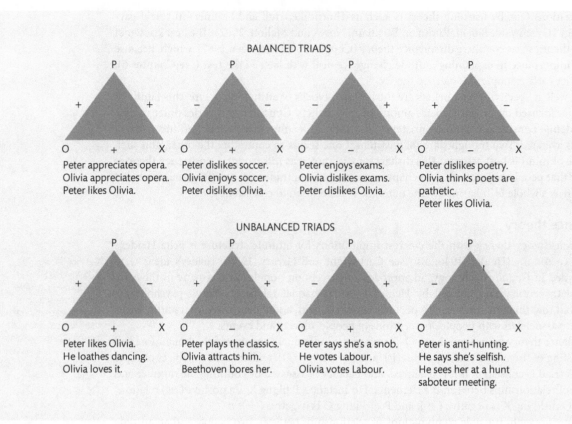

BALANCED TRIADS

Peter appreciates opera.
Olivia appreciates opera.
Peter likes Olivia.

Peter dislikes soccer.
Olivia enjoys soccer.
Peter dislikes Olivia.

Peter enjoys exams.
Olivia dislikes exams.
Peter dislikes Olivia.

Peter dislikes poetry.
Olivia thinks poets are
pathetic.
Peter likes Olivia.

UNBALANCED TRIADS

Peter likes Olivia.
He loathes dancing.
Olivia loves it.

Peter plays the classics.
Olivia attracts him.
Beethoven bores her.

Peter says she's a snob.
He votes Labour.
Olivia votes Labour.

Peter is anti-hunting.
He says she's selfish.
He sees her at a hunt
saboteur meeting.

Figure 5.1 Examples of balanced and unbalanced triads from Heider's theory of attitude change
In the balanced triads the relationships are consistent, in the unbalanced triads they are not

Sociocognitive model
Attitude theory highlighting
an evaluative component.
Knowledge of an object
is represented in memory
along with a summary of
how to appraise it.

component (e.g. Osgood, Suci and Tannenbaum, 1957). This simple idea resurfaces in a more complicated guise in Pratkanis and Greenwald's **sociocognitive model**, where an attitude is defined as 'a person's evaluation of an object of thought' (1989, p. 247). An attitude object (see Figure 5.2) is represented in memory by:

- an object label and the rules for applying that label;
- an evaluative summary of that object; and
- a knowledge structure supporting that evaluation.

For example, the attitude object we know as a 'shark' may be represented in memory as a really big fish with very sharp teeth (*label*); that lives in the sea and eats other fish and sometimes people (*rules*); is scary and best avoided while swimming (*evaluative summary*); and is a scientifically and fictionally well-documented threat to our physical well-being (*knowledge structure*). However, despite the cognitive emphasis, it was the evaluative component that Pratkanis and Greenwald highlighted.

The evaluative dimension of attitudes is of course a central focus of research on prejudice where the key problem is that members of one group harbour negative attitudes towards members of another group (Dovidio, Glick and Rudman, 2005; Jones, 1996; **see Chapter 10**). In the attitude literature, various terms have been used almost interchangeably in denoting this evaluative component, such as 'affect', 'evaluation', 'emotion' and 'feeling', suggesting an urgent need for the terminology to be tidied up and standardised (Breckler and Wiggins (1989a, 1989b). Recent research on affect and emotion (**discussed in Chapter 2**) has helped sort some of this out by theorising about the role of cognitive appraisals of stimuli in people's experience of

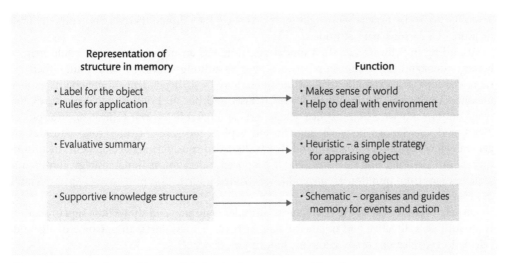

Figure 5.2 The sociocognitive model of attitude structure and function

This theory draws on research in social cognition and studies of memory. Just as physical objects or even people can be represented in memory, so too can an attitude object

Source: Based on Pratkanis and Greenwald (1989)

affect and emotion (e.g. Blascovich, 2008, Lazarus, 1991; see Keltner and Lerner, 2010). When we apply this knowledge to the study of an attitude, we can distinguish between *affect* (an emotional reaction to an attitude object) and *evaluation* (particular kinds of thought, belief and judgement about the object).

Decision making and attitudes

Do we perform cognitive algebra?

Information processing approaches emphasise how complex it is to acquire knowledge and to form and change our attitudes. According to information integration theory (Anderson, 1971, 1981; **see Chapter 2**), we use cognitive algebra to construct our attitudes from information we receive about attitude objects. People are sophisticated problem solvers and vigilant evaluators of new information. How we receive and combine this information provides the basis for attitude structure. The salience of some items and the order in which they are received become important determinants of the way in which they are processed. As new information arrives, people evaluate it and combine it with existing information stored in memory. For example, a warning from health authorities that a certain brand of food may cause serious illness may lead people to re-evaluate their attitude, change their behaviour and not eat that brand again.

In Norman Anderson's approach, we acquire and re-evaluate attitudes by using cognitive algebra. We 'mentally' average out the values attached to discrete bits of information that are collated and stored in memory about an attitude object. Ordinary people habitually use such mathematics: for example, if you think a friend is shy, energetic and compassionate, your overall attitude is an average of the evaluations you attach to those traits. You would calculate a different average for another friend who was outgoing, energetic and charismatic.

Attitudes and automatic judgements

As a challenge to classical attitude theory, Patricia Devine (1989) suggested that people's attitudes are underpinned by implicit and automatic judgements of which they are unaware. Because these judgements are automatic and unconscious, they are less influenced by *social*

Information processing
The evaluation of information; in relation to attitudes, the means by which people acquire knowledge and form and change attitudes.

Information integration theory
The idea that a person's attitude can be estimated by averaging across the positive and negative ratings of the object.

Cognitive algebra
Approach to the study of impression formation that focuses on how people combine attributes that have valence into an overall positive or negative impression.

desirability bias (i.e. how others might react). As such, they should therefore be a more reliable measure of a person's 'true' attitudes.

According to Schwarz (2000), a model of attitude as an implicit construct could help us better understand the relationship between people's attitudes and their behaviour. Others are more cautious. For example, implicit measures may be as dependent on context as explicit measures (attitudes), but in different ways (Glaser and Banaji, 1999). Implicit measures correlate only weakly with both explicit self-reports and overt behaviour (Hilton and Karpinski, 2000), and correlations between implicit and explicit measures of intergroup attitudes are generally low (Dovidio, Kawakami and Beach, 2001). In considering developments in attitude theory, van der Pligt and de Vries (2000) proposed a decision-making strategy continuum, which ranges from intuition at one end to controlled information processing (e.g. Anderson, 1971) at the other.

Dispute over the best way to characterise attitudes continues and shows little sign of abating. Is an attitude a directive and organised state of readiness (Allport), an outcome of algebraic calculation (Anderson) or an automatic judgement (Devine)?

Can attitudes predict behaviour?

Why study attitudes if scientists disagree about how best to define them? One answer is that attitudes may be useful for predicting what people will do – maybe if we change people's attitudes, we might be able to change their behaviour. Perhaps with tongue in cheek, Crano and Prislin have written in a recent review: 'Because attitudes predict behaviour, they are considered the crown jewel of social psychology' (2006, p. 360). As we shall see, a number of behavioural scientists have questioned this assumption.

For instance, Gregson and Stacey (1981) found only a small positive correlation between attitudes and self-reported alcohol consumption. Furthermore, there was no evidence of any benefits in focusing on attitude change rather than on economic incentives to control alcohol use (e.g. avoiding fines, increasing taxes). This sort of finding has caused some critics to question the utility of the concept of attitude: if attitude measures bear no relation to what people actually do, then what is the use of the concept? It is interesting that an early study of ethnic attitudes by LaPiere (1934) revealed a glaring inconsistency between what people do and what they say (see Box 5.1; **see also Chapter 10**).

Attitudes and behaviour
This voter is under surveillance. Will her selection reflect her own view, or might it be constrained by a prevailing norm?

Research classic 5.1
Do attitudes really predict behaviour?

The sociologist Richard LaPiere (1934) was interested in the difference between prejudiced attitudes towards Chinese in general and discriminatory behaviours towards a Chinese couple in particular. In the early 1930s, anti-Asian prejudice was quite strong among Americans. LaPiere embarked on a 10,000-mile sightseeing tour of the United States, accompanied by two young Chinese friends. They visited 66 hotels, caravan parks and tourist homes and were served in 184 restaurants. As they went from place to place, LaPiere was concerned that his friends might not be accepted but, as it turned out, they were refused service only once.

Six months after their trip, LaPiere sent a questionnaire to all the places they had visited, asking, 'Will you accept members of the Chinese race as guests in your establishment?' Of the 81 restaurants and 47 hotels that replied, 92 per cent said that they would *not* accept Chinese customers! Only 1 per cent said they would accept them, and the remainder checked 'Uncertain, depends on circumstances'. These written replies from the erstwhile hosts directly contradicted the way they had actually behaved.

This study was not, of course, scientifically designed – perhaps the people who responded to the letters were not those who dealt face-to-face with the Chinese couple; they might have responded differently in writing if they had been told that the couple was educated and well dressed; attitudes may have changed in the six months between the two measures. Nevertheless, the problem that LaPiere had unearthed provided an early challenge to the validity of the concept of attitude.

Following LaPiere's study, which vividly called into question the predictive utility of questionnaires, researchers have used more sophisticated methods to study the attitude–behaviour relationship; but still mainly found relatively low correspondence between questionnaire measures of attitudes and measures of actual behaviour. After reviewing this research, Wicker (1969) concluded that the correlation between attitudes and behaviour is seldom as high as 0.30 (which, when squared, indicates that only 9 per cent of the variability in a behaviour is accounted for by an attitude). In fact, Wicker found that the average correlation between attitudes and behaviour was only 0.15. This view was seized upon during the 1970s as damning evidence – the attitude concept is not worth a fig, since it has little predictive power. A sense of despair settled on the field (Abelson, 1972). Nevertheless, attitudes are still being researched (Banaji and Heiphetz, 2010; Fazio and Olson, 2003a), **and the topic commands two chapters of this book**.

What gradually emerged was that attitudes and overt behaviour are not related in a one-to-one fashion. There are conditions that promote or disrupt the correspondence between having an attitude and behaving (Doll and Ajzen, 1992; Smith and Stasson, 2000). For example, attitude–behaviour consistency can vary according to whether:

- an attitude is more rather than less accessible (see 'Attitude Accessibility');
- an attitude is expressed publicly, say in a group, or privately, such as when responding to a questionnaire;
- an individual identifies strongly or weakly with a group for which the attitude is normative.

Not all classes of social behaviour can be predicted accurately from verbally expressed attitudes. We look now at research that has explored why attitude–behaviour correspondence is often weak, and what factors may strengthen the correspondence.

Beliefs, intentions and behaviour

According to Martin Fishbein (1967a, 1967b, 1971), the basic ingredient of an attitude is affect, a position that reflects Thurstone's (1931) early definition. However, an attitude measure based

Table 5.1 A young man's hypothetical attitude towards contraceptive use: the strength and value of his beliefs

Attribute	Man's belief about woman using pill					Man's belief about man using condom				
	Strength of belief		Value of belief		Result	Strength of belief		Value of belief		Result
Reliability	0.90	×	+2	=	+1.80	0.70	×	−1	=	−0.70
Embarrassment	1.00	×	+2	=	+2.00	0.80	×	−2	=	−1.60
Side effects	0.10	×	−1	=	−0.10	1.00	×	+2	=	+2.00
Outcome					+3.70					−0.30

The strength of a belief, in this example, is the probability (from 0 to 1) that a person thinks that the belief is true. The value of a belief is an evaluation on a bipolar scale (in this case, ranging from +2 to −2).

entirely on a unidimensional, bipolar evaluative scale (such as good/bad) does not predict reliably how a person will later behave. Better prediction depends on an account of the interaction between attitudes, beliefs and behavioural intentions, and the connections of all of these with subsequent actions.

In this equation, we need to establish both how strong and how valuable a person's beliefs are: some beliefs will carry more weight than others in relation to the final act. For example, the strength or weakness of a person's religious convictions may be pivotal in their decision-making processes regarding moral behaviour – moral norms may play a very important role in attitude–behaviour relations (Manstead, 2000). Without this information, trying to predict an outcome for a given individual must inevitably be a hit-or-miss affair.

Consider the example in Table 5.1. A young, heterosexually active man might believe, strongly or not, that certain things are true about two forms of contraception, the pill and the condom. *Belief strength* (or expectancy) has a probability estimate, ranging from 0 to 1, regarding the truth; for example, he may hold a very strong belief (0.90) that the pill is a highly reliable method of birth control. Reliability of a contraceptive is a 'good' thing, so his *evaluation* (or value) of the pill is +2, say, on a five-point scale ranging from −2 to +2. Belief strength and evaluation interact, producing a final rating of +1.80. (Like Anderson, Fishbein's view incorporates the idea that people are able to perform cognitive algebra.)

Next, the young man might be fairly sure (0.70) that the condom is less reliable (−1), a rating of −0.70. Likewise, he thinks that using a condom is potentially embarrassing in a sexual encounter. His further belief that using a condom has no known side effects is not sufficient to offset the effects of the other two beliefs. Check the hypothetical algebra in Table 5.1. Consequently, the young man's intention to use a condom, should he possess one, may be quite low (perhaps he hopes that the women who cross his path use the pill!). Only by having all of this information could we be fairly confident about predicting his future behaviour.

This approach to prediction also offers a method of measurement, the expectancy–value technique. In subsequent work with his colleague Icek Ajzen, Fishbein developed the *theory of reasoned action* to link beliefs to intentions to behaviour (we return to this model later). Fishbein and Ajzen's work (Ajzen and Fishbein, 1980; Fishbein and Azjen, 1974) was a significant advance in understanding issues that had previously complicated the overall relationship between attitudes and behaviour. Predictions can be clarified when the inherent links are brought to the surface. Furthermore, behavioural predictions can be much improved if the measures of attitudes are specific rather than general.

Specific attitudes

Ajzen and Fishbein believed that success in predicting the way we behave is determined by asking whether we would perform a given act or series of acts. The key lies in asking questions that are quite specific rather than ones that deal with generalities.

Ajzen and Fishbein argued that much previous attitude research had suffered from either trying to predict specific behaviours from general attitudes or vice versa, so that low correlations were to be expected. This is, in essence, what LaPiere did. An example of a specific attitude predicting specific behaviour would be a student's attitude towards a psychology exam predicting how diligently he or she studies for that exam. In contrast, an example of a general attitude predicting a general class of behaviour would be attitudes towards psychology as a whole, predicting the behaviour generally relevant to learning more about psychology, such as reading magazine articles or talking with your tutor. How interested you are in psychology generally is not likely to be predictive of how well you prepare for a specific psychology exam.

In a two-year longitudinal study by Davidson and Jacard (1979), women's attitudes towards birth control were measured at different levels of specificity and used as predictors of their actual use of the contraceptive pill. The measures, ranging from very general to very specific, were correlated as follows with actual pill use (correlations in brackets): 'Attitude towards birth control' (0.08); 'Attitude towards birth control pills' (0.32); 'Attitude towards using birth control pills' (0.53); and 'Attitude towards using birth control pills during the next two years' (0.57). Thus, this last measure was the most highly correlated with actual use of the contraceptive pill. It indicates quite clearly that the closer the question was to the actual behaviour, the more accurately the behaviour was predicted. (See Kraus, 1995, for a meta-analysis of attitudes as predictors of behaviour.)

Meta-analysis
Statistical procedure that combines data from different studies to measure the overall reliability and strength of specific effects.

General attitudes

Fishbein and Ajzen (1975) also argued that we can predict behaviour from more general attitudes, but only if we adopt a multiple-act criterion. This criterion is a general behavioural index based on an average or combination of various specific behaviours. General attitudes usually predict multiple-act criteria much better than they predict single acts, because single acts are usually affected by many factors. For example, the specific behaviour of participating in a paper-recycling programme on a given day is a function of many factors, even the weather. Yet a person engaging in such behaviour may claim to be 'environmentally conscious', a general attitude. Environmental attitudes are no doubt one determinant of this behaviour, but they are not the only, or even perhaps the major, one.

Multiple-act criterion
Term for a general behavioural index based on an average or combination of several specific behaviours.

Reasoned action

The ideas outlined so far were integrated into a general model of the links between attitude and behaviour – the theory of reasoned action (Ajzen and Fishbein, 1980; Fishbein and Ajzen, 1974). The model encapsulated three processes of beliefs, intention and action and included the following components:

Theory of reasoned action
Fishbein and Ajzen's model of the links between attitude and behaviour. A major feature is the proposition that the best way to predict a behaviour is to ask whether the person intends to do it.

- *Subjective norm* – a product of what the person thinks others believe. Significant others provide direct or indirect information about 'what is the proper thing to do'.
- *Attitude towards the behaviour* – a product of the person's beliefs about the target behaviour and how these beliefs are evaluated (refer back to the cognitive algebra in Table 5.1). Note that this is an attitude towards behaviour (such as taking a birth control pill in Davidson and Jacard's study), not towards the object (such as the pill itself).
- *Behavioural intention* – an internal declaration to act.
- *Behaviour* – the action performed.

Usually, an action will be performed if (1) the person's attitude is favourable; and (2) the social norm is also favourable. In early tests of the theory, Fishbein and his colleagues (Fishbein and Feldman, 1963; Fishbein and Coombs, 1974) gave participants a series of statements about the attributes of various attitude objects: for example, political candidates. The participants estimated *expectancies* – that is, how likely it was that the object (candidate) possessed the various attributes – and gave the attributes a *value*. These expectancies and values were then used to predict the participants' feelings towards the attitude object, assessed by asking the participants how much they liked or disliked that object. The correlation between the scores and the participants' feelings was high, pointing to some promise for the model.

Other research reported that when people's voting intentions were later compared with how they actually voted, the correlations were:

- 0.80 in the 1976 American presidential election (Fishbein, Ajzen and Hinkle, 1980); and

- 0.89 in a referendum on nuclear power (Fishbein et al., 1980).

Overall if you know someone's very specific behavioural intentions then you are effectively almost there in terms of predicting what they will actually do – their behaviour. Meta-analyses of relevant research suggest this is the case but that some hurdles remain, for example to do with behavioural opportunities (Gollwitzer and Sheeran, 2006; Webb and Sheeran, 2006).

Planned behaviour: the role of volition

The theory of reasoned action (TRA) emphasises not only the rationality of human behaviour but also the belief that the behaviour is under the person's conscious control: for example, 'I know I can stop smoking if I really want to'. However, some actions are less under people's control than others.

Consequently, the basic model was extended by Ajzen (1989) to emphasise the role of volition. Perceived behavioural control is the extent to which the person believes it is easy or difficult to perform an act. The process of coming to such a decision includes consideration of past experiences, as well as present obstacles that the person may envisage. For example, Ajzen and Madden (1986) found that students, not surprisingly, want to get A-grades in their courses: A-grades are highly valued by the students (attitude), and they are the grades that their family and friends want them to get (subjective norm). However, prediction of actually getting an A will be unreliable unless the students' perceptions of their own abilities are taken into account.

Theory of planned behaviour
Modification by Ajzen of the *theory of reasoned action*. It suggests that predicting a behaviour from an attitude measure is improved if people believe they have control over that behaviour.

Ajzen has argued that perceived behavioural control can act on either the behavioural intention or directly on the behaviour itself. He referred to this modified model as the **theory of planned behaviour** (TPB). In a subsequent meta-analysis, Richard Cooke and Pascal Sheeran (2004) have referred to TPB as 'probably the dominant account of the relationship between cognitions and behaviour in social psychology' (2004, p. 159; also see Ajzen and Fishbein, 2005). The two theories, TRA and TPB, are not in conflict. The concepts and the way in which they are linked in each theory are shown in Figure 5.3.

In one study, Beck and Ajzen (1991) started with students' self-reports of the extent to which they had been dishonest in the past. The behaviour sampled included exam cheating, shoplifting and telling lies to avoid completing written assignments, actions that were quite often reported. They found that measuring the perception of control that students thought they had over these actions improved the accuracy of prediction of future actions, and, to some extent, the actual performance of the act. This was most successful in the case of cheating, which may well be planned in a more deliberate way than shoplifting or lying.

In another study, Madden, Ellen and Ajzen (1992) measured students' perceptions of control in relation to nine behaviours. These ranged from 'getting a good night's sleep' (quite hard to control) to 'taking vitamin supplements' (quite easy to control). The results were calculated to compare predictive power by squaring the correlation coefficient (i.e. r^2) between each of the two predictors (sleep and vitamins) and each of the outcomes (intentions and actions). Perceived control improved the prediction accuracy for both intentions and actions, and this improvement was substantially effective in predicting the action itself. These effects are evident in the steep gradient of the two lower lines in Figure 5.4, an outcome that has been confirmed in an independent study using a wide range of thirty behaviours (Sheeran, Trafimow, Finlay and Norman, 2002).

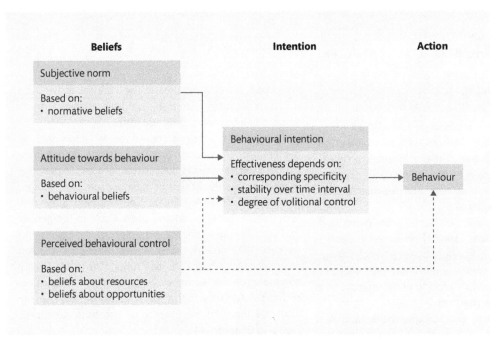

Figure 5.3 A comparison of the theory of reasoned action (TRA) and the theory of planned behaviour (TPB)

The solid lines show the concepts and links in the original theory of reasoned action; the dotted lines show an addition introduced in the theory of planned behaviour

Source: Based on Ajzen and Fishbein (1980); Madden, Ellen and Ajzen (1992)

Features of both models have been used to understand people's attitudes towards their health. Debbie Terry and her colleagues (Terry, Gallois and McCamish, 1993) have shown how Fishbein and Ajzen's concepts can be applied to the study of safe sex behaviour as a response to the threat of contracting HIV (see Box 5.2). Specifically, the target behaviour included monogamous relationships, non-penetrative sex and the use of condoms. All of the

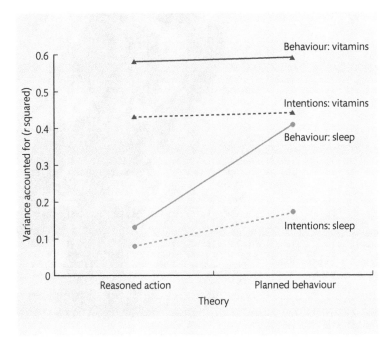

Figure 5.4 Theories of reasoned action and planned behaviour compared: the effect of including perceived behavioural control as a variable

Source: Based on data from Madden, Ellen and Ajzen (1992)

Social psychology in action 5.2
Reasoned action, planned behaviour and safe sex

TRA and TPB have proved useful in understanding and promoting responsible sexual behaviour

Social psychologists have increasingly turned their attention to promoting health practices such as avoiding the abuse of alcohol, tobacco and other substances; promoting dental hygiene; vaccinating against infectious diseases; participating in cervical smear tests; and using sun-screen products **(see also Chapter 6)**.

Another sphere of application has been the promotion of contraceptive practices to avoid unwanted pregnancies. Health professionals have also been concerned about the spread of HIV and contraction of AIDS. **(We noted in Chapter 2 that some people tend to underestimate the riskiness of their sexual practices.)**

In this context, social psychologists have mounted a concerted campaign of research promoting condom use, safe sex and monogamous relationships. Several researchers have explicitly recognised Fishbein and Ajzen's (Fishbein and Ajzen, 1974; Ajzen and Fishbein, 1980) theory of reasoned action as a model that helps to account for variability in people's willingness to practise safe sex (see Terry, Gallois and McCamish, 1993). One feature of this work has been to focus on establishing how much people feel they can actually exert control over their health. A woman with this sense of control is more likely to wear a seat belt, examine her breasts, use a contraceptive, have sex in an exclusive relationship, and discuss her partner's sexual and intravenous drug-use history.

Apart from a sense of control, other factors such as perceptions of condom proposers (those who initiate condom use), as well as the expectations and experience of safe sex, are implicated in initiating safe sex (Hodges, Klaaren and Wheatley, 2000). Coupled with these factors, cultural background also plays a role in the gender and sexuality equation. For example, Conley, Collins and Garcia (2000) found that Chinese Americans reacted more negatively than European Americans to the female condom proposer. Furthermore, Japanese Americans perceived the female condom proposer to be less sexually attractive than did the Chinese or European Americans **(see also Chapter 16)**.

A problem with practising safe sex with one's partner is that it is not a behaviour that comes completely under one individual's *volitional control*, whereas going for a run usually is. The theory of reasoned action, together with its extension, the theory of planned behaviour (see Figure 5.3), provides a framework for psychologists and other health professionals to target particular variables that have the potential to encourage safe sex, as well as other health behaviour.

Planned behaviour
The promotion of a health practice, such as breast self-examination, requires that a woman believes that she knows what to do and what to look for

variables shown in Figure 5.3 can be applied in this setting. In the context of practising safe sex, the particular variable of perceived behavioural control needs to be accounted for, particularly where neither of the sex partners may be fully confident of controlling the wishes of the other person. A practical question that may need to be examined is the degree of control that a woman might perceive she has about whether a condom will be used in her next sexual encounter.

In critically evaluating both TRA and TPB, Tony Manstead and Dianne Parker (1995) argued that the inclusion of 'perceived behavioural control' in TPB is an improvement on the original theory. In a meta-analysis by Armitage and Conner (2001), perceived behavioural control emerged as a significant variable and could account for up to 20 per cent of prospective actual behaviour.

TPB has also been applied to the prediction of driver behaviour in Britain (e.g. Parker, Manstead and Stradling, 1995; Conner, Lawton, Parker, Chorlton, Manstead and Stradling, 2007). Studies have measured both the intentions of drivers and their behaviours, such as speeding, cutting in, weaving recklessly and illegal overtaking on the inside lanes of a motorway. The study by Conner and his colleagues introduced actual behaviour measures – one a driving simulator, and the other real, on-road driving caught on a discreet camera. Their results suggest that the TPB can provide a basis for developing interventions designed to reduce speeding on the roads. The tendency to speed is based partly upon a driver's intentions to speed and partly on the absence of a moral norm not to speed (see below).

Aside from the usual variable associated with the TRA and TPB models, some researchers have pointed to the role of people's *moral values* in determining action (e.g. Gorsuch and Ortbergh, 1983; Manstead, 2000; Pagel and Davidson, 1984; Schwartz, 1977). For example, if someone wanted to find out whether we would donate money to charity, they would do well to find out whether acting charitably is a priority in our lives. In this specific context, Maio and Olson (1995) found that general altruistic values predicted charitable behaviour (donating to cancer research), but only where the context emphasised the *expression* of one's values. Where the context emphasised rewards and punishments (i.e. a utilitarian emphasis) values did not predict donating.

Habit is also a predictor of future behaviour in that an action can become relatively automatic (discussed in a later section in this chapter), and can operate independently of processes underlying TPB. Trafimow (2000) found that male and female students who were in the habit of using condoms reported that they would continue to do so on the next occasion. In effect, habitual condom users do not 'need' to use reasoned decisions, such as thinking about what their attitudes are or about what norms are appropriate. In a TPB study of binge drinking (Norman and Conner, 2006), the way that students viewed their drinking history could predict their future behaviour. For example, if Bill believes he is a binge drinker, he will attend less to his attitude towards alcohol abuse and will also feel that he has less control over how much he drinks.

Both the TRA and TPB models have implications for how we can strive for a healthy lifestyle (Connor, Norman and Bell, 2002; Stroebe, 2011). Likewise, in health psychology, **protection motivation theory** focuses on how people can make a start to protect their health, maintain better practices and avoid risky behaviour (see Box 5.3 and Figure 5.5).

Various issues to which these models have been applied include HIV prevention (Smith and Stasson, 2000), condom use and safer sex behaviour (Sheeran and Taylor, 1999), alcohol consumption (Conner, Warren, Close and Sparks, 1999), smoking (Godin, Valois, Lepage and Desharnais, 1992), and healthy eating (Connor, Norman and Bell, 2002). However, the models are not restricted to the health domain. For example, Fox-Cardamone, Hinkle and Hogue (2000) used TPB to examine antinuclear behaviour. Antinuclear attitudes emerged as significant predictors of either antinuclear intentions or behaviour. All three theories share the idea that motivation towards protection results from a perceived threat and the desire to avoid potential negative outcomes (Floyd, Prentice-Dunn and Rogers, 2000).

Protection motivation theory
Adopting a healthy behaviour requires cognitive balancing between the perceived threat of illness and one's capacity to cope with the health regimen.

Social psychology in action 5.3
Can we protect ourselves against major diseases?

According to statistics from the US Centers for Disease Control and Prevention, cardiovascular disease and cancer were by far the leading causes of death in the US in 2009; a statistic that prevails in most Western nations. It is well known that preventive behaviour for both diseases includes routine medical examinations, regular blood pressure readings, exercising aerobically for at least twenty minutes three times per week, eating a well-balanced diet that is low in salt and fat, maintaining a healthy weight and not smoking. It is a major challenge for health psychologists to find a model of health promotion that is robust enough to encourage people to engage in these preventative behaviours.

According to Floyd, Prentice-Dunn and Rogers (2000), protection motivation theory has emerged as just such a model. The model was developed initially to explain the effects of fear-arousing appeals on maladaptive health attitudes and behaviour, and was derived from Fishbein's theories of expectancy-value and reasoned action. Other components built into protection motivation theory included the effects of intrinsic and extrinsic reward (related to social learning theory) and Bandura's (1986, 1992) concept of self-efficacy, which in turn is closely related to that of *perceived behavioural control* in TPB (Ajzen, 1998).

From their meta-analysis of research based on sixty-five studies and more than twenty health issues, Floyd, Prentice-Dunn and Rogers argue that adaptive intentions and behaviour are facilitated by:

- an increase in the perceived severity of a health threat;
- the vulnerability of the individual to that threat;
- the perceived effectiveness of taking protective action; and
- self-efficacy.

In considering why Joe, for example, might either continue to smoke or decide to quit, protection motivation theory specifies two mediating cognitive processes:

1   *Threat appraisal* – smoking has intrinsic rewards (e.g. taste in mouth, nicotine effect) and extrinsic rewards (e.g. his friends think it's cool). These are weighed up against the extent to which Joe thinks there is a severe risk to his health (e.g. after reading the latest brochure in his doctor's waiting room) and that he is vulnerable (e.g. because a close relative who smoked died of lung cancer).

2   *Coping appraisal* – Joe takes into account response efficacy (whether nicotine replacement therapy might work) and self-efficacy (whether he thinks he can adhere to the regime).

The trade-off when Joe compares his appraisals of threat and coping determines his level of protection motivation and whether he decides to quit smoking (see Figure 5.5).

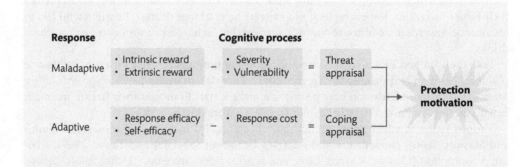

Figure 5.5 Mediating cognitive processes in protection motivation theory

This theory grew from psychological research into health promotion. Adopting a healthy practice will depend on several cognitive processes that lead to a balancing up of perceived threat versus the capacity to cope with a health regime

Source: Based on Floyd, Prentice-Dunn and Rogers (2000)

Self-efficacy
Expectations that we have about our capacity to succeed in particular tasks.

There is a reservation about TRA and TPB – it is assumed that attitudes are rational and socially significant behaviour is intentional, reasoned and planned. This may not always be true. How would you apply these theories to answer the second focus question?

Attitude accessibility

Most models of attitude feature a cognitive component, in that beliefs are the building blocks of the more general concept of attitude, and even approaches that emphasise an evaluative component agree on one matter: attitudes are represented in memory (Olson and Zanna, 1993).

Accessible attitudes are those that can be recalled from memory more easily and can therefore be expressed more quickly (Eagly and Chaiken, 1998). They can exert a strong influence on behaviour (Fazio, 1986) and are associated with greater attitude–behaviour consistency (Doll and Ajzen, 1992). They are also more stable, more selective in judging relevant information and more resistant to change (Fazio, 1995). There is some evidence that affective evaluations are faster than cognitive evaluations, suggesting more evaluative attitudes are more accessible in memory (Verplanken and Aarts, 1999; Verplanken, Hofstee and Janssen, 1998).

Most studies of attitude accessibility have focused on highly accessible attitudes, drawing on Fazio's (1995) model of attitudes as an association in memory between an object and an evaluation. The rationale behind Fazio's model is that the extent to which an attitude is 'handy' or functional and useful for the individual depends on the extent to which the attitude can be automatically activated in memory. The likelihood of automatic activation depends on the strength of the association between the object and the evaluation (Bargh, Chaiken, Govender and Pratto, 1992). Strong object–evaluation associations should therefore be highly functional because they help us make decisions.

Although the ideas behind attitude accessibility are intuitively appealing and supported by some research (e.g. Fazio, Ledbetter and Towles-Schwen, 2000), there is also some evidence that implicit measures (as object–evaluation associations) correlate only weakly with explicit self-reports, what people actually say (Hilton and Karpinski, 2000). We return to this topic later in this chapter when we examine how attitudes are measured.

As well as facilitating decision making, accessible attitudes orientate visual attention and categorisation processes (Roskos-Ewoldsen and Fazio, 1992; Smith, Fazio and Cejka, 1996), and free up resources for coping with stress (Fazio and Powell, 1997). How might accessible attitudes affect the way we categorise? Smith, Fazio and Cejka (1996) showed that, when choosing from a number of possible categories to describe an object, we are more likely to select an accessible one. For example, when participants rehearsed their attitudes towards dairy products, yoghurt was more likely to cue as a *dairy product*. On the other hand, if attitudes towards health food were experimentally enhanced, and therefore made more accessible in memory, yoghurt was more likely to cue as a *health food* (Eagly and Chaiken, 1998).

Fazio's studies confirmed earlier findings that perceptions of stimuli will probably be biased in the direction of an individual's attitude (Lambert, Solomon and Watson, 1949; Zanna, 1993). However, he also showed that costs are associated with highly accessible attitudes. Recall that accessible attitudes are stable over time. Thus, if the object of an attitude changes, accessible attitudes towards that object may function less well (Fazio, Ledbetter and Towles-Schwen, 2000). Accessibility can produce insensitivity to change – we have become set in our ways. Consequently, someone who feels negatively about a particular attitude object may not be able to detect if the 'object' has changed for better or perhaps worse (see Box 5.4).

Another way to conceptualise accessibility is in the language of *connectionism*. An accessible attitude is a cognitive node in the mind that is well connected to other cognitive nodes (thorough learning and perhaps conditioning), and so the focal attitude can be activated in many

Social psychology in action 5.4
Accessible attitudes can be costly

There may be costs associated with highly accessible attitudes. Fazio, Ledbetter and Towles-Schwen (2000) tested this idea in several experiments using computer-based morphing. Twenty-four same-sex digital facial photographs were paired so that one image in each pair was relatively attractive and one was not, based on earlier data. Five morphs (composites) of the images of each pair were created that varied in attractiveness determined by the percentage (e.g. 67 / 33, 50 / 50, 13 / 87) that each image contributed to a morph.

In part 1 of an experimental sequence, participants 'formed' attitudes that were either highly accessible (HA) or less accessible (LA). HA participants verbally rated how attractive each morph was, whereas LA participants verbally estimated the morph's probable physical height. Part 2 involved the detection of change in an image. Participants were told that they would see more faces, some of which were different photographs of people they had already seen, and they were to choose both quickly and accurately whether each image was the same or different from those seen earlier. HA participants were slower to respond than LA participants and also made more errors than LA participants. In an experimental variation, they also noticed less change in a morphed image.

All attitudes are functional and accessible attitudes even more so, since they usually deal with objects, events and people that are stable. However, if the attitude object changes over time then a highly accessible attitude may become dysfunctional – it is stuck in time.

different ways and along many different cognitive paths. According to Frank Van Overwalle and Frank Siebler:

> This allows a view of the mind as an adaptive learning mechanism that develops accurate mental representations of the world. Learning is modeled as a process of online adaptation of existing knowledge to novel information . . . the network changes the weights of the connections with the attitude object so as to better represent the accumulated history of co-occurrences between objects and their attributes and evaluations.

Van Overwalle and Siebler (2005, p. 232)

Attitude strength
If your home had been bulldozed how do you think you would feel?

Van Overwalle and Siebler suggest that a connectionist approach is consistent with: (1) dual-process models of attitude change **(see Chapter 6)**, and (2) the notion of algebraic weights placed on beliefs, introduced by Fishbein (see the example in Table 5.1).

Attitude strength and direct experience

Do strong attitudes guide behaviour? The results of a study of attitudes towards Greenpeace suggest so (Holland, Verplanken and Van Knippenberg, 2002). People with very positive attitudes towards Greenpeace were much more likely to make a donation to the cause than those with weak positive attitudes.

Almost by definition, strong attitudes must be highly accessible. They come to mind more readily and exert more influence over behaviour than weak attitudes. Fazio argued that attitudes are evaluative associations with objects, which makes his approach a one-component model. Associations can vary in strength from 'no link' (i.e. a non-attitude), to a weak link, to a strong link. Only an association that is strong allows the automatic activation of an attitude (Fazio, 1995; Fazio, Blascovich and Driscoll, 1992; Fazio and Powell, 1997; Fazio, Sanbonmatsu, Powell and Kardes, 1986; see Figure 5.6). As we go about our daily activities: 'we seamlessly and spontaneously evaluate the stimuli in our paths, including physical objects, people, words, pictures, faces, letters, and even odors' (Ferguson, 2007, p. 596).

Direct experience of an object and having a vested interest in it (i.e. something with a strong effect on your life) make the attitude more accessible and strengthen its effect on behaviour. For example, people who have had a nuclear reactor built in their neighbourhood will have stronger and more clearly defined attitudes regarding the safety of nuclear reactors. These people will be more motivated by their attitudes – they may be more involved in protests or more likely to move house.

Automatic activation
According to Fazio, attitudes that have a strong evaluative link to situational cues are more likely to come automatically to mind from memory.

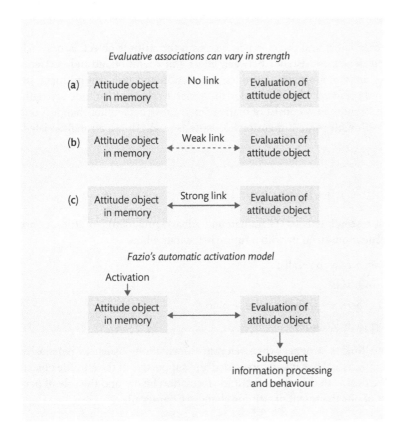

Figure 5.6 When is an attitude accessible?

A stronger attitude is more accessible than a weaker attitude. It can be automatically activated and will exert more influence over behaviour

As another example, consider attitudes towards doctor-assisted suicide (Haddock, Rothman, Reber and Schwarz, 1999). As subjective experience with this form of dying increased – its certainty, intensity and importance – the corresponding attitude about doctor-assisted suicide became stronger. It became more certain, intense and important.

The more often you *think* about an attitude, the more likely it is to resurface and influence your behaviour through easier decision making (Fazio, Blascovich and Driscoll, 1992). Powell and Fazio (1984) were able to make an attitude more accessible simply by asking on six different occasions what people's attitudes were as opposed to asking them only once. Accessing general attitudes can affect behaviour in specific situations. If the general attitude is never accessed, it cannot affect behaviour. Therefore, the activation step of Fazio's model is critical, since only activated attitudes can guide subsequent information processing and behaviour. Think of a sports coach priming a team by asking the question 'Which is the greatest team?' demanding a shouted response of 'We are!' and repeating this scenario a number of times before the match begins.

In addition to the role of strength, an attitude becomes more accessible as direct experience with the attitude object increases. Attitudes formed through actual experience are more consistently related to behaviour (Regan and Fazio, 1977; Doll and Ajzen, 1992). Suppose Mary has participated in several psychology experiments but William has only read about them. We can predict Mary's willingness to participate in the future more accurately than William's (Fazio and Zanna, 1978). Another example: your attitude to UFOs is far less likely to predict how you will act should you encounter one (!) than your attitude to lecturers is likely to predict your lecture room behaviour. Likewise, it would be reassuring to think that those people who had been caught driving with excessive blood alcohol levels would be less likely to drink and drive in the future. Unfortunately, this is not always the case.

Therefore, although direct experience seems appealing as an influence on attitude accessibility, establishing its actual effectiveness is a difficult task. We consider the role of direct experience again in the context of attitude formation in a later section in this chapter.

Apart from attitude accessibility and direct experience with the attitude object, issues such as attitude salience, ambivalence, consistency between affect and cognition, attitude extremity, affective intensity, certainty, importance, latitudes of rejection and non-commitment are common themes in attitude research that fall under the general rubric of 'attitude strength'. Not surprisingly, attitude strength may consist of many related constructs rather than just one (Krosnick et al., 1993). Although some dimensions of attitude strength are strongly related, most are not.

Reflecting on the attitude–behaviour link

Let us take stock of what research tells us (Glassman and Albarracín, 2006). As attitudes are being *formed,* they correlate more strongly with a future behaviour when:

- the attitudes are *accessible* (easy to recall);
- the attitudes are *stable over time*;
- people have had *direct experience* with the attitude object;
- people *frequently report* their attitudes.

The attitude–behaviour link is stronger when relevant information – such as persuasive arguments – is relevant to the actual behaviour, one-sided and supportive of the attitude object, rather than two-sided. We deal with the topic of attitude formation below, and the role of persuasive arguments is part of our treatment of attitude change (**Chapter 6**).

Moderator variables

Although it is difficult to predict single acts from general attitudes, prediction can be improved by the addition of a moderator variable that specifies conditions under which the attitude–behaviour relationship is stronger or weaker. Moderators include the situation, personality, habit, sense of control and direct experience. The attitude itself can also act as a moderator – for example an attitude that functions to emphasise a person's self-concept and central values has stronger attitude–behaviour correspondence than one that simply maximises rewards and minimises punishments (Verplanken and Holland, 2002; Maio and Olson, 1994). Ironically, moderator variables may turn out to be more powerful predictors of an action than the more general, underlying attitude. We consider two cases.

Moderator variable
A variable that qualifies an otherwise simple hypothesis with a view to improving its predictive power (e.g. A causes B, but only when C (the moderator) is present).

Situational variables

Aspects of the situation, or context, can cause people to act in a way that is inconsistent with their attitudes (Calder and Ross, 1973). Weak attitudes are particularly susceptible to context (Lavine, Huff, Wagner and Sweeney, 1998), and in many cases what tends to happen is that social norms that are contextually salient overwhelm people's underlying attitudes. For instance, if university students expect each other to dress in jeans and casual clothes, these expectations represent a powerful norm for how students dress on campus.

Norms have always been considered important in attitude–behaviour relations, but they have generally been separated from attitudes: attitudes are 'in here' (private, internalised cognitive constructs), norms are 'out there' (public, external pressures representing the cumulative expectations of others). This view of norms has been challenged by social identity theory (**see Chapter 11**), which sees no such distinction – attitudes can be personal and idiosyncratic but much more typically they are a normative property of a group and group identification causes one to internalise the group's normative properties, including its attitudes, as an aspect of self (e.g. Abrams and Hogg, 1990a; Hogg and Smith, 2007; Turner, 1991; **see Chapter 7**).

This idea has been applied to attitude–behaviour relations to argue that attitudes are more likely to express themselves as behaviour if the attitudes and associated behaviour are normative properties of a contextually salient social group with which people identify (Hogg and Smith, 2007; Terry and Hogg, 1996; Terry, Hogg and White, 2000). To test this, Terry and Hogg (1996) conducted two longitudinal questionnaire studies of students' intentions to take regular exercise and to protect themselves from the sun. These intentions were stronger when participants identified strongly with a self-relevant student peer group whom participants believed took regular exercise or habitually protected themselves from the sun (Figure 5.7).

Individual differences

Social psychologists tend to be divided into two camps – those who prefer situational explanations of social behaviour and those who prefer personality and individual difference explanations (Ross and Nisbett, 1991). Although this distinction has become less stark in recent years (Funder and Fast, 2010) it nevertheless has impacted attitude research. For example, Mischel (1968) argued that situational characteristics were more reliable predictors of behaviour than were personality traits (**see also the weak correlations reported between personality measures and leadership in Chapter 9**). Whereas Bem and Allen (1974) and Vaughan (1977) have shown that people who were consistent in their *answers* on a personality scale were more likely to be consistent in their *behaviour* across a variety of relevant situations than people who gave variable answers. For example, a high scorer on an extraversion–introversion scale would be more likely to behave in an extroverted manner and a low scorer in an introverted manner, across different social settings. On the other hand, those who were variable (mid-range scorers) in their answers on the scale would not behave consistently.

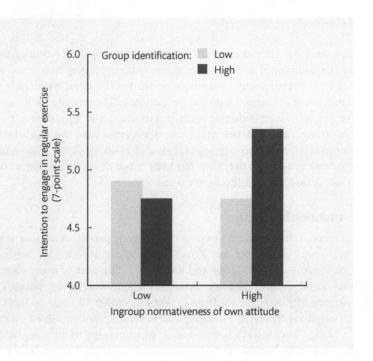

Figure 5.7 The role of norms and group identification in attitude–behaviour consistency

Students expressed a stronger intention to engage in regular exercise when they felt their attitudes towards exercise were normative of a student peer group with which they identified strongly

Source: Based on data by Terry and Hogg (1996)

It is therefore useful to know how people's behavioural *habits* are related to their *degree of control* over the behaviour (Langer, 1975; Petty and Cacioppo, 1981; Triandis, 1980; Verplanken, Aarts, van Knippenberg and Moonen, 1998) – the study of habits has experienced a recent revival (see Neal, Wood, Labrecque and Lally, 2012; Wood and Neal, 2007). Triandis (1977) proposed a model similar to Fishbein and Ajzen's, which included a habit factor to reflect the number of times a person had performed a particular action in the past. Smoking, for instance, is habitual for many people and is often partly due to a physiological and/or psychological dependency. Thus, the behaviour of smokers may bear little relationship to their attitudes towards cigarettes. Oskamp (1984) reported that about 70 per cent of smokers agreed that 'smoking is one of the causes of lung cancer', and that 'cigarette smoking causes disease and death'.

In a review of research on 'habit', Bas Verplanken and Henk Aarts (1999) concluded that the relationship between attitudes and behaviour and between intentions and behaviour were near zero when habits were strong but sizeable when habits were weak. However, psychologists are fiercely vigilant in protecting their theories! In this instance, Ajzen (2002) does not see an inconsistency between habitual behaviour and planned behaviour:

> The theory of planned behavior [and of reasoned action] does not propose that individuals review their behavioral, normative, and control beliefs prior to every enactment of a frequently performed behavior. Instead, attitudes and intentions – once formed and well-established – are assumed to be activated automatically and to guide behavior without the necessity of conscious supervision.
>
> Ajzen (2002, p. 108)

Mood as a moderator variable may be considered both a situational and a personality variable. Carolyn Semmler and Neil Brewer (2002) examined the effects of trial-induced mood on how jurors processed information and made decisions. They found that being sad did not affect a juror's judgement, despite an increase in irrelevant thought. However, angry jurors actually reported more irrelevant thoughts, detected fewer inconsistencies in the witness's testimony and judged the defendant more harshly.

If we replace 'mood' with terms like 'affect' and 'emotion', we invoke part of the three-component model of attitude structure discussed earlier. In this wider context, there has been considerable research into affect-based evaluations of an attitude object (e.g. 'I hate broccoli, but I love ice cream') especially in the context of persuasion and advertising (**see Chapter 6**).

Cognitive biases, one of which is self–other discrepancy (**see Chapter 4**), are also moderators of attitude–behaviour correspondence. Angela Paglia and Robin Room (1999) studied what more than 800 people expected to happen when they drank alcohol and also how readily available they thought alcohol should be. They found that support for tighter control over alcohol availability stems partly from what people expect to happen, both from their own drinking and from the drinking of others. There was a distinct self–other discrepancy: people expect alcohol to affect others more adversely than themselves! Furthermore, the greater the bias the greater the support for alcohol restriction.

Finally, some people are more focused than others on what has been called their *self-identity* – their sense of who they are as defined by the roles they occupy in society; although similar to social identity (**see Chapter 11**) self-identity is more focused on roles than group membership (Terry, Hogg and White, 1999; **also see Chapter 4**). Self-identity has been viewed as an influence on people's intentions to act, which is a component of the theory of planned behaviour, discussed above (Hagger and Chatzisarantis, 2006). In one study, people were more likely to express an intention to donate blood if being a blood donor was an important part of their self-identity (Charng, Piliavin and Callero, 1988).

Forming attitudes

Attitudes are learnt as part of the socialisation process (Fishbein and Ajzen, 1975; McGuire, 1969; Oskamp, 1977). They may develop through direct experiences or vicariously through interactions with others, or be a product of cognitive processes and thought. Generally, social psychologists have confined their work to understanding the basic psychological processes that underlie attitude formation rather than exploring how particular classes of attitude develop. The study of these processes usually involves laboratory experiments rather than survey or public opinion research.

Attitude formation
The process of forming our attitudes, mainly from our own experiences, the influences of others and our emotional reactions.

Behavioural approaches

Effects of direct experience

Many of the attitudes that people hold are the products of direct experience with attitude objects. There are several explanations for this process: mere exposure, classical conditioning, operant conditioning, social learning theory and self-perception theory.

Direct experience provides us with information about the attributes of an object, and helps to shape beliefs that influence how much we like or dislike the object (Fishbein and Ajzen, 1975). Even a mildly traumatic experience can trigger a negative attitude (Oskamp, 1977; Sargant, 1957), and make certain beliefs more salient than others. If your first visit to the dentist is painful, you may conclude that dentists hurt rather than help you, despite their friendly smile.

Mere exposure to an object on several occasions is likely to affect how we evaluate it – the mere exposure effect (Zajonc, 1968). The first time you hear a new song on the radio, you may find you neither strongly like nor dislike it, but with repetition your response in one direction or the other is likely to strengthen. However, the effect of continued repeated exposure diminishes. For example, increased liking for photos of people levelled off after about ten exposures (Bornstein, 1989). Mere exposure has most impact when we lack information about an issue. Sitting MPs, for example, usually have an advantage over other candidates in an election, simply because their names are more familiar.

Mere exposure effect
Repeated exposure to an object results in greater attraction to that object.

Classical conditioning
An intimate and relaxed setting induces a good mood. It is an easy step to associate this mood with someone who is immediately present, increasing mutual liking

Classical conditioning

Evaluative conditioning
A stimulus will become more liked or less liked when it is consistently paired with stimuli that are either positive or negative.

Repeated association may cause a formerly neutral stimulus to elicit a reaction that was previously elicited only by another stimulus. In the more specific case of evaluative conditioning, the degree of *liking* an object will change when it is consistently paired with other stimuli that are either positive or negative (De Houwer, Thomas and Baeyens, 2001). For example, children may initially be indifferent to politics but later vote as young adults for a party after years of exposure to a parent who has been an enthusiastic supporter – a classically conditioned response has become the basis of a subsequent political attitude. Classical conditioning may underlie the formation of a wide variety of attitudes (Zanna, Kiesler and Pilkonis, 1970). There is limited experimental evidence that both positive and negative attitudes towards otherwise neutral stimuli can form at a subliminal level, i.e. below conscious awareness (Krosnick, Betz, Jussim and Lynn, 1992; Olson and Fazio, 2002). However, a recent meta-analysis suggested caution about the strength of a subliminal effect pending further research (Hofmann, Hofmann, De Houwer, Perugini, Baeyens and Crombez, 2010).

Classical conditioning can be a powerful, even insidious, form of attitude learning. One study demonstrated the power of contextual stimuli by reinforcing some participants with soft drinks while they were reading a persuasive message (Janis, Kaye and Kirschner, 1965). Those given soft drinks were more persuaded by what they read than those who were not. In another study, participants listened to pleasant guitar music as an accompaniment to persuasive messages presented as folk songs. The songs proved more persuasive when accompanied by guitar music than without (Galizio and Hendrick, 1972). We may reasonably conclude that the positive feelings associated with the soft drinks or with guitar music became associated, via classical conditioning, with the persuasive messages.

Spreading attitude effect
A liked or disliked person (or attitude object) may affect not only the evaluation of a second person directly associated but also others merely associated with the second person.

An interesting corollary to this line of research is the spreading attitude effect. Eva Walther (2002) gives this example: Mary is at a conference where she notices Peter and Paul talking. She barely knows either one – they are affectively neutral. Then she sees Peter talking with Marc, someone she dislikes. First, Peter is now less likeable (evaluative conditioning); second, Paul is also less likeable (the spreading attitude effect). Peter's bad company has had a ripple effect on someone merely associated with him (in this case, Paul).

Instrumental conditioning

Behaviour that is followed by positive consequences is reinforced and is more likely to be repeated, whereas behaviour that is followed by negative consequences is not. For example, parents use verbal reinforcers to encourage acceptable behaviour in their children – quiet, cooperative play wins praise. There have been several studies of the effects of positive reinforcement on prosocial *behaviour,* such as rewarding when they behave generously – see the study by Rushton and Teachman (1978) for an example (**Chapter 13**, **Figure 13.3**). However, when they fight a reward is withheld or a punishment such as scolding is introduced. Instrumental learning can be accelerated or slowed by the frequency, temporal spacing and magnitude of the reinforcement (Kimble, 1961).When parents reward or punish their children they are shaping their *attitudes* on many issues, including religious or political beliefs and practices.

Adults' attitudes can also be shaped by verbal reinforcers. Chester Insko (1965) showed that students' responses to an attitude survey had been influenced by an apparently unrelated telephone conversation, which took place a week earlier, in which particular opinions were 'rewarded' by the interviewer responding with the reinforcer 'good'.

Both classical and instrumental conditioning emphasise the role of direct reinforcers in how behaviour is acquired and maintained. This is relevant to attitudes when we define an attitude as a class of behaviour, and becomes fairly straightforward if an attitude is further operationalised as an *evaluative response* (Fishbein, 1967a; Osgood, Suci and Tannenbaum, 1957).

Observational learning

Other psychologists view attitude formation as a *social* learning process, one that does not depend on direct reinforcers. Bandura (1973) and others concentrated on a process of **modelling** (**see also Chapters 12 and 14**), where one person's behaviour is a template for another's. Modelling requires observation: people learn new responses, not by directly experiencing positive or negative outcomes but by observing the outcomes of others' responses. Having a successful working mother, for instance, is likely to influence the future career and

Modelling
Tendency for a person to reproduce the actions, attitudes and emotional responses exhibited by a real-life or symbolic model. Also called *observational learning.*

Observational learning
So that's how you cook vegetables! Young children model their behaviour on significant adults

lifestyle choices of a daughter. Likewise, ethnic attitudes can be instilled in otherwise naive children if the models are significant adults in their lives. This can be seen in children who use ethnic slurs and insults, and claim to hate a certain ethnic group, but who are unable correctly to define the group or have no factual knowledge about its members (Allport, 1954b; **see also Chapter 11**).

Cognitive development

Other social psychologists prefer to think of attitude formation in terms of cognitive development. Cognitive consistency theories (such as balance; and cognitive dissonance, **treated in Chapter 6**) allow us to view attitude acquisition as an elaborative exercise of building connections (balanced or consonant) between more and more elements (e.g. beliefs). As the number of related elements increases, it is more likely that a generalised concept – an attitude – is being formed. Similarly, information integration theory can conceptualise attitude learning as a phenomenon in which more and more items of information about an attitude object have been processed (say, by averaging their weights).

A difference between cognitive and behavioural approaches is the relative weight that each gives to internal events versus external reinforcement. Although social cognition has become the dominant paradigm in social psychology (**Chapters 2 and 3**) we should not ignore some advantages of behavioural approaches. The latter are linked to the study of learning and often deal directly with developmental data (generated from studies of animals or children). Thus, learning theories continue to appeal to social psychologists who study attitude acquisition.

One interesting approach with both a behavioural and a perceptual flavour is Bem's (1972) **self-perception theory (see Chapter 4 for details)**. Bem proposed that people acquire knowledge about what kind of person they are, and thus their attitudes, by examining their own behaviour and asking: 'Why did I do that?' A person may act for reasons that are not obvious and then determine their attitude from the most readily available cause. For example, if you often go for long walks, you may conclude that 'I must like them, as I'm always doing that'. Bem's theory suggests that people act, and form attitudes, without much deliberate thinking.

Self-perception theory
Bem's idea that we gain knowledge of ourselves only by making self-attributions: for example, we infer our own attitudes from our own behaviour.

Sources of learning

Parents

An important source of your attitudes is the actions of other people around you. For children their parents are a powerful influence, involving all the kinds of learning mentioned above (classical conditioning, instrumental conditioning and observational learning). However, although the correlation between the *specific* attitudes of parents and their children is generally positive, it is also surprisingly weak; the correlation is stronger for *broad* attitudes (Connell, 1972).

Jennings and Niemi (1968) found a 0.60 correlation between high-school children's preferences for a particular political party and their parents' choices, and a correlation of 0.88 between parents' and children's choices of religion. Of course, such correlations may be constrained by parental opposition, a common experience of adolescents. Many high-school pupils deliberately adopt, or appear to adopt, attitudes that are inconsistent with their parents' merely to be contrary. In a longitudinal study of values, Kasser, Koestner and Lekes (2002) found strong links between childhood environmental factors, such as parenting behaviour, and later adult values. Restrictive parenting, for example, experienced at age five was reflected in higher conformity values and lower self-directed values in adulthood. Values are discussed later in this chapter.

Mass media

The mass media have a major influence on attitudes, and there is little question that visual media, in particular television, play an important part in attitude formation in children, particularly when attitudes are not strongly held (Goldberg and Gorn, 1974). A study by Chaffee, Jackson-Beeck, Durall and Wilson (1977) showed that, before age seven, American children got most of their political information from television and that this affected their views on politics and political institutions (Atkin, 1977; Rubin, 1978).

Among adults, MacKay and Covell (1997) reported a relationship between viewing sexual images of women in advertisements and holding attitudes sympathetic to sexual aggression **(see also Chapter 12)**. While the impact of television on adults is generally less clear-cut (Oskamp, 1984), some discernible trends occur on a larger scale. Kellstedt (2003) conducted an extensive statistical analysis of changes in Americans' racial attitudes over the last half-century. He found that media coverage does more than reflect public opinion – it has helped shape it. Long periods of liberalism have been followed by periods of conservatism, and these eras have responded to cues in the American media.

The impact of commercials on children's attitudes has also been investigated. Atkin (1980) found that children who watched a lot of television were twice as likely as those who watched a little to believe that sugar-coated sweets and cereals were good for them. In the same study, two-thirds of a group of children who saw a circus strong man eat a breakfast cereal believed it would make them strong too! These findings are of particular concern in the light of murders committed by young children (e.g. the murder in Liverpool in 1993 of 2-year-old James Bulger by two 10-year-old boys), and carried out in ways similar to those portrayed in certain films. **Media effects on aggression are discussed in Chapter 12.**

Concepts related to attitudes

Values

We have treated attitudes as a relatively high-level concept involving affect as a central dimension, with many theorists arguing that beliefs constitute an additional dimension. If we accept both views, an attitude is a set of integrated beliefs with an affective loading. From such an approach springs a further level of analysis, and another term, **values** (e.g. Bernard, Maio and Olson, 2003; Maio, 2010; Rohan, 2000).

Values
A higher-order concept thought to provide a structure for organising attitudes.

Values and attitudes are usually measured differently. Attitudes are measured to reflect varying degrees of favourability towards an object, whereas values are rated for their importance as guiding principles in life. An early emphasis on the global concept of values was the basis for a psychological test (Allport and Vernon, 1931) designed to measure the relative importance to a person of six broad classes of value orientation:

1 *theoretical* – an interest in problem solving, the basis of how things work;

2 *economic* – an interest in economic matters, finance and money affairs;

3 *aesthetic* – an interest in the arts, theatre, music, and so on;

4 *social* – a concern for one's fellows, a social welfare orientation;

5 *political* – an interest in political structures and power arrangements;

6 *religious* – a concern with theology, the afterlife and morals.

Milton Rokeach (1973) later suggested that values should be conceived less in terms of interests or activities and more as preferred goals (end-states). He distinguished between *terminal values* (e.g. equality and freedom) and *instrumental values* (e.g. honesty and ambition). A terminal value, such as equality, could have significant effects on the way someone might feel about racial issues, which is just what Rokeach found. From this viewpoint, a value is a higher-order concept having broad control over an individual's more specific attitudes. For example, measuring values can help to predict people's attitudes to the unemployed (Heaven, 1990), to industrial action (Feather, 2002), and to beliefs in a just world (Feather, 1991). When values are primed, we are more likely to make choices consistent with our values. For example, if information enhances our thoughts about the environment, we are more likely to behave in an environmentally friendly way (Verplanken and Holland, 2002).

Himmelweit, Humphreys and Jaeger (1985) conducted a longitudinal study, spanning almost a quarter of a century, of social psychological influences on voting in Britain. They found that specific attitudes were usually poor predictors, while broader sociopolitical values and party identifications were much better predictors. In another large-scale study by Hewstone (1986), this time of attitudes of French, Italian, German and British students towards European integration, general value orientation changes were seen to have some influence on changed attitudes towards integration.

According to Norm Feather (1994), values are general beliefs about desirable behaviour and goals, with an 'oughtness' quality about them. They both transcend attitudes and influence the form that attitudes take. Values offer standards for evaluating actions, justifying opinions and conduct, planning behaviour, deciding between different alternatives, engaging in social influence and presenting the self to others. Within the person, they are organised into hierarchies, and their relative importance may alter during a lifetime. Value systems vary across individuals, groups and cultures.

Feather (2002) tested some of these principles among a group of third-party participants in a study of an ongoing, major industrial dispute. Judgements about the quality of the behaviour (e.g. procedural fairness) of both the employer and the union were based on values such as authority, wealth, power, equality and being prosocial. Hofstede (1980) and S. H. Schwartz (1992), among others, have also explored the way that entire cultures can be characterised and differentiated by their underlying value systems **(see Chapter 16)**.

Can values predict behaviour? If the target behaviour is a specific act, it is very unlikely, given that a value is an even more general concept than an attitude. Although Bardi and Schwartz (2003) found correlations between some values and self-reported congruent behaviour (e.g. traditionalism and observing traditional holiday customs), they did not collect actual behavioural data.

Ideology

Ideology
A systematically interrelated set of beliefs whose primary function is explanation. It circumscribes thinking, making it difficult for the holder to escape from its mould.

Ideology overlaps to some extent with the term 'value'. It connotes an integrated and widely shared system of beliefs, usually with a social or political reference, that serves an explanatory function (Thompson, 1990). Most familiar to us are the religious and sociopolitical ideologies that serve as rallying points for many of the world's most intransigent intergroup conflicts **(see Chapters 10 and 11)**. Ideologies have a tendency to make the state of things as they are seem quite natural (the naturalistic fallacy), to justify or legitimise the status quo (Jost and van der Toorn, 2012; Jost & Hunyadi, 2002; Major, Quinton and McCoy, 2002), and to enhance hierarchical social relations (e.g. Sidanius, Levin, Federico and Pratto, 2001; Sidanius and Pratto, 1999). Ideologies also frame more specific values, attitudes and behavioural intentions (e.g. Crandall, 1994).

Philip Tetlock (1989) has proposed that terminal values, such as those described by Rokeach (1973), underlie many *political ideologies*. For example, Machiavellianism as an ideology, named after Machiavelli (a sixteenth-century Florentine diplomat considered by some to have been the first social scientist), is the notion that craft and deceit are justified in pursuing and maintaining power in the political world (Saucier, 2000). Ideologies can vary as a function of two characteristics:

1 They may assign different priorities to particular values: traditionally, we might expect liberals and conservatives to rank 'individual freedom' and 'national security' in opposite ways.

2 Some ideologies are pluralistic and others monistic. A pluralistic ideology can tolerate a conflict of values: for example, neoliberalism as a pluralistic ideology emphasises economic growth and also a concern with social justice. A monistic ideology will be quite intolerant of conflict, seeing issues in starkly simplistic terms (**see the discussion of authoritarianism in Chapter 10**). An example of a monistic ideology is Manicheism – the notion that the world is divided between good and evil principles.

Michael Billig (1991) has suggested that much of our everyday thinking arises from what he calls ideological dilemmas. Teachers, for example, face the dilemma of being an authority and yet encouraging equality between teacher and student. When conflict between values arises, it can trigger a clash of attitudes between groups. For example, Katz and Hass (1988) reported a polarisation of ethnic attitudes in a community when values such as communalism and individualism clashed.

Ideology, in the guise of ideological orthodoxy, has also been implicated in societal extremism. Ideology, because of its all-embracing explanatory function, provides an immensely comforting buffer against uncertainty; uncertainty about what to think, what to do, who one is, and ultimately the nature of existence (Hogg, 2007b, 2012; Solomon, Greenberg, Pyszczynski and Pryzbylinski, 1995; Van den Bos, 2009). It is only a short step to recognise that people will go to great lengths to protect their ideology and the group that defines it. One reason why religious ideologies are so powerful and enduring, and why religious fundamentalism arises, is precisely because organised religions are uncertainty-reducing groups that have sophisticated ideologies that define one's self and identity and normatively regulate both secular and existential aspects of life (Hogg, Adelman and Blagg, 2010).

According to **terror management theory** (e.g. Greenberg, Solomon and Pyszczynski, 1997; Pyszczynski, Greenberg and Solomon, 1999; Solomon, Greenberg and Pyszczynski, 1991) people may also subscribe to an ideology and defend their worldview as a way to buffer themselves against paralysing terror over the inevitability of their own death. Numerous studies have shown that making a person's own death salient leads to worldview defence.

Terror management theory
The notion that the most fundamental human motivation is to reduce the terror of the inevitability of death. Self-esteem may be centrally implicated in effective terror management.

Social representations

Researchers who work in a social representations tradition have a somewhat different perspective on attitudes. **In Chapter 3 we described social representations in detail.** First introduced by Serge Moscovici (1961) and based on earlier work by the French sociologist Emile Durkheim (1912/1995) on 'collective representations', social representations refer to the way that people elaborate simplified and shared understandings of their world through social interaction (Deaux and Philogene, 2001; Farr and Moscovici, 1984; Lorenzi-Cioldi and Clémence, 2001; Moscovici, 1981, 1988, 2000; Purkhardt, 1995).

Social representations
Collectively elaborated explanations of unfamiliar and complex phenomena that transform them into a familiar and simple form.

Moscovici has maintained that people's beliefs are socially constructed; they are shaped by what other people believe and say and they are shared with other members of one's community:

> Our reactions to events, our responses to stimuli, are related to a given definition, common to all the members of the community to which we belong.
>
> Moscovici (1983, p. 5)

From an attitudinal perspective, the important point is that specific attitudes are framed by, and embedded within, wider representational structures, which are in turn grounded in social groups. In this sense, attitudes tend to reflect the society or groups in which people live their lives.

This type of perspective on attitudes reflects a broader 'top-down' perspective on social behaviour, which has been a hallmark of European social psychology (**see Chapter 1**). It prompted the American social psychologist William McGuire (1986) to observe that 'the two movements serve mutually supplementary uses' in that the European concept of collective representations highlights how *alike* group members are, while the American individualist tradition highlights how *different* they are (see also Tajfel, 1972).

Social representations may influence the evaluative tone of attitudes 'nested' within them. For example, Pascal Moliner and Eric Tafani (1997) have argued that attitudes towards objects are based on the evaluative components of the representation of those objects, and that a change in attitudes towards an object may be accompanied by changes in the evaluative dimension of its representation.

Umbereen and her colleagues studied how Muslim and Christian students in the UK represented the second Iraq war, focusing on causal networks used by each group as explanations of the conflict (Rafiq, Jobanuptra and Muncer, 2006). Muslims and Christians agreed that there were causal links (sometimes bi-directional) between racism, religious prejudice and the history of conflict in the Middle East; however, Christians were more likely than Muslims to believe that the war was connected with a hunt for terrorist cells in Iraq – a reason consistently emphasised by then-US President G. W. Bush. Ironically, God's Will did not feature in either the Muslim or the Christian causal network!

Expectancy-value model
Direct experience with an attitude object informs a person how much that object should be liked or disliked in the future.

Likert scale
Scale that evaluates how strongly people agree/disagree with favourable/unfavourable statements about an attitude object. Initially, many items are tested. After item analysis, only those items that correlate with each other are retained.

Acquiescent response set
Tendency to agree with items in an attitude questionnaire. This leads to an ambiguity in interpretation if a high score on an attitude questionnaire can be obtained only by agreeing with all or most items.

Unidimensionality
A Guttman scale is cumulative: that is, agreement with the highest-scoring item implies agreement with all lower-scoring items.

Guttman scale
A scale that contains either favourable or unfavourable statements arranged hierarchically. Agreement with a strong statement implies agreement with weaker ones; disagreement with a weak one implies disagreement with stronger ones.

Measuring attitudes

Attitude scales

How should we measure attitudes; explicitly or implicitly? Some forms of attitude measurement can be completely explicit: people are simply asked to agree or disagree with various statements about their beliefs. Particularly in the early days of attitude research, in the 1930s, it was assumed that explicit measures would get at people's real beliefs and opinions. There was intense US media interest in predicting election results based on opinion polling (in particular, the Gallup Poll), and in establishing what election candidates believed and how they might act. The result was frenzied development of attitude questionnaires targeting a host of social issues. Several scales that were technically sophisticated for their time were developed by Thurstone, Likert, Guttman and Osgood, and are briefly described in Box 5.5.

In addition to scales based on summing scores across items, other researchers tried to get a better fit between a single item and a specific behaviour. We might ask, can this fit be improved if an attitude measure includes both an evaluative and a belief component? To this end, Fishbein and Ajzen (1974) developed the expectancy–value model, in which each contributing belief underlying an attitude domain is weighted by the strength of its relationship to the attitude object. The main elements of this model were described earlier in this chapter (see also Table 5.1). Despite some criticisms (see Eagly and Chaiken, 1993), this technique has had predictive success in a variety of settings – in marketing and consumer research (Assael, 1981), politics (Bowman and Fishbein, 1978), family planning (Vinokur-Kaplan, 1978), classroom attendance (Fredericks and Dossett, 1983), seat-belt wearing (Budd, North and Spencer, 1984), preventing HIV infection (Terry, Gallois and McCamish, 1993), and how mothers feed their infants (Manstead, Proffitt and Smart, 1983).

Using attitude scales today

Combinations of the Likert scale and the semantic differential have been used successfully to measure quite complex evaluations. For example, voters can be asked to evaluate various issues using a semantic differential scale. Then, using a Likert scale, they can be asked how they think

Research classic 5.5
Attitude scales

An enormous volume of research that measured people's attitudes towards social and political issues was stimulated by four early attitude scales.

Thurstone scale

When Thurstone (1928) published his landmark paper 'Attitudes can be measured', his approach was based on methods of psychophysical scaling in experimental psychology. In an innovative study of attitudes towards religion, more than 100 statements of opinion ranging from extremely favourable to extremely hostile were collected, statistically analysed and refined as a scale (Thurstone and Chave, 1929). Participants then classified the statements into eleven categories on a favourable–unfavourable continuum. Their responses were used to select a final scale of twenty-two items, two for each of the eleven points on the continuum, using items with the strongest of inter-judge agreement. Such a scale is then ready to measure other people's attitudes towards the issue. On a Thurstone scale a person's attitude score is calculated by averaging the scale values of the items endorsed.

Likert scale

A Thurstone scale is tedious to construct, and Likert (1932) developed a technique that produces a reasonably reliable attitude measure with relative ease. Respondents use a five-point response scale to indicate how much they agree or disagree with each of a series of statements. The points use labels such as 'strongly agree', 'agree', 'undecided', 'disagree', 'strongly disagree', ranging numerically from 5 to 1.

A person's score is summed across the statements and the total used as an index of the person's attitude. When developing a Likert scale, researchers find that responses to questions will not correlate equally with the total score. Those that do not correlate well are considered unreliable and dropped. Any ambiguous items – those that do not differentiate between people with differing attitudes – are dropped. The remainder constitute the final scale and, when the responses are summed, measure a person's attitude.

Where possible, items are selected so that for half of the items 'agree' represents a positive attitude and for the other half it represents a negative attitude. The scoring of the latter set of items is reversed (i.e. 5 becomes 1, 4 becomes 2, etc.) before the item scores are summed. This procedure controls acquiescent response set, a bias that otherwise could affect a variety of psychometric (such as personality) scales.

Guttman scale

A score on Thurstone and Likert scales does not have a unique meaning because two persons could receive the same score (averaged or summated) yet endorse quite different items. Guttman (1944) tried a different approach – a single, unidimensional trait can be measured by a set of statements that are ordered along a continuum ranging from least extreme to most extreme. Such a scale possesses unidimensionality. The statements vary from those that are easy to endorse to those that few people might endorse. Items on a Guttman scale are cumulative: acceptance of one item implies that the person accepts all other items that are less extreme. We could then predict a person's response to less extreme statements by knowing the most extreme item they will accept. Consider these items relating to the topic of inter-ethnic social contact – *I would accept people who are members of the immigrant ethnic group 'X':* . . . (1) *into my country* . . . (2) *into my neighbourhood* . . . (3) *into my house.* Agreement with (3) implies agreement with (1) and (2). Agreement with (2) implies agreement with (1), but not necessarily with (3). In practice, it is very difficult to develop a perfect unidimensional scale, which suggests that people respond on multiple dimensions rather than a single dimension.

Osgood's semantic differential

Osgood (Osgood, Suci and Tannenbaum, 1957) avoided using opinion statements altogether by focusing on the connotative meaning that people give to a word or concept. Studies of connotative meanings of words show that one of the major underlying dimensions is evaluation – the goodness or badness implied by the word. The word 'friend' tends to be thought of as *good* and the word 'enemy' as *bad.* According to Osgood, this evaluative dimension corresponds to our definition of an attitude. We should therefore be able to measure attitudes by having people rate a particular concept on a set of evaluative semantic scales. The concept of 'nuclear power' could be measured by responses on several evaluative (seven-point) scales (e.g. *good/bad, nice/awful, pleasant/unpleasant, fair/unfair, valuable/worthless*). An attitude score is averaged across the scales used. Osgood scales do not require writing attitude-relevant questions, and their reliability increases as more semantic scales are used. A disadvantage is that the measure can be too simple: it deals with evaluative meanings of a concept but not with opinions, which of course are the meat of the other classic scales.

each candidate stands on particular issues. Combining the two measures enables us to predict for whom they will vote (Ajzen and Fishbein, 1980).

The Likert scale has also contributed significantly to many modern questionnaires that start from the premise that the attitude being measured may be complex in having many underlying dimensions. The availability of powerful computer programs means that researchers are likely to choose from a variety of multivariate statistical methods such as factor analysis to analyse the underlying structure of questionnaire data.

Whereas Likert tested for unidimensionality in a fairly simple way by calculating item–total score correlations, factor analysis starts from a matrix based on correlations between all pairs of items making up the questionnaire scale. One then estimates whether a single general factor (or dimension), or more than one factor, is required to explain the variance in the respondents' pattern of responses to the questionnaire. For example, your attitudes towards your country's possession of nuclear weapons might depend on your reactions to war, nuclear contamination and relationships with other countries. Each of these might be measured on a different dimension and so the questionnaire could comprise several subscales (see Oppenheim, 1992).

Sometimes, factor analysis reveals substructures underlying a set of items that can be both interesting and subtle. In the development of a scale designed to measure 'sexism towards women', Glick and Fiske (1996) found evidence for two subscales – 'hostile sexism' and 'benevolent sexism' – pointing to covert ambivalence in their participants (**see Chapter 10**).

In this treatment of attitude scales we have not dealt with issues relating to developing an effective questionnaire. For example, the order in which questions are put can have subtle effects upon the way that people respond (Schwarz and Strack, 1991; for an overview of developing a sound questionnaire, see Oppenheim, 1992).

Physiological measures

Attitudes, particularly ones that have a strong evaluative or affective component, can also be measured indirectly by monitoring various physiological indices such as skin resistance (Rankin and Campbell, 1955), heart rate (Westie and DeFleur, 1959) and pupil dilation (Hess, 1965). Does your heart beat faster each time a certain person comes close? If so, we might surmise you have an attitude of some intensity!

Physiological measures have one big advantage over self-report measures: people may not realise that their attitudes are being assessed and, even if they do, they may not be able to alter their responses. This is why a polygraph or 'lie detector' is sometimes used in criminal investigations. Another physiological measure of attitudes that focuses more on whether the attitude is associated with avoidance-related feelings of threat or approach-related feelings of challenge is cortisol level in the blood or saliva (Blascovich and Tomaka, 1996; **see discussion affect and emotion in Chapter 2**). Cortisol has been used as an indicator of stress level: (a) when people's identity was under threat (Townsend, Major, Gangi and Mendes, 2011); and (b) when concerned about appearing prejudiced in an interracial encounter (Trawalter, Adam, Chase-Lansdale and Richeson, 2011).

However, physiological measures also have drawbacks since most are sensitive to variables other than attitudes (Cacioppo and Petty, 1981; also see Blascovich and Mendes, 2010; Blascovich and Seery, 2007). For example, skin resistance can change in the presence of novel or incongruous stimuli that may have nothing to do with the attitude in question. Similarly, heart rate is sensitive to task requirements – problem-solving tasks raise heart rate, while vigilance tasks (such as watching a VDU screen) usually lower it. Further, these measures provide limited information: they can indicate intensity of feeling but not direction. Two, totally opposed people who feel equally strongly about an issue cannot be distinguished.

Social neuroscience
Electrical activity in the brain may inform us of the nature and strength of a person's attitude

One measure that can distinguish between positive and negative attitudes is facial expression. Building on Darwin's suggestion that different facial expressions are used to convey different emotions **(see Chapter 15)**, Cacioppo and his colleagues (Cacioppo and Petty, 1979; Cacioppo and Tassinary, 1990) have linked facial muscle movements to underlying attitudes. They reasoned that people who agreed with a speech that they were listening to would display facial movements different from those of people who disagreed with the speech. To test this, they recorded the movements of specific facial muscles (associated with smiling or frowning) before and during a speech that advocated a conservative or a liberal view – either stricter or more lenient university regulations regarding alcohol or visiting hours. Before the speech, different patterns of muscle movement were associated with agreement compared with disagreement. These differences became more pronounced when people actually listened to the speeches. Thus, facial muscle movements provide a useful way of distinguishing people with favourable attitudes on a topic from those with unfavourable attitudes.

If attitudes, as internal states, can be inferred from external physiological indices such as heart rate and facial expression, why not take this one stage further and measure electrical activity in the brain. This idea underpins social neuroscience (e.g. Harmon-Jones and Winkielman, 2007; Lieberman, 2010; Ochsner, 2007; **see Chapter 2**), and in the context of attitude measurement the intensity and form of electrical activity and where it occurs in the brain should give an indication of what the attitude is.

For example, Levin (2000) investigated racial attitudes by measuring event-related brain potentials (ERPs) that indicate electrical activity when we respond to different stimuli. An ERP waveform includes several components, each providing evidence of different types of processing. In Levin's study, where white participants viewed a series of white and black faces, an ERP component indicated that white faces received more attention – suggesting that participants were processing their racial ingroup more deeply and the racial outgroup more superficially. This is consistent with other experimental evidence that people tend to perceptually differentiate ingroup members more than outgroup members – called the relative homogeneity effect **(see Chapter 11)**. In addition, there was greater ingroup evaluative bias shown by participants who were more prejudiced, assessed on an explicit attitude measure (Ito, Thompson and Cacioppo, 2004).

Social neuroscience
The exploration of the neurological underpinnings of the processes traditionally examined by social psychology.

Relative homogeneity effect
Tendency to see outgroup members as all the same, and ingroup members as more differentiated.

Measures of overt behaviour

We may also measure and infer attitudes by recording what people do. Sometimes, what they really do does not accord with what they *say* they do. For example, people's verbal reports of behaviours such as smoking, calories consumed and dental hygiene practices may not correspond very well to their actual physical condition. However, if we do not take what is said at face value, but instead consider the entire discursive event (what is said, how it is said, what non-verbal cues accompany the words, and the context in which it all happens), we can do a better job of inferring behaviour from what people say (**see Chapter 15**).

Unobtrusive measures

Unobtrusive measures
Observational approaches that neither intrude on the processes being studied nor cause people to behave unnaturally.

Counts of empty beer and whisky bottles in dustbins are examples of unobtrusive measures of attitudes towards alcohol in your neighbourhood, while chemists' records show which doctors prescribe new drugs. Bodily traces and archival records can furnish evidence of people's attitudes (Webb, Campbell, Schwartz and Sechrest, 1969). In a museum, the number of prints made by noses or fingers on a display case might show how popular the display was – and the height of the prints might indicate the viewers' ages! Public records and archival information can yield evidence about past and present community attitudes – for example the ebb and flow of authoritarianism and changes in prejudice (Simonton, 2003).

Changes in sex-role attitudes might be reflected in the roles of male and female characters in children's books. Library book withdrawals of fiction, not non-fiction, declined when television was introduced – suggesting one effect of television on people's behaviour. Will a book or play be more popular if it receives a favourable review? DVD rental stores' records of rental statistics also give an indication of trends in viewing preferences. These kinds of data are increasingly available in a world in which our every choice is monitored by web-based tracking systems that can even target advertisements at us based on our past behaviour – however, social psychologists have not as yet taken full advantage of this potential.

Non-verbal behaviour, **which we discuss in Chapter 15**, can also be used as an unobtrusive measure of people's attitudes. For example, people who like each other tend to sit closer together – so physical distance can be measured as an index of 'social distance' and tolerance of intimacy (Bogardus, 1925). Strangers in a waiting room who sit far apart from members of particular other groups are perhaps indicating intergroup antipathy, or maybe they are simply anxious about how to interact with a specific outgroup (Stephan and Stephan, 2000). Interpersonal distance can also measure fear. In one study (Webb, Campbell, Schwartz and Sechrest, 1969), adults told ghost stories to young children seated in a circle. The size of the circle of children grew smaller with each successive scary story!

Overall, however, unobtrusive measures are probably not as reliable as self-reported attitudes. Their value is that their limitations are different from those of standard measures. A researcher who wanted to be more confident of valid results would use both types and then correlate the data.

Bogus pipeline technique
A measurement technique that leads people to believe that a 'lie detector' can monitor their emotional responses, thus measuring their true attitudes.

We have discussed unobtrusive measures of behaviour in this section. Is it possible to have an obtrusive measure that will work? One instance is the bogus pipeline technique (Jones and Sigall, 1971), which is designed to convince participants that they cannot hide their true attitudes. People are connected to a machine said to be a lie detector and are told that it measures both the strength and direction of emotional responses, thus revealing their true attitudes and implying that there is no point in lying. Participants usually find this deception convincing and are less likely to conceal socially unacceptable attitudes such as racial prejudice (Allen, 1975; Quigley-Fernandez and Tedeschi, 1978), and socially undesirable or potentially embarrassing behaviours such as drinking in excess, snorting cocaine and having frequent oral sex (Tourangeau, Smith and Rasinski, 1997). So take care when you trial psychological equipment at the next university open day! In a study of whites' attitudes towards African-Americans, Nier (2005) used the bogus pipeline technique to compare implicit and explicit attitude measures (see next section). He reported similar results for both measures which suggests that a tendency to make a socially desirable response on matters of race rather than reveal one's 'true', potentially negative, attitude was reduced.

Measuring covert attitudes

Two terms have been used in this and related literature, 'implicit' and 'unobtrusive'. Although both methods are designed to measure attitudes, John Kihlstrom (2004) has made a conceptual distinction. Although it does not have a major impact on the discussion that follows, Kihlstrom argues that an unobtrusive method assesses an attitude that people are aware of but may be unwilling to reveal, whereas an implicit method assesses an attitude that people are not actually aware of.

Social psychologists have trialled a variety of implicit (or unobtrusive) measures to minimise the tendency for people to conceal their underlying attitudes by responding in socially desirable ways (Crosby, Bromley and Saxe, 1980; Devine, 1989; Gregg, Seibt and Banaji, 2006). We discuss three methods: detecting bias in language use, the priming of attitudes, and the implicit association test (IAT).

Bias in language use

Anne Maass and her colleagues (Franco and Maass, 1996; Maass, 1999; Maass, Salvi, Arcuri and Semin, 1989) have found that there are positive ingroup and negative outgroup biases in the way that language is used. People are more likely to talk in abstract than concrete terms about undesirable characteristics of an outgroup, and vice versa for desirable characteristics. Consequently, the ratio of abstract to concrete language usage, in relation to desirable versus undesirable characteristics, could be used as an index of prejudiced attitudes towards a particular group. Other techniques have involved the detailed analysis of discourse to reveal hidden attitudes (van Dijk, 1987, 1993; **see Chapter 15**) and likewise of non-verbal communication (Burgoon, Buller and Woodall, 1989; **see Chapter 15**). (What do you think of Rita's view of measuring attitudes in the third focus question?)

Attitude priming

Fazio and his colleagues (Fazio, Jackson, Dunton and Williams, 1995) used priming to explore how we make a judgement more quickly when an underlying attitude is congruent with a 'correct' response. While looking at a series of photos of black and white people, participants decided by pressing a button whether an adjective (from a series of positive and negative adjectives) that followed very quickly after a particular image was 'good' or 'bad'. White participants were slower in rating a positive adjective as good when it followed a black image, and black participants were slower in rating a positive adjective as good when it followed a white image.

Kawakami, Young and Dovidio (2002) used a similar rationale to explore how stereotypic judgements follow when a social category is invoked. Students participated and were either in a primed group or a control (non-primed) group. There were two phases:

1 *Priming the category 'elderly'.* A series of photographs of two different age sets, elderly people and college-age people, were shown to the primed group in random order on a computer screen, one at a time for 250 milliseconds. Each photograph was followed by the word *old?* and participants responded yes/no on either of two buttons.

Priming
Activation of accessible categories or schemas in memory that influence how we process new information.

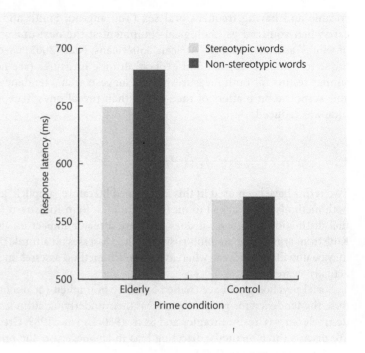

Figure 5.8 Priming the category 'elderly' can activate stereotypes

- The category 'elderly' was primed when participants chose whether persons in a series of photographs were *old* or not.
- The primed participants then decided whether word strings were real words or non-words. Half of the real words were age-stereotypic.

Source: Based on data from Kawakami, Young and Dovidio (2002)

2 *Activation of stereotypes.* Both groups were shown a list of strings of words (anagrams) and non-words and asked to respond yes/no if the word string was a real word or not. The real words were either age-stereotypic (e.g. serious, distrustful, elderly, pensioner) or not age-stereotypic (e.g. practical, jealous, teacher, florist).

There are two significant effects in the response latencies (time taken to respond) shown in Figure 5.8. First, the primed group took longer overall to respond than the control group. It is likely that the concept *elderly* activates a behavioural representation in memory of people who are mentally and physically slower than the young. The participants unwittingly slowed down when they responded. Second, the primed group (but not the control group) were a little quicker in responding to age-stereotypic words.

Implicit association test

Implicit association test
Reaction-time test to measure attitudes – particularly unpopular attitudes that people might conceal.

In a generally similar way to attitude priming, Greenwald and his colleagues (Greenwald et al., 2002; Greenwald, McGhee and Schwartz, 1998; also see Kihlstrom, 2004) developed the **implicit association test** (IAT) (see Box 5.6) using a computer display coupled with responding on a keyboard. Greenwald, McGhee and Schwartz aimed to reveal underlying negative interethnic attitudes, for example, by comparing the response latencies of American Japanese with American Koreans. The Japanese responded more quickly when a Japanese name was paired with a pleasant word, and the Koreans did the same when a Korean name was paired with a pleasant word. (Reflect on the fourth focus question at the beginning of this chapter).

In their review of implicit measures used in social cognition research, Fazio and Olson (2003b) noted that much of the data relating to the IAT is based on 'known-groups' – people who differ in an expected way. For example, when East Germans and West Germans responded more positively towards their respected ingroup (Kuhnen, Schiessl, Bauer, Paulig, Poehlmann et al., 2001). Fazio and Olson asked for more convincing evidence that the IAT has predictive validity (i.e. from IAT responses to actual behaviour). Fiedler,

Messner and Bluemke (2006) have added methodological concerns about the IAT as well, so the test's progress report at this stage is mixed. More recently, Greenwald and his associates responded with a meta-analysis of 122 studies comparing the predictive validity of both self-report and IAT measures (Greenwald, Poehlmann, Uhlmann and Banaji, 2009). As part of their research, they surmised that studies would differ in social sensitivity: those that were highly sensitive were likely subject to impression management. They concluded that:

- The topic domains reviewed varied considerably in social sensitivity from high (e.g. attitudes towards African Americans) to low (e.g. attitudes towards yoghurt).
- Within a socially sensitive domain, the predictive validity of IAT measures was clearly superior to that of self-report measures.

Impression management
People's use of various strategies to get other people to view them in a positive light.

Concluding thoughts

Attitudes have been treated as comprising three components: cognitive, affective and behavioural. Traditional research using questionnaires uses items about beliefs to measure the degree of affect (like or dislike) towards an attitude object. A well-researched questionnaire is usually based on a quantitative scale involving statistical analysis. Older questionnaire data were often not checked against real behavioural outcomes (such as the result of an election). More recently, some researchers versed in experimental methods in social cognition have shifted their focus towards using implicit measures, being less concerned with scaling individuals. They are much more interested in uncovering what people may try to conceal and in enlightening our understanding of how attitudes are structured and how they function. In Fazio and Olson's (2003b) review, implicit measures have some way to go to yield consistently valid and reliable results, but they hold promise for the future. Greenwald et al.'s analysis (2009) points to the likely superiority of the IAT, the currently most popular implicit measure, as a clear winner when a topic is socially sensitive.

We should also remember that the failure to detect an attitude does not imply that it does not exist; the way we have chosen to measure it may limit our capacity to unearth it. Furthermore,

Social psychology in action 5.6
The implicit association test

Cognitive research methods used in social cognition have produced an ingenious solution to the problem of measuring underlying attitudes in contexts where people may want to conceal what they really think – the implicit association test (IAT) (Greenwald, McGhee and Schwartz, 1998).

Based on the ideas that attitudes are associative mental networks and that associations are stronger if the attitude exists than if it doesn't, it follows that people will more quickly link concepts that are related than those that are not. So, if you dislike property developers, you will more quickly respond 'yes' to the word 'nasty' and 'no' to the word 'nice' than if you do not have a negative attitude towards developers. The IAT has participants press different keys on a keyboard or button box to match concepts (e.g. Algerian, lazy). What happens is that, where an attitude exists, the reaction is much faster when the concepts share a response key than when they do not.

The IAT has become remarkably popular in recent years as a technique for measuring prejudice in liberal Western societies such as the United States **(see Chapter 10)**. It appears to be internally consistent and well correlated with, and often superior to, other measures of prejudice and implicit attitudes (Cunningham, Preacher and Banaji, 2001; Greenwald et al., 2002). It seems that the test can even measure newly emergent negative attitudes towards very minimally defined laboratory groups (Ashburn-Nardo, Voils and Monteith, 2001).

an attitude may 're-emerge' after a period of time. Consider the very public expressions of racism in recent years by national figures in a number of countries. In the case of race, has an attitude re-emerged that was more prevalent in years gone by, or is it an overt expression of a commonly held attitude that runs counter to the usually expressed norm of equality? **Chapter 10 confronts some of these issues**.

Summary

- Attitudes have been a major interest of social psychologists for many years. They have been described as the most important concept in social psychology.

- Theories of attitude structure generally agree that attitudes are lasting, general evaluations of socially significant objects (including people and issues). Some emphasise that attitudes are relatively enduring organisations of beliefs and behavioural tendencies towards social objects.

- Attitude structure has been studied mostly from a cognitive viewpoint. Balance theory and the theory of cognitive dissonance **(see Chapter 6)** suggested that people strive to be internally consistent in their attitudes and beliefs.

- The link between attitudes and behaviour has been a source of controversy. The apparently poor predictive power of attitude measures led to a loss of confidence in the concept of attitude itself. Fishbein argued that attitudes can indeed predict behaviour. However, if the prediction concerns a specific act, the measure of attitude must also be specific.

- The interrelated theories of reasoned action and planned behaviour included the need to relate a specific act to a measure of the intention to perform that act. Other variables that affect the predicted behaviour are norms provided by other people and the extent to which the individual has control over the act.

- A strong attitude has a powerful evaluative association with the attitude object. It is more accessible in memory and more likely to be activated and the related behaviour performed. A more accessible attitude can involve a cost; high accessibility can lead to insensitivity to change in the attitude object.

- Attitudes that are accessible are more likely to be acted on.

- The prediction of behaviour from an attitude can be improved partly by accounting for moderator variables (situational and personality factors).

- Attitudes are learnt. They can be formed by direct experience, by conditioning, by observational learning and by drawing inferences from our own behaviour (self-perception).

- Parents and the mass media are powerful sources of attitude learning in children.

- A value is a higher-order concept that can play a guiding and organising role in relation to attitudes. Ideology and social representations are other related concepts.

- Measuring attitudes is both important and difficult. Traditional attitude scales of the 1930s are less frequently used today. While the response format of many modern measures is still based on the old Likert scale, the data are analysed by sophisticated statistical programs.

- A variety of physiological and behavioural indexes, both explicit and implicit, have been used to measure attitudes. The implicit association test has proved particularly popular and has gained traction when a more valid measure of a socially sensitive topic is required. Brain imaging technology is also being used to record neural processes correlated with implicit attitudes.

Key terms

Acquiescent response set
Attitude
Attitude formation
Automatic activation
Balance theory
Bogus pipeline
    technique
Cognition
Cognitive algebra
Cognitive consistency
    theories
Expectancy–value model
Guttman scale
Ideology
Implicit association test
Impression management

Information integration
    theory
Information processing
Likert scale
Mere exposure effect
Meta-analysis
Modelling
Moderator variable
Multiple act criterion
One-component attitude
    model
Priming
Protection motivation
    theory
Relative homogeneity
    effect

Self-efficacy
Self-perception theory
Social neuroscience
Social representations
Sociocognitive model
Spreading attitude effect
Terror management theory
Theory of planned behaviour
Theory of reasoned action
Three-component attitude
    model
Two-component attitude
    model
Unidimensionality
Unobtrusive measures
Values

Literature, film and TV

1984

George Orwell's 1949 novel about life in a fictional totalitarian regime, based on Stalin's Soviet Union. The book shows how such a regime controls all aspects of human existence, and has a particular emphasis on the crucial role of ideology. Through the creation of a new language, 'Newspeak', the regime is able to control thought and the way that people view the world. The book touches on the relationship between language and thought (**see Chapter 15**), and how language constrains and reflects what we can easily think about.

The Office

TV series in which David Brent (played by Ricky Gervais) and Gareth Keenan (played by Mackenzie Crook) are both prejudiced in old-fashioned and modern ways. Their antics are acutely embarrassing, and a wonderful illustration of how prejudiced attitudes reveal themselves in behaviour – all played out in a suburban British office environment.

A Few Good Men

1992 film directed by Rob Reiner, with Tom Cruise, Jack Nicholson, Demi Moore, Kevin Bacon and Kiefer Sutherland. Cruise and Moore are defence attorneys who have to find out what really happened in a murder at the Guantanamo Bay military base in Cuba. Different tactics are used to try to see through behaviour, and normative responses, to what people really know. The entire genre of courtroom dramas is often about the problem of discovering underlying attitudes and beliefs from what people say and do.

Pride and Prejudice

Jane Austen's classic 1813 novel about life and love in the genteel rural society of the day. The focal characters are Elizabeth and Darcy. One of the key features of this society is the possibility of misunderstanding based on the fact that there are strong normative pressures that inhibit the expression of one's true attitudes. The six-episode 1995 BBC mini-series adaptation of the book is a classic – Colin Firth's Mr Darcy in a wet shirt has become an unforgettable British TV moment.

Guided questions

1 What we do does not always follow from what we think. Why not?

2 What is the theory of *planned behaviour*? How can it be used to improve the predictive power of an attitude measure? Give an example from research.

3 Discuss the meaning of attitude accessibility and attitude strength. Illustrate your answer.

4 How are attitudes learnt?

MyPsychLab

5 Outline the connections between attitudes, values and ideology. Give an example of each. You can get a brief outline of the recent Hamas ideology in Chapter 5 of MyPsychLab at **www.mypsychlab.com** (watch *Israel Gaza Hamas recent history explained and Hamas ideology,* see http://www.youtube.com/watch?v=MdvN9s-YTic).

Learn more

Banaji, M. R., and Heiphetz, L. (2010). Attitudes. In S. T. Fiske, D. T. Gilbert, and G. Lindzey (eds), *Handbook of social psychology* (5th edn, Vol. 1, pp. 353–93). New York: Wiley. A completely up-to-date, comprehensive and detailed discussion of attitude research.

Bohner, G., and Dickel, N. (2011). Attitude and attitude change. *Annual Review of Psychology, 62,* 391–417.Topics include recent research on evaluative conditioning and on implicit and explicit models of attitude.

Eagly, A. H., and Chaiken, S. (2005). Attitude research in the 21st century: The current state of knowledge. In D. Albarracin, B. T. Johnson, and M. P. Zanna (eds), *The handbook of attitudes* (pp. 742–67). Mahwah, NJ: Erlbaum. Another excellent review from two of the leading attitude researchers.

Fazio, R. H., and Olson, M. A. (2007). Attitudes: Foundations, functions, and consequences. In M. A. Hogg, and J. Cooper (eds), *The SAGE handbook of social psychology: Concise student edition* (pp. 123–45). London: SAGE. A readable yet detailed overview of attitude theory and research.

Kihlstrom, J. F. (2004). Implicit methods in social psychology. In C. Sansone, C. C. E. Morf, and A. T. Panter (eds), *The SAGE handbook of methods in social psychology* (pp. 195–212). Thousand Oaks, CA: SAGE. A survey of methods used to assess people's unconscious (or implicit) attitudes, beliefs, and other mental states.

Maio, G., and Haddock, G. (2010). *The science of attitudes.* London: SAGE. A mid- to upper-level text dedicated to the science of attitudes – written by two leading attitude researchers.

Oppenheim, A. N. (1992). *Questionnaire design, interviewing and attitude measurement* (2nd edn). London: Pinter. A well-illustrated and comprehensive guide with easy-to-follow examples.

Robinson, J. P., Shaver, P. R., and Wrightsman, L. S. (eds) (1991). *Measures of personality and social psychological attitudes.* New York: Academic Press. A source-book of scales that have been used in social psychology and the study of personality.

Schwarz, N. (1996). Survey research: Collecting data by asking questions. In G. R. Semin, and K. Fiedler (eds), *Applied social psychology* (pp. 65–90). London: SAGE. A brief bird's-eye view of questionnaire design; with examples.

Terry, D. J., and Hogg, M. A. (eds) (2000). *Attitudes, behavior, and social context: The role of norms and group membership*. Mahwah, NJ: Erlbaum. A collection of chapters discussing attitudes and attitude phenomena from the perspective of group norms, group membership and social identity.

MyPsychLab

Use MyPsychLab to refresh your understanding, assess your progress and go further with interactive summaries, questions, podcasts and much more. To buy access or register your code, visit **www.mypsychlab.com.**

CHAPTER 8

Memory

ANY DAY, ANY DETAIL, ANY FACE: SHE CAN RECALL IT

A Hollywood actress who can remember every fact of her daily life over the past 40 years is baffling scientists.

She can remember every day of the past four decades as if it were yesterday. Ask Marilu Henner about a date in recent history – as many scientists have – and she will immediately volunteer the day of the week, the weather, what she was wearing and any public events she saw on television.

She is right more than 99 per cent of the time. She also appears to recall entire days from when she was 18 months old, playing with an older brother thus confounding experts who believe that children are fogged in 'infantile amnesia' until they are 2 and a half or more.

Henner, 59, who made her name in the American television comedy series, *Taxi*, during the late 1970s and early 1980s, is among a tiny group of people who can remember countless details of their lives and replay them as vividly as a high definition film.

They are blessed – or cursed – with hyperthymesia, a syndrome first described in an article in *Neurocase* in 2006 by a team of scientists from the University of California, Irvine.

Source: The Sunday Times, 2 February 2011.

WHAT YOU SHOULD BE ABLE TO DO AFTER READING CHAPTER 8

- Describe what is meant by 'memory' and describe the different types of memory process.
- Describe and understand theories of forgetting.
- Understand the term 'amnesia', be aware of different types of amnesia and understand the biological basis of the disorder.
- Distinguish between the processes of encoding and retrieval.
- Understand how memories are formed and can change over time (and how unreliable they can be).
- Be aware of the neural basis of learning and memory processes such as encoding and retrieval.

QUESTIONS TO THINK ABOUT

- What do we mean when we refer to 'memory'?
- Are there different types of memory?
- Why do we forget?
- Can memories be manipulated and, if so, how?
- Would you expect the brain mechanisms that are responsible for memory acquisition also to be responsible for retrieval? Why?
- Is memory capacity finite?
- Without memory, do we have personality?
- Where, in the brain, are memories stored? Can they be stored?

Memory: an introduction

Memory is the process of encoding, storing and retrieving information. **Encoding** refers to the active process of putting stimulus information into a form that can be used by our memory system. The process of maintaining information in memory is called **storage** and the active processes of locating and using information stored in memory is called **retrieval**.

When psychologists refer to the structure of memory, they are referring to two approaches to understanding memory – a literal one and a metaphorical one. Literally, memory may reflect the physiological changes that occur in the brain when an organism learns. Metaphorically, memory is viewed as a store or a process made up of systems and subsystems. These divisions may not necessarily have neurological meaning but they are useful metaphorical shorthand for describing aspects of memory. They are a way of explaining aspects of memory.

Types of memory

Research suggests that we possess at least four forms of memory: **sensory memory**, short-term memory, working memory and long-term memory (Baddeley, 1996). Sensory memory is memory in which representations of the physical features of a stimulus are stored for a very brief time, perhaps for a second or less. This form of memory is difficult to distinguish from the act of perception. The information contained in sensory memory represents the original stimulus fairly accurately and contains all or most of the information that has just been perceived. For example, sensory memory contains a brief image of a sight we have just seen or a fleeting echo of a sound we have just heard. Normally, we are not aware of sensory memory; no analysis seems to be performed on the information while it remains in this form. The function of sensory memory appears to be to hold information long enough for it to be transferred to the next form of memory, short-term memory.

Short-term memory (STM) refers to immediate memory for stimuli that have just been perceived. Its capacity is limited in terms of the number of items that it can store

and of its duration. For example, most people who look at the set of numbers

1492307

close their eyes and recite them back, will have no trouble remembering them. If they are asked to do the same with the following set they might have a little more trouble:

72523916584

Very few people can repeat 11 numbers. Even with practice, it is difficult to recite more than 7–9 independent pieces of information that you have seen only once. Short-term memory, therefore, has definite limits. However, there are ways to organise new information so that we can remember more than 7–9 items, but in such cases the items can no longer be considered independent.

Working memory (WM) is similar to short-term memory in that it involves short-term storage of information. But working memory is more than this in that it allows us to manipulate material in short-term memory. Remembering material while engaging in a different but related task, for example, illustrates working memory and you will find out more about this in a later section. If you had repeatedly recited the 11 numbers above until you had memorised them (rehearsal) you could have placed them in long-term memory. **Long-term memory** (LTM) refers to information that is represented on a permanent or near-permanent basis. Unlike short-term memory, long-term memory has no known limits and, as its name suggests, is relatively durable. If we stop thinking about something we have just perceived (that is, something contained in short-term memory), we may not remember the information later. However, information in long-term memory need not be continuously rehearsed. We can stop thinking about it until we need the information at a future time.

Some cognitive psychologists argue that no real distinction exists between short-term and long-term memory; instead, they see them as different phases of a continuous process. These psychologists object to the conception of memory as a series of separate units with information flowing from one to the next, as seen in Figure 8.1. Memory may be more complex than this model would have us believe, and the next sections explore the nature of sensory memory, short-term memory, working memory, long-term memory and other types of memory process.

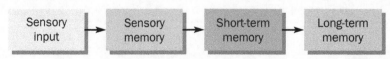

Figure 8.1 The information-processsing model of human memory.

Sensory memory

Under most circumstances, we are not aware of sensory memory. Information we have just perceived remains in sensory memory just long enough to be transferred to short-term memory. In order for us to become aware of sensory memory, information must be presented very briefly so that we can perceive its after-effects. Although we probably have a sensory memory for each sense modality, research efforts so far have focused on the two most important forms: iconic (visual) and echoic (auditory) memory.

Iconic memory

Visual sensory memory, called **iconic memory** (icon means 'image'), is a form of sensory memory that briefly holds a visual representation of a scene that has just been perceived. To study this form of memory, Sperling (1960) presented visual stimuli to people by means of a tachistoscope, an apparatus for presenting visual stimuli for extremely brief durations. Sperling flashed a set of nine letters on the screen for 50 milliseconds (ms). He then asked people to recall as many letters as they could, a method known as the whole-report procedure. On average, they could remember only four or five letters, but they insisted that they could see more. However, the image of the letters faded too fast for people to identify them all.

To determine whether the capacity of iconic memory accounted for this limitation, Sperling used a partial-report procedure. He asked people to name the letters in only one of the three horizontal rows. Depending on whether a high, middle or low tone was sounded, they were to report the letters in the top, middle or bottom line (see Figure 8.2). When the participants were warned beforehand to which line they should attend, they had no difficulty naming all three letters correctly. But then Sperling sounded the tone after he flashed the letters on the screen. The participants had to select the line from the mental image they still had: they had to retrieve the information from iconic memory. With brief delays, they

recalled the requested line of letters with perfect accuracy. For example, after seeing all nine letters flashed on the screen, they would hear the high tone, direct their attention to the top line of letters in their iconic memory, and 'read them off'. These results indicated that their iconic memory contained an image of all nine letters.

Sperling also varied the delay between flashing the nine letters on the screen and sounding the high, medium or low tone. If the delay was longer than 1 second, people could report only around 50 per cent of the letters. This result indicated that the image of the visual stimulus fades quickly from iconic memory. It also explained why participants who were asked to report all nine letters failed to report more than four or five. They had to scan their iconic memory, identify each letter and store each letter in short-term memory. This process took time, and during this time the image of the letters was fading. Although their iconic memory originally contained all nine letters, there was time to recognise and report only four or five before the mental image disappeared.

Echoic memory

Auditory sensory memory, called **echoic memory**, is a form of sensory memory for sounds that have just been perceived. It is necessary for comprehending many sounds, particularly those that constitute speech. When we hear a word pronounced, we hear individual sounds, one at a time. We cannot identify the word until we have heard all the sounds, so acoustical information must be stored temporarily until all the sounds have been received. For example, if someone says 'mallet', we may think of a kind of hammer; but if someone says 'malice', we will think of something entirely different. The first syllable we hear – 'mal' – has no meaning by itself in English, so we do not identify it as a word. However, once the last syllable is uttered, we can put the two syllables together and recognise the word. At this point, the word enters short-term memory. Echoic memory holds a representation of the initial sounds until the entire word has been heard; it seems to hold information for about four seconds (Darwin *et al.*, 1972).

Short-term memory (STM)

Short-term memory (STM) has a limited capacity, and most of the information that enters it is subsequently forgotten. Information in sensory memory enters STM, where it may be rehearsed for a while. The rehearsal process keeps the information in STM long enough for it to be transferred into long-term memory. After that, a person can stop thinking about the information; it can be recalled later, when it is needed.

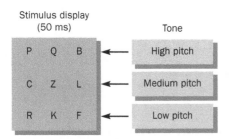

Figure 8.2 The critical features of Sperling's iconic memory study.

Source: Adapted from Sperling, G., The information available in brief visual presentations, *Psychological Monographs*, 1960, 74, 1–29.

This simple story is actually inaccurate. First of all, information does not simply 'enter short-term memory'. For example, most people who read the letters and put them in short-term memory have a number of strategies for achieving this. Some would have repeated the letters to themselves or would have whispered or moved their lips. We can say the names of these letters because many years ago we learned them. But that knowledge is stored in long-term memory. Thus, when we see some letters, we retrieve information about their names from long-term memory, and then we hear ourselves rehearsing those names (out loud or silently). The five letters above contain only visual information, their names came from long-term memory, which means that the information put into short-term memory actually came from long-term memory.

P X L M R

To illustrate this, try the following experiment. Study the symbols below, then look away from the book, and try to keep them in STM.

ζ☐δϱ☐

This task is extremely difficult because few people will have learned the names of these symbols. Because of this, there is no way of recording them in short-term memory. Figure 8.3 may, therefore, be a better description of the memory process than is Figure 8.1.

Information can enter short-term memory from two directions: from sensory memory or from long-term memory. When we are asked to multiply 7 by 19, information about the request enters our short-term memory from our sensory memory. Actually performing the task, though, requires that we retrieve some information from long-term memory. What does 'multiply' mean? What is a 7 and a 19? At the moment of the request, such information is not being furnished through our senses; it is available only from long-term memory. However, that information is not recalled directly from long-term memory. It is first moved into short-term memory and then enters conscious awareness.

Psychologists have long debated the number of memory stores that we have – some view humans as having a short-term memory store and a long-term memory store (the dual-store model), whereas others argue that the distinction between these two stores is blurred and that we have one flexible memory store that deals with short-term and long-term memory retrieval (single-store model). Dual-store models were (and are) based on a simple paradigm: participants recall items from a list; if they recall from the end of this list, these items were retrieved from STM; words recalled from the beginning of the list were retrieved from long-term memory.

To determine whether this distinction was supportable, Talmi *et al.* (2005) set up an fMRI experiment in which participants were asked to remember and then recognise words from a list, as their brain activation was measured. Recognition of items appearing early in the list was associated with activity in regions of the brain associated with long-term memory (the hippocampus and related structures); recognition of items appearing later in the list was not associated with activation in these areas, providing some neuroimaging support for the distinction between dual memory stores.

Working memory

The fact that short-term memory contains both new information and information retrieved from long-term memory has led some psychologists to prefer the term 'working memory' (Baddeley and Hitch, 1974; Baddeley, 1986). Working memory acts on material we have just perceived and allows us to manipulate this in the short-term. It allows us to keep a new telephone number 'alive' in memory long enough to dial it or allows us to perform that multiplication task mentioned in the earlier paragraph. In short, it represents our ability to remember what we have just perceived and to think about it in terms of what we already know (Baddeley, 1986; Logie, 1996).

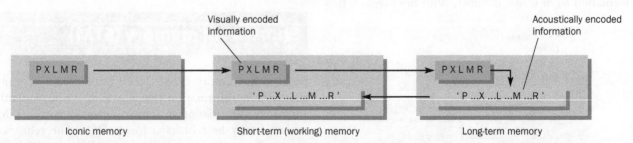

Figure 8.3 Relations between iconic memory, short-term memory and long-term memory. Letters are read, transformed into their acoustic equivalents and rehearsed as 'sounds' in the head. Information can enter short-term memory from both iconic memory and long-term memory. Visual information enters short-term memory from iconic memory, but what is already known about that information (such as names of letters) is moved from long-term memory to short-term memory.

We use it to remember whether any cars are coming up the street after looking left and then right, for example.

A widely used test of working memory is reading span (Daneman and Carpenter, 1980). One version involves asking people to read aloud and verify the truthfulness of sentences while, at the same time, trying to remember the last word of each sentence. This task, like many others of working memory, requires a person to maintain some information in memory (storage) while simultaneously manipulating other information (processing).

Another manipulation task in working memory might involve asking the participant to recite from memory a series of five letters forwards, backwards or in alphabetical order. After a delay, the participant is asked to match the number order of a given letter, according to the mental manipulation (e.g. forwards, backwards or alphabetical). So, if the letters B, M, T, E, I were presented and the participant was asked to alphabetise them, the number 4 (called a digit probe) should elicit the correct answer, M (because M is the fourth letter in the alphabetised string, B, E, I, M, T).

Although the terms 'short-term memory' and 'working memory' are sometimes used interchangeably, some psychologists make clear distinctions between them. Short-term memory has been referred to as information retained in long-term memory that is called on but not used in a sustained way. Working memory involves dual processing and actual manipulation of material in **mental space**, not simply the storage of material (Miyake, 2001). There is evidence that tests of working memory and short-term memory measure different processes (Kail and Hall, 2001).

The components of working memory

Working memory was a model devised in the 1970s and later developed extensively by the British psychologists Alan Baddeley and Graham Hitch. They regarded this type of memory as having three components which allowed us to store temporarily verbal material and visuospatial material, and to coordinate the storage of this material. The component which stores verbal material was originally called the **articulatory loop** although this term has been superseded by the term **phonological loop** (Baddeley and Logie, 1992). The component that allows storage of visuospatial material is called the **visuospatial scratchpad** and the coordinating system is called the **central executive**. The working memory 'system' is illustrated in Figure 8.4 and is described next.

Phonological working memory

When we see a printed word, we say it, out loud or silently. If it is said to ourselves, circuits of neurons that control articulation are activated. Information concerning

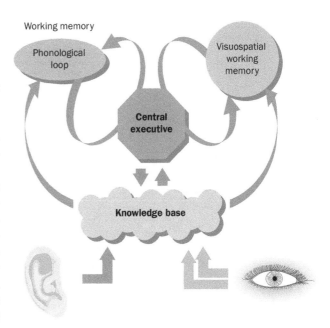

Figure 8.4 Logie's (1995) schematic drawing of the components of working memory.

Source: Adapted from Logie, R., *Visual Spatial Working Memory*, p. 127. © 1995. Reprinted by permission of Psychology Press Limited, Hove, UK.

this activity is communicated within the brain to circuits of neurons in the auditory system, and the word is 'heard'. Information is then transmitted back to the articulatory system, where the word is silently repeated. The loop continues until the person's attention turns to something else or until it is replaced with new information.

This articulatory or phonological loop allows the retention of verbal phonetic information (so it acts as a phonological store) and operates like the loop of an audiotape (hence, the name). Lists of long words are remembered more poorly than lists of short words, for example, because there is less room on the loop for lists of long words (so the words 'encyclopaedia', 'constellation' and 'antediluvian' would be more difficult to recall than would the words 'clock', 'parrot' and 'daisy'). However, because the loop also allows the rehearsal of information by **subvocal articulation** (such as subvocally rehearsing a telephone number), the loss of information from the phonological store can be avoided. According to Baddeley *et al.* (1975), the capacity of the phonological loop is determined by how much material the participant can rehearse in two seconds. (Figure 8.5 illustrates how the phonological loop is represented in the brain.)

However, the operation of the loop can be defective under certain circumstances. For example, Salame and Baddeley (1982) found that irrelevant speech played in the background while participants learned visually presented words interfered with the recall of these words, but the length of the words to be remembered had no significant

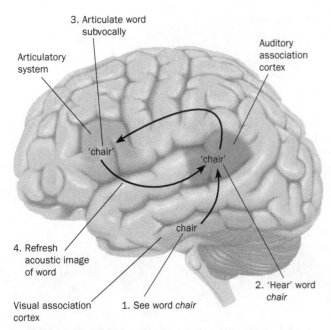

Figure 8.5 The articulatory loop. A hypothetical explanation of phonological working memory.

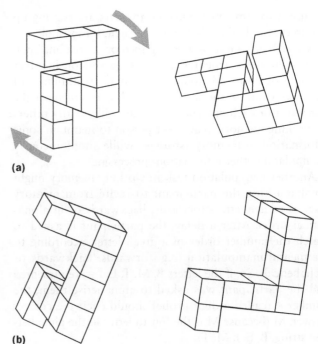

Figure 8.6 The mental rotation task. **(a)** The shape on the right is identical to the one on the left but rotated 80 degrees clockwise. **(b)** The two shapes are different.

Source: Adapted from Shepard, R.N. and Metzler, J., Mental rotation of three-dimensional objects, *Science*, 1971, 171, 701–3. © 1971. The American Association for the Advancement of Science.

effect on recall. However, the closer the irrelevant speech was to the words to be remembered, the greater the interference, suggesting that there was some interference in learning words while attending to the sound (or phonology) of similar ones. There is also evidence that non-speech-related material can have the same effect: even background noise can disrupt recall of verbal and arithmetical material (Banbury and Berry, 1998) (see Chapter 9).

Visuospatial working memory

Much of the information we process is non-verbal. We recognise objects, perceive their locations and find our way around our environment. We can look at objects, close our eyes and then sketch or describe them. We can do the same with things we saw in the past. The visuospatial scratchpad contains visual information either obtained from the immediate environment by means of the sense organs or retrieved from long-term memory.

An example of the ability to manipulate visual information in working memory comes from a famous experiment by Shepard and Metzler (1971). They presented people with pairs of drawings that could be perceived as three-dimensional constructions made of cubes. The participant's task was to see whether the shape on the right was identical to the one on the left; some were, and some were not. Even when the shapes were identical, the one on the right was sometimes drawn as if it had been rotated. For example, in Figure 8.6(a) the shape on the right has been rotated clockwise 80 degrees, but in Figure 8.6(b) the two shapes are different.

Shepard and Metzler found that people were accurate in judging whether the pairs of shapes were the same or different but took longer to decide when the right-hand shape was rotated. Participants formed an image of one of the drawings in their heads and rotated it until it was aligned the same way as the other one. If their rotated image coincided with the drawing, they recognised them as having the same shape. If they did not, they recognised them as being different. The data supported what the participants said – the more the shape was rotated, the longer it took for people to rotate the image of one of the shapes in working memory and compare it with the other one.

The central executive

The above elements – the phonological loop and the visuo–spatial scratchpad – do not work independently but have to be regulated and supervised, via the central executive subsystem (Baddeley, 1986). This central executive not only allocates mental resources to working memory tasks but also supervises the updating of what is in working memory.

How does working memory work?

Apart from allowing us to do the activities mentioned in the previous sections, working memory is also important for cognitive functions such as reading comprehension, academic ability and mathematics (Ashcraft and Kirk, 2001; Daneman and Hannon, 2001). Performance on a working memory span task involving numbers, for example, is a good predictor of spatial task performance (Kane *et al.*, 2001). Working memory performance is also a good predictor of reading comprehension or verbal ability if the working memory span tests involve verbal or numerical material (Daneman and Hannon, 2001; Hitch *et al.*, 2001; Shah and Miyake, 1996) (see Chapter 10).

According to the 'resource sharing model' of Daneman and Carpenter (the name given to it by Hitch *et al.*, 2001), a reading span task measures how flexibly we can allocate mental resources to the processing and storage of material. In practical terms, if a person is a good reader, reading sentences for their truthfulness uses up very few cognitive resources and, therefore, frees up more 'cognitive space' for other activities (in this example, storage of the last word in the sentences). If readers are poor, on the other hand, the opposite pattern is seen and they, therefore, show poor working memory performance (Yuill and Oakhill, 1991). Working memory capacity is thought to be one factor which determines good reading comprehension ability, although this view has been challenged – some psychologists argue that working memory deficits occur with language impairment, rather than causing it (Nation and Snowling, 1998, 1999). They note that even poor readers can remember as many one-, two- or three-syllable words as good readers.

Daneman and Carpenter's view of working memory (1980) has attracted much support and has been the dominant, explanatory view of working memory. An alternative model of working memory, however, argues that it is our control of attention that leads to successful working memory performance (Engle *et al.*, 1999). What counts is how much information can be stored, and this is determined by attention capacity. Thus, you should be able to predict people's performance on attention tasks from their working memory reading span tasks and there is some evidence to support this link.

A final alternative explanation argues that working memory depends on a person's ability to ignore irrelevant information rather than on their limited capacity to process information (Hasher and Zacks, 1988). In order to achieve this goal, there must be good inhibition of irrelevant information and a focus on only relevant material. It is a persuasive argument. Performance on working memory tasks depends on, among other factors, the ability to inhibit the interference produced by items encountered in early experimental trials (Lustig *et al.*, 2001). It appears to be one of the keys to successful working memory performance.

Primacy and recency effects

When individuals are asked to listen to a long list of words spoken one at a time and then write down as many as they can remember (a free recall task), most participants will remember the words at the beginning and the end of the list and forget the words in between. The tendency to remember the words at the beginning of the list is called the **primacy effect**; the tendency to remember words at the end of the list is called the **recency effect**. Two factors may account for these effects.

The primacy effect appears to be due to the fact that words earlier in a list have the opportunity to be rehearsed more than do words in the other parts of a list. This makes good sense – the first words get rehearsed more because, at the experiment's outset, these are the only words available to rehearse. The rehearsal permits them to be stored in long-term memory. As more and more words on the list are presented, short-term memory becomes fuller so that words that appear later in the list have more competition for rehearsal time. Because the first words on the list are rehearsed the most, they are remembered better.

As Atkinson and Shiffrin (1968) point out, because the words at the end of the list were the last to be heard, they are still available in short-term memory. Thus, when you are asked to write the words on the list, the last few words are still available in short-term memory even though they did not undergo as much rehearsal as words at the beginning of the list.

A way of testing this would be to create a delay between the presentation of the last stimulus and its recall. Postman and Phillips (1965), for example, inserted a delay of 15 seconds between the last item and recall and had their participants engage in another task. The effect was to abolish the recency effect because short-term memory was occupied and was not allowed to rehearse the last items in the list. When the delay involved no intervening activity, and so short-term memory was unoccupied by another task, the recency effect remained intact (Baddeley and Hitch, 1977). However, the abolition of both recency and primacy effects seems to depend on the nature of the intervening task. If people are told to count backwards for 20 seconds after the presentation of a word list, primacy and recency effects are still shown (Tzeng, 1973). The instructions given to people are also important. If people are instructed to repeat the list in the order they heard the words, the recency effect is abolished (Tulving and Arbuckle, 1963). If they are allowed to recall the list spontaneously, the recency effect remains.

Recency (and primacy) effects extend beyond the recall of artificial word lists. They have been reported for the recall of parking positions (Pinto and Baddeley, 1991), operas attended over a quarter of a century

(Sehulster, 1989), names of American presidents (Roediger and Crowder, 1976; Healy *et al.*, 2000) and hymn verses (Maylor, 2002). Baddeley and Hitch (1977) found that when rugby players were asked to recall the teams they played, they named the most recently played teams first and with greater accuracy.

The primacy and recency effects are important because they demonstrate that memory is not a random process. Information is not just plucked from the environment and stored away randomly in the brain. Instead, the processing of information is much more orderly; it follows predictable patterns and is dependent on the contributions of rehearsal and short-term memory.

The limits of short-term and working memory

How long does information remain in short-term or working memory? The answer may lie in a classic study by Lloyd and Margaret Peterson (Peterson and Peterson, 1959). The experimenters presented participants with a stimulus composed of three consonants, such as JRG. With rehearsal, the participants easily recalled it 30 seconds later. The Petersons then made the task more challenging: they prevented participants from rehearsing. After they presented the participants with JRG, they asked them to count backwards by three from a three-digit number they gave them immediately after they had presented the set of consonants. For example, they might present participants with JRG, then say, '397'. The participants would count out loud, '397... 394... 391... 388... 385', and so on until the experimenters signalled them to recall the consonants. The accuracy of recall was determined by the length of the interval between presentation of the consonants and when recall was requested (see Figure 8.7). When rehearsal was disrupted by backward counting – which prevented individuals from rehearsing information in short-term memory – the consonants remained accessible in memory for only a few seconds. After a 15–18-second delay between the presentation of the consonants and the recall signal, recall dropped to near zero.

What, then, is the capacity of short-term memory? Miller (1956), in a famous article entitled 'The magical number seven, plus or minus two', demonstrated that people could retain, on average, seven pieces of information in their short-term memory: seven numbers, seven letters, seven words or seven tones of a particular pitch. If we can remember and think about only seven pieces of information at a time, how can we manage to write novels, design buildings or even carry on simple conversations? The answer comes in a particular form of encoding of information that Miller called chunking, a process by

which information is simplified by rules which make it easily remembered once the rules are learned.

A simple demonstration illustrates this phenomenon. Read the ten numbers printed below and see whether you have any trouble remembering them.

1357924680

These numbers are easy to retain in short-term memory because we can remember a rule instead of ten independent numbers. In this case, the rule concerns odd and even numbers. The actual limit of short-term memory is seven chunks, not necessarily seven individual items. Thus, the total amount of information we can store in short-term memory depends on the particular rules we use to organise it.

In life outside the laboratory we are rarely required to remember a series of numbers. The rules that organise our short-term memories are much more complex than those that describe odd and even numbers. The principles of chunking can apply to more realistic learning situations. If we look at the following words:

> along got the was door crept locked slowly he until passage the he to which

and try to remember them, the task is difficult; there is too much information to store in short-term memory. If we repeat the process for the following group of words:

> He slowly crept along the passage until he got to the door, which was locked.

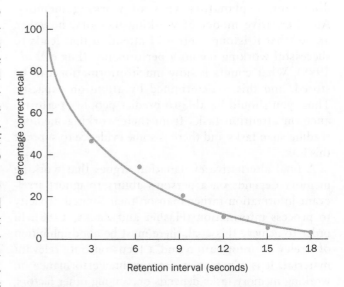

Figure 8.7 Limits of recall from working memory. Percentage correct recall of the stimulus as a function of the duration of the distractor task used in the study by Peterson and Peterson.

Source: Adapted from Peterson, L.M. and Peterson, J.M., Short-term retention of individual verbal items. *Journal of Experimental Psychology*, 1959, 58, 193–98.

we would be much more successful. Once the same fifteen words are arranged in a sequence that makes sense, they are not difficult to store in short-term memory.

The capacity of short-term memory for verbal material is not measured by the number of letters, syllables or words it can retain but by how much meaning the information offers: this is working memory and long-term memory working together. The first set of words above merely contains fifteen different words. However, when the items are related, we can store many more of them. We do not have to string fifteen words together in a meaningless fashion but can let the image of a man creeping down a passage towards a locked door organise the new information.

Loss of information from short-term memory

The essence of short-term memory is its transience; hence, its name. Information enters from sensory memory and from long-term memory, is rehearsed, thought about, modified and then leaves. Some of the information controls ongoing behaviour and some of it causes changes in long-term memory, but ultimately, it is lost from short-term memory. What causes it to leave? The simplest possibility is that it decays, it fades away. Rehearsal allows us to refresh information indefinitely, thus preventing the decay from eliminating the information.

However, the most important cause appears to be displacement. Once short-term memory has reached its capacity, either additional information will have to be ignored or some information already in short-term memory will have to be displaced to make room for the new information.

One of the best examples of displacement of information in short-term memory comes from an experiment conducted by Waugh and Norman (1965). The people in this study heard lists of sixteen digits. The last digit, accompanied by a tone, was called the probe digit. When people heard it, they had to think back to the previous occurrence of the same digit and tell the experimenter the digit that followed that one.

Look at the sequence of numbers listed below. The last one, a 9, was accompanied by a tone, which told the person that it was the probe. If you examine the list, you will see that the earlier occurrence of a 9 was followed by a 4. Thus, the target, or correct, response was 4.

2 6 7 5 1 3 7 2 6 3 9 4 5 8 1 9

Notice that the 4 is separated from the second 9 by three numbers (5, 8 and 1). Waugh and Norman presented many different lists in which the location of the correct

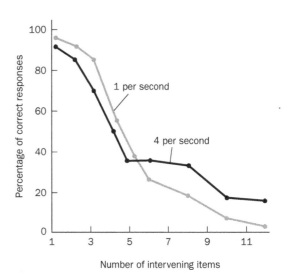

Figure 8.8 Displacement of information in short-term memory. The graph shows the percentage of correct responses as a function of intervening items presented at two different rates of time.
Source: Adapted from Waugh, N.C. and Norman, D.A., Primary memory. *Psychological Review*, 1965, 72, 89–104.

response varied. The distance between the target and the probe ranged from one to twelve items.

The study had two conditions. In one, the lists were presented rapidly, at four digits per second. In the other, they were presented slowly, at only one digit per second. The reason for this manipulation was to determine whether any effects they observed were caused by the mere passage of time rather than by displacement. They found that the more items that came between the target and the probe, the less likely it was that the target would be remembered. The critical variable seemed to be the number of items between the target and the probe, not the time that had elapsed (see Figure 8.8).

The results indicate that new information displaces old information in short-term memory. But at the longest delays (six or more intervening items), subjects performed more poorly when the items were presented slowly. Perhaps information in short-term memory does decay, but the effect is much less important than displacement.

Learning and encoding in long-term memory

What allows memory to move from short-term to long-term memory? Memory involves both active and passive processes. Sometimes, we use deliberate strategies to remember something (encode the information into long-term memory), for example, rehearsing the lines of a poem or memorising famous dates for a history exam. At other times, we simply observe and remember without any apparent effort, as when we tell a friend about an interesting experience we had. And memories can be formed even without our being aware of having learned something. What factors determine whether we can eventually remember an experience?

The consolidation hypothesis

The traditional view of memory is that it consists of a two-stage process (not counting sensory memory). Information enters short-term memory from the environment, where it is stored temporarily. If the material is rehearsed long enough, it is transferred into long-term memory. This transfer of information from short-term memory into long-term memory has been called consolidation (Hebb, 1949). Through rehearsal (for example, by means of the articulatory loop), the neural activity responding to sensory stimulation can be sustained; and if enough time passes, the activity causes structural changes in the brain. These structural changes are more or less permanent and solid (hence, the term 'consolidation'), and are responsible for long-term memory.

The **consolidation** hypothesis makes several assertions about the learning process. It asserts that short-term memory and long-term memory are physiologically different, and few investigators doubt that information that has just been perceived is stored in the brain in a different way from information that was perceived some time ago. However, some other features of the original consolidation hypothesis have been challenged. First, the hypothesis asserts that all information gets into long-term memory only after passing through short-term memory. Secondly, it asserts that the most important factor determining whether a particular piece of information reaches long-term memory is the amount of time it spends in short-term memory.

Levels of processing

Craik and Lockhart (1972) have pointed out that the act of rehearsal may effectively keep information in short-term memory but does not necessarily result in the establishment of long-term memories. They suggested that people engage in two different types of rehearsal: **maintenance rehearsal** and **elaborative rehearsal**. Maintenance rehearsal is the rote repetition of verbal information – simply repeating an item over and over. This behaviour serves to maintain the information in short-term memory but does not necessarily result in lasting changes. In contrast, when people engage in elaborative rehearsal, they think about the information and relate it to what they already know. Elaborative rehearsal

involves more than new information. It involves deeper processing: forming associations, attending to the meaning of the information, thinking about that information, and so on. Thus, we elaborate on new information by recollecting related information already in long-term memory. We are more likely to remember information for an examination by processing it deeply or meaningfully; simply rehearsing the material to be tested will not be effective.

Craik and Tulving (1975) gave participants a set of cards, each containing a printed sentence including a missing word, denoted by a blank line, such as 'The _____ is torn'. After reading the sentence, the participants looked at a word flashed on a screen, then pressed a button as quickly as possible to signify whether the word fitted the sentence. In this example, 'dress' will fit, but 'table' will not. The sentences varied in complexity. Some were very simple:

She cooked the _____.

The _____ is torn.

Others were complex:

The great bird swooped down and carried off the struggling _____.

The old man hobbled across the room and picked up the valuable _____.

The sentences were written so that the same word could be used for either a simple or a complex sentence: 'She cooked the chicken' or 'The great bird swooped down and carried off the struggling chicken'. All participants saw a particular word once, in either a simple or a complex sentence.

The experimenters made no mention of a memory test, so there was no reason for the participants to try to remember the words. However, after responding to the sentences, they were presented with them again and were asked to recall the words they had used. The experimenters found that the participants were twice as likely to remember a word if it had previously fitted into a sentence of medium or high complexity than if it had fitted into a simple one. These results suggest that a memory is more effectively established if the item is presented in a rich context – one that is likely to make us think about the item and imagine an action taking place.

Craik and Lockhart (1972) suggested that memory is a by-product of perceptual analysis. A central processor, analogous to the central processing unit of a computer, can analyse sensory information on several different levels. They conceived of the levels as being hierarchically arranged, from shallow (superficial) to deep (complex). A person can control the level of analysis by paying attention to different features of the stimulus. If a person focuses on the superficial sensory characteristics of a stimulus, then these features will be stored in memory. If the person focuses on the meaning of a stimulus and the ways in which it relates to other things the person already knows, then these features will be stored in memory. For example, consider the word:

tree

This word is written in black type, the letters are lower case, the bottom of the stem of the letter 't' curves upwards to the right, and so on. Craik and Lockhart referred to these characteristics as surface features and to the analysis of these features as **shallow processing**. Maintenance rehearsal is an example of shallow processing. In contrast, consider the meaning of the word 'tree'. You can think about how trees differ from other plants, what varieties of trees you have seen, what kinds of foods and what kinds of wood they provide, and so on. These features refer to a word's meaning and are called semantic features. Their analysis is called **deep processing**. Elaborative rehearsal is an example of deep processing. According to Craik and Lockhart, deep processing generally leads to better retention than does surface processing (see Figure 8.9). As you saw in Chapter 7, a deep approach to learning also improves a student's performance.

Encoding specificity

Encoding specificity refers to the principle that the way in which we encode information determines our ability to retrieve it later. For example, suppose that someone reads you a list of words that you are to recall later. The list contains the word 'beet', along with a number of terms related to music, such as 'melody', 'tune' and 'jazz'. When asked if the list contained the names of any vegetables, you may report that it did not. Because of the musical context, you encoded 'beet' as 'beat' and never thought of the tuberous vegetable while you were rehearsing the list (Flexser and Tulving, 1978). Many experiments have made the point that meaningful elaboration during encoding is helpful and probably necessary for the formation of useful memories.

Mnemonics and memory aids

When we can imagine information vividly and concretely, and when it fits into the context of what we already know, it is easy to remember later. **Mnemonic systems**

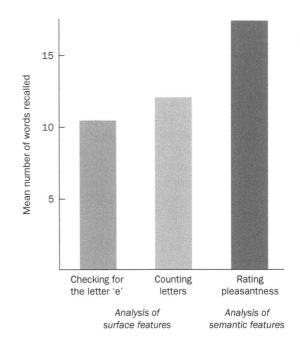

Figure 8.9 Shallow versus deep processing. Mean number of words recalled after performing tasks that required analysis of surface features or analysis of semantic features.

Source: Based on Craik, F.I.M. and Lockhart, R.S., Levels of processing: A framework for memory research. *Journal of Verbal Behavior*, 1972, 11, 671–84.

(from the Greek *mnemon*, meaning 'mindful') – special techniques or strategies consciously used to improve memory – make use of information already stored in long-term memory to make memorisation an easier task.

Mnemonic systems do not simplify information but make it more elaborate. More information is stored, not less. However, the additional information makes the material easier to recall. Mnemonic systems organise new information into a cohesive whole so that retrieval of part of the information ensures retrieval of the rest of it.

World memory champion 2011 Wang Feng

Source: World Memory Sports Council, www.worldmemorychampionships.com

Method of loci

In Greece before the sixth century BC, few people knew how to write, and those who did had to use cumbersome clay tablets. Consequently, oratory skills and memory for long epic poems (running for several hours) were highly prized, and some people earned their livings by using them. Because people could not carry around several hundred pounds of clay tablets, they had to keep important information in their heads. To do so, the Greeks devised the **method of loci**, a mnemonic system in which items to be remembered are mentally associated with specific physical locations (*locus* means 'place' in Latin).

To use the method of loci, would-be memory artists had to memorise the inside of a building. In Greece, they would wander through public buildings, stopping to study and memorise various locations and arranging them in order, usually starting with the door of the building. After memorising the locations, they could make the tour mentally, just as you could make a mental tour of your house to count the rooms. To learn a list of words, they would visualise each word in a particular location in the memorised building and picture the association as vividly as possible. For example, for the word 'love' they might imagine an embracing couple leaning against a particular column in a hall of the building. To recall the list, they would imagine each of the locations in sequence, 'see' each word, and say it. To store a speech, they would group the words into concepts and place a 'note' for each concept at a particular location in the sequence.

For example, if a person wanted to remember a short shopping list without writing it down and the list consists of five items: cheese, milk, eggs, soy sauce and lettuce, the person might first think of a familiar place, perhaps their house. Next, they would mentally walk through the house, visually placing different items from the list at locations – loci – in the house: a lump of cheese hanging from a coat rack, milk dripping from the kitchen tap, eggs lying in the hallway, a bottle of soy sauce on a dining chair, and a lettuce on the sofa (see Figure 8.10). Then, in the supermarket, the person mentally retraces his or her path through the house and notes what he or she has stored at the different loci.

Narrative stories

Another useful aid to memory is to place information into a **narrative**, in which items to be remembered are linked together by a story. Bower and Clark (1969) showed that even inexperienced people can use this method. The investigators asked people to try to learn twelve lists of ten concrete nouns each. They gave some of the people the following advice (p. 181):

Figure 8.10 The method of loci. Items to be remembered are visualised in specific, well-known places.

> A good way to learn the list of items is to make up a story relating the items to one another. Specifically, start with the first item and put it in a setting which will allow other items to be added to it. Then, add the other items to the story in the same order as the items appear. Make each story meaningful to yourself. Then, when you are asked to recall the items, you can simply go through your story and pull out the proper items in their correct order.

Here is a typical narrative, described by one of the subjects (list words are italicised):

> A *lumberjack* darted out of the forest, *skated* around a *hedge* past a colony of *ducks*. He tripped on some *furniture*, tearing his *stocking* while hastening to the *pillow* where his *mistress* lay.

People in the control group were merely asked to learn the lists and were given the same amount of time as the people in the 'narrative' group to study them. Both groups could remember a particular list equally well immediately afterwards. However, when all the lists had been learned, recall of all 120 words was far superior in the group that had constructed narrative stories.

Not all information can be easily converted to such a form, however. For example, if you were preparing to take an examination on the information in this chapter, figuring out how to encode it into lists would probably take you more time than studying and learning it by more traditional methods.

'Smart' drugs

In recent years, pharmaceutical companies have become excited at the possibility that drugs may help improve memory or reduce the decline in memory performance seen with normal ageing or in people with probable Alzheimer's disease, the major cause of dementia (there is more on memory and memory aids in ageing in Chapters 11 and 12). A less pressing but nonetheless novel issue is whether these drugs can enhance cognition in healthy individuals.

Drugs that claim to improve intellectual function have been called nootropics (from the Greek, *noos*, 'mind', and tropein, '*towards*'). Although the word was used to describe a specific drug that increased neurotransmitter activity (Nicholson, 1990), it is now used to refer to any drug that claims to improve cognitive function or protect neurons from injury or insult. These drugs are not excitants, tranquillisers or antipsychotics and they have few side effects (Gabryel and Trzeciak, 1994).

In a review of the effects of non-prescription compounds such as phosphaidylserin, citicoline, piracetam, vinpocetine, acetyl-L-carnitine and antioxidants on memory enhancement, McDaniel *et al.* (2002) concluded that the evidence provides little scientific support for the drugs' claims. However, they concede that it is possible that such drugs may be effective in certain circumstances. Although some studies appear to show positive benefits of drug administration on memory, closer observation of the data shows a more specific pattern of efficacy. A study of the drug Ginkgo-ginseng found an improvement in memory four weeks after drug administration to adults with normal memory (Wesnes *et al.*, 2000). This improvement was sustained for two weeks after the 12-week study. Scores on the memory tests, however, showed that the drug seemed to work only at a certain time of day. McDaniel *et al.* found that there was little difference in memory performance between the placebo and pill groups at 7.30 a.m. but there was a large and robust difference at 2.30 p.m. For almost all tests, performance in the pill group was better in the afternoon.

Long-term memory: episodic and semantic memory

Long-term memory contains more than exact records of sensory information that has been perceived. It also contains information that has been transformed – organised in terms of meaning. For example, the type of information that is personally meaningful to us (such as what we had for breakfast this morning or what we were doing last night) appears to be different from the type of information that is based on general knowledge (such as knowing the capitals of the world or the order in which Shakespeare wrote his plays). These two types of memory have been termed episodic and semantic memory, respectively, and the distinction was originally made by Tulving (1972). **Episodic memory** (or **autobiographical memory**) provides us with a record of our life experiences. Events stored there are autobiographical and there appears to be cross-cultural agreement on when such memories are acquired (even though cultures differ in terms of the type of memory encoded) (Conway *et al.*, 2005). **Semantic memory** consists of conceptual information such as general knowledge; it is a long-term store of data, facts and information. Our knowledge of what psychology is, the names of the authors of this book, the components of the human sensory systems and how neuroimaging has helped localise the process of working memory should form part of your semantic memory. Semantic memories can, of course, interact with episodic ones.

The distinction between episodic and semantic memory reflects the fact that we make different uses of things we have learned: we describe things that happened to us, or talk about facts we have learned. Tulving (1983, 1984) revised his original views of the two systems, suggesting that episodic memory is a part of semantic memory, not a separate, independent system, so the debate is ongoing.

One way of determining a distinction between them would be to show that brain regions involved in one are not as involved in the other. Studies of brain injury have highlighted the involvement of the left prefrontal cortex (PFC) in the retrieval of words in response to a cue (such as another word or a letter) and the temporal lobe in object naming and the retrieval of information about an object's characteristics (Martin and Chao, 2001). The processing of semantic information appears to involve a network of regions including the left prefrontal, parietal and posterior temporal cortex. When people are allowed to generate words to visually or auditorily presented cues, the posterior temporal cortex is activated regardless of whether the words are generated from the participants' native language or from their second language (Klein et al., 1999; Tatsumi et al., 1999).

Perhaps the most controversial data supporting the notion of semantic memory concerns stimulus specificity, the notion that one region of the brain is more involved than others in the perception or retrieval of certain categories of object. Well-known examples of this, as you saw in Chapter 6, are face recognition and the naming of inanimate and animate objects (Warrington, 1975; Warrington and Shallice, 1984; Warrington and McCarthy, 1987). Warrington's patients showed evidence of a dissociation between knowledge for living and non-living things. They were able to name non-living things but had considerable difficulty in naming living things, whether the stimuli to be named were verbal or nonverbal. In a later study, Warrington and Shallice (1984) interpreted their findings by suggesting that the two types of object-naming depended on different processing mechanisms. Living things would be processed primarily according to perceptual and visual features such as their size, colour, shape and so on, whereas non-living things would be processed according to their function.

Episodic memory across the ages

Based on a reading and understanding of the anatomical and physiological changes and reorganisation that occur in the brain during development – in childhood and old age – Shing et al. (2010) have proposed a new framework to understand how we develop episodic memory across the lifespan. Episodic memory – remembering of events in time and place that the person has experienced – appears susceptible to impairment in the very young and the very old (there is very little impairment before the age of 60 years). Shing suggests that there are two interacting processes at work: (1) a strategic component, which involves the control of memory formation and retrieval, from elaboration, organising memory at encoding and evaluating the result of retrieval; and (2) an associative component, which binds together the elements of memory to form a coherent representation. They argue that children's difficulties with episodic memory stem from problems with the

Memory – An international perspective

There seem to be real differences in the content of the autobiographical memories of people from different cultures. European Americans tend to recall their own roles in events and the feelings those events generated, whereas Asian Americans tend to recall details of social/group activities (Wang, 2004; Wang and Ross, 2005). One explanation for this is that American culture – at the most general level – is highly individualistic and emphasises and rewards autonomy and self-drive, whereas Asian cultures emphasise interdependence and the importance of social interaction/dependence.

To test this hypothesis, Wang (2008) asked Asian Americans to focus either on their American or their Asian background prior to recalling autobiographical memories. Those primed by the American condition recalled memories that were more self-focused and less social than were those whose Asian-ness had been primed. Participants who were not primed either way recalled the two types of content about equally.

Ji et al. (2009) hypothesised that Eastern cultures would make greater use of past information to make judgements about behaviour – presumably, because this provides more context in the same way that the background of a scene gives more context to the object in it. In an experiment where Canadian and Chinese participants were asked to read a description of a theft and then look at behaviours that had occurred near to the crime or at some time from it, Chinese participants placed more emphasis on distant events, considering them more relevant. They also recalled more detail about past events accurately than did the Canadians.

strategic component, which is mediated by the development of the PFC; older people's problems, however, stem from both and these are underpinned by changes in the PFC and medio-temporal lobes.

Neuroimaging data have generally supported the proposition that certain brain regions are specifically activated by specific stimuli, but do not explain why. Pictures of tools have been found to generate more brain activity in the left posterior temporal cortex than do pictures of other objects and animals (Martin *et al.*, 1996; Chao *et al.*, 1999). An area of the brain called the fusiform gyrus, as you saw in Chapter 6, is activated during face recognition but is not as consistently or significantly activated by other types of stimuli. Other stimuli which selectively activate certain brain regions are buildings and houses (Epstein and Kanwisher, 1998).

Explicit and implicit memory

Another distinction is made between explicit and implicit memory. **Explicit memory** refers to memory for information we were aware of learning. A simple example would be our recollection of the 12 times table: this is a task that most of us were instructed to remember explicitly. Recognition and recall of material in explicit memory require active recollection of material that has been studied (McBride and Dosher, 1997). For example, we might ask participants to recall freely as many words as they can after being presented with a long list of them, or to indicate which stimuli from an array of visual stimuli were previously seen. Under these conditions, participants are explicitly instructed to recall or to recognise.

Implicit memory, however, does not appear to rely on conscious awareness. Instead, it is memory for information that is incidentally or unintentionally learned and which does not rely on the recognition or recall of any specific learning episode (Schacter, 1987; Cleermans, 1993). It is sometimes referred to as being synonymous with procedural memory, the memory for knowing how to do things (like riding a bike, operating a computer keyboard, or playing a musical instrument). There is some question, however, over whether implicit and procedural memory are truly synonymous. Procedural memory implies that some conscious effort has been made towards learning a skill such as riding a bike or playing a musical instrument; implicit memory would assume that skills were learned without such conscious effort, which seems highly unlikely. Also, there seems to be little procedural input to performing a stem-completion task (described below), which taps implicit memory. There continues to be debate about the number of memory systems, and whether these memory systems are separate or different forms of the same system.

The acquisition of specific behaviours and skills is probably the most important form of implicit memory. Driving a car, turning the pages of a book, playing a musical instrument, dancing, throwing and catching a ball, sliding a chair backwards as we get up from the dinner table – all these skills involve coordination of movements with sensory information received from the environment and from our own moving body parts. We do not need to be able to describe these activities in order to perform them. We may not be aware of all the movements involved while we are performing them. Implicit memory may have evolved earlier than explicit memory.

A good example of learning without awareness is provided by an experiment conducted by Graf and Mandler (1984). These investigators showed people a list of six-letter words and had some of them engage in a task that involved elaborative processing: they were to think about each word and to decide how much they liked it. Other people were given a task that involved processing superficial features: they were asked to look at the words and decide whether they contained particular letters. Later, their explicit and implicit memories for the words were assessed. In both cases the basic task was the same, but the instructions to the subjects were different. People were shown the first three letters of each word. For example, if one of the words had been 'define', they would have been shown a card on which was printed 'def' (this is called a word-stem completion task). Several different six-letter words besides define begin with the letters 'def', such as 'deface', 'defame', 'defeat', 'defect', 'defend', 'defied' and 'deform', so there are several possible responses. The experimenters assessed explicit memory by asking people to try to remember the words they had seen previously, using the first three letters as a hint. They assessed implicit memory by asking the people to say the first word that came to mind that started with the three letters on the card.

Deliberate processing (shallow or deep processing) had a striking effect on the explicit memory task but not on the implicit memory task. When people used the three letters as cues for deliberate retrieval, they were much more successful if they had thought about whether they liked the word than if they simply paid attention to the occurrence of particular letters. However, when people simply said the first word that came to mind, the way they had studied the words had little effect on the number of correct words that 'popped into their heads' (see Figure 8.11).

In one experiment, Buchner and Wippich (2000) required participants either (1) to recognise from a list of new and old words, words that had been previously seen, or (2) to complete word stems using words that had previously been seen. This last implicit task was used in a famous study of amnesics' memory and no differences were found between amnesics and controls. When the researchers analysed the reliability of

Percentage recalled
40
20
Explicit recall
('Use letters as a cue')
Implicit recall
('First word that
comes to mind')
Semantic
(rate liking)
Superficial
(count letters)
Type of study of stimuli

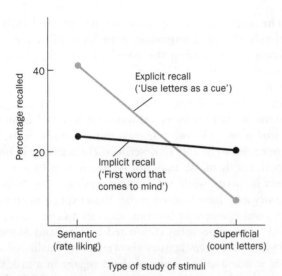

Figure 8.11 Explicit versus implicit memory. The graph shows the percentage of words recalled as a function of the type of study procedure. Deliberate processing improved performance of the explicit memory task but had little effect on the implicit memory task.

Source: Based on data from Graf, P. and Mandler, G., Activation makes words more accessible, but not necessarily more retrievable. *Journal of Verbal Learning and Verbal Behavior*, 1984, 23, 553–68.

these measures, the implicit measure was significantly less reliable than was the recognition measure. The study raises important questions about experiments which claim to show differences in memory performance based on implicit measures: it suggests that such differences may be due to methodological, rather than conceptual, reasons.

However, another study adopting a different method provides a different view. It puts forward the possibility that tests of explicit and implicit memory are dissociable because explicit tasks involve conceptual processing whereas implicit tasks involve perceptual processing. If both types of test are made conceptual, people may perform no differently on them (Brooks *et al.*, 2001).

Remembering

Remembering is an automatic process. The word 'automatic' means 'acting by itself'. But this definition implies that no special effort is involved. What is automatic is the retrieval of information from memory in response to the appropriate stimulus. What sometimes requires effort is the attempt to come up with the thoughts (the internal stimuli) that cause the information to be retrieved. In psychology experiments, retrieval can be measured in two basic ways: participants either recall material they have learned unprompted (free recall) or they are asked to identify material they had previously seen; this material is presented amongst stimuli that had not been seen (this is called a recognition memory paradigm).

The retrieval of implicit memories is automatic: when the appropriate stimulus occurs, it automatically evokes the appropriate response. Explicit memories can be retrieved automatically. Whisper your name to yourself. How did you manage to remember what your name is? How did you retrieve the information needed to move your lips in the proper sequence? Those questions cannot be answered by introspection. The information just leaps out at us when the proper question is asked (or, more generally, when the appropriate stimulus is encountered).

Reading provides a particularly compelling example of the automatic nature of memory retrieval. When an experienced reader looks at a familiar word, the name of the word occurs immediately, and so does the meaning. In fact, it is difficult to look at a word and not think of its name. Figure 8.12 contains a list of words that can be used to demonstrate a phenomenon known as the Stroop effect (Stroop, 1935; MacLeod, 1992). Look at the words in Figure 8.12 and, as quickly as you can, say the names of the colours in which the words are printed; do not read the words themselves.

Most people cannot completely ignore the words and simply name the colours; the tendency to think of the words and pronounce them is difficult to resist. The Stroop effect indicates that even when we try to suppress a well-practised memory, it tends to be retrieved automatically when the appropriate stimulus occurs.

blue blue blue green
green yellow red
yellow yellow blue
red green yellow
yellow green yellow
yellow red yellow
green blue yellow
red blue green green
blue blue green red

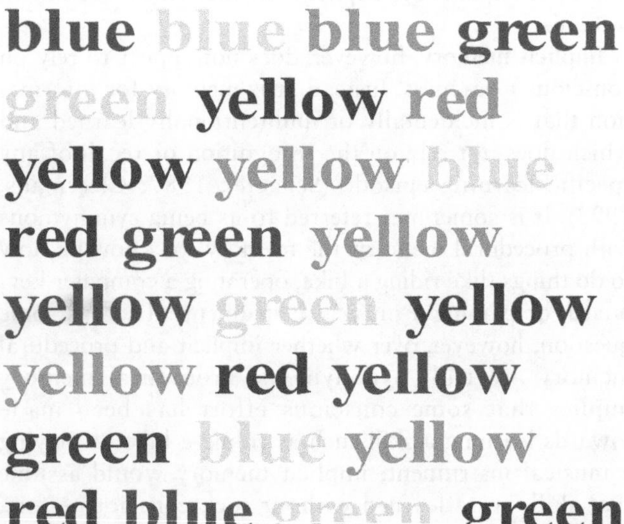

Figure 8.12 The Stroop effect. Name the colour in which the words are printed as quickly as you can; you will find it difficult to ignore what the words say.

But what about the fact that some memories seem to be difficult to recall? For most people, remembering information is effortless and smooth. It is something we do unconsciously and automatically – most of the time. Occasionally, though, our memory of a name or a place or something else fails. The experience is often frustrating because we know that the information is 'in there somewhere' but we just cannot seem to get it out. This is known as the **tip-of-the-tongue phenomenon** (you encountered the olfactory analogue, the tip-of-the-nose phenomenon, in Chapter 5). It was first studied carefully during the 1960s (Brown and McNeill, 1966), and since then we have learned a great deal about it (Jones, 1989; A.S. Brown, 1991). It is a common, if not universal, experience; it can occur about once a week and increases with age; it often involves proper names and knowing the first letter of the word; and is solved during the experience about 50 per cent of the time.

The active search for stimuli that will evoke the appropriate memory, as exemplified in the tip-of-the-tongue phenomenon, has been called recollection (Baddeley, 1982). Recollection may be aided by contextual variables, including physical objects, suggestions or other verbal stimuli. These contextual variables are called **retrieval cues**. The usefulness of these retrieval cues often depends on encoding specificity. Remember from the previous section that the encoding specificity principle states that information can only be retained if it has been stored and the way in which it is retrieved depends on how it was stored. One famous example is that of encoding and retrieving material above and under water. Godden and Baddeley (1975) asked skilled scuba divers to learn lists of words either under water or on land. The divers' ability to recall the lists was later tested in either the same or a different environment. The variable of interest was where subjects learned the list: in or out of the water. When lists were learned under water, they were recalled much better under water than on land, and lists learned on land were recalled better on land than in the water. The context in which information is learned or processed, therefore, influences our ability to recollect that information.

Reconstruction: remembering as a creative process

Much of what we recall from long-term memory may not be an accurate representation of what actually happened previously. One view of memory is that it is a plausible account of what might have happened or even of what we think should have happened. An early experiment by Bartlett drew attention to this possibility. This was Bartlett's view:

> Remembering is not the reexcitation of innumerable fixed, lifeless and fragmentary traces. It is an imaginative reconstruction, or construction, built out of the relation of our attitude towards a whole active mass of organised past reactions or experience and to a little outstanding detail which commonly appears in image or in language form. It is thus hardly ever really exact, even in the most rudimentary cases of rote recapitulation, and it is not at all important that it should be so. (*Source*: Bartlett, 1932, p. 213.)

Bartlett had people read a story or essay or look at a picture. Then he asked them on several later occasions to retell the prose passage or to draw the picture. Each time, the people 'remembered' the original a little differently. If the original story had contained peculiar and unexpected sequences of events, people tended to retell it in a more coherent and sensible fashion, as if their memories had been revised to make the information accord more closely with their own conceptions of reality. Bartlett concluded that people remember only a few striking details of an experience and that during recall they reconstruct the missing portions in accordance with their own expectations.

Many studies have confirmed Bartlett's conclusions and have extended his findings to related phenomena. Spiro (1977, 1980) found that people will remember even a rather simple story in different ways, according to their own conceptions of reality. Two groups of people read a story about an engaged couple in which the man was opposed to having children. In one version, the woman was upset when she learned his opinion because she wanted to have children. In the other version, the woman also did not want to have children. After reading the story, people were asked to fill out some forms. While collecting the forms, the experimenter either said nothing more about the story or 'casually mentioned' that the story was actually a true one and added one of two different endings: the couple got married and have been happy ever since, or the couple broke up and never saw each other again.

Two days, three weeks or six weeks later, the participants were asked to recall the story they had read. If at least three weeks had elapsed, people who had heard an ending that contradicted the story tended to 'remember' information that resolved the conflict. For example, if they had read that the woman was upset to learn that the man did not want children but were later told that the couple was happily married, people were likely to 'recall' something that would have resolved the conflict, such as that the couple had decided to adopt a child rather than have one of their own. If people had read that the woman also did not want children but were later told that the couple broke up, then they were likely to 'remember' that there was a difficulty with one set of parents. In contrast, people who had heard an ending that was consistent with the story they had read did not remember any extra facts; they did not need them to make sense of the story. For example, if they had heard that the couple disagreed about having a child and later broke up, no new 'facts' had to be added.

People were most confident about details that had actually not occurred but had been added to make more sense of the story. Thus, a person's confidence in the accuracy of a particular memory is not necessarily a good indication of whether the event actually occurred.

However, some researchers have criticised Bartlett's findings and some have even argued that Bartlett himself drew conclusions that were not warranted (Ost and Costall, 2002). Edwards and Middleton (1987), for example, have argued that the studies reported by Bartlett – these studies reported a form of memory called serial reproduction – did not assess the normal, everyday process of remembering. For example, participants in Bartlett's experiments wrote down alone what they could remember of a story read to them (rather than being retold to them, as you might expect in most everyday contexts). Others, such as Roediger *et al.* (2000), have argued that the material to be remembered was not particularly ecologically valid. One of the stories to be recalled, *The War of the Ghosts*, was quite exotic and unusual and not like everyday prose (Wynn and Logie, 1998; Roediger *et al.*, 2000), which made connections between parts of the story difficult to form. Bartlett did use more familiar material and found that participants made the typical reconstruction of the story. Bartlett's story is reproduced in Table 8.1, together with two recalled versions. Note the differences, and types of differences, between the actual story and the remembered one.

In an experiment in which the material to be remembered was relevant, Wynn and Logie (1998) quizzed undergraduates at two-month intervals about an incident at the beginning of the academic year and asked them to recall memories from that time. They found that memories were very resistant to change over time. However, although the study found that some distinctive memories could be accurately recalled, recent research suggests that memories can be very manipulable to the extent that false information introduced at recall can lead to this false information being incorporated into memory. The context in which memory and acquisition takes place can also influence our recall of events, as the next section shows.

Table 8.1 Two examples of *The War of the Ghosts* story. The first (a) is the original story; the second (b) is the same person's version of the story after eight days

(a) The War of the Ghosts

One night two young men from Egulac went down to the river to hunt seals, and while they were there it became foggy and calm. Then they heard war-cries, and they thought: 'Maybe this is a war-party.' They escaped to the shore, and hid behind a log. Now canoes came up, and they heard the noise of paddles, and saw one canoe coming up to them. There were five men in the canoe, and they said:

'What do you think? We wish to take you along. We are going up the river to make war on the people.'

One of the young men said: 'I have no arrows.'

'Arrows are in the canoe,' they said.

'I will not go along. I might be killed. My relatives do not know where I have gone. But you,' he said, turning to the other, 'may go with them.'

So one of the young men went, but the other returned home.

And the warriors went on up the river to a town on the other side of Kalama. The people came down to the water, and they began to fight, and many were killed. But presently the young man heard one of the warriors say: 'Quick, let us go home: that Indian has been hit.' Now he thought: 'Oh, they are ghosts.' He did not feel sick, but they said he had been shot.

So the canoes went back to Egulac, and the young man went ashore to his house, and made a fire. And he told everybody and said: 'Behold I accompanied the ghosts, and we went to fight. Many of our fellows were killed, and many of those who attacked us were killed. They said I was hit, and I did not feel sick.'

He told it all, and then he became quiet. When the sun rose he fell down. Something black came out of this mouth. His face became contorted. The people jumped up and cried.

He was dead.

(b) The War of the Ghosts

Two young men from Egulac went fishing. While thus engaged they heard a noise in the distance. 'That sounds like a war-cry,' said one, 'there is going to be some fighting.' Presently there appeared some warriors who invited them to join an expedition up the river.

One of the young men excused himself on the ground of family ties. 'I cannot come,' he said, 'as I might get killed.' So he returned home. The other man, however, joined the party, and they proceeded on canoes up the river. While landing on the banks the enemy appeared and were running down to meet them. Soon someone was wounded, and the party discovered that they were fighting against ghosts. The young man and his companion returned to the boats, and went back to their homes.

The next morning at dawn he was describing his adventures to his friends, who had gathered round him. Suddenly something black issued from his mouth, and he fell down uttering a cry. His friends closed around him, but found that he was dead.

Source: Bartlett, F.C., *Remembering*. London: Cambridge University Press, 1932.

Why do we remember the things that we do?

According to a review of the encoding and retrieval literature by Danker and Anderson (2010), it may be because the regions of the brain that are active during encoding are reactivated, partially, when we recall or retrieve.

In their review, they found that when neutral stimuli were associated with various sensory stimuli, the presence of these 'neutral' stimuli activated sensory and emotional regions in the brain. Similarly, when people encode material in a particular way, regions associated with different encoding strategies were reactivated. 'The process of remembering an episode,' they argue, 'involves literally returning to the brain state that was present during that episode' (p. 87). Interestingly, they also cite three studies of false memory which showed that false memory retrieval does not activate the region that is normally active during encoding.

Controversies in psychological science: How long does memory last?

The issue

In 1885, Hermann Ebbinghaus reported the results of the first experiment to determine the duration of memory. Using himself as a participant, Ebbinghaus memorised 13 nonsense syllables such as 'dax', 'wuj', 'lep' and 'pib'. He then studied how long it took him to relearn the original list after intervals varying from a few minutes up to 31 days. Figure 8.13 shows what he found. Much of what he learned was forgotten very quickly – usually within a day or two. But even after 31 days, he could still recall some of the original information.

Ebbinghaus's research dealt with remembering nonsense syllables and began a fruitful line of enquiry for psychologists interested in the length of time we can reasonably retain information before we begin to forget. For example, for how long might you remember the important experiences of your childhood? Or the information in this book? Or a well-known public event?

The evidence

Schmolck *et al.* (2000) looked at the effect of **retention interval** – the period between encoding and retrieval – on memory for the O.J. Simpson trial verdict, announced on 3 October 1995. College students were asked about how they heard the news about the verdict three days after the result, 15 months later and 32 months later. There was a significant difference between recall at 15 and at 32 months. After 15 months, about 50 per cent of recollections were accurate and only 11 per cent contained major errors; at 32 months, only 29 per cent of the recollections were accurate and 40 per cent contained major distortions. Figure 8.14 shows you how memory became distorted in these participants over time. There may be some value to this. There is neuroimaging evidence to suggest that the process of forgetting frees up regions of the brain: the forgetting of material that competes with more important information that we need to remember is associated with a decline in the activation of the PFC, for example (Kuhl *et al.*, 2007).

In a well-known study, Bahrick *et al.* (1975) investigated how much information about their classmates (such as faces

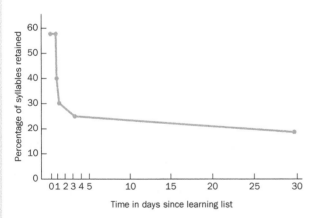

Figure 8.13 Ebbinghaus's (1885) forgetting curve.

Source: Adapted from Ebbinghaus, H., *Memory: A contribution to experimental psychology* (H.A. Ruger and C.E. Bussenius, trans.), 1885/1913. Teacher's College Press, Columbia University, New York.

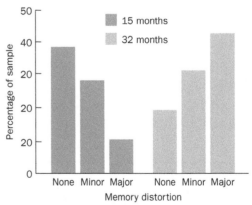

Figure 8.14 The degree of memory distortion (none, minor and major) for the O.J. Simpson trial verdict seen in Schmolck *et al.*'s study after 15 and 32 months.

Source: Schmolck, H., Buffalo, E.A. and Squire L.R., Memory distortions develop over time: Recollections of the O.J. Simpson trial verdict after 15 and 32 months. *Psychological Science*, 2000, 11(1), 39–45, reprinted by permission of Blackwell Publishers Ltd.

or names) graduates would remember 25 years after graduation. Bahrick found that the ability to recall classmates' names and to generate a name from a photo declined over time. The longer the retention interval (RI), the greater the decline. Recognition of faces and names and the matching of names to faces, however, was fairly robust. Ninety per cent of responses were correct over the first 15 years (although accuracy, again, declined when the RI became longer). Bahrick (1984) also reported that retention for Spanish learned at school declined in the first six years after graduating, stabilised for the next 35 years and then declined thereafter (see Figure 8.15).

Bahrick argued that the period of stability from 6 to 35 years represents a 'permastore'; this was a store of knowledge that was resistant to forgetting and which must have been learned deeply. An alternative interpretation, however, was suggested by Neisser (1984). He suggested that individuals have a schematic representation of a 'knowledge domain', that is, specific knowledge is not stored in a permanent way, but ways of representing that knowledge allow the retrieval of information. On the basis of this view, conceptual knowledge should be better retained (and retrieved) than would, say, straightforward facts.

Conway and co-workers (Conway *et al.*, 1991; Cohen *et al.*, 1992), measured students' retention of knowledge of cognitive psychology over 12 years (between 1978 and 1989) and found that memory declined in the first 36 months, then stabilised. However, the recall and recognition of proper names declined more rapidly than did memory for concepts. Why? If you accept Neisser's position, conceptual information should be better retained because memory is organised in such a way as to facilitate the retention of this type of information. Cohen (1990) further suggested that proper names lacked the semantic depth necessary for encoding concepts. Proper names did not need to be represented in abstract form and do not fall within a scheme of knowledge. In a follow-up study, Conway *et al.* (1992) found that coursework was a better predictor of retention than was exam performance because the learning for the former was distributed across the term whereas learning for the exam was, arguably, massed (being crammed).

Conway *et al.* (1997) found the better students seemed to 'remember' more of the answers in a multiple choice examination exam. For research methods courses, the same students 'knew' more, indicating that a **remember-to-know shift (R–K shift)** had occurred. Why, then, did better students not 'know' more after their lecture courses? One reason may be that the lecture courses contained more topics and that there was, therefore, greater variability in the types of knowledge domain to be learned (Conway *et al.*, 1997). Also, the research methods courses involved a large degree of repetition (as research methods courses do) and problem-solving is integral to the course: these factors might promote the R–K shift.

People's memory for their grades also declines with time (Bahrick *et al.*, 2008). One to 54 years after graduating, 276 participants were able to recall 3,025 of 3,967 grades. The better students made fewer errors. Of those who recalled their marks incorrectly, 81 per cent inflated the grade.

Conclusion

So, what can we conclude about long-term retention of knowledge? Non-schematic knowledge (such as the names of psychologists) declines more greatly than schematic knowledge (such as conceptual information). Better students also remember more of non-research methods psychology lecture courses and know more from research methods courses as well as recalling grades more accurately. One reason for this is that there is a shift from remembering to knowing, from episodic to semantic memory.

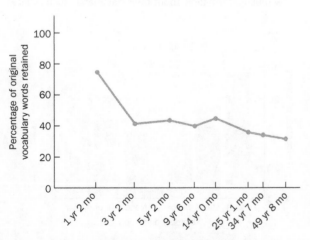

Figure 8.15 The forgetting curve for Spanish vocabulary.
Source: Adapted from Bahrick, H.P., Semantic memory content in permastore: Fifty years of Spanish learned in school. *Journal of Experimental Psychology: General*, 1984, 113, 1–29.

The malleability of memory

An experiment takes place in which participants are asked to read short passages of text and then, one day later in a telephone conversation, are asked questions about the content of the text and the context in which the reading occurred. Six weeks later, they are asked the same questions and also whether they remembered answers given in their telephone conversation. This experiment by Loftus and her colleagues (see Joslyn et al., 2001) found that while participants were remarkably good at remembering the correct answers they gave, they were significantly poor at remembering the questions they answered incorrectly. Perhaps the correct answers generated a positive mood or represented a more coherent memory.

This is one of several studies that indicate that our subjective beliefs about the context of content of memory can influence the recall of events. Research from social psychology and cognitive psychology shows how we can be misled into saying things or doing things we believe to be incorrect or which we are not sure about. The studies of Solomon Asch (described in Chapter 15) and Elizabeth Loftus (described below) show how malleable human behaviour can be, especially when we are faced with the pressure to conform.

Roediger et al. (2001) investigated whether conformity was simply a 'public' behaviour where a person wants to be seen to behave correctly and yet knows that their response is wrong, or a 'private' one, where the conversion in their belief is genuine. Studies of social psychology have shown that conformity is greater when participants make decisions in the company of others than when alone. Would the presence of another person who falsely claimed that an object had been in a room lead a participant also to claim that they remembered seeing an object in a room when no such object was present?

In one condition, a participant and a confederate watched slides of six household scenes featuring common household objects for either 15 or 60 seconds. In a collaborative recall task in which both individuals tried to recall as many objects in the scenes as they could, the confederate made occasional mistakes such as recalling items that were not in the slides. Some of these items were consistent with some of the items in the scene and other were not. After a short delay, the participant was asked to recall as many items from the scenes as they could. In a second condition, a similar experiment was carried out but no erroneous suggestions were made.

Participants in the company of those confederates who recalled objects that were not in the scenes recalled significantly more erroneous objects than did those in the control condition. This effect was magnified if people were exposed to the scenes for 15 seconds (presumably, reflecting the fact that such a short period leaves little time to monitor the scene and leads you to believe that there were objects presented that were not actually there). Participants who recalled these erroneous items were also more likely to report that they 'knew' the objects were in the scene rather than report they remembered seeing them.

Why were the participants influenced in this way? The authors interpret the results in terms of Johnson's source monitoring framework (Johnson et al., 1993). This argues that because we receive information from many sources, we can recall this material but misattribute it to earlier events. The collaborative recall part of the experiment may be an example of an early event acting as a source of memory interference where more recent memories interfere with current retrieval. The more consistent the confederates' recall is with that of the event or scene, the stronger the social contagion will be; the more distinctive the recall, the less likely social contagion is to occur.

This susceptibility has significant consequences for important areas of life, especially those which can have serious repercussions, such as eyewitness testimony.

Eyewitness testimony

On 4 October 1992, an El Al plane lost its engine after take-off from Amsterdam Schiphol Airport. It returned to the airport but lost height and crashed into an 11-storey apartment building. Ten months later, Crombag et al. (1996) questioned 193 individuals about the crash. The event was widely reported in the news but was not actually filmed. When individuals were asked if they saw the plane hit the building, 55 per cent said that they had (they had not been present at the time of the accident); 59 per cent said that the fire started immediately on impact. In a follow-up study, 68 per cent said they had seen the crash and 67 per cent of participants said that they saw the plane hit the building horizontally (in fact, it hit the building vertically).

This experiment and those of Loftus and her colleagues (Loftus, 1997) suggest that our recollections of events may not be infallible. Loftus, for example, has reported that the kinds of questions used to elicit information after an event has been experienced can have a major effect on what people remember. Loftus's research shows that even subtle changes in a question can affect people's recollections. For example, Loftus and Palmer (1974) showed people films of car accidents and asked them to estimate vehicles' speeds when they 'contacted/hit/bumped/collided/smashed' each other.

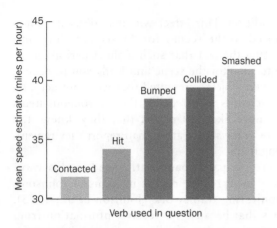

Figure 8.16 Leading questions and recall. Mean estimated speed of vehicles as recalled by people in the study of Loftus and Palmer (1974).

Source: Based on data from Loftus, E.F. and Palmer, J.C., Reconstruction of automobile destruction: An example of the interaction between language and memory. *Journal of Verbal Learning and Verbal Behavior*, 1974, 13, 585–89.

People's estimates of the vehicles' speeds were directly related to the force of the impact suggested by the verb, such as 'hit', that appeared in the question (see Figure 8.16). That is, the more expressive and dramatic the verb, the greater the estimated speed. In a similar experiment, people were asked a week after viewing the film whether they saw any broken glass at the scene (there was none). People in the 'smashed' group were most likely to say yes. Thus, a leading question that encouraged them to remember the vehicles going faster also encouraged them to remember that they saw non-existent broken glass. The question appears to have modified the memory itself.

Even very subtle leading questions can affect people's recollections. Loftus and Zanni (1975) showed people short films of an accident involving several vehicles. Some people were asked, 'Did you see a broken headlight?'; others were asked, 'Did you see the broken headlight?' The particular question biased the people's responses: although the film did not show a broken headlight, twice as many people who heard the article 'the' said that they remembered seeing one.

These are not the only examples of the ways in which memories can be altered. Individuals can be misled into thinking that a 'stop' sign was a 'give way' sign (Loftus *et al.*, 1978) and that a bare-handed thief wore gloves (Zaragoza and Mitchell, 1996). This misinformation effect is much stronger in older people (Jacoby *et al.*, 2005).

Experiments such as these have important implications for eyewitness testimony in courts of law. Wells and Seelau (1995) illustrate this point with the following examples:

What do these famous lines have in common? 'Beam me up, Scotty', 'Me Tarzan, you Jane', 'You dirty rat', 'Play it again, Sam', 'Elementary, my dear Watson'? Their fame, yes. But none of these lines was actually said. This highlights how our memory can be very malleable.

Source: Paramount Television/The Kobal Collection.

In 1984, Frederick Rene Dange was identified from a set of photographs and served 10 years in a Californian prison for rape, kidnapping, robbery and murder he did not commit. Dange was released in 1994 after a DNA test proved his innocence. In 1980, James Newsome was convicted of murder on the basis of eyewitness evidence. Fifteen years later, he was released after his fingerprints were submitted to new computer technology that implicated someone else as the murderer.

In a review of 205 cases of wrongful arrest, Rattner (1988) found that 52 per cent of these cases were associated with mistaken eyewitness testimony. In 1996, the National Institute of Justice found that 28 people had been wrongfully convicted based on eyewitness testimony (DNA evidence had exonerated the accused). Consequently, in 1998, the American Psychological Association issued a new series of rules and procedures designed to reduce errors made in considering eyewitness identification (Wells *et al.*, 1998).

Eyewitness identification

In a famous, historical case, Frye v. The United States (1923), the court ruled that scientific evidence was admissible only if it was generally accepted by the relevant scientific community. The judgment in a case called Daubert v. Merrell Dow Pharmaceuticals, Inc. 70 years later, however, ruled that judges would be the gatekeepers of scientific reliability in the US – they would judge the relevance, validity and reliability of scientific evidence. This makes the quality of evidence very important. Laypeople regard eyewitness reports as important to their evaluation of testimony (Shaw *et al.*, 1999). A survey of eyewitness testimony experts found that 98 per cent thought that testimony could be influenced by the way in which questions are worded, 98 per cent thought that police line-up instructions could affect identification, 87 per cent thought that eyewitnesses' confidence in their judgement is poorly correlated with the accuracy of the testimony, 83 per cent thought that memory loss is greatest immediately after witnessing the event and 80 per cent thought that eyewitness confidence is malleable and influenced by factors unrelated to accuracy, that exposure to a mugshot increases the likelihood of the face in the mugshot being selected from a later line-up, that children are more susceptible than adults to leading questions, and that eyewitnesses are better at recognising perpetrators of their own race (Kassin *et al.*, 2001).

According to forensic psychologists Gary Wells and Amy Bradfield (1999), 'There is increasing evidence that mistaken eyewitness identifications from line-ups and photospreads are the most frequent cause of juries convicting innocent persons.' They examined how information given to a witness before and after making a line-up identification affected the witness's confidence in making the correct identification. Giving positive post-identification feedback (such as telling the witness they identified the right suspect when they had not) inflates confidence in their identification, but also makes them think that their view of the suspect was better, that they identified the suspect more quickly and that they paid more attention when they witnessed the suspect.

In a twist to this type of experiment, Wells and Bradfield asked witnesses to think privately about how certain they were about their identification, how good their view was, how long they took to identify the suspect before being given false positive feedback. Another group of participants was given these instructions after receiving feedback and another was not instructed to think about its decision. In each case, the eyewitness had identified the wrong suspect.

The researchers found that when eyewitnesses were instructed to think about the decision prior to feedback, they were relatively unaffected by the false positive feedback. Those who were not instructed to think about their decision or were instructed to think after being given feedback showed a significant inflation in their confidence which also extended to other aspects of their testimony.

Interference

Although long-term memory is durable, it may also be susceptible to interference. The finding that some memories may interfere with the retrieval of others is well established. An early study by Jenkins and Dallenbach (1924) showed that people are less likely to remember information after an interval of wakefulness than after an interval of sleep, presumably because of new memories that are formed when one is awake.

Subsequent research soon showed that there are two types of interference in retrieval. Sometimes we experience **retroactive interference**: when we try to retrieve information, other information, which we have learned more recently, interferes. You may have a hard time recalling your old telephone number because a new one has replaced it. When memories that interfere with retrieval are formed after the learning that is being tested, we experience retroactive interference.

At other times, retrieval is impaired by **proactive interference**, in which our ability to recall new information is reduced because of information we learned previously. Figure 8.17 illustrates the experimental procedure used to examine the effects of proactive interference.

In this procedure, the experimental group learns the words in both list A and list B. The control group learns only the words in list B. Both groups then experience a retention interval before they are asked to recall the words in list B. If the experimental group recalls fewer words in list B during the test than does the control group, proactive interference is said to have occurred.

As reasonable and intuitive as the principle of interference may be, it has not gone unchallenged. Researchers agree that interference can affect retrieval, but some argue that the kinds of recall task people are asked to perform in the laboratory are most likely to be affected by interference. In real life, such effects may not be so powerful. For example, meaningful prose, such as the kind found in novels, is resistant to interference. That said, however, a recent study demonstrated that when participants watched either a violent, sexually explicit or neutral television show featuring nine adverts, recall of the advertisements immediately after the exposure and 24 hours later was poorer in the violent and sexual television conditions (Bushman and Bonacci, 2002). The effect was robust whether the television programme was liked or disliked and whether the participant was male or female. It seems as if some stimuli are powerful or exciting enough to interfere with our memory, even outside the laboratory.

Retroactive interference

Group	Initial learning	Retention interval	Retention test
Experimental	Learn A	Learn B	Recall A
Control	Learn A		Recall A

Proactive interference

Group	Initial learning		Retention interval	Retention test
Experimental	Learn A	Learn B		Recall B
Control	Learn B			Recall B

Figure 8.17 Retroactive and proactive interference illustrated.

State-dependent memory: the effect of mood on recall

Research suggests that recall of memory is better when people's moods or emotional states match their emotional states when they originally learned the material. This phenomenon is called **state-dependent memory**. The experimental procedure used in tests of state-dependent memory usually requires the manipulation of a person's mood by hypnosis (Bower, 1981), through drugs (Eich et al., 1975) or, more commonly, by the alteration of the environmental context, as exemplified by the scuba diver study described earlier (see page 271) (Godden and Baddeley, 1975). Next, the person is given a list of items to memorise. Later, when the person may or may not be experiencing the same mental or emotional state, they are asked to recall the items on the list. If the states match, recall is better.

Mood-dependent memory describes a context in which the person's mood at encoding and retrieval can affect the successful execution of these two processes (such as a well-liked song provoking memories of events experienced when the song was first heard). Although replications in which positive effects in mood-dependent memory are rare (Bower and Mayer, 1989), Eich (1995) suggests that when participants in these experiments experience strong/stable moods and are responsible for generating memory cues, mood-dependent memory is robust.

In one experiment, participants were asked to generate specific memories for events from autobiographical memory in response to common words (Eich et al., 1994). Two to three days later, participants were allowed to free recall the memories generated in the experiment. Eich et al. found that more events were recalled when the mood matched the mood at testing. In another set of experiments, Eich (1995) found that the transfer of infor-

mation from one environment to another is better if these environments feel similar. However, changes in the environment are not important if the moods at acquisition and reinstatement are the same. There is also evidence to suggest that individuals with mood disorders have a greater ability to discriminate between old and new stimuli if their moods at exposure and testing match (Eich et al., 1997).

Does this evidence suggest that mood-dependent memory is genuinely robust? Smith (1995) and Eich himself (1995) suggest that mood-dependent memory effects may be explained by other factors. Smith, for example, suggests that active memories or pre-existing mood generated at the time of acquisition could have cued a representation of the initial context of the original event.

State-dependent memory may be related to **place- or context-dependent memory**, illustrated by the Godden and Baddeley experiment above. The demonstration of place-dependent memory (PDM) depends on the event to be remembered, the nature of encoding and retrieval, the ease by which people can mentally reinstate themselves, and the retention interval (Smith, 1979, 1988; McDaniel et al., 1989; Wilhite, 1991). Reinstatement is important to PDM and refers to the process whereby the individual is placed in the same environment or is experiencing the same mood as when they originally encoded or generated information.

Because all of the factors listed above are important to PDM, the evidence for the phenomenon is mixed but generally supportive. In a meta-analysis of context-dependent memory studies in which retrieval and encoding were dependent on the explicit processing of aspects of the experimental environment, Smith and Vela (2001) found that context effects were very reliable. However, when people were encouraged to use non-contextual cues during encoding of material and its retrieval, the effects of environmental cues were reduced.

Accurate recall of memories of events experienced years previously has been found when the odours present at those events are re-presented some time later (Aggleton and Waskett, 1999; Chu and Downes, 2000), illustrating a form of state-dependent learning. Cann and Ross (1989) reported that the presence of a pleasant perfume at the presentation of a series of photographic slides led to better recognition if it was also presented at recall. Schab (1990) found that participants who learned and recalled in the presence of an ambient chocolate odour recalled more antonyms than did a control group or a group presented with an odour at encoding but not retrieval. In a subsequent experiment, odour-related words were no better recalled than neutral words although there was benefit to having the same odour present at encoding and recall. But the recall of memories may depend on the emotional nature of the odour. People report more unhappy memories in the presence of an unpleasant odour, for example, than they do in a pleasant one, and happier memories in the presence of a pleasant odour (Ehrlichman and Halpern, 1988).

Flashbulb memories

For British sports fans, it was a blessing; for those bored with wall-to-wall sport and physical activity involving sticks and running around in circles, it was a prompt for a collective groan. On 6 July 2005, the UK was told that London's bid to hold the 2012 Olympic Games was successful. Scenes of celebration ensued in Singapore and in London. The morning after, one of the authors was listening to the BBC's News and Sports radio station where the regular phone-in turned to discussing the logistics of holding the games and whether the capital would be up to it. At 9.50 a.m., the presenter, Michael Bannister, was about to introduce a guest when he read out an announcement from London Transport indicating that

Liverpool Street underground station in the financial district of London had been closed, due to a technical problem. Probably electrical, he said. This seemed unusual but, after 11 September 2001, nothing could be that unusual. The association with the 11 September attacks was prescient. It later transpired that bombs had been detonated in two London underground stations. A bus travelling near Tavistock Square, the home of the British Medical Association, had its roof blown off by another bomb. A total of 53 people were killed on 7 July 2005, including all of the British-born bombers.

The above recollection is an example of a **flashbulb memory** – the remembering of an event that is personally or socially important, novel, unexpected, vivid and has major long-term consequences. You will often hear people say that they knew exactly what they were doing when Kennedy was assassinated (Winograd and Killinger, 1983) in the same way that the author knew exactly where he was and what he was doing when news of the first of the 7 July London bombs exploding was heard.

The name 'flashbulb memories' was coined by Brown and Kulik (1977) to describe the vivid recollections from black and white respondents of the assassinations of Martin Luther King and President Kennedy. According to Brown and Kulik, the memory has a '"live" quality that is almost perceptual . . . like a photograph' (p. 74). Since Brown and Kulik's landmark paper was published, flashbulb memories have been reported for the death of the King of Belgium (Finkenauer et al., 1998), the death of spectators at the Hillsborough football stadium, England (Wright, 1993; Wright et al., 1998), the resignation of Margaret Thatcher as British prime minister (Conway et al., 1994; Wright et al., 1998), the Gulf War (Weaver, 1993), the assassination of Olaf Palme, the Swedish prime minister (Christianson, 1989), the 1986 American space shuttle disaster (Bohannon, 1988), the experience of being in an earthquake (Neisser et al., 1996b), the

Cutting edge: Humour improves memory, incidentally

A study from Japan has shown that participants' ability to draw pictures from memory depends on how humorous the pictures were (Takahashi and Inoue, 2009). The researchers presented students with pictures accompanied with a very humorous caption, a caption that was low in humour or a humour-free caption. Participants rated how funny they found the pictures and were then asked to draw as many of the pictures as they could in an unexpected memory test. Participants remembered the high-humour pictures better than the low-humour or neutral pictures. In a second experiment, participants were deliberately instructed to remember the pictures (explicit memory) or were not (incidental memory). In this experiment, degree of humour had no effect on memory in the explicit instructions condition; the effect was still seen in the implicit condition, suggesting that when individuals are specifically instructed to allocate memory resources to a task, the humorous nature of the stimulus becomes irrelevant because attention is directed elsewhere.

 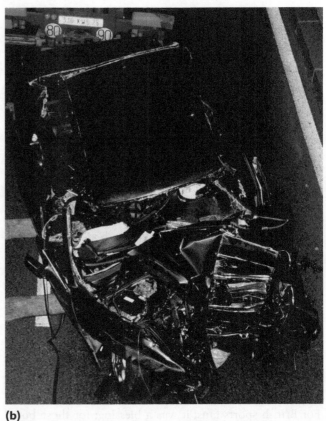

(a)   **(b)**

Flashbulb memories are thought to be generated by events that are important, unusual and personally meaningful. The attacks on the World Trade Center **(a)** and **(b)**, the car crash involving Dodi Fayed and Diana, Princess of Wales.
Source: © Press Association Images.

fall of the Berlin Wall, by East and West Germans (Bohn and Bernsten, 2007), and the death of Diana, Princess of Wales (Hornstein *et al.*, 2003).

According to Christianson (1992), 'people remember . . . public negative emotional events better than ordinary events thtat occurred equally long ago', suggesting that these events are not only more salient than others but also more accurate. Recently, there has been some debate on whether flashbulb memories are genuinely different from other types of memory. According to Brown and Kulik, flashbulb memories are of surprising or consequential events which are stored in the brain 'unchanged'; they also operate via a mechanism that is different from that which allows the formation of other types of memory. Wright (1993) and Wright *et al.* (1998), however, have conducted an extensive study of memories of the Hillsborough disaster and the resignation of Margaret Thatcher and suggest that flashbulb memories do not require a special mechanism. Furthermore, memories for these events may not even be vivid.

A problem with previous flashbulb memory research has been the absence of a 'control' group of memories: researchers have measured memories for flashbulb events over time but have not compared them with

memories for other events experienced roughly at the same time or before the memorable event. Addressing this problem, Talarico and Rubin (2003) examined under-graduates' recall of events when first hearing about the 11 September 2001 attacks on the World Trade Center, and of other everyday memories on 12 September. There is some debate in the flashbulb memory literature concerning the accuracy of recall of important events. Talarico and Rubin returned to the students one, six or 32 weeks later to test the accuracy and consistency of memory. There was a decline in the consistency of detail given for both types of event across time. Recall declined for both types of memory but flashbulb memories were recalled in a more narrative and coherent way. Emotion was unrelated to the consistency of recall but the more emotional the response, the greater the confidence in recalling details surrounding the event. The results suggest that while flashbulb memories are inconsistently recalled, their emotional impact makes people more confident about the perceived accuracy of their recall.

Hirst *et al.* (2009) asked 3,000 participants from the US to describe how they learned about the attacks on the World Trade Centre in 2001, one week, 11 months and/or 35 months after the attacks. They found that the forgetting rate for the event slowed after a year and that the emotional reactions to the event are remembered less well than are non-emotional aspects such as where they learned about the attack or from whom they learned the information.

Theories of flashbulb memories

What theory or theories can best account for flashbulb memories? Finkenauer *et al.* (1998) put the theories of Brown and Kulik (1977), and their own (called the emotional–integrative model), to the test by examining memories of the death of the King of Belgium on 13 August 1993. The experimenters' own model suggests that the appraisal of the event as novel and important leads to surprise. Surprise and the importance of the event to the person determine the intensity of the emotion experienced.

Finkenauer *et al.* noted that all the theories agreed that surprise and consequentiality are necessary for flashbulb memories. The degree of consequentiality influenced the degree of completeness and explicitness of the memory. Rehearsal of the memory for the event (thinking and talking about it) is also important. However, although the photographic model suggested that importance and feeling state were important determinants of flashbulb memories, these factors did not predict flashbulb memories.

Conway *et al.*'s (1994) model suggests that surprise and emotional feeling are determinants of flashbulb memories. However, Christianson and Engelberg's study (1999) of 203 participants' recall of the Estonia ferry disaster of September 1994 – in which 900 passengers died – found that fewer than one-third of respondents consistently reported their emotional state at the time of hearing of the disaster, suggesting that the recollection of emotional state is not a good predictor of memory consistency. This is consistent with Finkenauer *et al.*'s (1998) review of flashbulb memory models.

Finkenauer *et al.* suggest that the appraisal of an event as novel causes surprise; this then leads to the formation of a flashbulb memory. Appraisal of an event as important determines the intensity of the emotional response but this response does not directly affect the formation of flashbulb memories. Instead, the data suggest that emotional state triggers the rehearsal of remembered events which, in turn, strengthens memory.

The emotional–integrative model is a persuasive way of accounting for the factors necessary to determine a flashbulb memory. Because it is explicit, it is testable: you can generate hypotheses from the model and test them empirically. The evidence at the moment, however, suggests that flashbulb memories may not be special. Events may be memorable but they may not be memorable for the reasons originally given by the authors of flashbulb memories. Also, it seems as if the length of time since the flashbulb event was experienced is important to the amount of detail recalled.

The biological basis of memory

Much of what we know about the biology of human memory has been derived from studies of people who suffer from memory loss – amnesia – or from studies of animals in which amnesia is surgically induced to learn more about the specific brain mechanisms involved in memory (Parkin, 1996). But with the development of neuroimaging techniques, psychologists and neuroscientists have begun to outline the regions of the healthy brain that are active during the various memory processes of encoding, retrieval and working memory. Before reviewing this material, however, we need to go back to the beginning. To learning.

Before memory: learning

Before material can be remembered (and forgotten), it must first be learned. Learning involves three basic processes: the acquisition of material, its consolidation and its retrieval. Retrieval can involve free recall, where the participant is asked to remember previously presented stimuli, unaided by cues (or recognition) where the participant has, for example, to determine which of two stimuli had been previously presented (where one stimulus is a distractor and not experienced before and the other is the stimulus previously seen/heard/etc.).

During instrumental learning the organism identifies a link between a stimulus and the response (see Chapter 7). It learns that by making a certain number of behavioural responses or making these responses at certain intervals it will be rewarded (or reinforced; the reward reinforces the behaviour and encourages it to be repeated to achieve the same outcome). In classical conditioning, the organism learns that if two previously unassociated stimuli are paired often enough, then the response normally elicited by the first will also be elicited by the other (although before they were paired it would not have done this).

Learning seems to involve a strengthening of connections between neurons. The theory was proposed by Hebb (1949) in his famous book, *The Organization of Behaviour*. Hebb proposed that each psychologically important event is conceived of as the flow of activity in a neuronal loop. This loop is made up of the interconnections between dendrite, cell body and the synapses on these structures. The synapses in a particular path become functionally connected to form what Hebb called a cell assembly. The assumption he made was that if two neurons are excited together, they become linked functionally. If the synapse between two neurons is repeatedly activated as the postsynaptic neuron fires, then the structure or chemistry of the synapse changes. This change strengthens the connection between neurons.

Hebb proposed that short-term memory resulted from reverberation of the closed loops of the cell assembly; long-term memory is the more structural, lasting change in synaptic connections. This long-term change in structure is thought to reflect **long-term potentiation (LTP)**, a term which desribes the strengthening of neuronal connections via repeated stimulation (Lomo, 1966). Lomo found that if the axonal pathway from the entorhinal cortex to the dendate gyrus was repeatedly, electrically stimulated, then there was a long-term increase in the size of potentials generated by the postsynaptic neurons. LTP, therefore, was produced by the activation of synapses and the depolarisation of postsynaptic neurons. Psychologists agree that long-term memory involves more or less permanent changes in the structure of the brain (Fuster, 1995; Horn, 1998). But where and how?

Where are long-term memories formed?

Long-term potentiation seems to predominate in the hippocampus. If the hippocampus is stimulated, long-term physical changes are observed (Bliss and Gardner-Medwin, 1973). The entorhinal cortex provides inputs to the hippocampus. The axons from the entorhinal cortex pass through a part of the subcortex called the perforant path and form synapses with cells in the dendate gyrus, a part of the hippocampal formation.

The hippocampal formation itself is composed of two distinct structures: Ammon's horn (often referred to as the hippocampus) and the dendate gyrus. Ammon's horn comprises the substructures CA1, CA2 and CA3. CA1 is sometimes referred to as 'Sommer's sector'. There is also significant hippocampal output to the mammillary body via a tract called the fornix. Damage to each of these structures is sometimes associated with memory loss although the evidence for the involvement of the fornix is mixed (Calabrese *et al.*, 1995).

Translating this process into the behaviour seen in classical conditioning, the unconditioned stimulus (the puff of air) makes strong synaptic connections with the neurons which produce the unconditioned response (the blink). Presenting the conditioned stimulus (the tone) alone, generates weak synapses. But pairing the tone with the unconditioned stimulus leads to the conditioned stimulus forming very strong synaptic connections. The more often the pairing is made, the stronger the connection becomes. For this type of classical conditioning to occur, a functioning hippocampus appears to be necessary and the involvement of the structure would appear to be that of acquiring conscious knowledge of the relationship between the conditioned and unconditioned stimulus.

The hippocampus is also involved in learning the relationship between the unconditioned and conditioned stimulus when there is a delay between the presentation of each, a process called trace conditioning (Clark and Squire, 1998).

The consolidation of memory seems to be time-dependent. For example, the initial period and the few hours after the learning of UCS and CS pairings appears to be the moment when memory is consolidated. Therefore, interruption of the process at these times will impede consolidation (Bourtchouladze *et al.*, 1998). The first period of consolidation may be dependent on a different neurotransmitter system to that involved in the second. These are the NMDA and dopaminergic systems, respectively.

Chemical modulation of long-term potentiation

The most important excitatory neurotransmitter in the nervous system is glutamic acid or glutamate. One subtype of glutamate, N-methyl-D-aspartate (NMDA), appears to be important for producing long-term potentiation (LTP) (Abel and Lattal, 2001). NMDA receptors are found in the CA1 sector of the hippocampus; blocking activity in NMDA receptors prevents long-term potentiation in CA1 and the dendate gyrus. Blocking activity does not prevent or reverse LTP that has already occurred. The key process is the entry of calcium ions through ion channels, a phenomenon mediated by NMDA receptors.

When calcium enters an ion channel, changes in the structure of the neuron are produced by an enzyme, called a calcium-dependent enzyme, CDE (Lynch *et al.*, 1988). One CDE is called calpain which breaks down proteins in the spines of dendrites. Without this entry of calcium, LTP does not occur. Weak synapses, resulting from weak activation, do not lead to depolarisation that allows calcium ions to enter ion channels. Strong synapses that are activated do lead to this depolarisation, suggesting that the NMDA receptor is vital for the process of learning acquisition (Steele and Morris, 1999).

However, LTP can occur in other parts of the brain, apart from the hippocampus, and not all forms of LTP involve the NMDA receptors. So, although the hippocampus and the NMDA receptors seem to be prime mechanisms for LTP, they may not be the only ones. There are structures such as the amygdala, for example, that are involved in the conditioning of fear. Temporarily inactivating part of the amygdala, for example, can impair an organism's ability to learn to fear whereas inactivating the same area after conditioning has taken place still results in a fear response in the organism (Wilensky *et al.*, 1999). This finding suggests that this part of the amygdala may be involved in the acquisition, but not consolidation, of memory. The topic of fear conditioning is explored in more detail in Chapter 13.

One of the most important findings in the physiology of memory in recent decades has been that the hippocampal formation is essential for the formation or learning of new memories but it may not be involved in the long-term retention or retrieval of memory (Shors, 2004). What is unclear is why this dissociation should be.

Lee *et al.* (2004) have discovered that a type of gene, called *zif268*, is needed for the reconsolidation of context-dependent fear memory but another factor (called brain-derived neurotrophic factor or BDNF) is needed for initial consolidation. This shows how different physiological processes are involved in different aspects of memory formation: one type of factor is needed for immediate consolidation (but not reconsolidation) and another is involved in reconsolidation (but not immediate consolidation). The retrieval of fear memory also appears to recruit *zif268* but in another region of the brain – the anterior cingulate cortex (ACC) (Frankland *et al.*, 2004). Frankland *et al.* found that remote memory for fear was associated with anterior cingulate involvement in mice. Both the studies report changes in the brain during fear conditioning.

Studies of memory in animals have now associated around 47 specific genes with good memory performance. In research with human participants, genetic clusters were examined in participants who learned a series of semantically-unrelated words for immediate free recall and then completed an unexpected delayed free-recall test five minutes later (de Quervain and Papassotiropoulos, 2006). The genes that encoded a certain protein (ADCY8), and five others, were related to better memory performance and with greater activation in those brain regions involved in autobiographical memory and delayed recall (areas described below).

Amnesia

Damage to particular parts of the brain can permanently impair the ability to form new long-term memories while leaving language and perception intact. The inability to form new memories is called **anterograde amnesia**. The impairment in the ability to retrieve memories from before the brain injury is called **retrograde amnesia**. The brain damage can be caused by the effects of long-term alcoholism, severe malnutrition, stroke, head trauma or surgery. In general, people with anterograde amnesia can still remember events that occurred prior to the damage. They can talk about things that happened before the onset of their amnesia, but they cannot remember what has happened since. They never learn the names of people they subsequently meet, even if they see them daily for years.

One of the most famous cases of anterograde amnesia was patient HM (Scoville and Milner, 1957; Milner, 1970; Corkin *et al.*, 1981). HM's case is interesting because his amnesia was both severe and relatively pure, being uncontaminated by other neuropsychological deficits. At the age of nine, HM suffered a head injury after a bicycle accident which left him epileptic. In 1953, when HM was 27 years old, a neurosurgeon removed part of the temporal lobe on both sides of his brain because the drugs used to treat his epilepsy were not effective. The surgery cured the epilepsy, but it caused anterograde amnesia (this type of operation is no longer performed). HM died in 2009.

HM could carry on conversations and talk about general topics not related to recent events. He could also talk about his life prior to the surgery. However, he could not talk about anything that had happened since 1953. He lived in an institution where he could be cared for and spent most of his time solving crossword puzzles and watching television. HM was aware that he had a memory problem. For example, here is his response to a researcher's question:

Clearly, HM's problem lay in his ability to store new

Every day is alone in itself, whatever enjoyment I've had, and whatever sorrow I've had . . . Right now, I'm wondering. Have I done or said anything amiss? You see, at this moment everything looks clear to me, but what happened just before? That's what worries me. It's like waking from a dream; I just don't remember. (*Source:* Quoted in Milner, 1970, p. 37.)

information in long-term memory, not in his short-term memory. His verbal short-term memory was normal; he could repeat seven numbers forwards and five numbers backwards, which is about average for the general population. At first, investigators concluded that the problem was in memory consolidation and that the part of the brain that was destroyed during surgery was essential for carrying out this process. But subsequent evidence suggests that the brain damage disrupts explicit memory without seriously damaging implicit memory.

However, psychologists have questioned whether HM had a pure memory deficit, that is, one that prevents the acquisition or consolidation of new information for explicit recall but leaves other cognitive abilities (such as the ability to produce and comprehend language) intact (Mackay *et al.*, 1998). Mackay *et al.* cite studies in which participants described two meanings of ambiguous sentences presented visually (such as 'they talked about the problem with the mathematician') and compared these participants' performance with those of HM. HM's descriptions were 'less clear and concise and more repetitive than controls'. Independent judges also rated HM's descriptions as less grammatical and comprehensible.

Other investigators have found that people with anterograde amnesia can learn to solve puzzles, perform visual discriminations and make skilled movements that require hand–eye coordination (Squire, 1987). Clearly, their brains are still capable of undergoing the kinds of change that constitute long-term memory, but the people fail to remember having performed the tasks previously. For example, they may learn the task on one occasion. When, the next day, the experimenter brings them to the experimental apparatus and asks if they have ever seen it before, they say no. They have no explicit, episodic memory for having spent some time learning the task. But then they go on to perform the task well, clearly demonstrating the existence of implicit long-term memory.

Graf and Mandler (1984) showed lists of six-letter words to amnesic and non-amnesic people and asked them to rate how much they liked them. They then administered two types of memory test. In the explicit memory condition, they asked people to recall the words they had seen. In the implicit memory condition, they presented cards containing the first three letters of the words and asked people to say the first word that started with those letters that came into their minds. The amnesic people explicitly remembered fewer words than the non-amnesic people in the control group, but both groups performed well on the implicit memory task (see Figure 8.18).

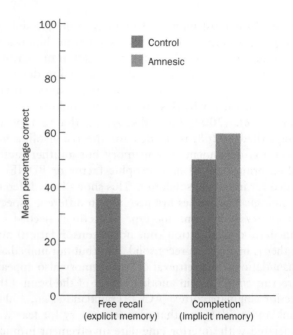

Figure 8.18 Explicit and implicit memory of amnesic patients and non-amnesic people. The performance of amnesic patients was impaired when they were instructed to try to recall the words they had previously seen but not when they were asked to say the first word that came into their minds.

Source: Adapted from Graf, P., Squire, L.R. and Mandler, G., The information that amnesic patients do not forget. *Journal of Experimental Psychology: Learning, memory and cognition*, 1984, 10, 164–78.

Psychology in action: Memory at the movies . . .

Common sense may be common (see Chapter 1) but does not make much sense in psychology. Sometimes people's misunderstandings of psychology, and science in general, can have serious consequences, such as distorting how mental illness and the mentally ill are viewed (see Chapter 18). In more light-hearted contexts, the misperception can seem comical. Films, television and novels exploit artistic licence to bend scientific facts sometimes to breaking point. An episode of the American sci-fi television programme, *The X Files*, had a protagonist confuse a technique used for measuring brain structure with one used for measuring brain activity. This protagonist was the medically qualified one. Even as this passage was being written, a journalist on a 24-hour television news channel is describing football supporters' reaction to a national football team manager as 'Pavlovian', thus misunderstanding Pavlov and, probably, football supporters.

Perhaps nowhere is artistic licence more vigorously exploited than in films. Baxendale (2004) has reviewed how films interpret and portray an important human phenomenon: memory loss. *The Bourne Supremacy, Total Recall, Memento, Men in Black, The Eternal Sunshine of the Spotless Mind* . . . several recent films have used amnesia as the hook with which to draw in

cinema-goers and the hook is not new. At least ten silent movies released before 1926 featured amnesic characters.

Amnesia is an organic disorder with a neurological or psychiatric basis. Fugue states (where people experience lack of consciousness but appear conscious and wander around oblivious to their condition, ending up in, for example, a bus depot) or states where people believe they are someone else (dissociative disorders) are rare, as are changes in personality and identity. Amnesic patients have normal intelligence, normal attention span but show a severe inability to process new information. The most common causes of amnesia are neurosurgery, infection or stroke. Many films routinely flout these known facts in the cause of entertainment and Baxendale highlights a few of these.

In terms of causes of amnesia, she finds that many movies attribute memory loss to car crashes and assault. When Santa falls from a sleigh in the film *Santa Who?* he loses his identity and autobiographical memory. This cause and effect, as Baxendale suggests, is highly unlikely. Everyday memory difficulties are also rarely seen (although they should be one of the defining features of the disorder) and amnesic characters pursue new careers and social networks,

Psychology in action: *Continued*

unimpeded by their cinematic affliction. Trained assassins are especially prone to developing this trait, as seen in *The Bourne Identity* and *The Long Kiss Goodnight*. (Although in an unusual and knowing twist, *The Bourne Identity Crisis* features a protagonist who forgets he is gay and becomes a trained assassin.)

Two other films, best forgotten, are *Clean Slate* and *50 First Dates*. In the former, the hero is able to form new memories while awake but, after sleeping, forgets all he has learned. In the latter, Adam Sandler attempts to seduce Drew Barrymore who forgets each meeting they have had. As Baxendale pointedly notes, 'Some viewers might envy Ms Barrymore's ability to forget her romantic encounters with Mr Sandler, but her affliction seems to be the result of a head injury rather than the unconscious suppression of traumatic memories.' Cinematic forgetfulness reaches its zenith – humorously and deliberately – in *Groundhog Day* where Bill Murray's character exists in a world in which he perpetually relives the previous day.

In terms of recovery, Baxendale notes how television and movies are enamoured of the 'two are better than one' philosophy of head injury – a bang on the head can produce memory loss but a second bang can restore it. This happens in the Tom and Jerry cartoons and films such as *Tarzan the Tiger* and *Singing in the Dark*. In real life, a second blow does not make an effective rehabilitation strategy.

There are some honourable exceptions to this filmic hall of dishonour. Christopher Nolan's innovative film *Memento*, for example, features a character played by Guy Pearce who has severe anterograde amnesia and tries to recall the events leading to his wife's death. This is relayed in a narrative played backwards, as the character tries to piece together clues to his life. The character does not suffer retrograde amnesia, does not lose his identity and suffers severe everyday memory problems (like HM who, apparently, inspired the story). He writes every detail he thinks is important, and which may help him understand the past, in a clearly visible place such as his body (if he used a notebook, he would forget about it and forget what he wrote in it).

Ironically, the film that does portray amnesia in the most realistic form, according to Baxendale, does not feature humans at all. It is *Finding Nemo* and the fish, Dory, has severe difficulty in learning and remembering new information, recalling names and knowing where she is going and why. 'Although her condition is often played for laughs,' Baxendale writes, 'poignant aspects of her memory loss are also portrayed, when she is alone, lost, and profoundly confused.' This reflects real-life, human amnesia.

Does the accurate or inaccurate portrayal of amnesia in films matter? After all, we don't always go to the cinema to confront a mirror raised to real life. We go to suspend disbelief. We go to see fish, toys and ants talking, to see a man in an unlikely, figure-hugging suit swinging from buildings by sticky strings spurting from his wrists, to cheer for a group of hobbits, to boo an asthmatic, black-helmeted villain, or to see a boy in spectacles racing on a broom in a flying contest. Reality becomes important, however, if the reality is meant to be accurately portrayed. Dustin Hoffman's character in *Rain Man*, for example, although an extreme example, is an attempt at a serious portrayal of the social debilitation experienced by a person with Asperger's Syndrome. (The man who inspired the Hoffman character appears in Chapter 12.)

The general lesson seems to be that if you expect to go to the cinema and see an accurate portrayal of memory loss then . . . well . . . forget it.

(a)

(b)

(a) Leonard Shelby, played by Guy Pearce in the film *Memento*, is one of the few successful cinematic portrayals of amnesia. The most successful, however, appears to be Dory **(b)**, in *Finding Nemo*.

Source: (a) Summit Entertainment/The Kobal Collection Ltd.; (b) W. Disney/Everett/Rex Features.

Amnesia is not an all-or-nothing phenomenon, however. Severe amnesia, for example, can leave facial familiarity recognition, the acquisition of school knowledge or knowledge of the meaning of words intact. The fact that amnesic patients can remember facts and describe experiences that occurred before the brain injury indicates that their ability to recall explicit memories acquired earlier is not severely disrupted. Of those parts of the brain necessary for establishing new explicit memories, the most important part seems to be the hippocampus, a structure located deep within the temporal lobe, and which forms part of the limbic system.

The role of the hippocampus in memory

The hippocampus, like many structures of the brain, is not fully mature at birth. In fact, it is not until a child is 2–3 years old that most of these structures are fully developed. As a result, many cognitive activities, such as the formation of semantic memories, are not particularly well developed until this age (Liston and Kagan, 2002). One reason that few people remember events that occurred during infancy may be the immaturity of the hippocampus.

The hippocampus receives information from all association areas of the brain and sends information back to them. In addition, the hippocampus has two-way connections with many regions in the interior of the cerebral hemispheres. Thus, the hippocampal formation is in a position to 'know' – and to influence – what is going on in the rest of the brain (Gluck and Myers, 1995). Presumably, it uses this information to influence the establishment of explicit long-term memories.

The structure appears to be very important for navigating or exploring our way around a spatial environment or in forming representations of the locations of objects (O'Keefe and Nadel, 1978). Morris et al. (1982), for example, placed rats in a pool of milky water that contained a platform just underneath the water. In order to avoid swimming constantly, the rats had to find the platform hidden beneath the milky water.

Eventually, through trial and error, the rats would find the platform. Then, the researchers performed a series of experimental ablations. One group of rats received lesions to the hippocampus, another received lesions to the cerebral cortex and another received no lesion. When the rats were then allowed into the pool, the pattern of behaviour seen in Figure 8.19 was observed. Notice how those rats with the hippocampus lesion had extremely poor navigation compared with the cortex lesion and control group. Similarly, when rats had learned that there was a platform under water and were then allowed to explore the water with the platform removed, those with an intact hippocampus would spend longer in the part of the maze where the platform had been previously positioned. Those rats with hippocampal lesions, however, did not engage in this 'dwell time' in the quadrant where the platform once was (Gerlai, 2001). This suggests an important role for the hippocampus in spatial learning.

Both rodents and primates show deficits in what has been called spatial memory (Redish and Touretzky, 1997). Spatial memory, the ability to encode and retrieve information about locations and routes is, like memory itself, not a unitary function. Kessels et al. (2001), for example, note that there is a difference between memory for routes and paths and the knowledge of spatial layouts which enables a person to find an object or a location. The role of the hippocampus in aspects of spatial memory has been well documented in animals, but O'Keefe and Nadel's view (1978) of hippocampal function has not gone unchallenged. Olton et al. (1979), for example, argued that the hippocampus was not exclusively responsible for spatial memory but was more involved in working memory. Tasks used in spatial memory tasks were, according to the theory, tests of short-term or working memory rather than spatial

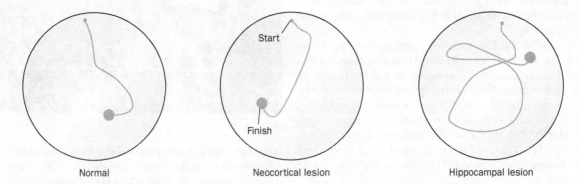

Figure 8.19 The effects of damaging a rat's hippocampus on its ability to find a platform in opaque water after having initially been trained to locate the platform successfully.

Source: Reprinted by permission from Macmillan Publishers Ltd: *Nature*, Place navigation impaired in rats with hippocampal lesions, 182(297), pp. 681–683 (Morris, R.G.M. *et al.* 1982), Copyright 1982.

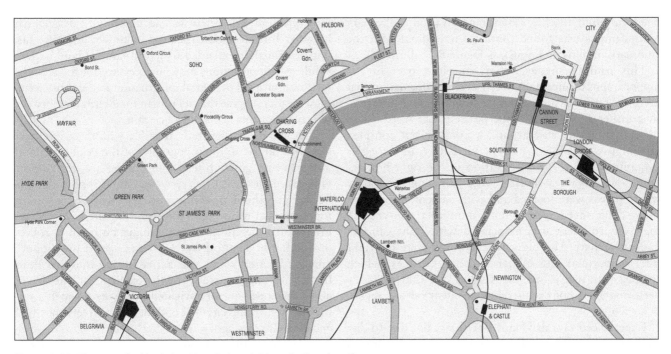

Figure 8.20 The route (in blue) that Maguire's taxi drivers had to describe.

Source: Maguire, E.A., Frackowiak, R.S.J. and Frith, C.D., Recalling routes around London: Activation of the right hippocampus in taxi drivers. *Journal of Neuroscience*, 1997, 17, 7103. © Society for Neuroscience.

memory: all required the organism to keep information in mind while they engaged in another behaviour that used such information and this is the feature that was disrupted by damage.

In a meta-analysis of 27 studies that reviewed the consequences of hippocampal dysfunction, Kessels *et al.* (2001) found that whereas mild or moderate impairments were found on tasks requiring integration of information or navigation around a maze, there was little effect on spatial working memory. There was, however, a large impairment on tests of positional memory such as locating Xs in an array of letters. The lesions in patients showing mild to severe impairment were invariably to the right hippocampus, a finding that is consistent with O'Keefe and Nadel's hypothesis (1978) that the right hippocampus is specialised for mapping spatial information.

Neuroimaging and memory

Although much of our knowledge about the brain mechanisms that underlie memory has been derived from animal studies or from studies of individuals with brain injury, neuroimaging studies provide evidence from healthy individuals, and suggest that different regions of the brain are more involved than others in performing different types of memory task (Cabeza and Nyberg, 2000; Fletcher and Henson, 2001). As Horn (1998) asked, 'If memory consists of a mark made in the brain by a particular experience, where is the mark and what is its nature?'

Spatial navigation

Maguire and her colleagues set up a novel and unusual experiment to see whether the hippocampus was active during spatial navigation (Maguire *et al.*, 1997). In their study, 11 London taxi drivers each with at least 14 years' experience of driving described the shortest legal route between two locations in London as a PET scanner observed brain activity study. You can see a map of the route in Figure 8.20.

The taxi drivers were also asked to recall famous London landmarks (an examination of topographical memory). The activation during these tasks was compared with that during the recall of sequences from famous films. When the drivers described the route from

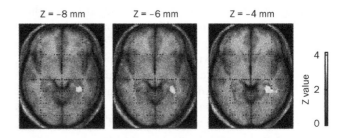

Figure 8.21 Areas of the brain activated by the recall of routes. Note the activation of the right hippocampus.

Source: Maguire, E.A., Frackowiak, R.S.J. and Frith, C.D., Recalling routes around London: Activation of the right hippocampus in taxi drivers. *Journal of Neuroscience*, 1997, 17, 7103. © Society for Neuroscience.

one location to another, significant activation of the right hippocampus was found (but was not found with the landmark or film conditions), as Figure 8.21 illustrates.

This finding suggests that the right part of the hippocampus is important to retrieval of information that involves recall of movement in complex environments. In another PET experiment, participants were asked to navigate their way around a familiar but complex virtual town, using a pair of virtual reality goggles (Maguire *et al.*, 1998). Activation of the right hippocampus was again associated with knowing accurately where places were located and with navigating between them. The speed with which individuals navigated their environment was associated with right caudate nucleus activity. Also activated, however, were the right inferior parietal and bilateral medial cortices, which suggests, as many imaging studies do, that memory performance is not exclusively dependent on one region or structure.

Experienced taxi driving is one thing, but day-to-day navigation is another. A recent study, however, examined untrained people's ability to navigate (drive) their way around a virtual London, as fMRI measured brain activation to see which regions of the brain were recruited during this type of task (Spiers and Maguire, 2007). Starting, turning and stopping were associated with activation in the premotor, parietal and cerebellar regions of the brain. Swerving and avoiding collisions were associated with occipital and parietal, as well as premotor and insula activation. The right prefrontal lobe was especially active when observing road traffic rules (supporting other studies you read about in Chapter 4 (and will read about further in Chapter 13) suggesting that these regions play a role in moral reasoning.

The picture is not consistent, however. Rosenbaum *et al.* (2005) noted that Maguire *et al.*'s data showed that activation was actually seen in the parahippocampal gyrus, not the hippocampus. They also describe results from their own fMRI study which found that participants who were engaged in the recall of well-rehearsed knowledge about a city's topography showed greatest activation in the parahippocampal gyrus (there was slight activation in the hippocampus) (Rosenbaum *et al.*, 2004).

A case study, reported by Rosenbaum *et al.* (2005), provides another source of evidence against the involvement of the hippocampus in topographical memory. They studied SB, a patient with probable Alzheimer's disease who had been a taxi driver in Toronto, Canada, for 40 years. His remote memory for spatial locations in Toronto was compared with two other retired taxi drivers (with different illnesses) and a healthy control group. His ability to spatially navigate between various Toronto landmarks was comparable to the other participants. His most pronounced deficit was an inability to distinguish between Toronto landmarks and unknown buildings (an impairment that extended to world-famous landmarks). While the hippocampus may be necessary for the acquisition and retrieval of spatial information in the short-term, these results suggest that its role in long-term memory for old environments is much less certain.

This and the earlier study, together with those of amnesics who can recall the topography of the neighbourhood in which they grew up (e.g. Teng and Squire, 1999), provides a challenge to the view that the hippocampus is needed for the acquisition and retrieval of long-term topographical memories. However, Maguire *et al.* (2006) investigated the effects of brain injury on recall of routes in London in a taxi driver with damage to the hippocampus, the area which was active during route recall in the earlier imaging study. In the experiment, the driver and a matched control navigated their way through a virtual version of the city of London, along streets they had encoded 40 years ago.

They found that the injury did not affect the driver's ability to orientate himself around the city, his knowledge of landmarks and the spatial relationships between them or his ability to navigate the town. However, the driver did have difficulty when navigating routes that were not A-roads (major road arteries). It was as if complex routes were more problematic for him. It is possible, therefore, that coarse recall of topography is not affected by the hippocampus but recall of detailed, complex spatial relations might be.

Working memory

The ability to manipulate information in memory over a short space of time seems to be the primary responsibility of the frontal lobes (Fletcher and Henson, 2001), regions which, apparently contrarily, also become active during the retrieval of material that has been retained over long periods. Fletcher and Henson (2001) distinguish between two types of measures in working memory tasks: maintenance and manipulation. Working memory maintenance tasks involve measuring the process of keeping information in mind; working memory manipulation tasks involve measuring the reorganisation of material that is kept in mind.

A typical maintenance task involves presenting a participant with between three and nine stimuli and asking them to indicate whether a single stimulus presented subsequently formed part of the original array. The letter-based version of this task is usually associated with significant increases in activation in the left hemisphere, especially the ventrolateral frontal cortex, parietal lobe and premotor area (Awh *et al.*, 1996). When the task involves information about spatial relations or objects rather than words, activity is greater in the right hemisphere. Often, the same regions activated by letters or words in the left hemisphere are also activated in the right by spatial/object stimuli (Smith *et al.*, 1996). When we maintain information in mind, there is sustained firing of neurons, especially in the PFC and, sometimes, the dorsolateral and intraparietal cortex – activation here is thought to predict better (or worse) working memory performance (Klingberg, 2010).

Remember from earlier that one type of working memory manipulation task involves presenting the participant with a series of five letters and then asking them to recite the letters forwards, backwards or in alphabetical order, in the mind. After a delay, the participant is asked to match the number order of a given letter, according to the mental manipulation (e.g. forwards, backwards or alphabetical). During the delay, there is usually activation seen in the ventrolateral and dorsolateral frontal cortex; during the reordering part of the task, activation is seen more in the dorsolateral part (D'Esposito *et al.*, 1999; Postle *et al.*, 1999).

At the neurotransmitter level, dopamine may be a key chemical. When training on working memory tasks occurs and two types of dopamine receptor are measured five weeks after this, one type (D2) remained unchanged in the cortex and subcortex but another (D1) declined in the cortex (McNab *et al.*, 2009). Agents which block dopamine can lead to better working memory performance (Vijayraghavan *et al.*, 2007).

Encoding and retrieval in episodic and semantic memory

Given that encoding and retrieval of information are two different cognitive tasks relating to the same function, you would expect these processes to have different underlying neural substrates. The left PFC is activated when we learn and encode material whereas the right side is activated when we try to recall this material (Tulving *et al.*, 1994; Nyberg *et al.*, 1996; Fletcher *et al.*, 1998a, b).

The encoding of episodic memory is associated with activity in regions including the prefrontal and medial-temporal cortex and the cerebellum (Cabeza and Nyberg, 2000). Studies have usually found left-sided activation during episodic memory encoding, especially during the encoding of verbal material. The encoding of non-verbal material tends to be associated with bilateral activity in the frontal cortex. The role of the left PFC in memory may be one of organising information: this part of the brain is responsible for our ability to group items on the basis of some characteristic or attribute. However, it is thought that the recollection of autobiographical memories also relies on the hippocampus (Piolini *et al.*, 2009).

Retrieval of episodic memory is consistently associated with prefrontal activation, sometimes in both cerebral hemispheres but usually in the right, although other regions are also activated depending on the type of material retrieved (Fletcher *et al.*, 1996; Nyberg *et al.*, 1996). Furthermore, there is evidence that the amygdala and the hippocampus contain neurons that encode our ability to recognise something and also when/where this something was originally seen. In one experiment, participants were asked to remember as many of 12 unique items, presented on a computer screen, as possible and also remember where on the screen they had seen them. The stronger the neurons' responses in the amygdala and hippocampus during encoding, the better the recall (Rutishauser *et al.*, 2008).

Remembering and long-term memory

Neuroimaging studies of long-term memory involve presenting the participants with several items that they are told to memorise (or given no memorisation instructions), and then asking them to recall the presented material some time later. Usually, the participant is asked to recognise the presented stimulus from a range of target and distractor stimuli. The process involves encoding and retrieval and neuroimaging research has highlighted the different brain regions involved in each type of process. If encoding is intentional or incidental, it is associated with left frontal cortex activation, as we have already seen. Simple retrieval of information is also associated with left frontal lobe activation (Fletcher and Henson, 2001).

If encoding and retrieval is successful, would greater brain activation be seen during encoding for those stimuli that were successfully encoded or for all stimuli regardless of how well they were retrieved? There is evidence from EEG studies that a specific type of electrical activity, called EEG theta, is greater during the encoding of successfully retrieved words than unsuccessfully retrieved ones (Klimesch *et al.*, 1997). In one neuroimaging study, Brewer *et al.* (1998) found that greater right frontal cortex activity was associated with successful encoding. Individuals were asked to view a series of indoor or outdoor scenes and decide whether each scene depicted outdoors or indoors. Thirty minutes later, they were given a recognition test and asked to indicate whether they remembered the scene, thought the scene was familiar but not well remembered or was forgotten. Memory for the scenes was predicted by frontal and parahippocampal activation with greater activation found for the remembered images.

Lateralisation of memory processes

A model called the HERA model has been proposed to account for the differences in brain activation seen during memory encoding and retrieval. HERA stands for Hemispheric Encoding-Retrieval Asymmetry, and the model argues that greater left than right frontal cortex activation is seen during episodic encoding whereas greater right than left frontal cortex activation is seen during episodic retrieval (Tulving *et al.*, 1994). The evidence reviewed above and more extensively in Fletcher and Henson (2001) and Cabeza and Nyberg (2000) suggests strong support for the model. In general, verbal encoding is associated with left frontal activation whereas right activation is more common during retrieval but, as we have seen, such areas as well as others can be bilaterally active during encoding and retrieval. Why?

Fletcher and Henson (2001) put forward some interesting possibilities. Two are statistical and methodological and hinge on (1) the type of statistical parameters a study sets for **statistical significance** in neuroimaging research (different studies may set different parameters) and (2) the small number of samples used in neuroimaging research. A further reason may be the lack of clarity over the precise definition of cognitive processes in memory studies. Setting aside questions regarding what is verbal and what is non-verbal (and whether these two categories could be considered unitary), there are also questions regarding the nature of encoding and retrieval. Not all studies use the same measures of encoding or retrieval; perhaps the inconsistencies in findings can, therefore, be attributed to these different methodological approaches.

The nature of the model is challengeable, however. Dobbins and Wagner (2005) presented participants with various stimuli and then presented three images

(two of which had been seen before) and asked them three different questions about each. The questions were 'Was this bigger before?' (the participant had to indicate whether an image previously seen had been bigger), 'Was it pleasant in the previous task?' (the participant was asked to indicate which of the stimuli was rated as pleasant or unpleasant in the previous task) and 'Is there a new item?' (the participant was asked to identify the image that had not been seen before). Two areas of the left PFC (specifically, the ventromedial/orbitofrontal cortex) were active in each of the retrieval conditions. There was greater activation in the anterior part of this region when participants retrieved conceptual information (pleasant condition) and in the posterior region during retrieval of conceptual and perceptual information (see Figure 8.22).

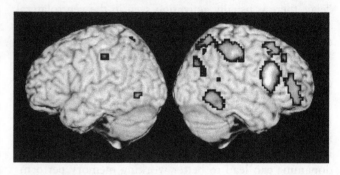

Figure 8.22 Domain-general and domain-sensitive prefrontal mechanisms.

Source: Dobbins, I.G. & Wagner, A.D. (2005) Domain-general and domain-sensitive prefrontal mechanisms for recollecting events and detecting novelty. *Cerebral Cortex*, 15, 1768-1778.

Chapter review

Sensory memory

- Memory is the process of encoding, storing and retrieving information. It exists in three forms: sensory, short-term/working and long-term. The characteristics of each differ, which suggests that they differ physiologically as well.
- Sensory memory provides temporary storage of information until the newly perceived information can be stored in short-term memory.
- Information in sensory memory lasts for only a short time. When a visual stimulus is presented in a brief flash, all of the information is available for a short time (iconic memory). If the viewer's attention is directed to one line of information within a few hundred milliseconds of the flash, the information can be transferred into short-term memory. Echoic memory

– sensory memory for sound – appears to operate similarly.

Short-term and working memory

- Short-term memory and working memory contain a representation of information that has just been perceived, such as a person's name or telephone number. Although the capacity of short-term memory is limited, we can rehearse the information as long as we choose, thus increasing the likelihood that we will remember it indefinitely.
- Information in short-term memory is encoded according to previously learned rules. Information in long-term memory determines the nature of the encoding.

- Working memory is different from short-term memory in that it allows the short-term storage and manipulation as opposed to simple storage of material in memory.
- Working memory comprises a phonological loop – a store of phonetic, verbal information – a visuospatial scratchpad – a store of spatial information and memories for movement – and a central executive responsible for supervising and updating the content of working memory.
- Short-term memory lasts for about 20 seconds and has a capacity of about seven items. We often simplify large amounts of information by organising it into 'chunks' of information, which can then be more easily rehearsed and remembered.
- When presented with a list of items, we tend to remember the items at the beginning of the list (the primacy effect) and at the end of the list (the recency effect) better than items in the middle of the list.
- The primacy effect occurs presumably because we have a greater opportunity to rehearse items early in the list and thus store them in long-term memory. The recency effect occurs because we can retrieve items at the end of the list from short-term memory.
- The existence of acoustical errors (rather than visual ones) in the task of remembering visually presented letters suggests that information is represented phonologically in short-term memory.
- Loss of information from short-term memory appears to be primarily a result of displacement; new information pushes out old information. However, a small amount of simple decay may also occur.

Learning and encoding in long-term memory

- Long-term memory refers to the very long-term retention of information and appears to consist of physical changes in the brain – probably within the sensory and motor association cortex.
- Consolidation of memories is likely caused by rehearsal of information, which sustains particular neural activities and leads to permanent structural changes in the brain.
- Short-term memories probably involve neural activity (which can be prolonged by rehearsal), whereas long-term memories probably involve permanent structural changes.
- Elaboration is important to learning. Maintenance rehearsal, or simple rote repetition, is usually less effective than elaborative rehearsal, which involves deeper, more meaningful processing.

- Encoding specificity states that the way in which material is stored depends on how the material is retrieved. The most durable and useful memories are encoded in ways that are meaningful.
- Some psychologists have argued that shallow processing is a less effective way of encoding information than is deep processing (levels of processing, therefore, determine the success of retrieval). Critics, however, point out that shallow processing sometimes produces very durable memories, and the distinction between shallow and deep has proved to be impossible to define explicitly.
- Mnemonic systems are strategies used to enhance memory and usually employ information that is already contained in long-term memory and visual imagery.

The organisation of long-term memory

- Episodic memory refers to memories of events and people that are personally meaningful to us; it is synonymous with autobiographical memory.
- Semantic memory refers to memory for knowledge and facts.
- Most psychologists believe that episodic and semantic memories are parts of different systems although this is controversial.
- Explicit memory refers to recollection of information that was deliberately encoded and retrieved; implicit memory refers to memory for information that is unintentionally learned.

Remembering

- Remembering is an automatic process, although we may sometimes work hard at generating thoughts that will help this process along.
- Forgetting information occurs primarily in the first few years after it is learned and the rate of forgetting decreases slowly thereafter. Once we have learned something and retained it for a few years, the chances are that we will remember it for a long time afterwards.
- Recalling a memory of a complex event entails a process of reconstruction that uses old information.
- Our ability to recall information from episodic memory is influenced by retrieval cues, such as the questions people are asked in courts of law to establish how an event occurred. Sometimes, the reconstruction introduces new 'facts' that we perceive as memories of what we previously perceived.

- Remembering is strongly influenced by contextual variables involving mood and emotion. Some evidence suggests that remembering is easier when an individual's mood during the attempt to recall information is the same as it was when that information was originally learned; this is called state-dependent memory.
- We also tend to remember the circumstances that we were in when we first heard of a particularly emotional event such as the death of a famous person, a natural disaster, or an invasion of one country by another; these are called flashbulb memories.
- Sometimes recollecting one memory is made more difficult by the information contained in another memory, a phenomenon known as interference.
- In retroactive interference, recently learned information interferes with recollection of information learned earlier.
- In proactive interference, information learned a while ago interferes with recently learned information.
- Although memory interference is demonstrated in the laboratory, it may not operate so obviously in real life. Prose and other forms of everyday language appear to be more resistant to interference.

Biological basis of memory

- Much of what we have learned about the biological basis of memory comes from studies involving humans with brain damage, from laboratory studies in which animals undergo surgical procedures that produce amnesia, and from neuroimaging studies of memory in healthy individuals.

- Learning seems to involve a strengthening of connections between neurons.
- Hebb proposed that short-term memory resulted from reverberation of the closed loops of the cell assembly; long-term memory is the more structural, lasting change in synaptic connections. This long-term change in structure is thought to reflect long-term potentiation (LTP), a term which describes the strengthening of neuronal connections via repeated stimulation.
- LTP is thought to originate in the hippocampus although it can occur elsewhere in the brain.
- A subtype of glutamate, N-methyl-D-aspartate (NMDA), appears to be important for producing long-term potentiation. NMDA receptors are found in the CA1 sector of the hippocampus; blocking activity in NMDA receptors prevents long-term potentiation in CA1 and the dendate gyrus.
- Anterograde amnesia refers to an inability to learn new memories after brain injury; these individuals can learn to perform many tasks that do not require verbal rules, such as recognising fragmentary pictures. Retrograde amnesia refers to the inability to retrieve remote memories.
- Patient HM showed an inability to store new information in long-term memory as a result of damage to the temporal lobes in general and the hippocampus in particular.
- The hippocampus is important for the learning of new material and for spatial navigation.
- The frontal cortex is involved in working memory and in the encoding and retrieval of material.

Suggestions for further reading

Baddley, A.D., Eysenck, M.W. and Anderson, M.C. (2009) *Memory.* Hove: Psychology Press.

Conway, M.A. (2009) Episodic memories. *Neuropsychologia,* 47, 2305–13.

Cotelli, M., Manenti, R., Zanetti, O. and Miniussi, C. (2012) Non-pharmacological intervention for memory decline. *Frontiers in Human Neuroscience,* 6, article 46.

Davachi, L. and Dobbins, I.G. (2008) Declarative memory. *Current Direction in Psychological Science,* 17 (2), 112–18.

Eichenbaum, H. (2012) *Cognitive Neuroscience of Memory: an introduction.* Oxford: Oxford University Press.

Eysenck, M.W. and Keane, M.T. (2010) *Cognitive Psychology: A student's handbook* (6th edn). Hove: Psychology Press.

Herrmann, D.J., Toder, C.Y., Gruneberg, M. and Payne, D.G. (2006) *Applied Cognitive Psychology: A textbook.* Hove: Psychology Press.

Klingberg, T. (2010) Training and plasticity of working memory. *Trends in Cognitive Sciences,* 14, 317–24.

Mecklinger, A. (2010) The control of long-term memory: Brain systems and cognitive processes. *Neurosciences and Biobehavioural Reviews,* 34, 1055–65.

O'Neill, J., Pleydell-Bouverie, B., Dupret, D. and Csicsvari, J. (2010). Play it again: Reactivation of waking experience and memory. *Trends in Neurosciences*, 33, 220–29.

Piolino, P., Desgranges, B. and Eustache, F. (2009) Episodic autobiographical memories over the course of time: cognitive, neuropsychological and neuroimaging findings. *Neuropsychologia*, 47, 2314–29.

Rosler, F., Ranganath, C., Roder, B. and Kluwe, R. (2009) *Neuroimaging in Human Memory*. Oxford: Oxford University Press.

Squire, L.R., Stark, C.F.L. and Clark, R.E. (2004) The medial temporal lobe. *Annual Review of Neuroscience,* 27, 279–306.

These are some excellent introductions to memory and aspects of memory.

CHAPTER 10

Language

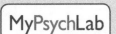

Explore the accompanying experiments, videos, simulations and animations on **MyPsychLab**. This chapter includes activities on:

- Morphemes
- Dyslexia detector
- The Wernicke-Geschwind model of language
- Handedness
- Check your understanding and prepare for your exams using the multiple choice, short answer and essay practice tests also available.

ALL CHILDREN SHOULD LEARN FOREIGN LANGUAGES, SAY PEERS

Angela Harrison, Education correspondent, BBC News

All children should learn a foreign language at primary and secondary school, a House of Lords committee has said.

The UK's attitude to languages has prevented its students from studying in Europe, according to the House of Lords' EU committee. Education Secretary Michael Gove also favours language learning from five.

Languages are not compulsory in English and Welsh secondary schools beyond the age of 14, although a review of the curriculum is under way in England.

Students in France, Germany and Spain were three times as likely as those in Britain to take part in an EU programme called Erasmus, where students can study or work abroad as part of their degree, the committee said.

Its inquiry follows a report from the European Commission last September which said that European universities had 'under-exploited potential' to contribute to Europe's prosperity and society.

Source: http://www.bbc.co.uk/news/education-17466166, 22 March 2012.

WHAT YOU SHOULD BE ABLE TO DO AFTER READING CHAPTER 10

- Define psycholinguistics and describe the nature of spoken language.
- Describe and explain the various models of reading.
- Describe various language disorders including the aphasias, the acquired dyslexias and developmental dyslexia and indicate what these tell us about normal language processing.
- Identify the neural mechanisms which might underlie different aspects of language such as speech perception, reading and speech comprehension.

QUESTIONS TO THINK ABOUT

- What is language?
- Why have humans evolved language?
- Can other primates learn language? Would this language approximate our own?
- What is the role of sound in understanding written and spoken language?
- What stages does language development go through?
- How do people learn to read? What is the best way of doing this?
- How do people learn to recognise words?
- What causes dyslexia?
- What are the effects of brain injury on reading, writing and speaking?
- Do all humans have the same central mechanism for producing language regardless of which language they speak?
- How are we able to comprehend language?

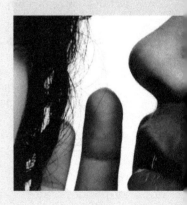

The use of language

Communication is probably one of the most important of all human behaviours. Our use of language can be private – we can think to ourselves in words or write diaries that are meant to be seen by no one but ourselves – but language evolved through social contacts among our early ancestors. Speaking and writing are clearly social behaviours: we learn these skills from other people and use them to communicate with them. An effective language system also abides by certain rules.

Although an exact definition is difficult to pin down (Harley, 2012), language can be characterised as a system of visual and/or vocal symbols which have meaning to the user and to the recipient. There are thought to be around 6,000 distinct languages in the world. The world's largest language is Chinese – it has more native speakers than any other – followed by English, Hindi/Urdu, Spanish and Arabic, as parts of Figure 10.1 and Table 10.1 show. The most popular foreign language is English (Montgomery, 2004) and Figure 10.2 shows the proportion of the population of selected European Union states which speak English (UK excluded).

We can use language to speak, write and read and we can also use it to remember and to think. Language also enables us to consider complex and abstract issues by encoding them in words and then manipulating the words according to specific rules. These rules are the subject of an area of study called **linguistics**.

Psycholinguistics: the study of language acquisition and meaning

The study of linguistics involves determining the 'rules' of language and the nature and meaning of written and spoken language. In contrast, **psycholinguistics**, a branch of psychology devoted to the study of verbal behaviour, examines the role of human cognition in language acquisition and comprehension: it is the integration of psychology and linguistics.

Psycholinguists are interested in how we acquire language – how verbal behaviour develops – and how we learn to speak from our interactions with others. In short, they are interested in the interaction between the structure and processing of language.

Psycholinguistics is a relatively recent, distinct branch of psychology although psychologists have studied language since the discipline's early experimental days. Wundt, for example, regarded as the father of psycholinguistics, argued that the sentence was the most basic

Table 10.1 Estimates of native speakers of the most popular languages in the world (in 1995)

	Language	No. of speakers (millions)
1	Chinese	1113
2	English	372
3	Hindi/Urdu	316
4	Spanish	304
5	Arabic	201
6	Portugese	165
7	Russian	155
8	Bengali	125
9	Japanese	123
10	German	102

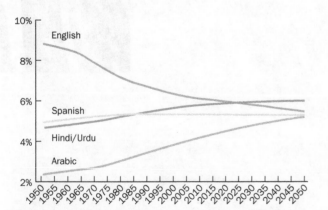

Figure 10.1 The projected survival and strength of the world's most successful languages.

Source: Reprinted with permission from 'The future of language' (Graddol, D.), *Science*, 303, 27 Feb., p. 1329. Copyright (2004) AAAS. Reprinted with permission from AAAS.

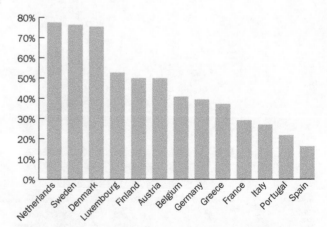

Figure 10.2 The percentage of the population of selected EU countries which speak English.

Source: Reprinted with permission from 'The future of language' (Graddol, D.), *Science*, 303, 27 Feb., p. 1330. Copyright (2004) AAAS. Reprinted with permission from AAAS.

element of speech production and comprehension. Speech production involved the transformation of thought process into sequences of speech segments; comprehension, on the other hand, was the reverse process. Wundt's view was not universally accepted. The linguist Hermann Paul, for example, argued that words, not sentences, were the building blocks of speech.

This essentially European debate became somewhat sterile during the 1920s and 1930s when the form of psychology championed by Wundt was usurped by behaviourism which, argued that psychology should concern itself only with observable behaviour (see Chapter 1). It was not until the 1950s that psychology began to take a renewed interest in the nature of language and, ironically, this interest was spurred by a linguist, Noam Chomsky. Chomsky's views of the nature of language are discussed later on in the chapter. This chapter reviews studies from psycholinguistics and cognitive psychology and introduces you to current understanding of the ways in which we produce and comprehend speech.

Perception of speech

Speech involves the production of a series of sounds in a continuous stream, punctuated by pauses and modulated by stress and changes in pitch. Sentences are written as sets of words, with spaces between them. Speech, however, is a more flexible means of communication than is writing. The sentences we utter are a string of sounds, some of which are emphasised (stressed), some are quickly glided over. We can raise the pitch of our voice when uttering some words and lower it when speaking others. We maintain a regular rhythmic pattern of stress. We pause at appropriate times, for example between phrases, but we do not pause after pronouncing each word. Thus, speech does not come to us as a series of individual words; we must extract the words from a stream of speech.

Recognition of speech sounds

The human auditory system is responsible for performing the complex task of enabling us to recognise speech sounds. The sound system of speech is called phonology. These sounds vary according to the sounds that precede and follow them, the speaker's accent and the stress placed on the syllables in which they occur. **Phonemes** are the elements of speech – the smallest units of sound that contribute to the meaning of a word. For example, the word 'pin' consists of three phonemes: /p/ + /i/ + /n/. It is important to note that phonemes are not the same as letters. The word 'ship', for example, has four letters but three phonemes: /sh/ + /i/ + /p/. Note that in linguistics

phonemes are flanked by two forward-slanting lines to indicate that they are phonemes and not letters. The first step in recognising speech sounds, therefore, is the identification of phonemes.

Production of speech

The production of speech is the result of a coordinated set of muscles found in the face, mouth and throat. Those responsible for producing some common words are illustrated in Figure 10.3.

One detectable and distinctive phonetic feature is **voice onset time,** the delay between the initial sound of a voiced consonant and the onset of vibration of the vocal cords. Voicing refers to the vibration of the vocal cords. The distinction between voiced and unvoiced consonants allows us to distinguish between /p/ (unvoiced) and /b/ (voiced), between /k/ (unvoiced) and /g/ (voiced), and between /t/ (unvoiced) and /d/ (voiced).

For example, although the difference between uttering 'pa' and 'ba' is subtle, it is discernible. Uttering 'pa' involves building up pressure in the mouth. When the lips are opened, a puff of air comes out. The 'ah' sound does not occur immediately, because the air pressure in the mouth and throat keeps air from leaving the lungs for a brief time. The vocal cords do not vibrate until air from the lungs passes through them. Uttering 'ba', however, does not involve the initial build-up of pressure. The vocal cords begin vibrating as soon as the lips open. The delay in voicing that occurs when uttering 'pa' is slight, only 0.06 seconds.

An experiment by Lisker and Abramson (1970) illustrates this point. They presented participants with a series of computer-generated sounds consisting of a puff followed by an 'ah'. The sounds varied only in one way: the amount of time between the puff and the 'ah'. When we speak, we make a puff for 'pa' but not for 'ba'. However, even though the computer always produced a puff, participants reported that they heard 'ba' when the delay was short and 'pa' when it was long. Participants discriminated between the phonemes /p/ and /b/ strictly according to the delay in voicing. The experiment demonstrates that the auditory system is capable of detecting very subtle differences.

Although the fundamental unit of speech, logically and descriptively, is the phoneme, research suggests that psychologically the fundamental unit is larger. For example, the two syllables 'doo' and 'dee' each consist of two phonemes. When spoken, the same phoneme, /d/, is heard at the beginning. However, when Liberman *et al.* (1967) analysed the sounds of the syllables, they found that the beginning phonemes were not the same. In fact, they could not cut out a section of a tape recording of the two syllables that would sound like /d/.

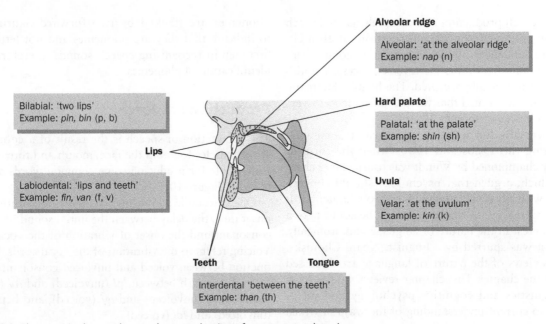

Figure 10.3 The areas in the vocal tract where production of consonants takes place.

Source: Payne, D.G. and Wenger, M.J., *Cognitive Psychology*. New York: Houghton Mifflin, 1998. Copyright © 1998 by Houghton Mifflin Company.

These results suggest that the fundamental unit of speech consists of groups of phonemes, such as syllables. The perception of a phoneme is affected by the sounds that follow it (Ganong, 1980). Using a computer to synthesise a novel sound that fell between those of the phonemes /g/ and /k/, Ganong reported that when the sound was followed by 'ift', the participants heard the word 'gift', but when it was followed by 'iss', they heard 'kiss'. These results suggest that we recognise speech sounds in pieces larger than individual phonemes.

Errors in speech production

As you will see later in this chapter, some individuals with damage to a specific part of the brain have an inability to produce speech or will produce meaningless speech. Speech errors or slips of the tongue, however, are not confined to the brain-damaged (Fromkin, 1988; Dell *et al.*, 1997) and some of these will be very familiar to you. Table 10.2 lists some of the common speech production errors made by normal individuals.

One obvious error is where the beginnings of words are transposed. So, for example, instead of saying 'dear old queen', you might say 'queer old dean'. This is an example of a Spoonerism, named after the Oxford don William A. Spooner who was noted for making such mistakes as saying 'noble tons of soil' instead of 'noble sons of toil'.

Speech errors are interesting because although they are errors they still follow the rules of grammar. For example,

one might confuse nouns in a sentence ('would you pass me that cupboard from the pepper') but you would not confuse a noun with a verb ('would you cupboard the pass from the pepper'). Errors thus reflect what we had intended to say rather than what we want to say (Levelt, 1989). Somehow, an error occurs between conception and execution.

When President Kennedy addressed his German audience with the inclusive pronouncement, 'Ich bin ein Berliner', what he actually said (to a Germanic ear) was – 'I am a cream pastry'. It is easy to see why we make such mistakes in languages which are unfamiliar, but why do you think that we make slips of the tongue in our native language?

Recognition of words: the importance of context

The perception of continuous speech involves different mechanisms from those used in the perception of isolated syllables. Because speech is full of hesitations, muffled sounds and sloppy pronunciations, many individual words can be hard to recognise out of context. For example, when Pollack and Pickett (1964) isolated individual words from a recording of normal conversations and played them back to other people, those people correctly identified the words only 47 per cent of the time. When they presented the same words in the context of

Table 10.2 Some common speech errors

1	**Errors at phonemic segments**
	Consonant anticipation: a reading list/a leading list
	Consonant deletion: speech error/peach error
	Vowel exchange: fill the pool/fool the pill
2	**Errors at phonetic features**
	Voicing reversal: big and fat/pig and vat
	Nasality reversal: cedars of Lebanon/cedars of Lemadon
3	**Errors at syllables**
	Syllable deletion: unanimity of opinion/unamity of opinion
	Syllable reversal: Stockwell and Schacter/Schachwell and Stockter
4	**Errors of stress (with the stressed syllable given in capital leters)**
	apples of the Origin/apples of the oRigin
	eCONomists: ecoNOMists, I mean, eCONomists
5	**Errors of word selection**
	Word exchange: tend to turn out/turn to tend out
	Word movement: I really must go/I must really go
6	**Errors at morphemes**
	Inflection morpheme error: cow tracks/tracks cows
	Derivational morpheme error: easily enough/easy enough
7	**Errors at phrases**
	A hummingbird was attracted by the red colour of the feeder/the red colour was attracted by a hummingbird of the feeder
	My sister went to the Grand Canyon/the Grand Canyon went to my sister
8	**Semantic and phonological word errors**
	Semantic substitution: too many irons in the fire/too many irons in the smoke
	Phonological substitution: white Anglo-Saxon Protestant/white Anglo-Saxon Prostitute
9	**Errors at morphologically complex words**
	Lexical selection error: it spread like wild fire/it spread like wild flower
	Exchange error: ministers in our church/churches in our minister

Source: Adapted from Fromkin, V.A., Speech production, in J. Berko Gleason and N.B. Ratner (eds) *Psycholinguistics*. Fort Worth: Holt, Rinehart & Winston (Wadsworth 1997 edition).

the original conversation, the participants identified and understood almost 100 per cent of them.

Understanding the meaning of speech

The meaning of a sentence (or of a group of connected sentences that are telling a story) is conveyed by the words that are chosen, the order in which they are combined, the affixes that are attached to the beginnings or ends of the words, the pattern of rhythm and emphasis of the speaker, and knowledge about the world shared by the speaker and the listener.

Syntax

The understanding of speech entails following the 'rules' of language. Words must be familiar and combined in specific ways. For example, the sentence, 'The two boys looked at the heavy box' is comprehensible; but the sentence, 'Boys the two looking heavily the box at' is not. Only the first sentence follows the rules of English grammar.

All languages have a **syntax**, or grammar, which is a set of rules governing the ways in which words are used to form sentences. They all follow certain principles, which linguists call syntactical rules, for combining words to form phrases, clauses or sentences (syntax, like synthesis, comes from the Greek *syntassein*, 'to put together'). Our understanding of syntax is automatic although learned. We are no more conscious of this process, for example, than a child is conscious of the laws of physics when he or she learns to ride a bicycle.

Word order

Word order is important in English. In the sentences 'The boy hit the ball' and 'The ball hit the boy', word order tells us who does what to whom. In English, the first noun of the sentence is the subject, the second noun is the object and the part in between is usually the verb. This structure is referred to as S–V–O word order (for subject–verb–object) and around 75 per cent of the world's languages possess this sentence structure (Bernstein and Berko, 1993). Other languages, however, have different orders. Japanese, for example, uses the S–O–V order and both Welsh and Arabic use V–S–O. The assignation of words into meaningful categories (such as noun, verb, adjective and so on) is called parsing, and parsing involves being able to identify word classes.

Word class

Word class refers to the grammatical categories such as noun, pronoun, verb and adjective, and words can be classified as function words or content words. Function words include determiners, quantifiers, prepositions and words in similar categories: 'a', 'the', 'to', 'some', 'and', 'but', 'when', and so on. Content words include nouns, verbs and most adjectives and adverbs: 'apple', 'rug', 'went', 'caught', 'heavy', 'mysterious', 'thoroughly', 'sadly'. Content words express meaning; function words express the relations between content words and thus are very important syntactical cues.

Affixes

Affixes are sounds that we add to the beginning (prefixes) or end (suffixes) of words to alter their grammatical function. For example, we add the suffix '-ed' to the end of a regular verb to indicate the past tense (drop/dropped); we add '-ing' to a verb to indicate its use as a noun (sing/singing as in 'we heard the choir sing' and 'the choir's singing was delightful'); and we add '-ly' to an adjective to indicate its use as an adverb (bright/brightly). We are quick to recognise the syntactical function of words with affixes like these. For example, Epstein (1961) presented people with word strings such as the following:

> a vap koob desak the citar molent um glox nerf
>
> A vapy koob desaked the citar molently um glox nerfs

The people could more easily remember the second string than the first, even though letters had been added to some of the words. Apparently, the addition of the affixes 'y', '-ed' and '-ly' made the words seem more like a sentence and they thus became easier to categorise and recall.

Semantics

The meaning of a word – its **semantics** – provides important cues to the syntax of a sentence (semantics comes from the Greek *sema*, 'sign'). For example, consider the following set of words: 'Frank discovered a flea combing his beard'. The syntax of this sentence is ambiguous. It does not tell us whether Frank was combing Frank's beard, the flea was combing the flea's beard, or the flea was combing Frank's beard. But our knowledge of the world and of the usual meanings of words tells us that Frank was doing the combing, because people, not fleas, have beards and combs.

Function words and content words

Function words (such as 'the', 'and', 'some') help us determine the syntax of a sentence; **content words** help us determine its meaning. For example, even with its function words removed the following set of words still makes pretty good sense: 'man placed wooden ladder tree climbed picked apples'. You can probably fill in the function words yourself and get 'The man placed the wooden ladder against the tree, climbed it, and picked some apples.'

Prosody

Prosody is a syntactic cue which refers to the use of stress, rhythm and changes in pitch that accompany speech. Prosody can emphasise the syntax of a word or group of words or even serve as the primary source of syntactic information. For example, in several languages (including English), a declarative sentence can be turned into a question by means of prosody. Read the following sentences at the top of the next page aloud to see how you would indicate to a listener which is a statement and which is a question.

We do this by intonation. In written communication, prosody is emphasised by punctuation marks. For example, a comma indicates a short pause, a full stop

You said that.

You said that?

indicates a longer one along with a fall in the pitch of voice, and a question mark indicates an upturn in the pitch of voice near the end of the sentence. These devices serve as only partial substitutes for the real thing. Because writers cannot rely on the cues provided by prosody, they must be especially careful to see that the syntax of their sentences is conveyed by other cues: word order, word class, function words, affixes and word meaning.

The relationship between semantics and syntax

Sentences can be read or heard semantically in more than one way. The linguist, Noam Chomsky (1957, 1965), suggested that language can partly be explained by reference to sentence grammar. Although Chomsky's ideas underwent several revisions, the 1965 version of his theory suggests that there are three grammars. The first – generative grammar – represents the rules by which a speaker's ideas can be transformed into a final grammatical form. These transformed ideas or thoughts are called deep structures (the second grammar). The final output is the surface grammar or structure which is the end spoken product.

The deep structure represents the kernel of what the person intended to say. In order to utter a sentence, the brain must transform the deep structure into the appropriate surface structure: the particular form the sentence takes.

Most psychologists agree that the distinction between surface structure and deep structure is important (Tanenhaus, 1988; Bohannon, 1993; Hulit and Howard, 1993). Individuals with a language disorder known as conduction aphasia have difficulty repeating words and phrases, but they can understand them. The deep structure of other people's speech appears to be retained, but not its surface structure.

What is meaning?

Words refer to objects, actions or relations in the world. Thus, the meaning of a word (its semantics) is defined by particular memories associated with it. For example, knowing the meaning of the word 'tree' means being able to imagine the physical characteristics of trees: what they look like, what the wind sounds like blowing through

their leaves, what the bark feels like, and so on. It also means knowing facts about trees: about their roots, buds, flowers, nuts, wood and the chlorophyll in their leaves. These memories are not stored in the primary speech areas but in other parts of the brain, especially regions of the association cortex. Different categories of memories may be stored in particular regions of the brain, but they are linked, so that hearing the word 'tree' activates all of them.

To hear a familiar word and understand its meaning involves first recognising the sequence of sounds that constitute the word. We must, therefore, have some form of memory store which contains the auditory representations of words. This store forms part of our auditory word recognition system. When we find the auditory entry for the word in our **mental lexicon** (lexicon means 'dictionary'), we must be able to access semantic information about this word. The region of the brain responsible for the auditory comprehension of words must somehow communicate with another region (or regions) which allows us to ascribe meaning to what we have just heard.

Is there a universal language?

Or, put less controversially, are there some features of language that are shared by most, if not all, languages? The answer seems to be yes. For example, all languages have nouns and words to represent states of action or states of being because we all need a way of referring to objects, people and events. Hockett (1960a, b) has suggested that all languages share similar features. These are listed in Table 10.3. Are there others that you think could be added to the list?

Gesture and communication

When we communicate orally, we often gesture and gesture was probably the evolutionary forerunner of vocal language. Some have argued that our language is gestural in nature, rather than acoustic (Gentilucci and Corballis, 2006). Ploog (2002) has hypothesised that we have two neural systems which mediate vocal behaviour. The first is in the cingulate cortex (and is found in non-humans) and the second is neocortical (seen in humans), which controls contralateral voluntary motor movement. The function of gesture appears manifold: it is used to express feeling, tone and meaning. Many of the gestures we make are intended to communicate an idea or thought or request. We point in order to direct people where to go; we beckon with our hands if we want someone to come near us; we have a number of gestures signifying disapproval of others.

Table 10.3 The features that Hockett regards as common to all languages

Universal	Description
Arbitrariness	There is no inherent connection between symbols and the objects they refer to
Broadcast transmission	Messages are transmitted in all directions and can be received by any hearer
Cultural transmission	Language is acquired through exposure to culture
Discreteness	A distinct range of possible speech sounds exists in language
Duality of structure	A small set of phenomes can be combined and recombined into an infinitely large set of meanings
Interchangeability	Humans are both message perceivers and message producers
Productivity	Novel messages can be produced according to the rules of the language
Semanticity	Meaning is conveyed by the symbols of the language
Specialisation	Sounds of a language are specialised to convey meaning (as compared with non-language sounds)
Total feedback	The speaker of a language has auditory feedback that occurs at the same time as the listener receives the message
Transitoriness	Linguistic messages fade quickly
Vocal–auditory channel	Means of transmission of the language is vocal-auditory

But can combining speech and gesture improve comprehension of another's intention? Kelly *et al.* (1999) set up a series of experiments in which they asked participants to watch video footage of a specially created scenario. For example, two characters, Adam and Bill, are going home when they meet each other in the street just outside their flat. Adam is on a bike and Bill is walking. Adam asks Bill if he had brought the burgers. Bill had not. Adam says to Bill that he had better get them. Bill protests that the burger bar is in another part of town. In one condition, Bill makes eye contact with Adam and gestures towards his friend's bike; in another, he maintains eye contact and just says the dialogue. In the experiment, participants are asked to indicate how they think the last person addressed in the scenario

would react to what had been communicated. All scenarios featured indirect requests; in none was a target mentioned (in the example here, a bike) or an intended action explicitly suggested.

The authors found that those in the gesture and speech condition were almost twice as likely to understand the nature of the indirect request than were those in the speech-only condition. The authors found a similar result in another experiment in which participants had to remember information spoken by a woman who made or did not make meaningful gestures (e.g. shooting a basketball) when describing her brother, a basketball player.

To investigate whether speakers gesture to help listeners better understand what they are saying, Alibali *et al.* (2001) observed the gestures made by individuals who were asked to narrate to a colleague the contents of an animated cartoon. In one part of the experiment, the listener was face-to-face with the gesturer and could see the speaker's gestures; in the other, a screen blocked the view of the speaker. The gestures were filmed by a hidden camera and were classified into two categories: representational gestures, those used to gesture meaning in speech, and beat gestures, those which conveyed no semantic content and were simple and rhythmic.

The rate of beat gestures was comparable in the visible and the blocked condition but the rate of representational gesture varied according to condition. Specifically, speakers used more representational gestures when the listeners could see them than when they could not.

The researchers suggest that these results support the semantic information hypothesis of gesture. This states that a speaker's visibility to the listener influences the production of meaningful gestures. We seem to gesture to convey meaning when we speak, even when our listeners cannot see these gestures.

There is some evidence that there is a common brain system mediating linguistic and non-linguistic (gestural) language. Enrici *et al.* (2011) examined the brain activation of people who looked at images where a communication was linguistic ('Let me pass the bottle') or 'extralinguistic' (a person in a picture gestured towards a bottle). Participants also looked at stimuli in which where they were told that a shelf was falling down or where this was made clear non-linguistically (the shelf was coming apart). Both types of task activated the superior temporal sulcus (STS), the junction of the temporal and parietal cortices and the medial prefrontal cortex (PFC). But areas involved in language (see a later section for a full description) were activated in the linguistic conditions but the sensory and motor areas of the brain were active when participants processed the extralinguistic, gestural stimuli.

Cutting edge: Finishing each others' sentences . . .

You like your partner for any number of reasons: their looks, their personality, the size of their intellect, their sense of humour. New research suggests that this romantic attachment might also be strengthened if you both use language in a similar way (Ireland *et al.*, 2011). In one experiment, researchers analysed the language use of both participants in a speed-dating event and examined whether this was associated with mutual attractiveness. It was: the greater the match between the participants' language style, the greater the likelihood of their both being romantically interested in each other. In a second experiment, the researchers examined language style in couples' instant messages by phone and internet. They found that similar language style predicted the stability of the relationship three months later. The greater the similarity, the greater the likelihood that they remained together.

The message seems to be that if you both end up finishing each others' sentences, you will be doing this for some time to come.

Psychology in action: Sex differences in communication

The prolific American linguist, Deborah Tannen, has reported some curious differences between men and women in the way they hold conversations and communicate with each other. Take the following example, from Tannen's book, *You Just Don't Understand* (1992):

> **'A married couple was in a car when the wife turned to her husband and asked, "Would you like to stop for a coffee?"'**
>
> **'No, thanks,' he answered truthfully. So they didn't stop.**
>
> **The result? The wife, who had indeed wanted to stop, became annoyed because she felt her preference had not been considered. The husband, seeing his wife was angry, became frustrated. Why didn't she just say what she wanted?**

This, according to Tannen's research, sums up one important difference between men's and women's language use: women often make a suggestion to start a negotiation. Men see it as a direct question to be answered directly. Another of Tannen's findings is that men's conversation can be a little like witnessing a verbal contest: it is a way of establishing dominance, not being pushed around, getting the upper hand. Women use conversation to encourage intimacy, closeness and support. Men are more independent, exemplified by a man's ability to make a unilateral decision which directly affects his partner without consulting her. Women try to win an argument by agreement – requests are formulated as proposals, not demands. Another difference is that men and women behave differently when dispensing advice and understanding – when a woman expresses a problem or difficulty, a man will suggest a solution, when what is usually desired is understanding and reassurance.

A recent meta-analysis of men's and women's talkativeness and the type of speech they engage in has found some surprising differences (Leaper and Ayres, 2007). The researchers examined degrees of affiliative speech – that used to affirm or positively engage with another person – and assertive speech – that used to advance a point of view, be direct and give information.

Women, as predicted, engaged in more affiliative speech (but did not act unassertively during exchanges) but there was no general difference between the sexes in terms of assertive speech. The authors found the following specific results:

- Men were more talkative and used assertive speech more.
- Men used assertive speech less during interactions with strangers than close relations.
- Men were more likely to give suggestions in speech and approached conversations in a task-oriented way.
- Women made more critical statements.
- Female undergraduates used more affiliative and less assertive speech, but there was no difference in non-students.
- When mothers and fathers were with their child, the mother would talk more.
- Men were more talkative than women in mixed-sex interactions but there was no sex difference when interactions were with the same sex.
- Women were more likely to use affiliative speech in same-sex than mixed sex interactions.
- Women disclosed more information than men but not in mixed-sex interactions.
- Women smiled more (and for longer in same-sex interactions).
- Men used assertive speech more in same-sex interactions (perhaps seeing the exchange as a form of competition).
- If a researcher was present, men used more assertive speech; when one was absent, the women did (although this finding was based on limited data).

Psychology in action: *Continued*

- Greater affiliative speech in women and greater talkativeness in men was more likely when research was done in a university laboratory.
- Women were more likely to discuss socioemotional-oriented topics; men discussed instrumental-oriented topics.
- Women were more assertive when interacting with children.
- Women used more affiliative speech when observed for brief periods (4–8 minutes), but not for 10–15 minutes or 20–300 minute periods.
- Talkativeness favouring men was greater in research published in top-tier journals.

The analysis suggests that sex differences in speech and the amount of speech can depend on a number of social and environmental factors, including the sex of the person the participant is interacting with, how long they interact, where they interact, how they interpret the situations they find themselves in, and whether they are students or non-students.

Do women have longer conversations? Friebel and Seabright (2011) examined the (anonymous) billing records of 3,103 mobile phone users in Italy and Greece. Over two years, women made fewer calls than did the men but the calls lasted 16 per cent longer. In a second study, they examined the length of time taken to deal with calls to a 'consumer services company' in Germany. They examined 92,000 days' worth of calls. Calls to women lasted 15 per cent longer than those to men. This did not affect productivity. The researchers noted that where sales could be measured, women sold slightly more.

Finally, a word about culture. If your first language is English you pay little thought to the sex or gender of the nouns you use. In English, nouns are neutral. In other languages, however, nouns are gendered. In French, for example, dogs, cats and Concorde are masculine (le chien, le chat, le Concorde) whereas apples, carrots and Rolex are feminine (la pomme, la carotte, une Rolex). Spanish and German are also gendered. You might not think this of much consequence but research suggests that these gendered words may influence how we think about them.

Boroditsky *et al.* (2003) examined how German and Spanish speakers described bridges. In German the word for bridge is a feminine noun; in Spanish it is masculine. They found that when the Germans spoke about bridges the structure was 'beautiful', 'elegant', 'fragile', 'pretty' and 'slender'. When the Spanish spoke about it, it was 'big', 'dangerous', 'long', 'strong' and 'sturdy'. Boroditsky *et al.* gave another group of French and Spanish speakers a memory test. Participants were asked to remember 24 inanimate objects which were given male or female names. The experiment was conducted in English. When the results were analysed, the nations remembered the objects best when the name given to them matched the gender of the word. The Spanish had especial problems in remembering a bridge if it was given a female name.

But the effect of language can be even more unwitting. Sera *et al.* (2002) asked French and Spanish participants to look at some objects and indicate whether a man or a woman should be the voice of these objects in a proposed animated film. Objects included a fork and a table (both feminine in French; masculine in Spanish). French speakers gave the fork a feminine voice more often than did the Spanish; conversely, the Spanish speakers chose a masculine voice.

Reading

Speech first developed as a means of communication between two or more people facing each other, or at least within earshot of each other, and probably occurred around 200,000 to 300,000 years ago. Indo-European languages (144 tongues), for example, seem to have a common root, as Figures 10.4 and 10.5 show.

The invention of writing, which made it possible for people to communicate across both space and time, was an important turning point in civilisation. The first system of writing appears to have been developed around 4000 BC in Sumeria (the location of present-day Iran and Iraq), apparently in response to the need to keep records of ownership and of business transactions. The earliest forms of writing were stylised drawings of real objects (pictographs), but most cultures soon developed symbols based on sounds. For example, Egyptian hieroglyphic writing used some symbols as pictographs but used others phonetically, to spell out people's names or words that denoted concepts not easily pictured (Ellis, 1992).

With the notable exception of Chinese (and other Asian writing systems based on Chinese), most modern languages use alphabetic writing systems in which a small number of symbols represent (more or less) the sounds used to pronounce words. For example, most European languages are represented by the Roman alphabet,

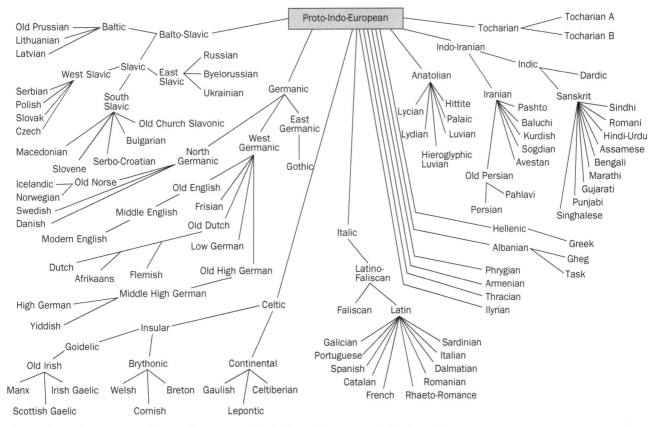

Figure 10.4 A language tree showing the suggested derivation of the most well-developed languages.

Source: from *Historical Linguistics: An Introduction*, MIT Press (Campbell, L. 1999) Fig. 6.1, p. 190, © 1999 Massachusetts Institute of Technology, by permission of The MIT Press and Edinburgh University Press, www.euppublishing.com.

originally developed to represent the sounds of Latin and subsequently adopted by tribes of people ruled or influenced by the Roman Empire. The Roman alphabet was adapted from the Greek alphabet, which in turn was adapted from the Phoenician alphabet. For example, the letter D has its origin in the Phoenician symbol 'daleth', which meant 'door'. At first, the symbol literally indicated a door, but it later came to represent the phoneme /d/. The Greeks adopted the symbol and its pronunciation but changed its name to delta. Finally, the Romans took it, altering its shape into the one we recognise in English today.

Scanning text

When we scan a scene, our eyes make rapid jumps called saccades. These same rapid movements occur during reading (a French ophthalmologist in the nineteenth century discovered saccadic eye movements while watching people read).

The study of eye movements is made possible by a device called an eye tracker. This device consists of an apparatus that holds a person's head in a fixed position and a special video camera that keeps track of the person's gaze by focusing on an eye and monitoring the position of the pupil. The person reads material presented by a computer on a video monitor.

Perception does not occur while the eyes are actually moving but during the brief fixations that occur between saccades. The average **fixation** has a duration of about 250 milliseconds, but their duration can vary considerably. Figure 10.6 shows the pattern of fixations made by both good and poor readers.

The ovals above the text indicate the location of the fixations (which occur just below the ovals, on the text itself), and the numbers indicate their duration (in milliseconds). The fixations of good readers were made in the forward direction; the poor readers looked back and examined previously read words several times (indicated by the arrows). In addition, the good reader took, on average, considerably less time to examine each word.

Familiar words tend to be skipped over more frequently than are visually similar non-words (Drieghe *et al.*, 2005). University students fixate on most words when they are asked to read text carefully enough to understand its meaning. They fixate on 80 per cent of the content words but only 40 per cent of the function words such as 'the' and 'and' (Just and Carpenter, 1980). Function words are generally shorter than content words,

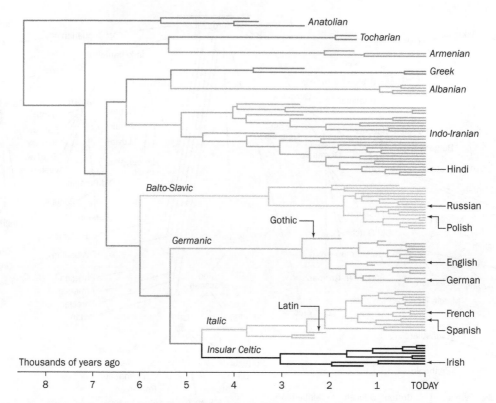

Figure 10.5 The origin of Indo-European languages. Atkinson et al's (2012) study of the evolution of words from 103 languages suggests that Indo-European languages originated in Anatolia (Turkey), approximately 9,000 years ago.

Source: from 'Mapping the Origins and Expansion of the Indo-European Language Family', *Science*, Vol. 337 no. 6097, pp. 957–960 (Bouckaert, R. 2012).

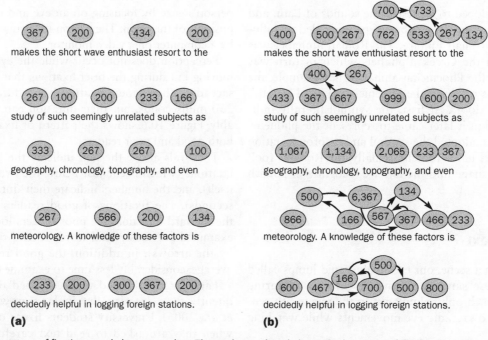

Figure 10.6 The pattern of fixations made by two readers. The ovals are placed above the locations of the fixations; the numbers within them indicate the durations of the fixations (in milliseconds). Arrows indicate backtracking to words already examined. **(a)** A good reader. **(b)** A poor reader.

Source: From Just, M.A. and Carpenter, P.A., *The Psychology of Reading and Language Comprehension* © 1987. Published by Allyn & Bacon, Boston, MA. Copyright © 1987 by Pearson Education. By permission of the publisher.

but the difference is not only a matter of size. Readers are more likely to skip over short function words such as 'and' or 'the' than over short content words such as 'ant' or 'run' (Carpenter and Just, 1983). For example, read the following sentence:

> I love Paris in the
>
> the springtime

You may not have noticed that second 'the' at the beginning of the second line and would have read the sentence as normal; we seem to be able to glide over function words such as 'the' without it detrimentally affecting the way in which we perceive and understand meaning.

As sentences are read, they are usually analysed word by word (Rayner and Pollatsek, 1989). Some words contribute more to our understanding than do others, and some sentences cannot make sense until we reach the end. The more unusual a word is, the longer a reader fixates on it. The word 'sable', for example, receives a longer fixation than the word 'table'. The word that follows an unusual word does not receive a longer-than-usual fixation, which indicates that the reader finishes processing the word before initiating the next saccade (Thibadeau et al., 1982). Readers also spend more time fixating on longer words. In fact, if word familiarity is held constant, the amount of time a word receives is proportional to its length (Carpenter and Just, 1983). In addition, Just et al. (1983) found that the amount of time that Chinese readers spent fixating on a Chinese character was proportional to the number of brush strokes used to make it. Because all Chinese characters are of approximately the same size, the increased fixation time appears to reflect the complexity of a word rather than the amount of space it occupies.

Phonetic and whole-word recognition

Most psychologists who study the reading process believe that readers have two basic ways of recognising words: phonetic and whole-word recognition. **Phonetic reading** involves the decoding of the sounds that letters or groups of letters make (in a similar way to which the units of speech are called phonemes, the units of written language are called **graphemes**). For example, the ability to pronounce nonsense words depends on our knowledge of the relation between letters and sounds in the English language. Such knowledge is used to 'sound the word out'. When we do this we apply **grapheme–phoneme correspondence** (GPC) rules: the rules which govern the ways in which we are able to translate written letters into the appropriate sounds. This is called **whole-word reading**: reading by recognising a word as a whole. But do we have to 'sound out' familiar, reasonably short words such

as 'table' or 'grass'? Probably not. Familiar words are perceived as whole words. However, consider this list of words: 'knave', 'shave', 'slave', 'have'. How did you pronounce the last word? You probably pronounced it to rhyme with 'slave'. This example illustrates that although whole-word reading would seem to be intuitively correct, our pronunciation of words can depend on the context in which words are used.

The process of reading

A relatively inexperienced reader will have to sound out most words and, consequently, will read rather slowly. Experienced, practised readers will quickly recognise most of them as individual units. In other words, during reading, phonetic and whole-word reading are engaged in a race. If the word is familiar, the whole-word method will win. If the word is unfamiliar, the whole-word method will lose and the phonetic method will have enough time to compete.

When we read a word, we must have some store of knowledge which allows us to identify words as words. In the same way that the auditory store was considered part of the auditory word recognition system, the visual store can be considered part of the visual word recognition system. But is our recognition of written words purely visual? Or can we read by 'ear'?

To answer this question, Rubenstein et al. (1971) presented individuals with three types of non-word (strings of letters which make invalid English words): **pseudowords**, which conformed to the rules of English but had no meaning (for example GANK), non-words which were pronounceable but illegally spelled (for example MIRQ), and non-words which were unpronounceable and illegally spelled (for example HTTR). The participants had to decide whether these words, presented on a computer screen, were real English words or not (this is called a lexical decision task). The experimenters found that participants took longest to reject the pseudowords, followed by illegally spelled pronounceable words, followed by illegally spelled unpronounceable words. In a second experiment, Rubenstein et al., included a set of words called **pseudohomophones**; these are words which are legally spelled, are pronounceable, sound like real words but have no meaning (for example PHICKS, which sounds like 'fix'). They would, therefore, pass an auditory word recognition system, but not the visual word recognition system. As predicted, pseudohomophones took longest to reject, followed by pseudowords.

Rubenstein et al. suggested that visual information is translated into a phonological code, a sound-based representation of the word, using grapheme to phoneme conversion. This representation is then checked by the auditory word recognition system which decides whether the word sounds like a real word or not. Pseudowords would fail this test – they do not sound like real words. Pseudohomophones, however, would pass because they do sound like real words. They, therefore, need to be checked by the visual word recognition system in order to determine whether the word is real. The visual word recognition system checks the orthography of a word (the way in which it is spelled). The recognition of words, therefore, involves phonic mediation: the conversion of written language into a sound-based representation.

Phonic mediation, however, appears to be necessary only for the recognition of unfamiliar words (Ellis, 1992). When we see a familiar word, we normally recognise it as a whole and say it aloud. If we see an unfamiliar word or a pronounceable non-word, we must try to read it phonetically. We recognise each letter and then sound it out, based on our knowledge of how letters are sounded out (phonetics).

Whole-word recognition is not only faster than phonetic decoding, but also essential in a language (such as English) in which spelling is not completely phonetic. In the following pairs of words:

cow/blow bone/one post/cost limb/climb

no single set of phonological rules can account for the pronunciation of both members of each pair (phonology refers to the relation between letters and the sounds they represent in a particular language). Yet all these words are familiar and easy to read. The ability to recognise words as wholes, therefore, may be necessary in order to read irregularly spelled words (although our 'have' example earlier on suggests how whole-word reading can fail).

Phonology, however, appears to be crucial for the development of language ability, as we will see later. Having good phonological skills appears to place children at an advantage linguistically. Gathercole and Baddeley (1990) found that 5-year-old children with good phonological skills were better at remembering nonsense words than were those with poor phonological skills. This ability to repeat nonsense words appears to be a good predictor of later, successful vocabulary acquisition (Gathercole et al., 1992). There is much debate over the best way to teach children how to learn to read, and psychologists have discovered much that teachers can use in their instruction.

The dual-route model of reading

The **dual-route model of reading** proposes that there are two routes that take the reader from spelling to sound (Coltheart, 1978; Morton and Patterson, 1980). The lexical route retrieves pronounced words from a lexicon, i.e. it 'looks up' words in an internal word pool which contains items learned through experience, a little like a personalised dictionary. This route is also known as the 'direct', 'lexical', 'lexico-semantic' or 'addressed' route: all refer to the same path. The sublexical route is the system which converts letters into sounds – a process called grapheme–phoneme correspondence. It 'translates' letters into sounds based on sound–letter associations that have been learned. Other terms for this route include indirect, assembled, sublexical and graphological. The lexical route would be able to identify all known words, regardless of whether they follow grapheme–phoneme correspondence rules; the sublexical route would be able to identify non-words using these rules (it would be able to recognise 'flound' as a non-word, for example, because the word follows normal grapheme–phoneme correspondence rules).

The model derived from studies of brain-injured patients who appear to rely more on one route than the other. People with a type of dyslexia called phonological dyslexia (see below), for example, appear to have access only to whole word forms (the direct, lexical route) and have difficulty in reading regularly spelled words (suggesting an impairment in the indirect, sublexical route). The reading of non-words is significantly worse than the reading of (familiar) words. An alternative to the dual-route model has argued that the same mechanisms underlie the reading aloud of words and non-words (such as 'nep' and 'cabe').

In a test of these competing models, Caccappoulo-van Vliet et al. (2004) described two patients with dementia who showed pure phonological dyslexia. These patients were unable to read non-words but they were able to read familiar, irregularly spelled words accurately. However, their phonological skills were intact, thus lending support to the dual-route model explanation of phonological dyslexia rather than the alternative (because phonological ability was generally unimpaired).

A meta-analysis of 35 neuroimaging studies of the dual-route model suggests that the two routes of reading can also be mapped in the healthy brain (Jobard et al., 2003). Access to the visual representation of words was found to rely on two routes, but there was no consistent brain region devoted to storing the shapes of word forms. Instead, a general region located at the occipitotemporal junction appeared to be involved in the initial segmentation or classification of word-like stimuli. The phonological route was subserved by parts of the temporal lobe and also regions involved in working memory (because of the process involved in matching letters and sounds). The so-called direct route, according to this review, recruited a pathway linking the occipitotemporal cortex with those involved in semantic processing (these regions are found in or around the temporal cortex).

Connectionism and the dual-route model

Are both routes in the dual-route model activated simultaneously during reading? One view holds that both systems operate in parallel and are in some form of race, the winner being the system which produces the best pronunciation. A second view holds that the two processes are pooled until a match is made that would prompt articulation. No clear agreement on this process has been reached, although a great deal of excitement in cognitive psychology and psycholinguistics has been roused by the possibilities of connectionism, a form of computer modelling of human cognitive function, in solving this problem. This approach argues that there are no qualitatively different processes involved in recognising words and that there is no localised lexicon.

Connectionism takes as its starting point the view that the brain, or our information processing system, operates in a similar way to a computer and can, therefore, be modelled. Such a model should be capable of learning (as our brain is). This idea, of course, is not new. Rosenblatt (1962) had developed a parallel processing machine which was capable of simple learning. Modern, computer-based models of human computation, however, were pioneered by Seidenberg and McClelland (1989). Their **parallel distributed processing (PDP)** model did away with the notion of dual routes and instead posited one route only which was non-lexical. Their model is an example of a computational model of behaviour because it translates units of behavioural phenomena into computations. Seidenberg and McClelland's model was a three-layer neural network which sought to read regular, exception and non-words from spelling to sound. The three layers were: features, letters and words. Perception within each of these layers was argued to occur in parallel so that the system could analyse features while it identified letters and attempted to name the word a stimulus might represent (Zorzi *et al.*, 1998).

However, the model has run into some difficulty. It cannot read non-words, for example, and it cannot simulate a form of dyslexia called surface dyslexia, which is described later in the chapter (Besner *et al.*, 1990; Coltheart *et al.*, 1993). The PDP model has been replaced by that of Plaut and colleagues (Plaut and McClelland, 1993; Plaut *et al.*, 1996) which seems to have met with some success in that it is at least capable of reading monosyllabic non-words but does not appear to account for the flexibility of human language (see Zorzi *et al.*, 1998, for a review). We will not say too much more about PDP and connectionism here.

Although the PDP model and connectionism are difficult concepts to grasp it is important to take note of them because there is great debate in psychology over the relevance and validity of connectionism in trying to explain the process of visual word recognition.

How children learn to read

Reading is an artificial activity and it must be taught to us (usually at an early age). A beginning reader has much of their work cut out because they have no vocabulary and no set of rules. Are there any cognitive skills (such as an awareness of rhyme or having an effective short-term memory) that can help develop the child's vocabulary and skills? Does reading develop naturally or in stages? And how can we best teach children to read?

To begin with, reading requires adequate sight, so a child would need to be visually competent. Of course, blind children can be taught Braille, but our concern here is with the development of visual word recognition and visual reading. The next important step is for the child to relate written letters or groups of letters to sounds. In some languages this is easier to do than it is in others. The rules needed to undertake this task are more complex in English, say, than in Finnish or Italian. Some of these rules will be simple – 'b' corresponds to /b/. Others are not – the 'c' in 'car' and 'mince' is sounded differently, for example. These general rules are called spelling-to-pronunciation correspondence rules or, more accurately, grapheme–phoneme correspondence rules. The essential feature of these rules is that the child must break up words into segments and put them back together again to form a pronounceable whole. This breaking and putting together again are called **segmentation** and **blending**, respectively, and are two tasks the beginning reader has great difficulty in undertaking.

According to Oakhill and Garnham (1988), the child's reading process is dependent on the development of a number of skills. Whether these skills give rise to reading, are associated with reading or develop from reading is an interesting psychological question that many developmental psychologists and psycholinguists have attempted to answer. However, this debate need not concern us here. What will concern us are the skills associated with reading development. Oakhill and Garnham's list includes the following features/skills: word consciousness, awareness of lower-level features, orthographic awareness, phonemic awareness and use of analogy.

- *Word consciousness*. Word consciousness or **lexical awareness** refers to the ability to understand that speech and writing are composed of different, distinct elements called words. Young children have difficulties in identifying word boundaries (where one ends and another begins), children with strong lexical awareness tend to develop better reading ability (Ryan *et al.*, 1977).

- *Awareness of lower-level features.* A young child has a limited sight vocabulary and what it does have will have been learned through breaking down the elements of words into manageable, processable pieces. English, although having an alphabet of 26 letters, has 45 phonemes. When Rozin *et al.* (1974) presented children with two words such as 'mow' and 'motorcycle' and asked them – auditorily – which one was 'mow', the maximum correct response varied from 50 per cent for suburban nursery children to 10 per cent for inner-city children.

- *Orthographic awareness.* The ability to recognise that writing systems have sets of rules that must be followed is called **orthographic awareness**. For example, in English, we know that some sequences of letters are acceptable (for example 'able') but know that others are not ('kqxg').

- *Phonological awareness.* Perhaps the most important skill a child needs in order to develop adequate reading ability is the capacity to appreciate sound and be able to identify letters with sounds (**phonological awareness**). Tests of phonological awareness would include finding the odd one out from two sets of spoken words such as: sun, sea, sock, rag; weed, need, peel, deed (Bradley and Bryant 1983; Bryant and Bradley, 1985). (These words rely on the child noting both the beginning and ending sounds of words.) Good performance at tasks such as these is a good predictor of later reading ability (Melby-Lervag *et al.*, 2012).

- *Use of analogy.* Sometimes, children will not use grapheme–phoneme correspondence rules to read a word because, to them, it looks like another word. For example, Marsh *et al.* (1977) asked children and adults to pronounce nonsense words such as 'tepherd'. This word, if pronounced according to GPC rules (with 'ph' pronounced as /f/) would be pronounced 'tefferd'. Children, however, pronounce it to rhyme with 'shepherd'. Adults do not. This is called children's use of analogy in reading.

The major ways in which children are taught to develop and use some or all of these skills are based on two systems: whole-word reading and phonics. Whole-word reading, as its name suggests, involves teaching the child to read whole words rather than analyse components of words and put them together to form whole words. This is sometimes called the look-and-say method because there is no room for segmentation of words. It is also called the meaning-based system because it encourages the child to think about the object the word

represents. Words are usually displayed singly on cards and classrooms might have objects and pictures with word-labels attached to them. This means that the child begins to generate a pool of words which they will then be able to read in books after a sufficient number of words has been learned. Whole-word reading is easier for the child because it does not rely on segmentation. It also, as we have already mentioned, encourages the child to think about word meaning. One disadvantage of the system, however, is its inability to teach children how to decode new or unfamiliar words because no rule-based system is learned. If one considers that the average adult has a reading vocabulary of 50,000 words, the number of words a child would have to learn would be impracticable.

The alternative approach is called phonics. This rule-based system teaches the child correspondences between letters and sounds (that is, GPC rules, segmentation and blending). There are many forms of this teaching system and most teach the children letter-to-sound correspondences first before exposing them to actual words. Recently, a year-long comparison of phonics versus standard teaching methods in a group of English children found that phonics was associated with a reduction in reading difficulties (Shapiro and Solity, 2008). The disadvantages of the system are that it cannot cope well with teaching the child irregular words and that 4–5-year-old children find the segmentation of phonemes difficult.

Many other teaching-of-reading systems exist. For example, one approach, the Initial Teaching Alphabet, reforms the orthography of irregular words by transforming them into regular words. Other approaches teach the child the letters of the alphabet first (success in which is a good predictor of reading ability). Another approach colour-codes letters in words. For example, a letter written in a certain colour can only be pronounced in one way. Yet another approach places marks underneath certain letters to indicate how they should be pronounced (the technical name for this is the 'diacritical marking system').

There is a close link between phonological skill and the ability to read. Some authors argue that is the key skill in the development of a child's reading ability. A study of 382 children from 21 primary schools in England found that phonological awareness was a significant predictor of later school success, including maths, reading and science performance, and teachers' positive assessments of the pupils (Savage *et al.*, 2007). 'Practically,' the authors conclude, 'screening of phonological awareness and basic reading skills by school staff in year 1 significantly enhances the capacity of schools to predict curricular outcomes in year 6' (p. 732). If this is so, one might hypothesise that if children are trained well in phonological awareness (an awareness of the sounds of words), they might develop better reading skills than those without the benefit of this training. Hatcher *et al.* (2004) tested this hypothesis by randomly assigning 410 British children of kindergarten age (4–5 years) to one of three teaching conditions or a control group. The conditions were Reading with Rhyme (a learning-to-read package with additional emphasis on rhyme), Reading with Phoneme (a learning-to-read package with additional emphasis on phoneme training such as syllable and word identification), and Reading with Rhyme and Phoneme (a combination of the first two). The control group was taught the standard reading programme. Measures of cognitive ability – including reading, arithmetic and literacy – were taken.

While children whose reading was progressing normally did not benefit significantly from the additional phonological training, children who had been identified as poor readers improved their reading skill and awareness of phonemes. The decline in reading ability was halted by the second school year in children who received phoneme training and by the third year in children who received the rhyme training.

Is there a 'best' approach amid these myriad of approaches? As you have seen, although some of the well-developed approaches have distinct advantages, all have certain disadvantages. However, one consistent predictor of later reading ability is successful phonological awareness. Pronunciation is also better if the phonetic aspects of speech are emphasised during the early stages of teaching. This may explain why developmental dyslexics often have good cognitive ability but have poor phonological processing skills, a topic we discuss in the section on language disorders below. If you were teaching a child to read, how would you start? What aspect of reading would you consider the most important to teach at the initial stages?

Understanding the meanings of words and sentences

The meanings of words are learned through experience. The meanings of content words involve memories of objects, actions and their characteristics; thus, the meanings of content words involve visual, auditory, somatosensory, olfactory and gustatory memories. These memories of the meanings of words are distributed throughout the brain. Our understanding of the meaning of the word 'apple', for example, involves memories of the sight of an apple, the way it feels in our hands, the crunching sound we hear when we bite into it, and the taste and odour we experience when we chew it. The understanding of the meanings of adjectives, such as the word 'heavy', involves memories of objects that are difficult or impossible to lift.

A phenomenon known as **semantic priming** gives us some hints about the nature of activation of memories triggered by the perception of words and phrases. Semantic priming is a facilitating effect on the recognition of words having meanings related to a word encountered earlier. A particular word can be more easily read if the word preceding it is related in meaning. If an individual sees the word 'bread', they will be more likely to recognise a fuzzy image of the word 'butter' or an image that is presented very briefly by means of a tachistoscope (Johnston and Dark, 1986). Presumably, the brain contains circuits of neurons that serve as 'word detectors' involved in visual recognition of particular words (Morton, 1979; McClelland and Rumelhart, 1981). Reading the word 'bread' activates word detectors and other neural circuits involved in memories of the word's meaning. Apparently, this activation spreads to circuits denoting related concepts, such as butter. Thus, our memories must be linked according to our experience regarding the relations between specific concepts.

Context effects, an example of top-down processing, have been demonstrated through semantic priming. Zola (1984), for example, asked people to read sentences such as the following:

1. Cinemas must have adequate popcorn to serve their patrons.

2. Cinemas must have buttered popcorn to serve their patrons.

while he recorded their eye movements with an eye tracker.

Zola found that individuals fixated for a significantly shorter time on the word popcorn in the second sentence. Because the word 'adequate' is not normally associated with the word 'popcorn', individuals reading the first sentence were unprepared for this word. However, 'buttered' is commonly associated with popcorn, especially in the context of a cinema. The context of the sentence, therefore, activated the word detector for 'popcorn', making the recognition of the word easier.

Semantic priming studies have also shed some light on another aspect of the reading process, the development of a mental model. It has been suggested that when a person reads some text, he or she generates a mental model of what the text is describing (Johnson-Laird, 1983). If the text contains a narrative, for example, the reader will imagine the scenes and actions that are being recounted. These issues of semantic priming and semantic networks are taken up in Chapter 11.

Cutting edge: Is it Ms or Mrs?

How important do you think a woman's surname is? According to a recent study from Tilburg University, more important than you might think (Noordewier et al., 2010).

In a series of studies, the researchers examined the effect of a woman keeping her maiden name, adopting her husband's surname or adopting a double-barrelled surname, on others' impressions. Women who kept their surname were more likely to judge themselves to be similar to the female stereotype than were those who did not. When people were asked to rate variously-surnamed women on a range of variables, women who adopted their married name were regarded as more caring, more dependent, less intelligent, more emotional, less competent and less ambitious than women who kept their maiden name. The converse was true for women who kept their maiden name: they were judged as more intelligent, more competent, less emotional, more independent and were judged to be similar to (unmarried) women who lived with a partner.

In a final study, in which people judged the suitability of job applicants, women who adopted their married name were not only less likely to be hired but, if they were, their salary would be lower.

Language acquisition by children

Perception of speech sounds by infants

Language development begins even before birth. Although the sounds that reach a foetus are somewhat muffled, speech sounds can still be heard. And some learning appears to take place prenatally (foetal learning is considered in more detail in Chapter 12). The voice that a foetus hears best and most often is obviously that of its mother. Consequently, a newborn infant prefers its mother's voice to that of others (DeCasper and Fifer, 1980). DeCasper and Spence (1986) even found that newborn infants preferred hearing their mothers reading a passage they had read aloud several times before their babies were born to hearing them read a passage they had never read before. Homae et al.(2011) using near infrared spectroscopy looked at infants' brain activity while they listened to no language, were read Japanese sentences aloud and then heard nothing again. There was activation seen in the temporal and frontal lobe during the last period but it was not as strong as in the first suggesting to the authors that the children had retained a 'memory' of the previous sound and that these brain regions underpin speech perception and could be activated even in children as young as 3 months old.

An infant's auditory system is well developed. Wertheimer (1961) found that newborns still in the delivery room can turn their heads towards the source of a sound. Babies 2 or 3 weeks of age can discriminate between the sound of a voice and other sounds. By the age of 2 months, babies can tell an angry voice from a pleasant one; an angry voice produces crying, whereas a pleasant one causes smiling and cooing.

One device used to determine what sounds a very young infant can perceive is the pacifier nipple, placed

Table 10.4 Examples of responses infants make to various speech sounds

Age of first occurrence	Response
Newborn	Is startled by a loud noise
	Turns head to look in the direction of sound
	Is calmed by the sound of a voice
	Prefers mother's voice to a stranger's
	Discriminates among many speech sounds
1–2 months	Smiles when spoken to
3–7 months	Responds differently to different intonations (e.g. friendly, angry)
8–12 months	Responds to name
	Responds to 'no'
	Recognises phrases from games (e.g. 'Peekaboo', 'How big is baby?')
	Recognises words from routines (e.g. waves to 'bye bye')
	Recognises some words

Source: From Berko Gleason, J., The Development of Language, 4th edn © 1997. Published by Allyn & Bacon, Boston, MA. Copyright © by Pearson Education. By permission of the publisher.

in the baby's mouth. The nipple is connected by a plastic tube to a pressure-sensitive switch that converts the infant's sucking movements into electrical signals. These signals can be used to turn on auditory stimuli. Each time the baby sucks, a particular sound is presented. If the auditory stimulus is novel, the baby usually begins to suck at a high rate. If the stimulus remains the same, its novelty wears off (habituation occurs) and the rate of sucking decreases. With another new stimulus, the rate of sucking again suddenly increases, unless the baby cannot discriminate the difference. If the stimuli sound the same to the infant, the rate of sucking remains low after the change.

Using this technique, Eimas *et al.* (1971) found that 1-month-old infants could tell the difference between the sounds of the consonants 'b' and 'p'. Like Lisker and Abramson (1970) in the study discussed earlier, they presented the sounds 'ba' and 'pa', synthesised by a computer. The infants, like the adult participants in the earlier study, discriminated between speech sounds having voice-onset times that differed by only 0.02 of a second. Even very early during post-natal development, the human auditory system is ready to make very fine discriminations. Table 10.4 lists some of the responses infants make to various types of speech sound.

The pre-speech period and the first words – An international perspective

The first sound that a baby makes is crying, a useful noise for attracting the attention of its carers. At about 1 month of age, infants start making other sounds, including 'cooing' (because of the prevalence of the 'ooing' sound). Often during this period, babies also make a series of sounds that resemble a half-hearted attempt to mimic the sound of crying (Kaplan and Kaplan, 1970).

At around 6 months, a baby's sounds begin to resemble those that occur in speech. Even though their babbling does not contain words – and does not appear to involve attempts to communicate verbally – the sounds that infants make, and the rhythm in which they are articulated, reflect the adult speech that babies hear. Mehler *et al.* (1988) found that 4-day-old infants preferred to hear a voice speaking French, their parents' native language. This ability to discriminate the sounds and rhythms of the language spoken around them manifested itself in the infants' own vocalisations very early on. Boysson-Bardies *et al.* (1984) had adult French speakers listen to recordings of the babbling of children from various cultures. The adults could easily distinguish the babbling of 8-month-old French infants from that of babies with different linguistic backgrounds.

A study by Kuhl *et al.* (1992) provides further evidence of the effect of children's linguistic environment on their language development. Native speakers learn not to distinguish between slight variations of sounds present in their language. In fact, they do not even hear the differences between them. For example, Japanese contains a sound that comes midway between /l/ and /r/. Different native speakers pronounce the sound differently, but all pronunciations are recognised as examples of the same phoneme. When native speakers of Japanese learn English, they have great difficulty distinguishing the sounds /l/ and /r/; for example, 'right' and 'light' sound to them like the same word. Presumably, the speech sounds that a child hears alter the brain mechanisms responsible for analysing them so that minor variations are not even perceived. The question is, when does this alteration occur? Most researchers have supposed that it happens only after children begin to learn the meanings of words, which occurs at around 10–12 months of age.

The experimenters presented two different vowel sounds, one found in English but not in Swedish and the other found in Swedish but not in English to 6-month-old infants in the US and Sweden. From time to time, they varied the sound slightly. The reactions of the Swedish infants and the American infants were strikingly different. Swedish infants noticed when the English vowel changed but not when the Swedish vowel changed; and American infants did the opposite. In other words, by the age of 6 months, the infants had learned not to pay attention to slight differences in speech sounds of their own language, but they were still able to distinguish slight differences in speech sounds they had never heard. Even though they were too young to understand the meaning of what they heard, the speech of people around them had affected the development of their perceptual mechanisms.

These results seem to support the **native language recognition hypothesis** – that infants have the ability to recognise words which belong to their native language (Moon *et al.*, 1993). Another hypothesis, the **general language discrimination hypothesis**, suggests that infants are capable of discriminating sentences from any two languages because they can extract sets of properties that these languages possess. The evidence above suggests that there is little support for this hypothesis. An alternative to these two hypotheses states that newborns are sensitive to prosody and can discriminate between languages on the basis of intonation and rhythm. This is called the rhythm-based language discrimination hypothesis (Nazzi *et al.*, 1998) and there is some support for this from studies in which infants were able to discriminate between English and Japanese but not English and Dutch.

Interestingly, there is evidence to suggest that the ability to discriminate between phonetic sounds successfully may change with age. Stager and Werker (1997) have reported that 8-month-old infants are capable of discriminating phonetic detail in a task in which 14-month-old infants cannot. The researchers suggest that this represents a reorganisation in the infant's language processing capacity: it shifts from the processes needed to learn syllables to the process needed to learn words. This is advantageous to the infant as it grows and has to put names to objects, events and situations. Because these activities are computationally complex and involve a huge increase in input, the amount of detail that needs to be processed is, therefore, limited.

Infant communication

Even before infants learn to talk, they display clear intent to communicate. Most attempts at pre-verbal infant communication fall into three categories: rejection, request (for social interaction, for an object or for an action) and comment (Sachs, 1993). Rejection usually involves pushing the unwanted object away and using facial expression and characteristic vocalisations to indicate displeasure. A request for social interaction usually involves the use of gestures and vocalisations to attract the caregiver's attention. A request for an object usually involves reaching and pointing and particular vocalisations. A request for an action (such as the one described above) similarly involves particular sounds and movements. Finally, a comment usually involves pointing out an object or handing it to the carer, accompanied by some vocalisation.

Infants babble before they talk. They often engage in serious 'conversations' with their carers, taking turns 'talking' with them. Infants' voices are modulated, and the stream of sounds they make sound as though they are using a secret language (Menn and Stoel-Gammon, 1993). At about 1 year of age, a child begins to produce words. The first sounds children use to produce speech appear to be similar across all languages and cultures: the first vowel is usually the soft 'a' sound of 'father', and the first consonant is a stop consonant produced with the lips – 'p' or 'b'.

Thus, the first word is often 'papa' or 'baba'. The next feature to be added is nasality, which converts the consonants 'p' or 'b' into 'm'. Thus, the next word is 'mama'. Mothers and fathers all over the world recognise these sounds as their children's attempts to address them. The first sounds of a child's true speech contain the same phonemes that are found in the babbling sounds that the child is already making; thus, speech emerges from pre-speech sounds. During the course of learning words from their carers and from older children, infants often invent their own protowords, unique strings of phonemes that serve word-like functions. The infants use these **proto-words** consistently in particular situations (Menn and Stoel-Gammon, 1993).

The development of speech sounds continues for many years. Some sequences are added very late. For example, the 'str' of string and the 'bl' of blink are difficult for young children to produce; they usually say 'tring' and 'link', omitting the first consonant. Most children recognise sounds in adult speech before they can produce them.

The two-word stage

At around 18–20 months of age, children start learning language by putting two words together, and their linguistic development takes a leap forward. It is at this stage that linguistic creativity begins.

As for first sounds, children's two-word utterances are remarkably consistent across all cultures. Children use words in the same way, regardless of the language their parents speak. Even deaf children who learn sign language from their parents put two words together in the same way as children who can hear (Bellugi and Klima, 1972). And deaf children whose parents do not know sign language invent their own signs and use them in orderly, 'rule-governed' ways (Goldin-Meadow and Feldman, 1977). Thus, the grammar of children's language at the two-word stage appears to be universal.

For many years, investigators described the speech of young children in terms of adult grammar, but researchers now recognise that children's speech simply follows different rules. Young children are incapable of forming complex sentences – partly because their vocabulary is small, partly because their short-term 'working' memory is limited (they cannot yet encode a long string of words), and partly because their cognitive development has not yet reached a stage at which they can learn complex rules of syntax (Locke, 1993).

Acquisition of adult rules of grammar

The first words that children use tend to be content words: these words are emphasised in adult speech and refer to objects and actions that children can directly observe (Brown and Bellugi, 1964). As children develop past the two-word stage, they begin to learn and use more and more of the grammatical rules that adults use. The first form of sentence lengthening appears to be the expansion of object nouns into noun phrases (Bloom, 1970). For example, 'that ball' becomes 'that a big ball'. Next, verbs are used more frequently, articles are added, prepositional phrases are mastered and sentences become more complex. These results involve the use of **inflections** and function words. Table 10.5 shows the approximate order in which children acquire some of these inflections and function words.

It is more difficult for children to add an inflection or function word to their vocabulary than to add a new content word because the rules that govern the use of inflections or function words are more complex than those that govern the use of most content words. In addition, content words usually refer to concrete objects or activities. The rules that govern the use of inflections or function words are rarely made explicit. A parent seldom says, 'When you want to use the past tense, add "-ed" to the verb', nor would a young child understand such a pronouncement. Instead, children must listen to speech and figure out how to express such concepts as the past tense.

Languages seem to differ significantly in terms of inflection. Of the 6,912 languages spoken in the world,

Table 10.5 The approximate order in which children acquire inflections and function words

Item		Example
1	Present progressive: *ing*	He is *sitting* down.
2	Preposition: *in*	The mouse is *in* the box.
3	Preposition: *on*	The book is *on* the table.
4	Plurals;– s	The *dogs* ran away.
5	Past irregular: e.g. *went*	The boy *went* home.
6	Possessive:– *'s*	The *girl's* dog is big.
7	Uncontractable copula *be*:	*Are* they boys or girls?
	e.g. *are, was*	*Was* that a dog?
8	Articles: *the, a, an*	He has *a* book.
9	Past regular: *-ed*	He *jumped* the stream
10	Third person regulars:-s s	She *ran* fast.
11	Third person irregular:	*Does* the dog bark?
	e.g. *has, does*	
12	Uncontractible auxiliary *be*:	*Is* he running?
	e.g. *is, were*	*Were* they at home?
13	Contractible copula *be*:	That's a spaniel.
	e.g. *'s, -re*	*They're* pretty.
14	Contractible auxiliary *be*:	He's doing it.
	e.g. *-'s, -'re*	*They're* running slowly.

Source: Adapted from Clark, H.H. and Clark, E.V., *Psychology and Language: An introduction to psycholinguistics*, 1977. © 1977, reprinted with permission of H.H. Clark & E.V. Clark.

each with its **median** number of 7,000 speakers, what is common to the languages spoken by the largest groups? Are there particular morphological, geographic or even social features these languages share that makes them so popular? Lupyan and Dale (2011) examined the structural properties of over 2,000 languages in an attempt to find an answer.

Their research uncovered universal features of the most widely spoken languages, spoken across the greatest geographical area: these had the simplest inflectional morphology and were the ones which used syntax, rather than modality, to indicate possession and provide evidence. The who-did-what-to-whom structure in these languages relied less on inflection/morphology and more on word order and the architecture of the language. One reason for the popularity of these languages, the authors argue, is that less complex morphology is easier to learn and, therefore, more economic to pass on to the next generation.

The most frequently used verbs in most languages are irregular. Forming the past tense of such verbs in English does not involve adding '-ed' (for example, go/went, throw/threw, buy/bought, see/saw). The past tense of such verbs must be learned individually. Because irregular verbs get more use than do regular ones, children learn them first, producing the past tense easily in sentences such as 'I came', 'I fell down', and 'she hit me'. Shortly after this period, they discover the regular past tense inflection and expand their vocabulary, producing sentences such as 'he dropped the ball'. But they also begin to say 'I comed', 'I falled down', and 'she hitted me'. Having learned a rule, they apply it to all verbs, including the irregular ones that they were previously using correctly. It takes children several years to learn to use the irregular past tense correctly again.

Children's rudimentary understanding, or at least recognition, of language and parts of speech seems to begin in the first few months of life. Children learn to assign meaning to words – decide whether they are nouns, verbs and so on – and use these words to form semi-structured sentences. That is, the child begins to follow the rules of grammar. Grammatical words tend to be phonetically and structurally smaller than lexical words – nouns, verbs and so on – and the commonest of them ('in', 'a', 'and') are used more frequently in conversation than are the most common lexical words. Does the child, therefore, show a preference for spoken grammatical or lexical words?

One study exposed 6-month-old infants to spoken lexical and grammatical words and measured their preference for each type of stimulus (Shi and Werker, 2001). The researchers found that the infants showed a preference for the lexical words. The authors suggest that although grammatical words are the most commonly used, lexical words may be more striking and acoustically interesting. Lexical words tend to be longer and have a more complex structure; mothers also tend to use lexical words in isolation (i.e. without the accompanying grammar). The preference for lexical words may help the child to give meaning to its world and act as a first essential step to developing more complex communication. It may be that children prefer and use lexical words first and then clamp them on to grammatical structures later.

Acquisition of meaning

The simplest explanation of why children use and understand language is that they hear a word spoken at the same time that they see (or hear, or touch) the object to which the word refers. After several such pairings, they add a word to their vocabulary. In fact, children first learn the names of things with which they interact, or things that change (and thus attract their attention).

For example, they are quick to learn words like 'biscuit' or 'blanket', but are slow to learn words like 'wall' or 'window' (Ross *et al.*, 1986; Pease *et al.*, 1993).

Fast mapping

This quick learning of new, content words has been called **fast mapping** (Carey and Bartlett, 1978; Markman, 1989). There is some debate over whether fast mapping is specific to language or whether it is generated by other, cognitive processes. For example, if fast mapping is seen only for words then this would suggest that the process is language based; if fast mapping can extend to other domains, this suggests that the process is underpinned by general cognitive abilities (such as the ability to memorise).

In two experiments, Markson and Bloom (1997) taught 3–4-year-old children and a group of university undergraduates to learn a word referring to an object ('kobi') and a fact about this object. In one experiment, participants were told that this was an object given to the experimenter by her uncle. The participants' ability to remember and identify the object was tested immediately after learning, one week after or one month after. Although the adults were better at remembering the object and object name than were the children, all children performed comparably well when asked to retrieve the word, identify the object about which facts were presented, and to identify the object given to the experimenter by her uncle. The study suggests that fast mapping may not necessarily be specific to language processing but is made possible by learning and memory mechanisms that are not specific to the language domain.

Waxman and Booth (2000) replicated Markson and Bloom's original finding but suggested that there is a crucial difference between the principles underpinning noun learning and fact learning. They introduced pre-school children to an unfamiliar object, such as those seen in Figure 10.7, and required them to associate it with a noun ('This is a koba') or a fact ('My uncle gave this to me'). The researchers then investigated whether (1) the children were able to map the word or fact correctly by choosing the 'koba' or 'the object the uncle gave to the experimenter', from a series of 10 familiar objects and (2) the children were able to extend their knowledge of the object by identifying the object from unfamiliar ones. In the second condition, the children were asked, 'Is this one a koba?' (word condition), or 'Is this the one my uncle gave me?' (fact condition). The children were able to map successfully using the word or the fact. However, there was a difference between the two conditions when children had to extend their knowledge – the children extended the noun to other, similar objects but did not extend the fact.

In another study, 2–4-year-old children were taught a novel name for an object ('My cat stepped on this

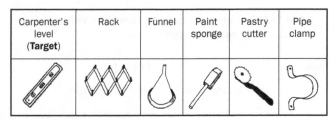

Figure 10.7 Some of the unfamiliar objects in Waxman and Booth's (2000) study.

Source: Waxman, S.R. and Booth, A.E., Principles that are invoked in the acquisition of words, but not facts. *Cognition*, 2000, 77, B33–B43. © 2000, with permission from Elsevier.

agnew') and given an arbitrary fact for a second, unfamiliar object (such as metal shelving brackets and Allen keys) (Behrend *et al.*, 2001). The children extended the novel name to more exemplars than they did facts, suggesting that some of the principles underpinning the learning of words and facts are different.

Overextension and underextension

Often a child may commit what are called errors of overextension or underextension. If a child has learned to identify a ball but says 'ball' when they see an apple or an orange, or even the moon, we must conclude that they do not know the meaning of 'ball'. This error is called **overextension** – the use of a word to denote a larger class of items than is appropriate. If the child uses the word to refer only to the small red plastic ball, the error is called an **underextension** – the use of a word to denote a smaller class of items than is appropriate. Table 10.6 lists some examples of children's overextensions while learning the meanings of new words.

Both overextensions and underextensions are normal; a single pairing of a word with the object does not provide enough information for accurate generalisation.

Carers often correct children's overextensions. The most effective type of instruction occurs when an adult provides the correct label and points out the features that distinguish the object from the one with which the child has confused it (Chapman *et al.*, 1986). For example, if a child calls a yo-yo a ball, the carer might say, 'That's a yo-yo. See? It goes up and down' (Pease *et al.*, 1993).

Bilingualism

If an individual can meet the communication demands of the self or the individual's culture in two or more languages, they are considered bilingual (Mohanty and Perregaux, 1997). **Bilingualism** is described as 'simultaneous' when two or more languages develop in childhood more or less simultaneously, spontaneously and naturally, and 'successive' when a second (and third) language is

Table 10.6 Some overextensions that children make while learning new words

Word	Original referent	Application
Mooi	Moon	Cakes, round marks on windows writing on windows and in books round shapes in books, round postmarks, letter *o*
buti	ball	Toy, radish, stone sphere at park entrance
ticktock	watch	All clocks and watches, gas meter, firehose wound on spool, bath scale round dial
baw	ball	Apples, grapes, eggs, squash, bell clapper, anything round
mem	horse	Cow, calf, pig, moose, all four-legged animals
fly	fly	Specks of dirt, dust, all small insects, child's own toes, crumbs of bread, a toad
wau-wau	dog	All animals, toy dog, soft house slippers, picture of an old man dressed in furs

Source: Adapted from Table 13.2 from *Psychology and Language: An introduction to psycholinguistics* by Herbert H. Clark and Eve V. Clark. © 1977, reprinted with permission of H.H. Clark & E.V. Clark.

learned after the first, such as learning a second language during puberty (Romaine, 1989).

Until relatively recently, it was thought that bilingualism was detrimental to cognitive performance such as lexical decision time: bilinguals were slower, committed more errors when naming pictures and had more tip-of-the tongue experiences. None of these is very much evident in conversation, however (Bialystok and Craik, 2010). The early studies, which compared Spanish–English bilinguals in America and English–Welsh bilinguals in Wales with monolinguals, showed that being able to speak two languages from childhood had negative consequences for intellectual development. However, these studies did not take into account socio-economic status, the degree of bilingualism or the skill in the second language (Lambert, 1977; Cummins, 1984). Rather than impairing cognitive ability, bilingualism appears to be beneficial to it (Perregaux, 1994).

Executive functions, for example, are much better performed by bilingual speakers – bilinguals sort cards by colour and shape and complete the Stroop task better (see Chapter 8) (Bialystok and Martin, 2004; Bialystok *et al.*, 2008). Vocabulary in both languages appears to be smaller, however, across the lifespan and in childhood (Bialystok *et al.*, in press). The reason for the better executive function performance appears to be that conflict resolution between two languages is a feature of executive function, and that the constant exercise of this conflict resolution enhances general executive function (Bialystok and Craik, 2010). It may even be a cognitive reserve, protecting against cognitive decline. One study, for example, has found that the age of onset of dementia is four years later for bilingual than monoligual speakers (Bialystok *et al.*, 2007).

Is there a language acquisition device?

According to Pinker (1984), 'In general, language acquisition is a stubbornly robust process; from what we can tell there is virtually no way to prevent it from happening, short of raising a child in a barrel.' The absence of barrels permitting, what shapes this linguistic learning process, and what motivates it?

There is vigorous controversy about why children learn to speak and, especially, why they learn to speak grammatically. Chomsky (1965) observed that the recorded speech of adults is not as correct as the dialogue we read in a novel or hear in a play; often it is ungrammatical, hesitating and full of unfinished sentences. In fact, he characterised everyday adult speech as 'defective' and 'degenerate'. If this speech is really what children hear when they learn to speak, it is amazing that they manage to acquire the rules of grammar.

The view that children learn regular rules from apparently haphazard samples of speech has led many linguists to conclude that the ability to learn language is innate. All a child has to do is to be in the company of speakers of a language. Linguists have proposed that a child's brain contains a **language acquisition device** which embodies rules of 'universal grammar'; because each language expresses these rules in slightly different ways, the child must learn the details, but the basics are already there in the brain (Chomsky, 1965; Lenneberg, 1967; McNeill, 1970).

The assertion that an innate language acquisition device guides children's acquisition of a language is part of a general theory about the cognitive structures responsible for language and its acquisitions (Pinker, 1990). The most important components are as follows:

- Children who are learning a language make hypotheses about the grammatical rules they need to follow. These hypotheses are confirmed or disconfirmed by the speech that they hear.
- An innate language acquisition device guides children's hypothesis formation. Because they have this device, there are certain types of hypothetical rule that they will never entertain and certain types of sentence that they will never utter.

- The language acquisition device makes reinforcement unnecessary; the device provides the motivation for the child to learn a language.
- There is a critical period for learning a language. The language acquisition device works best during childhood; after childhood, languages are difficult to learn and almost impossible to master.

Evaluation of the evidence for a language acquisition device

No investigator regards the first assertion – that children make and test hypotheses about grammatical rules – as tenable. Thus, we cannot simply ask children why they say what they do. Children's hypothesis-testing is a convenient metaphor for the fact that their speech sometimes follows one rule or another.

A more important – and testable – assertion is that the hypothesis testing is guided by the language acquisition device. The most important piece of evidence in favour of this assertion is the discovery of language universals: characteristics that can be found in all languages that linguists have studied. Some of the more important language universals include the existence of noun phrases ('the quick brown fox ...'); verb phrases ('... ate the chicken'); grammatical categories of words such as nouns and adjectives; and syntactical rules that permit the expression of subject–verb–object relations ('John hit Andy'), plurality ('two birds') and possession ('Rachel's pen').

However, the fact that all languages share certain characteristics does not mean that they are the products of innate brain mechanisms. For example, Hebb *et al.* (1973) observed that language universals may simply reflect realities of the world. When people deal with each other and with nature, their interactions often take the form of an agent acting on an object. Thus, the fact that all languages have ways of expressing these interactions is not surprising. Similarly, objects come in slightly different shapes, sizes and colours, so we can expect the need for ways (such as adjectives) to distinguish among them. It is not unreasonable to suppose that the same kinds of linguistic device have been independently invented at different times and in different places by different cultures. After all, archaeologists tell us that similar tools have been invented by different cultures all around the world. People need to cut, hammer, chisel, scrape and wedge things apart, and different cultures have invented similar devices to perform these tasks. We need not conclude that these inventions are products of a 'tool-making device' located in the brain. But even if some language universals are dictated by reality, others could

indeed be the result of a language acquisition device. For example, consider the following sentences, adapted from Pinker (1990):

> A1. Bill drove the car into the garage.
>
> A2. Bill drove the car.
>
> B1. Bill put the car into the garage.
>
> B2. Bill put the car.

Someone (such as a child learning a language) who heard sentences A1 and A2 could reasonably infer that sentence B1 could be transformed into sentence B2. But the inference obviously is false; sentence B2 is ungrammatical. The linguistic rules say that sentence A2 is acceptable but that sentence B2 is not very complex; and their complexity is taken as evidence that they must be innate, not learned. Pinker (1990, p. 206) concludes: 'The solution to the problem [that children do not utter sentence B2] must be that children's learning mechanisms ultimately do not allow them to make the generalisation.'

This conclusion rests on the assumption that children use rules similar to the ones that linguists use. How, the reasoning goes, could a child master such complicated rules at such an early stage of cognitive development unless the rules were already wired into the brain? But perhaps the children are not following such complex rules. Perhaps they learn that when you say 'put' (something) you must always go on to say where you put something. Linguists do not like rules that deal with particular words, such as put (something) (somewhere); they prefer abstract and general rules that deal with categories: clauses, prepositions, noun phrases and the like. But children learn particular words and their meanings – why should they not also learn that certain words must be followed (or must never be followed) by certain others? Doing so is certainly simpler than learning the complex and subtle rules that linguists have devised. It would seem that both complex and simple rules (or innate or learned ones) could explain the fact that children do not utter sentence B2.

The third assertion is that language acquisition occurs without the need of reinforcement, or even of correction. Brown and Hanlon (1970) recorded dialogue between children and parents and found that adults generally did not show disapproval when the children's utterances were ungrammatical and approval when they were grammatical. Instead, approval appeared to be contingent on the truth or accuracy of the children's statements. If there is no differential reinforcement, how can we explain the fact that children eventually learn to speak grammatically? It is undoubtedly true that adults rarely say, 'Good, you said that correctly', or, 'No, you said that wrongly'. However, adults do distinguish between grammatical and ungrammatical speech of children. A study by Bohannon and Stanowicz (1988) found that adults are likely to repeat children's grammatically correct sentences verbatim but to correct ungrammatical sentences. For example, if a child says, 'That be monkey', an adult would say, 'That is a monkey'. Adults were also more likely to ask for clarifications of ungrammatical sentences. Thus, adults do tend to provide the information children need to correct their faulty speech.

Chomsky's assertion about the defectiveness and degeneracy of adult speech is not strictly true, at least as far as it applies to what children hear. In fact, according to Newport *et al.* (1977), almost all the speech that a young child hears (at least, in industrialised English-speaking societies) is grammatically correct. If that is so, why should we hypothesise that a language acquisition device exists? Because, say some researchers, not all children are exposed to **child-directed speech** (that is, speech which adults use specifically when communicating with children). 'In some societies people tacitly assume that children aren't worth speaking to and don't have anything to say that is worth listening to. Such children learn to speak by overhearing streams of adult-to-adult speech' (Pinker, 1990, p. 218).

Pinker's statement is very strong; it says that children in some cultures have no speech directed towards them until they have mastered the language. It implies that the children's mothers do not talk to them and ignores the fact that older children may not be quite so choosy about their conversational partners. To conclude that such an extreme statement is true would require extensive observation and documentation of child-rearing practices in other cultures. One of the strongest biological tendencies of our species is for a mother to cherish, play with and communicate with her offspring. If there really is a culture in which mothers do not do so, we need better documentation.

In fact, children do not learn a language that they simply overhear. Bonvillian *et al.* (1976) studied children of deaf parents whose only exposure to spoken language was through television or radio. This exposure was not enough; although the children could hear and did watch television and listen to the radio, they did not learn to speak English. It takes more than 'overhearing streams of adult-to-adult speech' to learn a language. The way that parents talk to their children is closely related to the children's language acquisition (Furrow *et al.*, 1979; Furrow and Nelson, 1986). Thus, the question is, just how much instruction (in the form of child-directed speech) do children need?

The fact that parents do not often reward their children's speech behaviours with praise or tangible reinforcers (such as sweets) does not prove that reinforcement plays no role in learning a language. We humans are social animals; our behaviour is strongly affected by the behaviour of others. It is readily apparent to anyone who has observed the behaviour of children that the attention of other people is extremely important to them. Children will perform a variety of behaviours that get other people to pay attention to them. They will make faces, play games and even misbehave in order to attract attention. And above all, they will talk.

The final assertion – that the language acquisition device works best during childhood – has received the most experimental support. For example, Newport and Supalla (1987) studied the ability of people who were deaf from birth to use sign language. They found that the earlier the training began, the better the person was able to communicate. Johnson and Newport (1989) also found that native Korean and Chinese speakers who moved to the USA learned English grammar better if they arrived during childhood. The advantage did not appear to be a result of differences in motivation to learn a second language. Such results are consistent with the hypothesis that something occurs within the brain after childhood that makes it more difficult to learn a language.

Conclusion

Observational studies such as these do not prove that a cause-and-effect relation exists between the variables in question. Johnson and Newport (1989) suggest that people's age (in particular, the age of their brain) affects their language-learning ability. But other variables are also correlated with age. For example, the Korean and Chinese speakers who moved to the USA as children spent several years in school; and perhaps the school environment is a particularly good place to learn a second language. In addition, adults are generally more willing to correct the grammatical errors made by children than those made by adolescents or other adults; thus, children may get more tutoring. It is certainly possible that the investigators are correct, but their results cannot be taken as proof that the brain contains an innate language acquisition device.

In one sense, a language acquisition device does exist. The human brain is a language acquisition device; without it, languages are not acquired. The real controversy is over the characteristics of this language acquisition device. Is it so specialised that it contains universal rules of grammar and provides innate motivation that makes reinforcement unnecessary?

The issue is made more interesting, if controversial, if we consider the ability of other higher primates to learn language. Other higher primates such as gorillas or chimpanzees do not naturally produce language although they have their own system of communication. Their vocal apparatus is different from that of humans so it would be unrealistic to assume that they would be able to articulate human language. However, these animals are the ones that are genetically closest to us; similar brain asymmetries, especially in those parts of the brain which are thought to mediate language, are seen in humans and apes. Would it be possible to teach primates human language? Do higher primates also possess an innate language acquisition device but need an environmental prompt for such a device to start working? These questions form the basis of the following Controversies in Psychological Science section.

Controversies in psychological science: Can other primates acquire language?

The issue

The members of most species can communicate with one another. Even insects communicate: a female moth that is ready to mate can release a chemical that will bring male moths from miles away; a dog can tell its owner that it wants to go for a walk by bringing its lead in its mouth and whining at the door. But, until recently, humans were the only species that had languages – flexible systems that use symbols to express many meanings. But are other primates able to learn and use symbols in the same linguistic way that humans do?

The evidence

In the 1960s, Beatrice and Roger Gardner of the University of Nevada began Project Washoe (Gardner and Gardner, 1969, 1978), a remarkably successful attempt to teach sign language to a female chimpanzee named Washoe. Previous attempts to teach chimps to learn and use human language focused on speech (Hayes, 1952). These attempts failed because, as we noted above, chimps lack the control of tongue, lips, palate and vocal cords that humans have and thus cannot produce the variety of complex sounds that characterise human speech.

Gardner and Gardner realised this limitation and decided to attempt to teach Washoe a manual language – one that makes use of hand movements. Chimps' hand and finger dexterity is excellent, so the only limitations in their ability would be cognitive ones. The manual language the Gardners chose was based on ASL, the American sign language used by deaf people. This is a true language, containing function words and content words and having regular grammatical rules.

Washoe was 1 year old when she began learning sign language; by the time she was 4, she had a vocabulary of over 130 signs. Like children, she used single signs at first; then, she began to produce two-word sentences such as 'Washoe sorry', 'gimme flower', 'more fruit' and 'Roger tickle'. Sometimes, she strung three or more words together, using the concept of agent and object: 'You tickle me'. She asked and answered questions, apologised, made assertions – in short, did the kinds of things that children would do while learning to talk. She showed overextensions and underextensions, just as human children do. Occasionally, she even made correct generalisa-

tions by herself. After learning the sign for the verb 'open' (as in open box, open cupboard), she used it to say open faucet, when requesting a drink. She made signs to herself when she was alone and used them to 'talk' to cats and dogs, just as children will do. Although it is difficult to compare her progress with that of human children (the fairest comparison would be with that of deaf children learning to sign), humans clearly learn language much more readily than Washoe did.

Inspired by Project Washoe's success (Washoe died in 2007), several other investigators have taught primate species to use sign language. For example, Patterson began to teach a gorilla (Patterson and Linden, 1981) and Miles (1983) began to teach an orangutan. Washoe's training started relatively late in her life, and her trainers were not, at the beginning of the project, fluent in sign language. Other chimpanzees, raised from birth by humans who are native speakers of ASL, have begun to use signs when they are 3 months old (Gardner and Gardner, 1975).

Many psychologists and linguists have questioned whether the behaviour of these animals can really be classified as verbal behaviour. For example, Terrace et al. (1979) argue that the apes simply learned to imitate the gestures made by their trainers and that sequences of signs such as, 'please milk please me like drink apple bottle' (produced by a young gorilla) are nothing like the sequences that human children produce. Others have challenged these criticisms (Fouts, 1983; Miles, 1983; Stokoe, 1983), blaming much of the controversy on the method that Terrace and his colleagues used to train their chimpanzee.

Certainly, the verbal behaviour of apes cannot be the same as that of humans. If apes could learn to communicate linguistically as well as children can, then humans would not have been the only species to have developed language. The usefulness of these studies rests in what they can teach us about our own language and cognitive abilities. Through them, we may discover what abilities animals need to communicate as we do. They may also help us to understand the evolution of these capacities.

These studies have already provided some useful information. For example, Premack (1976) taught chimpanzees to 'read' and 'write' by arranging plastic tokens into 'sentences'. Each token represents an object, action or attribute such as colour or shape, in much the same way as words do. His first trainee, Sarah, whom he acquired when she was 1 year old,

Controversies in psychological science: *Continued*

THE WORLD WILL BE A DIFFERENT PLACE
ONCE YOU'VE SEEN IT THROUGH HIS EYES

PROJECT NIM

Source: Rex Features: C. Roads/Everett.

learned to understand complex sentences such as 'Sarah insert banana in pail, apple in dish'. When she saw the discs arranged in this order, she obeyed the instructions.

Chimpanzees can, apparently, use symbols to represent real objects and can manipulate these symbols logically. These abilities are two of the most powerful features of language. For Premack's chimpanzees, a blue plastic triangle means 'apple'. If the chimpanzees are given a blue plastic triangle and asked to choose the appropriate symbols denoting its colour and shape, they choose the ones that signify 'red' and 'round', not 'blue' and 'triangular'. Thus, the blue triangle is not simply a token the animals can use to obtain apples; it represents an apple for them, just as the word apple represents it for us.

Even though humans are the only primates who can pronounce words, several other species can recognise them. Savage-Rumbaugh (1990; Savage-Rumbaugh *et al.*, 1998) taught Kanzi, a pygmy chimpanzee, to communicate with humans by pressing buttons that contained symbols for words (see Figure 10.8).

Kanzi's human companions talked with him, and he learned to understand them. Although the structure of his vocal apparatus prevented him from responding vocally, he often tried to do so. During a three-month period, Savage-Rumbaugh and her colleagues tested Kanzi with 310 sentences, such as 'Put a

EVOLUTION BECOMES REVOLUTION

THE RISE OF THE PLANET OF THE APES

#apeswillrise   www.apeswillrise.com   COMING SOON

Source: Rex Features: 20th Century Fox/Everett.

Controversies in psychological science: *Continued*

Figure 10.8 One of the more famous primates studied for human language development was Nim Chimpsky (a play on Noam Chomsky). The story of this chimp's teaching, and its unusual instructors, was documented in the 2011 film, *Project Nim*.
Source: Science Photo Library Ltd: Susan Kuklin/Photo Researchers.

toothbrush in the lemonade'. Three hundred and two of these had never been heard by the chimpanzee before. Only situations in which Kanzi could not have been guided by non-verbal cues from the human companions were counted; often, Kanzi's back was to the speaker. He responded correctly 298 times. Table 10.7 presents specific examples of these sentences and the actions that Kanzi took.

Conclusion

The most successful attempts at teaching a language to other primates are those in which the animal and the trainer have established a close relationship in which they can successfully communicate non-verbally by means of facial expressions, movements and gestures. Such interactions naturally lead to attempts at communication; and if signs (or spoken words) serve to make communication easier and more effective, they will most readily be learned.

Table 10.7 Semantic relations comprehended by Kanzi, a pygmy chimpanzee

Semantic relations	N	Examples (spoken)
Action–object	107	*'Would you please carry the straw?'* Kanzi looks over a number of objects on the table, selects the straw, and takes it to the next room.
Object–action	13	*'Would you like to ball chase?'* Kanzi looks around for a ball, finds one in his swimming pool, takes it out, comes over to the keyboard, and answers 'Chase'
Object–location	8	*'Would you put out the grapes in the swimming pool?'* Kanzi selects some grapes from among several foods and tosses them into the swimming pool
Action–location	23	*'Let's chase to the A-frame,'* Kanzi is climbing in trees, has been ignoring things that are said to him. When he hears this he comes down rapidly and runs to the A-frame
Action–object–location	36	*'I hid the surprise by my foot,'* Kanzi has been told that a surprise is around somewhere, and he is looking for it. When he is given this clue, he immediately approaches the speaker and lifts up her foot
Object–action	9	*'Kanzi, the pine cone goes in your shirt,'* picks up a pine cone
Action–location–object	8	*'Go to the refrigerator and get out a tomato,'* Kanzi is playing in the water in the sink. When he hears this he stops, goes to the refrigerator, and gets a tomato
Agent–action–object	7	*'Jeannine hid the pine needles in her shirt,'* Kanzi is busy making a nest of blankets, branches and pine needles. When he hears this, he immediately walks over to Jeannine, lifts up her shirt, takes out the pine needles, and puts them in his nest
Action–object–recipient	19	*'Kanzi, please carry the cooler to Penny,'* Kanzi grabs the cooler and carries it over to Penny
Other–object–action –recipient; action–recipient –location; etc.	69	

Source: Savage-Rumbaugh, E.S., Language acquisition in nonhuman species, *Development Psychobiology*, 1990, 23, 599–620. Copyright © 1990, this material is used by permission of John Wiley & Sons, Inc.

Brain development and language

In his book *The Biological Foundations of Language*, Lenneberg (1967) argued that the functional lateralisation of language – one cerebral hemisphere's superiority for processing language – begins at the same time as the child begins to acquire language. Lenneberg thus argued that there was a sensitive period during which language should be acquired and lateralisation would develop.

Others (e.g. Krashen, 1973) argued that the hemispheres of the brain are equipotential at birth – each hemisphere is capable of undertaking the function for which the other becomes specialised. The **critical period** for lateralisation was complete by the age of 5 or 6 years. If lesions to the right hemisphere occurred before the age of 5 years, the child would show symptoms of aphasia, a disorder involving the inability to produce or comprehend speech. If damage occurred after the age of 5, no deficits in speech would arise suggesting that the normal left-for-language functional asymmetry had developed and was relatively complete. Krashen was involved in the study of an unusual case in which a young girl had been deprived of auditory stimulation and failed to develop normal language.

The case of 'Genie'

'Genie', real name Susan Wiley, was a 13-year-old girl who had been chronically abused since infancy. The girl's father had harnessed her to a potty in a room in the back of the family house since she was at least 20 months old and deprived her of any linguistic stimulation. She slept in a crib covered with wire mesh. Her father was intolerant of noise and would beat her whenever she made any sound. Her mother fed her a diet of baby food, cereals and, occasionally, boiled eggs. When eventually spotted by social workers, the girl was 4 feet 6 inches tall and weighed 4 stone. She could not eat solid food and had nearly two complete sets of teeth. She was 13 years and 9 months old.

Her most remarkable psychological feature was her almost complete lack of language. She could not talk and had a vocabulary of about 20 words (she could understand concepts such as 'red' 'blue', 'green'). Her speech production was limited to 'nomore', 'stopit' and other negatives. Following her discovery, she was admitted to the Children's Hospital in Los Angeles for treatment. Researchers were interested in how handicapped Genie's language had become and what possible recovery could be made from such gross linguistic impairment (Fromkin *et al.*, 1972/73; Curtiss, 1977). There had been isolated instances of 'accidental' cases of language deprivation before, such as Victor, the 'wild boy of Aveyron', who had been found in 1800, lurking naked in front of a cottage in the Languedoc region of France. He had spent his 12 years from infancy living in the woods, surviving on a diet of acorns and potatoes. He had had his throat cut

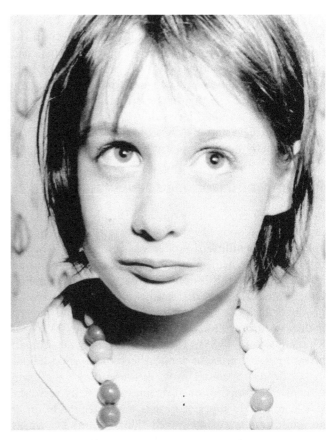

This is one of the few images of Genie (Susan Wiley) that is publicly available. It was reported that Genie had suffered sustained psychological and physical abuse from her father over a number of years which led to her showing highly maladaptive and delayed/impaired behaviour. It was this behaviour – a failure to use/develop language and interact normally with people- that led to the epithet 'wild child'. This is a term used to describe children who are literally abandoned, usually in the wild, and have no opportunity to develop language or social skills. Despite the best attempts of researchers to help rehabilitate Genie, her language did not improve significantly.
Source: Corbis: Bettmann.

as a toddler and been left to die. Victor had no language, and while he never learned to speak, he achieved a rudimentary ability to spell.

A year after she was discovered, Genie's language ability underwent marked improvement. Her ability to structure according to rules was the equivalent of a 20-year-old's, and her spatial ability placed her in the adult ability category. She could tell the difference between singular and plural words and positive and negative sentences and could understand some prepositions. Her speech was limited to one or two word sentences, however, eventually becoming very descriptive and concrete ('big rectangular pillow', 'very, very, very dark-green box'). The 'explosion' of language, normally expected after such dramatic improvements, never materialised.

It became clear that Genie could develop new but basic language skills. She made a dramatic recovery from the time of her discovery to the time when the scientists had to abandon their studies. Yet, her language never fully recovered, remaining steadfastly descriptive, almost at the level one would expect primates to achieve with intensive language training. Her study showed, however, the remarkable, devastating effects of language and auditory deprivation on the development of language ability.

Plasticity and language development

In a series of famous experiments, Dennis and Whitaker (1976) and Woods (1980) found that the incidence of aphasia, an inability to produce or comprehend speech, following right-hemisphere damage was greater during infancy than if the lesions had occurred later in life. Other authors suggest that left-hemisphere lesions would produce the greatest deficits in language and speech if they occurred after the age of 5 or 6 years (Vargha-Khadem et al., 1985). The evidence from the human literature was consistent with earlier experimental lesioning work in primates. This work found that if the brain of a monkey was lesioned during infancy, its recovery was significantly superior to that seen after the brain of an adult monkey was lesioned. This became known as the Kennard principle (named after Margaret Kennard who made the experimental observation): the notion that recovery from brain damage during infancy is better than from damage during adulthood.

Another source of data suggesting a critical period for the development of asymmetry comes from studies of hemispherectomy, where one hemisphere is removed for medical reasons, usually because of the growth of a large tumour or because of intractable epilepsy. In adults, left hemispherectomies result in fairly severe aphasia, but left hemispherectomies in children are associated with almost complete recovery of language function (Searleman, 1977).

What these data suggest is that the brain has a degree of plasticity when it is developing. That is, specialised functions have not developed in any sophisticated way in one or other hemisphere during early growth. After a specific age, however, this specialisation has begun, but one or other hemisphere can undertake the functions of the other if the other is damaged.

For example, studies have shown that early brain lesions in children between 13 and 36 months old are associated with a delay in the development of expressive vocabulary, especially if damage is to the left side. However, there seems to be little effect on the next stage of language development, sentence production (Vicari et al., 2000). If the damage occurs later, in adulthood, then it is hypothesised that the right hemisphere undertakes the language functions of the left (Hertz-Pannier et al., 1999). One study has found that injury to the left temporal lobe is associated with subsequent increased activation of the right frontal lobe during verbal fluency (Voets et al., 2006). MEG studies also suggest that lateralisation increases as a function of age (Ressel et al., 2008).

Is half a brain enough?

In a novel experiment to explore the nature of plasticity, Hertz-Pannier et al. (2002) studied six children who underwent left hemispherectomy for intractable epilepsy (epilepsy that cannot be controlled by drugs) and monitored their brain activity during language tasks before and after the surgery. They hypothesised that if the brain shows evidence of plasticity, then we might expect the right hemisphere to take over the language function of the left. They used fMRI to study the children at age 6 years and 10 months and found the typical left lateralisation for language tasks such as word generation; there was little right hemisphere activity.

Following surgery, receptive language recovered quickly but expressive language and reading was slower to recover. When fMRI scanning was undertaken again at 10 years 6 months, there was a shift in activity to the right hemisphere during expressive and receptive language tasks. The regions that were activated – the inferior frontal temporal and parietal cortices – were analogous to those in the left hemisphere prior to the surgery.

This activation in the right hemisphere is also seen in adults recovering from aphasia. For example, Cappa et al. (1997) found that activation in the right temporoparietal (TP) region during the acute phase of recovery predicted improvement in auditory comprehension later on. More recently, a group of researchers has found that a period of intensive training in a group of patients who had suffered a stroke destroying parts of the left frontal cortex and who had difficulty in comprehending speech, led to increased activation in the bilateral network of regions associated with language. There were also increases in right hemisphere regions.

A group of researchers from Germany compared the degree of brain activation and the degree of improvement in language function in eight patients who had suffered a stroke (Menke et al., 2009). Over two weeks and for three hours a day, patients were trained to name concrete words. Task performance was measured before the training, immediately after and eight months after. Language function improved considerably – from 0 per cent to 64 per cent accuracy across the study. The researchers also found, however, that success at the task was predicted by different brain regions depending on when testing took place. In the short-term, activation in the hippocampus and fusiform gyrus and in the right precuneus and cingulate gyrus predicted language success. At 8 months, right-sided activation in the equivalent of Wernicke's area was found, as was activation in other areas of the temporal lobe region.

The researchers suggest that the process of recovery is dynamic and conclude that their study shows that in the early stages, regions not particularly associated with language but associated with memory and attention are activated but in the later stages of recovery, the 'classical' language areas become more involved.

The picture is not entirely clear-cut, however. A different group of German researchers found that activation in the right frontal part of the brain predicted degree of improvement in patients who had suffered a stroke (Saur *et al.*, 2010). Language proficiency was measured by combining the scores from a battery of language tasks. They studied 21 stroke patients two weeks and eight months after language training.

Another case study highlights how successful language development could be following such radical surgery (Battro, 2000). Nico is an Italian boy who was born with left hemiplegia. He managed to walk by age 18 months but developed intractable epilepsy at 22 months. Drugs and selective lesioning of the brain failed to halt the epilepsy and so, as a last resort and with the permission of Nico's parents, surgeons performed a right hemidecortication when the boy was 3 years and 7 months.

Nico recovered well and he did not lose his speech. His IQ was 107 and he learned to develop the basics of spelling and grammar at the same age as normal children through the use of a computer. He is still behind other children in his ability to draw and has difficulty forming letters of the alphabet and numbers with the right hand. The outcome of Nico's surgery suggests that the right hemisphere may be what Popper and Eccles (1977) described as a 'minor brain'. Without it, Nico has learned to develop the important function of language although his 'right hemisphere' functions, such as drawing, are impaired.

The neuropsychology of language and language disorders

Neuropsychology aims to localise not only basic perceptual and sensory functions, such as touching, seeing, recognising objects and so on, but also quite sophisticated cognitive functions (see Chapters 1 and 4). The most extensively studied cognitive function is language, and our knowledge of the neuropsychology of language has come from three sources: studies of individuals with brain injury who show language impairment, individuals who do not develop language adequately, and neuroimaging studies in which activation of the brain in healthy

individuals is monitored while they complete language tasks. These sources indicate that the mechanisms involved in perception, comprehension and production of speech are located in different areas of the cerebral cortex.

Language disorders

Brain damage can result from a large number of factors and can cause a wide variety of impairments in cognitive function. Some of the most pronounced impairments are those related to language. Some language impairments result directly from brain injury, others do not but are likely to be the result of disorganised or abnormal brain activity or structure. The most common language disorders are called the aphasias. The key feature of the aphasias is the loss of language function; the patient is unable to produce or comprehend speech. Other important disorders of language are reading impairment (dyslexia) and stuttering and all three of these disorders are considered in the next sections.

Aphasia

Aphasia literally means 'total loss of language function', although patients with the disorder do not lose all language: they are able to perform some language tasks, for example, depending on the site of the brain injury. Because of this, the term 'dysphasia' is sometimes used (*dys-* means 'partial loss of'). There are different types of aphasia, and the most common are summarised in Table 10.9. Two of the most common types are non-fluent (Broca's) aphasia and receptive (Wernicke's) aphasia. The areas of the brain which, when damaged, cause these aphasias can be seen in Figure 10.9.

Speech production: evidence from non-fluent (Broca's) aphasia

In order to produce meaningful communication, we need to convert perceptions, memories and thoughts into speech. The neural mechanisms that control speech production appear to be located in the frontal lobes. Damage to a region of the motor association cortex in the left frontal lobe (Broca's area) disrupts the ability to speak: it causes **non-fluent (Broca's) aphasia**, a language disorder characterised by slow, laborious, non-fluent speech (it is also called expressive, production or motor aphasia). When trying to talk with patients who have non-fluent aphasia, most people find it hard to resist supplying the words the patients are groping for. But although these patients often mispronounce words, the ones they manage to produce are meaningful. They have something to say, but the damage to the frontal lobe makes it difficult for them to express these thoughts.

Table 10.9 (a) Types of aphasia, their primary symptoms and the site of the associated brain lesion

Type of aphasia	Primary symptoms	Brain lesion to
Sensory (Wernicke's) aphasia	General comprehension deficits, neologisms, word retrieval deficits, semantic paraphasias	Post-perisylvian region: posterio-superior temporal opercular supramarginal angular and posterior insular gyri; planum temporale
Production (Broca's) aphasia	Speech production deficit, abnormal prosody; impaired syntactic comprehension	Posterior part of the inferior frontal and precentral convolutions of the left hemisphere
Conduction aphasia	Naming deficits and impaired ability to repeat non-meaningful single words and word strings	Arcuate fasciculus, posterior parietal and temporal regions; left auditory complex, insula supramarginal gyrus
Deep dysphasia	Word repetition deficits; verbal (semantic) paraphasia	Temporal lobe, especially regions which mediate phonological processing
Transcortical sensory aphasia	Impaired comprehension, naming reading and writing, semantic irrelevancies in speech	Temporoparieto-occipital junction of the left hemisphere
Transcortical motor aphasia	Transient mutism and telegrammatic dysprosodic speech	Connection between Broca's area and the supplementary motor area; medial frontal lobe regions anterolateral to the left hemispheres frontal horn
Global aphasia	Generalised deficits in comprehension, repetiton, naming and speech production	Left perisylvian region, white matter, basal ganglia and thalamus

Source: G.N. Martin, *Human Neuropsychology*, 2nd edn, Pearson/Prentice Hall (2006).

Table 10.9 (b) Symptomatology of aphasia

Type	Site of damage	Spontaneous speech	Comprehension	Paraphasia	Repetition	Naming
Broca's		Non-fluent	Good	Common	Poor	Poor
Wernicke's		Fluent	Poor	Uncommon	Poor	Poor
Conduction		Fluent	Good	Common	Poor	Poor
Global		Non-fluent	Poor	Variable	Poor	Poor

Source: G.N. Martin, *Human Neuropsychology*, 2nd edn, Pearson/Prentice Hall (2006).

Below is a sample of speech from a man with Broca's aphasia, who is telling the examiner why he has come to the hospital. His words are meaningful but what he says is not grammatical. The dots indicate long pauses.

Lesions that produce non-fluent aphasia must be centred in the vicinity of Broca's area. However, damage restricted

'Ah . . . Monday . . . ah Dad and Paul [patient's name] . . . and Dad . . . hospital. Two . . . ah doctors . . . , and ah . . . thirty minutes . . . and yes . . . ah . . . hospital. And, er Wednesday . . . nine o'clock. And er Thursday, ten o'clock . . . doctors. Two doctors . . . and ah . . . teeth. Yeah, . . . fine.' (*Source*: Goodglass, 1976, p. 278.)

to the cortex of Broca's area does not appear to produce Broca's aphasia; the damage must extend to surrounding regions of the frontal lobe and to the underlying subcortical white matter (Damasio, 1989, Damasio *et al.*, 1996). Dronkers *et al.* (2007) used MRI to measure, in detail, the extent of the damage to the preserved brains of two of Broca's patients, including the famous Leborgne ('Tan').

They found that damage was much deeper than Broca reported (MRI was not available in his day) and other areas were also damaged including a large tract of fibre that connects the posterior and anterior language areas. Although damage to Broca's area can lead to transient impairment in speech production, it seems likely that damage to this fibre is necessary to produce severe speech difficulty.

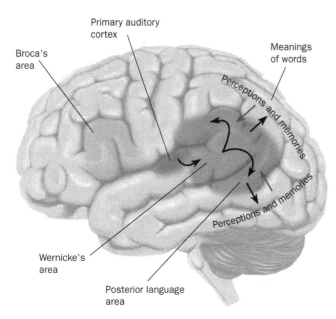

Broca's area

Primary auditory cortex

Meanings of words

Perceptions and memories

Perceptions and memories

Wernicke's area

Posterior language area

Figure 10.9 The dictionary in the brain relates the sounds of words to their meanings and permits us to comprehend the meanings of words and translate our own thoughts into words. Black arrows represent comprehension of words; red arrows represent translation of thoughts or perceptions into words.

Confusion about where – or what – Broca's area is exists even in the psychology literature today. One survey found that although 27 per cent of neuroimaging studies referred to Areas 44 and 45 as Broca's area, 52 per cent of the journal articles surveyed either did not define Broca's area or gave misleading or broad definitions of the region (Lindenberg *et al.*, 2007).

Wernicke (1874) suggested that Broca's area contains motor memories – in particular, memories of the sequences of muscular movements that are needed to articulate words. Talking involves rapid movements of the tongue, lips and jaw, and these movements must be coordinated with each other and with those of the vocal cords; thus, talking requires some very sophisticated motor control mechanisms. Because damage to the lower left frontal lobe (including Broca's area) disrupts the ability to articulate words, this region is the most likely candidate for the location of these 'programmes'. The fact that this region is located just in front of the part of the primary motor cortex that controls the muscles used for speech certainly supports this conclusion.

In addition to their role in the production of words, neural circuits located in the lower left frontal lobe appear to perform some more complex functions. Damage to Broca's area often produces **agrammatism**: loss of the ability to produce or comprehend speech that employs complex syntactical rules. For example, people with non-fluent aphasia rarely use function words. In addition, they rarely use grammatical markers such as

'-ed' or auxiliaries such as 'have' (as in 'I have gone'). A study by Saffran *et al.* (1980) illustrates this difficulty. The following quotations are from agrammatic patients attempting to describe pictures:

> Picture of a boy being hit in the head by a baseball: 'The boy is catch . . . the boy is hitch . . . the boy is hit the ball.' (p. 229)

> Picture of a girl giving flowers to her teacher: 'Girl . . . wants to . . . flowers . . . flowers and wants to . . . The woman . . . wants to . . . The girl wants to . . . the flowers and the woman.' (p. 234)

In an ordinary conversation, non-fluent aphasics seem to understand everything that is said to them. They appear to be irritated and annoyed by their inability to express their thoughts well, and they often make gestures to supplement their scanty speech. The striking disparity between their speech and their comprehension often leads people to assume that their comprehension is normal. Their comprehension, however, is not normal.

The agrammatism that accompanies non-fluent aphasia appears to disrupt patients' ability to use grammatical information, including word order, to decode the meaning of a sentence. Thus, their deficit in comprehension parallels their deficit in production. If they heard a sentence such as, 'The mosquito was swatted by the man', they would understand that it concerns a man and a mosquito and the action of swatting. Because of their knowledge of men and mosquitoes, they would have no trouble figuring out who is doing what to whom. But a sentence such as, 'The cow was kicked by the horse' does not provide any extra cues; if the grammar is not understood, neither is the meaning of the sentence.

Other experiments have shown that people with non-fluent aphasia have difficulty carrying out a sequence of commands, such as 'Pick up the red circle and touch the green square with it' (Boller and Dennis, 1979). This finding, along with the other symptoms described in this section, suggests that an important function of the left frontal lobe may be sequencing, both physically in terms of muscle movement (for example, the muscles of speech-producing words) and semantically in terms of sequencing actual words (for example, comprehending and producing grammatical speech). The frontal cortex may be important for allowing us to sequence stimuli correctly (see the section on working memory in Chapter 8). This sequencing role of the frontal cortex is returned to in the next chapter in relation to reasoning and in Chapter 13 in relation to organising social and emotional behaviour.

Speech comprehension: evidence from receptive (Wernicke's) aphasia

Comprehension of speech obviously begins in the auditory system, which is needed to analyse sequences of sounds and to recognise them as words. Recognition is the first step in comprehension. As we saw earlier in this chapter, recognising a spoken word is a complex perceptual task that relies on memories of sequences of sounds. This task appears to be accomplished by neural circuits in the upper part of the left temporal lobe – a region that is known as **Wernicke's area.**

Brain damage in the left hemisphere that invades Wernicke's area as well as the surrounding region of the temporal and parietal lobes produces a disorder known as **Wernicke's aphasia.** The symptoms of receptive aphasia are poor speech comprehension and production of meaningless speech (Wernicke's aphasia is also known as sensory or receptive aphasia). Unlike non-fluent aphasia, speech in receptive aphasia is fluent and unlaboured; the person does not strain to articulate words and does not appear to be searching for them. The patient maintains a melodic line, with the voice rising and falling normally. When you listen to the speech of a person with receptive aphasia, it appears to be grammatical. That is, the person uses function words such as 'the' and 'but' and employs complex verb tenses and subordinate clauses. However, the person uses few content words, and the words that he or she strings together just do not make sense. For example:

> Well this is . . . mother is away here working her work out o'here to get her better, but when she's looking, the two boys looking in other part. One their small tile into her time here. She's working another time because she's getting, too.
>
> (*Source*: Cookie Theft Picture Description from: Carroll, D. (1999) *Psychology of Language*, 3rd edn, Brooks/Cole Publishing Company.)

The failure of patients with Wernicke's aphasia to comprehend their own speech typically renders them unaware of their language processing problems and they will continue to participate in conversations, nodding in the appropriate places and taking turns to speak, blissfully unaware of their disorder.

Or this example of a conversation between a patient and a speech therapist:

> Therapist: What did you have (to eat)?
>
> PH: Today I haven't touched a/maiwa/d^/David. He had beastly tomorrow.
>
> Therapist: Was the food good?
>
> PH: Yes, it was fine. (*Source*: R.C. Martin, 2003.)

A commonly used test of comprehension for receptive aphasia assesses the patient's ability to understand questions by asking them to point to objects on a table in front of them. For example, they are asked to 'point to the one with ink'. If they point to an object other than a pen, they have not understood the request. When tested this way, people with severe Wernicke's aphasia show poor comprehension. In the Cookie Theft test (see box), the patient describes the scene on a card. The scene is a small boy stealing a cookie jar from a kitchen cupboard while his mother is washing dishes at a sink.

Because Wernicke's area is a region of the auditory association cortex, and because a comprehension deficit is so prominent in receptive aphasia, this disorder has been characterised as a receptive aphasia. Wernicke suggested that the region that now bears his name is the location of memories of the sequences of sounds that constitute words. This hypothesis is reasonable; it suggests that the auditory association cortex of Wernicke's area recognises the sounds of words, just as the visual association cortex in the lower part of the temporal lobe recognises the sight of objects.

Wernicke's aphasia, like non-fluent aphasia, actually appears to consist of several deficits. The abilities that are disrupted include recognition of spoken words, comprehension of the meaning of words, and the ability to convert thoughts into words. Recognition is a perceptual task; comprehension involves retrieval of additional information from long-term memory. Damage to Wernicke's area produces a deficit in recognition; damage to the surrounding temporal and parietal cortex produces a deficit in production of meaningful speech and comprehension of the speech of others.

Wise *et al.* (2001) have suggested that the term 'Wernicke's area' has become meaningless because different research groups delineate the area in different ways and impute to it different functions. They identified two regions within 'Wernicke's area' which seemed to perform different functions. One part responded to speech and non-speech sounds, including the sound of the speaker's voice. The posterior part of this, near the parietal lobe, was active during speech production. The second part identified was more lateral and responded to external sources of speech; it was also active during the recall of word lists. This suggests that the functions of both parts are compatible with a hypothesis which states that the first region is involved in mimicking sounds and the second is involved in the transient representation of heard or internally generated phonetic sequences.

If the region around Wernicke's area is damaged, but Wernicke's area itself is spared, the person will exhibit all of the symptoms of receptive aphasia except a deficit in auditory word recognition. Damage to the region surrounding Wernicke's area (the posterior language areas) produces a disorder known as **isolation aphasia,** an inability to comprehend speech or to produce meaningful speech accompanied by the ability to repeat speech and learn new sequences of words. The difference between isolation aphasia and Wernicke's aphasia is that patients with isolation aphasia can repeat what other people say to them; thus, they obviously can recognise words. However, they cannot comprehend the meaning of what they hear and repeat; nor can they produce meaningful speech of their own. Apparently, the sounds of words are recognised by neural circuits in Wernicke's area, and this information is transmitted to Broca's area so that the words can be repeated. However, because the posterior language area is destroyed, the meaning of the words cannot be comprehended.

Damage to other regions of the brain can disrupt particular categories of meaning in speech. For example, damage to part of the association cortex of the left parietal lobe can produce an inability to name the body parts. This disorder is called **autotopagnosia,** or 'poor knowledge of one's own topography' (a better name would have been autotopanomia, 'poor naming of one's own topography'). People who can otherwise converse normally cannot reliably point to their elbows, knees or cheeks when asked to do so, and they cannot name body parts when the examiner points to them. However, they have no difficulty understanding the meaning of other words.

Specific language impairment

Some children have difficulties in producing or understanding spoken language, in the absence of known brain injury. The 3–4 per cent who exhibit this impairment are said to show **specific language impairment.** Grammar

---

Psychology in action: The man who lost his language: the phenomenology of aphasia

On Tuesday, 28 July we went to a party in London. I drive home because John had had too much to drink. At a red light I glanced at him, and saw on his face the expression of a man crazed by an apocalyptic vision. He laughed it off: 'Is that what you go around saying at parties, "Good evening, you have a crazed apocalyptic look on your face?" ' If I had known what that look meant, it is theoretically possible that I might have saved him . . .

Source: Sheila Hale (2002) *The Man Who Lost His Language*, p. 30.

On the morning of the 30 July 1992, just before nine o'clock, Sir John Hale, art historian and prolific author, was found on his study floor, having the 'sweet witless smile of a baby' on his face and uttering only the words, 'the walls, the walls'. Hale had suffered a stroke. Sheila, his wife, had noted one of the signs just days before – a change in the musculature of his face. While most of the studies in this book emerge from academic journals, and are reported in the clinical way one would expect from such a source, Sheila Hale wrote a personal account of the disorder and its consequences, writing in careful and often touching detail about the day-to-day consequences of stroke and aphasia and how she coped with the virtual demolition of her husband's language.

Initially, John Hale was unable to speak or write or match written/spoken nouns to objects such as a razor, a chick, a pencil and some keys. He could surmise what people were saying from their gestures and tone of voice, laughing at jokes and following simple instructions. Reading for pleasure was difficult and he would turn over pages he could not follow. Curiously, he could understand academic journals and offprints which suggested a dissociation between reading for pleasure and reading for information. John was written off by his original consultant – at the time of the stroke, Hale was in his 60s and was felt to be unable to benefit from rehabilitation – but an independent neurologist suggested that his intelligence alone might help his recovery. Sheila Hale discovered a series of language puzzle books designed for Roald Dahl's wife, Patricia Neal – who had become aphasic following a stroke – by Valerie Eton Griffiths, and recruited family and friends to use them with her husband. At this point, he began introducing new sounds into his conversation: *the, da* or *whoah*. He could copy shapes and words and perform mental arithmetic but was unable to write words independently.

His speech therapist originally thought that John could not benefit from therapy – ironically, because he was too exuberant and that anyone with his degree of expressiveness would not be sufficiently motivated to help themselves through the difficult process of rehabilitation. This view changed when, at a dinner party, she lifted up her arm and asked John what it was: 'John said da *woahs*. Elizabeth said, "No, John, listen to yourself. Now listen to me: *ahm*". John said ahhhm. "No, John, you're saying *ahhhm*. It's not quite right, is it? What is this? This is my . . . ?" John said *ahm*' (Hale, 2002, p. 191).

Psychology in action: *Continued*

When Sheila asked the therapist how it could be that her husband could read German, English and French but not be able to write a sentence in any language, Elizabeth offered a series of illuminating metaphors: 'It is as though the road between Naples and Rome had been blown up. You can still travel between the two cities, but you have to make your way through the rubble to find an alternative route,' or 'The British Library has been shaken by an earthquake. The books have been hurled off the shelves. They're all mixed up and the catalogues can't be found. The books are like your words: there they are, but you have no means of finding them' (Hale, 2002, p. 195).

John's understanding of words was excellent and he could recognise written and spoken reversed letter words,

RICARDO WENT OUT SHOPPING TO BUY SOME FRUIT. HE BOUGHT A POUND OF *pears* . AND A LARGE JUICY WATER *melan* . HE ALSO WENT INTO THE OFF-LICENCE AND BOUGHT THREE BOTTLES OF *wine* . HE WALKED HOME ALONG BY THE *river* AND WATCHED THE MEN ROWING THE *boat* . A VERY BEAUTIFUL *girl* WAS SITTING ON A *bench* SO HE SAT NEXT TO HER. SHE HAD LONG BLONDE *hair* AND BIG BLUE *eyes* . RICARDO SAID 'GOOD *morning* IT'S A LOVELY *day* .' SHE TURNED TO HIM AND *smiled* SHOWING LOVELY WHITE *teeth* . RICARDO OFFERED HER ONE OF HIS *pears* . THEY TALKED HAPPILY FOR HALF AN HOUR AND THEN RICARDO ASKED HER OUT TO *dinner* . SHE AGREED AND THEY MET OUTSIDE THE *restaurant* AT 7.30PM.

April 11, 1996
Sheila, This splendid object, justifiably cost a seductive on the British £5! Who in did a famous series of linocuts and many other materials! In achieve the etching, engraving and drypoint.
~~Dad~~
John

Portrait of Trabuc
Vincent van Gogh, Dutch, 1853–1890
Oil on canvas, 24″ X 18¼″, 1889
Kunstmuseum Solothurn, Dübi-Müller-Stiftung

VAN GOGH IN SAINT-REMY AND AUVERS
An exhibition at The Metropolitan Museum of Art
05-07075-4 © 1986 MMA

20 September 1998
Dear Miranda,
    Thank you for the delicious dance on Friday. I was flattered to be on your party list and to partic...
    Love
    John

partic it
aejou
participate

Some examples of John Hale's writing and attempts at written comprehension. The photograph shows Hale with his wife, Sheila.

Source: S. Hale (2002) *The Man Who Lost His Language*. London: Penguin.

Psychology in action: *Continued*

real words and non-words; he could match synonyms, and words to pictures. However, phonological segmentation was a problem: when presented with the words 'map' and 'gap' he was unable to indicate which sound had changed. He knew that both were different. He could identify the number of letters in a word and could fill in blanks in a story but sometimes made dysgraphic errors, writing 'borg' for 'dog'.

Three years after his stroke, John was able to speak the words: *haaloo, bye, I, fine, wine, bus, bow, bell, more, my, house* and *horse*. Sometimes, when trying to say one of these words, he would say 'arm' instead. Two years later, Sheila described a typical morning: 'Over lunch he tells me about his morning. *Mmmmmm* means walking along minding his own business. *Arrrr-up!* With his left hand describing an arc means that he has crossed a bridge. He meets a friend: broad smile, greeting gestures; they go into a pub; mime of conversation: *bahbah-bahbahbah* – and drinking. Or John gets on a bus: sounds of changing gears, starting and stopping.'

Eventually, his non-language became less prosodic – he would introduce the words *um, oh, ah, aargh, gah, no* and *oh my God* to stem the mellifluous aphasic flow. He took great pains to find the right word, a struggle observed in the brain-injured patient, Lt Zasetsky by Luria (1972) in his book, *The Man with a Shattered World*. 'It was so hard to write,' Zasetsky wrote, 'At last, I'd turned up a good idea. So I began to hunt for words to describe it and finally I thought up two. But by the time I got to the third word, I was stuck . . . Finally, I managed to write a sentence expressing an idea I had . . . sometimes I'll sit over a page for a week or two . . . But I don't want to give it up. I want to finish what I've begun. So I sit at my desk all day, sweating over each word.'

One October evening, Sheila Hale wrote, 'I was too weak to resist a quick, forbidden glance into the future. And what I saw was a succession of meals, sitting across a table from a husband who was no more, or less, companionable than an affectionate dog' (Hale, 2002, p. 61). John Hale hid his despair well until, one afternoon, his wife found him with his head bowed and his left hand covering his face: 'When I put my arms around him, I felt the tears on his face. He was crying for the first time since I had known him.'

Hale's book is testament to the support, love and care that can help an individual with aphasia deal with extreme communication difficulty. Despite the impairment in his speech, John continued to be charming, garrulous and intelligent company. David Chambers summed up the positive aspects of Hale when writing the historian's obituary in *The Times*: 'for those in his company, the infinitely modulated exclamations, chuckles and ironical groans which accompanied his enchanting smile seemed almost to amount to conversation. Gregarious as ever, he proved that, even in aphasia, life can be exhilarating.'

---

and phonology are the most affected aspects, but intelligence is within the normal range. When a 6-year-old with adequate hearing but specific language impairment is asked to repeat the sentence, 'Goldilocks ran away from the three bears because she thought they might chase her,' she says, 'Doedilot when away from berd. Them gonna chate her' (Bishop, 1997). One study suggests that one cause of these problems may be impaired auditory perception (B.A. Wright *et al.*, 1997). These researchers found that the children were impaired when perceiving tones that were brief, but not tones that were long.

Some language impairments, however, seem to occur in the absence of such auditory impairment. These impairments arise from a child's inability to acquire the rules of language early (Gopnik, 1997). One example of such a language impairment is the inability to produce the past tense. For example, in the following statement,

'Everyday he walks eight miles. Yesterday he . . .'

Some children would not be able to supply the past tense for 'walk' to complete the second sentence. These problems are seen in children who have normal auditory acuity and non-verbal and psychosocial skills, and, although they may have other difficulties such as dyslexia and depression, none of these factors has been reliably associated with these specific language impairments.

In a review and theoretical analysis of these impairments, Gopnik (1997) has suggested there may be a strong genetic influence on their development because they tend to cluster in families and seem to occur in families cross-culturally. Gopnik suggests that this specific impairment in the use of complex grammatical rules is universal, although critics have argued that auditory/articulation problems or general problems with cognition may be the source of the impairment rather than a genetic, neural component. For example, children may leave off the /d/ sound when transforming an English word into the past tense. However, the problem does not seem to be specific to /d/ sounds. In languages where the past tense is transformed in a different way, the same specific language impairments have been observed. English, for example, has about four regular-form verbs; Greek has sixty. The number of mistakes in making past tenses seen in each language is proportional to the number of regular verbs they use. More to the point, as Gopnik notes, in French the final syllable is stressed so that it is not difficult to hear.

Speech and language disorders have been linked to chromosomes 3, 7, 13, 16 and 19. The genes underlying these are not fully identified, but one of these might be *FOXP2* located on chromosome band 7q31 (Fisher, 2005). Disruption of this gene leads to disruptions in articulation important for speech and seems to have evolved in the past 200,000 years. Striking evidence for this gene-linked disorder was found in a family where three generations were found to suffer from the impairment. Individuals with the genetic defect also have problems in expressing and understanding oral and written language. It is probably inaccurate to describe *FOXP2* as a 'language' gene, however, because it is also involved in other behaviour. To date, six chromosomes have been identified with links to specific learning impairment/dyslexia (Ramus, 2006).

Dyslexia

The term **dyslexia** refers to a disorder involving impaired reading and it is one of the most common language disorders seen in children and adults. The incidence of the disorder lies between 5 and 17.5 per cent (Shaywitz, 1998). Although boys are thought to be affected more than girls, the evidence is unclear (Flynn and Rahbar, 1994). Many different types of dyslexia have been described but there are two broad categories: acquired dyslexia and developmental dyslexia. Acquired dyslexia describes a reading impairment resulting from brain injury in individuals with previously normal language. Developmental dyslexia refers to a difficulty in learning

to read despite adequate intelligence and appropriate educational opportunity (Brunswick, 2009). The types of dyslexia and their symptoms are described in Table 10.10.

Acquired dyslexia

The most important forms of dyslexia which result from brain injury are visual word form dyslexia, phonological dyslexia, surface dyslexia and deep dyslexia. Visual word form dyslexia describes an inability to recognise words immediately but gradually with the naming of each letter (Warrington and Shallice, 1980). Sometimes a patient might commit a letter-naming mistake, pronouncing 'c, a, t ... cat' when the word to be read is 'mat'. The disorder is thought to result from a disconnection between the region of the left hemisphere which mediates the recognition of word forms (Speedie *et al.*, 1982) and the visual input system. Reading ability may rely on the perceptual and visual skills of the right hemisphere.

Phonological dyslexia refers to an inability to read pseudowords and non-words and is relatively rare (although phonological deficits are also seen in developmental dyslexia, described below). Phonological dyslexia provides evidence that whole-word reading and phonological reading involve different brain mechanisms and provides some support for the dual-route model of reading outlined earlier in the chapter (see Figure 10.10). Phonetic reading, which is the only way we can read nonwords or words we have not yet learned, entails some sort of letter-to-sound decoding. It also requires more than decoding of the sounds produced by single letters, because, for example, some sounds are transcribed as two-letter sequences (such as 'th' or 'sh') and the addition of the letter 'e' to the end of a word lengthens an internal vowel ('can' becomes 'cane').

Table 10.10 The dyslexias and the brain regions associated with them

Type of dyslexia	Primary symptoms	Brain regions implicated
Acquired dyslexia		
Visual word form dyslexia	Impaired sight reading; some decoding is possible	Disconnection between the angular gyrus of the dominant hemisphere and the visual input system
Phonological dyslexia	Deficits in reading pseudowords and non-words	Temporal lobe of the dominant hemisphere?
Surface dyslexia	Tendency to produce regularisation errors in the reading of irregular words	?
Deep dyslexia	Semantic substitutions, impaired reading of abstract words, inability to read non-words	Extensive damage to the dominant hemisphere
Developmental dyslexia	Impaired reading and spelling of words/ non-words/pseudowords, poor phonological processing skills, sequencing and short-term memory, some visuo-perceptual defects	Temporo-parietal regions of the dominant hemisphere

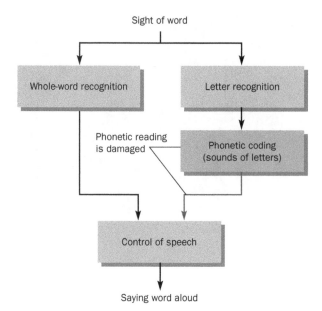

Figure 10.10 A hypothetical explanation of phonological dyslexia. Only whole-word reading remains.

Surface dyslexia is the inability to recognise and read words based on their physical characteristics. Individuals are able to apply the grapheme–phoneme correspondence rules, however (described earlier in the chapter), but have difficulties with irregular words, using inefficient spelling-to-sound strategies (so, 'yacht' is pronounced as it reads and sounds).

Deep dyslexia refers to a severe inability to read; concrete words can sometimes be read but are commonly replaced by semantically related words. For example, a patient would read 'sleep' when the word is 'dream' (Coltheart *et al.*, 1980). Abstract words are rarely pronounced accurately and neither are pronounceable non-words (indicating an inability to apply grapheme–phoneme correspondence rules).

Developmental dyslexia

The symptoms of developmental dyslexia resemble those of acquired dyslexias. Developmental dyslexia first manifests itself in childhood. It tends to occur in families, which suggests the presence of a genetic (and hence biological) component. For example, 33–66 per cent of parents with dyslexia will have children who develop the disorder. The percentage for parents without dyslexia is 6–16 per cent (Torppa *et al.*, 2010; Van Bergen *et al.*, 2011). If one or more parents has dyslexia then the child is said to be at 'familial risk' of dyslexia. A recent study compared a reading ability of those children with dyslexic parents who developed dyslexia, with children with dyslexic parents who did not develop dyslexia (van Bergen *et al.*, 2012). The dyslexic children were poor at naming the sounds of words, spelling and reading words

and pseudowords. The at-risk group which did not show evidence of dyslexia did slightly better but were worse than a normal reading control group. Interestingly, the study found that the parents' reading and their ability to name rapidly were strong predictors of the child's reading status.

A fairly constant factor in developmental dyslexia is poor awareness of the phonological features of sound, that is, poor phonological awareness (Stahl and Murray, 1994). The segmentation of words into sounds, being aware of alliteration, verbal repetition and verbal naming are all impaired in developmental dyslexia. For example, if children are asked to transpose the first sounds of the words 'mustard' and 'salad' (thereby producing 'sustard' and 'malad'), those with developmental dyslexia are unable to do this. Similarly, individuals with developmental dyslexia may be unable to perform phonological tasks such as indicating what is left when you take either the first or last sound away from a word such as 'mice'. This poor phonological awareness is independent of intelligence. Tanaka *et al.* (2010) found that when phonological processing was studied in high and low IQ children with poor reading ability, similar patterns of reduced brain activation was found in the left posteriotemporal and occipitotemporal parts of the brain (those normally activated by phonological processing).

Developmental dyslexia: possible neuropsychological causes

Visual pathway deficits

Some psychologists have argued that phonological impairments do not explain the persistent and severe nature of dyslexia (Hulme and Roodenrys, 1995). Reading is a complex task that requires phonology, memory and visual perception and there are various theories that attempt to explain developmental dyslexia in terms of dysfunctional neuronal systems in several areas of the brain (Habib, 2000). Stein and his colleagues (Stein, 1991; Stein and Walsh, 1997), for example, have suggested that developmental dyslexia is associated with poor visual direction sense, poor binocular convergence (described in Chapter 6), and visual fixation.

Stein's view argues that dyslexics are unable to process fast, incoming sensory information adequately. Most information from the retina to the cortex via the thalamus travels through one of three visual system pathways. One of these systems – the magnocellular (M) pathway – is thought to carry visual information about space, such as movement, depth and the relationships between the positions of stimuli. Some researchers have implicated a malfunctioning M pathway in dyslexia but have had difficulty in explaining why the defective pathway makes reading difficult.

(a)

(b)

(c)

(d)

According to Agatha Christie, the world's most successful writer: 'I myself, was always recognised . . . as the "slow" one in the family. It was quite true, and I knew it and accepted it. Writing and spelling were always terribly difficult for me. My letters were without originality. I was . . . an extraordinarily bad speller and have remained so until this day.'

Danny Glover **(a)**, Richard Branson **(b)**, Jay Leno **(c)** and Agatha Christie **(d)** . . . all very successful public figures. All are also dyslexic.
Source: (a) Frazer Harrison/Getty Images; (b) Chris Jackson/Getty Images; (c) Stephen Shugerman/Getty Images; and (d) Walter Bird/Getty Images.

Studies have shown that poor visual fixation, poor tracking from left to right and poor binocular convergence appear to hinder the development of normal reading (Eden *et al.*, 1994). In an fMRI study of developmental dyslexia and the ability to process visual motion, Eden *et al.* (1996) found that moving stimuli (such as dots) failed to activate the cortical area that is projected to by the magnocellular pathway (area V5). In competent readers, this area was activated in both hemispheres during the task. Furthermore, the presentation of stationary patterns did not produce different patterns of brain activation in dyslexic individuals and controls, suggesting that the dyslexic sample had difficulties specifically with attending to moving stimuli.

One hypothesis suggests that the M pathway plays an important role in selective attention. It acts as an attentional spotlight which focuses on important stimuli and ignores all the clutter surrounding these stimuli. Vidyasagar and Pammer (1999) put this hypothesis to the test. They asked 21 reading-impaired children and age-matched normal readers to complete a standard visual search task in which they had to locate a stimulus that was characterised by a combination of colour and form (for example, looking for a grey triangle in a background of grey circles). The greater the number of distractors in this task, the greater the number of errors made by the reading-impaired group. When there were fewer than 36 distractors, the impaired readers did as well as their age-matched counterparts. When the number increased to 70, a significantly greater number of errors were committed by the impaired reading group, suggesting to the authors that in the dyslexic group visual search mechanisms are compromised when a visual scene is cluttered. Because reading places great demands on the attentional spotlight – which detects the conjunction of features – an impairment in this process may be explained by deficits in the system that turns on and operates the spotlight.

A challenge was reported in a study which tested this explanation (Stuart et al., 2006). People with developmental dyslexia have an impairment in one of the two visual pathways, the magnocellular pathway, which means that they are not sensitive to rapidly changing stimuli. A deficit in the auditory equivalent means that they have difficulty in segmenting speech, making accurate phonological representations of what they read and making grapheme–phoneme correspondences. Stuart et al. measured auditory and visual contrast thresholds in adults with severe reading difficulties. This group showed normal ability to detect visual contrasts (and auditory contrasts). The data undermine the notion that the magnocellular pathway is defective in allowing a person to be sensitive to contrasts. Perhaps, the researchers suggest, the abnormality lies at the level of the interaction between this pathway and the other visual pathway, the parvocellular pathway.

Neural dysfunction

One of the consistent findings in neuroimaging studies of developmental dyslexia is that a decrease in blood flow is seen in temporal and inferior parietal areas, namely the areas involved in letter-to-sound conversion, the analysis of speech sounds and word form recognition (Brunswick et al., 1999; Aylward et al., 2003; Horwitz and Braun, 2004; Hoeft et al., 2006, 2007).

In a meta-analysis of 17 studies of brain activation in dyslexia, Richlan et al. (2009) found the following consistent effects: (1) underactivation of the posterior parts of left superior temporal gyrus; (2) underactivation of the supramarginal gyrus; (3) no dysfunction in the angular gyrus; (4) underactivation of the left inferior parietal lobe; (5) dysfunctional activation in the visual word form area; (5) overactivation in the left inferior frontal gyrus, premotor cortex and anterior insula; (6) no anomalies in the right hemisphere; and (7) no abnormalities in the cerebellum. The function of the fourth area in dyslexia is unclear and the activation in point five probably reflects

additional effort required to read in these participants. The failure to find any differences between typical and impaired readers in the cerebellum is at odds with individual studies which find such differences (see section below).

Some have argued that the degree of timing and progression of cortical activation may underpin reading difficulties, specifically in the parietal, temporal and frontal regions. Rezaie et al. (2011) used MEG to study the progression of brain activation in typical readers and children with reading difficulties who had to complete a visual word-recognition exercise. In the impaired group, activation was reduced in both hemispheres in the superior and middle temporal gyri but increased in the rostral middle, frontal and ventral occipitotemporal regions of the brain in both hemispheres. More interestingly, the peaks in the regions occurred simultaneously whereas in the typical group there was a progression of activation.

Cerebellar dysfunction

The cerebellum, best understood as the region which contributes to motor function, posture and balance, may also be implicated in developmental dyslexia. Nicolson et al. (1999) found that activation in the cerebellum was significantly lower in dyslexic than normal readers during the execution of familiar and novel motor tasks. The authors suggest that this cerebellar dysfunction affects the learning of new skills and the 'performance of automatic, overlearned skills'. Reading, they argue, is a complex behaviour composed of a number of interacting motor behaviours which need to be learned and improved over time. The dysfunctional cerebellum is not a cause of dyslexia but is a key structure in dyslexia.

Right-sided reduction in the front of the cerebellum has correctly predicted over 72 per cent of children with dyslexia: that is, the reduction in the region was correlated with poor reading (Eckert et al., 2003). Other studies find that activation is more diffuse in the cerebellum in dyslexic children who generate appropriate verbs to a noun (Baillieux et al., 2009). Bishop (2002) has argued that the development of the cerebellum depends on the degree of experience a person has with writing: a child with literacy problems is less likely to pick up a pen and use it frequently. Consequently, the cerebellum does not show the same strength of development seen in individuals who have a history of well-practised writing (Bishop, 2002).

Dyslexia across languages

Languages with fairly transparent reading systems, such as Italian, are less likely to present readers with difficulties. Paulesu et al. (2001) used PET to measure brain activation in French, English and Italian dyslexic participants and their respective control groups. Participants read either bisyllabic words or non-words aloud (an explicit reading task) or as they made decisions about specific physical features of letters in words (an implicit reading task). Activity in the same region in the left hemisphere was reduced in all three dyslexic groups. The region included the left middle, inferior and superior temporal cortex.

A recent study has extended the study of dyslexia in other languages to Chinese. In logographic Chinese, graphic forms (characters) are mapped onto syllables whereas in English, units (letters) are mapped onto phonemes. For this reason, when Chinese people engage in working memory tasks, there is activation in the areas responsible for visuospatial manipulation and the left middle frontal gyrus. There is the reading of complex shapes and characters and pronunciation must be memorised by rote. Earlier studies had associated impaired reading in logographic Chinese with anomalous activation in the left middle frontal gyrus (Siok *et al.*, 2004). In a follow-up study, Siok *et al.* (2008) found reduced activation in the same area in people identified as dyslexic in Chinese. This finding is important because it suggests that the brain regions implicated in dyslexia depend on whether the language is alphabetic (e.g. English, Italian and so on) or non-alphabetic. See Figure 10.11.

In a study of monolingual Chinese and English dyslexic participants who completed a word-matching task (in which two words or pictures had to be matched at either a superficial or a semantic level), Hu *et al.* (2010) found that less activation was found in the left angular gyrus and left middle frontal, posterior temporal and occipitotemporal regions of the brain, using fMRI. This reduction was found in English and Chinese dyslexic participants, although the normal readers showed differences in activation between each other.

In normal Chinese readers, there was increased activation in the left inferior frontal sulcus; in the English readers, there was increased activation in the posterior STS. These findings suggest that the neural activation seen in the dyslexic group was culturally independent – the decrease occurred in both cultures.

Failure of lateralisation

One model of developmental dyslexia suggests that dyslexic readers have delayed or reduced left hemisphere function or have no lateralised preference (Bishop, 1990; Galaburda *et al.*, 1994). There is evidence that function and structure are more symmetrical in dyslexic samples. When good and poor readers respond to visual or auditory stimuli, brain electrical activity is symmetrical in dyslexic readers but typically left-based in controls (Cohen and Breslin, 1984; Brunswick and Rippon, 1994; Rippon and Brunswick, 1998). A group of North

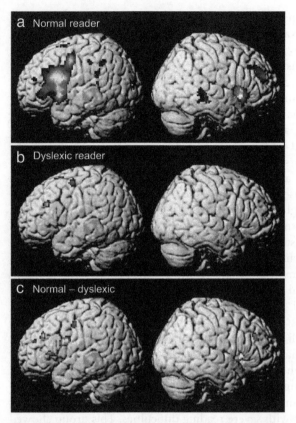

Figure 10.11 Brain regions showing significant activation in dyslexic and normal readers during a rhyme judgement task.
Source: Siok, W.T., Niu, Z., Jin, Z., Perfetti, C.A. and Tan, L.H. A structural–functional basis for dyslexia in the cortex of Chinese readers. *Proceedings of the National Academy of Sciences*, 2008, 105 (14), 5561–6.

American researchers has found that smaller and more symmetrical brain structures in 11–16 year old children were associated with considerable reading and language difficulties, and that larger, more asymmetric structures were associated with poor word reading, but not comprehension (Leonard *et al.*, 2006). The study also found, however, that 75 per cent of the children with developmental dyslexia showed asymmetry in a very important region for dyslexia: **planum temporale** (it was longer in the left, in contrast to some studies).

Word recognition and production: neuroimaging studies

Neuroimaging studies of normal readers generally conclude that the left hemisphere participates in language-related tasks more actively than does the right hemisphere and that specific regions of the left hemisphere are involved in the different components of language such as speech production, comprehension, processing of sound, meaning, and so on (Brunswick, 2004).

Petersen *et al.* (1988) were the first to conduct a PET investigation of language processing in healthy individuals. They found that the left posterior temporal cortex (including the primary auditory cortex and Wernicke's area) was significantly more active during passive listening of words than during a control condition. Repeating the nouns activated the primary motor cortex and Broca's area.

When people were asked to think of verbs that were appropriate to use with the nouns, even more intense activity was seen in Broca's area. Price *et al.* (1994) have also reported that greater activation in the left inferior and middle frontal cortices was found during performance of a lexical decision task whereas more temporal regions were activated during reading aloud and reading silently.

An important aspect of language analysis is, as you saw earlier in the chapter, phonological processing – the putting together of sounds to make meaningful words. Neuroimaging studies have found that when individuals discriminate between spoken words on the basis of phonetic structure, when they discriminate between consonants and when they make judgements about rhyme or engage in phonological memory tasks, activation in the left frontal cortex near Broca's area is found (Fiez *et al.*, 1995; Paulesu *et al.*, 1996; Zatorre *et al.*, 1996). Other studies report involvement of the temporal cortex and angular gyrus especially during tasks involving drawing analogies, repeating words and in reading words and pseudowords (Nobre *et al.*, 1994; Karbe *et al.*, 1998).

This evidence suggests that Broca's area and the frontal cortex are necessary for the phonetic manipulation of language but that the posterior temporal cortex is responsible for the perceptual analysis of speech (Zatorre *et al.*, 1996). However, the picture may be a little more complex. Binder *et al.* (1997) compared the analysis involved in the phonetic and semantic perception of aurally presented words with the analysis of non-linguistic stimuli such as tones. A large network of left-hemisphere regions was activated during the semantic analysis, including areas in the frontal, temporal and parietal cortex. Activation, therefore, was not limited to one specific region.

Damasio *et al.* (1996), in a comprehensive study of its kind, evaluated the effects of language processing in individuals with brain lesions in both hemispheres, inside and outside the temporal regions. Damasio *et al.* hypothesised that there is no single mediating site for all words, but there are separate regions within a larger network that are activated by different kinds of word. There were three categories of words: persons, non-unique animals and non-unique tools, each of which should be processed by different parts of the frontal and temporal lobe. Although 97 individuals showed normal language, 30 did not; 29 of these had brain injury to the left hemisphere. While impaired retrieval of words was associated with temporal cortex damage, abnormal retrieval of animal words was found in patients with left interior temporal lobe damage and abnormal retrieval of tools was associated with posterolateral inferior temporal cortex damage.

Because we cannot infer normal function from brain damage, Damasio *et al.* conducted a second experiment in which healthy individuals performed the same language tasks while undergoing a PET scan. Although all words activated the left temporal cortex, specific categories were associated with activation of specific regions of the brain. Naming of tools activated the posterior, middle and inferior temporal gyri, for example, and animal naming activated other parts of the inferior temporal cortex. These results are similar to those of Martin *et al.* (1996), which showed that different categories of words appeared to activate different parts of the brain. A recent study has even suggested that silently naming the use of tools activates Broca's area and the left premotor and supplementary motor area (Grafton *et al.*, 1997). This suggests that even the naming of a tool's use can activate those parts of the brain that would be activated during the actual movement involved in using those tools.

There is significant overlap between neuroimaging and lesion studies in what they reveal about localisation of language processes. However, in neuroimaging experiments, it is unclear whether the activation in specific regions is necessary for the aspects of language processing studied. According to Price *et al.* (2003), one method of determining the necessity of these areas is to examine lesion data and investigate whether lesions to different areas are associated with different deficits.

Price *et al.* used fMRI to study two patients with acquired dyslexia. One patient had damage to all of the left temporal regions that are usually activated during normal reading. He was able to read some highly imageable words but was unable to read pseudowords and made meaning errors when reading others (saying 'wrong' when trying to read the word 'error'). The pattern is consistent with deficits seen in deep or phonological dyslexia and suggests that he relies on semantics when translating written words into sounds. The second patient also showed left temporal lobe damage but the lesion did not affect the superior temporal lobe (but did affect the inferior and anterior region). She could read regular words and most pseudowords but had greater difficulty in reading irregularly spelled words, a pattern typical of surface dyslexia. She had difficulty in reading words that required semantic processing, suggesting that the areas damaged might be important for semantic processing.

The first patient was asked to read highly imageable words during scanning; the second was asked to read one of a triad of regular three-letter words. For example, the word BUS would appear under two identical words. The first patient showed activation in all the language areas one would expect to be activated during normal reading, except for the area damaged. The second patient activated all the typical language areas but showed a reduction in areas associated with semantic processing. On the basis of these single-case studies, Price *et al.* suggest that translating written words to sounds is mediated by the left midfusiform gyrus in the temporal cortex. But, when semantic processing is impaired, the posterior part of this region and left frontal areas tries to undertake the function of translating the written word into phonology via semantics.

In the first brain imaging study of the perception of British Sign Language (BSL), nine hearing and nine congenitally deaf individuals had their brain activity measured by fMRI during the perception of sentences presented in BSL (MacSweeney *et al.*, 2002). An analogous auditory task in English was completed by hearing individuals. Regardless of the modality of communication, there was activation in Broca's area and in Wernicke's area – both bilaterally – during the language perception tasks. However, differences did emerge between tasks in temporal and occipital areas. The auditory task in hearing individuals was associated with increased activity in the auditory cortices. This activation was not found during BSL. BSL, on the other hand, was associated with activity in an area called V5 at the junction of the temporal and occipital cortex. V5 is the region of the visual cortex which responds to movement and so activation here is consistent with what we know of the neurology of visual perception.

When hearing and deaf people's responses to BSL were explored, however, deaf signers showed greater activation in the left superior temporal cortex than did hearing signers. This result is intriguing because it suggests that the auditory cortex of the temporal lobe is active during an auditory language task in hearing individuals but that it may respond to visual input in congenitally deaf individuals.

This part of the temporal lobe has been described as a multi-modal language area (Buchel *et al.*, 1998) because it can be activated by language processed in different modalities. The MacSweeney study indicated that this was so for sign language. Buchel *et al.* observed a similar phenomenon when studying blind participants reading Braille. When people engaged in tactile reading, the posterior left temporal area (Area 37) was active. Buchel *et al.* proposed that this area in blind, Braille-reading participants promotes activity in other parts of the brain that allows participants access to words. However, this area was active only during written word recognition, not spoken word recognition.

Is there a visual word form area?

People with visual word form dyslexia are unable to recognise the form of words presented visually. Studies with healthy individuals have localised the ability to identify visual letter strings as words – visual word form – in the left fusiform gyrus. Consequently, this area has been known as the visual word form area (Warrington and Shallice, 1980) because it responds to the visual, rather than auditory, forms of words (Giraud and Price, 2001).

Neuroimaging studies show that the fusiform gyrus is active during the perception of word and word-like forms but it is less active during the perception of strings of letters that are unfamiliar such as consonant-string non-words (Buchel *et al.*, 1998). Polk and Farah (2002) found that the left ventral visual cortex was active during the recognition of pseudowords and words presented in normal case. Graves *et al.* (2010) suggested that this visual word form area also mediated word frequency effects – that is, it responds to classes of words that are either high or low frequency. They found increased activation in the inferior frontal gyrus, both sides of the anterior insula, the supplementary motor area and the left temporal lobe areas that were in or near the visual word form area. Activation here, they say, is evidence for whole-word processing whereas activation in the inferior frontal gyrus is evidence of this region's role in phonological processing.

Neuropsychological models of language: a summary

A recent review of neuropsychological models of language suggests that there are four competing and plausible frameworks for understanding the role of the brain in speech production and comprehension (Shalom and Poeppel, 2008).

1. *Price's (2000) model.* This is a descendant of the Broca–Wernicke–Lichtheim model embodied in the aphasia sections. The Broca–Wernicke–Lichtheim model is an umbrella term used to describe the way in which the brain organises language comprehension and production, and is named after three neuropsychological figures. Price's model suggests that acoustic analysis occurs in the superior temporal cortex, visual analysis in the posterior inferior frontal cortex and temporal cortex, and semantic representation in a network of frontal and temporal regions. She suggests that there are two routes to retrieving the sounds and sights of words – a non-semantic route (posterior superior temporal cortex) and a semantic route (via posterior/inferior temporal cortex). Speech planning is governed by the anterior part of Broca's area and actual output is the responsibility of the motor cortex.

Neuroimaging and language – An international perspective

Deep orthographies such as those found in English and French are a minefield of rules and linguistic irregularities. In English there are 1,120 ways of using graphemes (letters and strings of letters) to form 40 sounds (phonemes). Italian, on the other hand, has 33 graphemes representing 25 phonemes. When psychologists talk about the localisation of language, it is easy to forget that language is not a standard, unitary process but is heavily culture-bound. English, Russian and French, for example, all have different orthographical and phonological rules. Some authors have suggested that this explains the differences in word reading speed in English and Italian individuals (Italians are faster).

A recent meta-analysis of behavioural lateralisation studies (e.g. dichotic listening, visual field studies) of bilingualism has found differences between early and late bilinguals (Hull and Vaid, 2007). Early bilinguals (who acquired both languages before the age of 6) showed evidence of bilateral language representation; late bilinguals (who acquired language after the age of 6) showed greater left hemisphere dominance. In this second group, left hemisphere dominance was greater if participants were not proficient at the second language and if the second language was English.

Neuroimaging studies suggest more left hemisphere involvement in language by bilingual individuals and that similar cortical areas may be recruited during the processing of both languages. A study of French and English speakers, for example, found that performing language tasks in both languages was associated with activity in the left inferior frontal cortex (Klein *et al.*, 1995). Another study found that there was activation in different parts of Broca's area when people performed language tasks using a language learned in adulthood, but this activation was absent in those who had learned the language in childhood (Kim *et al.*, 1997). There was no difference in activation in Wernicke's area.

Some researchers have argued that such differences might reflect participants' proficiency in using language rather than the age at which the second language was acquired (Perani *et al.*, 1998). If there is an overlap in the language areas that mediate both tongues, this may be due to the similarity of the two languages spoken. Most studies, for example, have studied bilinguals who speak Indo-European languages (English, French, Italian and so on). Perani *et al.* (1996) compared brain activation in Italian–English speakers, where English was learned later in life, and Spanish–Catalan speakers, where Catalan was learned concomitantly with Spanish. Focal activity in the left hemisphere language regions was determined by expertise and not age of acquisition, a finding that has been replicated (Dehaene *et al.*, 1997; Chee *et al.*, 1999). Would the same overlap be seen if the two languages spoken were different in terms of syntax (meaning and grammar), morphology (physical construction of the language) and phonology (the sound of the language)?

To test this hypothesis, Klein *et al.* (1999) measured cerebral blood flow in seven native speakers of Chinese (Mandarin) who had acquired English during adolescence. Mandarin uses pitch and tone to a greater extent than does English. The participants' task was to repeat words in Mandarin and English and to generate a verb in response to a noun in Mandarin and English. All words were presented auditorily and participants were asked to respond vocally. Klein *et al.* (1999) found that an area in the left frontal cortex was activated during speech production in Mandarin and English. A similar area was found to be active during French and English language processing in a previous study of Klein *et al.*'s (1995). Such findings can even extend to speakers of four or more languages.

Breillman *et al.* (2004), for example, used fMRI to measure the response of six quadrilingual participants who were asked to generate appropriate verbs to nouns; if the word 'fish' was presented, the participant might respond with 'swim'. Participants had knowledge of four to five common languages (English, German, Italian, French or Spanish) and completed the verbal task in each of their languages. As previous studies would predict, the task was associated with left-sided activation but, curiously, this activation was more pronounced in the languages in which participants were least proficient. This suggests that when people speak languages in which they are proficient the brain expends less energy – the process is more automatic and requires fewer cognitive resources for this reason. If people are not proficient in a language, there has to be a greater attempt at producing and understanding that language; this, in turn, recruits greater neural resources in order for the process to succeed.

In two PET studies, Paulesu *et al.* (2000) asked six English and six Italian university students either to read aloud words and non-words (experiment 1) or to perform a feature detection task (experiment 2) which involved paying attention to physical aspects of words presented visually rather than to the words themselves. They were not asked to read the words in experiment 2. The authors found that, across both experiments, the Italian speakers showed greater activation in those areas responsible for processing phonemes (left temporal regions) whereas the English speakers showed greater activation in other areas of the temporal cortex and frontal cortex (areas activated during word retrieval and naming). The areas activated can be seen in Figure 10.12.

This study was the first to show cultural effects on brain function related to language in healthy individuals and suggests that the neurophysiological difference may underpin the behavioural findings from word reading speed studies.

The result is in keeping with studies of aphasia patients among different ethnic Chinese groups. Yu-Huan *et al.* (1990), for example, have reported that unilateral stroke

Neuroimaging and language – *Continued*

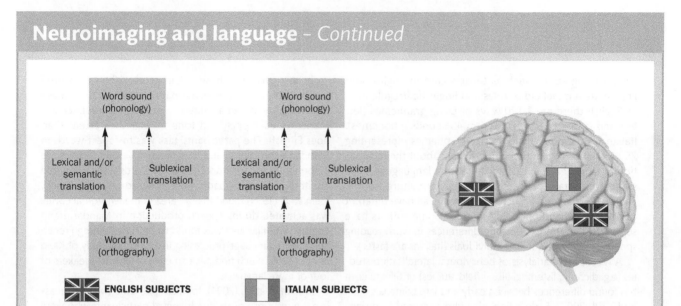

Figure 10.12 The different strategies used by English and Italian speakers are reflected in different types of brain activation.

Source: Fiez, J., Sound and meaning: How native language affects reading strategies. *Nature Neuroscience*, 2000, 3 (1), 3–5, reprinted by permission of the author and Nature Publishing Group.

leads to greater incidence of aphasia in dextrals with right-sided lesions (crossed aphasia) but only among the majority ethnic group called the Han. Crossed aphasia is rare among the minority ethnic group (the Uighur-Kazaks) and Wernicke's aphasia is generally rare in the Han. One explanation for this dissociation may lie in the way in which the languages of the groups differ: the Uighur-Kazak language is Indo-European-based and phonological in nature; the Han language, conversely, is non-phonetic ('ideographical') where one sound can have multiple meanings.

A similar distinction is found in Japanese. Phonetic-based symbols (Kana) and logographic symbols (Kanji) are used routinely in written Japanese. Left-sided lesions are associated with impaired Kana reading in Japanese participants but preserved Kanji reading (Sasanuma, 1975). When healthy individuals are exposed to the different symbols in a typical visual field experiment, a left visual field advantage for Kanji is reported, suggesting right hemisphere involvement (Elman *et al.*, 1981).

The emphasis in Price's model is on semantic processing.

2. *Friederici's (2002) model.* This model makes two claims. The first is that the temporal lobe is responsible for semantic identification (such as the retrieval of memorised semantic information) and the frontal lobe constructs semantic relationships. The second is that the structure of syntax is built before semantic processing occurs and that these two interact later on in the processing stream.

3. *Hickok and Poeppel's (2004) model.* This utilises the distinction drawn in visual processing between the ventral and the dorsal streams (see Chapter 6 and also in the dyslexia section). They propose a visual and an auditory stream. The visual stream has two sub-streams, one (ventral) projecting to the temporal lobe and which is responsible for visual object recognition (the 'what') and a dorsal one projecting to the parietal and frontal lobes, which are involved in the visual representations of spatial attributes of language (the

'where'). The auditory stream is analogously conceptualised in the same way. The model, however, has little to say about the role of Broca's area.

4. *Indefrey and Levelt's (2004) model.* This proposes that Wernicke's area is involved in lexical analysis and in the representation of words but the posterior middle temporal lobe is involved in the phonological aspects of retrieval. It sees word production as involving five main types of representation (from appreciating the idea that a stimulus is lexical, to the breakdown of phonological output into syllables to production) each of which is processed at different times (from 175 ms after stimulus onset to 600 ms).

Although each says something slightly different about language processing and how it occurs in the brain, there are similarities between them. They suggest that:

- memorisation (learning and retrieval) occurs in the temporal lobe;

- analysis occurs in the parietal lobe;
- synthesising (creating combinations of representations) occurs in the frontal lobe;

and that:

- the inferior parietal lobe, inferior frontal lobe and the whole of the temporal lobe are involved in phonological processing;
- the middle areas are involved in syntactic processing;
- inferior areas are involved in semantic processing.

Caveats and complications

Sex differences

Early neuroimaging studies showed greater left hemisphere activation in men when completing language tasks but a more symmetrical pattern of activation in women (Pugh *et al.*, 1996), but the literature is mixed. Knuas *et al.* (2004), for example, found greater leftward asymmetry in the planum temporale in women whereas Sommer *et al.*'s (2004) meta-analysis of 14 functional imaging studies comprising 377 men and 442 women found no evidence for a sex difference in brain activity during language processing. The most recent review has found no differences in proficiency between the sexes: there is an early advantage for girls but this disappears into adulthood (Wallentin, 2009). There is no consistent difference in brain activation or structure.

Language and the right hemisphere

The right side of the brain is not neglected in language. It takes on especial importance when the left hemisphere is damaged and may compensate for the language function lost after such damage. It is involved in the appreciation of metaphors (Bottini *et al.*, 1994) and in the processing of prosody and the affective tone of speech (Pell and Baum, 1997).

How good is the right hemisphere at processing language? And does it compensate well when the left hemisphere is damaged or removed during childhood? Evidence suggests that it does. Vanlancker-Sidtis (2004) examined the language and communication skills of an adult who had undergone a hemispherectomy at age 5. Consistent with what has previously been reported, the participant performed at normal levels on neuropsychological tests: he was able to pronounce, understand grammar and understand word and sentence meaning at the levels we would expect of a control participant. However, slight impairments were found on three tests: the patient had difficulty in pronouncing phonemically complex words, comprehending linguistic contrasts in prosody (i.e. understanding the difference between the pronunciation of 'moving van' and 'moving van' when the stress is on 'moving' or 'van') and in deciding whether one of two line drawings matched a sentence spoken by the experimenter.

Interestingly, these impairments in prosody did not manifest themselves in the patient's everyday life. He could converse, use humour and take turns when in conversation at a level which belied his surgery. The research suggests, however, that although removal of the 'language' hemisphere does not impair most language functions, specific testing picks up on specific deficits. The author, however, could not rule out the possibility that the patient was naturally left-handed, and, therefore, had 'right-hemisphere' speech.

Handedness

Handedness refers to the degree to which individuals preferentially use one hand for certain activities (such as writing, unscrewing a jar, throwing a ball). It can also refer to the strength of hand skill. It is found in a variety of species and in most primates (from old/new world monkeys to great apes). Evidence of handedness or laterality goes back two million years; we seem to be the most lateralised of the primates. The right-left hand ratio in chimps is 2:1; in humans, it is 9:1 (Hopkins and Cantaloupo, 2008).

Handedness may be relevant to language because left- and right-handers may have speech localised in different hemispheres. According to a pioneering study by Rasmussen and Milner (1977), 96 per cent of right-handers and 70 per cent of left-handers in their study had left-hemisphere speech. Other, recent estimates place the figures at 95.3 per cent and 61.4 per cent, respectively (Segalowitz and Bryden, 1983). There are more men who are left-handers than women (Papadatou-Pastoun *et al.*, 2008), possibly due to an X-linked allele.

The degree of activation in the right hemisphere during a word-generation task increases with the left-handedness of the participant (Knecht *et al.*, 2000a, b). Some psychologists have argued that human language evolved from gesture and that these gestures are 'behavioural fossils' accompanying speech. Corballis (1999), for example, argues that the proposition that language is gestural in origin might explain the relationship between handedness and cerebral asymmetry for language (of which, more later). Right-handers primarily gesture with their right hand (which may not be surprising), but left-handers (who have primarily left-hemisphere-based speech but show a more diverse pattern of localisation with some having speech in both hemispheres, or the right hemisphere) gesture with both hands.

The right shift theory

One theory of handedness suggests that the distribution of differences between the skills of both hands is determined by a single gene (Annett, 1985). Individuals who possess the rs+ allele have their hand distribution shifted to the right; their left hemisphere becomes dominant for speech. Individuals with the rs++ gene show an even greater shift to the right hand (these individuals are called homozygotes) whereas those with the rs+– gene show a lesser degree of hand dominance (these individuals are called heterozygotes). Those without the rs+ allele (who express the rs– genotype) will show no overall bias in hand dominance.

This theory is called the **right shift theory** because it suggests that a single gene shifts dominance to one hand (this oversimplifies a complex theory but it is basically correct). Annett's theory is important because it suggests a relationship between hand skill and language (and even cognitive) ability. For example, Annett's theory predicts that heterozygotes (those with the rs+– allele) will be more advantaged on some skills than others, and that homozygotes (those with the rs++ or the rs– – allele) and those with the rs+ gene absent, will be disadvantaged.

Annett and her colleagues (Annett and Manning, 1989; Annett, 1992) have shown that extreme left- and right-hand dominance in hand skill is associated with poorer reading ability than is intermediate hand skill. Annett (1993) also reported that children with intermediate hand skill were more likely to be selected for elite schools in the UK. Individuals with the least bias to dextrality perform better in terms of arithmetical ability and spatial skill (Annett and Manning, 1990; Annett, 1992).

However, research from other laboratories has not found unequivocal evidence for Annett's theory. For example, McManus et al. (1993) assessed the handedness and intellectual ability of medical students and examined differences between three degrees of right-handedness, from weak to strong preference. He found no evidence of cognitive advantage or disadvantage between weak, intermediate and strong right-handers. Similarly, Resch et al. (1997) administered a series of cognitive ability tests to 545 students whose hand preference they also measured. They found that although those at the left end of the handedness continuum showed the poorest spelling, non-verbal IQ and educational success, there was no significant difference between this group and an intermediate and right-handed group, whereas Annett's theory might predict that strong right-handers would also exhibit poorer language ability. Palmer and Corballis (1996) have also found no relationship between hand preference and reading ability in 11–13-year-old children. Instead, reading ability was predicted by the overall level of hand skill rather than by the skill difference between hands.

Others have criticised Annett's model for other reasons. For example, Provins (1997) argues that handedness is a product of motor learning and environmental pressure. What is genetically determined, Provins argues, is not handedness but the motor capacity which could produce left- and right-hand preference, depending on the environment. Other critics such as Corballis (1997) have queried whether a single gene locus for handedness is reasonable: although the data would seem to fit a single-gene model, most genes have several loci (see Chapter 3 and also Chapter 11 when we discuss the role of genetics in intelligence).

McManus (1985) has proposed that what is important is not hand skill, as Annett's model suggests, but hand preference. He proposes that a dextral allele (D) predisposes us towards right-hand preference while a chance allele (C) produces no directional bias. Individuals with the D allele (DD genotype) will develop a right-hand preference whereas those with the C allele (CC genotype) are equally likely to show left- or right-hand preference. Both models have attracted interest from researchers investigating the relationship between handedness and cognitive/language ability. Neither has fully explained this relationship but they provide an explanatory framework in which such relationships could operate.

Chapter review

Speech and comprehension

- Language can be defined as an orderly system of communication that involves the understanding or interpretation of vocal or written symbols.
- Phonemes are the basic elements of speech but research has also shown that the primary unit of analysis is not individual phonemes but groups of phonemes, perhaps syllables.
- Recognition of words in continuous speech is far superior to the ability to recognise them when they have been isolated. We use contextual information in recognising what we hear.

- Meaning is a joint function of syntax and semantics. All users of a particular language observe syntactical rules that establish the relations of the words in a sentence to one another. These rules are not learned explicitly. People can learn to apply rules of an artificial grammar without being able to say just what these rules are.
- The most important features that we use to understand syntax are word order, word class, function words, affixes, word meanings and prosody. Content words refer to objects, actions and the characteristics of objects and actions, and thus can express meaning even in some sentences having ambiguous syntax.
- Chomsky has suggested that speech production entails the transformation of deep structure (ideas, thoughts) into surface structure (actual sentence).
- Speech errors, although incorrect, follow syntactical rules; the errors lie in the content of the speech.

Reading

- Recognition of written words (reading) is a complex perceptual task which involves scanning text, perceiving and understanding symbols and sounding out these visual symbols.
- The eye-tracking device allows researchers to study people's eye movements and fixations and to learn from these behaviours some important facts about the nature of the reading process. For example, we analyse a sentence word by word as we read it, taking longer to move on from long words or unusual ones.
- Once a word has been perceived, recognition of its pronunciation and meaning takes place. Long or unfamiliar words are sounded out, that is, they are read phonologically by a process called phonic mediation.
- Short, familiar words are recognised as wholes. In fact, only whole-word reading will enable us to know how to pronounce words such as 'cow' and 'blow', or 'bone' and 'one', which have irregular spellings.
- The dual-route model of reading suggests that we have two routes for reading: one which does not rely on grapheme–phoneme correspondence rules and another which does.

Language acquisition by children

- Studies using the habituation of a baby's sucking response have shown that the human auditory system is capable of discriminating among speech sounds soon after birth.
- Human vocalisation begins with crying, then develops into cooing and babbling, and finally results in patterned speech. During the two-word stage, children begin to combine words creatively, saying things they have never heard.

- Child-directed speech is very different from that directed towards adults; it is simpler, clearer and generally refers to items and events in the present environment. As young children gain more experience with the world and with the speech of adults and older children, their vocabulary grows and they learn to use adult rules of grammar.
- Children seem to pay less attention to phonetic detail of language as they grow older, presumably because the process of acquiring vocabulary and understanding of objects and situations is computationally complex.
- Although the first verbs children learn tend to have irregular past tenses, once they learn the regular past tense rule (add '-ed'), they apply this rule even to irregular verbs they previously used correctly.
- A language acquisition device contains universal grammatical rules and motivates language acquisition. Although children's verbal performance can be described by complex rules, it is possible that simpler rules – which children could reasonably be expected to learn – can also be devised.
- Deliberate reinforcement is not necessary for language learning, but a controversy exists about just how important child-directed behaviour is.
- A critical period for language learning may exist which occurs between the ages of 5 and 14 years old; learning a new language after this is more difficult.
- Bilingualism refers to competence in two or more languages that are used to communicate with significant others. The languages activate similar brain areas, regardless of age of acquisition.
- Studies of other primates suggest that apes can be taught at least some of the rudiments of language.

Brain development and language

- Damage to either hemisphere is associated with better recovery of language when it occurs in childhood than adulthood.
- Some researchers have suggested that the lateralisation of language – left hemisphere dominance for language processing – is complete by around age 6; others argue that it continues until puberty.
- The ability of the brain to reorganise itself following injury in infancy and childhood, together with its ongoing development, is referred to as its plasticity.
- Children who have experienced surgical removal of an entire hemisphere, for medical reasons, do not experience significant impairments in function later in life.
- The ability of the child's brain to recover better than that of the adult's has been attributed to the ongoing

development of lateralisation as well as the capacity of the right hemisphere to undertake the role of the language functions if disrupted.

Neuropsychology of language and language disorders

- The effects of brain damage suggest that memories of the sounds of words are located in Wernicke's area and that memories of the muscular movements needed to produce them are located in Broca's area.
- Wernicke's area is necessary for speech perception and Broca's area is necessary for its production.
- Wernicke's aphasia (caused by damage that extends beyond the boundaries of Wernicke's area) is characterised by fluent but meaningless speech that is lacking in content words but rich in function words.
- Broca's aphasia (caused by damage that extends beyond the boundaries of Broca's area) is characterised by non-fluent but meaningful speech that is lacking in function words but rich in content words.
- Damage to the temporoparietal region surrounding Wernicke's area produces isolation aphasia – loss of the ability to produce meaningful speech or to comprehend the speech of others but retention of the ability to repeat speech.
- Dyslexia refers to an inability to read. There are two general types: acquired and developmental.
- Acquired dyslexia refers to reading disorders arising from brain injury and there are various types of dyslexia that result from brain injury such as deep dyslexia, phonological dyslexia and visual word form dyslexia. Although some regions of the

brain are known to be involved in these disorders, their exact neural basis is unknown.
- Developmental dyslexia refers to a disorder of reading that occurs without brain injury and manifests itself in delayed reading development. Phonological processing (the ability to break down words into sounds and appreciate how they relate to each other) is severely impaired in developmental dyslexia.
- No one knows the exact causes of developmental dyslexia. Theories include delayed or disorganised left hemisphere development, an impairment in the function of the magnocellular pathway, a dysfunctional cerebellum, an inability to scan text efficiently and neuronal degeneration in the temporal cortex.

Neuroimaging and language

- Neuroimaging studies of language production and comprehension suggest that no one brain region is involved in language processing. Instead, there is a complex mosaic of regions which contributes to language and which interacts in a way which we only partially understand.
- Evidence suggests that Broca's area and the frontal cortex is necessary for the phonetic manipulation of speech but that the temporal cortex is necessary for the perceptual analysis of speech.
- The language areas of men and women are differently activated, with more bilateral activation in women, but the evidence is inconsistent.
- Handedness also interacts with degree of language proficiency, but in slightly irregular ways. Most right- and left-handers have left-hemisphere speech.

Suggestions for further reading

Aitchison, J. (2011) *The Articulate Mammal*. London: Routledge.

Bialystok, E. and Craik, F.I.M. (2010) Cognitive and lingustic processing in the bilngual mind. *Current Directions in Psychological Science*, 19, 19–23.

Brunswick, N. (2009) *Dyslexia – A Beginner's Guide*. Oxford: Oneworld Publishers.

Brunswick, N. and Martin, G.N. (2006) The neuropsychology of language and language disorders. In G.N. Martin, *Human Neuropsychology* (2nd edn). Harlow: Prentice Hall.

Burling, R. (2005) *The Talking Ape: How language evolved*. Oxford: Oxford University Press.

Detuscher, G. (2010) *Through the Language Glass*. London: Arrow.

Diehl, R.L., Lotto, A.J. and Holt, L.L. (2004) Speech perception. *Annual Review of Psychology*, 55, 149–80.

Gentilucci, M. and Corballis, M.C. (2006) From manual gesture to speech: A gradual transition. *Neuroscience and Biobehavioral Reviews*, 30, 949–60.

Haesler, S. (2007) Programmed for speech. *Scientific American Mind*, 18, 3, 66–71.

Hale, S. (2002) *The Man Who Lost His Language*. London: Penguin.

Harley, T.A. (2012) *The Psychology of Language* (4th edn). Hove: Psychology Press.

Hugdahl, K. and Westerhausen, R. (2009) What is left is right: How speech asymmetry shaped the brain. *European Psychologist*, 14, 1, 78–89.

Tannen, D. (1992) *You Just Don't Understand: Women and men in conversation*. London: Virago.

Tannen, D. (1996) *Gender and Discourse*. Oxford: Oxford University Press.

This is a varied selection of books that describe and discuss some of the interesting aspects of language.

Chapter 11
Development of self-concept and gender identity

Learning outcomes

After reading this chapter, and with further recommended reading, you should be able to:

1. Recognise and define the different components of self-concept.

2. Critically evaluate the development of these different components and the factors that influence their development in children.

3. Critically describe children's understanding of their own and others' gender groups at different ages.

4. Outline the principles of the key theories that have been proposed to explain the development of gender identity.

5. Critically review the associated research that has been conducted for support of such theories.

Forms of self-awareness and identity

'I'm 5 years old . . . I'm a boy, and . . . I have brown hair, brown eyes . . . I'm fast! . . . I like to play, like all the time!' (5-year-old boy, in response to 'who are you?'; student's field notes)

'[I'd play with her cos] she's like me, we're both girls, we're like . . . the same . . .' (7-year-old white English girl in a London state primary school)

'I think she (pointing at the photo of a girl) won't like the same (food) as me cos only girls like to eat veggies!' (7-year-old English boy in a Greater London suburb)

- How has the 5-year-old boy described himself – would you say it is a superficial or deep description?
- Look at what the 7-year-old girl has said about her friend. Why is it important that her friend is a girl?
- Similarly, why does the 7-year-old boy infer such 'culinary habits' on specifically the opposite sex?

Introduction

The examples above are some of the typical responses from children of their age group in terms of how they would describe themselves to others or how they think about themselves and others. As we shall see later in the chapter, individual features (or 'attributes') such as those that the 5-year-old boy used in the form of age, gender, appearance and likes and dislikes tend to be some of the most prominent 'self-descriptions' by children at this age. Similarly, a clear preference for peers of the same sex, or making contrasting inferences about peers of their own and the opposite sex, as voiced by the two 7-year-olds, is fairly common among children at that age. Even adults would invariably draw on some of the individual and social group-based attributes and qualities to describe themselves. All of these are part and parcel of our senses of self and identity. In this chapter we first explore the definitions of self-concept and social identity. Then we move on to examine how the self-concept, and arguably the most dominant form of social identity – gender identity – develop across different stages of childhood, and the perspectives and theories that are used by academics to explain this development.

What are self-concept and social identity?

We have already had a glimpse of the 'ingredients' that make up a sense of self from the points of view of children. Let's spend a few moments on the question 'Who am I?' to explore this a little more.

STOP AND THINK

Consider the opening examples of children's answers to the question, 'Who am I?' What answer would you give now, as an adult, to the question, 'Who am I?'

It is quite likely that you would have thought about at least one of these items in your 'Who am I?' search: name, age, gender, birthplace and/or nationality, occupation, religion and parental status (if you have children). For some of us, it may be the case that one (or more) of the items on this list also makes us 'proud' (such as our job or being a parent). For others, an item or two may distinguish us as the same as (or different from) other people we know (such as our birthplace or nationality). Still others might have preferred to use abilities or interests, such as our dress sense, music taste or cooking and sporting skills, to mark ourselves out. Whatever they are on our 'Who am I?' list, and whether they are judged positively or negatively by others or ourselves, or in fact whether or not they can be observed by others, it is these characteristics, roles and ideas that we have built up and hold about ourselves that make up this jigsaw notion known as our self-concept.

Notice how some of these attributes, such as gender, age, race, ethnicity and nationality, are readily adopted by societies to categorise individuals into groups. Such groupings are often seen to share common characteristics, either external or internal, which we use to describe ourselves and others (as we have done in the exercise). However, we do not just describe each other; we also develop feelings towards our own group as well as other groups (such as a sense of belonging or preference, as we have seen in the case of the 7-year-old girl in the opening example). Moreover, sometimes, whether consciously or subconsciously, we make assumptions and evaluations of each other based on such group membership (as in the 7-year-old boy in the opening example), or how people think and behave in ways upheld as typical of members in such groups (such as being masculine or a 'typical man'). Our sense of social identity concerns all of these thinking (cognitive), feeling (affective) and behavioural components (Tajfel, 1978). The later part of the chapter will look closely at these concepts that concern the ever-important gender categories and associated identities.

As we have explored in the exercise and examples above, for many of us, those ingredients that build up our self-concepts and social identities serve as a kind of framework for thinking about our social world, structuring our experiences and guiding our social conduct and interpersonal interactions and relationships. Therefore, what we perceive of ourselves is highly central to our personality and behaviour. And we will see shortly how the self-concept forms very early in life and is influenced by a variety of factors, both cognitive and social, which makes it all the more important for us to try to understand its development.

Theories in the development of the self-concept

The influential theorist in self-concepts, Eleanor Maccoby (1980), once pointed out that a sense of self develops by 'degrees', in a gradual and cumulative manner. As every one of us develops ideas about who we are, those ideas are continually reviewed and

---

Definitions

Self-concept: ideas we have about ourselves, including our physical and mental qualities, and our emotional and behavioural attributes.
Social identity: a sense of identity derived from our membership of social groups, including categorising ourselves as members, feelings of belonging, and behaviour consistent with what is expected of group members.

revised through childhood in the light of our cognitive development and social experiences. For example, any fast-growing toddler will become more and more aware of her own behaviour as well as *others'* responses to it, and may form her own perceptions and evaluations of it. All these inputs are likely to play a role in shaping her later, more competent, realistic and reflective concept of herself as she grows.

Children's self-concepts through the years

Before delving into the stages of development in self-concept, and the factors that influence it in children, it is a good idea to explore what kinds of attributes and qualities children actually have about themselves at different ages. The first opening example in this chapter shows us some of the commonest kinds of description that children give in response to asking themselves the question 'Who am I?' This open-ended question has been one of the most popular, if simplest, means of obtaining children's self-descriptions.

Susan Harter, a prominent researcher in the 1980s, reviewed studies in which children were asked about themselves involving, among others, the 'Who am I?' question. What she noticed is an apparent developmental pattern in which children at different ages predominantly use different kinds of attributes and qualities to describe themselves. For the youngest children (aged 5 years or younger), observations based on their physical or external characteristics, such as appearance or activities, feature the most in their self-descriptions. For older children, there is often a shift towards more 'internal' descriptions, such as relationships with others or their inner feelings, beliefs and attitudes. For instance, in Rosenberg's (1979) study of 8- to 18-year-olds in Baltimore, when asked about what kind of person they would like to become, 36% of the 8-year-olds' answers were to do with interpersonal traits (e.g. 'shy', 'friendly') versus 69% of the 14–16-year-olds. The oldest group (up to 18 years old) also made far more use of the inner qualities that were only available to themselves and referred more to self-control (e.g. 'I don't show my feelings') when concerned with such emotions, motivations, wishes and secrets. Some of the popular features of self-descriptions at different ages are summarised in Table 11.1.

Table 11.1 Children's self-descriptions at different ages.

Age	Self-descriptions	Examples
5 years or under	Physical features or facts, overt preference or possessions	'I've red hair.' 'A girl.' 'I like milk.' 'I've got a bike.'
5–9 years	More character references and gradually interpersonal traits	'I'm happy.' 'I'm brave.' 'Sometimes I'm shy.'
Beyond 10 years	Increasing qualifiers for above by considering private self-knowledge	'I try not to be selfish but I find it hard sometimes.'

Of course, there may be a big difference between how particularly older children may describe themselves to a stranger, such as a researcher, and how they really think and feel about themselves (and later studies that have used methods other than self-reporting will be reviewed).

Also, as children get older, their increasingly complex language will enable them to express themselves more thoroughly. Nevertheless, such research gives us a taste of the increasing complexity of the developing child's self-concept. Indeed, the development of our self-concept as unique individuals, at least in Western cultures, is seen as a lengthy and complex journey, which goes through at least several stages throughout childhood, and probably even more over our lifetime (Maccoby, 1980). So, where, or at what age, is the starting point of this journey? And how does this self-understanding become more complex over time?

The emerging sense of self: early self-awareness

An awareness of the self, or the realisation and establishment that we simply 'exist' as our own individual entity, is the very first constituent that emerges of our self-concept. It has been argued that in early infancy children do not have this basic awareness – they do not perceive themselves as distinct beings – as separate from other beings, with their own unique appearance, properties or agency (meaning that they can cause an effect on other objects or actors in their physical and social world, that they can 'make things happen'). Such self-awareness can be illustrated using a simple visual cue recognition technique commonly known as the 'rouge test' (see the Research Methods box).

RESEARCH METHODS

Early sense of self

Developed initially for research with apes, Lewis and Brooks-Gunn (1978, 1979) carried out a simple experiment with young children by asking mothers unobtrusively to apply a spot of rouge to their child's nose. Later the children's reactions to their self-image were monitored when they were put in front of a mirror; the assumption was that if they were able to recognise the image was that of themselves – possessing a sense of self – they would reach for the spot on their nose where the rouge had been applied. This response was rarely observed before the age of 15 months, even though at 1 year old, children were amused by what they saw in the mirror – without paying any attention to the rouge – as if they were laughing at another child whose nose had been painted on! It was not until the second half of the second year that most of the children showed signs that they knew definitely the spot was of interest as it was on their *own* nose.

There are other techniques for assessing self-awareness that rely more on verbal indicators, such as asking some children to name or describe photographs of themselves (Bullock and Lutkenhaus, 1990) and examining their use of relevant terms like 'I' and 'me' (Bates, 1990). On the whole, these studies have found that, as with the rouge test, children's self-awareness (the recognition that the self exists as a separate and distinct individual with its own attributes), as the essential first stepping stone in the development of self-concept, is achieved by the end of the second year (see Figure 11.1).

• Do you think the rouge test is a good way of assessing a child's self-recognition?

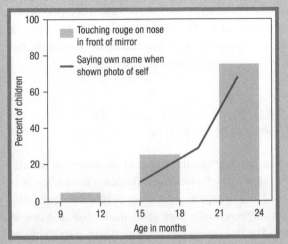

Figure 11.1 Self-recognition by the rouge test and self-naming from 9 to 24 months.

Source: Lewis and Brooks-Gunn (1978)

The key 'tool' of the rouge test is the mirror in which the infant recognises the reflection of his/her facial appearance. Could it be that familiarity with mirrors or emphasis on the *face* in social interactions may influence the development of this form of self-concept? A study by Keller et al. (2004) found that mutual eye contact and object stimulation (using objects to attract a child's attention) between parents and babies at 3 months predicted self-concept at 18–20 months and this might explain why infants of Cameroonian Nso farmers showed relatively low levels of self-recognition using the rouge test, compared with their Western counterparts. It is suggested that distal parenting (more object and face-to-face contexts), which is prevalent in the West and urban regions, facilitates this kind of (facial) recognition of others and self in infants compared with more proximal parenting (involving body stimulation and contact) in rural tribes.

Definition

Self-awareness: the first step in the development of self-concept; the recognition that we are distinct from others with physical and mental properties of our own.

The subjective or existential self

We have just seen how the earliest awareness of the self, the recognition that we exist as a separate and unique entity, has been studied in infancy. This early self-recognition was labelled as the 'self-as-subject', or the self 'I', by the pioneering American psychologist and philosopher,

William James (1892). This initial feature of the self as a 'subject' of experience is usually thought of in terms of its distinction from, or as a precursor to, the later feature of the self as an 'object' of knowledge (see the next section). James further articulated four conditions or elements for this existential self that refer to an awareness of: (1) our own agency in life events; (2) the uniqueness of our own experience as distinct from other people; (3) the continuity of our identity; (4) our own awareness, implying an element of self-reflexivity (that we are able to reflect on our awareness of the self).

Lewis (1990, 1991), of the rouge test, calls this aspect of the self the subjective self or existential self and argues that it endures through time and space, in line with James's original four elements. Even though, as we have explored in Lewis's studies, the child does not reach an elaborate understanding of the self until the second year of life, Lewis places the starting points of early existential understanding in the first few months of life. These early and basic starting points are rooted in numerous everyday interactions between the infant and the objects and people in their world. During such encounters, the infant learns that his actions can affect objects or people around him (their agency), that he is able to 'make' things happen, control objects and 'cause' others to respond. These can be very simple interactions such as an infant's attempts to move or manipulate a toy, or that, as he smiles, his mother smiles back or, when he cries, she coos and comforts. This is particularly true in the early months when parents spend a lot of time imitating the infant's behaviours, expressions and vocalisations (Meltzoff, 1990). It is through these experiences that the infant begins to separate the self from everything else (such as mother) and learn that this separate existence (as 'I') continues over time and across contexts.

The objective or categorical self

As cited earlier, James's configuration of the self consists of another key feature that he called the 'self-as-object', or the self as 'me'. This is more commonly known as the objective self or categorical self (Lewis, 1990). This aspect concerns the emerging process of defining the self in relation to the kinds of attributes and qualities that are commonly used to describe groupings of people, such as size, gender, ethnicity and relationship to others (as we explored briefly in the chapter's opening, with the concept of social identity, and will do so again later on). By this point of development, usually beyond 2 years

of age, children have achieved self-awareness, or the existential or subjective self, and they begin to be able to place themselves within, or to become aware that they can be seen by others in relation to, a great array of social categories (like gender and race) that human societies tend to use to define the individuals living among them.

The exact process of how, and the degree to which, children make use of human social categories to define themselves and each other will be detailed in the second part of this chapter ('Understanding of gender categories', pages 322–42). For now, it is important just to note the key distinction between the categorical 'me' and the existential 'I'. The categorical self does not refer to basic properties such as agency, but emphasises our 'roles' as commonly seen in the wider social world, and their associated attributes in relation to other members in society (such as being a girl versus being a boy, being a child versus being a grown-up).

The looking-glass self

It has been pointed out that a child's emerging existential self and the later objective self are influenced by social factors, particularly the child's understanding of his/her relationships with other people and of other people's perception of themselves. Cooley and Mead were two of the key theorists who initially conceptualised this close relationship between an individual child's understanding and others' understanding of the self formally (Cooley, 1902; Mead, 1934). This idea, termed the 'looking-glass self', refers to the way others hold up a 'social mirror' in which we may see ourselves as we are 'reflected' by them, and from there, we build up our senses of the self from the views we come to understand that others may have of us.

Definitions

Subjective or existential self: the recognition of the self that is unique and distinct from others, endures over time and space, and has an element of self-reflexivity.

Objective or categorical self: the recognition of the self as the person seen by others and defined by the attributes and qualities used to define groups of people.

Looking-glass self: the sense of self we develop as we respond to interactions with others and see how others react to us. We see ourselves reflected in other people's behaviour towards us.

Infant looking at himself in the mirror and reaching towards reflected image.
Source: Lam

Within this view, the importance of social interactions is emphasised as the tool through which the self and the social world are inextricably linked. Through repeated social exchanges, such as games and play, most of which involve the use of language, children gradually come to realise and adopt some of the perspectives that others have of them, and with such knowledge they also become more able to reflect on themselves. According to Cooley and Mead, a child cannot develop a sense of self without interactions with others, in order to learn how those others view the world and the people within it – including the child himself or herself.

Despite the idea of self as being a unique individual, self-concept is inextricably linked with others, where various social inputs come into play as the child develops her notion of what she is 'like' compared to others. This comparison process can be evaluative as well – it involves value-laden judgements about one's qualities. We will explore this side of the self below.

Self-esteem

Apart from the common attributes and social roles and categories we use to describe ourselves, we also have a more reflective and evaluative feature of our self-concept. Remember how in the first exercise of the chapter we reflected on the things about ourselves that make

us feel proud? Suffice it to say there are likely also things for which we do not feel very proud about ourselves. Children often reflect on and evaluate themselves, and such evaluations form an important part of their self-concept, their self-esteem.

Children's self-evaluations also go through stages of development, similar to the other features of the self. For instance, younger children tend to have more general or 'global' self-evaluations, such as how happy they are about themselves or how much they like the way they are. On entering early adolescence, their evaluations become increasingly differentiated, with separate judgements about their physical appearance, peer acceptance, and academic or athletic performance, and so forth. Susan Harter, as mentioned before with her work on children's self-descriptions, distinguished five areas in which children's self-evaluations may be measured: (1) scholastic competence – how competent the child considers herself to be at school; (2) athletic competence – the child's self-assessment of her competence in sporting activities;

Definition

Self-esteem: the evaluative and reflective features of our self-concept that can vary from high to low, and which draw in part on others' evaluations of ourselves.

(3) social acceptance – the child's self-assessment of popularity among her peers (see also the next chapter); (4) physical appearance – how good- or bad-looking the child thinks she is; (5) behavioural conduct – how acceptable the child thinks her behaviour is to others (Harter, 1987, 1990).

Harter also considers that our self-esteem functions as the discrepancy between two internal assessments of ourselves, our ideal self and our real self: that is, what we *would like* ourselves to be or think we *ought to be* versus what we think we *really are*. When there is little difference between the two selves, discrepancy is low, and self-esteem is generally high. When the discrepancy is high, self-esteem will be lower. The latter suggests that the child sees himself as failing to 'live up' to their ideals or standards. Obviously, such standards are not the same for everybody. A child who sees athletic competence as more important than academic competence and who does not do that well in his school work, but is reasonably sporty, will not suffer much from a low self-esteem. However, another child who achieves similar standards as the first child at school, but values academic competence as highly important, will have a lower self-esteem.

Developmentally, from junior school or later childhood at ages 8–10 onwards, children show increasing consistency (little fluctuation in the short term) in their self-esteem, and their judgements become increasingly more realistic, with an overall fall in self-esteem levels versus early childhood, as they are more and more aware of their positive as well as negative attributes (Harter, 2003). In the transition to adolescence, self-esteem becomes increasingly differentiated or 'compartmentalised' with newer areas (such as relationships and future career projections). Into adolescence, with the changing school (secondary or high school) environment accompanied by increased conflict in social roles, emotional changes and relationship complexity (Harter, 1998), a temporary decline in self-esteem is observed, although it tends to rise again towards adulthood with increasing maturity, control and coping ability (see also the Lifespan box for the continuity into adulthood). Social influences are a likely explanation, since older childhood self-judgements become increasingly closely matched with the evaluations of others (such as those by teachers; Marsh et al., 1998). The evaluations of others, therefore, function like elements of the looking-glass self, providing a reference point from which we reflect on ourselves and build up aspects of our self-concept. Here such influences bear more specifically on the evaluative aspects of the self.

Summing up: self-concept development

As we have seen, the child's self-concept, including self-esteem, is a highly significant part of her social development. This development seems to emerge from fairly rudimentary senses that gradually evolve into more complex understandings which are impacted by a multitude of factors, of which a few have been described above, most notably the social actors around the child, such as her parents and peers. The qualities, roles and evaluations taken on by the child also tend to become increasingly consistent with those expected by the social groups and institutions around her over time. In the next part of the chapter, we will draw attention to such relationships between the child's sense of self and one of the most pervasive systems involving a social group – gender.

LIFESPAN

Is self-esteem a stable psychological factor or does it change as we get older?

A paper published by Orth et al. in 2010 reports findings from the Americans' Changing Lives study, which followed up 3617 individuals (aged 25–40 years) for 16 years. The study collected data on, among other things, self-esteem, and the analysis revealed an interesting effect. Self-esteem increased fairly steadily during early to middle adulthood, before reaching a peak at around 60 years of age, then appeared to decline during older adulthood. When the authors investigated the data more closely, they found a few social group differences in the longer-term changes. For instance, women generally had lower self-esteem than men during young adulthood but, by older age, this difference gradually disappeared. There also appeared to be an effect of race, in that people who described themselves as 'black' saw a more dramatic fall in self-esteem towards late adulthood than did people who described themselves as 'white'. Education, too, played a part with more educated people reporting higher overall levels of self-esteem than less educated people, although for both groups their lifespan 'arcs' in self-esteem were the same (as in Figure 11.2).

- Why do you think is there a sharp fall in self-esteem around the age of 60 years for all the participants in this research study?

The authors noted that midlife is a time of relative stability in terms of work, family and romantic relationships. People increasingly occupy positions of power and status. This might in turn promote self-esteem. However, older adults may be experiencing a change in roles, such as an 'empty nest' (especially for women with their children leaving home), retirement and obsolete work skills in addition to health issues.

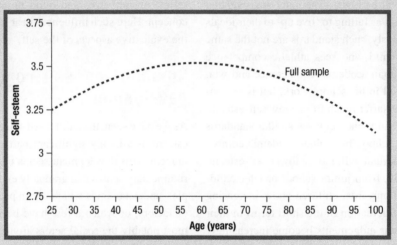

Figure 11.2 Changes in self-esteem through adulthood.

Source: Orth et al. (2010)

Understanding of gender categories: children's gender identity

We have seen how children gradually develop a sense of self across different ages. As the self-concept becomes more stable, children categorise and evaluate themselves and others along a wider range of social category systems, such as age, gender and race. As we have explored in the early part of the chapter, social categories are those groups in society that are seen to share common attributes, and social identities refer to the way we think and feel about, and behave towards, our own and others'

social groups. Among all the possible social identities we have, our sense of gender identity starts to develop very early in life. Indeed, Lewis and Brooks-Gunn (1979), whose work (the rouge test) we read earlier, argue that gender is among the earliest, if not the earliest, social category systems a child learns, and that knowledge about this system is concurrently developed in relation to the child's sense of self and others. We will first explore the child's basic understanding of gender in this section.

Development of gender identity

How do children understand that they are a boy or a girl? And when and how do they realise that they will grow up to be a man or a woman? How do they identify (or even endorse) those behaviours, attitudes and expectations considered to be appropriate for their own gender in their society? These are some of the questions we will address below.

Gender identity, just like self-concept, has different levels and aspects, which develop gradually in stages. Children appear able to differentiate people by gender very early. By 9 to 12 months, they respond differently to photographs of male versus female faces (e.g. Brooks-Gunn and Lewis, 1981; Fagot and Leinbach, 1993) and to male and female strangers in person (Smith and Sloboda, 1986). Soon after, from about 12–18 months, they acquire a set of verbal labels for these categories ('mummy', 'daddy'). However, at 2 years, many children still do not know how to answer if asked directly whether they are a boy or a girl. This is helped if they are shown stereotypical pictures of boys and girls and asked which one(s) refer to them (Thompson, 1975). Nevertheless, by 3 years of age, most children can correctly label themselves by their gender (Weinraub et al., 1984).

Kohlberg's cognitive-developmental theory (1966, explained more fully later) describes gender identity development as a three-step learning process that results from the child's attempt to understand sex-role behaviour. The three steps are: gender labelling (when the child is aware of his/her own sex but believes it can change); gender stability (when the child is aware that sex is stable over time, i.e. if I am a boy now, then I will still be a boy in a year's time); and gender constancy or consistency (when the child is aware that his/her sex remains the same, regardless of time or circumstance, i.e. even if I dress as a girl, I am still a boy).

The correct labelling of oneself and others by gender is only the first step towards an understanding of gender identity, and research shows that at the age of 3 children are very much reliant upon external physical characteristics in the 'here and now' as they identify each other. When children at this age are faced with 'deeper' questions about their gender, such as 'When you were a baby, were you a little girl or little boy?' or 'When you grow up, will you be a mummy or daddy?', many are very confused. This aspect of gender identity, known as gender stability, refers to the understanding that our gender group membership is a permanent part of ourselves that remains the same through time. This is usually achieved by around 4 years of age (Slaby and Frey, 1975). However, at this age, recognition of gender groups largely relies on stereotypical features. This can be easily demonstrated by an experimental procedure where, for example, the picture of a stereotypical-looking boy (with short hair and shorts) is presented, and only the stereotypical elements (hair and clothing) are switched into those stereotypical of a girl (with long hair and a dress; see Figure 11.3). Although the transformation is performed in front of the child and is not taxing on memory, many pre-schoolers are confused, and say that the boy in the picture is a girl after the switch (Emmerich et al., 1977; Gouze and Nadelman, 1980).

Non-pictorial methods, such as hypothetical questioning (e.g. 'Can you be a girl if you really want to be?', 'If a boy lets his hair grow very long, is he still a boy?') may also be used. When children acknowledge that gender stays the same despite changes in appearance, gender constancy is achieved, and this tends to occur after 5 years of age. It seems odd that children who understand the permanency of gender can somehow be 'fooled' by the superficial changes, even though research with children in both Western and Eastern cultures has charted this trend (Munroe et al., 1984). This may be because gender constancy requires knowledge of biological sex differences, and indeed constancy is achieved earlier in children who understand the genital differences (as a marker of sex differences to children) between the sexes (Bem, 1989).

The fulfilment of all of gender labelling, stability and constancy may seem like a major milestone in the young child's development, but it is only a basic part of gender identity. A larger part is learning about what is associated with 'being' a boy or a girl, what being a member of a gender group is supposed to mean in various social contexts. In fact, around the time of gender labelling, about 2½ years (Kuhn et al., 1978), children have already begun building up basic ideas about the activities, abilities or preferences and, later, attitudes and expectations that are appropriate for, or typical of,

Definitions

Gender stability: the understanding that gender group membership is normally stable and permanent over time.

Gender constancy: the understanding that gender group membership is unchanged despite changes in appearance.

Gender labelling: correct identification of 'male' or 'female' of oneself and others.

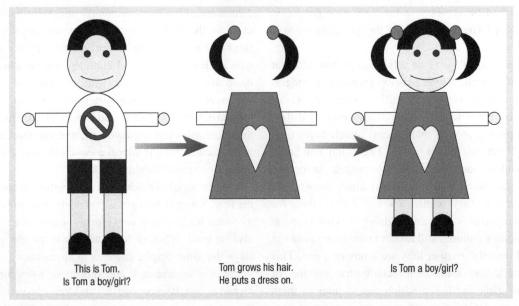

This is Tom.
Is Tom a boy/girl?

Tom grows his hair.
He puts a dress on.

Is Tom a boy/girl?

Figure 11.3 An example of the experimental transformation used for testing gender constancy in children.

their own and the other gender. These may surround adult daily activities, such as cooking and cleaning for women, repairing the house and car for men, or activities familiar to children, such as playing with dolls for girls and playing with trains for boys. Gender stereotypes also include beliefs about more subtle tendencies, such as 'girls cry and give kisses' and 'boys fight and don't cuddle'. Gender stereotyping also increases rapidly with age; before middle childhood (by the age of 5 years), children already associate various occupations and crude personality traits (such as 'strong', 'soft-hearted', 'cruel' and 'gentle') to men and women, and by the age of 8 to 9 years, their stereotypes are already very similar to those of adults (e.g. Best et al., 1977; Martin, 1993; Serbin et al., 1993).

Perhaps it is not surprising that children's stereotypes mimic those of adults. After all, in many societies, adults have clearly divided gender roles and stereotypes (most childcare is still conducted by women and men take on the heavier manual work, for instance) – children's beliefs may simply reflect the practical reality

they witness. However, gender roles have, at least in post-industrial societies, been changing a great deal whilst children's beliefs have not always caught on, but seem simply to exaggerate common stereotypes. Apart from that, what is startling is that stereotyped behaviours are shown in children earlier than stereotyped beliefs are expressed, as the following will review.

Children's preference for gender-stereotyped toys and games is apparent by about 18 to 24 months, before they are able to label gender categories reliably, and this continues well into middle childhood (O'Brien, 1992). By the age of 3, before gender stability, children begin to profess a preference for peers of their own gender for play and friendships, and actually interact more with them. When they are in school, their regular friendship groups are almost exclusively composed of those of

Definition

Gender stereotypes: beliefs about what is appropriate for or typical of one's own or the other gender group.

STOP AND THINK

- How typical do you rate yourself as a member of your gender group? Alternatively, how masculine or feminine do you see yourself?

- Did you see yourself as a 'boyish' (or 'girlish') child? What criteria did you use?

- Do you think children nowadays think and behave in more or less gender-stereotyped ways compared with when you were a child?

their own sex, and this continues well into adolescence (Maccoby, 1988, 1990). While boys tend to prefer to play outdoors in less structured large-group activities (such as football and play-fighting; see also the next chapter), girls tend to socialise in pairs or smaller groups, or engage in more structured 'traditional' games (such as skipping and hopscotch).

It is important to view the above evidence with caution. Much of the research involved observations of behaviours or interactions in homes, classrooms or playgrounds and required researchers' categorisation and interpretation, and thus a level of bias may have drawn from the inputs. Furthermore, some of the differences observed are often quite small and many studies of infants under 2 years of age have not found many consistent behavioural differences between boys and girls (see reviews by Owen Blakemore et al., 2009; Maccoby, 1998, 2000). Still, the division between boys and girls in social interactions and the same-sex preference in friendships are such prevalent social phenomena that we cannot deny that gender exerts a strong force on children's identity and relationships.

Taken together, gender is a system of social categories that permeates children's lives from very early on. Even before they learn the gender labels or grasp the idea of their permanency, stereotyped behaviours and thinking are already apparent. So, what may explain this pervasive phenomenon? There are myriad arguments that are centred upon either the 'nature' or 'nurture' side of the debate, whilst others focus on the role played by the child. We will explore some of the major theories in the following sections.

By school age, children's peer groups consist of mostly same-sex peers and this continues into adolescence.
Source: Lam

Biological explanations for gender identity

It is of little surprise that many researchers have located biological factors as being responsible for gender differences. Men and women are clearly different in terms of their genetic make-up and physiology, and some such inherent differences may underpin the psychological differences observed between boys and girls.

The basic genetic sex difference (the male has an XY pair and the female an XX pair of chromosomes) means differential sex hormone production before birth and later in adolescence (the male with more testosterone and the female with more oestrogen). This leads to different body and physical attributes, including the male's larger average size, relatively greater physical strength and lung capacity and, arguably, more aggressive instincts. According to most biological accounts, gender differences in social role patterns have taken shape through the course of evolution as an outcome of humans' adaptation to their environment, with men and women being 'equipped' with such physical characteristics and instinctual tendencies for different functions. For instance, the gender division of hunters and gatherers is a result of the male's size and strength being better suited for the demands of the former, with the female's childbearing and breastfeeding abilities making her the 'natural' caregiver or homemaker. Sex differences in psychological functioning are, however, less clear and probably overstated (Hyde, 2005). Whilst there appears to be an effect of social influences on the development of aspects of self-esteem (women generally score higher on behavioural conduct and moral-ethical self-esteem; Gentile et al., 2009), other studies seem to demonstrate biological influences – for example, where men are better at mental rotation tasks and women are better at verbal tasks (Hausmann et al., 2009). However, performance in mental rotation tasks can be improved with priming and practice (Ortner and Sieverding, 2008), and as males have been inducted and expected to perform more of these tasks, this suggests that social opportunities to engage in 'masculine' tasks are a potential factor other than biological sex.

Parental investment theory

Some theorists, namely the sociobiologists, have taken the above ideas further to explain the contemporary behaviours, relationship patterns and even status disparity between the sexes. The logic of their reasoning, termed the parental investment theory (Wilson, 1972, 1978; Archer, 1992; Kendrick, 1994), is set around the specifics of male–female reproduction, which is seen as the primary goal of human survival – to pass on one's own genes. Reproduction is less 'costly' biologically to the male since he does not carry the unborn offspring or give birth. However, he does not have the important advantage of the female in being certain that any offspring born to her will possess her genes – unless he remains with his mate to preclude her from mating with other males. Therefore a 'trade' is struck whereby the sexes each assess and offer the other their relevant attributes; he needs to assess her reproductive capacity to bear his offspring and offer a level of commitment towards providing for and protecting those offspring, while she takes time in turn to assess his suitability as a reproductive partner with the requisite strength and resources to protect and provide for her and their offspring.

Sociobiologists argue that the reproductive trade-off has led to differential ideas about what is attractive or 'sought after' in males and females. For instance, greater emphasis is placed on youthfulness and physical attractiveness for the female, whereas traits such as ambition and competitiveness, associated with the pursuit of conquest and territory and resource guarding, are more valued for the male (Buss, 1987). It is debatable whether, related to this trade-off, women really take greater care in their appearance than men do in modern societies if we consider such phenomena as the 'metrosexual' male, but as we saw earlier, research shows that boys do engage in more activities that command dominance and competitiveness than girls do (see also the next chapter on play-fighting). However, whether such behaviours have their origin in biological sex differences evolved through a *very* long history of environmental changes is harder to ascertain.

Definition

Parental investment theory: a theory used to explain gender differences on the basis of biological sex differences. The theory states that reproduction has different implications for males and females and that men and women therefore look for different traits in each other, which through the course of evolution have been adapted as the modern-day observed gender role, behaviour and status differences.

Biological evidence

In order to ensure that the biologically given sex differences underpin children's psychological and behavioural outcomes, some signs of the biological impact should be shown before the child experiences socialisation, to pinpoint that it is inherited biology rather than learnt characteristics that is responsible for their role differences. This requires research in early infancy and makes definitive evidence difficult to obtain, at least in humans, as we know from earlier in the chapter and previous chapters that from a young age the infant is already very receptive and responsive to the social world around them. Therefore, some of the early evidence has come from research on animals that manipulated the sex hormones of offspring through the pregnant mothers. One common practice was where scientists administered doses of testosterone to pregnant monkeys prenatally and monitored the development of their female offspring (e.g. Young, 1964). Many found that the offspring displayed more 'rough-and-tumble' play and aggression towards each other compared with female offspring who had not received testosterone.

Short of being able to do the same to human participants for obvious ethical reasons, a smaller number of studies on children who received abnormal amounts of sex hormones due to their mothers' conditions or accidents and errors in the medical sciences have shed light on the discussion. The earliest cases were reported by Money and Ehrhardt (1972) who examined girls with congenital adrenal hyperplasia (CAH), a condition resulting from exposure to excessive levels of androgen (a male sex hormone) before birth as a treatment given to mothers prone to miscarriages. The girls were born

Definition

Congenital adrenal hyperplasia: congenital adrenal hyperplasia can affect both boys and girls. People with congenital adrenal hyperplasia lack an enzyme needed by the adrenal gland to make the hormones cortisol and aldosterone. Without these hormones, the body produces more androgen – a type of male sex hormone. This causes male characteristics to appear early (or inappropriately). About 1 in 10 000–18 000 children are born with congenital adrenal hyperplasia (MEDLINE Plus, 2010).

with male genitalia that were corrected surgically, and were raised as girls. Follow-ups showed that they saw themselves as more 'tomboyish' and played less with other girls compared with a matched sample who had not received treatment. Further research showed that girls with CAH due to genetic defects were more likely to play with boys' toys and were reported by their parents as being less interested in girls' activities (Berenbaum and Snyder, 1995). Such reports have been replicated across countries, including the UK, USA, Japan and Sweden (see a review by Owen Blakemore et al., 2009). However, we should bear in mind that the knowledge of their daughters' medial history might have affected the parents' attitudes, perception or behaviour, though under the circumstances it would be unlikely that they actually encouraged the masculine behaviours rather than the opposite. For other research involving sex hormones, see also the case studies in Chapter 3, 'Research methods'.

Money and Ehrhardt (1972), who wrote about the CAH cases, also treated and reported on a high-profile case that, many years later, was to become one of the most controversial in the medical and psychological professions and beyond (see the 'Nature–nurture' box).

The true story of the twins makes a compelling case for the role that biology plays in developing gender identity. It would appear that no matter what interventions are put in place, we simply cannot avoid the effects of the genes and biological mechanisms we are born with. However, similar to the studies of the girls who were exposed to excess hormones prenatally, the parents knew the biological sex of the twin, who was also already in his second year when he underwent reconstructive surgery. Also, hormonal and psychological therapies continued to his adolescence, despite his unease about the visits to the medical and psychiatric professionals (as documented in media coverage). These events could have raised the child's doubts about his assigned gender and his parents' behaviours towards him. Finally, even when findings converge with prescriptions of the biological accounts, published cases such as this are rare.

In general, any evidence of the direct effects of hormonal manipulation and biological dysfunction on gender identity in humans is harder to obtain, even though some reviewers have observed in normally developing individuals that male sex hormones have the strongest effects on play, aggression (Collaer and Hines, 1995) and sexual orientation (Patterson, 1995). Still, is gender identity all about play, aggressive instincts and sex? Many limitations of the biological accounts, and in particular the parental investment theory, concern their narrow scope, centred upon dominance and sexual behaviour. Much of the focus was placed on male physical strength and 'innate' aggressiveness to explain dominance when, even among animals, dominance can be strategic and learned, and is not always associated with strength and aggressiveness (Sayer, 1982). Even if biological instincts are directly responsible for such behaviours, as we reviewed earlier, gender *identity* consists of much more than just behaviour. It includes complex cognitive and affective processes, some of which involve conscious decision making, such as identifying ourselves with others of our own gender group, forming stereotypes and expectations based on such memberships, all of which vary across societies and can change over time.

NATURE–NURTURE

Gender realignment: the well-known case of 'the boy without a penis'

Documented in several televised programmes and a popular book (*As Nature Made Him: The Boy who was Raised as a Girl*; see Colapinto, 2013), apart from academic articles, is the case of a boy who was one of a set of identical twins, followed initially by Money and Ehrhardt (1972). Born as a normal male, at 7 months of age Bruce had most of his penis burnt off during a spoiled routine circumcision. It was not until nearly a year later that the confused and upset parents referred themselves to Dr John Money, who advised them to have him undergo radical surgical reconstruction, followed by years of hormonal therapy, to ultimately become a girl. The surgery went ahead when Bruce was 17 months old and the case was soon hailed as a 'success' story of nurture overcoming nature to shape one child's gender identity, when Money's initial follow-ups reported a well-adjusted 'Brenda' with feminine characteristics, if energetic and a little 'tomboyish'. In fact, this was the first case of gender reassignment ever performed on a developmentally normal child – Money had routinely conducted the procedure originally on hermaphrodites (individuals born with both male and female sexual organs) – leading doctors around the world to perform many more reassignments on infants with injured or abnormal genitalia. Bruce was the ultimate 'real-life' experiment to prove it was nurture, not nature, that determines gender identity – particularly when his twin brother could be a perfect matched 'control' raised as a boy.

The reality was rather more complicated. Money's publications on the case ceased in the late 1970s. Decades later, when the twin, now 'David', was a grown-up and cast aside his anonymity to the media, the story of a truly harrowing childhood was recounted. John described how he felt awkward around girls, was not interested in girls' activities but in running, fighting and climbing, and was later teased by his peers for his masculine mannerisms. A follow-up of David's teens, by Milton Diamond (1982), a biologist by training, told a story of isolation and depression, with a great deal of uncertainty about his gender. But it was not until the disturbed 14-year-old became suicidal that his parents decided to reveal the truth on the advice of a local psychiatrist, and he soon embarked on the painful journey of reverting his identity back in line with his biological sex.

As an adult, David married, adopted children and later cooperated with Diamond and others to participate in a follow-up (Diamond and Signmundson, 1997) and further media coverage (see the websites at the end of the chapter). However, depression plagued his adolescence and adulthood, among other issues, such as marital and financial difficulties and a history of clinical depression in the family (which also affected his mother and twin brother, who committed suicide when David was 36). In 2004, at the age of 38, two days after his wife told him that she wanted to separate from him, David took his own life.

- Do you think the twin's troubled gender identity was a result of biology?
- What other factors might have influenced his gender development?

Social learning theories of gender identity

We have seen the effects of biological sex on gender identity as well as their limitations as a sole explanation. We have identified that, as different societies hold different conceptions of gender-appropriate thinking and behaviour that can change over time, it is plausible that the social environment plays a part in forming children's gender identity. Almost an antithesis to biological accounts, one other early approach, social learning theories (Bandura, 1969, 1977; Mischel, 1966, 1970), proposes that children are 'shaped' into gender roles by the behaviour of adults and other children, and as such children are recipients of social information about what is appropriate for their own gender group in their own culture.

According to the premises of social learning theories, gender identity is acquired (rather than pre-programmed by genes) as a product of the child's accumulated learning experiences and socialisation, and the socialising 'agents' are the key players in a child's life – adults, peers and the media being the key sources. Social learning operates through two complementary processes called *reinforcement* and *modelling*. For reinforcement,

Definition

Social learning theories: an approach that explains gender identity development in terms of the child's accumulating learning experiences from their social environment, particularly through modelling others' behaviour and being rewarded for adopting approved mannerisms.

the child is rewarded for behaving in gender-appropriate ways and 'punished' for behaving in gender-inappropriate ways, according to the gender roles in their culture. So-called 'rewards' and 'punishment' are metaphoric and often do not come in a tangible, overt manner (treats or reprimands). The socialising agents' attention or encouragement, or the lack or withdrawal of them, already serve as effective rewards or punishment (such as parents offering their children toys seen as appropriate for their gender, or being more engaging when they play with these toys, and less so when the children pick up toys seen as more appropriate for the opposite sex).

The agents themselves often also demonstrate gender-role-appropriate behaviours (and therefore serve as 'models' for how to perform such behaviours) as well as the consequences of conforming to the gender norms in that culture. There are many everyday examples of gender-role demonstrations (such as fathers and mothers performing gender-typical chores in the home, and televised commercials showing the popularity and enjoyment of children engaging with gender-stereotyped toys). These socialising agents' actions and responses will, whether consciously or unconsciously, lead to gender-role learning in the child, as we will explore below.

Adults as socialising agents

STOP AND THINK

Think back to your childhood: the daily routines that your parents engaged in (work, household duties and pastimes) and their interactions with you (caring roles and play). Then talk to some parents about their daily activities, or observe them, or (if you are a parent yourself) reflect on your daily activities with your children.

- How much of those are gender-typical behaviours?
- Do the father and mother take part in such behaviours to different extents?
- Has the pattern changed over the years?

Since its inception in the 1970s, the social learning approach to gender identity development has attracted a great deal of research, with the early period focusing on the behaviours and attitudes of adults towards children. For example, parents were observed to 'reward' gender-stereotyped behaviours and activities by infants of as young as 18 months, such as encouraging girls more for touching and cuddling than boys (Lewis, 1975),

Copying dad's behaviour is part of the gender-learning process.
Source: Lam

giving more encouragement to children for picking up gender-appropriate toys or engaging them for more gender-appropriate style of play or activities (e.g. Fagot, 1978; Caldera et al., 1989; Fagot and Hagan, 1991).

A series of studies since the 1970s, collectively known as the 'Baby X' experiments, illustrate some clear differences in the reactions towards, and expectations of, the same baby by adults simply due to her dress code or labelling by gender. Take the classic study by Will and colleagues (1976). The same baby girl was either dressed in blue and called 'Adam', or in pink and called 'Beth', when passed to some adult participants who were unaware of the purpose of the study. The adults were observed as they interacted with the infant, including their choice of toys (doll, train or 'gender-neutral' fish) that they handed to the baby. The results showed that the adults interacted differently with the baby depending on the colour of clothes and the name given ('Beth' was given the doll more often and received more smiles from the adults). Other Baby X studies vary in detail, such as the choice of toys, whether the baby was presented in person or via a video link, and the kinds of evaluation that adults had to make and so on, while retaining the same basic design. These studies reported similar patterns to that by Will et al. Both men and women were more likely to refer to the baby as 'big' and 'strong' when labelled as a boy versus 'small' and 'soft' when labelled as a girl (Rubin et al., 1974). They also encouraged the boy with more vigorous play and exploration, and treated the girl more gently and helped her more (Condry and Condry, 1976).

On the other hand, reviews of Baby X studies and similar research (Stern and Karraker, 1989; Golombok and Fivush, 1994; Maccoby, 2000; Golombok and Hines, 2002) noticed that some findings varied according to the kinds of measure used. Adults had less stereotypic responses if they were asked to evaluate the child's personality traits (e.g. how friendly or playful s/he was) compared with when they actually interacted with the child. This suggests that it is the adults' *behaviour* that bears out their existing gender stereotypes more, while their views (of the child) will be based more on the child's characteristics as they observed them.

Clearly, children do not only receive reinforcement through the behaviour and reactions of adults who hold gender-typed ideas. Even without such direct inputs, adults act as models of stereotyped behaviours which children observe and imitate. Studying children and their mothers, Fagot et al. (1992) reported that those with mothers who endorsed more traditional gender roles tended to gender-label objects earlier than those with mothers of more gender-egalitarian views. Reviewing a large body of work, it was noted that daily activity contexts (e.g. which parent does what at home) accounted for most of the variation in the modelling observed (Leaper, 2000). A recent study analysing parent–child (12-month-olds) interactions in Norway (Nordahl et al., 2014) has found noteworthy differences in mothers' and fathers' engagement. Fathers of boys showed more positive engagement than mothers of boys and fathers of girls, while mothers of both sexes were equally engaging. The researchers argue that child gender plays a greater role for fathers as they identify more with sons and perceive themselves as important role models to boys. On the other hand, mothers spend more time with their baby in the first year and have more experience and may be more organised and coherent with their emotional responses.

Therefore, the prior expectations and experiences of major adult role models can play a distinct role in how they interact with their young, who in turn may appropriate such behaviours. This is somewhat in line with a former meta-analysis (Lytton and Romney, 1991) that reported boys and girls to have similar experiences, if slightly more gender-stereotyped reinforcement by fathers (Lytton and Romney, 1991). This, in practice, is not really favouring social learning, as the majority of caregivers and educators are female. Theoretically speaking, if the strength of a child's gender identity was largely contingent on the rewards from, and his/her observations of, available adult models, then many children would have acquired a feminine identity. Moreover, whether through reinforcement or observation, what exactly is taken on board by the child, and how it gets 'translated' into gender-stereotyped behaviour, is far less clear-cut. Obviously, more forces are at work to foster gender development, and we will turn to these other agents next.

Peers as socialising agents

By middle childhood (by about age 5 and upwards), at least half of the child's waking hours will be spent in the social institution that is school, where most of the socialising agents are other children. All these agents bring with them their existing gender stereotypes as well as sharing such views (if sometimes also challenging those of each other), constructing and reproducing more. In fact, by 3 to 4 years of age, children already recognise the gender-appropriateness of play and activities, and criticise their peers for what they see as gender-inappropriate behaviour. The stereotypes that are re-created (such as 'daddies don't cook' and 'mummies don't drive cars') can in fact be even more rigid than those of adults (e.g. Fagot, 1977). As we saw earlier, both boys and girls like to play and associate more with those of their own sex. It is unsurprising that peers are such a dominant force in children's lives.

In a study that compared directly the behaviours of mothers, fathers and peers towards 3- to 5-year-olds' gender-appropriate and inappropriate play, Langlois and Downs (1980) found that peers had the strongest responses. Children were first instructed to play with highly gender-stereotyped toys for either boys or girls. Once the child was settled into play, the parent or peer was invited into the room to observe and interact with the child. Mothers displayed little differentiation in their responses towards their children, but fathers were rather more responsive towards gender-appropriateness; they were positive with their child in gender-appropriate play, but were more overtly hostile (making disparaging remarks or ridicule), particularly with sons, when they engaged in cross-gender play. Still, the peers' reactions towards gender-inappropriate play were the strongest of all, and also most negative when boys were playing with girls' toys.

Reviewing Baby X research, Stern and Karraker (1989) noted that, when children were asked to play with Baby X, they were more strongly influenced by information about the baby's alleged sex than were adults. The authors reason that, since children are themselves still learning about their own gender, they are prone to adopting more extreme attitudes. However, relatively recent reviews of other studies (e.g. Leman and Tenenbaum, 2014; Golombok and Hines, 2002; Owen Blakemore et al., 2009) have found few consistent differences in peer responses towards boys and girls, or towards gender-appropriate and inappropriate play or behaviour. Also similar to adult reinforcement and modelling, whether peers' responses translate later into more gender-stereotyped play and behaviour in children is difficult to study. Still, recent longitudinal research (Martin et al., 2013) found that the sex of school children's peers contributed the most to predict their friendships later, followed by activities (which are themselves gender-typed). So, it can be said that peers can both directly and indirectly influence children's gender development.

Researchers have also attempted to explore the real effects of agents by training adults or rewarding children to actively promote certain activities (such as cooperative play) and then measuring the children's behaviour at a later point. For example, Fagot (1985) found that girls were influenced by teachers and other girls, but not by boys, whereas boys were only influenced by other boys, and not by teachers or girls, preferring noisy rough-and-tumble play. This may be because cooperative activities involve 'feminine' behaviour (such as being quiet and sharing) to which girls are already more receptive than boys. In that case, children's 'selective' attention to different socialisation *content* (rather than socialising agents *per se*) should be studied. A recent study (Pahlke et al., 2014) has found that lessons fostering the ability to challenge sexism by teaching children aged 4–10 years to respond to undesirable/unfair bias (e.g. teasing about gender-role nonconformity) could lead to them being better able to identify sexism in the media and to respond to peers' sexist comments after a 6-month post-test period. This suggests that children are far from being passive vessels of gender and stereotyped information; they have the agency themselves also to either reproduce or resist stereotypes.

The media as a socialising agent

> **STOP AND THINK**
>
> When you next watch television with commercials, make notes of the behaviour and communication of the actors. How much of this can be called gender-stereotyped?

Since the beginning of the postwar years, the mass media, particularly televised media, have featured prominently in children's lives in industrialised countries. Children spend more time watching television and dealing in other digital media forms, particularly the internet, than they do interacting with their families and friends and even in school (Buckingham, 2003, 2013). Where the content of media is concerned, it is strongly stereotyped. Despite societal changes and political trends, in that adult broadcasters and actors of both sexes have become more equal in status, it is still the case that in series and commercials, even in children's programmes during primetime, many themes and roles are highly 'gendered', with some being more 'action-packed' or fantasy-based and others more sedentary or 'real-life', which might influence the viewing patterns of different children.

A study by Huston and colleagues has reported that, although the average time spent on watching television showed no sex differences, *what* boys and girls watched was very different from each other. Boys' interests were more uniform and 'action-oriented' and girls' were more diverse and 'people-oriented' (Huston et al., 1999). Later, Livingstone and Bovill (2001), in a large-scale European study, surveyed children's favourite shows between the ages of 6 and 16 years and found distinct developmental patterns of interests between boys and girls (Table 11.2). Both sexes were largely interested in cartoons until 9 or 10 years, when girls turned to soaps, and then this continued to 12–13 years before they turned to other series. In contrast, boys were equally likely to tune in to TV series or sports programmes at 12–13 years before sports became dominant from 15–16 years.

More recently, electronic media such as computer games and the internet have offered a highly attractive, or even addictive, source of entertainment (Larson, 2001). One study by Roberts and associates showed a consistent pattern where, between the ages of 8 and 18 years, boys spent three times as much time as girls did on video games (Roberts et al., 2004). This trend also held when comparing young adult male and female students (Li and Kirkup, 2007). If we consider the style and content or themes of popular video games (such as Super Mario, Call of Duty, and Football Manager 2010, all within the top 10 best-sellers on Amazon at time of writing), which are often masculine and action-oriented, these findings are perhaps not surprising. However, other games on the list include more feminine themes (such as Lego Harry Potter, Just Dance, and Dance on

Broadway), so the gaming industry may have become wise to the needs of girl players. A more recent survey of over 1200 students (Greenberg et al., 2010) reports that, while boys play more and have more motives (such as fantasy gratification) for play than girls do, their preference for physical games declines in late adolescence as motives start weakening from the middle years.

Since the 2000s, the focus has shifted towards children's and young people's use of the internet both as a source of information and, particularly more recently, as a space for online or 'virtual' social networking. There have been claims that online interactions and behaviour often reflect and reinforce gender norms (such as beauty ideals for girls or 'macho' personas for boys) that can shape young people's identity. Educational psychologist Catherine Steiner-Adair, in her studies with over 1000 children on the impact of technology (Steiner-Adair and Barker, 2013), found that it is clear that the internet has amplified the worst gender stereotypes that have been around, and she advocates teaching children to deconstruct those potentially harmful gender 'codes'. Indeed, in social media (such as Facebook) young men and women do tend to conform to social roles and norms consistent with their gender (Haferkamp et al., 2012).

The above findings are informative to the extent that they show children are selectively attending to media content that contains material appropriate for their own sex. Yet an obvious and critical issue remains about the nature of the relationship between viewing, game playing or internet use and gender identity. Earlier studies only established a tenuous relationship between the two (Durkin, 1985). It was observed that TV in the 1970s and 1980s portrayed women more negatively or in gender-stereotypic behaviour and rarely cast them in a starring role. It appears that, although some things have changed in terms of the newer gaming industry catering for girls, others have stayed the same in terms of the content of much of the televised media, particularly that for the teen market in terms of female under-representation (Gerding and Signorielli, 2014). It could be that already stereotyped children, just like their adult counterparts, simply prefer to engage with such material to find confirmation of their own views, and thus they are just responding to pre-existing preferences and tendencies (see the Cutting Edge box for how young people may interpret media information). However, because *selective* attention and modelling

Table 11.2 Favourite TV shows by age and gender: a European study.

Age	Boys	Girls
6–7 years	Cartoons	Cartoons
9–10 years	Cartoons	Soap operas
12–13 years	TV series, sports	Soap operas
15–16 years	Sports	TV series

Source: After Livingstone and Bovill (2001)

CUTTING EDGE

Teenagers constructing gender identity through media representations of romantic/sexual relationships and alcohol consumption

In a recently published paper in the *Sociology of Health and Illness*, a research team in Scotland (Hartley et al., 2014) report findings from 13- to 15-year-olds that explored how their relationships and drinking behaviour were shaped by the quest for appropriate gender identity. Contrary to most other social developmental studies, the researchers used a 'qualitative' non-statistical approach with relatively few (just over 80) participants. They engaged the students in group discussions and in-depth individual interviews that tapped into sensitive topics, including sexual behaviour, smoking, drinking and illegal drug use, and how such behaviours came to be interpreted by the participants and related to how they talked about their own behaviours.

On examining what forms of sexual/romantic behaviour and alcohol use are considered gender-appropriate, the students appeared to integrate media portrayals into their own notions of gender-appropriate behaviour. For instance, several students reported that the media directly influenced their relationship expectations, citing American sitcoms as sources of role models as well as portrayals of relationship – even though they were aware that such were unlike 'real life'. Also, while boys thought that girls learned 'perfect' unrealistic relationship expectations from TV or movies, girls suggested that boys derived their expectations from pornography. Although the media appeared to influence less their expectations of drinking, teenagers might drink to help them 'connect' with the opposite sex in ways which were shaped by what is gender-appropriate as learned from the media portrayals; they believed that certain kinds of drinking-related sexual behaviour

made them appear more or less feminine or masculine (e.g. boys being drunk related to promiscuous sex and physical aggression).

In sum, the processes of media influence seem to operate primarily through teenagers' presumptions about how their peers are influenced. Drawing on media content, they attempt to understand the roles and rules of relationships, and how one should behave, seemingly with the aim to belong and be accepted, by second-guessing their opposite-sex counterparts.

- **Why do you think that the researchers focused on sexual/romantic relationships and drinking to engage the teenagers in their study?**
- **What may be the reason that the teenagers believed that others (particularly the opposite sex) are more strongly affected by the media?**

As we read in the first part of this chapter on self-concepts, individuals become aware of their objective self, particularly in relation to common social categories such as gender as their social identity, through their relationships with others; Cooley's 'looking-glass self' suggests that people must consider themselves through the eyes of others. Moreover, the authors argue that, specific to their stage of development from childhood into adulthood, teenagers shift from largely single-sex to mixed-sex interactions (see the next chapter for details) and are increasingly required to negotiate their identities with a different peer group (i.e. the opposite sex). Finally, in the West, two of the most prevalent ways in which teenagers construct their identities in transition into adulthood (like rites of passage) are through the practices of drinking and engaging in sexual relationships. The authors further expected that these may demonstrate particular femininities and masculinities in particular social settings and interactions (as they indeed found from their data).

are happening, children should have some *cognition* (or awareness) of their own gender to guide them regarding *which* behaviour to take on board, and it is some of these processes that we will explore in the next approach.

Cognitive theories of gender identity

We have just considered the possibility that, in order for children to acquire a sense of gender identity, they ought to have some knowledge or awareness (cognition) of their own gender to steer them towards those agents of their own group. Indeed, the pioneer of the earliest cognitive theory of gender identity, Lawrence Kohlberg (1966), previously argued that 'our approach to the problems of sexual development starts directly with neither biology nor culture, but with cognition' (p. 82).

Drawing mainly on Piaget's school of thought (see Chapter 2, 'Theoretical perspectives'), Kohlberg (1966, 1969) saw gender identity development, like other cognitive development, as a constructive process; an active child is guided by reason or logic when dealing with gender-role knowledge. But where does this knowledge come from? 'How much' knowledge is needed for developing our sense of gender identity? According to Kohlberg, gender-role knowledge comes from children's encounters with the world around them – a process that he calls 'self-socialisation' (Maccoby and Jacklin, 1974). As for how much knowledge, we can find certain suggestions in Kohlberg's (1969) own cognitive-developmental theory. Interestingly, Kohlberg's theory also linked a child's cognitive capacity to his/her capacity for moral reasoning. These ideas and their role in managing behaviour in schools are explored in Chapter 15, 'Understanding bullying'.

Cognitive-developmental theory

Matching closely with Piaget's (1953) stage-based theory of intellectual development, Kohlberg expounded that the self-socialisation of gender identity develops gradually through three stages from early through middle childhood. In fact, the key milestones of the stages are concepts that we have earlier covered as gender labelling, stability and constancy, with each stage featured by a key (or rather, a lack of) cognitive skill (see Table 11.3). For example, in stage 2, the lack of conservation skills means that children are prone to being confused by physical transformation (as illustrated by the counter and liquid experiments in Chapter 3), including the transformation for testing gender constancy.

Unlike either the biological accounts or social learning theories, which see that the child's gender development is determined by her genes or the impact of socialising agents, this theory hinges on the assumption that the child's own role in seeking gender-role information is driven by her gender awareness and cognitive skills. Stage 3 skills are pivotal in Kohlberg's model because this is when the child is equipped with the fullest essential knowledge about her own gender group, that it is a differentiating, permanent and immutable part of her identity (gender labelling, stability and constancy all achieved).

> **Definition**
>
> Cognitive-developmental theory: a theory, derived by Kohlberg, that explains gender identity development by the child's developing cognitive skills in three stages, which underpin critical milestones in understanding about gender as gender labelling, gender stability and gender constancy.

Table 11.3 Stages in Kohlberg's (1969) cognitive-developmental theory.

Stage/age	Gender feature	Cognitive feature
Stage 1	Gender labelling	
2½–3½ years	Slow recognition of gender labels	Egocentrism
	Treat labels as personal terms	
Stage 2	Gender stability	
3½–4½ years	Gradually aware of gender durability	Poor conservation skills
	Dependent on physical cues	
Stage 3	Gender constancy	
4½–7 years	Understand gender is constant across time and contexts	Conservation skills achieved

Evidence supporting Kohlberg's theory has therefore come mainly from research that has identified a close relationship between the achievement of gender constancy and children's gender-appropriate or stereotyped behaviour or attitudes. For instance, Slaby and Frey (1975) examined pre-school children's level of gender constancy and attention towards same-gender models. They found that boys with a higher level of performance on gender constancy would pay more attention to male models than female ones, compared with those with a lower level of constancy. Similarly, Ruble et al. (1981) investigated the relationship between gender constancy and effects of commercials featuring gender-stereotyped toys. They found that gender constancy predicted children's responsiveness to the commercials, such that those who achieved constancy were more likely to play with the toys and judge that they were appropriate for their own gender compared with those who were not gender-constant.

Although such studies make a strong case for the importance of gender constancy, later research (e.g. Fagot, 1985; Carter and Levy, 1988) shows that, although gender constancy *helps* children to seek gender-appropriate information, it is not always *needed*. Indeed, as we reviewed earlier, gender-stereotyped tendencies (such as same-sex peer preference) are clearly apparent in pre-school – well before gender constancy is expected. Perhaps a lesser understanding of gender is already adequate. The next cognitive approach is one that takes this critical point into account.

Gender schema theories

Gender schema theorists do not dispute Kohlberg's point regarding the child's active role, but this relatively recent approach differs from his theory in its 'key' to explaining gender identity and stereotyping: simply, the knowledge of gender labels instead of acquiring gender constancy. Going by schema theorists (Bem, 1981; Martin and Halverson, 1981, 1983, 1987), once children can label social (gender) groups and crucially know to which group they belong (a boy or a girl), they

are readily motivated to search the social environment for information about behaviours or values consistent with that group (to be like others in it) which build up or enrich their *schema*. A schema is a system of beliefs (including stereotypes) about attributes associated with social groups. They provide a set of cognitive structures that help the child to form evaluations of and make assumptions about each other, objects and situations based on social group membership.

Accordingly, simply knowing one's own and others' gender (gender labelling) alone is sufficient to construct and develop gender schemas, and further development of gender identity and stereotypes builds on this knowledge base. However, it is important to bear in mind that in the beginning, the young child's schemas are very basic, based on a simple 'ingroup/outgroup' dichotomy and the most typical characteristics of each sex. Then the child learns more about the ingroup, including gradually a grasp of deeper, less superficial characteristics, which help build up part of his self-concept (a more coherent sophisticated sense of self as we read earlier) before he then begins to pay attention to the outgroup (see Martin and Halverson, 1981, 1987).

To demonstrate the workings of the schemas, an example using toy choice is used here (see Figure 11.4). The child perceiver might first identify a toy as gender-appropriate (or inappropriate) on his own liking of a new toy. Then, with the key knowledge of his own gender, the child will attend to it/prefer it more if it is deemed appropriate to the ingroup, or in the case of a new object predict that others of the *ingroup* will like it (if he does himself). The first mapping shows that, for a common, stereotyped toy like a car, the child knows that this item is designed 'for boys', hence the awareness of his own gender group leads him to decide that playing with this object is 'for him' (Martin and Halverson, 1981). A similar cognitive operation that depends on the child's awareness of his own gender may apply to thinking about a new, non-stereotyped toy (in the second mapping). Clearly, the child's own liking of any new toy will depend on how attractive it is to him. Yet if he has to 'guess' if *other* children may like it (an inference-making process), he may base his predictions on his own liking *in combination with the gender group membership* of himself in relation to those about whom he is making the predictions. Here, if the perceiver is a boy and he likes the toy, he may infer that, since he likes it, other boys should like it as much as he does (and girls less so) – even though the toy itself remains novel and non-stereotyped (as was found by Martin et al. (1995) with children as young as 4 years of age for a range of attractive and

---

Definition

Gender schema: a system of beliefs about the attributes and behaviours associated with gender that help the child to form evaluations of, and to make assumptions about, each other and social objects and situations based on gender group memberships.

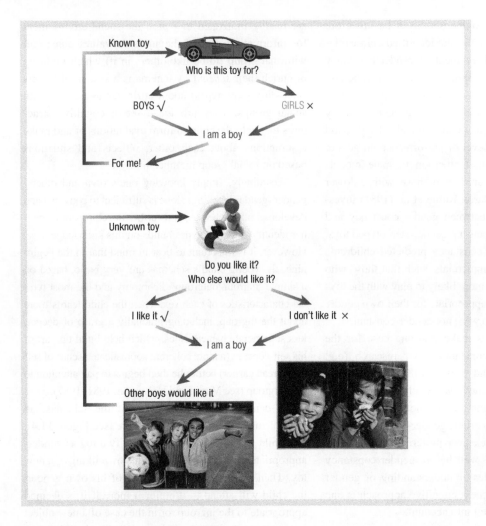

Known toy

Who is this toy for?

BOYS √   GIRLS ×

I am a boy

For me!

Unknown toy

Do you like it?
Who else would like it?

I like it √   I don't like it ×

I am a boy

Other boys would like it

Figure 11.4 The workings of gender schemas for known and novel toys.

Sources: (a) Martin and Halverson (1987); (b) Martin et al. (1995)

non-attractive novel toy objects). The child is said to be generalising his own attributes *selectively* to others of his gender ingroup, effectively generating new stereotypes for an otherwise gender-neutral object.

In the original study, children were asked how much they liked the toys and how much other 'boys' and 'girls' would like them. One may argue that, perhaps by articulating the gender group labels, children might have been 'primed' to think along gender divisions. However, later research (Lam and Leman, 2003) found that the 'gendercentric' thinking pattern still held when only photographs of boys and girls were shown (without articulating the terms). In fact, not only was such inference making applied to toys (which are of obvious interest to children anyway, or as a genre of social 'objects' toys are more susceptible to being assigned new stereotypes since many toys are advertised as 'for boys' or 'for girls'); but also the pattern has been found to apply to inference making about some foods (Lam and Leman, 2009).

Gender schemas influence things from gender-segregated play and playmate preference (e.g. Fagot, 1985; Martin et al., 1999; Leman and Lam, 2008) and recall of stereotypic information (e.g. Ruble and Stangor, 1986; Carter and Levy, 1988; Liben and Signorella, 1993), to preferred occupation and adult family preferences (Signorella and Hanson Frieze, 2008). The general trend is that children process faster, remember better and prefer material that is consistent with gender schemas (beliefs about what is gender-appropriate, such as stories or descriptions about boys and girls that are stereotypical in character or behaviour) and are less efficient or willing to deal with inconsistent information, or may even distort the material (e.g. 'misremembering' or fabricating book content, for instance; Frawley, 2008). Moreover, children perform better at tasks labelled as being 'for' their gender ingroup (Davies, 1986). This has considerable practical implications in such areas as education, as children not only actively organise their thinking and behaviour around what is expected of their gender ingroup, but also are more motivated to do well in a newly stereotyped task (simply because it is said to be 'for' their own sex).

A key strength of the schematic approach to gender identity is that it can account for the rigidity with which longstanding gender stereotypes are upheld by children. This is because the theories denote that once children are aware of their own gender group membership and start to build their gender schemas, they will already attend to and take on board more information that confirms stereotypic beliefs (and attune less to what deviates from them). This, in turn, enriches the schema further, and the child becomes even more stereotyped. This way, the child would be already attentive to the gender-appropriateness *already learned* about those attributes that are displayed or behaviours performed by a socialising agent, rather than the sex of the agent *per se* – which is where the social learning approach fell short in explaining. These tenets fit particularly well with the basic assumption of a cognitive approach that projects the child as an 'active' participant in constructing her own gender knowledge structures (the schemas). Furthermore, this construction will be increasingly susceptible to stereotypes in the environment, and this will in turn shape the child's behaviours and values, and inform their future decisions.

Despite the merits mentioned, there are at least several key limitations with this popular approach to accounting for the development of gender identity. The first concerns the cognitive school of theories in general. Even though it is empowering to conceptualise the child as active in formatting his/her own gender identity, the idea of 'self-socialisation' is at best vague. Even information such as 'cars are for boys' is taken for granted as just a common gender stereotype in the social environment to be 'picked up' by children. This leaves a 'black box' of unknowns like *how* children pick up this kind of information; the approach concentrates on what happens at the processing level, having assumed that the child already holds this information. Therefore we know relatively little about *what* the child's schemas actually contain (what beliefs or ideas), even though we know quite well *how* schemas are supposed to 'work' (as illustrated earlier).

However, it is well established (see Chapter 3) that cognitive development occurs within, and depends on, the social context of the child and his/her co-participants (cf. Vygotsky, 1978b), which is particularly important for developing social identities including gender identity

Gender-inappropriate play? Going by the schematic approach, the knowledge of gender stereotypes should mean that this girl would avoid the type of stereotypic toys she is enjoying.

Source: Lam

(Lloyd and Duveen, 1992). Furthermore, if general cognitive skills (such as labelling and conservation, which do not differ between boys and girls) determine gender-typed thinking and behaviour, we would expect similar stereotyping tendencies in boys and girls. However, this is not the case; as we saw earlier, boys and men tend to be more stereotypic than girls and boys, perhaps as a result of the father–son interaction from early in life. A recent study also shows that, when children were afforded the chance to predict the sex of gender-ambiguous characters (in drawings) in their own words (rather than using closed-ended dichotomised descriptions), they explained the reasons for their gender assignments in more unconventional than stereotypic terms, particularly in the case of younger, pre-school children (Tenenbaum et al., 2010). Perhaps to truly understand how children play an 'active' role in constructing gender identity, procedures such as this that give them their own 'voice' in research should be sought more.

Finally, with advances in technology including infant eye tracking since the 2000s, the research poses challenges for the basic premise of the approach. By 18 months, infants already attend more to gender-appropriate but novel toys (Campbell et al., 2000). Although we should exercise caution when interpreting observational data of pre-verbal infants, it is intriguing that infants who cannot reliably identify each other by gender can 'assign' gender to novel objects. Unless stereotypic toys possess properties 'intrinsically' appealing to boys and girls (such as in their textures), other (cognitive or non-cognitive) factors ought to be considered.

A combined approach: social cognitive theory

Mindful of the shortcomings of social learning and cognitive approaches, as reviewed above, Kay Bussey and Albert Bandura (1999, 2004) proposed a combined social cognitive theory of gender development that was an attempt to offer a more comprehensive account of children's gender identity development. Social cognitive theory describes a three-factor model of personal factors, environmental factors and behavioural patterns influencing gender development. Bussey and Bandura argue that we learn about gender through three routes: tuition, enactive experience and modelling. Gender *tuition* occurs when, for instance, a mother teaches her daughter how to bottle-feed a baby or when a father teaches his son the rules of football or the different types of car on the road.

Enactive experience describes the reaction of others to the child's behaviours, which facilitates gender development by reinforcing stereotyped behaviours and disapproving of or sanctioning non-stereotyped behaviours. Most commonly experienced, Bussey and Bandura argue, is *gender modelling*, where children learn about gender-stereotyped behaviours simply through observing other people.

As with the social learning approach that describes the development of aggression in young children, the social cognitive theory of gender development describes four factors influencing the learning potential of observed behaviour. Bussey and Bandura argue that observation of behaviour alone is not enough for the child to model it. In order for observations to have an effect on learning, four key cognitive processes must be activated: attention, memory, production and motivation. Therefore, children must first notice that the information is related to gender and be able to process and store this information in memory (see Chapter 6, 'Memory and intelligence'). Afterwards, the child must practise (produce) the behaviour they have learned and be rewarded for it (motivation). With all four processes successfully in place, an example of say, a girl's observation of her aunt making the tea while her uncle watches football with her brother will become a gender learning experience, which can be reinforced when she offers to help her aunt or when her uncle suggests that she help out so that he and her brother can catch up on a game.

Social cognitive theory is a complex model describing gender development in children that provides a framework for understanding the complicated interactive nature of personal and environmental factors and biological patterns of behaviours. According to the theory, children monitor their behaviour and their emotional reaction to that behaviour – does the girl matching her behaviour to her aunt's feel any sense of pride or shame in helping to make the tea while her brother watches the football? If the girl feels a sense of pride, she will add this experience to her developing sense of self-efficacy in attaining this gender-desirable role. This self-efficacy will then be reinforced and developed through further exposure to

Definition

Self-efficacy: a person's belief about how effectively he or she can control herself, her thoughts or behaviours, particularly when intended to fulfil a personal goal.

situations where she can practise (making the tea), through social modelling (seeing her mother and friends making the tea) and through social persuasion (seeing other fathers persuading women to make the tea whilst they watch sport on TV).

Gender identity development: synthesis and transaction

From what we have read of the major theoretical approaches, none alone can give a complete explanation for the complex and multidimensional 'jigsaw' that is the development of gender identity. It seems that there are biological forces in place that are irrepressible, where we simply cannot change some of the instincts and tendencies based on such forces. At the same time, it is clear that, from day one, the social forces are already at work. These operate through the way in which the child's life is structured by those closest to them. Their responses to, and expectations of, the child based on his or her gender can be both overtly and covertly conveyed, while at the same time the socialising agents themselves provide ready examples of gender-appropriate

behaviour. Meanwhile, the child is not a passive recipient 'imbued' by the action of their genes or people around them. Children actively seek and make sense of information about the gender groups available in their social environment and, from there, build and refine a complex system of thinking that will guide their further discovery. This is helped by the understanding of crucial concepts, such as the knowledge of which group they belong to. Clearly, none of these processes works in isolation. Figure 11.5 offers a model of 'transaction' between the factors and processes inherent in the child and those found in the environment with which the child interacts.

Transaction here refers to the continual interactions between forces derived from the child's own characteristics (be they the inborn biological sex or later self-concept constructed by the child) and the environment in which he or she is placed (which contains socialising agents). One crucial point is that each stage of development itself will lead on to spiralling interactions. Following the diagram, this is not so much because of the physical differences between the sexes from birth (which do influence some behavioural tendencies), but because of the psychological attributions made by socialising agents in the child's immediate environment, based on seeing such physical cues. Such attributions influence the way adults and peers behave towards the child, who is also actively making sense of their behaviour, to build up an early sense of self. The child, however, will continue to seek more information about gender groups and may find confirmation for the gender-relevant attributes from

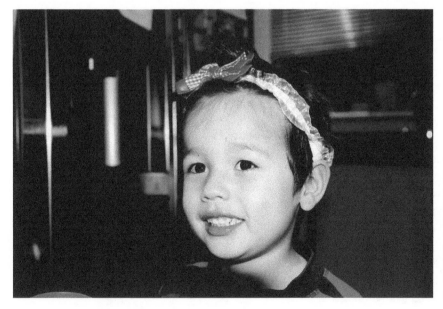

Figure 11.5 Gender-inappropriate play? Going by the schematic approach, the knowledge of stereotypes would mean that this boy would avoid the kind of stereotypic play or cross-dressing that he seems to be enjoying.

Source: Lam

the environment through the agents again. These inputs can then lead the child to differentiate further between the sexes in terms of these attributes.

Although it is in itself logical and plausible, the validity of transaction models such as this is difficult to test empirically, since it involves several interactions all happening at the same time. It is also difficult to apply the model to explain gender identity on an individual basis, especially in cases where a child has an 'atypical' identity. The Case Study box features one such case. What could possibly explain this kind of phenomenon?

It is noteworthy that, unlike the twins earlier, here is a case that concerns a boy who was born with the usual sets of male chromosomes, hormones and genitalia. It is then difficult to use biological explanations, unless there are unknown biological forces at work. The author raises the questions of how much hormones 'shape the brain' to be male or female and whether this development can be 'interrupted'. This opens up the possibilities of other kinds of input on gender identity. The parents apparently do not see the boy's gender identity as a 'problem' and

lead a 'normal' life. Can this be seen as their 'condoning' gender-inappropriate behaviour, contrary to what we read earlier about social learning theories, where adults actively reinforce gender-appropriateness? However, since we read that their son's feminine tendencies started by the age of 2, should the parents have intervened by actively 'shaping' him into a boy and referring him to professionals earlier? There are no simple answers to such questions, or indeed a 'right' solution to such cases, but what they do highlight, as the author argues, is the complex of biopsychological processes that form our gender development.

Summing up: gender identity development

Undoubtedly, gender provides one of the most, if not the most, pervasive systems of classification in societies, and one that permeates most aspects of adults' and children's lives. Since infancy, children already recognise the basic male–female distinctions, and from

CASE STUDY

Gender identity disorder (abridged from original article)

Mistakes in God's Factory

In 2005 a 12-year-old German boy became the world's youngest person to start hormone treatments for a sex change.

Kim P. is 14 years old. She's had enough of psychiatrists who ask weird questions. She's had enough of doctors who reject her case because this fashion-conscious girl – previously called 'Tim' in her patient file – unsettles them.

She was born as a boy. Her body, chromosomes and hormones were all undoubtedly masculine. But she felt otherwise. For Kim it was clear from the beginning that, as she says, 'I wound up in the wrong body.'

At the age of 2, Tim tried on his older sister's clothes, played with Barbies and said, 'I'm a girl.' Her parents thought it was a phase, but at the age of 4 Tim was still bawling after every haircut. At last he ran into his room with a pair of scissors and hollered that he wanted to

'cut off my thing!' and it was clear to his parents that the problem was serious. From then on, at home, Tim went by the name 'Kim'. By age 8 there was nothing boyish about her. She played typical girl games with other girls, went to their birthday parties and even dressed up for the ballet. Her teachers praised her exemplary social skills. When she was teased in the schoolyard and called names like 'tranny' or 'queer', she walked away.

'We always saw Kim as a girl, but not as a problem,' says the father. 'In fact, our life was surprisingly normal.' Normal until Kim was 12, and experienced the first signs of puberty. She was overcome by panic when her voice began to drop. She had no interest in becoming one of those brawny creatures with gigantic hands and deep voices who dressed like women but looked unfeminine. Only hormones could prevent Kim from turning into Tim again, and time was of the essence.

'Hormone treatment! Gender adjustment! How could you possibly do this to the child?' the family's paediatrician barked at the father – in Kim's presence.

Then came the sessions at the state psychiatric hospital, where Kim would sit in green rooms with high ceilings, playing with experimental blocks, while her parents answered endless questionnaires.

Kim's is a classic case, according to Bernd Meyenburg. Gender identity disorders are not rare among children, and they often appear as soon as a child starts to speak. The problem goes away in about a quarter of these children. In about 2 to 10% of the cases, though, early gender identity disorders lead to transsexualism.

'From a purely medical standpoint we are dealing with the mutilation of a biologically healthy body,' says Meyenburg. But in Kim's case, says Meyenburg, 'it would have been a crime to let her grow up as a man. There are very few people in whom it's so obvious.'

Meyenburg has been studying transsexuality since the 1970s. In those days, orthodox psychiatry believed that adverse social circumstances – namely the parents – were to blame when someone felt out of place in his or her biological gender.

Even Meyenburg was long convinced that severe emotional trauma in childhood caused transsexualism. 'On the other hand,' he says, 'depression isn't exactly rare in mothers. Wouldn't that mean there should be far more transsexuals?' Meyenburg points out another inconsistency: 'There are cases in which you could poke around in the parents' relationship as long as you wish and still find nothing.'

Gender development in human beings is a complex of bio-psychological processes, and when something goes wrong, not everyone understands. The medical community in particular tends to impose order. Developmental psychologists long believed that children were born emotionally neutral, and that a person's perceived gender affiliation was the result of social influence. Experts still think a lot of gender-specific behaviour is learned, but they also believe some of it is pre-wired in the womb. The extent to which androgen or oestrogen shapes the brain to be male or female is debatable; the age at which gender identity is established is unknown. Whether the development of an identity can be interrupted during early childhood isn't clear.

'Nowadays we believe that it's both,' says Meyenburg – 'environment and biology.'

'From an emotional standpoint, Kim comes across as a healthy, happy and balanced child,' Meyenburg wrote in his report. She had never behaved like a boy, not even for a short period of time. 'There is no doubt that her wish is irreversible, because it has been evident since very early childhood.'

In the past, Meyenburg was strictly opposed to hormone treatment before a child came of age. He began to question the wisdom of his own rules when one of his patients resisted his advice and ordered hormones over the internet. She went abroad at 17 and had a sex change operation for a few thousand euros. Meyenburg was angry at the time. Today this woman, a law student, is one of his happiest patients.

Now Meyenburg allows his young patients to enter hormone treatment early, before puberty complicates a sex change. 'They simply suffer less,' he says.

Kim is already much closer to realising her dream. The first letter of her name has been changed in her record, and her school now treats her as a girl. Thanks to the hormones, her breasts are developing, like those of other girls in her class. She's allowed to use the girls' locker room during gym class.

One thing hasn't completely changed for Kim, though – heckling in the schoolyard. But now her best friend sticks up for her. Kim says she feels good about herself in spite of the taunts. 'My girlfriends see me as a completely normal person,' she says.

'It's out of the question for me,' says Kim, who still wants to get rid of the parts of her body that remind her that she was born as Tim. By law, in Germany, she'll have to wait until she's 18 to take the next step. Meanwhile, she resorts to wearing tight pants.

'I just happen to be a girl,' says Kim. She keeps a piggybank in her bedroom filled with change she has been saving for the operation – since the age of 5. Once it's over, her new life will start. 'In Paris,' she says, 'where no one knows me.'

Source: Spiegel online magazine, 26 January 2007 (translated from the German)

- **What do you think is the explanation for Kim's gender identity?**
- **Do you agree with Bernd Meyenburg's assessment and decision to conduct hormone treatment (and later a sex change) on Kim?**
- **Do you think Kim will ever think of himself as a boy?**

there, a more sophisticated understanding about gender group memberships develops. Gender identity is a multidimensional construct in that it encompasses all of the cognitive, affective and behavioural components, and none of the purely biologically, socially or cognitively oriented approaches alone can explain this spectrum of developments. An inclusive approach in the form of transactions between the innate, individual and environmental elements offers the most reasonable account. It is, however, difficult to obtain empirical evidence for the simultaneous transactions, and many atypical cases of gender identity development remain unresolved.

SUMMARY

This chapter has covered the development of children's self-concept and, related to this, their gender identity. First, we saw that self-concept develops by degrees, from an infant's rudimentary awareness of their own existence as separate from that of others, to a more evaluative and reflective sense of the self as the child recognises how they may be perceived by others. Accordingly, through the ages, children's self-descriptions develop from ones about the more physical, observable and measurable features to ones derived from interpersonal relationships and inner qualities. Notably, this gradual development is likely to be influenced by the social interactions in which the child engages with those around them. Over time, their perceptions and evaluations become increasingly consistent with what is expected by others.

The chapter then looked at the part of a child's self-concept that is derived from gender group membership. We saw that, by the second year in life, infants respond differently to male and female stimuli and, soon after, they learn the gender labels to identify others and themselves, although this is based on superficial features – even when children learn that gender is a permanent part of the self. It is not until children grasp that gender remains constant despite outward changes in middle childhood that they have a fuller understanding of their membership. Still, gender encompasses other aspects, particularly the knowledge of stereotypes and gender-appropriate behaviour.

Three major theoretical approaches were put forward to explain the development of gender identity. The biological accounts propose that the different role, status and behavioural patterns between the sexes originate from biological differences evolved over time as humans adapted to environmental demands. In contrast, social learning theorists argue that children acquire gendered behaviour and values by modelling on and reinforcement by parents, peers and the media. Cognitive theories concentrate on the child's role in seeking and processing gender material from the environment and, in doing so, constructing their own gender identity. Each approach has its merits and empirical support; especially strong are the medical cases for the biological accounts, experiments showing different responses by adults or peers to the same child labelled differently or gender-appropriate and inappropriate behaviour for social learning, and studies showing the effects of schemas on gendered behaviour and recall for schema theories. Each approach also has its drawbacks, such as the narrow list of behaviours explained by biological factors, the issue of selective attention or modelling for social learning theories, and newer research into pre-labelling infants' differential responses to stereotyped toys. A transaction model was suggested which integrates the approaches, though the assessment of its validity requires further extensive research.

It is indeed the case that there are still plenty of 'unknowns' to be discovered about children's development of self-concept and gender identity. Questions remain, such as what in the social environment is 'most' significant in facilitating the development of self-concepts and gender identities – parents, peers, school or the media? What makes male–female distinctions so 'intrinsically' salient to begin with? How do we integrate the different biological, environmental and individual-child factors and cognitive processes to explain cases of atypical gender identity development? A great deal of work has discovered much of the crucial foundational knowledge and explicated the workings of each branch of factors and processes. The direction for future ventures in the area is to find out how these branches operate in conjunction with each other.

REVIEW QUESTIONS

1. What are the major milestones towards the child's establishment of a self-concept? What abilities does each of them require and reflect?
2. 'A child's gender identity is neither biologically determined, acquired through their social environment nor constructed by the child him or herself.' Evaluate the validity of this statement.
3. How important is self-esteem to our overall self-concept and what may influence its development?
4. What are the key factors that determine a child's sense of gender identity? Are some stronger than others?
5. Compare and contrast two major theoretical approaches that have been used to explain the development of gender identity.

RECOMMENDED READING

To understand the development of the looking-glass self, read:

Tice, D. M., & Wallace, H. M. (2005). The reflected self: Creating yourself as (you think) others see you. In M. R. Leary & J. P. Tangney (Eds.), *Handbook of Self and Identity* (91–105). New York: Guilford Press.

To understand more on the development of self throughout childhood and adolescence, read:

Harten, S. (2005). The development of self-representations during childhood and adolescence. In M. R. Leary & J. P. Tangney (Eds.), *Handbook of Self and Identity* (610–642). New York: Guilford Press.

For an in-depth discussion on self and identity development:

Fischer, K. W., & Harter, S. (2001). *The Construction of the Self: A Developmental Perspective*. New York: Guildford Press.

For a classic article covering a range of issues on gender development:

Maccoby, E. E. (2000). Perspectives on gender development. *International Journal of Behavioral Development*, 24, 398–406.

For an extensive nature–nurture debate on gender development:

Lipp, R. A. (2005). *Gender, Nature, and Nurture* (2nd Ed.). Mahwah, NJ: Lawrence Erlbaum Associates.

For more extensive, integrated reviews of research on gender development:

Leman, P. H., & Tenenbaum, H. R. (Eds.) (2014). *Gender and Development*. New York: Psychology Press.

Owen Blakemore, J. E. O., Berenbaum, S. A., & Liben, L. S. (Eds.) (2009). *Gender Development*. Hove: Psychology Press.

RECOMMENDED WEBSITES

The Max Planck Institute for Human Development has a number of research centres devoted to understanding our development of the self and self-concept:
http://www.mpib-berlin.mpg.de/index.en.htm

The SELF Research Centre (the Self-concept Enhancement and Learning Facilitation Group) based at Oxford University encompasses 450 members from 45 countries across six continents and a network of satellite centres producing research on enhancing positive self-concept:
http://www.self.ox.ac.uk/index.htm

For further information on issues relating to gender identity and research:
http://www.gires.org.uk

For media coverage of the Reimer case, the twin who was born a boy and raised as a girl, see these BBC sites:

http://www.bbc.co.uk/sn/tvradio/programmes/horizon/dr_money_prog_summary.shtml
http://www.bbc.co.uk/news/health-11814300

For current issues related to gender and development, particularly practical and global issues such as inequalities, *Gender and Development* is the only journal dedicated to this focus:

http://www.genderanddevelopment.org

CHAPTER 15

Social cognition and attitudes

Michael A. Hogg, Dominic Abrams and G. Neil Martin

Explore the accompanying experiments, videos, simulations and animations on **MyPsychLab**. This chapter includes activities on:

- Impression formation
- The actor-observer effect
- Unconscious stereotyping
- Cognitive dissonance
- Check your understanding and prepare for your exams using the multiple choice, short answer and essay practice tests also available.

WHAT WORKS BETTER: KEEP OFF THE GRASS OR SAVE THE PLANET?

Applying theories from social psychology to environmental problems, researchers at Arizona State University tested the power of social norms in influencing behaviour. Robert Cialdini, Ph.D., and two graduate students worked with a local hotel on a programme to encourage lodgers to reuse wet towels. The researchers randomly assigned cards with one of five different messages to 260 guest rooms, each with one of the following messages:

'Help the hotel save energy'

'Help save the environment'

'Partner with us to help save the environment'

'Help save resources for future generations'

'Join your fellow citizens in helping to save the environment'

The last message, which described a social norm, was the most successful . . . Next best were the messages urging environmental protection and the benefit to future generations . . . Least successful: The message emphasising the benefit to the hotel. Only one in five guests with that card reused their towels.

Source: http://www.apa.org/research/action/shaping.aspx.

WHAT YOU SHOULD BE ABLE TO DO AFTER READING CHAPTER 15

- Define social psychology and understand what social psychologists do.
- Understand how we process, store and use information about ourselves and other people.
- Understand the motives that influence how we form a conception of who we are.
- Understand how self-concept influences our perceptions and treatment of other people.
- Understand how we make inferences, especially causal inferences, about others' behaviour, and also about our own behaviour.
- Understand how attitudes are formed and changed

QUESTIONS TO THINK ABOUT

- Are the problems facing social psychology different from those in other branches of psychology?
- What makes social psychology similar to sociology, and what makes it similar to neuroscience?
- Does it matter where and when social psychology research is conducted?
- How quickly can you form a mental image of another person? What does the image contain? Is it purely visual, or does it capture something about their personality, group membership, or other 'social' information? How are such impressions formed?
- What determines whom you like and dislike? Why do you sometimes change your mind about a person?
- Why do you use stereotypes and is it possible to avoid them?
- Who would you trust to make an accurate judgement about your future prospects: a teacher, parent or yourself? What might influence the judgement made by each of these people?
- Try to persuade someone using a line of argument with which you personally disagree. Is persuasion simply a matter of using the right technique or are there other reasons why this is a difficult task? What tactics do you use, and why?

Social psychology

Most human activity is social. We spend most of our waking hours interacting with, thinking about, or being directly or indirectly influenced by other people. Our behaviour affects the way others think, feel and act and, in turn, their behaviour affects our thoughts, feelings and actions. Not for nothing is the great American social psychologist Elliot Aronson's best-selling book on social psychology called *The Social Animal* (latest edition published in 2011). Human interaction also structures the norms, conventions and institutions that make up the societies we live in.

The field of psychology that studies social behaviour is called social psychology. According to Gordon Allport (1968, p. 3), social psychology is the study of 'how the thoughts, feelings, and behaviour of individuals are influenced by the actual, imagined, or implied presence of others'. In the next two chapters we explore the way in which people, as individuals or in groups, affect one another. We examine the complex interplay of basic cognitive processes and cognitive structures that we use to process and store information, and the nature of human relations and interactions that occur in everyday life. In this chapter we focus on social cognition and attitudes – how people process and store social information, and how social information affects social behaviour. In Chapter 16 we focus on social interaction between individuals, between groups, and among people within groups.

Doing social psychology

To a large extent we are all social psychologists but rather than being empirical scientists, we are more like intuitive social psychologists (Heider, 1958). To get by in life we need to have a well-developed understanding of why people behave as they do, what causes particular behaviours, and what effect our behaviour has on others. These common-sense understandings are often quite accurate, but sometimes they are not. For example, we 'know' that 'birds of a feather flock together' (similarity leads to attraction), but we also 'know' that 'opposites attract'. So, which is correct? Many of us may also think that friendship between people from different racial groups should reduce prejudice – but does it? How can we be sure? Under what circumstances is someone most likely to help someone in distress? To get someone to do you a favour, should you first make a modest request that they will agree to and then scale it up to the real request, or should you first make an outrageously large request that nobody in their right mind would agree to and then scale it down?

To answer these questions, social psychologists use a wide range of scientific methods including laboratory experiments, field experiments, surveys, observation of naturally occurring behaviour, and the analysis of what people say and write. Controlled laboratory experiments predominate because they are so well suited to establishing the causes of behaviour. However, some research questions are difficult to address in the laboratory. For example, it would be difficult to study a riot or an established street gang in the laboratory. Can you think of any other experiment which you would think would be impossible to set up (you'll be surprised at some of the experiments psychologists have conducted . . .)? Social psychologists can be quite tenacious and inventive. One early researcher tried to instigate a riot in the laboratory by wafting smoke under the locked door of the laboratory – some groups of participants kicked the door open and disengaged the smoke generator, and other groups calmly discussed the possibility that they were being observed (French, 1944).

Social psychologists develop formal theories about human behaviour that, unlike common-sense theories, are carefully grounded in data from systematic and well-controlled research. These theories sometimes confirm common-sense knowledge, but sometimes they do not, and many theories are concerned with how people develop and use this common-sense social psychological knowledge in the first place.

Social cognition and social knowledge

At the heart of social behaviour is a our ability to make sense of a social situation in order to know what to expect and what to do. We often have ready-made explanations and interpretations of people and situations – explanations that are readily accessible in the society in which we live. In this way, people's social interpretations can vary from culture to culture, group to group, and across time. For example, Moscovici (1976) explored how Freudian concepts, such as unconscious motives, Oedipus complex, displacement and so forth, have become widely accepted and used in contemporary mass culture to account for people's behaviour. These **social representations** of the way people's minds work provide a framework for making sense of the world. This framework develops through many means, such as mass communication, informal conversation and adherence to prescriptions of scientific and religious movements and other group ideologies (Moscovici, 1983; also see Lorenzi-Cioldi and Clémence, 2001).

Social representations have far-reaching consequences for how we deal with one another. For example, whether insanity is considered to have a moral, biological, religious, physical or social cause will determine how it is responded to by policy-makers and the public (Jodelet, 1991). When Peter Sutcliffe, the British 'Yorkshire

Ripper', was convicted in 1981 in the UK of over 20 rapes and murders he was deemed to be 'criminal' rather than 'insane', and was therefore imprisoned rather than hospitalised. Such distinctions are dependent more on society's current social representations of good and evil, sanity and insanity than they are on objectively measurable criteria. However, criteria for diagnosing mental illness have progressed dramatically since then (see Chapter 18).

Against the background of particular social representations, values and norms, cognitive-inferential processes affect the way we understand, use and respond to our social environment (Augoustinos and Walker, 1995). For example, Echebarria-Echabe *et al.* (1994) examined how smokers and non-smokers account for the causes of smoking. Two representations appeared to be common: one which emphasised the psychological weakness of people who fall prey to the attractions of tobacco and another (defensive representation) which associated smoking with facilitative social factors and favourable stereotypes of smokers. When the potential conflict between non-smokers and smokers was made more salient, smokers became significantly more likely to adhere to the defensive representation.

Our ability to interpret social situations involves a range of basic cognitive–inferential processes, including memory for people, places and events; concept formation skills; and sensory and perceptual abilities. Social cognition rests on an array of basic cognitive–inferential processes and on the way in which social information is stored, structured and retrieved from memory. Fiske and Taylor have characterised the individual as a motivated tactician,

> a fully engaged thinker who has multiple cognitive strategies available and chooses among them based on goals, motives, and needs. Sometimes the motivated tactician chooses wisely, in the interests of adaptability and accuracy, and sometimes . . . defensively, in the interests of speed or self-esteem. (*Source*: Fiske and Taylor, 1991, p. 13.)

A central and dominant theme in social psychology has been the development of our understanding of social cognition – how people attend to, perceive, interpret, store and respond to social information.

Forming impressions of people

All of us form impressions of others: friends, neighbours, lecturers, foreigners – virtually everyone we meet. We assign all sorts of characteristics to them. We may, for example, think of someone as friendly or hostile, helpful or selfish. Note that these are terms that not only describe the type of person someone is, but which also critically evaluate them. One of the major tasks of social psychology is to understand how we form these impressions. In Solomon Asch's words, 'How do the perceptions, thoughts, and motives of one person become known to other persons?' (Asch, 1952, p. 143).To answer questions like this, psychologists study **impression formation**, the way in which we form impressions, often first impressions, of others and attribute specific characteristics to them.

Cognitive algebra

One perspective on impression formation argues that our evaluation of other poeple is critically important as it underpins fundamental judgements of danger and safety and thus approach–avoidance decisions. Impressions of people are largely evaluative. This process has been referred to as **cognitive algebra** (Anderson, 1978). This perspective argues that people intuitively represent traits in terms of their desirability: they effectively assign values to traits, e.g. $+1$, 0, -1, -2, and they integrate the value of traits they assign to a person in order to arrive at an overall evaluation of that person. This information can be integrated in three different ways:

- *summation* – the larger the number of positive traits the more positive the overall impression;
- *averaging* – a limited number of highly positive traits yields a more positive impression than lots of positive traits with many of them only marginally positive (marginal traits bring down the average);
- *weighted averaging* – not only are traits averaged, but some traits are considered more important than others in a particular context and are thus weighted more heavily. Research suggests that the weighted averaging model best characterises impression formation.

Several factors influence weighting. For example, the same information may be weighted differently if you are forming an impression of a potential friend rather than a potential colleague. Weightings of particular attributes may also be influenced by what other person attributes are present. The meanings of specific attributes, and overall meaning of a combination of attributes, may influence the meaning and the valence of a particular attribute. Generally, although attribute valence is important, so is the meaning of an attribute – when we evaluate someone as 'cruel' we not only evaluate that person negatively, but also know something about their behaviour. These and other considerations suggest people may not form impressions in such a piecemeal manner, but in a more holistic or gestalt manner that places a greater importance on the meaning of attributes. This idea underpins Asch's **configural model** of impression formation.

Asch's configural model

Over half a century ago, Asch (1946) noted that our impressions of others are formed by more complex rules than just a simple sum of the characteristics that we use to describe people. Asch was able to show that when we form impressions of other people, some perceptual features seem to have more influence than others in our final impression. For example, your impression of someone may be swayed by whether people are intelligent or not, and a friend's may be swayed by whether people are approachable or not. Kelly (1955) refers to these idiosyncratic views of what is most important in characterising people as **personal constructs**. In one context, intelligence may be a more relevant dimension than approachability (e.g. evaluating someone as a member of a research team), whereas in another context the opposite may be true (e.g., evaluating someone as a charity fund-raiser). Asch called characteristics that are disproportionately influential in impression formation **central traits**. Central traits are very useful for organising and summarising large amounts of diverse information about a person you encounter.

To demonstrate this, Asch (1946) provided participants with a list of traits describing a hypothetical person. Some received a list that included the trait 'warm', whereas others received an identical list, except that the trait 'warm' was replaced by 'cold'. Participants given the list including 'warm' were more likely to see the person as generous, happy and altruistic. But not all traits seemed to be so important. When the words 'polite' and 'blunt' were substituted for 'warm' and 'cold', no differences were observed in participants' impressions. Kelley (1950) replicated Asch's study in a more naturalistic setting where the target person was not hypothetical, but was a real person who really gave a guest lecture to a class. Kelley found the same results. Students who had had the lecturer described as 'cold' rated him to be more unsociable, self-centred, unpopular, formal, irritable, humourless and ruthless than did those who had had him described as 'warm'. Our perception of others seems to be based partially on central traits – which can vary from context to context, or from person to person.

Biases in impression formation

What determines whether a trait is central or not? One factor is the order in which information is available or is processed. Research suggests that the first information we process is the most important – there is a marked **primacy effect**. Getting to know someone takes time and usually requires many interactions. Perhaps the first time you saw someone was at a party when she was loud and boisterous, having a good time with her friends. But later, you learn that she is a mathematics student with excellent grades who is generally quite reserved. What is your overall impression of this person: loud and boisterous, or bright and shy? To determine whether first impressions might overpower later impressions, Asch (1946) presented one of the following lists of words to each of two groups of participants:

> Intelligent, industrious, impulsive, critical, stubborn, envious
>
> Envious, stubborn, critical, impulsive, industrious, intelligent

Notice that these lists contain the same words but in reverse order. After they saw the list, Asch asked the participants to describe the personality of the person having these characteristics. People who heard the first list evaluated the person much more favourably than people who heard the second list – a clear primacy effect.

Although sometimes more recent information can be influential (for example, when there is a lot of information and we are distracted), the general rule is that first impressions are most impactful and most enduring (Jones and Goethals, 1972).

The impressions we form of people are also disproportionately influenced by negative information. We tend to pay more attention to negative information, and although we like to think the best of people, bad impressions, once formed, are very difficult to change. By contrast, good impressions can easily change. One reason for this negativity bias is that people are probably especially sensitive to negative information because it can signify potential harm or danger (Skowronski and Carlston, 1989).

It will not surprise you to learn that sometimes there are social conventions and norms (sometimes legislation) that actually discourage us from forming impressions at all. For example, most of us would resist forming impressions based on race, gender or disability, particularly if we were serving on a selection panel for job applicants. People make an assessment of **social judgeability**, a perception of whether there is a legitimate and adequate basis for judging a specific person before forming an impression. Sometimes, merely believing you are in a position to make a judgement (but in reality you lack good evidence) results in your making unwarranted evaluations of other people (Leyens *et al.*, 1992).

Impressions are also influenced by physical appearance. Immediate first impressions, which as we have just seen can be quite enduring, are often based on what we see, because other information about people's 'character' is not yet available. According to Zebrowitz and Collins (1997), appearance-based first impressions can actually be surprisingly accurate. However, there are obvious pitfalls. For example, the tendency to form more favourable first impressions of physically attractive people may cause one to hire people who are delightfully decorative but not much good at getting the job done (Heilman and Stopeck, 1985). Also, a recent study of 11,370 convicted criminals found that those with the greatest tendency to control the impression formed of them were less likely to be antisocial, but were more likely to be convicted of serious crimes such as murder and sexual assault (C.G. Davis *et al.*, 2011). They also received longer sentences.

Schemas and categories

A central theme for social cognition is the concept of **schema** – although 'schemata' is the correct plural, social cognition theorists, perhaps embarrassingly, refer to 'schemas' (Fiske and Taylor, 1991). A schema is a mental framework or body of knowledge that organises and synthesises information about something. Schemas contain information about attributes and the relationship between attributes. We have schemas for specific people (for example, one's best friend), groups of people (for example, traffic wardens), ourselves, events (for example, how to order food at a restaurant), roles (for example, how the pilot of an aeroplane should behave in the cockpit), places and objects.

Schemas aid us in interpreting the world. The first time you visited your psychology professor in their office, for example, there were probably few surprises. Your 'professor' schema guided your expectations. However, you would probably be surprised if you saw that your professor's office was filled with skateboarding trophies, autographed photos of heavy metal bands, or dead animals mounted on the walls as hunting trophies. Such possessions are probably inconsistent with your impression of professors.

As an example of how schemas guide our interpretations, try to make sense of the following passage:

> The procedure is actually quite simple. First you arrange things into different groups. Of course, one pile may be sufficient depending on how much there is to do . . . It is important not to overdo things. That is, it is better to do too few things at once than too many. In the short run this may not seem important, but complications can easily arise. A mistake can be expensive as well.
> At first the whole procedure will seem complicated. Soon, however, it will become just another facet of life.
> (*Source*: Bransford and Johnson, 1972, p. 722).

Does this passage make sense to you? What if I tell you that the title of the passage is 'Washing Clothes'? Now you can interpret the passage easily. The sentences make perfect sense within the context of your schema for washing clothes. Not surprisingly, research has demonstrated that understanding is improved when people know the title of the passage before it is read (Bransford and Johnson, 1972). Imagine a time when you turned on the radio and a discussion or phone-in left you clueless as to the topic being talked about because the exchanges were so vague and generic that you could only make sense of them when the interviewer gave a reminder of the topic that was under discussion.

Categories, prototypes and exemplars

Once you categorise a person (as an individual or as a member of a particular group), the schema of that person or group is activated. Research suggests that schemas can be organised as prototypes (Cantor and Mischel, 1979) or as exemplars (Smith and Zárate, 1992). A prototype is an abstract fuzzy set of attributes that define the category, where no instance may actually embody the attributes. An exemplar is a specific instance of the category. For example, if your schema of French people is the actor Gérard Depardieu then you have an exemplar representation, whereas if what comes to mind is a general notion of baguettes, cafés, berets, striped jumpers, and so forth then you have a prototype representation. Note that both types of schema are equally accurate or inaccurate as a 'true' description of the category as a whole.

Social categories simplify the social world by reducing an infinite diversity of people to a more limited number of categories of people, each described by a schema – men, women, Catholics, Danes, doctors, and so forth. Categories only form and persist to the extent that they make sense of the world and one's place within it. Of course, any specific person can fit into many categories (e.g. someone can be a female, an Italian and an engineer), but the key point is that once a person is categorised the appropriate schema comes into play to influence perceptions, expectations and interaction.

Categories vary in inclusiveness. Highly inclusive categories have many members (for example, a nation) and thus tend to gloss over potentially important differences between people. More exclusive categories have fewer members (for example, a family). Although they capture differences more precisely, an exclusive category structure would produce too many categories – it is a too fine-grained segmentation of the world. In general, the most cognitively accessible social categories are **basic level categories** which are neither too inclusive nor too exclusive. Basic level categories are default categories that we first use to generate context-specific schemas of people – these are often based on visible cues such as skin colour, physiognomy, sex and dress (Zebrowitz, 1996).

However, many factors, including the social interactive context, our interaction goals and our own personal history, can influence basic level categories and what categorisation and associated schema comes into play in a particular context.

Schema acquisition and development

We tend to acquire and develop our schemas through exposure to instances of the category – face-to-face encounters, media presentations, second-hand accounts, and so forth. As one encounters more instances of a category one's schema is likely to become less exemplar-based and more prototype-based. Research suggests that such prototype-based schemas can become tightly organised into a single mental construct that is very rapidly activated in an all-or-nothing fashion by category cues (Schul, 1983). Such schemas are highly resistant to change (Fiske and Neuberg, 1990), which can be particularly problematic in the case of schemas of groups.

Group schemas and stereotypes

Schemas of social groups are particularly significant since they characterise large numbers of people in terms of a small number of properties that submerges the variety of differences that exist between people. Schemas of social groups are almost always shared among people in one group. For example British people often believe that Americans are 'brash', the French think the British are 'cold', and so forth. Shared schemas of social groups are best described as **stereotypes**. Because they are closely associated with prejudice, discrimination and intergroup relations, we will return to them in the next chapter (Leyens *et al.*, 1994).

According to Tajfel (1981), such stereotypes are learned early in childhood through normal socialisation rather than direct experience. Research suggests that children's use of stereotypes and expression of negative attitudes towards out-groups peak at around the age of 7 and then decline by 8 or 9 years of age. This may reflect cognitive developmental changes that affect the way children understand the meaning of categories and attributes, and changes in role-taking skills (Aboud, 1988; Durkin, 1995). Prejudice (a topic discussed in much greater depth in the next chapter) usually refers to a person's expression of negative views of and behaviours towards members of an ethnic group that differs from their own (Brown, 1995). A key component of prejudice is the belief that the ethnic or 'out-group' is highly dissimilar to the 'in-group' (the person's own social or racial group). Language is one important factor that can enhance or magnify perceived dissimilarities between groups and this is no more evident than when comparing different nationalities or cultures (Giles and Johnson, 1987; Giles and Coupland, 1991). Language is a communicative glue, bonding otherwise highly dissimilar individuals. Not only can it allow communication between the in-group members, it can also prevent or inhibit communication with out-group members.

Some of the best comedy comes from caricature – the exaggeration of stereotypes or stereotypical features. Two recent colourful examples are Sasha Baron-Cohen's creations, Borat and Bruno.
Source: Getty Images.

Automaticity of stereotypes

Images of another group (the out-group) are generally less favourable than images of one's own group (the in-group) and provide a relatively positive evaluation of oneself. For example, a stereotype that characterises an out-group as lazy and unmotivated is an excellent justification for an intergroup relationship where your own group has control over that group.

Once someone is categorised as a member of a particular group, the schema of that group (stereotype) influences the impression of that person. For example, if students believe that professors are pompous, boring and opinionated, then once you, as a student, categorise someone as a professor you will automatically tend to assume that they are pompous, boring and opinionated, and that impression will influence the entire interaction. The expectation may even, over a period of time, change the professor's behaviour to conform to your schema (Snyder, 1984).

Like other schemas, stereotypes are relatively automatically and unconsciously activated in particular contexts (Bargh, 1989) – they have the property of **automaticity**. Particular cues (for example, a Welsh accent) can automatically activate a categorisation (Welsh), which in turn automatically engages the appropriate stereotype. For example, in a classic study, Devine (1989) presented people with (negative) African-American primes (words like 'lazy', 'slavery', 'Negroes') far too quickly for people to be aware of them. She found that participants interpreted a subsequent neutral act, by someone merely called Donald, in ways that were consistent with negative stereotypes of African-Americans. Whether someone scored high or low on a racial prejudice scale did not affect susceptibility to preconscious priming – an effect that was replicated by Fazio *et al.* (1995). Other research has, however, shown that the effect is more marked for people who score high on unobtrusive measures of possessing racist attitudes (Lepore and Brown, 1997).

The property of automaticity has been exploited by the **implicit association test** (IAT; Greenwald *et al.*, 2002) which is able quite reliably to elicit our hidden prejudices. The test has been placed on the Web (http://implicit.harvard.edu/implicit/) – so you can discover if you are prejudiced, or rather, just how prejudiced you are.

Implicit biases or prejudice can be expressed towards various types of people, the obese for example (Teachman *et al.*, 2003). Beachgoers in Connecticut were given a newspaper article which stated that obesity was caused either by genetics or by overeating and lack of exercise. The IAT was then administered in which participants decided whether words paired with the adjective 'good' or 'bad' were appropriately paired. So, the pairing of 'thin people' with 'good' and 'fat people' with 'bad' would be expected to be responded to more quickly as an appropriate pairing than would 'fat people' and 'good'. Participants also completed a questionnaire measuring their attitudes towards obesity and obese people.

Although the participants claimed to hold no explicit biases towards fat people, their implicit responses suggested otherwise. People associated 'fat people' with more negative attributes (lazy, bad) than positive ones (motivated, smart). In line with Crandall's (1994) reasoning, this bias was greater when people had been previously primed to think that obesity was caused by controllable factors such as overeating and lack of exercise than when they saw it as being caused by uncontrollable genetic factors.

In a follow-up study, the implicit test was prefaced by stories which evoked sympathy towards fat people, or evoked sympathy towards people who use wheelchairs (what the researchers called a comparable 'stigmatised' group) or were neutral. Ninety women participated at Yale University. Reading empathic stories about fat people did not reduce implicit fat bias, compared with reading neutral stories. When overweight participants were added to this sample, there was evidence of in-group bias. Fat people were more likely to show less implicit bias after reading the empathetic material.

The results suggest that while people may claim that they do not hold negative (stereotypical) views of fat people, their implicit cognitions and behaviour suggest otherwise.

Leigh and Susilo (2009) exploited an unusual quirk of the Australian electoral system to see whether physical appearance implicitly influenced voting intentions. In the Northern Territory of Australia, photographs of candidates appear on ballot papers. In the study, the researchers examined whether the candidates' beauty and skin colour was associated with electoral success. They found that in areas with small indigenous populations, candidates with a lighter skin colour received more votes. In areas where there were high numbers of indigenous people, darker-skinned candidates were more successful. The effect of skin colour was more pronounced for people who were challengers for the position than for those who were incumbents. The candidates' beauty did not affect electoral success.

If stereotyping is largely an automatic process over which we have only limited conscious control, what can be done to combat it? One solution might be to make the category–stereotype link more conscious by thinking hard about it and suppressing the stereotype immediately it comes to mind. Over time, stereotype suppression might inhibit stereotype activation. An alternative view, which makes equal sense, is that the more you try to suppress the stereotype the firmer the cognitive or associative link between the category and the stereotype, and thus the more entrenched the automatic activation effect. Macrae *et al.* (1994) call this effect 'stereotype rebound'.

When good intentions backfire: stereotypes, influence and behaviour

A female assistant is working alongside her male boss on a complex decision task. Will he treat her any differently from a male assistant? Research by Vescio *et al.* (2005) examined the idea that powerful men use stereotypes to judge women when the stereotype seems contextually relevant and when they are focusing on the weakness of women in that context, that is, if the task is in an area in which women are stereotyped as weak.

Male and female students believed they were participating in an academic competition involving teams. Half the participants were led to believe that good leaders focused on eliminating weaknesses in their teams; the other half that good leaders focused on maximising strengths. Their task was to select from among four male and four female members those who should represent the team, and assign them roles of team captain, player and non-player. They were also asked to email an explanation for their decision to each member. The results showed that weakness-focused men, not women, used their stereotypes of subordinate women more strongly by assigning fewer valued positions in the group to those women. At the same time, these men praised the subordinate women more highly, as shown in Table 15.1. So these powerful men effectively acted in a patronising way towards subordinate women, denying them an opportunity for advancement but delivering positive messages to them.

Next Vescio and colleagues investigated how male leaders who patronised and focused on weakness might affect the behaviour of male and female subordinates. Being patronised makes people angry but, because women tend to avoid overtly aggressive responses, Vescio and colleagues predicted that low-power women may respond more passively to being patronised. In contrast, low-power men seemed likely to respond competitively, by endeavouring to perform better. A male leader assigned male or female participants a low-power role as a team member, and then either praised the member or did not, and assigned the member to a valued or devalued position in the group. Both male and

Table 15.1 Position assignment and praise of female subordinates as a function of leader's gender and social influence focus

| | Male leaders | | Female leaders | |
	Weakness focused	Strength focused	Weakness focused	Strength focused
Position assignment	3.79	4.47	4.76	4.58
Praise	4.42	3.84	3.69	3.62

Table 15.2 Performance as a function of position assignment, praise, and participant's gender

| | Valued position | | Devalued position | |
	Praised	Not praised	Praised	Not praised
Female participants	10.48	9.69	9.02	9.99
Male participants	10.00	10.19	11.86	10.5

female team members reported feeling angrier when they were patronised than when they were not but, as shown in Table 15.2, on a 23-item test males performed better after being patronised whereas females did not. As Vescio and colleagues conclude, leadership styles often focus on eliminating weaknesses, but people are likely to be more motivated and perform better, and less likely to be the unwitting victims of patronising stereotypes, when leaders focus on ways in which subordinate group members can promote the goals of the group.

Research shows that when people are negatively primed with an unflattering stereotype – women are poor at maths – the targeted sample has a reduced positive view of themselves and exhibit the stereotype they are primed with. Those unprimed do not show this behaviour. A study from the US has found that one particular anxiety, about maths, can influence children's judgements about stereotypical sex roles (Bellock *et al.*, 2010).

The researchers measured maths anxiety in first and second grade maths teachers in the US (over 90 per cent are women) and examined whether this affected children's performance and their sterotypes about the sexes (boys are good at maths, girls are good at reading). At the beginning of the year, there was no relationship between the teacher's maths anxiety and her children's performance. By the end of the year, however, there was: the more anxious the teacher, the more likely it was that girls (but not boys) endorsed the above stereotype. These girls' maths achievement was also lower than boys or girls who did not hold the stereotype. The teacher's ability could not explain these findings: if this were so, boys and girls would have shown similar declines.

Implicit attitudes: insights from neuroscience

A new field has emerged in psychology and neuroscience in the past decade which studies the relationship between brain structure and function, and social processes and behaviour. This field is called social neuroscience and it is well served by textbooks (such as those in the further reading list) and even its own journal. A significant part of research in this field has been devoted to the study of implicit processes, especially those implicit attitudes related to racism and other forms of prejudice (discussed in more detail in Chapter 16).

As implicit attitudes are expressed automatically and without conscious awareness, you might predict that the brain regions that are activated during implicit attitude expression are those which are primarily involved in automatic functions. There is considerable evidence for this and the focus of much of the attention has been on the amygdala (see Chapters 4 and 13). For example, Phelps *et al.* (2000) asked white Americans to view unfamiliar black and white women as fMRI recorded brain activation from the structure. They also measured participants' implicit and explicit attitudes to race. They found that activation in the amygdala to the black men was correlated with implicit, but not explicit, attitudes towards race. When black and white men who were famous and positively regarded were presented, the amygdala activation was eliminated, suggesting that the activation and implicit bias was a reflection of a fear of the unfamiliar. Hart *et al.* (2000), however, found activation to both black and white unfamiliar faces in black and white participants but that the activation declined when participants saw the same-race face but not the other-race face, suggesting to the authors that 'alarm signals from the amygdala attenuate more rapidly for same race than other race strangers' (p. 166).

In a twist on the normal paradigm, Cunningham *et al.* (2004) presented unfamiliar black and white faces subliminally and to conscious awareness as brain activation was measured. Amygdala activation was stronger when the black face was presented subliminally, suggesting an even greater degree of **automatic processing** in this structure. Activity in the anterior cingulate cortex (ACC) and dorsolateral prefrontal cortex (DlPFC), however, was correlated with a decline in activation in the amygdala suggesting (as Chapter 13 noted) that these regions acted as a break on – or controlled or modulated – the information sent by the amygdala.

Facing racial stereotypes

Physical appearance is a powerful cue to category membership. For example, we rely heavily on sex or skin colour to assign people to gender or racial/ethnic categories, and then generate stereotypical assumptions about their attributes and behaviours. We can even be quite discriminating in our perception of and reaction to physical appearance cues. For example, research in the US has shown that African-American prisoners who have more Afro-centric facial features receive more severe sentences than African-American prisoners with less Afro-centric features.

Blair *et al.* (2004) analysed the facial features of a random sample of black and white prison inmates who had been given equivalent sentences. They hypothesised that strongly Afro-centric facial features might unwittingly (or wittingly) influence sentencing decisions. They defined Afro-centric features as being typical of those seen in African-Americans – e.g. 'dark skin, wide nose, full lips'.

The sample comprised 216 black and white inmates at the Florida Department of Corrections and their facial photographs were presented to two groups of undergraduates who rated the degree to which facial features were typical of African-Americans. While there was little difference in the severity of the sentence given to the black and white prisoners, there were significant differences in the harshness of the sentence within the black sample. Those with stereotypically Afro-centric features were significantly more likely to have received harsher sentences than were those with less Afro-centric physical characteristics.

The results indicate that although bias and stereotyping were not evident in sentencing – black and white criminals with equivalent criminal histories were given comparable sentences – more subtle forms of stereotyping were significantly influencing sentencing decisions.

Cutting edge: He looks guilty

In an unusual study, Stillman *et al.* (2010) found that people were able to accurately estimate the degree of violence committed by sex offenders by looking at their faces only. In the experiment, 97 undergraduates saw photographs of 87 registered sex offenders for two seconds and were asked to rate how likely the person was to be violent on a four point scale. These judgements were then compared with the actual degree of violence shown in the criminal's offence. When judgements were accurate, the faces rated as violent were younger, had a heavier brow, looked more masculine and appeared physically strong.

However, errors were made and participants judged, incorrectly, that happy, well-groomed individuals were less likely to be violent and that angry and disgusted expressions on the faces would be associated with greater violence.

Stereotypes – An international perspective

Are there any features of stereotypes that transcend national boundaries? One model in social psychology – the stereotype content model – argues just that. One aspect of the model argues that there are two universally recognised stereotypical dimensions – competence and warmth. Another proposes that there may be an ambivalent stereotype – competent and cold or warm and incompetent. Cuddy et al. (2009) investigated whether these dimensions would be reflected in the stereotypes held by ten non-US nations, including seven European nations and three East Asian nations.

They were. The group found that the dimensions of competence and warmth characterised stereotypes of others. The group also found that out-groups were more likely to receive ambivalent descriptors (scoring high on one dimension and low on another). Groups of high status tend to be rated high on competence whereas very competitive groups tend to be rated as stereotypically less warm. So, whereas the nature of the stereotype can be seen to be universal, the expression of this stereotype varies cross-culturally.

Controversies in psychological science: Sexist humour – does it make you sexist?

Issue

People who express sexist attitudes – an antagonism towards women (perhaps, itself, a sexist definition) – tend to suppress them for external reasons rather than internal ones. That is, these views would violate some social norm and are, therefore, not expressed. Sexist jokes tend to re-enforce sexist beliefs. Highly sexist men are far more likely to accept a sexist norm after exposure to sexist jokes: when asked to pretend to be managers who had made sexist remarks to a woman employee, highly sexist men felt less guilty about it after reading sexist jokes than neutral ones (Ford et al., 2001). But can exposure to sexist humour create sexist beliefs?

Evidence

A group of US researchers asked participants to read a series of scenarios and pretend to empathise with people in them (Ford et al., 2008). In the scenario, participants were told that a discussion has taken place about workmates' favourite jokes. Some of these jokes were sexist (e.g. 'How can you tell if a blonde's been using the computer? There's Tippex on the screen'). The next scenario involved a discussion of views in which sexist beliefs were defended seriously. Finally, a vignette was presented in which the National Council of Women's aims were stated and its request for donations made clear. Participants were asked how much they would give to the organisation.

Highly sexist people exposed to sexist humour were less likely to give to the organisation. In a second experiment, the amount of money participants would cut from the organisation was measured. Sexist individuals exposed to sexist humour recommended greater budget cuts than those exposed to neutral comedy.

Conclusion

The moral of this story seems to be: exposure to some forms of comedy can harm your charity collecting.

Conceptual and historical issues in social psychology

So far, you have seen how social psychologists have studied basic social behaviours such as impression formation and stereotypes. That social psychologists study these topics and in an experimental way owes a lot to the branch's history and development. The empirical study of social behaviour emerged in the second half of the nineteenth century (with a group in Germany calling themselves students of Völkerpsychologie – folk psychology – who focused on the collective mind, in contrast to Wundt).

In the early 1900s, America superseded Germany as the powerhouse of social psychology – a process which was accelerated in the 1930s by an enormous influx of leading German social psychologists fleeing Nazism. The ensuing global conflict, the Second World War, then posed urgent applied social psychological questions that created an explosion of research activity that focused on, for example, small group processes (Lewin, 1951), attitudes and attitude change (Hovland et al., 1953) and prejudice (Adorno et al., 1950).

From the late 1940s, social psychology grew prodigiously, in terms of programmes, publications and profile within psychology. During the 1950s and early 1960s small group research flourished (for example, the study of group cohesion, leadership, communication networks, group influence – Shaw, 1976), as did the study of inter-personal relationships as social exchanges (Thibaut and Kelley, 1959), and the study of attitude change as the resolution of cognitive dissonance (Festinger, 1957). The mid-1960s through the 1970s was characterised by attri-bution theories that focused on how people, as intuitive scientists, develop causal explanations of their social world as a basis for behaviour (Kelley, 1973).

Generally speaking, there are two camps in social psy-chology: those who believe that group behaviour is not qualitatively different from individual or interpersonal behaviour (we can call them 'individualists') and those who believe it is ('collectivists'). The debate mostly bubbles along in the background, but from time to time it seems to become a major preoccupation. The 1960s was one such occasion, when social psychology seemed to be deep in crisis (Elms, 1975). Critics felt that the discipline was asking the wrong questions, providing inadequate explanations of trivial behaviours and using primitive methodologies. The resolution of the crisis had two contrasting prongs. Social psychologists in the USA developed social cognition (discussed extensively in this chapter) in a drive for better methodology and better theory (Fiske and Taylor, 1991), and social psychologists in Europe developed what they called a more social social psychology (Tajfel, 1984) in a drive for socially relevant research (for example, the study of prejudice and intergroup conflict) and theories that linked cognitive and social processes.

The late 1960s and early 1970s, therefore, saw the emergence of a crisis of confidence in social psychology. Social psychologists were concerned that social psy-chology was theoretically immature, methodologically unsophisticated, inappropriately dependent on scien-tific method, and focused too much on individuals and interpersonal interaction and too little on language and collective phenomena. Out of this angst arose a diversity of 'resolutions'. The two most successful are social cog-nition, with sophisticated methodologies and theories that continue to dominate social psychology (Nisbett and Ross, 1980; Fiske and Taylor, 1991; Devine *et al.*, 1994; Moskowitz, 2005), and social perspectives that focus on culture (Smith *et al.*, 2006), collective representations (Moscovici, 1976) and intergroup relations and social identity (Tajfel, 1984; Hogg and Abrams, 1988).

There is another set of responses that rejects tradi-tional social psychological methods, theories and research foci altogether, and instead focuses on subjectivity, lan-guage and qualitative methods (Potter and Wetherell, 1987; Edwards, 1997). Two recent trends in social psy-chology are evolutionary social psychology (Buss and Kenrick, 1998) and social neuroscience (Ochsner and Lieberman, 2001). The former focuses on the evo-lutionary and adaptive origins of social behaviours and social-cognitive processes. The latter maps social behaviours and social-cognitive processes onto functions, structures and processes within the brain.

Self and identity

Some of the most significant and influential schemas are those we have about ourselves. Not surprisingly, the self is an important focus for social psychological research – a review published in 1997 found that there had been 31,000 social psychological publications on the self over the pre-ceding 20 years (Ashmore and Jussim, 1997), and a journal exists dedicated to the topic (*Self and Identity*).

Self-knowledge

Knowledge about ourselves is very much like knowledge about other people. If you were asked who you were, how would you respond? You might say your name, that you are a student and perhaps that you are also an ath-lete or have a part-time job. Alternatively, you could talk about your family, your nationality, ethnicity or religion. There are many ways you could potentially describe your-self, all of which would reflect your **self-concept** – your knowledge, feelings and ideas about yourself. In its total-ity, the self is a person's distinct individuality. At the core of the self-concept is the **self-schema** – a mental frame-work that represents and synthesises information about who you are. The self-schema is a cognitive structure that organises the knowledge, feelings and ideas that consti-tute the self-concept.

Social psychologists believe that we have many differ-ent selves that can be more or less discrete and come into play in different contexts – the subjective experience of self is highly context dependent. Selves not only describe how we are, but also how we would like to be, called pos-sible selves (Markus and Nurius, 1986). Higgins (1987) takes this idea further in his **self-discrepancy theory**. He distinguishes between the actual self (how one really is), the ideal self (how one would like to be) and the 'ought' self (how one thinks one ought to be). The latter two are 'self-guides' which mobilise different types of self-related behaviours. The ideal self engages 'promotional' goals – we strive towards achieving the ideal, whereas the 'ought' self engages 'prevention' goals – we strive to avoid doing what we ought not to do (Higgins, 1998).

How do we learn who we are – how do we form self-schemas? Introspection is one way, but the overwhelmingly social nature of human existence means that we learn much more about ourselves from how others treat us, and from how we think others view us. Research on **self-fulfilling prophecies** shows that others' expectation about us can change the way we behave. For example,

Snyder (1984) reports a series of studies in which experimental participants behaved in a more extravert manner simply because others were primed with the false expectation that they, the participants, were extraverts. Expectations constrained participants to behave in a more extravert manner, and biased interpretations of neutral behaviour so it appeared more extravert. In this way participants gradually really did behave in a more extravert manner. Another example comes from research by Steele and Aronson (1995) into **stereotype threat**, which shows that because African-American students are aware of social expectations concerning academic underperformance, they can actually reduce effort and thus underperform.

Social impact on behaviour can affect self-conception because, according to self-perception theory (Bem, 1972), we often learn most about ourselves by simply observing how we behave. If there is no obvious coercion to behave as we do, then we assume that the behaviour reflects the type of person we are (see attribution theory, below). If you notice that you often drink coffee of your own free will you would be forgiven for deducing that you are the kind of person who likes coffee.

In addition to introspection and self-perception, another powerful source of self-knowledge is social comparison. According to **social comparison theory** (Festinger, 1954) people need to feel confident about the validity of their perceptions, attitudes, feelings and behaviours. This sense of validity often comes from the fact that other people who are similar to us agree with us. In this way, attitudes about ourselves may be grounded in belonging to groups of people who have similar views about who we are – views that reinforce and confirm our own self-attitudes.

Orientations of self-knowledge

We are all aware of two contrasting orientations to life – one in which we are adventurous, optimistic and approach-oriented (the glass is half full), and one in which we are more cautious, avoidant and defensively-oriented (the glass is half empty). This general distinction has recently been reconceptualised by **regulatory focus theory** (Higgins, 1997, 1998). Regulatory focus theory proposes that people have two separate self-regulatory systems, termed promotion and prevention, which are concerned with the pursuit of different types of goals.

The promotion system is concerned with the attainment of one's hopes and aspirations, termed ideals. It generates sensitivity to the presence or absence of positive events. People in a promotion focus adopt approach strategic means to attain their goals. For example, promotion-focused students are likely to seek ways to improve their grades, to find new challenges and to treat problems as interesting obstacles to overcome. Promotion-focused individuals are also especially likely to recall information relating to the pursuit of success by others (Higgins and Tykocinski, 1992) and are most inspired by positive role models, who emphasise strategies for achieving success (Lockwood et al., 2002). In addition, they tend to show especially high motivation and persistence on tasks that are framed in terms of gains and non-gains (Shah et al., 1998).

The prevention system is concerned with the fulfilment of one's duties and obligations, termed oughts. It generates sensitivity to the presence or absence of negative events. People in a prevention focus use avoidance strategic means to attain their goals. For example, prevention-focused students might be more concerned with avoiding new situations or new people, to concentrate more on avoiding failure rather than achieving the highest possible grade. Prevention-focused individuals are especially likely to recall information relating to the avoidance of failure by others (Higgins and Tykocinski, 1992) and are most inspired by negative role models, who highlight strategies for avoiding failure (Lockwood et al., 2002). In addition, they tend to show high motivation and persistence on tasks that are framed in terms of losses and non-losses (Shah et al., 1998).

The two self-regulatory systems can be activated either chronically or temporarily. Differences in chronic promotion and prevention focus can arise from differences in the quality of a child's relationship with a caregiver (Higgins and Silberman, 1998). Caregivers can initiate a chronic promotion focus by, for example, hugging and kissing a child for behaving in a desired manner (a positive event) and withdrawing love as discipline (absence of a positive event). Conversely, a chronic prevention focus will likely result if caregivers encourage a child to be especially alert to potential dangers (absence of a negative event) and punish and shout at a child when they behave undesirably (a negative event).

In addition to these chronic individual differences, regulatory focus can also change more quickly from situation to situation. Situational variability can be induced experimentally through, for example, task feedback or task instructions. In one study (E.T. Higgins et al., 1994), students were asked to report either on how their hopes and aspirations had changed over time (activating a promotion focus) or on how their sense of duty and obligation had changed over time (activating a prevention focus). The participants read about several episodes that occurred over the course of a few days in the life of another student. In each of these episodes the student was pursuing a desired goal by employing either approach strategic means ('Because I wanted to be at school for the beginning of my 8.30 psychology class which is usually excellent, I woke up early this morning'), or avoidance strategic means ('I wanted to take a class in photography at the community centre, so I didn't register for a class in Spanish that was scheduled at the same time'). Higgins et al. predicted that participants would recall better the episodes which described strategic means that were consistent with their induced self-regulatory focus. Consistent with this prediction, participants in a promotion focus recalled better the episodes in which the student used approach strategic means whereas participants in a prevention focus recalled better the episodes in which the student used avoidance strategic means.

One interesting line of research has applied the principles of regulatory focus theory to intergroup discrimination (Sassenberg et al., 2003). Participants with either a chronic or temporarily induced promotion or prevention focus were asked to distribute positive resources (money) or negative resources (withdrawal of money) between anonymous members of their own laboratory group (in-group) and anonymous members of another laboratory group (out-group).

Given that promotion-focused individuals have been shown to be especially sensitive to the presence or absence of positive outcomes whereas prevention-focused individuals are especially sensitive to the presence or absence of negative outcomes, Sassenberg et al. predicted that intergroup discrimination would be shown only when the available means for favouring the in-group were consistent with participants' chronic (or temporary) regulatory focus. Consistent with this prediction, participants discriminated under a promotion focus when positive but not negative resources had to be distributed and under a prevention focus when negative but not positive resources had to be distributed. In other words, under a promotion focus, group members focused on approaching positive in-group events and under a prevention focus group members focused on avoiding negative events.

Self-awareness

The above may give the impression that people spend all their time thinking about themselves, but this is not the case. People are not consciously aware of themselves all the time – if people were, then probably very little would ever get done. **Self-awareness** comes and goes for different reasons and with different consequences. Often we just get on with life without being particularly aware of ourselves, whereas at other times we can be obsessively self-absorbed or absolutely mortified over how others view us.

Duval and Wicklund (1972) believe that self-awareness is a state in which one is aware of oneself as an object, much as one might be aware of a tree or another person. Not surprisingly, standing in front of a mirror is a very effective way to become self-aware. Carver and Scheier (1981) argue that self-awareness can have at least two foci: the private self (one's private thoughts, feelings and attitudes) and the public self (how others see one, one's public image). Hence, self-awareness can also be raised simply by being in the presence of other people – for example, giving a public talk or performance. Private self-awareness

directs behaviour at matching one's internal standards, whereas public self-awareness directs behaviour at promoting a good impression in the eyes of others. In contrast to heightened self-awareness, reduced self-awareness can produce a sense of de-individuation (Zimbardo, 1970; Diener, 1980) that may be associated with disinhibited, impulsive and anti-normative behaviour.

Being self-aware causes one to exert effort to try to address any discrepancy between one's actual self and how one feels one would like to be or ought to be. According to self-discrepancy theory (Higgins, 1987), described above, failure to resolve a discrepancy between the actual and the ideal self produces dejection-related emotions (disappointment, dissatisfaction, sadness), whereas failure to resolve an actual, 'ought' discrepancy produces agitation-related emotions (anxiety, fear).

Types of self and identity

Actual and possible selves can take many different forms. The enormous variety of human existence offers us a dazzling kaleidoscope of different ways in which we can define and conceptualise our selves. However, since selves are largely grounded in human interaction, various forms of human interaction may produce a more limited number of types of self. In particular, researchers distinguish between selves and identities that are grounded in individuality, interpersonal relationships and group and category memberships.

Social identity theorists such as Hogg and Abrams (1988) and Tajfel and Turner (1986) distinguish between the personal self (personal identity: self defined in terms of idiosyncratic attributes or personal relationships) and the collective self (social identity: the self defined in terms of group attributes). Brewer and Gardner (1996) distinguish among individual self (defined by personal traits that differentiate one from all other people), relational self (defined by dyadic relationships), and collective self (defined by group memberships). From a more cultural perspective (see below), Markus and Kitayama (1991) distinguish between the independent self (self defined as autonomous and separate from other people) and the interdependent self (self defined in terms of specific relationships people have with others). These distinctions are certainly not the same as one another, but there is a general notion that people can define themselves perhaps as I, you and I, or we.

Social identity

Social identity theory distinguishes between personal self/ personal identity, and collective self/social identity (Tajfel and Turner, 1986; Hogg and Abrams, 1988). Social identity theorists believe that one's self-concept comprises a large array of different identities that fall into two broad types: personal identities that derive from our close inter-personal relationships (for example, friendships and romantic relationships) and our idiosyncratic character-istics (for example, being humorous), and social identities that derive from the social groups to which we belong (ethnicity, gender, profession, age group). Features of the immediate social context – situation, people, goals, activities and so forth – influence what aspect of the self-concept we experience and use to process information and plan action in that particular context.

Social identities are uniquely associated with group behaviours – for example, the stereotypes we spoke of above, but also other group behaviours such as conformity and discrimination (see Chapter 16). Social identities are attached to group memberships and derive their descriptive and evaluative properties from perceptions of the nature of the evaluative relations (for example, status) that exist between groups. In this way, intergroup relations influence self-conception. Social identity is associated with group and intergroup behaviours because the process of catego-rising ourselves and others as group members causes us to view ourselves and others only in terms of the defining attributes of membership of the relevant group, called the group prototype (Turner et al., 1987). This causes us to perceive and treat others stereotypically, and causes us and fellow group members to enact the defining features (per-ceptions, attitudes, feelings, behaviours) of our group.

Self-motives

What motivates the different ways that we may want to conceptualise ourselves? Research suggests that there are three general classes of motivations. One motive is self-assessment – a desire to find out the truth about ourselves, however disappointing or unfavour-able the truth may be (Trope, 1986). Another motive is self-verification – a desire to confirm what we already know about ourselves, by looking for self-consist-ent information (Swann, 1987). The third motive is self-enhancement – a desire to find out favourable things about ourselves (Kunda, 1990). Sedikides (1993) conducted a series of six experiments to compare the relative strength of these three motives, and concluded that self-enhance-ment is by far the strongest, with self-verification a distant second and self-assessment an even more distant third.

Because self-enhancement is so important, people have a formidable repertoire of strategies and tech-niques to construct or maintain a favourable self-concept (Baumeister, 1998). For example, they take credit for success but deny blame for failure; they forget failure feedback more readily than success feedback; they accept praise uncritically but receive criticism sceptically and dismiss it as being based on prejudice; and they self-inter-estedly interpret ambiguous self-attributes and perform a biased search of self-knowledge.

Self-esteem

The reason why people pursue self-enhancement is because it elevates **self-esteem**. Research overwhelmingly shows that it is adaptive for people to have a relatively positive sense of themselves, that there is a positivity bias and that a negative self-image can be quite dysfunctional (Taylor and Brown, 1988). People vary in their general level of self-esteem. People with higher self-esteem tend to pursue self-enhancement, whereas people with lower self-esteem tend to avoid self-derogation. Using the language of Higgins's (1998) regulatory focus theory, the former have a promotion orientation and the latter a prevention ori-entation. Although low self-esteem can be dysfunctional, research tends to discredit the popular belief that low self-esteem is associated with social problems such as violence (Baumeister et al., 1996). On the contrary, violence is more closely associated with narcissism – high self-esteem in conjunction with a feeling of being superior and special.

People may not pursue self-esteem for its own sake. Leary et al. (1995) suggest that self-esteem is an internal indicator of social acceptance and belonging – it is a 'soci-ometer'. The idea here is that the most basic human motive is to belong and to be properly socially connected. Feeling good about one's self – self-esteem – is an extremely power-ful indicator that one has succeeded in this pursuit.

Social inference

Causal attribution

As mentioned right at the start of this chapter, we are all intuitive social psychologists (Jones, 1990), using naive or common-sense psychological theories (Heider, 1958) to make sense of our social world. In order to interact with people and get on in life we need to have a basic under-standing of how people work – we need to know why people do what they do. This knowledge is essential if we are to be able to navigate our way through life in such a way that we can make good things happen for us and avoid bad things that might happen to us. The most powerful knowledge we can have about people is causal knowledge – if we know what causes people to behave in certain ways then we are able to predict and influence what people will do. For example, most of us know that if we are nice to people they are likely to agree to do small favours for us, and that people who feel threatened or cornered can often lash out aggressively. The explanation of how people develop a common-sense causal under-standing of human behaviour is called **attribution theory** (Hewstone, 1989). Strictly speaking, there are a number

Cultural differences in self and identity – An international perspective

The same person can experience self in an array of different personal or collective ways depending on context. There is, however, another tradition of research that focuses on enduring differences in self-conception that are grounded in cultural differences (Triandis, 1989; Markus and Kitayama, 1991; Oyserman *et al.*, 2002).

The key cultural difference is between individualistic and collectivist societies (Hofstede, 1980). Western societies such as the UK and US tend to be individualistic – they emphasise the unique individual and separateness from others, and encourage individual choice and loose ties among people. Eastern societies such as Japan and India tend to be collectivist – they emphasise group loyalty, relations among people and the collective good. According to Triandis *et al.* (1985), collectivist societies are associated with allocentrism (people who value cooperation, social support, equality and honesty), and individualistic societies with idiocentrism (people who strive for achievement, pleasure, social recognition and a comfortable life, and who experience anomie and a degree of social alienation).

More recently, Markus and Kitayama (1991) have identified the key cultural difference in self-conception to be between independent and interdependent self-construal. The independent construal emphasises the uniqueness of the self, its autonomy from others and self-reliance. Although other people have an influence on a person's behaviour, a person's self-concept is largely defined independently. The

interdependent construal emphasises the interconnectedness of people and the role that others play in developing an individual's self-concept. In the interdependent construal, what others think of the individual, or do to the individual, matter – the person is extremely sensitive to others and strives to form strong social bonds with them.

Students from India (a collectivist Eastern culture) judge the self to be more similar to others, whereas American students (members of an individualist culture) judge the self to be more dissimilar to others (Markus and Kitayama, 1991). Markus and Kitayama have also shown that Japanese students tend to associate positive feelings with interpersonal behaviours and tend not to associate such feelings with personal achievements. In contrast, American students tend to feel satisfaction in their accomplishments. In a similar vein, comparing workers' intentions to leave their organisations, Abrams *et al.* (1998) found that Japanese workers were influenced by the evaluations they expected from their friends, family and co-workers, whereas British workers were not.

Vignoles *et al.* (2000) note that despite cultural differences in self-conception, the need to have a distinctive and integrated sense of self is universal; however, self-distinctiveness means something different in individualist and in collectivist cultures. In the former it is the isolated and bounded self that gains meaning from separateness, whereas in the latter it is the relational self that gains meaning from its relations with others.

of variants of attribution theory that emphasise different aspects. Kelley's (1967) covariation model is probably the best established, and so we will focus on that.

Disposition versus situation

In deciding the causes of behaviour, the most important thing we need to know is whether the behaviour is a reflection of the person's disposition to behave in that way or a reflection of situational constraints that made them behave in that way. We need to assess the relative importance of situational and dispositional factors (Heider, 1958). **Situational factors** are stimuli in the environment. **Dispositional factors** are individual personality characteristics. One of the tasks of socialisation is to learn what behaviours are expected in various situations. Once we learn that in certain situations most people act in a specific way, we develop schemas for how we expect people to act in those situations. For example, when people are introduced, they are expected to look at each other, smile, say something like 'How do you do?' or 'It's nice to meet you', and perhaps offer to shake the other person's hand.

If people act in conventional ways in given situations, we are not surprised. Their behaviour appears to be dictated by social custom – by the characteristics of the situation.

As we get to know other people, we also learn what to expect from them as individuals. We learn about their dispositions – the kinds of behaviours in which they tend to engage across all sorts of situations. We learn to characterise people as friendly, generous, suspicious, pessimistic or greedy by observing their behaviour in a variety of situations. Sometimes, we even make inferences from a single observation (Krull and Erickson, 1995). If someone's behaviour is very different from the way most people would act in a particular situation, we attribute their behaviour to internal or dispositional causes. For example, if we see a person refuse to hold a door open for someone in a wheelchair, we assign that person some negative dispositional characteristics.

Kelley's covariation theory of attribution

Kelley (1967) has suggested that we attribute the behaviour of other people to external (situational) or internal (dispositional) causes on the basis of consideration of three aspects of the behaviour: its consensus, its consistency and its distinctiveness (Kelley, 1967; Kelley and Michela, 1980).

Consensual behaviour – a behaviour shared by many people – is usually attributed to external causes. The behaviour is assumed to be constrained or demanded by the situation. For example, if someone asks an acquaintance for the loan of a coin to make a telephone call, we do not conclude that the person is especially generous if they comply. The request is reasonable and costs little; lending the money is a consensual behaviour – most people would do it. However, if a person has some change but refuses to lend it, we readily attribute the behaviour to dispositional factors such as being a stingy or mean person.

We also base our attributions on **consistency** – on whether a person's behaviour occurs reliably in the same situation. For example, if you meet someone for the first time and notice that she speaks slowly and without much expression, stands in a slouching posture and sighs occasionally, you will probably conclude that she has a sad disposition. Now, suppose that after she has left, you mention to a friend that the young woman seems very passive. Your friend says, 'No, I know her well, and she's usually very cheerful.' With this new evidence about her behaviour you may reassess and wonder what happened to make her act so sad – was it something in the situation? If a person's pattern of behaviour is consistent, we attribute the behaviour to internal causes. Inconsistent behaviours lead us to seek external causes.

Finally, we base our attributions on **distinctiveness** – the extent to which a person performs a particular behaviour only in a particular situation. Behaviours that are distinctively associated with a particular situation are attributed to situational factors; those that occur in a variety of situations are attributed to dispositional factors. For example, suppose that your partner is always very attentive towards you and other people but seems very dismissive to you whenever a particular group of his friends are around. You are unlikely to conclude that he is a dismissive type of person; you are more likely to conclude that this particular group of friends has a bad influence on him. Because his dismissive behaviour occurs only under a distinctive circumstance (the presence of the group of friends), you attribute it to external causes. Table 15.3 summarises Kelley's ideas about the factors that determine internal or external attributions.

Implications and extensions of attribution theory

Attribution theory has a number of interesting implications and extensions. Earlier in this chapter we described how people can learn about themselves by investigating

Table 15.3 Kelley's theory of attribution

Principle	Attribution of external causality	Attribution of internal causality
Consensus	*High*. Person lends coin for telephone call, performing a socially acceptable behaviour	*Low*. Person refuses to lend coin and seems mean
Consistency	*Low*. Usually cheerful person acts sad and dejected; we wonder what event has caused the sadness	*High*. We meet a person who speaks slowly and slouches, and conclude that we have met a person who is sad by nature
Distinctiveness	*High*. A child is rude only when playing with a certain friend; we conclude that the friend is a bad influence	*Low*. A child acts impudently and says mean and nasty things to everyone they meet. We conclude that the child is rude

the causes of their behaviour. According to self-perception theory (Bem, 1972), if people can internally attribute their behaviour then they have gained knowledge about themselves.

Another intriguing idea, suggested by Schachter (1964), is that the emotions we experience have two distinct components: an undifferentiated state of generalised physiological arousal and a cognitive label attached on the basis of an attributional analysis of what caused the arousal. So, arousal in the presence of a snarling lion is experienced as fear whereas arousal in the presence of an attractive member of the opposite sex may be experienced as sexual desire or passion. If Schachter is right, then there are interesting therapeutic implications – for example, if someone who is anxious can be persuaded to reattribute their arousal to something amusing then anxiety could be transformed into happiness (Valins and Nisbett, 1972).

Schachter and Singer (1962) conducted an experiment that did indeed show that different emotions could be produced by different labels. Participants were injected with a drug that produces arousal and were told that the cause of the arousal was the drug, or they were not told anything. All participants then waited in a room with a euphoric or an angry confederate. Participants who had not been informed of the cause of the arousal attributed their arousal to the behaviour of the confederate and actually reported feeling euphoric or angry. This was a controlled laboratory experiment. Subsequent research has shown that the nature of physiological arousal associated with different emotions, particularly strong emotions, is often different and so the emotions are intrinsically different – emotions may be based less on cognitive labelling than Schachter first suggested (Reisenzein, 1983; Forsterling, 1988). However, anyone who has observed small children will know how easily tears can be changed to laughter by simply doing something funny to entertain the child.

Attributional biases

Although causal attribution is an important way in which people make sense of their world, it is quite clear that we do not rely on causal attributions all the time. If we did then we would be completely immobilised by cogitation. Attribution and other inferential processes help us to construct representations and theories of the world, and in many cases simple cues rapidly engage these fully-fledged interpretations. In other words, we often rely on fully-fledged schemas, such as stereotypes, as described in detail earlier in this chapter.

When we do perform causal attributions we are actually doing something quite complex. Formal science is all about understanding the causes of things, and we all know how difficult formal science is. Not surprisingly, lay attributions fall well short of the rigour of formal science. Although day-to-day attributions are adequate for our everyday social interactional needs, attributional accuracy is compromised by the nature of human information processing and social cognition – it is marked by an array of biases and errors (Nisbett and Ross, 1980).

Actor-observer effects and the fundamental attribution error

When attributing someone's behaviour to possible causes, an observer tends to overestimate the significance of dispositional factors and underestimate the significance of situational factors. This kind of bias is called the **fundamental attribution error** (Ross, 1977) or the correspondence bias (Gilbert and Malone, 1995). It also reflects essentialism (Haslam *et al.*, 1998) – a tendency to consider behaviour to reflect underlying and immutable, often innate, properties (essences) of people or the groups they belong to.

For example, if we see a driver make a mistake, we are more likely to conclude that the driver is careless than to consider that external factors (perhaps a crying baby in the back seat) may have been a temporary distraction.

The fundamental attribution error is remarkably potent (but see below). Even when evidence indicates otherwise, people seem to prefer dispositional explanations to situational ones. For example, consider a well-known study by Jones and Harris (1967). Students read essays that other students had either freely chosen or been instructed to write in support of or in opposition to Fidel

Castro. The students had to infer the writers' true attitude towards Castro. Where the writers had been free to choose, the students reasoned that those who wrote a pro-Castro essay were in favour of him, and those who wrote an anti-Castro essay were against him. Surprisingly, even when it was made quite clear that the writers had been instructed what essay to write, the students still believed that those who wrote a pro-Castro essay were in favour of him, and those who wrote an anti-Castro essay were against him. The students disregarded situational factors and made a dispositional attribution, thus committing the fundamental attribution error.

In contrast, when trying to explain our own behaviour, we are much more likely to attribute it to characteristics of the situation than to our own disposition. In other words, we tend to see our own behaviour as relatively variable and strongly influenced by the situation, whereas we see the behaviour of others as more stable and due to personal dispositions. When we try to explain our own behaviour, we are not likely to make the fundamental attribution error (Sande *et al.*, 1988). The fact that we tend to make different kinds of attributions for our own and others' behaviour is called the **actor–observer effect**.

A study of college-age male–female couples demonstrates the actor–observer effect (Orvis *et al.*, 1976). Each partner was asked separately to describe disagreements in the relationship, such as arguments and criticism. Each partner was also asked to explain his or her attribution of the underlying causes of the disagreements. When describing their own behaviour, each person tended to refer to environmental circumstances, such as financial problems or not getting enough sleep. However, when describing their partner's behaviour, participants often referred to specific negative personality characteristics, such as selfishness or low commitment to the relationship.

Why do we tend to commit the fundamental attribution error when we observe the behaviour of others but not when we explain the causes of our own behaviour? Jones and Nisbett (1971) suggested two possible reasons. First, we have a different focus of attention when we view ourselves. When we are doing something, we see the world around us more clearly than we see our own behaviour. However, when we observe someone else doing something, we focus our attention on what is most salient and relevant: that person's behaviour, not the situation in which they are placed.

A second possible reason for these differences in attribution is that different types of information are available to us about our own behaviour and that of other people. We have more information about our own behaviour and we are thus more likely to realise that our own behaviour is often inconsistent. We also have a better notion of which stimuli we are attending to in a given situation. This difference in information leads us to conclude that the behaviour of other people is consistent and thus is a product of their personalities, whereas ours is affected by the situation in which we find ourselves.

Even though we may be aware of the difference in attributions that we make as actors or observers, this does not seem to prevent the actor–observer effect. For example, Krueger et al. (1996) asked pairs of participants (one actor and one observer) to describe the actor on a series of trait adjectives and to rate the consistency of relevant behaviour. Participants then predicted one another's ratings. The actor–observer effect was obtained. Moreover, actors, but not observers, were aware that observers rated actors' behaviour as more consistent than actors themselves did.

The fundamental attribution error is also less 'fundamental' than was once thought – it is influenced by culture. As you might expect from our earlier comparison of individualist and collectivist cultures, it is more prevalent in the former than the latter types of society (Morris and Peng, 1994). People in individualist societies are more inclined to explain behaviour in terms of individual dispositions and free will, whereas people in collectivist societies are more inclined to explain behaviour in terms of social obligations and situational constraints.

The fundamental attribution error is also influenced by more immediate social contexts and individual goals. For example, Schmid and Fiedler (1998) examined closing speeches made by trainee lawyers and university students acting as prosecutors or defending lawyers. Prosecutors tended to attribute internal causality to the defendants, whereas defence lawyers tried to support negative intentional attributions to the victim. When an audience of laypeople was asked to judge the speeches, and recommend sentencing, its decisions reflected the attributions made in the speeches.

False consensus

Another attribution error is the tendency for people to believe that their own behaviour is widely shared and that their own views are consensual – an error called **false consensus**. For example, Sherman et al. (1984) found that male school students who smoked believed that a majority of their peers did so too, whereas non-smokers believed that a majority did not smoke. Obviously, both groups cannot be correct.

One explanation for false consensus is that people tend to surround themselves with similar others and thus actually encounter a disproportionate number of people who behave like they do (Ross, 1977). Thus, when people conclude that other people are more similar to themselves than they actually are, the error may be a result of a bias in selecting people to be with. Another possible explanation is that we dwell so much on our own behaviour that it effectively inhibits proper comparisons that might lead us to realise that others do not necessarily think or act as we do. A third possibility is that in order to have a stable perception of reality we need to believe that our perceptions, attitudes and behaviours are correct, and so we exaggerate the degree of consensual support we have. If you believe the world is flat, then it helps you believe this is true if you can believe that lots of other people agree with you (Marks and Miller, 1987). However, recent research suggests that this social projection of one's own beliefs involves the inclusion of others in the same social category as oneself (Spears and Manstead, 1990; Krueger and Clément, 1997), and it is increased when we are more self-attentive or self-conscious (Fenigstein and Abrams, 1993).

Self-serving biases

Some biases seem to be designed to protect or enhance our self-esteem or self-image (Hoorens, 1993) – these are called **self-serving biases**. These may take a number of forms, and sometimes we may not even be aware of them. For example, people seem to feel more positive about letters of the alphabet that are contained within their own names as compared with letters that do not appear in their name (the 'name letter effect'). Hoorens and Nuttin (1993) examined the name letter effect among children and university students. Participants tended to think these letters appeared more frequently in other words relative to non-name letters. Moreover, because of their association with oneself, 'mere ownership' of the name letters was sufficient to make them more attractive.

Self-serving biases of this type also find expression in the attributions we make. For example, when we attempt to attribute causes to our own behaviour – to explain the reasons for our actions – we tend to attribute our accomplishments and successes to internal causes and our failures and mistakes to external causes. Suppose that you receive an outstanding score on a test. If you are like most people, you will feel the high score is well deserved. After all, you are an intelligent individual who studied hard for the test. Your attributions reflect internal causes for the test score: you are bright and a hard worker. Now suppose that you fail the test – what sorts of attribution do you tend to make? Again, if you are like most people, you may blame your low score on the fact that it was a difficult, even unfair, test, or on the lecturer for being so picky about the answers they counted as wrong. Your attributions in this case blame external causes for the low score – the test's difficulty and the pickiness of your lecturer in marking it. One possible explanation for the self-serving bias is that people are motivated to protect and enhance their self-esteem (Sedikides and Gregg, 2003). Simply put, we protect our self-esteem when we blame failure on the environment and we enhance it when we give ourselves credit for our successes.

However, people differ in their **attributional style** – the extent to which they attribute their outcomes to stable and global causes (Metalsky et al., 1987). In general, people with a 'depressogenic' style are more likely to attribute their failures to these stable and global causes (for example, lack of ability that will affect performance in many ways), resulting in a sense of hopelessness and depression. On the other hand, there is some evidence that depressogenic attributional style is associated with very high levels of achievement among students, perhaps because such students actively test the limits of their capability, and set very high standards for themselves (Houston, 1994).

This sort of bias can also occur at the group level, where it is called the **ultimate attribution error**. People tend to attribute in-group failures and out-group successes to external factors such as luck, and in-group successes and out-group failures internally to properties of the groups and their members (Pettigrew, 1979). This clearly makes the group that you belong to, the in-group, appear much more positive than the group you do not belong to, the out-group, and thus is a self-serving bias.

Another self-serving attributional phenomenon is the belief in a just world – the belief that people get what they deserve in life (Lerner, 1977; Furnham, 2003). According to this idea, when misfortune or tragedy strikes, people tend to blame the victim instead of attributing the source of the problem to situational factors outside the victim's control. As a result, an innocent victim may be blamed for circumstances over which they had no control, and any suffering is seen as being deserved. Common examples of this include the tendency to blame unemployed people, destitute people, rape victims and even victims of genocide for their plight. People may also be complacent about HIV infection because they overly attribute it to risky behaviour by homosexuals (the belief that 'gays deserve AIDS') and thus not relevant to themselves (Ambrosio and Sheehan, 1991).

Although there is a sense in which the **belief in a just world** may reflect the fundamental attribution error, social psychologists believe it is also, and perhaps more importantly, a self-serving bias. By seeing people as bringing bad things on themselves by being bad people, we can reason that we are good, sensible people and thus these things will not happen to us. In this way the world appears more within our control and less fickle and unpredictable. An interesting twist, which is consistent with this idea, is self-blame. People may sometimes blame themselves for their plight in order to avoid the frightening conclusion that the world is a completely unpredictable place where anything may happen irrespective of what you do (Miller and Porter, 1983). Belief in a just world also varies across cultures. In a study of people from 12 countries, Furnham (1983) discovered that the susceptibility to the belief in a just world attribution error was positively correlated with wealth and social status. That is, across many countries (which included countries from both Eastern and Western cultures), a person was more likely to commit this kind of attributional error if they were wealthy and had high social status.

Attributional processes in relationships

People do not always engage in attributions in order to understand their world. However, people do tend to spend a great deal of time communicating their attributions, or negotiating with one another over their attributions. This is particularly the case in close interpersonal relationships (friendship and marriage), where attributions are communicated to fulfil a variety of functions – to explain, justify or excuse behaviour, or to attribute blame and instil guilt (Hilton, 1990).

Interpersonal relationships seem to go through three basic phases: formation, maintenance and dissolution. At each stage attributional communications can take a different form and serve different functions. During the formation stage, attributions reduce ambiguity and facilitate communication and an understanding of the relationship – they bring people together by providing a shared attributional framework. In the maintenance phase, the need to make attributions decreases because stable personalities and relationships have been constructed. The dissolution phase is characterised by an increase in attributions in order to regain an understanding of the relationship, or to deal with divergent attributions.

A notable feature of many interpersonal relationships is precisely this attributional conflict, where partners proffer divergent causal interpretations of behaviours, and disagree over what attributions to adopt. Often partners cannot even agree on a cause–effect sequence, one exclaiming, 'I withdraw because you nag', the other, 'I nag because you withdraw'.

Correlational studies show that happily married (or non-distressed) spouses tend to credit their partners for positive behaviours by citing internal, stable, global and controllable factors to explain them. Negative behaviours are explained away by ascribing them to causes viewed as external, unstable, specific and uncontrollable. Distressed couples behave in exactly the opposite way. In addition, it appears that while women engage in attributional thought about the relationship, men do so only when the relationship becomes dysfunctional. In this respect, and contrary to popular opinion, men may be the more diagnostic barometers of marital dysfunction.

Do attributional dynamics produce dysfunctional marital relationships, or do dysfunctional relationships distort the attributional dynamic? This important causal question has been looked at by Fincham and Bradbury (1987), who obtained responsibility attributions, causal attributions and marital satisfaction measures from 39 married couples on two occasions 10–12 months apart. Attributions made on the first occasion were found reliably to predict marital satisfaction 10–12 months later, but only for wives. Another longitudinal study (though only over a two-month period) confirmed that attributions do have a causal impact on subsequent relationship satisfaction. Subsequent, more extensive and better-controlled longitudinal studies have replicated these findings for both husbands and wives.

Srivastava *et al.* (2006) asked over 100 couples to indicate their satisfaction with their romantic relationship and investigated whether optimists were more satisfied (and whether partners of optimists were more satisfied). Both results were found: those who were most optimistic, and those partnered with very optimistic people, were significantly more likely to be satisfied with their relationship. A feature of this satisfaction that was important was perceived support – when they argued, partners who sought quick conflict resolution through conversation, for example, were more satisfied with the way in which the argument was resolved after a week had passed.

How long-term is this effect of optimism? When the researchers followed up couples after a year, it was men's overall optimism that predicted relationship success. Male optimists' relationships lasted longer than did non-optimists'.

Why is optimism so important? Srivastava *et al.* (2006) suggest that optimists may attribute a partner's negative outbursts or behaviour as temporary, reflecting a state-specific reaction rather than a global personality disposition. They may also focus more on a partner's positive characteristics, thus ignoring or playing down a partner's negative mood. They act as a more 'secure base' for their partners and thus provide much needed social support that is always there, unconditionally.

Heuristic judgements

Social cognition refers to ways in which we make inferences about people, social inferences, and the world we live in, and then store these inferences as schemas that guide our perception and judgement. An important basis for social inference is, as we have seen, to find causes for people's behaviour through attribution processes. However, as we have also seen, these processes are often not very accurate or reliable. Often we do not use attribution processes at all to make inferences about people, but instead use cognitive short-cuts or inferential rules called **heuristics**. Two of the most important heuristics that people use are representativeness and availability (Tversky and Kahneman, 1974).

The representativeness heuristic

When we meet someone for the first time, we notice their clothes, hairstyle, posture, manner of speaking, hand gestures and many other characteristics. Based on our previous experience, we use this information to make tentative conclusions about other characteristics that we cannot immediately discover. In doing so, we attempt to match the characteristics we can observe with schemas or stereotypes we have of different types or groups of people. If the person seems representative of one of these schemas, we conclude that they fit that particular category (Lupfer *et al.*, 1990). In making this conclusion, we use the **representativeness heuristic** – we classify an object into the category to which it appears to be the most similar.

The representativeness heuristic is based on our ability to categorise information. We observe that some characteristics tend to go together (or we are taught that they do). When we observe some of these characteristics, we conclude that the others are also present. Most of the time this strategy works; we are able to predict people's behaviour fairly accurately. Tversky and Kahneman (1974) describe someone called Steve: he is 'very shy and withdrawn, invariably helpful, but with little interest in people or in the world of reality. A meek and tidy soul, he has a need for order and structure, and a passion for detail'. Chances are you will infer that Steve is a librarian rather than a farmer, surgeon or trapeze artist – and you are probably quite likely to be correct. What we know about Steve seems to be quite representative of what we 'know' about librarians.

In relying on the representativeness heuristic we often subscribe to the **base-rate fallacy** – we overlook statistical information about the relative size of categories and therefore the probability that the person will belong to the category. If you described a person as being athletic and interested in surfing you are probably better off simply inferring she is Chinese than Australian (for every Australian there are 60 Chinese).

Learning to play the odds, so to speak, and so to avoid being misled by distinctive characteristics, is particularly important in certain intellectual endeavours. For example, doctors who are experienced in making diagnoses of diseases teach their students to learn and make use of the probabilities of particular diseases and not to be fooled by especially distinctive symptoms. In fact, Zukier and Pepitone (1984) posed a problem to first-year medical students and to residents who had completed their clinical training. The inexperienced students were tricked by the base-rate fallacy but the residents played the odds, as they had been taught to do.

The availability heuristic

When people attempt to assess the importance or the frequency of an event, they tend to be guided by the ease with which examples of that event come to mind – by how available these examples are to the imagination. This mental short-cut is called the **availability heuristic**. In general, the things we are able to think of most easily are more important and occur more frequently than things that are difficult to imagine. Thus, the availability heuristic works well – most of the time.

Some events are so vivid that we can easily picture them happening. We can easily picture getting mugged while walking through the heart of a large city at night or being involved in an aeroplane crash, probably because such events are often reported in the news and because they are so frightening. Thus, people tend to overestimate the likelihood of such misfortunes happening to them. Tversky and Kahneman (1982) demonstrated the effect of availability by asking people to estimate whether English words starting with 'k' were more or less common than words with 'k' in the third position (for example, 'kiss' versus 'lake'). Most people said that there were more words starting with 'k'. In fact, there are more than twice as many words having 'k' in the third position as those having 'k' in the first position. But because thinking of words that start with a particular letter is easier than thinking of words that contain the letter in another position, people are misled in their judgement.

Many variables can affect the availability of an event or a concept and thus increase its effect on our decision-making. For example, having recently seen a particular type of event makes it easier for us to think of other examples of that event. This phenomenon is called priming. Many first-year psychology students demonstrate this phenomenon when, after first learning the symptoms of various clinical disorders, they start 'discovering' these very symptoms in themselves.

Higgins et al. (1977) demonstrated the effects of priming on judging the personality characteristics of strangers. They had participants work on a task that introduced various descriptive adjectives. Next, the experimenters described an imaginary person, saying that he had performed such feats as climbing mountains and crossing the Atlantic in a yacht. Finally, they asked the participants to give their impressions of this person. Those participants who had previously been exposed to words such as 'adventurous' reported favourable impressions, whereas those who had been exposed to words such as 'reckless' reported unfavourable ones. The priming effect of the descriptive adjectives had biased their interpretation of the facts.

More recently, a group of US researchers found, rather surprisingly, that exposure to the Republican party flag increased positive attitudes to Republican beliefs (Carter et al., 2011). In two experiments, conducted during the 2008 US Presidential election and one year into Obama's administration, they exposed participants to the Republican flag and measured voting intentions and political attitudes and beliefs. Those exposed to the flag were more likely to be sympathetic to Republican beliefs and attitudes and expressed an intention to vote Republican despite the participants denying that such exposure would influence their thinking and this finding applied to both Democrat and Republican participants.

The availability heuristic also explains why personal encounters tend to have an especially strong effect on our decision-making. For example, suppose that you have decided to buy a new car. You have narrowed your choice down to two makes, both available for about the same price. You read an article in a consumer magazine that summarises the experiences of thousands of people who have purchased these cars, and their testimony shows clearly that one of them has a much better repair record. You decide to purchase that make, and mention the fact to a friend later that day. She says, 'Oh, no! Don't buy one of those. I bought one last year, and it has been nothing but trouble. I'd had it for only two weeks when it first broke down. I got it towed to a garage, and they had to order a part from the manufacturer. Since then, I've had trouble with the air conditioner and the transmission.' Would this experience affect your decision to buy that make of car?

Most people would take this personal encounter very seriously. Even though it consists of the experience of only one person, whereas the survey in the consumer magazine represents the experience of thousands of people, a vivid personal encounter is much more available and memorable than a set of statistics, and tends to have a disproportionate effect on our own behaviour (Borgida and Nisbett, 1977).

The cognitive accessibility of social information can also have dramatic effects on our behaviour and performance. Bargh et al. (1996) found that when participants had been primed with the stereotype of elderly people, they walked away from the experiment more slowly than unprimed participants. Dijksterhuis et al. (1998) extended this intriguing research to explore the effects of making specific individuals salient. Participants were first asked to unscramble some sentences that contained within them words that describe the traits associated with the elderly stereotype. This primed the elderly stereotype by making the attributes of elderly people more accessible in participants' minds. Next, half the participants were asked to make judgements about a specific elderly person, Princess Juliana, the 89-year-old Dutch Queen Mother. This made a specific 'exemplar' accessible. Participants were then directed to the lifts at the end of the corridor where another experimenter was waiting. The time taken for them to reach this second experimenter was recorded. In contrast to Bargh et al.'s (1996) results, when Princess Juliana was primed, participants walked significantly faster than when the general stereotype of elderly people had been primed.

These two studies illustrate that when general stereotypes are activated we may automatically adopt some of the stereotypical characteristics ourselves, but when images of specific extreme individuals are activated we automatically make a contrast between ourselves and the exemplar, making us react in opposition to the characteristics of the individual. We assimilate ourselves to stereotypes but contrast ourselves from individuals. For example, Dijksterhuis *et al.* (1998) also found that participants performed better on a test when the stereotype of professor had been primed than when the stereotype of a supermodel had been primed. However, they performed worse on the test when the specific example of Albert Einstein had been primed than when the specific example of Claudia Schiffer had been primed.

Attitudes and attitude change

The study of **attitudes** – relatively enduring sets of beliefs, feelings and intentions towards an object, person, event or symbol – is one of the most important fields of study in social psychology (Pratkanis *et al.*, 1989; Eagly and Chaiken, 1993). Some early definitions of social psychology actually defined social psychology as the study of attitudes.

The nature of attitudes

Many social psychologists believe that attitudes have three different components: affect, behavioural intention and cognition. The affective component consists of the kinds of feeling that an attitude object (person, activity, physical object) arouses. The behavioural intentional component consists of an intention to act in a particular way with respect to a particular object. The cognitive component consists of a set of beliefs about an object. Social psychologists have studied all three aspects of attitudes.

Affective components of attitudes

Affective components of attitudes can be very strong and pervasive. The bigot feels disgust in the presence of people from a certain religious, racial or ethnic group; the nature lover feels exhilaration from a pleasant walk through the woods. Like other emotional reactions, these feelings are strongly influenced by direct or vicarious classical conditioning (Rajecki, 1989).

Direct classical conditioning is straightforward. Suppose that you meet someone who seems to take delight in embarrassing you. She makes clever, sarcastic remarks that disparage your intelligence, looks and personality. Unfortunately, her remarks are so clever that your attempts to defend yourself make you appear even more foolish. After a few encounters with this person, the sight of her or the sound of her voice is likely to elicit feelings of dislike and fear. Your attitude towards her will be negative.

Vicarious classical conditioning undoubtedly plays a major role in transmitting parents' attitudes to their children. People are skilled at detecting even subtle signs of fear, hatred and other negative emotional states in people, especially when they know them well. Thus, children often vicariously experience their parents' prejudices and fears even if these feelings are unspoken. Children who see their parents recoil in disgust at the sight of members of some ethnic group are likely to feel the same emotion and thus, over time, develop the same attitude.

Simply being exposed repeatedly to an otherwise neutral object or issue over time may influence our attitude towards it – generally in a favourable direction. This attraction for the familiar is called the **mere exposure effect**. One of the first studies to demonstrate this effect used several neutral stimuli – towards which there were no positive or negative feelings – such as nonsense words, photographs of the faces of unknown people and Chinese characters (Zajonc, 1968). The more the participants saw the stimuli, the more they liked the stimuli later. Stimuli that were seen only once were liked more than ones never seen before. Even when the stimuli were flashed so briefly that they could not be recognised, participants usually preferred a stimulus that had been previously presented to a novel one that they could not recognise (Kunst-Wilson and Zajonc, 1980). The mere exposure effect probably reflects our tendency to feel positive about things that do not pose a threat to us. Our feelings towards a person, event or object will naturally improve if, on repeated exposure, we discover that no threat is posed.

Cognitive components of attitudes

We acquire most beliefs about a particular attitude object quite directly: we hear or read a fact or opinion, or other people validate our expressed beliefs. However, we can often develop fairly nebulous likes and dislikes (affect) and then develop our beliefs subsequently, to justify our feelings. For example, you may feel you dislike Honda cars, but really not have many beliefs about them. This affective orientation will guide the sorts of belief you subsequently hold about Hondas – you are more likely then to believe unfavourable than favourable things about Hondas. This illustrates an important point: although we can separate out different components of attitudes in order to describe them in a textbook, in reality they are inextricably linked.

We form and change our attitudes throughout our lives; however, children have an enormous task ahead of them: they come into the world with no attitudes, and so have very rapidly to learn attitudes in order to orient themselves to people, events and objects in their world. One way they do this is by simply imitating the behaviour of people who play an important role in their lives. Children usually repeat opinions expressed by their parents. In Northern Ireland, many children label themselves as Catholics or Protestants long before they know the values for which these religious organisations stand. Often they ask their parents, 'Are we Catholics or Protestants?' without considering whether they might have any choice in the matter. The tendency to identify with the family unit (and, later with peer groups) provides a strong incentive to adopt the group's attitudes.

Attitudes and behaviour

Attitudes have a behavioural intention component – a motivation or expressed intention to behave in some way or other that is consistent with the affective and cognitive components of an attitude. For example, many people have negative attitudes towards smoking and express the intention not to smoke. However, we all know that the expressed intention to behave according to an attitude certainly does not guarantee that we actually behave in that way – people who intend not to smoke often smoke. Intentions and behaviour are not the same thing.

People do not always behave as their expressed attitudes and beliefs would lead us to expect. In a classic example, LaPiere (1934) drove across the western United States with a Chinese couple. They stopped at over 250 restaurants and lodging places and were refused service only once. Several months after their trip, LaPiere wrote to the owners of the places they had visited and asked whether they would serve Chinese people. The response was overwhelmingly negative; 92 per cent of those who responded said that they would not. Clearly, their behaviour gave less evidence of racial bias than their expressed attitudes did. This study has been cited as evidence that attitudes do not always influence behaviour – indeed hundreds of studies of the relationship between attitudes and behaviour suggest, that on average, attitudes predict only 2–3 per cent of behaviour (Wicker, 1969). One way to think of this is that only two or three times out of 100 do people actually do what they say – perhaps we should not be quite so harsh on our politicians.

However, all is not lost. If it were, then commercial advertising would be a waste of time, as advertising largely tries to change behaviour by changing people's attitudes towards products. There are ways in which we can be much more accurate at predicting behaviour from attitudes. Attitude specificity is one important influence on attitude–behaviour congruence. If you measure a person's general attitude towards a topic, you will be unlikely to be able to predict their behaviour. Behaviours, unlike attitudes, are specific events. However, as the attitude being measured becomes more specific, the person's behaviour becomes more predictable.

For example, Weigel *et al.* (1974) measured people's attitudes towards a series of topics that increased in specificity from 'a pure environment' to 'the Sierra Club' (an American organisation that supports environmental

Table 15.4 Correlation between willingness to join or work for the Sierra Club and various measures of related attitudes

Attitude scale	Correlation
Importance of a pure environment	0.06
Pollution	0.32
Conservation	0.24
Attitude towards the Sierra Club	0.68

Source: Based on Weigel, R., Vernon, D.T.A. and Tognacci, L.N., Specificity of the attitude as a determinant of attitude–behavior congruence, *Journal of Personality and Social Psychology*, 1974, 30, 724 – 8.

causes). They used the participants' attitudes to predict whether they would volunteer for various activities to benefit the Sierra Club. A person's attitude towards environmentalism was a poor predictor of whether they would volunteer; their attitude towards the Sierra Club itself was a much better predictor (see Table 15.4). For example, a person might favour a pure environment but also dislike organised clubs or have little time to spare for meetings. This person would express a positive attitude towards a pure environment but would not join the club or volunteer for any activities to support it.

In another study, Davidson and Jacard (1979) monitored women's attitudes towards birth control as a predictor of use of the contraceptive pill over the next two years. They found that pill use over the next two years was most strongly predicted by a very specific measure of 'Attitude towards using birth control pills during the next two years' (a correlation of 0.57), and least strongly in contrast to the most general measure of 'Attitude towards birth control' (correlation of 0.08).

Reasoned action and planned behaviour

Probably the most systematic account of how attitudes and behaviour are related has been developed by Fishbein and Ajzen (see Ajzen, 1989) in their **theories of reasoned action** and of **planned behaviour**. Someone's intention to behave in a certain way is strengthened if (1) they have a positive attitude towards the behaviour, (2) they believe many people that matter also have a favourable attitude towards the behaviour, (3) they believe they have the resources and opportunity to engage in the behaviour, and (4) the intention is very specific to one particular behaviour. For example, consider someone who loves going to Wagnerian operas, all of whose friends also love going to Wagnerian operas, and who has a ticket to go to *The Ring*, which is on in his city tonight and who has nothing else to do tonight. If he expressed the strong intention of going to *The Ring* tonight which he is likely to do, then you can probably pretty accurately predict that this is what he will do. In contrast, consider someone who loves going to Wagnerian operas, but all of whose friends do not, and who has no ticket to the opera. He is unlikely to express a strong intention of going to *The Ring* tonight, and you are much less likely to know exactly what he will be doing.

D. Parker *et al.* (1995) surveyed almost 600 drivers in Britain, and found that they could quite accurately predict whether those drivers would engage in specific reckless driving behaviours, for example cutting in and reckless weaving, by measuring their attitudes towards the behaviour, the amount of support they perceived for this behaviour from their friends, and whether they had the resources and opportunity to behave in this way (for example, they had a car, they could get away with it, they had done it in the past and so knew what to do).

Attitude accessibility and attitude strength

Attitudes are cognitively represented in memory. Thus, like any other cognitive representations they are likely to have a greater influence on behaviour if they are readily accessible – easily and readily recalled. Indeed, research does show that attitudes affect behavioural intentions, and thus behaviour, more strongly if the attitudes are more accessible in memory (Doll and Ajzen, 1992). Our attitudes can also vary in strength. A strong attitude is one that has a strong associative link with the attitude object and thus, once activated, the attitude has a more automatic link with behavioural intentions and ultimately behaviour (Fazio *et al.*, 1986). So, for example, if you absolutely love chocolate and think about eating chocolate all the time then your attitude towards chocolate is strong and accessible and is probably a very good predictor of your intention to eat chocolate – an intention which probably maps tightly onto your behaviour. If, on the other hand, you quite like lobster and occasionally think about eating lobster then your attitude towards lobster is less strong and accessible, and is a poor predictor of your intentions and behaviour.

Social identity and norms

Another factor that influences the attitude–behaviour relationship is the extent to which an attitude is an important aspect of the kind of person we are. Self-defining attitudes, ones that define our identity, particularly our social identity as a group member, are more likely to be expressed as behaviour. More specifically, attitudes are more likely to express themselves as behaviour if the attitudes (and associated behaviour) are normative properties of a social group with which people identify (Terry and Hogg, 1996). To test this idea, Terry and Hogg (1996) measured attitudes and intentions relating to taking regular exercise and adopting

sun-protective behaviours. They found a much tighter attitude–intention link among student participants who identified strongly with a student peer group for whom they felt regular exercise and adopting sun-protective behaviour was a strong group-defining norm.

Attitude change and persuasion

People often attempt to persuade us to change our attitudes. Social psychological research on persuasion has taken its form from an early and highly influential programme of research by Hovland *et al.* (1953). Hovland and colleagues famously asked, 'Who says what to whom and with what effect?' – a question which identifies the three key aspects of persuasive communication: the source of the communication, the content of the message and the audience or target of the communication.

The source

Credibility and attractiveness are two aspects of the source of a message that have a major affect on persuasiveness. A message tends to be more persuasive if its source is credible. Source credibility is high when the source is perceived as knowledgeable and is trusted to communicate this knowledge accurately. For example, in one study, people developed a more favourable attitude towards different types of medicine when the information appeared in the prestigious medical journal *New England Journal of Medicine* than when it appeared in a mass-circulation tabloid (Hovland and Weiss, 1951). Research by Bochner and Insko (1966) showed that credible sources are not only more persuasive but they can also induce the greatest amount of attitude change. Bochner and Insko took advantage of the fact that their student participants believed that eight hours of sleep a night was required to maintain good health. They then exposed them to one of two sources of opinion, a high credibility Nobel Prize-winning sleep physiologist or a less credible YMCA instructor, who said that less sleep was optimal. Both sources shifted the students' attitudes when the sources advocated between seven and three hours' sleep, but when they advocated one or two hours the credible source was significantly more effective than the less credible source at changing attitudes.

Messages also have more impact when the source is physically attractive. For example, physically attractive people are more likely than physically unattractive people to persuade others to sign a petition (Chaiken, 1979). Individuals who are asked to endorse products for advertisers are almost always physically attractive or appealing in other ways. Since people tend to like people who are similar to them more than people who are not, similarity should have the same effect. However, this does not seem to be the case. People are more persuaded by similar others when the issue is a matter of taste (for example, musical preference), but more persuaded by dissimilar others when the issue is a matter of fact (for example, who won the Tour de France in a particular year) (Petty and Cacioppo, 1981).

The message

As you would expect, aspects of the message itself are important in determining its persuasive appeal.

For example, is an argument that provides only one side of an issue more effective than one that presents both sides? The answer depends on the audience. If the audience either knows very little about the issue or already holds a strong position with respect to it, one-sided arguments tend to be more effective. If the audience is well informed about the issue, however, a two-sided argument tends to be more persuasive (McAlister *et al.*, 1980).

Psychology in action: How not to throw in the towel

How effective are scare tactics embedded in the message in changing someone's attitude? Some research suggests that frightening messages are very effective and there is considerable research showing that negative messages are more effective than positive ones.

Leventhal *et al.* (1967) found that people were more likely to stop smoking when the message was accompanied by a graphic video of surgery on a patient affected by lung cancer. Other research finds the opposite. Janis and Feshbach (1953) found much more improvement in dental hygiene practices among participants who had been exposed to a low-fear message (facts about tooth decay and gum disease) than those exposed to a high-fear message (graphic visual images of disease).

Yet other research has shown that scare tactics may be effective in bringing about change, but only when combined with instructive information about how to change one's behaviour (Cialdini *et al.*, 1981). According to Janis (1967), a little bit of fear is good for motivation to attend to the message and to change one's attitudes and behaviours, but too much fear can distract us from the message so that we are unable to conceive of ways to put the message into action (Keller and Block, 1995).

Another example of the power of the message to change behaviour was highlighted in the vignette at the opening of the chapter. Goldstein *et al.* (2008) examined whether different types of messages left in people's hotel rooms would alter their towel recycling use. Great expense is spent on laundry by hotels, both financial and environmental. Could there be a way of persuading people to re-use their dirty towels? The researchers set up a field experiment in which hotel rooms hung signs which featured different messages. One featured what the researchers called a 'descriptive norm', e.g., 'JOIN YOUR FELLOW GUESTS IN HELPING TO SAVE THE ENVIRONMENT'. Almost 75 per cent of guests who are asked to participate in our new resource savings program do help by using their towels.' The other featured a standard signs about saving the environment, as illustrated in Figure 15.1.

Figure 15.1 The towel hanger used in Goldstein *et al.*'s experiment.

Source: Goldstein, N.J., Cialdini, R.B. & Griskevicius, V., 2008.

Guests who were provided with the first sign were significantly more likely to reuse their towels, as you can seen from the graph in Figure 15.2.

A similar change in behaviour was also observed in another context. Cialdini *et al.* (2006) examined whether the provision of different types of messages would affect

Psychology in action: *Continued*

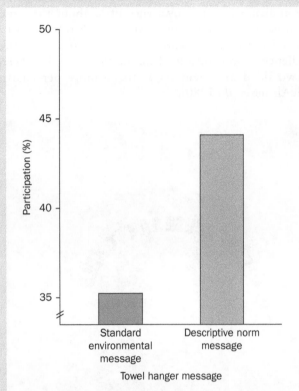

Figure 15.2 There was a significant difference in towel re-usage when the message on the towel hanger was changed.

people's tendency to thieve wood from Arizona's Petrified Forest National Park. They provided visitors with a plea to think about their behaviour and not steal but did so under two conditions: when messages were positively conveyed or negatively conveyed. In the positive condition, the message was: 'Please leave petrified wood in the forest' accompanied by a picture of a person holding a piece of wood and admiring it. In the negative condition, the message read: 'Please don't remove the petrified wood from the forest' accompanied by a drawing of a person stealing wood with a red circle and bar across him. In another manipulation, they exposed visitors to two milder messages which were descriptive but either mentioned that previous visitors had removed wood from the forest, changing its state, or had left the wood in the forest, preserving its natural state. When theft of wood was measured, those in the first manipulation were significantly less likely to steal whereas those in the second were more likely to steal.

The audience

Research on the audience or target of the communication identifies a number of factors that influence how easily persuaded people may be. One finding is that people who have very low or very high self-esteem are less easily persuaded than people with average self-esteem, because the former are either too anxious to pay attention or too self-assured to be influenced (Rhodes and Wood, 1992). There are no straightforward sex differences in persuadability, but complex interactions (Carli, 1990). For example, Covell *et al.* (1994) studied the effect of tobacco and alcohol advertisements on Canadian adult and adolescent males and females and discovered a sex difference among the adolescents only – female adolescents were more influenced than male adolescents by advertisements that were strongly image-oriented. As with sex, there is no clear relationship between age and persuadability – some research finds no age effect whereas other studies find that younger and older people are more easily persuaded than people in their middle years (Visser and Krosnick, 1998).

The process of attitude change through persuasion

Petty and Cacioppo (1986) have proposed the **elaboration likelihood model** to account for attitude change through persuasion (Figure 15.3). According to this model, persuasion can take either a central or a peripheral route. The central route requires a person to think critically about the argument being presented, to weigh its strengths and weaknesses, and to elaborate on the relevant themes. At issue is the substance of the argument, not its emotional or superficial appeal. The peripheral route, on the other hand, refers to attempts at persuasion in which the change is associated with positive stimuli – a professional athlete, a millionaire or an attractive model – which actually may have nothing to do with the substance of the argument. Selling products by associating them with attractive people or by implying that buying the product will result in emotional, social or financial benefits are examples of the use of peripheral attitude change techniques.

Very closely related to Petty and Cacioppo's distinction between central and peripheral route processing, is

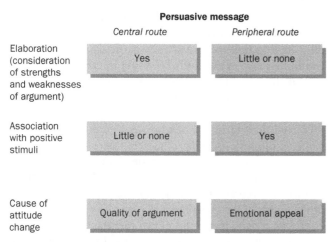

Persuasive message

	Central route	Peripheral route
Elaboration (consideration of strengths and weaknesses of argument)	Yes	Little or none
Association with positive stimuli	Little or none	Yes
Cause of attitude change	Quality of argument	Emotional appeal

Figure 15.3 The elaboration likelihood model of attitude change. Persuasive messages may centre either on a substantive argument that requires an individual to think about the argument's strengths and weaknesses (the central route) or on a superficial argument that is associated with positive stimuli (the peripheral route).

Chaiken's distinction between systematic and heuristic processing (Bohner *et al.*, 1995). People can systematically consider all aspects of a message, or they can very superficially rely on simple heuristics such as thinking that longer arguments or arguments with more statistical facts and figures must be more true, or that all messages from politicians are lies. People are more likely to resort to heuristic processing if they have limited time to process the message or if they are in a good mood. So, to change attitudes towards consumer products it is quite effective to bombard hurried people with advertisements that put them in a good mood and present statistical/scientific information from people dressed as scientists. This encourages heuristic processing and encourages the heuristic that messages backed by science must be true. One difference between the elaboration likelihood model and the heuristic–systematic model is that whereas a message is processed either centrally or peripherally at any one time, it can be processed systematically and heuristically at the same time.

Resistance to persuasion

Far more attempts at persuasion fail than succeed. Researchers have identified three major factors: reactance, forewarning and inoculation. Reactance refers to a tendency to resist persuasion, or even move one's attitudes in an opposite direction, when a deliberate persuasion attempt is detected. People do not like to have their personal freedom limited by being pressured to change their attitudes. When people are forewarned of an influence attempt they are less easily influenced, particularly as regards attitudes that are considered important. Forewarning allows people to generate defensive counterarguments to protect their attitudes.

Related to forewarning, is inoculation. Inoculation is a process where people are exposed to a weak version of a persuasive argument – much like inoculation against an illness. This allows people to build up resistance, in this case specific counterarguments, against the full-blown persuasive attempt. Research on inoculation was prompted by the way that American prisoners of war in the Korean War of the 1950s were easily brainwashed to denounce the American way of life and endorse Communism. It was thought that this had happened because the soldiers had never heard any attacks on the American way of life, and so were completely unprepared to protect their attitudes (McGuire, 1964). McGuire and Papageorgis (1961) conducted a study where student participants who strongly endorsed truisms such as 'It's a good idea to brush your teeth after every meal', were exposed to a strong attack on these truisms and then had their attitudes remeasured. Some participants were prepared for the attack by being provided with supporting arguments defending their position, some were inoculated by being exposed to a mild form of the attack, and some were not prepared at all. Supportive defence and inoculation reduced attitude change relative to no defence, but inoculation was significantly more effective.

What kinds of argument do you think would be effective in persuading you to change your attitude towards a prominent political figure? How would you describe these arguments in psychological terms? Based on social psychological knowledge about the relationship between attitudes and behaviour, what advice would you give an organisation that wanted to combat waste (for example, excessive paper use, excessive energy use)? Would you recommend changing employees' attitudes in order to change their behaviour?

Cognitive dissonance

Although we usually regard our attitudes as causes of our behaviour, our behaviour also affects our attitudes. Two major theories attempt to explain the effects of behaviour on attitude formation: cognitive dissonance and self-perception.

The oldest theory is cognitive dissonance theory, developed by Leon Festinger (1957). According to **cognitive dissonance theory**, when we perceive a discrepancy between our attitudes and behaviour, between our behaviour and self-image or between one attitude and another, an unpleasant state of anxiety, or dissonance, results. For example, a person may successfully overcome a childhood racial prejudice but may experience unpleasant emotional arousal at the sight of a racially mixed couple. The person experiences a conflict between the belief in their own lack of prejudice and the evidence of prejudice from their behaviour. This conflict produces dissonance, which is an aversive state that people are motivated to reduce. A person can reduce dissonance by (1) reducing the importance of one of the dissonant elements, (2) adding consonant elements, or (3) changing one of the dissonant elements.

Suppose that a student believes that he is very intelligent but he invariably receives poor grades in his courses. Because the obvious prediction is that intelligent people get good grades, the discrepancy causes the student to experience dissonance. To reduce this dissonance, he may decide that grades are not important and that intelligence is not very closely related to grades. He is using strategy 1, reducing the importance of one of the dissonant elements – the fact that he received poor grades in his courses. Or he can dwell on the belief that his lecturers were unfair or that his job leaves him little time to study. In this case, he is using strategy 2, reducing dissonance by adding consonant elements – those factors that can account for his poor grades and hence explain the discrepancy between his perceived intelligence and grades. Finally, he can use strategy 3 to change one of the dissonant elements. He can either improve his grades or revise his opinion of his own intelligence.

Induced compliance

Most of us believe that although we can induce someone to do something, getting someone to change an attitude is much harder. However, Festinger's theory of cognitive dissonance and supporting experimental evidence indicate otherwise. Under the right conditions, when people are coerced into doing something or are paid to do something, the act of **compliance** – simply engaging in a particular behaviour at someone else's request – may cause a change in their underlying attitudes.

Cognitive dissonance theory predicts that dissonance occurs when a person's behaviour has undesirable outcomes for self-esteem; there is a conflict between the person's belief in their own worth and the fact that they have done something that damages this belief. The person will then seek to justify the behaviour. For example, a poorly paid vacuum cleaner sales representative is likely to convince himself that the shoddy merchandise he sells is actually good. Otherwise, he must question why he works for a company that pays him poorly and requires him to lie to prospective customers about the quality of the product in order to make a sale. Conversely, an executive of one of the celebrity gossip magazines may know that the magazines she produces are sleazy, mindless drivel, but she is so well paid that she does not feel bad about producing them. Her high salary justifies her job and probably also provides her with enough self-esteem that she has decided that the public gets what it deserves anyway.

Festinger and Carlsmith (1959) verified this observation by having participants perform very boring tasks, such as putting spools on a tray, dumping them out, putting them

on the tray again, dumping them out again, and so on. After the participants had spent an hour on exercises like this, the experimenter asked each participant whether they would help out in the study by trying to convince the next person that the task was interesting and enjoyable. Some participants received $1 for helping out; others received $20. Control participants were paid nothing. The experimenters predicted that participants who were paid only $1 would perceive the task as being relatively interesting. They had been induced to lie to a 'fellow student' (actually, a confederate of the experimenters) for a paltry sum. Like the vacuum cleaner sales representative, they should convince themselves of the worth of the experiment to maintain their self-esteem. Poorly paid participants did in fact rate the task better than did those who were well paid (Figure 15.4). Clearly, our actions have an effect on our attitudes. When faced with inconsistency between our behaviour and our attitudes, we often change our attitudes to suit our behaviour.

Arousal and attitude change

Festinger's theory hypothesises that dissonance reduction is motivated by an aversive drive. A study by Croyle and Cooper (1983) obtained physiological evidence to support this hypothesis. The experimenters chose as their participants Princeton University students who disagreed with the assertion 'Alcohol use should be totally banned from the Princeton campus and eating clubs'. Each participant was induced to write an essay containing strong and forceful arguments in favour of the assertion or in opposition to it. While the participants were writing the essay, the experimenters measured the electrical conductance of their skin, which is known to be a good indicator of the physiological arousal that accompanies stress. Some participants were

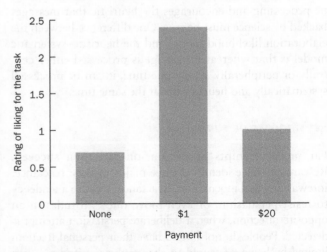

Figure 15.4 Effects of induced compliance. People who received $1 to lie about a boring task later indicated that they liked the task more than did people who received $20.

Source: Based on data from Festinger, L. and Carlsmith, J.M., Cognitive consequences of forced compliance. *Journal of Abnormal and Social Psychology*, 1959, 58, 203–10.

simply told to write the essay. Other participants were told that their participation was completely voluntary and that they were free to leave at any time; they even signed a form emphasising the voluntary nature of the task. Of course, all participants felt social pressure to continue the study, and all of them did. Those who were simply told to write the essay should have felt less personal responsibility for what they wrote and would therefore be expected to experience less cognitive dissonance than those who believed that they had exercised free choice in deciding to participate.

Participants in the 'free choice' condition who had written essays contradicting their original opinions showed both a change in opinion and evidence of physiological arousal. Those participants who were simply told to write the essay or who wrote arguments that they had originally agreed with showed little sign of arousal or attitude change (Figure 15.5).

Attitudes and expenditures

Festinger's theory of cognitive dissonance accounts for another relation between behaviour and attitudes: our tendency to value an item more if it costs us something. For example, some people buy extremely expensive brands of cosmetics even though the same ingredients are used in much cheaper brands. Presumably, they believe that if an item costs more, it must work better. Following the same

rationale, most animal shelters sell their stray animals to prospective pet owners, not only because the money helps defray their operating costs, but also because they assume that a purchased pet will be treated better than a free pet.

Aronson and Mills (1959) verified this phenomenon. The experimenters subjected female college students to varying degrees of embarrassment as a prerequisite for joining what was promised to be an interesting discussion about sexual behaviour. To produce slight embarrassment, they had the participants read aloud five sex-related words (such as prostitute, virgin and petting – remember that this research was conducted in the 1950s) to the experimenter, who was male. To produce more severe embarrassment, they had the women read aloud 12 obscene four-letter words and two sexually explicit passages of prose. The control group read nothing at all. The 'interesting group discussion' turned out to be a tape recording of a very dull conversation.

Festinger's theory predicts that the women who had to go through an embarrassing ordeal in order to join the group would experience some cognitive dissonance. They had suffered an ordeal in order to take part in an interesting discussion that turned out actually to be very dull. These negative and positive experiences are inconsistent and dissonance arousing, and should make them view the 'discussion' more favourably so that their effort would not be perceived as having been completely without value. The results were as predicted: the participants who had been embarrassed the most rated the discussion more favourably than did the control participants or those who had experienced only slight embarrassment. We value things at least partly by how much they cost us. One controversial implication is that people might value social goods like education and national parks more highly if they personally paid (more) for them.

Self-perception

Bem (1972) proposed an alternative to the theory of cognitive dissonance. Drawing on attribution theory, which we discussed earlier in this chapter, he defined self-perception theory in the following way:

> Individuals come to 'know' their own attitudes, emotions, and other internal states partially by inferring them from observations of their own overt behaviour and/or the circumstances in which this behaviour occurs. Thus, to the extent that internal cues are weak, ambiguous, or uninterpretable, the individual is functionally in the same position as an outside observer, an observer who must necessarily rely on those same external cues to infer the individual's inner states.

Bem noted that an observer who attempts to make judgements about someone's attitudes, emotions or other

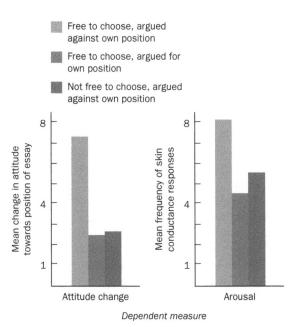

Figure 15.5 Physiological evidence for cognitive dissonance. Mean change in attitude towards the position advocated by the essay and mean frequency of skin conductance responses (a physiological index of arousal) in participants who argued for or against their own positions.

Source: Based on data from Croyle, R.T. and Cooper, J., Dissonance arousal: Physical evidence. *Journal of Personality and Social Psychology*, 1983, 45, 782–91.

internal states must examine the person's behaviour for clues. For example, if you cannot ask someone why they are doing something, you must analyse the situation in which the behaviour occurs to try to determine the motivation. Bem suggested that people analyse their own internal states in a similar way, making attributions about the causes of their own behaviour.

You will recall the experiment by Festinger and Carlsmith (1959) in which students who were paid only $1 later rated a boring task as more interesting than did those who were paid $20. How does self-perception theory explain these results? Suppose that an observer watches a participant who has been paid $1 to deliver a convincing speech to another student about how interesting a task was. Because being paid such a small sum is not a sufficient reason for calling a dull task interesting, the observer will probably conclude that the student actually enjoyed the task. Lacking good evidence for external causes, the observer will attribute the behaviour to a dispositional factor: interest in the task. Bem argued that the participant makes the same inference about themself. Because the participant was not paid enough to tell a lie, they must have enjoyed the task. The principal advantage of self-perception theory is that it makes fewer

assumptions than does dissonance theory; it does not postulate a motivating aversive-drive state.

But as Croyle and Cooper's (1983) experiment on essay writing showed, some conflict situations do produce arousal. Perhaps self-perception and cognitive dissonance occur under different conditions, producing attitude changes for different reasons. One factor that may determine whether dissonance or self-perception processes come into play involves the idea that attitudes have ranges of acceptable behaviour. For example, a pacifist might agree with using force to protect a helpless child from attack but would not agree with using force to react to a personal insult. According to Fazio *et al.* (1977), a pacifist who used force to protect a child might change his attitudes through self-perception (the behaviour falls within the latitude of acceptable behaviours), whereas a pacifist who struck out in retaliation for an insult would experience dissonance (the behaviour falls outside the latitude of acceptable behaviours). Using a slightly different logic, Cooper and Fazio (1984) suggest that when counter-attitudinal behaviour has undesirable consequences, we go through an attributional/self-perception process where we decide whether the behaviour was voluntary. If it was, then we experience dissonance.

Chapter review

Social psychology

- Social psychology is the study of how the thoughts, feelings and behaviour of people are influenced by the actual, imagined or implied presence of other people.
- Social psychologists employ the scientific method – they formulate theories of human behaviour and test them using a wide range of empirical methods.
- Social psychology has its roots in late-nineteenth-century German folk psychology. By the 1920s, America had taken the lead and social psychology was a branch of general psychology. The Second World War gave impetus to a focus on groups and attitudes. This was gradually replaced from the mid-1960s by a focus on individual cognition and inference in its social context. Contemporary social psychology is very diverse, embracing a wide range of emphases on social cognition, groups, intergroup relations, close relationships and attitudes.

Social cognition and social knowledge

- Social cognition refers to the way we process and represent the social world and our place in it. Social

cognition is governed by cognitive parsimony, but it is also motivated by our own goals.
- Impressions of people are strongly influenced by central traits, negative information and information that one encounters first (primacy effect).
- Our thoughts, feelings, perceptions and beliefs about the world are organised in mental frameworks, or schemas, which help us manage and synthesise information about our social world.
- Schemas can be tied closely to specific instances of a category (called exemplars) or they can be fuzzy abstractions of defining features (called prototypes).
- Schemas that are widely shared within a group, and are held about another group, are stereotypes.
- Schemas tend to be activated automatically once we have categorised a person, object or event.

Self and identity

- Our self-concept is based on schemas that organise and synthesise personal knowledge and feelings we have about ourselves.

- We often try to bring our behaviour, and thus our own self-conception, in line with how we would like to be, or we feel we ought to be.
- There are cultural and situational differences in the extent to which self-schemas are based on being an individual, a member of a group, or in a relationship with specific other people.
- Neuroimaging evidence suggests that our implicit attitudes and biases can be reflected in altered brain activation. For example, amygdala activation is found to images of black men when viewers expressed implicit, but not explicit, attitudes towards race.
- The way we conceptualise ourselves is most strongly motivated by a desire for an evaluatively positive self-concept that contributes to a sense of positive self-esteem.

Social inference

- In making attributions about the causes of another person's behaviour, we consider the relative contributions of dispositional and situational factors.
- In some circumstances we may gain an understanding of what sort of person we are and how we feel, by trying to discover what the causes of our behaviour might be.
- In making attributions about others' behaviour we tend to overestimate the role of dispositional factors and underestimate the role of situational factors (the fundamental attribution error); however, we do the opposite for our own behaviour.
- Attributions also tend to be self-serving. We attribute our own and our groups' good behaviours internally and bad behaviours externally. We also tend to think bad things happen to bad people and good things to good people.

- In making inferences about people we tend to rely on cognitive short-cuts or heuristics, such as how available something is to memory, and how superficially representative something is of a category.

Attitudes and attitude change

- Attitudes have affective, cognitive and behavioural intention components and may be learned through mere exposure to the object of the attitude, classical conditioning processes and imitation.
- Attitudes are poor predictors of behaviour unless very specific attitudes and very specific behaviours are measured. Prediction is even better if attitudes towards behaviours are measured, and if normative support is strong and opportunity and resources to perform the behaviour are available.
- To understand explicit attempts to change a person's attitude, we must consider both the source of the intended persuasive message and the message itself.
- A message tends to be persuasive if its source is credible or attractive and if it is pitched correctly at its intended audience.
- There are at least two routes to persuasion. The central route involves careful consideration of the message, whereas the peripheral route involves superficial reliance on heuristics such as the attractiveness of the message source.
- Cognitive dissonance is an aversive state that occurs when our attitudes and behaviour are inconsistent. Resolution of dissonance often involves changing attitudes in line with behaviour.
- Our own observations of our behaviour and situation also influence attitude development.

Suggestions for further reading

Aronson, E. (2011) *The Social Animal* (11th edn). New York: Freeman.

Cacioppo, J.T., Visser, P.S. and Pickett, C.L. (2012) *Social Neuroscience: People thinking about thinking people.* Cambridge, MA: MIT Press.

Fiske, S.T. and Macrae, N. (2012) *Sage Handbook of Social Cognition.* London: Sage.

Fiske, S.T. and Taylor, S.E. (2008) *Social Cognition: From brain to culture.* New York: McGraw-Hill.

Hogg, M.A. and Cooper, J. (eds) (2007) *Sage Handbook of Social Psychology.* London: Sage.

Hogg, M.A. and Vaughan, G.M. (2010) *Social Psychology* (5th edn). London: Pearson Education.

Moskowitz, G.B. (2005) *Social Cognition: Understanding self and others.* New York: Guilford.

Smith, P.B., Bond, M.H. and Kagitcibasi, C. (2006) *Understanding Social Psychology Across Cultures.* London: Sage.

Todorov, A., Fiske, S. and Prentice, D. (2011). *Social neuroscience: Toward understanding the underpinnings of the social mind.* Oxford: Oxford University Press.

Aronson's classic is a brilliant introduction to social psychology. The additional readings are very good reviews of attitudes.

CHAPTER 16

Interpersonal and group processes

Michael A. Hogg and Dominic Abrams and G. Neil Martin

JO YEATES'S LANDLORD CHRISTOPHER JEFFERIES 'GETTING ON WITH LIFE'

The landlord of Jo Yeates has said he is reaching the point where he can get on with his life again. Christopher Jefferies, who lived in the flat above the Bristol landscape architect, sued several newspapers for their 'lurid' coverage of his arrest on suspicion of her murder.

Vincent Tabak, 33, was last week convicted of murdering Miss Yeates. The 25 year old, originally from Ampfield in Hampshire, was found dead on Christmas Day last year.

Mr Jefferies, who lived above Miss Yeates and her boyfriend Greg Reardon in Canynge Road, Clifton, was arrested on suspicion of murder on 30 December. He spent three days in police custody and was eventually released from police bail in March. Miss Yeates's body was discovered on Christmas Day

Speaking to BBC Radio 4's *Today* programme about his ordeal with elements of the press and the police, Mr Jefferies said: 'It has taken up a whole year virtually of my life, that period of time has meant that everything else that I would normally be doing has been in abeyance.'

In July, the *Daily Mirror* and the *Sun* were fined for being in contempt of court by the High Court over their reporting of the police investigation. The *Daily Mirror* was fined £50,000 and the *Sun* £18,000.

Source: http://www.bbc.co.uk/news/uk-england-bristol-15551619, 2 November 2011.

WHAT YOU SHOULD BE ABLE TO DO AFTER READING CHAPTER 16

- Understand how people are influenced by individuals, authority, group norms and minorities.
- Know what affects people's performance of tasks in groups, and how groups make decisions and are influenced by leaders.
- Know why intergroup conflicts and prejudices are so difficult to change, and what underlies crowd behaviour and social movements.
- Understand some of the causes of human aggression, and what influences people's inclination to help others.
- Understand why we like who we do, and the path taken by love and close relationships.
- Appreciate the role of language, speech and non-verbal communication in social life, and what factors influence how we communicate.

QUESTIONS TO THINK ABOUT

- If someone ordered you to do something that caused serious harm to another person, would you do it?
- How does the presence of an audience affect the way you perform?
- Is there such a thing as team spirit? If so, which psychological processes are involved?
- What makes a great leader? What would ten such leaders have in common?
- If you try hard to suppress your prejudices, do you think they will gradually disappear?
- Can contact between racial groups reduce racial prejudice?
- Are men more aggressive than women?
- What sort of person are you attracted to, and why?
- Does attraction lead to love or vice versa?

Social influence

The social process responsible for attitude change (discussed in Chapter 15) is social influence. However, social influence is in fact a much wider topic because it also addresses changes in people's behaviour that are not associated with changed attitudes. Sometimes people simply do what people tell or ask them to do, without necessarily changing their underlying attitudes. A key distinction in the social influence literature is between compliance (a surface change in behaviour which is not associated with true underlying cognitive changes) and conformity (a deep-seated cognitive change, usually in response to the existence of self-defining group norms).

Compliance

Research on compliance focuses on the conditions under which people will go along with a request or do someone a favour. For example, how can you get someone to lend you some money, fix your car, pop down to the shops for you, fill out a questionnaire, and so forth? You simply want people to do what you request – you are not looking for deep-seated changes in their attitudes and values.

Ingratiation

One very effective method is **ingratiation**, which involves getting people to like you – flattery may not get you everywhere, but it is surprisingly effective. People are much more likely to agree to a request from someone they like or find attractive. One reason for this is that an attractive person, by association, makes the request appear more attractive. Advertisers regularly pay tribute to the effectiveness of association when they use attractive models and celebrities to endorse their products. For example, Smith and Engel (1968) showed two versions of an advertisement for a new car. One version included an attractive young woman and the other did not. When the participants subsequently rated the car, those who saw the advertisement with the attractive young woman rated the car as faster, more appealing, more expensive-looking and better designed.

Besides making products or opinions more attractive by being associated with them, attractive people are better able to get others to comply with their requests because people want to be liked by attractive people. People believe that being liked by attractive people makes them more desirable, too. Thus, people tend to emphasise their associations with attractive and important people. We have all encountered name-droppers who want us to think that they are part of a privileged circle of friends. This phenomenon is even demonstrated by fans of sports teams.

Cialdini *et al.* (1976) found that students were more likely to wear sweatshirts featuring their university name on the day after the university football team had won a game than after the team had lost. Also, Wann and Dolan (1994) have shown that spectators identify with, and are biased in favour of, fellow spectators who support the same team.

Although attractive people may influence our behaviour, it is possible that they may only influence our underlying attitudes when we do not consider the underlying message carefully. According to Petty and Cacioppo's (1986, 1996) elaboration likelihood model (see the section on attitude change in Chapter 15), people can process information either via a central or a peripheral route. Attractive people may influence us via the peripheral route, and can thus be less influential if we adopt central route processing.

Reciprocity

Another effective method for ensuring others will comply with your requests is first to do them a favour. This takes advantage of a powerful human expectation of **reciprocity** – the tendency to return favours others have done for us. When someone does something for us, we feel uncomfortable until we have discharged the debt. For example, if people invite us to their house for dinner, we feel obliged to return the favour in the near future. Owing a social debt to someone we do not like is especially distasteful. Often people will suffer in silence rather than ask for help from someone they dislike. Reciprocity is pervasive – every culture is known to have some form of the 'golden rule' (Cialdini, 1993). It establishes a basic guideline for behaviour in a wide range of situations, and its emergence in evolutionary history is considered to be crucial to the development of social life.

Reciprocity does not require that the 'favour' be initially requested or even wanted. The debt of obligation can be so strong that reciprocity can be exploited by people who want us to comply with their requests when we would otherwise not do so. For example, people trying to sell something often try to capitalise on the reciprocity rule by giving the potential customer a free sample. Once the person has accepted the 'gift', the sales representative tries to get them to return the favour by making a purchase. Many of us avoid accepting free samples because we dislike being manipulated into buying something we do not want.

Experiments conducted by social psychologists have confirmed the strength of reciprocity in human interactions. For example, Regan (1971) enlisted the participation of university students in an experiment that supposedly involved art appreciation. During a break in the experimental session, some participants were treated to a soft drink by another 'participant' (a confederate) or by the experimenter; others received nothing. After the experiment, the confederate asked each participant to purchase some raffle tickets he was selling. Compliance with the request was measured by the number of tickets each participant bought. The participants treated to a soft drink by the confederate purchased the most raffle tickets.

Multiple requests

A third technique for gaining compliance involves the use of multiple requests. The focal request is either preceded by a smaller request that everyone will agree to (called foot-in-the-door), or preceded by a much larger request that everyone will refuse (door-in-the-face), or accompanied by all sorts of sweeteners (low-balling).

To investigate the **foot-in-the-door tactic**, Freedman and Fraser (1966) sent a person posing as a volunteer worker to call on homeowners in a residential California neighbourhood. The volunteer asked the homeowners to perform a small task: to accept a 3-inch-square sign saying 'Keep California Beautiful' or 'Be a Safe Driver' or to sign a petition supporting legislation favouring one of these goals. Almost everyone agreed. Two weeks later, the experimenters sent another person to ask these people whether they would be willing to have public service billboards erected in front of their houses. To give them an idea of precisely what was being requested, the 'volunteer worker' showed the homeowners a photograph of a house almost completely hidden by a huge, ugly, poorly lettered sign saying 'Drive Carefully'. Over 55 per cent of the people agreed to this obnoxious request. In contrast, only 17 per cent of householders who had not been contacted previously (and asked to accept the smaller sign) agreed to have such a billboard placed on their property.

The foot-in-the-door tactic works even better when the focal request is preceded by a graded series of smaller requests leading up to the focal request (Dolinski, 2000). So, if you wanted to persuade someone to go out with you, it might be useful to get them first to agree to study with you in the library, and once they say yes, say, 'How about going for coffee?', and then once they agree, pose the focal request of asking them to go out with you.

The foot-in-the-door tactic probably works because once people have committed themselves to a course of action they are loath then to change their mind. Commitment probably increases compliance for several reasons. First, the act of complying with a request in a particular category may change a person's self-image. Through the process of self-attribution, people who accept a small sign to support safe driving may come to regard themselves as public-spirited – what sensible person is not in favour of safe driving? Thus, when they hear the billboard request, they find it difficult to refuse. After all, they are public-spirited, so how can they say

no? Saying no would imply that they did not have the courage of their convictions. Thus, this reason has at its root self-esteem. To maintain positive self-esteem, the person must say yes to the larger request.

Commitment may also increase compliance because the initial, smaller request changes people's perception of compliance in general. Evidence supporting this suggestion was provided by Rittle (1981). While sitting in a waiting room before taking part in an experiment, some adult participants were approached by an 8-year-old child who was having trouble operating a vending machine. Later, while answering a series of questions designed to disguise the true nature of the experiment, they were asked to rate their perceptions of how unpleasant it might be to provide help to other people. After the participants had answered all the questions and the study was apparently over, the interviewer asked them whether they would volunteer between 30 minutes and four hours of their time to participate in a research project. Participants who had helped the child rated helping as less unpleasant and were more willing to participate in the research project than were people who had not helped the child (see Figure 16.1).

The second multiple request tactic, the **door-in-the-face**, is the opposite of the foot-in-the-door. Here, the focal request is preceded by a much larger request that no one is likely to comply with. Cialdini *et al.* (1975) tested this tactic by approaching students with a huge

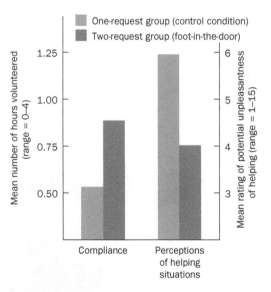

Figure 16.1 The effect of commitment on compliance and perceptions of the potential unpleasantness of helping situations. Mean number of hours volunteered (compliance) and mean rating of potential unpleasantness of volunteering, for control participants and participants who first helped a child.

Source: Based on data from Rittle, R.H., Changes in helping behaviour: Self versus situational perceptions as mediators of the foot-in-the-door technique. *Personality and Social Psychology Bulletin*, 1981, 7, 431–7.

request: 'Would you serve as a voluntary counsellor at a youth offenders' centre two hours a week for the next two years?' Virtually no one agreed. However, when the researchers then asked for a considerably smaller request, 'Would you chaperone a group of these offenders on a two-hour trip to the zoo?', 50 per cent agreed. When the second request was presented alone, less than 17 per cent complied. For the tactic to be effective, the final request should come from the same person who made the initial request. According to Cialdini and associates, participants perceive the scaled-down request as a concession by the influencer, and consequently they feel pressure to reciprocate. If some other person were to make the second request, reciprocation would not be necessary.

The final multiple request tactic is called **low-balling**. The effectiveness of low-balling depends on people's disinclination to change their mind once they have already made a commitment. For example, some of you may have had dealings with car sales agents. You are shown a beautiful car that you fall in love with and the agent commits you to purchasing the car which includes CD-player, GPS, air-conditioning, sunroof, electric windows and so forth, as well as all the various dealer costs. The agent now goes to get the paperwork ratified by their boss and comes back with the disappointing news that many of the 'extras' are not included. A rational choice would now be to decline to buy the car. However, because you are committed to your decision you are actually very likely still to purchase the car.

The effectiveness of low-balling was experimentally demonstrated by Cialdini et al. (1978). They asked half their participants to be in an experiment that began at 7 a.m. The other half were asked first to commit themselves to participating in an experiment, and then were informed that it would start at 7 a.m. The latter group, in the low-balling situation, complied more often (56 per cent) than the control group (31 per cent), and also tended to keep their appointments.

Even the once most powerful man in the world feels the need to obey authority: G.W. Bush's handwritten note at the UN on 14 September 2005, asking if he can go to the lavatory.
Source: REUTERS/Rick Wilking.

Obedience

Research confirms that people tend to comply with the requests of people in authority and to be swayed by their persuasive arguments, and that such obedience is generally approved of by society. Obedience can be quite mindless. Cohen and Davis (1981) cite the example of a physician who prescribed ear-drops for a hospitalised patient with an ear infection. His order read 'place in R ear'. Unfortunately, he apparently did not put enough space between the abbreviation for right (R) and the word ear – the nurse delivered the ear drops rectally. Neither she nor the patient thought to question such treatment for an earache. Other research in the US confirms that many medication errors occur because nurses overwhelmingly defer to doctors, even when the nurses have concerns about the wisdom or correctness of the doctors' directions (Lesar et al., 1997).

The classic study of blind obedience is a series of experiments performed by Stanley Milgram (1963), who advertised for participants in local newspapers in order to obtain as representative a sample as possible. The participants served as 'teachers' in what they were told was a learning experiment. A confederate (a middle-aged accountant) serving as the 'learner' was strapped into a chair 'to prevent excessive movements when he was shocked', and electrodes were attached to his wrist. The participants were told that 'although the shocks can be extremely painful, they cause no permanent tissue damage'.

The participant was then brought to a separate room housing an apparatus having dials, buttons and a series of switches that supposedly delivered shocks ranging from 15 to 450 volts. The participant was instructed to use this apparatus to deliver shocks, in increments of 15 volts for each 'mistake', to the learner in the other room. Beneath the switches were descriptive labels ranging from 'Slight shock' to 'Danger: severe shock'.

The learner gave his answers by pressing the appropriate lever on the table in front of him. Each time he made an incorrect response, the experimenter told the participant to throw another switch and give a larger shock. At the 300-volt level, the learner pounded on the wall and then stopped responding to questions. The experimenter told the participant to consider a 'no answer' as an incorrect answer. At the 315-volt level, the learner pounded on the wall again. If the participant hesitated in delivering a shock, the experimenter said, 'Please go on'. If this admonition was not enough, the experimenter said, 'The experiment requires that you continue', then, 'It is absolutely essential that you continue', and finally, 'You have no other choice; you must go on'. The factor of interest was how long the participants would continue to administer shocks to the hapless victim. A majority of participants gave the learner what they believed to be the 450-volt shock, despite the fact that the learner pounded on the wall twice and then stopped responding altogether (see Figure 16.2).

In a later experiment, when the confederate was placed in the same room as the participant and his struggling and apparent pain could be observed, 37.5 per cent of the participants – over one-third – obeyed the order to administer further shocks (Milgram, 1974). Thirty per cent were even willing to hold his hand against a metal plate to force him to receive the shock.

Milgram's experiments indicate that a significant percentage of people will blindly follow the orders of authority figures, no matter what the effects are on other people. Most people find this surprising. They cannot believe that for such a large proportion of people the social pressure to conform to the experimenter's orders is stronger than the participant's own desire not to hurt someone else. As Ross (1977) points out, this misperception is an example of the fundamental attribution error. People tend to underestimate the effectiveness of situational factors and to overestimate the effectiveness of dispositional ones. Clearly, the tendency to obey an authority figure is amazingly strong. However, one factor that can dramatically reduce obedience is social support for non-compliance. In one of his studies, Milgram had two confederates work with the participant. When the confederates were obedient, so was the participant – obedience increased to 92.5 per cent. However, when the confederates were disobedient so was the participant – obedience dropped dramatically to 10 per cent.

Understandably, much of the attention given to Milgram's research focused on its considerable ethical implications (Elms, 1995). Many people, psychologists and non-psychologists alike, have attacked his research on the grounds that it involved deception and too much emotional strain on the participants. Indeed, Milgram's

research helped prompt psychologists to strengthen ethical guidelines for conducting research with humans.

In his defence, however, it should be stressed that Milgram conducted an extensive debriefing at the end of each experimental session in which the true purpose of the experiment was explained to the participants. The participants were told that their behaviour was quite typical of the way most people responded to the situation posed by the experiment. In addition, the participants were later sent a detailed written report of the experimental procedure and a follow-up questionnaire asking them about their feelings regarding their participation. Eighty-four per cent of the participants said that they were glad to have participated in the experiment, and only 1.3 per cent indicated that they wished they had not participated.

An additional objection to Milgram's research is that people may have had to confront a disturbing aspect of their own behaviour – the self-realisation that they were capable of actions that they find reprehensible. Milgram replied that at least some of his participants considered their enhanced insight into their own behaviour to have been enough to justify their participation. Of course, Milgram could not guarantee that somebody, somewhere, who had participated in his research might not be deeply troubled by his participation. And therein lies another moral dilemma: to what extent is knowledge about behaviour, in general, and insight about one's own behaviour, in particular, to be avoided in case some people think that others might find this knowledge disturbing? That is not an easy question to answer and one that psychologists must grapple with each time they perform research such as that conducted by Milgram.

Milgram and obedience to authority in the twenty-first century

Most psychologists thought it would never happen but, in 2007, a psychologist from Santa Clara did it. On 3 January 2007, the American current affairs programme, *Primetime*, featured a replication of Milgram's study, conducted by Jerry Burger. The programme was timely. Milgram's findings have been thought to explain aberrations ranging from the Holocaust of the Second World War, to the Mai Lai massacre, to the torture and humiliation that was allowed to fester at Abu Ghraib. For decades, psychologists and others have debated whether Milgram's findings were of their time or whether, in this multimedia age, they could transcend temporal boundaries. But no psychologist has replicated Milgram's study for over 30 years (Blass, 2000) because professional societies' guidelines on the ethical treatment of participants would prevent such experiments from being conducted (Elms, 1995).

However, Burger (2009) alighted on a solution. Most of the controversy surrounding Milgram's studies focuses

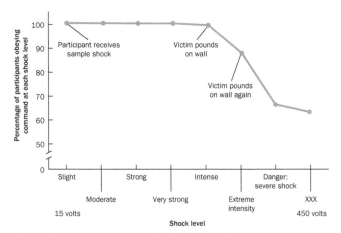

Figure 16.2 Data from one of Milgram's studies of obedience.

Source: From Baron, R.A. and Byrne, D., *Social Psychology: Understanding human interaction*, 8th edn © 1997. Published by Allyn & Bacon, Boston, MA. Copyright © by Pearson Education. By permission of the publisher.

on his fifth experiment. This is where participants were asked to administer shocks from between 15 and 450 volts to an unseen person. At 150 volts, the participants heard the cries of protest from the victim and the victim's expressions of pain. At up to 300 volts, the victim yelled that he was in pain. After 330 volts, he fell silent. Sixty-five per cent of people administered the shocks, at the experimenter's instigation, at the maximum voltage. The point at which participants began to become reluctant to give the shock was 150 volts. When psychiatrists, students and members of the public are asked at what point they would stop, 150 volts is their threshold (Milgram, 1974). This is an important figure because of those who reached this level, 79 per cent were prepared to continue to 450 volts, the maximum.

Burger used this fact to inform his replication. The assumption would be that if participants were willing to deliver a shock at this level, it is highly likely that they would have administered a higher shock (regardless of whether they said they would not). Burger carefully screened his participants, making sure that they had seen a clinical psychologist beforehand and that there was no indication of vulnerability. Participants were also informed, three times, that they could withdraw at any point and still keep the money they were promised for participating. They were told that the learner had also been offered the opportunity to leave at any point. Participants were told immediately after the experiment that the learner had received no shock (a long time elapsed in Milgram's study). In addition, the experimenter in Burger's study was a clinical psychologist who was instructed to stop immediately if any unacceptable signs of distress were observed. Twenty-nine men and 41 women participated. The experiment was run using an almost identical protocol to that in Milgram's studies. In one condition, participants saw another confederate refuse the experimenter's instructions.

Seventy per cent of participants were willing to go beyond the 150-volt limit and had to be prevented from doing so. Even when they saw a confederate refuse instructions they continued to deliver the shock, indicating that seeing others disobey did not inhibit the giving of punishment. There was no significant difference between men and women (Milgram's studies recruited, largely, men). And while those who reported being highly empathetic expressed a reluctance to continue earlier than did those who were less empathetic, this empathy did not prevent them from physically continuing with the experiment and delivering the shocks.

It seems as if, almost 30 years after Milgram's original experiment, people will behave in almost exactly the same way now as they did then. Of course, the jaded might ask whether we needed an experiment, Milgram's experiment, to tell us that people are inclined to obey authority. 'Of course not,' writes Blass (2009). 'What he did teach us is just how strong this tendency is – so strong, in fact, that it can make us act in ways contrary to our moral principles . . . Milgram showed that it does not take evil or aberrant persons to carry out actions that are reprehensible and cruel' (p. 40).

Conformity

Compliance and obedience produce changes in people's behaviour, but in general such changes do not correspond to a change in people's attitudes or other internal cognitive structures. These deeper changes are more likely to be wrought by group influence where we conform to what we perceive to be group norms (Turner, 1991).

Public Announcement

WE WILL PAY YOU $4.00 FOR ONE HOUR OF YOUR TIME

Persons Needed for a Study of Memory

• We will pay five hundred New Haven men to help us complete a scientific study of memory and learning. The study is being done at Yale University.

• Each person who participates will be paid $4.00 (plus 50c carfare) for approximately 1 hour's time. We need you for only one hour: there are no further obligations. You may choose the time you would like to come (evenings, weekdays, or weekends).

• No special training, education, or experience is needed. We want:

Factory workers	Businessmen	Construction workers
City employees	Clerks	Salespeople
Laborers	Professional people	White-collar workers
Barbers	Telephone workers	Others

All persons must be between the ages of 20 and 50. High school and college students cannot be used.

• If you meet these qualifications, fill out the coupon below and mail it now to Professor Stanley Milgram, Department of Psychology, Yale University, New Haven. You will be notified later of the specific time and place of the study. We reserve the right to decline any application.

• You will be paid $4.00 (plus 50c carfare) as soon as you arrive at the laboratory.

- -

TO:
PROF. STANLEY MILGRAM, DEPARTMENT OF PSYCHOLOGY, YALE UNIVERSITY, NEW HAVEN, CONN. I want to take part in this study of memory and learning. I am between the ages of 20 and 50. I will be paid $4.00 (plus 50c carfare) if I participate.

NAME (Please Print) . . . .

ADDRESS . . . .

TELEPHONE NO. . . . . Best time to call you . . . .

AGE . . . . . . OCCUPATION . . . . SEX . . . . . .
CAN YOU COME:

WEEKDAYS . . . . EVENINGS ! . . . . . WEEKENDS . . . .

A copy of the participant recruitment advert that Milgram used.
Source: TopFoto: The Granger Collection, New York.

The social psychology of attribution – An international perspective

People frequently talk of differences between the East and the West. Almost any psychological quirk in people from these two terrains can be attributed to one group having a 'Western' style of thinking or behaving and the other an 'Eastern' one. But is there any psychological evidence to support the cliché?

Interestingly, social psychology has provided some. Research on people's perception of the causes of behaviour has found a striking result: people from the West, largely the US, tend to explain others' behaviour in terms of people's characteristics, that is, they commit the fundamental attribution error. People from the East, on the other hand, such as East Asians, attribute people's behaviour to situational factors (Morris and Peng, 1994; Lee et al., 1996). In Morris and Peng's study, for example, the researchers analysed American and Chinese newspaper reports of mass murder and compared how often each nation attributed the murderers' actions to personal or situational characteristics. The US journalists tended to focus on negative personality characteristics of the murderers; the Chinese journalists focused more on situational/contextual factors.

Research also shows that the West, at least those living in the North American part of it, tends to hold single individuals responsible for actions whereas East Asians hold groups or communities responsible (Menon et al., 1999; Chiu et al., 2000). Chui et al. asked people to determine who was responsible when a pharmacist dispensed the incorrect medicine. Americans believed it was the specific pharmacist; Chinese participants believed it was the pharmacy as a unit. Americans also believe there are fewer reasons for the causes of people's behaviour than do other Asian nations, such as Korea (Choi et al., 2003).

In a recent study, European Americans and Asian Americans were asked to list their perceptions of consequences of various actions, including a shot in billiards and turning an area into a national park (Maddux and Yuki, 2006). When considering the consequences of taking a shot at billiards, the Asian Americans thought that a single shot would have a much greater impact on subsequent shots than did the European Americans. Japanese participants also listed more indirect consequences of creating a national park.

When the groups had to consider the consequences of a social act such as firing someone or causing an accident, the Japanese thought that these events would affect more people than did the Americans. They also felt more responsible, felt worse and were more likely to apologise to those affected.

The authors make an interesting extrapolation from their findings. The crime rate in Japan may be lower because the Japanese perceive their acts as affecting more people. The Japanese are also the only people to suffer from the culture-dependent psychological disorder, *taijin kyofusho* – an extreme fear of hurting or offending others and of being harshly judged by others. 'For East Asians,' the authors suggest, 'a sense of interdependence with others may extend farther outward in a temporal and physical manner, leading to a heightened sense of responsibility' (p. 680).

Norms

People, particularly in individualistic Western societies, often think that they are not very influenced by norms and conventions. Indeed, conforming is often viewed as undesirable, as an indication of a weak personality, a lack of individual autonomy, and so forth. In reality, almost everything we think and do is, to varying degrees, grounded in social norms and conventions. Language itself is a normative way of communicating and representing the world to ourselves and others. If people did not agree on how to construct sentences or on what sounds to use to refer to what objects, then communication would be impossible. What we eat, when we eat, what side of the road we drive on, how we behave in restaurants – these are all normative behaviours.

One of the earliest and most influential studies of how group **norms** emerge and then influence us was conducted by Sherif (1936). Sherif was able to show empirically how norms can arise out of social interaction, and then how these norms exert influence on behaviour. Sherif's study was based on a perceptual illusion, originally discovered by astronomers, called the **autokinetic effect**: a small stationary pin-point of light, when projected in an otherwise completely darkened room, appears to move. The illusion is so strong that even if someone is aware of the effect, the apparent movement often persists.

Sherif first placed participants in the room individually and asked each of them how far the light was moving at different times. The answers were quite variable; one person might see the light move 6 cm on average, whereas another might see it move an average of 300 cm. Next, Sherif had groups of three people observe the light together and call out their judgements of movement one after the other. Finally, the participants would again observe the light individually. The most interesting result of the study was that when people made their judgements together they very rapidly converged on a narrow range of judgements that was pretty close to the average of their individual judgements, and their subsequent individual judgements also fell within this narrow range. The group had established what Sherif referred to as a collective frame of reference – a group norm. Even when tested by themselves on a subsequent day, the group members still conformed to this frame of reference.

MacNeil and Sherif (1976) were able to show that even an arbitrary norm can have the same effect. They had a group with only one true participant and three confederates – the confederates made very extreme judgements that produced an extreme norm. MacNeil and Sherif gradually replaced all the confederates with real participants whose individual autokinetic judgements were nowhere near as extreme as the group norm – and yet, they still conformed tightly to the norm.

Sherif's autokinetic findings are not too surprising if we consider that the participants found themselves in an uncertain situation. It makes sense to use others' opinions or judgements as a frame of reference when you are not sure what is going on. But just how strongly do group norms influence individual behaviour when the situation is unambiguous – when we are certain that we perceive things as they really are? The answer to this question was provided in a series of elegant studies conducted by Asch (1951, 1952, 1955).

Majority influence

Asch's studies were less to do with the emergence of norms and more to do with how a numerical majority can influence a single person. Asch asked several groups of seven to nine students to estimate the lengths of lines presented on a screen. A sample line was shown at the left, and the participants were to choose which of the three lines to the right matched it (Figure 16.3). The participants gave their answers orally. In fact, there was only one true subject in each group; all the other participants were confederates of the experimenter. The seating was arranged so that the true subject answered last. On 12 of the 18 trials the confederates made unanimously incorrect responses. When this happened, about 25 per cent of true subjects remained unaffected, but the rest conformed to the erroneous majority on at least one trial. Five per cent conformed to all the incorrect judgements. Overall conformity occurred 33 per cent of the time when it could have occurred. Under control conditions, when the confederates responded accurately, fewer than 1 per cent of the true subjects' estimations were errors – the task was quite unambiguous.

Group pressure did not affect the participants' perceptions; it affected their behaviour. That is, the participants went along with the group decision even though the choice still looked wrong to them – and even though the other people were complete strangers. When they were questioned later, they said that they had started doubting

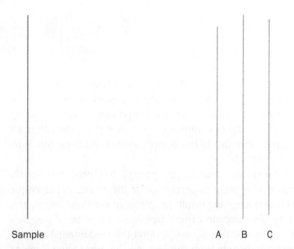

Sample   A   B   C

Figure 16.3 An example of the stimuli used by Asch (1951).

their own eyesight or had thought that perhaps they had misunderstood the instructions. The participants who did not conform felt uncomfortable about disagreeing with the other members of the group. The Asch effect shows how strong the tendency to conform can be. Faced with a simple, unambiguous task while in a group of strangers who showed no signs of disapproval when the participant disagreed with them, the vast majority of participants nevertheless ignored their own judgements and agreed with the obviously incorrect choice made by the other people.

Presumably, people conformed because they thought that the other members of the group might ridicule them, or at least secretly think badly of them, if they did not. If this is true then conformity should entirely disappear if participants could give their responses privately, without the other members of the group knowing what they had done. To investigate this, Deutsch and Gerard (1955) conducted an Asch-type study where participants gave their responses privately in cubicles. Conformity dropped but certainly did not disappear – it occurred at a rate of 23 per cent.

An interesting twist to the Asch paradigm was reported by a group of Japanese researchers (Mori and Arai, 2010). Instead of having confederates explicitly making (incorrect) judgements about a stimulus, the researchers were able to present stimuli on a half-transparent PowerPoint slide while participants wore sunglasses that were polarised so that they would filter green or magenta. These glasses affected the length of the lines visible on the screen because the magenta sunglasses allowed the top green part of the line to be seen as black and the green glasses prevented the perception of this colour (because the image and filter were green). In Asch's experiment, only men were tested. Mori and Arai tested men and women. Using this technique, women conformed to the majority decision but the men did not. The conformity did not rely on the uniformity of response from the majority (as was the case in the original experiment).

In research which sought to discover factors that would reduce conformity, probably the most important influence was the unanimity of the erroneous majority. Asch's original experiment employed a unanimous erroneous majority to obtain a conformity rate of 33 per cent. However, Asch also found that a correct supporter (i.e. a member of the majority who always gave the correct answer – and thus agreed with and supported the true participant) reduced conformity from 33 per cent to 5.5 per cent. Other experiments have confirmed that conformity is greatly reduced if the majority is not unanimous (Allen, 1975).

However, support itself may not be the crucial factor in reducing conformity. Any sort of lack of unanimity among the majority seems to be effective. For example, Asch found that a dissenter who was even more incorrect than the majority was equally effective. Allen and Levine (1971) conducted an experiment in which participants who were asked to make visual judgements were provided with a supporter who had normal vision, or a supporter who wore such thick glasses as to raise serious doubts about his ability to see anything at all, let alone accurately judge lines. In the absence of any support, participants conformed 97 per cent of the time. The 'competent' supporter reduced conformity to 36 per cent, but most surprising was that the 'incompetent' supporter reduced conformity as well, to 64 per cent.

The process of conformity

Why do people conform? Or rather, what is the process by which people conform? There are at least three reasons why people conform (Turner, 1991). The first is that people like to think their perceptions and attitudes are accurate and valid. So, if people are uncertain or find that others disagree with them, they may think they are wrong and feel a need to change their perceptions and attitudes in line with those of other people. This form of social influence is called **informational influence** (Deutsch and Gerard, 1955). It would have been present in the autokinetic studies, but not the Asch studies.

The second reason why people conform is that people like to be liked and approved of by others and therefore do not like to stand out as different, particularly when in the physical presence of other people. This form of social influence is called **normative influence** (Deutsch and Gerard, 1955). It would have been present in both the autokinetic studies and the Asch studies, but not in the Deutsch and Gerard study.

The third reason why people conform is that they feel a sense of belonging with the group defined by the norm – this is a process of **referent informational influence** (Turner, 1991), which is associated with social identity processes (Turner *et al.*, 1987; Hogg and Abrams, 1988). Group norms map out the defining attributes of a group. Thus, when people identify with the group they use the norms of the group to define themselves as group members. The process is fairly automatic – the group's norms are cognitively represented as a prototype (a fuzzy set of features that define the in-group and distinguish it from out-groups). When people categorise themselves as group members, they assimilate self to the relevant prototype and thus their behaviour is transformed so that it conforms to the prototype/norms. In the Sherif and Asch situations, other people's behaviour becomes a self-defining norm that is internalised to regulate one's own behaviour as a group member. Abrams *et al.* (1990) found that conformity in both the Sherif and the Asch paradigms was reduced when the source of influence was categorised as an out-group rather than an in-group.

The Stanford Prison experiment

On a par with the ethical vortex that is Milgram's obedience experiments is Philip Zimbardo's Stanford Prison experiment, another of social psychology's ground-breaking studies (Zimbardo, 1982). Zimbardo's involvement was motivated by several reported examples of guard brutality in US prisons. He sought to discover whether bad prison guards were inherently bad or were shaped by the situation in which they found themselves. In the original study, Zimbardo had the Palo Alto police arrest students, for various misdemeanours, assign them prisoner numbers and lock them up in a mocked-up real-life prison cell in a basement at Stanford University. Every attempt was made to ensure the authenticity of the prison environment (you can find out more details here: www.prisonexp.org). The students were randomly assigned to playing prisoners or guards. They knew the situation was not real but, as Zimbardo himself has noted, 'No one expected what happened'.

The experiment was meant to run for 14 days; it was stopped after less than a week. The researchers expected the prisoners to sit around, behind bars, reading books and playing guitars. But the prisoners began to rebel. On the second morning, they began protesting vocally and physically. It was at this point that the atmosphere changed. The guards became increasingly brutal, as if they were determined to demonstrate who had the real power in this context (remember that both groups were students). As the prisoners became increasingly humiliated, the guards' behaviour worsened. Faced with this authoritarian onslaught, the prisoners became increasingly compliant. This simply made the guards more sadistic. You can see how the guards' behaviour changed, and changed dramatically, in these quotes from one of the students who played a guard.

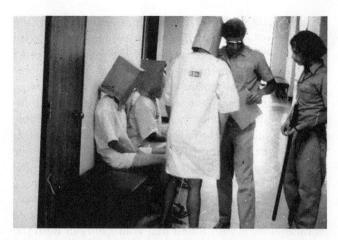

A still from the original Stanford Prison Experience.
Source: Philip G. Zimbardo, PhD.

Diary entry, before the experiment

As I am a pacifist and non-aggressive individual, I cannot forsee a time when I might maltreat other living things.

Day 3 of the study

This was my first chance to exercise the kind of manipulative power that I really like.

Day 5 of the study

I harass Sarge, who continues to stubbornly over-respond to commands. I have singled him out for special abuse both because he begs for it and because I simply don't like him.

Now, imagine if these were real prisoners and real guards, and maltreatment of prisoners was either condoned or not seen. What do you think would be likely to happen? The BBC 're-created' the experiments in 2003, not entirely to Zimbardo's satisfaction (see his interview in Cohen, 2004). But a real-life illustration emerged a few years ago with the revelation of the treatment of prisoners at the Iraqi prison, Abu Ghraib.

Minority influence

Conformity research tends to focus on the way that a numerical majority influences the attitudes and behaviour of a minority. A valid question arises then as to whether a minority can influence the majority – what facilitates **minority influence**. After all, everyday experience tells us that people do not always conform to majorities. Sometimes a minority can be persuasive. Indeed social change – from new trends and fashions to social movements and political revolutions – would not be possible if active minorities could not have influence over the masses

(Moscovici, 1976). Asch (1952) looked at this in one of his studies. He had 16 naive participants facing one confederate who gave incorrect answers. The participants found the confederate's behaviour ludicrous, and openly ridiculed him and laughed at him. Even the experimenter found the situation so bizarre that he could not contain his mirth and ended up laughing at the poor confederate. Clearly, in this context a minority was pretty ineffectual.

But in the Asch paradigm, who really is the majority and who the minority? Moscovici and Faucheux (1972) make the point that in a standard Asch experiment the hapless lone participant is faced by a small group of people who actually behave extremely bizarrely – in the real world, no one would make the judgements that the confederates make in the experiment. In reality, the majority is a minority, and the studies actually show how a minority viewpoint can be persuasive. This clever insight raises the question of how minorities are influential.

Because minorities have to combat a pervasive consensus that often has the support of a powerful elite, they need to adopt particular behavioural styles in order to be effective (Mugny, 1982). Minorities need to challenge the dominant consensus by providing an alternative viewpoint that is strongly consensual among minority members and has marked consistency across time. A consistent minority (1) disrupts the majority norm and thus produces uncertainty and doubt; (2) draws attention to itself as an entity; (3) conveys the existence of an alternative coherent point of view; (4) demonstrates certainty in, and unshakeable commitment to, its point of view; and (5) shows that the only solution to the conflict that has arisen is espousal of the minority viewpoint.

Minorities are also more effective if they are seen to have made significant personal or material sacrifices for their cause, to be acting out of principle rather than from ulterior motives, and to have some flexibility around their core message. There is also some evidence that minorities may be more effective if they are viewed by the majority as being a relevant in-group. This is usually difficult to bring about because, by definition, the majority protects itself by emphasising the out-group status of the minority. It can work, however, if the minority is able to establish its legitimate in-group credentials before it espouses a minority viewpoint (Crano and Alvaro, 1998) – in effect behaving like a wolf in sheep's clothing.

A consistent, but not rigid or inflexible, minority has what is called 'latent influence' that produces a **conversion effect**. Majority members cogitate about the minority position, but still conform to the majority position, until at a later point they suddenly appear to be converted to the minority's position and switch their allegiance and change their behaviour. This distinction between the majority having relatively surface influence and the minority having a deeper latent influence leading to conversion resembles to some extent the distinction made by social cognition and attitude researchers between peripheral and central route processing (Petty and Cacioppo, 1986) (discussed in Chapter 15).

Moscovici and Personnaz (1980) conducted an intriguing experiment to test the conversion and latent influence ideas. Participants called out the colour of a series of blue slides, which varied only in intensity, after they had heard a confederate who was described as either a member of the majority (82 per cent of people) or a member of a minority (18 per cent of people) describe the slide as green. Moscovici and Personnaz also had participants describe the chromatic after-image they saw when the slide had been removed – participants did not realise that the after-image of blue is yellow, and of green is purple. Participants exposed to majority influence (the confederate who was a member of the majority) showed a tendency to call the blue slides green, but their after-image was unaffected – it remained yellow, indicating that although they may have complied with the majority they certainly had not changed what they actually saw. Participants exposed to minority influence, however, continued to call the slides blue, but remarkably their after-image had shifted towards purple, and the effect had become a little stronger when they were tested individually at a later stage. Although they had not changed their surface behaviour, there was a deeper latent change in their perception as a consequence of minority influence.

People in groups

Human beings are unmistakably social creatures: a great deal of our lives is spent in the company of others. By itself, this is not an especially profound observation, but it leads to some interesting implications, particularly for social psychologists. We do not merely occupy physical space with other people. We affiliate psychologically and form groups with each other. A **group** is a collection of individuals who have a shared definition of who they are and what they should think, feel and do – people in the same group generally have common interests and goals. Groups are very diverse in size, form and longevity – they include ethnic groups, nations, organisations, departments, teams, clubs and even families. However, by the definition above, not all aggregations of people are groups in a psychological sense – a crowd of people shopping or some people standing at a bus stop are unlikely to be a group.

People aggregate, affiliate or form groups for all sorts of reasons. One set of reasons is very instrumental. Being in a group provides protection and allows people to do things that they cannot do alone. For example, it is probably better to walk down dangerous back streets in a crowd rather than alone, and a community can put up a barn more quickly than a lone individual. There are, however, some more basic psychological reasons for joining groups. A group of people with similar attitudes and behaviours to your own provides a wonderfully comforting sense of self-validation. Groups can reduce anxiety (Schachter, 1959), provide confirmation of the validity of one's perceptions (Festinger, 1954), and reduce uncertainty about one's self and one's place in the world (Hogg, 2000).

Baumeister and Leary (1995) believe that the need to belong is one of the most fundamental of all human motives. They may well be right. Williams and Sommer (1997) has shown in a series of vivid experiments that simply being ignored or excluded from social interaction can have quite profound effects. Indeed, many societies use ostracism or shunning as a potent punishment. In Williams and Sommer's studies, a naive participant ostensibly waiting with two other people (actually experimental confederates) for an experiment to begin is excluded by the confederates from a spontaneous game of passing a ball that they have found in the room. The participant showed signs of genuine distress – fidgeting, disengagement, displacement activities, and so forth.

The treatment of marginal group members and deviants

Many of the groups we are in, our in-groups, provide the psychological environment for the self and are therefore fundamental, or even primary, to our sense of who we are (Allport, 1954; Yzerbyt *et al.*, 2000). They matter psychologically so much to us that we can be inordinately concerned and upset if we feel marginalised or rejected by

In 2007, the UK saw its first 'run' on a bank. Within hours of rumours of the extent of the bank's debt, Northern Rock's customers began queuing to withdraw their money. Some claimed that such images fuelled greater panic and exacerbated the bank's problems.
Source: Getty Images: Peter Macdiarmid.

the group, and we can go to great lengths to protect the integrity of the group by treating deviant members harshly. For example, people are much more willing to derogate a deviant member of the in-group than a similarly deviant member of an out-group – a phenomenon known as the 'black sheep effect' (Marques *et al.*, 1988). Moreover, this effect is particularly strong when people identify strongly with their group (Branscombe *et al.*, 1993).

Marques *et al.* (2001) proposed that this effect reflects the operation of 'subjective group dynamics', whereby people try, psychologically, to sustain the sense of validity of their in-group's norms. In one experiment, Abrams *et al.* (2000) asked psychology students to evaluate normative or deviant group members who were either psychology students (in-group) or customs officers (out-group) who made statements about the UK's policy on asylum seekers. The norm for psychology students was to leave the existing policy unchanged, whereas the norm for customs officers was to advocate tighter restrictions. Two types of deviant were presented in each group. The anti-norm psychologist and anti-norm customs officer actually both expressed an identical (slightly restrictive) attitude which tended towards the views of the opposing group. Evaluations of these anti-norm members showed the classic black sheep effect. The out-group deviant was preferred over the in-group deviant. However, when the deviants expressed extreme positions that exaggerated the norm of their own group (i.e. a very restrictive customs officer and a very lenient psychologist) they were evaluated much more negatively, and positively, respectively. This pattern of results is shown in Figure 16.4.

The opposing reactions to the anti-norm and pro-norm deviants shows that people may be more concerned to ensure that they maintain the difference between in-group and out-group norms than to ensure that all members of

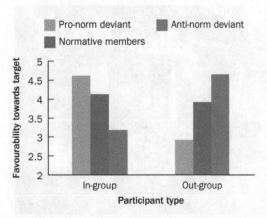

Figure 16.4 Favourability towards anti-norm and pro-norm deviants relative to normative members of the in-group and out-group.

Source: Based on Abrams, D., Marques, J.M., Brown, N.J. and Henson, M., Pro-norm and anti-norm deviance within and between groups. *Journal of Personality and Social Psychology*, 2000, 78, 911.

their group conform. Equally important is that people do not necessarily reject out-group members more than in-group members. They may favour out-group members who lend apparent support to the validity of in-group norms. Other research (Yzerbyt *et al.*, 1999; Hutchison and Abrams, 2003) shows that group members who identify more highly are likely to reject an anti-norm deviant from the stereotypical image of the group. All of this suggests that people are strongly motivated to sustain the idea that their in-group is a coherent entity.

Which is more important – the individual or the group?

There is evidence that people may store information about the individual and collective self in separate cognitive 'baskets' (Trafimow *et al.*, 1991), that is, when people think of their personal qualities they are unlikely also to think about their group memberships, and vice versa. This means it is possible to test whether the individual or collective self has primacy in terms of people's motivation. Despite evidence that people will defend their collective in-group norms, some researchers argue that the individual self-concept provides the most powerful motivational force for behaviour. Gaertner *et al.* (2002) proposed that the individual self has primacy both because the individual self is the unit of natural selection and because attributes of the self seem to remain stable over time, and changes occur only slowly over the lifespan, presumably because people defend their individual self against threatening feedback, and they selectively accept or pursue information that confirms their self-image as an individual.

A further possibility is that either the individual or collective self may have primacy, depending on the context. For example, Markus and Wurf (1987) assume that the self is defined by a 'working self-concept', which draws on the relevant attributes in relation to the current situation. More radically, Turner *et al.*'s (1987) self-categorisation theory holds that the context and situation have a very strong effect on how the self is defined. In particular, self is defined in terms of a social category to which one belongs relative to a category to which one does not belong within a situation. For example, at a football match people define themselves primarily in terms of which team they support (Cialdini *et al.*, 1976), whereas when taking part in an election they define themselves in terms of which party they support.

Gaertner and Insko (2000) showed that participants would allocate more money to the in-group than an out-group only if they believed their personal earnings could be influenced by other in-group members. In another set of studies Gaertner *et al.* (1999) showed that people whose individual self was threatened considered the threat to be more severe, felt more negative and angry and derogated the source of the threat more than did those who experienced a threat to the collective self. For example, in their experiment participants anticipated playing a game with an individual partner (dyad condition) or joined two others to play against another three-person group. Participants rated their initial feelings of anger, and then after completing an initial comprehension task, participants received positive or insulting feedback from the opposing person/team that they 'did well/seems to know what is going on', or 'did not do well, must be a little slow'. Participants then rated their feelings of anger again. Figure 16.5 shows that participants felt angrier when their individual self was insulted than when their collective self was insulted.

To compare evidence for these different views, Gaertner *et al.* (2002) conducted a meta-analysis (statistical summary across a series of different studies) to examine how people respond to threats to the individual and collective self, and how they respond to opportunities to enhance the self. In these experiments threats and enhancements were manipulated either by directing negative or positive feedback or linking positive or negative information to the individual or collective self. Across 37 different items of research evidence, Gaertner *et al.* found that people responded more strongly to both threats and enhancements of the individual self than to comparable threats to the collective self or the contextual self.

Social facilitation

You saw in the above discussion of social influence that the behaviour of other people has a powerful effect on our behaviour. Studies have shown that the mere presence of other people can affect a person's behaviour. Triplett (1897) published the first experimental study of **social facilitation** – the enhancement of a person's performance by the presence of other people. He had people perform simple tasks, such as turning the crank of a fishing reel. He found that his participants turned the crank faster and for longer if other people were present. Although many other studies found the same effect, some investigators reported just the opposite effect. If the task was difficult and complex, the presence of an audience impaired the participants' performance. We're all probably familiar with the sound of audience laughter accompanying a sitcom on television. More often than not, this laughter is real not canned and we know that – despite what people might say – people laugh more and find the comedy funnier if they watch or listen to the material with audience laughter present (Martin and Gray, 1996).

Zajonc (1965) has suggested an explanation for social facilitation. He claims that the presence of people who are watching a performer (or of people whom the performer perceives as watching) raises that person's arousal level and produces 'drive'. The increase in arousal has the effect of increasing the probability of performing dominant responses: responses that are best learned and most likely to occur in a particular situation. When the task is simple, the dominant response is generally the correct one (by definition an easy task is one which you get right all the time), so an audience improves performance. When the task is difficult the dominant response is generally not the correct one (by definition a difficult task is one which you get wrong all the time), so an audience impairs performance.

Subsequent experiments have supported Zajonc's explanation. For example, Martens (1969) tested the prediction that the presence of a group increases a person's level of arousal or drive. While participants performed a complex motor task alone or in the presence of ten people, the experimenter determined physiological arousal by measuring the amount of sweat present on the participants' palms. The presence of an audience produced a clear-cut effect: the participants who performed in front of other people had sweatier palms.

Markus (1978) tested the effects of an audience on task performance. She had student participants get undressed and then dress up in either their own clothes (an easy task where the dominant response is to get it right) or in unfamiliar clothing involving a special lab coat and special shoes (a difficult task where the dominant response is to make mistakes). Some participants did this alone whereas others did this while being watched. Relative to those who did the task alone, those who were being watched were faster on the easy task and slower on the difficult task – clear support for social facilitation.

Zajonc (1965) believed that the mere presence of other people produces arousal and drive. Baron (1986) proposed an alternative view. He argued that people are distracting and that trying to concentrate on a task while

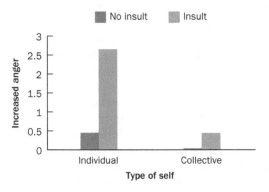

Figure 16.5 Increases in anger as a result of an insult to the individual or collective self.

Source: Based on Gaertner, L., Sedikides, C. and Graetz, K., In search of self-definition: Motivational primacy of the individual self, motivational primacy of the collective self, or collective primacy? *Journal of Personality and Social Psychology*, 1999, 76, 13.

being distracted causes arousal and drive. There is some support for this idea. Any form of distraction, for example loud noise, produces social facilitation effects – improved performance of easy tasks and degraded performance of difficult tasks. Baron has also suggested that perhaps the notion of arousal or drive is unnecessary. People have a limited capacity for attention. In order to perform a task successfully you need to attend to a range of cues and procedures. The presence of other people is an additional tax on attention, which people combat by narrowing their attention onto the task cues and procedures. Difficult tasks require more attention than easy tasks, and thus narrowing of attention causes you to fail to attend to some important cues – task performance deteriorates. Easy tasks require less attention, so narrowing of attention actually causes you to attend more to the task than you ordinarily would – task performance improves.

A final perspective on how being in the presence of other people affects task performance builds on the idea that people make you self-aware (Carver and Scheier, 1981; Higgins, 1987) (see also the section on 'Self awareness' in Chapter 15). Being self-aware motivates people to try to bring their actual self (their actual task performance) into line with their ideal self (how they would like or feel they ought to perform the task). Where the discrepancy is small, the additional motivation improves performance, but where the discrepancy is large and insurmountable, people tend to give up trying and task performance deteriorates.

Social loafing

Working together on a task, rather than merely being watched by others or simply being in the presence of others, can have additional effects: the presence of a group sometimes results in a decrease in effort, or **social loafing**. Thus, a group is often less than the sum of its individual members. Many years ago, Ringelmann (1913) measured the effort that people made when pulling a rope in a mock tug-of-war contest against a device that measured the exerted force. Presumably, the force exerted by eight people pulling together in a simple task would be at least the sum of their individual efforts or even somewhat greater than the sum because of social facilitation. However, Ringelmann found that the total force exerted was only about half what would be predicted by the simple combination of individual efforts. The participants exerted less force when they worked in a group.

The reduced performance could be due to at least two reasons. The people pulling on the rope could have distracted each other or interfered in other ways, or the people pulling the rope could simply have tried less hard – this is a distinction between **coordination losses** and **motivation losses** (Steiner, 1972). To tease these two possibilities apart, Ingham et al. (1974) replicated Ringelmann's study, but with two experimental conditions: one in which real groups of varying size pulled on a rope, and the other involving pseudo-groups with only one true participant and a number of confederates. The confederates were instructed only to pretend to pull on the rope while making realistic grunts to indicate exertion. The true participant was in the first position and so did not know that the confederates, who were behind, were not actually pulling. Participants in pseudo-groups pulled less strongly than participants pulling on their own. Because there was no coordination, there can be no loss due to poor coordination; the decrement can be attributed only to a loss of motivation. In real groups, there was an additional decrement in individual performance that can be attributed to coordination loss.

Scores of more recent studies have confirmed these results and have extended them to other behaviours, such as clapping, shouting, cheering and **brainstorming** (Williams et al., 2003). Formally defined, loafing is 'a reduction in individual effort when working on a collective task (in which one's outputs are pooled with those of other group members) compared to when working either alone or coactively' (Williams et al., 1993, p. 131).

Several variables have been found to influence the tendency to loaf. One of the most important of them is identifiability. Williams et al. (1981) asked participants to shout as loud as they could individually or in groups. Participants who were told that the equipment could measure only the total group effort shouted less loudly than those who were told that the equipment could measure individual efforts. The latter did not loaf – they shouted just as loudly in groups as they did alone. These results suggest that a person's efforts in a group activity are affected by whether other people can observe their individual efforts.

Another variable that determines whether social facilitation or social loafing occurs is individual responsibility. If a person's efforts are duplicated by those of another person (and if their individual efforts are not identifiable), the person is likely to exert sub-maximum effort. Harkins and Petty (1982) had participants work in groups of four on a task that required them to report whenever a dot appeared in a particular quadrant of a video screen. In one condition, each participant watched an individual quadrant and was solely responsible for detecting dots that appeared there. In the other condition, all four participants watched the same quadrant; thus, the responsibility for detecting dots was shared. Participants did not loaf when they were responsible for their own quadrants.

In a review of the social loafing literature, Karau and Williams (1993) noted that two variables – sex and culture – appear to moderate people's tendency to loaf. Although all people in different cultures are susceptible to social loafing, the effect is smaller for women than for men and for people living in Eastern cultures than for those living in Western cultures. Karau and Williams offer a reasonable explanation for this finding: both women and people living in Eastern cultures tend to be more group- or collectively-oriented in their thinking and behaviour than are men and people living in Western cultures. That is, women and people living in Eastern cultures tend to place greater importance on participating in group activities, which partially buffers them from social loafing effects.

Although research tends to show that loafing is the rule in groups, there are some studies which show that groups sometimes motivate people to work harder than they do alone. For example, Zaccaro (1984) had male and female participants construct 'moon tents' out of sheets of paper in two- or four-person co-active groups. The usual loafing effect emerged. However, other participants who believed they were competing against an out-group, and for whom the attractiveness and social relevance of the task was accentuated, behaved quite differently. The loafing effect was reversed: individuals performed at a higher rate in the larger group. This effect may represent **social compensation**, in which people work harder collectively than co-actively in order to compensate for anticipated loafing by others on important tasks or in important groups.

Why do people loaf? There are many reasons. For example, people are often anxious about having their performance evaluated, and so when their individual performance cannot be identified, they can avoid the possibility of evaluation by simply doing less. When their performance can be evaluated they are motivated to work harder in order to avoid an unfavourable evaluation. Another reason why people loaf may be because they feel that in a group they are dispensable – their effort is not really necessary to the group's overall performance because so many others are making a contribution.

Karau and Williams (1993; Williams *et al.*, 2003) have proposed an integrative model they call the **collective effort model**. It states that people will work hard on a collective task only to the degree that they expect their efforts to be instrumental in leading to outcomes that they value personally. Thus loafing will occur if people view the outcomes of the group performance or collective task as trivial or inconsistent with their own desires. Valued outcomes can be objective, say pay and rewards, or subjective such as personal satisfaction and feelings of growth, belonging or enjoyment. Even if people do value the outcomes, they will still loaf if they do not believe that their own efforts can help achieve those outcomes.

The collective effort model identifies a number of factors that moderate loafing. Because people work harder on collective tasks when they expect their effort to be instrumental in obtaining valued outcomes, loafing will be reduced when people: (1) believe their collective inputs can be evaluated; (2) work in smaller rather than larger groups; (3) view their contributions to the collective task as unique or important rather than redundant or trivial; (4) work on tasks that are meaningful, high in personal involvement, important to respected others, or intrinsically interesting; (5) work in cohesive groups or in situations that activate a salient group identity; (6) expect their co-workers to perform poorly; and (7) have a dispositional tendency to value collective outcomes.

Suppose that you have been asked by your psychology lecturer to organise a small group of class members to prepare a presentation. As the leader of the group, what steps might you take to prevent the individual members of your group from becoming social loafers?

Group decision-making

One of the most significant tasks that people perform in groups is decision-making. Group decision-making usually involves discussion that transforms a diversity of opinions into a single group decision.

Because it can be useful to predict what decision a group will come to from an initial distribution of diverse views (for example, juries, parliament, summits and other committees), research has identified a small number of explicit or implicit decision-making rules that groups can adopt, called **social decision schemes** (Davis, 1973). These are:

1 unanimity (discussion pressurises deviants to conform);

2 majority wins (discussion confirms the majority position, which is then adopted as the group position);

3 truth wins (discussion reveals the position that is demonstrably correct);

4 two-thirds majority (unless there is a two-thirds majority, the group is unable to reach a decision); and

5 first shift (the group ultimately adopts a decision consistent with the direction of the first shift in opinion shown by any member of the group).

If you know the decision rule that is being adopted, and you know the initial distribution of positions, then you can predict the group decision with a respectable degree of accuracy (Stasser and Dietz-Uhler, 2001).

Group decision-making involves social interaction, and so is subject to a range of effects that do not impact on individual decision-making, e.g. social facilitation and social loafing may affect the decision-making process.

Group remembering

For groups to make decisions they need to marshal a substantial amount of material that is stored in memory. Do groups facilitate or impede memory? Research shows that groups are better than individuals at recalling simple information – such as names of performers or capital cities (Clark and Stephenson, 1995). This is because the group can pool unshared information and can recognise what is true and what is false. However, in more complex memory tasks, like recalling a police interrogation, the group's memory tends to be a creative reconstruction rather than regurgitation of facts. Group remembering is often a constructive process, characterised by negotiation of an agreed joint account of some part of experience. Some individuals' memories will contribute to the developing consensus while others' will not. In this way the group shapes a version of the truth that gains its subjective veracity from the degree of consensus. The group in effect constructs a version of the truth that guides individuals about what to store as a true memory and what to discard as an incorrect memory.

Another way to look at group remembering is to focus not on what a group recalls, but on how a group stores information. Groups tend to have **transactive memory** structures (Moreland *et al.*, 1996). Within the group, different people specialise in remembering different things, but through interaction (transactions) all members of the group remember who is the memory specialist in different domains. Transactive memory has clear advantages in dealing with remembering large amounts of information. However, there are pitfalls. In the context of organisations, if someone leaves then their memory domain disappears and it can take a while for someone else to occupy that domain. The other side of the coin is that new members of organisations may take some time to learn the transactive memory structure of the organisation. In both cases, group processes are disrupted. Disruption can be minimised by making sure that people occupying important memory domains have 'understudies', and that new members are formally taught the transactive memory structure of the organisation.

Group polarisation

We often think of committees and other small decision-making groups as being cautious and conservative in making decisions. Indeed this is often the case – such groups arrive at group decisions that smooth out and average individual variability, which is precisely what one would expect from Sherif's (1936) research on group norms, described above. So, the social psychology community was most interested in Stoner's research (1961) – Stoner found that a group would actually make a more risky decision than the average of the positions held by the group members if the members themselves already leaned towards such a decision. Group discussion produced a risky shift.

Subsequent research has shown this phenomenon to be part of a more general tendency for a group decision to be more extreme than the mean of its members' positions, in the direction favoured by the mean – a phenomenon called **group polarisation** (Moscovici and Zavalloni, 1969). If the group leans towards taking a risk, group discussion will produce a more risky decision, if it leans towards caution then the group decision will be more cautious; if it leans towards joining the single European currency the decision will strongly favour joining; if it leans against joining it will be even more opposed; and so forth.

One important consequence of group polarisation is attitude change. For example, suppose that you join a local environmental group because you have a desire to protect the environment. After attending several meetings and discussing environmental issues with other group members, you may find that your pro-environment attitude has become even stronger: you are more of an environmentalist than you thought you were. The fact that group discussion can effect attitude change so powerfully has been documented in many psychology experiments. For example, Myers and Bishop (1970) found that the initial level of racial prejudice voiced by groups was altered through group discussion. Discussion caused the group with an initially low level of prejudice to become even less prejudiced and discussion caused the group with an initially high level of prejudice to become even more prejudiced.

What causes group discussion to lead to polarisation? Although several explanations have been offered, three seem the most plausible: those concerning informational and normative influence (Isenberg, 1986), and social identity processes (Turner *et al.*, 1989). Informational influence involves learning new information germane to the decision to be made. When you are in a group that is already slanted towards one decision, group discussion will bring to light new information that supports your position but that you have not heard before. This supportive novel information will strengthen commitment to your position, and across the members of the group this will encourage the group to endorse a more extreme decision.

Normative influence involves comparison of one's individual views with that of the group. Just as we discussed in the earlier section on conformity, people strive for social approval and do not like to stand out from the crowd. Discussion reveals what appears to be the socially desirable position, and thus members of the group strive to be seen by the other members of the group to be adhering to the 'popular' position. In this way the group becomes more extreme and is able to endorse a more extreme decision.

Social identity processes involve people in the group constructing a group norm to define their membership in the decision-making group and then conforming to that norm. If the group's mean initial position is relatively extreme, this implies that people who are not in the group (or who are in a specific out-group) are less extreme. In order to distinguish the group from 'other people', the in-group norm is perceptually polarised away from 'most other people'. The process of self-categorisation and depersonalisation associated with group identification (Turner *et al.*, 1987) causes people to conform to the polarised norm and thus endorse a polarised group decision. Research has supported this analysis by showing that group polarisation occurs only if people perceive the extreme mean to be a group norm rather than merely an aggregate of positions, and if they identify with the group defined by the norm (Mackie, 1986; Turner *et al.*, 1989; Abrams *et al.*, 1990).

Groupthink

Irving Janis has studied a related phenomenon that sometimes occurs in group decision-making – **groupthink**, the tendency to avoid dissent in the attempt to achieve group consensus (Janis, 1972, 1982). He developed the notion of groupthink after studying the poor decision-making that led President John F. Kennedy to order the ill-fated attempt to overthrow the Castro regime in Cuba in 1961. The decision to embark on the Bay of Pigs invasion was made by Kennedy and a small group of advisers. After studying the conditions that led to this decision and other important group decisions that altered the course of twentieth-century history (such as the 1941 Japanese attack on Pearl Harbor), Janis proposed his theory of groupthink.

The theory specifies the conditions necessary for groupthink as well as its symptoms and consequences (see Figure 16.6). The conditions that foster groupthink include a stressful situation in which the stakes are very high, a cohesive group of people who already tend to think alike and who are isolated from others who could offer criticism of the decision, and a strong group leader who makes their position well known to the group. In the Bay of Pigs example, the overthrow of one of America's arch-enemies was at stake, Kennedy's group of advisers were like-minded regarding the invasion and met in secret, and Kennedy was a forceful and charismatic leader who made his intentions to invade Cuba known to the group.

Janis also notes five symptoms of groupthink, all of which were present during the decision to invade Cuba: (1) group members share the illusion that their decision is sound, moral and right – in a word, invulnerable; (2) dissent from the leader's views are discouraged, further supporting the illusion that the group's decision is the right one; (3) instead of assessing the strengths and weaknesses of the decision, group members rationalise their decision, looking only for reasons that support it; (4) group members are closed-minded – they are not willing to listen to alternative suggestions and ideas; and (5) self-appointed 'mindguards' exist within the group who actively discourage dissent from the group norm.

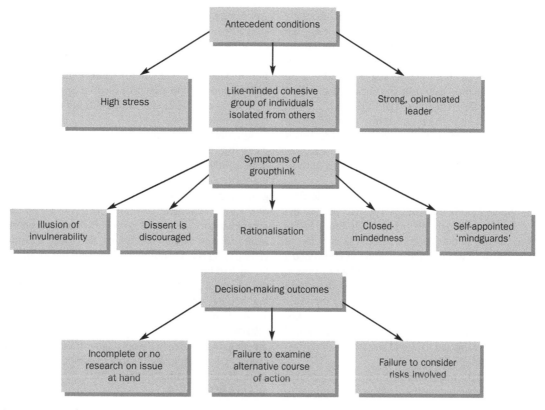

Figure 16.6 A summary of Janis's conception of groupthink.

Combined, these symptoms lead to flawed decision-making. They contribute to the tendency to conduct only incomplete or no research on the issue about which a decision is being made, to fail to examine alternative courses of action specified by the decision and, finally, to fail to consider potential risks inherent in the decision.

Janis argues that groupthink may be avoided by taking several precautions: (1) criticism by group members should be encouraged; (2) relevant input should be sought from appropriate people who are not members of the group; (3) the group should be broken down into sub-groups in which different ideas and opinions are generated and developed; and (4) the group leader should not overstate their position on the matter and should be on guard for rationalisation, closed-mindedness and illusions of invulnerability. An unlikely last word on this topic goes to former US President Ronald Reagan. He perceptively understood the dangers of groupthink: 'You risk becoming isolated. People tell you about what you want to hear and are reluctant to tell you about somebody who might not be pulling his weight or doing something hurtful to your administration. Not many people close to you are willing to say: "You're wrong".'

Psychology in action: The social psychology of drunkenness

How does alcohol affect your behaviour? Is it any different when you are alone or in a group? Are groups more risky or dangerous when they are drinking? Research into the effects of alcohol shows that individuals take more risks when they have been drinking. They are likely to be sexually irresponsible, aggressive, emotional, and to drive dangerously. Why?

According to Steele and Joseph's (1990) 'alcohol myopia' model, alcohol makes social behaviour more extreme because it blocks response conflicts by reducing cognitive constraints on affective preferences. Fromme et al. (1997) argued that drinkers maintain relatively automatic expectation of positive outcomes but they do not engage in systematic processing that is needed to evaluate potential negative outcomes. As a result, people become riskier in their choices. Research on groups suggests that people also change the way they view risks and social relationships when they make decisions in groups (Janis, 1972).

Curiously, almost all of the research into these effects of alcohol examines only the behaviour of individuals. This is surprising given that such a large proportion of alcohol consumption happens in social settings, often in groups of three or more people.

Abrams et al. (2006) investigated whether moderate alcohol intake affected students' attraction to risk. Half of the students consumed enough alcohol to bring them to the legal limit for driving in the UK and US (roughly two pints of beer or four glasses of wine). The other students consumed a placebo that tasted like alcohol but contained almost none. In one condition students were asked to complete tasks alone. In another condition students completed the same tasks together in groups of four. Members were asked to rate how attractive a series of 16 bets was to them and were told that they would be expected to spend some of their participation payment on these bets.

If group polarisation occurred, the group consensus should be more extreme than the average initial tendency of their individual members (Moscovici and Zavalloni, 1969). Given that alcohol myopia should make individuals risky, group polarisation should make them riskier still, so that the effect of alcohol is larger for groups than individuals. The group might also exhibit de-individuation, where group members become less self-conscious and less inhibited than individuals (Diener, 1980). Being in a group and drinking could add together to increase riskiness. A third possibility, group monitoring, argues that by sharing information, groups are often able to solve problems more reliably than their individual members (Laughlin and Ellis, 1986). The group monitoring hypothesis states that even when moderately intoxicated, group members will be able to attend to one another sufficiently to be reminded that perspectives other than their own should be considered during decision-making. This mutual monitoring within the group may compensate for the effects of alcohol on individuals' riskiness. Alcohol would make individuals but not groups riskier if group monitoring occurs.

Abrams and colleagues found the results supported the group monitoring hypothesis. Individuals found the bets significantly more attractive if they had consumed alcohol than if they were sober. However, when students were in groups, alcohol made no difference to the attractiveness of the bets. Adding further support to the group monitoring explanation is that whereas individuals completed the tasks more quickly after drinking alcohol (suggesting they were paying less attention), groups were significantly slower if they had been drinking alcohol. This fits with the idea that the groups were devoting time to monitoring and discussing their decisions.

Most people's drinking is likely to be moderate and relaxed social drinking, perhaps in the context of an informal meeting, or a drink after work. Under these circumstances it seems that groups might be able to compensate for the negative effects of alcohol on individuals' attentional capacities and loss of inhibition.

Leadership

Our discussion of groupthink has identified the important role of leaders in group decision-making. Indeed, it is very difficult to envisage groups without leaders. Almost all groups are structured into one or more people who have greater influence and take the lead, and others who are more influenced and act as followers. Leadership is endemic to group processes.

One approach to leadership focuses on the way that particular leadership styles are suited to different leadership situations – these are called **contingency theories** because they argue that the effectiveness of a particular style is contingent on situational factors. The best known of these is Fiedler's (1965) contingency theory. Fiedler believed that people differ in their leadership styles – some people are task-oriented and others relationship-oriented. Task-oriented leaders are authoritarian, value group success and derive self-esteem from task accomplishment rather than being liked by the group; relationship-oriented leaders are relaxed, friendly, non-directive and sociable, and gain self-esteem from happy and harmonious group relations. Fiedler also believed that leadership situations could be classified in terms of what he called situational control. At one extreme were situations in which leaders had legitimate authority, good leader–member relations and the task was well structured; at the other extreme, legitimacy was low, leader–member relations poor and the task poorly structured. Fiedler predicted that relationship-oriented leaders were more effective than task-oriented leaders except if situational control was either very high or very low, when task-oriented leaders would be more effective. There is general support for this analysis, except that critics have suggested that it is too static a view of leadership, and that it underplays the fact that leadership is very much a group process that involves the relationship between leaders and followers.

Leader–follower relations are a more central focus of **transactional theories of leadership**. For example, Hollander (1958) argues that for leaders to be effective they need to develop a relationship with the rest of the group that allows them to be innovative and to exert influence over the group. Hollander suggests that leaders need to accumulate what he calls idiosyncrasy credits. This can be done by (1) initially conforming closely to established group norms, (2) ensuring that the group feels it has democratically elected you as the leader, (3) making sure that you are seen to have the competence to fulfil the group's objectives, and (4) being seen to identify with the group, its ideals and its aspirations.

Another transactional model of leadership is **leader–member exchange (LMX)** theory (Graen and Uhl-Bien, 1995). To be effective, leaders need to establish very different individualised exchange relationships with different members of the group. However, in doing this, leaders need to be careful to treat all members with respect as valued group members, and not to create destructive internal divisions by showing too much preference for some members over others.

A development of transactional models of leadership focuses on **transformational leadership** (Bass, 1998). Transformational leaders' transactions with followers are characterised by charisma, inspirational motivation, intellectual stimulation and individualised consideration, which motivate followers to work for group goals that transcend immediate self-interest. Transformational leaders are those who respond positively to change and who actively induce change. Great leaders often do seem to behave in this way but critics worry that too much emphasis is now being placed on charisma as a personality attribute.

A different approach to the explanation of leadership has been proposed by social identity theorists (Hogg, 2001; Hogg and van Knippenberg, 2003). In groups, people tend to rest their evaluation and endorsement of leaders on the extent to which leaders match schemas they have of good leadership. However, where people identify strongly with a group that is important to self-definition, people's evaluations of their leaders are increasingly influenced by how prototypical of the group the leader is perceived to be.

There are many implications of this idea. For example, in very cohesive and salient groups with which people identify strongly, poor leaders (those who do not match effective leadership schemas) may prevail simply because they are highly prototypical of the group. Leaders are also presumably aware that they can increase their leadership effectiveness of such groups by being seen to be prototypical. They will engage in a rhetoric of prototypicality in which they talk up their own prototypicality (Reicher and Hopkins, 1996). Leaders of cohesive groups may behave differently as a function of how prototypical they are (van Knippenberg and van Knippenberg, 2003). Leaders who are highly prototypical are often aware that their prototypicality is not in question – they are thus able to be innovative and non-conformist. The prototypicality of less prototypical leaders still needs to be established – these leaders need to be much more conformist and thus less able to be innovative.

Crowds and social movements

Crowds are clearly group events; however, they seem to be somewhat different from other group phenomena we have discussed. We have all seen media coverage of football riots, and of crowd aggression in, for example, the Middle East and Northern Ireland, and many of us may have been involved in protests or demonstrations that have turned ugly. We are also familiar with vivid literary accounts of the great riots and demonstrations associated with the French and Russian revolutions. Crowds tend to

Negotiation, teamwork and leadership – An international perspective

From selling detergent to securing peace in Northern Ireland or the Middle East, the ability to negotiate with others is an important social skill. The outcome of a transaction or interaction can turn on not only how well you negotiate, but on how you work as a team and the leadership you show. A recent review by Gelfand et al. (2007) summarises how these three characteristics vary across nations and how this variation affects decisions.

Research on negotiation has shown that, in the US, people are more likely to show self-serving biases and make internal attributions about other negotiators' behaviour (Gelfand and Christakopoulou, 1999). North Americans are more likely to see conflicts as being about winning or violating an individual's rights (Gelfand et al., 2001), to share information directly with their colleagues during negotiation, and to achieve high goals that both parties want to attain (Adair et al., 2001). They are more likely to make concessions at the end of the negotiation than at the beginning (Hendon et al., 2003), and are most satisfied with a negotiation when their economic gains have been maximised (Ma et al., 2002).

Japanese negotiators, in contrast, see conflicts as a violation of duty but also as an opportunity to compromise (Gelfand et al., 2001). The Japanese, Russians and participants from Hong Kong are more likely to seek out information during a negotiation through a pattern of offers (Adair et al., 2001). Unlike US negotiators, Asian negotiators are more likely to make generous concessions early on in an exchange and gradually reduce these concessions as the negotiation goes on (Hendon et al., 2003). Unlike Americans, Estonians see a successful negotiation ending when both parties are the recipients of equivalent outcomes (Ma et al., 2002).

The ways in which teams operate and are perceived also differ across cultures. For example, Americans view their team less favourably if they – as individuals – do well but the team performs poorly. You don't see such an interpretation in Chinese participants (Chen et al., 1998). Taiwanese participants view their teams more negatively if membership changes often (compared with Australian participants, who don't) (Harrison et al., 2000). Individuals from collectivistic cultures are more likely to view teams as 'entities' and as 'acting as one' (Chiu et al., 2000). In Japan, indirect personal ties between group members are important for engendering trust amongst the team; in the US, this trust is fostered by team participants belonging to some shared membership category, such as the school they went to (Yuki et al., 2005). Teams of people from collectivistic cultures cooperate better and are more successful (Eby and Dobbins, 1997).

What if the team is made up of people from different cultures? The research suggests that these teams show considerable evidence of ethnocentrism and strong in-group biases (Von Glinow et al., 2004; Cramton and Hinds, 2005).

When the team leaders prevent communication breakdown, however, multicultural teams perform as well as monocultural teams (Ayoko et al., 2002). A person's culture/nation becomes important in team negotiations when either very few or very many members share the same background (Randel, 2003). Here, performance is worse than in more homogeneous groups (Thomas, 1999). Over time, however, Harrison et al. (2002) have found that this performance improves, presumably because team members have begun to familiarise themselves with each other and have learned about each other's behaviour. Also, the more heterogenous the team, the better the performance (compared with moderately varied teams) (Earley and Mosakowski, 2000).

Finally, we all know of leaders who seem capable of persuading others and of turning the minds of people who appear to hold entrenched, immutable opinions – Bill Clinton intervening to negotiate with the violently opposed political factions in Northern Ireland; Tony Blair persuading Bill Clinton to release ground troops in Kosovo which, ultimately, put an end to Milosevic's ethnic cleansing; Bob Geldof persuading a few popstars to sing a tune and then subsequently persuading millions to help feed the millions of starving in Africa and, more recently, persuading the eight richest nations in the world to tackle poverty in developing countries. (Of course, there are those whose persuasion is not as honourable or which leads to outcomes that are not as positive – such as those who can persuade young men that crashing a plane into a building or detonating a bomb on a tube train is a good idea or, more historically, Jim Jones, leader of the People's Temple – a Californian cult – who in 1978 ordered almost 800 people to commit suicide.)

Is there any trait that leaders such as this share? In individualistic cultures there is a tendency for leaders to use coercive power to achieve aims whereas in collectivistic cultures, the tendency is to use expert power. According to the Global Leadership and Organizational Behaviour Effectiveness Project (cleverly acronymed as GLOBE) which looked at 17,000 middle managers in 62 cultures, two traits stand out in good leaders: being charismatic and being a team-player (House et al., 2004). The best senior managers were described as innovative, visionary and courageous; those at a lower level were described as being attentive to subordinates and were good at team building.

Gelfand et al. (2007) note that charisma varies across nations. They cite the example given by Den Hartog and Verburg (1997). They found that a strong, ululating voice was described as enthusiastic in Latin American cultures, and therefore a vehicle for charisma, whereas a monotonous tone was described as worthy of respect and self-control in Asian cultures, a uniformity that was considered charismatic.

be volatile, unruly and often violent. They are, of course, not always like this – the crowds attending the funeral of Queen Elizabeth, the Queen Mother, in London in 2002 or those outside the Vatican hearing the Papal address, were certainly not. However, research on crowds has traditionally focused on the antisocial and violent portrayal of crowds. The assumption is that, sometimes, just being part of a crowd can be sufficient to transform our otherwise civil behaviour into unruly, violent acts.

Many social psychologists explain these acts in terms of de-individuation, in which one loses one's sense of individuality and personal responsibility. In collective settings, people 'blend' into the crowd, achieving a sense of anonymity that causes them to assume less responsibility for their actions (Diener, 1980). Consider a study of empathy towards strangers conducted by Zimbardo (1970). In one condition, young women were easily identifiable: they wore name tags and were called by their names. In another condition, a different group of young women were not so easily identifiable: they wore large coats and hoods without name tags and were never referred to by their names. The two groups of women were given chances to administer electric shocks to a stranger, who was actually a confederate of Zimbardo's. The young women who were unidentifiable gave nearly twice as many electric shocks to the stranger as did the young women whose identities were known. Thus, the amount of aggression Zimbardo observed in his participants was strongly correlated with the extent to which their identities were known, reinforcing the idea that antisocial behaviour observed in some groups is due to the loss of personal identity of its individual members.

People in crowds are not always antisocial, and crowds themselves are not always aggressive. De-individuation may not be an automatic consequence of crowds, or it may be a process that is less mechanically tied to antisocial behaviour. Taylor *et al.* (1994) characterise de-individuation as a process wherein one's personal identity – one's sense of self – is replaced by identification with the group's values and goals (see also Reicher *et al.*, 1995).

This idea has been more fully explored in terms of social identity theory, which we discussed earlier in this chapter. Reicher (1987, 2001) suggests that crowds are events where people from the same group, and thus with a common social identity, come together to achieve goals (which may or may not involve violence). The strong sense of common social identity ensures that people are highly attuned to the appropriate group norm, and thus conform tightly to it. There is no loss of identity or responsibility, no de-individuation, rather a change of identity. For Reicher, crowds are not fickle or irrational. They are group events in which there are clear limits to acceptable behaviour – limits set by the identity of the crowd. Local conditions and goals will influence how the crowd's social identity expresses itself within these limits. For example, Stott and colleagues have analysed the role of police behaviour in situations when football fans become violent, such as the 1998 World Cup Final, and conclude that the more heavy-handed the police are in their approach to policing the more violent and antagonistic the fans will be (e.g. Stott *et al.*, 2001; Stott and Adang, 2004).

This rational model of crowds links crowd action to various forms of social protest that may be part of a social movement. The key question in the study of social protest is what causes individual discontents or grievances to be transformed into collective action: how and why do sympathisers become mobilised as activists or participants? Klandermans (1997) argues that this involves the relationship between individual attitudes and behaviour (see Chapter 15). Sympathisers hold, by definition, sympathetic attitudes towards an issue yet these attitudes do not translate into behaviour. Participation also resembles a social dilemma (see below). Protest is generally for a social good (such as equality) or against a social ill (for example, pollution), and as success benefits everyone irrespective of participation but failure harms participants more, it is tempting to 'free ride' – to remain a sympathiser rather than become a participant.

When crowds go wrong: football hooliganism

Since the early 1970s European, but particularly English, football has become strongly associated with hooliganism. Football 'hooliganism' involves groups of people behaving in the same way. It is also a set of behaviours which is often associated in the popular mind with crowd behaviour, the popular image of a riot or other violent and antisocial collective event. Popular hysteria tends to characterise football hooliganism in terms of the familiar stereotypical image of football fans on the rampage (Murphy *et al.*, 1990).

De-individuation theories offer a group-oriented analysis of this phenomenon. A football match is a crowd context where people feel anonymous and unidentifiable; they lose their sense of individual identity and thus no longer feel that it is necessary to act in socially acceptable ways. This perspective assumes that people are fundamentally antisocial and aggressive, and that the only reason people do not ordinarily act in this way is that they are usually identifiable in a society whose norms strongly proscribe such behaviour. Hooliganism is primitive unsocialised behaviour which lies deep in all our psyches, and which is released in crowd settings like a football match. Although recognising the group context of hooliganism, this analysis is also rather individualistic. The crowd releases individual aggressive instincts – and in fact any (non-group) context that makes one feel de-individuated may have the same effect (for example, darkness, or clothing which conceals who we are). One problem with this analysis is that it cannot easily explain why most people at football matches do not indulge in hooliganism. Perhaps they are not de-individuated – but why? Perhaps they are de-individuated, but de-individuation does not inevitably produce hooliganism, in which case alternative or additional processes must operate to produce hooliganism.

A different, more genuinely group-oriented analysis of football hooliganism is provided by Marsh *et al.* (1978). According to their analysis, violence by football fans is actually orchestrated far away from the stadium and long before a given match. What might appear to be a motley crowd of supporters on match day can actually consist of several distinct groups of fans with different status. By participating in ritualised aggression over a period of time, a faithful follower can be 'promoted' into a higher group and can continue to pursue a 'career structure'. Rival fans who follow their group's rules quite carefully can avoid real physical harm to themselves or others. For example, chasing the opposition after a match ('seeing them off') need not necessarily end in violence since part of the agreed code is not actually to catch anyone. Seen in this light, football hooliganism is a kind of staged production and is not the example of an uncontrollable mob sometimes depicted by the media. When real violence does take place it tends to be both unusual and attributable to particular individuals.

Football hooliganism can also be understood in more broadly societal terms. For example, Murphy *et al.* (1990) described how football arose in Britain as an essentially working-class sport, and that by the 1950s working-class values to do with masculine aggression had already become associated with the game. Attempts by the government (seen as middle class) to control this aspect of the sport can backfire because these attempts merely enhance class solidarity and encourage increased violence that generalises beyond matches. This sort of explanation points towards an analysis in terms of intergroup relations and subcultural norms that prescribe and legitimate aggression. Fans derive a sense of who they are – a sense of identity – from being part of a group of supporters. Some people, particularly those with few other valued sources of identity, identify more strongly than others. The attitudinal, dress and behavioural norms of the group are strongly adhered to, particularly in situations where the group is very salient, for example, at or around a match when supporters of opposing teams are present in the stadium, in the streets and on public transport. The actual norms of the groups reflect the historical origins of the sport and the intrinsically competitive and masculine nature of the game. Football hooliganism is largely a display of controlled aggression and machismo that reflects strong identification with group norms (this sort of group-oriented analysis owes much to social identity theory).

Protestors marching after the riots in Paris of October/ November 2005, which led to debates on integration and discrimination in France, and to what extent French of North African descent could have a French national identity.
Source: Christophe Ena/Press Association Images.

Intergroup relations and prejudice

Our discussion of social protest leads neatly into this next topic. Social protest involves one group of people protesting against another group – often a minority group protesting against the government. It is a manifestation of intergroup relations. Sherif (1962, p. 5) has provided a classic definition of **intergroup relations**:

Intergroup relations refer to relations between two or more groups and their respective members. Whenever individuals belonging to one group interact, collectively or individually, with another group or its members in terms of their group identifications we have an instance of intergroup behaviour.

Relations between groups vary enormously from being relatively harmonious to being massively destructive, but almost always they tend to be characterised by some degree of competitive orientation that seeks to maintain the groups as distinctive entities. Because the extreme and harmful aspect of intergroup behaviour is so damaging (it includes war and genocide), research has tended to focus on that aspect and in particular on intergroup conflict and on the attitudinal aspect of hostile intergroup relations – prejudice.

Intergroup behaviour

Intergroup behaviour tends to be competitive and ethnocentric, that is, people tend to view all attributes of their group as being better than all attributes of any out-group they compare themselves with.

Realistic conflict and interdependence

One explanation of why and how this happens was developed on the basis of a series of three famous field experiments conducted by Sherif and his colleagues in 1949, 1953 and 1954 at summer camps for young boys in the US (see Sherif, 1966). The participants, 11-year-old boys, were randomly assigned to one of two cabins that were isolated from each other. Friends were split up to be in different cabins. During the first week, the boys in each cabin spent their time together as a group, fishing, hiking, swimming and otherwise enjoying themselves. The boys formed two cohesive groups, which they named the Rattlers and the Eagles. They became attached to their groups and strongly identified with them.

Next, the experimenters arranged a series of formal competitive events between the two groups. The best team was to win a trophy for the group and individual prizes for its members. As the competition progressed, the boys began taunting and insulting each other. Then the Eagles burned the Rattlers' flag and, in retaliation, the Rattlers broke into the Eagles' cabin and scattered or stole their rivals' belongings. Although further physical conflict was prevented by the experimenters, the two groups continued to abuse each other verbally and seemed to have developed a genuine hatred for each other – stereotypes and prejudices developed and were expressed verbally and physically.

Finally, in one of the studies the experimenters arranged for the boys to work together in order to accomplish shared goals that both groups valued but neither group could accomplish alone. The experimenters sabotaged the water supply for the camp and had the boys fix it; they had the boys repair a truck that had broken down; and they induced the boys to pool their money to rent a movie. After the boys worked on cooperative ventures, rather than competitive ones, the level of intergroup conflict diminished markedly.

To explain the results of these studies, Sherif developed **realistic conflict theory**. Sherif argued that the way people behave towards one another is strongly influenced by people's goals and their perception of the goal relations between people. When people have a common goal that requires interdependent action for its achievement, then people cooperate to help one another to achieve the goal, and this produces a sense of solidarity and oneness that underpins group formation. This is what happened in the first stage of the studies. When two groups have mutually exclusive goals, in other words when only one group can achieve the goal at the expense of the other group, then the groups compete and hinder each other from achieving their goal. This spawns mutual dislike, conflict and hostility. This is what happened in the second stage of the studies. When two groups have a common goal that

cannot be achieved by one group alone (called a superordinate goal), then the two groups cooperate to help one another to achieve the goal. This reduces hostility and generates more positive intergroup attitudes. This is what happened in the final stage of the studies.

Frustrated goals and relative deprivation

A key feature of realistic conflict theory is the argument that intergroup conflict rests on competitive goals that cause each group to impede or frustrate each other's attempts to achieve their goals. Collective goal frustration may contribute to hostile intergroup relations. This idea has its roots in Dollard *et al.*'s (1939) **frustration–aggression hypothesis**. When people's goals are frustrated they can feel a sense of anger (technically called an 'instigation to aggress') that can be dissipated only by aggression, often not directed at the cause of the frustration but at a scapegoat that is weak and vulnerable. According to Berkowitz (1962), frustration is most likely to translate into collective aggression against an outgroup when the instigation to aggress is associated with other generally aversive conditions, there are aggressive cues in the environment, and people are in the presence of others who are acting aggressively.

Generally, conflict between groups arises when a group has an acute feeling of being deprived. **Relative deprivation** can be most acute when a period of rising expectations (how things ought to be) and rising achievements (how things are) comes to an abrupt end because achievements suddenly drop off. This J-curve hypothesis (Davies, 1969) has been used to explain large-scale intergroup conflicts, for example, the French and Russian revolutions, and the rise of anti-Semitism in Europe after the economic crash of 1929.

Although relative deprivation can be based on diachronic (over time) comparisons between one's circumstances now and how they used to be, Runciman (1966) suggests that synchronic (here and now) self–other comparisons are much more immediate and powerful. These comparisons can be between one's self and individual others (interpersonal comparisons) or between one's own group and another group (intergroup comparisons). The former generates a sense of **egoistic relative deprivation** that is associated with stress, depression and demotivation. It is the latter that generates a sense of **fraternalistic relative deprivation** that is associated with collective protest, intergroup conflict, prejudice, and so forth (Vanneman and Pettigrew, 1972).

There are at least three conditions that seem to amplify the impact of fraternalistic deprivation on competitive intergroup behaviour: (1) people need to identify strongly with their group (Abrams, 1990); (2) people need to feel that their deprived state relative to another group rests not only on an unjust distribution of resources (distributive injustice), but also on unjust procedures (procedural injustice) (Tyler and Smith, 1998); and (3) there is a perception of real intergroup conflict over scarce resources (see our discussion of realistic conflict theory, above).

Humour, aggression and motivation: self-determination theory

According to self-determination theory (Deci and Ryan, 2000), autonomy motivation involves behaviour that includes making choices for oneself, acting according to values and principles that are respected and endorsed, and initiating behaviour in a proactive way. Control motivation, on the other hand, involves behaving according to the dictates of an external agency, under pressure and where behaviour is contingent on feedback from this agency. As you might expect, those expressing the former motivation would flourish; those with less autonomy and under greater control, would not.

There is evidence for this. People who are autonomous express greater well-being (Sheldon et al., 1996), have more positive romantic relationships (Knee et al., 2005) and perform better on tasks when they interact with others (Weinstein and Ryan, 2010). Weinstein et al. (2011) sought to see whether being primed with either of these orientations – primed autonomy and control – affected people's hostility and preference for hostile humour. In a series of four experiments, this is exactly what they found: people who had been primed with the control orientation found hostile humour (extracted from America's Funniest Home Videos) to be funnier (and less aversive). People who were high in trait hostility – and primed with the control condition – were particularly enamored with the hostile material. Both trait hostility and control priming also enhanced aggressive behaviour.

Social identity

Although competitive goals and a sense of relative deprivation certainly do encourage conflict and hostile intergroup attitudes and behaviour, there is also substantial evidence that the mere existence of social categories or groups can be sufficient to provide the framework for this behaviour. Tajfel et al. (1971) conducted an experiment in which school students were randomly assigned to groups (ostensibly on the basis of preferences for paintings by the artists Klee and Kandinsky, who were unknown to the students). The participants did not interact and did not know who was in their group or who was in the other group. Nevertheless they subsequently discriminated against the out-group by repeatedly allocating less money to the out-group than their own group (even though they personally did not benefit financially

from this allocation). This paradigm, the **minimal group paradigm**, and variants of it, have been used many hundreds of times over the last 35 years or so to replicate this effect – people who are categorised on a minimal, trivial and often random basis tend to show a competitive and discriminatory orientation towards an out-group.

It should be noted that minimal social categorisation can sometimes not produce discrimination. Experimental participants need to feel they belong to the minimal group, and this sense of belonging or identification is enhanced where people feel uncertain about themselves and their place in the social context (Hogg, 2000). Also, discrimination can disappear when participants, rather than allocating rewards, are asked to allocate punishments or withhold rewards – called the positive–negative asymmetry effect (Mummendey and Otten, 1998).

The initial minimal group finding was an important catalyst for the development, originally by Tajfel and then by Turner and his associates, of social identity theory (Tajfel and Turner, 1986; Turner et al., 1987; Hogg and Abrams, 1988; Hogg, 2006) (see also the section in Chapter 15 on self and identity). According to social identity theory, group and intergroup behaviour is associated with social identity (self-definition in terms of the defining attributes of an in-group), not personal identity (self-definition in terms of idiosyncratic traits or close interpersonal relationships). People cognitively represent social groups in terms of a fuzzy set of attributes (called a prototype) that simultaneously captures in-group similarities and intergroup differences. Prototypes are catered to specific contexts in order to maximise entitativity – the property of a group that makes it a distinct entity with sharp boundaries and clear consensual defining attributes. Self-inclusive social categories with high entitativity and clear prescriptive prototypes are very effective at reducing self-conceptual, attitudinal and behavioural uncertainty (Hogg, 2000).

When a particular intergroup categorisation seems best to account for what is going on in a particular situation it then becomes psychologically salient, that is, people categorise themselves and others in terms of the categorisation. Social categorisation causes people to view others and themselves not as unique individuals, but in terms of the relevant in-group or out-group prototype – a process called **depersonalisation** because perception is based on group membership and group attributes not individuality and personal attributes. Depersonalisation explains why, in intergroup contexts, we tend to see out-group members stereotypically, why we conform to in-group norms relating to perceptions, feelings, attitudes and behaviours, and why we tend to accentuate intergroup differences and intragroup similarities on all available and relevant dimensions of comparison. This cognitive aspect of social identity theory is called **self-categorisation theory** (Turner et al., 1987).

Because groups define and evaluate who we are, it is important that the groups we belong to have attributes that we consider to be evaluatively positive. Intergroup behaviour is a struggle for positive distinctiveness for our own group relative to relevant out-groups. This furnishes a favourable social identity, and this in turn contributes to an underlying sense of self-esteem. The struggle for positive social identity can be framed in terms of a struggle for status, with dominant groups protecting their high-status position of advantage and privilege, and subordinate groups striving to rectify their lower-status position and associated disadvantage. According to social identity theory, the form that this struggle takes depends upon people's perceptions of the nature of status relations between groups (Tajfel and Turner, 1986; Ellemers, 1993). The focus is largely on how lower-status groups respond to their social position.

Where status relations are considered legitimate but the boundaries between groups are believed to be permeable, members of lower-status groups pursue social mobility – they disidentify from their group and try to gain admittance for themselves and their immediate family to the higher-status group. This is almost always unsuccessful. It leaves people with a marginal social identity – rejected by their in-group and not accepted by the out-group. Where status relations are considered to be relatively legitimate and highly stable and boundaries are impermeable, lower-status group members pursue a strategy of social creativity. They try to improve their social identity by seeking a redefinition of in-group properties – different, more positive attributes and a re-evaluation of existing properties. They also focus on comparisons with groups who are even lower in status than their own. Finally, where people recognise the illegitimacy of their lower-status position, feel that status relations are unstable and can envisage ways to achieve a change in status relations, they engage in direct social competition. They go head-to-head with the higher-status groups – this can take the form of democratic political action, social protest or revolution and war.

The social identity analysis of intergroup behaviour has gathered substantial support as an account of the dynamics of intergroup behaviour. For example, regarding the role of self-esteem, Hunter et al. (1996) studied the intergroup relationship between Catholic and Protestant 16-year-olds in Northern Ireland. Participants first completed some measures of self-esteem and then evaluated the two groups. Self-esteem was then measured again. Among those who expressed in-group bias when they evaluated the groups (favouring their own group over the other), self-esteem was raised on dimensions such as honesty, academic ability and physical appearance.

Regarding the motivational role of uncertainty reduction, a series of experiments has shown that discrimination in the minimal group paradigm occurs only if people are categorised under conditions of subjective uncertainty that cause them to identify with the minimal group (Hogg, 2000). Regarding intergroup conflict, there is an entire literature in the area of language and social psychology which shows that **ethnolinguistic groups** (ethnic groups for whom language is a defining feature) thrive or perish depending on perceptions of the stability, legitimacy and permeability of status relations, exactly as predicted by social identity theory (Giles and Johnson, 1987). Finally, there is evidence that in-group prototypes do enhance entitativity and that people conform to such norms when they identify with their group (Abrams et al., 1990), and that this is associated with out-group stereotyping (Oakes et al., 1993; Leyens et al., 1994).

Ostracism

Research by Zadro et al. (2005) shows that people can feel worse when they are the target of ostracism (being excluded and ignored in the presence of others) than the target of a verbal dispute. Furthermore, those who are the source of the behaviour actually feel better when they ostracise you than when they target you with verbal dispute.

To demonstrate this, Zadro and colleagues conducted three role-playing experiments in which they constructed a mock train ride in the laboratory – three rows, one right behind the other, of three chairs. To further cue the 'train ride' aspect there were some of the usual signs found in trains, such as 'no smoking' and 'do not place your feet on the seats'. Student participants were randomly assigned the role of target or source – targets sat in the middle of rows and sources sat at the ends.

The scenario was described as one in which they were travelling home by train and the sources were cross with the target because he or she had not invited them to a party. In the ostracism condition the sources were told to express their anger by talking to one another across the target but ignoring the target. In the dispute condition they were told to express their anger by directly arguing with the target. The role-play lasted about five minutes, after which participants completed a questionnaire indicating how they felt – more specifically, to what extent they felt the four basic needs of belonging, control, self-esteem and meaningful existence were being met.

The results of the first study, with 35 students, showed that targets of ostracism felt all four needs were less satisfied than did targets of dispute – they felt less belonging, less control, lower self-esteem and less meaningful existence. Sources who used ostracism felt greater control than did sources who used dispute. The second study, with 57 participants, was virtually identical with some minor changes to increase the realism of the role-play. Once again targets of ostracism felt all four needs were less satisfied than did targets of dispute. The final study, with 138 participants, used a slightly different scenario – the target had refused to provide notes for the sources to catch up on a class they had missed – but was the same in other respects. Yet again, targets of ostracism felt all four needs were less satisfied than did targets of dispute – but here the difference was significant only on belonging and meaningful existence. In addition, sources of ostracism felt greater belonging and more superiority than did sources of dispute. This last study also had a control condition in which the target was explicitly included by the sources – as one would expect, inclusion caused both targets and sources to feel their needs were being better satisfied than did ostracism or dispute.

These studies by Zadro et al. (2005) are part of an extensive programme of research by Williams and his associates on the psychological effects of ostracism (Williams, 2001). These studies have used some very vivid paradigms – for example, in one paradigm a participant ostensibly waiting with two others for an experiment is initially included in a ball-tossing game and then excluded (e.g. Williams and Sommer, 1997). The reaction to ostracism underscores the fundamentally social nature of human existence and the way that our sense of self and of reality is grounded in social recognition. We feel isolated. What is astonishing is that this isolation can also make us feel, literally, cold. Zhong and Leonardelli (2008) found that when people were asked to recall an experience in which they felt socially isolated, they estimated the temperature of the room to be lower than did those who recalled an experience in which they were socially included. In a follow-up study, they manipulated exclusion directly. Participants played an online game of pass the ball with three other players. What the participants did not know is that some of them would not have the ball passed to them. They would be excluded. Those who were excluded found the room colder and expressed a greater desire for warm food and drink than did those who were included.

Recently, the effect of ostracism on the experience of pain was studied (Bernstein and Claypool, 2012). The research on the effect of ostracism on pain is mixed: some studies suggests that it increases pain sensitivity; others that it numbs the recipient. The cyberball manipulation leads people to be hypersensitive to pain but when they think about a future alone, it numbs them. Bernstein and Claypool, instead of using the cyberball task, asked people to imagine a future alone and, in the extreme scenario, 'devoid of any meaningful social relations'. They found that the more severe the future life exclusion, the greater the pain numbing; less severe future exclusion was associated with hypersensitivity to pain. They suggest that the hypersensitivity to the cyberball exclusion is adaptive and prosocial, a means of coping with ostracism. The future alone paradigm leads to maladaptive responses.

Prejudice

Intergroup attitudes are a core component of intergroup behaviour. Attitudes toward the out-group tend to be shared among the in-group members, and tend to devalue the out-group relative to the in-group – they are stereotypes and are a defining feature of prejudice. Indeed, **prejudice** can be defined as a shared attitude, generally negative, towards a social out-group, and thus towards members of that group purely on the basis of their membership in that group (see Chapter 11 for some discussion of the development of prejudice). Some of the most pernicious prejudices are those based on people's race, ethnicity, religion, age, sex, sexual orientation and mental and physical health. But people have a remarkable ability to be prejudiced against almost any group you care to mention – illustrated by the 2006 Oscar-winning film *Crash*. Like other attitudes, prejudices have a cognitive component. In this case the cognitive component is (as discussed in the social cognition section of Chapter 15) a stereotype or schema – a set of interrelated (and shared) beliefs about members of the group that influences perception once we categorise someone as being a member of the group. Again, like other attitudes, there is no guarantee that prejudice will be expressed as behaviour, but when it is, that behaviour is called **discrimination**.

Researchers at the universities of Colorado and Chicago have found that making stereotypes about people accessible influences a person's decision to shoot those individuals during a videogame (Correll et al., 2007). In the experiment, participants had to press a key indicating 'shoot' if they saw a person with a gun in the game they were playing. If the person was not carrying a gun, they were to press a key indicating 'don't shoot'. Half of the characters in the game were white, half were black. Before playing the game, people were asked to read newspaper articles in which armed robberies committed by either black or white felons were reported.

People who read about the black criminals were significantly more likely to shoot black targets in the videogame – regardless of whether these targets were armed or unarmed – than white (even armed) targets. So, by making stereotypical information accessible (the link between black people and violence), the researchers found that people's tendency to engage in stereotype-driven behaviour increased.

Theories of prejudice

Because prejudice is repugnant and can have such appalling effects, such as genocide, prejudice is often traced to individual differences and personality attributes. One of the most widely promulgated theories of prejudice is the **authoritarian personality** (Adorno et al., 1950). Children who are brought up in families where their parents use harsh disciplinarian methods to secure love and dependence develop a love–hate relationship with their parents, which is unendurably stressful. The stress is resolved by idealising their parents and all authority figures and redirecting their hatred onto weaker others. This resolution becomes a deep-seated and immutable personality syndrome, authoritarianism, which frames relations for the rest of the person's life. It predisposes people to be prejudiced. Another personality explanation has been proposed by Rokeach (1948), who argues that some people, for whatever reason, have a general cognitive style that is rigid and dogmatic. These people are predisposed to be prejudiced because they strive for a rigidly stratified social world, are resistant to belief change in the light of contradictory evidence, and are inclined to ground their beliefs in authority and orthodox belief systems.

An individual differences explanation of prejudice, called **social dominance theory**, has been proposed by Pratto *et al.* (1994). They describe a relatively sophisticated, but nonetheless 'individual differences', analysis of exploitative power-based intergroup relations. People who desire their own group to be dominant and superior to out-groups have a high social dominance orientation that encourages them to reject egalitarian ideologies, and to accept myths that legitimise hierarchy and discrimination. These kinds of people are more inclined to be prejudiced than are people who have a low social dominance orientation.

Critics of personality and individual differences explanations of prejudice (Pettigrew, 1958; Billig, 1976) note that prejudice is not a sporadic individual matter, but rather it is a collective behaviour engaged in by large numbers of people in a relatively coordinated and highly targeted manner. They also provide evidence that personality is actually a poor predictor of prejudice, and that the nature of intergroup relations is a better predictor. In general, most social psychologists now believe that prejudice is a part of intergroup behaviour and therefore needs to be understood as part of a theory of intergroup behaviour. Although prejudice, stereotypes and discrimination are expressed by individuals, they are genuinely intergroup phenomena: individuals are prejudiced because they belong to groups that have developed certain relations with one another that are characterised by unequal status and advantage, and by conflict and hatred (Brown, 1995).

Cognitive processes in prejudice

We have already see one way in which cognitive processes are involved in prejudice – the categorisation of people into in-group and out-group seems to lay the groundwork for intergroup behaviour and possible prejudice. It may do this because it affects self-conception: it encourages people to view themselves as group members and think of themselves in terms of social identity, which can be considered a type of self-schema. Social categorisation causes people to view out-group members in terms of stereotypes, and to behave in ways that favour the in-group and maintain the distinctiveness of in-group identity.

Another cognitive process that is involved in stereotyping and prejudice is illusory correlation. The availability heuristic involves people assuming that distinctive, easily imagined items occur more frequently (see Chapter 15). This phenomenon probably explains why people overestimate the rate of violent crime (because an act of violence is a frightening, distinctive event) and overestimate the relative numbers of violent crimes committed by members of minority groups (because members of minority groups tend to be more conspicuous). This tendency is an example of an **illusory correlation** – the perception of an apparent relation between two distinctive elements that does not actually exist or is enormously exaggerated (Hamilton and Gifford, 1976).

Another fallacy that promotes stereotyping is the **illusion of out-group homogeneity**. People tend to assume that members of other groups are much more similar than are members of their own group (Linville, 1982). This tendency is even seen between the sexes: women tend to perceive men as being more alike than women are, and men do the opposite (Park and Rothbart, 1982). The same is true for young people and old people (Linville *et al.*, 1989). However, this effect can sometimes be reversed so that people think their own group is more homogeneous than the out-group. Simon and Brown (1987) suggest that one situation in which this can happen is when the in-group is a minority group in terms of status. The reason for this is that solidarity and thus homogeneity may have a special value for minorities.

Stigma and disadvantage

One of the principal problems with prejudice is that it stigmatises and disadvantages entire groups of people: 'Stigmatised individuals possess (or are believed to possess) some attribute, or characteristic, that conveys a social identity that is devalued in a particular social context' (Crocker *et al.*, 1998, p. 505). The targets of prejudice and discrimination are members of stigmatised groups, and thus they are stigmatised individuals. Stigma persists for a number of reasons.

An fMRI study of stigma suggests that our unstated prejudices might be revealed by our brain activation. Krendl *et al.* (2006) asked 22 men to make explicit (do you like this person?) or implicit (is this a man or a woman?) judgements about people with well-established stigma (obesity, unattractiveness, transexuality, etc.). Areas of the brain normally activated by negative emotional

Cutting edge: The prejudice that dare not speak its name…

The way people speak affects how we behave towards them and think about them. Accents, whether regional or national, activate a store of stereotypes which may or not be accurate. We do not expect the Queen to sound like a cockney. Other accents may signify so-called class or competence or affect the credibility of the speaker.

A study from the University of Chicago asked native American English speakers to assess the truthfulness of innocuous statements made by people with mild or strong accents (Lev-Ari and Keysar, 2010). Mild accents were Polish, Turkish and German; strong accents were Italian,

Korean and (very accented) Turkish. Mild and strong versions were included to examine whether accent affected the difficulty of being understood. Statements included: 'Ants don't sleep'.

Native English speakers were less likely to believe statements that were spoken in a non-native accent. When the accent was brought to their attention as a possible source of bias, the effect disappeared for mild accents but remained for strong ones. Thus, accent, the authors conclude, 'might reduce the credibility of non-native job seekers, eyewitnesses, reporters and news anchors.'

---

stimuli, as well as regions involved in control and inhibition, were activated. However, when the most negatively perceived faces were judged in the implicit condition, activation was much greater in the amygdala and prefrontal cortex (PFC). Perhaps as one increased (in the amygdala), the other area responded to inhibit its activation.

A relatively positive sense of self can be gained by comparing others unfavourably with oneself. Stigma can legitimise inequalities of status and resource distribution that favour a dominant group – such groups are certainly going to ensure that the stigma remains in place, because it serves a system justification function (Jost and Hunyadi, 2002). Finally, people may need to stigmatise groups that have different world views from their own, because if one did not degrade and discredit out-groups in this way then the frail sense of certainty in, and controllability of, life that one gains from one's own world view would be shattered (Solomon *et al.*, 1991).

Members of stigmatised groups can experience **attributional ambiguity**. They can continually read prejudice and discrimination into innocuous behaviours and even into behaviours favouring them: Was I served first at the bar because I am black and the bartender was trying to conceal her hidden prejudice? Members of stigmatised groups can also suffer depressed self-esteem, self-worth and efficacy that can reduce motivation. For example, because stigmatised groups know exactly the negative stereotypes that others have of them, they experience what Steele *et al.* (2002) have called stereotype threat. Stigmatised individuals are aware that others may judge and treat them stereotypically, and thus, on tasks that really matter to them, they worry that through their behaviour they may even confirm the stereotypes. These concerns not only increase anxiety, but can also impair task performance. For example, an academically ambitious West Indian Briton, aware of stereotypes of intellectual inferiority, may be extremely anxious when

answering a question in class – she would be worried that the slightest mistake would be interpreted stereotypically. This anxiety may actually impact adversely on behaviour.

In general, however, although some stigmatised individuals are vulnerable to low self-esteem, diminished life satisfaction and, in some cases, depression, most members of stigmatised groups are able to weather the assaults and maintain a positive self-image (Crocker and Major, 1989). There are many ways in which people can do this. One way is to deny personal disadvantage. For instance, Crosby (1982) has identified the 'paradox of the contented female worker'. Women workers compare their salaries and working conditions with those of other women, which narrows the potential for recognising much larger sex-based inequalities in pay and conditions (Major, 1994).

Stereotype threat

Why do some groups in society underperform in particular areas – for example, academic underachievement of African-Americans, and mathematical and scientific underachievement of women? Coining the term 'stereotype threat', Steele and his colleagues argue that underachievement is a psychological response to stereotypes that characterise one's in-group (e.g. women) as inferior to a relevant outgroup (men) on a specific task (maths) in a specific domain (school) (Steele *et al.*, 2002). The negative stereotype is a cognitive and emotional burden that impedes performance and paradoxically actually produces an effect consistent with the negative expectation. Stereotype threat has two repercussions: anxiety about confirming the stereotype and thus being judged as possessing the negative attribute, and disengagement with the task and the domain. These two effects lead to underachievement (Steele, 1997; Aronson *et al.*, 1999).

Much of the original research had been conducted with African-American students in the American schooling system. For example, African-American students have been found to perform less well than their white counterparts in testing situations where negative stereotypes about African-Americans are relevant (Steele and Aronson, 1995). This may be due to the potential recognition that failure could confirm a negative stereotype of their in-group (and, by extension, the self). The stereotype threat effect has been investigated with different stigmatised groups and in several domains including white men's maths ability when compared to Asian-American men (traditionally associated with higher maths ability; Aronson et al., 1999) and children from low socio-economic backgrounds in academic testing situations (Croizet and Claire, 1998).

A principal aim of social psychological research into stereotype threat has been to discover what psychological variables (at both the social and individual levels) affect individuals' vulnerability to this effect. Some basic processes and issues have been identified, for example:

1 *Domain identification.* Stereotype threat only occurs in individuals for whom performing well in a given domain is important (Steele, 1997). Aronson et al. (1999) measured white male students' identification with maths and then asked them to complete a maths test either in the context of the stereotype that Asians are superior at maths (stereotype threat condition) or not (control condition). Performance on the maths test was significantly worse in the stereotype threat condition, but only for participants who identified highly with the maths domain (even when controlling for previous standardised aptitude test (SAT) scores). Interestingly, this study not only provides evidence for domain-specific identification but also demonstrates that stereotype threat can affect traditionally non-stigmatised groups (American white male students).

2 *Cognitive load.* It is possible that the stereotype threat effect is more pronounced when people are under high cognitive load as there is an extra pressure to disconfirm negative stereotypes. Spencer et al. (1999) examined this possibility in two experimental studies of high-achieving male and female American university students. Women are believed to experience stereotype threat in maths-related domains. Participants in the first study did a maths test that was either easy or difficult. There was no difference in the performance of male and female students on the easy test, but females performed significantly worse on the difficult test. The increased cognitive load of stereotype threat impeded performance on a task that also demanded greater cognitive capacity. In a second study, Spencer et al. showed that this gender difference in performance on the difficult test was accentuated when the test was explicitly introduced in terms of gender differences in maths ability. This finding lends further credibility to the idea

that performance differences do indeed result from stereotype threat rather than from real differences between males' and females' maths ability.

3 *Self-categorisation with the stereotyped group.* Research suggests that priming the social identity of the stigmatised group will automatically prime the negative stereotype and in turn affect performance in a stereotype-consistent manner. One study clearly demonstrates this effect in the maths performance of Asian-American women (Shih et al., 1999). In contrast to the negative connotations of being female in the maths domain, Shih et al. reasoned that Asian-American identity is associated with a positive stereotype of maths ability. Indeed, female Asian-Americans who were primed with their Asian-American identity significantly outperformed participants who were primed instead with their gender identity ('women').

4 *Individual level of identification with the stereotyped group.* Schmader (2002) demonstrated that the degree to which a person identifies with a relevant category also affects how strongly the stereotype influences their performance. White American students completed a maths test in either a gender-relevant domain or a gender-irrelevant domain. In the gender-irrelevant domain there was no difference between men's and women's performances on the test. However, in the gender-relevant domain, only the female participants who identified highly with their gender underperformed compared with males. Thus, vulnerability to stereotype threat seems to depend on whether people see themselves as representative of the stereotyped category.

Given the deleterious consequences of stereotype threat, is it possible to train people to combat or overcome stereotype threat? Aronson et al. (2002) conducted an intervention study to trial a method of helping students resist their responses to stereotype threat. African-American and Caucasian male and female undergraduates participated in a laboratory study ostensibly concerning a penpal mentoring system for younger students. They were randomly divided into three groups. A battery of attitude change techniques were used to teach them and help them internalise the idea that intelligence is malleable (intervention-specific group) or that people have different intelligence orientations (intervention-only group – in case intervention alone boosts performance). The third group was a no-intervention control. The results showed that several weeks after the lab session the students in the intervention-specific group (where the negative stereotype was challenged) reported greater academic identification and enjoyment and higher grades compared with the other intervention style and the control group. This was particularly the case for

African-American students whose academic performance and identification were depressed as a reaction to stereotype threat in the other conditions. It is interesting to note that there were no differences between groups on stereotype threat scores per se, suggesting that the specific intervention changed the participants' responses to stereotype threat and not their perceptions of it.

Modern forms of prejudice

Prejudice can express itself in many different ways. We are all familiar with what has been called old-fashioned prejudice – name-calling, abuse, persecution, assault and discrimination. This kind of expression of prejudice is now illegal and socially censured in all Western democratic societies, and so it is rarely encountered. Not surprisingly, research on racism in the US shows a dramatic reduction in expressed anti-black attitudes since the 1930s (Devine and Elliot, 1995).

However, it may not be so much that prejudice is vanishing but that it is changing its form. This new form of prejudice (the research focuses mainly on racism) has a number of different names – aversive racism, modern racism, symbolic racism, regressive racism or ambivalent racism (Gaertner and Dovidio, 1986; Hilton and von Hippel, 1996). However, the general idea is that people now experience a conflict between deep-seated emotional antipathy towards racial out-groups, and modern egalitarian values that exert pressure to behave in a non-prejudiced manner. The resolution of this conflict, which produces **modern racism** or subtle forms of racism, is achieved by avoidance and denial of racism – separate lives, avoidance of the topic of race, denial of being prejudiced, denial of racial disadvantage, and thus opposition to affirmative action or other measures to address racial disadvantage. Although this analysis is mainly focused on racism in the US, it can also apply to sexism (Swim *et al.*, 1995) and to racial attitudes in Europe (Pettigrew and Meertens, 1995).

Modern forms of prejudice can, by definition, be very difficult to detect, because people try to conceal their prejudices. To detect prejudice, researchers need to be ingenious in designing unobtrusive and indirect measures. Many different methods have been devised (Crosby *et al.*, 1980). For example, social cognition research shows that stereotypes can be automatically generated by categorisation, and categorisation can automatically arise from category primes (an accent, a face, a costume) (Bargh, 1989).

Another powerful unobtrusive measure of prejudice is to analyse the subtext of what people say. Racism can very subtly and quite unintentionally be embedded in the words we use, the way we express ourselves, and the way we communicate with and about racial out-groups (Potter and Wetherell, 1987; Edwards, 1997). For example, van Dijk (1987) found evidence of prejudice from a detailed analysis of spontaneous everyday talk among whites in the Netherlands and in southern California about other races (blacks, East Indians, North Africans, Hispanics, Asians). One hundred and eighty free-format interviews conducted between 1980 and 1985 were qualitatively analysed to show how racism is embedded in and reproduced by everyday discourse. People can use particular forms of language to communicate their prejudiced attitudes in ways that disarm the charge of being a racist. A common example is the disclaimer 'I'm not racist, but . . .' that can precede a clearly racist comment.

A more cognitive index of language and prejudice is the **linguistic intergroup bias** effect (Maass, 1999). Maass discovered that people tend to use concrete language that simply describes events when talking about positive out-group (and negative in-group) characteristics, but use much more general and abstract terms that relate to enduring traits when talking about negative out-group (and positive in-group) characteristics. In this way we can detect negative out-group attitudes: people start to become abstract and general when talking about their prejudices.

Can we reduce prejudice?

How can prejudice and intergroup conflict be reduced? Research suggests that propaganda, public service advertising and formal education have a limited effect – these methods are effective in conveying official societal expectations, but then, of course, they fail if they are conducted against a background of powerful and entrenched day-to-day informal endorsement of prejudice. So, are there any techniques that work and, if so, how?

On a larger scale, a popular view about how to reduce prejudice is the **contact hypothesis**: if people from different races could just get to know one another through coming together to interact then prejudice would disappear (Allport, 1954). Although this idea has immediate appeal, and indeed it was part of the scientific justification for the racial desegregation of the American schooling system in the 1950s, it is fraught with problems. For intergroup contact to work, people have to come together for prolonged equal-status, meaningful interaction that is pleasant and capable of changing stereotypes of entire groups not just attitudes towards the individuals with whom one interacts. Contact can often produce interracial friendships, but it rarely changes racial stereotypes. More often than not, contact can confirm and accentuate intergroup perceptions and further entrench stereotypes. There is often so much anxiety associated with intergroup encounters that groups avoid contact or find contact unpleasant and attribute this to the out-group (Stephan and Stephan, 2000).

Nevertheless, contact between members of different groups may promote positive attitudes. Indeed, a recent statistical survey of 515 studies of the effects of contact concluded that, all things being equal, contact does promote more positive intergroup relationships (Pettigrew and Tropp, 2006).

Contact may foster good interpersonal relationships ('decategorisation' of group members; Brewer and Miller, 1984), or it may foster a sense of common membership in a superordinate ingroup ('recategorisation'; Gaertner et al., 1993), or it may allow the recognition of positive features of other groups while preserving a sense of ingroup distinctiveness (mutual positive differentiation; Hewstone, 1996). Dovidio et al. (1997) asked sets of six participants to work first as two three-person groups. These groups then interacted and participants judged one another. Half of the participants were then encouraged to think of themselves as one larger (six-person) category. These recategorised participants were less likely to show evaluative preferences for their own sub-group, or to show a preference for self-disclosing to and helping members of their own sub-group.

Other research by S.C. Wright et al. (1997) has shown that that intergroup attitudes can improve if people witness or have knowledge of rewarding intergroup friendships between others – if my friend John has close out-group friends then maybe the out-group isn't quite as bad as I thought. Pettigrew (1998) concluded that friendship across group boundaries is an important way that contact allows people to learn about out-groups and to feel less anxious about future interaction with other members of these groups. This makes it more likely that people will generalise their positive feelings about an out-group friend to the out-group as a whole. Similar conclusions were reached by Brown and Hewstone (2005), who also emphasise the way that contact can influence emotions and feelings, and trust between groups, which in turn can promote more positive intergroup relationships.

Prejudices are intergroup psychological mechanisms for protecting and enhancing our self-image and our material well-being. Not surprisingly, threats to racial or cultural identity are unlikely to reduce prejudice. Thus, nations that try to assimilate ethnic minorities threaten those minorities and cause them to react to protect themselves, which in turn threatens the dominant majority and fuels prejudice. One strategy that does seem to help is pluralism or multiculturalism – a social policy that recognises cultural diversity within the confines of a common superordinate national identity (Hornsey and Hogg, 2000).

Many people are unaware of their stereotypes and preconceptions about members of other groups because (as noted in the social cognition section of Chapter

15) stereotypes are automatically linked to categories (Bargh, 1989). Although making people aware of their stereotypes can persuade people that their beliefs are unjustified, this can backfire if people then try too hard to suppress their stereotypes. In one study, participants were shown a picture of a skinhead and then wrote a passage about a day in the life of that person (Macrae et al., 1994). Half of the participants were instructed not to rely on stereotypes. Consistent with the instructions, participants in the no-stereotype condition used less stereotypical descriptions.

Next, participants were shown a picture of a second skinhead and were asked to write about a day in his life, but without suppression instructions. In this second stage, those who had been given the suppression instructions previously now showed a substantially increased use of stereotypical descriptions (see Table 16.1).

In a further experiment, compared with those in a control condition, participants who had first been in a suppress condition subsequently chose to sit further away from a chair they thought would be occupied by a skinhead. Macrae et al. reasoned that the effort involved in suppressing the stereotype actually makes the content of the stereotype more accessible. Thus, once a person is no longer actively suppressing the stereotype this content becomes 'hyperaccessible' (Wegner and Erber, 1992), resulting in a stereotype rebound effect (see also Plant and Devine, 2001).

The knack would seem to be to get people to have insight into their stereotypes – to understand them and see through them rather than merely to suppress them. The best solution may be to teach people to become less cognitively lazy and to take the time to reflect about their biases. For example, Langer et al. (1985) gave a group of children specific training in thinking about the problems of people with disabilities. They thought about such problems as the ways that a person with disabilities might drive a car and the reasons why a blind person might make a good newscaster. After this training, they were

Table 16.1 Ratings of passage stereotypically as a function of task instruction in Macrae et al., Experiment 1.

	Instruction	
Passage	Suppress stereotype	Control
1	5.54	6.95
2	7.83	7.08

Source: Macrae, C.N., Bodenhausen, G.V., Milne, A.B. and Jetten, J., Out of mind but back in sight: stereotypes on the rebound. Journal of Personality and Social Psychology, 1994, 67, 808–17. Copyright © 1994 by the American Psychological Association, reprinted with permission.

found to be more willing to go on a picnic with a person with disabilities than were children who did not receive the training. They were also more likely to see the specific consequences of particular disabilities rather than to view people with disabilities as 'less fit'. For example, they were likely to choose a blind child as a partner in a game of pin the tail on the donkey because they realised that the child would be likely to perform even better than a sighted child. Thus, at the individual level, people can learn to recognise their biases and to overcome their prejudices.

Devine (1989) proposed that even when a person has knowledge of a stereotype that is automatically linked to a category membership, the explicit application of a stereotype is a controllable process. It seems that people who are high and people who are low in prejudice towards a particular group may both share the same knowledge of the stereotype but low-prejudiced people may suppress or control the stereotype. However, the connection between categorising a person and applying a stereotype turns out to be complex. Lepore and Brown (1997) found that white British people's stereotypes of West Indians were similar regardless of whether participants were high or low scorers on a measure of prejudice.

The important message from this research is that even though people may share knowledge of a stereotype, they apply the stereotype differently when a categorisation is activated. That is, high-prejudiced people seem more likely to apply the negative aspects of the stereotype automatically, whereas low-prejudiced people are more likely to apply the positive aspects of the stereotype automatically.

What happens when a stereotype is activated directly at the same time as the category? For example, images conveyed by the music press often involve extreme representations of aggressive blacks (for example, rappers), or highly feminised and sexual images of women. It seems likely that such stereotypical images might override people's initial levels of prejudice. In line with this idea, Lepore and Brown (1997) found that when they primed participants with negative stereotype content (rather than just category labels) people who scored higher or lower on the prejudice scale were affected by the prime in the same way. Both sets of participants rated the target more negatively following the prime than when no prime was used. Thus, when the stereotype is activated directly, low- and high-prejudiced people apply negative stereotypical traits more readily.

With practice, stereotypes can be overcome: that is, when people either choose to, or are requested to, resist stereotypes over a period of time, the automatic associations they make with a particular category can be altered (Kawakami et al., 2000). The question is: how do low-prejudiced people sustain their low levels of prejudice in the face of pervasive social stereotypes? Monteith et al. (2002) argue that low-prejudiced people are especially sensitive to 'cues for control'. In essence, when automatic stereotype

activation results in a reaction that is inconsistent with the way we think we should respond, this results in a negative sense of self – a sense of guilt or unease. Over time, people learn that certain situational or other cues give advance warning that an undesired response is likely (for example, if race is mentioned in a conversation you might be alerted to the possibility that you could say something prejudicial).

Monteith et al. argued that when low-prejudiced individuals see images of black people linked with stereotypical content (for example, the statement 'this person spends a lot of time on the streets') this evokes guilt about the stereotypical association, and this in turn acts as a well-established cue for control.

In Monteith et al.'s research, participants who had completed measures of prejudice earlier in the year were asked to engage simultaneously in what they believed were two separate tasks. The first task was to decide whether pictures (of black and white people) had been presented before in the original format or as a mirror image. The second task was to decide what categories would best fit people described by a series of sentences (for example, the description 'this person has to do a lot of reading' fits the category 'college student'). Monteith et al. reasoned that if a picture of a black person happened to be presented in conjunction with a black stereotype description then this would constitute a cue for control among low-prejudiced people. Indeed, when these participants were presented with this combination of stimuli their decision times slowed down, relative to trials when the same sentences were paired with white faces. In contrast, participants who were high in prejudice were not expected to try to control their reactions, and in fact they responded with equal speed regardless of whether the black stereotypical sentences were paired with white or black faces. See Figure 16.7.

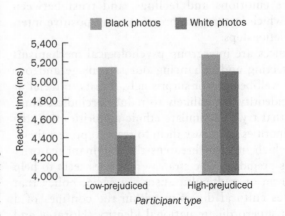

Figure 16.7 Reaction times as a function of race of photo and participant type.

Source: Based on Monteith, M.J., Ashburn-Nardo, L., Voils, C.I. and Czopp, A.M., Putting the brakes on prejudice: On the development and operation of cues for control. *Journal of Personality and Social Psychology*, 2002, 83, 1029–50.

But how is it that we sometimes make important errors when we make judgements about other people? Why do we have immediate, 'gut' reactions to people and events, and what are the advantages and pitfalls? If you were hired by an organisation to design and implement a strategy to reduce harmful ethnic prejudice among employees within the organisation, what would your strategy be?

Aggression and helping behaviour

Aggression

Human **aggression** is often considered to be an innate component of our biological inheritance, a behaviour which is a necessary part of the evolutionary process that ensures survival of the fittest (Lorenz, 1966). Chapter 13 described some of the basic functions of aggression. The ability to hurt others may well have these roots; however, social psychologists tend to be more interested in discovering situational factors that encourage or inhibit aggression and explain the huge diversity of human aggression (Baron and Richardson, 1994).

Many factors can cause aggression. When important goals are frustrated, people can feel angry and express this as aggression, particularly when there is an available target for aggression without fear of retaliation, and when the person who is frustrated has few other coping mechanisms available. According to social learning theory (Bandura, 1977), aggression can be learned by simply observing other people being reinforced for behaving aggressively. Aggression can also become more likely in a given situation if a person who has a tendency to respond aggressively is aroused, even if the arousal has nothing to do with anger (it could be arousal from a gym workout, a film, a sexual encounter).

People with a type A personality or elevated testosterone levels are also more likely to be aggressive. Testosterone is the male hormone, so, not surprisingly males tend to be more physically aggressive than females, but the hormonal cause can be very difficult to dissociate from the fact that men are typically socialised to be more aggressive than are females. There is little difference in verbal aggression between males and females (Harris, 1992). There is also evidence that disinhibition, caused perhaps by de-individuation, which we described earlier in this chapter, can increase the probability of aggression. Aggression, in the form of assaults in Minneapolis, has even been shown to increase with increasing temperature, peaking at around 25°C and then dropping off as it gets even hotter (Cohn and Rotton, 1997).

There are many paths to aggression – not surprisingly, aggression is an enduring problem for society. Consider the following scenario. A male with a type A personality and elevated testosterone is driving home in a hurry from the gym in traffic where people are successfully cutting in. He is in a large car with dark windows and the CD on full blast. What do you think might happen if you were driving rather slowly in front of him, or took rather a long time to pull away from the traffic lights?

Alcohol and aggression

Alcohol consumption is often associated with aggression. Research suggests that alcohol makes people more prone to social influence while at the same time less able to think through the consequences of their actions for themselves or others. Together this facilitates aggression when people drink in groups in societies that glorify aggression (Bushman and Cooper, 1990). Causal links are complex. For example, perhaps aggressive people like to go drinking in groups, and they would be aggressive even if they had not been drinking? However, controlled studies have shown that people who had consumed alcohol were more likely to act aggressively when encouraged by a confederate than were those who had consumed a placebo.

Media violence and aggression

Many people believe that the mass media, particularly films and television, have much to do with aggression. There is no denying that these media portray a great deal of aggression and in the majority of cases the aggression brings rewards to the aggressor – violence seems to pay. Social learning theory makes the clear prediction that much of the aggression in our society is caused or amplified by excessive violence on television and in films. However, research is inconclusive about the causal links (Phillips, 1986): perhaps aggressive people watch or pay more attention to media aggression, whereas non-aggressive people either do not watch media aggression or simply do not pay much attention to it. Similar arguments hold for the evidence that violent pornography is associated with more aggressive attitudes and behaviours towards women: perhaps misogynistic attitudes encourage men to view violent pornography rather than vice versa.

A new development in this field has been the popularity of video games of increasing gruesomeness and goriness. A recent debate in *Psychological Bulletin* (Anderson *et al.*, 2010; Bushman *et al.*, 2010; Ferguson and Kilburn, 2010) gives a flavour of the current debate concerning the potentially negative effects of playing these games. Anderson *et al.* (2010), for example, have argued that exposure to violent video games is associated with higher levels of aggressive behaviour, aggressive thinking, physiological arousal, lack of empathy and lower levels of prosocial behaviour, regardless of age or sex of the player. These effects are thought to be larger than the effects of TV and film violence (Polman *et al.*, 2008) but are also thought to be an overestimate because of publication bias – positive results are more likely to be published (Ferguson, 2007). Culture is also important – those countries with collectivist values and expect morality and a sense of self-discipline, such as Japan, are the least aggressive and report fewer murders and acts of violence (Bergeron and Schneider, 2005).

Prosocial and helping behaviour

Aggression is generally regarded as antisocial and undesirable. The flip side of this kind of behaviour is prosocial behaviour and behaviour oriented towards helping others. Just as aggression may have an evolutionary dimension, so does prosocial behaviour – cooperative helping behaviour among people is the foundation of human endeavour, and so it would be expected that over millions of years predispositions to behave in this way would have a selective advantage (Wilson, 2004). But again, as with the study of aggression, social psychologists are more concerned to identify situational factors that encourage people to behave prosocially and to help other people.

Cooperation and social dilemmas

Despite the possibility of an evolutionary advantage to cooperative prosocial behaviour, people are remarkably uncooperative. One popular research paradigm involves the **prisoner's dilemma** (Rapoport, 1976). In one variant of this, two obviously guilty suspects are questioned separately by detectives who have only enough evidence to convict them of a lesser offence. The suspects are separately offered a chance to confess, knowing that if one confesses but the other does not, the confessor will be granted immunity and the confession will be used to convict the other of the more serious offence. If both confess, each will receive a moderate sentence. If neither confesses, each will receive a very light sentence. The prisoners are faced by a dilemma as to whether to trust one another in order to obtain the best joint pay-off. Although mutual non-confession produces the best joint outcome, mutual suspicion and lack of trust almost always encourage both to confess. This finding has been replicated in hundreds of prisoner's dilemma experiments,

using a variety of experimental conditions and pay-off matrices (Dawes, 1991).

Many other **social dilemmas** involve a number of individuals or groups exploiting a limited resource (Kerr and Park, 2001) under conditions where, if everyone cooperates, an optimal solution for all is reached, but if everyone competes then everyone loses. These are called **commons dilemmas** because they are modelled on the 'tragedy of the commons'. English towns used to have common pasture on which people were free to graze their cattle. If all used it in moderation it would replenish itself and continually benefit them all. Imagine, however, 100 farmers surrounding a common that could support only 100 cows. If each grazed one cow, the common would be maximally utilised and minimally taxed. One farmer, however, might reason that if they grazed an additional cow, output would be doubled, minus a very small cost due to overgrazing – a cost borne equally by all 100 farmers. So this farmer adds a second cow. If all 100 farmers reasoned in this way they would rapidly destroy the common, thus producing the tragedy of the commons. The commons dilemma is an example of a replenishable resource dilemma. The commons is a renewable resource that will continually support many people provided that all people show restraint in 'harvesting' the resource. Many of the world's most pressing environmental and conservation problems are replenishable resource dilemmas – for example, rainforests and the world's population of ocean fish are renewable resources if harvested appropriately.

Another type of social dilemma is called a public goods dilemma. Public goods, such as public health, national parks, clean air and road networks, are provided for everyone. Because public goods are available to all, people are tempted to use them without contributing to their maintenance.

Experimental research on social dilemmas finds that when self-interest is pitted against the collective good, the usual outcome is competition and resource destruction even when appeals are made to cooperative and altruistic norms (Kerr, 1992). People can, however, act more cooperatively when they identify with the common good (Brewer and Kramer, 1986). In other words, when people derive their social identity from the entire group that has access to the resource, self-interest becomes subordinate to the common good (de Cremer and van Vugt, 1999). However, the same research indicates that when different groups, rather than individuals, have access to a public good, then the ensuing intergroup competition ensures ethnocentric actions which are far more destructive than mere self-interest. International competition over limited resources such as rainforests, whales and wetlands tragically accelerates their disappearance.

Another way in which social dilemmas can be resolved is by putting in place various structural solutions. These include a range of measures such as limiting the number of people accessing the resource (via permits), limiting the amount of the resource that people can take (via quotas), handing over management of the resource to an individual (a leader) or a single group, facilitating free communication among those accessing the resource, and shifting the pay-off to favour cooperation over competition. The problem with structural solutions is that they require an enlightened and powerful authority to implement measures, manage the bureaucracy and police violations. This can be hard to bring about (Rutte and Wilke, 1984).

Can the presence of a camera induce helpfulness? Van Rompay *et al.* (2009) recruited participants ostensibly to canvass their views of a Dutch bank. They were given a 'need for approval' scale to complete and then invited to an office at the researchers' university. In one office, there was a camera; in another, the camera was not present. After the participants had signed the informed consent form, the experimenter 'accidentally' dropped her papers. In the study, one of the questions participants answered was how willing they were to donate to charity. The remainder of items in the questionnaire were irrelevant. Thus, the researchers monitored public helpfulness (helping the researcher pick up her papers)

and private helpfulness (degree of willingness to donate to charity).

People were more likely to help the experimenter pick up her papers when a camera was present than when not. There was no effect of the camera on private helpfulness – those in the camera condition were no more likely to donate more to charity than were those in the camera-absent condition. Furthermore, the tendency to help was greatest in those participants scoring high in need for approval.

Bystander intervention

People sometimes find themselves in a situation where they witness an emergency where someone needs their help. When are people most likely to help and why?

In 1964 in New York City, a woman named Kitty Genovese was chased and repeatedly stabbed by an assailant, who took 35 minutes to kill her. The woman's screams apparently went unheeded by at least 38 people who watched from their windows. No one, it seemed, tried to stop the attacker; no one even made a quick, anonymous telephone call to the police. When the bystanders were questioned later, they could not explain their inaction. 'I just don't know,' they said.

As you can imagine, people were shocked by the bystanders' response to the Genovese murder. Commentators said that the apparent indifference of the

Controversies in psychological science: What did Kitty Genovese's witnesses really witness?

The issue

Kitty Genovese is probably the most well-known female 'participant' not only in social psychology, but psychology in general. The horrific ordeal she went through gave rise to a theory of social behaviour and intervention and sparked a series of now-famous experiments on the bystander effect, described in the text. Her murder was identified as a 'signal crime' – one that issued a warning about the breakdown in society's collective moral fabric (Innes, 2004). But was this research based on an enormous series of false premises? According to a review of the evidence by Manning *et al.* (2007), it was.

The evidence

These are the facts of Kitty Genovese's murder and the response to it:

In the early morning of 13 March 1964, Kitty Genovese was sexually assaulted and then murdered in the Kew Gardens dis-

trict of Queens in New York. According to almost all textbooks you will read which report the case, 38 people witnessed the assault and murder at some point from a nearby building but did nothing to intervene or alert the police. Curiously, although the case was reported in the local paper the next day, reference to the 38 witnesses only appeared in a newspaper, *The New York Times*, two weeks later, on 27 March – '38 who saw murder didn't call the police,' the story boldly surmised and went on: 'Apathy at stabbing of Queens woman shocks inspector.'

However, research by a local historian and lawyer, Joseph de May Jnr, began to cast doubt on this interpretation. He found that:

• not all of the 38 alleged witnesses were eyewitnesses – some only heard noise from the assault;

• the police were called immediately;

• despite reports that witnesses had seen Kitty Genovese for 30 minutes, this was impossible because, given the

Controversies in psychological science: *Continued*

geography and chronology of the assault, she could only have been visible for a few seconds;

- Kitty Genovese was still alive when the police arrived – she was not seen being murdered.

The story then becomes even more intriguing because no list of the 38 witnesses has ever been made available and the three witnesses in court said that their first glimpse of what transpired could not lead them to believe that what they were witnessing was a murder (Manning *et al.*, 2007). According to the District Attorney, only half a dozen people were found who saw something of relevance. None actually saw the stabbing and one reported shouting at the assailant. This scared him off. After this first attack, Kitty Genovese made her way around the corner of the building and tried to make her way to the entrance of her flat. She would have been out of sight of most witnesses. At the site of the second attack, the stairwell of 92–96 Austin Street, only one person could have seen what happened.

Despite reports to the contrary, some residents did try to contact the police. An affidavit sworn by a 15-year-old boy stated that his father called the police. At the appeal of the murderer in 1995, several of the residents stated that they had tried to call the police but were unsuccessful. There was no '911' service at that time and calls to the local police station were not always welcome. There were regular reports of trouble at a nearby bar and police found the constant

aggravation troublesome. This bar had closed earlier than usual on the night of Genovese's murder. One resident was even reported to have telephoned another resident, called the police and went to Genovese's side.

Conclusion

What does this curious collection of facts demonstrate? First, it clearly demonstrates that you should never believe what you read in the papers. The hoo-ha over the YK2 Millennium Bug and other spurious fears, many of which are detailed in Nick Davies's *Flat Earth News* (2008) (see also the Controversies in Psychological Science section in Chapter 2), provides further evidence in support of the recommendation. Misreporting, however, is alive and well. Recall the supposition, guesswork, accusations and rumour that surrounded Portugal resident Robert Murat and the media's assumption of his involvement in the disappearance of Madeleine McCann in 2007 and the hounding of Christopher Jefferies over the murder of his tenant, Joanne Yeates. Second, far from sounding the death knell of the responsible citizen and the intervening bystander, it appears to show that citizen intervention was in reasonably good health.

The case of Kitty Genovese may, in Manning *et al.*'s words, be 'a stubborn and intractable urban myth'. It illustrates explicitly the value of evaluating everything you read, including this CiPS section.

---

bystanders demonstrated that American society, especially in urban areas, had become cold and apathetic. Experiments performed by social psychologists suggest that this explanation is wrong – people in cities are not generally indifferent to the needs of other people. The fact that Kitty Genovese's attack went unreported is not remarkable because 38 people were present; it is precisely because so many people were present that the attack was not reported. Recent research, however, including a detailed review of the case suggests that this picture is not as clear-cut as it has usually been portrayed in textbooks. The Controversies in Psychological Science section reveals some remarkable facts about the case and undermines some persistent myths.

Darley and Latané have extensively studied the phenomenon of **bystander intervention** – the actions of people witnessing a situation in which someone appears to require assistance. Their experiments have shown that in such situations the presence of other people who are doing nothing inhibits others from giving aid. For example,

Darley and Latané (1968) staged an 'emergency' during a psychology experiment. Each participant participated in a discussion about personal problems associated with college life with one, two or five other people by means of an intercom. The experimenter explained that the participants would sit in individual rooms so that they would be anonymous and hence would be more likely to speak frankly. The experimenter would not listen in but would get their reactions later in a questionnaire. Actually, only one participant was present; the other voices were simply tape recordings. During the discussion, one of the people, who had previously said that he sometimes had seizures, apparently had one. His speech became incoherent and he stammered out a request for help.

Almost all participants left the room to help the victim when they were the only witness to the seizure. However, when there appeared to be other witnesses, the participants were much less likely to try to help. In addition, those who did try to help reacted more slowly if other people were thought to be present (see Figure 16.8).

Darley and Latané reported that the participants who did not respond were not indifferent to the plight of their fellow student. Indeed, when the experimenter entered the room, they usually appeared nervous and emotionally aroused, and they asked whether someone was helping the victim. The experimenters did not receive the impression that the participants had decided not to act; rather, they were still in conflict, trying to decide whether they should do something.

Thus, it seems that whether bystanders will intervene in a particular circumstance depends in part on how they perceive the situation. Latané and Darley (1970) have proposed a model describing a sequence of steps bystanders face when confronted with a potential emergency:

1 The event must come to their attention or be noticed.

2 They must assume some responsibility for helping the victim.

3 The possible courses of action must be considered and compared.

4 Finally, they must actually implement the chosen course of action.

Of course, this sequence takes place rapidly and without much awareness on the bystander's part, as is true of many situations to which we respond daily.

Unfortunately, at least from the perspective of the victim, obstacles may arise at any stage in this decision-making process, which make it unlikely that a bystander will intervene. In many cases, the bystander who is aware that others are available to help may not feel any personal responsibility to do so, a phenomenon called **diffusion of responsibility**. This factor is considered to be responsible for the finding that help is less likely to be offered when there are several bystanders present. In addition, the bystander may not feel competent to intervene or may be fearful of doing so; consequently, no action is taken. Shotland and Heinold (1985) staged an accident in which a person seemed to be bleeding. Bystanders who had received training in first-aid treatment were much more likely to come to the victim's aid, and they did so whether or not bystanders were present. Because they knew how to recognise an emergency and knew what to do, they were less likely to fear doing the wrong thing.

The last literature review of bystander intervention was conducted in 1981. An update was published by Fischer *et al.* (2011) who reviewed all studies from 1960 to 2010 which examined the determinants of intervening (a total of 7,700 participants). They found that people were found to be less likely to be bystanders if the situation was perceived as dangerous, if the perpetrators were present and the cost of intervening was physical rather than non-physical. The authors interpret their result in the context of an arousal–cost–reward model in which dangerous situations are recognised more quickly and are recognised as real emergencies and, therefore, increase arousal and helping. Bystanding was also attenuated when other bystanders provided physical support and if they were male and familiar.

Attraction and relationships

One of the most pervasive and immediate aspects of social life is our interpersonal relationships. It is, therefore, no accident that soap operas and celebrity magazines have a huge following, and they focus almost exclusively on close relationships – friendships, enmities, family life, romance, and so forth. For most of us, much of our day-to-day happiness or misery rests on how our personal relationships are faring.

Interpersonal attraction

One of the key features of our interpersonal relationships is whether we like someone or not, and whether they like us – **interpersonal attraction**. Many factors determine interpersonal attraction. Some factors are characteristics of the individuals themselves; others are determined by the socially reinforcing aspects of the environment. Interpersonal attraction is an important aspect of more enduring and closer relationships, such as friendships;

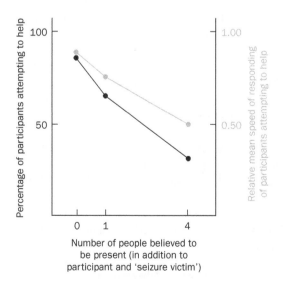

Figure 16.8 Bystander intervention. Percentage of participants attempting to help as a function of the number of other people the participants believed to be present.

Source: Based on data from Darley, J.M. and Latané, B., Bystander intervention in emergencies: Diffusion of responsibility. *Journal of Personality and Social Psychology,* 1968, 8, 377–83.

however, the bases of attraction can change as one moves through different stages of a relationship (Duck, 1992). Physical appearance and attitudinal similarity can be very important in the initial stages of a relationship, whereas deeper personality similarities and complementarities of needs may become more important later on.

Physical appearance

Despite such maxims as 'Beauty is in the eye of the beholder', 'Never judge a book by its cover' and 'Beauty is only skin-deep', research confirms that we tend to like physically attractive people more than physically less attractive people (Langlois *et al.*, 2000). Social reinforcement provides a likely explanation for this phenomenon. Someone who is seen in the company of an attractive person and is obviously favoured by this person is likely to be well regarded by other people.

Walster *et al.* (1966) studied the effects of physical appearance at a dance at which university students were paired by a computer. Midway through the evening, the experimenters asked the participants to rate the attraction they felt towards their partners and to say whether they thought they would like to see them in the future. For both sexes, the only characteristic that correlated with attraction was physical appearance. Intelligence, grades and personality variables had no significant effect.

When people first meet someone who is good-looking, they rate the person as probably holding attitudes similar to their own and tend to assume that they have a good personality, a successful marriage and high occupational status (Dion *et al.*, 1972). In fact, physically attractive people usually do possess many of these characteristics, probably because they receive favourable treatment from society (Hatfield and Sprecher, 1986).

However, among same-sex heterosexual individuals, physical appearance may have its drawbacks, especially if members of the other sex are involved. For example, consider a study in which females were shown photos of the same woman dressed either casually or provocatively and either talking or not talking to a man in the presence of his female companion (Baenninger *et al.*, 1993). The female participants rated the 'other woman' in the photos more negatively when she was provocatively dressed than when she was casually dressed. Thus, we seem to take into account the particular circumstances under which we meet another person – their sex and the other people who may be present – when making judgements about that person and their attractiveness.

Do women and men differ in terms of avoidance and anxiety when describing or perceiving their romantic relationships? A meta-analysis of 113 studies (comprising 66,132 individuals) has found that sex differences do exist but this is sample-dependent (Giudice, 2011). For example, in general men are higher in avoidance and lower in anxiety than are women. However, this difference is largest in community samples, smaller in students and smaller still when participants are recruited via the internet. There were also some national differences. Europe and the Middle East showed the largest sex differences; East Asian men were more avoidant but were no more or less anxious than women. Anxiety differences between the sexes peaked at young adulthood but avoidant behaviour increased throughout the lifetime.

Proximity

Not surprisingly, the mere physical proximity of one person to another is a potent facilitator of attraction (Sprecher, 1998). Festinger *et al.* (1950) found that the likelihood of friendships between people who lived in an apartment house was related to the distance between the apartments in which they lived: the closer the apartments, the more likely the friendship was. People were also unlikely to have friends who lived on a different floor unless their apartments were next to a stairway, where they would meet people going up or down the stairs.

Proximity enhances familiarity, and familiarity has been shown to increase liking. We tend to grow to like

---

Cutting edge: Risky business

We have all, at some point, behaved rather differently (and for various reasons) in front of a member of the opposite sex, but a new study has extended this to risk.

McAlvanah (2009) exposed participants to photographs of members of the same or different sex, before and after participants made a series of decisions about gambling outcomes. Participants exposed to a member of the opposite sex took many more risky gambles than did the control group. Attractiveness did not affect gambling decisions.

Attractiveness was found to have an effect on behaviour in a different study of interaction between men and women (Straaten *et al.*, 2009). Participants were asked to interact with another person who was high and low in attractiveness. Observers rated the participants' interaction in terms of how improved their fluency became, how positively they presented themselves, how much positive affect they showed, etc.

Men who rated themselves as similar in attractiveness to the confederate showed more of an increase in these behaviours – men low in attractiveness invested more in the interaction when meeting a confederate low in attractiveness, for example. Women's interaction was unrelated to the confederates' physical attractiveness.

things that become familiar to us over repeated exposure. Repetition generally increases our preference for a stimulus. This phenomenon applies to people as well. Even in the brief time it takes to participate in an experiment, familiarity affects interpersonal attraction. Saegert *et al.* (1973) had female university students participate in an experiment supposedly involving the sense of taste. Groups of two students (all were participants; no confederates this time) entered booths, where they tasted and rated various liquids. The movements of the participants from booth to booth were choreographed so that pairs of women were together from zero to ten times. Afterwards, the participants rated their attraction to each of the other people in the experiment. The amount of attraction the participants felt towards a given person was directly related to the number of interactions they had had – the more interactions, the more attracted they were to those persons (see Figure 16.9). And as you saw in Chapter 13, those who smile more are liked more.

Reciprocity

Liking follows the reciprocity principle – we tend to like those who like us. Dittes and Kelley (1956) led students in small discussion groups to believe, by way of anonymous written evaluations (actually written by the experimenters), that other group members either liked or disliked them. Results showed that students who believed they were liked were more attracted to the group than were those who believed they were disliked. More

recently, Sprecher (1998) found reciprocal liking to be one of the major determinants of interpersonal attraction.

However, people with low or high self-esteem respond differently. People with high self-esteem base their liking for others less strongly than do people with low self-esteem on whether other people like them. In addition, we tend to like others who grow to like us, and dislike those who initially like us and then cool off on us – this is called the **gain–loss hypothesis** (Aronson and Linder, 1965). There are two possible explanations for this effect. When rejection changes to acceptance, the anxiety over rejection is reduced so that we experience the pleasure of being liked. Alternatively, it is possible that we regard those who like us from the beginning as undiscriminating, and this reduces the value of their praise. Those who dislike us to begin with but then re-evaluate as they get to know us better are discerning people, so their praise is worth more.

Similarity and need complementarity

Another factor that influences interpersonal attraction is similarity – similarity in looks, interests and attitudes. Couples tend to be similar in attractiveness. In fact, couples who are mismatched in this respect are the most likely to break up (White, 1980). Although we might think that people would seek the most attractive partners that they could find, people tend to fear rejection and ridicule. Men especially tend to be afraid of approaching attractive women for this reason (Bernstein *et al.*, 1983).

Couples (and groups of friends) also tend to hold similar opinions. Presumably, a person who shares our opinions is likely to approve of us when we express them. Also, having friends who have similar opinions guarantees that our opinions are likely to find a consensus; we will not often find ourselves in the unpleasant position of saying something that invites disapproval from other people. Byrne (1971) confirmed, in a series of laboratory experiments, the important role of attitude similarity in relationships. The results were so reliable and consistent that Byrne formulated a 'law of attraction': attraction towards a person bears a linear relationship to the proportion of attitudes associated with the person. The more that other people agree with you, the more reinforcing they are and the greater your attraction to them. For example, if you suddenly discover that someone you are going out with likes the same obscure rock group as you, your liking for that person will suddenly increase.

Similarity of attitudes is not the only factor determining the strength of interpersonal attraction. Other kinds of similarity are also important, such as age, occupational status and ethnic background. Friends tend to have similar backgrounds as well as similar attitudes. In addition, liking can sometimes rest on dissimilarity. Winch (1958) suggested that under some circumstances, particularly in more developed relationships, people seek others who

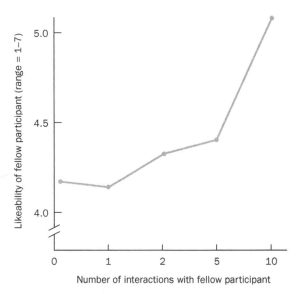

Figure 16.9 Familiarity, exposure and attraction. The rated likeability of a fellow participant as a function of number of interactions.

Source: Based on data from Saegert, S.C., Swap, W. and Zajonc, R.B., Exposure, context, and interpersonal attraction. *Journal of Personality and Social Psychology*, 1973, 25, 234–42.

have different qualities from ourselves and who can thus best satisfy our needs – we pursue **need complementarity**.

Loving

The relationships we have with others are generally marked by two different kinds of emotion: **liking**, a feeling of personal regard, intimacy and esteem towards another person, and **loving**, a combination of liking and a deep sense of attachment to another person. Loving someone does not necessarily entail romance. You may have several close friends whom you love dearly yet have no desire to be involved with romantically.

Romantic love, also called **passionate love**, is an emotionally intense desire for sexual union with another person (Hatfield, 1988). Feeling romantic love generally involves experiencing five closely intertwined elements: a desire for intimacy with another, feeling passion for that person, being preoccupied with thoughts of that person, developing feelings of emotional dependence on that person, and feeling wonderful if that person feels romantic love towards you and dejected if not.

'Falling in love' and 'being in love' are common expressions that people use to describe their passionate desires for one another. Passionate love may occur at almost any time during the life-cycle, although people involved in long-term cohabitation or marriages seem to experience a qualitatively different kind of love. The partners may still make passionate love to one another, but passion is no longer the defining characteristic of the relationship. This kind of love is called **companionate love** and is characterised by a deep, enduring affection and caring for another. Companionate love is also marked by a mutual sense of commitment, or a strong desire to maintain the relationship. How passionate love develops into companionate love is an unanswered question, although it is likely that the sort of intimacy that punctuates romantic love is still a major force in the relationship. An important feature of intimacy is self-disclosure, or the ability to share deeply private feelings and thoughts with another. Indeed, part of loving another is feeling comfortable sharing deeply personal aspects of yourself with that person.

Sternberg (1988b) has developed a theory of how intimacy, passion and commitment may combine to produce liking and several different forms of love (see Table 16.2). According to this theory, liking involves only intimacy, infatuation involves only passion, and empty love involves only commitment. Combining any two of these elements produces still other kinds of love. Romantic love entails both intimacy and passion but no commitment. Companionate love entails both intimacy and commitment but no passion. Fatuous love (a kind of love marked by complacency in the relationship) entails both passion and commitment but no intimacy. The highest form of love, consummate love, contains all three elements.

Sternberg's theory is descriptive. It characterises different kinds of love but it does not explain the origins of love. What function has love served in the evolution of our species? The answer can be summed up very succinctly: procreation and child-rearing. Although love of any kind for another person is not a necessary requirement for sexual intercourse, a man and a woman who love each other passionately are more likely to have sex than are a man and a woman who do not. And if their union produces a child, then love serves another function – it increases the likelihood that both parents will share in the responsibilities of child-rearing. Our capacity for loving, then, contributes in very practical ways to the continued existence of our species.

Maintaining and ending relationships

Research on the maintenance of relationships has mainly dealt with heterosexual marriages in Western societies. Marital satisfaction seems to rest on companionate love and role complementarity, coupled with a sense of security and a shared search for new excitements and stimulation.

Commitment, the desire or intention to continue in the relationship, is crucial. Highly committed partners have a greater chance of staying together (Adams and Jones, 1997), and the very idea of subjectively committing oneself to a relationship can be more important than the conditions that led to commitment (Berscheid and Reis, 1998). Commitment has also been linked to the level of marital satisfaction, pro-relationship behaviour and trust. Two longitudinal studies by Wieselquist et al. (1999) revealed that commitment-inspired acts, such as accommodation and willingness to sacrifice, are good indicators of someone's pro-relationship motives. This is a cyclical model: such acts in turn elicit the partner's trust and reciprocal commitment and subsequent dependence on the relationship.

Adams and Jones (1997) pinpointed three factors that contribute to an ongoing relationship: (1) personal dedication (positive attraction to a particular partner and

Table 16.2 Sternberg's theory of love

	Intimacy	Passion	Commitment
Non-love			
Liking	*****		
Infatuated love		*****	
Empty love			*****
Romantic love	*****	*****	
Companionate love	*****		*****
Fatuous love		*****	*****
Consummate love	*****	*****	*****

Source: After Sternberg, R.J., *The Triangle of Love*, New York: Basic Books, 1988.

relationship); (2) moral commitment (a sense of obligation, religious duty or social responsibility, as controlled by a person's values and moral principles); and (3) constraint commitment (factors that make it costly to leave a relationship, such as lack of attractive alternatives, and various social, financial or legal investments in the relationship). More informally, relationship maintenance depends on people's feelings that: (1) they want to continue the relationship; (2) they ought to continue it; (3) they must continue it.

The end of a relationship is heralded by four factors (Levinger, 1980): (1) a new life seems to be the only solution; (2) alternative partners are available; (3) there is an expectation that the relationship will fail; and (4) there is a lack of commitment to a continuing relationship. Rusbult and Zembrodt (1983) believe that once deterioration is identified, it can be responded to in any of four ways. A partner can take a passive stance and show loyalty by waiting for an improvement to occur, or neglect, by allowing the deterioration to continue. Alternatively, a partner can take an active stance and show 'voice' behaviour, by working at improving the relationship, or exit behaviour, by choosing to end the relationship.

Duck (1992) describes a **relationship dissolution model** of four phases that partners pass through when a break-up occurs. There is an intrapsychic phase that involves brooding and some needling of the partner. The next phase is the dyadic phase. The pair will discuss the relationship, identify problems and make attributions of blame. The third phase is the social phase. In saying that the relationship is near an end, the partners may negotiate with friends, both as a means of social support for an uncertain future and for reassurance of being right. The social network will probably take sides, pronounce on guilt and blame and, like a court, sanction the dissolution. The final grave-dressing phase involves elaborating an acceptable account of the relationship that preserves one's reputation for reliability in future relationships. This 'grave-dressing' activity seeks a socially acceptable version of the life and death of the relationship.

Attraction is usually seen as a positive thing, but to what extent is it likely to be an advantage or a problem if people within a workplace (classroom, office, military unit) are attracted to one another? How likely is this to happen, and why?

Non-verbal communication

Verbal communication is accompanied by a smorgasbord of non-verbal cues that are richly communicative (DePaulo and Friedman, 1998). **Non-verbal communication** provides information about feelings and intentions (for example, non-verbal cues are often reliable indica-

tors of whether someone likes you). It also can be used to regulate interactions (non-verbal cues can signal the approaching end of an utterance, or that someone else wishes to speak), to express intimacy (touching and mutual eye contact), to establish dominance or control (non-verbal threats) and to facilitate goal attainment (for example, pointing).

People tend to have less control over non-verbal than verbal communication, and people are often unaware that they are sending or receiving non-verbal cues. Non-verbal sensitivity improves with age, is more advanced among successful people, and is compromised among people with various psychopathologies. Are men or women better interpreters of body language? Sokolov *et al.* (2011) asked men and women to identify the emotion expressed in point-light displays of figures who knocked on a door. Women were more accurate in recognising anger in body posture but men were better at recognising happiness. When no emotion was expressed in the door-knocker, women were more accurate in identifying this neutral expression. Why should men be more accurate in identifying happiness, given that women are thought to be sensitive to positive emotion? The authors cite research showing that men produce greater brain activation to positive stimuli and are more sensitive to subtle expressions of happiness in faces and actions. They also note that the men in their study were young, of high social status and were well-educated and were, therefore, more sensitive to positive stimuli.

Because the eyes are often considered to be the windows of the soul, eye contact, now technically called **gaze**, communicates an enormous amount of information (Kleinke, 1986). For example, people gaze more at people they like, and lower-status people gaze more at higher-status people than vice versa except when a higher-status person wants to exert control over a lower-status person. Because white adults tend to gaze more when listening than when speaking, a speaker who increases gaze signals that they are about to stop speaking, and a listener who reduces gaze indicates that they are about to start speaking.

Touch appears to result in some significant and demonstrable changes in behaviour. Individuals interacting with others while holding a hot drink, for example, rate their confederate as warmer and more likeable than when the drink is cold (Williams and Bargh, 2008a). We also know that a light touch on a person's arm inclines them to spare small change to someone requesting it: 51 per cent will do so compared with the 29 per cent not touched (Kleinke, 1977). Touching another person significantly enhances their willingness to complete surveys, sign petitions or look after a large dog for 10 minutes – more people are willing to do so when touched (Willis and Hamm, 1980; Hornik, 1987; Gueguen, 2002; Gueguen and Fischer-Lokou, 2002). Touching also enhances person perception – librarians who touched students lightly were rated more favourably and tutors doing the same to their students were regarded as more patient and understanding (Steward and Lupfer, 1987).

Finally, how close people position themselves relative to other people, **interpersonal distance**, communicates intimacy and liking. Hall (1966) has identified four inter-personal distance zones: intimate (up to 0.50 m), personal (0.5–1.25 m), social (1.25–4 m) and public (4–8 m). Clearly, if you want to become intimate with someone you will stand close, and if that person would rather not be that intimate they will move away.

Chapter review

Social influence

- Compliance with a request can be strengthened by ingratiation, reciprocity, or making multiple requests to prepare the target for the focal request – foot-in-the-door, door-in-the-face, low-balling.
- People have a tendency to blindly obey orders from people in authority, even when the consequence of obedience is terrible suffering for others. Obedience drops dramatically when there is social support for disobedience.
- Social interaction, particularly when people are uncertain or are in need of social approval, produces group norms that subsequently regulate behaviour.
- People conform because they are unsure, in need of approval, or define themselves – their identity – in terms of a group that is defined by the norms.
- Although people usually conform to majorities, minorities can change attitudes and behaviour through a conversion process. To do this, minorities need to be internally consensual in repeatedly, but not dogmatically, promulgating the same message.

People in groups

- The presence of other people enhances the performance of a well-learned behaviour but interferes with the performance of complex or poorly learned behaviour.
- When a group of people must collectively perform a task, the effort of any one individual is usually less than we would predict had the individual attempted the task alone – a behaviour known as social loafing.
- Loafing is reduced among people who value their group and feel they must compensate for others' performances. It is also reduced when people feel more identifiable and when they feel the task is important.
- Groups often exist to make decisions. Effective group decision-making can be hampered by elements of the discussion leading to the decision. This can cause groups to make very extreme decisions (polarisation) or very bad decisions (groupthink).
- Groups often need to remember a great deal of information. One way to do this effectively is to have a transactive memory structure in which different individuals or different sub-groups are responsible for remembering different information, but all members of the group know who is responsible for what.
- Groups usually have leaders. Leadership effectiveness ultimately rests on whether the group perceives the leader as being legitimate, as having the requisite skills, as being a loyal and focal group member, and as having the appropriate relationships with followers.
- People in crowds can sometimes behave antisocially because they feel anonymous and not responsible for the consequences of their actions – they are de-individuated.
- Collective events can also change people's identities so that they identify with the identity of the crowd and conform strongly to group norms.

Intergroup relations and prejudice

- Intergroup relations exist whenever people belonging to one group interact collectively or individually with another group or its members in terms of their group identifications.
- Where groups have the same goal, but only one group can achieve the goal at the expense of the others, then intergroup relations become highly conflictual. Where groups have the same goal, but the goal can only be achieved by the groups working cooperatively together, intergroup relations are more harmonious.
- Where groups feel their goals are being frustrated by another group, or that they are deprived relative to another group, conflict and negative attitudes arise – the target is often a weaker scapegoat group.
- The framework of intergroup competition or hostility is also contained in the mere fact of the existence of different categories – in-groups and out-groups.
- Self-determination theory argues that when we make choices for ourselves and initiate behaviour proactively, we flourish. People who are autonomous have been found to express greater well-being, have more positive romantic relationships and perform better on tasks when they interact with others.

- People derive a sense of who they are – a social identity – from the groups they belong to, and thus they are prepared to protect these groups against other groups. Because groups define and evaluate one's identity, and thus self-concept, people strive to evaluate their groups more positively than other groups.
- Prejudice is an attitude, usually negative, towards a particular group. Its cognitive component is stereotypes, and its behavioural manifestation is discrimination.
- Stereotypes and prejudices may be strengthened because people inflate the co-occurrence of negative behaviours and distinctive groups, and also exaggerate the perceived homogeneity of out-groups.
- Some people may be more prejudiced than others, but generally we can all be prejudiced if the social conditions favour prejudice. Prejudice stigmatises and disadvantages other people, but prejudice can be difficult to detect where social norms and legislation outlaw blatant prejudice.
- Teaching people to think about members of other groups as individuals and to consider them in terms of their personal situations and characteristics can reduce prejudices and tendencies towards stereotyping.
- Although initially appealing, simply bringing different groups into contact with one another, so that they become familiar with one another, is not reliably effective in reducing prejudice.

Aggression and helping behaviour

- Arousal, frustration, disinhibition and elevated testosterone levels are all factors that can lead to human aggression.
- People can also learn to be aggressive by witnessing other people being reinforced for aggressive behaviour.
- Alcohol and media violence may also contribute to aggression.

- People often find it difficult to sacrifice their own personal short-term gains for long-term collective gains. This is the social dilemma that underpins many of the world's greatest environmental problems. Social dilemmas can be reduced when people feel themselves part of a community or group that accesses a resource. Leadership, resource management and limited access to a resource can also help.
- People often fail to help in an emergency (called bystander apathy) if there are many other potential helpers available or if they feel they do not have the resources to help. Misperception of norms can sometimes inhibit people from offering assistance in an emergency.
- Bystander intervention is facilitated if there are only few bystanders present and if they feel they have the resources (time, ability and so forth) to help.

Attraction and relationships

- We tend to be attracted to others who think positively of us, who are similar to us, who are physically attractive, and who live, work or play near us.
- Sternberg's theory of love describes how the elements of intimacy, passion and commitment are involved in the different kinds of love.
- The course of a relationship is strongly influenced by the degree of commitment the partners have to the relationship.

Non-verbal communication

- Speech is accompanied by non-verbal cues that are particularly important for communicating feelings and relationships, and for regulating conversation. Some of the most important non-verbal channels are gaze, facial expression, postures, gestures, touch and interpersonal distance.

Suggestions for further reading

Brown, R. (2010) *Prejudice: its social psychology* (2nd edn). London: Wiley-Blackwell.

Cacioppo, J. T. and Hawkley, L.C. (2009). Perceived social isolation and cognition. *Trends in Cognitive Sciences*, 13, 447–54.

Cialdini, R.B. (2007) *Influence: The psychology of persuasion*. New York: HarperCollins.

Krahne, B. (2010) *The social psychology of aggression* (2nd edn). London: Psychology Press.

Maio, G. and Haddock. G. (2012). *The psychology of attitudes and attitude change* (2nd edn). London: Sage.

Reicher, S.D., Haslam, S. A. and Platow, M. J. (2007) The new psychology of leadership. *Scientific American Mind*, 18, 3, 22–9.

Russell, N.J.C. (2011) Milgram's obedience to authority experiments: Origins and early evolution. *British Journal of Social Psychology*, 50, 140–62.

Special issue of *The Psychologist* on Milgram's obedience studies (2011), volume 24, issue 9.

Stangor, C. (2004) *Social Groups in Action and Interaction*. New York: Psychology Press.

Zimbardo, P. (2007) *The Lucifer Effect*. London: Ebury.

Some excellent items on interpersonal and group processes.

CHAPTER 6

Perception

MyPsychLab

Explore the accompanying
experiments, videos,
simulations and animations
on **MyPsychLab.**
This chapter includes
activities on:

- Facial perception
- Recognising the sex of a
  face
- Cues to depth
- The phi phenomenon
- Check your understanding
  and prepare for your exams
  using the multiple choice,
  short answer and essay
  practice tests also available.

One case that came back to me while I was writing was the curious one of
a man who was charged with sexual assault on a train.

He had been asleep, flown with wine, and when he woke up grabbed a
woman sitting across the carriage and started kissing her. She fought him
off and when the train stopped in a station he was arrested.

In conference, he kept saying, 'I thought she was my wife.' When we got
to court, the victim was the complete doppelganger of the wife – they
could have been identical twins. I called the wife and the jury acquitted.

Source: Clarissa Dickson-Wright (2007) *Spilling the Beans*, p. 87.

WHAT YOU SHOULD BE ABLE TO DO AFTER READING CHAPTER 6

- Define the term perception.
- Describe and understand how form, motion and space might be perceived.
- Describe the way in which the brain processes different types of visual information.
- Describe and understand the way in which we recognise faces and other types of stimuli.
- Understand the consequences of brain damage on visual perception and be aware of how these might help us to understand how the brain normally perceives.

QUESTIONS TO THINK ABOUT

- How do we assemble sensory cues from the environment and turn them into something meaningful?
- What is it about a face that makes it recognisable?
- How can we perceive a moving object as moving?
- How can we tell a moving car from a moving bus or train?
- Damage to which parts of the brain do you think would impair perception?
- Does the brain process different types of perception – form, space, motion, colour – differently?
- Are there stimulus-specific brain regions, ones that respond to specific classes of stimuli but not to others?

The nature of perception

Take a look around you – around the room or out the window. What do you see as you and your eyes move around? Shapes? Figures? Background? Shadows? Areas of light and dark? Your knowledge of the objects you see and their relative location is extensive, and you have a good idea of what they will feel like, even if you have not touched them. If the lighting suddenly changes (if lamps are turned on or off or if a cloud passes in front of the sun), the amount of light reflected by the objects in the scene changes too, but your perception of the objects remains the same – you see them as having the same shape, colour and texture as before. Similarly, you do not perceive an object as increasing in size as you approach it, even though the image it casts upon your retina does get larger. Form, movement and space are the essential elements of perception.

The brain receives fragments of information from approximately 1 million axons in each of the optic nerves. It combines and organises these fragments into the perception of a scene – objects having different forms, colours and textures, residing at different locations in three-dimensional space. Even when our bodies or our eyes move, exposing the photoreceptors to entirely new patterns of visual information, our perception of the scene before us does not change. We see a stable world, not a moving one, because the brain keeps track of our own movements and those of our eyes and compensates for the constantly changing patterns of neural firing that these movements cause.

Definition of perception

Perception is the process by which we recognise what is represented by the information provided by our sense organs. This process gives unity and coherence to this input. Perception is a rapid, automatic, unconscious process; it is not a deliberate one in which we puzzle out the meaning of what we see. We do not first see an object and then perceive it; we simply perceive the object. Occasionally we do see something ambiguous and must reflect about what it might be or gather further evidence to determine what it is, but this situation is more problem-solving than perception. If we look at a scene carefully, we can describe the elementary sensations that are present, but we do not become aware of the elements before we perceive the objects and the background of which they are a part. Our awareness of the process of visual perception comes only after it is complete; we are presented with a finished product, not the details of the process.

The distinction between sensation and perception is not easy to make; in some respects, the distinction is arbitrary. Probably because of the importance we give to vision and because of the richness of the information provided by our visual system, psychologists make a more explicit distinction between visual sensation and perception than they do for any other sensory system.

Perception of form

When we look at the world, we do not see patches of colours and shades of brightness. We see things – cars, streets, people, books, trees, dogs, chairs, walls, flowers, clouds, televisions. We see where each object is located, how large it is, and whether it is moving. We recognise familiar objects and also recognise when we see something we have never seen before. The visual system is able to perceive shapes, determine distances and detect movements; it tells us what something is, where it is located, and what it is doing.

Figure and ground

Most of what we see can be classified as either object or background. Objects are things having particular shapes and particular locations in space. Backgrounds are in essence formless and serve mostly to help us judge the location of objects we see in front of them. Psychologists use the terms **figure** and **ground** to label an object and its background, respectively. The classification of an item as a figure or as a part of the background is not an intrinsic property of the item. Rather, it depends on the behaviour of the observer. If you are watching some birds fly overhead, they are figures and the blue sky and the clouds behind them are part of the background. If, instead, you are watching the clouds move, then the birds become background. If you are looking at a picture hanging on a wall, it is an object. Sometimes, we receive ambiguous clues about what is object and what is background. For example, what do you see when you look at Figures 6.1 a, b and c?

One of the most important aspects of form perception is the existence of a boundary. If the visual field contains a sharp and distinct change in brightness, colour or texture, we perceive an edge. If this edge forms a continuous boundary, we will probably perceive the space enclosed by the boundary as a figure, as Figure 6.2 illustrates.

Organisation of elements: the principles of Gestalt

Most figures are defined by a boundary. But the presence of a boundary is not necessary for the perception of form.

(a)

(b)

(c)

Figure 6.1 **(a)** A drawing in which figure and ground can be reversed or 'flipped'. You can see either two faces against a white background or a goblet against a dark background. This a version of the Rubin vase, based on the work of the Swiss psychologist Edgar Rubin in the 1920s. Modern variants are illustrated by figures **(b)** (Wolverine or Batman?) and **(c)** (can you see the werewolf eating Wales?), both created by artist, Olly Moss (http://ollymoss.com).

Figure 6.3 shows that when small elements are arranged in groups, we tend to perceive them as larger figures. Figure 6.4 demonstrates illusory contours – lines that do not exist. In this figure, the orientation of the pie-shaped objects and the three 45-degree segments makes us perceive two triangles, one on top of the other. The one that looks like it is superimposed on the three black circles even appears to be brighter than the background.

In the early twentieth century, a group of psychologists, Max Wertheimer (1880–1943), Wolfgang Kohler (1887–1967) and Kurt Koffka (1886–1941), devised a theory of perception called Gestalt psychology (see Chapter 1) *Gestalt* is the German word for 'form'. They maintained that the task of perception was to recognise objects in the environment according to the organisation of their elements. They argued that in perception the whole is more

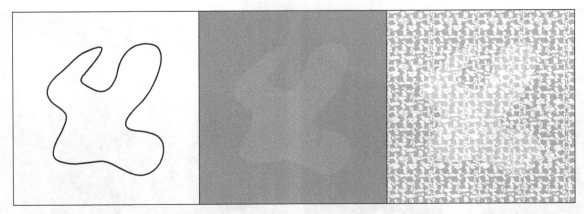

Figure 6.2 Form perception and boundaries. We immediately perceive even an unfamiliar figure when its outline is closed.

Figure 6.3 Grouping. We tend to perceive a group of smaller elements as a larger figure.

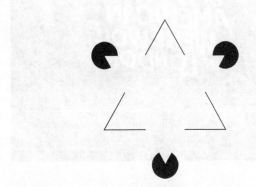

Figure 6.4 Illusory contours. Even when boundaries are not present, we can be fooled into seeing them. The triangle with its point down looks brighter than the surrounding area.

than the sum of its parts. Because of the characteristics of the visual system of the brain, visual perception cannot be understood simply by analysing the scene into its elements. Instead, what we see depends on the relations of these elements to one another (Wertheimer, 1912).

Elements of a visual scene can combine in various ways to produce different forms. Gestalt psychologists have observed that several principles of grouping can predict the combination of these elements. The fact that our visual system groups and combines elements is useful because we can then perceive forms even if they are fuzzy and incomplete. The real world presents us with objects partly obscured by other objects and with backgrounds that are the same colour as parts of the objects in front of them. The laws of grouping discovered by Gestalt psychologists describe the ability to distinguish a figure from its background.

The **adjacency/proximity principle** states that elements that are closest together will be perceived as belonging together (Wertheimer, 1912). Figure 6.5 demonstrates this principle. The pattern on the left looks like five vertical columns because the dots are closer to their neighbours above and below them than to those located to the right and to the left. The pattern on the right looks like five horizontal rows.

The **similarity principle** states that elements that look similar will be perceived as part of the same form. You can easily see the diamond inside the square in Figure 6.6.

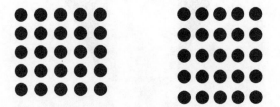

Figure 6.5 The Gestalt principle of proximity. Different spacing of the dots produces five vertical or five horizontal lines.

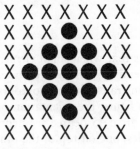

Figure 6.6 The Gestalt principle of similarity. Similar elements are perceived as belonging to the same form.

Good continuation is another Gestalt principle and refers to predictability or simplicity. For example, in Figure 6.7 it is simpler to perceive the line as following a smooth course than as suddenly making a sharp bend.

Often, one object partially hides another, but an incomplete image is perceived. The **law of closure** states that our visual system often supplies missing information and 'closes' the outline of an incomplete figure. For example, Figure 6.8 looks a bit like a triangle, but if you place a pencil on the page so that it covers the gaps, the figure undeniably looks like a triangle.

The final Gestalt principle of organisation relies on movement. The principle of common fate states that elements that move in the same direction will be perceived as belonging together and forming a figure. In the forest, an animal is camouflaged if its surface is covered with the same elements found in the background – spots of brown, tan and green – because its boundary is obscured. There is no basis for grouping the elements on the animal. As long as the animal is stationary, it remains well hidden. However, once it moves, the elements on its surface will move together, and the animal's form will quickly be perceived.

Models of pattern perception

Templates and prototypes

One explanation for our ability to recognise shapes of objects is that as we gain experience looking at things, we acquire templates, which are special kinds of visual

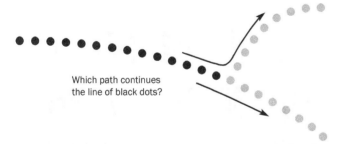

Figure 6.7 The Gestalt principle of good continuation. It is easier to perceive a smooth continuation than an abrupt shift.

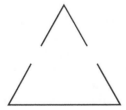

Figure 6.8 The Gestalt principle of closure. We tend to supply missing information to close a figure and separate it from its background. Lay a pencil across the gaps and see how strong the perception of a complete triangle becomes.

memories stored by the visual system. A **template** is a type of pattern used to manufacture a series of objects (Selfridge and Neisser, 1960). When a particular pattern of visual stimulation is encountered, the visual system searches through its set of templates and compares each of them with the pattern provided by the stimulus. If it finds a match, it knows that the pattern is a familiar one. Connections between the appropriate template and memories in other parts of the brain could provide the name of the object and other information about it, such as its function, when it was seen before, and so forth.

The template model of pattern recognition has the virtue of simplicity. However, it is unlikely that it could actually work because the visual system would have to store an unreasonably large number of templates. Despite the fact that you may look at your hand and watch your fingers wiggling about, you continue to recognise the pattern as belonging to your hand. How many different templates would your visual memory have to contain just to recognise a hand? Figure 6.9 illustrates this problem using the letter A.

A more flexible model of pattern perception suggests that patterns of visual stimulation are compared with **prototypes** rather than templates. Prototypes (Greek for 'original model') are idealised patterns of a particular shape; they resemble templates but are used in a much more flexible way. The visual system does not look for exact matches between the pattern being perceived and the memories of shapes of objects but accepts a degree of disparity; for instance, it accepts the various patterns produced when we look at a particular object from different viewpoints.

Most psychologists believe that pattern recognition by the visual system does involve prototypes, at least in some form. For example, you can probably identify maple trees, fir trees and palm trees when you see them. In nature, each tree looks different from all the others, but maples resemble other maples more than they resemble firs, and so on. A reasonable assumption is that your visual system has memories of the prototypical visual patterns that represent these objects. Recognising particular types of tree, then, is a matter of finding the best fit between stimulus and prototype.

Feature detection models

Some psychologists suggest that the visual system encodes images of familiar patterns in terms of **distinctive features** – collections of important physical features that specify particular items (Selfridge, 1959). We are better at distinguishing some stimuli from others. We are better at searching for the letter A among a series of Bs than we are searching for the letter B among a series of As; we are better at finding orange-coloured objects in a

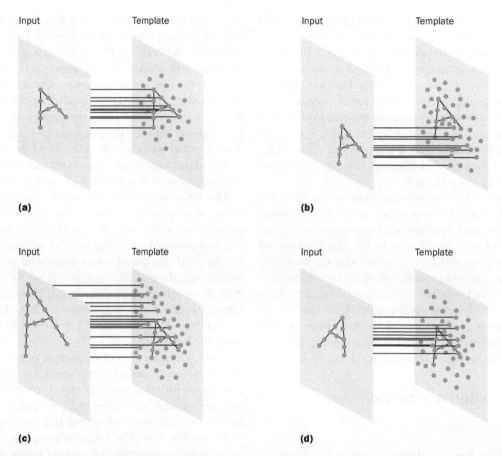

Figure 6.9 These four figures illustrate how template matching can fail. The position of the input may change **(b)**, its size may change **(c)** or its orientation may change **(d)**.

Source: Neisser, U., *Cognitive Psychology*. New York: Appleton-Century-Crofts, 1967. Reprinted with permission.

series of red ones than vice versa; we find it easier to find a tilted item in a series of vertical items than finding a vertical item in a series of tilted ones. Similarly, we are better at finding a mobile object in a series of stationary ones than a stationary one in a series of mobile ones. We can detect bumps in a display of bumpy and flat surfaces better than we can the absence of bumps, and we are better at finding a single stimulus in an array of different stimuli when there are many more different stimuli. It appears, then, that some stimuli have more distinctive features than others and this enhances discrimination.

Figure 6.10 contains several examples of the letter N. Although the examples vary in size and style, recognising them is not problematic because your visual system contains a specification of the distinctive features that fit the criterion for an N: two parallel vertical lines connected by a diagonal line sloping downward from the top of the left one to the bottom of the right one.

An experiment by Neisser (1964) supports the hypothesis that perception involves analysis of distinctive features. Figure 6.11 shows one of the tasks he asked people to do. The figure shows two columns of letters.

Figure 6.10 Distinctive features. We easily recognise all of these items as the letter N.

The task is to scan through them until you find the letter Z, which occurs once in each column.

You probably found the letter in the left column much faster than you did the one in the right column. Why? The letters in the left column share few features with those found in the letter Z, so the Z stands out from the others. In contrast, the letters in the right column have many features in common with the target letter, and thus the Z is 'camouflaged'.

The distinctive-features model appears to be a reasonable explanation for the perception of letters, but what

GDOROC	IVEMXW
COQUCD	XVIWME
DUCOQG	VEMIXW
GRUDQO	WEKMVI
OCDURQ	XIMVWE
DUCGRO	IVMWEX
ODUCQG	VWEMXI
CQOGRD	IMEWXV
DUZORQ	EXMZWI
UCGROD	IEMWVX
QCUDOG	EIVXWM
RQGUDO	WXEMIV
DRGOQC	MIWVXE
OQGDRU	IMEVXW
UGCODQ	IEMWVX
ODRUCQ	IMWVEX
UDQRGC	XWMVEI
ORGCUD	IWEVXM

Figure 6.11 A letter-search task. Look for the letter Z hidden in each column.

Source: Adapted from Neisser, J., Visual search. *Scientific American Mind*, 1964, 210, 94–102.

about more natural stimuli, which we encounter in places other than the written page? Biederman (1987, 1990) suggests a model of pattern recognition that combines some aspects of prototypes and distinctive features. He suggests that the shapes of objects that we encounter can be constructed from a set of 36 different shapes that he refers to as geons. Figure 6.12 illustrates a few geons and some objects that can be constructed from them. Perhaps, Biederman suggests, the visual system recognises objects by identifying the particular sets and arrangements of geons that they contain.

Even if Biederman is correct that our ability to perceive categories of common objects involves recognition of geons, it seems unlikely that the geons are involved in perception of particular objects. For example, it is difficult to imagine how we could perceive faces of different people as assemblies of different sets of geons. The geon hypothesis appears to work best for the recognition of prototypes of generic categories: telephones or torches in general rather than the telephone on your desk or the torch a friend lent you.

Biederman points out that particular features of figures – cusps and joints formed by the ends of line segments – are of critical importance in recognising drawings of objects, presumably because the presence of these joints enables the viewer to recognise the constituent geons. Figure 6.13 shows two sets of degraded images of drawings of five common objects. One set, (a), shows the locations of cusps and joints; the other, (b), does not. Biederman (1990) observed that people found the items with cusps and joints much easier to recognise.

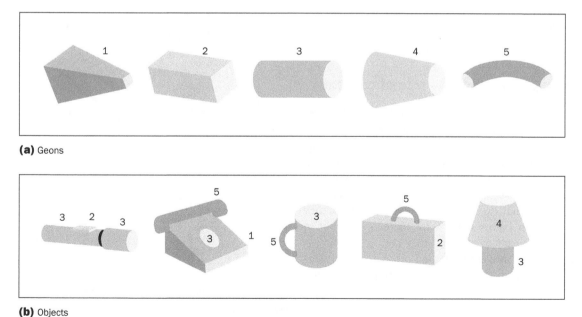

(a) Geons

(b) Objects

Figure 6.12 Geons for perception. **(a)** Several different geons. **(b)** The combination of two or three geons (indicated by the numbers) into common three-dimensional objects.

Source: Adapted from Biederman, I., Higher-level vision. In *An Invitation to Cognitive Science. Vol. 2: Visual Cognition and Action*, edited by D.N. Osherson, S.M. Kosslyn and J. Hollerbach. Cambridge, MA: MIT Press, 1990.

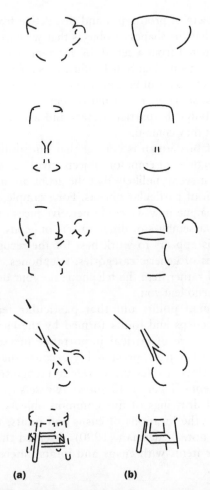

Figure 6.13 Incomplete figures. **(a)** With cusps and joints. **(b)** Without cusps and joints. Which set is easier to recognise?

Source: Adapted from Biederman, I., Higher-level vision. In *An Invitation to Cognitive Science. Vol. 2: Visual Cognition and Action*, edited by D.N. Osherson, S.M. Kosslyn and J. Hollerbach. Cambridge, MA: MIT Press, 1990.

Top-down processing: the role of context

We often perceive objects under conditions that are less than optimum; the object is in a shadow, camouflaged against a similar background or obscured by fog. Nevertheless, we usually manage to recognise the item correctly. We are often helped in our endeavour by the context in which we see the object. For example, look at Figure 6.14. What do you see? Can you tell what they are? Now look at Figure 6.15. With the elements put in context it is quite easy to see what they are.

Palmer (1975b) showed that even more general forms of context can aid in the perception of objects. He first

Figure 6.14 Simple elements that are difficult to recognise without a context.

Figure 6.15 An example of top-down processing. The context facilitates our recognition of the items shown in Figure 6.14.

Source: Adapted from Palmer, S.E., in *Explorations in Cognition*, D.A. Norman, D.E. Rumelhart and the LNR Research Group. San Francisco, CA: W.H. Freeman, 1975.

showed his participants familiar scenes, such as a kitchen. Next, he used a tachistoscope to show them drawings of individual items and asked the participants to identify them. A **tachistoscope** can present visual stimuli very briefly so that they are difficult to perceive (nowadays we would use a computer to perform the same function). Sometimes, participants saw an object that was appropriate to the scene, such as a loaf of bread. At other times, they saw an inappropriate but similarly shaped object, such as a letterbox (see Figure 6.16).

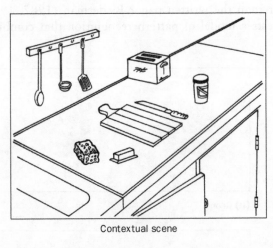

Contextual scene

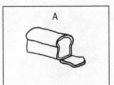

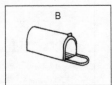

Target object (presented very briefly)

Figure 6.16 Stimuli from the experiment by Palmer (1975b). After looking at the contextual scene, participants were shown one of the stimuli below it very briefly, by means of a tachistoscope.

Source: Palmer, S.E., The effects of contextual scenes on the identification of objects. *Memory and Cognition*, 1975, 3, 519–26. Reprinted by permission of the Psychonomic Society, Inc.

Palmer found that when the objects fitted the context that had been set by the scene, participants correctly identified about 84 per cent of them. But when they did not, performance fell to about 50 per cent. Performance was intermediate in the no-context control condition, under which subjects did not first see a scene. Thus, compared with the no-context control condition, an appropriate context facilitated recognition and an inappropriate one interfered with it.

The context effects demonstrated by experiments such as Palmer's are not simply examples of guessing. That is, people do not think to themselves, 'Let's see, that shape could be either a letterbox or a loaf of bread. I saw a picture of a kitchen, so I suppose it's a loaf of bread.' The process is rapid, unconscious and automatic; thus, it belongs to the category of perception rather than to problem-solving, which is much slower and more deliberate. Somehow, seeing a kitchen scene sensitises the neural circuits responsible for the perception of loaves of bread and other items we have previously seen in that context.

Psychologists distinguish between two categories of information-processing models of pattern recognition: **bottom-up processing** and **top-down processing**. In bottom-up processing, also called data-driven processing, the perception is constructed out of the elements – the bits and pieces – of the stimulus, beginning with the image that falls on the retina. The information is processed by successive levels of the visual system until the highest levels (the 'top' of the system) are reached, and the object is perceived. Top-down processing refers to the use of contextual information – to the use of the 'big picture'. Presumably, once the kitchen scene is perceived, information is sent from the 'top' of the system down through lower levels. This information excites neural circuits responsible for perceiving those objects normally found in kitchens and inhibits others. Then, when the subject sees a drawing of a loaf of bread, information starts coming up through the successive levels of the system and finds the appropriate circuits already warmed up, so to speak.

In most cases, perception consists of a combination of top-down and bottom-up processing. Figure 6.17 shows several examples of objects that can be recognised only by a combination of both forms of processing. Our knowledge of the configurations of letters in words provides us with the contexts that permit us to organise the flow of information from the bottom up.

Direct perception: Gibson's affordances

In the chapter so far we have considered some of the mechanisms that underlie visual perception. But is this perception a response or a process? That is, is visual perception an active or passive process? We saw in an

Figure 6.17 Examples of combined top-down/bottom-up processing. The effect of context enables us to perceive the letters despite the missing or ambiguous features. Note that a given letter may be perceived in more than one way, depending on the letters surrounding it.

Source: Adapted from McClelland, I.J., Rumelhart, D.E. and Hinton, G.E., in *Parallel Distributed processing*. Vol. i: *Foundations*, edited by D.E. Rumelhart, J.L. McClelland and the PDP Research Group. © the Massachusetts Institute of Technology; published by the MIT Press, Cambridge, MA.

earlier section on cross-cultural differences that context is important for visual perception. The psychologist J.J. Gibson took this notion a step further. Over a period of 35 years, Gibson proposed a theory of perception which argued that perception was direct and did not depend on cognitive processes to bring together fragmented data (Gibson, 1950, 1966, 1979). Because of this, it is considered a direct theory of perception. Originally, Gibson was interested in distinguishing between unsuccessful and successful Second World War pilots. Some of the unsuccessful pilots were unable to land accurately and seemed unable to appreciate distance. However, Gibson found that even when these pilots were given training in depth perception – which may have remedied the problem – they continued to have difficulty.

According to Gibson, 'perceiving is an act, not a response; an act of attention, not a triggered impression; an achievement, not a reflex' (Gibson, 1979). Gibson's view of perception was that classical optical science ignored the complexity of real events. For example, it would focus on the effects of trivial, basic or simple stimuli on perceptual response. Gibson abandoned the depth/space perception view of the world and, instead, suggested that our perception of surfaces was more important. Surfaces comprised ground (which we discussed earlier) and texture elements in surfaces that would be attached or detached. Attached features would include bumps and indentations in the surface, such as rocks or trees; detached features would include items such as animals (which are detached from the surface).

Given the complex world in which we live, we must be able to perceive not just simple stimuli but stimuli which mean something more to us. We must decide whether an object is throwable or graspable, whether a surface can be sat upon and so on. We ask ourselves what can this object furnish us with, what does it afford us (Gibson, 1982)? These are the meanings that the environment has and Gibson called them **affordances**. Thus, Gibson highlighted the ecological nature of perception: we do not simply perceive simple stimuli but these stimuli mean something more in a wider, more complex context. This was a radical departure in visual perception because it implied that the perception of object meaning is direct. Perception involves determining whether something is capable of being sat upon or is throwable.

However, the theory is not without its problems. Costall (1995), for example, suggests that some affordances may not be able to afford. Imagine the ground covered in frost and a frozen lake. According to Gibson, the ground afforded walking. However, although the frosty ground does, the frozen lake may not. Similarly, although we might agree with Gibson that some surfaces are graspable or supporting we might disagree quite reasonably with the notion that surfaces are edible, for example, that they afford eating. Our decision that something is edible appears to rely on more than direct perception of surfaces.

Face perception

Although object perception is important to us, the perception of specific categories of stimuli may be even more important. One such category is 'faces'. Being able to recognise and identify faces is one of the most important social functions human beings can perform (Bruce, 1994). It helps us form relationships with people, spot faces in a crowd and provides us with potential non-verbal cues as to what a person is thinking or feeling (the role of emotion in facial expression is returned to in Chapter 13).

We can identify people better on the basis of the eyes than the mouth and both are more important than the nose (Bruce *et al.*, 1993), even when hairstyle, make-up and facial hair are removed or minimised. A three-dimensional image of a face – such as that seen in three-quarter profile – is better recognised than is a full-frontal photograph. Upright faces are better recognised and identified than are those upside down but there is a curious phenomenon called the 'Thatcher effect', first described by the British psychologist, Peter Thompson (1980). Take a look at the faces in Figure 6.18. They look fairly normal – you can easily identify the image as a face and, while you can see that the faces are inverted, the features appear to be in the right place, and are identifiable.

Now, turn the book upside down and look at the photographs again. It is a grotesque image, but only eyes and the mouth have been turned around (inverted) to create this effect. This is the Thatcher effect (so-called because Thompson created his stimuli using the face of the British Prime Minister).

Figure 6.18 The Thatcher effect – turn the page upside down to experience the effect.

Source: Grüter, T., Grüter, M. and Carbon, C-C. Neural and genetic foundations of face recognition and prosopagnosia. *Journal of Neuropsychology* (2008), 2, 79–97, figure 3.

Sex of the face

We can usually discriminate between faces more quickly on the basis of their users' sex than familiarity (Bruce *et al.*, 1987). Enlow (1982), for example, has suggested that men have larger noses and nasopharynxes, more prominent brows, a more sloping forehead and more deeply set eyes than do women. Shepherd (1989) noted that women had fuller cheeks and less facial hair (including eyebrows). Women are also thought to have smaller noses, a more depressed bridge of the nose, a shorter upper lip, and larger eyes with darker shadows, especially young women (Liggett, 1974).

When facial features are presented in isolation, eyes are the most reliable indicator of sex and the nose is the least reliable. With hair concealed, 96 per cent of participants were able to distinguish between faces based on sex (Burton *et al.*, 1993). When individual facial features or pairs of features (such as brow and eyes, nose and mouth) were presented to participants, the features which afforded the best opportunity to make sex discriminations were, in this order: brow and eyes, brow alone, eyes alone, whole jaw, chin, nose and mouth, and mouth alone (Brown and Perrett, 1993). These findings suggest that all facial features carry some information about sex (except the nose) but suggest that it is difficult to find even one or two features which distinguish absolutely between men's and women's faces. Some features, however, provide better clues than others.

Distinctiveness and attractiveness

Each of us finds different faces attractive: some of us find faces friendlier than others, some meaner and others more sexually alluring. Although individual differences exist at this, what seems like, subjective level, studies have shown that some features of the face are generally regarded as more attractive than others. Psychologists in the nineteenth century were interested in what makes a face attractive and constructed composites – averages of several different images – to produce a face which they believed was attractive (Galton, 1878; Stoddard, 1886). Recent work has provided a clearer account of what makes an attractive face; it has also helped to indicate which features of the face best allow us to remember a face or which make a face distinctive.

The distinctiveness of the face – defined as the deviation from the norm – is unrelated to attractiveness (Bruce *et al.*, 1994). Galton had hypothesised that averageness was attractiveness. That is, the more average-looking the face, the more attractive it was likely to be. This hypothesis was tested and challenged by Perrett *et al.* (1994), who compared the attractiveness ratings for average, attractive and highly attractive Caucasian female faces.

Perrett *et al.*, using special computer technology, constructed an average composite of photographs of 60 female faces. The 15 faces rated as most attractive from the original 60 were then averaged. Finally, the attractiveness of this average was enhanced by 50 per cent to provide a 'highly attractive' composite. Composites similar to those used in the experiment can be seen in Figure 6.19.

Caucasian raters found the 'attractive' composite more attractive than the average composite and the highly attractive composite more attractive than the 'attractive' composite, thus disconfirming Galton's hypothesis. Furthermore, when similar composites were made of Japanese women, the same results were obtained: both Caucasian and Japanese raters found the enhanced composite more attractive. What distinguished an average face from an attractive one?

The more attractive faces were those who had higher cheek bones, a thinner jaw and larger eyes relative to the size of the face. There was also a shorter distance between mouth and chin and between nose and mouth in the attractive faces.

Evolutionary psychologists argue that we are attracted to average faces because this behaviour evolved as a solution to attracting healthy mates – best to stick with what you know and can trust. An alternative view is that we are simply attracted to the familiar – a well-known psychological phenomenon. If this were true, we should be attracted to average-looking stimuli that are non-faces too. This is what Halberstadt and Rhodes (2000) found. They asked people to rate a selection of watches, birds and dogs for attractiveness and prototypicality (how typical they were of a category), or averageness. The researchers found that participants rated the average-looking stimuli as being the most attractive. One reason for this may be that we have a preference for averageness which 'reflects a more general preference for familiar stimuli'.

There is mixed evidence regarding the type of 'sexual' face that we like: some studies suggest that we prefer more feminised faces; others that we like masculinised ones (Johnston, 2006). The explanation for our preference for feminised faces is that they are more youthful, warm and honest; masculinised faces are colder, dominant and dishonest. Faces that are morphed to look younger are judged to be significantly more attractive (Ishi *et al.*, 2004). We also, naturally, spend more time looking at beautiful faces than unattractive ones, but a study from a group of US researchers has found that although women spend more time looking at beautiful male and female faces than they do unattractive ones, men spend longer than women looking at beautiful female faces (Levy *et al.*, 2008).

Women's preference for men's faces can change across the menstrual cycle (see Chapter 3). Penton-Voak and Perrett (2000) found that women in the follicular phase of their cycle were significantly more likely to prefer a masculine face than those in menses or in the luteal phase. Gangestad *et al.* (2004) found that women during the high-fertility portion of their menstrual cycle were more attracted to men who showed social presence and 'intrasexual competitiveness' than they were during their low-fertility days. Social presence was characterised by composure, having an athletic presence, maintaining eye contact, lack of self-deprecation, lack of downward gaze and 'lack of nice-guy self-presentation'. Direct intrasexual competitiveness was defined by behaviours that derogated competitors, lacked laughter and were directly sexually competitive. This preference only emerged when women wished short-term rather than long-term relationships, suggesting that a man's demeanour can significantly alter perceived attractiveness by women high in fertility, but this attraction may be short-lived.

One explanation for these findings is that during the fertile phase of the cycle, women are more likely to seek a sexual partner (and, potentially, a father for their child) who shows evidence of 'genetic benefits' (strength, assertiveness, etc.). This explanation is based on limited experimental data, however, and more direct behaviour – such as the interaction between men and women – has not been studied.

Although very masculine male faces are judged to be dominant, their owners are less likely to be judged suitable as a long-term partner by women than are owners of less masculine faces (Boothroyd *et al.*, 2007). Women at their most fertile preferred more symmetrical faces but this preference was found only when the women were seeking a short-term partner or if the women already had a partner (Little *et al.*, 2007), replicating Gangestad *et al*'s finding. The results suggest that this facial feature may maximise mating by encouraging short-term relationships. Symmetrical faces are usually judged to be more attractive than asymmetrical ones and there is evidence that facial symmetry in men and women is associated with perceived healthiness (Rhodes *et al.*, 2007) and self-reported extraversion (Pound *et al.*, 2007).

A directly gazing face is considered significantly more attractive than an indirectly gazing one. We also like objects more if we see a person smiling at them than if they show disgust. Furthermore, we are more likely to engage socially with people if they look at us directly. Strick *et al.* (2008) paired novel objects – pictures of unknown peppermint brands – with an attractive or unattractive face which looked straight at the participant or which averted its gaze. Participants rated the attractiveness of these objects. As predicted, objects paired with a directly gazing attractive face

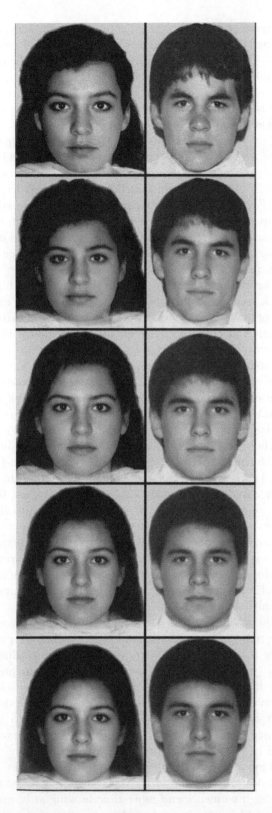

Figure 6.19 Faces similar to those used in Perrett *et al.*'s (1994) experiment. The faces are 'morphed' from averagely attractive (top two faces) to very attractive (bottom two faces). Most people rate the last two faces as most attractive.

Source: Reproduced with permission from © The British Psychological Society.

Cutting edge: Quarter back, nice front

Do successful athletes have more attractive faces? Williams *et al.* (2010b) asked female students from a Dutch University to rate the facial attractiveness of 30 players from the US's National Football League. The official measure of performance in this league is the quarterback's passer rating – number of touchdowns following a pass attempt, touchdown completions following passing, etc.

The attractiveness rating of the quarterback was significantly and positively correlated with their passer ratings, regardless of the player's age, ethnicity, height, weight or facial expression.

Why? One theory is that facial attractiveness is a measure of 'heritable fitness' and that these results specifically may be related to the degree of testosterone in the attractive, successful players – this is speculative; the amount of testosterone was not measured. The researchers argue that higher testosterone ratings may be associated with facial features that women find attractive.

were more positively evaluated than were objects paired with an indirectly gazing attractive face or an unattractive face.

Theories of face perception

The mechanisms that allow us to perceive faces are considered to be different from those that allow us to perceive objects; face perception has been thought of as 'special' (Farah *et al.*, 1998). Face perception involves a number of operations. We can perceive general characteristics such as the colour, sex and age of a face; we can perceive whether a face expresses anger, sadness or joy; we can distinguish familiar from unfamiliar faces. What model of face processing can account for these operations?

Bruce and Young (1986) suggested that face processing is made up of three functions: perception of facial expression, perception of familiar faces and perception of unfamiliar faces. Why does the model separate these functions? Bruce and Young reviewed extensive evidence which suggested that each of these functions is dependent on different cognitive abilities and that evidence from neuropsychology supported such a model. Current views of face processing argue that we exploit three strategies when we recognise faces. One strategy involves recognising the features of a face, a second involves recognising the relations between features in a face (configural processing) and a third suggests that we recognise the whole face (the holistic approach) (Gruter *et al.*, 2008). Configural processing works when faces are upright, but fails when they are inverted, à la the Thatcher effect. There is more on theories of face processing in a later section. Young and Bruce (2011) recently reflected on how well their model has endured. They note that the one factor they did not consider, and which should have been, was eye gaze.

Perception of space and motion

In addition to being able to perceive the forms of objects in our environment, we are able to judge quite accurately their relative location in space and their movements. Perceiving where things are and perceiving what they are doing are obviously important functions of the visual system.

Depth perception

Depth perception requires that we perceive the distance of objects in the environment from us and from each other. We do so by means of two kinds of cues: binocular ('two-eye') and monocular ('one-eye'). Binocular cues arise from the fact that the visual fields of both eyes overlap. Only animals that have eyes on the front of the head (such as primates, cats and some birds) can obtain binocular cues. Animals that have eyes on the sides of their heads (such as rabbits and fish) can obtain only monocular cues.

One monocular cue involves movement and thus must be experienced in the natural environment or in a motion picture. The other monocular cues can be represented in a drawing or a photograph. Most of these cues were originally discovered by artists and only later studied by psychologists (Zeki, 1998). Figure 6.20 shows the most important sources of depth cues.

Binocular cues

Convergence provides an important cue about distance. The eyes make **conjugate** movements so that both look at (converge on) the same point of the visual scene. If an object is very close to your face, your eyes are turned inwards. If it is farther away, they look more nearly straight ahead.

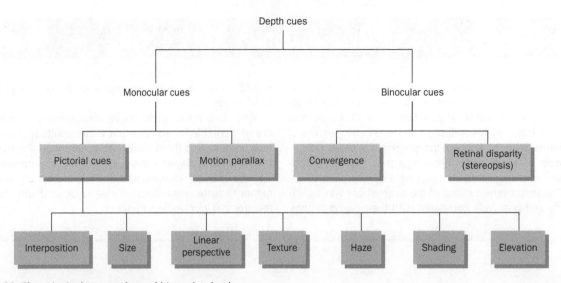

Figure 6.20 The principal monocular and binocular depth cues.

Source: From Margaret W. Matlin and Hugh H.J. Foley, *Sensation and Perception*, 3rd edn © 1992. Published by Allyn & Bacon, Boston, MA. Copyright © by Pearson Education. By permission of the publisher.

Thus, the eyes can be used like range finders. The brain controls the extraocular muscles, so it knows the angle between them, which is related to the distance between the object and the eyes. Convergence is most important for perceiving the distance of objects located close to us, especially those we can reach with our hands.

Another important factor in the perception of distance is the information provided by retinal disparity ('unlikeness' or 'dissimilarity'). Hold up a finger of one hand at arm's length and then hold up a finger of the other hand midway between your nose and the distant finger. If you look at one of the fingers, you will see a double image of the other one. Whenever your eyes are pointed towards a particular point, the images of objects at different distances will fall on different portions of the retina in each eye. The amount of disparity produced by the images of an object on the two retinas provides an important clue about its distance from us.

The perception of depth resulting from retinal disparity is called stereopsis. A stereoscope is a device that shows two slightly different pictures, one for each eye. The pictures are taken by a camera equipped with two lenses, located a few inches apart, just as our eyes are. When you look through a stereoscope, you see a three-dimensional image.

Monocular cues

One of the most important sources of information about the relative distance of objects is **interposition** (meaning 'placed between'). If one object is placed between us and another object so that the closer object partially obscures our view of the more distant one, we can immediately perceive which object is closer to us.

Obviously, interposition works best when we are familiar with the objects and know what their shapes should look like. Just as the Gestalt law of good continuation plays a role in form perception, the principle of good form affects our perception of the relative location of objects: we perceive the object having the simpler border as being closer. Figure 6.21(a) can be seen either as two rectangles, located one in front of the other (Figure 6.21(b)), or as a rectangle nestled against an L-shaped object (Figure 6.21(c)). Because we tend to perceive an ambiguous drawing according to the principle of good form, we are more likely to perceive Figure 6.21(a) as two simple shapes – rectangles – one partly hiding the other.

Another important monocular distance cue is provided by our familiarity with the sizes of objects. For example, if a car casts a very small image on our retinas, we will perceive it as being far away. Knowing how large cars are, our visual system can automatically compute the approximate distance from the size of the retinal image.

Figure 6.22 shows two columns located at different distances. The drawing shows **linear perspective**: the tendency for parallel lines that recede from us to appear to converge at a single point. Because of perspective, we perceive the columns as being the same size even though they produce retinal images of different sizes. We also perceive the segments of the wall between the columns as rectangular, even though the image they cast on the retina does not contain any right angles.

Texture, especially the texture of the ground, provides another cue we use to perceive the distance of objects sitting on the ground. A coarser texture looks closer, and a finer texture looks more distant. The earth's atmosphere, which always contains a certain amount of haze, can also

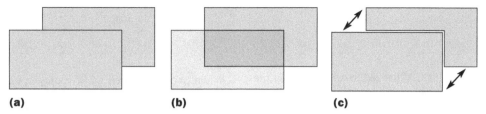

(a)   **(b)**   **(c)**

Figure 6.21 Use of the principle of good form in the perception of depth. The two objects shown in **(a)** could be two identical rectangles, one in front of the other, as shown in **(b)** or a rectangle and an L-shaped object, as shown in **(c)**. The principle of good form states that we will see the ambiguous object in its simplest (best) form – in this case a rectangle. As a result, the shape to the right is perceived as being partly hidden and thus further away from us.

Figure 6.22 Principle of perspective. Perspective gives the appearance of distance and makes the two columns look similar in size.

Figure 6.23 Cues from atmospheric haze. Variation in detail, owing to haze, produces an appearance of distance.
Source: Powerstock SuperStock, reprinted by permission.

supply cues about the relative distance of objects or parts of the landscape. Parts of the landscape that are further away become less distinct because of haze in the air. Thus, **haze** provides a monocular distance cue (see Figure 6.23).

The patterns of light and shadow in a scene – its **shading** – can provide us with cues about the three-dimensional shapes of objects. Although the cues that shading provides do not usually tell us much about the absolute distances of objects from us, they can tell us which parts of objects are closer and which are further away. Figure 6.24 illustrates the power of this phenomenon. Some of the circles look as if they bulge out towards us; others look as if they were hollowed out (dimpled). The only difference is the direction of the shading. Our visual system appears to interpret such stimuli as if they were illuminated from above. Thus, the top of a convex (bulging) object will be light and the bottom will be in shadow. If you turn the book upside-down, the bulges and dimples will reverse.

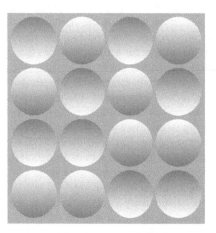

Figure 6.24 Depth cues supplied by shading. If the tops of the circles are dark, they look like depressions. If the bottoms are dark, they appear as bumps.

Psychology in action: CCTV and face perception

The increasing use of CCTV has led to an increase in the reliance on CCTV evidence in prosecutions but the quality of these images is very variable. According to a 2009 UK Home Office and police report, around 80 per cent of CCTV images are of no practical use because they are of such poor quality.

Lighting conditions, which are sometimes very poor in CCTV, affect face recognition significantly. For example, the ability to match faces (and even recognise familiar surfaces) is more accurate when lighting is from above, perhaps because it casts fewer shadows. Hill and Bruce (1996) suggest that lighting a face from the bottom reverses the brightness of facial areas such as the eye sockets and nostrils. In fact, lighting of this sort makes the face look like a negative. This study highlights an important point about face perception (and about the erroneous testimony described at the opening of the chapter). Our recognition of faces is not simply based on 'edge' information (contour). The shape of the face (viewpoint) and shading are also crucial in enabling us to make accurate recognition judgements.

Is recognition improved if the face is moving? After all, a moving image might give more information about shading, shape and contour than would a static one. Some researchers have reported that a moving image is more advantageous to accurate recognition than is a static one (Knight and Johnston, 1997; Pike et al., 1997). Others have found little improvement in recognition when moving and static images are compared (Christie and Bruce, 1998).

Recognition is enhanced by familiarity. Burton et al. (1999) took video footage of male and female university psychology lecturers caught on security cameras at the entrance to the psychology department. They then asked psychology and non-psychology students, as well as experienced police officers, to view this footage and then asked them to indicate which of the people in a set of high-quality photographs they had seen on tape. Psychology students made more correct identifications than did the non-psychology students or police officers, suggesting that previous familiarity with the target helps with recognition.

In the second experiment, the researchers looked at which specific bits of information the participants used to identify the target. They took the same video footage, but this time they either obscured the head, the body or the gait. Participants performed quite inaccurately when gait and body were obscured but were significantly worse at identifying the target when the head was obscured. Thus the advantage of familiarity – at least, in this experiment – was due to recognition of facial features rather than the way in which people walk or their body shape. Unusual gaits or shapes may produce different results.

When people watched CCTV footage of a person and then tried to match the image in the footage with either a single snapshot or an array of snapshots, people performed the task poorly (Bruce et al., 2001). However, when the participants knew the person in the footage – the targets were the participants' teachers or colleagues – they were significantly better at the task. Even in experiments where participants were made briefly familiar with the image they were exposed to, this period of familiarisation did not help the participant recognise the face.

According to Bruce et al. (2001), 'where a person is recognised on a CCTV image by someone familiar to them, these identifications should be taken very seriously, even if the CCTV image is of low quality'. They refer to the case of the London nail bomber, David Copeland, as an illustration of this finding. Copeland was responsible for killing three people and injuring 129 others in nail bomb explosions

The site of the bomb placed by David Copeland. Copeland was apprehended after a colleague recognised his face from CCTV footage shown on television. Research suggests that recognition of people seen in CCTV footage is significantly more accurate if these people are familiar. If the target person is not familiar, the likelihood of false positives (making an incorrect identification) increases.

Source: Metropolitan Police Service.

in three areas of London – Soho, Brick Lane and Brixton – in the spring of 1999. Copeland's final crime was committed in the Admiral Duncan pub in Soho, Central London. He left the pub at 6.05 p.m. The bomb exploded as Copeland made his way back to his hotel. Three people were killed, four required amputations and 26 suffered burns (Hopkins and Hall, 2000). Eighty minutes before the bomb was detonated Copeland's colleague had telephoned the police and told them that he thought the bomber identified on CCTV and publicised on television looked like his workmate. By that evening, police were planning a raid on Copeland's house.

These features are important to practical aspects of our lives, an example of which appears in the Psychology in Action section above.

Distance and location

When we are able to see the horizon, we perceive objects near it as being distant and those above or below it as being nearer to us. Thus, elevation provides an important monocular depth cue. For example, cloud B and triangle B in Figure 6.25 appear further away from us than do cloud A and triangle A.

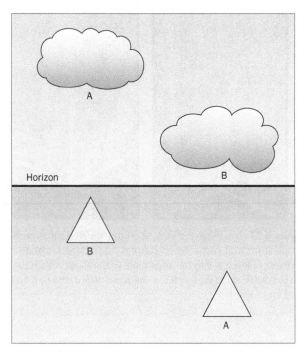

Figure 6.25 Depth cues supplied by elevation. The objects nearest the horizontal line appear furthest away from us.
Source: Adapted from Matlin, M.W. and Foley, H.J., *Sensation and Perception* (3rd edn). Boston, MA: Allyn & Bacon, 1992.

So far, all the monocular distance cues discussed have been those that can be rendered in a drawing or captured by a camera. However, another important source of distance information depends on our own movement. Try the following demonstrations. If you focus your eyes on an object close to you and move your head from side to side, your image of the scene moves back and forth behind the nearer object. If you focus your eyes on the background while moving your head from side to side, the image of the nearer object passes back and forth across the background. Head and body movements cause the images from the scene before us to change; the closer the object, the more it changes relative to the background. The information contained in this relative movement helps us to perceive distance.

The changes in the relative locations of the objects provide cues concerning their distance from the observer. The phenomenon is known as **motion parallax** (*parallax* comes from a Greek word meaning 'change').

Constancies of visual perception

An important characteristic of the visual environment is that it is almost always changing as we move, as objects move, and as lighting conditions change. However, despite the changing nature of the image the visual environment casts on our retinas, our perceptions remain remarkably constant.

Visual perception across cultures

From birth onwards, we explore our environment with our eyes. The patterns of light and dark, colour and movement, produce changes in the visual system of the brain. There is evidence, however, that perception is not absolute, that it varies across cultures. Ecological variables such as those associated with geography, cultural codes and education influence perception.

The visual stimulation we receive, particularly during infancy, affects the development of our visual system. If the environment lacks certain features – certain visual patterns – then an organism might fail to recognise the significance of these features if it encounters them later in life (Blakemore and Mitchell, 1973). But this is not the only type of environment that can influence perception.

There may also be differences in the cultural codes found in pictorial representations (Russell *et al.*, 1997). Although artists have learned to represent all the monocular depth cues (except for those produced by movement) in their paintings, not all cues are represented in the traditional art of all cultures. For example, many cultures do not use linear perspective. Does the absence of particular cues in the art of a particular culture mean that people from this culture will not recognise them when they see them in paintings from another culture?

It is quite rare for a member of one culture to be totally unable to recognise a depiction as a depiction (Russell *et al.*, 1997). However, Deregowski *et al.* (1972) found that when the Me'en tribe of Ethiopia, a culture unfamiliar with pictures, were shown a series of pictures from a children's colouring book, they would smell them, listen to the pages while flexing them, examine their texture but would ignore the actual pictures. They did recognise depictions of indigenous animals, suggesting that the familiarity of a pictorial depiction is important for recognition within cultures. Familiar objects are sometimes depicted in an exaggerated way. Aboriginal depictions of the crocodile, for example, are distorted: the trunk is seen from above and the head and tail from the side (Dziurawiec and Deregowski, 1992), although this finding may be attributable to the fact that such animals are difficult to draw.

There are other geographical influences on perception. People who live in 'carpentered worlds', that is worlds in which buildings are built from long, straight pieces of material that normally join each other in right angles, are more likely to be subject to the Müller–Lyer illusion. This illusion is shown in Figure 6.26. Look at the two vertical lines and decide which is longer.

Actually, the lines are of equal length. Segall *et al.* (1966) presented the Müller–Lyer illusion (and several others) to groups of subjects from Western and non-Western cultures. Most investigators believe that the Müller–Lyer illusion is a result of our experience with the angles formed by the intersection of walls, ceilings and floors (Redding and Hawley, 1993). The angled lines can be seen as examples of linear perspective (see Figure 6.27). In fact, Segall and his colleagues did find that people from 'carpentered' cultures were more susceptible to this illusion: experience with straight lines forming right angles appeared to affect people's perception.

Although the famous Müller-Lyer illusion can be demonstrated in modalities apart from vision (Mancini *et al.*, 2010), explanations for it have been based on an

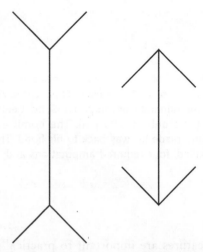

Figure 6.26 The Müller–Lyer illusion. The two vertical lines are actually equal in length, but the one on the left appears to be longer.

Figure 6.27 The impact of culture on the Müller–Lyer illusion. People from 'non-carpentered' cultures that lack rectangular corners are less likely to be susceptible to this illusion. Although the two vertical lines are actually the same height, the one on the right looks shorter.

understanding of the visual system. For example, people with damage to the extrastriate visual cortex in the occipital lobe are unable to perceive the illusion, fMRI data show activation of the bilateral lateral occipital cortex and the superior parietal cortex, and MEG research indicates that activation is seen at two times – once between 85 and 130 ms after the onset of the image and then again at 195–220 ms in the ventral visual pathway in the right temporal cortex, parietal and frontal cortex (Mancini *et al.*, 2011). The MEG data suggest that forming the representation of an object involves the lateral occipital and inferior temporal areas (Weidner *et al.*, 2010).

Mancini *et al.* (2011) used the stimulation technique, repetitive transcranial magnetic stimulation (rTMS), to examine whether these regions were involved in the Müller-Lyer illusion in the visual and haptic (somatosensory) domains. In the haptic domain, people moved their finger along a palpable version of the typical Müller-Lyer illusion but they were blindfold. Therefore, their only sensory feedback was tactile. When rTMS was applied over left and right occipito-temporal cortex, visual and haptic performance was impaired. Stimulation over the right or left superior parietal cortex did not affect the illusion.

These results suggest that the regions which allow for the processing of the illusion visually and haptically are both sides of the occipito-temporal cortex.

Brightness constancy

People can judge the whiteness or greyness of an object very well, even if the level of illumination changes. If you look at a sheet of white paper either in bright sunlight or in shade, you will perceive it as being white, although the intensity of its image on your retina will vary. If you look at a sheet of grey paper in sunlight, it may in fact reflect more light to your eye than will a white paper located in the shade, but you will still see the white paper as white and the grey paper as grey. This phenomenon is known as **brightness constancy**.

Form constancy

When we approach an object or when it approaches us, we do not perceive it as getting larger. Even though the image of the object on the retina gets larger, we perceive this change as being due to a decrease in the distance between ourselves and the object. Our perception of the object's size remains relatively constant.

The unchanging perception of an object's size and shape when it moves relative to us is called **form constancy**. Psychologists also refer to size constancy, but size is simply one aspect of form. In the nineteenth century, Hermann von Helmholtz suggested that form constancy was achieved by **unconscious inference**, a mental computation of which we are unaware. We know the size and shape of a familiar object. Therefore, if the image it casts upon our retina is small, we perceive it as being far away; if the image is large, we perceive it as being close. In either case, we perceive the object itself as being the same size.

Controversies in psychological science: How does language influence visual perception?

The issue

One of the greatest controversies in psychology (and anthropology) is whether language influences perception. Words for shades of light and colour seem to be more limited in some cultures than others. The Inuit, for example, have more than one name for various shades of snow, whereas Africans have different words for different shades of sand, presumably because these features form a crucial part of the culture's environment. The language we use to describe what we see may directly affect our perception of stimuli.

The evidence

In the mid-nineteenth century, the British statesman William Gladstone noted that Homer's Ancient Greek classics, *The Iliad* and *The Odyssey*, had no reference to blue or orange or green. The sea, in fact, was described as 'wine-dark' or violet and the sky was never described as blue; oxen were described as purple. Black was most common (170 references),

followed by white (100), *eruthros*/red (13), *xanthos*/yellow (10) and violet (6). Oddly, *chloros* – which gives its name to chlorophyll – was used for non-green objects. Did the Greeks did not perceive these colours? Magnus (1880) investigated this hypothesis by gathering both linguistic and perceptual data. He sent questionnaires and colour chips to Western residents of European colonies and asked them to test the abilities of the native people to distinguish among the various colours. He assumed that language would reflect perceptual ability. If a language did not contain words to distinguish between certain colours, then the people who belonged to that culture would not be able to distinguish these colours perceptually.

Magnus was surprised to discover very few cultural differences in people's ability to perceive various colours. Linguistic differences did not appear to reflect perceptual differences. The issue emerged again in the mid-twentieth century with the principle of **linguistic relativity**. Briefly stated, this principle asserts that language used by the members of a particular culture is related to these people's thoughts and perceptions. The

Controversies in psychological science: *Continued*

best-known proponent of this principle, Benjamin Whorf, stated that 'the background linguistic system . . . of each language is not merely a reproducing instrument for voicing ideas but rather is itself a shaper of ideas, the program and guide for the individual's mental activity, for his analysis of impressions, for his synthesis of his mental stock-of-trade' (Whorf, 1956, p. 212). This became known as the **Sapir–Whorf hypothesis** – the idea that language can determine thought (Kay and Kempton, 1984).

Proponents of linguistic relativity suggested that colour names were cultural conventions – that members of a given culture could divide the countless combinations of hue, saturation and brightness (defined in Chapter 5) that we call colours into any number of different categories (Kay *et al.*, 1997). Each category was assigned a name, and when members of that culture looked out at the world, they perceived each of the colours they saw as belonging to one of these categories.

Two anthropologists, Berlin and Kay, examined this hypothesis in a linguistic study of a wide range of languages. They found the following eleven primary colour terms: black, white, red, yellow, green, blue, brown, purple, pink, orange and grey (Berlin and Kay, 1969; Kay, 1975; Kay *et al.*, 1991). The authors referred to these as focal colours. Not all languages used all eleven (as English does). In fact, some languages used only two: black and white (Heider, 1972). Others, such as Russian, had two words for blue (see below).

If a language contained words for three primary colours, these colours were black, white and red. If it contained words for six primary colours, these were black, white, red, yellow, green and blue. Berlin and Kay suggested that basic colour terms would be named more quickly than non-basic colour terms, that basic terms would be more salient, that is, they would be elicited first if you asked people to name colours spontaneously, and that basic terms would be more common in written communications such as texts. In fact, people do respond more quickly to basic than they do to non-basic colour terms across a range of languages; when asked to write down a list of as many colour words in five minutes as possible and draw a line under the last words written, every minute, basic terms invariably appear at the beginning of the list (Corbett and Davies, 1997). Similarly, Heider (1971) found that both children and adults found it easier to remember a colour chip of a focal colour (such as red or blue) than one of a non-focal colour (such as turquoise or peach).

In a famous cross-cultural study, Heider (1972) studied members of the Dani culture of New Guinea. The language of the Dani people has only two basic colour terms: *mili* ('black')

and *mola* ('white'). Heider assembled two sets of colour chips, one containing focal colours and the other containing non-focal colours. She taught her participants arbitrary names that she made up for the colours. Even though the participants had no words in their language for any of the colours, the group learning names for focal colours learned the names faster and remembered them better.

Categorical perception of colour refers to our ability to discriminate between two colours that seem to fall along a continuum. However, speakers of Berinmo (Papua New Guinea) and Himba do not distinguish a boundary between green and blue, which suggests that categorical perception is not universal. Roberson *et al.* (2008) tested this hypothesis in a group of native Korean- and English-speaking adults. Koreans distinguish between *yeondu* and *chorok*. The boundary between the two was described as 'green' by English speakers. Korean speakers were faster at discriminating between colours marked as a boundary in Korean but not English, but not at distinguishing between colours that fell within a colour category. The faster participants showed categorical perception only when stimuli appeared in the right visual field; slower participants showed categorical perception in both visual fields, suggesting that categorical perception may be verbally mediated by the left hemisphere.

Russian has two colour names for blue – *siniy* (dark) and *soleuboy* (light). To see whether this distinction affected perception, Winawer *et al.* (2007) asked Russian speakers to look at three squares – one at the top, two on the bottom. The task was to tell which of the two at the bottom was the same colour as the one on top (there was always one). If the top squares were dark and the odd one out light, then response time was quicker; the closer the hue of the odd one out to the other two squares, the longer the response time. But if the odd one out was two shades lighter and the upper square was dark but on the border with light, response time was shorter than if the odd one out was two shades darker. No such effect was found with English speakers suggesting that the Russians reacted to the blue shade differently.

A similar effect has been observed in English. Gilbert *et al.* (2006) had participants look at a cross in the middle of a circle made of coloured squares. One square was differently coloured to the rest. Participants were asked to indicate whether the square was to the left or the right of the cross. See Figure 6.28. When the odd-one-out was very different in colour, reaction time was quick. No surprise there. However, when the odd-one-out was across the green-blue border compared to the other squares and when it was

Controversies in psychological science: *Continued*

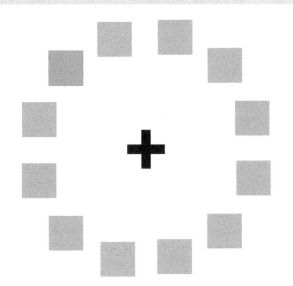

Figure 6.28 Gilbert *et al.*'s (2006) stimuli from their study demonstrating the Sapir–Whorf hypothesis even in English.

presented on the right, response time was shorter. The effect was not as pronounced on the left side.

Brain imaging research with Mandarin Chinese has also supported the Sapir–Whorf hypothesis. Tan *et al.* (2008) measured brain activation as participants saw two coloured squares and had to indicate whether they were the same or different. There were two conditions. In one, the colours were easy to name in Mandarin Chinese; in the second, the colours were just as recognisable but were hard to name. Both conditions activated identical areas in the occipital cortex and frontal gyrus. However, when the colours were easy to name activation was stronger in other regions (left posterior temporal gyrus and inferior parietal lobule, which are involved in word-finding) compared to when they were hard to name. This suggests, according to the authors, that language areas of the brain are involved in visual perception decisions.

Conclusion

Colour is a difficult topic to study cross-culturally. The evidence suggests, however, that although there are cultural variations in the number of colour words used, there seems to be cross-cultural agreement on the colours considered as 'basic'.

Form constancy also works for rotation. The drawing in Figure 6.29(a) could be either a trapezoid or a rectangle rotated away from us. However, the extra cues clearly identify the drawing in Figure 6.29 (b) as a window, and experience tells us that windows are rectangular rather than trapezoidal; thus, we perceive it

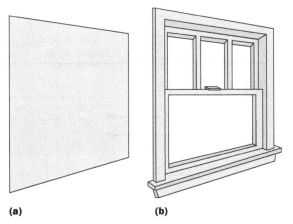

(a)   **(b)**

Figure 6.29 Form constancy. **(a)** This figure can be perceived as a trapezoid. **(b)** Because we recognise this figure as a window, we perceive its shape as rectangular.

as rectangular. Obviously, this effect will not be seen in members of cultures that do not have buildings fitted with rectangular windows (or seen by people unfamiliar with the object).

The process just described works for familiar objects. However, we often see unfamiliar objects whose size we do not already know. If we are to perceive the size and shape of unfamiliar objects accurately, we must know something about their distance from us. An object that produces a large retinal image is perceived as big if it is far away and small if it is close. Figure 6.30 illustrates this phenomenon. Although the two letterboxes are exactly the same size, the one that appears to be further away looks larger. If you turn the book upside-down and look at the figure again, the appearance of depth is greatly diminished, and the two letterboxes appear to be approximately the same size.

Perception of motion

Detection of movement is one of the most primitive aspects of visual perception. This ability is seen even in animals whose visual systems do not obtain detailed

Figure 6.30 Effect of perceived distance. Although both letterboxes are exactly the same size, the upper one looks larger because of the depth cues (perspective and texture) that surround it. If you turn the book upside-down and look at the picture, thus disrupting the depth cues, the letterboxes look the same size.

images of the environment. Of course, our visual system can detect more than the mere presence of movement. We can see what is moving in our environment and can detect the direction in which it is moving.

Adaptation and long-term modification

One of the most important characteristics of all sensory systems is that they show adaptation and rebound effects. For example, when you stare at a spot of colour, the adaptation of neurons in your visual system will produce a negative after-image if you shift your gaze to a neutral background; and if you put your hand in some hot water, warm water will feel cool to that hand immediately afterwards.

Motion, like other kinds of stimuli, can give rise to adaptation and after-effects. Tootell *et al.* (1995) presented participants with a display showing a series of concentric rings moving outwards, like the ripples in a pond. When the rings suddenly stopped moving, participants had the impression of the opposite movement – that the rings were moving inwards. During this time, the experimenters scanned the participants' brains to measure their metabolic activity. The scans showed increased activity in the motion-sensitive region of the visual association cortex, which lasted as long as the illusion did. Thus, the neural circuits that give rise to this illusion appear to be located in the same region that responds to actual moving stimuli.

Interpretation of a moving retinal image

As you read this book, your eyes are continuously moving. Naturally, the eye movements cause the image on your retina to move. You can also cause the retinal image to move by holding the book close to your face, looking

straight ahead and moving it back and forth. In the first case, when you were reading normally, you perceived the book as being still. In the second case, you perceived it as moving. Why does your brain interpret the movement differently in these two cases? Try another demonstration. Pick a letter on this page, stare at it and then move the book around, following the letter with your eyes. This time you will perceive the book as moving, even though the image on your retina remains stable. Thus, perception of movement requires coordination between movements of the image on the retina and those of the eyes.

Obviously, the visual system must know about eye movements in order to compensate for them in interpreting the significance of moving images on the retina. Another simple demonstration suggests the source of this information. Close your left eye and look slightly down and to the left. Gently press your finger against the outer corner of the upper eyelid of your right eye and make your right eye move a bit. The scene before you appears to be moving, even though you know better. This sensation of movement occurs because your finger – not your eye muscles – moved your eye. When your eye moves normally, perceptual mechanisms in your brain compensate for this movement. Even though the image on the retina moves, you perceive the environment as being stationary. However, if the image moves because the object itself moves or because you push your eye with your finger, you perceive movement (see Figure 6.31).

In general, if two objects of different size are seen moving relative to each other, the smaller one is perceived as moving and the larger one as standing still. We perceive people at a distance moving against a stable background and flies moving against an unmoving wall. Thus, when an experimenter moves a frame that encloses a stationary dot, we tend to see the dot move, not the frame. This phenomenon is also encountered when we perceive the moon racing behind the clouds, even though we know that the clouds, not the moon, are moving.

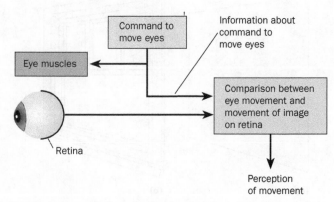

Figure 6.31 A schematic representation of the brain mechanisms responsible for the interpretation of a moving retinal image. This system must compensate for eye movements.

Perception and the environment – An international perspective

There is a small amount of evidence to suggest that differences in visual perception exist between Western people and those from East Asia – Westerners tend to perceive objects more analytically and in a more focused way; East Asians are more likely to attend to the context in which objects appear (i.e. they perceive a scene 'holistically') (Choi and Nisbett, 1998; Chua *et al.*, 2005a).

In one study where American and Japanese participants were asked to describe an underwater scene, Americans were more likely to describe objects in the water but the Japanese reported 60 per cent more information about the background environment (Masuda and Nisbett, 2001). In a different scenario, Americans were also able to identify an object (a tiger) more accurately than were the Japanese when it appeared against a different background from that in which it was originally seen. Why does this focal v. context effect occur? One reason might be the types of eye movement made by different cultures.

To test this hypothesis, Chua *et al.* (2005) asked American and Chinese participants to view scenes in which objects appeared against complex backgrounds. The eye movement of participants as they viewed the object and scene were then tracked. Compared with the Chinese, Americans focused on specific objects and more quickly. The Chinese made more **saccades** – eye movements – to the background.

The researchers suggest that this effect could partly be explained by socialisation. East Asians grow up and live in complex social networks in which paying attention to context is important (perhaps more important than focusing on individual objects or people); Westerners, however, are educated to value individuality and independence (and eye movement is, therefore, directed accordingly). This extends even to cultural products. An analysis of advertising and popular texts in Western and Asian (Korea, Japan, China)/Mexican cultures found that the latter were more individualistic and less collectivistic (Morling and Lamoreaux, 2008).

Similar cultural effects can occur when rating facial expressions. Participants in one experiment were asked to rate the degree of emotion shown in cartoons depicting happy, sad, angry or neutral facial expressions. These faces were surrounded by other people expressing the same or different emotion (Masuda *et al.*, 2008). The surrounding stimuli influenced the ratings of Japanese participants significantly more than they did Westerners. This was evidenced by eye-tracking data. The Japanese spent more time looking at the surrounding stimuli than did the Westerners. The lack of self-absorption of Japanese participants was also seen in an experiment in which people completed a verbal fluidity task – where there was an opportunity to cheat – in front of a mirror (Heine *et al.*, 2008). North Americans were more self-critical and less likely to cheat in front of the mirror; the Japanese participants were unaffected by the presence of a mirror.

Different nations and different cultures as well as groups within those nations and cultures can also produce art that can be as similar as it is different. Masuda *et al.* (2008) analysed the artistic styles in a total of 365 Western and 218 Eastern landscapes and 286 and 151 portrait paintings. Eastern landscape art was more likely to place the horizon higher than was Western art, which created more space for field information. For portrait paintings, the size of the models was smaller in the Eastern sample; conversely, the Western sample was less likely to include more background.

In a second study, groups of American and Taiwanese, Korean, Japanese and Chinese students were asked to draw and photograph landscapes and portraits. The use of context was greater in both types of stimuli in the Eastern sample. It was more likely to draw the horizon in a high position and draw more objects. It was also more likely to use the zoom function to minimise the size of the model in portrait photographs and make the context larger. Finally, American and East Asians students were asked to rate their preference for portrait photographs where the model and the background varied. Japanese participants were significantly less likely to prefer narrow backgrounds and larger models.

The findings are consistent with those of other studies. Miyamoto *et al.* (2006) took photographs of significant cultural institutions in the US and Japan. These included schools, post offices, hotels, etc. The institutions in Japan featured more objects and were visually more complex.

Why do these differences occur? Masuda *et al.* (2008) cite Cohen *et al's* insider/outsider view of how we organise information about the world (Cohen and Gunz, 2002; Cohen *et al.*, 2007). The insider is dominant in the West – this person dwells on his/her own private experiences and sees the world from his/her point of view. The outsider views the world from the point of view of an outsider looking at the self. It seems as if these roles can change. For example, people who have been exposed to Japanese scenes for a few minutes notice more context than those who are exposed to American scenes (Miyamoto *et al.*, 2006).

Does language affect our understanding of spatial relations?

You saw in the Controversies in Psychological Science section on colour and language how culture/language can influence visual perception. An even more intriguing interaction can occur when people are asked to describe directions, and more intriguing still is the community which has helped illuminate this anomaly and which is described by Deutscher (2010). The Guugu Yimithirr is a population of around 1,000 who dwell 30 miles north of Cookstown in North East Australia and have a particularly well-known claim to fame.

When Captain Cook disembarked there in 1770 and encountered a strange animal, he was told that it was a 'kanguroo'. Later explorers were baffled, however, because none of the Aborigines encountered had heard of such an animal and, by all accounts, thought they were being taught the English word for it. Fifty years later another naval explorer, Phillips King, arrived and was told that the bouncy animal was 'minnor' or 'meenuah'. What created this confusion? And which was correct? The answer came in 1971 when an anthropologist called John Haviland discovered that the Guugu Yimithirr described one type of kangaroo as gangurru. The name given by them to other types of kangaroo was a variant of what was told to King – the word meant 'meat' or 'edible animal'. They distinguished between the two types.

But the Guugu Yimithirr also have an unusual way of constructing other expressions: spatial relations. When we give directions, we do so using one of two frames of refer-ence. If someone wants to find out where the nearest coffee shop is, you would either say 'After the newsagent, turn left and then, after the hairdresser's, turn right' or 'After the newsagent, turn west, then head north and turn north east'. The first, the one most people use, is ego-centric and the two axes of right and left depend on the orientation of the body. The second type depends on geographical coordi-nates (which is, objectively, more accurate but needs to be computed and is, therefore, less easy to use day-to-day).

The peculiarity of the Guugu Yimithirr is that they use this form, not the ego-centric form, to describe spatial relations. They have no word for left, right, in front of or behind when referring to object location. Instead, they use cardinal directions – north, south, east and west. This means that any direction is given in relation to what is seen in front of them. If a person described the movement of an actor on a television programme, then the directions would depend on the position of the television (not the actor). If the television was moved, the type of direction would move. If they read a book, a character would be said to be to the west of a woman; if the book was rotated, the man would be to the north of the woman. Even memories are recalled in this way. (A similar phenomenon is seen in the Tzeltal highland tribe of South East Mexico – they describe directions in relation to downhill, uphill and across.) They do understand the concepts of left and right in English.

This form of thinking might suggest that they have a different way of constructing reality and the external world. Let's see. Take a look at the Figure 6.32 and remem-ber the position of the objects on the table. Do that now.

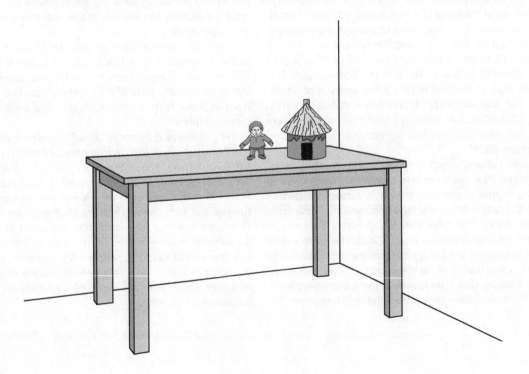

Figure 6.32

Now look at Figure 6.33 and again remember the position of the objects. Do that now.

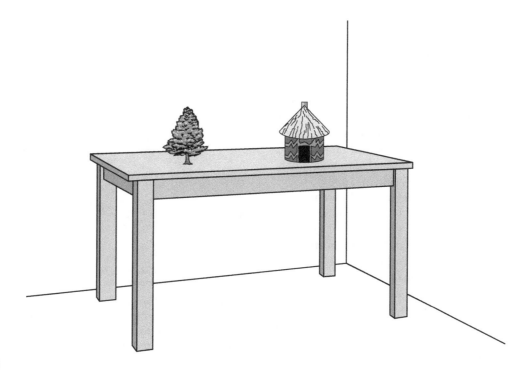

Figure 6.33

Finally, without looking at the two figures you have just seen, look at Figure 6.34 and indicate where you think the tree should go based on your memory of its position in the previous figure.

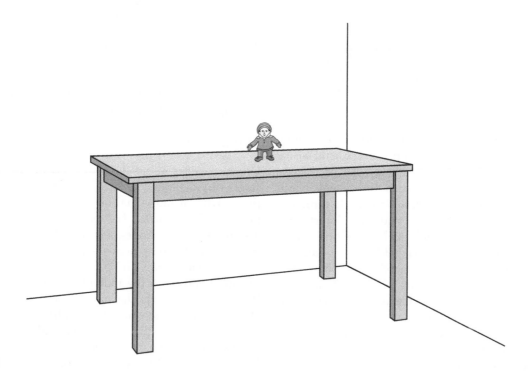

Figure 6.34

Not too difficult was it? Quite obvious, in fact. Except, to a member of the Guugu Yimithirr, there was nothing obvious about it. In fact, they would have placed the tree to the right of the doll, not the left as you did. The reason for this is that the tables in the first two figures were not in the same orientation – the second was rotated 180 degrees. They, therefore, located the tree to the south of the doll, taking into account the rotation which we ignored. The way in which they constructed and communicated spatial relations affected their memory and their decision to locate the tree. Language had affected reality.

This finding has been replicated using real tables placed in different rooms (Levinson *et al.*, 2002), although others have queried this finding (Li and Gleitman, 2002).

A final note about language and space. A recent study exploited the fact that different languages have different writing systems (Bergen and Lau, 2012). Mandarin Chinese is written left to right and top to bottom. In Taiwan, letters are written top to bottom but right to left. In Bergen and Lau's experiment Mandarin Chinese, Taiwanese and English speakers were asked to arrange the development of, for example, a frog from tadpole onwards. The stages of development were depicted on cards which the participants would arrange. The experimenters found that the English speakers plotted time from left to right, as did the majority of Mandarin Chinese speakers. The Taiwanese participants, however, were just as likely to plot time from left to right, as they were top to bottom. Some also depicted the stages going from right to left, suggesting that the way in which time is spatially represented can be influenced by writing system.

Brain mechanisms of visual perception

Although the eyes contain the photoreceptors that detect areas of different brightnesses and colours, perception takes place in the brain. The optic nerves send visual information to the thalamus, which relays the information to the primary visual cortex located in the occipital lobe at the back of the brain (see Chapters 4 and 5). In turn, neurons in the primary visual cortex send visual information to two successive levels of the visual association cortex. The first level, located in the occipital lobe, surrounds the primary visual cortex. The second level is divided into two parts, one in the middle of the parietal lobe and one in the lower part of the temporal lobe. Figure 6.35 illustrates the various regions involved in visual perception.

Visual perception by the brain is often described as a hierarchy of information processing. According to this scheme, circuits of neurons analyse particular aspects of

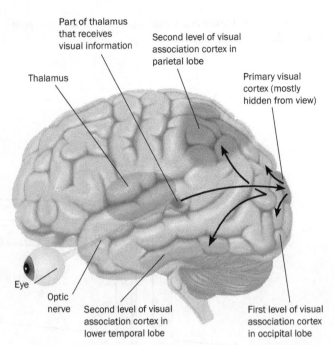

Figure 6.35 The visual system of the brain. Arrows represent the flow of visual information. Sensory information from the eye is transmitted through the optic nerve to the thalamus, and from there it is relayed to the primary visual cortex. The results of the analysis performed there are sent to the visual association cortex of the occipital lobe (first level) and then on to that of the temporal lobe and parietal lobe (second level). At each stage, additional analysis takes place.

visual information and send the results of their analysis on to another circuit, which performs further analysis. At each step in the process, successively more complex features are analysed. Eventually, the process leads to the perception of the scene and of all the objects in it. The higher levels of the perceptual process interact with memories: the viewer recognises familiar objects and learns the appearance of new, unfamiliar ones. Deprivation of the visual system or damage to it during the early years of development can have significant consequences for visual function.

The primary visual cortex

Our knowledge about the characteristics of the earliest stages of visual analysis has come from investigations of the activity of individual neurons in the thalamus and primary visual cortex. For example, Hubel and Wiesel inserted microelectrodes – extremely fine wires having microscopically sharp points – into various regions of the visual system of cats and monkeys to detect the action potentials produced by individual neurons (Hubel and Wiesel, 1977, 1979). The signals detected by the microelectrodes are electronically amplified and sent to a recording device so that they can be studied later.

After positioning a microelectrode close to a neuron, Hubel and Wiesel presented various stimuli on a large screen in front of the anaesthetised animal. The anaesthesia makes the animal unconscious but does not prevent neurons in the visual system from responding. The researchers moved a stimulus around on the screen until they located the point where it had the largest effect on the electrical activity of the neuron. Next, they presented the animal with stimuli of various shapes in order to learn which ones produced the greatest response from the neuron.

From their experiments, Hubel and Wiesel (1977, 1979) concluded that the geography of the visual field is retained in the primary visual cortex. That is, the surface of the retina is 'mapped' on the surface of the primary visual cortex. However, this map on the brain is distorted, with the largest amount of area given to the centre of the visual field. The map is actually like a mosaic. Each piece of the mosaic (usually called a module) consists of a block of tissue, approximately 0.5 × 0.7mm in size and containing approximately 150,000 neurons.

All of the neurons within a module receive information from the same small region of the retina. The primary visual cortex contains approximately 2,500 of these modules. Because each module in the visual cortex receives information from a small region of the retina, that means that it receives information from a small region of the visual field – the scene that the eye is viewing. If you looked at the scene before you through a straw, you would see the amount of information received by an individual module. Hubel and Wiesel found that neural circuits within each module analysed various characteristics of their own particular part of the visual field, that is, of their **receptive field**. Some circuits detected the presence of lines passing through the region and signalled the orientation of these lines (that

is, the angle they made with respect to the horizon). Other circuits detected the thickness of these lines. Others detected movement and its direction. Still others detected colours.

Because each module in the primary visual cortex receives information about only a restricted area of the visual field, the information must be combined somehow for perception to take place. This combination takes place in the visual association cortex.

The visual association cortex

The first level of the visual association cortex, which surrounds the primary visual cortex, contains several subdivisions, each of which contains a map of the visual scene. Each subdivision receives information from different types of neural circuit within the modules of the primary visual cortex. One subdivision receives information about the orientation and widths of lines and edges and is involved in perception of shapes. Another subdivision receives information about movement and keeps track of the relative movements of objects (and may help compensate for movements of the eyes as we scan the scene in front of us). Yet another subdivision receives information concerning colour (Zeki, 1993; Milner, 1998). You can see these subdivisions in Figure 6.36.

The two regions of the second level of the visual association cortex put together the information gathered and processed by the various subdivisions of the first level. Information about shape, movement and colour is combined in the visual association cortex in the lower part of the temporal lobe. Three-dimensional

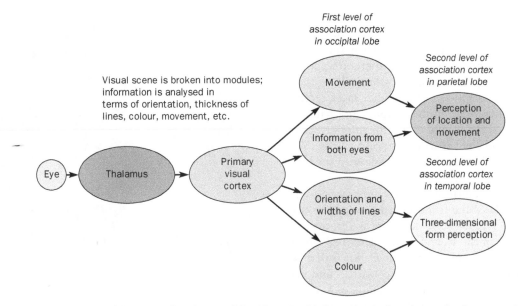

Figure 6.36 Schematic diagram of the types of analysis performed on visual information in the primary visual cortex and the various regions of the visual association cortex.

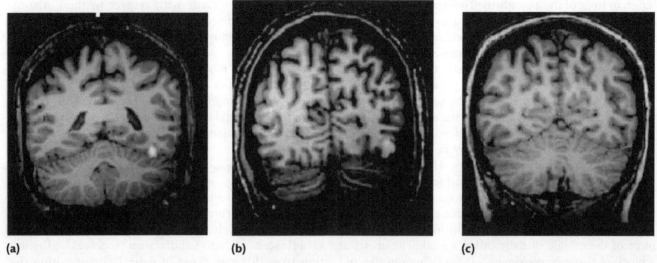

Figure 6.37 The areas involved in face processing, as illustrated by neuroimaging scans: the frontal gyrus **(a)**, the interior occipital gyrus **(b)** and the superior temporal sulcus **(c)**.

form perception takes place here. The visual association cortex in the parietal lobe is responsible for perception of the location of objects. It integrates information from the first level of the visual association cortex with information from the motor system and the body senses about movements of the eyes, head and body.

The 'special' case of faces: evidence from neuroimaging

You saw in an earlier section, that faces are thought to be special stimuli in visual perception. Their specialness has been enhanced by evidence that there are specific brain regions that appear to respond selectively to them. For example, the perception of unfamiliar faces recruits a specific set of brain areas in the occipital and temporal lobe – these include the frontal gyrus, the inferior occipital gyrus (IOG) and the superior temporal sulcus (STS) (Natu and O'Toole, 2011), which you can see in the brain scans in Figure 6.37.

Within these regions, there are thought to be face-selective regions: the middle of the frontal gyrus, called the **fusiform face area** (FFA) (as seen in Figure 6.38), and the occipital face area in the second region described earlier, for example. Neuroimaging studies have shown that the face-specific effects in the STS are not consistent and may depend on whether the stimulus is dynamic or static. If the stimulus is moving, activation here is more consistent (Fox *et al.*, 2009).

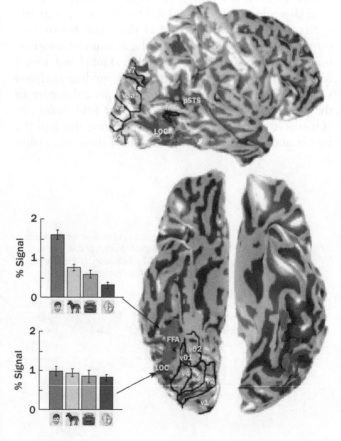

Figure 6.38 Some of the areas of the brain responding to faces and other animate and inanimate objects (Fox *et al.*, 2009).

Haxby *et al.* (2000) have proposed that the brain's involvement in face processing can be explained by a distributed neural model. Specifically, they suggest that first, there are core areas dedicated to face processing specifically, and these areas are the ones described above. Second, there are regions which process the invariant features of the face – such as the position of the eyes, nose, mouth and so on – and these are the fusiform gyrus and the IOG. Features of the face which can change, such as its expression or gaze, are processed by the posterior STS.

In terms of more complex features of processing, they suggest that connections between the lateral frontal gyrus and the anterior temporal lobe mediate our ability to code personal identity in a face, as well as the name associated with it and the biography of the person. The superior temporal sulcus is connected to the intra-parietal sulcus and this region allows us to direct our attention to faces. Other regions, such as the amygdala, insula and limbic system, mediate the ability to extract emotion from a face.

The recognition of famous faces appears to recruit the fusiform gyrus and the anterior or middle temporal cortex with personally familiar faces recruiting even more areas for reasons described below. The FFA adapts fairly quickly to repeated presentations – so activation becomes less when we see the same face over and over again. However, this activation re-starts when our viewpoint of the face changes (Andrews and Ewbank, 2004; Ewbank and Andrews, 2008).

At the specific level of familiar faces – the faces which we know intimately such as a friend or family member – Gobbini and Haxby (2007) have proposed the **familiar face recognition model** which is based on fMRI studies of people's responses to the faces of their friends, family and children. Processing familiar faces is much more complex than processing an unfamiliar face or a famous one because the emotional and autobiographical baggage which accompanies such a face is greater. Gobbini and Haxby have argued that knowledge of the traits of the individual's face and the ability to evaluate the mental state of the face of a familiar person is mediated by an area called the anterior paracingulate cortex. Biographical and semantic information associated with the face is mediated by the anterior temporal cortex. Autobiographical memories associated with the face activate the precuneus and posterior cingulate cortex, with emotion mediated by the typical regions already described above.

Brain damage and visual perception

Schneider (1969) had proposed that there were two major visual system pathways: a geniculostrate pathway which was responsible for identifying stimuli and discriminating between patterns, and a retinotectal pathway which was responsible for locating objects in space. Schneider's theory has since been modified, although the idea that different brain regions are responsible for the perception of an object's qualities and its location is valid.

Ungerleider and Mishkin (1982), for example, suggested that different parts of the brain were involved in object identification and object location: the appreciation of an object's qualities was the role of the inferior temporal cortex; the ability to locate an object was the role of the posterior parietal cortex. Primates with posterior parietal cortex lesions make consistent errors in accurately reaching out for or grasping objects although their ability to discriminate between objects is intact. Similar damage in humans also results in difficulties performing visuospatial tasks such as estimating length and distance (Von Cramon and Kerkhoff, 1993; Jeannerod *et al.*, 1994).

The parietal cortex (see Chapter 4) plays an important role in visually guiding movement and in grasping or manipulating objects (Sakata, 1997). Importantly, Ungerleider and Mishkin distinguished between a ventral and dorsal pathway or stream which projected from the primary visual cortex (PVC) to these areas. Thus, although originating in the PVC, the two pathways were independent and projected to different areas of the brain (to the occipitotemporal and the posterior half of the parietal cortex, respectively). The ventral stream was later extended to the ventrolateral and dorsolateral prefrontal cortex (ALPFC) (Kravitz *et al.*, 2011).

Goodale and Milner (1992) and Milner and Goodale (1995) developed this idea that what was important was not 'what' and 'where', but 'what' and 'how'. In Ungerleider and Mishkin's model, the ventral stream processed the 'what' component of visual perception (identification of an object) whereas the dorsal stream processed the 'where' component (the spatial location of an object). Goodale and Milner's research has focused on the 'what' and 'how' areas. The brain regions representing these streams can be seen in Figure 6.39.

Goodale and Milner have made an extensive study of DF, a woman with substantial bilateral damage to the occipital cortex (but sparing the PVC) resulting from carbon monoxide poisoning (Goodale and Milner, 1992; Milner and Goodale, 1995). DF is unable to discriminate between geometric shapes and is unable to recognise or identify objects, despite having no language or visual sensory impairment (Milner *et al.*, 1991). That is, she exhibits visual form agnosia (agnosia is described in more detail in a later section). DF is able to respond to objects. For example, she can place her hand into a slot of varying orientations or grasp blocks (Goodale *et al.*, 1991). However, when she is asked to estimate the orientation of the slot or the width of the box by verbally reporting or by gesturing, she is unable to do so. Why?

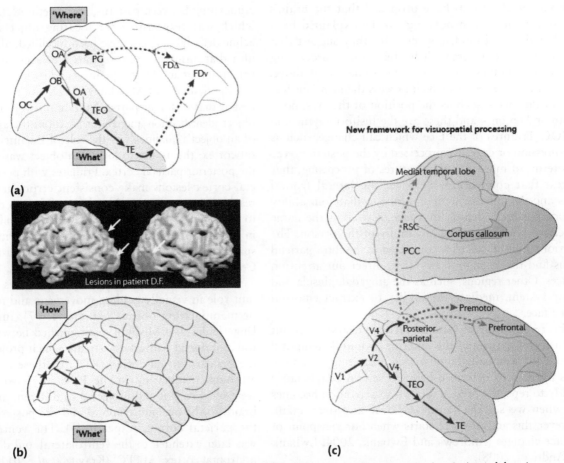

Figure 6.39 Pathways in the brain that were originally thought to mediate where a stimulus is perceived and what is **(a)** and how a stimulus is perceived **(b)** based on findings from patients such as DF (see brain scans in the middle). The two brain figures on the right **(c)** show how the ventral ('what') stream has been extended to include some of the frontal areas of the brain (Kravitz et al., 2011).

DF may be using the intact visuomotor processing system in the parietal cortex to perform the grasping and orientation tasks (Milner and Goodale, 1995; Milner, 1998). The guidance of motor behaviour relies on a primitive dorsal stream in the parietal cortex which is spared in DF. This is why the execution of her motor behaviour is accurate. When asked to indicate which of two boxes is a rectangle and which is a square, she can respond correctly when holding the boxes but less correctly when making a verbal response (Murphy et al., 1996). DF would make partial movements towards one of the boxes before correcting herself. When these initial reaches were analysed, they showed the same level of accuracy as if she had verbally reported which box was which. Did DF monitor the size of her anticipatory grip before making a decision?

There is evidence that she does. When asked to look at a series of lines of varying orientation and then copy them on a separate piece of paper, DF would outline the line in the air before making a copy. When asked not to do this, her copies were still relatively accurate. She found the task

easier if she imagined herself drawing the line: when she was asked to copy the line immediately – thereby preventing rehearsal from taking place – she failed (Dijkerman and Milner, 1997). DF must have generated a motor image of the lines to allow her to accomplish this task, a behaviour which would have been made possible by intact functioning of the frontal and parietal lobes.

On the basis of DF's behaviour, research from neuroimaging studies of motor movement and vision, and animal lesions to parietal and occipital areas, Milner and Goodale (1995) propose that the dorsal stream sends information about object characteristics and orientation that is related to movement from the primary visual cortex to the parietal cortex. Damage to the ventral stream, which projects to the inferior temporal cortex, is what is responsible for DF's inability to access perceptual information. The dorsal stream is automatic, non-conscious and involves visually guided action, not spatial perception whereas the ventral stream produces the representations that are available to conscious experience.

Some have argued (Kravitz *et al.*, 2011) that the dorsal stream is in fact three streams with one mediating spatial working memory (see Chapter 8), another mediating visually guided action and a third, spatial navigation. These go to the parieto-PFC, parieto-premotor cortex and parieto-medial temporal cortex, respectively. This is a challenge to the 'what' and 'how' model because Kravitz *et al.* argue that the different streams support different functions because of the cortical areas they project to.

Projections to the primary visual cortex

Two specific pathways – the parvocellular (P) and magnocellular (M) pathways – run from the retina to the cortex and terminate in different layers of the primary visual cortex (V1). Other layers of V1 project to other dorsal and ventral stream areas. Layers 2 and 3 of V1, for example, provide input to the ventral stream areas whereas layer 4B sends input to dorsal stream areas. Layer 4B also receives input from the M and P pathways and projects to areas such as V5, a region known to be involved in motion perception. Many other circuits such as this are made within the visual system but comparatively little is known about how functionally relevant such connections are or how different types of cell contribute to the circuitry. One study has shown that different types of neurons in area V1 receive different signals from the M and P pathways and forward this information to other specific cortical areas (Yabuta *et al.*, 2001). The results of the study suggest that if two types of cell project to different layers, perhaps each type carries different types of information in the cortical visual system.

Perceptual disorders

When the brain is damaged and visual perception is impaired, the patient is said to exhibit a **perceptual disorder**. There are several perceptual disorders and each is associated with damage to different parts of the visual system. It is important to note that these disorders are strictly perceptual, that is, there is no underlying impairment in sensation (patients retain visual acuity and the ability to tell light from dark and so on). The basic visual sensory system itself is, therefore, unimpaired. Three of the most important perceptual disorders are blindsight, agnosia and spatial neglect. Each is important in its own way because they demonstrate how brain damage can affect different aspects of visual perception.

Blindsight

When the primary visual cortex is damaged, a person becomes blind in some portion of the visual field. Some individuals, however, can lose substantial areas of the PVC and yet show evidence of perceiving objects despite being 'cortically blind'. This phenomenon is called **blindsight** (Weiskrantz, 1986, 1997) because although patients are unable to see properties of objects they are aware of other aspects such as movement of objects. Moving objects are better detected than still ones, objects can be located if they are pointed at and they can detect movement and colour, despite being 'unable' to see the stimuli. (There are equivalent phenomena in the auditory and somatosensory systems called deaf hearing and blindtouch.)

The earliest case of blindsight was reported at the beginning of the last century (Riddoch, 1917). Riddoch was an army medical officer who had made a study of soldiers whose primary visual cortex had been damaged by gunshot wounds. Although none of the patients could directly describe objects placed in front of them (neither shape, form nor colour), they were conscious of the movement of the objects, despite the movement being 'vague and shadowy'. This suggested to Riddoch that some residual visual ability in the PVC remained which allowed the perception of object motion but no other aspect of visual perception. Some patients need to be prompted to 'guess' (Blindsight Type 1) whereas others will report vague sensations (Blindsight Type 2) although both types claim that they cannot see anything. That the PVC is damaged led to the hypothesis that this area was responsible for conscious visual perception (Radoeva *et al.*, 2008).

Since Riddoch's study, several other cases of blindsight have been reported, notably Larry Weiskrantz's famous patient, DB (Weiskrantz, 1986). DB had undergone surgery for a brain tumour, which necessitated removal of the area of the visual cortex in the right occipital lobe. This surgery resulted in a scotoma – an area of complete blindness in the visual field. DB could indicate whether a stick was horizontal or vertical, could point to the location of an object when instructed, and could detect whether an object was present or absent. Other tasks presented greater difficulty: DB could not distinguish a triangle from a cross or a curved triangle from a normal one. The most intriguing feature of DB's behaviour, however, was a lack of awareness of the stimuli presented. According to DB, he 'couldn't see anything' when test stimuli were seen. Why could DB, and patients like DB, make perceptual decisions despite being unaware of visual stimuli?

One hypothesis suggests that perceptual tasks can be completed successfully because stray light emitted by stimuli makes its way from the intact field of vision because it reflects from surfaces outside the eye area – what is called extraocular scatter (Cowey, 2004). The stray light hypothesis, however, appears to be an unlikely explanation because DB is able to make perceptual decisions in the presence of strong ambient light which reduces the amount of stray light emitted by stimuli. More to the point, this theory does not explain how DB can still make decisions based on the spatial dimensions of objects.

An alternative hypothesis is that the ability is attributable to the degrading of normal vision, possibly due to the presence of some residual striatal cortex ('islands' of PVC cortex that are undamaged) (Wessinger et al., 1999). Implicit in this hypothesis is the notion that residual abilities are not attributable to the functioning of another visual system pathway. There are ten known pathways from the retina to the brain (Stoerig and Cowey, 1997). As you have seen, there appear to be two distinct pathways in the visual system which mediate different aspects of vision. The visual location of objects, for example, is thought to be a function of a system which includes the superior colliculus, the posterior thalamus and areas 20 and 21, whereas the analysis of visual form, pattern or colour is thought to be a function of the geniculostriate system which sends projections from the retina to the lateral geniculate nucleus, then to areas 17, 18 and 19, and then to areas 20 and 21. Blindsight could, therefore, conceivably be due to a disconnection between these two systems. Again, there are arguments against this hypothesis.

Curiously, DB, although unable to 'see' objects when presented to him, even 30 years after his deficit was first studied, appears to be aware of a visual 'after-image' after a stimulus on a monitor is switched off (Weiskrantz et al., 2002). The colour and spatial structure of the stimulus can be described, a phenomenon that is correlated with increased PFC activity (Weiskrantz et al., 2003). It is unclear whether this ability is due to spared striate cortex, however, because DB has surgical clips which prevent him from undergoing an MRI scan which would demarcate the preserved cortex.

Visual agnosia

Patients with posterior lesions to the left or right hemisphere sometimes have considerable difficulty in recognising objects, despite having intact sensory systems. We saw an example of this in an earlier section when we discussed the perceptual impairments seen in patient DF. This disorder is called agnosia (literally 'without knowledge'), a term coined by Sigmund Freud. Agnosia can occur in any sense (tactile agnosia refers to the inability to recognise an object by touch, for example) but **visual agnosia** is the most common type (Farah, 1990; Farah and Ratcliff, 1994).

The existence of specific types of agnosia is a controversial topic in perception and neuropsychology. A distinction is usually made between two types of visual agnosia: associative and apperceptive. **Apperceptive agnosia** is the inability to recognise objects whereas **associative agnosia** is the inability to make meaningful associations

to objects that are visually presented. Some neuropsychologists have argued that the boundaries between these two types are 'fuzzy' (DeRenzi and Lucchelli, 1993), and other sub-types of visual agnosia have been suggested (Humphreys and Riddoch, 1987a). Apperceptive agnosics have a severe impairment in the ability to copy drawings, as patient DF did. Associative agnosics, conversely, can copy accurately but are unable to identify their drawings. For example, Humphreys and Riddoch's patient, HJA, spent six hours completing an accurate drawing but was unable to identify it when he had finished. Figure 6.40 shows you an example of HJA's drawings.

There has been considerable debate concerning the specificity of visual object agnosia, that is, whether some patients are able to recognise some categories of object but not others (Newcombe et al., 1994). The commonest dissociation is seen between living and non-living things. Generally, it has been found that recognition of living objects (such as animals) is less accurate in agnosic patients than is recognition of non-living objects (Warrington and Shallice, 1984; Silveri et al., 1997). To determine whether different brain regions were responsible for this dissociation, Martin et al. (1996) conducted a PET study of healthy individuals' brain activity as the subjects named pictures of tools or animals. Both categories of words were associated with activation in the visual cortex and Broca's area (because the participants saw and spoke) but some areas were activated by the naming of animals (left occipital region) and others by the naming of tools (right premotor regions).

Some psychologists, however, have argued that these studies do not show differences between the categories

Figure 6.40 The drawing of a building by HJA reflects great attention but he was unable to name it. The line drawings beneath are of very simple objects but HJA was unable to name them.

Source: Humphreys and Riddoch (1987). *To See or Not to See*. Andover: Psychology Press, reprinted by permission of Cengage/Thomson Learning.

of object but between the ways in which these two different types of stimulus are presented. Parkin and Stewart (1993), for example, have suggested that it is more difficult to recognise drawings of animate than inanimate objects. An inanimate object, such as a cup, is a lot less detailed than an animate object, such as a fly. The dissociation seen in agnosic patients, therefore, may be due to the complexity and/or familiarity of the perceived stimulus. Stewart *et al.* (1992) have suggested that when these artefacts are controlled for, these dissociations disappear. However, the issue continues to be controversial. Sheridan and Humphreys (1993), for example, have shown that patients show such dissociations even under well-controlled conditions and a recent review suggests that specific brain regions may mediate the recognition of objects from different semantic categories (Gainotti, 2000).

Prosopagnosia

A more category-specific form of agnosia is **prosopagnosia**. Some individuals with damage to specific areas of the posterior right hemisphere (and sometimes left and right hemispheres) show an impairment in the ability to recognise familiar faces. This condition is known as prosopagnosia ('loss of knowledge for faces'). Some patients are unable to recognise famous faces (Warrington and James, 1967) or familiar people such as spouses (DeRenzi,

Barry Wainwright, who suffers from prosopagnosia: 'If I look at a photograph of myself, I don't know it's me. I don't recognise my wife or my seven children, either, even when I'm looking right at them.'

Source: Guardian News & Media Ltd: Fabio De Paola.

1986). This disorder, while rare, can have dramatic effects on a person's everyday life. For example, here are some comments from patients with prosopagnosia on how their condition affects them (Yardley *et al.*, 2008):

> 'I was getting off a bus and somebody got on it and grabbed me, and I pushed them out of the way and it was only when they opened their mouth that I realized it was my own mother.'
>
> 'Sometimes if I see someone and I'm not sure if I know them I just try and keep out of their way and hope they don't see me, 'cause I don't know how to act.'
>
> 'The condition makes me less interested in the social events, the partying, the getting to know lots of people, because that just gives me a whole set of things I'll get wrong.'
>
> 'I'd try, spend three days chatting up some girl and then cut her dead in the street without knowing that I'd done it.'

Much of the recent neuropsychological work on face recognition has exploited neuroimaging techniques in order to determine whether different regions of the human brain respond to faces selectively. One controversy in the area surrounds whether such selective activation is specific to faces or to some other perceptual aspect of faces, such as whether they appear in greyscale or in two-tone. Kanwisher *et al.* (1998), for example, found that the brain region which you encountered in the earlier section, the human fusiform face area (HFFA), was significantly activated when people viewed upright and inverted greyscale faces. Inverted two-tone faces, however, were associated with significantly reduced brain activation. The results suggest that the HFFA does not respond specifically to low-level features of faces (if it did, the inverted and upright two-tone faces would have produced similar activation) but does respond to face stimuli. The authors acknowledge, however, that this may not be the only brain region specialised for face processing.

Current neuroimaging data make HFFA one of the strong contenders for the role of the brain's primary face processor, as an earlier section showed. However, could the selectivity of this area be because we are expert at recognising faces and that the area responds to familiar stimuli which we are expert at identifying? Rhodes *et al.* (2004) set up two experiments in which people were either trained or were not trained to recognise Lepidoptera (moths and butterflies). Brain activation was monitored using fMRI while participants viewed faces and Lepidoptera. In the second experiment, experts in identifying moths and butterflies passively watched examples of the species while brain activity was recorded. In the first experiment, the FFA was more significantly activated when people watched faces than Lepidoptera, regardless of whether people had been trained to recognise examples of the species. In the second experiment, activation was greater in the FFA when the butterfly experts watched faces than Lepidoptera. There was no overlap in the areas activated by faces and moths and butterflies. The results suggest that the FFA contains neurons that allow 'individuation' of (i.e. discrimination between) faces.

Spatial neglect

Patients with lesions in the right parietotemporal cortex sometimes have difficulty in perceiving objects to their left (Vallar, 1998). In fact, in 80 per cent of patients with right hemisphere stroke, patients are unable to attend automatically to any stimuli in left space (Halligan and Marshall, 1994). This is called **spatial neglect** (or unilateral spatial hemineglect) and occurs on the side of the body that is contralateral to the side of the brain damage (the regions damaged can be seen in Figure 6.41). Neglect for the left

side is more common than right neglect (which would be caused by damage to the left hemisphere).

Patients exhibiting spatial neglect behave as if half of the world does not exist. They may forget to attend to their clothing on the left-hand side, neglect food on the left side of the plate or ignore the left-hand side of their newspaper (Halligan and Cockburn, 1993; Halligan and Marshall, 1994).

Spatial neglect patients show a characteristic pattern of behaviour on visuospatial tests. For example, if they are required to bisect lines of varying length, they will err to the right. If they are presented with an array of stimuli (such as small lines) and asked to mark off as many as possible, they mark off those on the right-hand side but fail to mark off those on the left, as seen in Figure 6.42.

Similarly, neglect patients, when asked to draw (or mentally imagine a scene) fail to draw or report details from the left side of the object or image (Guariglia *et al.*, 1993; Halligan and Marshall, 1994). Sometimes, patients will transfer details from the left to the right-hand side, as seen in Figure 6.43. This is called **allesthesia** or **allochiria** (Meador *et al.*, 1991).

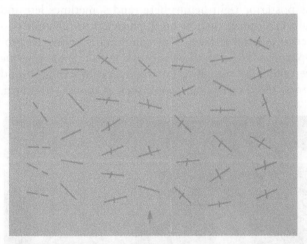

Figure 6.42 The line cancellation task. Spatial neglect patients consistently neglect one side of the display (in this example, the left side).

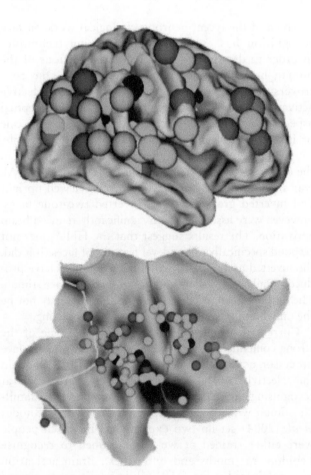

Figure 6.41 The areas of the brain damaged in spatial neglect patients.

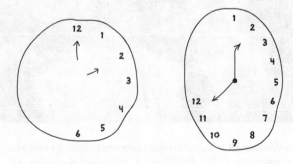

Figure 6.43 The famous clock-drawing task at which spatial neglect patients are impaired. Patients either neglect the numerals on the left side completely or bunch them up on the right.

The examples shown in Figures 6.45(a) and 6.45(b) illustrate the profound consequences that brain damage can have on perceptual behaviour, not just in terms of behavioural impairment but also in terms of disruption to a patient's life and work.

The reasons for spatial neglect are unclear (see Halligan and Marshall, 1994, and Mozer *et al.*, 1997, for a discussion).

Psychology in action: How does brain injury affect artists?

Losing the ability to speak, to recall information, or to organise and plan everyday life efficiently are all unwelcome intruders in the world of the normally functioning. But what if the disrupted function is essential to the person's life and provides him or her with a livelihood? Beethoven composed symphonies, Evelyn Glennie plays exceptional xylophone, Stevie Wonder is an accomplished keyboardist; even James Joyce managed to produce *Ulysses* and *Finnegan's Wake* despite his chronic sight loss (although this is thought to explain some of Joyce's eccentric text). None of these, however, despite their sensory losses, sustained brain injury. Chatterjee (2004) has reviewed the type of effects brain injury has on an artist's performance and output.

The loss of the ability to perceive colour is clearly one of the most challenging problems for an artist who exploits his or her chromatic palette. Sacks (1995) describes an artist who developed an injury leaving him **achromatopsic** – the artist's world appeared 'dirty grey' and he reported being unable to imagine colours (or even being able to dream in colour). Before the accident leading to the injury, the patient painted colourful, abstract creations; after the accident, the paintings became figurative and abstract. Contrast, figure and form were good as was the patient's ability to understand and describe colour but his use of colour became haphazard.

Unilateral spatial neglect has more intriguing, if predictable, consequences. Jung (1974) described four early cases of painters who developed neglect following brain injury. One, the German artist Lovis Corinth, had suffered a right hemisphere stroke. His painting changed dramatically: the contours on the left of his work disappeared and details became misplaced. Blanke *et al.* (2003) reported the case of a 71-year-old artist who could colour the right side of her paintings normally and evenly but paid minimal attention to the left. Figure 6.44 gives an example of the patient's art following injury. Neglect for colour was greater than neglect for form in the majority of the patient's paintings. Painter IK showed right neglect where entire canvasses would be created in exuberant colour but the right side lacked detail and form (Marsh and Philwin, 1987).

Perhaps the most famous example of unilateral spatial neglect is the Italian film director, Federico Fellini, whose disorder was reported by Cantagallo and Della Sala (1998). At the age of 73, Fellini suffered a stroke in the middle cerebral artery of the right parietal lobe that caused left extrapersonal

Drawing showing left colour neglect
Arrow indicates the middle of the page.

Figure 6.44 The colour neglect seen in a drawing by Blanke *et al.'s* patient.

Source: Plate 6.2 from *Human Neuropsychology*, 2nd edn, Pearson/Prentice Hall (Martin, G.N., 2006). Image kindly provided by Dr Olaf Blanke.

spatial neglect that persisted for two months. As well as being a celebrated film director, Fellini was an accomplished cartoonist and his completion of neglect tests was peppered with his cartoonish embellishments. His original cartoons showed neglect of the left side. Figures 6.45(a) and 6.45(b) illustrate some of Fellini's attempts.

Fellini's neglect did not appear to be representational (he could imagine both sides of his visual field) and he was completely aware of his deficits. Unlike patients in previous reports, his increased awareness did not lead to a decrease in his neglect (Guariglia *et al.*, 1993).

As Fellini did, some artists can recover their ability to attend to the left to some extent; sometimes they will use broader strokes than normal or may be more expressive, as the painters Loring Hughes and Lovis Corinth found.

Psychology in action: *Continued*

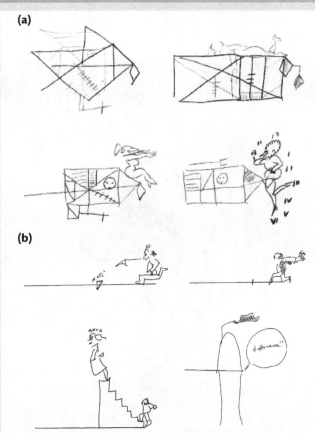

(a)

(b)

Figure 6.45 Italian film director Federico Fellini developed spatial neglect after suffering a stroke. As well as being a director, Fellini was also a talented cartoonist and he doodled comically on his psychological tests. **(a)** and **(b)** Examples of Fellini's spatial neglect test performance.

Source: Chatterjee, A. A madness to the methods of cognitive neuroscience? *Journal of Cognitive Neuroscience*, 2005, 17, 6, 847–9, © by the Massachusetts Institute of Technology.

At least neglect patients can recognise their creations. Some patients with visual agnosia are unable to do this. Wapner *et al.* (1978) report the case of a 73-year-old amateur artist who developed visual agnosia following a stroke. The artist would draw extremely laboriously but failed to recognise what he drew. He could identify the general shape of the object and describe its function, and even tried to identify it from its parts, but could not put a label to it. His agnosia was perceptual, rather than conceptual, because he would sometimes describe the functions of parts of the object he drew (e.g. what a telephone was for).

Agnosic patients can sometimes imagine the objects they would like to draw. Botez *et al.* (1985), however, report the case of a 38-year-old teacher and amateur charcoal drawer who was unable to imagine people, places or objects following dilation of one of the brain's chambers. Copying objects presented little problem but when the object was removed from sight, her drawings became simple and schematic. When she was given the name of an object to draw, she could not do this competently.

Perception seems the most likely casualty in the artist's battle with brain damage but there are some cases of impairment to other functions which led to some unusual artistic consequences. The Bulgarian artist Zlatio Boiyadjiev exhibited a natural, pictorial style prior to the development of aphasia (Zaimov *et al.*, 1969). After the aphasia, his art became bold, rich and colourful, full of striking, energetic lines and replete with bizarre imagery. Another artist with aphasia, the Polish artist RL (an Assistant Professor in Lublin), was known for highly symbolic paintings. Following aphasia, he produced very well-executed charcoal drawings, self-portraits and landscapes (Kaczmarek, 1991). No matter how hard he tried, he never did recover the symbolism of his art that existed before the aphasia.

Chapter review

Perception of form

- Perception of form requires recognition of figure and ground. The Gestalt organisational laws of proximity, similarity, good continuation and common fate describe some of the ways in which we distinguish figure from ground even when the outlines of the figures are not explicitly bounded by lines.

- One hypothesis suggests that our brain contains templates of all the shapes we can perceive. We compare a particular pattern of visual input with these templates until we find a fit. A second hypothesis suggests that our brain contains prototypes, which are more flexible than simple templates. Some psychologists believe that prototypes are collections of distinctive features (such as the two parallel lines and the connecting diagonal of the letter N).

- Perception involves both bottom-up and top-down processing. Our perceptions are influenced not only by the details of the particular stimuli we see, but also by their relations to each other and our expectations. Thus, we may perceive a shape either as a loaf of bread in the kitchen or as a letterbox alongside a country road, for example.
- We can usually distinguish male and female faces on the basis of eyes, mouth and nose but rarely on the basis of single features alone.
- Lighting, form and contour significantly influence our ability to recognise faces correctly.

Perception of space and motion

- Because the size and shape of a retinal image vary with the location of an object relative to the eye, accurate form perception requires depth perception – perception of the locations of objects in space.
- Depth perception comes from binocular cues (from convergence and retinal disparity) and monocular cues (from interposition, size, linear perspective, texture, haze shading, elevation and the effects of head and body movements).
- The Sapir–Whorf hypothesis suggests that language can strongly affect the way we perceive the world although there is not much research to support it. It is possible that experience with some environmental features, such as particular geographical features or buildings composed of straight lines and right angles, has some influence on the way people perceive the world.
- We perceive the brightness of an object relative to that of objects around it; thus, objects retain a constant brightness under a variety of conditions of illumination. In addition, our perception of the relative distance of objects helps us maintain form constancy.
- Because our bodies may well be moving while we are visually following some activity in the outside world, the visual system has to make further compensations. It keeps track of the commands to the eye muscles and compensates for the direction in which the eyes are pointing.
- Movement is perceived when objects move relative to one another. In particular, a smaller object is likely to be perceived as moving across a larger one. Movement is also perceived when our eyes follow a moving object, even though its image remains on the same part of the retina and supplies important cues about an object's three-dimensional shape.

- There is evidence that language can influence the understanding and use of spatial relations. Members of the Guugu Yimithirr community, for example, describe the position and relations between objects in a different way to people from the West.

Brain mechanisms of visual perception

- Visual information proceeds from the retina to the thalamus, and then to the primary visual cortex (PVC). The PVC is organised into modules, each of which receives information from a small region of the retina.
- Neural circuits within each module analyse specific information from their part of the visual field, including the orientation and width of lines, colour and movement.
- The different types of information analysed by the neural circuits in the modules of the PVC are sent to separate maps of the visual field in the first level of the visual association cortex. The information from these maps is combined in the second level of the visual association cortex: form perception in the base of the temporal lobe and spatial perception in the parietal lobe.
- The brain seems to contain visual systems which process (1) features of objects and (2) the space indication of objects. The first, the ventral stream, projects from the PVC to the inferior temporal cortex; the second, the dorsal stream, projects from the PVC to the posterior parietal cortex.
- While it was once thought that the fusiform face area was the most important brain region for face processing, fMRI research suggests that processing of different types of faces (familiar/unfamiliar; famous/not famous) depends on other brain areas.
- Visual agnosia is the inability to perceive objects accurately (apperceptive agnosia) or assign meaning to visually presented objects (associative agnosia). Prosopagnosia is the inability to identify familiar faces and results from bilateral or unilateral posterior brain damage.
- The agnosic deficits seen in patient DF may be due to an intact dorsal stream but an impaired ventral stream.
- Blindsight refers to the ability to perform visual perceptual tasks despite a lack of awareness of the perceived stimuli; it is normally associated with damage outside the primary visual cortex.
- Spatial neglect is the inability to attend to stimuli in one half of space. Patients usually neglect the left-hand side as a result of right parietotemporal cortex damage (that is, the deficit is contralesional – occurs on the opposite side to the brain damage).

Suggestions for further reading

Chatterjee, A. (2004) Neuropsychology of art. *Neuropsychologia*, 42, 1568–83.

Conway, B.R. and Livingstone, M.S. (2007) Perspectives on science and art. *Current Opinion in Neurobiology*, 17, 476–82.

Daw, N. (2012) *How vision works: the physiological mechanisms behind what we see.* Oxford: Oxford University Press.

Detuscher, G. (2010) *Through the Language Glass.* London: Arrow.

Goldstein, E.B. (2009) *Sensation and Perception.* (8th edn). Belmont, CA: Thompson.

Gregory, R.L. (2009) *Seeing through illusions.* Oxford: Oxford University Press.

Gruter, T. (2006) Picture this – how does the brain create images in our minds? *Scientific American Mind*, 17, 1, 18–23.

Gruter, T., Gruter, M. and Carbon, C-C. (2008) Neural and genetic foundations of face recognition and prosopagnosia. *Journal of Neuropsychology*, 2, 79–97.

Hatfield, G. and Allred, S. (2012) *Visual experience: Sensation, cognition and constancy.* Oxford: Oxford University Press.

Hole, G. and Bourne, V. (2010) *Face processing.* Oxford: Oxford University Press.

Johnston, V.S. (2006) Mate choice decisions: The role of facial beauty. *Trends in Cognitive Sciences*, 10, 1, 10–13.

Kravitz, D.J., Saleem, K.S., Baker, C.I. and Mishkin, M. (2011) A new neural framework for visuospatial processing. *Nature Reviews Neuroscience*, 12, 217–30.

Martin, G.N. (2006) *Human Neuropsychology* (2nd edn). Harlow: Prentice Hall Europe.

Mather, G (2011) *Essentials of Sensation and Perception.* London: Routledge.

Ramachandran, V.S. and Rogers-Ramachandran, D. (2007) Paradoxical perceptions. *Scientific American Mind*, 18, 2, 18–20.

Regier, T. and Kay, P. (2009) Language, thought and color: Whorf was half right. *Trends in Cognitive Sciences*, 13, 439–6.

Young, A.W. and Bruce, V. (2011) Understanding person perception. *British Journal of Psychology*, 102, 959–74.

Some very good readings on visual perception and its disorders.

CHAPTER 5

AN INTRODUCTION TO PERCEPTION

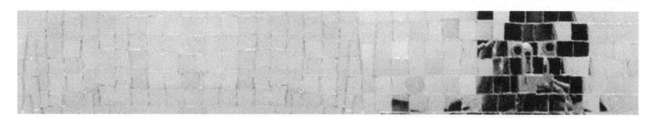

LEARNING OBJECTIVES

By the end of this chapter, you should be able to:

- Distinguish between perceptual and cognitive processes.
- Discuss how the familiarity effect relates to both late and early processes.
- Identify how the principles of familiarity, recency and expectancy operate in perception.
- Distinguish between the Old Look and New Look schools in perception.
- Detail the principles of Bruner's perceptual readiness theory (1957).
- Understand the significance of illusions for theories of perception.

CHAPTER CONTENTS

'It only attacks when the moon is aglow' The Beast of Burnley

Camping out in the woods with school friends was a rite of passage during the summer holidays. Stocked to the brim with incredibly unhealthy sweets and fizzy pop with neither a piece of fruit nor a decent toothbrush in sight, you set about bedding down for the night after a full day's open air fun. Some time after the obligatory exchange of ghost stories, and just before the last comforting square of chocolate has been consumed, an eerie sound fills the tent. For once, this isn't one of your companions letting off 'steam' but something rather more sinister. 'What the hell was that?' 'Oh, it'll be a cow – I saw a whole bunch of them in the next field this afternoon.' 'It's a rabid sheep! I knew one was going to attack me one day after eating all that lamb.' 'I heard that there's a beast that roams these parts, my dad told me the story of the Beast of Burnley just before I left. He especially told me to look out for strange shadows moving in front of the tent.' At that point, the torch batteries fail and more than one scream can be heard over the Burnley moorland . . .

When we don't know what a stimulus is, how do we estimate it? How does what we've experienced before colour our judgement? What happens when a stimulus is completely ambiguous, even after staring at it for what seems like hours? Answers to these and other related questions will be addressed in this chapter, although we may never know the true identity of the Beast of Burnley . . .

REFLECTIVE QUESTIONS

1. How much of what you see and hear is caused by your environment and how much is caused by you? Do you tend to interpret the world in terms of what is most familiar, what has been seen most recently or what is more expected? How might these different influences interact with one another?

2. Have you ever looked at something and done a double take? What happens when you see something you don't understand? How do you know when something doesn't look right and how do you try to resolve these ambiguities in our environment? When we experience multiple interpretations of the same thing, what does this tell us about how we perceive the world?

Introduction and preliminary considerations

Having considered the particularities of visual encoding, visual sensory memory and visual masking, the intention now is to examine broader questions about the nature of human perception. We will be concerned with the degree to which perception is governed, not so much by what is out there, but by what the person brings to the task. Basic questions exist over the extent to which our perceptions of the world are governed by our experience of the world and as we will see, according to one fairly radical perspective, it is claimed that our perceptions of the world are built up from knowledge of previous experience of it.

Clearly such a presupposition stands in stark contrast with the naïve realist view of perception as set out by Neisser (1967; and described previously, see Chapter 3). By the naïve realist view, our perceptions of the world are taken to mirror the world, but if we admit that our perceptions of the world are affected by our past experience of it, then something has to give – something more than mirroring is going on. An entailment of this is that everyone's experience of the world is unique, but if this is true, then how can it be that we all perceive the same world? On the one hand, we all happily admit that our experiences of the world are different – two people cannot be at exactly the same point in space at the same time. On the other hand, we must also admit that there is some common ground for how else could we successfully communicate among ourselves? We need to consider these issues very carefully.

Initially we will survey some basic points about human perception that have emerged in the literature, and then move on to examine some basic effects that have been taken to reflect general characteristics of the human perceptual system. Some of the evidence comes from the literature on word recognition, but the aim is to take from these studies evidence for general principles of perception. We will consider, in turn, **familiarity effects, recency effects** and **expectancy** or **set effects**.

> familiarity effects Empirical findings that reveal how familiarity influences our perceptions of the world.
>
> recency effects In perception research, experimental findings that reveal how the recency with which a stimulus has been encountered influences the perception of the stimulus. In memory research, how items towards the end of a list of to-be-remembered items are well recalled.
>
> expectancy (set) effects Empirical findings that reveal how expectancy can influence our perceptions of the world.

Distinguishing perception from cognition

Before getting too engrossed in the details, it is important to set the work within a general framework for thinking. To provide a context for appreciating the relevant data, it is useful to consider some general theoretical issues first. One very useful framework for thinking was provided by Fodor (1983) and is captured by his modularity of mind hypothesis (see Chapter 2). A schematic representation of Fodor's architecture of the mind is provided in Figure 5.1, and this clearly shows that each of the five senses is decomposed into its own sub-set of input modules. Following sensory encoding, the input modules act as the interface between the world and the mind of the observer.

Here the distinction between the proximal and distal stimulus will, again, turn out to be useful. To reiterate: the proximal stimulus is the stimulation of the sense organs, while the distal stimulus is the actual physical thing that gave rise to proximal stimulus. So the brown leather chair is the distal stimulus and the corresponding pattern of light that impinges on the retinae is the proximal stimulus.

Initially, the stimulus energy (i.e., the proximal stimulus) that arrives at the epithelium (i.e., the surface of the body) is encoded by the sensory transducers. The eventual stimulus information is then passed on to the input modules, which in turn generate outputs that feed into the central processors. The central processors then function to try to make sense of the sense data. The central processors attempt to identify the distal stimulus that gave rise to the proximal stimulus. In very broad strokes, this is the general view of processing set out by Fodor in his modularity of mind hypothesis (1983; see Chapter 2).

Figure 5.1 also maps the distinction between **perception** and **cognition** onto the functional distinction between, respectively, the operation of the input modules on the one hand, and the operation of the central processes on the other. At a stretch, we could also cite Turvey's concurrent and contingent model here (see Chapter 4), since the peripheral and central nets in his model bear a certain resemblance to the input and central mechanisms, respectively. There is a division between relatively dumb peripheral mechanisms and the relatively clever central mechanisms.

Couched in this way the framework for thinking rests upon a seemingly simple distinction between perception and cognition. As an act of simplification, in the figure a line has been drawn between the perceptual mechanisms (the input modules) and cognitive processes (the central processors). Of course, whether it is at all sensible to accept such a clean division between perception and cognition is something that will preoccupy us throughout this chapter. It should come as no surprise to learn that many have taken issue with this distinction: it is controversial and it continues to be hotly debated (see Pylyshyn, 1999, and commentaries). Controversy surrounds such questions as: Can we sensibly distinguish properties of the perceptual system from properties of the cognitive system? Is there a useful distinction to be drawn between perceiving and conceiving? Is the 'seeing' vs. 'deciding' distinction valid? These questions will be addressed as discussion proceeds.

Despite such concerns, we will adopt Fodor's theory (see Chapter 2) as a useful starting point because it provides such a very clear framework for thinking about many fundamental issues in cognitive psychology. Ultimately, though, the psychological validity of the model stands or falls by whether it can adequately account for the data. We will therefore need to examine the sorts of empirical claims that the model makes about human information processing and see whether these stand up to scrutiny.

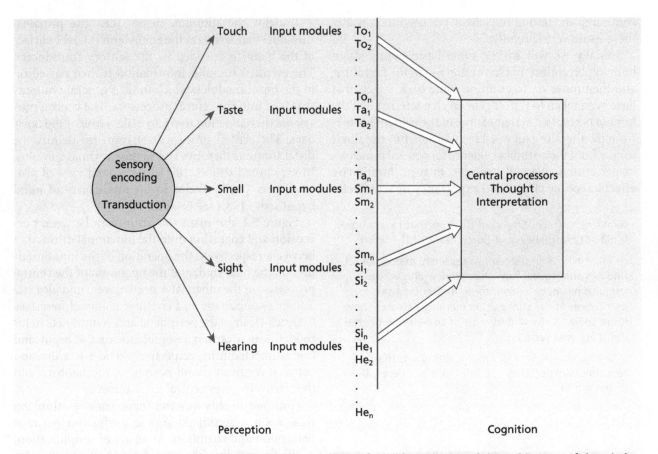

Touch   Input modules   To₁
                          To₂
                           .
                           .
                          Toₙ
Taste   Input modules   Ta₁
                          Ta₂
                           .
                           .
                          Taₙ
Smell   Input modules   Sm₁
                          Sm₂
                           .
                           .
                          Smₙ
Sight   Input modules   Si₁
                          Si₂
                           .
                           .
                          Siₙ
Hearing Input modules   He₁
                          He₂
                           .
                           .
                          Heₙ

Sensory encoding Transduction

Central processors
Thought
Interpretation

Perception   Cognition

Figure 5.1 A schematic representation of Fodor's (1983) modularity of mind hypothesis and the architecture of the mind

Among the many characteristics of input modules that Fodor (1983) outlined, he asserted that input modules are **informationally encapsulated** (p. 64). By this he means that once a module receives input, it produces a corresponding output that 'is largely insensitive to what the perceiver presumes or desires' (p. 68). So regardless of what the perceiver hopes to see or hear or feel, etc., the input modules operate according to certain principles that are insensitive to these higher-order considerations. The assumption is that a perceiver is built so as generally to 'see what's there, not what it wants or expects to be there' (p. 68).

A complementary way of thinking about this is that the **processing** that goes on in the input modules is **bottom-up** or *stimulus driven*. Higher-order knowledge does not influence processing at this stage – the input modules operate in a purely feedforward manner and there is no feedback from central processes to the input modules (see Chapter 4). Input modules merely slavishly operate on the proximal stimulus and produce an output that approximates to the best first guess as to what is out there. They produce a first stab as to what the corresponding distal stimulus might be.

The input modules operate in a purely feedforward manner and there is no feedback from the central processors. Think of it this way: you (an input module) are working in a parcel sorting office and have been asked to separate out very large parcels from those that could possibly fit through a standard letter box. In making such a distinction you are merely operating on one set of criteria (such as size and volume) and your decisions are not based on what is contained in the parcels. Identifying what is in the parcels is up to someone else – someone who cannot alter your decisions in any way whatsoever.

So according to this view the input modules (the perceptual mechanisms) produce the best first guess as to what sort of object may have given rise to this pattern of input. In contrast, it is the job of the central processors (the cognitive mechanisms) to assign meaning to this input and so make sense of the sense data. The central mechanisms make a more informed judgement as to what the distal stimulus actually is by taking into account what the input modules are signalling and what the person knows about the world. By this view, the perceptual mechanisms operate quite independently of any cognitive influence. It therefore follows that perception and cognition are different and can be studied – to a certain extent – independently of one another. What we have here is a very clear statement of the distinction between perception and cognition.

Although there is something of a philosophical flavour to what is being discussed, as we shall see, there are empirical consequences that follow from holding such views. In this regard, initially we will continue to adhere to the tradition that has concentrated on trying to ascertain the degree to which a particular experimental effect reflects characteristics of encoding mechanisms (the perceptual system) as opposed to characteristics of more central decision mechanisms (the cognitive system). In pre-empting a very involved discussion of the evidence, though, we begin by considering the general modularity framework for thinking in some more detail. Moreover, before any congratulations are offered over novelty and originality, it should be stated at the outset that similar ideas have been around since the turn of the last century enshrined in the 'classic sensation-interpretation doctrine' associated with Wundt and Titchener (see Rock, 1983, p. 299).

Pinpoint question 5.1

According to Fodor (1983), which mechanisms are responsible for (a) your reading the sentence 'your in-laws are coming to visit' and (b) either jumping for joy or weeping openly?

perception According to Fodor (1983), operations associated with the input modules.

cognition According to Fodor (1983), operations associated with the central processes.

informationally encapsulated A property of a processing module (Fodor, 1983) in which its operations are determined locally by information contained within the module.

bottom-up processing Processes driven by the stimulus in a feed-forward fashion.

Drawing a distinction between the perceptual system and the cognitive system

To frame the present discussion we will freely use the phrase the **perceptual system** as being shorthand for the underlying mechanisms that produce an internal representation of the input stimulus (this will be known as the **perceptual representation**). In the preceding material, the perceptual system has been variously discussed in terms of encoding/peripheral/early mechanisms. In contrast, the **cognitive system** will be used as shorthand for the underlying mechanisms that operate on the perceptual representation to provide an interpretation of the input stimulus (the higher-order/later/central mechanisms). By this view the perceptual system operates so as to take the proximal stimulus and generate an internal representation of this. This perceptual representation is then amenable to further interpretative analysis that is undertaken by the cognitive system. (The nature of the perceptual representation will be discussed in more detail as we proceed.)

The purpose of the cognitive system is to take the perceptual representation and to assign an interpretation to it: the cognitive system generates a specification of the distal stimulus given the proximal stimulus as contained in the perceptual representation. Continuing in this vein, the eventual percept contains a specification of both the physical characteristics of the input together with a decision about what the distal stimulus actually is. There is a perceptual record of the stimulus which has been produced by the perceptual system and there is an interpretation of what this record specifies as supplied by the cognitive system.

For perception to work properly we want the perceptual system to deliver a representation that is a truthful record of the environment – something that is also known as a **veridical representation**. In other words, ideally the mapping between the proximal stimulus (the input) and the distal stimulus (an entity in the real world) should be correct. For example, if a tiger is currently present in the immediate environment then the perceptual system should deliver a

For example . . .

You might be surprised to read about fictional superheroes in these pages, but it turns out that the cry, 'Is it a bird? Is it a plane? No, it's Superman!' could be interpreted as multiple decisions (of varying success) of the cognitive system as to what could possibly be that flying distal stimulus in the sky creating the related retinal proximal stimulation.

representation that leads the cognitive system to decide that there is a tiger present in the immediate environment. It should do this as quickly and effectively as possible. Clearly the perceptual system must be pretty good at this because we humans have survived despite not being the strongest or fastest predators on the planet.

Within the present framework for thinking, the observer's perceptual representation is assumed to contain a specification of patches of brown and black colours that, in combination, add up to a coherent tiger-like shape – it contains a record of the physical attributes of the proximal stimulus. Importantly, though, such a representation must allow the cognitive system to decide quickly that this representation signifies the presence of the tiger. Optimally, the perceptual system should be providing the cognitive system with a veridical (i.e., truthful) record of the environment that provides a very good basis upon which the cognitive system can decide what is out there.

These ideas will be fleshed out in more detail as we proceed, but for now we need to consider whether the evidence collected from experiments that we will review reflect the operation of perceptual mechanisms (as just described) or whether they are more indicative of the operation of interpretative (cognitive) mechanisms. We have drawn upon a rather simple distinction between (i) the perceptual system that encodes the proximal stimulus in such a way that a perceptual representation is generated and (ii) the cognitive system that provides an interpretation of the perceptual representation. The fundamental question now is whether we can marshal evidence that supports this distinction in such a way that the characteristics of these two systems are made clear.

When cast in these terms, there is a clear link with the material in the previous chapter. A similar aim was behind the experiments of Broadbent and Gregory (1967a) in their attempt to establish whether perceptual defence – the apparent failure to perceive threatening words – was due to a change in perceptual sensitivity or a change in response bias. Indeed the signal detection theory parameters of sensitivity (d') and bias (β) came to prominence on the understanding that effects on measures of sensitivity reflected some aspect of the perceptual system and that effects on measures of bias reflected some aspect of the cognitive system. To be clear, the simple logic is that any d' effect is associated with perceptual mechanisms whereas any β effect is associated with interpretative/decisional mechanisms that constitute the cognitive system.

Much of the early work that we will review here was concerned with trying to tie down whether effects could be used to adjudicate between perceptual and cognitive mechanisms. More generally, this kind of issue is critical because if we take some observation (or more generally an experimental effect such as perceptual defence) to be indicative of an interpretation placed on some stimulus, then what we are admitting is that the observation reveals very little (even possibly nothing) about perception. The effect is more likely telling us something about how we interpret the world and we should set this aside from issues regarding the operation of the perceptual system.

> **perceptual system** Mechanisms responsible for the generation of an initial internal representation of a stimulus.
>
> **perceptual representation** Stimulus representation derived through the operation of the perceptual mechanisms.
>
> **cognitive system** Interpretative mechanisms.
>
> **veridical representation** An internal record of an external stimulus that is a truthful specification of it.

Familiarity and perception

Let us return to our tiger example to carry the discussion forward. In recognising the patches of brown and black as signifying the presence of a 'tiger', the visual input has been assigned to a particular mental category. In this way stored knowledge of the world allows us to make sense of the data from the senses. The phrase **mental category** will be discussed in much more detail later (see Chapter 12), but, for now, it can be used as shorthand for stored knowledge about the nature of a class of things. Recognising a given stimulus means assigning the perceptual representation of the proximal stimulus to a mental category. Of course, you will be unable to do this if the stimulus is unfamiliar because, by definition, you have no mental categories for unfamiliar things. Critically, though, this does not mean that you will be unable to perceive an unfamiliar stimulus.

For instance, you have probably never come across the letter string NEBRUE before but this does not mean that you cannot perceive it. Patently, therefore, there is an important sense in which perception and interpretation are different. The perceptual system generates a perceptual representation of NEBRUE, but the cognitive system fails to generate a very meaningful interpretation of the input. Here the interpretation

(a)

(b)

Figure 5.2 Seeing vs. recognising
Examples of (a) easy to describe, and (b) difficult to describe figures.

Source: Kanizsa, G. (1985). Seeing and thinking. *Acta Psychologica*, 59, 23–33 (fig. 1, p. 24). Reproduced with permission from Elsevier.

assigned to the marks on the page may be nothing other than an attempted pronunciation of the letters. Hence, NEBRUE is seen but it is not recognised.

To cement this particular point, consider Figure 5.2 (taken from Kanizsa, 1985). In the upper half of the figure are various geometric shapes. In a hypothetical case one participant (the sender) is presented with these and must get a second participant (the receiver) to reproduce these but the sender may only describe the figures to the receiver. The claim is that this task is relatively straightforward because both participants can easily relate these to familiar mental categories such as a black equilateral triangle, a small ring on a blue background, and so on. However, if the sender is now presented with the blob-like configurations in the lower half of the figure, the task becomes incredibly difficult.

The more cynical among you might be thinking that all of this is simply common sense so what is the point in discussing it? Well, what the example should make clear is that, as Kanizsa (1985) stated, 'there is no difference between the two situations with regard to the visual aspect as such' (p. 25). Both sets of marks on the page are clearly visible and can therefore be easily seen. However, in the former case the marks on the piece of paper constitute familiar shapes and in the latter they do not. Here, therefore, there is apparently a very clear-cut distinction between perceiving and conceiving. The process of seeing is the same for both familiar and unfamiliar cases, yet something else appears to be going on when we are confronted by familiar entities as compared with unfamiliar entities.

Consideration of this kind of point leads us seamlessly on to a discussion of familiarity effects in perception.

Familiarity and word recognition

Intuitively it may seem that familiar things are easier to perceive than unfamiliar things, and this is indeed what is implied on a superficial understanding of what familiarity effects in perception reveal. However, as our discussion of perceptual defence showed, we need to tread carefully and be much more analytic in our approach. Does familiarity really affect perception? Are familiarity effects indicative of the operation of the perceptual system? or do they tell us more about the operation of the cognitive system?

To address these questions, psychologists have been preoccupied with experiments on word recognition. As Michaels and Turvey (1979) noted, since the time of Cattell (1886), it has been known that words are more accurately identified from a briefly presented display than are random letter strings. One obvious reason for this is that words are simply more familiar than a random string of letters. Upon reflection, however, words and random letter strings differ on several other things as well – such as meaningfulness and, possibly, pronounceability (see Pollatsek, Well, & Schindler, 1975, for a brief review). So the above so-called **word recognition advantage** may not be solely due to words being simply more familiar than random letter strings; other factors may be at play and may be confounded with our familiarity variable.

Given such difficulties in comparing the perception of words with the perception of random letter strings, an alternative has been to just consider the perception of different types of words, where the different word types are defined according to their *frequency of occurrence in the language*. We can therefore control items by matching them on meaningfulness and pronounceability, but can also allow them to differ on their frequency (e.g., 'fable' vs. 'table'). It will generally be the case that a given word will be more meaningful and pronounceable than a random string of letters so to overcome such confounds it is better to examine the perceptibility of words that differ in familiarity. In the simplest case we can compare the perceptibility of common vs. rare words (cf. Broadbent & Gregory, 1967a).

As Broadbent and Gregory (1971) stated, one advantage of doing this sort of experiment with words is that we have an objective measure of how familiar the items are because there exist norms that contain actual frequency counts of words taken from large samples of written and transcribed spoken language. For instance, a very famous word count is the Kučera and Francis (1967) word count, and if you look at this particular set of word norms you will discover that THE is the most common word and ZOOMING and ZOOMS languish towards the bottom of the table. Indeed, the existence of such word norms and the ability to control systematically for stimulus frequency is one very good reason that words have been so intensively studied in experiments on perception.

This is not to argue that such experiments cannot be carried out with other forms of stimulus materials, but merely that it has proved easiest to carry them out with words. Indeed, a possible confusion – that must be avoided – is that the results of the experiments recounted here *only* reflect properties of the human word recognition system. Well, some of the effects are peculiar to the perception of words, but originally the experiments were motivated by a desire to understand more general properties of the perceptual system.

The **word frequency effect** is our first indication of a familiarity effect in perception. Broadbent and Gregory (1967a) began their paper with the statement that, 'It is, of course, normal to find that words common in the language are more easily perceived than are words which are uncommon' (p. 579), but two different sorts of accounts of this frequency effect have been contrasted. According to the first, the understanding is that the effect reflects sensory mechanisms – for instance, that 'sensory mechanisms are selectively adjusted so as to collect more evidence about the occurrence of probable events (than rare events)' (Broadbent & Gregory, 1971, p. 1: material in parentheses added). In contrast, and according to the second class of theories, the frequency effect reflects a decision or response bias located at a later, more central stage of processing. The basic question is therefore: is the word frequency effect telling us something about the perceptual system or is it telling us something about the cognitive system? Is the word frequency effect a so-called perceptual effect?

Pinpoint question 5.2

Why are rare words a better control than non-words when examining the processing of familiar words?

Sensory/perceptual accounts of the effects of familiarity

So the central issue is whether the word frequency effect (in particular) and familiarity effects (in general) reflect characteristics of either the perceptual system or those of the cognitive system. To get a better handle on this, let us reconsider the notion of a line detector and also assume that different detectors exist for lines of any orientation (one for horizontal lines, one for vertical lines, one for a rightward diagonal, one for a leftward diagonal, and so on). Therefore we might describe the letter V as one rightward diagonal and one leftward diagonal joined at the base. Let us also assume that in the corresponding hypothetical world, horizontal and vertical lines are more plentiful than diagonal lines. Consequently, horizontal and vertical lines will be more familiar than diagonal lines. How might an organism evolve to take advantage of this? Well, on a sensory account the organism may well have acquired more receptive fields for horizontal and vertical lines than for diagonal lines. In this regard the sensory mechanisms have been selectively adjusted throughout the evolutionary history of the organism to take advantage of the basic statistical nature of the world.

Alternatively, or indeed in addition to this, the perceptual mechanisms could be tuned throughout the course of the developmental history of the individual. Evidence for this idea comes from the work of Blakemore and Cooper (1970). In brief, they reared two kittens in highly constrained visual environments such that one kitten was only exposed to vertical lines and edges and the other kitten was only exposed to horizontal lines and edges. Later, recordings were taken of single neurons inside the brains of these kittens. Generally speaking, when orientation-selective cells were found (neural line detectors of the type already discussed), all were found to have preferred orientations of within 45° of the orientation to which the kitten had been first exposed. No cells were found that were linked to directions orthogonal (at right angles) to the original exposed orientation. Indeed simple behavioural tests revealed that the kittens were essentially blind to lines and edges in the non-preferred direction. So Kitty H reared in a horizontal world could see horizontal but not vertical lines. Kitty V reared in a vertical world could see vertical but not horizontal lines.

More provocative are the claims that such perceptual tuning can take place over much shorter time spans. Here it is not so much that an individual possesses disproportionately more feature analysers of a particular type than another (i.e., vertical line detectors over horizontal line detectors), but that particular feature analysers become more highly tuned than do others. To take an example from the concurrent and contingent account of processing (Turvey, 1973; see Chapter 4), the peripheral nets for familiar stimuli operate much more quickly than do those for unfamiliar stimuli. Hence they deliver their outputs to the central nets much sooner than do those for unfamiliar stimuli. Over time, therefore, the peripheral nets for familiar stimuli are 'tuned up' in the sense that they become 'well oiled' in delivering fast outputs. Such tuning does not take place for unfamiliar stimuli because they are encountered much less often.

As we will see shortly, there are also other accounts of perceptual tuning in which such processes arise under the control of the participant. It is not so much that the perceptual system passively changes as a consequence of being exposed to environmental influences but that the participant actively takes control over the operation of perceptual analysis. Such accounts as these are particularly controversial because they stand in complete contrast to the stimulus-driven, modular account of processing described in Figure 5.1. So, in contrast to such sensory accounts of familiarity effects (i.e., the perceptual mechanisms for familiar instances perform better than those for rare instances), the alternative is to consider decision or response bias accounts.

Decisional/post-perceptual accounts of familiarity

Let us assume that each line detector has a threshold such that when the relevant line falls within the detector's receptive field, activation accrues at the detector (in the manner described in Chapter 4). When this activation exceeds the threshold, the detector fires and the line is identified. In this sort of system it is possible to think that each line detector has its threshold set at a particular level which is given by the probability of how often its corresponding line is encountered. So lines that are highly probable (say, horizontal and vertical lines) give rise to lower thresholds than lines that are rare (say, the diagonal lines).

What this means is that a detector with a lower threshold will fire more easily (or more quickly) than one with a higher threshold because the detector with a lower threshold needs less activation to fire (see Figure 5.3). Lowering the threshold implies that a much more liberal criterion is applied to detecting when the critical stimulus is present. So more probable lines will be detected more easily than will less probable lines. Less evidence needs to be present for detection of a probable line than an improbable line because of the difference in the respective threshold levels of activation on the corresponding line detectors.

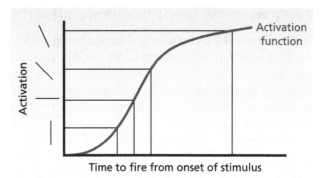

Figure 5.3 Schematic representation of various line detectors and their different thresholds
The *y* axis reflects the amount of activation provided by an input stimulus. The different line detectors are ordered according to the amount of activation that is needed for them to 'fire'. The understanding is that the thresholds, in this example, reflect how frequently the actual lines have been encountered. So the vertical line detector has a lower threshold than the others because vertical lines have been encountered the most often.

At one level the argument is quite subtle because there is a distinction being drawn between encoding and deciding/responding. By the sensory account, familiar items are encoded more quickly and/or more accurately than are unfamiliar items. By the later decision/response account, all items are encoded in the same fashion, it is just that familiar items are categorised more quickly than unfamiliar items. A decision about a familiar item is reached more quickly than a decision about an unfamiliar item because the observer is using a less stringent criterion for category membership for familiar than unfamiliar items. So, to use the language of signal detection theory, a purely sensory account predicts an effect on d'. d' values for familiar items should be greater than unfamiliar items by the sensory account. The noise and the signal + noise distributions are far apart for familiar items and close together for unfamiliar items. In contrast, the decision/response bias account predicts an effect on β and now the difference between familiar vs. unfamiliar items should be reflected in β. Participants should miss more unfamiliar than familiar items.

Pinpoint question 5.3

In a city, which do you think would have the lower threshold – the smell of car fumes or alpine air – and why?

Explaining the word frequency effect

In the same way that we discuss different line detectors for lines of different orientations, we can discuss word detectors for different words. In this way we assume that each familiar word has its own word detector and each has a threshold set by the frequency of occurrence of the word in the language. In discussing such a framework for thinking about word recognition, Broadbent and Gregory (1971) located the word frequency effect at the level of central and not sensory mechanisms; that is, they located the familiarity effect in word recognition at the level of the word detectors. They argued that the word frequency effect reflects the fact that word detectors for common words have lower thresholds and hence need less evidence to fire, than do the detectors for rare words. By extension, they argued that familiarity effects, in general, reflect the operation of central decision mechanisms rather than perceptual encoding operations.

Active vs. passive theories of perception

On the basis of this kind of word frequency effect, Broadbent (1977) introduced a more general framework for thinking about perception by contrasting **active theories** of perception with **passive theories**. For him the word frequency effect is indicative of a passive mechanism in which judgements are made about evidence for relevant stimuli that accrues at the level of corresponding stimulus detectors (i.e., word detectors). Word detectors with lower thresholds fire more quickly than do detectors with higher thresholds. The contrasting view is that active mechanisms are responsible for the effect. For instance, it could be that the participant has, in a sense, the ability to alter the perceptual system in line with knowledge and expectations about the world. By this view, the person is able to take control over the perceptual system to such an extent that they can selectively tune the perceptual encoding of common over rare stimuli. We will return to the distinction between active and passive views of perception later and we will explore more thoroughly active accounts of perception. For now, though, we need only note the distinction. Bearing this in mind, we can reconsider familiarity effects that have been documented in the literature.

Familiarity effects reflect late processes

In using the term 'late' in the present context, the intended reference is with respect to accounts in which there are stages of information processing that are arranged in a sequence such that certain processes come into play later than do others. We can then discriminate early from later stages of processing in much the same way that Turvey (1973) distinguished peripheral from central nets. According to the general framework sketched in Figure 5.1, sensory encoding operates (early) prior to any (later) decisional or response processes. The relevant distinction here is between perceptual and post-perceptual processes. By this view, a 'late' process refers to a post-perceptual process and an 'early' process refers to some form of perceptual/ encoding process. As we have seen, Broadbent and Gregory (1967a) favoured a post-perceptual account of the word frequency effect which has its locus at a relatively late stage of processing.

Evidence that familiarity effects in perception do not reflect properties of sensory encoding was discussed by Hochberg (1968). In a critical experiment, on each trial he presented a pair of letter strings printed either side of a central fixation point for a very brief interval. Each letter string was presented vertically, not horizontally (see Figure 5.4). On each trial the participant simply had to say whether the letter strings were identical or not. This is known as a simultaneous **same/different judgement task** or more simply a *same/different task*. Each pair of letters was repeatedly presented over trials and the display duration was incremented slightly over trials. This was continued until the participant made a correct judgement. So as the exposure duration increased, the perceptibility of the letter strings also increased.

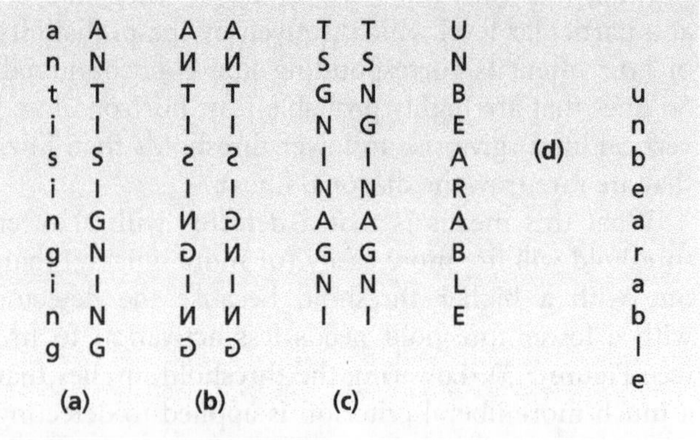

Figure 5.4 Examples of the letter string stimuli that Hochberg (1968) used in his same/different matching experiments

Source: Hochberg, J. E. (1968). In the mind's eye. In R. N. Haber (Ed.), *Contemporary theory and research in visual perception* (fig. 16, p. 327). New York: Holt Rinehart & Winston.

What Hochberg found was that there was no difference in performance across different types of letter strings when the strings of letters were spaced closely together (i.e., positioned closely side by side). That is, participants were unaffected by whether the strings were meaningful or pronounceable as compared to when the strings were meaningless and unpronounceable. Judgements were also unaffected by whether the individual letters were printed in normal or reversed print (see Figure 5.4). If the letter strings were spaced far apart (or the strings were presented sequentially with one string being presented and then removed before the other), matching was better for words than illegible or unpronounceable letter strings. According to Hochberg, under these conditions the task demanded temporary storage of the letters for comparison purposes. Now the results showed that familiarity aided the formation of memory traces for the words but not non-words.

What these data suggest therefore is that when the task judgement could be carried out at the level of sensory analysis (i.e., when the strings were spaced close together), the familiarity of the materials was of no consequence. It was therefore concluded that the effect of familiarity in perception is located at the level of central and not sensory mechanisms. Indeed such a conclusion gained further support in the more recent replication and extension carried out by Pollatsek et al. (1975) (see Figure 5.5). → See 'What have we learnt?', below.

Familiarity effects reflect early processes

Having considered the evidence that suggests a late locus of the effects of familiarity, we now turn to the contrasting evidence that suggests an earlier locus. Two examples will be considered in this regard. The first

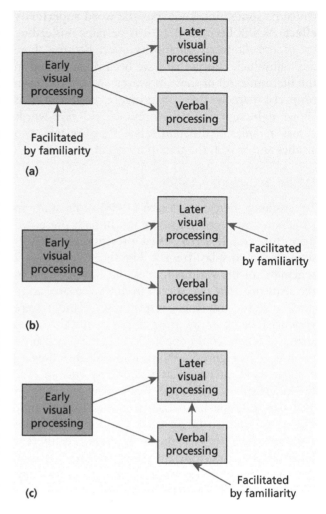

Figure 5.5 Familiarity effects in word perception
Various ideas concerning where, in the processing system, familiarity exerts its influence (taken from Pollatsek *et al.*, 1975).

Source: Pollatsek, A., Well, A. D., & Schindler, R. M. (1975). Familiarity affects visual processing of words. *Journal of Experimental Psychology: Human Perception and Performance, 1,* 328–338 (fig. 1, p. 337). Reproduced with permission from APA.

→ What have we learnt?

The view that emerges from consideration of this body of work on familiarity effects in processing of letter strings is that any such effects reflect the operation, not of sensory encoding mechanisms, but of more central processes concerning storage, comparison and decision. More recently, though, other data have been collected and these suggest that not all effects of familiarity in word recognition are the same. Therefore there may indeed be grounds for arguing that sensory analysis can be influenced by the familiarity of the stimulus.

Remember, what we are trying to do here is ascertain what processing mechanisms are responsible for particular behavioural effects – are familiarity effects (like the word frequency effect) indicative of perceptual or cognitive mechanisms?

concerns something known as the **word superiority effect**. As will become clear, it is perhaps misleading to discuss *the* word superiority effect because there are many such effects that have been documented in the literature. All of these, however, share a common property, namely that performance with words is shown to be superior to performance with non-words across a range of different tasks. Here we take two studies and look at them in more detail.

Doyle and Leach (1988)

For instance, Doyle and Leach (1988) ran a study in which on trial a central fixation was initially presented prior to a rapid serial visual presentation (RSVP) sequence of display frames. Figure 5.6 provides a schematic of the various frames and timings used in the sequence. The two special frames were labelled as interval X and interval Y, respectively. X and Y were very brief, being in the order of 25 ms, and the target string of letters could appear in either interval on a given trial. As Figure 5.6 shows, immediately following each of these intervals was a rapid sequence of four masking displays. Collectively this sequence was known as a **dynamic mask**. In each frame of the dynamic mask, and at each target letter position, a different nonsense character was presented. Across the different frames of the masks different nonsense characters were presented and this created an impression of random characters rapidly changing in shape as the sequence unfolded.

All the participant had to do was to indicate whether the target letter string was presented in interval X or interval Y. Such a paradigm is known as a **two-alternative forced choice** (a 2AFC) task. The participant is forced (okay, 'encouraged') to make a decision about one of two alternatives. In this case, what participants actually did was to rate their confidence on a four-point scale as to how sure they were that the target occurred in interval X or that it occurred in interval Y.

Part of the reason that this is such a clever experiment is that the participants were not being tested on their ability to identify the target letter strings; they were being tested on their ability to perceive where in the sequence the target appeared. In this regard, an important manipulation was that on half the trials the target letter string was a word and on half the trials the target string was a non-word. If participants had been tested on their ability to identify the letter strings then any difference in performance across familiar words and unfamiliar non-words may have been due to good guessing on the word trials. If the target is HOME and all you saw was HOM*, then why not guess HOME. In contrast, in their actual task Doyle and Leach (1988) measured perception of the letter strings in such a way that any influence of familiarity could only show up indirectly.

Indeed, the central result was that, generally speaking, judgements for words were more accurate than were judgements for non-words. Participants were more accurate in locating which interval a word occurred in than they were in locating the interval in which a non-word occurred in. There was a word superiority effect because participants were more accurate on word than non-word trials. More critical, though, was that the effect was revealed in measures relating to d' and, as was explained above, this effect was therefore taken to reflect perceptual sensitivity and not response bias. → See 'What have we learnt?', page 155.

Merikle and Reingold (1990)

The second example of a 'perceptual' familiarity effect in word recognition is taken from a paper by Merikle

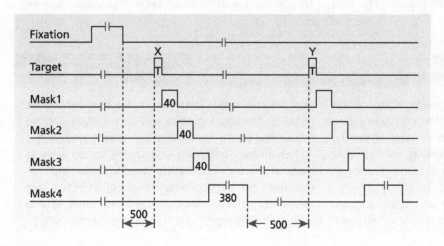

Figure 5.6 Schematic representation of the RSVP displays that Doyle and Leach (1988) used in their experiments

The target occurred either before the pattern mask located at X or before the pattern mask located at Y. A target never appeared at both positions within a trial.

Source: Doyle, J. R., & Leach, C. (1988). Word superiority in signal detection: Barely a glimpse, yet reading nonetheless. *Cognitive Psychology, 20*, 283–318 (fig. 1, p. 301). Reproduced with permission from Elsevier.

In summary, what we have here is an effect of familiarity that shows that familiar items (words) are more easily detected than are unfamiliar items (non-words). This effect cannot be attributed to participants lowering some response criterion for words relative to non-words (better guessing on word trials) because the effects were revealed in d' rather than β. The effect of word familiarity seems to be operating at the level of an early perceptual encoding stage of processing. We may conclude that at some perceptual level the processing of familiar items is facilitated relative to unfamiliar items.

In terms of real life, the suggestion is the following: assume you are standing on a railway platform and aimlessly watching the trains go by. What the experimental evidence suggests is that you are more likely to detect the presence of a friend or relative on a train that moves past than someone you barely know. This is even though the presence of your friend is completely unexpected! The implication of the work of Doyle and Leach (1988) is that such an effect actually does reflect something about perceptual encoding. Familiar items are more easily encoded than are unfamiliar items.

and Reingold (1990). They ran a series of experiments, only one of which will be mentioned here. On a given trial and following the offset of fixation display presented to both eyes, a forward mask of a random string of letters was presented to the right eye for 50 ms. There was then a short pause followed by presentation of the target field to the left eye, which itself was followed by the mask being re-presented to the right eye. In the experiment under consideration the target frame duration was set at 50 ms. On half the trials, the target field contained a target letter string and on the remaining half trials the target field was blank.

For their first response on each trial participants merely had to report whether or not a target string was presented. This requirement was taken to define the **detection task**. In addition, in a second *lexical decision task*, participants then had to respond whether the target string was a word or a non-word. The experiment extends the basic methodology that Cheesman and Merikle (1984) developed, as we discussed in Chapter 4. Critically on the trials in which a target string was presented, a word appeared on a random half of the trials. On the remaining trials the target was a non-word. From the participant's viewpoint, the experiment may have seemed a little odd because even on trials when they thought no target had been present they still were expected to make a lexical decision response!

The data from the detection responses showed that detection performance was better for words than non-words; that is, there was again a robust word superiority effect. Participants were more accurate in deciding that a target string rather than a blank frame had been presented when the target string was a word than when it was a non-word. Again this result was

found when comparing scores computed as a variant of d'. Hence the conclusion was that stimulus familiarity did affect stimulus detection at the level of perceptual mechanisms. The findings could not be explained adequately in terms of a difference in bias in responding to words relative to non-words because of the effect being manifest through differences in d' and not β. Word familiarity seems to exert an influence at a relatively early perceptual encoding stage of processing. Such evidence converges on the same conclusion as that put forward by Doyle and Leach (1988).

The findings on the lexical decision responses were equally provocative. Again measures of sensitivity were computed as a function of whether participants were correct in their detection decisions. The data were broken down as to whether participants scored a hit or a miss on the detection task. Now it was found that participants generally performed well when they detected the target string (on hit trials). If they detected the target then they could judge reasonably well if it was a word or a non-word. A different pattern arose on trials where the participants missed the target. Now they were reasonably accurate in making a word response, but they were essentially guessing when the target was a non-word. If participants failed to detect the target, they were still reasonably good at responding that it might have been a word. Critically therefore, as Merikle and Reingold (1990) stated, 'only familiar stimuli were perceived when participants failed to detect a stimulus but that both familiar and unfamiliar stimuli were perceived following stimulus detection' (p. 582). The fact that participants could perform above chance with words that they were unable to detect was taken to show that some form of knowledge about words had been accessed without participants being consciously aware of this. Such an effect therefore is another indication of semantic activation without conscious awareness – see Chapter 4.

Collectively, the data from the detection and lexical decision tasks reported by Merikle and Reingold (1990), has shown that stimulus familiarity affects both perceptual and interpretative stages of processing. Familiar stimuli were detected better than unfamiliar stimuli. In addition, familiar stimuli, but not unfamiliar stimuli, were seen to engage with cognitive mechanisms concerned with stored knowledge. In this regard, there is a rather clear indication of how *word* familiarity operates: perceptual mechanisms are apparently tuned to the detection of familiar over unfamiliar stimuli. Furthermore, familiar stimuli apparently engage interpretive process in a way that unfamiliar stimuli do not. → See 'What have we learnt?', below.

Pinpoint question 5.4

If a word superiority effect shows up for the measure of d' rather than β, does this mean perceptual or response mechanisms are responsible?

mental category Stored knowledge regarding the nature of a class of objects or entities.

word recognition advantage For example, the finding that words are more accurately recognised from a briefly presented display than strings of random letters. More generally, where performance with words is better than with any other form of strings of letters.

word frequency effect Differences observed in word processing as a result of the frequency of occurrence in natural language. Common words are typically dealt with more effectively than rare words.

active theories A phrase used to refer to theories of perception in which the person can exert some control over how they perceive the world.

passive theories A phrase used to refer to theories of perception in which the person has no control over their perceptions of the world.

same/different judgement task Experimental paradigm where, on each trial, participants are required to compare two stimuli and respond as to whether they are the same or whether they differ from one another.

word superiority effect Generally speaking, when performance with words is superior relative to performance with non-words.

dynamic mask A mask that changes over time.

two-alternative forced choice Paradigm in which participants are required to choose between one of two possible alternatives on every trial.

detection task An experimental task in which the participant simply has to respond on every trial as to whether a stimulus is present or not.

→ What have we learnt?

Initially the early work on familiarity effects was taken to show that familiarity operates at a level after sensory analysis is complete. In this regard the familiarity effects were interpreted as showing decision/response biases. Given this, it was concluded that familiarity exerts its influence at a post-perceptual stage of processing and therefore such effects tell us relatively little (perhaps nothing) about the nature of the perceptual system. The more recent studies, in contrast, have demonstrated quite convincingly that (at least where words are concerned) familiarity can exert an influence at an earlier perceptual stage of processing. Word familiarity conveys a benefit at the level of sensory analysis.

This is not to argue that the earlier and more recent data sets contradict one another. On the contrary, what seems to have emerged is that certain tasks have revealed familiarity effects that do not reflect the operation of perceptual mechanisms, and as such they suggest that the corresponding familiarity effects arise through the operation of post-perceptual mechanisms. Other tasks have quite clearly revealed how familiarity influences sensory analysis. On these grounds, it is most sensible to conclude that familiarity effects can arise at various stages throughout the processing system. Importantly, there is evidence to suggest that sensory mechanisms may become particularly attuned to familiar stimuli.

Recency and expectancy

From a common-sense point of view it seems reasonable to claim that what observers actually perceive is, to large measure, determined by what they expect to perceive. You get on a bus and you expect to see an adult bus driver sat behind the wheel. Such a claim is enshrined in studies of expectancy on perception. In contrast, effects of recency on perception are studied on the assumption that a stimulus is more readily perceived if it has recently been encountered than if it has not. This probably has nothing to do with common sense, but the idea is that if you have just seen next door's dog rummaging in the hedge, then you will most probably see next door's dog next time you glance up and look at the bundle of fur in the garden. In examining effects of recency and expectancy on perception we will begin by considering experimental evidence that has been used to back up such intuitive, common-sense claims about the nature of human perception. However, we need to assess carefully whether there is any empirical evidence for such claims.

Other studies are then considered that have attempted to establish the locus of such effects in the human information processing system. So in the same way that research was directed to trying to find out where in the processing system familiarity was exerting its influence, we now must consider where recency and expectancy exert theirs. We can ask whether effects of recency and expectancy are located at perceptual or post-perceptual stages of processing. To address these issues much of the evidence comes from studies of the perception of so-called **ambiguous figures** and it is to these that the discussion now turns.

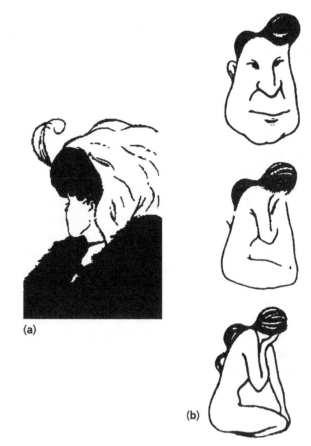

(a)

(b)

Figure 5.7 Perceptually ambiguous figures
(a) The now classic, ambiguous figure: Boring's old/young woman. (b) Examples of the nude/face figure. Ambiguity, varying from male to female, changes down the page, with the middle figure being the most ambiguous.

Source: (a) Fisher, G. H. (1966). Materials for experimental studies of ambiguous and embedded figures. *Research Bulletin*, No. 4. Department of Psychology, University of Newcastle upon Tyne. Reproduced with permission.

The perception of ambiguous figures

Let us begin this discussion with a consideration of a classic stimulus in perceptual psychology known as an ambiguous figure. One of the most famous of these is that shown in Figure 5.7a and this has come to be known as Boring's (1930) figure of a young/old woman. If you're having trouble seeing either, the choker on the neck of the young woman is the mouth of the older woman. As Figure 5.7b also shows, it is quite possible to generate a set of figures that vary along an ambiguity continuum. At one end of the continuum is a figure that unambiguously depicts a face of a man and at the opposite end is a figure that unambiguously depicts a young woman. The central figure is ambiguous. Being able to vary figural ambiguity in this way has proved

to be a critical factor in studies of expectancy and recency in perception.

In an early study Leeper (1935) initially presented participants with an unambiguous version of Boring's figure and then went on to examine how the participants would interpret a subsequent presentation of the corresponding ambiguous figure. A central result was that participants tended to report resolving the ambiguity in terms of the interpretation of the unambiguous figure they had previously been given. So if they had been presented with the young woman version of the figure, they then interpreted the ambiguous figure as depicting a young woman. This was taken as evidence of how previous experience can affect present perceptions – participants tended to report the most recently accounted interpretation of the stimulus.

In a much later study Rock and Mitchener (1992) provided other evidence relevant to the general idea that expectancy affects perception. Now participants were chosen so that they were completely naïve with respect to ambiguous figures. That is, the participants had no previous knowledge of ambiguous figures and were therefore unaware that such figures could have more than one interpretation. Rock and Mitchener ran two conditions: in the *uninformed condition* participants were just asked to report what they saw when presented with an ambiguous figure. It is well established that in free viewing conditions informed participants first report one interpretation of the stimulus and then, at some time later, this flips or reverses and they then report the other interpretation of the stimulus. This is known as **ambiguous figure reversal**. Indeed with prolonged viewing the different interpretations alternate repeatedly (and why this happens has been the topic of some concern: see Horlitz & O'Leary, 1993). Nevertheless, in the uninformed condition, only one-third of the participants reported seeing the figures reverse. That is, they typically reported one, but not both interpretations of the figures.

In a second, *informed condition* participants were now presented with the ambiguous figures and were told that the figures could be seen in either of two different ways. In this way participants were instilled with an expectancy over the nature of the stimuli – each participant had been told that the figures could be seen in more than one way. Now all of the participants reported both interpretations and all reported that the figures reversed with prolonged viewing. Rock and Mitchener were very keen to underline how the contrast between performance across the two conditions provided further evidence of how knowledge affects perception – if participants did not know that the figures could be given either of two different interpretations, then they generally perceived the figure in a particular way and maintained that reading of the stimulus. In contrast, when the participants were informed about the nature of the ambiguity they were able to assign both interpretations and generate two quite different percepts.

Research focus 5.1

Flip-flopping: children's responses to ambiguous figures

Being students of psychology, we are all probably very suspicious of whatever kind of stimulus somebody shows us in a lab. We might get people to look at faces in the hope that this will reveal something about race bias or we might show individuals artificial creatures to see whether it can tell us something about face processing. Therefore, when we present our participants with ambiguous figures, it's likely that they already have some prior experience with such figures and know all about the different interpretations of the images. In addition, some of the participants will be eager to please as well! To avoid such confounds, Mitroff, Sobel and Gopnik (2006) were interested in children's responses to ambiguous figures since it's likely that children will approach them in a naïve (in the nicest sense of the word) fashion.

Data from 34 children aged 5–9 were analysed in the experiment. Mitroff et al. (2006) used a classic ambiguous figure known as the duck/rabbit, in addition to more unambiguous versions of the same picture (see Figure 5.8). Children were asked to report

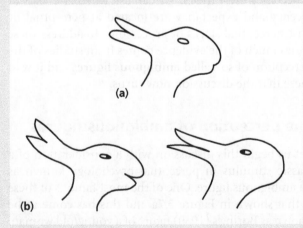

Figure 5.8 Fair game
The consequences of a duck and rabbit mating – the infamous ambiguous dabbit (or ruck) shown in (a). Unambiguous versions are shown in (b).

Source: Mitroff, S. R., Sobel, D. M., & Gopnik, A. (2006). Reversing how to think about ambiguous figure reversals: Spontaneous alternating by uninformed observers. *Perception*, 35, 709–715 (fig. 1, p. 711). Reproduced with permission from Pion Limited, London.

what they saw when presented with the ambiguous figure. If children reported both interpretations during the initial phase of the experiment, then this was considered a *spontaneous reversal*. Following the first presentation, participants were shown the unambiguous version to spoil the fun, and then were presented with the ambiguous figure again. If participants reported both interpretations in this second phase, this was labelled an *informed reversal*.

Only 12 of the initial 34 children were reported as experiencing spontaneous reversal, and of the remaining 22 children, 20 reported seeing multiple interpretations following instructions, thereby giving rise to a larger percentage of informed reversals. Importantly, Mitroff et al. (2006) also conducted further tests with the children to assess their theory of mind, that is, the extent to which they were aware of other people's feelings and perspectives. Specifically, children who reported spontaneous reversals performed particularly well on one particular test, in which the child had to report where in a fictitious village one member thought another person was situated: 'John thinks that Mary is at the park' (Mitroff et al., 2006, p. 712).

Mitroff et al. (2006) concluded that the data do not sit well with a purely bottom-up account of ambiguous figure reversal, in which the observer experiences neural saturation in relation to one interpretation so as switches over to the other interpretation. This is because bottom-up effects do not account for failures to reverse spontaneously. Neither does the data fit with a purely top-down account, in which the person has to know about the ambiguous nature of the figure prior to exposure. This is because top-down effects do not account for spontaneous reversals. A link between theory of mind and spontaneous reversals is suggested, although some children achieved one without the other. Perhaps the interpretation of ambiguous figures just got a little bit more ambiguous!

Source: Mitroff, S. R., Sobel, D. M., & Gopnik, A. (2006). Reversing how to think about ambiguous figure reversals: Spontaneous alternating by uninformed observers. *Perception, 35*, 709–715.

Attempting to disentangle effects of recency from those of expectancy

Taken together these experiments provide evidence in support of the common-sense ideas that recency and expectancy affect perception. Of course the data are silent on where such recency and expectancy effects may be located, but we will return to this issue shortly. In simple terms, the original Leeper study concerned how recency may affect perception, and the later Rock and Mitchener study examined how expectancy affects perception. In a further important study, Epstein and Rock (1960) examined the perception of ambiguous figures in a bid to see whether recency or expectancy was the overriding factor in determining the current perception.

On a typical trial, the participant was presented with a sequence of stimuli where each stimulus apart from the last was an unambiguous version of Boring's figure. The different versions of the figure were presented in an alternating sequence (i.e., old, young, old, young, . . .). Let us assume the last unambiguous figure to be presented in the sequence was of the old woman. However, the actual sequence ended when the ambiguous version was now presented. As a consequence, participants could not predict when the sequence would end but when the last figure was presented they had to report whether they saw the old or young woman. If they reported 'old' it was assumed that their report had been influenced by recency – the most recently presented version of the figure influenced their report of the ambiguous figure. However, if they reported 'young' then it was assumed that expectancy and not recency had influenced their report. The young version is the one that was predicted (i.e., expected) on the basis of the alternating sequence. Epstein and Rock found that current interpretations of the ambiguous figure tended to reflect an effect of recency. Participants reported the interpretation consistent with the figure most recently presented (in our case, old) and not the one that was expected on the basis of the alternation (in our case, young).

Unfortunately, as is the tendency with these kinds of things, ensuing research has tended to cloud the picture. For instance, in a later paper, Girgus, Rock and Egatz (1977) reported a failure to find any effect of recency on the perception of ambiguous figures. In an initial exposure phase participants were presented with a series of pictures and they had to rate each of them for attractiveness. In the experimental condition two unambiguous versions of a standard ambiguous figure were included in this exposure sequence of pictures. In the control condition these two pictures were replaced by neutral pictures. The whole series of pictures were repeatedly shown to the participants five times.

→ What have we learnt?

The evidence for effects of recency on the perception taken from the work on ambiguous figures is slight. Indeed, the fragility of such effects has been emphasised most clearly by Wilton (1985). In a series of experiments he was able to demonstrate that recency can be shown to influence the interpretation of ambiguous figures but in ways that remain unclear. Indeed the manner in which this factor operates in concert with others is still quite mysterious. So whereas the effects of familiarity in perception have been relatively straightforward to deal with, the picture is far from clear regarding the evidence for recency effects in perception.

What we are trying to do here is focus on what might be termed the common-sense view of perception that associates all so-called perceptual effects with the operations of the perceptual system. The claims are as follows:

1. Familiar things are easier to perceive than are unfamiliar things.
2. More recently encountered things are easier to perceive than are things encountered less recently.
3. You perceive what you want to; what you expect to perceive.

We need to assess the evidence both in terms of trying to elevate such common-sense notions to the level of scientific fact and also in terms of trying to locate where in the processing system the factors are having their influence. We have addressed point 1 and concluded that the evidence for point 2 is, so far, equivocal. We will turn to point 3 in a moment. Before that, though, we need to acknowledge that a much stronger case can be built for effects of recency in perception from studies with other kinds of materials. It is to these that we now turn.

The main measure of interest was the number of experimental and control participants that spontaneously reported seeing the ambiguous figure reverse when this was presented in a 60 second test phase subsequent to the exposure phase. The results revealed that there was no difference across the two conditions because, respectively, 7 out of 12 and 8 out of 12 participants reported reversals in the experimental and control groups. So it was concluded that the recent exposure of the two different interpretations of the ambiguous figures did not materially affect the tendency to report these interpretations at test. → See 'What have we learnt?', above.

Recency and repetition priming

The mixed results in trying to establish an effect of recency on the interpretations of ambiguous figures should not distract us from the very robust effects of recency found in studies of repetition priming. Although there are many different kinds of repetition effects to be found in the literature, let us define the standard repetition effect as showing that the identification of a given stimulus is improved if it is repeated. Stated thus, it is easy to see how familiarity can be construed in terms of repetition over the long term: more familiar items have been encountered more often. So again there is a possible problem in trying to disentangle repetition from familiarity. A considerable amount of literature on repetition priming concerns single word recognition. However, comparable experiments using a variety of other materials do exist, and, in the current context, the study by Benton and Moscovitch (1988) is of some importance.

Benton and Moscovitch (1988)

Consider their Experiment 1. In their lexical decision task on each trial participants were presented visually with a single string of letters and they had to respond as quickly and as accurately as they could to whether the string corresponded to a word or not. Here reaction times (RTs), recorded in ms, and accuracy were the main measures of interest. (There are 1,000 milliseconds in a second, so 500 ms is half a second.) On a random half of trials a word was presented and on the remaining trials a non-word was presented. Participants pressed one response key to signal 'word' and a different key to signal 'non-word'. Within the experimental blocks of trials, however, some of the stimuli were repeated.

Three different sorts of repetitions were examined. On Lag 0 trials the stimulus on trial n was immediately repeated on trial $n + 1$ (the same target string was repeated on the next trial), and as such there was no lag between the repeated item. On Lag 4 trials the stimulus on trial n was repeated on trial $n + 5$ (there were 4 intervening trials between the first and second presentations of the target string); on Lag 15 trials the stimulus on trial n was repeated on trial $n + 16$ (there were 15 intervening trials between the first and second presentations of the target string). Table 5.1 provides examples.

Table 5.1 Schematic representation of various trial dependencies in the lexical decision task carried out by Benton and Moscovitch (1988).

Trial	Lag 0 – Word repetition	Lag 0 – Non-word repetition	Lag 4 – Word repetition	Lag 4 – Non-word repetition	Lag 15 – Word repetition	Lag 15 – Non-word repetition
1	**HOUSE**	VOWEL	**HOUSE**	HOLLY	**HOUSE**	**CRIPE**
2	**HOUSE**	DRIFT	SWAER	BERRY	AREA	CASTLE
3	LAND	SMALE	FICK	**CRIPE**	KILM	CANNON
4	FORM	ASILE	GRIGH	RADIO	YEAR	GINO
5	TILT	QUIET	LAWN	WENT	ULIM	HIDDEN
6	FROST	**CRIPE**	**HOUSE**	NIGBIPS	BIONE	ITEM
7	SORG	**CRIPE**	BIRDS	TOAST	WIBE	GRID
8	NOUR	GHOST	GOUR	**CRIPE**	YOST	SOCKS
9	GLUM	MOUSE	ROUGH	SWIND	HOST	WENT
10	FIRE	FRIN	HIFT	TABLE	FLOOR	MONTH
11	DORL	SWIRL	MASK	VIXE	BAND	YOUR
12	SIPH	GRAFT	AMOCK	FINT	MUG	LOOR
13	NOUGHT	KRINE	DEOY	LIPE	UNTIL	MIST
14	ABLE	DOWN	FRION	CHRIM	WERN	MINT
15	DREN	SPRITE	BORT	SLAPE	RENT	OVEN
16	GLOT	MOVE	RIFLE	CLOSE	BELT	CAVO
17	ZERO	NICE	STRIPE	VIOL	**HOUSE**	**CRIPE**

Each column contains a possible sequence of trials. The actual types of repetitions co-occurred in a block of trials. Here they are separated out for illustrative purposes only. On each trial a letter string was presented and the participant simply had to press one key as a word response and a different key for a non-word response. The first and second stimulus presentations are shown in **bold**.

In an additional face/non-face discrimination task participants again made a binary decision on each trial, but now the stimulus was either a proper photograph of a face or a doctored photograph of a face. With these latter stimuli – known as non-faces – the internal features of a face had been rearranged by switching the position of the eyes, nose and mouth. The structure of the face/non-face task was the same as the lexical decision task with the same sorts of repetition trials being included. See Figure 5.9 for a particularly gruesome example of this sort of non-face.

With this design it is possible to see how familiarity and repetition can be examined separately. The non-words and non-faces were completely unfamiliar to the participants. In addition, although each face was easily classified as a being a face, the actual faces were unfamiliar to the participants. Finally, each word was familiar in its own right. So across these different types of stimuli familiarity varied, but each stimulus type was examined in the various repetition conditions.

The results of the experiment were striking. First there was a large repetition effect for stimulus type on Lag 0 trials. Participants were facilitated in responding on these trials relative to when the stimulus was not

repeated. In addition, repetition effects were found for words at all three lags. To be clear, in this experiment a repetition effect was observed if the average RT on repeated trials was shorter than the average RT on trials where the stimulus was presented for the first time. So for words there was a very large repetition effect on immediate repetition trials – of the order of 100 ms – this reduced on Lag 4 trials (to about 60 ms) and reduced again on Lag 15 trials (to about 40 ms). In this way the data revealed an effect of recency that dissipated with time. The repetition effect decreased as a function of recency – the more recently the stimulus word had been presented, the quicker participants were to make the classification response.

For all of the other unfamiliar stimuli the repetition effect was only statistically significant on Lag 0 trials. Here there was a strong recency effect but this was very short-lived. If any other stimulus intervened between the two presentations of the item the repetition effect was abolished. So the overall contrast between performance with words and the other items shows that the repetition effects for words reflects things other than perceptual processes – things relating to knowing the particular items used. Participants were generally

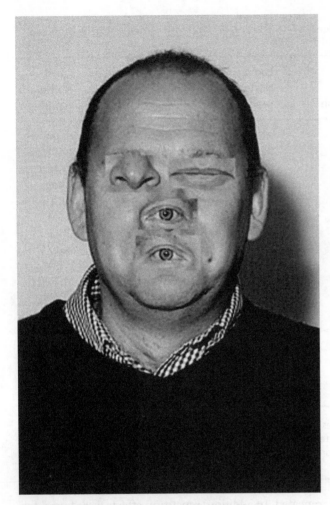

Figure 5.9 Beauty is in the eye of the beholder
A non-face stimulus akin to those used by Benton and Moscovitch (1988).

facilitated on repeated word trials because they possessed stored knowledge about these particular stimuli prior to the experiment. This suggests that the word repetition effects reflected, in part, a memory component – performance was facilitated because of some form of memory representation of the actual items used.

How might this be? Well, on the understanding that there exist word detectors, of the sort described by Broadbent and Gregory (1971), then the presentation of a particular word results in the lowering of the threshold on its own particular detector. A consequence of this lowering of the threshold is that less evidence is required for the detector to fire next time the word is presented. The fact that the repetition effect dissipated with lag can be interpreted as showing that the detection threshold returns relatively to its original baseline level gradually over time.

Although analogous face detectors may exist, only unfamiliar faces were used in the experiment. Therefore such putative mechanisms could play no role – there are no face-specific face detectors for unfamiliar faces. Consistent with this idea is that the long-lasting repetition effects were only found with words and not the face stimuli. This gives further credence to the idea that the longer-term repetition effects reflect some property of some form of long-term memory representations (i.e., word-specific detector). Such longer-term repetition effects only occur with familiar stimuli. Nevertheless all stimulus types produced an immediate repetition effect. This immediate repetition effect was taken to reflect the facilitation of perceptual encoding processes.
→ See 'What have we learnt?', page 163.

→ See 'What have we learnt?', page 163.

> **Pinpoint question 5.5**
>
> **What's the definition of a repetition effect?**

Expectancy and set

In many respects the notions of familiarity and recency relate, essentially, to stimulus factors on the grounds that both can be objectively quantified. The experimenter can either choose materials that vary in frequency of occurrence in everyday life, or can carefully control the recency of exposure of a given stimulus. This is not to argue that there can be no control over a participant's expectancies, but that it is a much more difficult subjective factor to gain control over. For instance, it is possible simply to tell a participant to expect certain stimuli during an experiment, but it is something of an act of faith to assume that the participant then sets up the desired expectancy during the task.

Such concerns are critical because now we are turning to a particularly radical version of the claim that past experience together with current stimulation determines our perceptions of the world. In this regard psychologists have considered how it might be that observers' mental states can affect their perceptions (we approach this important topic in a different way in Chapter 16). The naïve default position is that if an observer is *set to* or *expects to* perceive a stimulus of a particular type then this will materially affect how the observer perceives the world. For instance, even the slightest evidence consistent with the stimulus will be taken as evidence of the stimulus (Cherry, 1978, p. 276). Indeed Rock, Hall and Davis (1994) discussed this sort of issue in describing some general principles regarding the perception of ambiguous figures.

Benton and Moscovitch (1988) described evidence for repetition effects that were taken to reflect facilitation of perceptual encoding processes and other repetition effects that were taken to reflect an additional benefit due to stored knowledge. Most important are the data that suggest that recency does influence perceptual encoding mechanisms. If either a letter string or an unfamiliar face were immediately repeated then its recognition was facilitated relative to cases where different stimuli occurred on successive trials. On these grounds, there is evidence to suggest that the perceptual system is sensitised to detect items that have recently been encountered.

However, it should be borne in mind that the effects are not as profound as might have been assumed on the basis of certain traditional ideas found in the literature. The perceptual effects are very short-lived indeed and only survive for a matter of seconds (as gauged by the time between successive trials). The more pronounced repetition effects with words than faces, reported by Benton and Moscovitch (1988), seem to reflect the operation of later interpretative mechanisms linked to stored knowledge. When these are stimulated, any contingent facilitation is much longer lasting than when unfamiliar stimuli are repeated. Yet again therefore the evidence suggests that some of the effects being reported reflect particular properties of the human word recognition system and we need to be mindful about this when attempting to draw conclusions about the perceptual system in general.

According to them, for reversals to occur the participant must know that the figure is ambiguous, and they must also be aware of exactly what the alternative interpretations of the figure actually are. These claims are about **mental set** but theorists have also discussed the notion of **instructional set** and it is to this that we turn first.

Instructional set

According to Hochberg (1978), 'if the viewer is *set* to expect a particular *kind* of material, he will see it better at a shorter exposure' (p. 165). The basic idea that instructional set can be an important determiner of perception is perhaps best conveyed by the following simple example. In Figure 5.10 two patterns are provided and both contain well-known symbols – one a letter and the other a number. One implication of this is that, prior to knowing about the constitution of the patterns, you may well have been unable to see the E and the 3. However, as soon as you were informed about the inclusion of the symbols you were *set* to find them. How instructional set affects perception has been the topic of much debate. Rather critically, though, we need to be clear about whether such effects reflect perceptual or later decision mechanisms. We cannot dispute the fact that such factors produce effects, but we do need to be clear exactly what it is in functional terms that the effects are telling us.

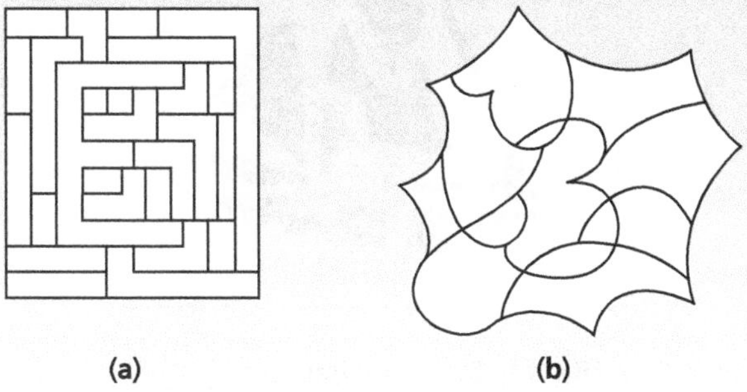

(a)   **(b)**

Figure 5.10 Embedded figures
Examples of hidden figures. As a hint, a letter is embedded in (a) and a digit in (b).

Source: Cherry, C. (1978). *On human communication* (fig. 7.8, p. 278). Cambridge, Massachusetts: The MIT Press. Reproduced with permission.

What sort of instructional set would help to see the number in this sentence?

Mental set

With instructional set, participants are specifically told to focus on some particular stimulus characteristic and to report on this. However, of some additional interest are cases where the effects of set are shown unintentionally. Several examples are worthy of comment. The first such example is a study by Bruner and Postman (1949). This has been discussed as providing evidence for a set effect in perception (Steinfeld, 1967), but it is instructive to think about whether the evidence is so clear-cut. The data clearly show an effect of past experience on perception but we will need to consider carefully whether this evidence really is indicative of an effect of mental set.

Bruner and Postman (1949) presented participants with brief visual displays, each of which contained a depiction of a playing card. An ascending **staircase method** of presentation was used in which each display was presented three times at 10, 30, 50, 70, 100, 150, 200, 250, 300, 400, 500, 600, 700, 800, 900 and 1,000 ms. (The staircase refers to the increments in display duration over trials and, given that the display duration increased monotonically over trials, the staircase is ascending.) At each exposure participants had to report what they had seen. What the participants did not know was that some of the stimuli contained what were known as incongruous cards, that is, cards in which the suit was presented in the wrong colour (e.g., the six of spades in red, see Figure 5.11). The basic results were straightforward and showed that for each display duration normal cards were recognised more accurately than were the incongruous cards.

This general pattern of results was taken to reflect an influence of set, that is, participants had difficulties in perceiving the incongruous cards because these stimuli violated their expectations about how playing cards should be. Indeed on some trials participants reported seeing compromise stimuli. For instance, the red six of spades was reported to have been presented in 'brown', or in 'purple', 'lighter than black', 'blacker than red', etc. Again these sorts of errors have been discussed as being a compromise between the actual stimulus and the expected stimulus (Gordon, 1989). However, it is difficult to see why these particular effects reflect something particular about expectancy rather than familiarity. Normal cards are more familiar than incongruous cards, hence the effects might be just as easily explained via familiarity as expectancy. So how might we distinguish between these two factors?

Well, ideally we need to use unfamiliar stimuli, but induce a particular mental set in the participants. Exactly this sort of manipulation was carried out by Steinfeld (1967). Here three independent groups of participants were tested. In Group A participants were read a short story about a sinking ocean liner. Group B participants were read a story completely unrelated to the ocean liner story and Group C participants were read no story. In the test phase all participants were shown a fragmented figure that was difficult to see as a ship (see Figure 5.12). The measure of interest was how long participants needed to view the figure before seeing it as a ship. The central result was that Group A participants took considerably less time to report seeing the ship than did the other two groups.

Figure 5.11 Okay, who dealt this hand?
Examples of the sorts of playing card stimuli used by Bruner and Postman (1949) in their experiments on the perception of incongruity.

Figure 5.12 Life is full of possibilities
The sort of fragmentary figures used in the experiments by Steinfeld (1967).

Source: Leeper, R. (1935). A study of a neglected portion of the field of learning: The development of sensory organization. *Journal of Genetic Psychology, 46*, 41–75 (fig. 1, p. 49). Reproduced with permission of the Helen Dwight Reid Educational Foundation.

→ **What have we learnt?**

In his recent review of set effects in perception, Pashler (1998) was very circumspect in his conclusions. From his review of the literature he concluded that the effects, such as they are, are very limited. At the most, the effects are generally consistent with the following idea. What expectancy does do is allow for the selective exclusion of noisy and irrelevant information when making judgements about stimuli that are difficult to otherwise perceive, such as in cases where the important stimuli are briefly presented and masked or they are presented in other forms of irrelevant noise.

More generally the claim is not that 'the perception of an object is changed or that an object is perceived . . . as something other than itself' but that expectancy can improve the efficiency with which a more precise description of the actual stimulus will be derived (Huang & Pashler, 2005, p. 156). So whereas an unexpected stimulus might be coded as being a short line oriented at *approximately* 45° to the right, the corresponding expected stimulus would be coded as being a short line oriented at exactly 45° to the right. What expectancy can do, therefore, is improve the precision with which a veridical – a truthful and more exact – description of a stimulus can be derived.

These data are important because the test stimulus was completely unfamiliar to the participants yet prior exposure to a relevant story induced a particular perceptual organisation of the stimulus. The data are clear in and of themselves, but it is not so transparent as to where to locate this set effect. That is, Steinfeld's result might reflect some form of perceptual 'tuning' of encoding processes (Steinfeld, 1967, p. 520), or the effect might reflect later decision or response processes. The point is that, unless we can locate where particular effects of associated variables may be operating, it is impossible to claim with any certainty that they inform about perception. → See 'What have we learnt?', above.

More general conclusions

More generally, the foregoing discussion has been based on adopting the distinction between the perceptual system and the cognitive system. It has been assumed that the perceptual system is responsible for generating a perceptual representation of the proximal stimulus. The perceptual system comprises mechanisms concerned with encoding the proximal stimulus into a form that allows the cognitive system to arrive at a sensible interpretation of what is actually out there. The discussion has focused on some general principles that are assumed to underpin the operation of the perceptual system. Implicit in the discussion has been a certain presupposition about how human perception operates with regard to how it might be that past experience critically affects our perceptions of the world. This discussion has been set against the generally accepted ideas that (i) familiar items are easier to perceive than unfamiliar items, (ii) more recently experienced items are easier to perceive than not-so-recent items, and (iii) expected items are easier to perceive than unexpected items.

In each case, though, more detailed questions have been asked about whether the related effects reflect the operation of perceptual rather than cognitive/interpretative mechanisms. Most of the evidence has favoured accounts that locate the effects at later rather than earlier stages of processing. It has been accepted that in many respects the effects reflect decisional processes in which certain interpretations of the stimulus are favoured over others. In the absence of any further context '?able' is taken to signal the presence of 'table' rather than 'fable' merely because 'table' is more likely. The perceptual representation is ambiguous with respect to whether 'fable' or 'table' is really out there. The interpretation of this representation is biased towards 'table' because of its familiarity. In contrast, expectancy would favour 'fable' given the context. 'A short story leading to a moral conclusion is usually known as a ?able'.

In such passive accounts of processing the perceptual system merely runs off a perceptual representation of the stimulus and the rest is left to interpretative mechanisms that are located at later processing stages. Accordingly, it is at these post-perceptual stages of processing that the effects of familiarity, recency, expectancy and set are located. All of the effects are therefore post-perceptual in nature and all of this fits very well with the strictly modular account of processing discussed by Fodor (1983) and set out in Figure 5.1. By that account the input modules are 'largely insensitive to what the perceiver presumes or desires', and as was noted above, the perceiver is built so as generally to 'see what's there, not what it wants or expects to be there' (p. 68). Perceptual analysis is insulated from higher-order factors and cannot be altered by how the participant construes the world. So much for only seeing what you want to see.

In contrast, and perhaps more provocative, are the claims that even perceptual encoding can be altered by the participant's knowledge of the world. Several such effects have been described here and the data do indicate that perceptual mechanisms are differentially sensitive to the familiarity, recency and expectancy of the stimuli. How might this be? Well, it has been suggested that such effects reflect the fact that the perceptual system can be selectively tuned to collect evidence of a particular type. In addition, or indeed alternatively, there is the idea that such factors influence the selective uptake of information such that irrelevant sources of stimulation can be filtered out or excluded from further analysis (see Pashler, 1998).

These points are subtle but can be clarified by considering these sentiments expressed by Huang and Pashler (2005, p. 156) regarding the role that attention plays in perceptual processing: 'paying attention to a red object will not make it redder or brighter, but will only make the redness more precise and the related judgment more accurate'. An implication is that a similar conclusion applies in thinking about how familiarity, recency and expectancy operate in perception. It is not that they fundamentally alter the manner in which perceptual analysis takes place, rather they can improve the precision with which a stimulus is analysed.

This is indeed a very far cry from the rather strong statements about how perceptual analyses can be controlled or changed by the participant on a whim. To appreciate this fully, though, it is important to see how ideas about subjective factors in perception have sparked much controversy throughout the history of experimental cognitive psychology.

Pinpoint question 5.7

How do the effects of recency, familiarity and expectancy manifest themselves in perception?

---

ambiguous figures A stimulus that has more than one interpretation and there is no obvious reason as to which is the 'correct' one.

ambiguous figure reversal The point at which an ambiguous figure switches between two different interpretations.

---

mental set A person's frame of mind or expectancies about an up-and-coming stimulus.

instructional set An expectation towards a certain kind of stimulus, usually as a result of explicit guidance by the experimenter.

staircase method A psychological procedure whereby the limits of performance are assessed by an experimenter systematically increasing or decreasing a parameter over trials.

The Old Look/New Look schools in perception

So far it has been suggested, according to the modular view sketched in Figure 5.1, that the perceptual system operates in very much a feedforward manner: the input modules passively produce outputs that are then operated upon by the central (cognitive) mechanisms. However, such a passive view of perception stands in stark contrast to one traditional and important alternative.

In the late 1940s several perceptual theorists began to emphasise how inner states such as needs, emotions and values might contribute to a participant's perceptions. This particular school of thought became known as the **New Look** approach to perception and a basic premise here was that the affective (emotional) state of the observer plays a fundamental role in determining that observer's perceptions of the world. This is a very broad acceptance of the view that knowledge of the world fundamentally determines perception. To arrive at a reasonable appreciation of this so-called *New Look approach* it is useful to know what the **Old Look** looked like (so to speak). In this regard, and according to Swets (1973), the Old Look comprised, primarily, the Gestaltists who concentrated on the stimulus determinants of perception (the physical nature of the stimulus) and not subjective factors. So to best understand the New Look we need to first consider the Old.

The Old Look: Gestalt theory

A central feature of Gestalt theory is its emphasis on trying to establish what is the correct unit of perceptual analysis. Whereas we might focus on the nature of primitive (i.e., elemental) perceptual features (such as short lines and edges) and their corresponding feature detectors (such as our now good friend the line detector), Gestalt theorists focused on the distinction

Figure 5.13 The whole is different from the sum of its parts
Examples of how the global aspects of different figures may be the same but that their local aspects differ.

Source: Haber, R. N., & Hershenson, M. (1979). *The psychology of visual perception* (fig. 8.10, p. 191). London: Holt, Rinehart and Winston. Reproduced with permission from Ralph Haber.

Figure 5.14 Do not attempt this at home
One of the authors providing an example of the difference between figure and ground. In this case, though, the figure is on the ground.

between the perceptual whole and its parts. They stressed that it is the relations between the parts and their overall arrangement that is most important: our perceptual impressions are governed by interpreting wholes and not parts. Although the classic phrase here is that 'the whole is more than the sum of its parts', Gestalt theorists emphasised a slightly different take, namely that the whole is *different from* the sum of its parts. Less catchy perhaps, but just as theoretically important, is, as Haber and Hershenson (1979) stated, the whole has unique attributes that are independent from the nature of its parts.

Figure 5.13 provides a schematic example of this. The four elements in each figure are arranged in such a way that the impression is of a global square. Moreover the impression of the square is maintained even though the nature of the elements can change. The same impression of a square is conveyed when triangles or unfilled circles are substituted as parts. If such a transposition of parts does not alter the impression of the whole, then it is clear that the whole is independent of the nature of its parts. The perception of the whole is not fundamentally dependent on the nature of its parts. In this way the notion of primitive perceptual features and their assumed detectors plays no critical role in the theory. The theory is more concerned with global aspects of perception than elemental details.

The Gestalt laws of perceptual organisation

In addition to this emphasis on the correct level of perceptual analysis, Gestalt theory also set out principles concerning perceptual organisation. These are typically referred to as the **Gestalt laws** of perceptual organisation and they define how it is that unrelated parts are assembled into perceptible wholes. In this regard, the notion of figure/ground segregation is

central. The account focuses on perceptual principles that give rise to assumed plausible segregations of the stimulus array that at first blush distinguish objects from their backgrounds. The Gestalt laws of grouping provide useful rules of thumb as to how best to divide the array into discrete objects. So the distinction is between objects (figures) segregated from the background (ground). (Figure 5.14 provides an example of where one figure, falling off a bike, was photographed against a background, which in this case was thankfully sand.)

At a more general level, the account is that there are certain principles of perceptual encoding that operate to provide a 'best first guess' as to which aspects of the stimulus information correspond to meaningful chunks (perhaps even objects) in the input. These principles can be applied to any form of input without regard to whether the environment is familiar or not. The laws of grouping merely offer suggestions as to how best to divide up the input into separate chunks: the decision as to what sort of objects are present is left to the more central (interpretive) processes to work out. Several laws of grouping were put forward during the first half of the twentieth century and these relate to how stimuli give rise to certain sorts of interpretations and not others. It seems that the perceptual system exhibits certain preferences in choosing certain forms of organisation over others. Such sentiments as these are best conveyed by concrete examples.

Figure 5.15 illustrates the points for us. In (a) the dots in the matrix are spaced evenly from one another, hence there is no clear organised percept that emerges.

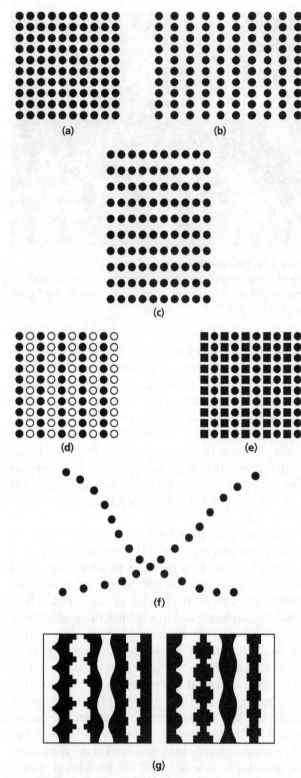

Figure 5.15 Examples of the Gestalt laws of perceptual organisation
See text for further details.

Source: (g) Gordon, I. E. (1989). *Theories of visual perception* (1st ed., fig 3.3, p. 54). Chichester, England: John Wiley & Sons.

However, when the factor of **proximity** is acting, elements are organised in groups by the closeness of the elements – so in Figure 5.15(b) the dots are grouped into columns and not rows, whereas the opposite is true in Figure 5.15(c). Grouping may also be determined by the **similarity** of the elements such as in Figure 5.15(d) and (e) where the elements group respectively by common colour and common form respectively. In both cases the elements organise themselves into columns.

Various other factors relate to something known as good continuations: common fate, direction, good curve. These are conveyed with respect of Figure 5.15(f). Closure and symmetry are related factors and these are illustrated in Figure 5.15(g). In summarising the factors, Robertson (1986, p. 164; see Figure 5.16, taken from Palmer, 1992) also discussed the idea of objective set by which certain organisations can be induced by prior experience (but here we are beginning to blur the distinction between stimulus determinants and subjective factors). However, she related that Gestalt theorists did discuss the subjective factors of experience or habit as defining predispositions to organise stimuli in particular ways. At the time, however, this was of marginal interest given the emphasis on stimulus and not participant variables.

The Principle of Prägnanz

The main point of the Gestalt approach was to describe principles of organisation that gave rise to certain predepositions about how best to organise the proximal stimulus into meaningful wholes. To this end the Gestaltists also derived the **Principle of Prägnanz**. In its original form the principle was that 'perceptual organization will always be as "good" as the prevailing conditions allow' (Koffka, 1935/1963) and here the term 'good', although undefined, related to the application of stimulus factors such as regularity, similarity, symmetry, simplicity and so on. More generally, this principle of Prägnanz has been interpreted as a statement of the **minimum principle** (Hochberg & McAllister, 1953), namely, that of all the possible organisations consistent with a proximal stimulus the preferred one will be the one that is the simplest. We shall discuss the minimum principle in much greater depth later. For now it is most sensible to just describe the material rather than analyse it in depth.

Gestalt theory and the brain

A different aspect of Gestalt theory also warrants a mention. This is that the theory presupposed that

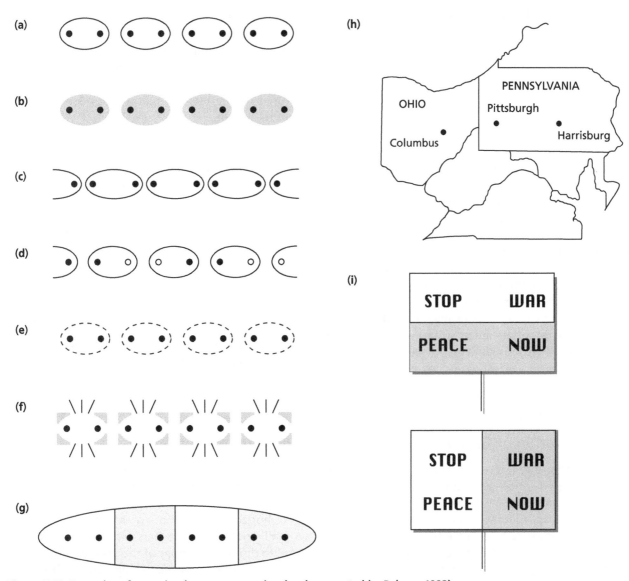

Figure 5.16 Examples of grouping by common region (as documented by Palmer, 1992)
Elements that fall within the same common region group together. Grouping by common region also seems to override grouping by proximity (c) and grouping by similarity (d). In (f) the notion of a region can be defined by illusory contours is shown. In (h) and (i), real-world examples are provided. In (i) different meanings are induced according to how the words are grouped together.

Source: Palmer, S. E. (1992). Common region: A new principle of perceptual grouping. *Cognitive Psychology, 24*, 436–447 (fig. 2, p. 439). Reproduced with permission from Elsevier.

perceptual organisation came about because the brain is structured to pick up the holistic properties of the stimulus as given by configural cues such as symmetry and closure. In this regard, the theory was fleshed out at the level of assumed electrical field properties of the brain. When a given stimulus acted as an input to sensory analysis the brain in turn resonated to the structural aspects of the stimulus and eventually settled on a pattern of activity that reflected 'an equilibrium involving minimum energy load' (van der Helm, 2000, p. 774). Given that almost no one now takes this theoretical excursion seriously, there is little point in dwelling too long on the details (for a very readable account, though, see Gordon, 1989). Despite the fact that there is little interest in the neural aspect of the theory, the Gestalt laws have had a profound and enduring impact on thinking about human perception. They remain the topic of much contemporary research and, in this regard, Figure 5.16 provides examples of a more recently described principle of perceptual organisation (taken from Palmer, 1992). Before we move on, it is important to appreciate one last aspect of Gestalt theory.

Mental copies and perceptual organisation

This is that if we accept that the Gestalt principles of organisation do play a central role in perception, then we have further grounds for arguing against the idea that, fundamentally, the internal representation of the proximal stimulus is something other than a mere copy of sensory stimulation. To reiterate, whereas in vision it is tempting to discuss the notion of a retinal copy of a visible stimulus, this fails to capture, in an important sense, the nature of perceptual representation. If we accept that the Gestalt laws provide something of an account of why certain interpretations are preferred over others, then it is difficult to see how this can be merely due to generating a copy of the stimulus.

Perceptual organisation implies that the input is structured in such a way that certain relations between the parts are specified and others are not. Figure 5.15(c) is structured according to rows and not columns so there is a fundamental sense in which the rows are captured by the internal representation whereas the columns are not.

This sort of idea will be returned to shortly but in the current context it is possible to classify the Old (Gestaltist) Look as being essentially a passive view of perception in which encoding principles are applied to any stimulus independently of its nature and of the mental state of the participant. By this view the operation of the perceptual system cannot be altered or influenced by prior knowledge. To understand this, however, we need to contrast the Old Look with the New.

Pinpoint question 5.8

What is a defining principle of the 'Old Look' Gestalt accounts of perception?

Research focus 5.2

The gestation of Gestalt: how infants learn to group perceptually

Babies are pretty interesting things. To see directly into their perceptions and cognitions would be truly a phenomenal step in uncovering how mental faculties develop. Clearly, given the concerns in this chapter, it is interesting to ask how it is that babies develop a sense of Prägnanz. The problem is, of course, getting some sort of meaningful response from infants, apart from the occasional giggle and stream of milky sick.

Quinn and Bhatt (2006) argued that one way to examine perceptual grouping in babies is to adopt a familiarisation–novelty preference paradigm (after Fantz, 1964). Here, ickle participants are presented with an initial stimulus until they become familiar with it. Then two new stimuli are presented, one that is similar to the familiar stimulus and a novel stimulus. By measuring looking time, if the infant looks longer at the novel stimulus, then the idea is that the baby has a representation of the familiar object such that the novel stimulus can be distinguished from it.

Over a series of experiments, Quinn and Bhatt (2006) tested both 3–4- and 7–8-month-old children. In the first experiment, infants were presented with

solid bars organised in vertical columns or horizontal rows, and also with a 4×4 grid of squares which could either be filled in to represent the same vertical or horizontal organisation. Infants could either be familiarised with the bars first and then compared to different versions of the grid, or presented with the grid first and then compared to different versions of the bars – see Figure 5.17(a). According to looking times, infants preferred the novel stimulus in both cases, indicating grouping by lightness since the filled-in squares formed one (perceptual) group and the unfilled squares formed another. Quinn and Bhatt (2006) then ruled out the idea that the use of identical shapes facilitated perceptual organisation in the first experiment by defining rows and columns according to random squares and diamonds – see Figure 5.17(b). Again, on the basis of looking times, infants preferred the novel stimulus, again indicating grouping by lightness. However, in a third experiment – Figure 5.17(c) – when form became the grouping attribute that distinguished familiar from novel test stimuli, infants did not as readily show a preference for the novel stimulus.

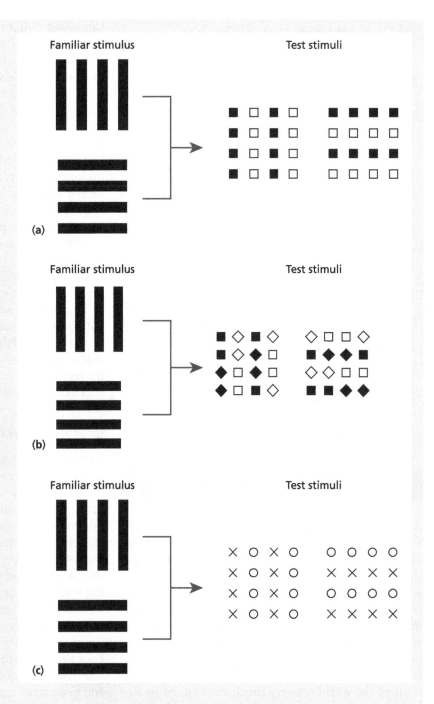

Figure 5.17 Examples of the sorts of displays used by Quinn and Bhatt (2006)

Source: Quinn, P. C., & Bhatt, R. S. (2006). Are some Gestalt principles deployed more readily than others during early development? The case of lightness versus form similarity. *Journal of Experimental Psychology: Human Perception and Performance, 32*, 1221–1230 (fig. 1, p. 1223, fig. 2, p. 1225, fig. 3, p. 1226). Reproduced with permission from APA.

Quinn and Bhatt (2006) concluded that grouping according to lightness is a much stronger cue for perceptual organisation in infants than form, which raises the question why? Well, the authors go on to suggest that form grouping is slowly learnt while lightness grouping might be acquired much earlier for the infant. So you need to give those gurgling and smelly humans a little more credit, as at 8 months old they are well on their way to developing some incredibly complex perceptual grouping mechanisms. Sounds exhausting – no wonder they sleep all the time.

Source: Quinn, P. C., & Bhatt, R. S. (2006). Are some Gestalt principles deployed more readily than others during early development? The case of lightness versus form similarity. *Journal of Experimental Psychology: Human Perception and Performance, 32*, 1221–1230.

New Look The idea that our perceptions of the world are influenced by our knowledge, expectations, beliefs, needs and desires about the world.

Old Look A passive view of perception in which encoding principles are applied to any stimulus independently of its nature and irrespective of the mental state of the participant.

Gestalt laws A set of statements backed up by demonstrations of how it is that the perceptual system groups elements (the parts) into coherent wholes. Collectively the laws specify principles of perceptual organisation.

proximity As pointed out by Gestaltists, elements that are close together tend to group together.

similarity As pointed out by Gestaltists, elements that are similar tend to group together.

principle of Prägnanz As pointed out by Gestaltists, perceptual elements tend to cohere into 'good' groupings.

minimum principle The idea that of all possible perceptual organisations, the one that will be selected will be the simplest.

The New Look

A pivotal figure in the New Look theoretical movement was Jerome Bruner (see collected papers in Anglin, 1974) and of particular interest is his seminal paper written in 1957. His theoretical approach is worthy of some detailed consideration because it provides a very good summary of some key ideas that are implicated in many attempts to understand human perception. It also allows us to reconsider the difference between passive and active views of perception.

The general New Look approach is that our perceptions of the world are very much determined by our knowledge, expectations, beliefs, needs and desires about the world. Perceptual defence (see discussion in Chapter 4) is one example taken to justify this claim, but many other examples exist. An important and early study was carried out by Bruner and Goodman (1947). They tested participants individually and the task was to alter the size of a spot of light so that it matched a comparison disc. The discs varied in size and varied in nature. Generally participants were reasonably good in their estimates of size when the discs were neutral but this changed dramatically when the discs were replaced with coins. Now participants generally overestimated the size of the coins and these estimates tended to increase with the value of the coins.

More unfortunate, though, is the realisation that the findings were further complicated by socio-economic factors. The participants in the experiment were 10-year-old children and half were classified as rich and half were classified as poor. When the size ratings were broken down according to the socio-economic class of the children, a rather upsetting result emerged. Although both sets of children overestimated the size of the coins, the poor children's estimates were more extreme than those of the rich children. Moreover the poor children's overestimates increased quite dramatically with the value of the coins: this was not true of the rich children's estimates.

Regardless of what the correct interpretation of these data is, the impact of the study was profound and the findings formed the foundations for the idea that *need* and *value* fundamentally determine our perceptions of the world. Such a view was clarified further in Bruner's later *perceptual readiness* theory.

Bruner's perceptual readiness theory

Central is the idea of a **perceptual cue** as defined as a property of the proximal stimulus. For Bruner the act of perception is taking the information provided by proximal cues and assigning this to a mental category. Fundamentally this means that perception implies the existence of certain mental categories. For instance, this might mean taking this particular spot of light on the retina and assigning it to the category 'a visual impression'. More generally it would mean being able to interpret the spot of light as (say) arising from the usherette's torch in a cinema. What we have here is a claim that perception means going from perceptual cues to mental categories. As Bruner (1957, p. 125) asserted, 'all perceptual experience is necessarily the end product of a categorization process'.

By assigning a given input to a mental category the implication is that the act of perception is said to 'go beyond' the information given. So as soon as you draw the perceptual inference that the spot of light indicates the presence of the usherette's torch, you can begin to draw certain other inferences about properties of the distal object that are plausible – in this sense, you have gone beyond the information that is the spot of light that was given. For instance, you can make predictions about the size of the torch in relation to the usherette's body and the fact that it will contain a switch for operating it and so on. As Bruner stated, such inferences imply **predictive veridicality**. The act of perception implies that the observer can go on to make predictions about the unseen environment on the basis of what has already been seen. The usefulness of such predictions depends on how elaborate the corresponding mental categories are. So a torch expert will begin to make far more sophisticated predictions about the 'spot of light' than the novice.

These are very important points because they begin to show how it is that perception is intimately tied up with prediction. By this view the perceptual system is taken to provide the observer with a representation of the world that is useful for prediction. So the perceptual representation of the brown and black striped 'tiger-like' shape will also provide some indication of the position of this object relative to the observer. This can then be used as a basis to decide to run or stay very still indeed! (See Allport, Tipper, & Chmiel, 1985, p. 109.) Predictions about what to do next are based on the information transmitted by the perceptual system. As a consequence it is important that whatever information is conveyed, is done so in a manner that makes it easy for the cognitive system to work on. The cognitive system must arrive at a reasonable interpretation of the outside world quickly and effectively (especially where perceiving tigers is concerned!).

In addition, Bruner discussed the notion of the accessibility of mental categories. That is, classifying 'the spot of light' as 'the usherette's torch' depends to some degree on the accessibility of the latter category. By the perceptual readiness account, the accessibility of a given category depends on essentially two factors, namely (i) the expectancies that the observer has of the likelihood of certain events, and (ii) the observer's needs. So the usherette's torch category will be highly accessible within the cinema rather than outside the cinema and it will be more easily accessed if you arrive late for the film and the cinema appears full than if you arrive in plenty of time and the cinema is not full. These notions of accessibility refer to the 'readiness' in 'perceptual readiness'.

> **perceptual cue** An aspect of the proximal stimulus that is used to infer what the distal stimulus is.
>
> **predictive veridicality** Going beyond the information provided by the current stimulus representation so as to predict future events.

Perception as a process of unconscious inference

Aside from the notion of category accessibility, central to the account is the notion of a **perceptual inference**. Much like Sherlock Holmes goes about solving a case, the perceptual system is seen to engage in taking a series of cues (clues) provided by the sensory stimulation and figuring out how best to interpret these cues. Perceptual inferences are made in assigning these cues to these categories. From registering this particular spot of light you draw the inference that it arises from the usherette's torch. Given that such inference making is not a conscious activity, we have the notion of perception being based on making **unconscious inferences**. This is very much in line with the traditional view of perception which is typically traced back to Helmholtz (1867/1962) – that perceptual processes act as though solving a problem by taking various cues and forming the best hypothesis as to the most likely distal stimulus that gave rise to the proximal stimulus.

The likelihood principle

In this regard, we have a different principle of perception from the minimum principle given to us by the Gestalt theorists. This alternative is known as the **likelihood principle** – 'sensory elements will be organized into the most probable object or event (distal stimulus) in the environment consistent with the sensory data (the proximal stimulus)' (Pomerantz & Kubovy, 1986, pp. 36–9). As Gregory (1970) stated, 'We are forced . . . to suppose that perception involves betting on the most probable interpretation of sensory data, in terms of the world of objects' (p. 29). Pylyshyn (1999) went even further and stated that, according to the New Look, perception involves a cycle of hypothesis and test whereby an initial best guess is made on the basis of some set of cues together with the current subjective state of the observer, this is checked against the stimulus information and, if needs be, the hypothesis is refined, reformulated and re-checked.

There are many fundamental issues here. For instance, ensuing arguments focused on various distinctions such as that between perception and cognition, between observation and inference (Fodor, 1984), between stimulus-driven and knowledge-based processes, between peripheral and central processes, etc. We will consider some of these as the discussion proceeds. However, the New Look approach only really makes sense in the view that, in general, the proximal stimulus is fundamentally ambiguous. The New Look approach is based on what has come to be known as a **poverty of the stimulus** argument (Fodor, 1985).

The poverty of the stimulus argument

By the poverty of the stimulus argument, the claim is that each proximal stimulus is an impoverished version of what is actually out there. In vision the perceptual system operates upon 2D impressions of a 3D world, and this may lead to problems and difficulties. For instance, given the right lighting conditions and angle of regard, a square patch of light may appear to signify the presence of a tilted oblong (Broadbent, 1971, p. 12). In the above example, featuring 'The Two Ronnies', 'four candles' and 'fork handles' may be indistinguishable in the absence of further disambiguating information, such as being in a home furnishing store as opposed to a garden centre. These sorts of examples are taken to show that any given proximal stimulus may be consistent with a number of different states of the environment (Broadbent, 1971, p. 12). Such a claim does not have universal support and it has been categorically denied by Gibson (1986) and the many followers of the direct perception school of thought. Consideration of the ensuing, rather heated debate would lead us in a direction away from cognitive accounts of perception. Interested readers may be entertained by the fray by consulting Fodor and Pylyshyn (1981) and Turvey, Shaw, Reed and Mace (1981).

Perhaps consideration of a classic example – known as the Necker cube (see Figure 5.18) – will help cement these ideas. This figure is inherently ambiguous because various actual objects could produce such a 2D projection – you are either looking down on a wire cube or looking up at one. More generally, though, it is claimed that every proximal stimulus is inherently ambiguous because it could have arisen from any one of an indefinite number of distal causes. The basic claim is that, in general, the proximal stimulus is

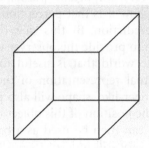

Figure 5.18 The classic Necker cube figure

an impoverished specification of the distal stimulus, and because of this the perceptual system necessarily engages in some form of inference-making. On the basis of this evidence (this sensory stimulation, i.e., a spot of light) your best guess is that this particular object (the distal stimulus, i.e., the usherette's torch) is actually out there in the real world. You make an inference about the nature of the distal object on the basis of the perceptual cues provided in the proximal stimulus. The argument is that if the information available at the senses uniquely specified the distal stimulus, then there would be no need for perceptual inference-making, as Gigerenzer and Murray (1987) rightly point out (p. 69).

Pinpoint question 5.9

'Let him have it, Chris', was the (alleged) sentence uttered by Derek Bentley as he and an armed Chris Craig were cornered on the roof top of a building in Croydon by police after they were disturbed while planning to rob a warehouse. Why was this spoken utterance ambiguous?

Perceptual inference-making

It is very easy to get confused here and, as Pinpoint question 5.9 demonstrates, perceptual ambiguity in some extreme cases can mean the difference between

You saw the whole of the cube: spatial neglect and Necker drawings

When a brain-damaged individual falls into the hands of a psychologist, they are often asked to perform a number of weird and wonderful tasks in order to assess their mental capacities. One such type of brain damage is spatial neglect and one such type of task is to draw a Necker cube. Typically, individuals with spatial neglect will fail to draw one half of the visual scene, typically the half of the scene opposite (or **contralateral**, as we like to say in the trade) to the side of the brain that has received the damage. Seki, Ishiai, Koyama, Sato, Hirabayashi and Inaki (2000) were particularly interested in why certain individuals with spatial neglect could successfully complete a drawing of the Necker cube while others couldn't.

An impressive sample of 100 right-handed patients with right hemisphere stroke was used in the study. This meant that these individuals would show neglect in the left side of space. Participants were split into two groups according to the severity of their neglect (mild and severe) and were also administered a test of verbal intelligence. Individuals were then asked to go ahead and draw a Necker cube with no time restrictions.

Upon a close examination of exactly how each individual drew the Necker cube, Seki et al. (2000) found that verbal IQ was positively correlated to the number of correct vertices the patient drew. Importantly, while verbal IQ did not appear to be a factor in determining the number of correct vertices for patients with mild neglect, a fair verbal IQ for those individuals with severe neglect helped to maintain performance at mild neglect levels. That is, it was only the combination of poor verbal IQ and severe neglect that caused the problem in drawing the Necker cube. This is clearly represented in Figure 5.19(b), in which the left halves of the cube and flower are missing.

Seki et al. (2000) concluded that both the severity of the spatial neglect and the verbal intelligence of the patient play critical roles in determining performance in post-trauma tasks such as those reported

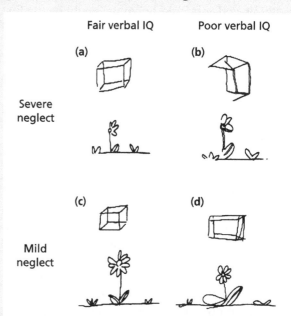

Figure 5.19 Drawings of various figures by individuals suffering from spatial neglect
Verbal intelligence can overcome drawing problems in patients with spatial neglect. The left-side neglect of a Necker cube in severe neglect patients appears to be more apparent for individuals with poor verbal IQ (b) relative to fair verbal IQ (a). Those with mild neglect and fair verbal IQ (c) perform relatively well at these tasks.

Source: Seki, K., Ishiai, S., Koyama, Y., Sato, S., Hirabayashi, H., & Inaki, K. (2000). Why are some patients with severe neglect able to copy a cube? The significance of verbal intelligence. *Neuropsychologia, 38*, 1466–1472 (fig. 5, p. 1470). Reproduced with permission from Elsevier.

here. Therefore, not only is the Necker cube an interesting stimulus from a standard cognitive point of view, but it can also tell us something about the abilities of individuals who have suffered brain trauma. Not bad for a collection of 12 lines, really.

Source: Seki, K., Ishiai, S., Koyama, Y., Sato, S., Hirabayashi, H., & Inaki, K. (2000). Why are some patients with severe neglect able to copy a cube? The significance of verbal intelligence. *Neuropsychologia, 38*, 1466–1472.

life and death – Derek Bentley was eventually convicted and sent to the gallows. Typically, when inference-making is discussed, the implication is that someone is engaged in some form of difficult problem-solving

activity such as completing a crossword puzzle. The aim here is to go from a set of clues to filling in the letters in the crossword. For example, given the clue 'Coin used as an image of worship (4)', one way to proceed is simply to think of different coins whose names are four letters long. So the (bottom-up) inference is that the solution is a name of a coin that is four letters in length. The word length ('4') initiates the hypothesis-and-test cycle. So 'dime' might be the first hypothesis but then 'cent' fits this description as well and the current input is ambiguous with respect to both of these (top-down) predictions. However, an alternative hypothesis can be considered and this comes from knowledge about how crosswords work. Here the idea is to rearrange the particular letters of COIN and test out these possibilities. In doing this, a much more plausible solution is discovered.

This example stresses how problem solving can involve inference-making, generating hypotheses and testing these against the evidence. However, the example also emphasises conscious processes in which participants would be able to provide a running commentary of how they were proceeding while engaged in the task. This is quite unlike the sort of problem solving that is taken to characterise perception. The idea that perception is like problem solving must not be taken to imply that perceptual analysis is dependent on being aware of the underlying processes. As Gregory (1980) stated, 'Much of human behaviour controlled by perception can occur without awareness: consciousness is seldom, if ever, necessary' (p. 196). So the problem-solving terminology applied to perceptual analysis describes the way in which the underlying processes are assumed to operate, by analogy.

The overarching point is that the perceptual system is faced with the problem of deciding which distal stimulus gave rise to this particular proximal stimulus. The argument goes that it achieves a solution by a process of unconscious inference-making. Certain plausible hypotheses are made about the possible link between the proximal and distal stimuli and these are then tested out against the available sensory evidence.

This will become much clearer if we consider what a perceptual inference might look like and here we can turn to an abridged example taken from Gigerenzer and Murray (1987, p. 63). They defined a perceptual inference in terms of something they call a **probabilistic syllogism**. Any syllogism contains a series of statements that are divided into initial premises and a final conclusion. So an example of a perceptual inference is taken to include:

- *a major premise*: concurrent stimulation of the same right-hand position on both retinae is *normally* associated with a luminous object being present in the left visual field

- *a minor premise*: there is currently stimulation of these right-handed retinal locations
- *a conclusion*: a luminous object is currently present in the left side of space.

Gigerenzer and Murray (1987) stated that, according to the traditional Hemholtzian view of inference-making in perception, the major premise is a generalisation learned by experience, but it seems also quite possible that the premise could specify some constraint that has evolved over the emergence of the human visual system – for example, shadows cast on the ground tend to provide information about the actual position of the light source. Now of course these sorts of constraints could be learnt but they could also reflect evolutionary adaptations.

The major premise also contains the important hedge 'normally', and this gives licence to the term 'probabilistic' in 'probabilistic syllogism'. The assumption is that perceptual inferences are not water-tight and can only provide best first guesses as to the nature of the environment. Indeed the fact that the visual system can be fooled by visual illusions shows that the perceptual system is fallible: the initial inferences made about the sensory data are often incorrect.

Lessons from perceptual illusions

Optimally, the perceptual system should be providing the cognitive system with an accurate (veridical) record of the environment that unambiguously specifies what is out there. However, outside this 'best of all possible worlds' scenario, the truth is that the perceptual system is fallible and mistakes do arise. Indeed there is a vast literature on how the perceptual system may be fooled by various kinds of perceptual illusions (see Wade, 1982) and some of these (see Figure 5.20) are extraordinarily compelling. The existence of such illusions provides clear examples of mismatches between our perceptions of the external world and the actual nature of the external world. Indeed examples such as these again stand in contrast to the naïve realist view of perception in which our internal world simply mirrors the external world. Our perceptions of the world cannot be mere copies because if they were then there would be no such things as perceptual illusions. There really is no need to conclude that the stick bends merely because it is half submerged in water. Even though the perceptual representation specifies a bent stick, the real world contains a straight stick. The stick appears to be bent even though we know that the stick is straight. In this case, and despite knowledge to

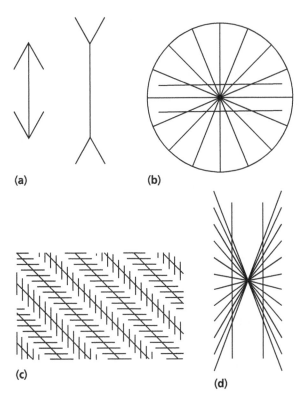

Figure 5.20 A cornucopia of visual illusions
(a) The Muller–Lyer illusion: the right vertical line appears longer than the left. (b) The two parallel, horizontal lines appear to bow. (c) The long diagonal lines appear not to be parallel. (d) The two parallel, vertical lines appear to bow.

Sources: (a) Robinson, J. O. (1972). *The psychology of visual illusion* (fig. 2.1, p. 21, fig. 3.3, p. 67, fig. 3.19, p. 73 and fig. 3.33, p. 7). London: Hutchinson. Reproduced with permission.
(b–d) Palmer, S. E. (1992). Common region: A new principle of perceptual grouping. *Cognitive Psychology*, *24*, 436–447 (fig. 7, p. 445). Reproduced with permission from Elsevier.

the contrary, the world appears differently from what it actually is. So what are such apparent anomalies telling us?

The understanding here is that the perceptual system has evolved in such a way that it delivers as truthful a representation of the environment as possible given certain facts about the nature of the world together with physical constraints embodied in the central nervous system. For instance, our ability to perceive the depth of surfaces relative to our angle of regard is in part driven by the fact that we have two eyes that are symmetrically positioned relative to the midline of our bodies. This is a rather obvious physiological constraint. In addition, we can only detect certain wavelengths of light (contained in the visible spectrum) and we cannot hear dog whistles, even if we'd want to. The perceptual system operates within such physical constraints that, according to evolutionary theory, reflect a sensitivity to those properties of the world that have adaptive significance to us as biological organisms.

More interesting, perhaps, is the possibility that the perceptual system has evolved in such a way that it reflects particular properties about real-world structure (i.e., objects). In this regard, Marr (1982) considered a number of processing constraints that likely reflect properties of the nature of objects such that they are cohesive and may be rigid. Points on the surface of an object that are adjacent will likely stimulate adjacent retinal cells. Hence the firing of two adjacent retinal cells implies two sources of light that arise from a single object. In this way the sorts of perceptual inferences that characterise the perceptual analysis stage (about contour extraction and figure/ground segregation) can

For example . . .

Physiological constraints do not just restrict laboratory experiments – they also have been used and abused in the outside world too. For example, **presbycusis** is the common complaint suffered by many older individuals who lose sensitivity in higher frequency regions (low frequency sounds are rumbles and booms, high frequency sounds are shrills and whistles). According to one article from *The New York Times* (Vitello, Hammer & Schweber 2006), presbycusis was manipulated in two different social contexts. In the first devious manoeuvre, annoying high frequency sounds, which younger people could

hear but older people could not, were installed around bus stops and other favourite haunts of the adolescent to disperse large groups in public settings. In a second, equally devious manoeuvre, the kids decided to use similar high frequency sounds as ring tones, such that they could remain in the loop regarding phone calls and text messages in class without that ancient, grey-haired teacher at the front being able to hear what was happening. Touché!

Source: Vitello, P., Hammer, K., & Schweber, N. (2006, June 12). A ring tone meant to fall on deaf ears. *The New York Times*.

make clever suggestions about the sorts of structures out there that correspond to objects. Gregory (1970) provides some further examples. The critical point, though, is that, in some cases, such knowledge (as embodied in the processing constraints) may not apply equally well in all cases.

Consider the classic Muller–Lyer figure shown in Figure 5.20(a). The figure on the right is typically interpreted as a receding corner of a room whereas the figure on the left is interpreted as a protruding corner of a room. The so-called fins attached to the line ends are taken by the visual system to correspond to cues to distance as to how far the edge is from the viewer. In the real world the cues indicate that the respective edges are at different distances from the viewer. So if a metre-tall fencing post is situated one metre from the viewer and there is another situated 10 metres away, the latter gives rise to a smaller retinal image than the former – the more distant post 'looks smaller' than the nearer one. More formally, Emmert's rule states that 'the image of an object is inversely proportional to distance' (Rock, 1983, p. 302). So as Rock stated, in

applying the rule, 'the greater the perceived distance of the image, the larger the object must be' (p. 302). To compensate for this the visual system is said to invoke **size constancy/invariance**. Merely because objects recede into the distance does not mean that they decrease in size, so to preserve the idea that objects retain their size this perceptual inference is built into the system. However, the violation of size constancy can also lead to some interesting holiday photos (see Figure 5.21).

According to Gregory (1970), it is the misapplication of size constancy that gives rise to the Muller–Lyer illusion. In the right-hand version of Figure 5.20(a) the edge appears further away than it does in the left-hand version, hence the system tries to compensate for this by producing an impression of a line that is longer than it actually is (on the right) and a line that is shorter than it actually is (on the left). It would be disingenuous to convey that this is the only account of the illusion – it is not (see Robinson, 1972) – but the example is nevertheless intriguing. It shows how arguments have been made to try to substantiate the claim

Figure 5.21 Violations of size constancy make for great holiday photos
Source: Alamy Images/Peter Jordan.

Figure 5.22 A visually confusing scene (from Kanizsa, 1969)

Source: Kanizsa, G. (1969). Perception, past experience and the 'impossible experiment'. *Acta Psychologica*, *31*, 66–96 (fig. 18, p. 85). Reproduced with permission from Elsevier.

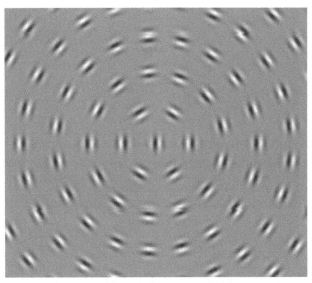

Figure 5.23 An example of how isolated elements cohere to form the impression of surfaces and contours

Source: Achtman, R. L., Hess, R. F., & Wang, Y.-Z. (2003). Sensitivity for global shape detection. *Journal of Vision*, *3*, 616–624 (fig. 2j, p. 619). Copyright © The Association for Research in Vision and Ophthalmology (AVRO). Reproduced with permission.

that knowledge about the physical world may form the basis of perceptual analysis, and, moreover, that there are clear cases where such knowledge is misapplied.

Indeed, this sort of consideration has been brought to the fore on several occasions by Kanizsa (1969, 1985). For instance, in Figure 5.22 the impression is that the sails of the boats are nearer than the fishing rod despite everything we know about fishing rods and their size in relation to the size of a sail. In this way it is seen that certain perceptual inferences are drawn that starkly contradict common sense – in this case it seems that the visual system prefers to interpret larger objects as nearer (Kanizsa, 1969).

> **Pinpoint question 5.10**
>
> **Why don't perceptual illusions support a naïve view of perception?**

Modularity revisited

If this inference-making view of perception is accepted, then one sensible way to proceed is to try to figure out what sorts of perceptual inferences there are. One first approximation to an answer is provided by the Gestalt laws. For instance, the fact that these elements line up in a systematic way suggests that they form part of a single edge or contour (see Figure 5.23, taken from Achtman, Hess & Wang, 2003). A more detailed account, though, has been put forward by Fodor (1983, 1985).

We have already discussed the notion of a perceptual module in the Fodorian sense and how this may be characterised by *information encapsulation*. That is, each module has access only to a limited module-specific store of knowledge. So for instance, the speech processing module would most likely have access to information regarding word boundaries and properties of the sound signal specific to speech, the visual module concerning figure/ground segregation would have access to information regarding the nature of contours and edges, and so on. The critical thing, however, is that both modules are limited in only having access to information within their respective domains. The speech module has no access to information about edges and the figure/ground module has no access to information about spoken words.

In addition, neither module has access to semantic/conceptual knowledge about what a cat is or what /cat/ (the spoken form of 'cat') means. Although these ideas are contentious, one simple way of thinking about perceptual modules, and the perceptual system in general, is that it takes sensory data and generates some form of representation of this in terms of a specification of a segregation between objects and background without any commitment to what the objects are. For ease of exposition this has been referred to here as a perceptual representation. The perceptual representation therefore is a structured representation

Figure 5.24 Yet another example of a fragmentary figure

Source: Leeper, R. (1935). A study of a neglected portion of the field of learning: The development of sensory organization. *Journal of Genetic Psychology, 46*, 41–75 (fig. 1, p. 49). Reproduced with permission of the Helen Dwight Reid Educational Foundation.

in which the stimulus information has been divided up into plausible figures and plausible ground – it specifies 'the arrangement of things in the world' (Fodor, 1983, p. 42). It is the work of the central systems to now generate a plausible interpretation of this perceptual representation.

'Seeing' vs. 'Seeing as'

A very useful distinction in this context is between 'seeing' and 'seeing as'. This can be most easily grasped by considering Figure 5.24. Initially you probably see just a jumble of black blobs on a white background – we see the blobs and we see them *as* blobs. However, it is also possible to see the blobs as a man riding a horse. In both cases it is appropriate to discuss the perceptual representation as merely specifying individual black blobs. In the first case our interpretation of the figure is essentially black blobs on a white background. In the second case our interpretation is that the figure depicts, albeit in a very impoverished way, a man riding a horse. The claim is that the perceptual representation underlying these different interpretations is the same – the seeing is the same in both cases. What changes is the interpretation – the seeing as.

Bottom-up vs. top-down modes of processing

In contrast to this analysis, in the New Look approach even perceptual processes (i.e., the seeing) are influenced by general knowledge. Here the basic idea is that knowledge of the world in large part determines our perceptions of it to the extent that it will fundamentally alter the perceptual representation. So if we need to eat we will actually begin to see food. The differences between the two theoretical approaches can be better

understood in terms of the difference between stimulus-driven and knowledge-driven processes or alternatively between bottom-up and top-down processes. To reiterate: stimulus-driven/bottom-up processes are those that are essentially put in motion by the stimulus – it is difficult not to state that such processes are automatically invoked by the physical nature of the stimulus. The ace of hearts automatically produces activation in the red detectors (see Figure 5.11). In contrast, knowledge-driven or top-down processes 'control and structure information delivered by input processes' (Gordon, 1989, p. 137).

So whereas in the modular account inferences work from the bottom up, inferences in the New Look operate from the top down. To invoke top-down processes in perception seems to allow for the possibility that the act of seeing can be fundamentally altered by our desires, needs, wants, expectations, etc. So the New Look account of perception is active, not passive, and as Broadbent (1977) stated, the implication is that the central mechanisms essentially interrogate the input, 'testing hypothetical models of the world against the sensory evidence' (p. 113). Perhaps the most extreme form of top-down processing is that implemented in the re-entrant model of Di Lollo and colleagues in which the pattern information represented at the level of the pattern layer over-writes the current representation of the input in the working space (see Chapter 4). However, less extreme forms of top-down processing are possible (see Figure 5.25). Figure 5.25 is taken from Gregory (1998) and sets out a framework for thinking about perception that encompasses the New Look. By this view, top-down processes may be invoked when an error in interpreting the proximal stimulus occurs.

perceptual inference Certain plausible hypotheses are made about the possible link between the proximal and distal stimuli and these are then tested out against the available sensory evidence.

unconscious inference A perceptual inference that operates unconsciously.

likelihood principle The idea that 'sensory elements will be organized into the most probable object or event (distal stimulus) in the environment consistent with the sensory data (the proximal stimulus)' (Pomerantz & Kubovy, 1986, pp. 36–9).

poverty of the stimulus The assumption that the proximal stimulus is a very poor under-specification of what the distal stimulus is.

contralateral Opposite side to the side being considered.

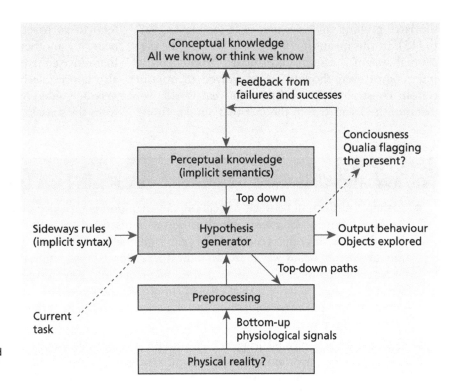

Figure 5.25 Gregory's (1998) schematic representation of the organisation and operation of the human perceptual system

Source: Gregory, R. L. (1998). Brainy minds. *British Medical Journal, 317,* 1693–1695 (fig. 3, p. 1694). Reproduced with permission from BMJ Publishing Group.

---

probabilistic syllogism A collection of statements in which the major premise and minor premise lead to a likely conclusion.

presbycusis Loss of high frequency sensitivity in hearing traditionally associated with aging.

size constancy/invariance The perceptual inference that an object retains its size regardless of the size of its image on the retina. The ability to discount absolute size in identifying shape.

Concluding comments

So where does this leave us? Well, it appears that we have two alternative accounts of inference-making in perception. By the modularity of mind view (Fodor, 1983) each perceptual module contains certain principles of operation (these define the corresponding perceptual inferences) that are applied to any stimulus in a bid to parse the input into plausible objects, from the bottom up. The input modules feed forward the first best guess as to the nature of the stimulus. The eventual perceptual representation is then operated upon by the central mechanisms that offer an interpretation of the input (e.g., a few random black blobs on the page, a huntsman on a horse). In contrast to

this, and according to the New Look, the actual perceptual analysis is driven by the mental categories that the participant possesses in a top-down fashion. If I am hungry enough, any large yellow 'M' in the high street will do.

The central dilemma remains. This revolves around whether or not our knowledge of the world can influence stimulus coding in such a way that our perceptions primarily reflect our wants, needs and desires instead of what is really out there. In considering this dilemma we have attempted to base the discussion on an apparently clear distinction between a passive (Old Look) account of perception and an active (New Look) account. However, a more complicated view has emerged from consideration of the issues. Indeed, as Broadbent (1977) stated, there is possibly a better framework for thinking about perception.

By this view there is an initial perceptual analysis stage that is passive and which takes evidence that arrives at the senses and then goes on to *suggest* possible interpretations of the environment. This is then followed by a stage in which the most promising interpretation is followed by active interrogation of sensory stimulation to check for the presence of features that have yet to be detected. According to Navon (1981) it is useful therefore to distinguish between *suggestion* as the label for the 'flow of information from the environment into the perceptual system' and *inquiry* as the label for the later probing of the evidence (Broadbent, 1977, p. 115). By this means it is possible to see how the perceptual system is essentially insulated from cognitive interference even though it has evolved to honour certain constraints that exist in the real world. For instance, it is sensitive to the fact that similar things tend to go together and that similar things that are near one another go together, and that similar things that move coherently together go together, etc. We can also appreciate how the interpretation of a stimulus may be guided by the selective uptake of information from the senses.

CHAPTER SUMMARY

- A simple distinction between perception and cognition is provided and this mapped onto the difference between input modules and central processes as discussed by Fodor (1983) in his modularity of mind hypothesis. In this respect, perception is informationally encapsulated such that the outputs from the input modules do not in any way reflect an individual's expectations, wants, desires or needs. In contrast, higher-order influences such as wishes or desires only come into play during the operation of central processes, when the system is trying to understand (interpret) the sense data. The perceptual system (and the concomitant perceptual representation) therefore may be said to be veridical (truthful), although the interpretations of this representation may not be.

- Even though it is possible to perceive a stimulus without necessarily being able to recognise it, familiarity clearly plays an important role in perception. However, in order to assess whether familiarity impacts upon perception or cognition, word recognition experiments have been particularly useful (Broadbent & Gregory, 1967a). The word frequency effect is perhaps the most obvious manifestation of how familiarity impacts on perception: common words are more easily perceived than are rare words.

- Nevertheless, it is not clear whether frequency effects come about through an enhancement of sensory mechanisms (i.e., perception) or whether central and more response-based mechanisms (i.e., cognition) are responsible. Blakemore and Cooper (1970) found that kittens raised in environments in which only vertical or horizontal lines were present were essentially blind to orientations to which they had not been exposed. Such data support a perceptual account of familiarity. Alternatively, familiar stimuli might be thought of as having a lower threshold than unfamiliar stimuli, thereby supporting a decisional account of familiarity. Perceptual and decisional accounts may be distinguished using signal detection theory and the observation of an effect of familiarity on d' or β, respectively.

- In accounting specifically for the word frequency effect, empirical support has been garnered for accounts that argue for the locus of this effect at a perceptual (early) level and those that argue for a post-perceptual (late) level. For example, using a same/different paradigm, Hochberg (1968) showed that the ability to respond same/different was equivalent for meaningful and meaningless letter strings when they were placed close together. The idea here was that when such judgements could be made at the level of sensory analysis, then familiarity was not important. Consequently, such effects had to exist at the level of post-perceptual processes.

- However, additional evidence supporting the perceptual nature of familiarity effects is provided by research into word superiority. Doyle and Leach (1988) asked participants on which of two intervals either a word or non-word appeared given very fast rates of presentation. A word superiority effect was found – i.e., perceptual report of words was better than for non-words – and the effect was manifest in d' (a measure of sensitivity), thereby supporting a perceptual account of familiarity. Merikle and Reingold (1990) also found a word superiority effect in visual masking studies on d' providing further support for this claim.

- Our sensory world is also influenced by what we expect to experience and how recently we have encountered certain events. The study of ambiguous figures (such as the classic old/young woman) helps to compare the relative contribution of these two factors. Epstein and Rock (1960) presented participants with an alternating sequence of unambiguous old or young woman pictures followed by a target ambiguous figure. If recency was the most important factor influencing judgement, then participants should interpret the ambiguous figure according to the last picture. If expectancy was more important, then participants should interpret the ambiguous figure according to the expected pattern of the previous stimuli. While support for recency over expectation was provided, more recent evidence (Girgus, Rock, & Egatz, 1977; Wilton, 1985) has called this conclusion into question.

- Ideas related to the effects of recency are also represented by the literature on repetition priming, in which stimulus identification is improved if a stimulus is repeated (Humphreys, Besner, & Quinlan, 1998). Benton and Moscovitch (1988) examined the interaction between familiarity and repetition. For unfamiliar stimuli such as non-words, repetition only had a very short-lived effect. For familiar stimuli such as words, repetition had a longer-lasting effect. Therefore, although perception is sensitive to recently encountered stimuli, the role of long-term representations such as those associated with familiar stimuli also seems to influence judgement.

- Expectancy can influence perception in many different forms. Instructional set refers to explicit commands influencing a participant's perception (Hochberg, 1970). In contrast, mental set is where a participant is implicitly put in mind of a certain perception (Steinfeld, 1967). In sum then, familiarity, recency and expectancy are all thought to influence perception, although it is hard to disentangle these influences and also hard to locate the actual site of these effects (Huang & Pashler, 2005).

- Notions of participant factors influencing current perception stand in contrast to the 'Old Look' Gestalt school. The Gestalt laws or principles of perceptual organisation such as proximity and similarity were used to explain how individuals derive perceptual representations without reference to beliefs, desires, expectations, etc. A more overriding principle is that of the principle of Prägnanz – 'perceptual organization will always be as "good" as the prevailing conditions allow' (Koffka, 1935/1963).

- In contrast, the New Look school of perception (Bruner, 1957) did, however, acknowledge that our prior knowledge, needs and experience of the world heavily influence what we currently perceive. Perceptual readiness was put forward as a concept by which the individual was able to assign perception to mental categories and consequently go beyond the sense data to make inferences about what else might be out there (predictive veridicality).

- In the (Old Look) minimum principle, of all possible organisations the one that will be selected will be the simplest. In contrast, in the (New Look) likelihood principle it is the organisation that is most likely that will be selected. Also associated with the New Look school is that idea that individuals engage in a form of perceptual hypothesis testing regarding their environment. These kinds of perceptual inferences can be important when our sensory input is impoverished.

- Such a binary Old Look vs. New Look distinction may not be that helpful after all and if we are to make significant progress in understanding perception then aspects of both active and passive modes of operation will need to be considered (cf. Broadbent, 1977).

ANSWERS TO PINPOINT QUESTIONS

5.1 Perception and input modules are responsible for (a) the first initial reading of the sentence. Cognition and central mechanisms are responsible for (b) its interpretation.

5.2 It is better to compare rare words with familiar words rather than random letter strings, since potential confounds such as meaningfulness and pronounceability are controlled for.

5.3 The smell of car fumes should have a lower threshold in the city because of its increased familiarity.

5.4 Traditionally, it has been accepted that an effect of d' implies operations at the level of perceptual mechanisms.

5.5 A repetition effect is where responses to the repeated presentation of a stimulus is facilitated

▶

relative to a case where the stimulus is not repeated.

5.6   Look between words rather than within the words themselves (. . . instructional se**t wo**uld help . . .).

5.7   More recent, more familiar and more expected stimuli will be identified more effectively than distant, rare and unexpected stimuli.

5.8   The Old Look Gestalts posit a passive view of perception in which encoding is driven by basic grouping mechanisms rather than the mental state of the person.

5.9   'Let him have it, Chris' could have been referring to Chris handing over the gun, or it could have been an encouragement to shoot at the police.

5.10 Perceptual illusions have multiple interpretations and as such perception cannot simply be based on simple copying operations.

CHAPTER 7

Learning and behaviour

LUCK CAN CHANGE YOUR LIFE

Ms V is a compulsive gambler. It wrecked her marriage and drained her wallet long ago. Her kids don't like her because she is always barely scraping by – and borrowing money from them – waiting for the next big win that she hopes will give her all the cash she needs to escape her current mess.

How did it all begin? The answer lies in the schedules of reinforcement. At college, one of her boyfriends liked to bet on the horses and V went along one day. She bet £10 on a filly named Flo and won £300. What a rush! Luck brought her a giant reinforcer without much effort – with no 'down side' in sight. Her boyfriend was excited, too. V saved the money and went back to the track several more times over the next several weeks – sometimes alone, sometimes with her boyfriend – making more £10 bets. Most lost. A few made small wins. But the betting was exciting, and there was lots of sensory stimulation when her horse took one of the front positions.

When V's £300 was about half gone, she bet on a long shot with big odds. No one expected Viceroy to win, but V put down £75 on a hunch. Viceroy . . . won by a nose. V walked away with £4,500 in her pocket. Early periods of generous reinforcement can have a big effect on our later behavioural decisions.

Source: adapted from Baldwin and Baldwin, 1998.

WHAT YOU SHOULD BE ABLE TO DO AFTER READING CHAPTER 7

- Describe the concept of habituation and the phenomena of classical conditioning and operant learning.
- Understand the principles underlying classical conditioning.
- Understand the principles underlying operant conditioning.
- Describe and explain conditioned aversions.
- Apply the principles of learning theory to behaviour.
- Describe some of the factors that influence academic learning.

QUESTIONS TO THINK ABOUT

- Do different aspects of learning have different underlying principles? Is learning to ride a bike governed by different principles from those used for learning to find your way around college or university or learning a foreign language?
- Does all learning have to be intentional? Can you learn something without knowing it or without wanting to learn it?
- Is learning a process that depends on innate ability, the ability to adopt successful learning strategies or both?
- What factors do you think enhance and promote the process of learning?
- What psychological factors can enhance (or impair) your academic learning?
- In what way is the brain like a computer (and vice versa)?

The purpose of learning

Behaviours that produce favourable consequences are repeated and become habits, but those that produce unfavourable consequences tend not to recur (Ouellette and Wood, 1998). In other words, we learn from experience. **Learning** is an adaptive process in which the tendency to perform a particular behaviour is changed by experience. As conditions change, we learn new behaviours and eliminate old ones.

This chapter considers three kinds of learning: habituation, classical conditioning and operant conditioning. All three involve cause-and-effect relations between behaviour and the environment. We learn which stimuli are trivial and which are important, and we learn to make adaptive responses and to avoid maladaptive ones. We learn to recognise those conditions under which a particular response is useful and those under which a different response is more appropriate. The types of learning described in this chapter serve as the building blocks for more complex behaviours, such as problem-solving and thinking, which we consider in later chapters.

Learning, however, cannot be truly observed in a direct sense; it can only be inferred from changes in behaviour. The influential field of behaviourism (see Chapter 1) which dominated experimental psychology in the early twentieth century demanded that only observable behaviour could be valid subject matter for psychologists. However, even the founding father of behaviourism, John B. Watson, argued that there could be two categories of observable behaviour: explicit behaviour, which is directly observable to the eye, and implicit behaviour, which could be measured by special equipment (an example would be the measurement of bodily response using psychophysiological recording equipment).

But not all changes in behaviour are caused by learning. For example, your performance in an examination or the skill with which you operate a car can be affected by your physical or mental condition, such as fatigue, fearfulness or distraction. Moreover, learning may occur without noticeable changes in observable behaviour taking place. In some cases, learning is not apparent – at least, not right away – from our observable behaviour. In other cases, we may never have the opportunity to demonstrate what we have learned. For example, although you may have received training in how to conduct an orthogonally rotated factor analysis in your computer's statistics package, you may never need to demonstrate the results of your learning again. In still other cases, you may not be sufficiently motivated to demonstrate something you have learned. For example, a tutor might pose a question in a seminar but although you know the answer, you do not say anything because you get nervous when speaking in front of others.

Learning takes place within the nervous system. Experience alters the structure and chemistry of the brain, and these changes affect the individual's subsequent behaviour. Performance is the behavioural change (or new behaviour) produced by this internal change.

Habituation

Many events may cause us to react automatically. For example, a sudden, unexpected noise causes an **orienting response**: we become alert and turn our heads towards the source of the sound. However, if the noise occurs repeatedly, we gradually cease to respond to it; we eventually ignore it. **Habituation**, learning not to respond to an unimportant event that occurs repeatedly, is the simplest form of learning. Even infants a few months old show evidence of habituation (see Chapter 12).

From an evolutionary perspective, habituation makes adaptive sense. If a once-novel stimulus occurs again and again without any important result, the stimulus has no significance to the organism. Obviously, responding to a stimulus of no importance wastes time and energy.

The simplest form of habituation is temporary, and is known as short-term habituation. Imagine entering a new room in an inhabited house. It is likely that you will perceive the distinctive odour of the room. Eventually, however, you begin not to notice the odour; you will have become habituated. If you return to the same house the next day, however, you will perceive that distinctive smell again but if you stay in the room for long enough, you will again become habituated.

Classical conditioning

Unlike habituation, **classical conditioning** involves learning about the conditions that predict that a significant event will occur. We acquire much of our behaviour through classical conditioning. For example, if you are hungry and smell a favourite food cooking, your mouth is likely to water. If you see someone with whom you have recently had a serious argument, you are likely to experience again some of the emotional reactions that occurred during the encounter. If you hear a song that you used to listen to with a loved one, you are likely to experience a feeling of nostalgia. If you listen to a piece of music that can be distinctly identified by nation, then people will buy more of that nation's wine. How does such classical conditioning take place?

Imagine that you have an uninflated balloon directly before you. Someone starts inflating the balloon with a pump; the balloon gets larger and larger. What are you likely to do? You will probably grimace and squint your eyes as you realise that the balloon is about to burst in your face.

Now consider how a person learns to flinch defensively at the sight of a tightly stretched balloon. Suppose that we inflate a balloon in front of a young boy who has never seen one before. The boy will turn his eyes towards the enlarging balloon, but he will not flinch. When the balloon explodes, the noise and the blast of air will cause a defensive startle reaction: he will squint, grimace, raise his shoulders and suddenly move his arms towards his body. A bursting balloon is an important stimulus, one that causes an automatic, unlearned defensive reaction.

We will probably not have to repeat the experience many times for the boy to learn to react the way we all do – flinching defensively before the balloon actually bursts. A previously neutral stimulus (the over-inflated balloon), followed by an important stimulus (the explosion that occurs when the balloon bursts), can now trigger the defensive flinching response by itself. The defensive flinching response has been classically conditioned to the sight of an over-inflated balloon. Two stimuli have become associated with each other.

Pavlov's serendipitous discovery

In December 1904, the Russian physiologist Ivan Pavlov was awarded the Nobel Prize in physiology and medicine for his work on the digestive system. Invited to Stockholm to accept the award and to deliver an acceptance speech, the 55-year-old Pavlov did not speak of his pioneering work on digestion (Babkin, 1949). Instead, his address, entitled 'The first sure steps along the path of a new investigation', focused on his more recent work involving conditional reflexes or 'involuntary' responses. Pavlov's new line of research was to take him far from the research for which he was awarded the Nobel Prize, and today he is remembered more for his work in psychology than in physiology. But it was while studying the digestive system that Pavlov stumbled on the phenomenon that was to make a lasting impact on psychology (Windholz, 1997).

Pavlov's chief ambition as a physiologist was to discover the neural mechanisms controlling glandular secretions during digestion. He measured the secretions during the course of a meal by inserting a small tube in a duct in an animal's mouth and collecting drops of saliva as they were secreted by the salivary gland. During each of the test sessions, he placed dry food powder inside the dog's mouth and then collected the saliva. All went well until the dogs became experienced subjects. After several testing sessions, the dogs began salivating before being fed, usually as soon as they saw the laboratory assistant enter the room with the food powder. What Pavlov discovered was a form of learning in which one stimulus predicts the occurrence of another. In this case, the appearance of the laboratory assistant predicted the appearance of food.

Rather than ignoring this phenomenon or treating it as a confounding variable that needed to be controlled, Pavlov designed experiments to discover exactly why the dogs were salivating before being given the opportunity to eat. He suspected that salivation might be triggered by stimuli that were initially unrelated to eating. Somehow, these neutral stimuli came to control what is normally a natural reflexive behaviour. After all, dogs do not naturally salivate when they see laboratory assistants.

To do so, he placed an inexperienced dog in a harness and occasionally gave it small amounts of food powder. Before placing the food powder in the dog's mouth, Pavlov sounded a bell, a buzzer or some other auditory stimulus. At first, the dog showed only a startle response to the sound, perking its ears and turning its head towards the sound. The dog salivated only when the food powder was placed in its mouth. But after only a dozen or so pairings of the bell and food powder, the dog began to salivate when the bell rang. Placing the food powder in the dog's mouth was no longer necessary to elicit salivation; the sound by itself was sufficient. Pavlov showed that a neutral stimulus can elicit a response similar to the original reflex when the stimulus predicts the occurrence of a significant stimulus (in this case, food powder).

This type of learning is called classical or **Pavlovian conditioning**. Pavlov demonstrated that conditioning occurred only when the food powder followed the bell within a short time. If there was a long delay between the sound and the food powder or if the sound followed the food powder, the animal never learned to salivate when it heard the sound. Thus, the sequence and timing of events are important factors in classical conditioning. Classical conditioning provides us with a way to learn cause-and-effect relations between environmental events. We are able to learn about the stimuli that warn us that an important event is about to occur. Obviously, warning stimuli must occur prior to the event about which we are being warned.

Figure 7.1 shows the basic classical conditioning procedure – the special conditions that must exist for an organism to respond to a previously neutral stimulus.

A stimulus, such as food, that naturally elicits reflexive behaviour, such as salivation, is called an **unconditional stimulus (UCS)**. The reflexive behaviour itself is called the **unconditional response (UCR)**. If, for a certain dog, a bell signals food, then the bell may also come to elicit salivation through classical conditioning. Another dog

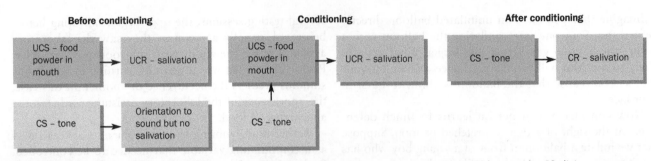

Figure 7.1 Basic components of the classical conditioning procedure. Prior to conditioning, the UCS but not the CS elicits a response (the UCR). During conditioning, the CS is presented in conjunction with the UCS. Once the conditioning is completed, the CS alone elicits a response (the CR).

may hear the sound of an electric can opener just before it is fed, in which case that sound will come to elicit salivation. A neutral stimulus paired with the UCS that eventually elicits a response is called a **conditional stimulus (CS)**. The behaviour elicited by a CS is called a **conditional response (CR)**. In the case of Pavlov's dogs, food powder was the UCS: it elicited the UCR, salivation.

At first, when Pavlov presented the sound of the bell or buzzer, the dogs did not salivate; the sound was merely a neutral stimulus, not a CS. However, with repeated pairings of the sound and the food powder, the sound became a CS, reliably eliciting the CR – salivation.

The biological significance of classical conditioning

Salivation is an innate behaviour and is adaptive because it facilitates digestion. Through natural selection, the neural circuitry that underlies salivation has become part of the genetic endowment of many species. Pavlov's experiments demonstrated that an innate reflexive behaviour, such as salivation, can be elicited by novel stimuli. Thus, a response that is naturally under the control of appropriate environmental stimuli, such as salivation caused by the presence of food in the mouth, can also come to be controlled by other kinds of stimulus.

Classical conditioning accomplishes two functions. First, the ability to learn to recognise stimuli that predict the occurrence of an important event allows the learner to make the appropriate response faster and perhaps more effectively. For example, hearing the buzz of a wasp near your head may make you duck and avoid being stung. Seeing a rival increases an animal's heart rate and the flow of blood to its muscles, makes it assume a threatening posture, and causes the release of hormones that prepare it for vigorous exercise.

The second function of classical conditioning is even more significant. Through classical conditioning, stimuli that were previously unimportant acquire some of the properties of the important stimuli with which they have been associated and thus become able to modify behaviour. A neutral stimulus becomes desirable when it is associated with a desirable stimulus or it becomes undesirable when it is associated with an undesirable one. In a sense, the stimulus takes on symbolic value. For example, we respond differently to the sight of a stack of money and to a stack of paper napkins. The reason for the special reaction to money is that money has, in the past, been associated with desirable commodities, such as food, clothing, cars, electrical equipment and so on.

Basic principles of classical conditioning

Classical conditioning involves several learning principles, including acquisition, extinction, spontaneous recovery, stimulus generalisation and discrimination.

Acquisition

In laboratory experiments, a single pairing of the CS with the UCS is not usually sufficient for learning to take place. Only with repeated CS–UCS pairings does conditional responding gradually appear. The learning phase of classical conditioning, during which the CS gradually increases in frequency or strength, is called **acquisition**.

In one study (Trapold and Spence, 1960), a tone (CS) was paired with a puff of air into the eye (UCS). The puff of air caused the participants' eyes to blink automatically (UCR). Conditioning was measured as the percentage of trials in which conditional eyeblinks (CR) occurred. Note that at the beginning of the experiment, the tone elicited very few CRs. During the first 50 trials, the percentage of CRs increased rapidly but finally stabilised.

Two factors that influence the strength of the CR are the intensity of the UCS and the timing of the CS and UCS. The intensity of the UCS can determine how quickly the CR will be acquired: more intense UCSs usually produce more rapid learning. For example, rats will learn a conditioned fear response faster if they receive higher levels of a painful stimulus (Annau and Kamin, 1961).

Classical conditioning of a salivary response in dogs occurs faster when the animals are given larger amounts of food (Wagner *et al.*, 1964). Generally speaking, the more intense the UCS, the stronger the CR.

The second factor affecting the acquisition of the CR is the timing of the CS and UCS. Classical conditioning occurs fastest when the CS occurs shortly before the UCS and both stimuli end at the same time. In his experiments on salivary conditioning, Pavlov found that one half-second was the optimal delay between the onset of the CS and the onset of the UCS. With shorter or longer delays between the CS and UCS, conditioning generally was slower and weaker (see Figure 7.2).

Extinction and spontaneous recovery

Once a classically conditioned response has been acquired, what happens to that response if the CS continues to be presented but is no longer followed by the UCS? This procedure, called **extinction**, eventually eliminates the CR. Returning to our classically conditioned eyeblink response, suppose that after we reduce the intensity of the UCS, we stop presenting the UCS (the puff of air). However, we do continue to present the CS (the tone).

It is important to realise that extinction occurs only when the CS occurs but the UCS does not. For example, the eyeblink response will extinguish only if the tone is presented without the puff of air. If neither stimulus is presented, extinction will not occur. In other words, the subject must learn that the CS no longer predicts the occurrence of the UCS – and that cannot happen if neither stimulus is presented.

Once a CR has been extinguished, it may not disappear from the organism's behaviour permanently. Pavlov demonstrated that after responding had been extinguished, the CR would often suddenly reappear the next time the dog was placed in the experimental apparatus. Pavlov referred to the CR's reappearance after a 'time out' period as **spontaneous recovery**. He also found that if he began presenting the CS and the UCS together again, the animals would acquire the CR very rapidly – much faster than they did in the first place.

Stimulus generalisation and discrimination

No two stimuli are exactly alike. Once a response has been conditioned to a CS, similar stimuli will also elicit that response. The more closely the other stimuli resemble the CS, the more likely they will elicit the CR. For example, Pavlov discovered that once a dog learned to salivate when it heard a bell, it would salivate when it heard a bell having a different tone or when it heard a buzzer. This phenomenon is called **generalisation**: a response produced by a particular CS will also occur when a similar CS is presented. Of course, there are limits to generalisation. A dog that learns to salivate when it hears a bell will probably not salivate when it hears a door close in the hallway.

In addition, an organism can be taught to distinguish between similar but different stimuli – a phenomenon called **discrimination**. Discrimination training is accomplished by using two different CSs during training. One CS is always followed by the UCS; the other CS is never followed by the UCS. For example, suppose that we regularly direct a puff of air at an animal's eye during each trial in which a low-pitched tone (CS+) is sounded, but on trials in which a high-pitched tone (CS−) is sounded, we present no air puff. At first, increased amounts of blinking will occur in response to both stimuli (generalisation). Gradually, however, fewer and fewer blinks will occur after the CS− but they will continue to be elicited by the CS+ (see Figure 7.3). Discrimination, then, involves learning the difference between two or more stimuli. An animal learns that differences among stimuli are important – it learns when to respond to one stimulus and when not to respond to a different stimulus.

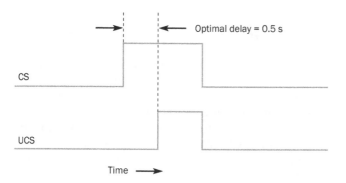

Figure 7.2 The timing of the CS and UCS in classical conditioning. The CS precedes the UCS by a brief interval of time, and both stimuli end simultaneously.

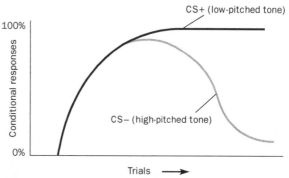

Figure 7.3 Behaviour produced through discrimination training. The CS+ is always followed by the UCS (a puff of air directed towards the eye); the CS− is always presented without the UCS.

Conditional emotional responses

Many stimuli are able to arouse emotional responses, such as feelings of disgust, contempt, fear, anger, sadness, tenderness, longing or sexual desire. Many of these stimuli, such as a place, a phrase, a song or someone's voice and face, originally had no special significance. But because these stimuli were paired with other stimuli that elicited strong emotional reactions, they came, through classical conditioning, to take on emotional significance.

If you read or hear words such as 'enemy', 'ugly', 'bitter' or 'failure', you are likely to experience at least a weak negative emotional response. In contrast, the words 'gift', 'win', 'happy' and 'beauty' may elicit positive responses. These words had no effect on you before you learned what they meant. They took on their power through being paired with pleasant or unpleasant events or perhaps with descriptions of such events.

Phobias

Many people are troubled by behaviours that they wish they could stop or by thoughts and fears that bother them. Phobias are unreasonable fears of specific objects or situations, such as spiders, cars or enclosed spaces. We will look at phobias in more detail in Chapter 18. Presumably, at some time early in life, the person having the phobia was exposed to the now-feared object in conjunction with a stimulus that elicited pain or fear. For example, being stuck in a hot, overcrowded lift with a group of frightened and sweating fellow passengers might be expected to lead to a fear of lifts or perhaps even to produce a fully-fledged phobia.

Classical conditioning can occur even without direct experience with the conditional and unconditional stimuli. For example, a child of a parent who has a snake phobia can develop the same fear simply by observing signs of fear in his or her parent. The child need not be attacked or menaced by a snake. In addition, people can develop phobias vicariously – by hearing about or reading stories that vividly describe unpleasant episodes. The imaginary episode that we picture as we hear or read a story (UCS) can provide imaginary stimuli (CSs) that lead to real conditional emotional responses (CRs).

The case of Little Albert

A famous example of an experimentally induced learned phobia is that of Little Albert. John B. Watson (you came across his work and ideas in Chapter 1) believed that behaviour had to be observable in order to be measured. He was excited by Pavlov's finding that dogs could be conditioned to respond in a specific way to a previously neutral stimulus. He and Rosalie Rayner set up the first experiment in which fear was experimentally conditioned in a human being (Watson and Rayner, 1920).

At the age of 9 months, a healthy infant called Albert B was shown to have no fear of live animals such as rats and rabbits (Albert is for ever known in textbooks as Little Albert; his real name may have been Douglas Merritte – Beck *et al.*, 2009). When a steel bar was unexpectedly struck by a claw hammer, however, he became distressed and frightened. Watson and Rayner attempted to condition fear of a previously unfeared object (a white rat) in Little Albert by pairing it with a feared stimulus (the noise of the hammer hitting the bar). They paired the rat with the noise seven times in two sessions, one week apart. When the rat was presented on its own, Albert became distressed and avoided the rat. Five days later, Albert was exposed to a number of other objects such as familiar wooden blocks, a rabbit, a dog, a sealskin coat, white cotton, the heads of Watson and two assistants and a Santa Claus mask. Albert showed a fear response to the rabbit, the dog and the sealskin coat. The initial conditioned response had generalised to some objects but not others.

Watson and Rayner's experiment is famous for two reasons. The first is the successful attempt at experimentally conditioning fear in a human being; the second is the number of inaccuracies reported in articles and textbooks describing the experiment (Harris, 1979). These include inaccurate information about Albert's age, the conditioned stimulus and the list of objects that Albert was believed to be frightened of after conditioning (the list includes fur pelt, a man's beard, a cat, a puppy, a glove, Albert's aunt and a teddy bear). These inaccuracies teach a valuable lesson, and that is the wisdom of consulting original sources of information. Because the study of Albert is part of psychology's history, details become distorted when information is passed down from textbook to textbook. This is a form of memory distortion described in more detail in the next chapter.

What is learned in classical conditioning?

Research shows that for classical conditioning to occur, the CS must be a reliable predictor of the UCS (Rescorla, 1991). Imagine yourself as the subject in a classical conditioning demonstration involving a tone as the CS, a puff of air into your left eye as the UCS and an eyeblink as the CR. Your psychology lecturer asks you to come to the front of the class and seats you in a comfortable chair.

Occasionally, a tone sounds for a second or two, and then a brief but strong puff of air hits your eye. The puff of air makes you blink. Soon you begin to blink during the tone, before the puff occurs. Now consider all the other stimuli in the seminar room – your tutor explaining the demonstration to the group, your colleagues' questions, squeaks from students moving in their chairs, and so on. Why don't any of these sounds become CSs? Why do you blink only during the tone? After all, some of these stimuli occur at the same time as the puff of air. The answer is that among the stimuli present during the demonstration, only the tone reliably predicts the puff of air. All the other stimuli are poor forecasters of the UCS. The neutral stimulus becomes a CS only when the following conditions are satisfied:

1 The CS must regularly occur prior to the presentation of the UCS.

2 The CS does not regularly occur when the UCS is absent.

Consider another example. The smell of food is more likely to elicit feelings of anticipation and excitement about supper if you are hungry than is the smell of your mother's cologne because the smell of the food is the best predictor of a meal about to be served. Similarly, the sound of footsteps behind you as you are walking is more apt to make you afraid than the sound of a car passing by or the wind blowing in the trees because the footsteps are better predictors of being mugged or threatened with danger.

It also appears that conditioned responses are more common to novel than familiar stimuli. Pavlov had observed that a novel CS was more successfully paired with a UCS than was a familiar one. This phenomenon is known as **latent inhibition** (Lubow, 1989), and because familiar stimuli are associated less successfully with conditioning than are novel ones, this effect is called the **CS pre-exposure effect** (because participants will have already been pre-exposed to the CS). Similarly, when an organism is presented with the UCS (which may be novel) before it is used as a UCS in the experiment proper, the link between CS and UCS is weaker. This is called the **UCS pre-exposure effect** (Randich and LoLordo, 1979).

Why does latent inhibition occur? No one quite knows for sure, but one explanation is related to the degree of exposure to the stimulus. A familiar CS is familiar to individuals by being in the environment; because the CS is part of the environment of context then the CS becomes merged into the context of the conditioning. To use a description from signal detection theory (see Chapter 5), the signal-to-noise ratio is weak – the CS sends a weak signal because it cannot be distinguished from the context very well.

Neurobiological correlates of Pavlovian conditioning

In an experiment to determine the brain regions involved in Pavlovian fear conditioning, participants were exposed to lights that signalled the appearance of a painful electric shock (conditioned stimulus, CS) or ones that did not (Knight *et al.*, 1999). fMRI was used to monitor differences in brain activation. As training and learning progressed, the amount of neuronal activity seen during the warning CS increased in a part of the brain called the anterior cingulate, in the front of the brain. When the light and shock were not paired (i.e. they were not associated), this activation did not occur. Although the researchers suggest that this part of the brain may not be neccessary for learning fear, it does facilitate the learning of fear. Another crucial structure for fear conditioning is the amygdala. You will discover more about its role in fear recognition and conditioning in Chapter 13.

After behaviourism

Pavlov's work greatly influenced his colleagues abroad, especially the pioneers of behaviourist thinking such as John B. Watson. Behaviourism was a robust and experimentally strict discipline whose principles were laid out

Cutting edge: Decoding the brain: Morse code

The 1990s British detective series, *Morse*, featured an opening signature tune in which a clue to the culprit's identity was revealed in Morse code (you see what they did there). A study by German and American researchers has examined how learning Morse code affects brain activation (Schmidt-Wilcke *et al.*, 2010). fMRI was used to study the ability to decipher Morse code in 16 healthy volunteers. Areas known to be involved in memory and language were particularly activated during Morse code deciphering. The density of grey matter also increased in the left occipitotemporal lobe in learners compared with the control group.

by Watson in the first and second decades of the twentieth century. It viewed behaviour and learning in terms of stimulus and response and, as the next evolution of behaviourism described in the next section shows, reinforcement. The inner mind or introspective self-reports played no part in behaviourist thinking: these were unverifiable and held the same status as superstition to the behaviourist. Both stimulus and response could be observed and the effect of one on the other recorded. Behaviourism left a unique and historical legacy that is seen in almost all experimental work undertaken in psychology today; its effects were such that modern psychology has absorbed its principles and aims.

The torch-bearers of behaviourism, however, began to modify elements of its thinking in the mid-twentieth century and although the effects of these modifications made no significant or lasting impact on psychology by themselves, the attempts at modification did because other, more dominant approaches to studying behaviour arose from them. Two influential psychologists, whose specific work did not have a long-lasting effect on the way psychology is studied, but did bequeath a way of thinking about learning and behaviour, were Clark L. Hull (1884–1952) and Edward Chase Tolman (1886–1959).

Hull's computational approach to learning

Of all the learning theories reviewed in this chapter, Hull's is probably the most ambitious and complicated of them. In his two published books, *Principles of Behaviour* (1943) and *A Behaviour System* (1952), Hull made extremely detailed predictions about behaviour that could occur in specific situations. The books contained 153 theorems that ranged from considering how we learn to discriminate, to moving in space, to how we acquire our values, and Hull's aim was to develop a system whereby behaviour could be predicted from specified independent variables (IVs). You can quickly appreciate why the approach is seen as ambitious and complicated.

Hull organised his system by considering what Watson's behaviourism did not wish to: **intervening variables**, the variables that could modify the relationship between stimulus and response. In Hull's system, analysis of behaviour comprised four stages:

Stage 1   Analysis of the IVs from which behaviour was predicted.

Stage 2   Computing values for intervening variables.

Stage 3   Computing values at this stage, using values at stage 2.

Stage 4   Analysis of the dependent variables (DVs).

In summary, the stage process argued that knowing the values of an independent variable at stage 1 meant

computing values of the intervening variables at stage 2, using these computed values to compute those at stage 3 and from this predict the outcome (or the dependent variable). Figure 7.4 summarises the main points of the system.

The number of independent variables were limitless and could range from direct stimulation (the brightness of light or the loudness of noise) to events that preceded the moment of study (such as degree of exercise taken or the amount of food consumed) to experiential episodes (such as the number of times a person had responded to the stimulus before). To produce a response (the DV), the IV would interact with the intervening variables at stages 3 and 4.

These intervening variables were not directly observable and were hypothetical states (you might see why Watson's behaviourism would have rejected Hull's approach). According to Hull, there were two types of intervening variable: habit strength and drive. A simple definition of each would be: habit strength is the strength of the connections that had been learned between a stimulus and a response after reinforced practice had occurred; drive is a state of activation that propels an organism to seek stimulation (a reduction in the drive would serve as a reward). (You will find out more about these concepts and their validity in Chapter 13.) A drive represents a temporary state which is produced when the body has been deprived of something it needs, such as food, water, relief from pain, and so on. The greater the reward, therefore, the greater the reduction in drive: a slice of bread would not significantly reduce the drive for food, but a four course meal might. The greater the number of times a response was followed by

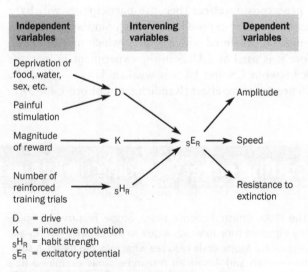

D   = drive
K   = incentive motivation
$_sH_R$ = habit strength
$_sE_R$ = excitatory potential

Figure 7.4 A simplified version of Hull's system.

Source: Adapted from Hill W.F., *Learning: A survey of psychological interpretation,* 7th edn. Published by Allyn & Bacon, Boston, MA. Copyright © 1997 by Pearson Education. By permission of the publisher.

reinforcement, the greater the formation of habit strength and the connections between a stimulus and its response. Hull also suggested another variable, incentive motivation, which would account for the organisms's response to rewards of increasing size.

As the above cursory description of the system suggests, Hull's theory was complex and followed detailed mathematical formulae. His second book contained 133 theorems which, for good measure, followed on from 17 postulates and 15 corollaries. The apparent beauty and strength of Hull's system was that one variable could be computed from another using these formulae. Where the system failed, however, was in using the values from a single experiment to predict later behaviour: this often did not work. Hull later stated that the values were meant to be regarded as illustrations rather than as fixed numbers and that, of course, values would vary across individuals. While Hull's work has not had the direct influence and impact on later theory of some other schools of learning and behaviour, it represented an ambitious and laudable attempt at pinning down behaviour to values that could be computed and used to predict later behaviour.

Tolman and the cognitive map

Like Hull, Tolman argued that there was more to the study of learning and behaviour than simply recording the stimulus and measuring the response. Tolman's view was that a theory of behaviour should consider the cognitive variables that intercede between stimulus and response: our thoughts, beliefs, attitudes, motivation to succeed and so on are all important determinants of our response to a stimulus.

Tolman's approach was called purposive behaviourism and although, like the behaviourism it followed, it concerned itself with objective and observable behaviour and the external influences that could change it, it was also concerned with the cognitive processes that guided or gave rise to that behaviour. Behaviour had a purpose; it was executed to achieve a goal, hence, purposive behaviourism.

According to Tolman, the behaviour that we engage in to achieve our goals is underpinned by our cognitions. Our cognitive processing can be measured by observing the way in which a person behaves or has experienced specific stimuli. For example, we might learn that chilli con carne tastes nicer with added ginger, cinnamon and three, rather than two, red chillies, so we make the chilli again adding these ingredients. None or any might make the chilli nicer but if none do, we experiment again either by adding or subtracting ingredients. Our experience – our cognitions – modifies our behaviour.

Tolman's most famous illustration of learning and the cognitions that lead to a response is that of reward location. If an organism finds a way of locating a reward, it may eventually find a different, more efficient method, of locating it. If you imagine yourself in a strange town centre for the first time, your first successfully navigated route to a shop may be the longest, or least efficient one. With increasing knowledge of the environment, you will eventually find the shortest, quickest route to the shop you want.

In Tolman's experiment, rats were allowed to run on a table and through an enclosed alleyway which led to various elevated pathways at the end of one of which was some food (Tolman *et al.*, 1946). When the rat had learned the location of the food, the alleyway was removed and replaced with new routes which went in different directions. Figure 7.5 shows you the difference between the two conditions.

Tolman *et al.* found that, in the second condition, the rats did not take the route they had previously learned in order to obtain the food. Instead, they took a short-cut towards the direction of the food. According to Tolman, the rat had learned a 'cognitive map' of the routes and chose the shortest one. Although this seems eminently plausible, Tolman did not seem to consider that the rat may have taken the shortest route because the smell of the food led the rodent to it.

This objection aside, Tolman's influence was important because it rejected the stiff stimulus–response (S–R) approaches of behaviourism and encouraged an emphasis on the cognitive variables that shape behaviour. The essential principles of the approach can be seen in much of modern-day experiments on transfer of learning: the principle whereby learning in one environment can be

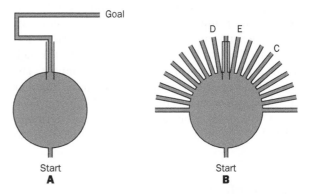

Figure 7.5 The two pathways used in Tolman's experiment. In the first, the rat takes the longer route in order to find the food. In the second, the original route is blocked and 18 new routes made available. The rats chose the tunnel marked C (that corresponding most closely to the location of the food), rather than D or E, the routes closest to that originally taken.

Source: Hill W.F., *Learning: A survey of psychological interpretation*, 7th edn. Published by Allyn & Bacon, Boston, MA. Copyright © 1997 by Pearson Education. By permission of the publisher.

successfully transferred to a different one. Work in virtual reality technology, for example, has been able to present participants with 'virtual' versions of environments which participants can navigate and explore before encountering the actual environment, thereby assisting navigation in the real version (Wilson *et al.*, 1999).

Wilson *et al.* (1996) found that severely disabled children who explored this computer simulation were able to point successfully to objects in the real building when they later encountered it. A group of undergraduates who guessed the location of the objects, without having had the benefit of exposure to the computer simulation, performed less accurately.

Tolman died just before the beginning of what is called in psychology, 'the cognitive revolution' (see Chapter 1). However, his approach was a precursor to the cognitive revolution and prompted other disciplines, such as linguistics, to consider cognitive variables in their study. While Tolman's ideas were superseded to some extent by developments in cognitive psychology, his work could be seen as the bedrock on which cognitive psychology's general approach is based.

Operant conditioning

Habituation and classical conditioning teach us about stimuli in the environment: we learn to ignore unimportant stimuli, and we learn about those that predict the occurrence of important ones. These forms of learning deal with relations between one stimulus and another. In contrast, **operant conditioning** tells about the relations between environmental stimuli and our own behaviour; it is also called instrumental learning. The term 'operant' refers to the fact that an organism learns through responding – through operating on the environment. The principle behind operant conditioning is already familiar to you: when a particular action has good consequences, the action will tend to be repeated; when a particular action has bad consequences, the action will tend not to be repeated.

The law of effect

Operant conditioning was first discovered in the basement of a house in Cambridge, Massachusetts, by a 24-year-old man who would later become one of the twentieth century's most influential educational psychologists, Edward L. Thorndike. Thorndike placed a hungry cat inside a 'puzzle box'. The animal could escape and eat some food only after it operated a latch that opened the door. At first,

the cat engaged in random behaviour: mewing, scratching, hissing, pacing and so on. Eventually, the cat would accidentally activate the latch and open the door. On successive trials, the animal's behaviour would become more and more efficient until it was operating the latch without hesitation. Thorndike called this process 'learning by trial and accidental success'.

Thorndike explained that the cat learned to make the correct response because only the correct response was followed by a favourable outcome: escape from the box and the opportunity to eat some food. The occurrence of the favourable outcome strengthens the response that produced it. Thorndike called this relation between a response and its consequences the law of effect.

The impact of Thorndike's discovery of the law of effect on the early development of scientific psychology would be difficult to overstate. It affected research in the study of learning in one very important way: it stimulated an enormous number of experimental studies aimed at understanding behaviour–environment interactions, a line of research that is known today as behaviour analysis. Nowhere was this effect more evident than in the work of B.F. Skinner.

Skinner and operant behaviour

Although Thorndike discovered the law of effect, Harvard psychologist Burrhus Frederic Skinner championed the laboratory study of the law of effect and advocated the application of behaviour analysis and its methods to solving human problems (Skinner, 1953, 1971; Mazur, 1994). He devised objective methods for studying behaviour, invented apparatus and methods for observing it, and created his own philosophy for interpreting it (Bolles, 1979). Moreover, he wrote several books for the general public, including a novel, *Walden Two*, that showed how his discoveries might be used for improving society (Skinner, 1948).

One of Skinner's most important inventions was the **operant chamber** (or Skinner box), an apparatus in which an animal's behaviour can be easily observed, manipulated and automatically recorded (as seen in Figure 7.6).

For example, an operant chamber used for rats is constructed so that a particular behaviour, such as pressing on a lever, will occasionally cause a pellet of food to be delivered. An operant chamber used for pigeons is built so that a peck at a plastic disc on the front wall will occasionally open a drawer that contains some grain. Behaviour analysts who study human behaviour use special devices suitable to the unique characteristics of their human subjects (Baron *et al.*, 1991). In this case, instead of giving their participants some food, they give them points (as in a video game) or points exchangeable for money.

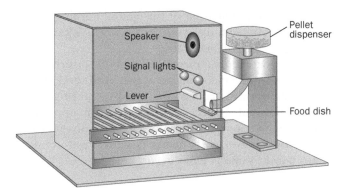

Figure 7.6 An operant chamber. (This operant chamber is used for lever pressing by rats.)

"It's a rather interesting phenomenon. Every time I press this lever, that post-graduate student breathes a sigh of relief."

Behaviour analysts manipulate environmental events to determine their effects on response rate, the number of responses emitted during a given amount of time. Events that increase response rate are said to strengthen responding; events that decrease response rate weaken responding. To measure response rate, Skinner devised the **cumulative recorder**, a device that records each response as it occurs in time.

The invention of the operant chamber and the cumulative recorder represent clear advances over Thorndike's research methods because subjects can (1) emit responses more freely over a greater time period, and (2) be studied for longer periods of time without interference produced by the experimenter handling or otherwise interacting with them between trials. Under highly controlled conditions such as these, behaviour analysts have been able to discover a wide range of important behavioural principles.

The three-term contingency

Behaviour does not occur in a vacuum. Sometimes a response will have certain consequences; sometimes it will not. Our daily behaviour is guided by many different kinds of discriminative stimuli – stimuli that indicate that behaviour will have certain consequences and thus sets the occasion for responding. For example, consider answering the telephone. The phone rings, you pick it up and say 'hello' into the receiver. Most of the time, someone on the other end of the line begins to speak. Have you ever picked up a telephone when it was not ringing and said, 'hello'? Doing so would be absurd, because there would be no one on the other end of the line with whom to speak. We answer the phone (make a response) only when the phone rings (the preceding event) because, in the past, someone with whom we enjoy talking has been at the other end of the line (the following event). Skinner referred formally to the relationship among these three items – the preceding event, the response and the following event – as the **three-term contingency** (see Figure 7.7).

The preceding event – the **discriminative stimulus** – sets the occasion for responding because, in the past, when that stimulus occurred, the response was followed by certain consequences. If the phone rings, we are likely to answer it because we have learned that doing so has particular (and generally favourable) consequences. The response we make – in this case, picking up the phone when the phone rings and saying 'hello' – is called an operant behaviour. The following event – the voice on the other end of the line – is the consequence of the operant behaviour.

Operant behaviour, therefore, occurs in the presence of discriminative stimuli and is followed by certain

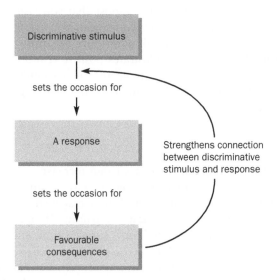

Figure 7.7 The three-term contingency.

consequences. These consequences are contingent upon behaviour, that is, they are produced by that behaviour. In the presence of discriminative stimuli, a consequence will occur if and only if an operant behaviour occurs. In the absence of a discriminative stimulus, the operant behaviour will have no effect. Once an operant behaviour is established, it tends to persist whenever the discriminative stimulus occurs, even if other aspects of the environment change (Nevin, 1988; Mace *et al.*, 1990). Of course, motivational factors can affect a response. For example, you might not bother to answer the telephone if you are doing something you do not want to interrupt.

Reinforcement, punishment and extinction

Behaviour analysts study behaviour–environment interactions by manipulating the relations among components of the three-term contingency. Of the three elements, the consequence is the most frequently manipulated variable. In general, operant behaviours can be followed by five different kinds of consequence: positive reinforcement, negative reinforcement, punishment, response cost and extinction. These consequences are always defined in terms of their effect on responding.

Positive reinforcement

Positive reinforcement refers to an increase in the frequency of a response that is regularly and reliably followed by an appetitive stimulus. An appetitive stimulus is any stimulus that an organism seeks out. If an appetitive stimulus follows a response and increases the frequency of that response, we call it a positive reinforcer. For example, the opportunity to eat some food can reinforce a hungry pigeon's pecking of a plastic disc. Money or other rewards (including social rewards) can reinforce a person's behaviour. Suppose that you visit a new restaurant and really enjoy your meal. You are likely to visit the restaurant several more times because you like the food. This example illustrates positive reinforcement. Your enjoyment of the food (the appetitive stimulus) reinforces your going to the restaurant and ordering dinner (the response).

Negative reinforcement

Negative reinforcement refers to an increase in the frequency of a response that is regularly and reliably followed by the termination of an aversive stimulus. An aversive stimulus is unpleasant or painful. If an aversive stimulus is terminated (ends or is turned off) as soon as a response occurs and thus increases the frequency of that response, we call it a negative reinforcer. For example, after you have walked barefoot across a stretch of hot pavement, the termination of the painful burning sensation negatively reinforces your response of sticking your feet into a puddle of cool water.

It is important to remember that both positive and negative reinforcement increase the likelihood that a given response will occur again. However, positive reinforcement involves the occurrence of an appetitive stimulus, whereas negative reinforcement involves the termination of an aversive stimulus. Negative reinforcement is thus not the same as punishment.

Punishment

Punishment refers to a decrease in the frequency of a response that is regularly and reliably followed by an aversive stimulus. If an aversive stimulus follows a response and decreases the frequency of that response, we call it a punisher. For example, receiving a painful bite would punish the response of sticking your finger into a parrot's cage. People often attempt to punish the behaviour of their children or pets by scolding them.

Although punishment is effective in reducing or suppressing undesirable behaviour in the short term, it can also produce several negative side effects: unrestrained use of physical force (for example, child abuse) may cause serious bodily injury. Punishment often induces fear, hostility and other undesirable emotions in people receiving punishment. It may result in retaliation against the punisher. Through punishment, organisms learn only which response not to make. Punishment does not teach the organism desirable responses.

Reinforcement and punishment are most effective in maintaining or changing behaviour when a stimulus immediately follows the behaviour. It may occur to you that many organisms, particularly humans, can tolerate a long delay between their work and the reward that they receive for it. This ability appears to contradict the principle that reinforcement must occur immediately. However, the apparent contradiction can be explained by a phenomenon called conditioned reinforcement.

Why is immediacy of reinforcement or punishment essential for learning? The answer is found by examining the function of operant conditioning: learning about the consequences of our own behaviour. Normally, causes and effects are closely related in time; you do something, and something immediately happens, good or bad. The consequences of our action teach us whether to repeat that action. Events that follow a response by a long delay were probably not caused by that response.

It is important not to confuse punishment with negative reinforcement. Punishment causes a behaviour to decrease, whereas negative reinforcement causes a behaviour to increase.

Response cost

Response cost refers to a decrease in the frequency of a response that is regularly and reliably followed by the termination of an appetitive stimulus. Response cost is a form of punishment. For example, suppose that you are enjoying a conversation with an attractive person that you have just met. You make a disparaging remark about a political party. Your new friend's smile suddenly disappears. You quickly change the topic and never bring it up again. The behaviour (disparaging remark) is followed by the removal of an appetitive stimulus (your new friend's smile). The removal of the smile punishes the disparaging remark.

Response cost is often referred to as time-out from positive reinforcement (or simply time-out) when it is used to remove a person physically from an activity that is reinforcing to that person.

As we have just seen, there are four types of operant conditioning – two kinds of reinforcement and two kinds of punishment – caused by the occurrence or termination of appetitive or aversive stimuli. Another way to change behaviour through operant conditioning is extinction, which involves no consequence at all. See Figure 7.8.

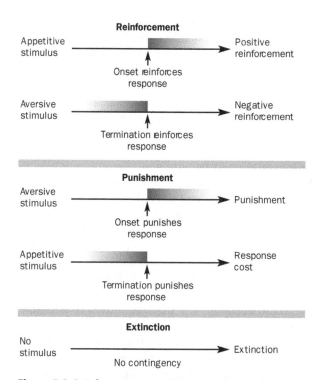

Figure 7.8 Reinforcement, punishment and extinction produced by the onset, termination or omission of appetitive or aversive stimuli. The upward-pointing arrows indicate the occurrence of a response.

Extinction

Extinction is a decrease in the frequency of a previously reinforced response because it is no longer followed by a reinforcer. Behaviour that is no longer reinforced decreases in frequency: it is said to extinguish. For example, a rat whose lever pressing was reinforced previously with food will eventually stop pressing the lever when food is no longer delivered. People soon learn to stop dropping money into vending machines that don't work. A young boy will stop telling his favourite 'knock-knock' joke if no one laughs at it any more.

Extinction is not the same as forgetting. Forgetting takes place when a behaviour is not rehearsed (or a person does not think about a particular memory) for a long time. Extinction takes place when an organism makes a response that is no longer reinforced. If the organism does not have an opportunity to make that response, it will not extinguish. For example, if you go out of town for a few weeks, you will not forget how to operate the vending machine where you often buy a bar of chocolate. However, if you put money in the machine and do not receive anything in return, your response will extinguish.

Other operant procedures and phenomena

The basic principles of reinforcement, punishment and extinction described above are used in other operant procedures to teach an organism a new response, to teach it when or when not to respond, or to teach it how to respond in a particular way.

Shaping

Most behaviour is acquired through an organism's interaction with reinforcing and punishing events in its environment. In fact, Skinner developed a technique, called **shaping**, to teach new behaviours to his subjects. Shaping involves reinforcing any behaviour that successively approximates the desired response. Imagine that we want to train a rat to press a lever when a red light is lit (the discriminative stimulus) in an operant chamber. Although the rat has used its paws to manipulate many things during its lifetime, it has never before pressed a lever in an operant chamber. And when it is first placed in the chamber, it is not likely to press the lever even once on its own.

The lever on the wall of the chamber is attached to an electrical switch that is wired to electronic control equipment or a computer. A mechanical dispenser can automatically drop pellets of food into a dish in the chamber. Thus, the delivery of a food pellet can be made dependent on the rat's pressing the lever.

Before we can shape lever pressing, we must make the rat hungry. We do so by letting the animal eat only once a day. When we know that it is hungry, we place the animal in the operant chamber and then train it to eat the food pellets as they are dispensed from the pellet dispenser. As each pellet is delivered, the dispenser makes a clicking sound. This sound is important. No matter where the rat is in the operant chamber, it can hear the sound, which indicates that the food pellet has been dispensed. Once the rat is hungry and has learned where to obtain food, we are ready to shape the desired response. We make the operation of the pellet dispenser contingent on the rat's behaviour. We start by giving the rat a food pellet for just facing in the direction of the lever. Next, we wait until the rat makes a move towards the lever. Finally, we give the rat a piece of food only if it touches the lever. Soon, our rat performs like Thorndike's cats: it makes the same response again and again.

Shaping is a formal training procedure, but something like it also occurs in the world outside the laboratory. A teacher praises poorly formed letters produced by a child who is just beginning to print. As time goes on, only more accurately drawn letters bring approval. The method of successive approximations can also be self-administered. Consider the acquisition of skills through trial and error. To begin with, you must be able to recognise the target behaviour – the behaviour displayed by a person having the appropriate skill. Your first attempts produce behaviours that vaguely resemble those of a skilled performer, and you are satisfied by the results of these attempts. In other words, the stimuli that are produced by your behaviour serve as reinforcers for that behaviour. As your skill develops, you become less satisfied with crude approximations to the final behaviour; you are satisfied only when your behaviour improves so that it more closely resembles the target behaviour. Your own criteria change as you become more skilled. Skills such as learning to draw a picture, catching a ball or making a bed are all behaviours that are acquired through shaping. After all, when a child learns these skills, they first learn behaviours that only approximate the final level of skill that they will attain. This process is perfectly analogous to the use of changing criteria in training an animal to perform a complex behaviour.

Intermittent reinforcement

So far, we have considered situations in which a reinforcing stimulus is presented after each response (or, in the case of extinction, not at all). But usually not every response is reinforced. Sometimes a kind word is ignored; sometimes it is appreciated. Not every fishing trip is rewarded with a catch, but some are, and that is enough to keep a person trying.

The term **intermittent reinforcement** refers to situations in which not every occurrence of a response is reinforced.

The relation between responding and reinforcement usually follows one of two patterns: each response has a certain probability of being reinforced, or responses are reinforced after particular intervals of time have elapsed. Probability-based patterns require a variable number of responses for each reinforcer. Consider the performance of an archer shooting arrows at a target. Suppose that the archer hits the bull's-eye one-fifth of the time. On average, he will have to make five responses for every reinforcement (hitting the bull's-eye); the ratio of responding to reinforcement is five to one. The number of reinforcers the archer receives is directly proportional to the number of responses he makes. If he shoots more arrows (that is, if his rate of responding increases), he will receive more reinforcers, assuming that he does not get tired or careless.

Behaviour analysts refer to this pattern of intermittent reinforcement as a ratio schedule of reinforcement. In the laboratory, the apparatus controlling the operant chamber may be programmed to deliver a reinforcer after every fifth response (a ratio of five to one), after every tenth, after every two hundredth, or after any desired number. If the ratio is constant – for example if a reinforcer is programmed to be delivered following every tenth response – the animal will respond rapidly, receive the reinforcer, pause a little while and then begin responding again. This type of ratio schedule is called a **fixed-ratio schedule** (specifically, a fixed-ratio 10 schedule).

If the ratio is variable, averaging a particular number of responses but varying from trial to trial, the animal will respond at a steady, rapid pace. For example, we might programme a reinforcer to be delivered, on average, after every 50 responses. This type of ratio schedule is called a **variable-ratio schedule** (specifically, a variable-ratio 50 schedule). A slot machine is sometimes programmed to deliver money on a variable-ratio schedule of reinforcement. Variable in this instance means that the person cannot predict how many responses will be needed for the next pay-off.

The second type of pattern of reinforcement involves time. A response is reinforced, but only after a particular time interval has elapsed. Imagine that you wanted to know what the weather was going to be like because your friends are due to visit, but the weather where they are is quite snowy. In order to keep abreast of the weather, you listen to the half-hourly bulletin on your local radio station. This pattern of intermittent reinforcement is called an interval schedule of reinforcement. After various intervals of time, a response will be reinforced. If the time intervals are fixed, the animal will stop responding after each reinforcement. It learns that responses made immediately after reinforcement are never reinforced. Then it will begin responding a little while before the next reinforcer is available. This type of interval schedule is called a **fixed-interval schedule**.

If the time intervals are variable, an animal will respond at a slow, steady rate. That way, it will not waste energy on useless responses, but it will not miss any opportunities for reinforcement either. This type of interval schedule is called a **variable-interval schedule**. In a variable-interval 60-second schedule of reinforcement, a reinforcer would be delivered immediately following the first response after different time intervals had elapsed. The interval might be 30 seconds at one time, and 90 seconds at another, but, on the average, it will be 60 seconds. An animal whose behaviour is reinforced by this schedule would learn not to pause immediately after a reinforcer was delivered. Instead, it would steadily respond throughout the interval, regardless of the length of the interval.

Schedules of reinforcement are important because they show us that different reinforcement contingencies affect the pattern and rate of responding. Think about your own behaviour. How would you perform in subjects in which your grades were determined by a mid-term and a final exam, or by weekly quizzes, or by unannounced quizzes that occur at variable intervals? What kind of schedule of reinforcement is a salesperson on while waiting on potential customers?

Some people work at a slow, steady rate, but others work furiously after long periods of inactivity. Can it be that in the past their work habits were shaped by different schedules of reinforcement?

Resistance to extinction and intermittent reinforcement

A response that has been reinforced intermittently is more resistant to extinction. A response that has been continuously reinforced is much less likely to be so resistant. Baldwin and Baldwin (1998) illustrate this by citing the example of two girls who were prone to throwing temper tantrums. Connie (for it is she) received continuous reinforcement for her tantrums by her parents. Whenever she would throw a tantrum, her parents would pay her attention. Paula (for it is she), however, received only intermittent reinforcement – her parents had two other children and would only pay attention to her tantrums about once in every six episodes. This, as you now know, is a typical variable-ratio 6 method of reinforcement.

When they joined school, the teacher expressed unhappiness at the tantrums and suggested that the parents undertake a programme of extinction: they were asked to ignore all tantrums. What happened? On the first day of extinction, Connie actually experienced more tantrums (20 per cent more – Lerman and Iwata, 1995) but this dropped to zero in the next few days. Paula's behaviour, on the other hand, was less resistant to extinction. It took two to three weeks for the tantrums gradually to reduce. She continued to throw tantrums long after Connie had stopped.

Why? Well, Connie's behaviour changed because previously continuously reinforced behaviour was now not reinforced at all. Her behaviour received no reinforcement and because her tantrums did not attract the necessary attention, they stopped. They increased on the first day because Connie believed she had to produce more behaviour to receive her reinforcement. When she realised that this behaviour would not be reinforced, she stopped. Paula's behaviour, however, had previously been intermittently reinforced (every sixth tantrum) and so the new schedule had little effect on her tantrums because she had become accustomed to receiving no reinforcement for her behaviour. On the first day of the programme, therefore, she behaved as she normally would because it was pretty much like normal. Her extinction was gradual and longer than Connie's because it took a longer period to realise that reinforcement was completely absent rather than intermittent.

Generalisation and discrimination

In classical conditioning, generalisation means that stimuli resembling the CS also elicit the CR. In operant conditioning, generalisation means that stimuli resembling a discriminative stimulus also serve as discriminative stimuli for a particular response.

In operant conditioning, as in classical conditioning, generalisation can be reduced through discrimination training. In classical conditioning, discrimination means that CRs occur only in response to certain CSs and not to other, similar stimuli. In operant conditioning, discrimination means that responding occurs only when a particular discriminative stimulus is present – one that was present while responding was reinforced in the past. Responding does not occur when discriminative stimuli associated with extinction or punishment are present.

Obviously, recognising certain kinds of similarities between different categories of stimuli is a very important task in our everyday lives. When we encounter a problem to solve – for example, diagnosing a puzzling disease or improving a manufactured product – we attempt to discover elements of the situation that are similar to those we have seen in other situations and try to apply the strategies that have been successful in the past. That is, we try to generalise old solutions to new problems.

Discriminative stimuli can exert powerful control over responding because of their association with the consequences of such responding. In or out of the laboratory, we learn to behave appropriately to environmental conditions. For example, we usually talk about different things with different people. We learn that some friends do not care for sports, so we do not talk about this topic with them because we will receive few reinforcers (such as nods or smiles). Instead, we discuss topics that have interested them in the past.

Conditioned reinforcement and punishment

We have studied reinforcement mainly in terms of primary reinforcers and primary punishers. **Primary reinforcers** are biologically significant appetitive stimuli, such as food when one is hungry. **Primary punishers** are biologically significant aversive stimuli, such as those that produce pain. Behaviour can also be reinforced with a wide variety of other stimuli: money, a smile, kind words, a pat on the back, or prizes and awards. These stimuli, called **conditioned (or secondary) reinforcers**, acquire their reinforcing properties through association with primary reinforcers. Because it can be exchanged for so many different kinds of primary reinforcers in our society, money is the most common conditioned reinforcer among humans. That money is a conditioned reinforcer can be demonstrated by asking yourself whether you would continue to work if you could no longer exchange money for food, drink, shelter and other items.

Similarly, **conditioned punishers** acquire their punishing effects through association with aversive events. For example, the sight of a flashing light on top of a police car serves as a conditioned punisher to a person who is driving too fast because such a sight precedes an unpleasant set of stimuli: a lecture by a police officer and a ticket for speeding.

A stimulus becomes a conditioned reinforcer or punisher by means of classical conditioning. That is, if a neutral stimulus occurs regularly just before an appetitive or aversive stimulus, then the neutral stimulus itself becomes an appetitive or aversive stimulus. The primary reinforcer or punisher serves as the UCS because it produces the UCR – good or bad feelings. After classical conditioning takes place, these good or bad feelings are produced by the CS – the conditioned reinforcer or punisher. Once that happens, the stimulus can reinforce or punish behaviours by itself. Thus, operant conditioning often involves aspects of classical conditioning.

Conditioned reinforcement and punishment are very important. They permit an organism's behaviour to be affected by stimuli that are not biologically important in themselves but that are regularly associated with the onset or termination of biologically important stimuli. Indeed, stimuli can even become conditioned reinforcers or punishers by being associated with other conditioned reinforcers or punishers. The speeding ticket is just such an example. If an organism's behaviour could be controlled only by primary reinforcers and punishers, its behaviour would not be very flexible. The organism would never learn to perform behaviours that had only long-range benefits. Instead, its behaviour would be controlled on a moment-to-moment basis by a very limited set of stimuli. Conditioned reinforcers and punishers, such as money, grades, smiles and frowns, allow for behaviour to be altered by a wide variety of contingencies.

Conditioning of complex behaviours

The previous sections considered rather simple examples of reinforced behaviours. But people and many other animals are able to learn very complex behaviours. Consider the behaviour of a young girl learning to print letters. She sits at her school desk, producing long rows of letters. What kinds of reinforcing stimuli maintain her behaviour? Why is she devoting her time to a task that involves so much effort?

The answer is that her behaviour produces stimuli – printed letters – which serve as conditioned reinforcers. In previous class sessions, the teacher demonstrated how to print the letters and praised the girl for printing them herself. The act of printing was reinforced, and the printed letters that this act produces come to serve as conditioned reinforcers. The child prints a letter, sees that it looks close to the way it should, and her efforts are reinforced by the sight of the letter. Doing something correctly or making progress towards that goal can provide an effective reinforcer.

This fact is often overlooked by people who take a limited view of the process of reinforcement, thinking that it has to resemble the delivery of a small piece of food to an animal being taught a trick. Some people even say that because reinforcers are rarely delivered to humans immediately after they perform a behaviour, operant conditioning cannot play a major role in human learning. This assertion misses the point that, especially for humans, reinforcers can be very subtle events.

Aversive control of behaviour

Your own experience has probably taught you that punishment can be as effective as positive reinforcement in changing behaviour. Aversive control of behaviour is common in our society, from fines given to speeding motorists to the prison sentences given to criminals. Aversive control of behaviour is common for two main reasons. First, it can be highly effective in inducing behaviour change, producing nearly immediate results. A person given a fine for jumping a red light is likely, at least for a short while, to heed the sign's message. The very effectiveness of punishment as a means of behaviour change can serve as an immediate reinforcer for the person doing the punishing.

Secondly, society cannot always control the positive reinforcers that shape and maintain the behaviour of its members. However, it can and does control aversive stimuli that may be used to punish misconduct. For example, suppose that a young person's peers encourage antisocial behaviours such as theft. Society has no control over reinforcers provided by the peer group, but it can control stimuli to punish the antisocial behaviours, such as fines and imprisonment.

Escape and avoidance

Negative reinforcement teaches organisms to make responses that terminate aversive stimuli. These responses can make a stimulus cease or the organism can simply run away. In either case, psychologists call the behaviour an **escape response**: the organism endures the effects of the aversive stimulus until its behaviour terminates the stimulus. In some cases, the animal can do more than escape the aversive stimulus; it can learn to do something to prevent it occurring. This type of behaviour is known as an **avoidance response**.

Avoidance responses usually require some warning that the aversive stimulus is about to occur in order for the organism to be able to make the appropriate response soon enough. Imagine that you meet a man at a party who backs you against the wall and engages you in the most boring conversation you have ever had. In addition, his breath is so bad that you are afraid you will pass out. You finally manage to break away from him (an escape response). A few days later, you attend another party. You begin walking towards the buffet table and see the same man (discriminative stimulus) standing nearby. You decide that you will get some food later and turn away to talk with some friends at the other end of the room (an avoidance response).

As you saw earlier, phobias can be considered to be **conditioned emotional responses** – fears that are acquired through classical conditioning. But unlike most classically conditioned responses, phobias are especially resistant to extinction. If we classically condition an eyeblink response in a rabbit and then repeatedly present the CS alone, without the UCS (puff of air), the response will extinguish. However, if a person has a phobia for cockroaches, the phobia will not extinguish easily even if they encounter cockroaches and nothing bad happens. Why does the response persist?

Most psychologists believe that the answer lies in a subtle interaction between operant and classical conditioning. The sight of a cockroach makes a person with a cockroach phobia feel frightened, that is, they experience an unpleasant conditional emotional response. The person runs out of the room, leaving the cockroach behind and reducing the unpleasant feelings of fear. This reduction in an aversive stimulus reinforces the avoidance response and perpetuates the phobia.

Conditioning of flavour aversions

You have probably eaten foods that made you sick and now avoid them on the basis of their flavour alone. The association of a substance's flavour with illness, which is often caused by eating that substance, leads to **conditioned flavour–aversion learning**.

The study of flavour-aversion learning is important not only because it is a real-life experience, but also because it has taught psychologists about unique relations that may exist between certain CSs and certain UCSs. Just as punishment is a result of classical conditioning where a species-typical defensive response becomes classically conditioned to a discriminative stimulus, conditioned flavour aversions are acquired in the same way. The flavour is followed by a UCS (sickness) that elicits the unpleasant responses of the autonomic nervous system (ANS), such as cramping and retching. Then, when the animal encounters the flavour again, the experience triggers unpleasant internal reactions that cause the animal to stop eating the food.

Many learning researchers once believed that nearly any CS could be paired with nearly any UCS to produce nearly any CR. However, in a now classic experiment, Garcia and Koelling (1966) showed that animals are more prepared to learn some types of relation among stimuli than others.

In the first phase of their experiment, Garcia and Koelling permitted rats to drink saccharine-flavoured water from a tube. Each lick from the tube produced three CSs: taste, noise and bright lights. This phase ensured that rats were equally familiar with each of the CSs. In the next phase, the rats were divided into four groups, each experiencing either 'bright-noisy' water or 'tasty' water. Each CS was paired with illness or electric shock.

After several trials, the experimenters measured the amount of saccharine-flavoured water the rats consumed. They found that the rats learned the association between flavour and illness but not between flavour and pain produced by electric shock. Likewise, the rats learned the association between the 'bright-noisy' water and shock-induced pain but not between the 'bright-noisy' water and illness. The results make sense; after all, the animal has to taste the flavour that makes it ill, not hear it, and in the world outside the laboratory, a particular flavour does not usually indicate that you are about to receive an electric shock.

This experiment draws two important conclusions: (1) rats can learn about associations between internal sensations (being sick) and novel tastes, and (2) the interval between the two stimuli can be very long. These facts suggest that the brain mechanisms responsible for a conditioned flavour aversion are different from the ones that mediate an aversion caused by stimuli applied to the outside of the body (such as a painful foot shock). It appears that conditioned flavour aversions serve to protect animals from poisonous foods by enabling them to learn to avoid eating them. Because few naturally occurring poisons cause sickness immediately, neural mechanisms that mediate conditioned flavour aversions must be capable of learning the association between events that are separated in time. Most other cause-and-effect relations involve events that occur close in time; hence the neural mechanisms that mediate an organism's ability to learn about them operate under different time constraints.

Some animals have eating habits quite different from those of rats; they eat foods that they cannot taste or smell. For example, some birds eat seeds that are encased in a tasteless husk. They do not have teeth, so they cannot break open the husk and taste the seed. Thus, they cannot use odour or taste as a cue to avoid a poison. However, Wilcoxon et al., (1971) found that quail (a species of seed-eating birds) can form a conditioned aversion to the sight of food that earlier made them sick. People can also acquire conditioned flavour aversions. A friend of mine often took trips on aeroplanes with her parents when she was a child. Unfortunately, she usually got airsick. Just before take-off, her mother would give her some spearmint-flavoured chewing gum to help relieve the pressure on her eardrums that would occur when the plane ascended. She developed a conditioned flavour aversion to spearmint gum. In fact, the odour of the gum still makes her feel nauseated.

Conditioned flavour aversions, like most learning situations, involve both classical and operant conditioning. From one point of view, we can say that the aversive stimuli produced by the poison punish the behaviour of eating a particular food. That is, the flavour serves as a discriminative stimulus for a punishment contingency (operant conditioning). However, it also serves as a conditioned stimulus for a classical conditioning situation: the flavour is followed by a UCS (the poison) that elicits unpleasant responses of the ANS, such as cramping and retching. Then, when the animal encounters the flavour at a later date, it experiences unpleasant reactions that cause it to leave the source of the stimulus and avoid the food.

Psychology in action: Flavour aversions

Because conditioned flavour aversions can occur when particular flavours are followed by feelings of nausea, even several hours later, this phenomenon has several implications for situations outside the laboratory. An unfortunate side effect of chemotherapy or radiation therapy for cancer is nausea. Besides killing the rapidly dividing cells of malignant tumours, both chemotherapy and radiation kill the rapidly dividing cells that line the digestive system and thus cause nausea and vomiting.

Knowing what we know about conditioned flavour aversions, we might predict that chemotherapy or radiation therapy would cause a conditioned aversion to the foods a patient ate during the previous meal. Bernstein (1978) showed that this prediction is correct. She gave ice cream to some cancer patients who were about to receive a session of chemotherapy and found that several months later, 75 per cent of these patients refused to eat ice cream of the same flavour. In contrast, control subjects who did not taste it before their chemotherapy said that they liked it very much. Only one trial was necessary to develop the conditioned flavour aversion. Even when patients have a clear understanding that the drugs are responsible for their aversion and that the food is really wholesome, they still cannot bring themselves to eat it (Bernstein, 1991). Thus, a conditioned food aversion is not a result of cognitive processes such as reasoning or expectation.

Questionnaires and interviews reveal that cancer patients develop aversions to the foods that they normally eat even if their treatment sessions occur several hours after the previous meal (Bernstein et al., 1982; Mattes et al., 1987). When patients receive many treatment sessions, they are likely to develop aversions to a wide variety of foods. Because a treatment that produces nausea may cause the development of a conditioned flavour aversion to the last thing a person has eaten, Broberg and Bernstein (1987) attempted to attach the aversion to a flavour other than one that patients encounter in their normal diets. Cancer patients ate either a coconut or root beer Lifesaver (a sweet) after the last meal before a chemotherapy session. The experimenters hypothesised that the unique flavour would serve as a scapegoat, thus preventing a conditioned aversion to patients' normal foods. The procedure worked; the patients were much less likely to show an aversion to the food eaten during the last meal before the treatment.

Conditioned flavour aversions can also have useful applications. For example, psychologists have applied conditioned aversions to wildlife control. In regions where coyotes have been attacking sheep, they have left chunks of dog food laced with an emetic drug wrapped in pieces of fresh sheep-skin. The coyotes eat the bait, become sick and develop a conditioned aversion to the smell and taste of sheep (Gustavson and Gustavson, 1985). These methods can help protect endangered species as well as livestock. Mongooses have been introduced into some islands in the Caribbean, where they menace the indigenous population of sea turtles. Nicolaus and Nellis (1987) found that a conditioned aversion to turtle eggs could be established in mongooses by feeding them eggs into which an emetic drug had been injected.

Evidence suggests that for some species, conditioned flavour aversions can become cultural traditions. Gustavson and Gustavson (1985) reported that after adult coyotes had developed a conditioned aversion to a particular food, their offspring, too, avoided that food. Apparently, the young coyotes learned from their mothers what food was fit to eat. However, Nicolaus et al. (1982) found that adult racoons having a conditioned aversion to chickens did not teach their offspring to avoid chickens. In fact, after seeing the young racoons kill and eat chickens, the adults overcame their aversion and began preying on chickens again.

Applications of operant conditioning to human behaviour

Instructional control

Human behaviour is influenced not only by reinforcement but also by the interactions of reinforcement with rules, that is, verbal descriptions of the relation between behaviour and reinforcement. In fact, much of our everyday behaviour involves following rules of one sort or another. Cooking from a recipe, following directions to a friend's house, and obeying the speed limit are common examples. Because rules have the potential to influence our behaviour in almost any situation, behaviour analysts are interested in learning more about how rules and reinforcement interact.

One way to investigate this interaction is to give subjects rules that are false, that is, rules that are inaccurate descriptions of the behaviour required for reinforcement (Galizio, 1979; Baron and Galizio, 1983). In such experiments, people may behave in accordance with either the rule or the reinforcement requirement. Other researchers have shown that people sometimes generate their own rules about the consequences of their behaviour (Lowe, 1979). Lowe argues that our ability to describe verbally the consequences of our behaviour explains why humans often respond differently from other animals when placed under similar reinforcement contingencies (Lowe et al., 1983). When exposed to fixed-interval schedules, animals do not behave immediately after each reinforcement. As time passes, though, responding gradually increases until the next reinforcer is delivered. Humans, on the other hand, tend to follow one of two strategies: responding very slowly or responding very rapidly. Those people who respond slowly often describe the schedule as interval-based and they respond accordingly. Those who respond rapidly usually describe the schedule as ratio-based – which it is not – and they respond accordingly. Thus, the language one uses may indeed exert some control over one's own behaviour.

Stimulus equivalence

Stimulus equivalence refers to the emergence of novel behaviour without direct reinforcement of that behaviour (Fields, 1993; Fields et al., 1995). Imagine that you were asked to learn the relationship among a group of symbols: A, B and C. Suppose further that after training without reinforcement, you discovered that A = B and A = C. How then would you respond to the following question: does B = C? You would probably reason that if A = B and A = C, then B, too, is equal to C. But notice that you were never trained or received any direct reinforcement for learning that B = C. Rather, the equivalent relationship between B and C emerged from your previous learning; hence, the term 'stimulus equivalence'.

Stimulus equivalence is an important area of research because it represents one way we learn to use and understand symbols, such as language. For example, let A represent a picture of a dog, B represent the spoken word 'dog', and C represent the printed word 'dog'. Suppose that we teach a child to point to the picture of the dog (A) and say the word 'dog' (B). In this case, the child learns that A = B and B = A. Next, suppose that we teach the child to point to the picture of the dog (A) when he sees the printed word 'dog' (C). The child learns that A = C and that C = A. What we are really interested in, though, is whether the child will have learned that the spoken word 'dog' (B) is equivalent to, or means the same thing as, the printed word 'dog' (C).

This is precisely what children learn under these circumstances, even though the equivalent relationship, B = C, has not been directly trained (Sidman and Tailby, 1982). Rather, it emerged as a consequence of the child's learning history. Understanding how stimulus equivalence develops is likely to lead to a better understanding of language development.

Drug use and abuse

Soon after Skinner outlined the principles of operant behaviour, others were quick to apply them to the study of drug action and drug-taking (Thompson and Schuster, 1968). In fact, Skinner's three-term contingency is now partly the basis of an entirely separate discipline of pharmacology known as behavioural pharmacology, the study of how drugs influence behaviour. In this field, the terms 'discriminative stimuli', 'responding' and 'consequences' translate into drugs as discriminative stimuli, the direct effects of drugs on behaviour, and the reinforcing effects of drugs, respectively. Perhaps the most interesting discovery in behavioural pharmacology is the finding that most psychoactive drugs function as reinforcers in both humans and animals.

When administered as a consequence of responding, these drugs will induce and maintain high rates of responding (Griffiths et al., 1980). There is a very high correlation between drugs that will maintain animal responding in experimental settings and those that are abused by humans (Griffiths et al., 1980). Cocaine, for example, maintains very high rates of responding and drug consumption, to the point that food and water consumption decreases to life-threatening levels. Unlimited access to cocaine in rhesus monkeys can lead, in some cases, to death. These findings have allowed psychologists to study the abuse potential of newly available drugs in order to predict their likelihood of becoming drugs of abuse. The realisation that drugs are reinforcers has, in turn, led behavioural pharmacologists to treat cocaine dependence in people successfully by scheduling reinforcement for non-drug-taking behaviour (S.T. Higgins et al., 1994).

Just as the telephone ringing can serve as a discriminative stimulus for you answering it, the stimulus effects of drugs can also exert control over human behaviours that are reinforced by non-drug stimuli. People become more sociable under the influence of alcohol not only because the drug reduces their inhibitions, but also because people have some successful social interactions while under the drug's effects. These interactions reinforce their sociability. In fact, many laboratory studies have shown that certain drugs actually increase social responding and social reinforcement (Higgins *et al.*, 1989).

Observation and imitation

Normally, we learn about the consequences of our own behaviour or about stimuli that directly affect us. We can also learn by a less direct method: observing the behaviour of others.

Evidence suggests that imitation does seem to be an innate tendency. Many species of birds must learn to sing the song of their species; if they are raised apart from other birds of their species, they will never sing or they will sing a peculiar song that bears little resemblance to that of normally raised birds (Marler, 1961). However, if they hear the normal song played over a loudspeaker, they will sing it properly when they become adults. They have learned the song, but clearly there were no external reinforcement contingencies; nothing in the environment reinforced their singing of the song.

Classically conditioned behaviours, as well as operantly conditioned behaviours, can be acquired through observation. For example, suppose that a young girl sees her mother show signs of fear whenever she encounters a dog. The girl herself will likely develop a fear of dogs, even if she never sees another one. In fact, Bandura and Menlove (1968) reported that children who were afraid of animals – in this case, dogs – were likely to have a parent who feared dogs, but they usually could not remember having had unpleasant direct experiences with them. We tend to imitate, and feel, the emotional responses of people we observe (see Chapter 13).

Under normal circumstances, learning by observation may not require external reinforcement. In fact, there is strong evidence that imitating the behaviour of other organisms may be reinforcing in itself. However, in some cases in which the ability to imitate is absent, it can be learned through reinforcement. For example, Baer *et al.* (1967) studied three severely retarded children who had never been seen to imitate the behaviour of other people. When the experimenters first tried to induce the children to do what they themselves did, such as clap their hands, the children were unresponsive. Next, the experimenters tried to induce and reinforce imitative behaviour in the children. An experimenter would look at a child, say 'do this', and perform a behaviour. If the child made a similar response, the child was immediately praised and given a piece of food. At first, the children were physically guided to make the response. If the behaviour to be imitated was clapping, the experimenter would clap their hands, hold the child's hands and clap them together, and then praise the child and give them some food.

The procedure worked. The children learned to imitate the experimenters' behaviours. More importantly, however, the children had not simply learned to mimic a specific set of responses. They had acquired the general tendency to imitate. When the researchers performed new behaviours and said 'do this', the children would imitate them.

Controversies in psychological science: Is the brain like a computer?

The issue

In his editorial of an issue of the journal *Perception*, Gregory (1998) asked, 'Is the brain a computer?' If a computer is anything that solves problems, then 'yes', says Gregory, 'the brain is a computer'. Similarly, if perception is problem-solving (such as being able to perceive an object from poor amounts of sensory data), then the visual brain is also a computer.

The evidence

Although cognitive psychology has a history that dates back to the early part of the twentieth century, most of its philosophy and methodology has developed since the 1960s.

During this time, the best-known physical device that performs functions similar to those of the human brain has been the general-purpose serial computer. Thus, it is the computer that provided (and still provides) much of the inspiration for the models of human brain function constructed by cognitive psychologists.

Modern general-purpose computers consist of four major parts:

- Input and output devices (or, collectively, I/O devices) permit us to communicate with the computer – to give it instructions or data and to learn the results of its computations.

Controversies in psychological science: *Continued*

- Memory permits information to be stored in the computer. This information can contain instructions or data we have given the computer or the intermediate steps and final results of its calculations.
- A central processor contains the electronic circuits necessary for the computer to perform its functions – to read the information received by the input devices and to store it in memory, to execute the steps specified by the instructions contained in its programs, and to display the results by means of:
- The output devices.

Modern general-purpose computers can be programmed to store any kind of information that can be coded in numbers or words, can solve any logical problem that can be explicitly described, and can compute any mathematical equations that can be written. Therefore, in principle, at least, they can be programmed to do the things we do: perceive, remember, make deductions, solve problems. The power and flexibility of computers seem to make them an excellent basis for constructing models of mental processes.

For example, psychologists, linguists and computer scientists have constructed computer-inspired models of visual pattern perception, speech comprehension, reading, control of movement and memory (Rolls, 1997, 2008), as well as robots which can mimic aspects of behaviour. Some of these are more successful than others. The computer Deep Blue, for example, played a six-game chess match against the World Chess Champion Gary Kasparov in 1997, and won by two games to one (the players drew three times). The advantage that such a computer has is its speed of processing; its disadvantage is that its depth of understanding is limited and not as sophisticated as that of humans. It can be programmed with all the moves in chess that are known to date, but it may not understand why those moves may work. While speed is one of a computer's advantages – and at this they are far superior to humans: chips are faster than neurons – its disadvantage is seen clearly in exercises such as language translation, at which its performance is generally execrable. It can understand grammar and it may understand specific words, but it has no sense of the meaning of a sentence. Sentences such as 'He was killing time' are problematic for it. We understand this to mean occupying our time while we wait; a computer may understand this to mean murdering a clock.

Artificial intelligence

The construction of computer programs that simulate human mental functions is called artificial intelligence. The aim of such enterprises is to try to clarify the nature of mental functions. For instance, to construct a program and simulate perception and classification of certain types of pattern, the investigator must specify precisely what the task of pattern perception requires. If the program fails to recognise the patterns, then the investigator knows that something is wrong with the model or with the way it has been implemented in the program. The investigator revises the model/program, tries again, and keeps working until it finally works (or until they give up the task as being too ambitious). So far, no program is advanced enough to deal with more than a small fraction of the patterns a human can recognise.

Ideally, the task of discovering what steps are necessary in a computer program to simulate some human cognitive abilities tells the investigator the kinds of process the brain must perform. However, there is usually more than one way to accomplish a particular goal. Critics of artificial intelligence have pointed out that even if it is entirely possible to write a program that performs a task that the human brain performs – and comes up with exactly the same results – the computer may perform the task in an entirely different way. In fact, some say, given the way that computers work and what we know about the structure of the human brain, the computer program is guaranteed to work differently.

Serial computers work one step at a time and each step takes time. A complicated program will contain more steps and will take more time to execute. But we do some things extremely quickly that computers take a very long time to do. One of the best examples is visual perception. We can recognise a complex figure about as quickly as we can a simple one. For us, it takes about the same amount of time to recognise a friend's face as it does to identify a simple triangle. The same is not true at all for a serial computer. A computer must 'examine' the scene through an input device something like a television camera. Information about the brightness of each point of the picture must be converted into a number and stored in a memory location. Then the program examines each memory location, one at a time, and does calculations that determine the locations of lines, edges, textures and shapes. Finally, it tries to determine what these shapes represent. Recognising a face takes much longer than recognising a triangle.

If the brain were a serial device, its maximum speed would probably be around ten steps per second, considering the rate at which neurons can fire (Rumelhart *et al.*, 1986). This rate is extremely slow compared with modern serial computers. Obviously, when we perceive visual images, our brain does not act like a serial device.

Controversies in psychological science: *Continued*

Parallel processing and neural networks

Instead, the brain appears to be a **parallel processor**, in which many different modules (collections of circuits of neurons) work simultaneously at different tasks. A complex task is broken down into many smaller ones, and separate modules work on each of them. Because the brain consists of many billions of neurons, it can afford to devote different clusters of neurons to different tasks (see Chapters 4 and 6). With so many things happening at the same time, the task gets done quickly.

Recently, psychologists have begun to devise models of mental functions that are based, very loosely, on the way the brain seems to be constructed. These models are called **neural networks**, and the general approach is called **connectionism**. One area of psychology where neural networks have been applied is language (see Chapter 10).

Computer simulation specialists have discovered that when they construct a network of simple elements interconnected in certain ways, the network does some surprising things. The elements have properties like those of neurons. They are connected to each other through junctions similar to synapses. Like synapses, these junctions can have either excitatory or inhibitory effects. When an element receives a critical amount of excitation, it sends a message to the elements with which it communicates, and so on. Some of the elements of a network have input lines that can receive signals from the 'outside', which could represent a sensory organ or the information received from another network. Other elements have output lines, which communicate with other networks or control muscles, producing behaviour. Thus, particular patterns of input can represent particular stimuli, and particular patterns of output can represent responses.

Investigators do not construct physical networks. Instead, they write computer programs that simulate them. The programs keep track of each element and the state of each of its inputs and outputs and calculate what would happen if a particular pattern of input is presented. Neural networks can be taught to 'recognise' particular stimuli. They are shown a particular stimulus, and their output is monitored. If the response on the output lines is incorrect, the network is given a signal indicating the correct response. This signal causes the strength of some of the junctions to be changed, just as learning is thought to alter the strength of synapses in the brain. After several trials, the network learns to make correct responses.

If the network uses a sufficiently large number of elements, it can be trained to recognise several different patterns, producing the correct response each time one of the patterns is shown to it. In addition, it will even recognise the patterns if they are altered slightly, or if only parts of the patterns are shown. Thus, neural networks can recognise not only particular patterns but also variations on that pattern. Thus, they act as if they had learned general prototypes, not specific templates. For example, they may learn that the letter A reproduced in Times Roman font is the same as an A reproduced in Palatino font.

Conclusion

So, does the brain work like a computer? The answer seems to be that it does, but not like the most familiar kind of computer, which cognitive psychologists first used as a basis for constructing models of brain function. The brain appears to be a parallel processor made up of collections of neural networks. Neural networks' attempts to simulate the functions of the brain have not met with considerable success (which is not surprising given the complexity of that organ). Most simulations have been of the very basic, perceptual kind. It is interesting to speculate that a strong artificial intelligence position on the nature of simulating brain function would effectively result in the creation of a conscious computer. How likely do you think this is?

Learning in practice: being a student

So far, we have considered some of the important theories of learning that have made an impact on psychology and in applied contexts. Other elements of the learning process are covered in the Chapter 8 on memory. The remainder of this chapter examines how various factors can affect academic learning and success. It explores how the use of different teaching methods can influence learning as might the type of material taught. It also considers how specific variables such as personality, learning style, group study and confidence can influence successful understanding of learned material.

Deep v. shallow learning

Perhaps the most consistently studied – and reliable – dichotomy in the psychology of learning is deep and shallow processing (or learning). In shallow learning, there is an emphasis on remembering facts, rather than on understanding them; in deep learning, there is an emphasis on knowing and understanding material, rather than on the straightforward process of remembering it.

For example, in the 1990s researchers suggested that learning could be conceptualised in five ways (Saljo, 1991; adapted from Hartley, 1998):

1 Learning is a means of acquiring knowledge.

2 Learning is a means of storing (remembering) information that could be used later.

3 Learning is the acquisition of facts, knowledge and methods.

4 Learning is the making sense of, or abstracting meaning from, material.

5 Learning is a process that assists the interpretation or understanding of reality.

Researchers found that those students who were classified as 'shallow' learners were most likely to adopt the first two of these learning strategies; 'deep' learners were more likely to adopt the last two. To examine whether 'depth' could be taught, Norton and Crowley (1995) studied the effect of incorporating workshops into a first-year psychology course on students' learning strategies. When the performance of those who attended all the workshops was compared with those who attended one or two or none, there was no increase in deep processing in the conscientious students. However, those who stayed with the workshops adopted a less shallow processing style as the course progressed. The results demonstrated that by encouraging students to think, to interpret and to discuss concepts and ideas – rather than asking them to learn their material by rote – this process could make them less shallow learners.

The idea was first proposed and demonstrated empirically in Sweden in the 1970s. Marton and Saljo (1976), for example, characterised deep learners as those who would agree with statements such as:

- I try to get the principal ideas.
- I try to find the main points of a chapter.

Whereas shallow learners were likely to agree with statements such as:

- I try to concentrate on remembering as much as possible.

That is, the deep learners tried to glean meaning from material whereas the shallow learners tried to remember the information. When a group of students was given a 1,400-word article on curriculum reform in Swedish universities and asked to summarise the author's main argument in one or two sentences, the results were – in light of what you now know – predictable. None of the students who were classified as shallow learners (based on their responses to a questionnaire) was able to do this; those classified as deep learners did this faultlessly.

In an article by Gibbs (1992) cited in Hartley (1998), the author lists factors which could encourage shallow processing and those which could foster deep learning. Here are some of those factors:

- Factors encouraging surface learning:
  - heavy workload;
  - excess course material;
  - reduced opportunity to study a subject in depth;
  - lack of choice in subject areas and methods of studying those subjects;
  - assessment that is threatening and anxiety-provoking.

- Factors encouraging deep learning:
  - project work;
  - learning by doing;
  - problem-based learning;
  - work that does not rely solely on remembering;
  - work that allows reflection;
  - independent learning;
  - rewarding understanding and penalising memorisation;
  - involving students in the choice of assessment method.

So, the message that seems to be clear and consistent from research is: in the contexts studied, having a 'deep' approach to study is better than one driven by a need to remember.

Learning style

Psychologists have devised various ways of measuring students' learning styles and investigating whether students on different courses learn in different ways. One of these measures is the Student Process Questionnaire (SPQ) (Biggs, 1987), a 42-item measure of a deep approach to learning (evaluating material critically; reading widely; engaging in discussion), a surface approach to learning (e.g. rote learning) and an achieving approach to learning (where the student has a strong intention to succeed and obtain high grades). In a study of how chemistry students' learning style changes across their course (Zeegers, 2001), the deep approach to learning was the one most closely related to good grade outcome but the achieving approach was the one most likely to undergo fluctuations across the course. Students expressed less achievement-driven behaviour as the course progressed, suggesting that striving for high grades became less important as their education progressed. The surface approach increased in the first year of study but stabilised thereafter. Older students were significantly more likely to engage in deep learning and also show high achievement motivation. These students also received higher grades and completed more units on their courses.

Cutting edge: Cheaters profiled

As a psychology student, you will probably have received a number of imprecations regarding the evils of plagiarism. This is important counsel because using someone else's words without crediting them is theft (and also not very clever). You may even have used the software, TurnItIn (TIN), which tells you the proportion of your work which overlaps significantly with published sources or sources in its archive (such as past students' essays and lab reports).

Despite the strong advice, and this software, some students continue to cheat. Is there something special about these students that distinguishes them from the honest?

Williams *et al.* (2010) examined the personality characteristics of self-reported student cheaters and found that they were more likely to express the Dark Triad–Machiavelianism (being cynical, amoral and manipulative), narcissism (being arrogant, self-centred and self-enhancing) and psychopathy (having an erratic lifestyle and being manipulative, callous and antisocial), as well as being low in agreeableness and conscientiousness. When the researchers examined these traits more closely, only psychopathy was found to be a significant predictor. Those scoring high on this trait were more likely to cheat. This finding was confirmed in a naturalistic study using TIN – those who were found to plagiarise, according to the software, were more likely to show psychopathy.

There was also a relationship between cheating and poor verbal ability. Self-reported cheating was higher in men than women but this sex difference disappeared when plagiarism was measured directly via TIN.

Changes in students' views about their learning

The perception and understanding of material learned across a degree changes. A study at Princeton University found that the instructor's way of expressing him/herself, information about the course and an absence of criticism about the course from others was significantly related to post-course evaluations in general (Babad *et al.*, 1999). The features that predicted evaluations at introductory level were not those that predicted evaluations at advanced level 4. The only consistent feature was that workload and mark leniency were weak predictors of course selection.

Features on advanced courses which predicted evaluation were interesting readings, having an interesting course and instructor's knowledge and expertise. None of the personality factors – such as the lecturer's sense of humour or approachability – predicted these students' evaluations of their course. Only for the introductory students was there a relationship between the instructor's humour and the post-course evaluation.

The study appears to show that as students progress through their degree, what they value in a course changes. They become more concerned with academic substance and less with 'lighter' features such as the instructor's sense of humour. At the beginning of their education, first year students are sampling the many different things that university or college has to offer. The instructor's sense of humour and expression was important to first year students, but advanced students valued the quality of their courses and teaching, such as the content of courses and how well they were taught and prepared. The authors argue that the respondents in their sample may not be representative (because Princeton undergraduates have different course structures to those of others) but suggest that the results could be generalised to similar institutions.

A study from the University of Missouri-Columbia found that by graduation, students placed less emphasis on extrinsic factors (such as earning money, gaining popularity and how they looked) and more on intrinsic factors (valuing community, intimacy and growth) (Sheldon, 2005). The greater the shift to intrinsic values, the greater the sense of psychological well-being students felt as they progressed through college. You might find that the findings of these studies mirror your own experience as a psychology student.

A study of Belgian undergraduates' evolution of their learning style has found that whereas some learning styles change markedly as the students progress, others are more variable (Donche *et al.*, 2010). The study found that first year students learned in a more undirected way than did third year students with third year students showing greater evidence of meaning-directed (i.e., deep) learning. However, the researchers note that even final year students were likely to adopt a reproduction-oriented learning style (reproducing what they have learned/revised without accompanying deep learning). They suggest that this could be one flexible strategy which helps students: a combination of meaning-oriented and reproduction-oriented learning.

Probably one of the most challenging (i.e., difficult) courses you will take in psychology will be research methods. But are there predictors of good research methods performance, beyond mathematical ability? A study from South Africa suggest that there are (Payne and Israel, 2010). They examined predictors of performance in a research design and analysis course in 80 students. Secondary school performance and age were the best predictors, but among the non-demographic characteristics were self-efficacy, help-seeking and having a reflective learning style. Those more proficient in maths were better at the course.

Personality and academic success

An analysis of 109 studies examining the relationship between psychosocial and study skill factors, grade success and student retention (how likely students are to stay on their course) has shown that there is a moderately significant relationship between remaining in college and (i) keeping academic goals, (ii) a person's capability to assess the ability to succeed academically and (iii) good academic skills. The best predictors of grade success are motivation to achieve and the student's ability to assess accurately his/her ability to succeed (Robbins *et al.*, 2004). The results seem to tally with those from the workplace where highly motivated employees and those capable of self-evaluation are those who are most successful.

However, personality may be a better predictor of academic performance than grades or other factors. Openness to experience and agreeableness have been found to be significant predictors of academic success, but extraversion, neuroticism and conscientiousness have not (you will find a detailed description of these personality types in Chapter 14) (Farsides and Woodfield, 2003). Of all the variables studied, however, a non-personality factor – seminar attendance – was the strongest predictor of success. This said, a **meta-analysis** of studies exploring the relationship between personality and academic performance found that one personality variable in particular was important (Poropat, 2009). In a sample totalling over 70,000 participants from secondary and tertiary education the greatest correlation – it predicted performance better than did intelligence – was between performance and conscientiousness.

Chamorro-Premuzic *et al.* (2008) found that the personality characteristics of the lecturer interact with the students' own and these influence perceptions of teaching. Students tended to prefer lecturers with personalities similar to their own, unless they were neurotic. Particularly, they preferred lecturers who were emotionally stable and conscientious.

Variations in a number of personality traits can interact with other variables to influence academic performance (Ackerman *et al.*, 2011). Caprara *et al.* (2011) examined whether openness to experience and conscientiousness, as well as self-efficacy, influenced academic performance in 412 Italian children in a longitudinal study conducted from 13 to 19 years.

They found that openness and self-efficacy at age 13 predicted academic performance in junior school, regardless of socioeconomic status. Grades at junior school contributed to self-efficacy beliefs at 16 and these beliefs predicted later academic success (regardless of previous grades). Conscientiousness had an indirect influence on achievement as its effect was mediated by self-efficacy.

Confidence

One variable that might mediate the relationship between learning style and academic success is confidence. A small number of studies has shown that the relationship between a person's confidence in performing well and actual performance, however, may not be that great. Studies of students have shown that those who do best are those that do not express over-generous levels of confidence: the more modestly self-assessed students performed best. Conversely, those who rate their confidence in their ability highly tend not to do as well as their self-image would predict. In one study of students from university courses in Israel, the Netherlands, Palestine, Taiwan and the US, confidence ratings were seen to be nation-dependent in some cases (Lundeberg *et al.*, 2000).

Palestinian students expressed greatest confidence in their ability (whether they were actually correct or incorrect in answering questions). Taiwan students were the least confident but were better able to discriminate between their performance when they knew they were right and when they were wrong. That is, their confidence rating was higher when they got the answer right, and lower when they got the answer wrong. Other countries such as the US, the Netherlands and Israel showed comparable performance and confidence scores. There was no significant difference between men or women in their confidence ratings and the relationship between this and performance.

There are aspects of learning that can be positively influenced by confidence, however. Participants who scored higher in conscientiousness and openness tend to be more confident about their reading and writing ability (Pulford and Sohal, 2006). Agreeableness and perfectionism predicted confidence in numeracy skills. People who expressed least confidence in speaking tended to be introvert, female, low on conscientiousness and were not especially motivated to be organised. Confidence in the ability to manage time was found in participants who were conscientious, extravert and motivated to be organised. All three personality traits predicted Grade Point Average in the first year (the greater the trait expressed, the higher the GPA).

The best way to understand a textbook

This textbook should provide you with enough basic information and further reading for you to understand important concepts, theories and findings in psychology research, to write your essays, sit your course exams or complete your course projects. But are there specific ways of reading this textbook that can maximise your learning?

According to research by Slotte and Lonka (1999), there is. They studied 226 high school students' methods of taking notes from a philosophical textbook, the content of which would be examined formally before students enrolled on a course. Half of the sample were asked to review their notes during note-taking; the other half were not given any explicit instructions. The quality and quantity of the notes was then analysed and correlated with exam performance.

They found that reviewing notes during essay writing was associated with good performance on questions that required comprehension of the text and deep, detailed knowledge. However, reviewing these notes did not help with drawing original conclusions about the text. Importantly, they note that students summarising the text in their own words with their own subheadings and structure performed better than those students who took verbatim notes or took notes in the exact order in which the material appeared in the text. This finding suggests that deeper understanding (and better performance) comes from having read and understood material in a text. The key to this is being able to express the text's ideas in your own words. If you have not done this, you haven't understood the text.

Is learning by note-taking from this book different from note-taking from a lecture? A meta-analysis suggests that the relationship between note-taking and encoding of information in a text or during a lecture is significant but modest (Kobayashi, 2005). Inexperienced students benefited more from note-taking than did experienced ones, possibly because the latter could perform successfully without substantial note-taking. Taking notes from a visual presentation was less effective than taking notes from an audio source, presumably because paying attention to the lecture together with meeting the mechanical demands of note-taking interfered with the writing.

Studying psychology – An international perspective

You might think that most psychology students study similar topics over similar periods of time across the world. In a sense, this is right but some countries teach psychology in different ways; some have only recently developed psychology degrees; some teach psychology to achieve a particular end such as training in educational psychology. How does the teaching of psychology differ across the world?

In Australia, psychology departments exist in almost all universities (in 2006 only three did not have one) (Wilson and Provost, 2006). Like those in the UK, departments in the older universities evolved from philosophy departments in the early twentieth century. Again, like the UK, the 1980s saw an expansion of Australian institutes calling themselves universities and thus offering university psychology degrees (the parallel in the UK is the transmogrification of the polytechnics into universities in the early 1990s). Like the UK, courses are accredited by a professional organisation (the Australian Psychological Society). Psychology students in Australia can study three types of psychology degrees: a three-year degree that does not prepare the student to practise psychology; a four-year degree, which does and involves the writing of a thesis and the study of ethics; and graduate degrees.

Courses are slightly different in Italy. Here, in 2006, students could study for a three-year degree, which qualifies them to practise as a 'psychological assistant' in a restricted range of areas (Prandini and McCarthy, 2006), or a five-year degree which involves an additional two years of study which qualifies the student to practise. The student then pursues a graduate programme in a specific area to specialise further. All public school teachers in Italy have to complete a postgraduate course which involves training in psychology (Prandini and McCarthy, 2006).

Surprisingly for a country that is the birthplace of modern psychology, Germany only established its first professional curriculum in psychology in 1941 (Hodapp and Langfeldt, 2006). In the 1960s, there were 18 universities offering psychology to 2,000 students taught by 31 professors. In the 1980s, there were 30 universities teaching 18,000 students. By 2006, there were around 43 universities with 450 professors teaching 32,000 students (Hodapp and Langfeldt, 2006). Approximately 70 per cent of students are women, a figure that is echoed in the UK. German universities are changing and as of 2004, a Diplom qualification now entitles students to work in a profession related to psychology. As with all the degrees mentioned so far, the emphasis in German education is on teaching skills that will enable students to apply scientific principles to human behaviour.

The large number of departments in Germany, and other countries, isn't seen elsewhere. Greece, for example, in 2006 had four psychology departments offering two types of 'undergraduate' degree: a Ptychion (Bachelor's) degree, lasting four years, and a Master's degree (Metaptychiako Diploma) in

▶

an area such as clinical, school/educational or organisational psychology – this can last up to three years and involves internship at a relevant institution (Georgas, 2006).

The compactness of provision in Greece contrasts with Russia: 100 psychology departments have been established in the past decade (Karandashev, 2006). In 2006, students at Russian universities could study for four (Bachelor's degree) or five years (Specialist degree), in programmes regulated by the Ministry of Education (Karandashev, 2006). The four-year course trains students in general psychology; the five-year course prepares them for professional work. While Russia has divested itself of its communist shackles (partly), China has not. Psychology became an independent university discipline in China in 1960 but, following the 'Cultural Revolution' of 1966–76 and the resultant closure of all universities, psychology was attacked as pseudoscience (Zhang and Xu, 2006).

Since 1980, however, psychology has clawed its way back into the university curriculum and is now one of the most popular science subjects (Zhang and Xu, 2006).

Finally, and interestingly given the politically fractious times in which we live, what of Iran? Iran was no academic late-developer: it was running courses in psychology in the 1920s. In 2006, 19 universities offered psychology courses, with the BS (Bachelor of Science) degree being awarded after four years of study (Alipour, 2006). Unlike some other countries, the psychological associations in Iran do not accredit courses. Around 34,000 psychology students were studying in Iran and specialising in four fields: general, clinical, exceptional children and industrial psychology (Alipour, 2006). Very interestingly, in 2003, the Islamic Iranian parliament passed a law that granted equal status to medical and psychological counselling services.

Chapter review

Habituation and classical conditioning

- Habituation screens out stimuli that experience has shown to be unimportant. This form of learning allows organisms to respond to more important stimuli, such as those related to survival and reproduction.
- Classical conditioning occurs when a neutral stimulus occurs just before an unconditional stimulus (UCS) – one that automatically elicits a behaviour. The response that an organism makes in response to the unconditional stimulus (the UCR) is already a natural part of its behaviour; what the organism learns to do is to make it in response to a new stimulus (the conditional stimulus, or CS). When the response is made to the CS, it is called the conditional response, or CR.
- The relationship between the conditional stimulus and unconditional stimulus determines the nature of the conditional response. Acquisition of the conditional response is influenced by the intensity of the unconditional stimulus and the delay between the conditional stimulus and unconditional stimulus.
- Extinction occurs when the conditional stimulus is still presented but is no longer followed by the unconditional stimulus; the conditional response may show spontaneous recovery later, even after a delay.

- Generalisation occurs when stimuli similar to the conditional stimulus used in training elicit the conditional response.
- Discrimination involves training the organism to make a conditional response only after a particular conditional stimulus occurs.
- Classical conditioning can also establish various classes of stimuli as objects of fear (phobia) or of sexual attraction (fetishes). For classical conditioning to occur, the conditional stimulus must not only occur immediately before the unconditional stimulus, but it must also reliably predict the occurrence of the unconditional stimulus.

After behaviourism

- Hull's theory of learning reduced behaviour to numerical values; using these values Hull's system sought to predict behaviour.
- Tolman's theory of learning argued that stimulus–response models were too simplistic and suggested the concept of intervening variables – variables which mediated the relationship between a stimulus and the response to it. Tolman's research led to the coining of the term cognitive map to describe our ability to manipulate three-dimensional environments in the mind.

Operant conditioning

- The law of effect specifies a relation between behaviour and its consequences. If a stimulus that follows a response makes that response become more likely, we say that the response was reinforced. If the stimulus makes the response become less likely, we say that it was punished. The reinforcing or punishing stimulus must follow the behaviour almost immediately if it is to be effective.
- The process of operant conditioning helps adapt an organism's behaviour to its environment.
- Skinner described the relation between behaviour and environmental events as a three-term contingency: in the presence of discriminative stimuli, a consequence will occur if and only if an operant response occurs.
- A reinforcer is an appetitive stimulus that follows an operant response and causes that response to occur more frequently in the future.
- A punisher is an aversive stimulus that follows an operant response and causes it to occur less frequently in the future.
- If an aversive stimulus is terminated after a response occurs, the response is reinforced through a process called negative reinforcement. The termination of an appetitive stimulus can punish a response through a process called response cost.
- Extinction occurs when operant responses are emitted but not reinforced, which makes sense because organisms must be able to adapt their behaviour to changing environments.
- Complex responses, which are unlikely to occur spontaneously, can be shaped by the method of successive approximations.
- Various types of schedule of reinforcement have different effects on the rate and pattern of responding. When a response is reinforced intermittently, it is more resistant to extinction, probably because an intermittent reinforcement schedule resembles extinction more than a continuous reinforcement schedule does.
- Discrimination involves the detection of essential differences between stimuli or situations so that responding occurs only when appropriate.
- Generalisation is another necessary component of all forms of learning because no two stimuli, and no two responses, are precisely the same. Thus, generalisation embodies the ability to apply what is learned from one experience to similar experiences.
- The major difference between classical conditioning and operant conditioning is in the nature of the contingencies: classical conditioning involves a contingency between stimuli (CS and UCS), whereas operant conditioning involves a contingency between the organism's behaviour and an appetitive or aversive stimulus. The two types of conditioning complement each other. The pairings of neutral stimuli with appetitive and aversive stimuli (classical conditioning) determine which stimuli become conditioned reinforcers and punishers.

Conditioning of complex behaviours

- Much behaviour is under the control of aversive contingencies, which specify particular behaviours that are instrumental in either escaping or avoiding aversive stimuli.
- In conditioned flavour aversions, there is a delay between tasting a poison and getting sick; the rule that a reinforcing or punishing stimulus must immediately follow the response cannot, therefore, apply.
- We are able to acquire both operantly and classically conditioned responses through observation and imitation; we can learn to modify and combine responses learned in other contexts to solve new problems. This is referred to as insight.
- Behaviour analysts argue that behaviour is governed by external causes, such as discriminative stimuli and environmentally based reinforcers and punishers; cognitive psychologists maintain that behaviour is controlled by internal causes, such as thoughts, images, feelings and perceptions.

Factors influencing learning in an academic context

- Research has shown that various factors can influence academic learning, including personality, learning style, group study, the type of learning materials and the style of teaching.
- Students normally begin courses by adopting superficial learning styles geared towards achieving grades and covering the basics; as they progress, learning becomes deeper and more thoughtful.
- While beginning students evaluate courses based on superficial factors, such as the lecturer's sense of humour, more advanced students value the lecturer's knowledge and the quality of the learning materials more.
- The key to understanding material in textbooks is to underline the parts that you consider relevant first and then to write these parts in your own words.

Suggestions for further reading

Learning – general reading

Malott, R.W. and Trojan, E.A. (2008) *Principles of Behaviour* (6th edn). Boston, MA: Prentice Hall.

Martin, G.L. and Pear, J. (2007) *Behaviour modification: What is it and how to do it.* Boston, MA: Prentice Hall.

Olson, M. and Hergenhahn, B.R. (2009) *Introduction to the theories of learning* (8th edn). Boston, MA: Prentice Hall.

Terry, S. (2009) *Learning and Memory* (4th edn). Boston, MA: Allyn & Bacon.

Good, comprehensive accounts of the psychology of learning.

Learning – specific reading

Beck, H.P., Levinson, S. and Irons, G. (2009) Finding Little Albert. *American Psychologist*, 64, 605–14.

Harris, B. (1979) Whatever happened to Little Albert? *American Psychologist*, 34, 2, 151–60.

Hartley, J. (1998) *Learning and Studying.* London: Routledge.

Pashler, H., McDaniel, M., Rohrer, D. and Bjork, R (2009). Learning styles. *Psychological Science in the Public Interest*, 9, 105–19.

Staddon, J.E.R. and Cerutti, D.T. (2003) Operant conditioning. *Annual Review of Psychology*, 54, 115–44.

Watson, J.B. and Rayner, R. (1920) Conditioned emotional reactions. *Journal of Experimental Psychology*, 3, 1–14.

Watson and Rayner's original article on conditioned human fear is a classic of its kind – the first scientific study of conditioning of fear in a human being. Apart from its historical interest, it is also useful to read in order to avoid the mistakes highlighted in Harris's incisive review.

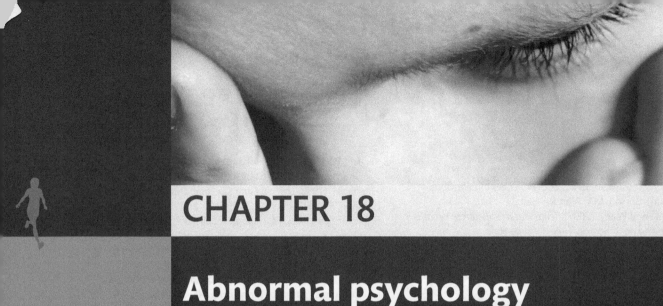

CHAPTER 18

Abnormal psychology

MyPsychLab

Explore the accompanying experiments, videos, simulations and animations on **MyPsychLab**.

This chapter includes activities on:

- Perspectives on mental disorders
- Hierarchy of anxiety
- Genetic causes of schizophrenia
- Mood disorders
- Check your understanding and prepare for your exams using the multiple choice, short answer and essay practice tests also available.

JK ROWLING REVEALS HER THOUGHTS OF SUICIDE AS A YOUNG SINGLE MOTHER

Linda Johnston

While the 42-year-old author has spoken before of her battle with depression, it is the first time she has admitted that she considered ending her life.

At the time, she was living on state benefits after having separated from her then husband and was living in a cramped and unheated flat in Edinburgh with her baby daughter.

Rowling, whose Potter novels have sold more than 400 million copies, said: 'We're talking suicidal thoughts here, we're not talking "I'm a little bit miserable."'

'Two weeks later I had a phone call from my regular GP who had looked back over the notes . . . She called me back in and I got counselling through her. She absolutely saved me because I don't think I would have had the guts to do it twice.'

She said, 'I have never been remotely ashamed of having been depressed – never. What's to be ashamed of? I went through a really rough time and I am quite proud that I got out of that.'

Source: The Herald, 24 March 2008.

WHAT YOU SHOULD BE ABLE TO DO AFTER READING CHAPTER 18

- Define the term 'mental illness'.
- Explain the aim of classification of mental disorders and define mental abnormality.
- Describe the most important treatment approaches to mental disorders.
- Describe the symptoms and causes of major mental disorders.
- Evaluate theories of mental disorder.
- Evaluate treatment approaches to mental disorder.

QUESTIONS TO THINK ABOUT

- What makes an abnormal behaviour abnormal?
- Which term makes the best sense: mental disorder or mental illness?
- How, and in what ways, are mental illnesses different from 'physical' ones?
- Are mental illnesses categorical or do they fall along a continuum?
- Do all mental disorders have a biological basis?
- What are the best treatments for mental illness? Do you think some treatment approaches are more appropriate than others?

Classification and diagnosis of mental disorders

Abnormal psychology is the area of psychology which studies and treats mental disorder. Mental disorders are disorders of thought, feeling or behaviour and are characterised by behaviourally deviant features. Their causes may be genetic, environmental, cognitive or neurobiological.

Some of these disorders you will be familiar with – depression and anxiety, for example. Others will not be so familiar, such as **paraphilia** and conversion disorder. Although the symptoms described for each disorder may apply to healthy individuals who exhibit a 'bad mood' or who are under stress, these disorders represent a severe impairment in functioning. Clinical depression is not the same as the 'low' we sometimes feel in life, and generalised anxiety disorder does not represent the stress we feel before an exam or speaking in public.

The term 'mental disorder' refers to a clinical impairment characterised by abnormal thought, feeling or behaviour. Some mental disorders, especially the less severe ones, appear to be caused by environmental factors or by a person's perception of these factors, such as stress or unhealthy family interactions. In contrast, many of the more severe mental disorders appear to be caused by hereditary and other biological factors that disrupt normal thought processes or produce inappropriate emotional reactions. The descriptions of mental disorders in this chapter necessarily make distinctions that are not always easy to make in real life; the essential features of the more important mental disorders are simplified here for the sake of clarity. In addition, many of the cases that clinicians encounter are less clear-cut than the ones included here and are thus not so easily classified.

To understand, diagnose and treat psychological disorders, some sort of classification system is needed. The need for a comprehensive classification system of psychological disorders was first recognised by Emil Kraepelin (1856–1926), who provided his version in a textbook of psychiatry published in 1883. The classification most widely used today still retains a number of Kraepelin's original categories.

What is 'abnormal'?

Mental disorders are characterised by abnormal behaviour, thoughts and feelings. The term 'abnormal' literally refers to any departure from the norm. Thus, a short or tall person is 'abnormal', and so is someone who is especially intelligent or talented. Albert Einstein was 'abnormal', as were Oscar Wilde and Pablo Picasso. The term 'abnormal' is often used pejoratively – it is used to refer to characteristics that are disliked or feared – but this is not the way in which it is used when describing mental illness. The most important feature of a mental disorder, however, may not be whether a person's behaviour is abnormal – different from that of most other people – but whether it is maladaptive. Mental disorders cause distress or discomfort and often interfere with people's ability to lead useful, productive lives. They often make it impossible for people to hold down jobs, raise families or relate to others socially.

The causes of mental disorders

What causes mental disorders? In general, they are caused by an interaction between hereditary, cognitive and environmental factors. In some cases, the genetic component is strong and the person is likely to develop a mental disorder even in a very supportive environment. In other cases, the cognitive and environmental components are strong. A complete understanding of mental disorders requires that scientists investigate genetic, cognitive and environmental factors. Once genetic factors are identified, the scientist faces the task of determining the physiological effects of the relevant genes and the consequences of these effects on a person's susceptibility to a mental disorder. Understanding the cognitive factors involved in mental disorders requires identification of the origins of distorted perceptions and maladaptive thought patterns. And environmental factors encompass more than simply a person's family history or present social interactions; they also include the effects of prenatal health and nutrition, childhood diseases and exposure to drugs and environmental toxins.

Different psychologists and other mental health professionals approach the study of mental disorders from different perspectives, each of which places more or less emphasis on these factors. The perspectives differ primarily in their explanation of the aetiology, or origin, of mental disorders. Some of these perspectives are described next.

The psychodynamic perspective

According to the psychodynamic perspective, based on Freud's early work (see Chapter 14), mental disorders originate in intrapsychic conflict produced by the three warring factions of the mind: the id, ego and superego. For some people, the conflict becomes so severe that the mind's defence mechanisms are ineffective, resulting in mental disorders that may involve, among other symptoms, extreme anxiety, obsessive thoughts and compulsive behaviour, depression, distorted perceptions and patterns of thinking, and paralysis or blindness for which there is no physical cause. The id, ego and superego are hypothetical constructs, not physical structures of the brain (see Chapter 14). But Freud and his followers often spoke as if these structures and their functions were real. Even today, psychodynamic theorists and practitioners approach mental disorders by emphasising the role of intrapsychic conflict in creating psychological distress and maladaptive behaviour.

The medical perspective

The medical perspective has its origins in the work of the ancient Greek physician Hippocrates. Hippocrates formulated the idea that excesses in the four humours (black bile, yellow bile, blood and phlegm) led to emotional problems. Other physicians, Greek and Roman, extended Hippocrates' ideas and developed the concept of mental illness – illnesses of the mind. Eventually, specialised institutions or asylums were established where people with mental disorders were confined. Early asylums were ill-run and the patients' problems were poorly understood and often mistreated. During the eighteenth and nineteenth centuries, massive reforms in the institutional care of people with mental disorders took place. The quality of the facilities and the amount of compassion for patients improved, and physicians, including neurosurgeons and psychiatrists, who were specifically trained in the medical treatment of mental disorders, were hired to care for these patients.

Today, the medical perspective is the dominant perspective in the treatment of mental disorders. Individuals with mental disorders are no longer confined to mental institutions. Instead, they are treated on an out-patient basis with drugs that are effective in abating the symptoms of mental disorders. Usually, only those people with very severe mental problems are institutionalised. The **medical model**, as the medical perspective is properly called, is based on the idea that mental disorders are caused by specific abnormalities of the brain and nervous system and that, in principle, they should be approached the same way as physical illnesses. As we shall see, several mental disorders, including schizophrenia, depression and bipolar disorder, are known to have specific biological causes and can be treated to some extent with drugs. We shall also see that genetics play a pivotal role in some of these disorders.

However, not all mental disorders can be traced so directly to physical causes. For that reason, other perspectives, which focus on the cognitive and environmental factors involved in mental disorders, have emerged.

The cognitive behavioural perspective

In contrast to the medical perspective, the cognitive behavioural perspective holds that mental disorders are learned maladaptive behaviour patterns that can best be understood by focusing on environmental factors and a person's perception of those factors. In this view, a mental disorder is not something that arises spontaneously within a person. Instead, it is caused by the person's interaction with their environment. For example, a person's excessive use of alcohol or other drugs may be negatively reinforced by the relief from tension or anxiety that often accompanies intoxication.

According to the cognitive behavioural perspective, it is not merely the environment that matters: what also counts is a person's ongoing subjective interpretation of the events taking place in their environment. Therapists operating from the cognitive behavioural perspective therefore encourage their clients to replace or substitute maladaptive thoughts and behaviours with more adaptive ones.

The humanistic and sociocultural perspective

Proponents of the humanistic perspective (see Chapter 14) argue that proper personality development occurs when people experience unconditional positive regard. According to this view, mental disorders arise when people perceive that they must earn the positive regard of others. Cultural variables influence the nature and extent to which people interpret their own behaviours as normal or abnormal. What is considered perfectly normal in one culture may be considered abnormal in another. Moreover, mental disorders exist that appear to occur only in certain cultures – a phenomenon called **culture-bound syndrome**. These are discussed in the International perspective section on pages 710–712.

Classification of disorders

Mental disorders can be classified in many ways, but the two systems most commonly used in the world are those presented in the American Psychiatric Association's *Diagnostic and Statistical Manual (of Mental Disorders)*

IV (DSM-IV TR) (2000) and the World Health Organization's *International Classification of Diseases* 10 (ICD-10)(1992). DSM-IV TR was originally devised by American psychologists for the classification of mental disorders, whereas ICD-10 was devised as an international classification system for all diseases. These two are more alike than different, although differences do exist (Andrews *et al.*, 1999). Table 18.1 lists the classifications in DSM-IV TR, with several subclassifications omitted for the sake of simplicity.

Table 18.1 Summary of the DSM-IV classification scheme for axes I and II

Axis I – Major clinical syndromes

Disorders usually first appearing in infancy, childhood or adolescence	Any deviation from normal development, including mental retardation, autism, attention deficit disorder with hyperactivity, excessive fears, speech problems and highly aggressive behaviour
Delirium, dementia, amnestic and other cognitive disorders	Disorders due to deterioration of the brain because of ageing, disease, such as Alzheimer's disease (which was discussed in Chapter 11), or ingestion or exposure to drugs or toxic substances (such as lead)
Psychoactive substance abuse disorders	Psychological, social or physical problems related to abuse of alcohol or other drugs (Psychoactive substance use and abuse was discussed in Chapters 3, 4 and 16 and is also discussed in this chapter.)
Schizophrenia and other psychotic disorders	A group of disorders marked by loss of contact with reality, illogical thought, inappropriate displays of emotion, bizarre perceptions and usually some form of hallucinations or delusions
Mood disorders	Disorders involving extreme deviations from normal mood, including severe depression (major depression), excessive elation (mania), or alteration between severe depression and excessive elation (bipolar disorder)
Anxiety disorders	Excessive fear of specific objects (phobia); repetitive, persistent thoughts accompanied by ritualistic-like behaviour that reduces anxiety (obsessive-compulsive behaviour); panic attacks; generalised and intense feelings of anxiety; and feelings of dread caused by experiencing traumatic events such as natural disasters or combat
Somatoform disorders	Disorders involving pain, paralysis or blindness for which no physical cause can be found. Excessive concern for one's health, as is typical in persons with hypochondriasis
Factitious disorders	Fake mental disorders, such as Munchausen syndrome, in which the individual is frequently hospitalised because of their claims of illness
Dissociative disorders	Loss of personal identity and changes in normal consciousness, including amnesia and multiple personality disorder, in which there exist two or more independently functioning personality systems
Sexual and sex identity disorders	Disorders involving fetishes, sexual dysfunction (such as impotence or orgasmic dysfunctions), and problems of sexual identity (such as transsexualism)
Eating disorders	Disorders relating to excessive concern about one's body weight, such as anorexia nervosa (self-starvation) and bulimia (alternating periods of eating large amounts of food and vomiting) (Eating disorders were discussed in Chapter 13.)
Sleep disorders	Disorders including severe insomnia, chronic sleepiness, sleepwalking, narcolepsy (suddenly falling asleep) and sleep apnoea (Sleep disorders were discussed in Chapter 9.)
Impulse control disorders	Disorders involving compulsive behaviours such as stealing, fire setting or gambling
Adjustment disorders	Disorders stemming from difficulties adjusting to significant life stressors, such as death of a loved one, loss of a job or financial difficulties, and family problems, including divorce (Some adjustment disorders, as they pertain to difficulty in coping with life stressors, were discussed in Chapter 17.)
Axis II – Personality disorders	Personality disorders are long-term, maladaptive and rigid personality traits that impair normal functioning and involve psychological stress. Two examples are antisocial personality disorder (lack of emphathy or care for others, lack of guilt for misdeeds, antisocial behaviour and persistent lying, cheating and stealing) and narcissistic personality disorder (inflated sense of self-worth and importance and persistent seeking of attention)

DSM-IV TR classification

The DSM-IV TR is the latest version of a scheme that was devised to provide a reliable, universal set of diagnostic categories having criteria specified as explicitly as possible. DSM-V is due to replace this in 2013/14. The DSM-IV TR describes an individual's psychological condition using five different criteria, called **axes**. Individuals undergoing evaluation are assessed on each of the axes. Axis I contains information on major psychological disorders that require clinical attention, including disorders that may develop during childhood. Personality disorders are found on Axis II. Diagnoses can be made that include both Axis I and Axis II disorders, and multiple diagnoses can occur on either axis alone. For example, major depression and alcohol dependence are both Axis I disorders, and both disorders may characterise one individual at any one period of time. A person's psychological condition may be due to several different psychological disorders described in the DSM-IV TR, just as one person may suffer simultaneously from several different physical disorders.

Axes III to V provide information about the life of the individual in addition to the basic classification provided by Axes I and II. Axis III is used to describe any physical disorders, such as skin rashes or heightened blood pressure, accompanying the psychological disorder. Axis IV specifies the severity of stress that the person has experienced (usually within the last year). This axis details the source of stress (for example, family or work) and indicates its severity and approximate duration. Axis V describes the person's overall level of psychological, social or occupational functioning. The purpose of Axis V is to estimate the extent to which a person's quality of life has been diminished by the disorder. Ratings are made on a 100-point global assessment of functioning (GAF) scale, with 100 representing the absence or near absence of impaired functioning, 50 representing serious problems in functioning, and 10 representing impairment that may result in injury to the individual or to others.

The DSM-IV TR provides a systematic means of providing and evaluating a variety of personal and psychological information about any one specific individual. Alcohol dependence (Axis I) often leads to marital problems, which may also be partially associated with an antisocial personality disorder (Axis II). Marital problems may lead to a divorce and these problems and the divorce are themselves stressors (Axis IV) that may subsequently contribute to an episode of major depression (Axis I). Alcohol dependence may eventually lead to physical problems, such as cirrhosis of the liver (Axis III). These problems, now acting in concert, are likely to lead to an increased impairment in overall life functioning (Axis V) so that the individual has only a few friends, none of them close, and is unable to keep a job. The evaluation of this person might be summarised as follows:

Axis I:	Alcohol dependence
Axis II:	Antisocial personality disorder
Axis III:	Alcoholic cirrhosis of the liver
Axis IV:	Severe – divorce, loss of job
Axis V:	GAF evaluation = 30 (a very serious impairment of functioning)

How valid and reliable is the DSM?

Although the DSM-IV TR is the most widely used classification system for mental disorders, it is not without its problems. Reflecting the fact that the DSM-IV TR has been strongly influenced by psychiatrists, the DSM-IV TR tends to be more consistent with the medical perspective on mental disorders. This means that diagnosis and treatment based on the DSM-IV TR emphasise biological factors, which, in turn, means that potential cognitive and environmental determinants may be overlooked.

Another potential problem with the DSM-IV TR (and perhaps with any classification scheme) is questionable reliability. Reliability in this context means what it did in the context of psychological testing (discussed in Chapter 2) – consistency across applications. If the DSM-IV TR was perfectly reliable, users would be able to diagnose each case in the same way. But evaluating psychological disorders is not so easy. Using the DSM-IV TR is not like using a recipe; it is more like navigating your way through an unfamiliar city using only a crude map. Using this map, you may or may not reach your destination. Mental disorders do not have distinct borders that allow a mental health professional to diagnose a disorder in a person with 100 per cent accuracy all of the time. Some critics argue, for example, that DSM encourages the making of false-positive judgements – claiming a disorder exists when there only exists a moderate, normal disruption in behaviour. For example, one in four cases of bereavement might be diagnosed as major depressive disorder when these people are undergoing a natural, event-specific change in mood (Wakefield *et al.,* 2007).

Personality disorder is one of the most commonly used diagnoses (Verheul and Widiger, 2004), but critics have highlighted inconsistencies in how each type of personality disorder is rated – one type has five or eight criteria that have to be met but only two of the types have any published rationale for the criteria (Widiger and Trull, 2007). These authors also note that the approach to diagnosing personality disorders is now polythetic – that is, four out of five criteria need to be met, rather than all. Widiger and Trull suggest that each diagnostic category might be scored along a 5-point scale and this may be one solution.

This is why evidence suggests that actuarial (statistical) analysis of symptoms is better than clinical analysis (Aegisdottir *et al.,* 2006). Specific indicators such as sex, age, test scores, medical history and so on (actuarial measures) are superior to expert 'experience' and knowledge of previous cases. You might guess that this name comes from the world of insurance (hence, actuary) and you'd be right: the actuarial method was used to assess how long a person would live (using statistics such as age, sex, height, weight, etc.) and to set levels of insurance.

Of course, not every individual will follow the pattern predicted by these statistics (not every overweight, short, old man will live longer than a slim, tall woman) but as a general guide they are a useful statistical predictor of groups of people's behaviour as a whole. In the clinical realm, Aegisdottir *et al.* (2006)'s meta-analysis found that actuarial method was 13 per cent more accurate. Reasons for the success include its reliability – a decision is based on the same criteria and not based on the subjective impression of the clinician who may be influenced by irrelevant variables or not pay attention to relevant ones. Most clinicians, however, adopt the clinical method, despite the advantages of the actuarial method. People are always more persuaded by the importance of narrative than the importance of statistics (as Chapter 2 showed).

There will probably always be dangers in classifying mental disorders. No classification scheme is likely to be perfect, and no two people with the same diagnosis will behave in exactly the same way. Yet once people are labelled, they are likely to be perceived as having all the characteristics assumed to accompany that label; their behaviour will probably be perceived selectively and interpreted in terms of the diagnosis.

An experiment by Langer and Abelson (1974) illustrated how labelling can affect **clinical judgements**. A group of psychoanalysts were shown a videotape of a young man who was being interviewed. Half of the psychoanalysts were told that the man was a job applicant, while the other half were told that he was a patient. Although both groups of clinicians watched the same man exhibiting the same behaviour, those who were told that he was a patient rated him as being more disturbed, that is, less well adjusted.

It is easy to lapse into the mistaken belief that, somehow or other, labelling disorders explains why people are like they are. Diagnosing a psychological disorder only describes the symptoms of the disorder; it does not explain its origins. To say that someone did something 'because he's schizophrenic' does not explain his behaviour. We need to be on guard against associating the names of disorders with people rather than with their symptoms. It is more appropriate to talk about 'someone who displays the characteristics of schizophrenia' than to say that 'he's a schizophrenic'.

According even to DSM-IV TR's defenders, 'the most ridiculed aspect of DSM classification system is its ever-expanding size' (Wakefield, 2001), and commentators have remarked that each new edition of the manual brings with it a new classification of a behaviour as a mental illness. Some view this enlargement as enlightenment and a recognition of a behaviour as a serious mental problem, illness or psychiatric condition. Others see the expansion as overinclusive, overeager and as inappropriately labelling odd or eccentric behaviour as deviant or as an illness without sufficient scientific evidence for doing so (Houts and Follette, 1998). New disorders are invented, according to critics, and previously accepted behaviours are labelled as disorders, in effect creating a 'social invention of mental disorders' (Houts, 2001).

Houts (2001), one of DSM's fiercest critics, refers to sleep disorders as an example of this invention and over-inclusiveness. Until DSM-III-R, sleep disorders were not considered mental disorders. 'It is as though sleep problems became mental disorders overnight sometime in 1987,' he notes. Other behaviours which Houts argues are inappropriately classed as mental disorder include **frotteurism** (touching or rubbing up against another in a sexual way without consent), kleptomania (compulsive theft), dyscalculia (a disorder of mathematical thinking), pathological gambling and voyeurism. There is also the 'wastebasket' category of 'sexual disorder not otherwise specified' which represents exactly what it says: any sexual behaviour considered deviant by a psychiatrist that does not meet the criteria of the other disorders.

DSM-V is undergoing its final revisions as this text is going to press. There appear to be two major changes in store for clinicians and patients. One is that some disorders are being removed and replaced with a 'continuum' rather than a discrete diagnostic category. For example, Asperger's Syndrome may no longer appear as a discrete disorder but will fall along an autism 'spectrum'. This change of approach has been broadly welcomed.

The second change, more controversially, is the inclusion of disorders previously regarded as normal behaviour. For example, one proposal is that children's temper tantrums will become 'Disruptive Mood Dysregulation Disorder', normal grief will become 'Major Depressive Disorder', and so on. Criticism of this approach – pathologising the normal – has beset DSM since its inception. However, critics, even those involved in chairing previous DSM revisions, such as Allen Frances, have offered excoriating assessments of this new set of diagnoses (you can find his objections here: http://www.huffingtonpost.com/allen-frances/dsm-5_b_2227626.html.

Furthermore, the reliability of the new diagnostic criteria, even according to the DSM's own committee, is mediocre at best, poor at worst (Freedman *et al.*, 2013). For example, the committee notes: 'Independent interviews by two different clinicians trained in the diagnoses, each prompted by a computerized checklist, assessment of agreement across different academic centers, and a pre-established statistical plan are now employed for the first time in the DSM Field Trials' (Freedman *et al.*, 2013, p1). But a close analysis of the results indicates that there is poor agreement between these two clinicians. The next edition of *Psychology* will make (even more?) interesting reading.

The need for classification

Because labelling can have negative effects, some people, such as Szasz (1960, 1987), have suggested that we should abandon all attempts to classify and diagnose mental disorders. In fact, Szasz has argued that the concept of mental illness has done more harm than good because of the negative effects it has on those people who are said to be mentally ill. Szasz notes that labelling people as mentally ill places the responsibility for their care with the medical establishment, thereby relieving such people of responsibility for their mental states and for taking personal steps towards improvement. As you will see in the next section, the lay view of mental illness is not positive and almost consistently ill-informed. Children's television programmes have referred to unlikeable or eccentric characters using terms related to mental illness (see Chapter 1). A later section in this chapter on soldiers' attitudes to seeking mental health help after a tour of duty cites a study which found that over 50 per cent of soldiers who meet screening criteria for various mental health problems said that their leadership/unit would have less confidence in them and that they would be seen as weak if they sought help (Hoge *et al.*, 2004). People who feel stigmatised by being labelled with the name of a mental illness feel more rejected, devalued and are up to seven times more likely to experience low self-esteem than are those who do not regard the diagnosis as a stigma (Link *et al.*, 2001; Perlick *et al.*, 2001).

However, proper classification has advantages for a patient. One advantage is that, with few exceptions, the recognition of a specific diagnostic category precedes the development of successful treatment for that disorder. Treatments for diseases such as diabetes, syphilis, tetanus and malaria were found only after the disorders could be reliably diagnosed. A patient may have a multitude of symptoms, but before the cause of the disorder (and hence its treatment) can be discovered, the primary symptoms must be identified. For example, Graves's disease is characterised by irritability, restlessness, confused and rapid thought processes and, occasionally, delusions and hallucinations. Little was known about the endocrine system during the nineteenth century when Robert Graves identified the disease, but we now know that this syndrome results from oversecretion of thyroxine, a hormone produced by the thyroid gland. Treatment involves prescription of antithyroid drugs or surgical removal of the thyroid gland, followed by administration of appropriate doses of thyroxine. Graves's classification scheme for the symptoms was devised many years before the physiological basis of the disease could be understood. But once enough was known about the effects of thyroxine, physicians were able to treat Graves's disease and strike it off the roll of mental disorders.

On a less dramatic scale, different kinds of mental disorder have different causes, and they respond to different types of psychological treatment and drugs. If future research is to reveal more about causes and treatments of these disorders, we must be able to classify specific mental disorders reliably and accurately.

Another important reason for properly classifying mental disorders is prognosis. Some disorders have good prognoses; the patients are likely to improve soon and are unlikely to have a recurrence of their problems. Other disorders have progressive courses; patients are less likely to recover from these disorders. In the first case, patients can obtain reassurance about their futures; in the second case, patients' families can obtain assistance in making realistic plans.

Lay knowledge of mental illness

In 2000, a protest group in the US called StigmaBusters successfully lobbied the TV channel, ABC, to pull a show, *Wonderland*, which portrayed people with mental illness as being dangerous or unpredictable (Corrigan *et al.*, 2005). Lay understanding of mental illness is not good. Many people either know little or nothing about the symptoms or treatment of mental illness or

The boxer Frank Bruno's admission to a psychiatric hospital for depression was treated in two versions of the UK's best-selling daily newspaper, *The Sun*. This was the second edition, printed because of the complaints generated by the first in which the boxer was described as 'Bonkers Bruno'.

Source: The Sun/NI Syndication. Copyright© News Group Newspapers Ltd.

misunderstand mental illness and assume that mentally ill people behave in ways that they, in reality, do not. Landlords who believe the stereotype of the mentally ill are less likely to offer accommodation or are more likely to offer poor accommodation (Page, 1995) and employers are likely to believe the mentally ill are incapable of working effectively (Page, 1995). Fear of mental illness also appears to have increased in the past 40 years (Phelan *et al.*, 2000), and this is the subject below.

Jorm (2000) found that members of the public had difficulty in recognising mental disorders correctly, with schizophrenia often mistaken for depression. Patients with depression are often incorrectly described as having a physical disorder (rather than a physiological one). Misunderstanding of the term schizophrenia is probably the commonest, as a raft of European surveys has shown. Knowledge of aetiology is similarly questionable, with most people believing that depression and schizophrenia are caused by social or environmental stressors. These are important aetiological factors, Jorm argues, but environmental stressors in schizophrenia are triggers rather than causes. The public's view of the medication used to treat mental illness is almost uniformly negative, contrary to the views of clinicians and to evidence from randomised controlled trials showing the relative success of these drugs in reducing symptoms. When the public is asked why their views of drugs are negative, side effects and dependence on the drugs are usually cited. Natural remedies (such as vitamins) are regarded more positively.

Educational strategies designed to teach people more about the reality of mental illness, via books, flyers, films and DVDs, for example, lead to short-term improvements in attitude but have no long-term effect (Penn *et al.*, 1999; Corrigan *et al.*, 2001). The greater the prejudice against the mentally ill, the more resistant people are to education. Face-to-face contact is slightly better. When people are confronted with the subject of their prejudice – and realise that they are not violent, unpredictable or inhuman – their attitude becomes more positive (Corrigan *et al.*, 2001). This attitude becomes even more positive when the stigmatised person has been moderately stereotyped (Reinke *et al.*, 2004).

The public's attitude to mental health, therefore, is not positive but can campaigns designed to change negative attitudes achieve their aim? Mehta *et al.* (2009) analysed changes in attitude in over 2,000 respondents across three years – from 2000 to 2003. Participants from England and Scotland were included. The survey included 26 items such as 'mental illness is an illness like any other', 'virtually anyone can become mentally ill', 'people with mental illness are a burden on society', and participants agreed or disagreed on a 5-point scale.

The study found that attitudes became more negative for 17 of the items in England and four in Scotland. There was no increase in positive attitude in either country.

Why was there a difference between countries? The authors argue that the Scottish government's 'see me' campaign (www.seemescotland.co.uk), which is designed to convey positive messages to the public about mental illness, had an effect. This began in 2000 and is ongoing. The cinema advertising, leafleting in prisons, schools, libraries and so on, they argue, may have exerted a beneficial effect (although this appears to have reduced the degree of negative attitudes, rather than increase the degree of positive attitudes).

Mental illness – An international perspective

The two manuals used by psychiatrists to diagnose mental disorder are the *Diagnostic and Statistical Manual of Mental Disorders* IV (DSM-IV TR; American Psychiatric Association, 2000) and *International Classification of Diseases* 10 (ICD-10; World Health Organization, 1992). Because these manuals are standard reference works for the diagnosis of mental illness, there is an implication that symptoms can be grouped together to form a disorder in any culture. The DSM-IV TR, for example, lists 350 disorders which should apply across cultures. In a survey of papers submitted to six prestigious psychiatry journals over a three-year period only 6 per cent of papers came from areas outside Europe and America. This 6 per cent represents 90 per cent of the world's population. Could mental disorder be culture-dependent? Are these diagnostic manuals too Western-based? Might a mental disorder in one culture be classed as normal behaviour in another?

Some clinicians have argued that we cannot apply Western diagnostic criteria such as those in DSM to other cultures (Hinton and Kleinman, 1993). This cultural relativism argues that behaviour considered abnormal in one culture may be considered normal in another. In addition, a behaviour classed as one type of mental disorder in one culture may be classed as a different one in a different culture. These two problems are generic in diagnosing mental illness across cultures. The DSM-IV TR recognises the latter problem in its appendix which contains details of 25 culture-based syndromes. The authors responsible for the DSM and ICD have ▶

Mental illness – *Continued*

also attempted to address the problem of cultural relativism by conducting extensive cross-cultural investigations on the generalisability of mental disorder diagnosis. How culture-bound, therefore, are mental disorders? Tanaka-Matsumi and Draguns (1997) have found that depression, for example, is common across most cultures. A World Health Organization (WHO) study of depression in Switzerland, Canada, Japan and Iran (World Health Organization, 1983) found that 76 per cent of individuals diagnosed as depressed exhibited symptoms of sadness, joylessness, anxiety, tension and lack of energy. Levels of guilt, however, showed large variation between cultures. Iran reported the lowest levels (22 per cent of respondents), followed by Japan (45 per cent), Canada (58 per cent) and Switzerland (68 per cent). There was also within-culture variation. For example, the two Japanese cities studied (Nagasaki and Tokyo) showed different degrees of depression, with more core symptoms reported in Nagasaki.

A study of British and Turkish outpatients found that Turkish patients reported more somatic complaints (insomnia, hypochondria) whereas the British patients reported more psychological complaints such as guilt and pessimism (Ulusahin *et al.*, 1994).

Suicidal ideation (thoughts about suicide) and suicide are also symptoms of depression which show cultural variation. In a study of the suicide rates among 15–24-year-olds in a large number of countries including Egypt, Jordan, Kuwait, Syria, the Scandinavian countries, eastern Europe, Japan, Singapore and Sri Lanka, the Arabic states (Egypt, Jordan, etc.) had the lowest suicide rates whereas Scandinavia, eastern Europe and some Asian countries had the highest (Barraclough, 1988). The highest reported rates were for Sri Lanka (47 suicides per 100,000 of the population) and Hungary (38.6 per 100,000). The exact reasons for these high rates are unknown. Some have suggested that the weakening of family structure or religious values is responsible; others suggest that endemic group violence is responsible in Sri Lanka and a fear of failure is responsible in Hungary, but these are vague, general reasons which could apply to other countries (Jilek-Aal, 1988). Paris (1991) has also cautioned that suicide and suicide attempts fluctuate across space and time and that such fluctuation may not be detected in epidemiological surveys of suicide.

Schizophrenia has been subject to three major cross-cultural studies over 25 years in 20 research centres from 17 countries. The aim of such exhaustive research has been to collect data, standardise the instruments used for measuring schizophrenic symptoms and conduct follow-up assessments (Jablensky, 1989). If different countries have different ways of measuring schizophrenia, for example, then a higher or lower incidence of the disorder may not reflect actual incidence but differences in the ways in which schizophrenia is diagnosed. The 1979 study conducted by the World Health Organization

(1979) found that the prognosis (outcome) for schizophrenia was better in developing countries (Colombia, Nigeria, India) than in developed countries (US, UK, Denmark). Schizophrenia was diagnosed as being more chronic in the most well-educated people, but only in developing countries. Later studies indicated that the outcome for schizophrenia was worse in countries such as India.

One of the most comprehensive cross-cultural studies examined 1,379 schizophrenic patients in 12 centres from 10 countries: Denmark (Aarhus), India (Agra and Chandigarh), Columbia (Cali), Ireland (Dublin), Nigeria (Fbadai), Russia (Moscow), the UK (Nottingham), Japan (Nagasaki), the Czech Republic (Prague) and the US (Honolulu, Hawaii and Rochester, New York). In each of the countries, the incidence rates were comparable (Jablensky *et al.*, 1992).

A disorder which does present some cross-cultural problems is anxiety (Tseng *et al.*, 1990). Here, there is great cultural variability in terms of the degree of generalised anxiety reported. Tseng *et al.* (1986) asked psychiatrists in Beijing, Tokyo and Honolulu to diagnose the mental disorder of Chinese patients recorded on videotape. The Beijing psychiatrists diagnosed the patients as exhibiting neurasthenia; the others diagnosed adjustment reaction. When Japanese and American psychiatrists were asked to diagnose patients with social phobia, the Japanese psychiatrists showed greater agreement in their diagnosis of Japanese social phobics than did their American counterparts (Tseng *et al.*, 1990).

Results like these suggest that cultural variations exist in the diagnosis of some mental disorders. Perhaps because anxiety is a more vague syndrome than is depression or schizophrenia, it ought not to be surprising that great variation exists between cultures in diagnosing this disorder. When more specific anxiety disorders are examined, such as object phobia, some cross-cultural agreement occurs (Davey, 1992; Davey *et al.*, 1998). In their study of the nature of object phobia in Japanese, British, American, Scandinavian, Indian, Korean and Hong Kong individuals, Davey *et al.* (1998) reported that there was broad agreement on the stimuli considered phobia-related. This consistency suggests that, at least for some anxiety disorders, there is universality.

Slightly more problematical for diagnostic manuals such as the DSM and ICD are culture-bound syndromes (Simons and Hughes, 1985). Although the DSM-IV TR lists 25 of these, it does not provide any criteria for them. Anorexia, which is not explicitly defined as culture-bound in the DSM-IV TR, seems to predominate in Western countries although there are reports of the disorder appearing in Asia (Lee, 1995). Three culture-bound syndromes are Koro, Taijin Kyofusho and anthropophobia (Tanaka-Matsumi and Draguns, 1997). Koro is found in men in southern China or Southeast Asia and refers to a belief that genitals are withdrawn into the abdomen and a fear of death provoked by a female ghost

Mental illness – *Continued*

(Tseng *et al.*, 1992). Taijin Kyofusho is a Japanese disorder similar to social phobia. However, individuals with this disorder have a specific fear of offending others by blushing, emitting offensive odours, staring inappropriately and presenting improper facial expressions (Tanaka-Matsumi, 1979). Anthropophobia seems to be the Chinese equivalent and involves the fear of being looked at.

It seems evident that although there is agreement between cultures about what constitutes a diagnosis for some mental disorders, there is clear variation for others. Anxiety, for example, seems to show the greatest variation, and depression and schizophrenia the least. Furthermore, there are some mental disorders which are culture-bound.

The treatment of mental disorders

The evolution of interventions

Mental disorder and its treatment has a long history. In the past, people suffering from mental disorder have been regarded with awe or fear; others whom we would now probably classify as paranoid schizophrenics were seen as instruments through whom gods or spirits were speaking. More often, they were considered to be occupied by devils or evil spirits and were made to suffer accordingly. The earliest known attempts to treat mental disorders involved trephining, or drilling holes in a person's skull. Presumably, the opening was made to permit evil spirits to leave the victim's head. In prehistoric times, this procedure was performed with a sharp-edged stone; later civilisations, such as the Egyptians, refined the practice. Signs of healing at the edges of the holes in prehistoric skulls indicate that some people survived these operations. An example is seen in Figure 18.1.

Many painful practices were directed at people's presumed possession by evil spirits. Individuals who were thought to be unwilling hosts for evil spirits were subjected to curses or insults designed to persuade the demons to leave. If this approach had no effect, exorcism was tried to make the person's body an unpleasant place for devils to reside. Other rituals included beatings, starving, near-drowning and the drinking of foul-tasting concoctions. The delusional schemes of psychotics often include beliefs of personal guilt and unworthiness. In a society that accepted the notion that there were witches and devils, these people were ready to imagine themselves as evil. They confessed to unspeakable acts of sorcery and welcomed their own persecution and punishment.

Until the eighteenth century, many Europeans accepted the idea that devils and spirits were responsible for peculiar

behaviours in some people. But a few people believed that these disorders reflected diseases and that they should be treated medically, with compassion for the victim. Johann Wier, a sixteenth-century physician, was among the first to challenge the practice of witchcraft. He argued that most people who were being tortured and burned for practising witchcraft in fact suffered from mental illness. The Church condemned his writings as heretical and banned them. However, even within the Church some people began to realise that the prevailing beliefs and practices were wrong.

As belief in witchcraft and demonology waned, the clergy, the medical authorities and the general public began to regard people with mental disorders as ill. Torture and persecution eventually ceased. However, the

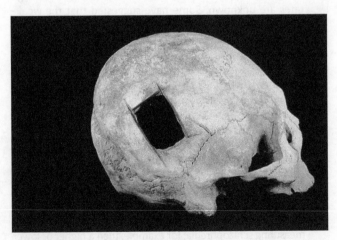

Figure 18.1 Among the earliest biological approaches to the treatment of mental disorders was the ancient practice of trephining, in which a hole was made in the skull to allow evil spirits to escape from the person's head.
Source: Loren McIntyre/Woodfin Camp & Associates, Inc.

lives of mentally ill people did not necessarily become better. The unfortunate ones were consigned to various asylums established for the care of the mentally ill. Most of these mental institutions were inhumane. Patients were often kept in chains and sometimes wallowed in their own excrement. Those who displayed bizarre catatonic postures or who had fanciful delusions were exhibited to the public for a fee. Many of the treatments designed to cure mental patients were little better than the tortures that had previously been used to drive out evil spirits. Patients were tied up, doused in cold water, bled, made to vomit, spun violently in a rotating chair and otherwise assaulted.

Mistreatment of the mentally ill did not go unnoticed by humanitarians. A famous and effective early reformer was Philippe Pinel (1745–1826), a French physician. In 1793, Pinel was appointed director of La Bicêtre, a mental hospital in Paris. Pinel believed that most mental patients would respond well to kind treatment. As an experiment, he removed the chains from some of the patients, took them out of dungeons and allowed them to walk about the hospital grounds. The experiment was a remarkable success; an atmosphere of peace and quiet replaced the previous noise, stench and general aura of despair. Many patients were eventually discharged. Pinel's success at La Bicêtre was repeated when he was given charge of Salpêtrière Hospital. Some mentally ill people eventually recover – or at least get much better – without any treatment at all. But if a person was put in a mental institution that existed prior to Pinel's time, they had little chance to show improvement.

The development of modern treatment

The modern history of specific treatments for mental disorders probably began with Franz Anton Mesmer (1734–1815), an Austrian physician who practised in Paris in the late eighteenth and early nineteenth centuries. He devised a theory of 'magnetic fluxes', according to which he attempted to effect cures by manipulating iron rods and bottles of chemicals. In reality, he hypnotised his patients and thereby alleviated some of their symptoms. As a result, hypnosis was first known as mesmerism.

In 1815, there were approximately 2,000 individuals institutionalised in mental asylums in England. The number had increased a century later when 100 or so asylums in England and Wales housed an average of 1,000 patients. In America, at the same time, the number housed was between 1,500 and 3,000. Dr William Black, a nineteenth-century English physician, kept a list of the causes of insanity of those individuals admitted to the Bethlem asylum, the largest madhouse in the UK at the time (it was also known as Bedlam).

A French neurologist, Jean Martin Charcot (1825–93), began his investigations of the therapeutic uses of hypnosis when one of his students hypnotised a woman and induced her to display the symptoms of a conversion reaction (hysteria). Charcot examined her and concluded that she was a hysterical patient. The student then woke the woman, and her symptoms vanished. Charcot had previously believed that hysteria had an organic basis, but this experience changed his opinion, and he began investigating its psychological causes.

Just before Freud began private practice, he studied with Charcot in Paris and observed the effects of hypnosis on hysteria. Freud's association with Charcot, and later with Breuer, started him on his life's study of the determinants of personality and the origins of mental illness. He created the practice of psychoanalysis. Some modern psychiatrists and psychologists still use some of his therapeutic methods to treat their clients.

Current treatment: the eclectic approach

Most therapists adopt a general, **eclectic approach** to the treatment of mental disorders. The eclectic approach (from the Greek *eklegein*, to 'single out') involves the therapist using whatever methods they feel will work best for a particular client at a particular time. Such therapists are not strongly wedded to particular theoretical orientations; instead, they seek the particular form of therapy that will best solve a particular client's problems. This often means combining aspects of several different treatment approaches according to a particular client's problem and personal circumstances. For example, Acierno *et al.* (1993) have shown that combinations of therapies are more effective in treating panic disorder than is any one alone.

Types of treatment

Psychoanalysis and psychodynamic therapy

Sigmund Freud is given credit for developing psychoanalysis, which is a form of therapy aimed at providing the client with insight into their unconscious motivations and impulses (see Chapter 14). Freud's theory of personality suggests that unconscious conflicts based on the competing demands of the id (representing biological urges), the superego (representing the moral dictates of society) and the ego (representing reality) often lead to anxiety. The source of these conflicts, according to Freud, can usually be traced back to unacceptable, often sexually based, urges from early childhood: repressed impulses and feelings that lead to conscious anxiety.

The purpose of therapy is to create a setting in which clues about the origins of intrapsychic conflicts are most likely to be revealed by the client. These clues are revealed in clients' dreams, physical problems, memory (or failure to remember certain things), manner of speech and cognitive and emotional reactions to therapy. Then, by exposing the client to these clues, they will gain insight into the problem.

While the psychoanalyst's primary role is interpretation, the client's main job is to provide the psychoanalyst with something to interpret: descriptions of their fears, anxieties, thoughts or repressed memories. This is not an easy task for the client to accomplish because the client unconsciously invokes one or more defence mechanisms, which (as you recall from Chapter 14), prevent anxiety-provoking memories and ideas from reaching conscious awareness. Together, the psychoanalyst and client work for insight into the client's problems.

Psychoanalytic techniques

Freud used free association to encourage the client to speak freely, without censoring possibly embarrassing or socially unacceptable thoughts. Freud achieved this goal in two ways. First, the client was encouraged to report any thoughts or images that came to mind, without worrying about their meaning. Secondly, Freud attempted to minimise any authoritative influence over the client's disclosures by eliminating eye contact. He usually sat in a chair at the head of a couch on which the client reclined.

Among the topics clients are encouraged to discuss are their dreams. Dream interpretation, the evaluation of the underlying meaning of dream content, is a hallmark of psychoanalysis (Freud, 1900). But even dream content is subject to some censoring, according to Freud, so that the analyst must be able to distinguish between the dream's manifest content (the actual images and events that occur within the dream) and latent content (the hidden meaning or significance of the dream). The manifest content masks the latent content because the latent content is anxiety-provoking and causes the person psychological discomfort.

Insight is not achieved quickly, nor do clients always find it easy to disclose private aspects of their personal lives. For example, a client may have to confront the reality of being abused as a child, or of being unloved, or of feeling peculiar, inferior or out of place. Although the client wishes to be cured, they do not look forward to the anxiety and apprehension that may result from recalling painful memories. The client often becomes defensive at some point during therapy, unconsciously attempting to halt further insight by censoring their true feelings, a process Freud called **resistance**.

Over a period of months or even years of therapy sessions taking place as often as several times a week, the client gradually becomes less inhibited, and the discussion begins to drift away from recent events to the more distant shores of early childhood. As the client relives aspects of childhood, they may begin to project powerful attitudes and emotions onto the therapist, a process called **transference**. The client may come to love or hate the therapist with the same intensity of the powerful emotions experienced in childhood towards parents or siblings.

Freud reasoned that the analyst, being human too, could just as easily project his or her emotions onto the client, a process he called counter-transference. Unlike transference, Freud believed **counter-transference** to be unhealthy and undesirable. To be effective, the analyst must remain emotionally detached and objective in their appraisal of the client's disclosures. For this reason, he argued that the analyst, in order to understand their own unconscious conflicts, should undergo complete analysis with another therapist.

Modern psychodynamic therapy

Psychoanalysis is now often referred to as **psychodynamic therapy** to reflect differences between modern psychoanalytic approaches and the original form of Freudian psychoanalysis. For example, although modern forms of psychodynamic therapies still focus on achieving insight into the unconscious, they tend to place less emphasis on sexual factors during development and more upon social and interpersonal experiences. Contemporary therapists also are more likely to address concerns and issues in the client's present life than to examine childhood experiences exclusively.

Modern psychodynamic therapists also view the ego as playing a more active role in influencing a person's thoughts and actions. Instead of viewing the ego as functioning merely to seek ways to satisfy the demands of the id and superego, they believe it to be a proactive component in one's overall psychological functioning. In other words, compared with Freud, modern psychodynamic therapists see the ego as having more control over the psyche. Thus, people receiving psychodynamic therapy are seen as being less constrained by the mind's unconscious forces than Freud thought them to be.

One modern form of psychodynamic therapy, time-limited therapy, takes 25–30 sessions with the therapist to complete (Strupp, 1993). The goal of time-limited therapy is to understand and improve the client's interpersonal skills through interpretation of transference processes. This therapy is based on Freud's belief that our early experiences with others influence the dynamics of our current relationships. Time-limited therapy focuses on the schemata that a client has about interpersonal relationships and attempts to modify those that are incorrect or that otherwise prevent the client from developing fulfilling relationships with others.

Evaluation

Evaluating the effectiveness of psychoanalysis or psychodynamic therapy is difficult because only a small proportion of people with mental disorders qualify for this method of treatment. To participate in this kind of therapy, a client must be intelligent, articulate and motivated enough to spend three or more hours a week working hard to uncover unconscious conflicts. In addition, they must be able to afford the therapist's fees, which are high. These qualifications rule out most psychotics, as well as people who lack the time or money to devote to such a long-term project. Furthermore, many people who enter this kind of therapy become dissatisfied with their progress and leave. In other cases, the therapist encourages a client to leave if they decide that the client is not cooperating fully. Thus, those who actually complete a course of therapy do not constitute a random sample, and we cannot conclude that this kind of therapy works just because a high percentage of this group is happy with the results. Those who have dropped out ought also to be counted.

Another problem in evaluating psychoanalysis and psychodynamic therapy is that therapists have a way to 'explain' their failures: they can blame them on the client (Eysenck, 1985). If the client appears to accept an insight into their behaviour but the behaviour does not change, the insight is said to be merely 'intellectual'. This escape clause makes the argument for the importance of insight completely circular and, therefore, illogical: if the client gets better, the improvement is due to insight; but if the client's behaviour remains unchanged, real (as opposed to 'intellectual') insight did not occur.

Humanistic therapies

Client-centred therapy

In the 1940s, Carl Rogers (1902–87) developed the first **humanistic therapy**, creating a major alternative to psychoanalysis. The aim of humanistic therapy is to provide the client with a greater understanding of their unique potential for personal growth and self-actualisation. Humanistic therapies proceed from the assumption that people are good and have innate worth. Psychological problems reflect some type of blocking of one's potential for personal growth; humanistic therapy aims to realise this potential.

Rogers found the formalism of psychoanalysis too confining and its emphasis on intrapsychic conflict too pessimistic (Tobin, 1991). His discontent led him to develop his own theory of personality, abnormal behaviour and therapy. His **client-centred therapy** is so named because of the respect given the client during therapy: the client decides what to talk about without direction or judgement from the therapist. The client takes ultimate responsibility for resolving the client's problems. The client, not a method or theory, is the focus of the therapy.

Rogers believed that the cause of many psychological problems can be traced to people's perceptions of themselves as they actually are (their real selves) as differing from the people they would like to be (their ideal selves). Rogers called this discrepancy between the real and the ideal perceptions of the self incongruence. The goal of client-centred therapy is to reduce **incongruence** by fostering experiences that will make attainment of the ideal self possible. Because the client's and not the therapist's thoughts direct the course of therapy, the therapist strives to make those thoughts, perceptions and feelings more noticeable to the client. This is frequently done through reflection, sensitive rephrasing or mirroring of the client's statements. For example:

> *Client*: I get so frustrated at my parents. They just don't understand how I feel. They don't know what it's like to be me.
>
> *Therapist*: You seem to be saying that the things that are important to you aren't very important to your parents. You'd like them now and then to see things from your perspective.

By reflecting the concerns of the client, the therapist demonstrates empathy, or the ability to perceive the world from another's viewpoint. The establishment of empathy is key in encouraging the client to deal with the incongruence between the real and the ideal selves.

For Rogers (1951), the 'worth and significance of the individual' is a basic ground rule of therapy. This theme is represented in therapy through unconditional positive regard, in which the therapist tries to convey to the client that his or her worth as a human being is not dependent on anything they think, do or feel.

In client-centred therapy, the therapist totally and unconditionally accepts the client and approves of them as a person so that the client can come to understand that their feelings are worthwhile and important. Once the client begins to pay attention to these feelings, a self-healing process begins. For example, a client usually has difficulty at first expressing feelings verbally. The therapist tries to understand the feelings underlying the client's confused state and to help them put those feelings into words. Through this process, the client learns to understand and heed their own drive towards self-actualisation.

Evaluation

Unlike many other clinicians, who prefer to rely on their own judgements concerning the effectiveness of their techniques, Rogers himself stimulated a considerable amount of research on the effectiveness of client-centred therapy. He recorded therapeutic sessions so that various techniques could be evaluated. One researcher, Truax (1966), obtained permission from Rogers (and his clients) to record some therapy sessions, and he classified the statements made by the clients into several categories. One of the categories included statements of improving mental health, such as 'I'm feeling better lately' or 'I don't feel as depressed as I used to'. After each of the patients' statements, Truax noted Rogers's reaction to see whether he gave a positive response. Typical positive responses were 'Oh, really? Tell me more' or 'Uh-huh. That's nice' or just a friendly 'Mm'. Truax found that of the eight categories of client statements, only those that indicated progress were regularly followed by a positive response from Rogers. Not surprisingly, during their therapy, the clients made more and more statements indicating progress.

This study attests to the power of social reinforcement and its occurrence in unexpected places. Rogers was an effective and conscientious psychotherapist, but he had not intended to single out and reinforce his clients' realistic expressions of progress in therapy. (Of course, he did not uncritically reinforce exaggerated or unrealistic positive statements.) This finding does not discredit client-centred therapy. Rogers simply adopted a very effective strategy for altering a person's behaviour. He used to refer to his therapy as non-directive; however, when he realised that he was reinforcing positive statements, he stopped referring to it as non-directive because it obviously was not.

Behavioural and cognitive behavioural therapies

The fundamental assumption made by behavioural therapists is that people learn maladaptive or self-defeating behaviour in the same way as they learn adaptive behaviour. Undesirable behaviour, such as nail-biting or alcohol abuse, is the problem, not just a reflection of the problem.

The methods that behavioural therapists use to induce behaviour change are extensions of classical and operant conditioning principles and work quite successfully.

In classical conditioning, a previously neutral stimulus (ultimately the conditional stimulus, CS) comes to elicit the same response as a stimulus (unconditional stimulus, UCS) that naturally elicits that response because the CS reliably predicts the UCS (see Chapter 7). According to Joseph Wolpe (1958), one of the founders of behavioural therapy, many of our everyday fears and anxieties become associated with neutral stimuli through coincidence. Going to the dentist may evoke fear because the last time that you went you were not given enough anaesthetic and the drilling hurt. Although the dental surgery is usually not painful, you associate the dentist with pain because of your past experience. The next sections describe some of the more specific behavioural and cognitive behavioural approaches.

Systematic desensitisation

One behavioural therapy technique, developed by Wolpe, has been especially successful in eliminating some kinds of fear and phobia. This technique, called **systematic desensitisation**, is designed to remove the unpleasant emotional response produced by the feared object or situation and replace it with an incompatible one – relaxation.

The client is first trained to achieve complete relaxation. The essential task is to learn to respond quickly to suggestions to feel relaxed and peaceful so that these suggestions can elicit an immediate relaxation response. Next, client and therapist construct a hierarchy of anxiety-related stimuli.

Finally, the conditional stimuli (fear-eliciting situations) are paired with stimuli that elicit the learned relaxation response. For example, a person with a fear of spiders is instructed to relax and then to imagine hearing from a neighbour that she saw a spider in her garage. If the client reports no anxiety, they are instructed to move to the next item in the hierarchy and to imagine hearing a neighbour say that there is a tiny spider across the street; and so on. Whenever the client begins feeling anxious, they signal to the therapist with some predetermined gesture such as raising a finger. The therapist instructs the client to relax and, if necessary, describes a less threatening scene. The client is not permitted to feel severe anxiety at any time. Gradually, over a series of sessions (the average is 11), the client is able to get through the entire list, vicariously experiencing even the most feared encounters.

Whereas practitioners of systematic desensitisation are careful not to permit their clients to become too anxious, practitioners of a procedure called **flooding** attempt to rid their clients of their fears by arousing them intensely until their responses diminish through habituation and they learn that nothing bad happens. The therapist describes, as graphically as possible, the most frightening encounters possible with the object of a client's phobia. The client tries to imagine the encounter and to experience intense fear (thereby 'flooding' the client's mind with anxious thoughts). In some cases, the client actually encounters the object of their fear, in which case the treatment is called *in vivo* (live) **implosion therapy**. Of course, the client is protected from any adverse effects of the encounter (or the encounter is imaginary), so there are no dangerous consequences. Eventually, the fear response begins to subside, and the client learns that even the worst imaginable encounter can become tolerable. In a sense, the client learns not to fear their own anxiety attack, and avoidance responses begin to extinguish.

Aversion therapy

In **aversion therapy**, a negative reaction to a neutral stimulus is caused by pairing it with an aversive stimulus (UCS). Aversion therapy attempts to establish an unpleasant response (such as a feeling of fear or disgust) to the object that produces the undesired behaviour. For example, a person with a **fetish** for women's shoes might be given painful electrical shocks while viewing colour slides of women's shoes. Aversion therapy has also been used to treat drinking, smoking, transvestism, **exhibitionism** and overeating. This technique has been shown to be moderately effective (Marshall *et al.*, 1991). However, because the method involves pain or nausea, the client's participation must be voluntary, and the method should be employed only if other approaches fail or are impractical.

The use of aversive methods raises ethical issues, particularly when the individual is so severely impaired that they are unable to give informed consent to a particular therapeutic procedure. It would seem reasonable that aversive methods involving stimuli such as electric shock should be used as the last resort. In a method called **covert sensitisation**, instead of experiencing a punishing stimulus after performing a behaviour, the client imagines that they are performing an undesirable behaviour and then imagines receiving an aversive stimulus.

Behaviour modification

Behaviour modification, a general term describing therapy based on operant conditioning principles (see Chapter 7), involves altering maladaptive behaviour by rearranging the contingencies between behaviour and its consequences. Increases in desirable behaviour can be brought about through either positive or negative reinforcement, and undesirable behaviour can be reduced through either extinction or punishment.

In its infancy, behaviour modification was applied chiefly to patients with schizophrenia (described in detail later) and the mentally retarded (Lindsley, 1956; Ayllon and Azrin, 1968; Neisworth and Madle, 1982). The use of operant conditioning principles has been extended to a wide array of behaviours and circumstances, for example weight management, anorexia nervosa, bed-wetting, smoking and compliance with medical regimens (Kazdin, 1994).

Token economies

The behaviour–analytic approach has been used on a large scale in mental institutions with generally good success. Residents are often asked to do chores to engage them in active participation in their environment. In some instances, other specific behaviours are also targeted as desirable and therapeutic, such as helping residents who have more severe problems. To promote these social behaviours, therapists have designed **token economies**. A list of tasks is compiled, and residents receive tokens as rewards for performing the tasks; later, they can exchange these tokens for snacks, other desired articles or various privileges. The tokens become conditioned reinforcers for desirable and appropriate behaviours. The amount of time spent performing the desirable behaviours was high when reinforcement contingencies were imposed and low when they were not.

Although token economies are based on a simple principle, they are very difficult to implement. A mental institution includes patients, caretakers, housekeeping staff and professional staff. If a token economy is to be effective, all staff members who deal with residents must learn how the system works; ideally, they should also understand and agree with its underlying principles. A token economy can easily be sabotaged by a few people who believe that the system is foolish, wrong or in some way threatening to themselves. If these obstacles can be overcome, token economies work very well.

Modelling

Humans (and many other animals) have the ability to learn without directly experiencing an event. People can imitate the behaviour of other people, watching what they do and, if the conditions are appropriate, performing the same behaviour. This capability provides the basis for the technique of **modelling**. Behaviour therapists have found that clients can make much better progress when they have access to a model providing examples of successful behaviours to imitate.

Social skills training

With social skills training, the client is taught to behave in a desirable and socially appropriate way and this has been used extensively in individuals with schizophrenia (see below) and Asperger's syndrome (Chapter 12). They might do this by engaging in **assertiveness training**, which teaches the client to be more direct about their feelings (Oltmans and Emery, 1998). A part of assertiveness training might be **role-playing**, in which the client is taught to act out or rehearse social skills by adopting the identity of another, socially skilled person.

Cognitive behavioural therapy

The first attempts at developing psychotherapies based on altering or manipulating cognitive processes emerged during the 1970s. These attempts were undertaken by behavioural therapists who suspected that maladaptive behaviour, or, for that matter, adaptive behaviour, could be due to more than only environmental variables. They began exploring how their clients' thoughts, perceptions, expectations and self-statements might interact with environmental factors in the development and maintenance of maladaptive behaviour.

The focus of **cognitive behavioural therapy (CBT)** is on changing the client's maladaptive thoughts, beliefs and perceptions. Like behaviour therapists – and unlike most insight psychotherapists – cognitive behaviour therapists are not particularly interested in events that occurred in the client's childhood. They are interested in the here and now and in altering the client's behaviour so that it becomes more functional. Although they employ many methods used by behavioural therapists, they believe that when behaviours change, they do so because of changes in cognitive processes.

There are many ways in which CBT can be applied to mental disorder. Attribution retraining, for example, involves retraining the client to alter their perception of causes of events or behaviour (attributions are perceived causes). One way in which this can be achieved is by requesting the client to adopt a more scientific approach to their beliefs. For example, it is common in depression for a depressed person to attribute causes for failure to themselves but to attribute successes to others. Attribution retraining should encourage the client to change these 'faulty' attributions and make them more realistic. One form of CBT designed to treat depression requires the patient to assess whether their view of themselves and others is distorted based on a considered analysis of their lives. This approach, based on the clinical work of Beck (1967, 1976; Beck and Emery, 1985), is considered in the section on depression below (see page. 752).

Another CBT approach, **rational-emotive therapy**, was developed in the 1950s by Albert Ellis, a clinical psychologist, and is based on the belief that psychological problems are caused by how people think about upsetting events and situations. In contrast to the other forms of CBT, rational-emotive therapy did not grow out of the tradition of behaviour therapy. Ellis asserts that psychological problems are the result of faulty cognitions; therapy is therefore aimed at changing people's beliefs. Rational-emotive therapy is highly directive and confrontational. The therapist tells their clients what they are doing wrong and how they should change.

According to Ellis and his followers, emotions are the products of cognition. A significant activating event (A) is followed by a highly charged emotional consequence (C), but it is not correct to say that A has caused C. Rather, C is a result of the person's belief system (B).

Therefore, inappropriate emotions (such as depression, guilt and anxiety) can be abolished only if a change occurs in the person's belief system. It is the task of the rational-emotive therapist to dispute the person's beliefs and to convince them that those beliefs are inappropriate. Ellis tries to show his clients that irrational beliefs are impossible to satisfy, that they make little logical sense and that adhering to them creates needless anxiety, self-blame and self-doubt. The following are examples of the kinds of ideas that Ellis believes to be irrational:

> The idea that it is a necessity for an adult to be loved or approved by virtually every significant person in the community.
>
> The idea that one should be thoroughly competent, adequate, and goal-oriented in all possible respects if one is to consider oneself as having worth.
>
> The idea that human unhappiness is externally caused and that people have little or no ability to control their lives.
>
> The idea that one's past is an all-important determinant of one's present behaviour.
>
> The idea that there is invariably a right, precise, and perfect solution to human problems and that it is catastrophic if this perfect solution is not found. (*Source*: Ellis, 1973, pp. 152–3.)

In a review of research evaluating the effectiveness of rational-emotive therapy, Haaga and Davison (1989) concluded that the method has been shown to reduce general anxiety, test anxiety and unassertiveness. Rational-emotive therapy has appeal and potential usefulness for those who can enjoy and profit from intellectual teaching and argumentation. The people who are likely to benefit most from this form of therapy are those who are self-demanding and who feel guilty for not living up to their own standards of perfection. People with serious anxiety disorders or with severe thought disorders, such as schizophrenia and other psychoses, are unlikely to respond to an intellectual analysis of their problems.

Many therapists who adopt an eclectic approach use some of the techniques of rational-emotive therapy with some of their clients. In its advocacy of rationality and its eschewing of superstition, the therapy proposes a common-sense approach to living. However, many psychotherapists disagree with Ellis's denial of the importance of empathy in the relationship between therapist and client.

Evaluation

Psychotherapists of traditional orientations have criticised behavioural therapy for its focus on the symptoms of a psychological problem to the exclusion of its root causes. Some psychoanalysts even argue that treatment of just the symptoms is dangerous. In their view, the removal of one symptom of an intrapsychic conflict will simply produce another, perhaps more serious, symptom through a process called **symptom substitution**.

There is little evidence that symptom substitution occurs. It is true that many people's behavioural problems are caused by conditions that existed in the past, and often these problems become self-perpetuating. Behavioural therapy can, in many cases, eliminate the problem behaviour without delving into the past. For example, a child may, for one reason or another, begin wetting the bed. The nightly awakening irritates the parents, who must change the bed sheets and the child's pyjamas. The disturbance often disrupts family relationships. The child develops feelings of guilt and insecurity and wets the bed more often. Instead of analysing the sources of family conflict, a therapist who uses behavioural therapy would install a device in the child's bed that rings a bell when they begin to urinate. The child awakens and goes to the bathroom to urinate and soon ceases to wet the bed. The elimination of bed-wetting causes rapid improvement in the child's self-esteem and in the entire family relationship. Symptom substitution does not appear to occur (Baker, 1969).

Although cognitive behavioural therapists believe in the importance of unobservable constructs such as feelings, thoughts and perceptions, they do not believe that good therapeutic results can be achieved by focusing on cognitions alone. They, like their behaviour-analytic colleagues, insist that it is not enough to have their clients introspect and analyse their thought patterns. Instead, therapists must help clients to change their behaviour. Behavioural changes can cause cognitive changes. For example, when a client observes that they are now engaging in fewer maladaptive behaviours and more adaptive behaviours, the client's self-perceptions and self-esteem are bound to change as a result. Therapy is more effective when attention is paid to cognitions as well as to behaviours.

Psychology in action: How instructions to express reduce distress

Imagine having experienced severe distress or trauma. You may have been physically attacked, robbed or sexually assaulted. Anecdotal evidence suggests that it is best to talk about these events to another person – this allows you to express your feelings about the event that you had previously kept to yourself. It is a form of catharsis, people will say. They might be right.

A novel medicine treatment for trauma has been emotional disclosure (ED) through expressive writing. ED involves asking an individual who has suffered severe trauma or distress to express how they feel about the distress or trauma by writing about it and to write or think about why they feel in the way that they do. This ostensibly simple technique has been found to improve coping, physical health, emotional health and immune system functioning in extremely distressed individuals (Smyth, 1998).

The pioneers of this technique, James Pennebaker and his colleagues (Pennebaker et al., 1988; Pennebaker and Francis, 1996; Pennebaker, 1997), have published several studies showing that when distressed individuals are asked to write down their thoughts and express their emotions, these individuals required fewer visits from the doctor than did those who wrote about trivial topics. Individuals also showed an improvement in their immune system functioning. The participants in these studies were people suffering real distress – Holocaust survivors, the bereaved and the recently unemployed.

Replications by different groups are positive, but mixed. Some improvement in physical health beyond the 'treatment' period has been reported (Lepore, 1997) and survivors of trauma who create narratives about their distress feel better than those who do not (Foa et al., 1995). Arthritic patients who wrote about the emotionally negative aspects of their illness saw an improvement in their condition (Kelley et al., 1997). Sloan and Marx (2004) randomly assigned 49 women who reported having experienced at least one traumatic event and who showed at least moderate levels of post-traumatic stress disorder to a disclosure condition – where they wrote about a traumatic event in prose as emotionally as possible – or a control condition where no writing occurred. Participants in the disclosure condition reported fewer psychological and physical symptoms a month after testing. The only improvement that was 'clinically' significant, however, was a reduction in depressive symptoms.

A study investigating the effects of ED in patients suffering serious illness found that it had little effect in reducing distress, but patients who had little social contact with others or who found that the opportunities for expressing emotions to others were limited benefited greatly from the process. Zakowski *et al.* (2004) randomly assigned 104 gynaecological and prostate cancer patients to an ED condition, where patients wrote about their trauma for 20 minutes a day for three days, or a non-ED condition (writing about a non-emotional topic). Those in the ED condition who had little opportunity for expressing emotion in social contexts benefited significantly from the ability to write about their illness. The lack of a reduction in stress is comparable to findings from studies of breast cancer which report similarly negative findings (Stanton and Danoff-Burg, 2002). The authors suggest that the benefits of writing in cancer patients might be better revealed in more objective, physical measures rather than subjective, self-report measures.

Some researchers have hypothesised that the benefits of expressive writing arise from the changes in thinking that such writing encourages (Pennebaker, 1997). When individuals write about cause and effect in their expressive writing and show insight into their distress, physical and psychological health improves – their thoughts become more methodically organised (Pennebaker *et al.*, 1997).

Undergraduates who wrote about their stressful thoughts and feelings on entering university showed significantly better working memory performance at the end of the experiment (Klein and Boals, 2001). More 'cognitive' than 'emotion' words were used at a later session (compared with earlier sessions). The researchers suggest that this supports Smyth's (1998) contention that if writing moderates health by changing cognition, changes in tests measuring cognition should be closely associated with the writing process. In a second experiment, students were asked to write about intrusive negative thoughts. They showed significant improvements in working memory than did those who wrote about a positive event or a trivial one.

This last finding suggests that the improvements may be due to the removal of intrusive negative thoughts, rather than intrusive thoughts per se (positive thoughts, for example, which may have been on people's minds, did not place significant strains on working memory). Of course, this study focused on one type of working memory task and did not measure health outcomes, but the authors hypothesise that the improvements in health as a result of expressive writing may be due to the improvements in working memory capacity.

Other forms of psychotherapy

Group therapy

Group psychotherapy, in which two or more clients meet simultaneously with a therapist to discuss problems, became common during the Second World War. The stresses of combat produced psychological problems in many members of the armed forces, and the demand for psychotherapists greatly exceeded the supply. What began as an economic necessity became an institution once the effectiveness of group treatment was recognised.

Because most psychological problems involve interactions with other people, treating these problems in a group setting may be worthwhile. Group therapy provides four advantages that are not found in individual therapy:

1 The group setting permits the therapist to observe and interpret actual interactions without having to rely on clients' descriptions, which may be selective or faulty.

2 A group can bring social pressure to bear on the behaviours of its members. If a person receives similar comments about their behaviour from all the members of a group, the message is often more convincing than if a psychotherapist delivers the same comments in a private session.

3 The process of seeing the causes of maladaptive behaviour in other people often helps a person to gain insight into their own problems. People can often learn from the mistakes of others.

4 Knowing that other people have problems similar to one's own can bring comfort and relief. People discover that they are not alone.

The structure of group therapy sessions can vary widely. Some sessions are little more than lectures, in which the therapist presents information about a problem common to all members of the group, followed by discussion. For example, in a case involving a person with severe mental or physical illness, the therapist explains to family members the nature, treatment and possible outcomes of the disorder. Then the therapist answers questions and allows people to share their feelings about what the illness has done to their family. Other groups are simply efficient ways to treat several clients at the same time. Most types of group therapy involve interactions among the participants.

Family therapy and couples therapy

In **family therapy**, a therapist meets with (usually) all the members of a client's family and analyses the ways in which individuals interact. The therapist attempts to get family members to talk to each other instead of addressing all comments and questions to them. As much as possible, the family therapist tries to collect data about the interactions – how individuals sit in relation to each other, who interrupts whom, who looks at whom before speaking – in order to infer the nature of interrelationships within the family. For example, there may be barriers between certain family members; perhaps a father is unable to communicate with one of his children. Or two or more family members may be so dependent on each other that they cannot function independently; they constantly seek each other's approval and, through overdependence, make each other miserable.

After inferring the family structure, the therapist attempts to restructure it by replacing maladaptive interactions with more effective, functional ones. The therapist suggests that perhaps all members of the family must change if the client is to make real improvement. They get family members to 'actualise' their transactional patterns – to act out their everyday relationships – so that the maladaptive interactions will show themselves. Restructuring techniques include forming temporary alliances between the therapist and one or more of the family members, increasing tension in order to trigger changes in unstable structures, assigning explicit tasks and homework to family members (for example, making them interact with other members), and providing general support, education and guidance. Sometimes, the therapist visits the family at home. For example, if a child in a family refuses to eat, the therapist will visit during a mealtime in order to see the problem acted out as explicitly as possible.

Behavioural therapists have also applied their methods of analysis and treatment to families. This approach focuses on the social environment provided by the family and on the ways in which family members reinforce or punish each other's behaviour. The strategy is to identify the maladaptive behaviours of the individuals and the ways these behaviours are inadvertently reinforced by the rest of the family. Then the therapist helps the family members find ways to increase positive exchanges and reinforce each other's adaptive behaviours. A careful analysis of the social dynamics of a family often reveals that changes need to be made not in the individual showing the most maladaptive behaviours but in the other members of the family.

All couples will find that they disagree on some important issues. These disagreements necessarily lead to conflicts. For example, they may have to decide whether to move to accommodate the career of one of the partners, they will have to decide how to spend their money, and they will have to decide how to allocate household chores. Their ability to resolve conflict is one of the most important factors affecting the quality and durability of their relationship (Schwartz and Schwartz, 1980).

Controversies in psychological science: Does psychotherapy work?

The issue

Evaluation of therapies and therapists is an important issue. It has received much attention, but almost everyone who is involved agrees that too little is known about the efficacy of psychotherapeutic methods, partly because psychotherapeutic effectiveness is difficult to study. The most well-known psychotherapies, their goals and methods of intervention are summarised in Table 18.2. Given that there are at least 400 types of therapy and over 150 classified mental disorders (Garfield and Bergin, 1994), achieving some consistency across studies is difficult.

Several other factors make it extremely difficult to evaluate the effectiveness of a particular form of therapy or an individual therapist. These include measurement – there are no easily applied, commonly agreed criteria for mental health; and self-selection – clients choose whether to enter therapy, what type of therapy to engage in and how long to stay in therapy, which makes it nearly impossible to establish either a stable sample population or a control group. Self-selection means that certain kinds of people are more likely than others to enter a particular therapy and stick with it, which produces a biased sample. Lack of a stable sample and of a control group makes it difficult to compare the effectiveness of various kinds of therapy. Many patients change therapists or leave therapy altogether. What conclusions can we make about the effectiveness of a therapy by looking only at the progress made by the clients who remain with it?

Controversies in psychological science: *Continued*

Yet another problem with scientific evaluation of psychotherapy is the question of an appropriate control group. The effects of therapeutic drugs must be determined through comparison with the effects of placebos (innocuous pills that have no effects on people's thoughts and behaviour) to be sure that the improvement has not occurred merely because the patient thinks that a pill has done some good. Placebo effects can also occur in psychotherapy: people know that they are being treated and get better because they believe that the treatment should lead to improvement. Also, given the assumption that these therapies have the power to do good, there may be the possibility that they also have the power to do harm (Barlow, 2010; Dimidjian and Hollon, 2010). Given these problems, what can we say about the efficacy of psychotherapy?

The evidence

In a pioneering, controversial paper on psychotherapeutic evaluation, Eysenck (1952) examined 19 studies assessing the effectiveness of psychotherapy. He reported that of the people who remained in psychoanalysis as long as their therapists thought they should, 66 per cent showed improvement. Similarly, 64 per cent of patients treated eclectically showed an improvement. However, 72 per cent of patients who were treated only custodially (receiving no psychotherapy) in institutions showed improvement. In other words, people got better just as fast by themselves as they did in therapy.

Subsequent studies were not much more supportive. Some investigators, including Eysenck, concluded that it was unethical to charge a person for psychotherapy because there was little scientific evidence for its effectiveness. Many forms of therapy have never been evaluated objectively because their practitioners are convinced that the method works and deem objective confirmation unnecessary.

Figure 18.2 summarises Smith *et al.*'s (1980) well-known meta-analysis of 475 studies comparing the outcome effectiveness of psychodynamic, gestalt, client-centred,

Table 18.2 Summary of the basic assumptions, goals and methods involved in traditional forms of psychotherapy

Type of therapy	Basic assumptions	Primary goals	Typical method of analysis or intervention
Psychoanalysis	Behaviour is motivated by intra-psychic conflict and biological urges	To discover the sources of conflict and resolve them through insight	Free association, dream interpretation, interpretation of transference, resistance, memory, and manner of speech
Psychodynamic	Behaviour is motivated by both unconscious forces and inter-personal experiences	To understand and improve interpersonal skills	Interpretation of transference and modification of client's inappropriate schemata about interpersonal relationships
Humanistic and gestalt	People are good and have innate worth	To promote personal growth and self-actualisation and to enhance client's awareness of bodily sensations and feelings	Reduce incongruence through reflection, empathy, unconditional positive regard and techniques to enhance personal awareness and feelings of self-worth
Behavioural and cognitive behavioural	Behaviour is controlled largely by environmental contingencies, people's perception of them, or their combination	To change maladaptive behaviour and thinking patterns	Manipulate environmental variables, restructure thinking patterns and correct faulty thinking or irrational beliefs
Family/couples	Problems in relationships entail everybody involved in them	To discover how interactions influence problems in individual functioning	Analysis of patterns of family/couple's interaction and how others reinforce maladaptive and adaptive thinking and behaving

Controversies in psychological science: *Continued*

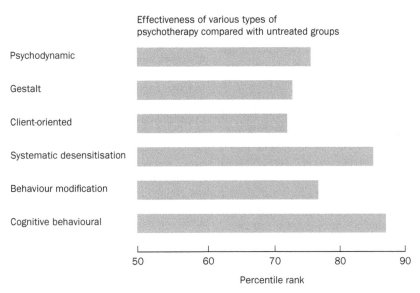

Effectiveness of various types of
psychotherapy compared with untreated groups

Figure 18.2 Effectiveness of psychotherapy. The results of Smith *et al.*'s meta-analysis comparing the effectiveness of different therapies.

systematic desensitisation, behaviour modification and cognitive behavioural therapies. Relative to no therapy, each of these therapies was shown to be superior in helping people with their problems. As you can see, behavioural and cognitive therapies tended to exceed others in effectiveness, although these differences were often small. More recent research has confirmed these results, indicating that almost all people who enter behavioural or cognitive behavioural therapy tend to improve with regard to the reason that brought them to therapy (Robinson *et al.*, 1990).

Several studies have suggested that the ability to form understanding, warm and empathetic relationships is one of the most important traits that distinguish an effective therapist from an ineffective one (Beutler *et al.*, 1994). For example, Strupp and Hadley (1979) enlisted a group of lecturers on the basis of their reputation as warm, trustworthy, empathetic individuals. The lecturers (from the departments of English, history, mathematics and philosophy) were asked to hold weekly counselling sessions for students with psychological difficulties. Another group of students was assigned to professional psychotherapists, both psychologists and psychiatrists, and a third group received no treatment at all. Most of the students showed moderate depression or anxiety.

Although there was much variability, with some individual students showing substantial improvement, students who met with the lecturers did as well as those who met with the professional therapists. Both groups did

significantly better than the control subjects who received no treatment. These results suggest that sympathy and understanding are the most important ingredients in the psychotherapeutic process, at least for treatment of mild anxiety or depression. In such cases, the therapists' theories of how mental disorders should be treated may be less important than their ability to establish warm, understanding relationships with their clients.

In one meta-analysis, Westen and Morrison (2001) scrutinised studies from nine clinical psychology and psychiatric journals published between 1990 and 1999. To be eligible for inclusion, studies had to test the efficacy of a specific psychosocial treatment against a waiting-list control group and an alternative therapy, have had a follow-up of at least 12 months, include valid measures of outcome and be experimental in nature. Thirty-four studies met these inclusion criteria.

The authors found substantial improvement in mental health in up to half of the patients. The majority of patients, however, did not show sustained improvement at one to two years' follow-up, especially those who are depressed or generally anxious. Half of patients who complete a course of treatment will benefit from it, whereas the figure drops to 40 per cent if a patient simply enters treatment (but may not continue). The long-term treatment success for panic disorder is good, but the authors found that the depressed or anxious patient will maintain mild to significant levels of symptoms after treatment. The authors note that follow-up studies at two years were non-existent. In the four studies that did conduct such a follow-up, a quarter of depressed patients who did not abuse alcohol or drugs and were not suicidal will improve two years after treatment. Psychotherapy for panic disorder treatment was the most effective, with 46 per cent of patients showing sustained improvement.

The strict exclusion/inclusion criteria in the study is a plus and a negative. On the plus side, the studies reviewed are carefully selected and well-controlled experimental studies. On the negative side, few studies were included and complications such as co-morbidity (the appearance of one disorder with another) were not addressed because patients in the selected studies suffered exclusively from one disorder. The future should see the inclusion of studies employing other therapies.

Conclusion

The success of psychotherapy (which includes CBT as well as the other, humanistic therapies) rests on the type of therapy applied. There are some negative outcomes: an estimated 9–13 per cent of clients worsen after psychotherapy (Beutler and Clarkin, 1990) and it is ineffective for dealing with other physical illnesses, such as cancer (Coyne *et al.*, 2007, 2009). The application of psychotherapy to schizophrenia has been associated with a deterioration in the client's condition (Lambert and Bergin, 1994). Also, some problems may be inappropriate for psychotherapy: criminal or antisocial behaviour, for example. For some other problems, however, such as depression, psychotherapy may be quite effective when combined with other treatments.

Biological treatments

The most common biological treatment for mental illness is pharmacological. Psychopharmacological interventions are aimed at treating psychological problems by using chemical agents.

There are four major classes of drugs used to treat mental disorders: antipsychotic drugs, antidepressant drugs, antimanic drugs and anti-anxiety drugs. We discuss the application and effectiveness of these drugs in the sections describing mental disorders.

Some people with depression do not respond to antidepressant drugs, but a substantial percentage of these people improve after a few sessions of **electroconvulsive therapy** (ECT) in which electrodes are applied to a person's head and a brief surge of electrical current is passed through them. Because antidepressant medications are generally slow-acting, taking ten days to two weeks for their therapeutic effects to begin, severe cases of depression are often treated with a brief course of ECT to reduce the symptoms immediately. These people are then maintained on an antidepressant drug.

There are several problems with ECT treatments. An excessive number of ECT treatments has been associated with permanent memory loss (Squire *et al.*, 1981) with little enduring effect on cognitive performance (Calev *et al.*, 1995; Barnes *et al.*, 1997). Nowadays, ECT is usually administered only to the right hemisphere, in order to minimise damage to people's verbal memories, and is used only when the patient's symptoms justify it. Because ECT undoubtedly achieves its effects through the

biochemical consequences of the seizure, pharmacologists may discover new drugs that can produce rapid therapeutic effects without ECT's deleterious ones. Once this breakthrough occurs, ECT can be abandoned.

One other biological treatment for mental disorders is even more controversial than electroconvulsive therapy: psychosurgery or neurosurgery (Fenton, 1998). **Psychosurgery** involves the treatment of a mental disorder, in the absence of obvious organic damage, through brain surgery. In contrast, brain surgery to remove a tumour or diseased neural tissue or to repair a damaged blood vessel is not psychosurgery, and there is no controversy about these procedures.

Psychosurgery has its origins in the late 1930s when, at a conference at University College London, the results of frontal lobectomies on two chimpanzees, Becky and Lucy, were presented. The surgery resulted in an increase in calmness and passivity in the chimps. Egas Moniz, a 59-year-old Portuguese professor of neurology, one of the audience at the meeting, suggested that this technique might also be appropriate for humans. Late in 1935, the first frontal lobotomy operations were performed. While treating some symptoms, such as those in chronic schizophrenia, the prefrontal lobotomies were found to have serious side effects, such as apathy and severe blunting of emotions, intellectual impairments and deficits in judgement and planning ability. Nevertheless, the procedure was used for a variety of conditions, most of which were not improved by the surgery. Approximately 40,000 prefrontal lobotomies were performed in the US alone, most of them between 1935 and 1955. A simple procedure,

A few surgeons have continued to refine the technique of psychosurgery and now perform a procedure called a **cingulotomy**, which involves cutting the cingulum bundle, a small band of nerve fibres that connects the prefrontal cortex (PFC) with parts of the limbic system (Ballantine *et al.*, 1987). Cingulotomies have been shown to be effective in helping some people who suffer from severe compulsions (Tippin and Henn, 1982). In a recent study, Baer *et al.* (1995) conducted a long-term follow-up study of 18 people who underwent cingulotomy for severe obsessive-compulsive disorder. For each of these people, other forms of therapy – drug therapy and behavioural therapy – had been unsuccessful in treating their symptoms. However, after their surgeries, the people in Baer's study showed marked improvements in their functioning, decreased symptoms of depression and anxiety, and few negative side effects.

Drug therapy is the preferred biological treatment for mental disorders although it represents only a possible treatment, not a cure. Usually, the drugs are effective only to the extent that the people for whom they are prescribed actually use them. In some cases, people forget to take their drugs, only to have the disordered symptoms return. In other cases, people take their drugs, get better, and stop taking the drugs because they feel that they are no longer 'sick'. In this case, too, the symptoms soon return. For some people, this cycle repeats itself endlessly. Table 18.3 lists some of the drugs commonly used to treat mental disorders.

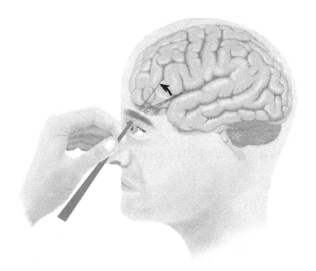

Figure 18.3 'Ice pick' prefrontal lobotomy. The sharp metal rod (a leucotome) is inserted under the eyelid and just above the eye so that it pierces the skull and enters the base of the frontal lobe.

Source: Adapted with permission from Freeman, W., *Proceedings of the Royal Society of Medicine*, 1949, 42 (suppl.), 8–12. Reprinted by permission of The Royal Society of Medicine.

called 'ice pick' prefrontal lobotomy by its critics, was even performed on an out-patient basis, as seen in Figure 18.3. The development of antipsychotic drugs and the increasing attention paid to the serious side effects of prefrontal lobotomy led to a sharp decline in the use of this procedure during the 1950s. Today it is no longer performed.

Table 18.3 Drugs commonly used to treat mental disorders

Therapeutic function	Class of drugs	Generic name	Trade name
Antipsychotic	Soporific	Chlorpromazine	Thorazine
	Non-soporific	Acetophenazine	Tindal
	Phenothiazines	Thioridazine	Mellaril
		Fluphenazine	Permitil
		Trifluoperazine	Stelazine
		Perphenazine	Trilafon
	Butyrophenones	Haloperidol	Haldol
Antidepressant	Tricyclics	Imipramine	Tofranil
	Monoamine oxidase inhibitors	Amitryptiline	Elavil
		Phenelzine	Nardil
	Serotonin reuptake inhibitors	Fluoxetine	Prozac
			Miltown
Anti-anxiety	Propanediols	Meprobamate	
	Benzodiazepines	Chlordiazepoxide	Librium
		Diazepam	Valium
Antimanic	Lithium salts	Lithium carbonate	Eskalith

Mental disorders

The previous section described each of the major approaches to treating mental disorder. This section reviews some of the most important mental disorders. Each major class of disorder is described according to its symptoms, its possible causes and the current treatment approach.

Anxiety, somatoform and dissociative mental disorders

Anxiety, somatoform and dissociative mental disorders are often referred to as neuroses. Most neuroses are strategies of perception and behaviour that have become distorted or exaggerated. They are characterised by pathological increases in anxiety or by defence mechanisms applied too rigidly, resulting in mental processes that are maladaptive. Neurotic people are anxious, fearful, depressed and generally unhappy. However, unlike people who are afflicted with psychoses, they do not suffer from delusions or severely disordered thought processes. Furthermore, they almost universally realise that they have a problem. Most neurotics are only too aware that their strategies for coping with the world are not working. Neurotic behaviour is usually characterised by avoidance rather than confrontation of problems.

Anxiety disorders

Several important types of mental disorders are classified as anxiety disorders, which have fear and anxiety as their most prominent symptoms. **Anxiety** is a sense of apprehension or doom that is accompanied by certain physiological reactions, such as accelerated heart rate, sweaty palms and tightness in the stomach. Anxiety disorders are the most common psychological disorders and the reported rate of anxiety disorder is twice as high in European women than in men (Weiller *et al.*, 1998). Five of the most important anxiety disorders are generalised anxiety disorder, panic disorder, phobic disorder, obsessive-compulsive disorder and post-traumatic stress disorder.

The most common of these are agoraphobia, panic disorder and generalised anxiety disorder, all of which are described next, together with possible aetiology. There seems to be national variation in the prevalence of these disorders. Generalised anxiety disorder is more frequent in cities such as Paris and Berlin, for example, whereas it is low in Manchester and Groningen (the Netherlands). Panic disorder appears to be more common in Manchester and agoraphobia in Groningen (Weiller *et al.*, 1998).

Generalised anxiety disorder (GAD)

Description

The principal characteristic of **generalised anxiety disorder (GAD)** is excessive worry about all matters relating to the individual's life: health, money, work, relationships and so on. According to DSM-IV TR, these worries must be present on most days and will have occurred over a period of at least six months. The anxious individual finds it difficult to control the worry and shows at least three symptoms out of the following: restlessness, being easily fatigued, difficulty concentrating, irritability, muscle tension and sleep disturbance. Around 12 per cent of anxiety disorders are GAD (American Psychiatric Association, 2001) and most individuals with GAD also experience depression which sometimes makes a clear-cut diagnosis of GAD difficult.

Anxious individuals spend considerably longer making decisions. For example, Tallis *et al.* (1991) asked a group of controls and clinically anxious individuals to respond if a target was present on a computer monitor. Although there was no difference between controls and anxious individuals when the target was present, the anxious group took significantly longer to make a decision when the target was absent. This finding demonstrates that anxious individuals seem to attend more to tasks that require them to make absolutely correct decisions.

Aetiology

Several models exist which try to explain GAD; some of these also apply to other mental disorders but this section limits itself to those which account for GAD explicitly. One explanation (Borkovec, 1994) suggests that GAD arises from the individual's drive to set and anticipate a set of goals that are desirable. In this context, the anxiety arises when a history of a frustrated failure to achieve affects the perception of cues associated with these goals. Anxiety is reflected in the individual's need to anticipate all possible outcomes, for fear of failing or not achieving.

Eysenck (1992) has argued that although Berkovec's model [described in full in Berkovec (1994)] might explain pathological worry, it does not explain normal worry. Eysenck's model attempts to explain both by suggesting that worry or anxiety serves as an 'alarm function' which brings information concerning threat-related stimuli into awareness. In a sense, worry acts as a behaviour that will prepare an individual for future behaviour; it prompts the individual to anticipate future situations and their solutions.

Although older than Eysenck's, Gray's (1982) model suggests a similar mechanism but ties it to neurophysiology and certain brain systems. According to Gray, anxiety is evoked by signals of punishment, lack of reward, novel stimuli and innate fear stimuli. The individual detects such threats by means of a **behavioural inhibition system (BIS)** which also generates the anxiety. An important function of the BIS is that it helps the organism (Gray's theory applies to humans and other animals) to evaluate the threat content of a stimulus or event. The neurophysiology of the system is vast and complicated, involving neuroanatomical and neurochemical interaction between a number of brain regions. The BIS is thought to be represented by the septum and hippocampal formation.

Two-factor model

The two-factor model of anxiety suggests that individuals exhibit a vulnerability to anxiety owing to high trait anxiety and poor coping skills. There is a strong correlation between neuroticism and almost all major anxiety disorders (Andrews et al., 1989; Andrews, 1991). There also seems to be a loss of control exhibited by anxious individuals and anxiety is often preceded by stressful life events (Last et al., 1984), as Borkovec's model also suggests. Individuals with panic disorder and GAD have been found to rate their parents as less caring and as overprotective (Silove et al., 1991), indicating perhaps one cause of the perceived lack of control. High trait anxiety individuals have been found to be very similar to clinically anxious patients in terms of their perception that events are out of their control and in terms of parental overprotection (Bennett and Stirling, 1998).

Information-processing models

A number of studies have suggested that individuals high in trait anxiety and those suffering GAD exhibit **attentional biases**. That is, they are significantly biased towards responding to threat- or anxiety-related material. Anxious people are more vigilant when reacting to threatening faces than non-threatening faces, for example (Bradley et al., 1999). There are various ways of measuring this attentional bias and three of the most common measures are the dot probe, the emotional Stroop test and the interpretation of ambiguous sentences (Eysenck et al., 1991; Wells and Mathews, 1994).

The dot probe task involves the presentation of two words, one above the other, on a computer monitor.

Individuals are asked to read aloud the word at the top; this word is either neutral or is an anxiety- or threat-related word. After a short pause, the individual is presented with either another pair of words or a dot where the top or bottom word appeared. The individual has to press a key when such a dot appears. MacLeod and his colleagues (MacLeod et al., 1986; Matthews et al., 1990) have reported that latencies are shorter for anxiety-related words in GAD patients.

Similar biases are reported for the emotional Stroop task. In this, individuals have to read the colour in which a word is written. These words are either neutral or anxiety-related. GAD patients and individuals high in trait anxiety exhibit a bias towards the anxiety-related words, although the effects found with the Stroop are not as robust as those seen in the dot probe (Williams et al., 1996). Finally, anxious individuals have a tendency to interpret ambiguous sentences such as 'The two men watched as the chest was opened' as threatening, that is, they interpret the chest as being a person's torso rather than a large box (Eysenck et al., 1991).

Each model of GAD has some merit; that Eysenck's and Gray's models flag anxiety as indicating an alarm system that prepares an individual for future action suggests that anxiety results from excessive monitoring for and detection of threat. The findings from attentional bias studies support this view. Why the anxiety should be produced by this appraisal in some individuals and not in others, however, is still unclear. Borkovec's model is useful in that it specifies previous non-reward and frustration as a cause of being unable to achieve goals. Gray's model is useful because it ties this appraisal down to one neuropsychological system.

Treatment

The most common form of treatment for GAD is psychopharmacological, with drug administration sometimes coupled with CBT. The drugs used to combat anxiety disorder are called **anti-anxiety drugs** or **anxiolytics**.

The anxiolytics include barbiturates, benzodiazepines and antidepressants. Barbiturates are sedatives and include drugs such as Phenobarbital. However, because they are highly toxic and foster dependence, they are not widely used. Benzodiazepines are anticonvulsant and sedative drugs, and are the most widely prescribed. Two common benzodiazepines are chlordiazepoxide (Librium) and diazepam (Valium), both of which are low in toxicity.

A meta-analysis of 65 studies comparing CBT and/or pharmacological interventions with a control condition for the treatment of GAD, found that CBT was a significantly better treatment than was no treatment (Mitte, 2005). When studies directly compare CBT with drug intervention, there was no significant difference in efficacy.

Panic disorder

Description

Panic has been described as a fear of fear (Foa *et al.*, 1984). Individuals who experience panic are threatened by the presence or the potential presence of fear-related physical states. People with **panic disorder** suffer from episodic attacks of acute anxiety – periods of acute and unremitting terror that grip them for lengths of time lasting from a few seconds to a few hours. The lifetime prevalence rate for panic disorder is estimated to be about 4 per cent (Katerndahl and Realini, 1993). Panic attacks (without agoraphobia, which is the anxiety disorder we discuss next) are equally likely to appear in men and women (Clarke, 1992). The disorder usually has its onset in young adulthood; it rarely begins after age 35 (Woodruff *et al.*, 1972).

Panic attacks include many physical symptoms, such as shortness of breath, sweating, racing heartbeat (trachycardia), physical tension, cognitive disorganisation, dizziness and fear of loss of support (jelly legs). The individual feels as if he or she is about to collapse and is on the point of death. Such catastrophic thoughts and feelings only exacerbate the physical symptoms and so the individual becomes involved in a self-fulfilling prophecy.

Between panic attacks, people with panic disorder tend to suffer from **anticipatory anxiety** – a fear of having a panic attack (Ottaviani and Beck, 1987). Because attacks can occur without apparent cause, these people anxiously worry about when the next one might strike them. Sometimes, a panic attack that occurs in a particular situation can cause the person to fear that situation. The anxiety we all feel from time to time is significantly different from the intense fear and terror experienced by a person gripped by a panic attack, as the case study below illustrates.

Aetiology

Genetic models

There seems to be a hereditary component to panic disorders: the concordance rate for the disorder is higher between identical twins than between fraternal twins (Torgerson, 1983). Almost 30 per cent of the first-degree relatives (parents, children and siblings) of a person with panic disorder also have panic disorder (Crowe *et al.*, 1983). According to Crowe *et al.*, the pattern of panic disorder within a family tree suggests that the disorder is caused by a single, dominant gene.

Panic attacks can be triggered in people with histories of panic disorder by giving them injections of lactic acid (a by-product of muscular activity) or by having them breathe air containing an elevated amount of carbon dioxide (Woods *et al.*, 1988; Cowley and Arana, 1990).

People with family histories of panic attack are more likely to react to sodium lactate, even if they have never had a panic attack previously (Balon *et al.*, 1989). Some researchers believe that what is inherited is a tendency to react with alarm to bodily sensations that would not disturb most other people.

Clark's model

The most comprehensive (and cognitive) model of panic disorder is that proposed by David Clark. Clark (1986, 1988) argues that panic attacks are produced by the **catastrophic misinterpretation** of bodily events. Slight changes in bodily sensation are interpreted as symptomatic of a physical threat which makes the individual anxious. The more anxious the individual becomes, the more intense the bodily sensations become (the self-fulfilling prophecy referred to above). According to Clark's model, two processes contribute to the maintenance of this misinterpretation. The first is hypervigilance: the individual repeatedly checks for changes in bodily sensations; the second is avoidance strategies: the individual avoids those behaviours they feel will exacerbate the bodily sensations. For example, a person who is afraid that he is about to have a heart attack will avoid exercise (although this prevents the individual from discovering that exercise will not cause a heart attack).

Seligman (1988), however, has argued that the catastrophic misinterpretation theory is questionable on the grounds that the realisation that death will not accompany panic attacks will eventually dawn on these patients. Seligman suggests an alternative suggestion based on **evolutionary preparedness**, the notion that we are evolutionarily predisposed to respond in a specific way to some stimuli because it is to our advantage to do so (Seligman, 1971). Panic, in this context, is the individual's response to biologically prepared bodily sensations. However, as Power and Dalgleish (1997) argue, the failure to realise that death does not follow bodily sensations arises because individuals avoid situations and stimuli that would induce such bodily sensations in the first place. Seligman's formulation may not, therefore, be necessary (for the reason he suggests).

Interestingly, some patients maintain that they do not misinterpret their bodily sensations catastrophically and some are more difficult to convince that these sensations will not lead to death (McNally, 1990). These findings point to a degree of variation in panic disorder patients. The anxiety sensitivity hypothesis (Reiss and McNally, 1985), for example, suggests that some individuals are more anxiety-sensitive than others. The degree of sensitivity depends on pre-existing beliefs about the harmfulness of bodily sensations. These pre-existing beliefs predispose the individual to interpret bodily events negatively and erroneously. This leads to panic.

Treatment

Treatment for panic disorder can be both cognitive behavioural or pharmacological. CBT, for example, is effective at reducing panic attacks. Such therapy would involve breathing and relaxation techniques, **cognitive restructuring** (altering misconceptions about the consequences of bodily sensations) and eliciting bodily sensations in the individual to demonstrate the non-harmful nature of such changes (Craske *et al.*, 1997). Antidepressants and anxiolytics are sometimes used to treat panic attacks with some success. Some individuals react badly to the drugs, however, and while they treat the anxiety generated during panic, they do not address the core problem of catastrophic misinterpretation.

Phobic disorders

Phobias – named after the Greek god Phobos, who frightened his enemies – are irrational fears of specific objects or situations. Because phobias can be highly specific, clinicians have coined a variety of inventive names, some of which are summarised in Table 18.4.

Most individuals have one or more irrational fears of specific objects or situations, and it is difficult to draw a line between these fears and phobic disorders. If someone is afraid of spiders but manages to lead a normal life by avoiding them, it would seem inappropriate to say

that the person has a mental disorder. Similarly, many otherwise normal people are afraid of speaking in public. The term 'phobic disorder' should be reserved for people whose fear makes their life difficult. The DSM-IV TR recognises three types of phobic disorder: agoraphobia, social phobia and simple phobia.

Agoraphobia

Agoraphobia (*agora* means 'marketplace' in Ancient Greek) is a fear of open spaces and is the most serious and common of the phobic disorders. It occurs in between 50 and 80 per cent of phobic disorders (Matthews *et al.*, 1981). It is reported three times as often in women as in men. Onset is sudden and individuals are usually in their early twenties (Clarke, 1992). The term was coined by Westphal in 1871 to describe four (male) cases who feared open spaces.

Most cases of agoraphobia are considered to be caused by panic attacks and are classified with them. Agoraphobia associated with panic attacks is defined as a fear of 'being in places or situations from which escape might be difficult (or embarrassing) or in which help might not be available in the event of a panic attack . . . As a result of this fear, the person either restricts travel or needs a companion when away from home' (American Psychiatric Association, 2001). Agoraphobia can be severely disabling. Some people with this disorder have stayed inside their house for years, afraid to venture outside. Supermarkets and queuing are especially anxiety-provoking for agoraphobics. Features of supermarket layout such as stairways and diminished access, for example, are regarded as anxiety-provoking by agoraphobic individuals (Jones *et al.*, 1996).

Social phobia

Social phobia is an exaggerated 'fear of one or more situations . . . in which the person is exposed to possible scrutiny by others and fears that he or she may do something or act in a way that will be humiliating or embarrassing' (American Psychiatric Association, 2001). Most people with social phobia are only mildly impaired, but the situations in which they can operate may be severely curtailed. Social phobics, like patients with GAD, seem to bias their attention towards threat-related stimuli (Rapee and Heimberg, 1997).

At the core of the disorder seems to be conflict regarding the internal representation of their appearance and external indicators which evaluate them negatively. Rapee and Heimberg, therefore, proposed that socially phobic individuals allocate excessive attentional resources towards mental representations of how they are perceived by their audience. In a study in which high and

Table 18.4 Name and description of some common phobias

Name	Object or situation feared
Acrophobia	Heights
Agoraphobia	Open spaces
Ailurophobia	Cats
Algophobia	Pain
Astraphobia	Storms, thunder, lightning
Belonophobia	Needles
Claustrophobia	Enclosed spaces
Haematophobia	Blood
Monophobia	Being alone
Mysophobia	Contamination or germs
Nyctophobia	Darkness
Ochlophobia	Crowds
Pathophobia	Disease
Pyrophobia	Fire
Siderophobia	Railways
Syphilophobia	Syphilis
Taphophobia	Being buried alive
Triskaidekaphobia	Thirteen
Zoophobia	Animals, or a specific animal

low anxious social phobic individuals gave a five-minute speech in front of an audience that was behaving positively (smiling) or negatively (frowning), Veljaca and Rapee (1998) found that highly anxious individuals were better at detecting negative audience behaviours whereas the low anxiety individuals were better at detecting the positive behaviours. Social phobics also interpret ambiguous social events more negatively, and interpret mildly negative, unambiguous events more catastrophically than do people suffering from anxiety, or a group of healthy controls (Stopa and Clark, 2000).

Specific phobia

Specific phobia includes all other phobias, such as fear of snakes, darkness or heights. These phobias are often caused by a specific traumatic experience and are the easiest of all types of phobia to treat. The Epidemiological Catchment Area (ECA) Study found that insects, mice, snakes and bats were the more frequently cited feared /disgust-provoking stimuli (Robins and Regier, 1994). Animals are a common phobia. Davey (1992), for example, reported that one-third of women and one-quarter of men reported having a spider phobia.

The lifetime prevalence rate for simple phobia is estimated to be about 14 per cent for women and about 8 per cent for men (Robins and Regier, 1991), but approximately one-third of the population sometimes exhibit phobic symptoms (Goodwin and Guze, 1984).

Aetiology

Animal phobias are sometimes surprising because in Europe, for example, there are no indigenous lethally poisonous spiders, although spider phobias are common. One explanation for this anomaly is that we fear animals that have potentially lethal consequences; we are, therefore, predisposed to fear them. This is the preparedness hypothesis (Seligman, 1971) which we encountered in the section on panic disorder. Evidence for this hypothesis comes in the form of the deliberate conditioning of fear

of spiders. These conditioning experiences are the most difficult to extinguish – more difficult than non-threatening stimuli (Ohman *et al.*, 1985; McNally, 1987).

However, Seligman's theory has its problems. For example, if we are adaptively predisposed to fear the stimuli producing simple phobias, what adaptive purpose does a fear of snails, moths and slugs serve? As McNally (1995) points out, we can ascribe adaptive significance to a fear of any object if we are creative enough. One theory suggests that phobias develop from a pairing of a phobic object with an aversive stimulus so that phobic stimuli become phobic by association. However, only 40–50 per cent of animal phobias appear to be accounted for in this way. Davey (1992) also reported that only eight out of 118 spider phobics recall having a traumatic experience with spiders.

Matchett and Davey (1991) suggest an alternative explanation: that some stimuli become the object of phobia because of our inherent fear of contamination or disease. Animals (such as spiders, slugs, cockroaches) become feared because they seem disgusting and we would reject them as food on the basis of this disgust (although some individuals would be immune to such disgust responses; snails are considered a delicacy in certain parts of Europe). In fact, sensitivity to disgust may be an important determinant of the level of fear (Webb and Davey, 1993). To investigate whether some animal phobias were disgust- or fear-related, Davey *et al.* (1998) conducted a cross-cultural study of phobia in seven countries. An analysis of the data suggested that phobic stimuli could be divided into one of three categories: fear-irrelevant (for example, chicken, hamster, cow), fear-relevant (for example, lion, bear, alligator) and disgust-relevant (for example, cockroach, spider, maggot, worm). Disgust was consistent across cultures (although there were some cross-cultural differences with Indian respondents reporting lower levels of fear to the disgust stimuli and Japanese respondents showing higher levels of fear). This finding suggests that not all stimuli may be feared for the same reasons (perhaps the term 'simple phobia' is too simplistic, as Curtis *et al.* (1998) suggest).

Cutting edge: How specific is specific phobia?

Some innovative work in neuroimaging has found that as an object a person fears come closer to them, activity is increased in an area of the brain called the bed of the nucleus stria terminalis. When a person holds a feared object, such as a snake, however, and moves it closer to their own person, activation is found in the ventromedial prefrontal cortex

(VPC) (Nili *et al.*, 2010; Somerville *et al.*, 2010). The studies suggest that our brain has a network of regions and structures that allows us to appraise threat-related objects, determine our reaction to them and to overcome our fear of them.

Mobbs *et al.*, (2010) have now shown, using fMRI, that when a tarantula is placed closer to a person's foot (seen

▶

Cutting edge: *Continued*

via a live video feed), a series of brain regions become activated as feelings of threat increase. These include the periaqueductal gray, the amygdala and the stria terminalis. The amygdala and terminalis activation increased as the spider moved closer to the participant. As the spider moved away, activation became more pronounced in the orbitofrontal cortex (OFC). See Figure 18.4.

But are such regions activated to every phobia? Or do some phobias have features not shared by others? Animal phobias, for example, are known to activate the amygdala, insula and anterior cingulate cortex (ACC) (Shin and Liberzon, 2010). DSM-IV lists five distinct types: blood-injection-injury, animal, situational, natural environment and 'other', some of which have different behavioural and physiological responses to others.

Lueken *et al.* (2011) used fMRI and galvanic skin response (GSR) to compare two groups of phobics: those with ophiadanophobia (snake; animal) and those with dental phobia (blood-injection-injury) as participants watched a fear-inducing video of their feared stimulus/situation.

The fear of snakes was associated with increased activation in the amygdala, insula, thalamus and in GSR. The dental phobics, however, showed activation in the PFC and OFC and less GSR. These data suggests that these two phobias differ, with different underlying neural characteristics.

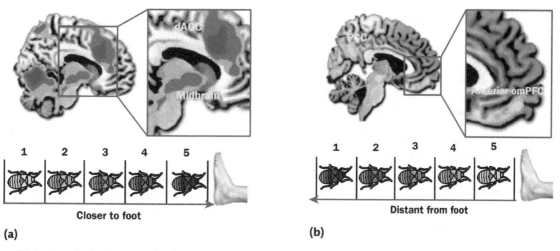

Figure 18.4 How the brain responds when it sees an approaching object it fears. ACC = anterior cingulate cortex, dACC = dorsal anterior cingulate cortex, PCC = posterior cingulate cortex, omPFC = orbitomedial prefrontal cortex.

Treatment

Phobias are sometimes treated by systematic desensitisation (described in the general section on treatment) or modelling. Bandura (1971), for example, has described a modelling session with people who had a phobic fear of snakes. The therapist himself performed the fearless behaviour at each step and gradually led participants into touching, stroking and then holding the snake's body with gloved and bare hands while the experimenter held the snake securely by head and tail. If a participant was unable to touch the snake following ample demonstration, they were asked to place their hand on the experimenter's and to move their own hand down gradually until it touched the snake's body. After participants no longer felt any apprehension about touching the snake under these secure conditions, anxieties about contact with the snake's head area and entwining tail were extinguished. The therapist again performed the tasks fearlessly, and then he and the participant performed the responses jointly. As participants became less fearful, the experimenter gradually reduced his participation and control over the snake, until eventually participants were able to hold the snake in their lap without assistance, to let the snake loose in the room and retrieve it, and to let it crawl freely over their body. Progress through the graded approach tasks was paced according to the participants' apprehensiveness. When they reported being able to perform one activity with little or no fear, they were eased into a more difficult interaction. This treatment eliminated fear of snakes in 92 per cent of those who participated.

Modelling is successful for several reasons. Participants learn to make new responses by imitating those of the therapist and their behaviour in doing so is reinforced. When they observe a confident person approaching and touching a feared object without showing any signs of emotional distress, they probably experience a vicarious extinction of their own emotional responses. In fact, Bandura (1971, p. 684) reports that 'having successfully overcome a phobia that had plagued them for most of their lives, subjects reported increased confidence that they could cope effectively with other fear-provoking events', including encounters with other people.

CBT has also been applied to agoraphobia (Ost *et al.*, 1993). In an experiment in which the effect of exposure (graded exposure to the phobic stimuli) was compared with exposure and CBT (combating negative thoughts and dysfunctional attitudes), Burke *et al.* (1997) found no difference in the effectiveness of the two therapies at six months following the therapy: both were equally effective. Similar combinations have also been found to be effective for social phobia (Scholing and Emmelkamp, 1996).

A recently developed treatment has taken the idea of exposure but added a technological element: virtual reality (VR) technology. This has many practical benefits. The fear of flying, for example, would be more efficiently treated using simulated or virtual stimuli rather than taking sufferers to airports. This approach is evaluated in the Psychology in Action section.

Psychology in action: Virtual planes can relieve real fear of flying

The fear may be more common than people imagine. According to one German study, 15 per cent of respondents reported having a fear of flying and around 60 per cent of those try to cope with this fear by drinking alcohol or taking tranquillisers (Wilhelm and Roth, 1997).

In many cases, treatment may take the form of CBT which exposes the patient to the fear-eliciting stressor with the aim of attenuating the fear that such stressors cause. For example, a patient may be exposed to real aeroplanes or may be walked around a stationary plane. Recently, however, psychologists have harnessed new technology to help people combat their fear of flying: virtual reality or VR (Klein, 1998). VR technology allows researchers to simulate events, locations or stimuli effectively using computer software. Consequently, it is a very convenient and inexpensive approach to treatment.

Rothbaum *et al.* (2000) randomly assigned 49 patients who expressed a fear of flying to one of three conditions: VR training, standard exposure therapy or no therapy where patients were on a waiting list for treatment.

The VR training involved exposing the participant to a virtual aircraft (sitting in it while it took off and landed); standard exposure involved direct exposure to an airport and a stationary plane. Both experimental conditions were preceded by four sessions of anxiety management. Patients received treatment over eight weeks and a post-treatment flight was set up after this period to examine the efficacy of the VR treatment, as measured by willingness to fly and self-reported anxiety about the first flight.

Both VR and standard exposure treatments were better than the control condition in reducing fear of flying. The beneficial effects of exposure were still seen at a six-month follow-up. Ninety-three per cent of VR patients and 93 per cent of standard exposure patients had flown after treatment. The results show that VR may be an inexpensive and more convenient way of reducing the fear of flying than is actual exposure to real aeroplanes. If given the choice, patients indicated that they would opt for the VR treatment rather than real exposure.

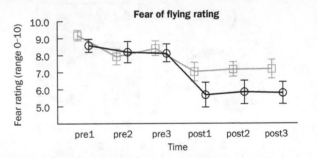

Figure 18.5 Fear of flying scores for people in the VR exposure group (black line) and the relaxation group (orange line).

Source: Muhlberger, A., Herrmann, M.J., Wiedemann, G., Ellgring, H. and Pauli, P., Repeated exposure of flight phobics to flights in virtual reality. *Behaviour Research and Therapy*, 2001, 39, 1033–50. Copyright 2000, with permission from Elsevier.

Exposure to VR also appears to be more effective at reducing flight anxiety than is relaxation therapy, a common psychological intervention that some flyers adopt. Muhlberger *et al.* (2001) found that while exposure to VR flights increased feelings of fear, these feelings gradually attenuated and to a greater extent than they did in people undergoing relaxation training. Both approaches reduced flight anxiety, but VR was better, as Figure 18.5 shows.

Virtual reality technology of this kind has now been successfully used to treat arachnophobia (Carlin *et al.*, 1997) and claustrophobia (Botella *et al.*, 1998). As with all treatments, its success is measured by its long-term effects. A recent 12–month follow-up study suggests that VR flight exposure has lasting effects on anxiety relief. Rothbaum's team followed up 24 patients who were either exposed to actual planes and an airport or to VR flying. As you saw in the section at the beginning, both interventions were successful at the first testing point. The follow-up study showed that the initial improvements were maintained. The results suggest that a very short-term treatment that imposes fewer practical demands than real exposure to planes and airports can have sustainable benefits.

Post-traumatic stress disorder (PTSD)

Description

Post-traumatic stress disorder (PTSD) is a relatively new anxiety disorder (it made its first appearance in DSM-III in 1980) and refers to anxiety that follows a traumatic event. This event poses a threat to the individual's life or the lives of others. Symptoms of the disorder include the re-experiencing of feelings related to the event (such as intrusive memories, thoughts and images related to the event), avoidant behaviour (such as denial and emotional numbing) and arousal (such as hypervigilance for trauma-related information). A recent analysis suggests that the symptoms can be grouped into four types: intrusions, avoidance, dysphoria and hyperarousal (Yufik and Simmons, 2010). Sadness, guilt and anger are also associated with the disorder (Shore *et al.*, 1989). These latter symptoms are important because PTSD seldom appears alone but with other disorders or additional diagnoses (McFarlane, 1992; Bleich *et al.*, 1997). PTSD is a controversial inclusion in DSM-IV TR because its validity has been challenged. Some researchers point to the ease with which PTSD symptoms can be faked (Burges and McMillan, 2001).

The prevalence rate is around 25–30 per cent in the general population, and rape is associated with the greatest prevalence (Green, 1994). Other events which can produce PTSD are road traffic accidents (Stallard *et al.*, 1998; Murray *et al.*, 2002), bank robberies (Kamphuis and Emmelkamp, 1998), war (Fontana and Rosenheck, 1993) and natural or human-made disasters (Freedy *et al.*, 1994). Onset of the disorder may be delayed by many years (Blank, 1993). As with GAD and panic disorder, there is a greater Stroop interference for words related to the trauma (Thrasher *et al.*, 1994).

The emergency services, especially its members who respond to disasters, may be more prone to developing the disorder because of the type of work they engage in. In the UK, ambulance drivers answer more calls than do the police and fire service combined. It might be expected, therefore, that the incidence of PTSD is high (between 10 and 20 per cent). Clohessy and Ehlers (1999) found that 21 per cent of the 56 ambulance drivers in the UK they studied met DSM-IV TR criteria for PTSD. Predictors of the severity of the post-traumatic stress were poor coping strategy, efforts to suppress intrusive thoughts and dwelling on previous distressing events.

In a study of 96 victims of physical or sexual assault, Dunmore *et al.* (1999) found that some factors were common to both onset and maintenance whereas others were specific to onset. Factors associated with both were appraising the event and the consequences of the event (dwelling on the assault and its aftermath) and adopting poor coping strategies (such as avoidance). Factors which were related to onset were feeling detached during the assault and being unable to perceive positive responses from others. The researchers suggest that these cognitive factors may contribute to PTSD in a number of ways. They may prevent recovery by encouraging poor coping strategy or by generating a sense of immediate threat.

Aetiology

Horowitz's (1979, 1986) model suggests that information about the trauma in PTSD is processed because of a mechanism called completion tendency. Completion tendency refers to the need for new information to be integrated into existing patterns of thought and memory. Power and Dalgleish (1997) describe how there is first a stunned reaction to the traumatic event and then a feeling of information overload as the individual realises the enormity of the trauma. Such information cannot be accommodated by existing mental schemata, and defence mechanisms, such as denial and numbing, provide a means of coping with this lack of accommodation. Completion tendency, however, insists on keeping the memory of the event alive (Horowitz calls this 'active memory') through flashbacks and nightmares. The anxiety results from the vacillation between these two processes: defence mechanisms and completion tendency. Although an honourable attempt at explaining PTSD, Power and Dalgleish (1997) query whether the model explains some features of the disorder. Why do only some individuals develop PTSD, for example? And why is PTSD delayed in some individuals?

An alternative model suggests that in PTSD the individual's beliefs about the world have been shattered. The individual is thought to view themselves as personally invulnerable, and that the world is meaningful and comprehensible (Janoff-Bulman, 1989, 1992). This structure is shattered after the traumatic event which gives rise to PTSD. The process by which this structure breakdown occurs, however, is not explained by the model.

Treatment

Various forms of treatment have been attempted with PTSD with varying success (Shalev *et al.*, 1996; Foa and Meadows, 1997). Debriefing appears to be ineffective (Deahl *et al.*, 1994) but drug treatment meets with mixed success (O'Brien and Nutt, 1998). Treatment based on exposure seems to be effective (Foa and Meadows, 1997).

Obsessive-compulsive disorder (OCD)

Description

Individuals with **obsessive-compulsive disorder** (OCD) suffer from obsessions – thoughts that will not leave them – and **compulsions** – behaviours that they cannot keep from performing. In one study, impaired control of mental activities, checking, urges involving loss of motor control and feeling contaminated were found to be the major classes of obsession and compulsion among a large sample of American college students (Sternberger and Burns, 1990). The lifetime prevalence rate is estimated to be about 2.5 per cent (Robins and Regier, 1991; Bebbington, 1998).

Unlike people with panic disorder, people with OCD have a defence against anxiety – their compulsive behaviour. Unfortunately, the need to perform this compulsive behaviour often becomes more and more demanding of their time until it interferes with their daily life. Obsessions are seen in many mental disorders, including schizophrenia. However, unlike persons with schizophrenia, people with OCD recognise that their thoughts and behaviours are senseless and wish that they would go away. The types of obsession and compulsion seen in these individuals are summarised in Table 18.5.

Consider the case of Sergei, a 17-year-old ex-student:

Only a year ago, Sergei seemed to be a normal adolescent with many talents and interests. Then, almost overnight he was transformed into a lonely outsider, excluded from social life by his psychological disabilities. Specifically, he was unable to stop washing. Haunted by the notion that he was dirty – in spite of the contrary evidence of the senses – he began to spend more and more of his time cleansing himself of imaginary dirt. At first his ritual ablutions were confined to weekends and evenings and he was able to stay in school while keeping them up, but soon they began to consume all his time, forcing him to drop out of school, a victim of his inability to feel clean enough. (*Source*: Rapoport, 1989, p. 63.)

There are two principal kinds of obsession: obsessive doubt or uncertainty, and obsessive fear of doing something prohibited (Salkovskis *et al.*, 1998). Uncertainties, both trivial and important, preoccupy some people with OCD almost completely. Others are plagued with the fear that they will do something terrible – swear aloud in church, urinate in someone's living room, kill themselves or a loved one, or jump off a bridge – although they seldom actually do anything antisocial. And even though they are often obsessed with thoughts of killing themselves, fewer than 1 per cent of them actually attempt suicide.

Most compulsions fall into one of four categories: counting, checking, cleaning and avoidance. For example, people might repeatedly check burners on the stove to see that they are off and windows and doors to be sure that they are locked. Some people wash their hands hundreds of times a day, even when they become covered with painful sores. Other people meticulously clean their homes or endlessly wash, dry and fold their clothes. Some become afraid to leave home because they fear contamination and refuse to touch other members of their families. If they do accidentally become 'contaminated', they usually have lengthy purification rituals.

Aetiology

Several possible causes have been suggested for OCD. Unlike simple anxiety states, this disorder can be understood in terms of defence mechanisms. Some cognitive investigators have suggested that obsessions serve as devices to occupy the mind and displace painful thoughts.

Cognitive researchers also point out that persons with OCD believe that they should be competent at all times, avoid any kind of criticism at all costs, and worry about being punished by others for behaviour that is less than perfect (Sarason and Sarason, 1993). Thus, one reason people who have OCD may engage in checking behaviour is to reduce the anxiety caused by fear of being perceived by others as incompetent or to avoid others' criticism that they have done something less than perfectly.

Family studies have found that OCD is associated with a neurological disorder called **Gilles de la Tourette's syndrome**, which appears during childhood (Janowic, 1993). Gilles de la Tourette's syndrome is characterised by muscular and vocal tics, including making facial grimaces, squatting, pacing, twirling, barking, sniffing, coughing, grunting or repeating specific words (especially vulgarities). It is not clear why some people with the faulty gene develop Gilles de la Tourette's syndrome early in childhood and others develop OCD later in life.

Treatment

There are usually two forms of treatment employed in OCD. The first is behavioural therapy in which the individual may be exposed to the object, situation or event that provokes the ritualistic behaviour (Emmelkamp, 1993). One example may be to deliberately dirty the hands of an individual who ritualistically washes their hands 20 or 30 times a day and not allow them to wash their hands (Rapoport, 1989). This type of therapy

Table 18.5 The number and percentage of obsessive and compulsive symptoms reported by 70 children and adolescents diagnosed with obsessive-compulsive disorder

	Reported symptom at initial interview	
Obsessions	**Number**	**%**
Concern with dirt, germs or environmental toxins	28	40
Something terrible happening (fire, death or illness of self or loved one)	17	24
Symmetry, order or exactness	12	17
Scrupulosity (religious obsessions)	9	13
Concern or disgust with bodily wastes or secretions (urine, stools, saliva)	6	8
Lucky or unlucky numbers	6	8
Forbidden, aggressive or perverse sexual thoughts, images or impulses	3	4
Fear might harm others or oneself	3	4
Concern with household items	2	3
Intrusive nonsense sounds, words or music	1	1
Compulsions	**Number**	**%**
Excessive or ritualised handwashing, showering, bathing, toothbrushing or grooming	60	85
Repeating rituals (going in or out of a door, up or down from a chair)	36	51
Checking (doors, locks, cooker, appliances, emergency brake on car, homework)	32	46
Rituals to remove contact with contaminants	16	23
Touching	14	20
Measures to prevent harm to self or others	11	16
Ordering or arranging	12	17
Counting	13	18
Hoarding or collecting rituals	8	11
Rituals of cleaning household or inanimate objects	4	6
Miscellaneous rituals (such as writing, moving, speaking)	18	26

Source: Rapoport, J.L., The biology of obsessions and compulsions, *Scientific American* (international edition), 1989 (March), p. 63. Copyright © 1989 by Scientific American, Inc. All rights reserved.

has met with some success in serious cases of OCD. However, behavioural treatment appears to be more successful at eliminating compulsive than obsessive behaviour (Emmelkamp, 1993). Drug treatment appears to eliminate both successfully. These drugs are two sero-tonin-specific reuptake inhibitors (described in more detail in the section on depression below) and act by increasing the amount of the neurotransmitter, serotonin, in the brain.

Somatoform and dissociative disorders

The primary symptoms of somatoform disorder are a bodily or physical (*soma* means 'body') problem for which there is no physiological basis. The two most important somatoform disorders are somatisation disorder and conversion disorder.

Somatisation disorder

Somatisation disorder occurs mostly among women and involves complaints of wide-ranging physical ailments for which there is no apparent biological basis (the complaints must include at least 13 symptoms from a list of 35, which fall into the following categories: gastrointestinal symptoms, pain symptoms, cardiopulmonary symptoms, pseudoneurological symptoms, sexual symptoms and female reproductive symptoms). This disorder used to be called hysteria. The older term derives from the Greek word *hysteria*, meaning 'uterus', because of the ancient belief that various emotional and physical ailments in women could be caused by the uterus wandering around inside the body, searching for a baby.

It is true that somatisation disorder is seen almost exclusively in women; however, modern use of the term 'hysteria' does not imply any gynaecological problems. Moreover, this disorder is rare even among women: Regier *et al.* (1988) found that the incidence of somatisation disorder in a sample of over 18,000 people was less than

1 per cent in women and non-existent in men. Somatisation disorder is often chronic, lasting for decades.

Conversion disorder

Conversion disorder is characterised by physical complaints that resemble neurological disorders but have no underlying organic pathological basis. The symptoms include blindness, deafness, loss of feeling, and paralysis. According to the DSM-IV TR, a conversion disorder must have some apparent psychological reason for the symptoms; the symptoms must occur in response to an environmental stimulus that produces a psychological conflict, or they must permit the person to avoid an unpleasant activity or to receive support and sympathy. Unlike somatisation disorder, conversion disorder can afflict both men and women.

Somatisation disorder consists of complaints of medical problems, but the examining physician is unable to see any signs that would indicate physical illness. In contrast, a patient with conversion disorder gives the appearance of having a neurological disorder such as blindness or paralysis. Psychophysiological disorders (also called psychosomatic disorders) are not the result of fictitious or imaginary symptoms; they are real, organic illnesses caused or made worse by psychological factors. For example, stress can cause gastric ulcers, asthma or other physical symptoms; ulcers caused by stress are real, not imaginary. Successful therapy would thus require reduction of the person's level of stress as well as surgical or medical treatment of the lesions in the stomach.

Dissociative disorders

In dissociative disorders, anxiety is reduced by a sudden disruption in consciousness, which in turn produces changes in one's sense of identity. Like conversion disorder, the term 'dissociative disorder' comes from Freud. According to psychoanalytical theory, a person develops a dissociative disorder when a massive repression fails to keep a strong sexual desire from consciousness. As a result, the person resorts to dissociating one part of their mind from the rest.

The most common dissociative disorder is psychogenic amnesia, in which a person 'forgets' all their past life, along with the conflicts that were present, and begins a new one. The term 'psychogenic' means 'produced by the mind'. Because amnesia can also be produced by physical means – such as epilepsy, drug or alcohol intoxication, and brain damage – clinicians must be careful to distinguish between amnesias of organic and psychogenic origin.

A psychogenic fugue is a special form of amnesia in which a person deliberately leaves home and starts a new life elsewhere (fugue means 'flight'). You read about this in the memory at the movies section in Chapter 8.

Dissociative identity disorder is a very rare, but very striking, dissociative disorder that is marked by the presence of two or more separate personalities within the individual, either of which may be dominant at any given time. Only about 100 cases of dissociative identity disorder have been documented, and some investigators believe that many, if not most of them, are simulations, not actual mental disorders.

An interesting example of dissociative identity disorder is the case of Billy Milligan as told in the book *The Minds of Billy Milligan* (Keyes, 1981). Milligan was accused of rape and kidnapping but was deemed not guilty by reason of insanity. His psychiatric examination showed him to have 24 different personalities. Two were women and one was a young girl. There was a Briton, an Australian and a Yugoslav. One woman, a lesbian, was a poet, while the Yugoslav was an expert on weapons and munitions, and the Briton and Australian were minor criminals. Dissociative identity disorder has received much attention; people find it fascinating to contemplate several different personalities, most of whom are unaware of each other, existing within the same individual. Bliss (1980) suggests that dissociative identity disorder is a form of self-hypnosis, established early in life and motivated by painful experiences. In fact, the overwhelming majority of people diagnosed as having multiple personality disorder report having been physically abused when they were a child (Kluft, 1984).

Personality disorders

The DSM-IV TR classifies abnormalities in behaviour that impair social or occupational functioning as personality disorders. There are several types of personality disorder which the DSM has grouped into three clusters. Cluster A, for example, refers to the 'eccentric cluster' of schizotypal and paranoid personality disorder; Cluster B (the dramatic cluster) includes the narcissistic and antisocial personality disorders; and Cluster C (the anxious cluster) includes avoidant and dependent personality disorders (Van Velzen and Emmelkamp, 1996). Another general cluster accounts for other personality disorders not covered by these clusters. Because there are so many personality disorders, this chapter focuses on just one in depth: antisocial personality disorder. Table 18.6 provides a description of the several other personality disorders.

Table 18.6 Descriptions of various personality disorders

Personality disorder	Description
Paranoid	Suspiciousness and extreme mistrust of others; enhanced perception of being under attack by others
Schizoid	Difficulty in social functioning - poor ability and little desire to become attached to others
Schizotypal	Unusual thought patterns and perceptions; poor communication and social skills
Histrionic	Attention-seeking; preoccupation with personal attractiveness; prone to anger when attempts at attracting attention fail
Narcissistic	Self-promoting; lack of empathy for others; attention-seeking; grandiosity
Borderline	Lack of impulse control; drastic mood swings; inappropriate anger; becomes bored easily and for prolonged periods; suicidal
Avoidant	Oversensitivity to rejection; little confidence in initiating or maintaining social relationships
Dependent	Uncomfortable being alone or in terminating relationships; places others' needs above one's own in order to preserve the relationship; indecisive
Obsessive-compulsive	Preoccupation with rules and order; tendency towards perfectionism; difficulty relaxing or enjoying life
Passive-aggressive	Negative attitudes; negativity is expressed through passive means; complaining, expressing envy and resentment towards others who are more fortunate
Depressive	Pervasive depressive cognitions and self-criticism; persistent unhappiness; feelings of guilt and inadequacy

Source: Adapted from Carson, R.C., *et al.*, *Abnormal Psychology and Modern Life*, 10th edn. Published by Allyn & Bacon, Boston, MA. Copyright © 1996 by Pearson Education. By permission of the publisher.

Antisocial personality disorder and psychopathy

Antisocial personality disorder refers to a failure to conform to standards of decency, repeated lying and stealing, a failure to sustain long-lasting and loving relationships, low tolerance of boredom and a complete lack of guilt. The first edition of the DSM used the term 'sociopathic personality disturbance', which was subsequently replaced by the present term, 'antisocial personality disorder'. Most clinicians still refer to such people as psychopaths or sociopaths but this is probably incorrect. There is good evidence, for example, that antisocial personality disorder/sociopathy and psychopathy are different disorders; the former is characterised by antisocial behaviour, usually criminal, whereas the latter is characterised by these antisocial activities plus other, more emotive factors such as lack of empathy for others, remorselessness and manipulativeness.

Description

Psychopaths commit more offences than the average criminal (Hare, 1981; Kosson *et al.*, 1990) and are significantly more violent. Hare and McPherson (1984) report that psychopaths are convicted of three-and-a-half times more violent crime than are non-psychopathic criminals. Because of data such as these, psychologists have made attempts to identify the chronic psychopathic offender early on in life, although these studies have met with mixed success (Lynam, 1996; Raine *et al.*, 1996).

The diagnostic criteria of the DSM-IV TR include evidence of at least three types of antisocial behaviour before age 15 and at least four after age 18. The adult forms of antisocial behaviour include inability to sustain consistent work behaviour; lack of ability to function as a responsible parent; repeated criminal activity, such as theft, pimping or prostitution; inability to maintain enduring attachment to a sexual partner; irritability and aggressiveness, including fights or assault; failure to honour financial obligations; impulsiveness and failure to plan ahead; habitual lying or use of aliases; and consistently reckless or drunken driving. In addition to meeting at least four of these criteria, the person must have displayed a 'pattern of continuous antisocial behaviour in which the rights of others are violated, with no intervening period of at least five years without antisocial behaviour'. The lifetime prevalence rate for antisocial personality disorder, according to DSM-IV TR, is about 3 per cent for men and less than 1 per cent for women.

Cleckley (1976) has listed 16 characteristics of antisocial personality disorder, seen in Table 18.7. Cleckley's list of features provides a good picture of what most psychopaths are like. They are unconcerned for other people's feelings and suffer no remorse or guilt if their actions hurt others. Although they may be superficially charming, they do not form real friendships; thus, they often become swindlers or confidence artists. Both male and female psychopaths are sexually promiscuous from an early age, but these encounters do not seem to mean much to them. Female psychopaths tend to marry early, to be unfaithful to their husbands, and soon become separated or divorced.

Table 18.7 Cleckley's primary characteristics of antisocial personality disorder

1   Superficial charm and good 'intelligence'
2   Absence of delusions and other signs of irrational thinking
3   Absence of 'nervousness'
4   Unreliability
5   Untruthfulness and insincerity
6   Lack of remorse or shame
7   Inadequately motivated antisocial behaviour
8   Poor judgement and failure to learn by experience
9   Pathological egocentricity and incapacity for love
10   General poverty in major affective reactions
11   Specific loss of insight
12   Unresponsiveness in general interpersonal relations
13   Fantastic and uninviting behaviour
14   Suicide rarely carried out
15   Sex life impersonal, trivial and poorly integrated
16   Failure to follow any life plan

Source: Cleckley, H., *The Mask of Sanity*, pp. 337–8. St Louis, MO: C.V. Mosby, 1976. Reprinted with permission.

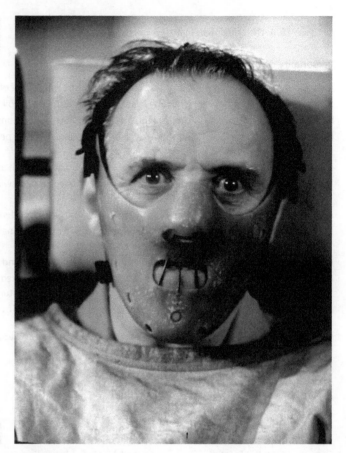

Not a typical psychopath.
Source: Everett Collection/Rex Features.

They tend to marry other psychopaths, so their husbands' behaviour is often similar to their own. Psychopaths habitually tell lies, even when there is no apparent reason for doing so and even when the lie is likely to be discovered. They steal things they do not need or even appear to want. When confronted with evidence of having lied or cheated, psychopaths do not act ashamed or embarrassed and usually shrug the incident off as a joke.

Psychopaths do not easily learn from experience; they tend to continue committing behaviours that get them into trouble. They also do not appear to be driven to perform their antisocial behaviours; instead, they usually give the impression that they are acting on whims. When someone commits a heinous crime such as a brutal murder, normal people expect that the criminal had a reason for doing so. However, criminal psychopaths are typically unable to supply a reason more compelling than 'I just felt like it'. They do not show much excitement or enthusiasm about what they are doing and do not appear to derive much pleasure from life. Although they are capable of understanding the difference between right and wrong, the consequences of immoral behaviour and the possession of this knowledge is unimportant to them (Cima *et al.*, 2010).

Aetiology

Cleckley (1976, p. 371) suggested that the psychopath's defect 'consists of an unawareness and a persistent lack of ability to become aware of what the most important experiences of life mean to others . . . The major emotional accompaniments are absent or so attenuated as

to count for little.' Some investigators have hypothesised that this lack of involvement is caused by an unresponsive autonomic nervous system (ANS). If a person feels no anticipatory fear of punishment, they are perhaps more likely to commit acts that normal people would be afraid to commit. Similarly, if a person feels little or no emotional response to other people and to their joys and sorrows, they are unlikely to establish close relationships with them.

Many experiments have found that psychopaths do show less reactivity in situations involving punishment. For example, Hare (1965) demonstrated that psychopaths show fewer signs of anticipatory fear. All participants in Hare's study watched the numerals 1 to 12 appear in sequential order in the window of a device used to present visual stimuli. They were told that they would receive a very painful shock when the numeral 8 appeared. Psychopathic subjects showed much less anticipatory responsiveness than did normal control subjects or non-psychopathic criminals.

According to Hare (1996, p. 46), 'In some respects, it is as if psychopaths lack a central organiser to plan and keep track of what they think and say'. The part of the brain that is more responsible than any other for monitoring, organising and integrating sensory input and behaviour, is the frontal cortex. People with damage to the frontal cortex have also been shown to exhibit irregularities in ANS functioning such as a lack of heart rate responsiveness and GSR in contexts that require an assessment of risk.

Over many years, Adrian Raine, James Blair and others in the UK and US have published controversial data linking frontal lobe dysfunction with psychopathic behaviour and antisocial personality disorder. In general, psychopaths tend to show less activity or less volume in this area, a region known to mediate some aspects of emotional and social behaviour (see Chapter 13). In what they describe as a study showing the 'first evidence for a structural brain deficit in antisocial personality disorder' (APD), Raine et al. (2000) compared the brain volume of 21 community volunteers having the DSM-IV TR ratified APD with control groups and found that prefrontal brain volume of the APD group was 11 per cent less than other groups. They also showed little autonomic response when undertaking the social stressor task – they had their behaviour videotaped as they talked about their faults.

A recent review of neuroimaging findings from psychopathy has highlighted the importance of four areas of the brain: the OFC, the amygdala, the anterior/posterior cingulate and nearby limbic structures (Anderson and Kiehl, 2012). A study of white matter volume in the brains of psychopaths and non-psychopaths has found a reduction in the connections between the frontal lobe and the thalamus. At the level of function, connections between the prefrontal lobe, the amygdala and the parietal lobe were reduced in the psychopaths (Motzkin et al., 2011). When psychopaths had to make decisions regarding moral violations, activity in the ventromedial PFC and temporal cortex was reduced compared to a control group (Herenski et al., 2010).

To date, neuroimaging studies have focused on 'unsuccessful' psychopaths, i.e. those who have been caught and jailed. It has been suggested that successful psychopaths – those who are not caught and jailed – are behaviourally very similar to their incarcerated counterparts but are physiologically different (Widom, 1978). Ishikawa et al. (2001) recruited people from temporary employment agencies and administered the Hare Psychopathy Checklist to determine the degree of psychopathy in the sample. The researchers found that, when compared with the control group, the successful psychopaths showed heightened heart rate activity and performed better than the unsuccessful psychopaths at a test of frontal lobe function. The authors suggest that this reactivity reflects the successful psychopath's greater awareness of changes in the social environment – they are better than unsuccessful psychopaths at assessing or making risky

decisions; unsuccessful psychopaths show little ANS reaction to risk and it may be this lack of feedback from the ANS that leads to their slipping up.

Treatment

There is no standard, effective treatment for APD or psychopathy and the treatments used have normally been designed for other purposes such as anger management or reducing deviant sexual behaviour (Oltmans and Emery, 1998). Whereas evidence suggests that there is some temporary effect on the behaviour, the effect does not generalise to other settings in the long term. One predictor of success, when it does happen, is a person's adherence to a treatment programme: the more successful complete the programme (Reid and Gacono, 2000).

Schizophrenic disorders

Schizophrenia, the most common psychosis, includes several types, each with a distinctive set of symptoms. There is some controversy over whether schizophrenia is a unitary disorder with various sub-types or whether each sub-type constitutes a distinct disorder. Because the prognosis differs for the various sub-types of schizophrenia, each would appear to differ at least in severity. An individual may, at different times, meet the criteria for different sub-types, although the diagnosis of schizophrenia seems valid and reliable (Mason et al., 1997).

Description

Schizophrenia refers to a group of psychological disorders involving distortions of thought, perception and emotion, bizarre behaviour and social withdrawal. Around eight to 40 cases per 1,000 are reported per year worldwide and the disorder appears to recognise no cultural or international boundaries. It is higher in urban areas and there is a lifetime risk of 0.7 per cent of developing the illness (and this is greater in men). It is highest in people of lowest socio-economic status, has its onset in adolescence or early adulthood, and genetic factors account for 80 per cent of the disorder's appearance (Tandon et al., 2008a). Schizophrenia is probably the most serious of the mental disorders. It tends to manifest itself in the patient's mid-twenties, although there will have been evidence of subtle clinical symptoms and decline of function prior to this – the so-called prodromal stage of the illness (Addington et al., 2007).

Descriptions of symptoms in ancient writings indicate that the disorder has been around for thousands of years (Jeste *et al.*, 1985). The word 'schizophrenia' literally means 'split mind', although it is commonly misinterpreted as 'split personality'. The schizophrenic does not suffer from split personality or multiple personality (those are other mental disorders) but from disordered thought and affect. The man who invented the term, Eugen Bleuler (in 1911), intended it to refer to a break with reality caused by such disorganisation of the various functions of the mind that thoughts and feelings no longer worked together normally.

Many studies of people who become schizophrenics in adulthood have found that they were different from others even in childhood. One study obtained home movies of people with adult-onset schizophrenia that showed them and their siblings when they were children (Walker and Lewine, 1990). Although the schizophrenia did not manifest itself until adulthood, viewers of the films (six graduate students and one professional clinical psychologist) did an excellent job of identifying the children who were to become schizophrenic. The viewers commented on the children's poor eye contact, relative lack of responsiveness and positive affect, and generally poor motor coordination.

There are also degrees of cognitive impairment seen in schizophrenia. Verbal fluency – the ability to name as many objects beginning with a particular letter or belonging to the same category – appears to be impaired in schizophrenic individuals (Gruzelier *et al.*, 1988), although the category version of this test appears to be better performed (Joyce *et al.*, 1996). Semantic memory and performance on 'frontal lobe' tasks is also impaired in schizophrenic individuals (Shallice and Burgess 1991; Tamlyn *et al.*, 1992).

The prognosis for schizophrenia is described by the 'law of thirds'. Approximately one-third of the people who are diagnosed as having it will require institutionalisation for the rest of their lives. About one-third show remission of symptoms and may be said to be cured of the disorder. The final third are occasionally symptom-free (sometimes for many years) only to have the symptoms return, requiring more treatment and perhaps even institutionalisation. It has the worst prognosis of the psychiatric illnesses apart from dementia (Jobe and Harrow, 2010). After about five years, however, the illness stabilises and does not worsen.

Schizophrenia is characterised by two categories of symptoms: positive and negative. **Positive symptoms** include thought disorders, hallucinations and delusions. A **thought disorder** – a pattern of disorganised, irrational thinking – is probably the most pronounced symptom of schizophrenia. People with schizophrenia have great difficulty arranging their thoughts logically and sorting out plausible conclusions from absurd ones. In conversation, they jump from one topic to another as new associations come up. Sometimes, they utter meaningless words or choose words for their rhyme rather than for their meaning. **Delusions** are beliefs that are obviously contrary to fact. **Delusions of persecution** are false beliefs that others are plotting and conspiring against oneself. **Delusions of grandeur** are false beliefs in one's power and importance, such as a conviction that one has god-like powers or has special knowledge that no one else possesses. **Delusions of control** are related to delusions of persecution; the person believes, for example, that they are being controlled by others through such means as radar or tiny radio receivers implanted in their brain.

The third positive symptom of schizophrenia is **hallucinations**, which are perceptions of stimuli that are not actually present. The most common schizophrenic hallucinations are auditory, but such hallucinations can also involve any of the other senses. The typical schizophrenic hallucination consists of voices talking to the person. Sometimes, they order the person to act; sometimes, they scold the person for their unworthiness; sometimes, they just utter meaningless phrases. Sometimes, those with schizophrenia may also hear a voice that keeps a running commentary on their behaviour, or they hear two or more voices.

In contrast to the positive symptoms, the **negative symptoms** of schizophrenia are known by the absence of normal behaviours: flattened emotional response, poverty of speech, lack of initiative and persistence, inability to experience pleasure, and social withdrawal.

Types of schizophrenia

The DSM-IV TR identifies four types of schizophrenia: undifferentiated, catatonic, paranoid and disorganised. Most cases of schizophrenia, however, do not fit exactly into one of these categories. Many individuals are diagnosed with **undifferentiated schizophrenia**, that is, the patients have delusions, hallucinations and disorganised behaviour but do not meet the criteria for catatonic, paranoid or disorganised schizophrenia. In addition, some patients' symptoms change after an initial diagnosis, and their classification changes accordingly.

Catatonic schizophrenia (from the Greek *katateinein*, meaning 'to stretch or draw tight') is characterised by various motor disturbances, including catatonic postures – bizarre, stationary poses maintained for many hours – and waxy flexibility, in which the person's limbs can be moulded into new positions, which are then maintained. Catatonic schizophrenics are often aware of all that goes on about them and will talk about what happened after the episode of catatonia subsides.

The pre-eminent symptoms of **paranoid schizophrenia** are delusions of persecution, grandeur or control. The word 'paranoid' has become so widely used in ordinary language that it has come to mean 'suspicious'. However, not all paranoid schizophrenics believe that they are being persecuted. Some believe that they hold special powers that can save the world or that they are Christ, or Napoleon or the president of the USA.

Paranoid schizophrenics are among the most intelligent of psychotic patients, so, not surprisingly, they often build up delusional structures incorporating a wealth of detail. Even the most trivial event is interpreted in terms of a grand scheme, whether it is a delusion of persecution or one of grandeur. The way a person walks, a particular facial expression or movement, or even the shapes of clouds can acquire special significance. An example of a case study of paranoid schizophrenia appears in the Psychology in Action section.

Psychology in action: Treating paranoid schizophrenia

Bill McClary, a 25-year-old unemployed man, did not go to the therapist willingly. His sister Coleen, with whom he had been living for 18 months, suggested that Bill receive professional help for behaviour that had become increasingly unusual. He would spend most of his time in social isolation, daydreaming, talking to himself and saying things that did not make sense. Although most people engage in such behaviour at some time, Bill's was constant and this is what worried his sister.

On seeking professional help, Bill appeared quiet and hesitant. During therapy, he was friendly but shy and ill-at-ease. It was only later that his therapist learned of even stranger and unusual behaviour reported by Bill's brother Roger.

It transpired that Bill had had occasional but not long-lasting heterosexual and homosexual relationships. After moving in with his sister, he became convinced that people were talking about him, especially about his sexuality. He came to believe that a group of conspirators had implanted microphones and cameras in the house to spy on his sexual encounters with men. These recordings were released as a film which Bill believed had grossed $50 million at the box office; this money was used to fund the activity of the Irish Republican Army in Northern Ireland and he would often feel deeply guilty and responsible for the deaths there because his money was used to buy arms and ammunition.

Bill also heard voices discussing his sexual behaviour in unpleasant terms. Often, these discussions would involve an element of punishment, such as 'He's a faggot; we've got to kill him'. The successfully released film was called *Honour Thy Father* and Bill's name in the film was Gay Talese. Although Bill did not acknowledge the fact, this name actually belonged to a real novelist who wrote about organised crime. He maintained that his photograph had appeared on the cover of *Time* magazine in the previous year with the name Gay Talese printed clearly on it.

Bill was the youngest of four children born to Irish-American parents. He was very close to his mother and his father blamed him for the break-up of his marriage; he was often excluded from his father's activities. At the age of 12, Bill's father fell ill and Bill remembered wanting to see him dead. His school work was good and he eventually became a bank clerk – a stop-gap job while he thought of which career to pursue. He was quiet and polite but eccentric; he resigned after two years to become a lift operator, a job which afforded even more thinking time, but he was sacked after a year for being disorganised. He moved in with his mother shortly after this but because each made the other anxious, he moved out and moved in with his sister, her husband and their three children. It was at this point that Bill's unusual behaviour became noticeable.

Bill did not seem to enjoy life very much – he did not like interacting with others, was ambivalent about relationships and described sex in very impersonal terms. Initial therapy sessions targeted Bill's indifference and time-keeping and his sister was advised to ignore inappropriate behaviour. If he missed breakfast, then he would not have a snack cooked for him at eleven, as had previously happened. This strategy and others like it resulted in Bill keeping time and domestic appointments. He enjoyed helping his niece with her homework and so this pleasant activity was encouraged. Eventually, his schedule approached those of the house and he began to help more with domestic chores. Mumbling and lack of social contact was tackled next. The therapist advised Bill to move to one area of the house whenever he felt the need to mumble and talk to himself. This was partly but not totally successful. His shyness with other people was tackled by asking Bill to rehearse mentally conversations that might occur with other people.

When the 'film fantasy' was made aware to the therapist, however, Bill was prescribed thioridazine, a standard antipsychotic medication. This was successful in reducing the self-talk but his delusions remained. To try and eliminate these delusions, Bill was told to visit a local library and find the cover of *Time* with his photograph on. This he did and obviously did not find such a cover. However, he believed that the covers had been switched by conspirators. He was told to go to two more libraries but he was still convinced that the covers had been switched. Over the next few weeks, he began to believe that he might just have imagined the *Time* incident and his delusions managed to recede a little.

Source: Oltmans et al. (1995).

Disorganised schizophrenia is a serious progressive and irreversible disorder characterised primarily by disturbances of thought. People with disorganised schizophrenia often display signs of emotion, especially silly laughter, that are inappropriate to the circumstances. Also, their speech tends to be a jumble of words: 'I came to the hospital to play, gay, way, lay, day, bray, donkey, monkey' (Snyder, 1974, p. 132). This sort of speech is often referred to as a word salad.

Aetiology

Research into the causes of all kinds and forms of schizophrenia throughout this century and the last reflects the challenge that psychologists face in attempting to understand how psychological and biological factors interact to influence behaviour. Schizophrenia appears to result from one or more inherited, biological predispositions that are activated by environmental stress. In fact, this is currently the predominant view of schizophrenia. Figure 18.8 summarises pre- and post-natal risk factors.

Genetic causes

The heritability of schizophrenia, or more precisely the heritability of a tendency towards schizophrenia, has now been firmly established by both twin studies and adoption studies. Identical (monozygotic, MZ) twins are much more likely to be concordant for schizophrenia than are fraternal (dizygotic, DZ) twins, and the children of parents with schizophrenia are more likely themselves to become schizophrenic, even if they were adopted and raised by non-schizophrenic parents (Kety *et al.*, 1968; Farmer *et al.*, 1987). Twin studies of schizophrenia compare the concordance rates of MZ twins with the concordance rates of siblings of different genetic relatedness who were reared either together or apart. The risk of one MZ twin developing the disorder if the other has it is between 50 and 70 per cent; in DZ twins, this is between

9 and 18 per cent. If both of a child's parents are affected, it has a 40–60 per cent of chance of developing the illness (Tanda *et al.*, 2008b).

If a person has been diagnosed with schizophrenia, there exists the possibility that other family members have the disorder, too. It is important to note that although the likelihood of developing schizophrenia increases if a person has schizophrenic relatives, this disorder is not a simple trait, like eye colour, that is inherited. Even if both parents are schizophrenic, the probability that their child will develop schizophrenia is 30 per cent or less.

Current findings provide strong evidence that schizophrenia is heritable, and they also support the conclusion that carrying a 'schizophrenia gene' does not mean that a person will necessarily become schizophrenic (see Figure 18.6). These figures suggest that the environment may be an important trigger for the activation of the biological predisposition.

Several chromosomal regions have been identified as being involved in schizophrenia, around 20 (Lewis *et al.*, 2003), and the total number of genes linked with the disorder is 4,000, a quarter of all known genes (Keshavan *et al.*, 2008). The specific genes involved are likely to be *Sp21-22* and *22q 11-12*.

Neurochemical causes

Two classes of drug have been found to affect the symptoms of schizophrenia. Cocaine and amphetamine can cause symptoms of schizophrenia, both in schizophrenics and in non-schizophrenics; antipsychotic drugs, on the other hand, can reduce them. Because both types of drug affect neural communication in which dopamine serves as a transmitter substance, investigators have hypothesised that abnormal activity of these neurons is the primary cause of schizophrenia. That is, the **dopamine hypothesis** states that the positive symptoms of schizophrenia are produced by overactivity of synapses that use dopamine as a transmitter substance.

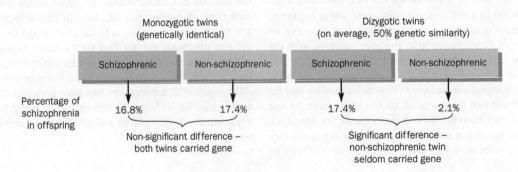

Figure 18.6 Heritability of schizophrenia. An explanation for evidence that people can have an unexpressed 'schizophrenia gene'.

Amphetamine and related substances make naturally occurring schizophrenia worse: paranoids become more suspicious, disorganised schizophrenics become sillier and catatonics become more rigid or hyperactive. Davis (1974) injected an amphetamine-like drug into schizophrenic patients whose symptoms had abated. Within one minute, each patient's condition changed 'from a mild schizophrenia into a wild and very florid schizophrenia'.

Chlorpromazine and other antipsychotic drugs are remarkably effective in alleviating the positive symptoms of schizophrenia but produce little consistent improvement in the negative symptoms. Hallucinations diminish or disappear, delusions become less striking or cease altogether, and the patient's thought processes become more coherent. These drugs are not merely tranquillisers; for example, they cause a patient with catatonic immobility to begin moving again as well as cause an excited patient to quieten down. In contrast, true tranquillisers such as Librium or Valium only make a schizophrenic patient slow-moving and lethargic.

Amphetamine, cocaine and the antipsychotic drugs act on synapses – the junctions between nerve cells – in the brain. One neuron passes on excitatory or inhibitory messages to another by releasing a small amount of transmitter substance from its terminal button into the synaptic cleft. The chemical activates receptors on the surface of the receiving neuron, and the activated receptors either excite or inhibit the receiving neuron. Drugs such as amphetamine and cocaine cause the stimulation of receptors for dopamine. In contrast, antipsychotic drugs block dopamine receptors and prevent them from becoming stimulated. The focus of the drugs appears to be the D2 receptor in the striatum: around 70 per cent of these receptors are occupied by antipsychotic medication which blocks their action (Lidow *et al.*, 1998). Cocaine, conversely, activates this receptor.

Neurological causes

Ventricular enlargement/tissue loss

Weinberger and Wyatt (1982) found that the ventricles in the brains of schizophrenic patients were, on average, twice as large as those of normal subjects. This enlargement has been confirmed in 50 studies (Lewis, 1990); MRI studies further indicate that the medial temporal lobes may be affected (Chua and McKenna, 1995), although there appears to be a reduction in whole-brain size together with an increase in the occipital areas of the ventricles (Lawrie and Abukmeil, 1998). The most consistent finding is a reduction in the lateral or third ventricle (Keshavan *et al.*, 2008; Tanda *et al.*, 2008a).

There is a loss of total brain volume as well as reduced grey matter in the temporal lobe, the PFC and the thalamus (Keshavan *et al.*, 2008). The caudate nucleus is larger in those who respond to treatment (Keshavan *et al.*, 2008). There is more surface contraction in the prefrontal cortex in prodromal patients who go on to develop the disorder than in those who do not (Sun *et al.*, 2009), as can be seen in Figure 18.7.

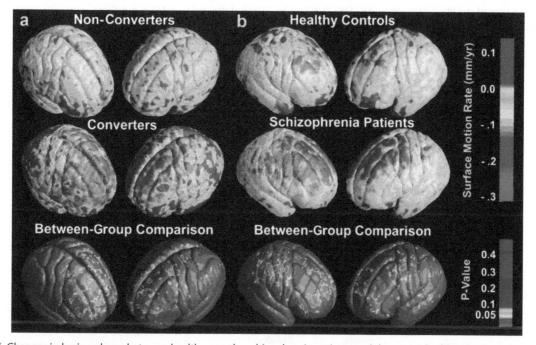

Figure 18.7 Changes in brain volume between healthy people, schizophrenic patients and those at risk of developing schizophrenia who later go on to develop (or not develop) the disorder.

The prefrontal cortex

The PFC and medial temporal lobe have been identified as areas with abnormalities – either structural or functional – in schizophrenia, with hypofrontality or reduced frontal lobe activity being the most commonly reported. The involvement of these areas may explain the working memory and declarative memory problems in schizophrenia (Karlsgodt *et al.*, 2010). Keefe *et al.* (1995) found that schizophrenic patients performed poorly at keeping information in working memory over 30-second and 60-second delay periods, a frontal lobe function. Executive function and episodic memory performance, in general, is poor (Reichenberg and Harvey, 2007). These abnormalities are milder in the relatives of schizophrenic patients (Reichenberg and Harvey, 2007). It has also been found that the degree of impaired activation depends on the severity of the symptoms (Sanz *et al.*, 2009).

PET studies of schizophrenic patients suggest that there is a decrease in dopamine receptors in the PFC (Okubo *et al.*, 1997) and a decrease of N-acetyl aspartate in the frontal and temporal lobe (Keshavan *et al.*, 2008). There is also evidence that the neuronal density in the PFC is 17 per cent higher compared with patients with Huntington's chorea and patients with schizophrenia-related disorders (Selemon *et al.*, 1995). These researchers suggested that this 'squashing' of neurons results from abnormal brain development and may account for the frontal lobe deficits.

Crow (1998, 2002) has controversially suggested that a deficit in the functional lateralisation of the brain, especially the lateralisation of language, may be the cause of schizophrenia, although the evidence for this is mixed. A recent study found a significant reduction in the superior (top) part of the left temporal lobe in schizophrenic patients as well as a general reduction in the size of the temporal lobe, although this last finding was not statistically significant (Highley *et al.*, 1999). The researchers also found a relationship between this asymmetrical reduction and the time of onset of the disorder: the later the onset, the greater the reduction. Another study, this time of frontal lobe asymmetry, found that the planum temporale and Sylvian fissure were less lateralised in schizophrenic patients (Sommer *et al.*, 2001). As you saw in Chapter 10, asymmetry of these structures is associated with language processing.

Neurodevelopmental impairment

According to Weinberger (1996): 'Schizophrenia is related to a defect in brain development. This defect predisposes to a characteristic pattern of brain malfunction in early adult life and to symptoms that respond to antidopaminergic drugs.' See Figure 18.8. Impaired or delayed development may be a risk factor, and is linked to the development of specific genes, abnormalities in DNA leading to the deletion or duplication of some DNA sequences, prenatal complications and changes in brain structure (Walker *et al.*, 2010). Structural abnormalities in the brain and abnormal migration of neurons in the foetal brain also been cited as risk factors (Connor *et al.*, 2009).

Cognitive and environmental causes

Family and expressed emotion

A study carried out in Finland has suggested that being raised by a 'mentally healthy' family helps to protect against the development of schizophrenia (Tienari *et al.*,

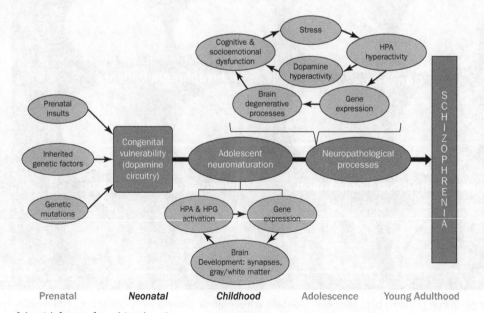

Figure 18.8 Some of the risk factors for schizophrenia

1987). The researchers examined the children of schizophrenic mothers who had been adopted away early in life. Following interviews and psychological tests, the families who adopted the children were classified as well-adjusted, moderately maladjusted or severely maladjusted. The children adopted by the well-adjusted families were least likely to show signs of mental disturbance, including schizophrenia. These findings suggest that the environment may be either an important cause or mediator of schizophrenia.

The personality and communicative abilities of either or both parents appear to play an influential role in the development of schizophrenic symptoms in children. Several studies have shown that children raised by parents who are dominating, overprotective, rigid and insensitive to the needs of others later develop schizophrenia (Roff and Knight, 1981). In many cases, a parent may be verbally accepting of the child yet in other ways reject them, which establishes a conflict for the child called a **double-bind**. For example, a mother may encourage her son to become emotionally dependent on her yet continually reject him when he tries to hug her or sit on her lap.

Another environmental factor which could account for the development of schizophrenia is **expressed emotion** or EE (Hooley et al., 1996). Brown et al. (1966; Brown, 1985) identified a category of behaviours of families of individuals recovering from schizophrenia that seemed to be related to the patients' rates of recovery. They labelled this variable expressed emotion, which consists of expressions of criticism, hostility and emotional overinvolvement by the family members towards the patient. Patients living in a family environment in which the level of expressed emotion was low were more likely to recover, whereas those in families in which it was high were likely to continue to exhibit schizophrenic symptoms. Perceived criticism also appears to be important: in depressed patients, perceived criticism predicted a relapse in the mental disorder more reliably than did actual criticism (Hooley and Teasdale, 1989); mood disorder patients with high-EE families appear to be more non-verbally negative than patients from low-EE families (Simoneau et al., 1998).

Jenkins and Karno (1992) report that over 100 studies have investigated expressed emotion in countries ranging from North America, England, Denmark, and Italy to France, Spain, Germany, Taiwan, India, Egypt and Australia. Despite differences in the ways that people of different cultures perceive mental illness and express themselves, expressed emotion does not seem to be culture-bound. Two elements appear to be common to all cultures: critical comments and emotional overinvolvement. If these elements are present in families of schizophrenics at low levels, patients are likely to recover

quickly; if they are present at high levels, patients are less likely to recover quickly. Expressed emotion has been found to increase with illness duration and patients are more likely to relapse if they come from high-EE families (Hooley, 2010).

Treatment

The commonest form of treatment for schizophrenia is psychopharmacological. The only effective means of treating the disorder is by D2 antagonists. These **antipsychotic** drugs help to reduce the effects of schizophrenia apparently by blocking dopamine receptors in the brain. Presumably, overactivity of dopamine synapses is responsible for the positive symptoms of schizophrenia, which is why treatment is effective at combating the positive symptoms but has limited success in combating the negative symptoms (Keshavan et al., 2008). Although dopamine-secreting neurons are located in several parts of the brain, most researchers believe that the ones involved in the symptoms of schizophrenia are located in the cerebral cortex and parts of the limbic system near the front of the brain. There is evidence that the education of the family/patient about the disorder reduces the likelihood of a relapse and that social skills training also improves outcome (Keshavan et al., 2008).

A different system of dopamine-secreting neurons in the brain is involved in the control of movement. Occasionally, this system of neurons degenerates in older people, producing Parkinson's disease. Symptoms of this disorder include tremors, muscular rigidity, loss of balance, difficulty in initiating movement and impaired breathing that makes speech indistinct. In severe cases the person is bedridden.

The major problem with antipsychotic drugs is that they do not discriminate between these two systems of dopamine-secreting neurons. The drugs interfere with the activity of both the circuits involved in the symptoms of schizophrenia and the circuits involved in the control of movements. Consequently, when a person with schizophrenia begins taking an antipsychotic drug, they often exhibit a movement disorder. Fortunately, the disorder is usually temporary and soon disappears.

However, after taking the antipsychotic drug for several years, some people develop a different, more serious, movement disorder known as **tardive dyskinesia** (tardive means late developing; dyskinesia refers to a disturbance in movement), an often irreversible and untreatable syndrome characterised by continual involuntary lip smacking, grimacing and drooling (Cummings and Wirshing, 1989).

Clozapine, an antischizophrenic drug, is more effective than other antipsychotic drugs in helping cases of almost untreatable schizophrenia (Kane et al., 1988). It improves the symptoms of about 30–50 per cent of those people who have not responded to traditional antipsychotic drugs. Because about 2 per cent of those taking clozapine suffer an inhibition of white blood cell production, which can be fatal, weekly blood tests have to be conducted. Prognosis is worse for patients on long-term antipsychotic medication (Chouinard and Chouinard, 2008).

The positive symptoms of the illness have been addressed using CBT. One aim of the CBT is to improve the patient's social skills by changing his/her cognition. A meta-analysis of social skills training in schizophrenia found that they led to improvements in the acquisition of skills, assertiveness, social interactions and a general reduction in symptoms (Kurtz and Mueser, 2009). More modest improvements are seen in social activities such as behaving appropriately at a supermarket.

Mood disorders

Everyone experiences moods varying from sadness to happiness to elation. We are excited when our team wins a game, saddened to learn that a friend's father has had a heart attack, thrilled at news of a higher than expected grade in an exam, and devastated by the death of a loved one. Some people, though, experience more dramatic mood changes than these. Significant shifts or disturbances in mood that affect normal perception, thought and behaviour are called mood disorders. They may be characterised by a deep, foreboding depression or by a combination of depression and euphoria.

Mood disorders are primarily disorders of emotion. The most severe mood disorders are bipolar disorder and major depression. **Bipolar disorder** is characterised by alternating periods of mania (wild excitement) and depression. **Major depression** involves persistent and severe feelings of sadness and worthlessness accompanied by changes in appetite, sleeping and behaviour. The lifetime prevalence rates for major depression are about 13 per cent for males and about 21 per cent for females (Kessler et al., 1994).

A less severe form of depression is called **dysthymic disorder**. The term comes from the Greek words *dus*, 'bad' and *thymos*, 'spirit'. The primary difference between this disorder and major depression is its relatively low severity. Similarly, **cyclothymic disorder** resembles bipolar disorder but is much less severe.

Mania

Mania (the Greek word for madness) is characterised by wild, exuberant, unrealistic activity unprecipitated by environmental events. During manic episodes, people are usually elated and self-confident; however, contradiction or interference tends to make them very angry. Their speech (and, presumably, their thought processes)

becomes very rapid. They tend to flit from topic to topic and are full of grandiose plans, but their thoughts are not as disorganised as those of people with schizophrenia. Manic patients also tend to be restless and hyperactive, often pacing around ceaselessly. They often have delusions and hallucinations, typically of a nature that fits their exuberant mood. Impairments in 'frontal lobe' function such as set-shifting, verbal memory and sustained attention have been reported (Clark et al., 2002), and the experience of the disorder has been related to an oversensitive frontal cortex (Harmon-Jones et al., 2002).

Author, creativity researcher and manic-depressive, Kay Jamison.
Source: Getty Images.

Depression knows no social or intellectual barriers. Lewis Wolpert, Professor of Developmental Biology, Winston Churchill, British Prime Minister (both pictured here) and the late Stuart Sutherland, Professor of Psychology, have all suffered from major depression or bipolar disorder.

Sources: Colin McPherson (l); PA Photos/Empics (r).

The usual response that manic speech and behaviour evokes in another person is one of sympathetic amusement. In fact, when an experienced clinician starts to become amused by a patient, the clinician begins to suspect the presence of mania. Because very few patients exhibit only mania, the DSM-IV TR classifies all cases in which mania occurs as bipolar disorder. Patients with bipolar disorder usually experience alternate periods of mania and depression. Each of these periods lasts from a few days to a few weeks, usually with several days of relatively normal behaviour between. Around 40 per cent of bipolar disorder patients will have been diagnosed with major depression previously (Bowden, 2001). During the depressive and manic period, there appear to be cognitive impairments such as delayed verbal memory whereas during the depressed period, there is decreased verbal fluency (Kurtz and Gerraty, 2009), Even according to DSM-IV TR, 'the specific diagnostic categories are meant to serve as guidelines to be informed by clinical judgement and are not meant to be used in a cookbook fashion'. Many therapists have observed that there is often something brittle and unnatural about the happiness during the manic phase, as though the patient is making themselves be happy to ward off an attack of depression. Indeed, some manic patients are simply hyperactive and irritable rather than euphoric.

Depression

Description

> It was the worst experience of my life. More terrible even than watching my wife die of cancer. I am ashamed to admit that my depression felt worse than her death but it's true. I was in a state that bears no resemblance to anything I had experienced before. I was not just feeling very low. I was seriously ill. I was totally self-involved, negative and thought about suicide most of the time. I could not think properly let alone work, and wanted to remain curled up in bed all day.

These were the opening words of Professor Lewis Wolpert, Professor of Developmental Biology at University College London in his book, *Malignant Sadness*. Depressed people are extremely sad and are usually full of self-directed guilt, but not because of any particular environmental event. Depressed people cannot always state why they are depressed. Around 17 per cent of people will experience a major episode of depression at some point in their lives (Kessler *et al.*, 1994) and a similar percentage experiences disability at work due to the illness (Goldberg and Steury, 2001). Beck (1967) identified five cardinal symptoms of depression: (1) a sad and apathetic mood; (2) feelings of worthlessness and hopelessness; (3) a desire to withdraw from other people; (4) sleeplessness and loss of appetite and sexual desire; and (5) change in activity level, to either lethargy or agitation. Major depression must be distinguished from grief, such as that caused by the death of a loved one. People who are grieving feel sad and depressed but do not fear losing their minds or have thoughts of self-harm. Because many people who do suffer from major depression or the depressed phase of bipolar disorder commit suicide, these disorders are potentially fatal. The fatality rate by suicide for major depression is estimated at 15 per cent (Guze and Robins, 1970). According to Elizabeth Wurtzel, author of *Prozac Nation*:

> one day, you realise that your entire life is just awful, not worth living, a horror and a black blot on the white terrain of human existence. One morning, you wake up afraid you are going to live ... for all intents and purposes, the deeply depressed are just the walking, waking dead.

The 'walking, waking dead', according to the World Health Organization (2002b), account for 4.4 per cent of the world's disease burden, a percentage similar to that for ischaemic heart disease and asthma and pulmonary disease combined. According to one study, depressive disorders are likely to be the second most common diseases by the year 2020 (Brown, 2001). Successful treatment, therefore, is vital. Interventions can reduce the burden of depression by as much as 10–30 per cent (Chisholm *et al.*, 2004).

The UK Office for National Statistics estimates that 2.6 million people suffered depression in England in 2000 (Thomas and Morris, 2003), 72 per cent of whom were girls/women and 20 per cent of whom were aged between 35 and 44 years. The direct cost to the National Health Service was estimated at almost £370 million. The total cost, which includes economic costs such as days taken off work and disability benefit, was estimated to be £9 billion. The cost of treatment, therefore, was a drop in the ocean compared to the other costs involved. Some 109.7 million working days were lost through depression and 2,615 deaths resulted from the disorder.

A Canadian study of 1,281 employees who had claimed depression-related absences from work found that 60 per cent who claimed disability benefit took antidepressants. Those who took the recommended drugs and at the right dosage were less likely to claim long-term disability benefits or to leave work completely. The researchers estimated that early intervention would reduce the appearance of depression by three weeks, representing a financial saving of $3,500 per person. If early intervention

had occurred in people who started taking the drugs 30 days after the start of the first episode of depression, savings of around $539,000 could have been made.

Of course, perhaps more important than the financial cost is the human, psychological cost. As Thomas and Morris (2003) conclude (p. 518), 'the intangible elements of pain and suffering of people with depressive disorders and their families and the effects on quality of life cannot be quantified in monetary terms'.

Aetiology

Cognitive causes

People with mood disorders do not have the same outlook on life as others. Specifically, they make negative statements about themselves and their abilities: 'Nobody likes me', 'I'm not good at anything', 'What's the point in even trying, I'll just mess it up anyway'. Because they are so negative about themselves, depressed people are particularly unpleasant to be around. The problem is that the depressed individual is caught in a vicious circle: negative statements strain interpersonal relationships, which result in others withdrawing or failing to initiate social support, which, in turn, reinforces the depressed individual's negative statements (Klerman and Weissman, 1986).

Beck (1967, 1991) suggested that the changes in affect seen in depression are not primary but instead are secondary to changes in cognition. That is, the primary disturbance is a distortion in the person's view of reality. For example, a depressed person may see a scratch on the surface of their car and conclude that the car is ruined; or a person whose recipe fails may see the unappetising dish as proof of their unworthiness; or a nasty letter from a creditor is seen as a serious and personal condemnation. According to Beck, depressed people's thinking is characterised by self-blame (things that go wrong are always their fault), overemphasis on the negative aspects of life (small problems are blown out of proportion) and failure to appreciate positive experiences (pessimism). This kind of pessimistic thinking involves negative thoughts about the self, about the present and about the future, which Beck collectively referred to as the **cognitive triad**. In short, depressed people blame their present miserable situation on their inadequacies and a lack of hope for improving the situation in the future.

The negative view of the self and events, however, seems to be time-specific. Depressed individuals who are asked to describe themselves 'right now' use negative terms, but use less negative terms when they describe how they usually feel (Brewin *et al.*, 1992). Depressed patients are also likely to be negative when discussing things globally but not when discussing specific issues (Wycherley, 1995).

Beck's original model argued that cognition caused the emotional disorder, but his later reformulation of the theory suggested that cognition is part of a set of interacting mechanisms that include biological, psychological and social factors (Kovacs and Beck, 1978). In the reformulation, Beck argued that people might be predisposed to develop depression under certain circumstances. He called this a diathesis–stress theory. Central to the theory is that there is a set of schema – a stored collection of knowledge that affects encoding and understanding of all other processed information – which, when activated, sets off a series of negative thoughts and experiences. If the schema is depressogenic – characterised by depressive features – then an event which might activate these schemata leads to the person processing information very negatively. However, if a person is not exposed to these triggers, they will think or behave no more depressively than a person who does not possess depressogenic schemata. A study of undergraduates found that students with dysfunctional attitudes – those who were identified as having depressogenic schemata – felt more depressed after learning they had been refused a place at a university of their choice than when learning that they had, a pattern not seen in students whose attitudes were not dysfunctional (Abela and D'Allessandro, 2002).

Beck also distinguished between two types of depression: sociotropic depression in which the abnormal belief derived from a dependence on others, and autonomous depression in which the individual was goal-oriented and relied little on others. The evidence for these two types as distinct varieties of depression, however, is mixed (Power and Dalgleish, 1997).

Another causal factor in depression appears to involve the attributional style of the depressed person (Abramson *et al.*, 1978, 1989). According to this idea, it is not merely experiencing negative events that causes people to become depressed: what is more important are the attributions people make about why those events occur. People who are most likely to become depressed are those who attribute negative events and experiences to their own shortcomings and who believe that their life situations are never going to get any better. A person's attributional style, then, serves as a predisposition or diathesis for depression. In other words, people prone to depression tend to have a hopeless outlook on their life: 'I am not good at anything I try to do and it will never get any better. I am always going to be a useless person.' According to this view, depression is most likely when people with pessimistic attributional styles encounter significant or frequent life stressors (Abramson *et al.*, 1989). The pessimistic attributions are then generalised to other, perhaps smaller, stressors, and eventually a deep sense of hopelessness and despair sets in. Thus, the original formulation of the theory was called the helplessness theory whereas the later reformulation became known as the hopelessness theory.

Such people also appear to suffer a double dose of hopelessness. Not only do they perceive negative outcomes as being their own fault, but they also perceive positive outcomes as being due to circumstance or to luck. In addition, they apply pessimistic attributions to a wide range of events and experiences and apply positive attributions only to a very narrow range of events and experiences, if any.

However, there is mixed evidence for a strong version of the hopelessness attribution theory. Swendsen (1998) reported that attributional style did not predict immediate depressed or anxious mood in a group of 91 individuals who were asked to report negative events, cognitions, anxiety and depression five times a day for one week. However, attributional style did predict 'individual' specific causal attributions made to negative events. Similar findings have been reported in other studies (Kapci, 1998). Lynd-Stevenson (1996, 1997) reports that hopelessness does not mediate the relationship between attributional style and depression but that there is a mediating effect when measures of hopelessness are relevant to the individual's ongoing life (in Lynd-Stevenson's sample's case, hopelessness related to unemployment). Attributional style, therefore, seems to apply only in certain, relevant contexts.

Genetic causes

Like schizophrenia, the mood disorders appear to have a genetic component. People who have first-degree relatives with a serious mood disorder are ten times more likely to develop these disorders than are people without afflicted relatives (Rosenthal, 1970). Furthermore, the concordance rate for bipolar disorder is 72 per cent for MZ twins, compared with 14 per cent for DZ twins. For major depression, the figures are 40 per cent and 11 per cent, respectively (Allen, 1976). Thus, bipolar disorder appears to be more heritable than major depression, and the two disorders appear to have different genetic causes. Recent studies, however, have cast doubt on the heritability of major depressive disorder (Andrew *et al.*, 1998).

Neurochemical causes

Drug treatments for depression (which are described in detail below) have shed some light on the biochemical causes of schizophrenia. Antidepressants such as imipramine, for example, stimulate synapses that use two transmitter substances, norepinephrine and serotonin. Other drugs such as reserpine, which is used to treat high blood pressure, can cause episodes of depression. Reserpine lowers blood pressure by blocking the release of norepinephrine in muscles in the walls of blood vessels, thus causing the muscles to relax. However, because the drug also blocks the release of norepinephrine and serotonin in the brain, a common side – effect is depression. This side effect strengthens the argument that biochemical factors in the brain play an important role in depression.

Such data have suggested a biological amine theory of depression: depression results from a depletion in the monoamines, dopamine, norepinephrine or serotonin. The serotonin hypothesis is a variant of this general theory. The serotonin hypothesis suggests that this neurotransmitter (the lack of it) may be more involved in depression because blocking reuptake of serotonin is more effective than blocking norepinephrine. Given that most antidepressants augment serotonin (perhaps by different mechanisms), perhaps the involvement of other neurotransmitters is peripheral.

In addition to the amines, levels of the neurotransmitter gamma amino butyuric acid (GABA) have been found to be lower in the cerebrospinal fluid (CSF) and plasma of individuals with unipolar depression (Brambila *et al.*, 2003). When depressed individuals are given drugs which increase the level of serotonin at serotonergic neurons or are given ECT, the decrease in GABA concentration seen in the occipital cortex is reversed (Sanacora *et al.*, 2002, 2004). The roles of the two classes of GABA (the a and b classes) in depression, however, are unclear.

Neuropathological causes

In a neuroimaging study, activity in the PFC near the top of the corpus callosum was reduced in individuals with unipolar and bipolar depression (Drevets *et al.*, 1997). This part of the PFC is called the ACC and a specific region within the cingulate – which has been called subgenual region sg24 – is less active in people with mood disorder, as Figure 18.9 shows.

Drevets *et al.* found that the volume of this region was lateralised to the left hemisphere, which is consistent with the data and model of normal emotion (described in Chapter 13). These findings were subsequently replicated in a group of people with severe mood disorder (Hirayasu *et al.*, 1999).

When Drevets and his colleagues went on to explore the cellular nature of this region in people with mood disorder, they found the typical reduction in sg24 but also a reduction in the density of cells and in the number of glial cells (see Ongur *et al.*, 1998). A further study, using a larger sample, found that same pattern of cell reduction in a group of individuals with major and bipolar depression but only in a subset with a family history of the disorder (Torrey *et al.*, 2000). These cells carry neurotransmitter receptors and help to transport neurotransmitters, which may explain why their reduction is associated with depression; the reduction might also

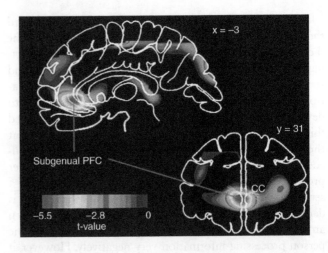

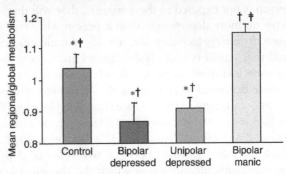

* p<0.025 control vs. depressed; † p<0.01 depressed vs. manic; ‡ p<0.05 control vs. manic

Figure 18.9 Decreases in activation in the prefrontal cortex seen in individuals with mood disorders.

Source: Drevets, W.C., Neuroimaging and neuropathological studies of depression: Implications for the cognitive-emotional features of mood disorders. *Current Opinion in Neurobiology*, 2001, 11, 240–49. Copyright 2001, with permission from Elsevier.

explain why this area is seen as smaller in people with depression and bipolar depression.

Studies have also implicated a dysfunction in the hypothalamus (Swaab *et al.*, 2005; Bao *et al.*, 2008). For example, cortisol levels (the glucocorticoid you read about in the stress section of Chapter 17) are thought to be worse in the morning than in the afternoon (and depressed people are at their worst in the morning). Levels of cortisol are higher in depressed individuals than controls and an increase in the number of neurons in the hypothalamus that release corticotrophin-releasing hormone (CRH) is found in these patients; the level of CRH in CSF is also higher and people on cortisol-increasing drugs report symptoms of depression. Serotonin is reduced in the presence of CRH and, as the principal action of antidepressants is to make more serotonin available in the brain, these two factors may be linked.

Geography

Some studies suggest that depression and psychosis are more common in urban than rural areas but others report no such difference. To attempt to determine whether such a difference was real and consistent, Sundquist *et al.* (2004) followed up the entire Swedish population aged between 25 and 64 years who had been admitted to hospital with a diagnosis of depression and psychosis. Level of urbanisation was defined by population density.

They found that those patients who lived in the most densely populated areas were 68–77 per cent more likely to be at risk of developing psychosis and 12–20 per cent more likely to be at risk of developing depression than were patients who lived in the least densely populated areas.

Why such a difference should emerge is unknown. It may be that living in densely populated areas produces more adverse living circumstances, such as stressful events and little social support.

Suicide – An international perspective

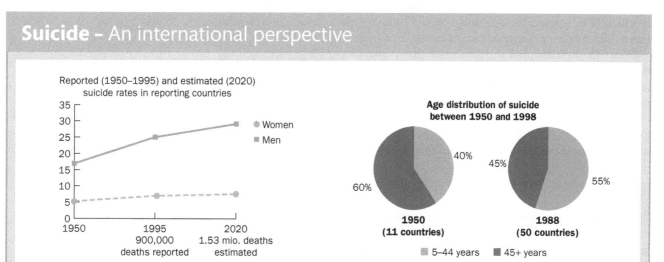

Figure 18.10 World Health Organization statistics for suicide rates across the world.
Source: World Health Organization.

Migration, low intelligence and substance use may separately be important risk factors for depression and suicide. In some countries, suicide rates have increased by over 60 per cent in between 1950 and 2000 and you can see this pattern and the international incidence in Figures 18.10(a) and 18.10(b).

A study of immigration into Estonia, which had been part of the Soviet Union until independence in 1991 and had, therefore, a significant Russian population (about 30 per cent of the population were Russians in 1989), found that while the rate of suicide was lower in the Russian minority during Soviet rule, this pattern changed during the period of stabilisation following independence (Varnik *et al.*, 2005). The rate was higher than that found in Estonians in Estonia or in Russians in Russia, reflecting a change in status from privileged minority to non-privileged minority. The rates converged in 1998, suggesting to the authors that this may reflect the efforts by the Estonian government to integrate the Russian minority.

In a separate study of Swedish servicemen, Gunnell *et al.* (2005) found that of 987,308 Swedish men followed up for up to 26 years risk of suicide was 2–3 times higher in men with the lowest cognitive test scores compared to those with the highest. The greatest suicide risk emerged from the test of logic – this was the test correlating most significantly with suicide. Perhaps this reflects an inability to solve problems in real life; problems which, if left unresolved, lead to self-harm and death.

Suicide attempts in adolescence are associated with heavy or frequent drinking and illegal drug-taking (Shaffer and Pfeffer, 2001; Gould *et al.*, 2003). A group of Norwegian researchers monitored the correlation between substance use and suicide in two surveys (in 1992 and 2002) of 23,000 13-19-year-olds (Rossow *et al.*, 2005). There was a significant relationship between increased substance use and suicide, but only in girls. For boys, the effect of substance use seemed to be less pronounced in 2002 than in 1992. For both sexes, the substance most significantly associated with suicide attempts was alcohol.

Treatment

The two principal treatments for clinical depression are cognitive therapy and antidepressant medication.

Cognitive (behavioural) therapy

Beck's cognitive therapy begins by arguing that the negative beliefs held by depressed individuals are seen as conclusions based on faulty logic (Beck, 1967). A depressed person concludes that they are 'deprived, frustrated, humiliated, rejected or punished' (Beck et al., 1979, p. 120). Beck views the cognitions of the depressed individual in terms of a cognitive triad: a negative view of the self ('I am worthless'), of the outside world ('The world makes impossible demands on me') and of the future ('Things are never going to get better').

Even when confronted with evidence that contradicts their negative beliefs, depressed individuals often find an illogical means of interpreting good news as bad news (Lewinsohn et al., 1980). For example, a student who receives an A grade on an exam might attribute the high grade to an easy, unchallenging exam rather than to their own mastery of the material. The fact that few others in the class received a high grade does little to convince the depressed person that they deserve congratulations for having done well. The depressed student goes on believing, against contrary evidence, that the good grade was not really deserved.

Once the faulty logic is recognised for what it is, therapy entails exploring means for correcting the distortions. The therapist does not accept the client's conclusions and inferences at their face value. Instead, those conclusions resulting from faulty logic are discussed so that the client may understand them from another perspective, changing their behaviour as a result.

Meta-analyses suggest that CBT can be a very effective means of combating depression and may even be more effective than tricyclic antidepressants (see below) in the long term (Hensley et al., 2004).

Antidepressant drugs

Tricyclic antidepressants

Antidepressant drugs are a class of drugs used to treat the symptoms of major depression and the most common of these are listed in Table 18.8. **Antimanic drugs** are used to

Table 18.8 Some of the drugs used to treat depression

Substance	Generic name	Example
Norepinephrine-reuptake inhibitors (Tertiary amine tricyclics)	Amitriptyline	Elavil
	Clomipramine	Anafranil
	Doxepin	Adapin, Sinequa
	Imipramine	Tofranil
	Trimipramine	Surmontil
Norepinephrine-reuptake inhibitors (Secondary amine tricyclics)	Amoxapine	Asendin
	Desipramine	Norpramin, Pertofrane
	Maprotiline	Ludiomil
	Nortriptyline	Pamelor
	Protriptyline	Vivactil
Serotonin-reuptake inhibitors	Fluoxetine	Prozac
	Fluvoxamine	Luvox
	Paroxetine	Paxil
	Sertraline	Zoloft
	Venlafaxine	Effexor
Atypical antidepressants	Bupropion	Wellbutrin
	Nefazodone	Serzone
	Trazodone	Desyrel
Monoamine oxidase inhibitors	Phenelzine	Nardil
	Tranylcypromine	Parnate
	Selegiline	Eldepryl

Source: From Goodman and Gilman's The Pharmacological Basis of Therapeutics, 9th edn (Hardman, J.G. and Limberd, L.E., eds), 'Drugs and the treatment of psychiatric ___: psychosis and anxiety' (Baldessarini, R.J.). Reproduced with permission of The McGraw-Hill Companies.

treat the symptoms of bipolar disorder and mania. The earliest used antidepressant drugs were derived from the family of chemicals known as **tricyclics**, which refers to their 'three-ring' chemical structure (Lickey and Gordon, 1983).

Although the biology of depression is not well understood, the most widely accepted theory is that depression may result from a deficiency of the catecholamine neurotransmitters norepinephrine and serotonin. Each of these neurotransmitters may be involved in different types of depression, although researchers are not sure how. Antidepressant drugs seem to slow down the reuptake of these neurotransmitters by presynaptic axons. Although tricyclic antidepressants do not work for all people, about 60–80 per cent of those whose depression has brought despair to their lives gradually return to normal after having been placed on tricyclics for two to six weeks (Hughes and Pierattini, 1992). Unfortunately, tricyclics have many side effects, including dizziness, sweating, weight gain, constipation, increased heart rate, poor concentration and dry mouth.

Monoamine oxidase inhibitors (MAOIs)

Another class of antidepressants, introduced in the late 1950s, is the **monoamine oxidase inhibitors (MAOIs)**, which take one to three weeks to begin alleviating depression. MAOIs prevent enzymes in the synaptic gap from destroying dopamine, norepinephrine and serotonin that have been released by presynaptic neurons. These drugs can have many side effects, many of them fatal. The **tyramine cheese reaction**, for example, arises from the eating of foods containing tyramine such as some wines, milk products, coffee and chocolate. Because the monoamine oxidase does not oxidise tyramine, tyramine displaces epinephrine at epinephrine receptors. This produces severe hypertension and blurred vision, impotence, insomnia and nausea. It can also be fatal if leading to a haemorrhage. MAOIs also have been shown to be more effective in treating atypical depressions such as those involving hypersomnia (too much sleep) or mood swings (Hughes and Pierattini, 1992).

Serotonin-specific reuptake inhibitors (SSRIs)

A relatively new class of drugs is **serotonin-specific reuptake inhibitors (SSRIs)**, which, as their name suggests, block the reuptake of serotonin in nerve cells. As a result, the common feature of all SSRIs is that they enhance the transmission of serotonin. Perhaps the most common SSRI is fluoxetine (Prozac), first authorised for medical use in 1988. Fluoxetine inhibits the reuptake of serotonin, leaving more of that neurotransmitter in the synaptic cleft to stimulate post-synaptic receptors, and is the drug of first choice when tricyclic drug treatment has failed. SSRIs produce fewer negative side-effects than do tricyclics and the MAOIs, although some individuals do experience headache, gastrointestinal

discomfort, insomnia, tremor and sexual dysfunction. There is evidence, however, that antidepressants have no clinical advantage over placebo in minor depression (Barbui *et al.*, 2011).

Recent pharmacological treatments

Two developments in the psychopharmacology of depression have been second generation (atypical) depressants which block either norepinephrine reuptake or dopamine reuptake, and **dual-action antidepressants** which block certain serotonin receptors while inhibiting its reuptake. An example of the former, nefazdone, was released in 1995; an example of the latter, mirtazapine, was released in 1997. Neither type of drug has been authorised in all European countries and, because of their youth, little research is available evaluating their long-term efficacy.

The important factor in assessing the effect of antidepressant medication is the maintenance phase of the treatment. In the initial period of drug-taking, there is an acute phase in which the acute symptoms begin to stabilise. This period can last up to three months (Hirschfeld, 2001). The next period extends between the end of the acute period and the end of the depression itself, a period that can take up to 6–12 months. The danger is that if patients had stabilised in the acute phase, then they would have medication withdrawn. According to Hirschfeld (2001), however, around one-third to one-half of people who successfully stabilise in the acute phase, will relapse if medication is not sustained, hence the importance of monitoring behaviour closely during this period.

Lithium carbonate

Lithium carbonate is most effective in the treatment of bipolar disorders or simple mania (Young and Newham, 2006). People's manic symptoms usually decrease as soon as their blood level of lithium reaches a sufficiently high level (Gerbino *et al.*, 1978). In bipolar disorder, once the manic phase is eliminated, the depressed phase does not return. People with bipolar disorder have remained free of their symptoms for years as long as they have continued taking lithium carbonate. This drug can have some side effects, such as a fine tremor or excessive urine production; but in general, the benefits far outweigh the adverse symptoms. However, an overdose of lithium is toxic, which means that the person's blood level of lithium must be monitored regularly. Psychotherapy has also been associated with some benefits, but this treatment is more successful for depression than mania (Scott, 2006).

The major difficulty with treating bipolar disorder is that people with this disorder often miss their 'high'. When medication is effective, the mania subsides along with the depression. But most people enjoy at least the initial phase of their manic periods, and some believe that they are more creative at that time. In addition, many of these people say that they resent having to depend on a chemical 'crutch'. As a consequence, many people suffering from bipolar disorder stop taking their medication. Not taking their medication endangers the lives of these people because the risk of death by suicide is particularly high during the depressive phase of bipolar disorder.

Chapter review

Classification and diagnosis of mental disorders

- Psychologists and other mental health professionals view the causes of mental disorders from several different perspectives:
  - The psychodynamic perspective argues that mental disorders arise from intrapsychic conflict that overwhelms the mind's defence mechanisms.
  - The medical perspective asserts that mental disorders have an organic basis, as physical illnesses do.
  - The cognitive behavioural perspective maintains that mental disorders are learned patterns of maladaptive thinking and behaving.
  - The humanistic perspective suggests that mental disorders arise from an oversensitivity to the demands of others and because positive regard from others is conditional on meeting those demands.
  - The sociocultural perspective focuses on how cultural variables influence the development of mental disorders and people's subjective reactions to them.
- The two major manuals for diagnostic mental disorder are the *Diagnostic and Statistical Manual of Mental Disorders* IV (American Psychiatric Association, 2000) and the *International Classification of Diseases* 10 (World Health Organization, 1992).
- There is strong cross-cultural agreement for the diagnosis of disorder such as schizophrenia, although anxiety and social phobia are not as uniformly diagnosed; there are also culture-bound disorders which are not universal.
- Research indicates that lay people continue to show poor understanding of the symptoms, possible causes and treatment of mental illness.

Treatment of mental disorders

- Historically, people suffering from emotional or behavioural problems were believed to be possessed by demons or were accused of being witches. They were often subjected to torture, including trephining, in which a small hole was punctured in the skull of the afflicted person to allow demonic spirits to escape. Mental patients in sixteenth- and seventeenth-century asylums encountered abject humiliation. Philippe Pinel, a French physician, is often credited with changing the asylum environment in the late eighteenth century.
- Modern therapy adopts an eclectic approach – the borrowing of methods from different treatments and blending them in a way that will work best in treating the patient's problem. There are, however, different types of treatment approaches that have specific characteristics.
- Insight psychotherapy is based primarily on conversation between therapist and client. The oldest form of insight psychotherapy, psychoanalysis, was devised by Freud.
- Psychoanalysis attempts to discover the forces that are warring in the client's psyche and to resolve these inner conflicts by bringing to consciousness the client's unconscious drives and the defences that have been established against them. Insight is believed to be the primary source of healing.
- Humanistic therapy emphasises conscious, deliberate mental processes.
- Client-centred therapy is based on the premise that people are healthy and good and that their problems result from faulty thinking. Instead of evaluating themselves in terms of their own self-concepts, they judge themselves by other people's standards. This tendency is rectified by providing an environment of unconditional positive regard in which clients can find their own way to good mental health.
- The range of people that may benefit from insight therapy is limited and narrow. In general, those most likely to benefit are those who are intelligent and able to articulate their problems. Insight psychotherapies are not effective with persons with serious mental disorders such as schizophrenia. There are also difficulties with evaluating their effectiveness.

- Behavioural therapists attempt to use the principles of classical and operant conditioning to modify behaviour – fears are eliminated or maladaptive behaviours are replaced with adaptive ones.
- Systematic desensitisation uses classical conditioning procedures to condition relaxation to stimuli that were previously producing fear. In contrast, implosion therapy attempts to extinguish fear and avoidance responses. Aversion therapy attempts to condition an unpleasant response to a stimulus with which the client is preoccupied, such as a fetish.
- The most formal system of therapy based on operant conditioning involves token economies, which arrange contingencies in the environment of people who reside in institutions.
- Some operant treatment is vicarious – people can imagine their own behaviour with its consequent reinforcement or punishment.
- Modelling involves using others as role models for behaviour.
- The major problem with behaviour therapy is the failure of patients to transfer behaviour outside the therapy setting. Techniques to promote generalisation include the use of intermittent reinforcement and recruitment of family and friends as adjunct therapists.
- Cognitive behavioural therapies attempt to change overt behaviour and unobservable cognitive processes.
- Rational-emotive therapy is based on the assumption that people's psychological problems stem from faulty cognitions. Its practitioners use many forms of persuasion, including confrontation, to encourage people to abandon faulty cognitions in favour of logical and healthy ones.
- Beck has developed ways to help depressed people correct errors of cognition that perpetuate self-defeating thoughts.
- Group therapy is based on the belief that certain problems can be treated more efficiently and more effectively in group settings.
- Practitioners of family therapy, couples therapy and some forms of group behaviour therapy observe people's interactions with others and attempt to help them learn how to establish more effective patterns of behaviour. Treatment of groups, including families and couples, permits the therapist to observe clients' social behaviours, and it uses social pressures to help convince clients of the necessity for behavioural change. It permits clients to learn from the mistakes of others and to observe that other people have similar problems, which often provides reassurance.

- The effectiveness of psychotherapeutic methods is difficult to assess: outcomes are difficult to measure objectively, ethical considerations make it hard to establish control groups for some types of disorder, and self-selection and drop-outs make it impossible to compare randomly selected groups of participants. Research suggests that behavioural therapy and cognitive behavioural therapy are effective.
- Biological treatments for mental disorders include drugs, electroconvulsive therapy and psychosurgery.
- Research has shown that treatment of the positive symptoms of schizophrenia with antipsychotic drugs, of major depression with antidepressant drugs and of bipolar disorder with lithium carbonate are the most effective ways to alleviate the symptoms of these disorders.
- Tricyclic antidepressant drugs can also alleviate severe anxiety that occurs during panic attacks and agoraphobia and can reduce the severity of obsessive-compulsive disorder.
- Although electroconvulsive therapy is an effective treatment for depression, its use is reserved for cases in which rapid relief is critical because the seizures may produce brain damage.
- The most controversial treatment, psychosurgery, is rarely performed today. Its only accepted use, in the form of cingulotomy, is for treatment of crippling compulsions that cannot be reduced by more conventional means.

Mental disorders

Anxiety, somatoform and dissociative mental disorders

- Anxiety disorders refer to mental disorders which are characterised by excessive worry or fear and include generalised anxiety disorder, panic disorder, simple phobia, obsessive-compulsive disorder and post-traumatic stress disorder.
- Generalised anxiety disorder is characterised by excessive worry about all aspects of life; the most explanatory models suggest that anxiety serves as an alarm function preparing an organism for future action. It is best treated by anxiolytic (anti-anxiety) drugs.
- Panic disorder results from a fear of fear. A patient misinterprets bodily sensations catastrophically.
- Cognitive behavioural therapy and anti-anxiety drugs are effective treatments.
- Social phobia refers to an excessive pathological fear of speaking or performing in public.

- Agoraphobia, the most common phobia, is the fear of open spaces. Simple phobia is a fear of specific stimuli such as spiders and snakes.
- Recent research has applied virtual reality technology (exposure to computer-simulated events, objects or locations) to the treatment of the fear of flying and fear of spiders, with long-term success.
- Post-traumatic stress disorder refers to anxiety generated by an astonishing event or trauma (such as natural catastrophe, war or rape).
- Somatoform disorders include somatisation disorder and conversion disorder.
- Somatisation disorder refers to complaints of symptoms of illness without underlying physiological causes. Almost all people with this disorder are women.
- Conversion disorder involves specific neurological symptoms, such as paralysis or sensory disturbance, that are not produced by a physiological disorder.
- Dissociative disorders include psychogenic amnesia (with or without fugue) – a withdrawal from a painful situation or from intolerable guilt; multiple personalities – the adoption of several distinct and complete personalities.

Personality disorders

- Antisocial personality disorder refers to a pathological impairment in social and personal behaviour. It is also known as psychopathy or sociopathy, but antisocial personality is qualitatively different from psychopathy. Psychopaths are indifferent to the effects of their behaviour on other people, are impulsive, fail to learn from experience, are sexually promiscuous, lack commitment to a partner and are habitual liars. Some psychopaths are superficially charming and psychopathy tends to run in families.
- Evidence suggests that the frontal lobe is either dysfunctional or smaller in psychopaths.
- There is a significant association between psychopathy and alcohol abuse.

Schizophrenic disorders

- Schizophrenia is a mental illness characterised by distortions of thought, perception and emotion.
- The main positive symptoms of schizophrenia include thought disorders; delusions of persecution, grandeur and control; and hallucinations. The main negative symptoms include withdrawal, apathy and poverty of speech.
- DSM-IV TR classifies schizophrenia into several sub-types, including undifferentiated, catatonic, paranoid and disorganised.

- Recent research suggests that a low level of expressed emotion (including critical comments and emotional overinvolvement) by family members facilitates the recovery of a patient with schizophrenia.
- Positive symptoms of schizophrenia can be made worse in schizophrenic patients by drugs that stimulate dopamine synapses (cocaine and amphetamine) and can be reduced or eliminated by drugs that block dopamine receptors (antipsychotic drugs).
- These findings have led to the dopamine hypothesis, which states that schizophrenia is caused by an inherited biochemical defect that causes dopamine neurons to be overactive.
- Enlargement of the ventricles is a consistent finding in schizophrenic patients and is unrelated to drug use; there is also evidence of reduced frontal lobe activation.
- Some researchers have suggested that lateralisation of function does not occur normally in schizophrenia.
- More recent studies indicate that schizophrenia can best be conceived of as two different disorders.
- The positive symptoms are produced by overactivity of dopamine neurons and can be treated with antipsychotic drugs. These positive symptoms are associated with limbic and sublimbic neural activation during verbal hallucination and verbal disorganisation.
- The negative symptoms, which do not respond to these drugs, are caused by brain abnormality. Investigators have found direct evidence of brain damage by inspecting CT scans of living patients' brains.
- Researchers have suggested three possible causes of the brain abnormality: a virus that triggers an autoimmune disease, which causes brain damage later in life; a virus that damages the brain early in life; and obstetric complications.

Mood disorders

- Mood disorders refer to a severe disturbance in emotion.
- Bipolar disorder consists of alternating periods of mania and depression; major depression consists of depression alone.
- Beck has noted that although mood disorders involve emotional reactions, these reactions may be, at least in part, based on faulty and negative cognition. Others such as Abramson and co-workers suggest that depressed individuals are characterised by a negative attributional style which promotes helplessness and hopelessness.
- Heritability studies strongly suggest a biological component to mood disorders. This possibility receives support from the finding that biological treatments effectively reduce the symptoms of these disorders, while

- reserpine, a drug used to treat hypertension, can cause depression.
- Biological treatments include lithium carbonate for bipolar disorder and electroconvulsive therapy and antidepressant drugs (including monoamine oxidase inhibitors and tricyclic antidepressants) for depression.

- Neuroimaging research has shown that an area in the frontal cortex, sg24, is smaller in people suffering from depression.
- Recently developed drugs for depression, called serotonin-specific reuptake inhibitors, act by preventing reuptake of serotonin and blocking serotonin receptors.

Suggestions for further reading

Abnormal psychology – general reading

Bentall, R.P. and Beck, A.T. (2004) *Madness Explained: Psychosis and human nature.* New York: Penguin.

Butcher, J.N., Mineka, S. and Hooley, J. (2009) *Abnormal Psychology* (14th edn). Boston, MA: Prentice Hall.

Kramer, G.P., Bernstein, D.S. and Phares, V. (2009) *Introduction to Clinical Psychology* (7th edn). Boston, MA: Prentice Hall.

Kring, A., Davison, G.C., Neale, J.M. and Johnson, S. (2009) *Abnormal Psychology* (11th edn). Chichester: Wiley.

Nevid, J., Rathus, S. and Greene, B. (2010) *Abnormal Psychology in a Changing World* (7th edn). Boston, MA: Allyn & Bacon.

Oltmans, T.F. and Emery, R.E. (2010) *Abnormal Psychology* (6th edn). Upper Saddle River, NJ: Prentice Hall.

Abnormal psychology is one of the most popular areas of study in psychology. As a result, there are many good textbooks which are in their sixth editions (and beyond). The books listed here are very good introductions to the general area of mental disorder and are recommended for more information on topics covered in this chapter.

Specific mental illnesses

Arkowitz, H. and Lillienfeld, S.O. (2007) The best medicine? *Scientific American Mind*, 18, 5, 80–83.

Special issue of *Current Directions in Psychological Science* on schizophrenia, 2010, vol 19.

Tandon, R., Keshavan, M.S. and Nasrallah, H.A. (2008) Schizophrenia, 'Just the facts': What we know in 2008, Part 1: Overview. *Schizophrenia Research*, 100, 4–19.

Tandon, R., Keshavan, M.S. and Nasrallah, H.A. (2008). Schizophrenia, 'Just the facts': What we know in 2008, Part 2; Epidemiology and etiology. *Schizophrenia Research*, 100, 1–18.

A number of books treat mental disorders separately, and the texts and papers here are some of the best covering anxiety, depression and schizophrenia.

Case studies and papers in mental illness

Jamison, K.R. (1993) *Touched with Fire.* New York: Free Press.

Jamison, K.R. (1995) *The Unquiet Mind.* London: Picador.

Jamison, K.R. (2004) *Exuberance.* New York: Knopf.

Meyer, R.G., Chapman, L.K. and Weaver, C.M. (2009) *Case Studies in Abnormal Behaviour* (8th edn). Boston, MA: Allyn & Bacon.

Oltmans, T.F., Martin, M. Neale, J.M. and Davison, G. (2006) *Case Studies in Abnormal Psychology* (7th edn). Chichester: Wiley.

Sutherland, S. (1987) *Breakdown.* London: Weidenfeld & Nicolson.

Wolpert, L. (1999) *Malignant Sadness: The anatomy of depression.* London: Faber.

The impact of mental disorder (on the individual and on the people around the individual) is seen vividly in personal accounts of mental illness. These books present case studies of mental disorder but from slightly different perspectives. Oltmans *et al.*'s book complements the DSM-IV TR and presents case studies of each of the major disorders listed in the manual. Sutherland's book is remarkable. It is an account of bipolar disorder suffered by the late Stuart Sutherland and recounts the various treatments and therapies he underwent in a search for a cure. He describes the events surrounding the disorder with often painful honesty, and the account is made all the more provocative by the fact that Sutherland was Professor of Psychology at the University of Sussex. Wolpert, another distinguished academic, suffered from major episodes of depression. In his book, he describes the episodes vividly and reviews current understanding of the disorder and its treatment.